ICD-10-CM/PCS CODING

THEORY AND PRACTICE

2021/2022 Edition

Elsevier
3251 Riverport Lane
St. Louis, Missouri 63043

ICD-10-CM/PCS CODING: THEORY AND PRACTICE, 2021/2022 EDITION ISBN: 978-0-323-76414-8

Access to the 2022 coding updates can be found in the "Content Updates" section located in your Evolve Resources.

Notices

Previous editions copyrighted 2019, 2018, 2017, 2016, 2015, 2014, 2013, and 2012.

International Standard Book Number: 978-0-323-76414-8

Senior Content Strategist: Brandi Graham
Senior Content Development Manager: Luke E. Held
Senior Content Development Specialist: Joshua S. Rapplean
Publishing Services Manager: Julie Eddy
Senior Project Manager: Abigail Bradberry
Senior Book Designer: Maggie Reid

Printed in Canada

Last digit is the print number: 9 8 7 6 5 4 3 2 1

Development of This Edition

SUBJECT MATTER EXPERT

Patricia Cordy Henricksen, MS, CHCA, CPC-I, CPC, CCP-P, ACS-PM
AAPC-Approved ICD-10-CM Trainer
Auditing, Coding, and Education Specialist
Soterion Medical Services
Lexington, Kentucky

Foreword

It is an honor to have an opportunity to share with you my thoughts and feelings about *ICD-10-CM/PCS Coding: Theory and Practice.*

This user-friendly book takes the mystery out of ICD-10-CM/PCS coding and meets the needs of not only students but also busy instructors. The approach is straightforward, clear, concise, and complete. This book contains the latest in coding assignments and covers a wide variety of coding applications by the use of exercises within the text and the accompanying Student Workbook on Evolve. The use of color illustrations and photographs further enhances the book and will keep the reader interested.

This is the definitive ICD-10-CM/PCS coding text!

Carol J. Buck
Author/Instructor

Preface

Authoritatively referenced and easy to use for teaching, *ICD-10-CM/PCS Coding: Theory and Practice* is the first coding resource designed with instructors and students in mind. This comprehensive guide presents reliable coverage of ICD-10-CM/PCS in a systematic, straightforward format that guides students through the coding process. With clear examples, challenging review questions, and outstanding instructor support, this innovative resource is not only a valuable coding tool but also a time-saving teaching tool!

ICD-10-CM/PCS Coding: Theory and Practice is intended for those who are learning to code, as well as for experienced professionals who wish to have a reference and/or learn the ICD-10-CM/PCS coding system. Unlike other books in this area, *ICD-10-CM/PCS Coding: Theory and Practice* sets out to help students (1) understand why coding is essential and necessary, (2) understand the basics of the health record, and (3) fully understand the rules, guidelines, and functions of ICD-10-CM/PCS coding. This book can be used in medical insurance, billing, and coding educational programs; in health information management programs; and as a useful reference to practitioners in the field.

The accompanying workbook has been moved to Evolve, but still includes the practice exercises that help students apply the guidelines and select principal diagnoses, while different types of operative reports provide more practice in assigning procedure codes.

As a publisher of an ICD-10 coding textbook, we are caught between a rock and a hard place when it comes to publishing in August because the updated *ICD-10-CM Official Guidelines for Coding and Reporting* are not made available until August. It is important to check the companion Evolve website for the most current guidelines and for any addenda that may result due to changes in the guidelines.

ORGANIZATION

The organization of *ICD-10-CM/PCS: Theory and Practice* follows the most logical way to learn this material. The early chapters focus on history, the health record as the foundation for coding, and the *Official Guidelines for Coding and Reporting*. A coder must have a basic understanding of this foundational content before moving on to more complicated material. Specifically, Chapter 4 covers the basic steps of ICD-10-CM coding and the correct process for locating codes in the ICD-10-CM manual.

Chapters 9 through 26 cover each chapter of the ICD-10-CM code book. These chapters are sequenced in this book for the following reasons. The assignment of codes for signs, symptoms, infectious diseases, and Z codes may be applied to all chapters in the ICD-10-CM code book; therefore these are the first coding chapters in this book. Each of these chapters follows a very specific template that will help students learn and instructors teach this complex material, beginning with the corresponding coding guidelines from the *ICD-10-CM Official Guidelines for Coding and Reporting*. This reinforces the importance of the guidelines in accurate code assignment. Following this is a section on anatomy and physiology, with full-color illustrations of the body system discussed in the chapter. This allows for more informed decision making when selecting the correct code and also provides an important review of anatomy and physiology. Key disease conditions are covered and illustrated with examples.

Within each coding chapter is a separate list of Z codes. Z codes are used in all sections of the ICD-10-CM code book, and this list gives students, instructors, and practitioners easy reference to the correct Z codes for each section.

Featured in select chapters are common medications and treatments for the related disease conditions. It is important to become familiar with common medications to identify chronic illnesses that may be documented in the health record.

Procedures are another important section of the coding chapters. Common and complex procedures relating to the diagnoses are covered in this section using ICD-10-PCS.

DISTINCTIVE FEATURES

- Full-color design with illustrations. This helps important content such as anatomy and physiology stand out and come alive and provides visual reinforcement of key concepts.
- Numerous and varied examples and exercises within each chapter. These exercises break the chapter into manageable segments and help students gauge learning while reinforcing important concepts.
- Partial answer keys for the textbook and student workbook on Evolve are available in the Evolve Student Resources for instant feedback to enhance student learning.

ADDITIONAL RESOURCES

Get the most out of your course with these additional learning and teaching resources (Refer to the front inside cover of this text for registration instructions to access these comprehensive online resources.).

TEACH Instructor Resources on Evolve

- TEACH is the complete curriculum manual, giving instructors everything necessary to enhance an ICD-10-CM course and save time!
  - **Lesson plans** tie together related content in the textbook, workbook, and instructor resources and reduce preparation time.
  - **Lecture slides and notes** presented in PowerPoint guide instructors through class presentations.
  - **Answer keys** for every exercise, chapter review, and test bank question enable fast, efficient student assessment.
  - **Test banks** help prepare exams instantly with chapter-specific test banks presented in ExamView.
- **Instructor Content Updates**.

Evolve Learning Resources

- This companion website contains helpful material that will extend your studies beyond the classroom.
- 30-day access to TruCode® Encoder Essentials. We've included 30-day access to TruCode® Encoder Essentials, with every new *ICD-10-CM/PCS Coding, Theory and Practice, 2021/2022 Edition* book purchase.
  - When ready to activate **(we recommend at the end of the course)**, scratch off the gray sticker at the bottom right of the inside front cover of the main text to reveal an access code.
  - Next, access http://evolve.elsevier.com/trucode
  - Enter the access code when prompted on screen. **Access codes will only be valid during the current coding year, and once entered access will be limited to 30 days.**
  - **NOTE:** It is recommended that you only activate your TruCode® Encoder Essentials access as a CAPSTONE at the end of your course, after you have completed all of the text exercises using your print coding manuals.

- TruCode® Instructions and Practice Exercises. For more specific instructions and practice using TruCode® Encoder Essentials, click the *TruCode® Instructions and Practice Exercises* asset on the main *ICD-10-CM/PCS Coding* Evolve site. Answers for the TruCode® Practice Exercises are only available in the TEACH Instructor Resources on Evolve.
- Coding Tips and Links. *Official Guidelines for Coding and Reporting,* AHIMA How to Interpret Standards of Ethical Coding, content updates, and coding links help you stay current with this ever-changing field.
- Student Workbook on Evolve. Apply the textbook content and prepare for employment with this study guide! The workbook contains:
  - Application activities that give students hands-on practice applying ICD-10-CM coding to actual health records.
  - Case studies that illustrate common scenarios students will encounter on the job.
  - Partial answer key in the Evolve Student Resources.
- Interactive Operative Reports. These OR reports can be found in most of the disease chapters. Please see the Evolve Companion site for further details. By coding these OR reports, the student will become more familiar with the documentation that is used by surgeons and will get practice translating the documentation into ICD-10-PCS codes. A special thanks to mtsamples.com for allowing us to use some of their sample reports.

Contents

1

The Rationale for and History of Coding

CHAPTER OUTLINE

LEARNING OBJECTIVES

1. Describe the application of coding
2. Define nomenclature and classification
3. Identify the historical timeline of coding
4. Describe different coding organizations and credentials
5. Recognize the importance of the Standards of Ethical Coding
6. Define compliance as it relates to coding
7. Explain confidentiality as it applies to coding

ABBREVIATIONS/ACRONYMS

AAPC American Academy of Professional Coders

A&P anatomy and physiology

AHA American Hospital Association

AHIMA American Health Information Management Association

CCA Certified Coding Associate

CCS Certified Coding Specialist

CCS-P Certified Coding Specialist—Physician Based

CDIP Certified Documentation Improvement Practitioner

CEUs continuing education units

CIC Certified Inpatient Coder

CMS Centers for Medicare and Medicaid Services

COC Certified Outpatient Coder

CPC Certified Professional Coder

CRC Certified Risk Adjustment Coder

DRGs diagnosis-related groups

HCC Hierarchical Condition Categories

HIPAA Health Insurance Portability and Accountability Act

ICD-10-CM *International Classification of Diseases, 10th Revision, Clinical Modification*

ICD-10-PCS *International Classification of Diseases, 10th Revision, Procedure Coding System*

IS *information systems*

MS-DRG Medicare Severity diagnosis-related group

NCHS National Center for Health Statistics

OIG Office of the Inspector General

RHIA Registered Health Information Administrator

RHIT Registered Health Information Technician

SNOMED Systematized Nomenclature of Medicine

UR utilization review

WHO World Health Organization

BACKGROUND OF CODING

What Is Coding, and What Are Its Applications?

As a student in this field, you will often be asked these questions. Why does one study this subject? What type of work does a "coder" do? Basically, medical coding consists of translating **diagnoses** and **procedures** into special alphanumeric characters for the purpose of statistically capturing data. This process is done for us every day in all aspects of daily life. If you buy a banana at the grocery store, the cash register captures that banana as a number, which, in turn, provides data on the number of bananas sold in that store or by that grocery chain; it also yields data of importance to the store on replenishing their inventory, details regarding what time of year the greatest number of bananas are sold, and so forth.

Translation of a disease and/or a procedure into an ICD-10 code is not as simple as it may seem. This process requires a thorough knowledge of anatomy and physiology, disease processes, medical **terminology**, laboratory values, pharmacology, surgical procedures, and last but not least, a myriad of coding rules and guidelines. Diseases and procedures are translated into a coding system known as the *International Classification of Diseases, 10th Revision, Clinical Modification* ICD-10-CM and ICD-10-PCS. This **classification** system has been used worldwide and has been clinically modified for the United States.

Coded data is used for many purposes, including research and planning. For example, a healthcare provider or facility could use this data to find out how many cases of appendicitis were treated in a year. This information could be used by a healthcare facility in decisions about the possible purchase of more equipment, the addition of an operating room, the hiring of additional staff, or by the provider to gain additional skills. Since the implementation of DRGs—now known as MS-DRGs—coded data are also used for **reimbursement** (payment) purposes, and they are increasingly used for risk management and quality improvement, as well as in nursing clinical pathways. Coded data were important from the start, but use of this data for reimbursement has elevated the importance of accurate coding.

Capture of health data through ICD-10 codes that are used worldwide has proved useful for the study of patterns of disease, disease epidemics, causes of mortality, and treatment modalities. Without the use of a classification system, comparison of data would be impossible.

Nomenclature and Classification

A nomenclature and a classification of diseases are required for development of a coding system. A **nomenclature** is a system of names that are used as preferred terminology, in this case, for diseases and procedures. Often, diseases in different areas of the country or in different countries are identified by dissimilar terminology, which makes the capture of comparative statistical data next to impossible. For example, another name for "amyotrophic lateral sclerosis" is "Lou Gehrig's disease," which is also known as a "motor neuron disease." Nomenclatures of disease were first developed in the United States around 1928. The Systematized Nomenclature of Medicine (SNOMED), published by the College of American Pathologists, is the most up-to-date system in current use.

Classification systems group together similar items for easy storage and retrieval. Within a classification system, items are arranged into groups according to specific criteria. The history of classification systems goes back as far as Hippocrates. During the 17th century, London Bills of Mortality represented the first attempts of scientists to gather statistical data on disease. The ICD-10-CM classification system is a closed system that comprises diseases, injuries, surgeries, and procedures. In a closed classification system a disease, condition, or procedure can be classified in only one place.

HISTORY OF CODING

Classification systems date back to Bertillon's Classification of Causes of Death, which was developed in 1893. This system was adopted by the United States in 1898 under the recommendation of the American Public Health Association. System revisions were scheduled to take place every 10 years, and the classification was maintained by the World Health Organization (WHO). Revisions became known as the International Classification of Causes of Death. Over the years, this system has been changed to allow its use not only in mortality (death) reporting but in morbidity (disease condition) reporting as well. Since its inception, this classification has been revised 10 times. The Clinical Modification (CM) was developed in 1977 by the United States to more accurately capture morbidity data for study within the United States, as well as information on operative and diagnostic procedures that were not included in the original publication of ICD.

Currently, most countries are using ICD-10, which was published in 1993 by the WHO. ICD-10-CM has been clinically modified for use in the United States and was implemented on October 1, 2015. The final rule for adoption of ICD-10-CM and ICD-10-PCS was released in January of 2009.

Work on ICD-10 was begun in 1983. The tabular volume was published in 1992, and the instructional volume followed in 1993; the Alphabetic Index was published in 1994. In 1994, the United States began the process of determining whether a clinical modification (CM) would be necessary. A draft version was made available in 2002, updated in July 2007, and updated again in 2009, and was updated yearly until it was implemented. The latest version can be found at the National Center for Health Statistics website.

Clinical modifications made to ICD-10 allow a higher level of specificity. Since 1999, ICD-10 has been used in the United States for the reporting of mortality data. A total of 90 countries, including Canada and Australia, are currently using ICD-10.

ICD-10 may be updated biannually in April and October. Updates contain additional codes, revised codes, and codes that are deleted. These updates are published in the ***Federal Register*** (the official daily publication for rules, proposed rules, and notices of U.S. federal agencies and organizations) as a proposed rule and then as a final rule. They are available at the Centers for Medicare and Medicaid Services (CMS) website (www.cms.gov). It is of the utmost importance that code books and coding software (**encoder**) be updated to ensure that coding is accurate and to facilitate accurate reimbursement. The ICD-10 Coordination and Maintenance Committee meets twice a year and is used as a forum for proposals to update ICD-10. This committee serves in an advisory capacity. Two federal agencies are responsible for maintenance of ICD-10. The classification of diagnoses is the responsibility of the NCHS (National Center for Health Statistics), and the classification of procedures is the responsibility of CMS (Centers for Medicare and Medicaid Services). The Coordination and Maintenance Committee meetings are open to the public and comments are encouraged. The meeting is also available by webcast and toll-free dial-in access. All comments and recommendations are evaluated before a final decision on new codes is issued.

The development and maintenance of the guidelines of ICD-10-CM is the responsibility of the National Center for Health Statistics (NCHS), CMS, the American Hospital Association (AHA), and the American Health Information Management Association (AHIMA), which are also known as the Cooperating Parties. Many publications provide coding advice and information, but only one publication is official. This publication, *AHA Coding Clinic for ICD-10-CM* (referred to as *Coding Clinic*), which is published quarterly by the AHA, provides coding advice and guidelines that have been approved by the Cooperating Parties and must be followed by coders.

CODING ORGANIZATIONS AND CREDENTIALS

Coders come from a variety of educational backgrounds. Many coders have attended 4-year college programs in Health Information Administration; others have completed 2-year college programs in Health Information Technology. Some community colleges offer programs geared only to medical coding. Whatever their background, most coders take certification examinations to earn **credentials** (which are certificates that recognize a course of study taken in a specific field and acknowledge that competency is required) and become members of a professional organization. Many employers include a requirement for certification as part of their coding job description.

Coders can work in a variety of settings; most often, they are employed by hospitals, physician offices, outpatient surgical centers, long-term care facilities, and insurance companies. It is predicted that the demand for coding professionals will far exceed the number of coders in the workforce.

The two most well-known professional associations for coders are AHIMA (www.ahima.org) and the American Academy of Professional Coders (AAPC) (www.aapc.com). Both of these organizations offer a variety of coding credentials. AHIMA, which has been in existence for over 75 years, has undergone several name changes along the way to keep up with the ever-changing technological skills, educational requirements, and roles of its members. It boasts a membership of over 103,000. Traditionally, this organization has provided support for facility coders, but in recent years, it has expanded to include coders who provide services in physician's offices and outpatient settings. AHIMA offers the following credentials:

CCA	Certified Coding Associate
CCS	Certified Coding Specialist
CCS-P	Certified Coding Specialist—Physician Based
CDIP	Certified Document Improvement Practitioner
CHDA	Certified Health Data Analyst
CHPS	Certified in Healthcare Privacy and Security
RHIT	Registered Health Information Technician
RHIA	Registered Health Information Administrator

AAPC has over 190,000 credentialed members and was started in 1981. It was founded to assist coders in providing services to physicians and offers the following credentials:

CDEO	Certified Documentation Expert - Outpatient
CIC	Certified Inpatient Coder
COC	Certified Outpatient Coder
COC-A	Certified Outpatient Coder-Apprentice
CPB	Certified Professional Biller
CPC	Certified Professional Coder
CPCO	Certified Professional Compliance Officer
CPC-A	Certified Professional Coder-Apprentice
CPMA	Certified Professional Medical Auditor
CPPM	Certified Physician Practice Manager
CRC	Certified Risk Adjustment Coder

The CRC credential is for a Certified Risk Adjustment Coder. These coders must be familiar with Hierarchical Condition Categories (HCC), which are the basis for reimbursement for Medicare Advantage plans (Medicare Part C) since 2004.

To obtain credentials from either organization, a coder must sit for a certification examination and complete college coursework in several areas such as medical terminology and anatomy and physiology. To maintain their credentials, coders must earn continuing education units (CEUs). The number of CEUs required is dependent on the credential(s) of the coder (Table 1-1).

CODING ETHICS

Along with providing credentials, both AHIMA and AAPC have set standards for Coding **Ethics**, which are reprinted in Figures 1-1 and 1-2. (Please see the Evolve companion website for "How to Interpret the Standards of Ethical Coding.") Members of these organizations are expected to abide by these coding standards. A coder who is asked to disregard a guideline to facilitate payment should decline on the basis of these standards, by which coders are bound.

TABLE 1-1 CREDENTIALS AND CONTINUING EDUCATION UNIT REQUIREMENTS

Credential	Organization Offering Credential	Education Required	CEUs Required per 2-Year Cycle
CCA	AHIMA	High school diploma or equivalent	20
CCS	AHIMA	High school diploma or equivalent	20
CCS-P	AHIMA	High school diploma or equivalent	20
CIC	AAPC	High school diploma or equivalent	
COC	AAPC	High school diploma or equivalent and 2 years coding experience	36
COC-A	AAPC	High school diploma or equivalent	36
CPB	AAPC	High school diploma or equivalent	
CPC	AAPC	High school diploma or equivalent and 2 years coding experience	36
CPC-A	AAPC	High school diploma or equivalent	36
CPMA	AAPC	High school diploma or equivalent	
CPPM	AAPC	High school diploma or equivalent	
CRC	AAPC	High school diploma or equivalent	
RHIT	AHIMA	2-Year degree in accredited HIM program	20
RHIA	AHIMA	4-Year degree in accredited HIM program	30

Standards of Ethical Coding

Coding professionals should:

1. Apply accurate, complete, and consistent coding practices that yield quality data.
2. Gather and report all data required for internal and external reporting, in accordance with applicable requirements and data set definitions.
3. Assign and report, in any format, only the codes and data that are clearly and consistently supported by health record documentation in accordance with applicable code set and abstraction conventions and requirements.
4. Query and/or consult as needed with the provider for clarification and additional documentation prior to final code assignment in accordance with acceptable healthcare industry practices.
5. Refuse to participate in, support, or change reported data and/or narrative titles, billing data, clinical documentation practices, or any coding-related activities intended to skew or misrepresent data and their meaning that do not comply with requirements.
6. Facilitate, advocate, and collaborate with healthcare professionals in the pursuit of accurate, complete, and reliable coded data and in situations that support ethical coding practices.
7. Advance coding knowledge and practice through continuing education, including but not limited to meeting continuing education requirements.
8. Maintain the confidentiality of protected health information in accordance with the Code of Ethics.
9. Refuse to participate in the development of coding and coding-related technology that is not designed in accordance with requirements.
10. Demonstrate behavior that reflects integrity, shows a commitment to ethical and legal coding practices, and fosters trust in professional activities.
11. Refuse to participate in and/or conceal unethical coding, data abstraction, query practices, or any inappropriate activities related to coding and address any perceived unethical coding-related practices.

Revised and approved by the House of Delegates 12/16

FIGURE 1-1. AHIMA's Standards of Ethical Coding.

AAPC Code of Ethics

It shall be the responsibility of every AAPC member, as a condition of continued membership, to conduct themselves in all professional activities in a manner consistent with ALL of the following ethical principles of professional conduct:

- Integrity
- Respect
- Commitment
- Competence
- Fairness
- Responsibility

Adherence to these ethical standards assists in ensuring public confidence in the integrity and professionalism of AAPC members. Failure to conform professional conduct to these ethical standards, as determined by AAPC's Ethics Committee, may result in the loss of membership with AAPC.

FIGURE 1-2. AAPC's Code of Ethical Standards.

Access the AAPC website for more detailed explanation of the ethical principles outlined in their Code of Ethics.

COMPLIANCE

Compliance is defined as "acting according to certain accepted standards or, in simple terms, abiding by the rules." In health care, this requires following the rules and guidelines as set forth by the government through Medicare and Medicaid and all professional organizations which a facility or provider may belong to or is participating with, and following the policies and procedures of that organization.

Compliance officers and programs are found in many industries. It wasn't until after the passage of the Health Insurance Portability and Accountability Act of 1996 (HIPAA) that compliance officers became a standard presence in healthcare facilities. HIPAA gave additional funding to the U.S. Department of Health and Human Services, the Office of the Inspector General (OIG), and the U.S. Department of Justice to increase penalties for healthcare fraud and abuse. Ongoing investigations in healthcare institutions across the United States are exploring violations of the False Claim Act and other laws.

As explained in an article by Joette Hanna that appeared in the *Journal of AHIMA*, entitled "Constructing a Coding Compliance Plan,"[2] several steps must be taken if a coding department wishes to ensure that it is in compliance. Coding departments must do the following:

- Abide by AHIMA's Standards of Ethical Coding
- Develop coding policies and procedures
- Develop a working relationship with the billing department
- Develop a coding compliance work plan
- Conduct coding audits
- Develop an action plan based on audit results

Likewise, a practice brief published by AHIMA in 2001, entitled "Developing a Coding Compliance Policy Document,"[3] states that the following bulleted items should be included in a coding compliance plan:

- Policy statement regarding the commitment of the organization to correct assignment and reporting of codes
- The Official Coding Guidelines used by the facility
- The people responsible for code assignment
- What needs to be done when clinical information is not clear enough to assign codes
- If there are payer-specific guidelines, where these may be found
- A procedure for correcting codes that have been assigned incorrectly

- Plan for education on areas of risk as identified by audits
- Identification of essential coding resources that are available and to be used by coding professionals
- Procedure for coding new and/or unusual diagnoses or procedures
- A policy for which procedures will be reported
- Procedure for resolving coding/documentation disputes with physicians
- Procedure for processing claim rejections
- Procedure for handling requests for coding amendments
- Policy that requires coders to have available coding manuals and not just encoder
- Process for review of coding on those records coded with incomplete documentation

CONFIDENTIALITY

Employees in a healthcare setting must be aware of the confidentiality of the information surrounding them. When they take the Hippocratic Oath, physicians swear to maintain patient confidentiality. Likewise, in the Patient Bill of Rights as prepared by the AHA, the patient's right to privacy is stated. The Code of Ethics of the AHIMA also addresses confidentiality when it says, "Members will promote and protect the confidentiality and security of health records and information."

Coders must read a patient's personal medical information before they can code the encounter and/or patient admission. It is important that this information not be shared with anyone, including other employees, unless they have a legitimate need to know to perform their job; patient information should never be discussed in a place where any visitor could overhear.

CHAPTER REVIEW EXERCISE

Write the correct answer(s) in the space(s) provided.

1. What does a coder do?

____

2. What coding system is currently used in the United States for diagnosis coding?

____

3. What does the CM of ICD-10-CM stand for?

____

4. List three uses for coded data.

1. ______________________________

2. ______________________________

3. ______________________________

5. What payment system does Medicare use for inpatient reimbursement?

____

6. Describe the difference between a nomenclature and a classification system.

____

7. What nomenclature of disease is used in the United States?

____

8. Define a closed classification system.

____

9. When was the International Classification of Diseases first adopted by the United States?

____

10. When and how often is this system (ICD-10-CM) updated?

____

11. What four groups constitute the Cooperating Parties?

1. ____

2. ____

3. ____

4. ____

12. Who publishes official coding advice and guidance?

____

13. What organizations award coding credentials?

____

14. What is another word that is used in the industry for "following the rules"?

____

15. If you were coding a neighbor's record, would it be okay for you to tell your other neighbors the reason the patient was hospitalized?

____

16. What does HIPAA stand for?

____

17. Most industrialized countries do not use ICD-10.
A. True
B. False

18. The federal agency responsible for the maintenance of ICD-10-CM PCS is The Center for Disease Control.
A. True
B. False

CHAPTER GLOSSARY

Classification: grouping together of items as for storage and retrieval.

Compliance: adherence to accepted standards.

Credential: degree, certificate, or award that recognizes a course of study taken in a specific field and that acknowledges the competency required.

Diagnosis: identification of a disease through signs, symptoms, and tests.

Encoder: coding software that is used to assign diagnosis and procedure codes.

Ethics: moral standard.

Federal Register: the official daily publication for rules, proposed rules, and notices of U.S. federal agencies and organizations.

Nomenclature: system of names that are used as the preferred terminology.

Procedure: a diagnostic or therapeutic process performed on a patient.

Reimbursement: payment for healthcare services.

Terminology: words and phrases that apply to a particular field.

REFERENCES

1. American Health Information Management Association: Destination 10: healthcare organization preparation for ICD-10-CM and ICD-10-PCS. *J AHIMA* 75:56A–556D, 2004.
2. Hanna J: Constructing a coding compliance plan. *J AHIMA* 73:48–56, 2002.
3. AHIMA Coding Practice Team: Developing a coding compliance policy document (AHIMA practice brief). *J AHIMA* 72:88A–888C, 2001.

2

The Health Record as the Foundation of Coding

CHAPTER OUTLINE

The Health Record

Sections of the Health Record

- Administrative Data
- Clinical Data

Uniform Hospital Discharge Data Set (UHDDS) Reporting Standards for Diagnoses and Procedures

- Principal Diagnosis
- Principal Procedure
- Other Diagnoses

Coding From Documentation Found in the Health Record

The Use of Queries in the Coding Process

- When to Query
- How to Query
- Query Format
- Query Retention Policy
- Leading Query
- Who to Query
- Elements of a Query Form

Chapter Review Exercise

Chapter Glossary

References

LEARNING OBJECTIVES

1. Explain the purpose of the various forms or reports found in a health record
2. Define "principal diagnosis"
3. Define "principal procedure"
4. Identify reasons for assigning codes for other diagnoses
5. List the basic guidelines for reporting diagnoses/procedures
6. Identify types of documentation acceptable for assigning codes
7. Explain the query process

ABBREVIATIONS/ACRONYMS

AHQA American Health Quality Association

BPH benign prostatic hypertrophy

CBC complete blood count

CC chief complaint

CMS Centers for Medicare and Medicaid Services

CPT *Current Procedural Terminology*

COPD chronic obstructive pulmonary disease

DOB date of birth

ED Emergency Department

EEG electroencephalogram

EGD esophagogastroduodenoscopy

EKG electrocardiogram

ER Emergency Room

GERD gastroesophageal reflux disease

H&P history and physical

ABBREVIATIONS/ ACRONYMS—*cont'd*

HPI history of present illness

ICD-10-CM *International Classification of Diseases, 10th Revision, Clinical Modification*

ICU intensive care unit

MAR medication administration record

MRA magnetic resonance angiography

MRI magnetic resonance imaging

MS-DRGs Medicare Severity diagnosis-related groups

MVP mitral valve prolapse

NPI National Provider Identifier

OP Report operative report

POA present on admission

SOAP Subjective/Objective/Assessment/Plan

TJC The Joint Commission

TPR temperature, pulse, and respiration

UHDDS Uniform Hospital Discharge Data Set

UPIN Unique Physician Identification Number

THE HEALTH RECORD

A health record must be maintained for every individual who is assessed or treated. Although Edna Huffman's classic *Health Information Management*[1] book is no longer in print, her definition of the purpose and use of a health record still holds true today. She states, "The main purpose of the medical record is to accurately and adequately document a patient's life and health history, including past and present illnesses and treatments, with emphasis on the events affecting the patient during the current episode of care." Huffman goes on to say, "The medical record must be compiled in a timely manner and contain sufficient data to identify the patient, support the diagnosis or reason for health care encounter, justify the treatment and accurately document the results." According to Abdelhak's *Health Information: Management of a Strategic Resource*,[2] the health record serves five purposes:

1. Describes the patient's health history
2. Serves as a method for clinicians to communicate regarding the plan of care for the patients
3. Serves as a legal document of care and services provided
4. Serves as a source of data
5. Serves as a resource for healthcare practitioner education

The patient's health record in today's environment may be maintained in several formats or **hybrids**. The traditional health record consists of documentation on paper prepared by **healthcare providers** that describes the condition of the patient and the plan and course of treatment. As the world advances through electronic forms of documentation, paper notes become more and more obsolete. Some paper documentation and some transcribed or electronically stored documentation may be available. Many facilities have actually achieved a predominantly electronic health record. One of the advantages of storing the record electronically is that many users are able to access the record at the same time. Whether in electronic, paper, or hybrid form, documentation serves as the basis of a health record.

The Centers for Medicare and Medicaid Services (CMS) has provided physicians with *General Principles of Medical Record Documentation*.[3]

- Medical records should be complete and legible
- The documentation of each patient encounter should include:
  - Reason for encounter and relevant history
  - Physical examination findings and prior diagnostic test results
  - Assessment, clinical impression, and diagnosis
  - Plan for care
- Date and legible identity of the observer
- The rationale for ordering diagnostic and ancillary services (if not documented, should be easily inferred)
- Past and present diagnoses should be accessible for treating and/or consulting physician

- Appropriate health risk factors should be identified
- Patient's progress, response to changes in treatment, and revision of diagnosis should be documented
- *Current Procedural Terminology* (CPT) and *International Classification of Diseases, 10th Revision, Clinical Modification* (ICD-10-CM) codes reported on health insurance claim forms should be supported by documentation in the medical record

SECTIONS OF THE HEALTH RECORD

Every facility has its own policies and procedures regarding the organization of the health record. Records will differ slightly depending upon the course of the patient's condition and treatment. If a record were to be organized similarly to a novel that tells a story, the elements discussed in the next sections would be included.

Administrative Data

- Demographic
- Personal data
- Consents

Information contained in this section will facilitate identification of the patient. Some of the UHDDS data elements included are personal identification, date of birth (DOB), sex, race, residence, admit date, and discharge date. See Figure 2-1.

Clinical Data

- Emergency room record (when applicable) (see Figure 2-2)
- Admission history and physical (see Figure 2-3)
- Physician orders (see Figures 2-4 and 2-5)
- Progress notes recorded by healthcare providers (see Figure 2-6, *A* and *B*)
- Anesthesia forms (when applicable) (see Figure 2-9)
- Operative report (when applicable) (see Figure 2-10)
- Recovery room notes (when applicable)
- Consultations (when applicable)
- Laboratory test results (when applicable) (see Figure 2-8)
- Radiology report (when applicable) (see Figure 2-11)
- Miscellaneous ancillary reports (when applicable)
- Discharge summary (see Figure 2-12)

Data are collected from the health record as mandated by governmental and nongovernmental agencies. The Joint Commission (TJC) places data requirements and time frames for documentation within the health record. The federal government and state licensing agencies may have similar requirements. Medical staff bylaws often include these documentation requirements. In 1974, the Uniform Hospital Discharge Data Set (UHDDS) mandated that hospitals must report a common core of data. Since that time, the requirements have been revised and will continue to change as necessary. The UHDDS required data elements are listed in Figure 2-1.

Emergency Room Record

The emergency room record is a mini health record. It contains a **chief complaint (CC)**, which is the reason, in the patient's own words, for presentation to the hospital. It contains a history, physical examination, laboratory results, radiology reports (if applicable), plan of care, physician orders, and documentation of any procedures performed. Last but not least, it contains a list of working diagnoses and information on the disposition of the patient. See Figure 2-2 for a sample of an ED (Emergency Department, or also called ER for Emergency Room) record.

Uniform Hospital Discharge Data Set

01. **Personal identifier**
02. **Date of birth (month, day, and year)**
03. **Sex**
04. **Race and ethnicity**
05. **Residence (usual residence, full address, and zip code [nine-digit zip code, if available])**
06. **Hospital identification number**
    Three options are given for this institutional number, with the Medicare provider number as the recommended choice. The federal tax identification number of the American Hospital Association number is preferred to creating a new number.
07. **Admission date (month, day, and year)**
08. **Type of admission (scheduled or unscheduled)**
09. **Discharge date (month, day, and year)**
10. **Attending physician identification (NPI)**
11. **Operating physician identification (NPI)**
12. **Principal diagnosis**
    The condition established after study to be chiefly responsible for occasioning the admission of the patient to the hospital for care.
13. **Other diagnoses**
    All conditions that coexist at the time of admission or that develop subsequently that affect the treatment received and/or the length of stay. Diagnoses that relate to an earlier episode and have no bearing on the current hospital stay are excluded.
14. **Qualifier for other diagnoses**
    A qualifier is given for each diagnosis coded under "other diagnoses" to indicate whether the onset of the diagnosis preceded or followed admission to the hospital. The option "uncertain" is permitted.
15. **External cause-of-injury code**
    Hospitals should complete this item whenever there is a diagnosis of an injury, poisoning, or adverse effect.
16. **Birth weight of neonate**
17. **Procedures and dates**
    a. All significant procedures are to be reported. A significant procedure is one that (1) is surgical in nature, (2) carries a procedural risk, (3) carries an anesthetic risk, or (4) requires specialized training.
    b. The date of each significant procedure must be reported.
    c. When multiple procedures are reported, the principal procedure is designated. The principal procedure is one that was performed for definitive treatment rather than one performed for diagnostic or explanatory purposes or was necessary to take care of a complication. If two procedures appear to be principal, then the one most related to the principal diagnosis is selected as the principal procedure.
    d. The UPIN of the person performing the principal procedure must be reported.
18. **Disposition of the patient**
    a. Discharged home (not to home health service)
    b. Discharged to acute care hospital
    c. Discharged to nursing facility
    d. Discharged to home to be under the care of a home health service
    e. Discharged to other health care facility
    f. Left against medical advice
    g. Alive, other; or alive, not stated
    h. Died
19. **Patient's expected source of payment**
    a. Primary source
    b. Other source
20. **Total charges**
    List all charges billed by the hospital for this hospitalization. Professional charges for individual patient care by physicians are excluded.

FIGURE 2-1. Uniform Hospital Discharge Data Set elements.

Date: Room: Time in room: AM/PM

Hx source: (Patient) / spouse / family / friend / EMS / other ☐ History & ROS limited by medical or other condition

Time seen ___ (AM)/PM

PMH: None **PSH:** None

Renal Tx - now advanced nephropathy
Lupus nephritis DM perpt last Cr = 8
htn
cluster HA
SLE
fibromyalgia
s/p cholecystectomy

CC:

HPI: 51 y/o ♀ c lupus c failing renal tx (perpt last Cr 8), recent dle on 7/14/06 for rejection of tx, now presents c 1 d h/o trouble speaking. Pt has had trouble getting words out x 2 weeks. Now c acute stuttering since this am, 9AM ⊕ HA - same pain frontal, band like Ⓑ eye pain. On Gabapentin x 2 weeks ⊕ cough, ⊕ chills ⊕ twitching x 1 month, ⊕ diplopia ... 2 weeks

Meds: None See triage/nursing sheet
calcitriol, FeSO4, Prograf
aranesp, Nexium, Toprol
gabapentin, folic acid, Furosemide
phoslo, Prednisone
nifedical, Azathioprine
MVI

FH: (None) / CAD / CVA / Cancer / DM / HTN / **Other:**

Allergies: NKDA / (other:) Zantac, Bactrim, anti seizure med?

SH: Tobacco: (None) / Current / Past / ______ Pack-year

Alcohol: (None) / Occ / Mod / Heavy:

Drugs: (None) / Current / Past / Type: ______

Lives In: (Home (family)) / Home (alone) / NH / Homeless/Other

ROS: CIRCLE ALL THAT APPLY, CROSS OUT NEGATIVE COMPLAINTS OR SYSTEMS, LIST OTHERS

Gen	Eyes	ENT	Resp	CV	GI	GU	Skin	MS	Psych	Neuro	All/IM
~~Fever~~	Blur vision	Hearing prob	Cough	~~Chest pain~~	(Abd pain) chronic	~~Dysuria~~	~~Rash~~	~~Neck pain~~	~~Depression~~	~~HA~~	Allergies
~~Chills~~	~~Less vision~~	Rhinitis	~~Wheezing~~	~~DOE~~	~~N/V/D~~	~~Flank pain~~	~~Itching~~	(Back pain) lower	Hallucination	(Weakness)	Hives
Weight loss	(Diplopia)	Nose bleed	(Dyspnea)	(Edema)	Melena	~~Vag bleed~~	~~Bruising~~	Arm pain	Suicidal	Gait prob	Poor healing
Weakness	(Pain)	Throat pain	Hemoptysis	Palpitations	~~Rectal blood~~	Discharge	Wounds:	Leg pain	Homicidal	(Speech prob)	
	Photophobia	Voice change	Pleuritis	Lightheaded	~~Vomit blood~~	Testicle pain					

Heme	Endo
Anemia	Weight loss
~~Bruising~~	Polyuria
Bleeding	Polydipsia
Lymph nodes	

Other ROS: dry mouth; Ⓑ eye pain x 2 weeks; ⊕ diplopia - occasional

LMP: ______ ☐ All other systems reviewed are negative Pain Score (1-10): ______

PE: ☒ VS reviewed BP: 147/88 HR: 82 RR: 16 T: 98.5 **O2 sat:** 97 % on RA Normal/Hypoxia

Gen	Appearance	NAD pt stuttering. Not in respiratory distress. Cushingoid
Eyes	Conjunctiva	(Normal)
	Pupils	Normal EOM (Normal) Fundi Normal
ENT	Head/Face	(Atrauma)
	Ear	(Normal)
	Nose	(Normal)
	Oropharynx	(Normal)
Resp	Effort	(Normal)
	Auscultation	(Normal)
CV	Auscultation	(Normal)
	Jugular	(Normal)
	Edema	None 2+ edema to mid calf
GI	Bowel sound	(Normal) obese - n
	Palpation	(NT / ND) Ⓛ LQ scar where transplant
	Rectal exam	Normal
GU	CVA Tender	None
	External	Normal
	Pelvic	Normal
Skin		(Normal)
MS	Extremity	Normal
	Neck	Normal
	Back	Normal
Lymph	Neck: Normal	Groin: Normal Axilla: Normal
Psych	Judgment	Normal Orientation: (0 x 3)
	Mood/Affect	Normal Speech: Normal
Neuro	CN: II - XII	(Normal) Gait: Normal
	Motor	Normal Cerebellar: Normal
	DTRs	Normal Sensation: (Normal)

Labs: 5.0 > 10.6 / 34.2 < 182; AG 18; 143 | 101 | (66) / 3.7 | 24 | (7.8) < (137); 9.1 | 6.5 | 0.2 | 25 / 3.5 | 14 < 91; INR 0.9; aPTT 0.8

Pt stuttering spontaneously resolves & then recurs
⊕ tremulous occasional having full body twitching - stops when pt. hold extremities
strength 4/5 Ⓑ LE
⊕ Rhomberg. pt very unsteady when closes her eyes
Reflexes 1+ throughout

______ Resident/PA/NP ID #

______ Resident/PA/NP

MEDICAL RECORD

FIGURE 2-2. Emergency Room record.

MEDICAL DECISION MAKING

PLAN

Head CT
labs

Differential Dx:

1. Stroke
2. uremia
3. infection
4. drug side effect

1745 Renal (XH) 39842 called. will come to consult.

☑ Discussed history, plan or diagnosis with other provider.
☑ Prior medical records reviewed.
☑ Nursing / EMS notes reviewed.
☐ The patient was given: *IM / IV* medications or *IV fluids.*
☐ Patient referred for further care.

Radiology Results: ☐ ED interpretation ☐ Discussed with Radiologist

CT - No CT evidence of acute ischemia

EKG/Rhythm: NSR / Arrythmia: ______

ATTENDING PHYSICIAN NOTE: Time seen: 1100 AM / PM (circled PM)

☐ I was present with the resident/midlevel during the patient's history and physical and discussed their management with the resident. I have reviewed the resident's note above and agree with the documented findings and plan of care.
☑ I saw and evaluated the patient. I reviewed the resident/midlevel's note above and agree, in addition to/except that:

Additional findings:

s/p Renal Tx
c [illegible]
⊖ [illegible]
→ [illegible]

Procedure / Progress Note: Time:______ AM / PM **Consult:**______ Called: ______ AM / PM

No acute neurologic [illegible]
pt accepted to medicine for uremia

Provider: ______

Procedures: Central Venous / Intubation / LP / Suture / Chest tube / Nasal Pack / Sedation / Splint / I&D / Other: ______

Diagnosis:

1. Uremia
2. ______
3. ______
4. ______
5. ______
6. ______

☐ **See procedure documentation**
☐ **See additional documentation**

Critical Care Time: ______ minutes

Dispo: Discharge / Admit (circled) / Transfer / AMA
Condition: Stable / Good (circled) / Fair / Serious / Expired

Admission/Transfer Location: ______
Discharge time: ______ AM / PM Date:

Attendings: ______

MEDICAL RECORD

FIGURE 2-2, cont'd. Emergency Room record.

Admission History and Physical Examination

Admission history and physical documentation normally contains the following elements:

- Chief complaint (CC)
- History of the present illness (HPI)
- Past medical history
- Family medical history
- Social history
- Review of systems
- Physical examination
- Impression/Assessment
- Plan

See Figure 2-3 for an example of a history and physical form (H&P). The history and physical needs to be performed and documented within 24 hours of admission for an inpatient encounter.

Physician Orders

This is the area of the record in which the attending **physician**, as well as physician **consultants**, gives directives to the house staff and to nursing and ancillary services. Physician orders are dated, timed, and signed and become part of the record. Verbal orders by physicians are guided by medical staff regulations. See Figure 2-4 for an example of handwritten physician orders and Figure 2-5 for an electronic physician order.

Progress Notes

Progress notes are records of the course of a patient's hospital care. They are usually written by the attending physician (Figure 2-6, *A*). Academic medical centers may have notes written by medical students, interns, and residents, as well as attending physicians and consultants. Some facilities have integrated progress notes, which allow individuals from several disciplines to write in the same area of the record. An integrated progress note may include notes written by dietitians, physical therapists, respiratory therapists, and nurses.

Progress notes written by the attending physician are recorded on a daily basis; the frequency of such note taking is governed by medical staff regulations. These notes describe how the patient is progressing and put forth the plan of care for the patient. In an electronic patient record, these notes may be dictated and transcribed or typed by physicians themselves. Physicians are usually taught to document progress notes according to the SOAP format. SOAP stands for the following:

Subjective—The problem in the patient's own words (chief complaint)
Objective—The physician identifies the history, physical examination, and diagnostic test results
Assessment—Where the subjective and objective combine for a conclusion
Plan—Approach the physician is taking to solve the patient's problem

See Figure 2-6, *B,* for an example of a progress note written in SOAP format.

Nursing Notes

If nursing notes are not integrated, they are often found in their own section of the record on forms that lend themselves to the type of information nurses are required to document. Nursing notes usually consist of an admission note, graphic charts, medication/treatment records, and temperature, pulse, and respiration (TPR) sheets. See Figure 2-7 for an example of an electronic medication administration record (MAR) and Figure 2-8 for an example of laboratory results.

Anesthesia Forms

The anesthesiologist is required to write preanesthesia and postanesthesia notes. The anesthetic agent, amount given, administration technique used, duration of the procedure, amount of blood loss, fluids given, and any complications or additional procedures

Text continued on p. 22

ADMISSION NOTE

M.D.: Pager:

Date: Time:

Chief Complaint:
twitching

History of Present Illness:
This is a 51 year old woman with a history of lupus, lupus nephritis, and cadaveric renal transplant in 2000 who now presents with 2 weeks of worsening twitching. The patient describes starting neurontin for headaches approximately 3 weeks ago. She subsequently noted first subtle twitching of an extremity or her face. The movements have progressed to include difficulty speaking, dysarthria ("I couldn't say what I was thinking") and difficulty walking.

The patient has also noticed worsening fatigue, a change in her skin ("It's ashy") and worsening edema (including LE and peri-orbital).

On Friday the patient called the transplant nurse who recommended she come to the Emergency room. There, she was seen by neuro, who felt most of her symptoms were most likely related to worsening renal failure with gabapentin. They also noted b/l ptosis and findings suggestive of a peripheral neuropathy.

The patient reports no improvement in symptoms since arrival.

ED Course:
As above.

Primary MD:

Emergency Contact:

Code Status:

Review of Systems: (circled) positive ~~ABC~~ negative

Constitutional:
~~Fevers,~~ ~~Chills,~~ ~~Night Sweats,~~ (Fatigue) Weight Loss, Weight Gain, Heat Intolerance, Cold Intolerance

Neuro:
(Headache) ~~Seizures,~~ ~~Syncope,~~ ~~Lightheaded,~~ ~~Vertigo,~~ ~~Dizziness,~~ ~~Tremor,~~ ~~Weakness,~~ ~~Numbness,~~ ~~Tingling~~

HEENT:
~~Vision change,~~ (Diplopia) Cataracts, Glaucoma, Hearing Loss, Tinnitus, Sinusitis, ~~Sore Throat,~~ Polydipsia, Lymphadenopathy

CV:
~~Chest Pain,~~ ~~Palpitations,~~ ~~Orthopnea,~~ PND Claudication, Exercise Intolerance

Respiratory:
~~SOB,~~ Pleuritic Pain, Wheezing, ~~Cough~~ ~~Sputum,~~ Hemoptysis

GI:
~~Abdominal Pain,~~ ~~Nausea,~~ ~~Vomiting,~~ ~~Diarrhea,~~ ~~Constipation,~~ Jaundice, ~~Melena,~~ BRBPR, Dysphagia, Odynophagia, Reflux, Hematemesis

GU:
~~Dysuria,~~ Frequency, Urgency, Hesitancy, Incontinence, Hematuria, polyuria
LMP ________________

Skin/Skeletal:
(Rashes) (Bruising) Joint Stiffness/Pain, Myalgias

Psych:
~~Depression,~~ Mood Changes, SI, HI, Plan

X All other systems negative

FIGURE 2-3. History and physical.

Continued

M.D.: Pager:

Date: Time:

Past Medical History:
Lupus diagnosed 1991, h/o lupus arthritis and muscle pain
- No prior lupus involvement in brain
- No recent flairs

Social History:

Tobacco: none

Alcohol: none

Illicits: none

Residence: lives with daughter

Occupation: owned her own hair salon, now not working

Family: son and daughter in area

Other:

Allergies:
Zantac –> decreased muscle tone

Medications:
Imuran 150mg po qd
Prednisone 10mg po qd
Prograf 4mg po bid
nexium 40mg po qd
stresstab + zinc
folate 1mg po qd
Fe 300mg po tid
Toprol XL 100mg po qd
Calcitriol 0.5mg po q.o.d.
PhosLo 2 tab po TID
Aranesp 100 q.o.week
Lasix 40mg po bid
Clonidine 0.1mg po bid

Family History:
Mo - Kidney stones
No lupus, no renal failure

T_c afeb / T_m	HR 72	BP 140/80
RR 20 / Pain 0	SaO_2 98%	FiO_2 None
Wt	I/O	Dexi / Stool

FIGURE 2-3, cont'd. History and physical.

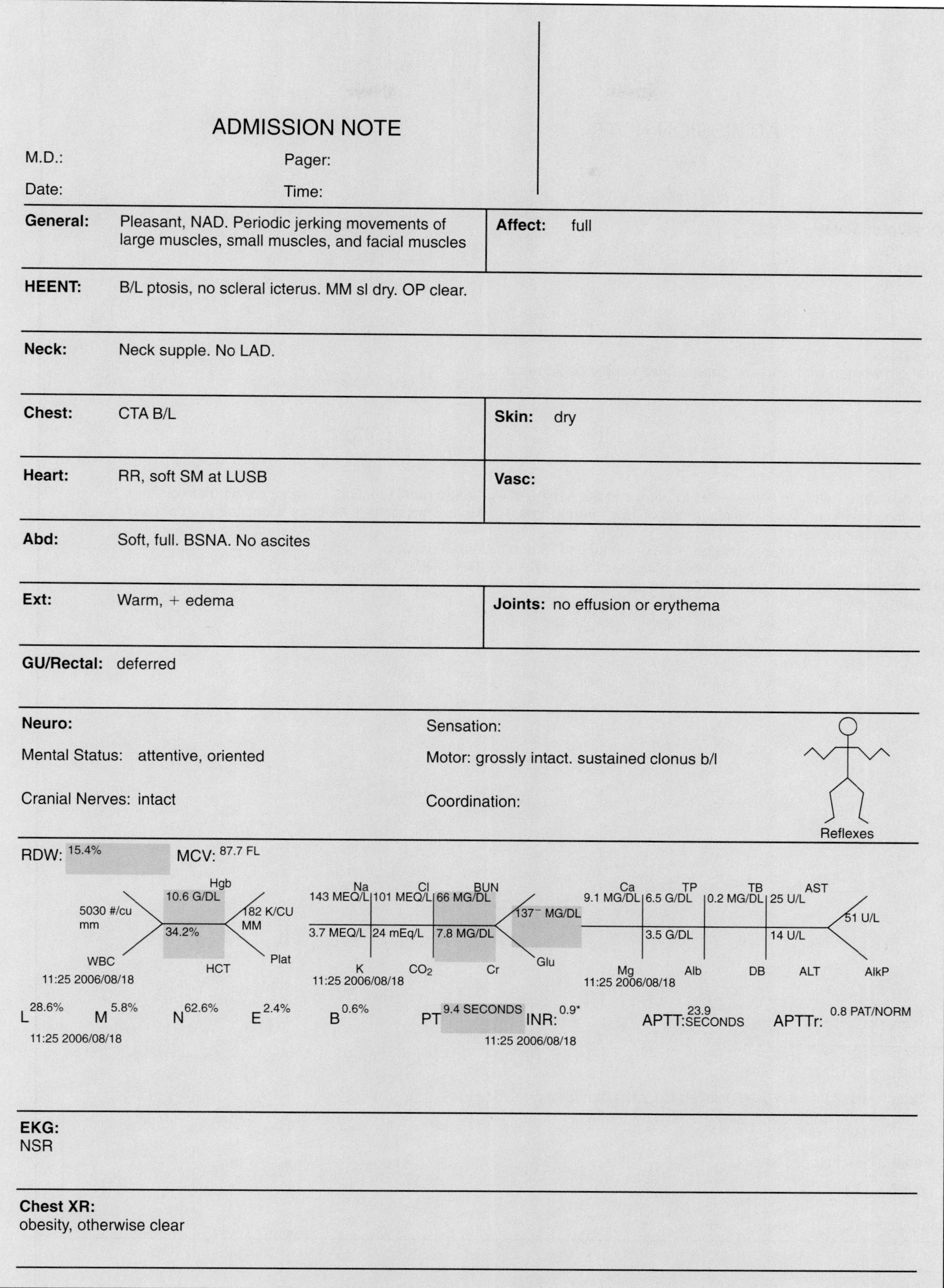

ADMISSION NOTE

M.D.: Pager:

Date: Time:

General: Pleasant, NAD. Periodic jerking movements of large muscles, small muscles, and facial muscles

Affect: full

HEENT: B/L ptosis, no scleral icterus. MM sl dry. OP clear.

Neck: Neck supple. No LAD.

Chest: CTA B/L

Skin: dry

Heart: RR, soft SM at LUSB

Vasc:

Abd: Soft, full. BSNA. No ascites

Ext: Warm, + edema

Joints: no effusion or erythema

GU/Rectal: deferred

Neuro:

Mental Status: attentive, oriented

Cranial Nerves: intact

Sensation:

Motor: grossly intact. sustained clonus b/l

Coordination:

Reflexes

RDW: 15.4% MCV: 87.7 FL

WBC 5030 #/cu mm; Hgb 10.6 G/DL; HCT 34.2%; Plat 182 K/CU MM

11:25 2006/08/18

Na 143 MEQ/L; Cl 101 MEQ/L; BUN 66 MG/DL; K 3.7 MEQ/L; CO_2 24 mEq/L; Cr 7.8 MG/DL; Glu 137⁻ MG/DL

11:25 2006/08/18

Ca 9.1 MG/DL; TP 6.5 G/DL; TB 0.2 MG/DL; AST 25 U/L; Mg [blank]; Alb 3.5 G/DL; DB [blank]; ALT 14 U/L; AlkP 51 U/L

11:25 2006/08/18

L 28.6% M 5.8% N 62.6% E 2.4% B 0.6%

11:25 2006/08/18

PT 9.4 SECONDS INR: 0.9* APTT: 23.9 SECONDS APTTr: 0.8 PAT/NORM

11:25 2006/08/18

EKG:
NSR

Chest XR:
obesity, otherwise clear

FIGURE 2-3, cont'd. History and physical.

Continued

ADMISSION NOTE

M.D.: Pager:

Date: Time:

Radiographic Data:

Impression

51 year old woman with worsening renal failure and muscle twitching.

Plan:

1. Neuro-Muscle twitching is likely due to uremia in the setting of worsened renal function. Suspect contribution of gabapentin, which can cause twitching and is correlated in time. Plan is to start dialysis Monday. Continue prograf (can stop monday per renal).
2. Renal-Continue prograf, nephrovite, phoslo. Renal diet. Renal has seen patient.
3. Rheum-Continue Imuran. No evidence of acute flair, but check ESR & CRP. Continue prednisone.
4. HTN-Continue clonidine, toprol, nifedipine qd.
5. Dispo-See PMD.

DVT Prophylaxis? heparin 5000 units sq bid, stop Sun for dialysis Monday

1. Trembling paralysis

2. Renal failure, unspecified

3. HTN [Hypertension]

4. Lupus nephritis

Date:

FIGURE 2-3, cont'd. History and physical.

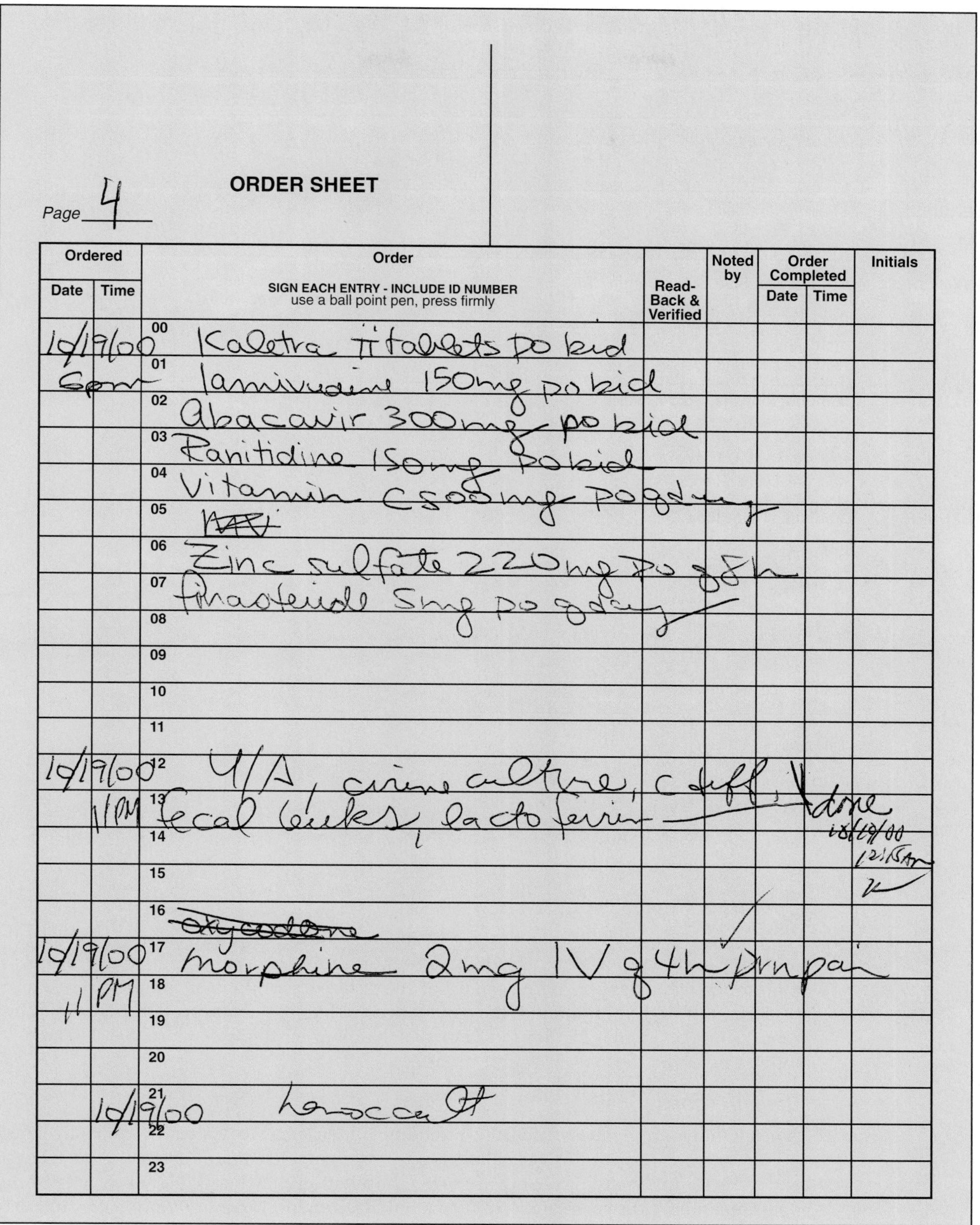

Page 4

ORDER SHEET

Ordered			Order	Read-Back & Verified	Noted by	Order Completed		Initials
Date	Time		SIGN EACH ENTRY - INCLUDE ID NUMBER use a ball point pen, press firmly			Date	Time	
10/19/00		00	Kaletra ii tablets po bid					
	6pm	01	lamivudine 150mg po bid					
		02	abacavir 300mg po bid					
		03	Ranitidine 150mg po bid					
		04	Vitamin C 500mg po qday					
		05	~~NAV~~					
		06	Zinc sulfate 220mg po q8h					
		07	finasteride 5mg po qday					
		08						
		09						
		10						
		11						
10/19/00		12	U/A, urine culture, c diff,					
	11PM	13	fecal leuks, lactoferrin					done
		14						10/19/00
		15						12:15Am
		16	~~oxycodone~~					
10/19/00		17	morphine 2mg IV q4h prn pain					
	11PM	18						
		19						
		20						
	10/19/00	21	[illegible]					
		22						
		23						

FIGURE 2-4. Handwritten physician orders.

Cumulative Order Summary

Orders: ____________________

Med Rec No: ____________________

Location: ____________________ Birth date: __________ Age: _____

Atn: ______________________________ Sex: _____

ALLERGIES:	Swelling-dexamethasone			
Ord #	**Order name/description**	**Start date**	**Ord status**	**Stop date**
001BXMXJH	**Immunofixation-Electro, Serum LAB** Entered DT/TM: ____________________ Auth prescriber: ____________________ Auth prescriber number: ____________	__________	1 or more final results received	
001BXMXJJ	**Immunoglobulins, Serum LAB** Entered DT/TM: ____________________ Auth prescriber: ____________________ Auth prescriber number: ____________	__________	1 or more final results received	
001BXNBHF	**Transfuse Red Blood Cells** Start date: ________, urgency: when available, transfuse 2 consent obtained units. Transfuse each unit over 2 hours, in dialysis. When the patient is ready and the product is available, call or fax blood bank for delivery. with dialysis ________ Entered DT/TM: ____________________ Auth prescriber: ____________________ Auth prescriber number: ____________	__________	Completed	____________

FIGURE 2-5. Electronic physician order.

performed by the anesthesiologist must be documented. See Figure 2-9 for an example of anesthesia documentation.

Operative Report

An operative report (OP Report) must be included in the health record for patients who undergo surgical procedures. The operative report should include a preoperative diagnosis, a postoperative diagnosis, dates, names of surgeons, descriptions of findings, procedures performed, and the condition of the patient at completion of the procedure. The operative report must be written or dictated immediately following the procedure. See Figure 2-10 for a sample of a dictated operative report.

Consultations

Consultations are requested by the attending physician who wishes to gain an expert opinion on treatment of a particular aspect of the patient's condition that is outside the expertise of the attending. A preoperative consultation may be requested as part of the determination of the surgical risk of the patient. Information acquired during consults may be integrated within progress notes or recorded on a separate consult report.

Laboratory, Radiology, and Pathology Reports

Laboratory data are often captured electronically. Laboratory data would include such items as complete blood count (CBC), urinalysis, and metabolic levels. Radiology reports are

Text continued on p. 32

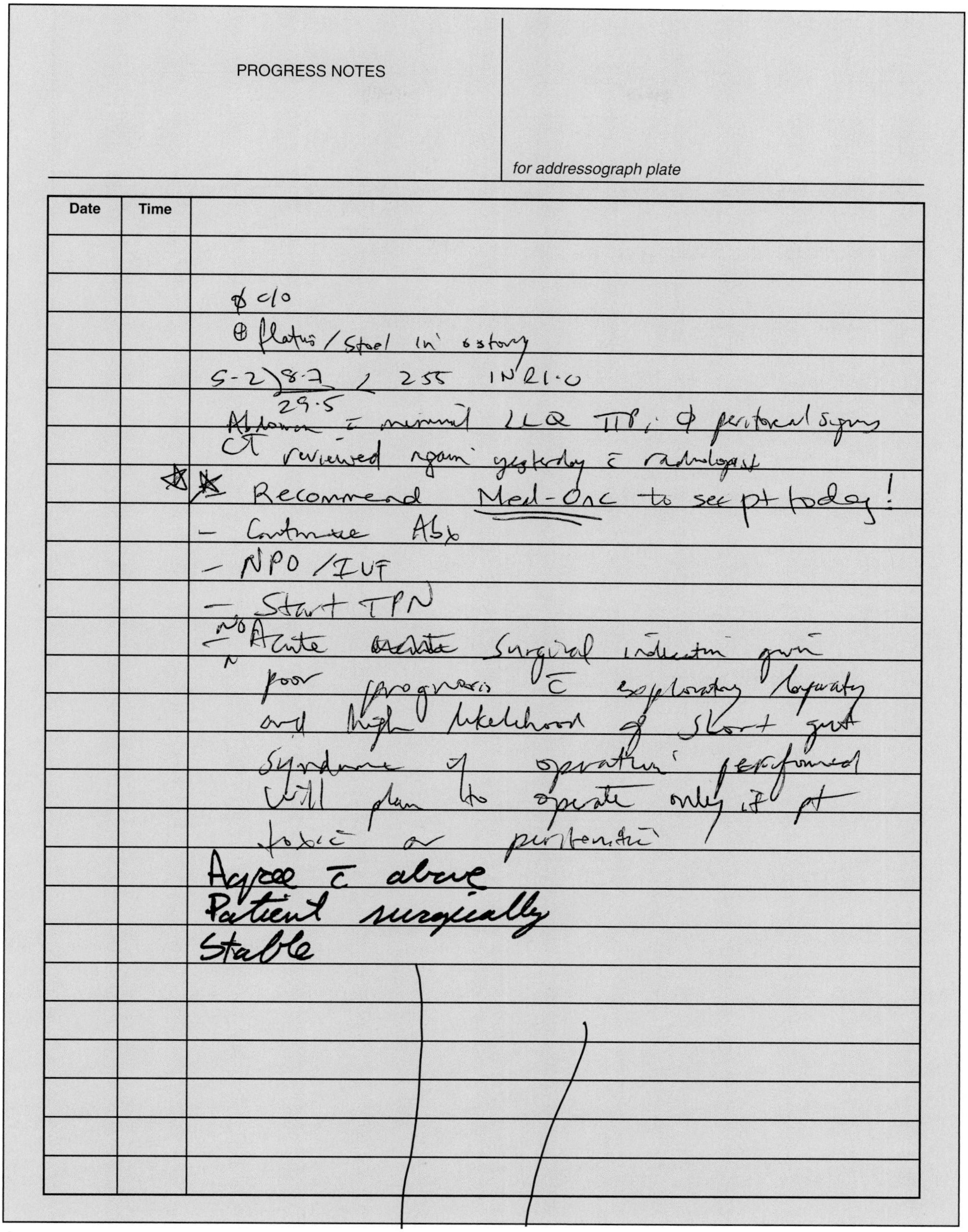

PROGRESS NOTES

for addressograph plate

Date	Time	
		ø c/o
		⊕ flatus / stool in ostomy
		S-2) 8.7 / 29.5 < 255 INR 1.0
		Abdomen c̄ minimal LLQ TTP; ø peritoneal signs
		CT reviewed again yesterday c̄ radiologist
		✱ Recommend Med-Onc to see pt today!
		– Continue Abx
		– NPO / IVF
		– Start TPN
		– No Acute surgical indication given poor prognosis c̄ exploratory laparotomy and high likelihood of short gut syndrome if operation performed. Will plan to operate only if pt toxic or peritonitic
		Agree c̄ above
		Patient surgically Stable

A

FIGURE 2-6. **A,** Progress notes.

Continued

Page 1

Patient information

[can use hospital plate]

Inpatient Progress Note

Evaluation type: ☒ Followup care ☐ Discharge note

Meds
Lepirudin
Protonix
Odansetron
Dilaudid PCA
Aspart Insulin Sliding Scale

Clinical information

S| Tearful; c/o pain in abd.

O| VS: 37.1 18 95 108/71 97%

(-)icterus

ABD: distended (mod).
Well appearing incision
c/d/i c̄ steristrips

EXT: ⊖edema

Assessment & plan:

HD#10 c̄ Budd Chiari 2° PCV s/p surgical shunt (mesocaval) c̄ bx.

- cont. current management bridging anticoag c̄ Lepirudin given h/o HIT until ~~ok to start~~ Coumadin c̄ therapeutic INR

Assistant: ______ (Signature) ______ (Print) MD #: ______ Date: ______
(If involved) ☐ Fellow ☐ Resident ☐ NP ☐ PA

Attending: ______ (Signature) ______ (Print) MD #: ______ Date/time ______

(7/03)

B

FIGURE 2-6, cont'd. **B,** SOAP progress note.

Medication Administration Record

Med Rec No: ______________________
Visit ID No: ______________________

Location: ________________ Age: ______ Sex: _______

Atn DR: ____________________ Birthday: ___________

ALLERGIES: Swelling-dexamethasone

Scheduled

Medications	Doses	Comments
Routine **Hydroxychloroquine enteral** 200 mg PO bid routine. Administer with food or milk. **Start:** __________ **Stop:** __________	**Ord #: 001BXCBQV** **(Continued...)** Performed __________ 13:00 __________ (RN) Performed __________ 22:00 __________ (RN)	
Routine **Labetalol enteral** 400 mg PO bid, routine **Start:** __________ **Stop:** __________	**Ord #: 001BXTZQD** Not performed– __________ 13:00 __________ (RN) Physician request... Canceled	
Routine **Levothyroxine enteral** 100 mcg PO daily routine **Start:** __________ **Stop:** __________	**Ord #: 001BXBJST** Performed __________ 13:00 __________ (RN)	
Routine **Lisinopril enteral** 40 mg PO daily routine **Start:** __________ **Stop:** __________	**Ord #: 001BXTKKD** Performed __________ 13:00 __________ (RN)	

FIGURE 2-7. Medication administration record.

Laboratory Results

Component	Low range	High range	Range units	16:00:00
Sodium	135	148	mEq/L	140
Potassium, serum	3.5	5.0	mEq/L	4.3
Chloride	99	111	mEq/L	104
Urea-nitrogen	7	22	mg/dL	11
Glucose	60	99	mg/dL	91*
Creatinine, serum	0.5	1.2	mg/dL	0.5
Calcium	8.4	10.5	mg/dL	9.6
Total protein	6.0	8.2	g/dL	7.4
Albumin	3.5	5.3	g/dL	4.6
Total bilirubin	0.1	1.2	mg/dL	0.3
Alanine amino trans	0	31	U/L	5
Aspartate amino tran	0	31	U/L	16
Alkaline phosphatase	100	320	U/L	92
CO_2	21	31	mEq/L	27
Anion gap	11	20	mEq/L	13
Sun/creat ratio				22
Ast/alt ratio				3.2
Est Gfr (Afr Amer)			mL/min/A	Text*
Est Gfr (non-Afr-Am)			mL/min/A	Text*

FIGURE 2-8. Laboratory results.

Anesthesia Preoperative Assessment

PLEASE WRITE LEGIBLY

PROCEDURE FEMORAL INTRAMEDULLAR ROD

DIAGNOSIS (Rt) Leg Shortening

MEDICATIONS

None

for addressograph plate

ALLERGIES (drug/environmental/food) NKDA

PAIN HISTORY ☒ Negative
Intensity (0-10) ____
Location ____
Affect quality of life? ☐ Y ☐ N
Pain meds effective? ☐ Y ☐ N
Alleviating / Aggravating factors ____
Quality: Sharp / dull / other ____
Onset / duration ____

Anesthesia Issues ☐ Negative
☐ Difficult Airway
☐ By exam ☐ By history
☐ TMJ problems
☐ Snoring (circled) ☐ OSA mild
☐ Hoarseness
☐ Nasal obstruction
☐ Stridor/croup
☐ Fam Hx Anesth Problems
☐ Malignant Hyperthermia
☐ Obesity
☐ Post-op nausea/vomiting
☐ Organ transplant ____

Cardiovascular ☒ Negative
☐ Myocard infarct: Date ____
☐ Hypertension
☐ Arrhythmia: type ____
☐ Pacemaker ☐ AICD
☐ Angina: ☐ stable ☐ unstable
☐ CHF: Date ____ EF ___ %
☐ Valve disease: ____
☐ Mod ☐ Severe
☐ Peripheral vascular disease
☐ Past cardiac surgery
☐ Angioplasty
☐ Deep vein thrombus
☐ Pulmonary embolus
☐ Heart murmur
☐ Stress test/cardiac cath
Detail results below

Denies cyanosis or diaphoresis c̄ Activity

Pulmonary ☒ Negative
☐ Smoking hx ☐ current ___ ppd
☐ Asthma
☐ Hospitalized ☐ Steroid use
☐ Recent wheezing
☐ COPD/BPD
☐ Cough: active / chronic
☐ Other

Renal ☒ Negative
☐ Renal insufficiency
☐ Dialysis
☐ Other

Hepatic ☒ Negative
☐ Hepatitis
☐ Cirrhosis
☐ Other

Endocrine ☒ Negative
☐ Diabetes
☐ Thyroid
☐ Steroid usage
☐ Other

Infections ☐ Negative
☐ SBE prophylaxis
☐ HIV ☐ Sepsis ☐ URI
☐ VRE
☐ MRSA: contact / resp.

Immunized to date

Neurologic ☒ Negative
☐ Seizure
☐ Elevated ICP ☐ Shunt
☐ Spinal cord injury
☐ CVA/TIA
☐ Cerebral palsy
☐ Mental retardation
☐ Chronic pain
☐ Neuropathy/paresthesia
☐ Myopathy/muscular dystrophy
☐ Syncope
☐ Hearing loss
☐ Blind: right / left
☐ Other

Gastrointestinal ☒ Negative
☐ GE reflux / hiatal hernia
☐ Bowel obstruction ☐ Ascites
☐ Ulcers
☐ GI bleed
☐ Dysphagia
☐ Other

Hematol/Onc ☒ Negative
☐ Sickle cell disease ☐ Trait
☐ Coagulopathy
☐ Anemia
☐ Past transfusion
☐ Refuses transfusion
☐ Tumor ____
☐ Chemo/Rad therapy

Obstetrics ☐ Negative
☐ Preeclampsia/eclampsia
☐ Placenta previa/abruptio
☐ LMP 7/9/06 ☐ HCG ____
☐ Other

Drug Use ☒ Negative
☐ ETOH ☐ Daily
☐ Never ☐ Occasional
☐ IVDA ☐ Cocaine
☐ Other

Activity Level
☐ Bedridden
☐ Assistance with self-care
☐ <1 flight of stairs
☐ 1–3 flights of stairs
☒ >3 flights of stairs
☒ Able to lie flat one hour

Pediatrics ☐ Negative
☐ Prematurity
☐ Congenital abnl.
☐ Apnea
☐ Passive smoking
☐ Other

FTVD in China

Day of Surgery:
NPO since 10 p.m.

DETAILS OF PRESENT ILLNESS AND PAST MEDICAL HISTORY

16 y.o. ♀ for leg length shortening, ∅ PMH.

PREVIOUS SURGERY AND ANESTHESIA ☒ NONE

140 | 104 | 11 / 4.3 | 27 | 0.5 < 91 4.7 > 12.4 / 37.4 < 232 hcg ⊖

LABS / ECG

BP Range (R) 109/60 (L) 103/54 P 86 R ____ T 36.9 WT 46.4 (lbs/kg) HT 5′ 0″ (in/cm) Room Air Sat 100% Age 16 M/(F)

HISTORY PERFORMED BY: ____ ID Number ____ DATE ____ TIME ____

CHART COPY page 1 of 2

FIGURE 2-9. Anesthesia record.

PRE-ANESTHESIA / PRE-OPERATIVE ASSESSMENT
PAGE 2

PLEASE WRITE LEGIBLY

for addressograph plate

Physical Examination

HEENT Normocephaly, NO oral lesions MP=I
Neck: supple c FROM midline trachea
Cardiovascular RRR $S_1 S_2$ NO murmurs or clicks.
Lungs Bil CTA
Pain sites / Pertinent other A OX3 accompanied by Father NAD.
NPO p 12mn Instructions and directions to CAOS were given to pt's Father instruction to avoid NSAIDS preop were given as well to Father

Physical exam performed by: ______ ID Number ______ Date ______ Time ______

ANESTHESIA ATTENDING PRE-ANESTHESIA ASSESSMENT AND CONSENT

Medical record and laboratory data reviewed ☑ Patient examined ☑

Patient is appropriate for the planned anesthesia:
General ☑ Spinal ☐
Regional block ☐ Epidural/caudal ☑
Monitored anesthesia care ☐ Other ☐ ______
Special monitoring ☐

Planned post-operative care: PACU ☑ ICU ☐ Other ☐

ASA STATUS | 1 (marked) | 2 | 3 | 4 | 5 | 6 | E |

Airway Assessment:
Oral excursion: FB 1☐ 2☐ 3☐ 4☐
T-M distance: FB 1☐ 2☐ 3☐ 4☐ Class I
Dentition: Upper nl☐ dentures☐ caps☐ decayed☐ loose☐
Lower nl☐ dentures☐ caps☐ decayed☐ loose☐
Mallampati: I☐ II☐ III☐ IV☐
Neck Extension: nl☐ 7☐ 77☐
Flexion: nl☐ 7☐ 77☐

16 yo ♂ for Ⓡ leg shortening
Ⓡ leg length discrepancy
otherwise healthy ⊖ heart/lung hx
ASA I for GOTA / epidural for postop analgesia
NO Ad
NO meds

☐ Informed consent not obtained due to the emergent condition of the patient.

The plan for anesthesia and postoperative pain management, their alternatives, and the risks and benefits of these plans and alternatives have been explained to me and my questions have been answered to my satisfaction. I give my consent.

Signature of Patient / Parent / Guardian, Health Care Agent ______ Telephone consent witness ______ Signature of health care provider securing consent ______

Anesthesiologist Signature ______ **ID Number** ______ **Date** ______ **Time** ______

SURGICAL ATTENDING PRE-OPERATIVE ASSESSMENT–to be completed by surgeon if used as a surgical history and physical

CHIEF COMPLAINT ______

FAMILY HISTORY ______ SOCIAL HISTORY ______

Pre-operative history, physical exam, and pertinent laboratory data reviewed by me with amendments as follows: ☐ NONE

Preoperative diagnosis: ______

Planned procedure: ______

Surgeon Signature ______ **ID Number** ______ **Date** ______ **Time** ______

CHART COPY

page 2 of 2

FIGURE 2-9, cont'd. Anesthesia record.

Continued

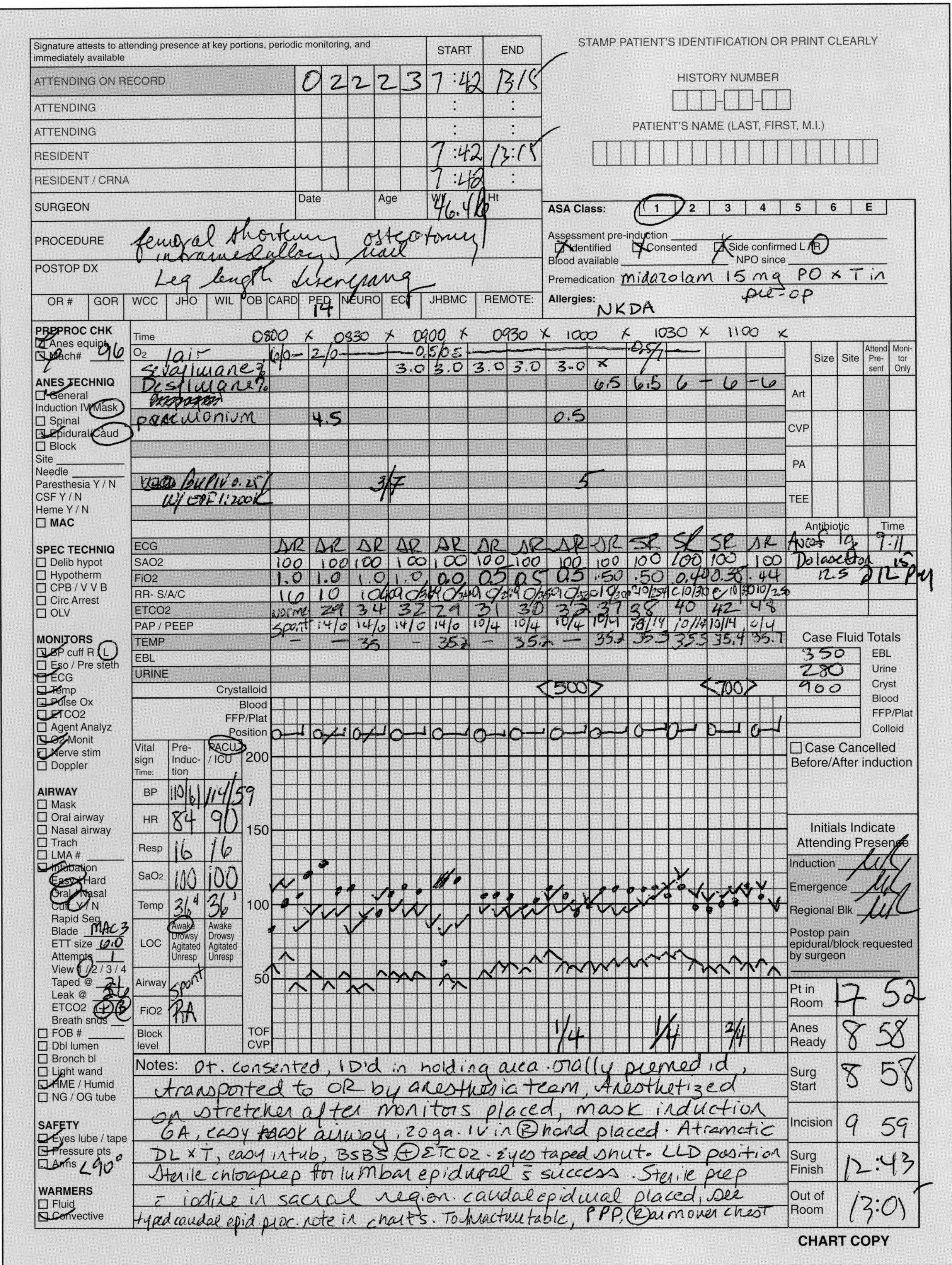

Signature attests to attending presence at key portions, periodic monitoring, and immediately available

		START	END
ATTENDING ON RECORD	02223	7:42	13:15
ATTENDING		:	:
ATTENDING		:	:
RESIDENT		7:42	13:15
RESIDENT / CRNA		7:42	:
SURGEON	Date	Age	Wt 46.4 kg	Ht

STAMP PATIENT'S IDENTIFICATION OR PRINT CLEARLY

HISTORY NUMBER

PATIENT'S NAME (LAST, FIRST, M.I.)

ASA Class: (1) 2 3 4 5 6 E

Assessment pre-induction: ☒ Identified ☒ Consented ☒ Side confirmed L / (R)

Blood available ___ NPO since ___

Premedication: midazolam 15 mg PO x T in pre-op

Allergies: NKDA

PROCEDURE: femoral shortening osteotomy intramedullary nail

POSTOP DX: Leg length discrepancy

OR # | GOR | WCC | JHO | WIL | OB | CARD | PED 14 | NEURO | ECT | JHBMC | REMOTE:

PREPROC CHK: ☒ Anes equip ☒ Mach# 96

ANES TECHNIQ: ☒ General; Induction IV / (Mask); ☐ Spinal; ☒ Epidural / (Caud); ☐ Block; Site; Needle; Paresthesia Y / N; CSF Y / N; Heme Y / N; ☐ MAC

SPEC TECHNIQ: ☐ Delib hypot ☐ Hypotherm ☐ CPB / V V B ☐ Circ Arrest ☐ OLV

MONITORS: ☒ BP cuff R (L) ☐ Eso / Pre steth ☒ ECG ☒ Temp ☒ Pulse Ox ☒ ETCO2 ☐ Agent Analyz ☒ O2 Monit ☒ Nerve stim ☐ Doppler

AIRWAY: ☐ Mask ☐ Oral airway ☐ Nasal airway ☐ Trach ☐ LMA # ☒ Intubation; Easy / Hard; Oral / Nasal; Cuff Y / N; Rapid Seq; Blade MAC 3; ETT size 6.0; Attempts 1; View (1) / 2 / 3 / 4; Taped @ 21; Leak @ ; ETCO2 (+); Breath snds (+); ☐ FOB # ☐ Dbl lumen ☐ Bronch bl ☐ Light wand ☒ HME / Humid ☐ NG / OG tube

SAFETY: ☒ Eyes lube / tape ☒ Pressure pts ☒ Arms < 90°

WARMERS: ☐ Fluid ☒ Convective

Time: 0800 x 0830 x 0900 x 0930 x 1000 x 1030 x 1100 x

O2	1 air	1/0 — 2/0		0.5/0.5					0.5/1				
Sevoflurane %			3.0	3.0	3.0	3.0	3.0	x					
Desflurane %								6.5	6.5	6	6	6	
pancuronium		4.5					0.5						
bupiv 0.25% w/ epi 1:200k			3/7				5						
ECG	AR	AR	AR	AR	AR	AR	AR	AR	SR	SR	SR	SR	AR
SAO2	100	100	100	100	100	100	100	100	100	100	100	100	100
FiO2	1.0	1.0	1.0	1.0	0.0	0.5	0.5	0.5	.50	.50	0.40	0.35	.44
RR- S/A/C	16	10	[illegible]										
ETCO2	normal	29	34	32	29	31	30	32	37	38	40	42	48
PAP / PEEP	spont	14/0	14/0	14/0	14/0	10/4	10/4	10/4	10/4	10/4	10/4	10/4	0/4
TEMP	—	—	35	—	35.2	—	35.2	—	35.2	35.3	35.3	35.4	35.1
EBL													
URINE													
Crystalloid						<500>					<700>		

Blood; FFP/Plat; Position

Vital sign	Pre-Induction	PACU / ICU
BP	110/61	114/59
HR	84	90
Resp	16	16
SaO2	100	100
Temp	36.4	36.1
LOC	(Awake) Drowsy Agitated Unresp	Awake Drowsy Agitated Unresp
Airway		spont
FiO2		RA
Block level		

200 / 150 / 100 / 50; TOF CVP: 1/4, 1/4, 2/4

	Size	Site	Attend Present	Monitor Only
Art				
CVP				
PA				
TEE				

Antibiotic	Time
Ancef 1g	9:11
Dolasetron 12.5	15 / 2:12 PM

Case Fluid Totals

350	EBL
280	Urine
900	Cryst
	Blood
	FFP/Plat
	Colloid

☐ Case Cancelled Before/After induction

Initials Indicate Attending Presence: Induction [initials]; Emergence [initials]; Regional Blk [initials]; Postop pain epidural/block requested by surgeon

Pt in Room	7 52
Anes Ready	8 58
Surg Start	8 58
Incision	9 59
Surg Finish	12:43
Out of Room	13:01

Notes: Pt. consented, ID'd in holding area. Orally premed'd, transported to OR by anesthesia team, Anesthetized on stretcher after monitors placed, mask induction GA, easy mask airway, 20ga. IV in (R) hand placed. Atraumatic DL x T, easy intub, BSBS (+) ETCO2. Eyes taped shut. LLD position Sterile chloraprep for lumbar epidural c̄ success. Sterile prep c̄ iodine in sacral region. caudal epidural placed, see typed caudal epid. proc. note in charts. To fracture table, PPP, (R) arm over chest

CHART COPY

FIGURE 2-9, cont'd. Anesthesia record.

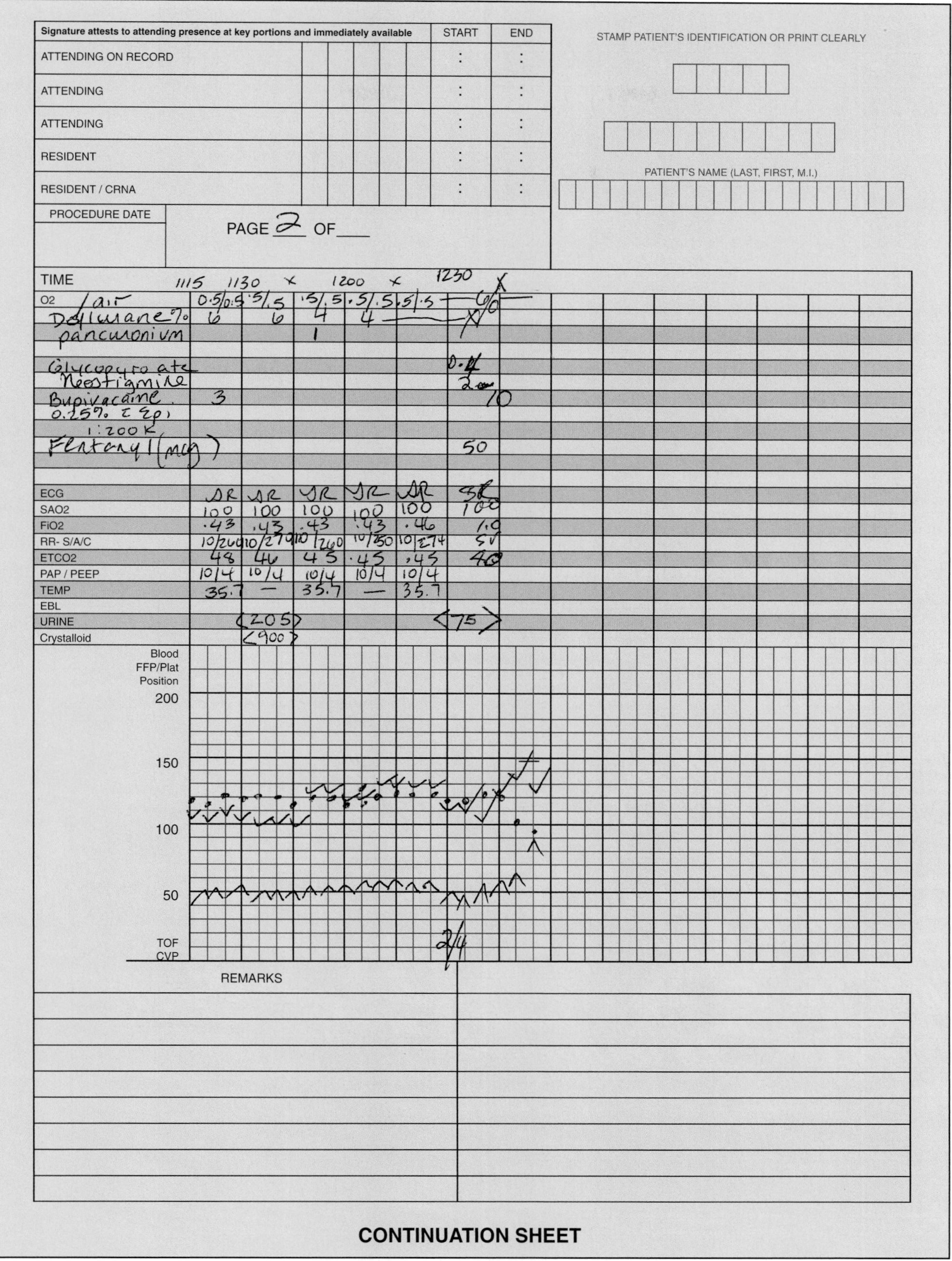

Signature attests to attending presence at key portions and immediately available	START	END
ATTENDING ON RECORD	:	:
ATTENDING	:	:
ATTENDING	:	:
RESIDENT	:	:
RESIDENT / CRNA	:	:

STAMP PATIENT'S IDENTIFICATION OR PRINT CLEARLY

PATIENT'S NAME (LAST, FIRST, M.I.)

PROCEDURE DATE

PAGE 2 OF ___

TIME	1115	1130	×	1200	×	1230	X
O2 /air	0.5/0.5	.5/.5	.5/.5	.5/.5	.5/.5		0/0
Desflurane %	6	6	4	4			X
pancuronium			1				
Glycopyrrolate						0.4	
Neostigmine						2	
Bupivacaine 0.25% c Epi 1:200K	3					10	
Fentanyl (mcg)						50	
ECG	SR	SR	SR	SR	SR	SR	
SAO2	100	100	100	100	100	100	
FiO2	.43	.43	.43	.43	.46	1.0	
RR- S/A/C	10/260	10/279	10/260	10/250	10/274	SV	
ETCO2	48	46	45	.45	.45	40	
PAP / PEEP	10/4	10/4	10/4	10/4	10/4		
TEMP	35.7	—	35.7	—	35.7		
EBL							
URINE		<205>				<75>	
Crystalloid		<900>					

REMARKS

CONTINUATION SHEET

FIGURE 2-9, cont'd. Anesthesia record.

Continued

Patient name ______________________________ History # ________________

TIME	pH	pCO2	pO2	HCO3	Na	K	Ca	Glu	HGB				

AS A Physical Status Classification
1: A normal, healthy patient
2: A patient with mild systemic disease
3. A patient with severe systemic disease
4: A patient with severe systemic disease that is a threat to life
5. A moribund patient, not expected to survive without the operation
6: A declared dead patient for organ donation
E: An emergency operation

SYMBOLS		POSITION	TABLE FLAT	OTHER POS.
NIBP	X	Supine		Sitting
PULSE	•—•	Prone		Lithotomy
ART BP	╪	Lateral L down		Jackknife
MAP	><	Lateral R down		

CRITERIA FOR DISCHARGE DIRECTLY TO NURSING UNIT	CRITERIA MET	RETURN TO BASELINE
Level of consciousness–awake, alert appropriately conversant or baseline		
Return to usual pattern of mobility or as appropriate per procedure		
BP within normal range. There is no evidence of severe hyper- or hypotension		
Pulse rate (60–100 adults / 80–150 pediatrics) and rhythm regular or baseline		
Respiratory rate: 12–20 (>3 years); 20–40 (<3 years) and pattern normal		
Oxygen saturation >93% or comparable to baseline		
Ability to swallow secretions or baseline		
Dressings, tubes and drains intact with amount of drainage appropriate for procedure		

DISCHARGE TO: Signature Dr. # Date Time

Intraop and Post Anesthesia Notes: Stable during procedure
fuctomed/extubated in OR
after reversal of paralysis —
Given c̄ 2/4 twitches on TOF
(+) sust. tetanus, following commands, strong
hand grip.
Alert/awake to PACU O2 FM. Spont vent.
Mild pain (R) leg. Epidural had just been
redosed + is now connected to infusion.
Report given. No complications

☒ Responsibility for patient management and monitoring after transport and report transferred to: PACU / ICU / Other ________

Signature ________ Provider No. ________ Date ________ Time ________

☐ Transfer of care accepted in ICU:

Signature ________ Provider No. ________ Date ________ Time ________

FIGURE 2-9, cont'd. Anesthesia record.

Operative Report

PATIENT NAME: Sonia Sample
ROOM NUMBER: 222 West
MR NUMBER: 12-34-56

DATE OF PROCEDURE: 04/22/00
PREOPERATIVE DIAGNOSIS: Acute cholecystitis
POSTOPERATIVE DIAGNOSIS: Acute cholecystitis
NAME OF PROCEDURE: 1. Laparoscopic cholecystectomy
2. Intraoperative cystic duct cholangiogram
SURGEON:
ASSISTANT:
ANESTHESIOLOGIST:
ANESTHESIA: General
DESCRIPTION OF THE OPERATION:

The patient was placed in the supine position under general anesthesia. The oral gastric tube was placed. The Foley catheter was placed. The patient received appropriate antibiotics. The abdomen was prepped with iodine and draped in the usual fashion. Using a midline subumbilical incision, we entered the subcutaneous fat to find the aponeurosis of the rectus abdominis. Two stay sutures were placed 0.5 cm from the midline bilaterally and we left on these sutures, creating an opening in the linea alba.

Under direct vision, the catheter was placed. The Hasson cannula was placed in the abdominal cavity and all was normal except an acute necrotizing and probably gangrenous gallbladder. There were multiple omental adhesions. Three other trocars were placed in the right subcostal plane in the midline, midclavicular line, and midaxillary line using a #10, #5, and #5 mm trocar, respectively. The gallbladder was punctured and emptied of clear white bile indicating a hydrops of the gallbladder. It was grasped at its fundus and at Hartmann's pouch retracted cephalad and to the right, respectively. We found the cystic duct and the cystic artery after circumferential dissection and isolated the cystic duct completely.

When we were sure that this structure was a deep cystic duct, the clip was placed at this most distal aspect to make an opening immediately proximally and we placed a Reddick cholangiocatheter into it via #14 gauge percutaneous catheter. The cholangiogram showed normal arborization of the liver radicals. Normal bifurcation of the common hepatic duct. Normal common hepatic duct. Long large cystic duct. The common bile duct had numerous stones within it. They could not be emptied from the common bile duct. There was good flow into the duodenum.

The impression was choledocholithiasis. This was corroborated by the radiologist. The decision was made to prepare the patient most probably for endoscopic retrograde cholangiopancreatography postoperatively, and no further intervention of the common bile duct was done in this setting.

The cholangiocatheter was removed. An attempt was made to milk the bile out but no stones came out. Three clips were placed on the proximal aspect of the cystic duct and the duct was then cut distally. The artery was isolated and double clipped proximally and single clipped distally and cut in the intervening section. We then peeled the gallbladder off the gallbladder bed with some difficulty because of the intense edema and inflammation. It was then removed from the liver bed completely. Cautery, suctioning and irrigation were used copiously to create a bloodless field. A last check was made and there was no bleeding and no bile leaking. A #15 Jackson-Pratt type drain was placed into Morrison's pouch and brought out through the lateral most port. We then removed, with great difficulty, the gallbladder from the umbilicus. Because of its enormous size and a 3 cm stone within it that was very difficult to macerate, the opening of the umbilicus had to be enlarged.

As this was done, we removed the gallbladder completely and sent it for pathologic section. Two separate figure-of-eight 0 PDS were used to close the abdominal fascia. The Jackson-Pratt drain was then sutured in place with 2.0 nylon. The skin was closed throughout with subcuticular 3-0 PDS after copious irrigation of the subcutaneous plane. Mastisol and Steri-Strips were placed on the wound. The patient remained stable although she did have bigeminy during surgery and was on a Lidocaine drip. She will be going to the intensive care unit but as she left, she was extubated in the recovery room and was fully alert. She is moving all limbs.

I will discuss with the gastroenterologist postoperative endoscopic retrograde cholangiopancreatography.

SPECIMEN: Gallbladder.

____
Surgeon

FIGURE 2-10. Operative report.

Radiology Report

EXAM DATE:
HISTORY NUMBER:
AGE: SEX: RACE:
REQUESTER:

EXAM: MHM 1006-MRI, brain w/wo cont w/diff
RESULT:
SYMPTOMS: Acute change in mental status.
MEDICAL/SURGICAL HISTORY: Pancreatic cancer, bacteremia.
SUSPECTED DIAGNOSIS: Mets.

TECHNIQUE: Sagittal T1, axial T2, axial FLAIR, and post-contrast axial and coronal T1 through brain. Magnevist (0.1 mmol/kg) injected intravenously without complication. Diffusion images obtained.

FINDINGS:
Minimal cerebral atrophy with expected ventricular dilatation appropriate for age.

Minimal scattered foci of increased T2 signal are noted in the periventricular and subcortical white matter and brainstem, cerebellar peduncles which are nonspecific but likely reflective of small vessel ischemia. Old lacunar infarcts noted in the posterior limb of the right internal capsule/right thalamus.

No evidence of mass, hemorrhage, midline shift, or abnormal enhancement. Ventricles and sulci are normal in size, shape, and position. No abnormal intra or extra axial fluid collection. Normal flow voids in carotid and basilar arteries. Normal scalp, calvarium, orbits. Trace ethmoid and maxillary sinus disease. Minimal left mastoiditis.

IMPRESSION:
Minimal cerebral atrophy with expected ventricular dilatation appropriate for age.

Chronic ischemic disease.
Old lacunar infarcts.

Minimal left mastoiditis.

FIGURE 2-11. Radiology report.

increasingly captured electronically, and the physician may often find the actual image available electronically. Pathology reports consist of a gross description of the tissue removed and microscopic evaluation that includes the diagnosis. See Figures 2-8 and 2-11 for examples of these types of reports.

Discharge Summary

The discharge summary (Figure 2-12) is a summary of the patient's stay in the hospital. It should include the following:

- History of the present illness
- Past medical history
- Significant findings
- Pertinent laboratory data
- Procedures performed or treatment rendered
- Final diagnosis
- Discharge instructions; medications and the condition of the patient on discharge

Discharge Summary

PATIENT NAME: Sonia Sample
MR NUMBER: 12-34-56

ADMISSION DATE: 04/19/00
DISCHARGE DATE: 04/27/00
ADMITTING IMPRESSION: Acute abdominal pain, rule out diverticulitis.
HISTORY OF PRESENT ILLNESS:
The patient is a 57-year-old white female who has history of hypertension, valvular heart disease, and cardiomyopathy, who was seen in the emergency room with complaints of acute abdominal pain. On evaluation, she was found to be very tender in the abdomen. She had white blood cell count of 19,000 and was admitted with a diagnosis of rule out diverticulitis.
HOSPITAL COURSE:
CT scan of the abdomen was consistent with cholecystitis and ultrasound of the gallbladder was consistent with cholelithiasis. She was cleared for surgery by cardiologist and was treated preoperatively with intravenous antibiotics, intravenous fluids, and pain medication. On 4/22/00, the patient underwent laparoscopic cholecystectomy. On 4/26/00, she underwent an endoscopic retrograde cholangiopancreatography. The postoperative course was remarkable for some shortness of breath, otherwise the patient was doing well. She remained very stable, afebrile, and was discharged home.
DISCHARGE DIAGNOSES
1. Cholelithiasis with acute cholecystitis; status post laparoscopic cholecystectomy
2. Mitral valve disorder
3. Hypertensive heart disease with history of angiopathic cardiomyopathy

MEDICATIONS
1. Cozaar
2. Hytrin
3. Lasix
4. Potassium
5. Lanoxin

DIET: The patient is to be on a low-fat diet.
ACTIVITIES: The patient is to be ambulating at home p.r.n.
FOLLOW-UP: Follow-up in two weeks.
Medications, diet, activities, and follow-up have all been discussed with the patient and she showed a good understanding

____
Attending Physician

FIGURE 2-12. Discharge summary.

EXERCISE 2-1

Choose the correct answer option or write the correct answer(s) in the space(s) provided.

1. Every patient encounter must have a health record.
A. True
B. False

2. The operative report should be written or dictated immediately following the procedure.
A. True
B. False

3. List five purposes of a health record.

1. ____

2. ____

3. ____

4. ______________________________

5. ______________________________

4. Name an advantage of an electronic patient record.

____

5. Name the nonfederal organization that requires reporting of data collected from the health record.

____

6. List five elements required by the UHDDS.

1. ______________________________

2. ______________________________

3. ______________________________

4. ______________________________

5. ______________________________

7. Where in the record would you find the chief complaint?

____

8. If a physician was treating a patient with an antibiotic, where in the record would you look to see that treatment had been discontinued?

____

9. Where in the record would you expect to see how the patient was progressing on a daily basis?

____

10. Where in the record might you look to find how much blood was lost during surgery?

____

UNIFORM HOSPITAL DISCHARGE DATA SET (UHDDS) REPORTING STANDARDS FOR DIAGNOSES AND PROCEDURES

It is the responsibility of a coder to extract from the health record the diagnoses for which a patient is being treated and the procedures that have been performed. The extracting of data from the health record may also be referred to as **abstracting**. To complete this task, a coder must rely on definitions as developed by UHDDS for principal diagnosis, secondary diagnoses, principal procedure, and secondary procedures for inpatient encounters.

Principal Diagnosis

The **principal diagnosis** is defined as the condition established after study to be chiefly responsible for occasioning the admission of the patient to the hospital for care. This definition is one, if not the most important, concept that a coder must understand and apply. The principal diagnosis, along with the principal procedure, determines the assignment of the Medicare Severity diagnosis-related groups (MS-DRGs), which, in turn, affects reimbursement. Physicians are often not aware of this definition or how it is applied; therefore, the coder must take care to select the correct principal diagnosis after record review.

EXAMPLE

A patient presents to the emergency room with a cough and fever. After the chest x-ray is reviewed, it is determined that the patient has pneumonia, and the patient is admitted for treatment.

The principal diagnosis is pneumonia.

EXAMPLE

A patient presents to the emergency room with acute abdominal pain. After the patient is evaluated, he is taken to the OR for an appendectomy. The pathology report reveals an acute appendicitis, which is confirmed by the physician in the discharge summary.

The principal diagnosis is acute appendicitis.

Sometimes, the principal diagnosis is not as easily identifiable as it is in the previous two examples. There may be a secondary diagnosis that utilizes more resources during a patient stay but is not the principal diagnosis.

EXAMPLE

A patient is admitted for coronary artery bypass surgery with a diagnosis of coronary artery disease. The surgery is successful, and on the fourth postoperative day, pneumonia develops. The pneumonia is severe, and the patient goes into respiratory failure and must be intubated and treated in the intensive care unit (ICU). The patient remains in the ICU for 10 days because he cannot be weaned from the ventilator. The patient undergoes a tracheostomy procedure and is discharged to a rehab facility.

The principal diagnosis is coronary artery disease, even though most of the treatment was focused on pneumonia and respiratory failure.

Principal Procedure

These are the guidelines that should be followed for selection of the principal procedure.

Selection of Principal Procedure:
The following instructions should be applied in the selection of principal procedure and clarification on the importance of the relation to the principal diagnosis when more than one procedure is performed:

1. Procedure performed for definitive treatment of both principal diagnosis and secondary diagnosis.
   a. Sequence procedure performed for definitive treatment most related to principal diagnosis as principal procedure.
2. Procedure performed for definitive treatment and diagnostic procedures performed for both principal diagnosis and secondary diagnosis.
   a. Sequence procedure performed for definitive treatment most related to principal diagnosis as principal procedure.
3. A diagnostic procedure was performed for the principal diagnosis and a procedure is performed for definitive treatment of a secondary diagnosis.
   a. Sequence diagnostic procedure as principal procedure, since the procedure most related to the principal diagnosis takes precedence.
4. No procedures performed that are related to principal diagnosis; procedures performed for definitive treatment and diagnostic procedures were performed for secondary diagnosis.
   a. Sequence procedure performed for definitive treatment of secondary diagnosis as principal procedure, since there are no procedures (definitive or nondefinitive treatment) related to principal diagnosis.

Other Diagnoses

UHDDS requires reporting of other diagnoses that have significance for the specific hospital encounter. Reportable diagnoses are "conditions that coexist at the time of admission, or develop subsequently or affect the treatment received and/or the length of stay. Diagnoses which relate to an earlier episode which have no bearing on the current hospital stay are to be excluded."

Other diagnoses are defined as additional conditions that affect patient care because they require one or more of the following:

- Clinical evaluation, or
- Therapeutic treatment, or
- Diagnostic procedures, or

- Extended length of hospital stay, or
- Increased nursing care and/or monitoring

Second only to an understanding and application of the definition of "principal diagnosis" is the definition of when to code "other diagnoses." Once again, the importance of these secondary diagnoses comes into play in the MS-DRG reimbursement system. Other diagnoses may be identified as complications and/or **comorbidities** under the MS-DRG system, which may affect payment.

Clinical Evaluation

If the condition of a patient is being clinically evaluated, the coder would expect to see some testing and clinical observations, or perhaps a consultation.

EXAMPLE

During the course of a hospital stay, a patient develops low sodium levels. The physician makes note of this condition and documents that continued laboratory values will be watched. This would constitute clinical evaluation.

Therapeutic Treatment

Medications, physical therapy, and surgery are forms of therapeutic treatment.

EXAMPLE

The physician documents in the patient's past medical history that the patient has a history of a seizure disorder. The medication list contains the drug Dilantin. The fact that the patient is currently being treated for a seizure disorder with this medication constitutes a reportable secondary diagnosis. Physicians often list conditions in the patient's past medical history for which he or she is currently being treated. The coder should be familiar with medications and the conditions they treat.

Diagnostic Procedures

Often in the course of an inpatient hospital stay, physicians are trying to determine the cause of a sign, symptom, or patient complaint; in these cases, tests are often done to determine the underlying cause. A few examples of types of diagnostic procedures are provided here:

- EKG or ECG (electrocardiogram)
- EEG (electroencephalogram)
- EGD (esophagogastroduodenoscopy)
- Colonoscopy
- Echocardiogram
- MRI (magnetic resonance imaging)
- MRA (magnetic resonance angiography)
- X-rays

EXAMPLE

A patient presents to the emergency room with pain in the leg after a fall down the stairs. An x-ray is performed that reveals a fracture of the tibia.

Extended Length of Hospital Stay

In some cases, a patient is ready to be discharged from the hospital, but develops a condition that requires more intensive investigation, monitoring, or watchful waiting; this may require an additional night's stay.

Increased Nursing Care and/or Other Monitoring

A patient may have a decubitus ulcer that requires no physician treatment but does require more intensive nursing care. It is important to remember that if the physician does not document the diagnosis for which care is being rendered, the coder must query the physician before adding the code.

Previous Conditions

Often, in a discharge summary or a history and physical, a physician will list diagnoses and/or procedures from previous admissions that are not applicable to the current hospital stay. These conditions are generally not reported.

EXAMPLE A patient is admitted with acute bronchitis. The patient was admitted 2 years ago for an appendectomy and has a history of shingles. In the discharge summary, the physician documents acute bronchitis, status post appendectomy, and a history of shingles. In this case, the only diagnosis to be coded is acute bronchitis.

Reporting of Coexisting Chronic Conditions

Often, patients may have multiple chronic conditions when they are admitted to a hospital. These chronic conditions may not be specifically treated with medications or procedures; however, they are reported because they may be evaluated and/or monitored, or affect the way a patient is treated.

EXAMPLE A patient is admitted with benign prostatic hypertrophy (BPH) for a transurethral prostatectomy. The anesthesiologist in the preoperative note documents that the patient has mitral valve prolapse and requires antibiotics prior to undergoing dental procedures. The fact that the patient has mitral valve prolapse and requires antibiotics is a significant factor for the anesthesiologist. This condition is under clinical evaluation by the anesthesiologist and is being treated simultaneously. Therefore, both BPH and mitral valve prolapse (MVP) are reported.

EXAMPLE A patient is admitted with acute appendicitis. The anesthesiologist and the preoperative consultation indicate that the patient has a history of chronic obstructive pulmonary disease (COPD). The acute appendicitis and the COPD are coded. COPD is a chronic condition that affects patients for the rest of their lives. This, in turn, affects the monitoring and evaluation of this patient.

Integral versus Nonintegral Conditions

Conditions that are an **integral** part of the disease process are not coded.

EXAMPLE A patient is admitted to the hospital with a cough. After performing a diagnostic evaluation, the physician determines that the patient has pneumonia. Coughing is a symptom of pneumonia and is not coded.

EXAMPLE A patient is admitted to the hospital with fever and an elevated white blood count. A blood culture comes back positive, and the physician determines that the patient has sepsis. In this case, only the sepsis is coded; fever and an elevated white blood count are all symptoms of sepsis and are therefore not coded.

Likewise, conditions that are NOT an integral part of the disease process may be coded. Additional conditions that may **not** be associated routinely with a disease process should be coded when present.

EXAMPLE A patient is admitted to the hospital with a metastatic brain cancer for surgical removal. The patient's history reveals that he has had lung cancer that was surgically removed and now is presenting with seizures, metastatic brain cancer, and headache. Brain cancer is the principal diagnosis, and seizures and history of lung cancer are coded as secondary diagnoses; headache is not reported because it is a symptom of metastatic brain cancer.

Abnormal Findings

Abnormal findings (laboratory, x-ray, pathologic, and other diagnostic results) should not be assigned codes and reported unless the provider indicates their clinical significance. If the findings are outside the normal range and the provider has ordered other tests to evaluate the condition or prescribed treatment, it is appropriate to query the provider as to whether the abnormal finding should be assigned codes.

EXERCISE 2-2

Write the correct answer(s) in the space(s) provided.

1. What is the most important definition a coder should know?

____

2. What determines an MS-DRG?

____

3. What is the principal diagnosis in the following scenario?
A patient is admitted to the hospital with extreme indigestion. A workup ensues, and the patient is found to have GERD (gastroesophageal reflux disease). Three days later, on the day of discharge, the patient is unable to speak. After undergoing MRI, the patient is found to have had a stroke.

____

4. A patient is admitted to the hospital with an asthma attack. On his last admission 3 years ago, the diagnosis was community-acquired pneumonia. Is the pneumonia coded, and why or why not?

____

5. List five reasons why a secondary diagnosis might be reported.

1. ______________________________

2. ______________________________

3. ______________________________

4. ______________________________

5. ______________________________

6. The physician documents seizure disorder in the patient's past medical history. The patient is receiving Tegretol, according to the list of medications. Should the seizure disorder be coded, and why or why not?

____

7. A patient has urinary retention after undergoing surgery documented in progress notes. The attending writes an order for the nursing staff to record urine output. The nurse inserts a Foley catheter. Should the urinary retention be coded, and if so, why or why not?

____

8. If a patient is not on any drugs for Parkinson's, should a code be assigned for this diagnosis and why or why not?

____

9. If a patient presents with diarrhea and vomiting and the attending physician determines this to be gastroenteritis, what diagnosis/diagnoses should be assigned?

____

10. Which is the principal procedure, when a diagnostic procedure is performed for the principal diagnosis and a therapeutic procedure is performed for definitive treatment of a secondary diagnosis?

____

CODING FROM DOCUMENTATION FOUND IN THE HEALTH RECORD

The usual advice given to a new coder is to begin to code a record by reading the discharge summary. This, in theory, is the summation of what took place during this patient's hospital admission. The discharge summary is similar to a synopsis of a book. By reading this document, the coder should be able to determine the principal diagnosis. However, the caveat is that the documenting physician may not be aware of the definition of a principal diagnosis and may list a diagnosis that does not meet the requirements of this definition.

Following a review of the discharge summary, the coder should move to the ER record (if applicable), which is the beginning of the patient's story. This will reveal the patient's chief complaint. The chief complaint is expressed in the words of the patient and gives the reason why he or she is presenting to the ER. The ER record generally provides to the coder the **admission diagnosis**. The admitting diagnosis may be a symptom, and after examination, a working diagnosis may become apparent. By the time the patient leaves the ER to go to the floor, the emergency room physician will have a working diagnosis or will be aware of a symptom that needs additional workup. If this diagnosis is not clear from the ER record, the admission orders should be reviewed for a diagnosis that is listed as the reason for admission.

If no ER record is available, or after the coder has read the ER record, he or she should move on to the admission history and physical (H&P). Generally, the progress notes are reviewed, followed by the OR reports, laboratory results, radiology reports, consults, and orders. Some documents such as the discharge summary, operative report, or pathology report may not be available at the time of coding. Hospitals may have a policy on whether an inpatient record should be coded without these reports or put on hold until the reports are completed. The following examples show documentation inconsistencies. When documentation inconsistencies are present the attending should be queried for clarification.

EXAMPLE

The ER form has a listing of common medical conditions. The ER physician will circle any pertinent diagnoses. The physician has circled ESRD (end-stage renal disease) on the ER form. Throughout the body of the health record, no documentation of ESRD is found, nor does any documentation state that the patient is on dialysis or that the patient is awaiting a transplant. The only documentation in the chart is for chronic renal insufficiency (CRI).

- Differences in coding: N18.6 versus N18.9

EXAMPLE

Throughout a patient's inpatient chart, it is documented that the patient has a history of pneumonia. This is also documented in the past medical history.

No chest x-ray was performed. Physical exam showed that the lungs were clear. On the discharge summary, pneumonia is documented instead of history of pneumonia.

- Differences in coding: J18.9 versus Z87.01

EXAMPLE

Throughout a patient's chart, documentation of ESLD (end-stage liver disease) is found, along with the fact that the patient is awaiting a liver transplant. The patient has a history of cirrhosis and hepatitis C.

One progress note reads:

Cirrhosis/hep C/ESKD (end-stage kidney disease)

No documentation in the chart describes any abnormal kidney function. It appears that the physician may have meant to write ESLD instead of ESKD.

It is acceptable to code from any documentation provided by a physician. Physicians (individuals qualified by education and legally authorized to practice medicine) may be referred to as attendings, consulting physicians, interns, and residents. Physicians may include surgeons, anesthesiologists, oncologists, internists, hospitalists, intensivists, family practitioners, and interventionalists. Medical students have not completed their education and are not included in the category of physician. Some medical staff bylaws may accept documentation by other healthcare providers such as nurse practitioners or physician assistants.

Some confusion has arisen as to what exactly may be coded from radiology and pathology reports. The coder cannot assign codes from these reports without obtaining documentation by the attending. For example if the attending physician documents lung mass and the pathologist documents carcinoma of the lung, this would be conflicting documentation and the attending must clarify. Additional details (e.g., area of fracture, location of mass) related to confirmed diagnoses may be taken from the x-ray report. For example if the physician has already documented an ulnar fracture, the coder may pick up additional details on the site of the fracture from the radiology report.

THE USE OF QUERIES IN THE CODING PROCESS

In 2001, AHIMA published a Practice Brief entitled *Developing a Physician Query Process,*[4] which describes the goal of the query process as "to improve physician documentation and coding professionals' understanding of the unique clinical situation, not to improve reimbursement." A well-established and managed query process ensures data integrity. This Practice Brief was updated in October 2008 with a new Practice Brief entitled *Managing an Effective Query Process.*[5]

In February of 2013 a new Practice Brief entitled "Guidelines for Achieving a Compliant Query Practice" was issued. This brief was written to help clarify previous practice briefs, and it serves to augment what has been previously stated; Updated in 2019, where applicable, it supersedes previous guidance.

Each facility should prepare its own policies and procedures regarding the query process. In the October Practice Brief, AHIMA details many items that may be included in a facility policy.

When to Query

The 2013 "Guideline" Practice Brief lists reasons for which a query could be generated. Generally a query should be initiated if the documentation is conflicting, imprecise, incomplete, illegible, ambiguous, or inconsistent.

- Documentation describes or is associated with clinical indicators without a definitive relationship to an underlying diagnosis.

EXAMPLE

The patient presents to the ER from the nursing home with hypotension, fever, elevated WBC, and a high respiratory rate. The ER physician documents pneumonia. The query would be for sepsis because the patient has clinical evidence of meeting SIRS criteria.

- Documentation includes clinical indicators, diagnostic evaluation, and/or treatment not related to a specific condition or procedure.

EXAMPLE

A patient presents with a cough and fever. A chest x-ray is ordered for the patient, and the patient is started on clindamycin. No diagnosis is documented. A query would be generated for a diagnosis for the antibiotics.

- Documentation provides a diagnosis without underlying clinical validation.

EXAMPLE

The patient presents to the ER with abdominal pain, gastroenteritis, and hypokalemia. In the discharge summary, the physician documents hyperkalemia. The coder may generate a query to address this conflict. Depending on the policies of the facility, this conflict may need to be addressed through a physician advisor.

- Documentation is unclear for present on admission.

EXAMPLE

On day two of the hospital stay the physician documents UTI and begins antibiotics. It would be appropriate to query the physician for present on admission.

How to Query

The physician may be queried either verbally or in writing. Verbal queries should be documented at the time of discussion or immediately after, and they should contain the same format as written queries and contain the same clinical indicators as would be in a written query. It is suggested that the query be maintained as part of the medical record, and if the physician response is on the form and not in the medical record, the form should be part of the permanent health record. If the query is not maintained in the health record, organizations should maintain copies as part of a business record. Queries should not be leading. A leading query is one that is not supported by the clinical information in the record and/or one that directs a provider to a specific diagnosis or procedure. The use of the term *possible* is discouraged when querying. Even though the guidelines allow assigning codes to most possible conditions, the term is too broad to be used in the query format.

Query Format

Queries may be written in open-ended or multiple-choice format, and in some circumstances the use of yes/no queries may be acceptable. All queries must be supported by pertinent clinical indicators.

Multiple-choice query options should include reasonable options as supported by clinical indications. It is acceptable to provide a new diagnosis in the options list (this is not considered introducing new information). When using this format, additional options such as "clinically undetermined" or "not clinically significant" are suggested.

Yes/no queries should also include options such as "clinically undetermined" or "not clinically significant." Yes/no queries should be used in the following circumstances.

- To determine present on admission (POA)
- To inquire or further specify a diagnosis that is already in the documented in the record, such as findings in diagnostic reports
- To establish a cause-and-effect relationship between documented conditions (e.g., manifestation/etiology, complications and conditions/diagnostic findings)
- To resolve conflicting documentation from multiple providers

Query Retention Policy

Each facility should have a policy regarding the retention of queries. The best practice would be to have the practitioner's response to the query in the health record. This response may be an addendum, which should be timely written and should include the current date and time and the reason for this additional documentation.

Leading Query

It is unacceptable to lead a provider to document a particular response. As mentioned previously, a leading query is one not supported by clinical indicators found in the record, or one that directs the provider to document a particular diagnosis or procedure. In the Practice Brief *Guidelines for Achieving a Compliant Query Practice,* AHIMA has provided examples of compliant and noncompliant queries. These can be found at http://journal.ahima.org/2013/02/01/physician-query-examples/.

Who to Query

The query should be directed to the provider who supplied the documentation in question. This may mean that the query is directed to a consultant, anesthesiologist, or surgeon, among others. Abnormal lab finding queries should be addressed to the attending physician. If there is conflicting documentation between a consultant and an attending physician, the attending physician should be queried for clarification.

Elements of a Query Form

A query should contain the following elements:

- Date of query
- Patient name
- Medical record number
- Account number
- Admission date/date of service
- Specific question needing clarification along with clinical indicators
- Identification of the coder asking the question
- Contact information for the coder initiating the query
- Area for response from provider
- Place for provider signature and date of response
- Instruction for documentation or any correction or addendum in the body of the record

Queries can be forms (Figure 2-13) placed in charts, faxes, and/or electronic communications transmitted via secure e-mail or IT messaging. Facility policy will control where queries are maintained. It is preferable that they become part of the official health record, whether paper or electronic.

It is not advised to use sticky notes, scratch paper, or any note that can be removed and discarded. It is acceptable to use a single query form for multiple queries.

CHAPTER REVIEW EXERCISE

Write the correct answer(s) in the space(s) provided or choose the correct answer option.

1. When coding a record, where is the best place to begin?

____

2. If the discharge summary includes a list of diagnoses, should the coder choose the first in the list as the principal diagnosis?

A. Yes

B. No

3. What does TJC stand for?

____

4. What does UHDDS stand for?

____

5. Which report in the record must be on the record within 24 hours?

____

6. What does the term "integral" mean?

____

7. Where in the record would a coder find the admitting diagnosis?

____

8. Name one reason why a coder would query a physician.

____

PHYSICIAN QUERY FORM

Patient Name: ____________________

Patient Number: ____________________

Admission Date: ____________________ Discharge Date: ________

Query Date: ____________________

Dear Dr. ____________________:

In order to assign the most appropriate codes that reflect the conditions of your patient, more clarification is required.

From a coding perspective "urosepsis" is a nonspecific term. It may mean that the patient has an infection localized in the urinary tract, or it may signify that the urinary tract infection has now become generalized sepsis. Please document in the space below or write an addendum to the patient's record the diagnosis that best represents your use of the term "urosepsis."

Physician Response:

____

____

____

____

____

____________________ ________

Physician signature Date

Thank you.

Coder Name: ____________________ Contact #: ________

FIGURE 2-13. Physician query form.

9. The best place in the record to find the patient's history is in the ________________

________________________________.

10. The beginning of the patient's story is usually the discharge summary.

A. True

B. False

11. It is permissible for a coder to use documentation provided by an interventionalist.

A. True

B. False

12. Once a physician answers a coding question, it should be thrown in the trash.
    A. True
    B. False
13. Physician queries should have only enough room for a physician to sign and date.
    A. True
    B. False
14. When a coding question is asked, it is very important that the financial impact of the response is included.
    A. True
    B. False
15. It is important that the date and the identity of the physician be included for every note.
    A. True
    B. False
16. It is important for the record to include documentation that supports a code used in billing.
    A. True
    B. False
17. Documentation from a physician consultant cannot be used to assign codes.
    A. True
    B. False
18. A principal diagnosis is one of the elements that determine an MS-DRG.
    A. True
    B. False
19. An example of a diagnostic procedure is an MRI.
    A. True
    B. False
20. Surgery can be a form of therapeutic treatment.
    A. True
    B. False

CHAPTER GLOSSARY

Abstracting: extracting data from the health record.

Admission diagnosis: diagnosis that brings the patient to the hospital. This will often be a symptom.

Chief complaint: the reason, in the patient's own words, for presenting to the hospital.

Comorbidities: preexisting diagnoses or conditions that are present on admission.

Consultant: healthcare provider who is asked to see the patient to provide expert opinion outside the expertise of the requester.

Healthcare provider: person who provides care to a patient.

Hybrid: a combination of formats producing similar results (i.e., paper and electronic records).

Integral: essential part of a disease process.

Physician: licensed medical doctor.

Principal diagnosis: the condition established after study to be chiefly responsible for occasioning the admission of the patient to the hospital for care.

Progress notes: daily recordings by healthcare providers of patient progress.

REFERENCES

1. Huffman E: Health Information Management, ed 10, Berwyn, IL, 1994, Physicians' Record Company, p 30.
2. Abdelhak M, Grostick S, Hanken MA, et al, editors: Health Information: Management of a Strategic Resource, ed 2, St. Louis, 2001, WB Saunders.
3. Medicare 1995 Documentation Guidelines: General Principles of Medical Record Documentation, 1995, Centers for Medicare and Medicaid Services, U.S. Department of Health and Human Services.
4. Prophet S: Developing a physician query process (AHIMA practice brief). *J AHIMA* 72:88I–88M, 2001.
5. AHIMA: Managing an effective query process. *J AHIMA* 79:83–88, 2008.

3

ICD-10-CM Format and Conventions

CHAPTER OUTLINE

LEARNING OBJECTIVES

1. Identify the format of the ICD-10-CM code book
2. Explain and apply the conventions and guidelines

ABBREVIATIONS/ ACRONYMS

CPT *Current Procedural Terminology*

ICD-10-CM *International Classification of Diseases, 10th Revision, Clinical Modification*

ICD-10-PCS *International Classification of Diseases, 10th Revision, Procedure Coding System*

NEC not elsewhere classifiable

NOS not otherwise specified

WHO World Health Organization

ICD-10-CM Official Guidelines for Coding and Reporting (2021-2022)

Please refer to the companion Evolve website for the most current 2021-2022 guidelines.

FY2021-2022

The Centers for Medicare and Medicaid Services (CMS) and the National Center for Health Statistics (NCHS), two departments within the U.S. Federal Government's Department of Health and Human Services (DHHS) provide the following guidelines for coding and reporting using the International Classification of Diseases, 10th Revision, Clinical Modification (ICD-10-CM). These guidelines should be used as a companion document to the official version of the ICD-10-CM as published on the NCHS website. The ICD-10-CM is a morbidity classification published by the United States for classifying diagnoses and reason for visits in all health care settings. The ICD-10-CM is based on the ICD-10, the statistical classification of disease published by the World Health Organization (WHO).

These guidelines have been approved by the four organizations that make up the Cooperating Parties for the ICD-10-CM: the American Hospital Association (AHA), the American Health Information Management Association (AHIMA), CMS, and NCHS.

These guidelines are a set of rules that have been developed to accompany and complement the official conventions and instructions provided within the ICD-10-CM itself. The instructions and conventions of the classification take precedence over guidelines. These guidelines are based on the coding and sequencing instructions in the Tabular List and Alphabetic Index of ICD-10-CM, but provide additional instruction. Adherence to these guidelines when assigning ICD-10-CM diagnosis codes is required under the Health Insurance Portability and Accountability Act (HIPAA). The diagnosis codes (Tabular List and Alphabetic Index) have been adopted under HIPAA for all healthcare settings. A joint effort between the healthcare provider and the coder is essential to achieve complete and accurate documentation, code assignment, and reporting of diagnoses and procedures. These guidelines have been developed to assist both the healthcare provider and the coder in identifying those diagnoses that are to be reported. The importance of consistent, complete documentation in the medical record cannot be overemphasized. Without such documentation accurate coding cannot be achieved. The entire record should be reviewed to determine the specific reason for the encounter and the conditions treated.

The term encounter is used for all settings, including hospital admissions. In the context of these guidelines, the term provider is used throughout the guidelines to mean physician or any qualified health care practitioner who is legally accountable for establishing the patient's diagnosis. Only this set of guidelines, approved by the Cooperating Parties, is official.

The guidelines are organized into sections. Section I includes the structure and conventions of the classification and general guidelines that apply to the entire classification, and chapter-specific guidelines that correspond to the chapters as they are arranged in the classification. Section II includes guidelines for selection of principal diagnosis for non-outpatient settings. Section III includes guidelines for reporting additional diagnoses in non-outpatient settings. Section IV is for outpatient coding and reporting. It is necessary to review all sections of the guidelines to fully understand all of the rules and instructions needed to code properly.

Section I. Conventions, general coding guidelines and chapter specific guidelines

The conventions, general guidelines and chapter-specific guidelines are applicable to all health care settings unless otherwise indicated. The conventions and instructions of the classification take precedence over guidelines.

A. Conventions for the ICD-10-CM

The conventions for the ICD-10-CM are the general rules for use of the classification independent of the guidelines. These conventions are incorporated within the Alphabetic Index and Tabular List of the ICD-10-CM as instructional notes.

1. The Alphabetic Index and Tabular List

The ICD-10-CM is divided into the Alphabetic Index, an alphabetical list of terms and their corresponding code, and the Tabular List, a structured list of codes divided into chapters based on body system or condition (Figures 3-1 and 3-2). The Alphabetic Index consists of the following parts: the Index of Diseases and Injury, the Index of External Causes of Injury, the Table of Neoplasms and the Table of Drugs and Chemicals.

See Section I.C.2. General guidelines

See Section I.C.19. Adverse effects, poisoning, underdosing and toxic effects

2. Format and Structure:

The ICD-10-CM Tabular List contains categories, subcategories and codes. Characters for categories, subcategories and codes may be either a letter or a number. All categories are 3 characters.

A three-character category that has no further subdivision is equivalent to a code. Subcategories are either

Disease, diseased *(Continued)*
breast (*see also* Disorder, breast) N64.9
cystic (chronic) – *see* Mastopathy, cystic
fibrocystic – *see* Mastopathy, cystic
Paget's
female, unspecified side C50.91-
male, unspecified side C50.92-
specified NEC N64.89
Breda's – *see* Yaws
Bretonneau's (diphtheritic malignant angina) A36.0

FIGURE 3-1. Alphabetic Index entry for Paget's disease, female breast.

● **C50.9 Malignant neoplasm of breast of unspecified site**
● **C50.91 Malignant neoplasm of breast of unspecified site, female**
❑ **C50.911 Malignant neoplasm of unspecified site of right female breast**
❑ **C50.912 Malignant neoplasm of unspecified site of left female breast**
❑ **C50.919 Malignant neoplasm of unspecified site of unspecified female breast**

FIGURE 3-2. Tabular List entry for Paget's disease, female breast.

4 or 5 characters. Codes may be 3, 4, 5, 6 or 7 characters. That is, each level of subdivision after a category is a subcategory. The final level of subdivision is a code. Codes that have applicable 7th characters are still referred to as codes, not subcategories. A code that has an applicable 7th character is considered invalid without the 7th character.

The ICD-10-CM uses an indented format for ease in reference.

3. **Use of codes for reporting purposes**
   For reporting purposes only codes are permissible, not categories or subcategories, and any applicable 7th character is required.

In the Alphabetic Index of ICD-10-CM a dash (-) is used to indicate that there are further characters that need to be assigned for a valid code. In Figures 3-1 and 3-2, note that C50.91 would be an invalid code. A sixth digit is necessary to identify left, right, or unspecified breast. All codes must be assigned to the final level of subdivision. A valid code is at least three characters, but could be four, five, six, or seven characters.

4. **Placeholder character**
   The ICD-10-CM utilizes a placeholder character "X". The "X" is used as a placeholder at certain codes to allow for future expansion. An example of this is at the poisoning, adverse effect and underdosing codes, categories T36-T50.

   Where a placeholder exists, the X must be used in order for the code to be considered a valid code (Figure 3-3).
5. **7th Characters**
   Certain ICD-10-CM categories have applicable 7th characters. The applicable 7th character is required for all codes within the category, or as the notes in the Tabular List instruct. The 7th character must always be the 7th character in the data field. If a code that requires a 7th character is not 6 characters, a placeholder X must be used to fill in the empty characters (see Figure 3-3).

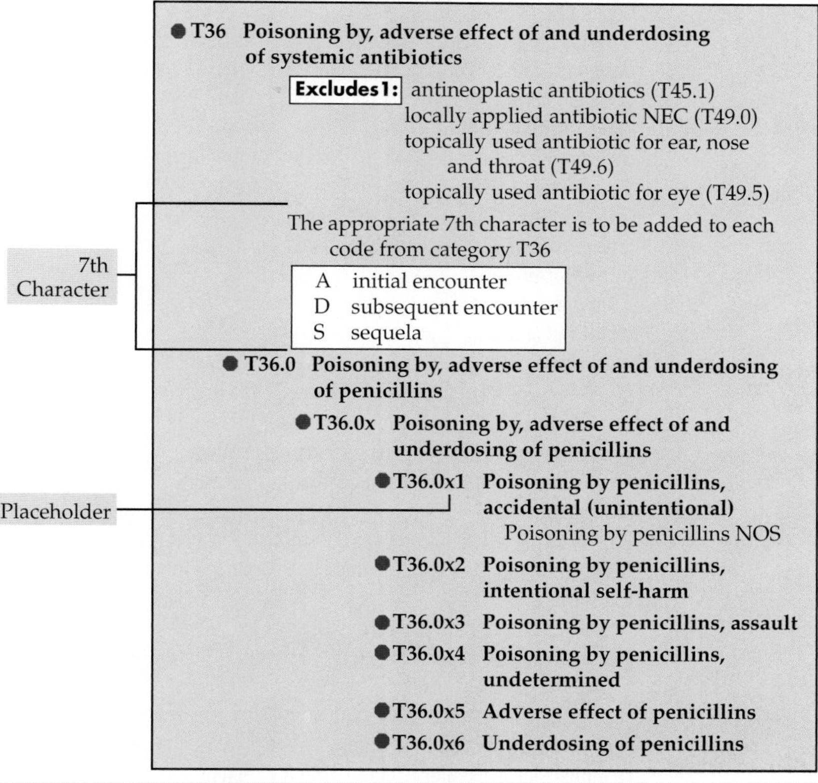

FIGURE 3-3. Placeholder in ICD-10-CM, 7th character.

6. Abbreviations

a. Alphabetic Index abbreviations

NEC "Not elsewhere classifiable"
This abbreviation in the Alphabetic Index represents "other specified". When a specific code is not available for a condition, the Alphabetic Index directs the coder to the "other specified" code in the Tabular List.

NOS "Not otherwise specified"
This abbreviation is the equivalent of unspecified.

b. Tabular List abbreviations

NEC "Not elsewhere classifiable"
This abbreviation in the Tabular List represents "other specified". When a specific code is not available for a condition, the Tabular List includes an NEC entry under a code to identify the code as the "other specified" code.

NOS "Not otherwise specified"
This abbreviation is the equivalent of unspecified.

7. Punctuation

[ ] Brackets are used in the Tabular List to enclose synonyms, alternative wording or explanatory phrases. Brackets are used in the Alphabetic Index to identify manifestation codes.

( ) Parentheses are used in both the Alphabetic Index and Tabular List to enclose supplementary words that may be present or absent in the statement of a disease or procedure without affecting the code number to which it is assigned. The terms within the parentheses are referred to as nonessential modifiers. The nonessential modifiers in the Alphabetic Index to Disease apply to subterms following a main term except when a nonessential modifier and a subentry are mutually exclusive, the subentry takes precedence. For example, in the ICD-10-CM Alphabetic Index under the main term Enteritis, "acute" is a nonessential modifier and "chronic" is a subentry. In this case, the nonessential modifier "acute" does not apply to the subentry "chronic."

: Colons are used in the Tabular List after an incomplete term which needs one or more of the modifiers following the colon to make it assignable to a given category.

8. Use of "and"

See Section I.A.14. Use of the term "And".

9. Other and Unspecified codes

a. "Other" codes

Codes titled "other" or "other specified" are for use when the information in the medical record provides detail for which a specific code does not exist. Alphabetic Index entries with NEC in the line designate "other" codes in the Tabular List. These Alphabetic Index entries represent specific disease entities for which no specific code exists so the term is included within an "other" code.

b. "Unspecified" codes

Codes titled "unspecified" are for use when the information in the medical record is insufficient to assign a more specific code. For those categories for which an unspecified code is not provided, the "other specified" code may represent both other and unspecified.

See Section I.B.18, Use of Signs/Symptoms/Unspecified Codes

10. Includes Notes

This note appears immediately under a three character code title to further define, or give examples of, the content of the category.

11. Inclusion terms

List of terms is included under some codes. These terms are the conditions for which that code is to be used. The terms may be synonyms of the code title, or, in the case of "other specified" codes, the terms are a list of the various conditions assigned to that code. The inclusion terms are not necessarily exhaustive. Additional terms found only in the Alphabetic Index may also be assigned to a code.

12. Excludes Notes

The ICD-10-CM has two types of excludes notes. Each type of note has a different definition for use but they are all similar in that they indicate that codes excluded from each other are independent of each other.

a. Excludes1

A type 1 Excludes note is a pure excludes note. It means "NOT CODED HERE!" An Excludes1 note indicates that the code excluded should never be used at the same time as the code above the Excludes 1 note. An Excludes1 is used when two conditions cannot occur together, such as a congenital form versus an acquired form of the same condition. An exception to the Excludes1 definition is the circumstance when the two conditions are unrelated to each other. If it is not clear whether the two conditions involving an Excludes1 note are related or not, query the provider. For example, code F45.8, Other somatoform disorders, has an Excludes1 note for "sleep related teeth grinding (G47.63)," because "teeth grinding" is an inclusion term under F45.8. Only one of these two codes should be assigned for

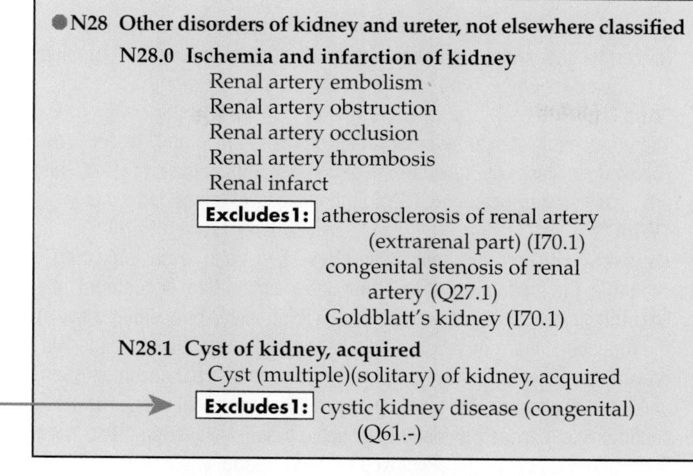
●N28 **Other disorders of kidney and ureter, not elsewhere classified**
N28.0 Ischemia and infarction of kidney
Renal artery embolism
Renal artery obstruction
Renal artery occlusion
Renal artery thrombosis
Renal infarct
Excludes1: atherosclerosis of renal artery (extrarenal part) (I70.1)
congenital stenosis of renal artery (Q27.1)
Goldblatt's kidney (I70.1)
N28.1 Cyst of kidney, acquired
Cyst (multiple)(solitary) of kidney, acquired
Excludes1: cystic kidney disease (congenital) (Q61.-)

FIGURE 3-4. Example of Excludes1 note.

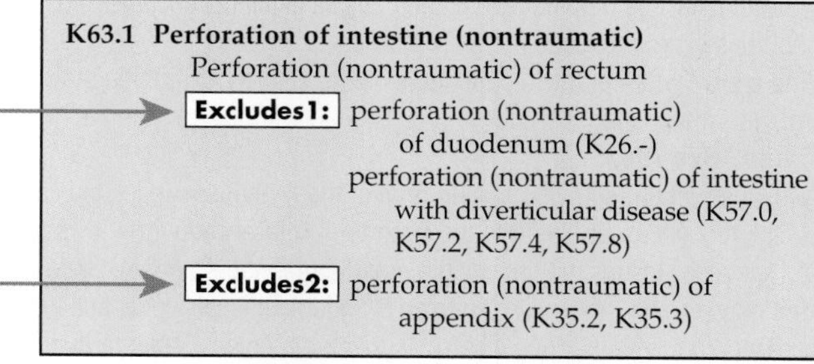
K63.1 Perforation of intestine (nontraumatic)
Perforation (nontraumatic) of rectum
Excludes1: perforation (nontraumatic) of duodenum (K26.-)
perforation (nontraumatic) of intestine with diverticular disease (K57.0, K57.2, K57.4, K57.8)
Excludes2: perforation (nontraumatic) of appendix (K35.2, K35.3)

FIGURE 3-5. Example of Excludes1 and Excludes2 notes.

teeth grinding. However, psychogenic dysmenorrhea is also an inclusion term under F45.8, and a patient could have both this condition and sleep-related teeth grinding. In this case, the two conditions are clearly unrelated to each other, and so it would be appropriate to report F45.8 and G47.63 together.

b. Excludes2

A type 2 Excludes note represents "Not included here". An Excludes2 note indicates that the condition excluded is not part of the condition represented by the code, but a patient may have both conditions at the same time. When an Excludes2 note appears under a code, it is acceptable to use both the code and the excluded code together, when appropriate (see Figure 3-5).

13. Etiology/manifestation convention ("code first", "use additional code" and "in diseases classified elsewhere" notes)

Certain conditions have both an underlying etiology and multiple body system manifestations due to the underlying etiology. For such conditions, the ICD-10-CM has a coding convention that requires the underlying condition be sequenced first, if applicable, followed by the manifestation. Wherever such a combination exists, there is a "use additional code" note at the etiology code, and a "code first" note at the manifestation code. These instructional notes indicate the proper sequencing order of the codes, etiology followed by manifestation.

In most cases the manifestation codes will have in the code title, "in diseases classified elsewhere." Codes with this title are a component of the etiology/manifestation convention. The code title indicates that it is a manifestation code. "In diseases classified elsewhere" codes are never permitted to be used as first-listed or principal diagnosis codes. They must be used in conjunction with an underlying condition code and they must be listed following the underlying condition. See category F02, Dementia in other diseases classified elsewhere, for an example of this convention.

There are manifestation codes that do not have "in diseases classified elsewhere" in the title. For such codes, there is a "use additional code" note at the etiology code and a "code first" note at the manifestation code, and the rules for sequencing apply.

In addition to the notes in the Tabular List, these conditions also have a specific Alphabetic Index entry structure. In the Alphabetic Index both conditions are listed together with the etiology code first followed by the manifestation codes in brackets. The code in brackets is always to be sequenced second.

An example of the etiology/manifestation convention is dementia in Parkinson's disease. In the Alphabetic Index, code G20 is listed first, followed by code F02.80 or F02.81 in brackets. Code G20 represents the underlying etiology, Parkinson's disease, and must be sequenced first, whereas codes F02.80 and F02.81 represent the manifestation of dementia in diseases classified elsewhere, with or without behavioral disturbance.

"Code first" and "Use additional code" notes are also used as sequencing rules in the classification for certain codes that are not part of an etiology/manifestation combination.

See Section I.B.7. Multiple coding for a single condition.

14. "And"

The word "and" should be interpreted to mean either "and" or "or" when it appears in a title.

For example, cases of "tuberculosis of bones", "tuberculosis of joints" and "tuberculosis of bones and joints" are classified to subcategory A18.0, Tuberculosis of bones and joints.

15. "With"

The word "with" or "in" should be interpreted to mean "associated with" or "due to" when it appears in a code title, the Alphabetic Index (either under a main term or subterm), or an instructional note in the Tabular List. The classification presumes a causal relationship between the two conditions linked by these terms in the Alphabetic Index or Tabular List. These conditions should be coded as related even in the absence of provider documentation explicitly linking them, unless the documentation clearly states the conditions are unrelated or when another guideline exists that specifically requires a documented linkage between two conditions (e.g., sepsis guideline for "acute organ dysfunction that is not clearly associated with the sepsis"). For conditions not specifically linked by these relational terms in the classification or when a guideline requires that a linkage between two conditions be explicitly documented, provider documentation must link the conditions in order to code them as related.

The word "with" in the Alphabetic Index is sequenced immediately following the main term or subterm, not in alphabetical order.

16. "See" and "See Also"

The "see" instruction following a main term in the Alphabetic Index indicates that another term should be referenced. It is necessary to go to the main term referenced with the "see" note to locate the correct code.

A "see also" instruction following a main term in the Alphabetic Index instructs that there is another main term that may also be referenced that may provide additional Alphabetic Index entries that may be useful. It is not necessary to follow the "see also" note when the original main term provides the necessary code.

17. "Code also" note

A "code also" note instructs that two codes may be required to fully describe a condition, but this note does not provide sequencing direction. The sequencing depends on the circumstances of the encounter.

18. Default codes

A code listed next to a main term in the ICD-10-CM Alphabetic Index is referred to as a default code. The default code represents that condition that is most commonly associated with the main term, or is the unspecified code for the condition. If a condition is documented in a medical record (for example, appendicitis) without any additional information, such as acute or chronic, the default code should be assigned (Figure 3-6).

19. Code assignment and Clinical Criteria

The assignment of a diagnosis code is based on the provider's diagnostic statement that the condition exists. The provider's statement that the patient has a particular condition is sufficient. Code assignment is not based on clinical criteria used by the provider to establish the diagnosis.

Several publishers have a variety of ICD-10-CM and ICD-10-PCS code books available. Physicians use CPT codes to bill for services and procedures—and therefore will not use ICD-10-PCS. Expert versions may contain reimbursement edits, color-coded information, Medicare code edits, and age and sex edits. Some books are updated with replacement pages

Failure, failed *(Continued)*
respiration, respiratory J96.90
 with
  hypercapnia J96.92
  hypoxia J96.91
 acute J96.00
  with
   hypercapnia J96.02
   hypoxia J96.91
 acute and (on) chronic J96.20
  with
   hypercapnia J96.22
   hypoxia J96.21
 center G93.89

FIGURE 3-6. Alphabetic Index default code for respiratory failure.

quarterly and may include references to *Coding Clinic* articles. At the beginning of a code book, information is usually provided that explains the conventions used in that version.

The **ICD-10-CM** code book is also divided into two parts: an Alphabetic Index and a Tabular List. The Alphabetic Index lists terms and corresponding codes in alphabetic order. The main index is the Index to Diseases and Injuries, and there is an additional index to External Causes of Injury. There are two tables located in the main index: the Neoplasm Table and the Table of Drugs and Chemicals. The Tabular List is an alphanumeric listing of codes that are divided into chapters based on body system or conditions.

There is an additional book for procedures, which is entitled **ICD-10-PCS**.

Format of Tabular List of Diseases and Injuries

In ICD-10-CM, the Tabular List of Diseases and Injuries consists of 22 chapters (Table 3-1). Most of the chapters are based on body systems; however, some are based on conditions. Within each chapter, codes are divided as follows:

- Blocks
- Categories
- Subcategories

Blocks

Each chapter in ICD-10-CM is divided into blocks. A block is a group of three-character categories that represent diseases or conditions that are similar (Table 3-2).

Categories

In ICD-10-CM, the first character of a three-character **category** is a letter, and each letter is associated with a particular chapter except for D and H. The letter D can be found in ICD-10-CM Chapters 2 and 3, the letter H can be found in both ICD-10-CM Chapters 7 and 8, and ICD-10-CM Chapter 19 uses two letters, S and T. The second and third characters are numbers. Most three-character categories are divided into four- or five-character subcategories. If a three-character category is not subdivided, it is a valid three-character code.

TABLE 3-1 ICD-10-CM TABLE OF CONTENTS FOR TABULAR LIST

ICD-10-CM Tabular List of Diseases and Injuries
Certain Infectious and Parasitic Diseases (A00-B99)
Neoplasms (C00-D49)
Diseases of the Blood and Blood-Forming Organs and Certain Disorders Involving the Immune Mechanism (D50-D89)
Endocrine, Nutritional, and Metabolic Diseases (E00-E89)
Mental and Behavioral Disorders (F01-F99)
Diseases of the Nervous System (G00-G99)
Diseases of the Eye and Adnexa (H00-H59)
Diseases of the Ear and Mastoid Process (H60-H95)
Diseases of the Circulatory System (I00-I99)
Diseases of the Respiratory System (J00-J99)
Diseases of the Digestive System (K00-K95)
Diseases of the Skin and Subcutaneous Tissue (L00-L99)
Diseases of the Musculoskeletal System and Connective Tissue (M00-M99)
Diseases of the Genitourinary System (N00-N99)
Pregnancy, Childbirth, and the Puerperium (O00-O9A)
Certain Conditions Originating in the Perinatal Period (P00-P96)
Congenital Malformations, Deformations, and Chromosomal Abnormalities (Q00-Q99)
Symptoms, Signs, and Abnormal Clinical and Laboratory Findings (R00-R99)
Injury, Poisoning, and Certain Other Consequences of External Causes (S00-T88)
External Causes of Morbidity (V00-Y99)
Factors Influencing Health Status and Contact with Health Services (Z00-Z99)
Codes for special purposes (U00-U85)

TABLE 3-2 BLOCKS FOR THE NERVOUS SYSTEM CHAPTER OF ICD-10-CM

G00-G09	Inflammatory diseases of the central nervous system
G10-G14	Systemic atrophies primarily affecting the central nervous system
G20-G26	Extrapyramidal and movement disorders
G30-G32	Other degenerative diseases of the nervous system
G35-G37	Demyelinating diseases of the central nervous system
G40-G47	Episodic and paroxysmal disorders
G50-G59	Nerve, nerve root, and plexus disorders
G60-G65	Polyneuropathies and other disorders of the peripheral nervous system
G70-G73	Diseases of myoneural junction and muscle
G80-G83	Cerebral palsy and other paralytic syndromes
G89-G99	Other disorders of the nervous system

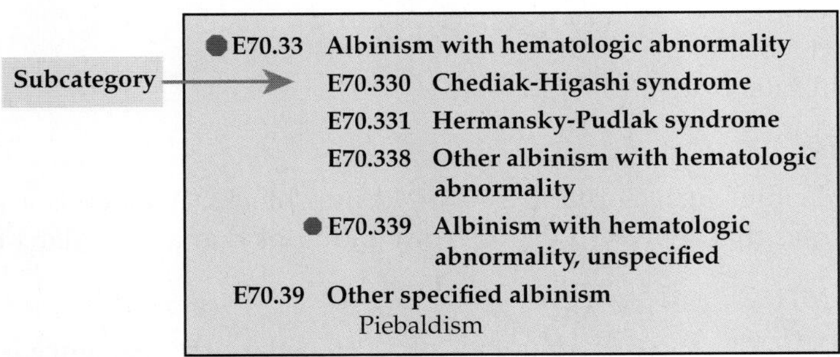

FIGURE 3-7. Example of subcategory in ICD-10-CM.

Subcategories

In ICD-10-CM, subcategories can be either four or five characters; every subdivision after a category is a **subcategory** (Figure 3-7). Subcategory characters can be either letters or numbers. Codes in ICD-10-CM can be three to seven characters in length. The last level of subdivision becomes the final code. The final character may be a number or a letter.

EXERCISE 3-1

Identify the following as a chapter, block, category, or subcategory.

1. Diseases of Veins, Lymphatics Vessels, and Lymph Nodes of NEC (I80-I89) __________
2. Diseases of the Circulatory System (I00-I99) __________
3. I81 Portal vein thrombosis __________
4. I82 Other venous embolism and thrombosis __________
5. I82.0 Budd-Chiari syndrome __________

Placeholder Character

The letter *x* in ICD-10-CM is a placeholder. It is most often used in the fifth character position and in certain six-character code positions. These placeholders are to be used for future code expansion. When a placeholder is required the *x* must be used for the code to be considered valid.

EXAMPLE

T36.0x1A, Poisoning by penicillins, accidental, initial encounter

Some categories have seventh-characters, and this seventh character is required for all codes in that category. These seventh-characters are widely used in Chapter 19, Injury, poisoning, and certain other consequences of external causes. If a code in these categories is not six characters in length, a placeholder of *x* must be added before the seventh character.

EXAMPLE

Sprain of ribs, subsequent encounter, S23.41xD.

EXERCISE 3-2

Using Figure 3-8, select the appropriate seventh-character.

1. Displaced transverse fracture of the shaft of the right ulna, subsequent encounter for closed fracture with nonunion, S52.221 __________
2. Displaced transverse fracture of the shaft of the right ulna, initial encounter for closed fracture, S52.221 __________
3. Displaced transverse fracture of the shaft of the right ulna, initial encounter for open fracture type IIIB, S52.221 __________
4. Displaced transverse fracture of the shaft of the right ulna, subsequent encounter for open fracture type IIIB with a nonunion, S52.221 __________
5. Displaced transverse fracture of the shaft of the right ulna, subsequent encounter for open fracture type IIIB with a malunion, S52.221 __________

Format of Alphabetic Index to Diseases and Injuries

The Alphabetic Index in ICD-10-CM contains the following:

- The Index to Diseases and Injuries
  - Neoplasm Table
  - Table of Drugs and Chemicals
- Index to External Causes

Index to Diseases and Injuries

Three levels of indentation are used in the Alphabetic Index. These include the following:

- Main terms
- Subterms
- Carryover lines

The **main terms** are identified by bold print and are set flush with the left margin of each column (Figure 3-9). Alphabetization rules apply in locating main terms and subterms in the Alphabetic Index. Numerical entries appear first under the main term or subterm (Figure 3-10). Main terms usually are identified by disease conditions and nouns. The main term is not a body part or site.

EXAMPLE

The patient has been admitted with deep vein thrombosis. The main term is "thrombosis." "Deep" is a location and "vein" refers to a body part. When looking in the Alphabetic Index, you will look up Thrombosis, subterm vein, with subterm deep.

EXAMPLE

The patient is being treated for adhesive bursitis of the shoulder. The main term is "bursitis." "Adhesive" describes the type of bursitis and "shoulder" is a body part.

● **S52 Fracture of forearm**

Note: A fracture not identified as displaced or nondisplaced should be coded to displaced

A fracture not designated as open or closed should be coded to closed

The open fracture designations are based on the Gustilo open fracture classification

Excludes1 traumatic amputation of forearm (S58.-)

Excludes2 fracture at wrist and hand level (S62.-)

The appropriate 7th character is to be added to all codes from category S52

A	initial encounter for closed fracture
B	initial encounter for open fracture type I or II initial encounter for open fracture NOS
C	initial encounter for open fracture type IIIA, IIIB, or IIIC
D	subsequent encounter for closed fracture with routine healing
E	subsequent encounter for open fracture type I or II with routine healing
F	subsequent encounter for open fracture type IIIA, IIIB, or IIIC with routine healing
G	subsequent encounter for closed fracture with delayed healing
H	subsequent encounter for open fracture type I or II with delayed healing
J	subsequent encounter for open fracture type IIIA, IIIB, or IIIC with delayed healing
K	subsequent encounter for closed fracture with nonunion
M	subsequent encounter for open fracture type I or II with nonunion
N	subsequent encounter for open fracture type IIIA, IIIB, or IIIC with nonunion
P	subsequent encounter for closed fracture with malunion
Q	subsequent encounter for open fracture type I or II with malunion
R	subsequent encounter for open fracture type IIIA, IIIB, or IIIC with malunion
S	sequela

● **S52.0 Fracture of upper end of ulna**

Fracture of proximal end of ulna

Excludes2 fracture of elbow NOS (S42.40-)
fractures of shaft of ulna (S52.2-)

● **S52.00 Unspecified fracture of upper end of ulna**

Ex: For category S52.00 CC codes S52.00[B,C]: S52.001-S52.009[B,C], S52.021-S52.109[B,C], S52.121-S52.189[B,C], S52.201-S52.209[A,B,C], S52.211-S52.219[A], S52.221-S52.266[A,B,C], S52.271-S52.279[B,C], S52.281-S52-309[A,B,C], S52.311-S52.319[A], S52.321-S52.516[A,B,C], S52.531-S52.616[A,B,C], S52.691-S52.92X[A,B,C], S59.001-S59.099[A], S59.201-S59.299[A], S62.90X[B]

For S52.00[K,M,N,P,Q,R]: See S02.0[K]

● ■ **S52.001 Unspecified fracture of upper end of right ulna** K, M, N, P, Q, R, **B, C, C-S, B, C**

● ■ **S52.002 Unspecified fracture of upper end of left ulna K, M, N, P, Q,** R, **B, C, C-S, B, C**

● ■ **S52.009 Unspecified fracture of upper end of unspecified ulna K, M, N, P, Q,** R, **B, C, C-S, B, C**

FIGURE 3-8. Example of 7th character.

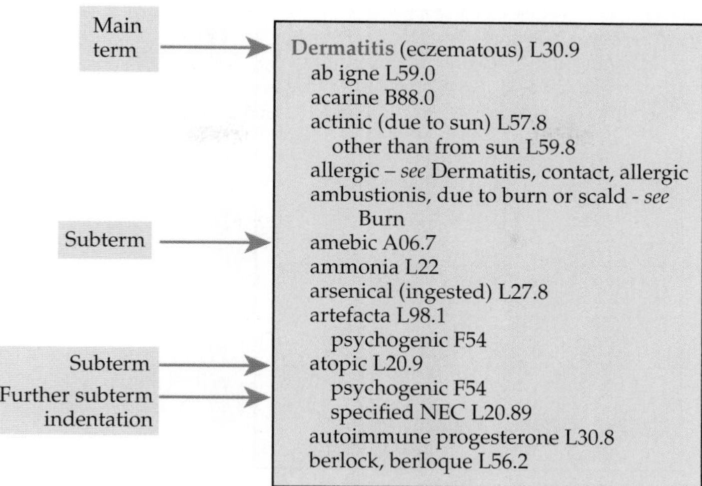

FIGURE 3-9. Various levels of indentation in the index. The bold term is the main term.

Deficiency, defective Q89.9
3-beta hydroxysteroid dehydrogenase E25.0
11-hydroxylase E25.0
21-hydroxylase E25.0
abdominal wall, congenital Q79.59
antibody immunodeficiency D80.9

FIGURE 3-10. Numerical entries in the Alphabetic Index.

EXERCISE 3-3

Underline the main terms to be located in the Alphabetic Index in the following diagnosis statements.

1. Decubitus ulcer of the heel ______________
2. Acute anterior wall myocardial infarction ______________
3. Respiratory anthrax ______________
4. Endometriosis of the ovary ______________
5. Gouty arthritis ______________

The subterms are indented to the right under the main term. They are not bolded and begin with a lowercase letter. **Subterms** modify the main term and sometimes are called essential modifiers. These terms provide greater specificity to the disease or injury. It is possible for a subterm to be followed by additional subterm(s). These additional subterms are indented even farther to the right than are subterms (refer to Figure 3-9).

Some subterms are called **connecting words**. This means that there is a relationship between a main term or a subterm and an associated condition or etiology. Connecting words "with" and "without" are located before any other subterms (Figure 3-11). Additional connecting words include the following:

- Associated with
- Due to
- In
- With
- With mention of

Abscess (connective tissue) (embolic) (fistulous) (infective) (metastatic) (multiple) (pernicious) (pyogenic) (septic) L02.91
with
diverticular disease (intestine) K57.80
with bleeding K57.81
large intestine K57.20
with
bleeding K57.21
small intestine K57.40
with bleeding K57.41
small intestine K57.00
with
bleeding K57.01
large intestine K57.40
with bleeding K57.41
lymphangitis - code by site under Abscess

FIGURE 3-11. Connecting term "with" follows the main term.

Fenestration, fenestrated - *see also* Imperfect, closure
aortico-pulmonary Q21.4
cusps, heart valve NEC Q24.8
pulmonary Q22.3
pulmonic cusps Q22.3

FIGURE 3-12. Carryover line.

EXERCISE 3-4

Using the Alphabetic Index only, assign codes to the following conditions.

1. Asthma due to detergent ______
2. Cholelithiasis with acute cholecystitis ______
3. Parkinsonism associated with neurogenic orthostatic hypotension ______
4. Lymphadenitis due to diphtheria. ______
5. List the subterms for coryza. ______

Carryover lines are used when an entry will not fit on a single line. These are indented to the right even farther than a subterm to avoid confusion (Figure 3-12).

CODING CONVENTIONS

Coding **conventions** are addressed by the Official Guidelines for Coding and Reporting in ICD-10-CM. It is important for coders to understand these conventions so that accurate assignment of codes can be ensured. It is important to remember that the instructions and conventions of the classification take precedence over guidelines.

Conventions include some of the following:

- Abbreviations
- Punctuation/symbols
- Instructional notes
- Linking terms
- Cross-references

Mycosis, mycotic B49
cutaneous NEC B36.9
ear B36.9
in
aspergillosis B44.89
candidiasis B37.84
moniliasis B37.84
fungoides (extranodal) (solid organ) C84.0-
mouth B37.0
nails B35.1
opportunistic B48.8
skin NEC B36.9
specified NEC 848.8
stomatitis B37.0
vagina, vaginitis (candidal) B37.3
Mydriasis (pupil) H57.04
Myelatelia Q06.1
Myelinolysis, pontine, central G37.2

FIGURE 3-13. The Index entry for mycosis, skin "not elsewhere classifiable" (NEC) is assigned code B36.9.

Abbreviations

In ICD-10-CM, the two main abbreviations are

- NEC—not elsewhere classifiable
- NOS—not otherwise specified

The abbreviation NEC stands for not elsewhere classifiable, which represents "other specified." If a code for a specific condition is not available in the Index, the Index will direct the coder to the "other specified" code in the Tabular. Likewise, in the Tabular the NEC represents "other specified" (Figure 3-13).

NOS is a Tabular List abbreviation that means "unspecified" (Figure 3-14). These codes are to be used only when the documentation in the health record does not provide adequate information. The unspecified code often appears as the code following the main term in the Alphabetic Index. The subterms should be reviewed to determine whether a more specific code is available.

Punctuation

Brackets

Brackets are used in the Tabular List to enclose synonyms, alternative wording, or explanatory phrases (Figure 3-15). Brackets are used in the Alphabetic Index to identify manifestation codes (Figure 3-16). The code in brackets is always sequenced second.

Parentheses

Parentheses are used in both the Alphabetic Index and the Tabular List to enclose supplementary words. The presence or absence of these terms does not affect code assignment, so they are called nonessential modifiers. A **nonessential modifier** is a term that is enclosed in parentheses following a main term or a subterm, whose presence or absence has no effect on code assignment. These are "take it or leave it" terms. Sometimes, the subterm can be found among the nonessential modifiers (Figures 3-17 and 3-18).

If the diagnostic statement is "double pneumonia," (see Figure 3-17), since "double" is a nonessential modifier, it is assigned the same code as "pneumonia" J18.9. The word "double" makes absolutely no difference in assignment of the code for "double pneumonia."

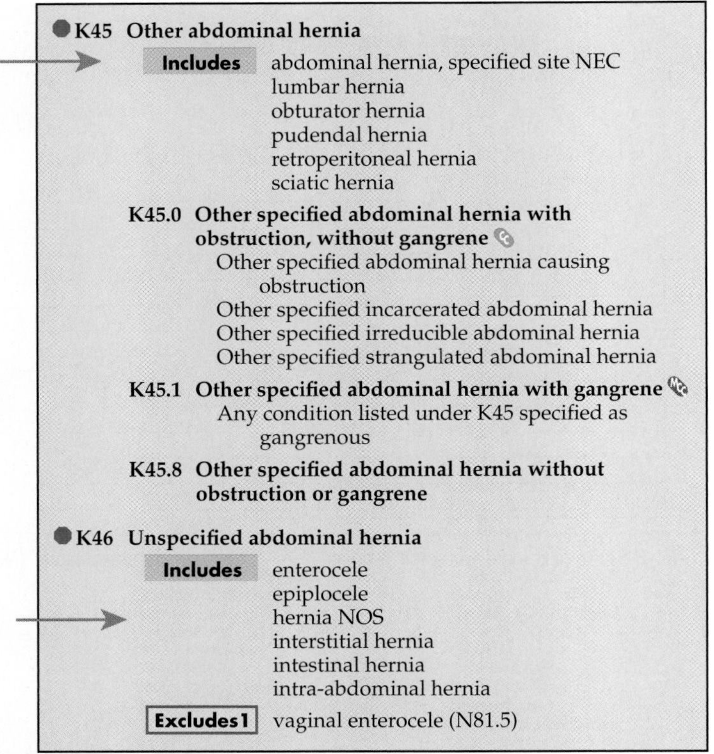

K45 Other abdominal hernia

Includes abdominal hernia, specified site NEC
lumbar hernia
obturator hernia
pudendal hernia
retroperitoneal hernia
sciatic hernia

K45.0 Other specified abdominal hernia with obstruction, without gangrene
Other specified abdominal hernia causing obstruction
Other specified incarcerated abdominal hernia
Other specified irreducible abdominal hernia
Other specified strangulated abdominal hernia

K45.1 Other specified abdominal hernia with gangrene
Any condition listed under K45 specified as gangrenous

K45.8 Other specified abdominal hernia without obstruction or gangrene

K46 Unspecified abdominal hernia

Includes enterocele
epiplocele
hernia NOS
interstitial hernia
intestinal hernia
intra-abdominal hernia

Excludes1 vaginal enterocele (N81.5)

FIGURE 3-14. Examples of NEC and NOS from the Tabular.

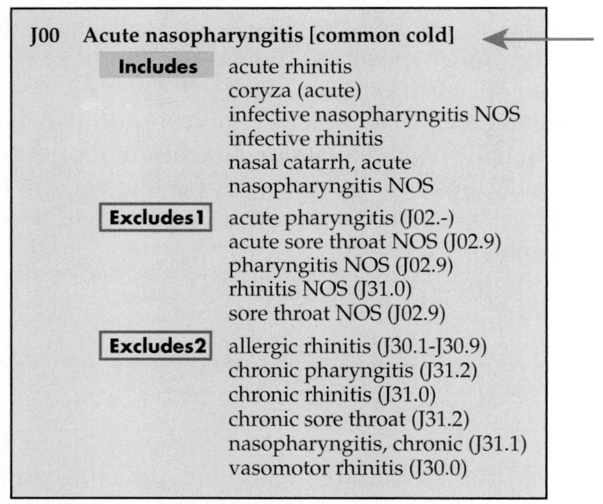

J00 Acute nasopharyngitis [common cold]

Includes acute rhinitis
coryza (acute)
infective nasopharyngitis NOS
infective rhinitis
nasal catarrh, acute
nasopharyngitis NOS

Excludes1 acute pharyngitis (J02.-)
acute sore throat NOS (J02.9)
pharyngitis NOS (J02.9)
rhinitis NOS (J31.0)
sore throat NOS (J02.9)

Excludes2 allergic rhinitis (J30.1-J30.9)
chronic pharyngitis (J31.2)
chronic rhinitis (J31.0)
chronic sore throat (J31.2)
nasopharyngitis, chronic (J31.1)
vasomotor rhinitis (J30.0)

FIGURE 3-15. Brackets for synonyms or alternative wording.

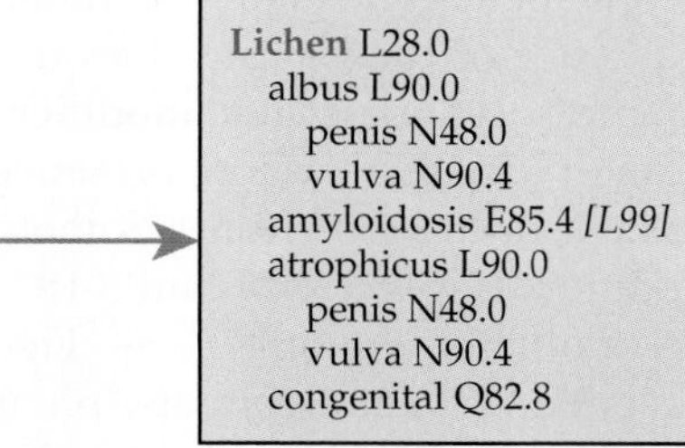

Lichen L28.0
albus L90.0
penis N48.0
vulva N90.4
amyloidosis E85.4 *[L99]*
atrophicus L90.0
penis N48.0
vulva N90.4
congenital Q82.8

FIGURE 3-16. Brackets for manifestation codes.

Pneumonia (acute) (double) (migratory)
(purulent) (septic) (unresolved)
J18.9
with
influenza—*see* Influenza, with,
pneumonia
lung abscess J85.1
due to specified organism - *see*
Pneumonia, in (due to)

FIGURE 3-17. The use of parentheses in the Index for the diagnosis of pneumonia.

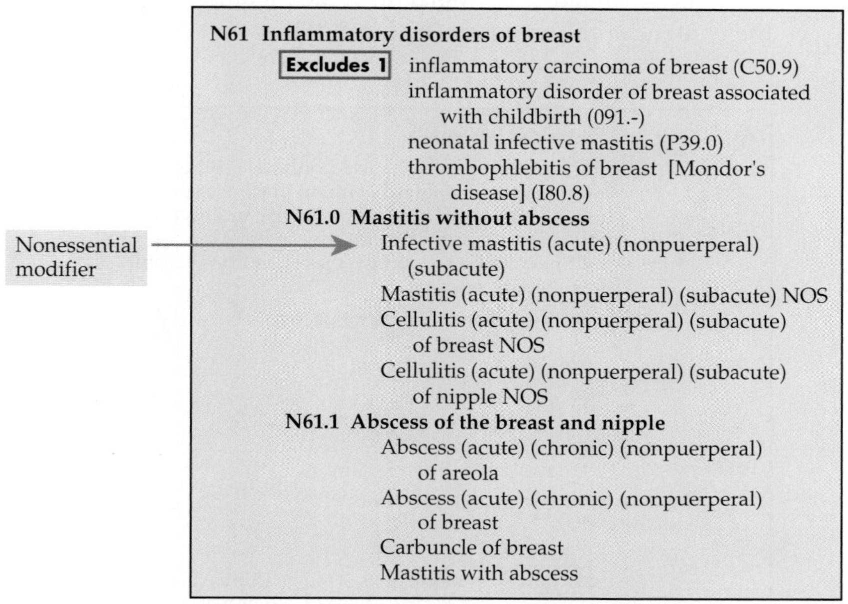

N61 Inflammatory disorders of breast
Excludes 1 inflammatory carcinoma of breast (C50.9)
inflammatory disorder of breast associated with childbirth (091.-)
neonatal infective mastitis (P39.0)
thrombophlebitis of breast [Mondor's disease] (I80.8)
N61.0 Mastitis without abscess
Infective mastitis (acute) (nonpuerperal) (subacute)
Mastitis (acute) (nonpuerperal) (subacute) NOS
Cellulitis (acute) (nonpuerperal) (subacute) of breast NOS
Cellulitis (acute) (nonpuerperal) (subacute) of nipple NOS
N61.1 Abscess of the breast and nipple
Abscess (acute) (chronic) (nonpuerperal) of areola
Abscess (acute) (chronic) (nonpuerperal) of breast
Carbuncle of breast
Mastitis with abscess

FIGURE 3-18. The nonessential modifier in the Tabular.

● ***I52 Other heart disorders in diseases classified elsewhere***
Code first underlying disease, such as:
congenital syphilis (A50.5)
mucopolysaccharidosis (E76.3)
schistosomiasis (B65.0-B65.9)
Excludes1 heart disease (in):
gonococcal infection (A54.83)
meningococcal infection (A39.50)
rheumatoid arthritis (M05.31)
syphilis (A52.06)

FIGURE 3-19. Colon used within an "Excludes" note.

EXERCISE 3-5

Using the Alphabetic Index, locate the following main terms, and identify whether the bolded subterm is an essential or a nonessential modifier.

1. **Immature** cataract ______________
2. **Nuclear** cataract ______________
3. **Essential** hypertension ______________
4. **Filarial** infestation ______________
5. **Thyrotoxic** exophthalmos ______________

Colons

Colons are used in the Tabular List. They are used after a term that requires one or more modifiers that follow the colon to make it assignable to a particular category (Figure 3-19).

Instructional Notes

General notes may be found in the Alphabetic Index and the Tabular List. These notes provide additional information (Figure 3-20). Other types of instructional notes are Inclusion; Exclusion; code first; use additional code; and code, if applicable, any causal condition first.

Inclusion Notes

An "Includes" note is an instructional note that appears immediately under a three-character code title or category. The purpose of the Includes note is to give examples or further define the content of the category (Figure 3-21).

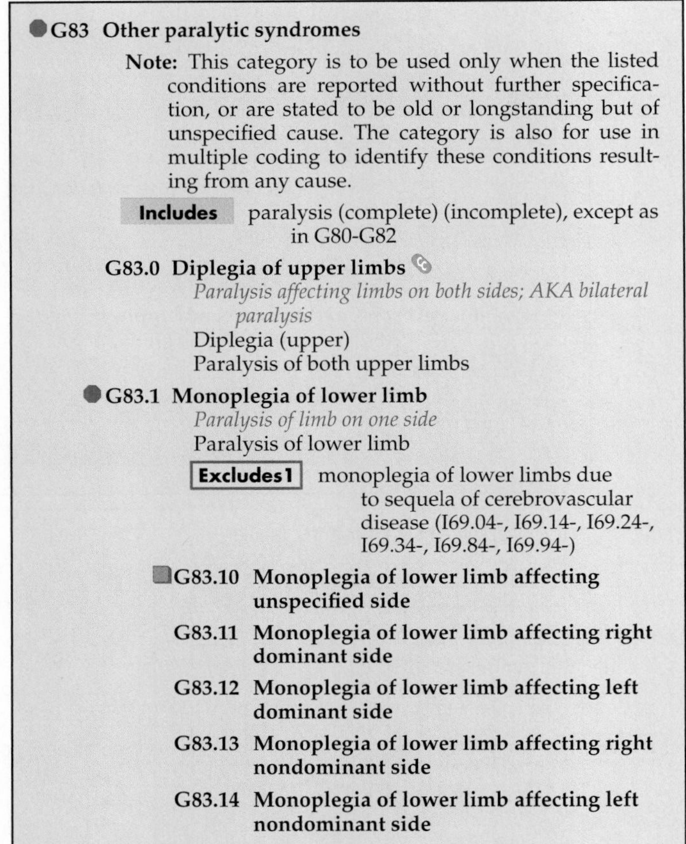

G83 Other paralytic syndromes

Note: This category is to be used only when the listed conditions are reported without further specification, or are stated to be old or longstanding but of unspecified cause. The category is also for use in multiple coding to identify these conditions resulting from any cause.

Includes paralysis (complete) (incomplete), except as in G80-G82

G83.0 Diplegia of upper limbs

Paralysis affecting limbs on both sides; AKA bilateral paralysis

Diplegia (upper)

Paralysis of both upper limbs

G83.1 Monoplegia of lower limb

Paralysis of limb on one side

Paralysis of lower limb

Excludes1 monoplegia of lower limbs due to sequela of cerebrovascular disease (I69.04-, I69.14-, I69.24-, I69.34-, I69.84-, I69.94-)

G83.10 Monoplegia of lower limb affecting unspecified side

G83.11 Monoplegia of lower limb affecting right dominant side

G83.12 Monoplegia of lower limb affecting left dominant side

G83.13 Monoplegia of lower limb affecting right nondominant side

G83.14 Monoplegia of lower limb affecting left nondominant side

FIGURE 3-20. General notes found in the Tabular.

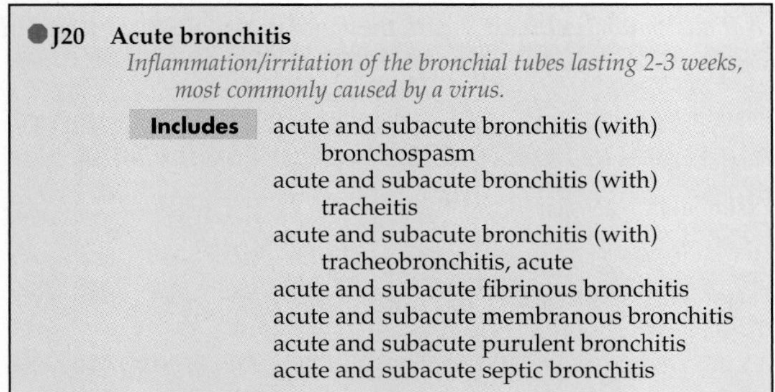

J20 Acute bronchitis

Inflammation/irritation of the bronchial tubes lasting 2-3 weeks, most commonly caused by a virus.

Includes acute and subacute bronchitis (with) bronchospasm

acute and subacute bronchitis (with) tracheitis

acute and subacute bronchitis (with) tracheobronchitis, acute

acute and subacute fibrinous bronchitis

acute and subacute membranous bronchitis

acute and subacute purulent bronchitis

acute and subacute septic bronchitis

FIGURE 3-21. This "Includes" note is found under category J20.

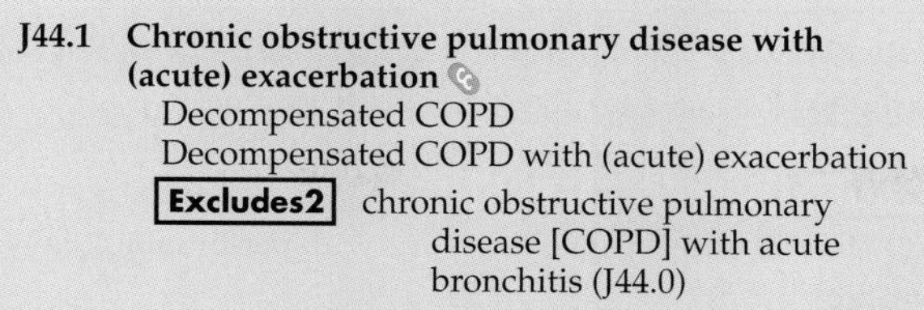

J44.1 Chronic obstructive pulmonary disease with (acute) exacerbation
Decompensated COPD
Decompensated COPD with (acute) exacerbation
Excludes2 chronic obstructive pulmonary disease [COPD] with acute bronchitis (J44.0)

FIGURE 3-22. Inclusion terms.

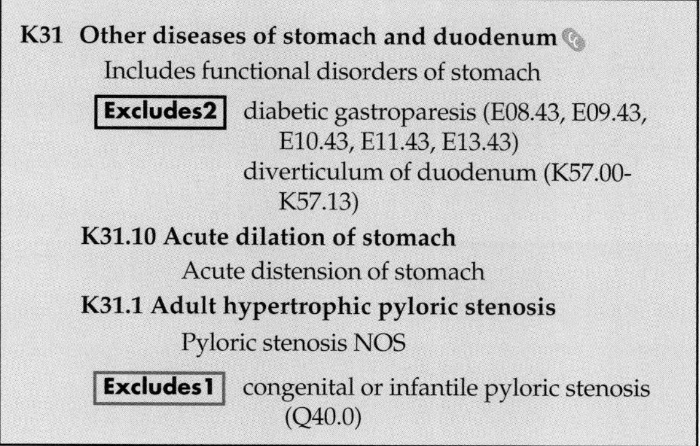

K31 Other diseases of stomach and duodenum
Includes functional disorders of stomach
Excludes2 diabetic gastroparesis (E08.43, E09.43, E10.43, E11.43, E13.43)
diverticulum of duodenum (K57.00-K57.13)
K31.10 Acute dilation of stomach
Acute distension of stomach
K31.1 Adult hypertrophic pyloric stenosis
Pyloric stenosis NOS
Excludes1 congenital or infantile pyloric stenosis (Q40.0)

FIGURE 3-23. Example of Excludes1 note.

Inclusion Terms

According to the guidelines, Inclusion terms are a list of terms that are found under some fourth- and fifth-character codes (Figure 3-22). These terms may be synonyms or various other conditions that are assigned to the code. Inclusion terms do not necessarily constitute a comprehensive list. Additional terms found only in the Alphabetic Index and not in the Tabular List may be assigned a code without mention in the Inclusion terms. In these instances, the Index should be trusted.

Exclusion Notes

ICD-10-CM has two types of "Excludes" notes:

- Excludes1
  An Excludes1 note is used to indicate that two conditions cannot occur together. If a certain condition is excluded, it means it cannot be coded here (Figure 3-23). According to the *Official Coding Guidelines for Coding and Reporting,* an exception can be made if the two conditions are unrelated to each other. If it is not clear whether the two conditions involved are related or not, the provider should be queried.

EXAMPLE

The 3-week-old infant presents to the hospital with projectile vomiting. The doctor diagnoses the patient with congenital pyloric stenosis. Code K31.1 excludes congenital pyloric stenosis, directing the coder to Q40.0

- Excludes2
  An Excludes2 note is used to indicate that the condition is not represented by the code, "not included here." In the case of the Excludes2 note, it would be acceptable to use two codes as appropriate (Figure 3-24).

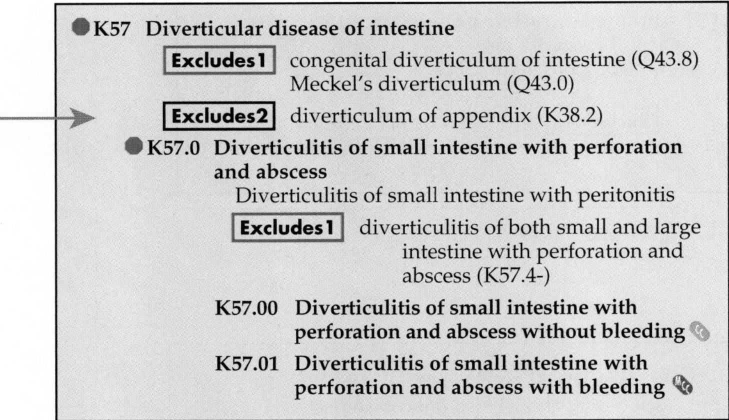

●K57 **Diverticular disease of intestine**
Excludes1 congenital diverticulum of intestine (Q43.8)
Meckel's diverticulum (Q43.0)
Excludes2 diverticulum of appendix (K38.2)
●K57.0 **Diverticulitis of small intestine with perforation and abscess**
Diverticulitis of small intestine with peritonitis
Excludes1 diverticulitis of both small and large intestine with perforation and abscess (K57.4-)
K57.00 **Diverticulitis of small intestine with perforation and abscess without bleeding**
K57.01 **Diverticulitis of small intestine with perforation and abscess with bleeding**

FIGURE 3-24. Example of Excludes2 note.

EXAMPLE

Patient presents to the hospital with stomach pain. The doctor diagnoses the patient with diverticulitis of the colon and the appendix. This would require two codes, one for the colon and one for the appendix. See the Excludes2 note under K57, which states Excludes2 diverticulum of appendix (K38.2).

EXERCISE 3-6

Using the Tabular List, answer the following questions.

1. Is bronchitis due to fumes and vapors assigned code J40? ________
   If not, what code is assigned? ________
2. Is chronic sinusitis assigned code category J01? ________
   If not, what code is assigned? ________
3. Is gangrenous tonsillitis assigned to code category J03? ________
   If not, what code is assigned? ________
4. Is hypertensive cardiomegaly included in code category I11? ________
   If not, what code is assigned? ________
5. Is aseptic peritonitis included in code category K65? ________
   If not, what code is assigned? ________

Etiology and Manifestation Convention

Some disease conditions may have both an underlying **etiology** (cause or origin of a disease or condition) as well as many body system **manifestations** that are the direct cause of the underlying etiology. In ICD-10-CM the underlying condition is sequenced first, followed by the manifestation. There will be two sets of instructions for these conditions. The etiology code will have an instruction to use an additional code, while the manifestation code will have a note to code first the etiology code (Figure 3-25). In Figure 3-25, under the code category F02 for Dementia, the instructions advise to code first the underlying condition. If the patient had Alzheimer's, code category G30 (Figure 3-26) would become the first sequenced code, and the instructional note under G30 likewise advises the coder to assign an additional code for dementia. In most cases the manifestation codes will have in the title "in diseases classified elsewhere" (Figure 3-27). When this terminology is used, these codes are NEVER to be used first. These codes must be sequenced after the underlying condition code. If the manifestation code does not have "in diseases classified elsewhere" in the title but does have a "use additional code" note, the same sequencing rules apply as for "in diseases classified elsewhere."

● **F02 Dementia in other diseases classified elsewhere**

Code first the underlying physiological condition, such as:

Alzheimer's (G30.-)
cerebral lipidosis (E75.4)
Creutzfeldt-Jakob disease (A81.0-)
dementia with Lewy bodies (G31.83)
dementia with Parkinsonism (G31.83)
epilepsy and recurrent seizures (G40.-)
frontotemporal dementia (G31.09)
hepatolenticular degeneration (E83.0)
human immunodeficiency virus [HIV] disease (B20)
Huntington's disease (G10)
hypercalcemia (E83.52)
hypothyroidism, acquired (E00-E03.-)
intoxications (T36-T65)
Jakob-Creutzfeldt disease (A81.0-)
multiple sclerosis (G35)
neurosyphilis (A52.17)
niacin deficiency [pellagra] (E52)
Parkinson's disease (G20)
Pick's disease (G31.01)
polyarteritis nodosa (M30.0)
prion disease (A81.9)
systemic lupus erythematosus (M32.-)
traumatic brain injury (S06.-)
trypanosomiasis (B56.-, B57.-)
vitamin B deficiency (E53.8)

Includes Major neurocognitive disorder in other diseases classified elsewhere

Excludes2 dementia in alcohol and psychoactive substance disorders (F10-F19, with .17, .27, .97)
vascular dementia (F01.5-)

FIGURE 3-25. Instruction note to code first underlying condition.

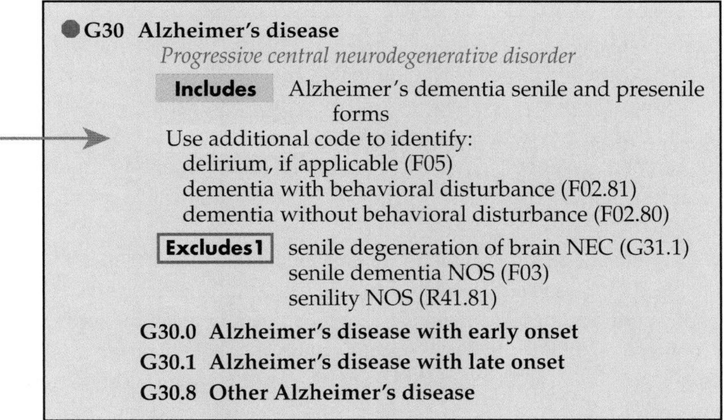

● **G30 Alzheimer's disease**

Progressive central neurodegenerative disorder

Includes Alzheimer's dementia senile and presenile forms

Use additional code to identify:
delirium, if applicable (F05)
dementia with behavioral disturbance (F02.81)
dementia without behavioral disturbance (F02.80)

Excludes1 senile degeneration of brain NEC (G31.1)
senile dementia NOS (F03)
senility NOS (R41.81)

G30.0 Alzheimer's disease with early onset
G30.1 Alzheimer's disease with late onset
G30.8 Other Alzheimer's disease

FIGURE 3-26. Use additional code note.

G99.0 Autonomic neuropathy in diseases classified elsewhere

Code first underlying disease, such as:

amyloidosis (E85.-)
gout (M1A-, M10.-)
hyperthyroidism (E05.-)

Excludes1 diabetic autonomic neuropathy (E08-E13 with .43)

FIGURE 3-27. Example of manifestation code "in diseases classified elsewhere."

Amyloid heart (disease) E85.4 *[I43]*
Amyloidosis (generalized) (primary) E85.9
  with lung involvement E85.4 *[J99]*
  familial E85.2
  genetic E85.2
  heart E85.4 *[I43]*
  hemodialysis-associated E85.3
  liver E85.4 *[K77]* ←
  localized E85.4
  neuropathic heredofamilial E85.1
  non-neuropathic heredofamilial E85.0
  organ limited E85.4
  Portuguese E85.1
  pulmonary E85.4 *[J99]*
  secondary systemic E85.3
  skin (lichen) (macular) E85.4 *[L99]*
  specified NEC E85.8

FIGURE 3-28. Manifestation code in brackets.

● **M10 Gout**
Accumulation of uric acid that results in swollen, red, hot, painful, stiff joints.
Acute gout
Gout attack
Gout flare
Gout NOS
Podagra
Use additional code to identify:
  Autonomic neuropathy in diseases classified elsewhere (G99.0)
  Calculus of urinary tract in diseases classified elsewhere (N22)
  Cardiomyopathy in diseases classified elsewhere (I43)
  Disorders of external ear in diseases classified elsewhere (H61.1-, H62.8-)
  Disorders of iris and ciliary body in diseases classified elsewhere (H22)
  Glomerular disorders in diseases classified elsewhere (N08)
Excludes2 chronic gout (M1A-)

FIGURE 3-29. Instructional note to use additional code.

● **D89.81 Graft-versus-host disease**
Code first underlying cause, such as:
  complications of transplanted organs and tissue (T86.-)
  complications of blood transfusion (T80.89)
Use additional code to identify associated manifestations, such as:
  desquamative dermatitis (L30.8)
  diarrhea (R19.7)
  elevated bilirubin (R17)
  hair loss (L65.9)

FIGURE 3-30. Instructional note to code first underlying cause.

In the Alphabetic Index, manifestation codes will be listed together with the etiology code first followed by the manifestation code in brackets. The code in brackets is always sequenced second (Figure 3-28).

When there is not an etiology/manifestation combination but the terms "code first underlying cause" and "use additional code" are used, the same sequencing rules apply (Figure 3-30).

EXAMPLE

A patient with idiopathic gout of the right foot has an associated calculus of the urinary tract, M10.071, N22 (Figure 3-29).

EXAMPLE

Patient has an ulcer of the right ankle due to diabetes, type 2. The ulcer shows exposure of the fat layer. E11.622, L97.312, codes must be sequenced in this order.

Code category L97 includes an instructional note to code first any associated underlying condition.

EXAMPLE

Patient has a urinary tract infection due to *Escherichia coli*, must be sequenced in this order, N39.0, B96.20.

The "use additional code" note instructs the coder to assign an additional code for the organism (Figure 3-31).

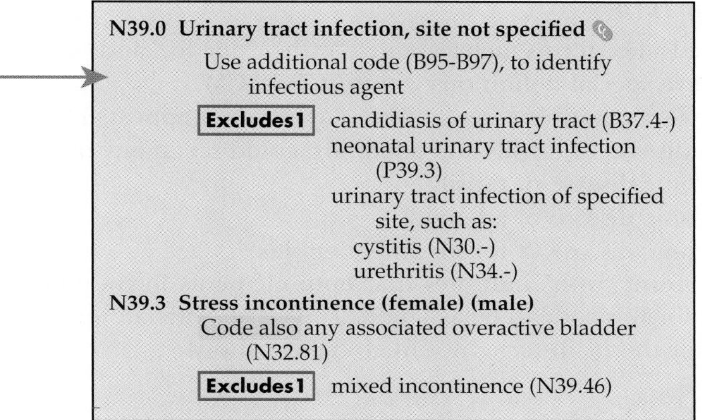

N39.0 Urinary tract infection, site not specified
Use additional code (B95-B97), to identify infectious agent
Excludes1 candidiasis of urinary tract (B37.4-)
neonatal urinary tract infection (P39.3)
urinary tract infection of specified site, such as:
cystitis (N30.-)
urethritis (N34.-)
N39.3 Stress incontinence (female) (male)
Code also any associated overactive bladder (N32.81)
Excludes1 mixed incontinence (N39.46)

FIGURE 3-31. Instructional note to use an additional code.

Diabetes, diabetic (mellitus) (sugar) E11.9
with
amyotrophy E11.44
arthropathy NEC E11.618
autonomic (poly)neuropathy E11.43
cataract E11.36
Charcot's joints E11.610
chronic kidney disease E11.22
circulatory complication NEC E11.59
complication E11.8
specified NEC E11.69
dermatitis E11.620
foot ulcer E11.621
gangrene E11.52
gastroparesis E11.43
glomerulonephrosis, intracapillary E11.21
glomerulosclerosis, intercapillary E11.21
hyperglycemia E11.65
hyperosmolarity E11.00
with coma E11.01
hypoglycemia E11.649
with coma E11.641

FIGURE 3-32. Diabetes with hypoglycemia.

EXERCISE 3-7

Using the Tabular List and instructional notes, assign and sequence the following code(s).

1. See category G30 and assign code(s) for a patient who has Alzheimer's disease and dementia with behavioral disturbances. ______________
2. See code E84.0 and assign code(s) for a patient with cystic fibrosis and pseudomonas. ______________
3. See category J13 and assign code(s) for a patient with a lung abscess who also has pneumonia due to streptococcus pneumoniae. ______________
4. See code N40.1 and assign code(s) for a patient with hyperplasia of the prostate with urinary retention. ______________
5. See code I85.11 and assign code(s) for a patient with bleeding esophageal varices and cirrhosis of the liver. ______________

Linking Terms

As in the Index, terms such as "and," "with," "due to," and "in" are used to link terms. These terms have special definitions within ICD-10-CM.

The term "and" means "and" or "or" when it appears in a title. The code category J35, chronic disease of tonsils and adenoids, could mean any of the following:

- Chronic disease of tonsils
- Chronic disease of adenoids
- Chronic disease of tonsils and adenoids

The term "with" indicates that both elements in the title must be present and documented for this code to be assigned. The word "with" in the Alphabetic Index is sequenced right after the main term, not in alphabetical order.

EXAMPLE

Type 2 diabetes with hypoglycemia and coma is assigned E11.641.

Cross-References

Cross-reference terms are used in the Alphabetic Index to instruct a coder to look elsewhere prior to code assignment. These terms include *"see,"* *"see also,"* "*see* category," and "*see* condition" (Figure 3-33).

The term "see" is a mandatory instruction that advises the coder to go to another main term (Figure 3-34).

The term "see also" instructs the coder about the possibility that a better main term may appear elsewhere in the Alphabetic Index. If the specific diagnosis cannot be completely identified by the subterms, it may be necessary to follow the "see also" instruction (Figure 3-35).

Hereditary - *see* condition
Heredodegeneration, macular - *see* Dystrophy, retina
Heredopathia atactica polyneuritiformis G60.1
Heredosyphilis - *see* Syphilis, congenital
Herlitz' syndrome Q81.1
Hermansky-Pudlak syndrome E70.331

FIGURE 3-33. Under the main term "Hereditary," mandatory instructions are given to *"see"* condition.

Angioblastoma - *see* Neoplasm, connective tissue, uncertain behavior

FIGURE 3-34. Cross-reference to *"see"* another main term.

Hydrarthrosis - *see also* Effusion, joint
gonococcal A54.42
intermittent M12.40
ankle M12.47-
elbow M12.42-
foot joint M12.47-
hand joint M12.44-
hip M12.45-
knee M12.46-
multiple site M12.49
shoulder M12.41-
specified joint NEC M12.48
wrist M12.43-
of yaws (early) (late) (*see also* subcategory M14.8-) A66.6
syphilitic (late) A52.77
congenital A50.55 *[M12.80]*

FIGURE 3-35. *"See also"* instruction to go to the main term "Effusion."

A "code also" note instructs the coder that two codes may be required to fully describe a condition. "Code also" notes do not give sequencing instruction.

Default Codes

In the ICD-10-CM Alphabetic Index, if a code is listed next to the main term, it is the default code. A default code may represent a condition that is most commonly associated with the main term or is the unspecified term for that condition. For example, if pneumonia is documented in a medical record and no additional information or specificity is supplied, such as aspiration or viral, the default code is J18.9.

Syndromes

To code syndromes, the guidance supplied by the Alphabetic Index must be followed. Should there be no guidance in the Index, codes should be assigned for all the manifestations of the syndrome that have been documented. Additional codes for manifestations that are not an integral part of the disease process may also be assigned when the condition does not have a unique code.

EXERCISE 3-8

Using the Alphabetic Index, answer the following questions.

1. Locate the main term "arthropathy" in the Index. Is there another term for "arthropathy" that may be located in the Index, and if so, what is the term? ______________
2. Locate the main term "climacteric" in the Index. Is there another term for "climacteric" that may be located in the Index, and if so, what is the term? ______________
3. Locate the main term "lathyrism" in the Index. Is there another term for "lathyrism," and if so, what is the term? ______________
4. Locate the main term "enteric" in the Index. Is there another term for "enteric" that may be located in the Index, and if so, what is the term? ______________
5. Locate the main term "late effect "in the Index. Is there another term for "late effect" that may be located in the Index, and if so, what is the term? ______________

CHAPTER REVIEW EXERCISE

Match the term, symbol, or punctuation with the appropriate description.

______ **1.** Stands for "not otherwise specified"

______ **2.** Used in both the Index and the Tabular to enclose supplementary words that may be present or absent in the statement of a disease or procedure, without affecting the code number to which it is assigned

______ **3.** This note appears immediately under a three-character code title to further define, or give examples of, the content of the category

______ **4.** A note under a code indicates that the terms excluded from the code are to be coded elsewhere

______ **5.** A word that should be interpreted to mean either "and" or "or" when it appears in a title

______ **6.** Stands for "not elsewhere classifiable"

A. Omit code
B. ( )
C. NOS
D. Includes
E. NEC
F. See category
G. See also
H. Etiology
I. Excludes
J. And
K. Use additional code

Using ICD-10-CM, Volume 1, Tabular List, locate the first pages of Chapter 10, and answer the following questions about the chapter.

7. The name of the chapter: ______
8. The name of the first section block: ______
9. The description of the first category: ______
10. The description of the first subcategory: ______
11. What note at the beginning of the chapter applies to the entire chapter? ______
12. What instructional note applies to category J01? ______
13. What Excludes note applies to the first section block? ______

Underline the main terms to be located in the Alphabetic Index in the following diagnostic statements.

14. Profound anemia ______
15. Chronic prostatitis ______
16. Mild protein-calorie malnutrition ______
17. Granuloma lung ______
18. Pain in shoulder ______

Using the Alphabetic Index, locate the following main terms and identify whether the bolded subterm is an essential or a nonessential modifier.

19. **Cortical** cataract ______
20. **Senile** cataract ______
21. **Contact** dermatitis ______
22. **Classical** migraine ______
23. **Congential** strabismus ______

Using the Alphabetic Index, answer the following questions.

24. Locate the main term "acrochondrohyperplasia" in the Index. Is there another term for "acrochondrohyperplasia" that may be located in the Index, and if so, what is the term? ______________

25. Locate the main term "malarial" in the Index. Is there another term for "malarial" that may be located in the Index, and if so, what is the term? ______________

Using the Tabular List, answer the following questions.

26. Is decompensated chronic obstructive pulmonary disease with acute exacerbation assigned J44.9? ______________
If not, what code is assigned? ______________

27. Is rupture of the esophagus assigned code K22.3? ______________
If not, what code is assigned? ______________

Using the Tabular List and instructional notes, assign and sequence the following code(s).

28. See category G31 and assign code(s) for a patient who has Pick's disease with behavioral disturbances. ______________

29. See code L62 and assign code(s) for a patient with pachydermoperiostosis with nail dystrophy of the right hand. ______________

30. Assign code(s) for a patient with atherosclerosis of the left lower extremity with a left ankle ulcer with fat layer exposed. ______________

CHAPTER GLOSSARY

Carryover line: used when an entry will not fit on a single line.

Category: a single three-digit code that describes a disease or a similarly related group of conditions.

Connecting words: subterms that denote a relationship between a main term or a subterm and an associated condition or etiology.

Conventions: general rules for use in classification that must be followed for accurate coding.

Etiology: cause or origin of a disease or condition.

ICD-10-CM: *International Classification of Diseases, 10th Revision, Clinical Modification.*

ICD-10-PCS: *International Classification of Diseases, 10th Revision, Procedure Coding System.*

Main term: term that identifies disease conditions or injuries, it is identified in bold print and set flush with the left margin of each column in the Alphabetic Index.

Manifestation: symptom of a condition that is the result of a disease.

NEC: abbreviation for "not elsewhere classifiable" that means "other specified."

Nonessential modifier: term that is enclosed in parentheses; its presence or absence does not affect code assignment.

NOS: abbreviation for "not otherwise specified" that means "unspecified."

Section: consists of a group of three-character categories that represent diseases or conditions that are similar.

See: a mandatory cross-reference that advises the coder to go to another main term.

See also: cross-reference that instructs the coder about the possibility that there may be a better main term elsewhere in the Alphabetic Index.

Subcategory: a fourth-character code that provides additional information or specificity.

Subclassification: a fifth-character code that provides even greater specificity.

Subterms: give more specific information about a main term. Subterms identify site, type, or etiology of a disease condition or injury. Also, modifiers that are indented to the right of the main term.

4

Basic Steps of Coding

CHAPTER OUTLINE

LEARNING OBJECTIVES

1. Assign a diagnosis or procedure from the Alphabetic Index using main terms, subterms, and essential modifiers
2. Explain the necessity of referencing the Alphabetic Index and the Tabular List
3. Describe basic steps of coding
4. Explain how to use both the Alphabetic Index and the Tabular List

ABBREVIATIONS/ ACRONYMS

CC chief complaint
DS discharge summary
ER Emergency Room
OR Operating Room

BASIC STEPS OF CODING

1. Review the health record.
2. Identify the diagnoses and procedures to be coded.
3. Identify the principal diagnosis and the principal procedure.
4. Identify main term(s) in the Alphabetic Index.
5. Review any subterms under the main term in the Alphabetic Index.
6. Follow any cross-reference instructions, such as "see also."
7. Verify in the Tabular List the code(s) selected from the Alphabetic Index.
8. Refer to any instructional notation in the Tabular List.
9. Assign codes to the highest level of specificity.
10. Assign codes to the diagnoses and procedures, reporting all applicable codes, and sequence in accordance with the guidelines.

REVIEW OF THE HEALTH RECORD

As described in Chapter 2 of this textbook, the first step in coding the **principal diagnosis** (condition established after study to be chiefly responsible for occasioning admission of the patient to the hospital for care) or first-listed diagnosis, other reportable diagnoses, and procedures is review of the health record.

The discharge summary (DS), if available, may be the first document to be reviewed for code selection. The coder reads the summary to understand the highlights of this encounter. The **discharge summary** is a synopsis of the events included in a patient's hospital stay. Most pertinent information is contained in the discharge summary. A physician should list the diagnoses and the procedures that were performed during this encounter. The coder should not solely rely on the discharge summary to capture all diagnoses and procedures that occurred during this encounter.

For many reasons, the discharge summary is not the only document from which codes are captured.

- Coders may not have a discharge summary at the time of coding.
- If the patient is in the hospital for a long stay, often the attending physician will focus only on those diagnoses that were treated during the latter part of the stay.
- Physicians list conditions that are not currently under treatment and that appear only in the patient's history.
- Likewise, physicians describe diagnoses as "history of" when, in fact, they represent conditions that are being currently treated.

Most coders start the coding process as they begin their document review. A coder is continually trying to determine the principal diagnosis during the record review. Clues to determination of the principal diagnosis can be found in the ER record or in the admitting orders. Physicians, in their admitting orders, give a reason for admitting the patient. When evaluating an ER record, a coder first looks for the **chief complaint** (CC), which is the reason in the patient's own words for presenting to the hospital.

EXAMPLE

CC: I have a bad cough, fever, and headache, and my throat is so sore I can't even swallow liquids.

As the coder continues the review of the ER document, the ER physician provides a diagnosis for admission to the hospital. The **admitting diagnosis** is the condition that requires the patient to be hospitalized. This condition may be a sign or a symptom that requires testing and evaluation to determine a diagnosis. In the previous example, the ER physician might document, "Admit patient to the hospital for possible pneumonia and dehydration." In this case, the pneumonia has not yet been confirmed, but the dehydration is known.

A **differential diagnosis** occurs when a patient presents with a symptom that could represent a variety of diagnoses. During the patient's stay a variety of studies may be conducted to rule out or confirm the differential diagnoses.

EXAMPLE

A patient presents with abdominal pain, and the physician suspects that this might represent appendicitis, gastroenteritis, or cholecystitis. Appendicitis, gastroenteritis, and cholecystitis are differential diagnoses.

A coder continues on through the health record, reviewing all progress notes, operative reports, anesthesiology notes, and consults to arrive at all diagnoses and procedures that need to be captured or reported.

The second most important concept that a coder must remember (after the definition of principal diagnosis and principal procedure) is that once a term has been located in the Alphabetic Index, the code must then be verified in the Tabular Index. This is not the case in ICD-10-PCS, in which you do not need to refer to the Index before referring to the tables.

ALPHABETIC INDEX

The **Alphabetic Index** consists of an Alphabetic Index to Diseases and an Alphabetic Index to Procedures. In ICD-10-PCS, the purpose of the Alphabetic Index is to locate the appropriate table.

Locate the Main Term in the Index to Diseases

Once the coder begins to establish diagnoses and procedures, the first task in selecting a code is to locate the **main term**, which is always identified by bold type, in the Alphabetic Index.

EXAMPLE

Using pneumonia as the diagnosis, locate this term in the Alphabetic Index. The code for pneumonia is J18.9 (Figure 4-1).

EXERCISE 4-1

Assign codes to the following diagnoses:

1. Aspiration pneumonia ____________
2. Pneumonia due to *Klebsiella pneumoniae* ____________
3. Mycoplasma pneumonia ____________
4. Varicella pneumonia ____________
5. Viral pneumonia ____________

After the main term, "pneumonia," in the Alphabetic Index, is a list of **nonessential modifiers** (words in parentheses). Remember that nonessential modifiers have no effect on the main term. They are "take it or leave it" terms. Sometimes, the subterm that a coder is searching for can be found among the nonessential modifiers.

EXAMPLE

Double pneumonia is coded to J18.9.
Acute pneumonia, J18.9.
Purulent pneumonia, J18.9. (See Figure 4-1.)

In locating the main term, the coder must remember that main terms are usually identified by disease conditions and nouns. They are not body parts or sites. If a physician documents *Klebsiella pneumoniae* pneumonia, the noun is the main term and the one to be located in the Alphabetic Index. To find *Klebsiella pneumoniae* in the Alphabetic Index, the coder goes to "pneumonia" and looks for the subterm, *"Klebsiella"* (Figure 4-2).

Subterms are modifiers of main terms, and in contrast to nonessential modifiers, they do have an effect on the appropriate code assignment. To determine the main term, the coder must decide what condition the patient has (in this case, pneumonia), which is the main term; subterms are modifiers of the main term, which in this case is *Klebsiella pneumoniae.*

EXAMPLE

If a patient has a diagnosis of hiatal hernia, the main term is "hernia," and the subterm is "hiatal."
The main terms usually are nouns and/or disease conditions. The main terms below are underlined.
Gastric <u>upset</u>
Chronic <u>mastoiditis</u>
<u>Herpes</u> simplex

Sometimes, a main term may be found under more than one Index entry (Figure 4-3). This is most often true of **eponyms** (a disease or syndrome named for a person). Adjectives and anatomic sites do appear as main terms, but they instruct the coder to see the condition (Figure 4-4).

EXAMPLE

Diagnosis of ischial fracture: The Index for "ischial" would direct the coder to go to the condition or, in this case, fracture.
Ischium, ischial—*see* condition

Nonessential modifiers

Main Term

Code for pneumonia

Subterm

Pneumonia (acute) (double) (migratory) (purulent) (septic) (unresolved) J18.9
with
lung abscess J85.1
due to specified organism - *see* Pneumonia, in (due to)
influenza -*see* Influenza, with, pneumonia
adenoviral J12.0
adynamic J18.2
alba A50.04
allergic - see also Pneumonitis, hypersensitivity J82.89
alveolar - *see* Pneumonia, lobar
anaerobes J15.8
anthrax A22.1
apex, apical - *see* Pneumonia, lobar
Ascaris B77.81
aspiration J69.0
due to
aspiration of microorganisms
bacterial J15.9
viral J12.9
food (regurgitated) J69.0
gastric secretions J69.0
milk (regurgitated) J69.0
oils, essences J69.1
solids, liquids NEC J69.8
vomitus J69.0
newborn P24.81
amniotic fluid (clear) P24.11
blood P24.21
liquor (amnii) P24.11
meconium P24.01
milk P24.31
mucus P24.11
food (regurgitated) P24.31
specified NEC P24.81
stomach contents P24.31
postprocedural J95.4
atypical NEC J18.9
bacillus J15.9
specified NEC J15.8
bacterial J15.9
specified NEC J15.8
Bacteroides (fragilis) (oralis) (melaninogenicus) J15.8
basal, basic, basilar - *see* Pneumonia, by type
bronchiolitis obliterans organized (BOOP) J84.89
broncho-, bronchial (confluent) (croupous) (diffuse) (disseminated) (hemorrhagic) (involving lobes) (lobar) (terminal) J18.0
allergic (eosinophilic) J82.89
aspiration - *see* Pneumonia, aspiration
bacterial J15.9
specified NEC J15.8
chronic - *see* Fibrosis, lung
diplococcal J13
Eaton's agent J15.7
Escherichia coli (E. coli) J15.5
Friedländer's bacillus J15.0
Hemophilus influenzae J14
hypostatic J18.2
inhalation (*see also* Pneumonia, aspiration

Pneumonia *(Continued)*
due to fumes or vapors (chemical) J68.0
of oils or essences J69.1
Klebsiella (pneumoniae) J15.0
lipid, lipoid J69.1
endogenous J84.89
Mycoplasma (pneumoniae) J15.7
pleuro-pneumonia-like-organisms (PPLO) J15.7
pneumococcal J13
Proteus J15.6
Pseudomonas J15.1
Serratia marcescens J15.6
specified organism NEC J16.8
staphylococcal - *see* Pneumonia, staphylococcal
streptococcal NEC J15.4
group B J15.3
pneumoniae J13
viral, virus - *see* Pneumonia, viral
Butyrivibrio (fibriosolvens) J15.8
Candida B37.1
caseous - *see* Tuberculosis, pulmonary
catarrhal - *see* Pneumonia, broncho
chlamydial J16.0
congenital P23.1
cholesterol J84.8
cirrhotic (chronic) - *see* Fibrosis, lung
Clostridium (haemolyticum) (novyi) J15.8
confluent - *see* Pneumonia, broncho
congenital (infective) P23.9
due to
bacterium NEC P23.6
Chlamydia P23.1
Escherichia coli P23.4
Haemophilus influenzae P23.6
infective organism NEC P23.8
Klebsiella pneumoniae P23.6
Mycoplasma P23.6
Pseudomonas P23.5
Staphylococcus P23.2
Streptococcus (except group B) P23.6
group B P23.3
viral agent P23.0
specified NEC P23.8
croupous - *see* Pneumonia, lobar
cryptogenic organizing J84.116
cytomegalic inclusion B25.0
cytomegaloviral B25.0
deglutition - *see* Pneumonia, aspiration
desquamative interstitial J84.117
diffuse - *see* Pneumonia, broncho
diplococcal, diplococcus (broncho-) (lobar) J13
disseminated (focal) - *see* Pneumonia, broncho
Eaton's agent J15.7
embolic, embolism - *see* Embolism, pulmonary
Enterobacter J15.6
eosinophilic, acute J82.89
eosinophilic, chronic J82.81
Escherichia coli (E. coli) J15.5
Eubacterium J15.8
fibrinous - *see* Pneumonia, lobar
fibroid, fibrous (chronic) - *see* Fibrosis, lung
Friedländer's bacillus J15.0

FIGURE 4-1. Alphabetic Index entry for "pneumonia."

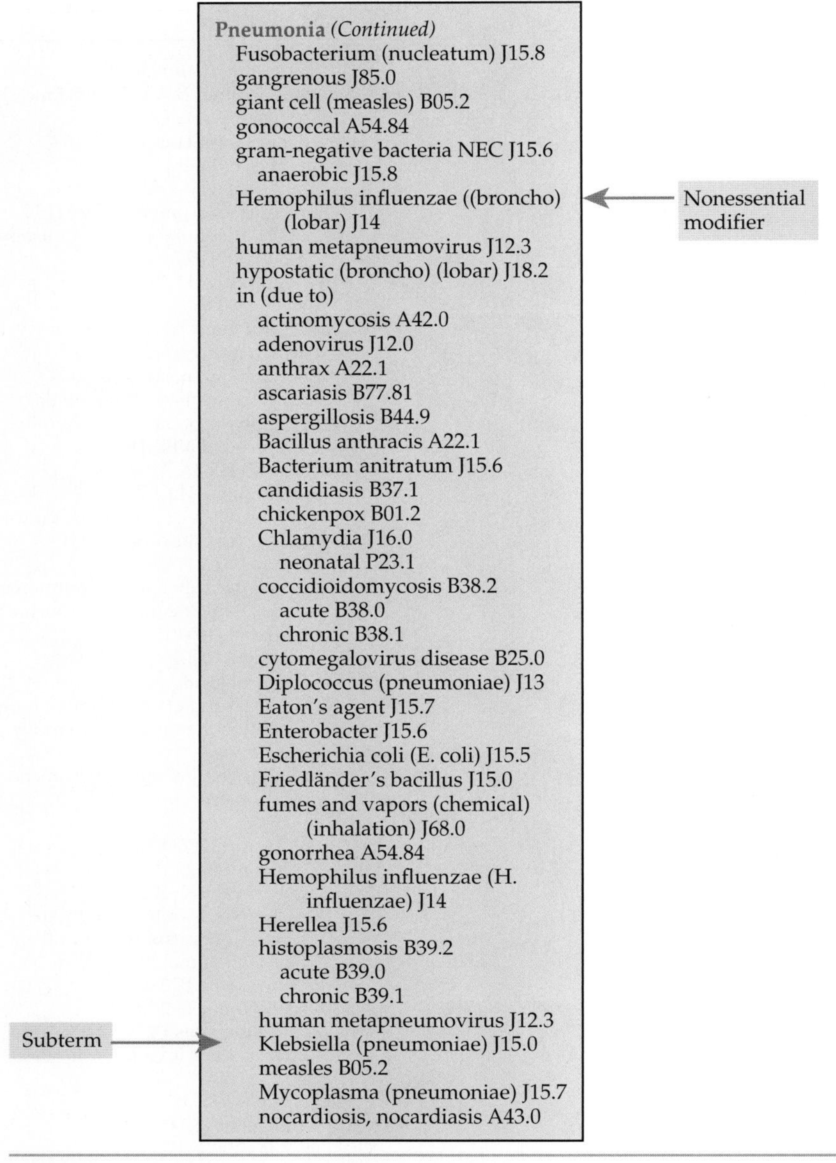

Pneumonia (Continued)
Fusobacterium (nucleatum) J15.8
gangrenous J85.0
giant cell (measles) B05.2
gonococcal A54.84
gram-negative bacteria NEC J15.6
anaerobic J15.8
Hemophilus influenzae ((broncho) (lobar) J14
human metapneumovirus J12.3
hypostatic (broncho) (lobar) J18.2
in (due to)
actinomycosis A42.0
adenovirus J12.0
anthrax A22.1
ascariasis B77.81
aspergillosis B44.9
Bacillus anthracis A22.1
Bacterium anitratum J15.6
candidiasis B37.1
chickenpox B01.2
Chlamydia J16.0
neonatal P23.1
coccidioidomycosis B38.2
acute B38.0
chronic B38.1
cytomegalovirus disease B25.0
Diplococcus (pneumoniae) J13
Eaton's agent J15.7
Enterobacter J15.6
Escherichia coli (E. coli) J15.5
Friedländer's bacillus J15.0
fumes and vapors (chemical) (inhalation) J68.0
gonorrhea A54.84
Hemophilus influenzae (H. influenzae) J14
Herellea J15.6
histoplasmosis B39.2
acute B39.0
chronic B39.1
human metapneumovirus J12.3
Klebsiella (pneumoniae) J15.0
measles B05.2
Mycoplasma (pneumoniae) J15.7
nocardiosis, nocardiasis A43.0
Nonessential modifier
Subterm

FIGURE 4-2. Example of subterm "Klebsiella," under "pneumonia."

EXAMPLE

Chronic otitis media—look up "chronic" in the Alphabetic Index.
Chronic—*see* condition

The term *"see"* is a mandatory direction to look elsewhere in the Alphabetic Index.

Sometimes the Index will direct the coder to *see also*. This instruction means that if the term cannot be located under the Index entry, the user should go to the suggested Index entry.

The general rule that main terms identify disease conditions has some exceptions. One of these exceptions is Z codes, which can be found under main terms such as "admission," "examination," and "status." These will be fully covered in Chapter 9 on Z codes. Likewise, obstetric conditions can be found under main terms such as "pregnancy" and "puerperal" and will be covered in Chapter 22 in the section on obstetrics and gynecology. There is also a main term for Sequelae that can be used to identify residuals of various disease conditions and complications.

Diverticulum, diverticula (multiple) K57.90
appendix (noninflammatory) K38.2
bladder (sphincter) N32.3
congenital Q64.6
bronchus (congenital) Q32.4
acquired J98.09
calyx, calyceal (kidney) N28.89
cardia (stomach) K31.4
cecum - *see* Diverticulosis, intestine, large
congenital Q43.8
colon - *see* Diverticulosis, intestine, large
congenital Q43.8
duodenum - *see* Diverticulosis, intestine, small
congenital Q43.8
epiphrenic (esophagus) K22.5
esophagus (congenital) Q39.6
acquired (epiphrenic) (pulsion) (traction) K22.5
eustachian tube – *see* Disorder, eustachian tube, specified NEC
fallopian tube N83.8
gastric K31.4
heart (congenital) Q24.8
ileum - *see* Diverticulosis, intestine, small
jejunum - *see* Diverticulosis, intestine, small
kidney (pelvis) (calyces) N28.89
with calculus - *see* Calculus, kidney
Meckel's (displaced) (hypertrophic) Q43.0

Eponym as the subterm

Meckel's diverticulitis, diverticulum (displaced) (hypertrophic) Q43.0

Eponym as the main term

FIGURE 4-3. Example of multiple Alphabetic Index entries for Meckel's diverticulum.

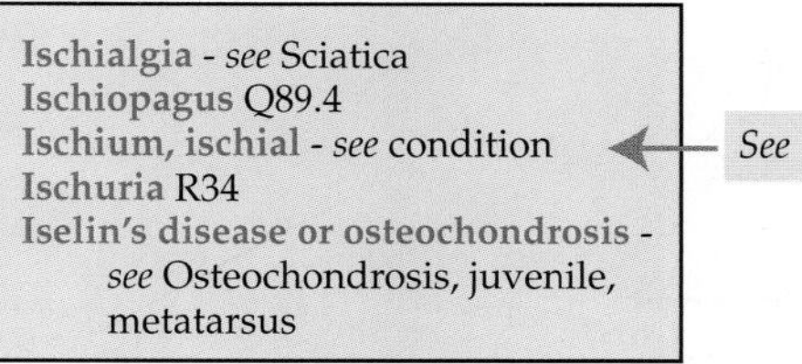
Ischialgia - *see* Sciatica
Ischiopagus Q89.4
Ischium, ischial - *see* condition
Ischuria R34
Iselin's disease or osteochondrosis - *see* Osteochondrosis, juvenile, metatarsus

FIGURE 4-4. Example of an anatomic site instructing coder to *see* condition.

EXERCISE 4-2

Underline all main terms to be located in the Alphabetic Index.

1. Esophageal reflux
2. Tourette's disease
3. Iatrogenic thyroiditis
4. Infantile eczema
5. Coronary artery disease
6. Congestive heart failure
7. Rheumatoid arthritis
8. Atrial fibrillation

TABULAR LIST

Once the code has been selected from the Alphabetic Index, it must then be verified in the **Tabular List**. Sometimes a code that is selected from the Alphabetic Index does not seem to match what is described in the Tabular List. If this is the case, the coder should review the Alphabetic Index and the Tabular List for all exclusion notes and other instructional notes. It may require that the coder browse the category in the Tabular List for a more representative code. It also may require that the coder access *Coding Clinic* for any advice on how to code a specific diagnosis.

EXAMPLE

Documentation in the chart describes the patient as having anorexia. She has been admitted to the psychiatric unit of the hospital.
Look up "Anorexia" in the Alphabetic Index, R63.0.
Go to the Tabular List and review the Excludes notes.
Because this is a psychiatric admission, reviewing the codes excluded may assist in assigning the correct code.

The rule of never coding directly from the Alphabetic Index without reviewing the Tabular also applies to never coding from instructional notes within the Tabular without first reviewing the actual Tabular Listing of the code.

CHAPTER REVIEW EXERCISE

Using the Alphabetic Index and the Tabular List, code all the following diagnoses and underline the main term.

1. Acute nontransmural myocardial infarction ____________
2. *Clostridium difficile* enteritis ____________
3. Refractory megaloblastic anemia ____________
4. Acute suppurative appendicitis ____________
5. Stage 3 pressure ulcer of the sacrum ____________
6. Abdominal aortic aneurysm ____________
7. Colon obstruction ____________
8. Intractable epilepsy with status epilepticus ____________
9. Paroxysmal supraventricular tachycardia ____________
10. Streptococcal group A pneumonia ____________
11. Deep vein thrombosis of the right femoral vein ____________
12. Chronic laryngotracheitis ____________
13. Dysphagia ____________
14. Adhesive bursitis of the right shoulder ____________
15. History of cardiovascular disease in the family ____________

CHAPTER GLOSSARY

Admitting diagnosis: the condition that requires the patient to be hospitalized.

Alphabetic Index: the index found in the ICD-10-CM book for both disease conditions and procedures.

Chief complaint: the reason, in the patient's own words, for presenting to the hospital.

Differential diagnosis: when a symptom may represent a variety of diagnoses.

Discharge summary: a review of the patient's hospital course. This summary details the reason for admission or tests or procedures performed and how the patient responded.

Eponym: term for a disease, structure, procedure, or syndrome that has been named for a person.

Main term: term that identifies disease conditions or injuries; it is identified in bold print and set flush with the left margin of each column in the Alphabetic Index.

Nonessential modifier: term that is enclosed in parentheses; its presence or absence does not affect code assignment.

Principal diagnosis: condition established after study to be chiefly responsible for occasioning admission of the patient to the hospital for care.

Subterm: gives more specific information about a main term. Subterms identify site, type, or etiology of a disease condition or injury. Also, modifiers that are indented to the right of the main term.

Tabular List: section of the ICD-10-CM book that contains the code listing, along with exclusion or inclusion notes.

5

General Coding Guidelines for Diagnosis

CHAPTER OUTLINE

LEARNING OBJECTIVES

1. Apply ICD-10-CM Official Guidelines for Coding and Reporting
2. Sequence ICD-10-CM diagnosis codes as directed by coding guidelines or ICD-10-CM conventions
3. Determine whether signs, symptoms, or manifestations require separate code assignments
4. Assign ICD-10-CM diagnosis codes for sequela

ABBREVIATIONS/ ACRONYMS

AHA American Hospital Association

AHIMA American Health Information Management Association

CMS Centers for Medicare and Medicaid Services

DHHS U.S. Department of Health and Human Services

HIPAA Health Insurance Portability and Accountability Act

ICD-10-CM *International Classification of Diseases, 10th Revision, Clinical Modification*

NCHS National Center for Health Statistics

ICD-10-CM OFFICIAL GUIDELINES FOR CODING AND REPORTING

The ICD-10-CM Official Guidelines for Coding and Reporting were developed by the Cooperating Parties to provide further guidance regarding coding and sequencing that is not provided in the ICD-10-CM manual. These guidelines do not cover every situation and have been formatted in a manner that will allow for expansion as new guidelines are developed. The guidelines may be changed each year, and changes may have greater impact in some years than in others.

In this chapter, the coder will review the general guidelines and coding examples as applicable. The convention guidelines with examples were presented in Chapter 3, "ICD-10-CM, Format and Conventions." Chapter-specific guidelines are provided and explained in the respective disease or body system chapter.

Disease, diseased *(Continued)*
breast (*see also* Disorder, breast) N64.9
cystic (chronic) – *see* Mastopathy, cystic
fibrocystic – *see* Mastopathy, cystic
Paget's
female, unspecified side C50.91-
male, unspecified side C50.92-
specified NEC N64.89
Breda's – *see* Yaws
Bretonneau's (diphtheritic malignant angina) A36.0

FIGURE 5-1. Alphabetic Index entry for Paget's disease, female breast.

● **C50.9 Malignant neoplasm of breast of unspecified site**
● **C50.91 Malignant neoplasm of breast of unspecified site, female**
❑ **C50.911 Malignant neoplasm of unspecified site of right female breast**
❑ **C50.912 Malignant neoplasm of unspecified site of left female breast**
❑ **C50.919 Malignant neoplasm of unspecified site of unspecified female breast**

FIGURE 5-2. Tabular List entry for Paget's disease, female breast.

GENERAL CODING GUIDELINES

General coding guidelines apply to all healthcare settings and to the entire ICD-10-CM classification system.

In the Alphabetic Index of ICD-10-CM a dash (-) is used to indicate that there are further characters that need to be assigned for a valid code. In Figures 5-1 and 5-2, note that C50.91 would be an invalid code. A sixth character is necessary to identify left, right, or unspecified breast. All codes must be assigned to the final level of subdivision. A valid code is at least three characters, but could be four, five, six, or seven characters.

ICD-10-CM Official Guidelines for Coding and Reporting (2021-2022)

Please refer to the companion Evolve website for the most current 2021-2022 guidelines.

Section I. Conventions, general coding guidelines and chapter specific guidelines

The conventions, general guidelines and chapter-specific guidelines are applicable to all health care settings unless otherwise indicated. The conventions and instructions of the classification take precedence over guidelines.

B. General Coding Guidelines

1. Locating a code in the ICD-10-CM

To select a code in the classification that corresponds to a diagnosis or reason for visit documented in a medical record, first locate the term in the Alphabetic Index, and then verify the code in the Tabular List. Read and be guided by instructional notations that appear in both the Alphabetic Index and the Tabular List.

It is essential to use both the Alphabetic Index and Tabular List when locating and assigning a code. The Alphabetic Index does not always provide the full code. Selection of the full code, including laterality and any applicable 7th character can only be done in the Tabular List. A dash (-) at the end of an Alphabetic Index entry indicates that additional characters are required. Even if a dash is not included at the Alphabetic Index entry, it is necessary to refer to the Tabular List to verify that no 7th character is required.

2. **Level of Detail in Coding**
   Diagnosis codes are to be used and reported at their highest number of characters available. ICD-10-CM diagnosis codes are composed of codes with 3, 4, 5, 6 or 7 characters. Codes with three characters are included in ICD-10-CM as the heading of a category of codes that may be further subdivided by the use of fourth and/or fifth characters and/or sixth characters, which provide greater detail.

   A three-character code is to be used only if it is not further subdivided. A code is invalid if it has not been coded to the full number of characters required for that code, including the 7th character, if applicable.

EXERCISE 5-1

Using the Alphabetic Index and the Tabular List, assign the appropriate code(s).

1. Ankylosis right ankle
   Code from Alphabetic Index ________________
   Code following verification in Tabular List ________________
2. Hairy-cell leukemia in remission
   Code from Alphabetic Index ________________
   Code following verification in Tabular List ________________
3. Traumatic spiral fracture shaft of left humerus
   Code from Alphabetic Index ________________
   Code following verification in Tabular List ________________
4. Bilateral carpal tunnel syndrome
   Code from Alphabetic Index ________________
   Code following verification in Tabular List ________________

3. **Code or codes from A00.0 through T88.9, Z00-Z99.8**
   The appropriate code or codes from A00.0 through T88.9, Z00-Z99.8 must be used to identify diagnoses, symptoms, conditions, problems, complaints or other reason(s) for the encounter/visit.
4. **Signs and symptoms**
   Codes that describe symptoms and signs, as opposed to diagnoses, are acceptable for reporting purposes when a related definitive diagnosis has not been established (confirmed) by the provider. Chapter 18 of ICD-10-CM, Symptoms, Signs, and Abnormal Clinical and Laboratory Findings, Not Elsewhere Classified (codes R00.0-R99) contains many, but not all codes for symptoms.
   See Section I.B.18 Use of Signs/Symptoms/Unspecified Codes

EXAMPLE Pyrexia of unknown origin, R50.9.

5. **Conditions that are an integral part of a disease process**
   Signs and symptoms that are associated routinely with a disease process should not be assigned as additional codes, unless otherwise instructed by the classification.
6. **Conditions that are not an integral part of a disease process**
   Additional signs and symptoms that may not be associated routinely with a disease process should be coded when present.

EXAMPLE Hematuria due to calculus of kidney, N20.0 (The hematuria is integral to the calculus).

EXAMPLE Ascites due to cirrhosis of the liver, K74.60, R18.8.

Chapter 18 of ICD-10-CM contains most but not all codes used to identify signs and symptoms.

Signs and symptoms codes are acceptable to code:

- When no definitive diagnosis has been established
- When they are not an integral part of the disease process
- When directed by the classification to assign an additional code
- When a sign or symptom affects the patient's condition or treatment given

It is not acceptable to code signs or symptoms:

- When a definitive diagnosis has been established
- When they are an integral part of the disease process

EXERCISE 5-2

Answer the following questions.

1. List two common symptoms of gallstones. ______________
2. List the symptom most commonly associated with costochondritis. ______________
3. List two common symptoms of urinary tract infection. ______________
4. A patient has osteoarthritis and anemia. The anemia is integral to the osteoarthritis.
   A. True
   B. False
5. A patient has dyspnea caused by congestive heart failure. Dyspnea should be assigned as an additional code.
   A. True
   B. False

Assign codes to the following conditions.

6. Nocturia due to benign prostatic hypertrophy ______________
7. Anorexia due to acute appendicitis ______________
8. Seizure due to glioblastoma multiforme right temporal lobe ______________
9. Fever due to pneumonia ______________
10. Headaches of undetermined etiology ______________

7. **Multiple coding for a single condition**
   In addition to the etiology/manifestation convention that requires two codes to fully describe a single condition that affects multiple body systems, there are other single conditions that also require more than one code. "Use additional code" notes are found in the Tabular List at codes that are not part of an etiology/manifestation pair where a secondary code is useful to fully describe a condition. The sequencing rule is the same as the etiology/manifestation pair, "use additional code" indicates that a secondary code should be added, if known.
   For example, for bacterial infections that are not included in chapter 1, a secondary code from category B95, Streptococcus, Staphylococcus, and Enterococcus, as the cause of diseases classified

elsewhere, or B96, Other bacterial agents as the cause of diseases classified elsewhere, may be required to identify the bacterial organism causing the infection. A "use additional code" note will normally be found at the infectious disease code, indicating a need for the organism code to be added as a secondary code (Figure 5-3).

"Code first" notes are also under certain codes that are not specifically manifestation codes but may be due to an underlying cause. When there is a "code first" note and an underlying condition is present, the underlying condition should be sequenced first, if known (Figure 5-4).

"Code, if applicable, any causal condition first", notes indicate that this code may be assigned as a principal diagnosis when the causal condition is unknown or not applicable. If a causal condition is known, then the code for that condition should be sequenced as the principal or first-listed diagnosis.

Multiple codes may be needed for sequela, complication codes and obstetric codes to more fully describe a condition. See the specific guidelines for these conditions for further instruction.

EXAMPLE

Acute pyelonephritis due to *Escherichia coli (E. coli)*, N10, B96.20.

EXERCISE 5-3

Assign codes to the following conditions.

1. Dementia due to Alzheimer's, early onset ______________
2. Hypertensive retinopathy, bilateral ______________
3. Cellulitis of left lower leg due to group A *streptococcus* ______________
4. Acute prostatitis due to *Escherichia coli* ______________
5. Anemia due to chronic kidney disease, stage 3 ______________

8. Acute and Chronic Conditions

If the same condition is described as both acute (subacute) and chronic, and separate subentries exist in the Alphabetic Index at the same indentation level, code both and sequence the acute (subacute) code first (Figure 5-5).

N10 Acute pyelonephritis

Acute infectious interstitial nephritis
Acute pyelitis
Acute tubulo-interstitial nephritis
Hemoglobin nephrosis
Myoglobin nephrosis

Use additional code (B95-B97), to identify infectious agent

FIGURE 5-3. Instruction to use additional code.

● *H28 Cataract in diseases classified elsewhere*

Code first underlying disease, such as:
hypoparathyroidism (E20.-)
myotonia (G71.1-)
myxedema (E03.-)
protein-calorie malnutrition (E40-E46)

Excludes1 cataract in diabetes mellitus (E08.36, E09.36, E10.36, E11.36, E13.36)

FIGURE 5-4. Code first note.

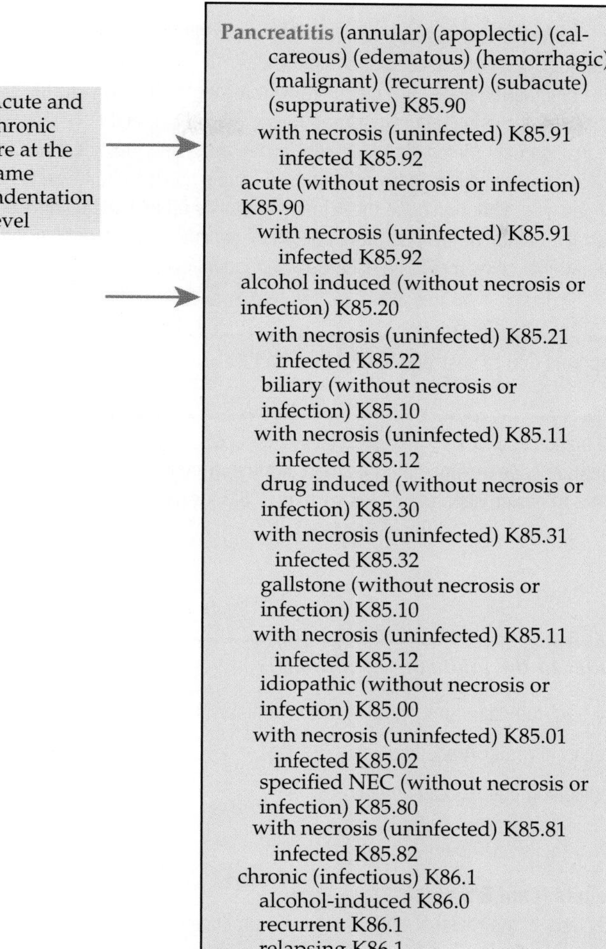
Acute and chronic are at the same indentation level

Pancreatitis (annular) (apoplectic) (calcareous) (edematous) (hemorrhagic) (malignant) (recurrent) (subacute) (suppurative) K85.90
- with necrosis (uninfected) K85.91
  - infected K85.92
- acute (without necrosis or infection) K85.90
  - with necrosis (uninfected) K85.91
    - infected K85.92
  - alcohol induced (without necrosis or infection) K85.20
    - with necrosis (uninfected) K85.21
      - infected K85.22
  - biliary (without necrosis or infection) K85.10
    - with necrosis (uninfected) K85.11
      - infected K85.12
  - drug induced (without necrosis or infection) K85.30
    - with necrosis (uninfected) K85.31
      - infected K85.32
  - gallstone (without necrosis or infection) K85.10
    - with necrosis (uninfected) K85.11
      - infected K85.12
  - idiopathic (without necrosis or infection) K85.00
    - with necrosis (uninfected) K85.01
      - infected K85.02
  - specified NEC (without necrosis or infection) K85.80
    - with necrosis (uninfected) K85.81
      - infected K85.82
- chronic (infectious) K86.1
  - alcohol-induced K86.0
  - recurrent K86.1
  - relapsing K86.1

FIGURE 5-5. Subterms for acute and chronic.

EXAMPLE

Acute and chronic pancreatitis, K85.90, K86.1.

EXAMPLE

Acute and chronic cholecystitis, K81.2.
Separate subterms are included for "acute" and "chronic," but a subterm for "acute and chronic" is also provided.

EXAMPLE

Acute and chronic otitis media, H66.90.
Separate subterms are provided for "acute" and "chronic," but they use the same code.

EXERCISE 5-4

Assign and sequence codes to the following conditions.

1. Subacute and chronic appendicitis __________
2. Acute and chronic bronchitis __________
3. Acute and chronic pyelonephritis __________
4. Acute on chronic renal failure __________
5. Acute on chronic respiratory failure __________

9. Combination Code

A combination code is a single code used to classify:
Two diagnoses, or

A diagnosis with an associated secondary process (manifestation)
A diagnosis with an associated complication

Combination codes are identified by referring to subterm entries in the Alphabetic Index and by reading the inclusion and exclusion notes in the Tabular List.

Assign only the combination code when that code fully identifies the diagnostic conditions involved or when the Alphabetic Index so directs. Multiple coding should not be used when the classification provides a combination code that clearly identifies all of the elements documented in the diagnosis. When the combination code lacks necessary specificity in describing the manifestation or complication, an additional code should be used as a secondary code.

EXAMPLE

Chronic pyelonephritis due to vesicoureteral reflux, N11.0.

EXAMPLE

Pseudomonas pneumonia, J15.1.

The combination code includes the infection and the organism responsible for the infection *(Pseudomonas)*. It would be incorrect to assign separate codes such as J18.9 for pneumonia and B96.5 to identify the *Pseudomonas* organism.

EXERCISE 5-5

Assign codes to the following conditions.

1. Urinary tract infection (urogenital) due to candidiasis ______________
2. Streptococcal group A pneumonia ______________
3. Food poisoning due to *Salmonella* ______________

10. Sequela (Late Effects)

A sequela is the residual effect (condition produced) after the acute phase of an illness or injury has terminated. There is no time limit on when a sequela code can be used. The residual may be apparent early, such as in cerebral infarction, or it may occur months or years later, such as that due to a previous injury. Examples of sequela include scar formation resulting from a burn, deviated septum due to a nasal fracture, and infertility due to tubal occlusion from old tuberculosis. Coding of sequela generally requires two codes sequenced in the following order: The condition or nature of the sequela is sequenced first. The sequela code is sequenced second.

An exception to the above guidelines are those instances where the code for the sequela is followed by a manifestation code identified in the Tabular List and title, or the sequela code has been expanded (at the fourth, fifth or sixth character levels) to include the manifestation(s). The code for the acute phase of an illness or injury that led to the sequela is never used with a code for the late effect.

See Section I.C.9. Sequelae of cerebrovascular disease
See Section I.C.15. Sequelae of complication of pregnancy, childbirth and the puerperium
See Section I.C.19. Application of 7th characters for Chapter 19

The coding of sequela of injuries is discussed in Chapter 25 with the assignment of the 7th character of S to indicate sequela. The importance in this chapter is to become aware of and be able to recognize when a sequela is present.

EXERCISE 5-6

Write the term(s) that represent the sequela and its cause in the following cases on the lines provided, and assign the appropriate codes.

1. Keloid scar left forearm, resulting from second-degree burns; injury occurred 1 year ago

Sequela: ____ Code: ______________

Cause: ____ Code: ______________

2. Traumatic arthritis in the right ankle joint due to previous nondisplaced lateral malleolar fracture
Sequela: ______________________ Code: __________
Cause: ______________________ Code: __________

3. Oropharyngeal phase dysphagia due to CVA 3 months ago
Sequela: ______________________ Code: __________
Cause: ______________________ Code: __________

11. Impending or Threatened Condition

Code any condition described at the time of discharge as "impending" or "threatened" as follows:

If it did occur, code as confirmed diagnosis.

If it did not occur, reference the Alphabetic Index to determine if the condition has a subentry term for "impending" or "threatened" and also reference main term entries for "Impending" and for "Threatened."

If the subterms are listed, assign the given code.

If the subterms are not listed, code the existing underlying condition(s) and not the condition described as impending or threatened.

Occasionally, conditions will be treated and documented as impending conditions. According to the guidelines, if the diagnosis has been confirmed, it should be coded as an active and current condition. If it is impending or threatened rather than active and current, check the Alphabetic Index to see whether a code is available that describes the impending condition. If no code is available, code the existing underlying condition(s) or symptoms.

EXAMPLE Impending myocardial infarction, I20.0 (Look up the main term, impending).

EXAMPLE Impending fracture of the humerus due to multiple myeloma, C90.00.

12. Reporting Same Diagnosis Code More than Once

Each unique ICD-10-CM diagnosis code may be reported only once for an encounter. This applies to bilateral conditions when there are no distinct codes identifying laterality or two different conditions classified to the same ICD-10-CM diagnosis code.

13. Laterality

Some ICD-10-CM codes indicate laterality, specifying whether the condition occurs on the left, right or is bilateral. If no bilateral code is provided and the condition is bilateral, assign separate codes for both the left and right side. If the side is not identified in the medical record, assign the code for the unspecified side.

When a patient has a bilateral condition and each side is treated during separate encounters, assign the "bilateral" code (as the condition still exists on both sides), including for the encounter to treat the first side. For the second encounter for treatment after one side has previously been treated and the condition no longer exists on that side, assign the appropriate unilateral code for the side where the condition still exists (e.g., cataract surgery performed on each eye in separate encounters). The bilateral code would not be assigned for the subsequent encounter, as the patient no longer has the condition in the previously-treated site. If the treatment on the first side did not completely resolve the condition, then the bilateral code would still be appropriate.

EXAMPLE Primary osteoarthritis both hips, M16.0.

14. Documentation by Clinicians Other than the Patient's Provider

Code assignment is based on the documentation by patient's provider (i.e., physician or other qualified healthcare practitioner legally accountable for establishing the patient's diagnosis). There are a few exceptions, such as codes for the Body Mass Index (BMI), depth of non-pressure chronic ulcers, pressure ulcer stage, coma scale, and NIH stroke scale (NIHSS) codes, code assignment may be based on medical record documentation from clinicians who are not the patient's provider (i.e., physician or other qualified healthcare practitioner legally accountable for establishing the patient's diagnosis), since this information is typically documented by other clinicians involved in the care of the patient (e.g., a dietitian often documents the BMI, a nurse often documents the pressure ulcer stages, and an emergency medical technician often documents the coma scale). However, the associated diagnosis (such as overweight, obesity, acute stroke, or pressure ulcer) must be documented by the patient's provider. If there is conflicting medical record documentation, either from the same clinician or different clinicians, the patient's attending provider should be queried for clarification.

For social determinants of health, such as information found in categories Z55-Z65, Persons with potential health hazards related to socio-economic and psychosocial circumstances, code assignment may be based on medical record documentation from clinicians involved in the care of the patient who are not the patient's provider since this information represents social information, rather than medical diagnoses. Patient self-reported documentation may also be used to assign codes for social determinants of health, as long as the self-reported information is signed-off by and incorporated into the health record by either a clinician or provider. The BMI, coma scale, and NIHSS codes and categories Z55-Z65 should only be reported as secondary diagnoses.

EXAMPLE The dietitian documents a BMI of 32. The physician documents obesity (adult patient), E66.9, Z68.32.

15. Syndromes
Follow the Alphabetic Index guidance when coding syndromes. In the absence of Alphabetic Index guidance, assign codes for the documented manifestations of the syndrome. Additional codes for manifestations that are not an integral part of the disease process may also be assigned when the condition does not have a unique code.

EXAMPLE Female infant with Aicardi syndrome. Patient has the characteristic features of absence of the corpus callosum and infantile spasms, Q04.0, G40.822.

16. Documentation of Complications of Care
Code assignment is based on the provider's documentation of the relationship between the condition and the care or procedure, unless otherwise instructed by the classification. The guideline extends to any complications of care, regardless of the chapter the code is located in. It is important to note that not all conditions that occur during or following medical care or surgery are classified as complications. There must be a cause-and-effect relationship between the care provided and the condition, and an indication in the documentation that it is a complication. Query the provider for clarification, if the complication is not clearly documented.

EXAMPLE Patient is seen in the clinic for routine post-surgical aftercare. Patient had appendectomy 5 days ago. Patient was treated for a UTI, Z48.815, Z90.49, N39.0.

There is no documentation that indicates that the urinary tract infection is a complication of the patient's recent surgery.

EXAMPLE Patient was seen in the ER for dehiscence of external abdominal wound following appendectomy, T81.31×A, Y83.6, Z90.49.

17. Borderline Diagnosis
If the provider documents a "borderline" diagnosis at the time of discharge, the diagnosis is coded as confirmed, unless the classification provides a specific entry (e.g., borderline diabetes). If a borderline condition has a specific index entry in ICD-10-CM, it should be coded as such. Since borderline conditions are not uncertain diagnoses, no distinction is made between the care setting (inpatient versus outpatient). Whenever the documentation is unclear regarding a borderline condition, coders are encouraged to query for clarification.

EXAMPLE The patient is seen in the clinic for borderline diabetes, R73.03.

EXAMPLE

The physician documented that the patient has borderline pulmonary hypertension, I27.2.

18. Use of Sign/Symptom/Unspecified Codes

Sign/symptom and "unspecified" codes have acceptable, even necessary, uses. While specific diagnosis codes should be reported when they are supported by the available medical record documentation and clinical knowledge of the patient's health condition, there are instances when signs/symptoms or unspecified codes are the best choices for accurately reflecting the healthcare encounter. Each healthcare encounter should be coded to the level of certainty known for that encounter.

If a definitive diagnosis has not been established by the end of the encounter, it is appropriate to report codes for sign(s) and/or symptoms(s) in lieu of a definitive diagnosis. When significant clinical information isn't known or available about a particular health condition to assign a more specific code, it is acceptable to report the appropriate "unspecified" code (e.g., a diagnosis of pneumonia has been determined, but not the specific type). Unspecified codes should be reported when they are the codes that most accurately reflect what is known about the patient's condition at the time of that particular encounter. It would be inappropriate to select a specific code that is not supported by the medical record documentation or conduct medically unnecessary diagnostic testing in order to determine a more specific code.

EXERCISE 5-7

Assign codes to the following conditions.

1. Impending delirium tremens ____________
2. Threatened miscarriage ____________
3. Impending myocardial infarction ____________
4. Impending fracture of femur due to severe osteoporosis ____________
5. Impending stroke. Patient presented with dysarthria. ____________
6. Physician documents sacral pressure ulcer. Nursing documentation indicates stage 3. ____________
7. Patient is being treated for blackheads and cystic acne. ____________
8. Pain, bilateral knee joints ____________
9. Borderline hypertension ____________
10. Physician documents that the patient (adult) is overweight. ____________
    BMI is documented as 29.0 by dietitian.

19. Coding for Healthcare Encounters in Hurricane Aftermath

a. Use of External Cause of Morbidity Codes

An external cause of morbidity code should be assigned to identify the cause of the injury(ies) incurred as a result of the hurricane. The use of external cause of morbidity codes is supplemental to the application of ICD-10 -CM codes. External cause of morbidity codes are never to be recorded as a principal diagnosis (first-listed in non-inpatient settings). The appropriate injury code should be sequenced before any external cause codes. The external cause of morbidity codes capture how the injury or health condition happened (cause), the intent (unintentional or accidental; or intentional, such as suicide or assault), the place where the event occurred, the activity of the patient at the time of the event, and the person's status (e.g., civilian, military). They should not be assigned for encounters to treat hurricane victims' medical conditions when no injury, adverse effect or poisoning is involved. External cause of morbidity codes should be assigned for each encounter for care and treatment of the injury, External cause of morbidity codes may be assigned in all healthcare settings. For the purpose of capturing complete and accurate ICD-10-CM data in the aftermath of the hurricane, a healthcare setting should be considered as any location where medical care is provided by licensed healthcare professionals.

b. Sequencing of External Causes of Morbidity Codes

Codes for cataclysmic events, such as a hurricane, take priority over all other external cause codes except child and adult abuse and terrorism and should be sequenced before other external cause of injury codes. Assign as many external cause of morbidity codes as necessary to fully explain each cause. For example, if an injury occurs as a result of a building collapse during the hurricane, external cause codes for both the hurricane and the building collapse should be assigned, with the external cause code for hurricane being sequenced as the first external cause code. For injurie incurred as a direct result of the hurricane, assign the appropriate code(s) for the injuries, followed by the code X37.0-, Hurricane (with the appropriate 7th character), and any other applicable external cause of injury codes. Code X37.0- also should be assigned when an injury is incurred as a result of flooding caused by a levee breaking related to the hurricane. Code X38.-, Flood (with the appropriate 7th character), should be assigned when an injury is from flooding resulting directly from the storm. X36.0- , Collapse of a dam or man-made structure, should not be assigned when the cause of the collapse is due to the hurricane. Use of code X36.0- is limited to collapses of man-made structures due to earth surface movements, not due to storm surges directly from a hurricane.

c. Other External Causes of Morbidity Code Issues

For injuries that are not a direct result of the hurricane, such as an evacuee that has incurred an injury as a result of a motor vehicle accident, assign the appropriate external cause of morbidity code(s) to ;describe the cause of the injury, but do not assign code X37.0-, Hurricane. If it is not clear whether this injury was a direct result of the hurricane, assume the injury is due to the hurricane and assign code X37.0-, Hurricane, as well as any other applicable external cause of morbidity codes. In addition to code X37.0-, Hurricane, other possible applicable external cause of morbidity codes. In addition to code X37.0-, Hurricane, other possible applicable external cause of morbidity codes include:

- W54.0-, Bitten by dog
- X30-, Exposure to excessive natural heat
- X312-, Exposure to excessive natural cold
- X38-, Flood

d. Use of Z codes

Z codes (other reasons for healthcare encounters) may be assigned as appropriate to further explain the reasons for presenting for healthcare services, including transfers between healthcare facilities. The ICD-10-CM Official Guidelines for Coding and Reporting identify which codes may be assigned as principal or first-listed diagnosis only, secondary diagnosis only, or principal/first-listed or secondary (depending on the circumstances). Possible applicable Z codes include:

- Z59.0, Homelessness
- Z59.1, Inadequate housing
- Z59.5, Extreme poverty
- Z75.1, Person awaiting admission to adequate facility elsewhere
- Z75.3, Unavailability and inaccessibility of healthcare facilities
- Z75.4, Unavailability and inaccessibility of other helping agencies
- Z76.2, Encounter for health supervision / care of other healthy infant and child
- Z99.12, Encounter for respirator (ventilator) dependence during power failure

The external cause of morbidity codes and the Z codes listed above are not an all-inclusive list. Other codes may be applicable to the encounter based upon the documentation. Assign as many codes as necessary to fully explain each healthcare encounter. Since patient history information may be very limited, use any available documentation to assign the appropriate external cause of morbidity and Z codes.

SELECTION OF PRINCIPAL DIAGNOSIS

Section II. Selection of Principal Diagnosis

The circumstances of inpatient admission always govern the selection of principal diagnosis. The principal diagnosis is defined in the Uniform Hospital Discharge Data Set (UHDDS) as "that condition established after study to be chiefly responsible for occasioning the admission of the patient to the hospital for care."

The UHDDS definitions are used by hospitals to report inpatient data elements in a standardized manner. These data elements and their definitions can be found in the July 31, 1985, Federal Register (Vol. 50, No, 147), pp. 31038-40.

Since that time the application of the UHDDS definitions has been expanded to include all non-outpatient settings (acute care, short-term, long-term care, and psychiatric hospitals; home health agencies; rehab facilities; nursing homes, etc). The UHDDS definitions also apply to hospice services (all levels of care).

In determining principal diagnosis the coding conventions in the ICD-10-CM, the Tabular List and Alphabetic Index take precedence over these official coding guidelines.

(See Section I.A., Conventions for the ICD-10-CM)

The importance of consistent, complete documentation in the medical record cannot be overemphasized. Without such documentation the application of all coding guidelines is a difficult, if not impossible, task.

A. Codes for symptoms, signs, and ill-defined conditions

Codes for symptoms, signs, and ill-defined conditions from Chapter 18 are not to be used as principal diagnosis when a related definitive diagnosis has been established.

EXAMPLE

Right lower quadrant abdominal pain due to acute appendicitis. The code for the abdominal pain is R10.31 (from Chapter 18), and it is due to acute appendicitis. The only code necessary is K35.80, for acute appendicitis.

B. Two or more interrelated conditions, each potentially meeting the definition for principal diagnosis.

When there are two or more interrelated conditions (such as diseases in the same ICD-10-CM chapter or manifestations characteristically associated with a certain disease) potentially meeting the definition of principal diagnosis, either condition may be sequenced first, unless the circumstances of the admission, the therapy provided, the Tabular List, or the Alphabetic Index indicate otherwise.

EXAMPLE

The patient had severe dehydration and hypokalemia that were treated with IV fluids and IV potassium supplements, E86.0, E87.6, or E87.6, E86.0.

C. Two or more diagnoses that equally meet the definition for principal diagnosis

In the unusual instance when two or more diagnoses equally meet the criteria for principal diagnosis as determined by the circumstances of admission, diagnostic workup and/or therapy provided, and the Alphabetic Index, Tabular List, or another coding guidelines does not provide sequencing direction, any one of the diagnoses may be sequenced first.

EXAMPLE

The patient was admitted with an exacerbation of her chronic obstructive pulmonary disease and decompensation of her congestive heart failure. Either J44.1 or I50.9 could be selected for the principal diagnosis, and the other code would be a secondary diagnosis code.

D. Two or more comparative or contrasting conditions.

In those rare instances when two or more contrasting or comparative diagnoses are documented as "either/or" (or similar terminology), they are coded as if the diagnoses were confirmed and the diagnoses are sequenced according to the circumstances of the admission. If no further determination can be made as to which diagnosis should be principal, either diagnosis may be sequenced first.

EXAMPLE

Peptic ulcer disease versus cholecystitis, K27.9, K81.9, or K81.9, K27.9.

E. A symptom(s) followed by contrasting/comparative diagnoses

GUIDELINE HAS BEEN DELETED EFFECTIVE OCTOBER 1, 2014

F. Original treatment plan not carried out

Sequence as the principal diagnosis the condition, which after study occasioned the admission to the hospital, even though treatment may not have been carried out due to unforeseen circumstances.

EXAMPLE

The patient was admitted for cholecystectomy because of cholelithiasis. The patient was noted to be having an exacerbation of congestive heart failure (CHF), so the surgery was canceled and IV Lasix was administered to treat the CHF, K80.20, I50.9, Z53.09. No procedure code would be assigned because the procedure was canceled before it was started.

G. Complications of surgery and other medical care

When the admission is for treatment of a complication resulting from surgery or other medical care, the complication code is sequenced as the principal diagnosis. If the complication is classified to the T80-T88 series and the code lacks the necessary specificity in describing the complication, an additional code for the specific complication should be assigned.

EXAMPLE

The patient was admitted for dehiscence of external abdominal incision, T81.31xA, Y83.9.

H. Uncertain Diagnosis

If the diagnosis documented at the time of discharge is qualified as "probable," "suspected," "likely," "questionable," "possible," or "still to be ruled out," "compatible with," "consistent with," or other similar terms indicating uncertainty, code the condition as if it existed or was established. The bases for these guidelines are the diagnostic workup, arrangements for further workup or observation, and initial therapeutic approach that correspond most closely with the established diagnosis.

Note: This guideline is applicable only to inpatient admissions to short-term, acute, long-term care and psychiatric hospitals.

EXAMPLE

Possible adenovirus meningitis, A87.1.

In the chapter specific guidelines, there are four exceptions to the uncertain diagnosis guideline.

- Code A92.5 Zika virus should only be assigned for confirmed cases
- Code B20 AIDS should only be assigned for confirmed cases
- Code J09.X- Avian influenza should only be assigned for confirmed cases
- Code J09.X- H1N1 influenza should only be assigned for confirmed cases

I. Admission from Observation Unit

1. Admission Following Medical Observation

When a patient is admitted to an observation unit for a medical condition, which either worsens or does not improve, and is subsequently admitted as an inpatient of the same hospital for this same medical condition, the principal diagnosis would be the medical condition which led to the hospital admission.

EXAMPLE

The patient was admitted for medical observation because of chest pain. After further investigation and testing, it was determined that the patient had a NSTEMI, and the patient was admitted for inpatient care, I21.4.

2. Admission Following Post-Operative Observation

When a patient is admitted to an observation unit to monitor a condition (or complication) that develops following outpatient surgery, and then is subsequently admitted as an inpatient of the same hospital, hospitals should apply the Uniform Hospital Discharge Data Set (UHDDS) definition of principal diagnosis as "that condition established after study to be chiefly responsible for occasioning the admission of the patient to the hospital for care."

J. Admission from Outpatient Surgery

When a patient receives surgery in the hospital's outpatient surgery department and is subsequently admitted for continuing inpatient care at the same hospital, the following guidelines should be followed in selecting the principal diagnosis for the inpatient admission:

- If the reason for the inpatient admission is a complication, assign the complication as the principal diagnosis.
- If no complication, or other condition, is documented as the reason for the inpatient admission, assign the reason for the outpatient surgery as the principal diagnosis.
- If the reason for the inpatient admission is another condition unrelated to the surgery, assign the unrelated condition as the principal diagnosis.

EXAMPLE

The patient was admitted following an outpatient esophagogastroduodenoscopy for gastroesophageal reflux. The patient went into atrial fibrillation in the recovery room and was admitted to inpatient status. The physician documents that the atrial fibrillation is a complication of the procedure, I97.89, I48.91, K21.9, Y83.8, Y92.238, 0DJ08ZZ.

K. Admission/Encounters for Rehabilitation

When the purpose for the admission/encounter is rehabilitation, sequence first the code for the condition for which the service is being performed. For example, for an admission/encounter for rehabilitation for right-sided dominant hemiplegia following a cerebrovascular infarction, report code I69.351, Hemiplegia and hemiparesis following cerebral infarction affecting right dominant side, as the first-listed or principal diagnosis.

If the condition for which the rehabilitation service is no longer present, report the appropriate aftercare code as the first-listed or principal diagnosis unless the rehabilitation service is being provided following an injury. For rehabilitation services following active treatment of an injury, assign the injury code with the appropriate seventh character for subsequent encounter as the first-listed or principal diagnosis. For example, if a patient with severe degenerative osteoarthritis of the hip underwent hip replacement and the current encounter/admission is for rehabilitation, report code Z47.1, Aftercare following joint replacement surgery, as the first-listed or principal diagnosis. If the patient requires rehabilitation post hip replacement for right intertrochanteric femur fracture, report code S72.141D, Displaced intertrochanteric fracture of right femur, subsequent encounter for closed fracture with routine healing, as the first-listed or principal diagnosis.

See Section I.C.21.c.7, Factors influencing health status and contact with health services, Aftercare.

See Section I.C.19.a. for additional information about the use of 7th characters for injury codes.

EXAMPLE

Patient is admitted for rehabilitation due to recent cerebrovascular infarction with oropharyngeal dysphagia, I69.391, R13.12

REPORTING ADDITIONAL DIAGNOSES

Section III. Reporting Additional Diagnoses

GENERAL RULES FOR OTHER (ADDITIONAL) DIAGNOSES

For reporting purposes the definition for "other diagnoses" is interpreted as additional conditions that affect patient care in terms of requiring:

clinical evaluation; or
therapeutic treatment; or
diagnostic procedures; or
extended length of hospital stay; or
increased nursing care and/or monitoring.

The UHDDS item #11-b defines Other Diagnoses as "all conditions that coexist at the time of admission, that develop subsequently, or that affect the treatment received and/or the length of stay. Diagnoses that relate to an earlier episode which have no bearing on the current hospital stay are to be excluded." UHDDS definitions apply to inpatients in acute care, short-term, long term care and psychiatric hospital setting. The UHDDS definitions are used by acute care short-term hospitals to report inpatient data elements in a standardized manner. These data elements and their definitions can be found in the July 31, 1985, Federal Register (Vol. 50, No, 147), pp. 31038-40.

Since that time the application of the UHDDS definitions has been expanded to include all non-outpatient settings (acute care, short-term, long-term care, and psychiatric hospitals; home health agencies; rehab facilities; nursing homes, etc). The UHDDS definitions also apply to hospice services (all levels of care).

The following guidelines are to be applied in designating "other diagnoses" when neither the Alphabetic Index nor the Tabular List in ICD-10-CM provide direction. The listing of the diagnoses in the patient record is the responsibility of the attending provider.

A. Previous conditions

If the provider has included a diagnosis in the final diagnostic statement, such as the discharge summary or the face sheet, it should ordinarily be coded. Some providers include in the diagnostic statement resolved conditions or diagnoses and status-post procedures from previous admission that have no bearing on the current stay. Such conditions are not to be reported and are coded only if required by hospital policy.

However, history codes (categories Z80-Z87) may be used as secondary codes if the historical condition or family history has an impact on current care or influences treatment.

EXAMPLE The patient is being treated for congestive heart failure and has a history of allergy to shellfish. A code is available for history of shellfish allergy, but it would not be necessary to assign this code unless facility policy directs the coder to do so. Some physicians list allergies and previous surgeries as diagnoses, I50.9.

EXAMPLE The patient is being treated for prostate cancer. A significant family history of prostate cancer has been reported, C61, Z80.42.

B. Abnormal findings

Abnormal findings (laboratory, x-ray, pathologic, and other diagnostic results) are not coded and reported unless the provider indicates their clinical significance. If the findings are outside the normal range and the attending provider has ordered other tests to evaluate the condition or prescribed treatment, it is appropriate to ask the provider whether the abnormal finding should be added.

Please note: This differs from the coding practices in the outpatient setting for coding encounters for diagnostic tests that have been interpreted by a provider.

EXAMPLE Potassium is noted to be low on laboratory testing. Potassium 20 mEq was ordered.
Query the physician regarding the significance of the abnormal lab value and subsequent treatment.

C. Uncertain Diagnosis

If the diagnosis documented at the time of discharge is qualified as "probable," "suspected," "likely," "questionable," "possible," or "still to be ruled out," "compatible with," "consistent with," or other similar terms indicating uncertainty, code the condition as if it existed or was established. The bases for these guidelines are the diagnostic workup, arrangements for further workup or observation, and initial therapeutic approach that correspond most closely with the established diagnosis.

Note: This guideline is applicable only to inpatient admissions to short-term, acute, long-term care and psychiatric hospitals.

EXAMPLE Suspected aspiration pneumonitis, J69.0.

CHAPTER REVIEW EXERCISE

Select the correct answer for each of the following:

1. Conditions that are integral to a disease or condition should be coded as additional diagnoses.
   A. True
   B. False
2. When separate codes are used to identify acute and chronic conditions, the chronic code is sequenced first.
   A. True
   B. False
3. Reliance on only the Alphabetic Index or only the Tabular List can lead to errors in code assignments and less specificity in code selection in ICD-10-CM.
   A. True
   B. False
4. A patient has anemia due to chronic renal failure. The anemia is integral to the chronic renal failure.
   A. True
   B. False
5. A patient has right lower quadrant abdominal pain due to acute appendicitis. The abdominal pain should be assigned as an additional code.
   A. True
   B. False
6. In the inpatient setting, it is acceptable to code diagnoses that have not yet been confirmed but that are questionable or suspected at the time of discharge (with the exceptions of AIDS and avian and H1N1 influenza and Zika virus).
   A. True
   B. False
7. If the discharge diagnosis was abdominal pain due to acute appendicitis, abdominal pain would be coded as the principal diagnosis.
   A. True
   B. False

Assign codes to the following conditions.

8. Cerebral infarction due to thrombosis right carotid artery
   Code from Alphabetic Index ____________
   Code following verification in Tabular List ____________
9. Supervision of high-risk pregnancy (second trimester) due to history of stillbirth
   Code from Alphabetic Index ____________
   Code following verification in Tabular List ____________
10. Spastic hemiplegia affecting right dominant side
    Code from Alphabetic Index ____________
    Code following verification in Tabular List ____________

Identify integral and nonintegral conditions by answering the following questions.

11. List two common symptoms of kidney stones. ____________
12. List two common symptoms associated with rheumatoid arthritis. ____________
13. List two common symptoms of acute renal failure. ____________

Assign and sequence codes to the following conditions.

14. Acute and chronic cystitis ____________
15. Acute on chronic oophoritis ____________
16. Dementia due to Alzheimer's ____________
17. Viral gastroenteritis with diarrhea and vomiting ____________
18. Fever and headache due to viral meningitis ____________
19. Constrictive pericarditis due to old tuberculosis infection of the heart ____________
20. Mild intellectual disability due to previous acute poliomyelitis ____________

CHAPTER GLOSSARY

This chapter is unique in that the glossary definitions are not provided within the chapter. These terms are used within the guidelines without definition. The glossary definitions are provided in this section for quick reference.

Acute: a short and relatively severe course.

Chronic: persistent over a long period.

Combination code: a single code used to classify two diagnoses; or a diagnosis with an associated secondary process (manifestation); or a diagnosis with an associated complication.

Conventions: general rules for use in classification that must be followed for accurate coding.

Etiology: cause or origin of a disease or condition.

Manifestation: symptom or condition that is the result of a disease.

Residual condition or effect: when the acute phase of an illness or injury has passed, but a residual condition or health problem remains.

Sequelae: residual conditions or effects; time when the acute phase of an illness or injury has passed, but residual conditions or health problems remain.

Sign: objective evidence of a disease or of a patient's condition as perceived by the patient's examining physician.

Subacute: somewhat acute; between chronic and acute.

Symptom: subjective evidence of a disease or of a patient's condition as perceived by the patient.

6

Introduction to ICD-10-PCS

CHAPTER OUTLINE

Format and Organization of ICD-10-PCS
- Alphabetic Index and Tables

Medical and Surgical Section

ICD-10-PCS Coding Guidelines

Chapter Review Exercise

Chapter Glossary

LEARNING OBJECTIVES

1. Identify the format of ICD-10-PCS, Alphabetic Index, and PCS Tables
2. Define the root operations for the medical and surgical section of ICD-10-PCS
3. Define the approaches that are used in the medical and surgical section of ICD-10-PCS
4. Apply and assign the correct ICD-10-PCS codes in accordance with the conventions and ICD-10-PCS Coding Guidelines

ABBREVIATIONS/ ACRONYMS

CAS computer assisted surgery

ICD-10-CM *International Classification of Diseases, 10th Revision, Clinical Modification*

ICD-10-PCS *International Classification of Diseases, 10th Revision, Procedure Coding System*

NEC not elsewhere classifiable

NOS not otherwise specified

PTCA percutaneous transluminal coronary angioplasty

HISTORY OF ICD-10-PCS

In 1992, the Centers for Medicare and Medicaid Services (CMS) funded a project to replace Volume 3 of ICD-9-CM, which was outdated and could not be expanded to classify procedures with more specific detail. 3M Health Information Systems was awarded a contract to develop a new system for procedural coding, ICD-10-PCS (Procedure Coding System). ICD-10-PCS was initially released in 1998. Since that time, it has been updated to incorporate changes that were made to ICD-9-CM, Volume 3. CMS is responsible for the maintenance of ICD-10-PCS. (Information about ICD-10-PCS is available on the CMS website.)

The ICD-10 Procedure Coding System was developed with four characteristics in mind:

1. Completeness—Each procedure should have its own code.
2. Expandability—New procedure codes should be easily added (unlimited number of codes).
3. Multiaxial—Each code character should have the same meaning across and within body systems.
4. Standardized terminology—ICD-10-PCS will include definitions for terminology used, and multiple meanings will not be associated with the same term.

Other principles followed in the development of ICD-10-PCS include:

- Diagnostic information is not included in the procedure description.
- A "not otherwise specified" (NOS) option is *not* available.

- The "not elsewhere classifiable" (NEC) option is limited.
- All procedures are defined to a high level of specificity.

Of interest is that ICD-10-PCS is used only in the United States. There is no international procedure classification with the ICD-10 classification system.

FORMAT AND ORGANIZATION OF ICD-10-PCS

ICD-10-PCS is different from ICD-10-CM because, instead of a Tabular Listing, there are Tables that are used to assign procedure codes. In ICD-10-PCS, there is an Alphabetic Index that can be used to direct the coder to a specific Table. Most entries in the Alphabetic Index include the first three or four characters of a procedure code. There are some exceptions where the entire code may be displayed.

All ICD-10-PCS codes are seven characters (no decimal points are used), with each character representing a particular aspect of the procedure. ICD-10-PCS codes are alphanumeric, and each character is represented by a letter or a number, which is referred to as a "value." There are 34 possible values for each character, the numbers 0-9, and letter A-H, J-N and P-Z. The letters I and O are not used in ICD-10-PCS.

Alphabetic Index and Tables

The ICD-10-PCS code book contains the Alphabetic Index and PCS Tables. Once you have become familiar with the table structure, it may not be necessary to even use the index, which is structured in a way that follows the organization of the tables but may only identify the first three or four characters of the procedure code. The two types of main terms that are listed in the Alphabetic Index are:

- Based on the root operation or general type of procedure
- Common procedure terms

EXAMPLE

Alphabetic Index Entry for Appendectomy (Figure 6-1).

In this example, there are two possible tables, 0DBJ and 0DTJ. The root operation, excision or resection, needs to be determined to find the right table and to assign characters 4 through 7 for the appropriate code.

Appendectomy (the surgical removal of the appendix) via open approach.

The root operation is resection, because all of the appendix is removed without replacement. In the Alphabetic Index, under *Resection,* go to Table 0DT (see Figure 6-2) and assign Characters 4 through 7. Character 4 is *J,* for the appendix. Character 5 is *Open.* Character 6 is *Z,* for no device, and Character 7 is *Z,* for no qualifier. Therefore, the ICD-10-PCS code for appendectomy *is 0DTJ0ZZ.*

CHARACTER 1 SECTION	CHARACTER 2 BODY SYSTEM	CHARACTER 3 OPERATION	CHARACTER 4 BODY PART	CHARACTER 5 APPROACH	CHARACTER 6 DEVICE	CHARACTER 7 QUALIFIER
Medical and Surgical	Gastrointestinal System	Resection	Appendix	Open	No Device	No Qualifier
0	D	T	J	0	Z	Z

Appendectomy
see Excision, Appendix **0DBJ**
see Resection, Appendix **0DTJ**
Appendicolysis *see* Release, Appendix **0DNJ**
Appendicotomy *see* Drainage, Appendix **0D9J**

FIGURE 6-1. Alphabetic Index entry for appendectomy.

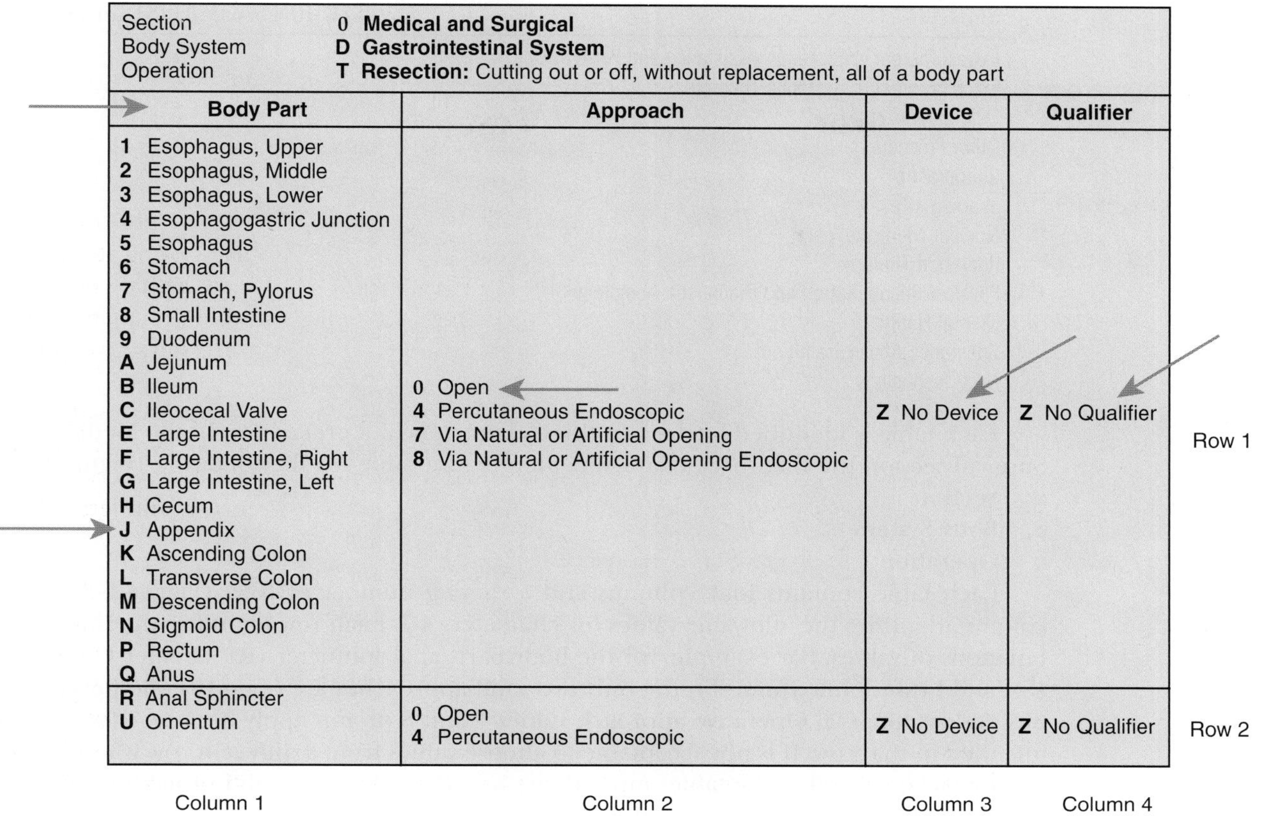

Section	0 **Medical and Surgical**		
Body System	D **Gastrointestinal System**		
Operation	T **Resection:** Cutting out or off, without replacement, all of a body part		
Body Part	**Approach**	**Device**	**Qualifier**
1 Esophagus, Upper 2 Esophagus, Middle 3 Esophagus, Lower 4 Esophagogastric Junction 5 Esophagus 6 Stomach 7 Stomach, Pylorus 8 Small Intestine 9 Duodenum A Jejunum B Ileum C Ileocecal Valve E Large Intestine F Large Intestine, Right G Large Intestine, Left H Cecum J Appendix K Ascending Colon L Transverse Colon M Descending Colon N Sigmoid Colon P Rectum Q Anus	0 Open 4 Percutaneous Endoscopic 7 Via Natural or Artificial Opening 8 Via Natural or Artificial Opening Endoscopic	Z No Device	Z No Qualifier
R Anal Sphincter U Omentum	0 Open 4 Percutaneous Endoscopic	Z No Device	Z No Qualifier

FIGURE 6-2. Table ODT for resection of gastrointestinal system.

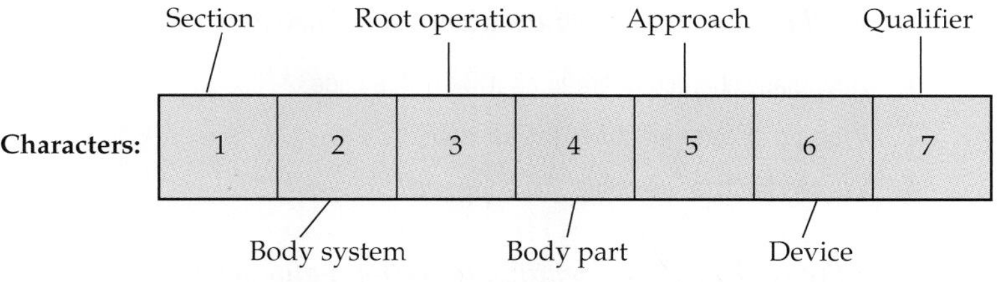

FIGURE 6-3. Characters of an ICD-10-PCS code in the Medical and Surgical Section.

In order to understand an ICD-10-PCS code, you need to know what each of the seven characters represent. See Figure 6-3 for the ICD-10-PCS code structure and the meaning of each character within the Medical and Surgical Section, which is the largest section in the PCS code book and where the majority of our procedure codes will be assigned from. The character value for the Medical and Surgical section is 0 (the number "zero," not the letter O).

The PCS Tables are divided into 17 sections that classify the type of procedure within each section. The first character of an ICD-10-PCS code identifies the section that describes the category where the code is located. Sections 1 through 9 are medical- and surgical-related sections. Sections B through D and F through H represent ancillary sections of ICD-10-PCS. The 17 sections and the corresponding section values are as follows:

SECTION	SECTION VALUE/FIRST CHARACTER
Medical and Surgical	0
Obstetrics	1
Placement	2
Administration	3
Measurement and Monitoring	4

SECTION	SECTION VALUE/FIRST CHARACTER
Extracorporeal or Systemic Assistance and Performance	5
Extracorporeal or Systemic Therapies	6
Osteopathic	7
Other Procedures	8
Chiropractic	9
Imaging	B
Nuclear Medicine	C
Radiation Therapy	D
Physical Rehabilitation and Diagnostic Audiology	F
Mental Health	G
Substance Abuse Treatment	H
New Technology	X

Each table is identified by the first three characters of a procedure. In the Medical and Surgical section the first three characters identify the value for the following (Figure 6-2):

- Section
- Body System
- Operation

Each table contains four columns and a varying number of rows (Figure 6-2). Each column identifies the allowable values for characters 4-7. Each row identifies the valid combinations of values. For example, for the body parts anal sphincter (R), Greater Omentum (S), and Lesser Omentum (T), the only two valid approaches are open (0) and percutaneous endoscopic (4). Operative approach values 7 and 8 do not apply because they are not included in that row. It is not acceptable to choose values from a different row when assigning a procedure code. The tables must always be used to assign a valid procedure code.

EXERCISE 6-1

Answer the following questions about the characters in an ICD-10-PCS code.

1. How many characters are in an ICD-10-PCS code? ______________

2. Which character identifies the approach? ______________

3. Which character identifies the body part? ______________

Using the ICD-10-PCS, identify the section value for the following.

4. Radiation oncology ______________

5. Administration ______________

6. Other procedure ______________

7. Obstetrics ______________

8. Mental health ______________

Using the Alphabetic Index only, identify the appropriate table for the following procedures.

9. Cholecystectomy ______________

10. Replacement, right knee ______________

11. Tracheostomy ______________

12. Mental health medication management ______________

13. Transfusion of platelets via peripheral vein ______________

Using the table in Figure 6-2, answer the following questions.

14. 0DTR8ZZ is a valid code.

A. True

B. False

15. 0DT80ZZ is a valid code.
   A. True
   B. False

16. A biopsy of the esophagus would be coded using Table 0DT.
   A. True
   B. False

MEDICAL AND SURGICAL SECTION

Body Systems

A **body system** defines an anatomic region or a general physiological system on which a procedure is performed. Some body systems may be further divided into multiple body systems. For example, the cardiovascular/circulatory system is divided into the following body systems:

- Heart and great vessels
- Upper arteries
- Lower arteries
- Upper veins
- Lower veins

The body systems or the second character for the Medical and Surgical section are as follows:

CHARACTER	BODY SYSTEM
0	Central nervous system
1	Peripheral nervous system
2	Heart and great vessels
3	Upper arteries
4	Lower arteries
5	Upper veins
6	Lower veins
7	Lymphatic and hemic system
8	Eye
9	Ear, nose, sinus
B	Respiratory system
C	Mouth and throat
D	Gastrointestinal system
F	Hepatobiliary system and pancreas
G	Endocrine system
H	Skin and breast
J	Subcutaneous tissue and fascia
K	Muscles
L	Tendons
M	Bursae and ligaments
N	Head and facial bones
P	Upper bones
Q	Lower bones
R	Upper joints
S	Lower joints
T	Urinary system
U	Female reproductive system
V	Male reproductive system
W	Anatomical regions, general
X	Anatomical regions, upper extremities
Y	Anatomical regions, lower extremities

According to the guidelines (B2.1a and B2.1b), the procedure codes in the general anatomical regions body systems should only be used when the procedure is performed on an anatomical region rather than a specific body part. Also when body systems are designated as upper and lower, if the body part is located above the diaphragm it is upper, and if the body part is located below the diaphragm it is considered lower.

EXERCISE 6-2

Using reference material if necessary, answer the following questions about ICD-10-PCS.

1. The thoracic nerve is in what body system? ______________
2. The lacrimal gland is in what body system? ______________
3. The cystic duct is in what body system? ______________

Root Operations

The root operation, or the third character, identifies the main objective and/or the intent of the procedure performed. There is a specific definition for each root operation. Although this is part of the standardization of terminology for ICD-10-PCS, it may not be the terminology used by physicians. According to the guidelines it is the coder's responsibility to determine what the documentation in the medical record equates to in the PCS definitions. Physicians are not expected to use terminology in the same way that has been defined by PCS. For example, a TURP (transurethral resection of the prostate) includes the word resection. In PCS resection means the cutting out/off without replacement all of a body part. A TURP is not a resection of the whole body part (prostate), so it would be coded to an excision (cutting out/off without replacement some of a body) in PCS. It would be the coder's responsibility to determine this by reading the OR report and being knowledgeable about the surgical procedure. There are 31 root operations for the Medical and Surgical section. The character value for the root operation is in parentheses following the root operation term, and an example of a procedure that fits the root operation is in parentheses following the definition. The root operation character value is consistent throughout this section. There are no combination procedure codes in ICD-10-PCS. Each procedure performed during an operative episode with a distinct objective is coded separately (see guidelines for coding multiple procedures B3.2).

Root operations that remove some/all of a body part:

- **Destruction (5):** physical eradication of all or a portion of a body part by the direct use of energy, force, or a destructive agent (ablation of endometriosis)
- **Detachment (6):** cutting off all or a portion of the upper or lower extremities (above-knee amputation)
- **Excision (B):** cutting out or off, without replacement, a portion of a body part (partial nephrectomy)
- **Extraction (D):** pulling or stripping out or off all or a portion of a body part by the use of force (bone marrow biopsy)
- **Resection (T):** cutting out or off, without replacement, all of a body part (total lobectomy of lung)

Root operations that remove solid, fluids, or gases from a body part:

- **Drainage (9):** taking or letting out fluids and/or gases from a body part (paracentesis)
- **Extirpation (C):** taking or cutting out solid matter from a body part (thrombectomy)
- **Fragmentation (F):** breaking solid matter in a body part into pieces (extracorporeal shockwave lithotripsy)

Root operations that involve cutting or separation only:

- **Division (8):** cutting into a body part without draining fluids and/or gases from the body part in order to separate or transect a body part (osteotomy)
- **Release (N):** freeing a body part from an abnormal physical constraint (lysis of adhesions)

Root operations that put in, put back, or move some or all of a body part:

- **Reattachment (M):** putting back in or on all or a portion of a separated body part to its normal location or other suitable location (reattachment of finger)
- **Reposition (S):** moving to its normal location, or other suitable location, all or a portion of a body part (fracture reduction)
- **Transfer (X):** moving, without taking out, all or a portion of a body part to another location to take over the function of all or a portion of a body part (pedicle skin flap)
- **Transplantation (Y):** putting in or on all or a portion of a living body part taken from another individual or animal to physically take the place and/or function of all or a portion of a similar body part (kidney transplant)

Root operations that alter the diameter/route of a tubular body part:

- **Bypass (1):** altering the route of passage of the contents of a tubular body part (CABG)
- **Dilation (7):** expanding an orifice or the lumen of a tubular body part (PTCA)
- **Occlusion (L):** completely closing an orifice or lumen of a tubular body part (tubal ligation)
- **Restriction (V):** partially closing an orifice or lumen of a tubular body part (Nissen fundoplication)

Root operations that always involve a device:

- **Change (2):** taking out or off a device from a body part and putting back an identical or similar device in or on the same body part without cutting or puncturing the skin or a mucous membrane (changing a gastrostomy tube)
- **Insertion (H):** putting in a nonbiological appliance that monitors, assists, performs, or prevents a physiological function but does not physically take the place of a body part (insertion of pacemaker lead)
- **Replacement (R):** putting in or on biological or synthetic material that physically takes the place and/or function of all or a portion of a body part (total knee replacement)
- **Removal (P):** taking out or off a device from a body part (removing a chest tube)
- **Revision (W):** correcting, to the extent possible, a malfunctioning or displaced device (adjustment of knee prosthesis)
- **Supplement (U):** putting in or on biological or synthetic material that physically reinforces and/or augments the function of a portion of a body part (herniorrhaphy with mesh)

Root operations that involve examination only:

- **Inspection (J):** visually and/or manually exploring a body part (diagnostic arthroscopy)
- **Map (K):** locating the route of passage of electrical impulses and/or locating functional areas in a body part (cardiac mapping)

Root operations that include other repair:

- **Control (3):** stopping, or attempting to stop, postprocedural or other acute bleeding (control of post-prostatectomy hemorrhage, control of intracranial subdural hemorrhage, control of bleeding duodenal ulcer, control of retroperitoneal hemorrhage)
- **Repair (Q):** restoring, to the extent possible, a body part to its normal anatomic structure and function (herniorrhaphy)

The root operation repair is used when the root operation for the procedure performed cannot be classified to a more specific root operation.

Root operations that include other objectives:

- **Alteration (0):** modifying the natural anatomic structure of a body part without affecting the function of the body part (breast augmentation)
- **Creation (4):** putting in or on biological or synthetic material to form a new body part that to the extent possible replicates the anatomic structure or function of an absent body part (creation of vagina in a male, creation of right and left atrioventricular valve from common atrioventricular valve)
- **Fusion (G):** joining together portions of an articular body part rendering the articular body part immobile (spinal fusion)

Terms such as *incision* or *anastomosis* are not root operations, as they are always integral to another procedure. The identification and determination of the correct root operation is vital to the selection of the appropriate table.

EXERCISE 6-3

Without using reference material, answer the following questions about ICD-10-PCS.

1. Modifying the natural anatomic structure of a body part without affecting the function of the body part is
   A. alteration
   B. fusion
   C. creation
   D. repair
2. Cutting off all or a portion of the upper or lower extremities is
   A. destruction
   B. fragmentation
   C. detachment
   D. resection
3. Completely closing an orifice or lumen of a tubular body part is
   A. bypass
   B. restriction
   C. dilation
   D. occlusion
4. Freeing a body part from an abnormal physical constraint is
   A. reposition
   B. division
   C. release
   D. transfer
5. Taking or letting out fluids and/or gases from a body part is
   A. extirpation
   B. fragmentation
   C. extraction
   D. drainage
6. Stopping, or attempting to stop, postprocedural or other acute bleeding is
   A. inspection
   B. control
   C. mapping
   D. alteration
7. Taking out or off a device from a body part is
   A. replacement
   B. removal
   C. revision
   D. change
8. Moving to its normal location or other suitable location all or a portion of a body part is
   A. reposition
   B. release
   C. transfer
   D. transplantation
9. Cutting out or off, without replacement, a portion of a body part is
   A. resection
   B. excision
   C. destruction
   D. extraction
10. Cutting into a body part without draining fluids and/or gases from the body part in order to separate or transect a body part is
   A. reattachment
   B. release
   C. transfer
   D. division

11. Putting in or on biological or synthetic material that physically reinforces and/or augments the function of a portion of a body part is
- **A.** restriction
- **B.** insertion
- **C.** supplementation
- **D.** revision

12. Visually and/or manually exploring a body part is
- **A.** creation
- **B.** fusion
- **C.** inspection
- **D.** mapping

Body Part

The body part, the fourth character, identifies the specific body part on which the procedure was performed. Each body system will have corresponding body parts. Look at the various tables within the ICD-10-PCS code book to get an idea about the body parts that are body part values (Figure 6-4).

According to the guidelines (B4.1a, B4.1b, B4.2, and B4.3), if a procedure is performed on a portion of a body part that does not have a separate body part value, code the body part value corresponding to the whole body part. If the prefix "peri" is combined with a body part to identify the site of a procedure, the procedure is coded to the body part names (e.g., perirenal is coded to kidney body part). When a specific branch of a body part does not have its own body part value in PCS, the body part is coded to the closest proximal branch that has a specific body part value. If an identical procedure is performed on bilateral body parts and a bilateral body part value exists for that body part, a single procedure code is assigned. If no bilateral body part value exists, each procedure is coded separately using the appropriate body part value.

Section	0 **Medical and Surgical**		
Body System	B **Respiratory System**		
Operation	5 **Destruction:** Physical eradication of all or a portion of a body part by the direct use of energy, force, or a destructive agent		
Body Part	**Approach**	**Device**	**Qualifier**
1 Trachea **2** Carina **3** Main Bronchus, Right **4** Upper Lobe Bronchus, Right **5** Middle Lobe Bronchus, Right **6** Lower Lobe Bronchus, Right **7** Main Bronchus, Left **8** Upper Lobe Bronchus, Left **9** Lingula Bronchus **B** Lower Lobe Bronchus, Left **C** Upper Lung Lobe, Right **D** Middle Lung Lobe, Right **F** Lower Lung Lobe, Right **G** Upper Lung Lobe, Left **H** Lung Lingula **J** Lower Lung Lobe, Left **K** Lung, Right **L** Lung, Left **M** Lungs, Bilateral	**0** Open **3** Percutaneous **4** Percutaneous Endoscopic **7** Via Natural or Artificial Opening **8** Via Natural or Artificial Opening Endoscopic	**Z** No Device	**Z** No Qualifier
N Pleura, Right **P** Pleura, Left **T** Diaphragm	**0** Open **3** Percutaneous **4** Percutaneous Endoscopic	**Z** No Device	**Z** No Qualifier

FIGURE 6-4. Table for destruction of respiratory system.

Approaches

The approach, the fifth character, identifies the operative approach or the method used to reach the operative site. There is a specific definition for each approach. Although this is part of the standardization of terminology for ICD-10-PCS, it may not be the terminology used by physicians. There are seven approaches for the Medical and Surgical section (Figure 6-5). An example is included in parentheses following the definition. The character value and definition for the approaches are as follows:

CHARACTER	APPROACH
0	**Open:** cutting through the skin, mucous membrane, and any other body layers necessary to expose the site of the procedure (abdominal hysterectomy)
3	**Percutaneous:** entry, by puncture or minor incision, of instrumentation through the skin, mucous membrane, and any other body layers necessary to reach the site of the procedure (needle biopsy liver)
4	**Percutaneous endoscopic:** entry, by puncture or minor incision, of instrumentation through the skin, mucous membrane, and any other body layers necessary to reach and visualize the site of the procedure (laparoscopic cholecystectomy)
7	**Via natural or artificial opening:** entry of instrumentation through a natural or artificial external opening to reach the site of the procedure (endotracheal intubation)
8	**Via natural or artificial opening endoscopic:** entry of instrumentation through a natural or artificial external opening to reach and visualize the site of the procedure (colonoscopy)
F	**Via natural or artificial opening with percutaneous endoscopic assistance:** cutting through the skin, mucous membrane, and any other body layers necessary to expose the site of the procedure, and entry, by puncture or minor incision, of instrumentation through the skin, mucous membrane, and any other body layers necessary to aid in the performance of the procedure (laparoscopic-assisted vaginal hysterectomy)
X	**External:** procedures performed directly on the skin or mucous membrane and procedures performed indirectly by the application of external force through the skin or mucous membrane (tonsillectomy)

The approach is determined by the following three components for procedures performed on an internal body part:

- Access location—specifies the external site through which the site of the procedure is reached, either through skin, mucous membrane, or external orifices
- Method—specifies how the external access location is entered
- Type of instrumentation—specifies the specialized equipment used to perform the procedure

According to the guidelines, procedures performed using an open approach with percutaneous endoscopic assistance are coded to open approach. External approach includes procedures performed within an orifice on structures that are visible without the aid of any instrumentation. Another example of an external approach is when a procedure is performed indirectly by using external force through the intervening body layers (e.g., closed reduction of a fracture). Procedures that are performed percutaneously via a device placed for the procedures are coded to percutaneous approach.

Computer and Robotic-Assisted Surgery

Advances in computer technologies have made it possible for computers to be utilized in the performance of diagnostic and therapeutic procedures. **Computer assisted surgery (CAS)** is an adjunct procedure that allows increased visualization and more precise navigation during surgery. CAS may be useful with surgical planning by using preoperative and intraoperative images. The computers identify particular landmarks and then establish spatial relationships between locations on the computer images with the actual corresponding anatomic locations on the patient. Navigation is real-time tracking of instruments during the procedure.

Robotic-assisted surgery is a minimally invasive technique that utilizes robotic arms to manipulate the surgical equipment and tools. A physician sits at a console and controls the joysticks that guide the robot in the performance of the surgical procedure. Unlike CAS, robotic-assisted procedures include the actual performance of the procedure. To identify

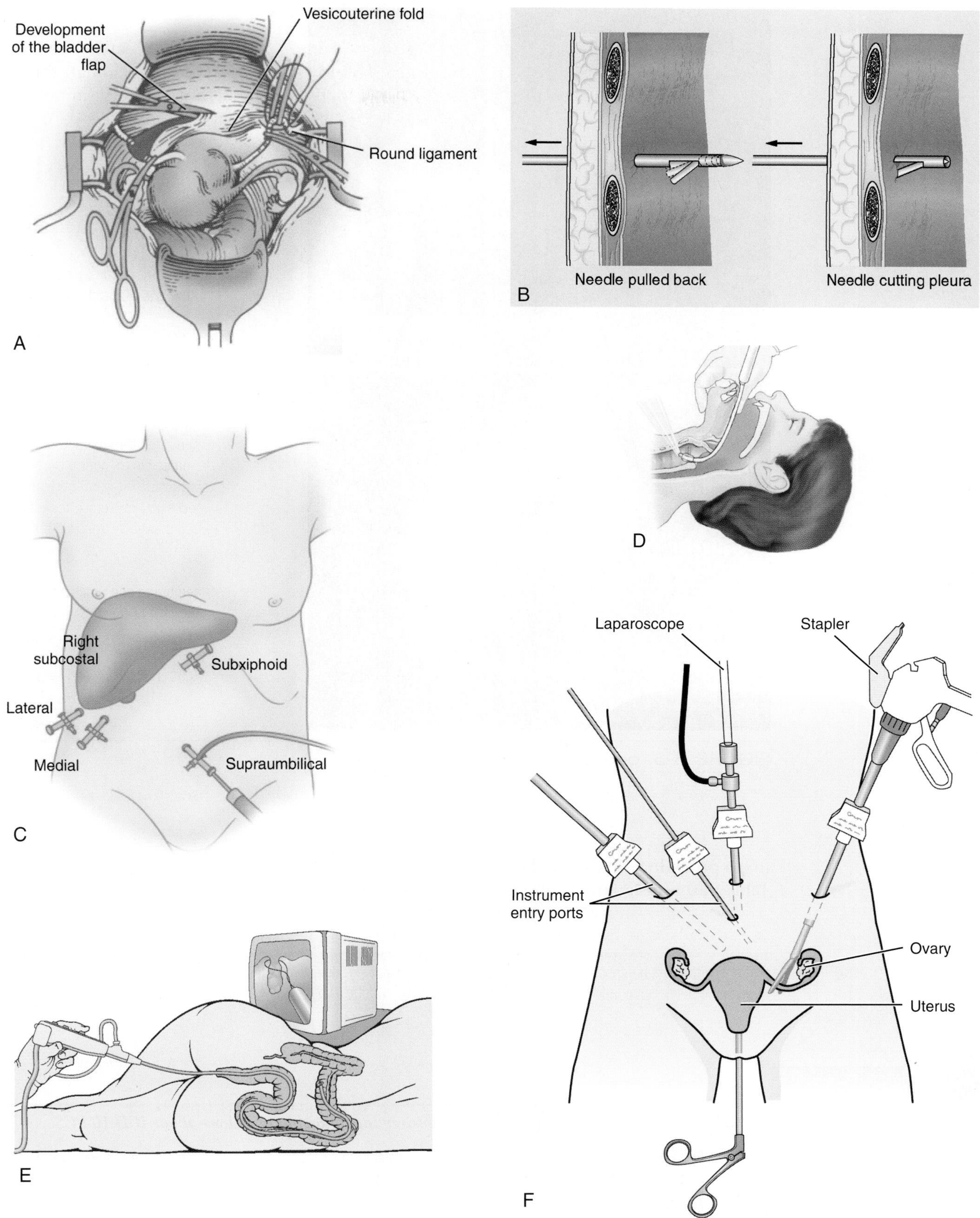

FIGURE 6-5. Surgical approaches. **A,** Open. **B,** Percutaneous. **C,** Percutaneous endoscopic. **D,** Via natural opening. **E,** Via natural opening endoscopic. **F,** Via natural opening with percutaneous endoscopic assistance.

Continued

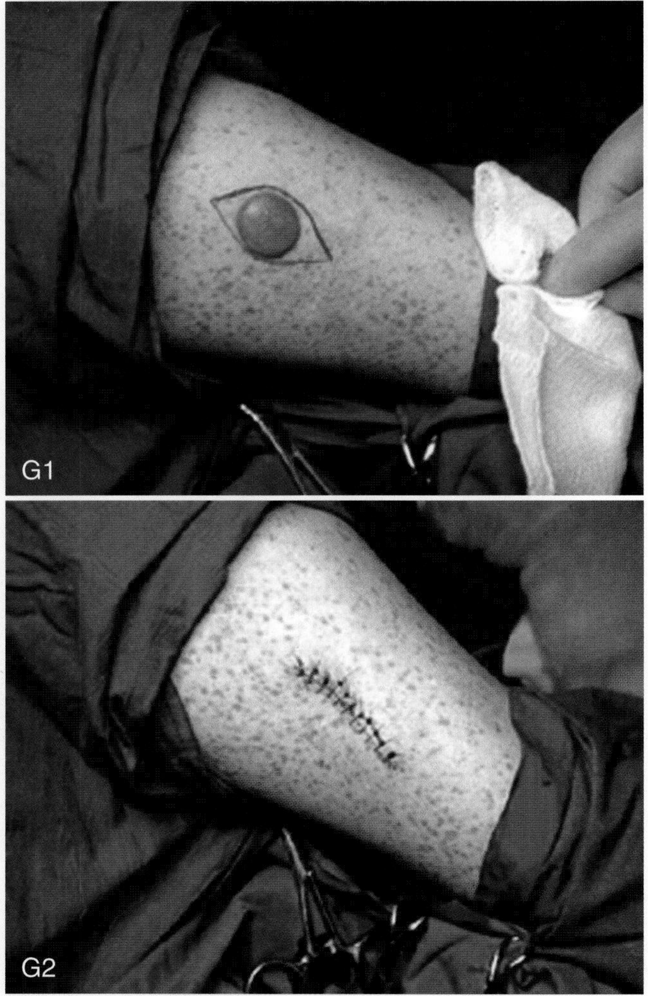

FIGURE 6-5, cont'd **G,** External.

that a procedure was assisted by computer or robotic technologies, an additional code from Table 8E0 is assigned (Figure 6-6).

EXAMPLE

Patient with prostate cancer had a robotic-assisted laparoscopic radical prostatectomy including seminal vesicles with diagnostic pelvic lymphadenectomy (total of three nodes), C61, 0VT04ZZ, 0VT34ZZ, 07BC4ZX, 8E0W4CZ.

EXERCISE 6-4

Without the use of reference material, answer the following questions about ICD-10-PCS.

1. Entry of instrumentation, by puncture or minor incision, through the skin, mucous membrane, and any other body layers necessary to reach the site of the procedure is
   A. open
   B. percutaneous
   C. percutaneous endoscopic
   D. open with percutaneous endoscopic assistance

2. Cutting through the skin, mucous membrane, and any other body layers necessary to expose the site of the procedure is
   A. open
   B. percutaneous
   C. percutaneous endoscopic
   D. open with percutaneous endoscopic assistance
3. Procedures performed directly on the skin or mucous membrane and procedures performed indirectly by the application of external force through the skin or mucous membrane are
   A. percutaneous
   B. open
   C. via natural or artificial opening
   D. external

Device

The device, the sixth character, identifies a device that remains after the procedure is completed. There are four types of devices:

- Biological or synthetic material that takes the place of all or a portion of a body part
- Biological or synthetic material that assists or prevents a physiological function
- Therapeutic material that is not absorbed by, eliminated by, or incorporated into a body part
- Mechanical or electronic appliances used to assist, monitor, take the place of, or prevent a physiological function

The root operations *change, insertion, removal, replacement, revision,* and *supplement* always involve a device. Materials that are part of a procedure—such as clips, ligatures, and sutures—are not considered devices. There is a value for other devices (Y; Figure 6-7), which can be used until more specific devices are added to the ICD-10 coding procedural system.

When no device is used in a procedure, the value Z (none) is assigned as the sixth character. There are a couple of resources available in the ICD-10-PCS code book to assist

SECTION: 8 OTHER PROCEDURES
BODY SYSTEM: E PHYSIOLOGICAL SYSTEMS AND ANATOMICAL REGIONS
OPERATION 0 OTHER PROCEDURES: Methodologies which attempt to remediate or cure a disorder or disease

Body Region	Approach	Method	Qualifier
1 Nervous System U Female Reproductive System	X External	Y Other Method	7 Examination
2 Circulatory System	3 Percutaneous X External	D Near Infrared Spectroscopy	Z No Qualifier
9 Head and Neck Region W Trunk Region	0 Open 3 Percutaneous 4 Percutaneous Endoscopic 7 Via Natural or Artificial Opening 8 Via Natural or Artificial Opening Endoscopic	C Robotic Assisted Procedure ← E Fluorescence Guided Procedure	Z No Qualifier
9 Head and Neck Region W Trunk Region	X External →	B Computer Assisted Procedure	F With Fluoroscopy G With Computerized Tomography H With Magnetic Resonance Imaging Z No Qualifier
9 Head and Neck Region W Trunk Region	X External	C Robotic Assisted Procedure	Z No Qualifier
9 Head and Neck Region W Trunk Region	X External	Y Other Method	8 Suture Removal

FIGURE 6-6. Table 8E0, which shows computer and robotic assisted methods.

Section	0 **Medical and Surgical**		
Body System	0 **Central Nervous System**		
Operation	2 **Change:** Taking out or off a device from a body part and putting back an identical or similar device in or on the same body part without cutting or puncturing the skin or a mucous membrane		
Body Part	**Approach**	**Device**	**Qualifier**
0 Brain E Cranial Nerve U Spinal Canal	X External	0 Drainage Device Y Other Device ←	Z No Qualifier

FIGURE 6-7. Table for change in central nervous system.

in the assignment of any devices. Although these resources are not a comprehensive listing, they can be helpful.

- Device Key
- Device Aggregation Table

The device key is a listing of common devices, including the brand names, with the corresponding ICD-10-PCS terms to assist in the assignment of the appropriate device value. For example, annuloplasty ring should be coded to the ICD-10-PCS value for "synthetic substitute" device.

The device aggregation table includes information to correlate a specific device along with root operation and body system to a general device term.

EXERCISE 6-5

Without the use of reference material, answer the following questions about ICD-10-PCS.

1. Sutures are considered a device.
   A. True
   B. False

2. A device is left in place after completion of the procedure.
   A. True
   B. False

3. The root operation insertion always involves a device.
   A. True
   B. False

Qualifier

The qualifier, the seventh character, identifies a unique value for an individual procedure. A qualifier may indicate that a procedure was done for diagnostic purposes (Figure 6-8); in coronary artery bypass procedures, the qualifier identifies the origin of the bypass (Figure 6-9).

EXAMPLE

Diagnostic thoracentesis, left pleura cavity (removal of fluid from pleural cavity), 0W9B3ZX.

The root operation is drainage, taking or letting out fluids and/or gases from a body part.

In the Alphabetic Index, under the term thoracentesis, it says to see Drainage, Anatomical Regions.

Under the term drainage, pleural cavity, go to Table 0W9 (Figure 6-10) and assign Characters 4 through 7. Character 4 is B for the pleural cavity, left. Character 5 is percutaneous because a thoracentesis is usually done percutaneously. Character 6 is Z, no device, and Character 7, is X because the procedure was diagnostic.

SECTION	BODY SYSTEM	ROOT OPERATION	BODY PART	APPROACH	DEVICE	QUALIFIER
Medical and Surgical	Anatomical Regions	Drainage	Pleural Cavity, Left	Percutaneous	No Device	Diagnostic
0	W	9	B	3	Z	X

Section 0 **Medical and Surgical** Body System K **Muscles** Operation B **Excision:** Cutting out or off, without replacement, a portion of a body part			
Body Part	**Approach**	**Device**	**Qualifier**
0 Head Muscle **1** Facial Muscle **2** Neck Muscle, Right **3** Neck Muscle, Left **4** Tongue, Palate, Pharynx Muscle **5** Shoulder Muscle, Right **6** Shoulder Muscle, Left **7** Upper Arm Muscle, Right **8** Upper Arm Muscle, Left **9** Lower Arm and Wrist Muscle, Right **B** Lower Arm and Wrist Muscle, Left **C** Hand Muscle, Right **D** Hand Muscle, Left **F** Trunk Muscle, Right **G** Trunk Muscle, Left **H** Thorax Muscle, Right **J** Thorax Muscle, Left **K** Abdomen Muscle, Right **L** Abdomen Muscle, Left **M** Perineum Muscle **N** Hip Muscle, Right **P** Hip Muscle, Left **Q** Upper Leg Muscle, Right **R** Upper Leg Muscle, Left **S** Lower Leg Muscle, Right **T** Lower Leg Muscle, Left **V** Foot Muscle, Right **W** Foot Muscle, Left	**0** Open **3** Percutaneous **4** Percutaneous Endoscopic	**Z** No Device	**X** Diagnostic **Z** No Qualifier

FIGURE 6-8. Table for excision of muscles.

EXAMPLE

Partial right laparoscopic nephrectomy for known malignant neoplasm.

The root operation is excision, cutting out or off, without replacement, a portion of a body part.

Under the term nephrectomy, excision, go to Table 0TB (Figure 6-11), and assign Characters 4 through 7. Character 4 is 0 for kidney, right. Character 5 is percutaneous endoscopic because the procedure was performed laparoscopically. Character 6 is Z, no device, and Character 7 is Z because the procedure was a definitive procedure for a known malignancy so it was not diagnostic.

Partial right laparoscopic nephrectomy, 0TB04ZZ

SECTION	BODY SYSTEM	ROOT OPERATION	BODY PART	APPROACH	DEVICE	QUALIFIER
Medical and Surgical	Urinary System	Excision	Kidney, Right	Percutaneous Endoscopic	No Device	No Qualifier
0	T	B	0	4	Z	Z

ICD-10-PCS CODING GUIDELINES

The ICD-10-PCS guidelines are available at the Centers for Medicare and Medicaid (CMS) website. The guidelines are divided into four parts:

A. Conventions
B. Medical and Surgical Section Guidelines
- Body system
- Root operation
- Body part
- Approach
- Device

C. Obstetrics Section Guidelines
D. New Technology Section Guidelines
E. Selection of Principal Procedure

There are many guidelines for ICD-10-PCS. Within the ICD-10-PCS guidelines, examples are given.

Section Body System Operation	**0 Medical and Surgical** **2 Heart and Great Vessels** **1 Bypass**: Altering the route of passage of the contents of a tubular body part		
Body Part	**Approach**	**Device**	**Qualifier**
0 Coronary Artery, One Artery **1** Coronary Artery, Two Arteries **2** Coronary Artery, Three Arteries **3** Coronary Artery, Four or More Arteries	**0** Open	**8** Zooplastic Tissue **9** Autologous Venous Tissue **A** Autologous Arterial Tissue **J** Synthetic Substitute **K** Nonautologous Tissue Substitute	**3** Coronary Artery **8** Internal Mammary, Right **9** Internal Mammary, Left **C** Thoracic Artery **F** Abdominal Artery **W** Aorta
0 Coronary Artery, One Artery **1** Coronary Artery, Two Arteries **2** Coronary Artery, Three Arteries **3** Coronary Artery, Four or More Arteries	**0** Open	**Z** No Device	**3** Coronary Artery **8** Internal Mammary, Right **9** Internal Mammary, Left **C** Thoracic Artery **F** Abdominal Artery
0 Coronary Artery, One Artery **1** Coronary Artery, Two Arteries **2** Coronary Artery, Three Arteries **3** Coronary Artery, Four or More Arteries	**3** Percutaneous	**4** Intraluminal Device, Drug-eluting **D** Intraluminal Device	**4** Coronary Vein
0 Coronary Artery, One Artery **1** Coronary Artery, Two Arteries **2** Coronary Artery, Three Arteries **3** Coronary Artery, Four or More Arteries	**4** Percutaneous Endoscopic	**4** Intraluminal Device, Drug-eluting **D** Intraluminal Device	**4** Coronary Vein
0 Coronary Artery, One Artery **1** Coronary Artery, Two Arteries **2** Coronary Artery, Three Arteries **3** Coronary Artery, Four or More Arteries	**4** Percutaneous Endoscopic	**8** Zooplastic Tissue **9** Autologous Venous Tissue **A** Autologous Arterial Tissue **J** Synthetic Substitute **K** Nonautologous Tissue Substitute	**3** Coronary Artery **8** Internal Mammary, Right **9** Internal Mammary, Left **C** Thoracic Artery **F** Abdominal Artery **W** Aorta

FIGURE 6-9. Table for bypass of heart and great vessels.

Section Body System Operation	**0 Medical and Surgical** **W Anatomical Regions, General** **9 Drainage**: Taking or letting out fluids and/or gases from a body part		
Body Part	**Approach**	**Device**	**Qualifier**
0 Head **1** Cranial Cavity **2** Face **3** Oral Cavity and Throat **4** Upper Jaw **5** Lower Jaw **6** Neck **8** Chest Wall **9** Pleural Cavity, Right **B** Pleural Cavity, Left **C** Mediastinum **D** Pericardial Cavity **F** Abdominal Wall **G** Peritoneal Cavity **H** Retroperitoneum **K** Upper Back **L** Lower Back **M** Perineum, Male **N** Perineum, Female	**0** Open **3** Percutaneous **4** Percutaneous Endoscopic	**Z** No Device	**X** Diagnostic **Z** No Qualifier

FIGURE 6-10. Table for drainage of anatomical region.

Section Body System Operation	**0 Medical and Surgical** **T Urinary System** **B Excision**: Cutting out or off, without replacement, a portion of a body part		
Body Part	**Approach**	**Device**	**Qualifier**
0 Kidney, Right **1** Kidney, Left **3** Kidney Pelvis, Right **4** Kidney Pelvis, Left **6** Ureter, Right **7** Ureter, Left **B** Bladder **C** Bladder Neck	**0** Open **3** Percutaneous **4** Percutaneous Endoscopic **7** Via Natural or Artificial Opening **8** Via Natural or Artificial Opening Endoscopic	**Z** No Device	**X** Diagnostic **Z** No Qualifier
D Urethra	**0** Open **3** Percutaneous **4** Percutaneous Endoscopic **7** Via Natural or Artificial Opening **8** Via Natural or Artificial Opening Endoscopic **X** External	**Z** No Device	**X** Diagnostic **Z** No Qualifier

FIGURE 6-11. Table for excision of urinary system.

ICD-10-PCS Coding Guidelines (2021/2022)

See the CMS website at www.cms.gov for the Introduction to the ICD-10-PCS Coding Guidelines.

A. *Conventions*

A1. ICD-10-PCS codes are composed of seven characters. Each character is an axis of classification that specifies information about the procedure performed. Within a defined code range, a character specifies the same type of information in that axis of classification.
Example: The fifth axis of classification specifies the approach in sections 0 through 4 and 7 through 9 of the system.

A2. One of 34 possible values can be assigned to each axis of classification in the seven-character code: they are the numbers 0 through 9 and the alphabet (except I and O because they are easily confused with the numbers 1 and 0). The number of unique values used in an axis of classification differs as needed.
Example: Where the fifth axis of classification specifies the approach, seven different approach values are currently used to specify the approach.

A3. The valid values for an axis of classification can be added to as needed.
Example: If a significantly distinct type of device is used in a new procedure, a new device value can be added to the system.

A4. As with words in their context, the meaning of any single value is a combination of its axis of classification and any preceding values on which it may be dependent.
Example: The meaning of a body part value in the Medical and Surgical section is always dependent on the body system value. The body part value 0 in the Central Nervous body system specifies Brain and the body part value 0 in the Peripheral Nervous body system specifies Cervical Plexus.

A5. As the system is expanded to become increasingly detailed, over time more values will depend on preceding values for their meaning.
Example: In the Lower Joints body system, the device value 3 in the root operation Insertion specifies Infusion Device and the device value 3 in the root operation Replacement specifies Ceramic Synthetic Substitute.

A6. The purpose of the alphabetic index is to locate the appropriate table that contains all information necessary to construct a procedure code. The PCS Tables should always be consulted to find the most appropriate valid code.

A7. It is not required to consult the index first before proceeding to the tables to complete the code. A valid code may be chosen directly from the tables.

A8. All seven characters must be specified to be a valid code. If the documentation is incomplete for coding purposes, the physician should be queried for the necessary information.

A9. Within a PCS table, valid codes include all combinations of choices in characters 4 through 7 contained in the same row of the table. In the example below, 0JHT3VZ is a valid code, and 0JHW3VZ is *not* a valid code.

Section: 0 Medical and Surgical
Body System: J Subcutaneous Tissue and Fascia

Operation: H Insertion: Putting in a nonbiological appliance that monitors, assists, performs, or prevents a physiological function but does not physically take the place of a body part

BODY PART	APPROACH	DEVICE	QUALIFIER
S Subcutaneous Tissue and Fascia, Head and Neck V Subcutaneous Tissue and Fascia, Upper Extremity W Subcutaneous Tissue and Fascia, Lower Extremity	0 Open 3 Percutaneous	1 Radioactive Element 3 Infusion Device Y Other Device	Z No Qualifier
T Subcutaneous Tissue and Fascia, Trunk	0 Open 3 Percutaneous	1 Radioactive Element 3 Infusion Device V Infusion Pump Y Other Device	Z No Qualifier

A10. "And," when used in a code description, means "and/or", except when used to describe a combination of multiple body parts for which separate values exist for each body part (e.g., Skin and Subcutaneous Tissue used as a qualifier, where there are separate body part values for "Skin" and "Subcutaneous Tissue"). *Example*: Lower Arm and Wrist Muscle means lower arm and/or wrist muscle.

A11. Many of the terms used to construct PCS codes are defined within the system. It is the coder's responsibility to determine what the documentation in the medical record equates to in the PCS definitions. The physician is not expected to use the terms used in PCS code descriptions, nor is the coder required to query the physician when the correlation between the documentation and the defined PCS terms is clear.
Example: When the physician documents "partial resection" the coder can independently correlate "partial resection" to the root operation Excision without querying the physician for clarification.

B. *Medical and Surgical Section Guidelines (section 0)*

B2. Body System

General guidelines

B2.1a. The procedure codes in Anatomical Regions, General, Anatomical Regions, Upper Extremities and Anatomical Regions, Lower Extremities can be used when the procedure is performed on an anatomical region rather than a specific body part or on the rare occasion when no information is available to support assignment of a code to a specific body part.
Examples: Chest tube drainage of the pleural cavity is coded to the root operation Drainage found in the body system Anatomical Regions, General. Suture repair of the abdominal wall is coded to the root operation Repair in the body system Anatomical Regions, General. Amputation of the foot is coded to the root operation Detachment in the body system Anatomical Regions, Lower Extremities.

B2.1b. Where the general body part values "upper" and "lower" are provided as an option in the Upper Arteries, Lower Arteries, Upper Veins, Lower Veins, Muscles and Tendons body systems, "upper" or "lower" specifies body parts located above or below the diaphragm respectively.
Example: Vein body parts above the diaphragm are found in the Upper Veins body system; vein body parts below the diaphragm are found in the Lower Veins body system.

B3. Root Operation

General guidelines

B3.1a. In order to determine the appropriate root operation, the full definition of the root operation as contained in the PCS Tables must be applied.

B3.1b. Components of a procedure specified in the root operation definition or explanation as integral to that root operation are not coded separately. Procedural steps necessary to reach the operative site and close the operative site, including anastomosis of a tubular body part, are also not coded separately.
Examples: Resection of a joint as part of a joint replacement procedure is included in the root operation definition of Replacement and is not coded separately. Laparotomy performed to reach the site of an open liver biopsy is not coded separately. In a resection of sigmoid colon with anastomosis of descending colon to rectum, the anastomosis is not coded separately.

Multiple procedures

B3.2. During the same operative episode, multiple procedures are coded if:

a. The same root operation is performed on different body parts as defined by distinct values of the body part character.
Examples: Diagnostic excision of liver and pancreas are coded separately. Excision of lesion in the ascending colon and excision of lesion in the transverse colon are coded separately.

b. The same root operation is repeated in multiple body parts, and those body parts are separate and distinct body parts classified to a single ICD-10-PCS body part value.
Examples: Excision of the sartorius muscle and excision of the gracilis muscle are both included in the upper leg muscle body part value, and multiple procedures are coded. Extraction of multiple toenails are coded separately.

c. Multiple root operations with distinct objectives are performed on the same body part.
Example: Destruction of sigmoid lesion and bypass of sigmoid colon are coded separately.

d. The intended root operation is attempted using one approach, but is converted to a different approach.
Example: Laparoscopic cholecystectomy converted to an open cholecystectomy is coded as percutaneous endoscopic Inspection and open Resection.

Discontinued or incomplete procedures

B3.3. If the intended procedure is discontinued or otherwise not completed, code the procedure to the root operation performed. If a procedure is discontinued before any other root operation is performed, code the root operation Inspection of the body part of anatomical region inspected.
Example: A planned aortic valve replacement procedure is discontinued after the initial thoracotomy and before any incision is made in the heart muscle, when the patient becomes hemodynamically unstable. This procedure is coded as an open Inspection of the mediastinum.

Biopsy procedures

B3.4a. Biopsy procedures are coded using the root operations Excision, Extraction, or Drainage and the qualifier Diagnostic.
Examples: Fine needle aspiration biopsy of fluid in the lung is coded to the root operation Drainage with the qualifier Diagnostic. Biopsy of bone marrow is coded to the root operation Extraction with the qualifier Diagnostic. Lymph node sampling for biopsy is coded to the root operation Excision with the qualifier Diagnostic.

Biopsy followed by more definitive treatment

B3.4b. If a diagnostic Excision, Extraction, or Drainage procedure (biopsy) is followed by a more definitive procedure, such as Destruction, Excision or Resection at the same procedure site, both the biopsy and the more definitive treatment are coded.
Example: Biopsy of breast followed by partial mastectomy at the same procedure site, both the biopsy and the partial mastectomy procedure are coded.

Overlapping body layers

B3.5. If the root operations Excision, Extraction, Repair or Inspection are performed on overlapping layers of the musculoskeletal system, the body part specifying the deepest layer is coded.
Example: Excisional debridement that includes skin and subcutaneous tissue and muscle is coded to the muscle body part.

Bypass procedures

B3.6a. Bypass procedures are coded by identifying the body part bypassed "from" and the body part bypassed "to." The fourth character body part specifies the body part bypassed from, and the qualifier specifies the body part bypassed to.
Example: Bypass from stomach to jejunum, stomach is the body part and jejunum is the qualifier.

B3.6b. Coronary artery bypass procedures are coded differently than other bypass procedures as described in the previous guideline. Rather than identifying the body part bypassed from, the body part identifies the number of coronary arteries bypassed to, and the qualifier specifies the vessel bypassed from.
Example: Aortocoronary artery bypass of the left anterior descending coronary artery and the obtuse marginal coronary artery is classified in the body part axis of classification as two coronary arteries, and the qualifier specifies the aorta as the body part bypassed from.

B3.6c. If multiple coronary artery sites are bypassed, a separate procedure is coded for each coronary artery that uses a different device and/or qualifier.
Example: Aortocoronary artery bypass and internal mammary coronary artery bypass are coded separately.

Control vs. more definitive root operations

B3.7. The root operation Control is defined as, "Stopping, or attempting to stop, postprocedural or other acute bleeding." If an attempt to stop postprocedural or other acute bleeding is unsuccessful, and to stop the bleeding requires performing a more definitive root operation, such as Bypass, Detachment, Excision, Extraction, Reposition, Replacement, or Resection, then the more definitive root operation is coded instead of Control.
Example: Resection of spleen to stop bleeding is coded to Resection instead of Control.

Excision vs. Resection

B3.8. PCS contains specific body parts for anatomical subdivisions of a body part, such as lobes of the lungs or liver and regions of the intestine. Resection of the specific body part is coded whenever all of the body part is cut out or off, rather than coding Excision of a less specific body part.
Example: Left upper lung lobectomy is coded to Resection of Upper Lung Lobe, Left rather than Excision of Lung, Left.

Excision for graft

B3.9. If an autograft is obtained from a different procedure site in order to complete the objective of the procedure, a separate procedure is coded, except when the seventh character qualifier value in the ICD-10-PCS table fully specifies the site from which the autograft was obtained.
Examples: Coronary bypass with excision of saphenous vein graft, excision of saphenous vein is coded separately. Replacement of breast with autologous deep inferior epigastric artery perforator (DIEP) flap, excision of the DIEP flap is not coded separately. The seventh character qualifier value Deep Inferior Epigastric Artery Perforator Flap in the Replacement table fully specifies the site of the autograft harvest.

Fusion procedures of the spine

B3.10a. The body part coded for a spinal vertebral joint(s) rendered immobile by a spinal fusion procedure is classified by the level of the spine (e.g., thoracic). There are distinct body part values for a single vertebral joint and for multiple vertebral joints at each spinal level.
Example: Body part values specify Lumbar Vertebral Joint, Lumbar Vertebral Joints, 2 or More and Lumbosacral Vertebral Joint.

B3.10b. If multiple vertebral joints are fused, a separate procedure is coded for each vertebral joint that uses a different device and/or qualifier.
Example: Fusion of lumbar vertebral joint, posterior approach, anterior column and fusion of lumbar vertebral joint, posterior approach, posterior column are coded separately.

B3.10c. Combinations of devices and materials are often used on a vertebral joint to render the joint immobile. When combinations of devices are used on the same vertebral joint, the device value coded for the procedure is as follows:

- If an interbody fusion device is used to render the joint immobile containing bone graft or bone graft substitute, the procedure is coded with the device value Interbody Fusion Device
- If bone graft is the *only* device used to render the joint immobile, the procedure is coded with the device value Nonautologous Tissue Substitute or Autologous Tissue Substitute
- If a mixture of autologous and nonautologous bone graft (with or without biological or synthetic extenders or binders) is used to render the joint immobile, code the procedure with the device value Autologous Tissue Substitute

Examples: Fusion of a vertebral joint using a cage style interbody fusion device containing morsellized bone graft is coded to the device Interbody Fusion Device. Fusion of a vertebral joint using a bone dowel interbody fusion device made of cadaver bone and packed with a mixture of local morsellized bone and demineralized bone matrix is coded to the device Interbody Fusion Device.

Fusion of a vertebral joint using both autologous bone graft and bone bank bone graft is coded to the device Autologous Tissue Substitute.

Inspection procedures

B3.11a. Inspection of a body part(s) performed in order to achieve the objective of a procedure is not coded separately.
Example: Fiberoptic bronchoscopy performed for irrigation of bronchus, only the irrigation procedure is coded.

B3.11b. If multiple tubular body parts are inspected, the most distal body part (the body part furthest from the starting point of the inspection) is coded. If multiple non-tubular body parts in a region are inspected, the body part that specifies the entire area inspected is coded.
Examples: Cystoureteroscopy with inspection of bladder and ureters is coded to the ureter body part value.

Exploratory laparotomy with general inspection of abdominal contents is coded to the peritoneal cavity body part value.

B3.11c. When both an Inspection procedure and another procedure are performed on the same body part during the same episode, if the Inspection procedure is performed using a different approach than the other procedure, the Inspection procedure is coded separately.
Example: Endoscopic Inspection of the duodenum is coded separately when open Excision of the duodenum is performed during the same procedural episode.

Occlusion vs. Restriction for vessel embolization procedures

B3.12. If the objective of an embolization procedure is to completely close a vessel, the root operation Occlusion is coded. If the objective of an embolization procedure is to narrow the lumen of a vessel, the root operation Restriction is coded.
Examples: Tumor embolization is coded to the root operation Occlusion, because the objective of the procedure is to cut off the blood supply to the vessel.

Embolization of a cerebral aneurysm is coded to the root operation Restriction, because the objective of the procedure is not to close off the vessel entirely, but to narrow the lumen of the vessel at the site of the aneurysm where it is abnormally wide.

Release procedures

B3.13. In the root operation Release, the body part value coded is the body part being freed and not the tissue being manipulated or cut to free the body part.
Example: Lysis of intestinal adhesions is coded to the specific intestine body part value.

Release vs. Division

B3.14. If the sole objective of the procedure is freeing a body part without cutting the body part, the root operation is Release. If the sole objective of the procedure is separating or transecting a body part, the root operation is Division.
Examples: Freeing a nerve root from surrounding scar tissue to relieve pain is coded to the root operation Release. Severing a nerve root to relieve pain is coded to the root operation Division.

Reposition for fracture treatment

B3.15. Reduction of a displaced fracture is coded to the root operation Reposition and the application of a cast or splint in conjunction with the Reposition procedure is not coded separately. Treatment of a nondisplaced fracture is coded to the procedure performed.
Examples: Casting of a nondisplaced fracture is coded to the root operation Immobilization in the Placement section.
Putting a pin in a nondisplaced fracture is coded to the root operation Insertion.

Transplantation vs. Administration

B3.16. Putting in a mature and functioning living body part taken from another individual or animal is coded to the root operation Transplantation. Putting in autologous or nonautologous cells is coded to the Administration section.
Example: Putting in autologous or nonautologous bone marrow, pancreatic islet cells or stem cells is coded to the Administration section.

Transfer procedures using multiple tissue layers

B3.17. The root operation Transfer contains qualifiers that can be used to specify when a transfer flap is composed of more than one tissue layer, such as a musculocutaneous flap. For procedures involving transfer of multiple tissue layers including skin, subcutaneous tissue, fascia or muscle, the procedure is coded to the body part value that describes the deepest tissue layer in the flap, and the qualifier can be used to describe the additional tissue layer(s) in the transfer flap.
Example: A musculocutaneous flap transfer is coded to the appropriate body part value in the body system Muscles, and the qualifier is used to describe the additional tissue layer(s) in the transfer flap.

Excision/Resection followed by replacement

B3.18. If an excision or resection of a body part is followed by a replacement procedure, code both procedures to identify each distinct objective, except when the excision or resection is considered integral and preparatory for the replacement procedure.
Examples: Mastectomy followed by reconstruction, both resection and replacement of the breast are coded to fully capture the distinct objectives of the procedures performed. Maxillectomy with obturator reconstruction, both excision and replacement of the maxilla are coded to fully capture the distinct objectives of the procedures performed. Excisional debridement of tendon with skin graft, both the excision of the tendon and the replacement of the skin with a graft are coded to fully capture the distinct objectives of the procedures performed. Esophagectomy followed by reconstruction with colonic interposition, both the resection and the transfer of the large intestine to function as the esophagus are coded to fully capture the distinct objectives of the procedures performed.
Examples: Resection of a joint as part of a joint replacement procedure is considered integral and preparatory for the replacement of the joint and the resection is not coded separately.
Resection of a valve as part of a valve replacement procedure is considered integral and preparatory for the valve replacement and the resection is not coded separately.

B4. Body Part

General guidelines

B4.1a. If a procedure is performed on a portion of a body part that does not have a separate body part value, code the body part value corresponding to the whole body part.
Example: A procedure performed on the alveolar process of the mandible is coded to the mandible body part.

B4.1b. If the prefix "peri" is combined with a body part to identify the site of the procedure, and the site of the procedure is not further specified, then the procedure is coded to the body part named. This guideline applies only when a more specific body part value is not available.
Examples: A procedure site identified as perirenal is coded to the kidney body part when the site of the procedure is not further specified. A procedure site described in the documentation as peri-urethral, and documentation also indicates that it is the vulvar tissue and not the urethral tissue that is the site of the procedure, then the procedure is coded to the vulva body part. A procedure site documented as involving the periosteum is coded to the corresponding bone body part.

B4.1c. If a procedure is performed on a continuous section of a tubular body part, code the body part value corresponding to the furthest anatomical site from the point of entry.
Example: A procedure performed on a continuous section of artery from the femoral artery to the external iliac artery with the point of entry at the femoral artery is coded to the external iliac body part.

Branches of body parts

B4.2. Where a specific branch of a body part does not have its own body part value in PCS, the body part is typically coded to the closest proximal branch that has a specific body part value. In the cardiovascular body systems, if a general body part is available in the correct root operation table, and coding to a proximal branch would require assigning a code in a different body system, the procedure is coded using the general body part value.
Examples: A procedure performed on the mandibular branch of the trigeminal nerve is coded to the trigeminal nerve body part value. Occlusion of the bronchial artery is coded to the body part value of Upper Artery in the body system Upper Arteries, and not to the body part value Thoracic Aorta, Descending in the body system Heart and Great Vessels.

Bilateral body part values

B4.3. Bilateral body part values are available for a limited number of body parts. If the identical procedure is performed on contralateral body parts, and a bilateral body part value exists for that body part, a single procedure is coded using the bilateral body part value. If no bilateral body part value exists, each procedure is coded separately using the appropriate body part value.
Examples: The identical procedure performed on both fallopian tubes is coded once using the body part value Fallopian Tube, Bilateral. The identical procedure performed on both knee joints is coded twice using the body part values Knee Joint, Right and Knee Joint, Left.

Coronary arteries

B4.4. The coronary arteries are classified as a single body part that is further specified by number of arteries treated. One procedure code specifying multiple arteries is used when the same procedure is performed, including the same device and qualifier values.
Examples: Angioplasty of two distinct coronary arteries with placement of two stents is coded as Dilation of Coronary Artery, Two Arteries with Two Intraluminal Devices.
Angioplasty of two distinct coronary arteries, one with stent placed and one without, is coded separately as Dilation of Coronary Artery, One Artery with Intraluminal Device, and Dilation of Coronary Artery, One Artery with no device.

Tendons, ligaments, bursae and fascia near a joint

B4.5. Procedures performed on tendons, ligaments, bursae and fascia supporting a joint are coded to the body part in the respective body system that is the focus of the procedure. Procedures performed on joint structures themselves are coded to the body part in the joint body systems.
Examples: Repair of the anterior cruciate ligament of the knee is coded to the knee bursae and ligament body part in the bursae and ligaments body system. Knee arthroscopy with shaving of articular cartilage is coded to the knee joint body part in the Lower Joints body system.

Skin, subcutaneous tissue and fascia overlying a joint

B4.6. If a procedure is performed on the skin, subcutaneous tissue or fascia overlying a joint, the procedure is coded to the following body part:

- Shoulder is coded to Upper Arm
- Elbow is coded to Lower Arm
- Wrist is coded to Lower Arm
- Hip is coded to Upper Leg
- Knee is coded to Lower Leg
- Ankle is coded to Foot

Fingers and toes

B4.7. If a body system does not contain a separate body part value for fingers, procedures performed on the fingers are coded to the body part value for the hand. If a body system does not contain a separate body part value for toes, procedures performed on the toes are coded to the body part value for the foot.
Example: Excision of finger muscle is coded to one of the hand muscle body part values in the Muscles body system.

Upper and lower intestinal tract

B4.8. In the Gastrointestinal body system, the general body part values Upper Intestinal Tract and Lower Intestinal Tract are provided as an option for the root operations Change, Inspection, Removal and Revision. Upper Intestinal Tract includes the portion of the gastrointestinal tract from the esophagus down to and including the duodenum, and Lower Intestinal Tract includes the portion of the gastrointestinal tract from the jejunum down to and including the rectum and anus.
Example: In the root operation Change table, change of a device in the jejunum is coded using the body part Lower Intestinal Tract.

B5. Approach

Open approach with percutaneous endoscopic assistance

B5.2a. Procedures performed using the open approach with percutaneous endoscopic assistance are coded to the approach Open.

Example: Laparoscopic-assisted sigmoidectomy is coded to the approach Open.

Percutaneous endoscopic approach with extension of incision

B5.2b. Procedures performed using the percutaneous endoscopic approach, with incision or extension of an incision to assist in the removal of all or a portion of a body part or to anastomose a tubular body part to complete the procedure, are coded to the approach value Percutaneous Endoscopic.

Examples: Laparoscopic sigmoid colectomy with extension of stapling port for removal of specimen and direct anastomosis is coded to the approach value Percutaneous Endoscopic.

Laparoscopic nephrectomy with midline incision for removing the resected kidney is code to the approach value Percutaneous Endoscopic.

Robotic-assisted laparoscopic prostatectomy with extension of incision for removal of the resected prostate is coded to the approach value Percutaneous Endoscopic.

External approach

B5.3a. Procedures performed within an orifice on structures that are visible without the aid of any instrumentation are coded to the approach External.

Example: Resection of tonsils is coded to the approach External.

B5.3b. Procedures performed indirectly by the application of external force through the intervening body layers are coded to the approach External.

Example: Closed reduction of fracture is coded to the approach External.

Percutaneous procedure via device

B5.4. Procedures performed percutaneously via a device placed for the procedure are coded to the approach Percutaneous.

Example: Fragmentation of kidney stone performed via percutaneous nephrostomy is coded to the approach Percutaneous.

B6. Device

General guidelines

B6.1a. A device is coded only if a device remains after the procedure is completed. If no device remains, the device value No Device is coded. In limited root operations, the classification provides the qualifier values Temporary and Intraoperative, for specific procedures involving clinically significant devices, where the purpose of the device is to be utilized for a brief duration during the procedure or current inpatient stay. If a device that is intended to remain after the procedure is completed requires removal before the end of the operative episode in which it was inserted (for example, the device size is inadequate or a complication occurs), both the insertion and removal of the device should be coded.

B6.1b. Materials such as sutures, ligatures, radiological markers and temporary post-operative wound drains are considered integral to the performance of a procedure and are not coded as devices.

B6.1c. Procedures performed on a device only and not on a body part are specified in the root operations Change, Irrigation, Removal and Revision, and are coded to the procedure performed.

Example: Irrigation of percutaneous nephrostomy tube is coded to the root operation Irrigation of indwelling device in the Administration section.

Drainage device

B6.2. A separate procedure to put in a drainage device is coded to the root operation Drainage with the device value Drainage Device.

F. Selection of Principal Procedure

The following instruction should be applied in the selection of principal procedure and clarification on the importance of the relation to the principal diagnosis when more than one procedure is performed:

1. Procedure performed for definitive treatment of both principal diagnosis and secondary diagnosis.
   a. Sequence procedure performed for definitive treatment most related to principal diagnosis as principal procedure.
2. Procedure performed for definitive treatment and diagnostic procedures performed for both principal diagnosis and secondary diagnosis.
   a. Sequence procedure performed for definitive treatment most related to principal diagnosis as principal procedure.
3. A diagnostic procedure was performed for the principal diagnosis and a procedure is performed for definitive treatment of a secondary diagnosis.
   a. Sequence diagnostic procedure as principal procedure, since the procedure most related to the principal diagnosis takes precedence.
4. No procedures performed that are related to principal diagnosis; procedures performed for definitive treatment and diagnostic procedures were performed for secondary diagnosis.
   a. Sequence procedure performed for definitive treatment of secondary diagnosis as principal procedure, since there are no procedures (definitive or nondefinitive treatment) related to principal diagnosis.

EXERCISE 6-6

With the use of reference material, answer the following questions about ICD-10-PCS.

1. It is acceptable to choose a valid code directly from the tables.
   A. True
   B. False
2. Procedures that are performed using an open approach with percutaneous endoscopic assistance are coded to an open approach.
   A. True
   B. False
3. Body systems designated as "upper" contain body parts above the heart.
   A. True
   B. False
4. When a patient is having a hip replacement, a code for the resection of a joint is assigned in addition to the joint replacement code.
   A. True
   B. False
5. Procedures performed on the distal end of the humerus are coded to the Arm body part value.
   A. True
   B. False
6. A closed reduction of a fracture is coded to the manipulation approach.
   A. True
   B. False
7. It is acceptable to choose a valid code directly from the index.
   A. True
   B. False
8. Body systems designated as "lower" contain body parts below the diaphragm.
   A. True
   B. False
9. If the intended procedure is discontinued, code to the root operation that was intended.
   A. True
   B. False
10. If the identical procedure is performed on contralateral body parts, and a bilateral body part value is available for that body part, a single code with the bilateral body part should be assigned.
    A. True
    B. False
11. When used in a code description, the term *and* means "and/or."
    A. True
    B. False
12. It is acceptable to use a general body part value when the specific body part cannot be determined.
    A. True
    B. False
13. The body site for perirenal is "peritoneum."
    A. True
    B. False
14. A temporary postoperative wound drain is considered a device when assigning a ICD-10-PCS code.
    A. True
    B. False
15. Exploration or inspection of a body part that is integral to the performance of the procedure is not coded separately.
    A. True
    B. False

16. A bone marrow transplant is coded to the root operation transplant.
    A. True
    B. False
17. The root operation to stop postprocedural bleeding is control.
    A. True
    B. False
18. Procedures performed on the skin are coded to the body part values in the body system Skin and breast.
    A. True
    B. False
19. A device is only coded if the device remains after the procedure is completed.
    A. True
    B. False
20. The resection of tonsils is coded to an open approach.
    A. True
    B. False

CHAPTER REVIEW EXERCISE

Complete the following review exercises.

1. It is not acceptable to choose a valid code directly from the tables.
   A. True
   B. False
2. The resection of tonsils is coded to an external approach.
   A. True
   B. False
3. The body site for perirenal is kidney.
   A. True
   B. False
4. When a patient is having a knee replacement, a code for the resection of a joint is not assigned but is coded to the joint replacement.
   A. True
   B. False
5. A device is only coded if the device remains after the procedure is completed.
   A. True
   B. False
6. The root operation replacement always involves a device.
   A. True
   B. False
7. The approach for a laparoscopic cholecystectomy is percutaneous endoscopic.
   A. True
   B. False
8. The entry by puncture or minor incision, of instrumentation through the skin, mucous membrane, and any other body layers necessary to reach the operative site is an open approach.
   A. True
   B. False
9. All ICD-10-PCS codes have six characters.
   A. True
   B. False
10. The AMA is responsible for the maintenance of ICD-10-PCS.
    A. True
    B. False

11. Which of the following is a characteristic of ICD-10-PCS?
    A. Codes have a decimal point.
    B. Codes are similar to ICD-10-CM codes.
    C. There are 34 possible values for a character.
    D. The number of codes is limited.
12. The first character of an ICD-10-PCS code represents
    A. Body part
    B. Approach
    C. Section
    D. Device

Locate the following terms in the Alphabetic Index and identify the characters listed in the Index.

13. Brachytherapy, prostate __________
14. Fragmentation, right ureteral stone __________
15. Kidney transplant, left __________
16. Resection, adrenal glands __________
17. PPN via central vein __________

Assign the appropriate ICD-10-PCS codes to the following procedures in accordance with the coding guidelines.

18. Open partial nephrectomy, left __________
19. Therapeutic thoracentesis, right pleural cavity __________
20. Open lysis of adhesions, gallbladder __________

CHAPTER GLOSSARY

It is important to note that most of these definitions are as defined by ICD-10-PCS.

Alteration: modifying the natural anatomic structure of a body part without affecting the function of the body part (breast augmentation).

Body system: an anatomic region or a general physiological system on which a procedure is performed.

Bypass: altering the route of passage of the contents of a tubular body part (CABG).

Change: taking out or off a device from a body part and putting back an identical or similar device in or on the same body part without cutting or puncturing the skin or a mucous membrane (change gastrostomy tube).

Computer assisted surgery (CAS): adjunctive procedure that allows increased visualization and more precise navigation while remaining minimally invasive.

Control: stopping, or attempting to stop, postprocedural bleeding or other acute bleeding (control of post-prostatectomy hemorrhage, control of bleeding duodenal ulcer, control of retroperitoneal hemorrhage).

Creation: putting in or on biological or synthetic material to form a new body part that to the extent possible replicates the anatomic structure or function of an absent body part (creation of vagina in a male, creation of right and left atrioventricular valve from common atrioventricular valve)

Destruction: physical eradication of all or a portion of a body part by the direct use of energy, force, or a destructive agent (ablation of endometriosis).

Detachment: cutting off all or a portion of the upper or lower extremities (above-knee amputation).

Dilation: expanding an orifice or the lumen of a tubular body part (PTCA).

Division: cutting into a body part without draining fluids and/or gases from the body part in order to separate or transect a body part (osteotomy).

Drainage: taking or letting out fluids and/or gases from a body part (paracentesis).

Excision: cutting out or off, without replacement, a portion of a body part (partial nephrectomy).

External: procedures performed directly on the skin or mucous membrane and procedures performed indirectly by the application of external force through the skin or mucous membrane (tonsillectomy).

Extirpation: taking or cutting out solid matter from a body part (thrombectomy).

Extraction: pulling or stripping out or off all or a portion of a body part by the use of force (bone marrow biopsy).

Fragmentation: breaking solid matter in a body part into pieces (extracorporeal shockwave lithotripsy).

Fusion: joining together portions of an articular body part, rendering the articular body part immobile (spinal fusion).

Insertion: putting in a nonbiological appliance that monitors, assists, performs, or prevents a physiological function but does not physically take the place of a body part (insertion of pacemaker lead).

Inspection: visually and/or manually exploring a body part (diagnostic arthroscopy).

Map: locating the route of passage of electrical impulses and/or locating functional areas in a body part (cardiac mapping).

Occlusion: completely closing an orifice or lumen of a tubular body part (tubal ligation).

Open: cutting through the skin, mucous membrane, and any other body layers necessary to expose the site of the procedure (abdominal hysterectomy).

Percutaneous: entry, by puncture or minor incision, of instrumentation through the skin, mucous membrane, and any other body layers necessary to reach the site of the procedure (needle biopsy liver).

Percutaneous endoscopic: entry, by puncture or minor incision, of instrumentation through the skin, mucous membrane, and any other body layers necessary to reach and visualize the site of the procedure (laparoscopic cholecystectomy).

Reattachment: putting back in or on all or a portion of a separated body part to its normal location or other suitable location.

Release: to free a body part from an abnormal physical constraint (lysis of adhesions).

Removal: taking out or off a device from a body part (remove chest tube).

Repair: restoring, to the extent possible, a body part to its normal anatomic structure and function (herniorrhaphy).

Replacement: putting in or on biological or synthetic material that physically takes the place and/or performs the function of all or a portion of a body part (total knee replacement).

Reposition: moving to its normal location, or other suitable location, all or a portion of a body part (fracture reduction).

Resection: cutting out or off, without replacement, all of a body part (total lobectomy of lung).

Restriction: partially closing an orifice or lumen of a tubular body part (Nissen fundoplication).

Revision: correcting, to the extent possible, a malfunctioning or displaced device (adjustment of knee prosthesis).

Robotic-assisted surgery: minimally invasive technique that utilizes robotic arms to manipulate the surgical equipment and tools.

Supplement: putting in or on biological or synthetic material that physically reinforces and/or augments the function of a portion of a body part (herniorrhaphy with mesh).

Transfer: moving, without taking out, all or a portion of a body part to another location to take over the function of all or a portion of a body part (pedicle skin flap).

Transplantation: putting in or on all or a portion of a living body part taken from another individual or animal to physically take the place and/or function of all or a portion of a similar body part (kidney transplant).

Via natural or artificial opening: entry of instrumentation through a natural or artificial external opening to reach the site of the procedure (endotracheal intubation).

Via natural or artificial opening endoscopic: entry of instrumentation through a natural or artificial external opening to reach and visualize the site of the procedure (colonoscopy).

Via natural or artificial opening with percutaneous endoscopic assistance: cutting through the skin, mucous membrane, and any other body layers necessary to expose the site of the procedure, and entry, by puncture or minor incision, of instrumentation through the skin, mucous membrane, and any other body layers necessary to aid in the performance of the procedure (laparoscopic-assisted vaginal hysterectomy).

7

General Coding Guidelines for Other Medical- and Surgical-Related Procedures and Ancillary Procedures

CHAPTER OUTLINE

LEARNING OBJECTIVES

1. Apply the conventions and ICD-10-PCS Coding Guidelines
2. Define the root operations/types for each section of ICD-10-PCS
3. Define the approaches for each section of ICD-10-PCS
4. Understand the purpose of the new technology section
5. Assign procedure codes using ICD-10-PCS

ABBREVIATIONS/ ACRONYMS

CT computerized tomography
ECMO extracorporeal membrane oxygenation
ECT electroconvulsive therapy
ICD-10-PCS *International Classification of Diseases, 10th Revision, Procedure Coding System*
MRI magnetic resonance imaging
PET positron emission tomography

ICD-10-PCS Coding Guidelines (2021-2022)

Please refer to the companion Evolve website for the most current 2021-2022 guidelines.

Transplantation vs. Administration

B3.16 Putting in a mature and functioning living body part taken from another individual or animal is coded to the root operation Transplantation. Putting in autologous or nonautologous cells is coded to the Administration section.
Example: Putting in autologous or nonautologous bone marrow, pancreatic islet cells or stem cells is coded to the Administration section.

EXAMPLE

Nonautologous bone marrow transplant via central venous line in patient with multiple myeloma, C90.00, 30243G4.

Obstetric Section Guidelines (section 1)

C. Obstetrics Section

Products of conception

C1 Procedures performed on the products of conception are coded to the Obstetrics section. Procedures performed on the pregnant female other than the products of conception are coded to the appropriate root operation in the Medical and Surgical section.
Example: Amniocentesis is coded to the products of conception body part in the Obstetrics section. Repair of obstetric urethral laceration is coded to the urethra body part in the Medical and Surgical section.

EXAMPLE Amniocentesis was performed to screen for genetic and chromosomal abnormalities, Z13.79, 10903ZU.

Procedures following delivery or abortion

C2 Procedures performed following a delivery or abortion for curettage of the endometrium or evacuation of retained products of conception are all coded in the Obstetrics section, to the root operation Extraction and the body part Products of Conception, Retained. Diagnostic or therapeutic dilation and curettage performed during times other than the postpartum or post-abortion period are all coded in the Medical and Surgical section, to the root operation Extraction and the body part Endometrium.

EXAMPLE D&C for retained products of conception following a spontaneous abortion at 8 weeks' gestation, O03.4, Z3A.08 10D17ZZ.

Radiation Therapy Section Guidelines (section D)

D. Radiation Therapy Section

Brachytherapy

D1.a. Brachytherapy is coded to the modality Brachytherapy in the Radiation Therapy section. When a radioactive brachytherapy source is left in the body at the end of the procedure, it is coded separately to the root operation Insertion with the device valve Radioactive Element.
Example: Brachytherapy with implantation of a low dose rate brachytherapy source left in the body at the end of the procedure is coded to the applicable treatment site in section D, Radiation Therapy, with the modality Brachytherapy, the modality qualifier value Low Dose Rate, and the applicable isotope value and qualifier value. The implantation of the brachytherapy source is coded separately to the device value Radioactive Element in the appropriate insertion table of the Medical and Surgical section. The Radiation Therapy section code identifies the specific modality and isotope of the brachytherapy, and the root operation Insertion code identifies the implantation of the brachytherapy source that remains in the body at the end of the procedure.
Exception: Implantation of Cesium-131 brachytherapy seeds embedded in collagen matrix to the treatment site after resection of brain tumor is coded to the root operation Insertion with the device value Radioactive Element, Cesium-131 Collagen Implant. The procedure is coded to the root operation Insertion only, because the device value identifies both the implantation of the radioactive element and a specific brachytherapy isotope that is not included in the Radiation Therapy section tables.

D1.b. Separate procedure to place a temporary applicator for delivering the brachytherapy is coded to the root operation Insertion and the device value Other Device.
Examples: Intrauterine brachytherapy applicator placed as a separate procedure from the brachytherapy procedure is coded to Insertion of Other Device, and the brachytherapy is coded separately using the modality Brachytherapy in the Radiation Therapy section. Intrauterine brachytherapy applicator placed concomitantly with delivery of the brachytherapy dose is coded with a single code using the modality Brachytherapy in the Radiation Therapy section.

New Technology Section Guidelines (section X)

E. New Technology Section

General guidelines

E1.a Section X codes fully represent the specific procedure described in the code title, and do not require additional codes from other sections of ICD-10-PCS. When section X contains a code title which fully describes a specific new technology procedure, and is the only procedure performed, only the Section X code is reported for the procedure. There is no need to report an additional code in another section of ICD-10-PCS.

Examples: XW04321 Introduction if Ceflazidime-Avibactam Anti-infective into Central Vein, Percutaneous Approach, New Technology Group 1, can be coded to indicate that Ceflazidime-Avibactam Anti-Infective was administered via a central vein. A separate code from table 3E0 in the Administrative section of ICD-10-PCS is not coded in addition to this code.

E1.b When multiple procedures are performed, New Technology section X codes are coded following the multiple procedures guideline.
Examples: Dual filter cerebral embolic filtration used during transcatheter aortic valve replacement (TAVR), X2A5312 Cerebral Embolic Filtration, Dual Filter in Innominate Artery and Left Common Carotid Artery, Percutaneous Approach, New Technology Group 2, is coded for the cerebral embolic filtration, along with an ICD-10-PCS code for the TAVR procedure.
Magnetically controlled growth rod (MCGR) placed during a spinal fusion procedure, a code from table XNS, Reposition of the Bones is coded for the MCGR, along with an ICD-10-PCS code for the spinal fusion procedure.

EXAMPLE

Introduction of Ceftazidime-Avibactam Anti-infective into Central Vein, Percutaneous Approach, XW04321, New Technology Group 1, can be coded to indicate that Ceftazidime-Avibactam Anti-infective was administered via a central vein. A separate code from table 3E0 in the Administration section of ICD-10-PCS is not coded in addition to this code.

OTHER MEDICAL- AND SURGICAL-RELATED PROCEDURES

The other medical- and surgical-related procedure sections of ICD-10-PCS include the following sections:

SECTION VALUE	DESCRIPTION
1	Obstetrics
2	Placement
3	Administration
4	Measurement and Monitoring
5	Extracorporeal or Systemic Assistance and Performance
6	Extracorporeal or Systemic Therapies
7	Osteopathic
8	Other procedures
9	Chiropractic

Obstetrics

Obstetrics include only those procedures that are performed on the products of conception. The term "**products of conception**" refers to all physical components of a pregnancy, including the fetus, amnion, umbilical cord, and placenta, regardless of gestational age. Procedures performed on a pregnant female other than on the products of conception are coded in the Medical and Surgical section. All ICD-10-PCS codes are seven characters, each character representing a particular aspect of the procedure. The meanings of the obstetric procedure characters are as follows:

CHARACTER	REPRESENTS
1	Section
2	Body system
3	Root operation
4	Body part
5	Approach
6	Device
7	Qualifier

Obstetric codes are found in Section 1, so they have a first-character value of 1. The second-character value for body system is Pregnancy. The third character identifies the root operation. There are a total of 12 root operations in the Obstetrics section. Ten of these are taken from the Medical and Surgical section and that includes:

CHARACTER	REPRESENTS
2	Change
9	Drainage
D	Extraction
H	Insertion
J	Inspection
P	Removal
Q	Repair
S	Reposition
T	Resection
Y	Transplantation

This section includes two additional root operations:

- **Abortion (A):** artificially terminating a pregnancy
- **Delivery (E):** assisting the passage of the products of conception from the genital canal

The fourth character classifies the body part. Body part values in this section are:

- Products of conception
- Products of conception, retained
- Products of conception, ectopic

The fifth character identifies the approach; these are defined in the Medical and Surgical section. The sixth character is for the device. The seventh character identifies various qualifiers, such as type of extraction, type of cesarean section, and so on.

EXAMPLE

Manually assisted delivery, 10E0XZZ

SECTION	BODY SYSTEM	ROOT OPERATION	BODY PART	APPROACH	DEVICE	QUALIFIER
Obstetrics	Pregnancy	Delivery	Products of Conception	External	No Device	No Qualifier
1	0	E	0	X	Z	Z

The root operation, Delivery, applies only to manually-assisted, vaginal delivery and is defined as assisting the passage of the products of conception from the genital canal. Cesarean deliveries are coded in this section to the root operation extraction.

EXERCISE 7-1

Answer the following questions or assign ICD-10-PCS codes.

1. Obstetric procedures are any procedure performed on a pregnant woman.
   A. True
   B. False
2. In ICD-10-PCS, "abortion" is defined as "the spontaneous termination of a pregnancy."
   A. True
   B. False
3. Low cesarean section would be identified by the fifth character, the approach.
   A. True
   B. False
4. Vaginal delivery using vacuum extraction ____________
5. Low cesarean section ____________

Placement

Placement codes include procedures for putting a device in or on a body region for the purpose of protection, immobilization, stretching, compression, or packing. All ICD-10-PCS codes are seven characters, each representing a particular aspect of the procedure. The meanings of the placement procedure characters are as follows:

CHARACTER	REPRESENTS
1	Section
2	Body system
3	Root operation
4	Body region
5	Approach
6	Device
7	Qualifier

Placement codes are found in Section 2, so they have a first-character value of 2. The second-character value, for body system, is either anatomical region or body orifice. The third character identifies the root operation. The root operations in the placement section include only those procedures performed without making an incision or a puncture. Two of these are taken from the Medical and Surgical section and that includes:

CHARACTER	REPRESENTS
0	Change
5	Removal

Section 2 includes five additional root operations:

- **Compression (1):** putting pressure on a body region
- **Dressing (2):** putting material on a body region for protection
- **Immobilization (3):** limiting or preventing motion of a body region
- **Packing (4):** putting material in a body region or orifice
- **Traction (6):** exerting a pulling force on a body region in a distal direction

The fourth-character value classifies body region or natural orifice. The fifth-character value identifies the approach; and because all placement procedures are performed directly on the skin or mucous membranes, or indirectly by applying external force, the approach value is always X, for external. The sixth-character value classifies device. The seventh character is for a qualifier, but it is not used in the Placement section at this time, so the value is always no qualifier (Z).

EXAMPLE

Cast to right lower arm, 2W3CX2Z

SECTION	BODY SYSTEM	ROOT OPERATION	BODY REGION	APPROACH	DEVICE	QUALIFIER
Placement	Anatomical Region	Immobilization	Lower Arm, Right	External	Cast	No Qualifier
2	W	3	C	X	2	Z

Splints and braces that are placed in the inpatient setting are coded in this section. If a fitting for a device such as a splint or brace is performed in the rehabilitation setting, the codes from the F0D table are assigned.

Administration

Administration codes include procedures for putting in or on a therapeutic, prophylactic, protective, diagnostic, nutritional, or physiological substance. All ICD-10-PCS codes are seven characters, each representing a particular aspect of the procedure. The meanings of the administration procedure characters are as follows:

CHARACTER	REPRESENTS
1	Section
2	Body system
3	Root operation
4	Body system/region
5	Approach
6	Substance
7	Qualifier

Administration codes are found in Section 3, so they have a first-character value of 3. The second character has three values: physiological systems and anatomical regions, circulatory system, or indwelling device. The third-character value identifies the root operation. Section 3 has three root operations:

- **Introduction (0):** putting in or on a therapeutic, diagnostic, nutritional, physiological, or prophylactic substance except blood or blood products
- **Irrigation (1):** putting in or on a cleansing substance
- **Transfusion (2):** putting in blood or blood products

The fourth-character value classifies body system/region. This identifies the site where the substance is administered. The fifth-character value identifies the approach, and each approach is defined in the Medical and Surgical section. Percutaneous is the approach for procedures that are introduced intradermally, subcutaneously, and intramuscularly (e.g., injections). The sixth-character value specifies the substance introduced. The seventh character is for a qualifier that indicates whether the substance used was autologous or nonautologous or to further specify the substance. **Autologous** means originating from the recipient, rather than from a donor, or transferred from the same individual's body, (e.g., a skin graft is taken from one part of the body and transferred to another part of the body on the same individual).

EXAMPLE

Administration of RBCs, nonautologous via peripheral vein, 30233N1

SECTION	BODY SYSTEM	ROOT OPERATION	BODY SYSTEM/ REGION	APPROACH	SUBSTANCE	QUALIFIER
Administration	Circulatory	Transfusion	Peripheral Vein	Percutaneous	Red Blood Cells	Nonautologous
3	0	2	3	3	N	1

EXERCISE 7-2

Answer the following questions or assign ICD-10-PCS codes.

1. Irrigation is a root operation that is found in the Placement section.
   A. True
   B. False
2. Immobilization is limiting or preventing motion of a body region.
   A. True
   B. False
3. In the Administration section, Character 6 identifies the substance being introduced.
   A. True
   B. False
4. Transfusion of platelets, nonautologous via central vein ______________
5. Introduction of tube feedings into stomach via previously placed PEG ______________

Measurement and Monitoring

Measurement and monitoring codes include procedures for determining the level of a physiological or physical function. All ICD-10-PCS codes are seven characters, each representing a particular aspect of the procedure. The meanings of the measuring and monitoring procedure characters are as follows:

CHARACTER	REPRESENTS
1	Section
2	Body system
3	Root operation
4	Body system
5	Approach
6	Function/Device
7	Qualifier

Measurement and monitoring codes are found in Section 4, so they have a first-character value of 4. The second character has two values, for either physiological systems or physiological devices. The third-character value identifies the root operation. Section 4 has two root operations:

- **Measurement (0):** determining the level of a physiological or physical function at a point in time
- **Monitoring (1):** determining the level of a physiological or physical function repetitively over a period of time

The fourth-character value identifies the body system being measured or monitored. The fifth-character value identifies the approach, and each is defined in the Medical and Surgical section. The sixth-character value specifies the physiological or physical function monitored. The seventh character is a qualifier used to further specify the body part or a variation of the procedure performed.

EXAMPLE

Holter monitoring, 4A12X45

SECTION	BODY SYSTEM	ROOT OPERATION	BODY SYSTEM	APPROACH	FUNCTION/ DEVICE	QUALIFIER
Measurement and Monitoring	Physiological Systems	Monitoring	Cardiac	External	Electrical Activity	Ambulatory
4	A	1	2	X	4	5

Extracorporeal or Systemic Assistance and Performance

Extracorporeal or systemic assistance and performance codes are used when equipment outside of the body is used to assist or perform a physiological function. All ICD-10-PCS codes are seven characters, each representing a particular aspect of the procedure. The meanings of the extracorporeal assistance and performance procedure characters are as follows:

CHARACTER	REPRESENTS
1	Section
2	Body system
3	Root operation
4	Body system
5	Duration
6	Function
7	Qualifier

Extracorporeal assistance and performance codes are found in Section 5, so they have a first-character value of 5. The second-character value is for physiological systems.

The third-character value identifies the root operation. The section has three root operations:

- **Assistance (0):** taking over a portion of a physiological function by extracorporeal means such as intra-aortic balloon pump to support cardiac output.
- **Performance (1):** completely taking over a physiological function by extracorporeal means such as total mechanical ventilation or cardiopulmonary bypass.
- **Restoration (2):** returning, or attempting to return, a physiological function to its original state by extracorporeal means

Restoration defines only external cardioversion and defibrillation procedures. Failed cardioversion procedures are also included in the definition of restoration and are coded the same as successful procedures.

The fourth-character value classifies the body system to which the extracorporeal assistance or performance is applied. The fifth-character value identifies the duration of the procedure. The sixth-character value specifies the physiological function assisted or performed during the procedure. The seventh character is a qualifier that specifies the type of equipment used, if any.

EXAMPLE

Mechanical ventilation, continuous for 48 hours, 5A1945Z

SECTION	BODY SYSTEM	ROOT OPERATION	BODY SYSTEM	DURATION	FUNCTION	QUALIFIER
Extracorporeal Assistance and Performance	Physiological Systems	Performance	Respiratory	24-96 consecutive hours	Ventilation	No Qualifier
5	A	1	9	4	5	Z

Extracorporeal or Systemic Therapies

Extracorporeal or systemic therapy codes are used when equipment outside of the body is used for a therapeutic purpose that does not involve the assistance or performance of a physiological function. All ICD-10-PCS codes are seven characters, each representing a particular aspect of the procedure. The meanings of the extracorporeal therapies procedure characters are as follows:

CHARACTER	REPRESENTS
1	Section
2	Body system
3	Root operation
4	Body system
5	Duration
6	Qualifier
7	Qualifier

Extracorporeal or systemic therapy codes are found in Section 6, so they have a first-character value of 6. The second-character value is for physiological systems. The third-character value identifies the root operation. Section 6 has ten root operations:

- **Atmospheric control (0):** extracorporeal control of atmospheric pressure and composition
- **Decompression (1):** extracorporeal elimination of undissolved gas from body fluids
- **Electromagnetic therapy (2):** extracorporeal treatment by electromagnetic rays
- **Hyperthermia (3):** extracorporeal raising of body temperature
- **Hypothermia (4):** extracorporeal lowering of body temperature
- **Perfusion (B):** extracorporeal treatment by diffusion of therapeutic fluid
- **Pheresis (5):** extracorporeal separation of blood products
- **Phototherapy (6):** extracorporeal treatment by light rays
- **Shock wave therapy (9):** extracorporeal treatment by shock waves

- **Ultrasound therapy (7):** extracorporeal treatment by ultrasound
- **Ultraviolet light therapy (8):** extracorporeal treatment by ultraviolet light

Hyperthermia can be used to treat temperature imbalance as well as an adjunct radiation treatment for cancer. When performed to treat temperature imbalance, the procedure is coded to this section.

When performed for cancer treatment, whole-body hyperthermia is classified as a modality qualifier in the radiation oncology section.

The fourth character identifies the body system to which the extracorporeal therapy is performed. The fifth character identifies the duration of the procedure. The sixth-character value is not specified and always has the value no qualifier. The seventh character is a qualifier used for the root operations of pheresis and ultrasound therapy. The duration value for single and/or multiple is assigned based on whether the treatment is a continuous (single) treatment or administered in separate treatment sessions (multiple).

EXAMPLE

Plasmapheresis, single, 6A550Z3

SECTION	BODY SYSTEM	ROOT OPERATION	BODY SYSTEM	DURATION	QUALIFIER	QUALIFIER
Extracorporeal Therapies	Physiological Systems	Pheresis	Circulatory	Single	No Qualifier	Plasma
6	A	5	5	0	Z	3

EXERCISE 7-3

Answer the following questions or assign ICD-10-PCS codes.

1. Hypothermia procedure is a type of extracorporeal therapy.
   A. True
   B. False
2. Measurement is defined as determining the level of physiological or physical function repetitively over a period of time.
   A. True
   B. False
3. Extracorporeal therapy uses equipment outside the body for a therapeutic purpose that does not involve the assistance or performance of a physiological function.
   A. True
   B. False
4. In the extracorporeal assistance and performance section, the definition for *performance* is "completely taking over a physiological function by extracorporeal means."
   A. True
   B. False
5. When a fifth-character is used for extracorporeal therapies, this specifies the duration of the patient's hospital stay.
   A. True
   B. False
6. Swan Ganz (pulmonary artery output monitoring) ______________
7. External cardioversion ______________
8. Hemodialysis, intermittent ______________

Osteopathic

Osteopathic codes are used for osteopathic procedures. All ICD-10-PCS codes are seven characters, each representing a particular aspect of the procedure. The meanings of the procedure characters for the Osteopathic section are as follows:

CHARACTER	REPRESENTS
1	Section
2	Body system
3	Root operation
4	Body region
5	Approach
6	Method
7	Qualifier

Osteopathic codes are found in Section 7, so they have a first-character value of 7. The second character is for anatomical regions, and the third character identifies the root operation.

Section 7 has only one root operation:

- **Treatment (0):** manual treatment to eliminate or alleviate somatic dysfunction and related disorders

The fourth character identifies the body region on which the osteopathic treatments are performed. The fifth character identifies the approach, which is always external. The sixth character specifies the method by which the treatment is performed. The seventh character is for a qualifier, but it is not specified in the osteopathic section at this time, so the value is always None (Z).

EXAMPLE

Indirect osteopathic treatment to the lumbar region, 7W03X4Z

SECTION	BODY SYSTEM	ROOT OPERATION	BODY REGION	APPROACH	METHOD	QUALIFIER
Osteopathic	Anatomical Regions	Treatment	Lumbar	External	Indirect	None
7	W	0	3	X	4	Z

Other Procedures

Other procedure codes are used for a variety of other procedures (e.g., acupuncture, suture removal, and in vitro fertilization). All ICD-10-PCS codes are seven characters, each representing a particular aspect of the procedure. The meanings of the other procedure characters are as follows:

CHARACTER	REPRESENTS
1	Section
2	Body system
3	Root operation
4	Body region
5	Approach
6	Method
7	Qualifier

Other procedure codes are found in Section 8, so they have a first-character value of 8. The second character is for physiological systems and anatomical region, and the third character identifies the root operation.

The section has only one root operation:

- **Other procedures (0):** methodologies that attempt to remediate or cure a disorder or disease

The fourth character specifies the body region on which the procedure is performed. The fifth character identifies the approach, and each is defined in the Medical and Surgical section. The sixth-character value specifies the method by which the procedure is performed. The seventh character is to identify various qualifiers necessary to provide more information about a specific procedure.

EXAMPLE

Suture removal, left calf, 8E0YXY8

SECTION	BODY SYSTEM	ROOT OPERATION	BODY REGION	APPROACH	METHOD	QUALIFIER
Other Procedures	Physiological Systems and Anatomical Regions	Other Procedures	Lower Extremity	External	Other Method	Suture Removal
8	E	0	Y	X	Y	8

Chiropractic

All ICD-10-PCS codes for chiropractic procedures are seven characters, each representing a particular aspect of the procedure. The meanings of the chiropractic procedure characters are as follows:

CHARACTER	REPRESENTS
1	Section
2	Body system
3	Root operation
4	Body region
5	Approach
6	Method
7	Qualifier

Chiropractic codes are found in Section 9, so they have a first-character value of 9. The second character identifies anatomical regions, and the third character identifies the root operation.

Section 9 has only one root operation:

- **Manipulation (B):** manual procedures that involve a directed thrust to move a joint past the physiological range of motion without exceeding the anatomical limit

The fourth character specifies the body region on which the chiropractic manipulation is performed. The fifth character identifies the approach, which is always external. The sixth-character value specifies the method by which the manipulation is performed. The seventh character is for a qualifier, but it is not specified in the chiropractic section at this time, so the value is always None(Z).

EXAMPLE

Chiropractic treatment to cervical spine, short lever specific contact, 9WB1XHZ

SECTION	BODY SYSTEM	ROOT OPERATION	BODY REGION	APPROACH	METHOD	QUALIFIER
Chiropractic	Anatomical Regions	Manipulation	Cervical	External	Short Lever Specific Contact	None
9	W	B	1	X	H	Z

EXERCISE 7-4

Answer the following questions or assign ICD-10-PCS codes.

1. The approach for chiropractic manipulation is always external.
   A. True
   B. False
2. Acupuncture can be coded in the Other Procedures section of ICD-10-PCS.
   A. True
   B. False
3. Any root operation in the Medical and Surgical section can be used in the Osteopathic section.
   A. True
   B. False
4. The approach for an osteopathic treatment is always external.
   A. True
   B. False
5. Robotic-assisted laparoscopic hysterectomy (code the robotic assistance only) ____________
6. Chiropractic manipulation to abdomen, indirect visceral ____________

ANCILLARY SECTIONS

The ancillary sections of ICD-10-PCS include the following:

SECTION VALUE	DESCRIPTION
B	Imaging
C	Nuclear Medicine
D	Radiation Therapy
F	Physical Rehabilitation and Diagnostic Audiology
G	Mental Health
H	Substance Abuse Treatment

Imaging

Imaging procedures include plain radiography, fluoroscopy, CT, MRI, and ultrasound. All ICD-10-PCS codes are seven characters, each representing a particular aspect of the procedure. The meanings of the imaging procedure characters are as follows:

CHARACTER	REPRESENTS
1	Section
2	Body system
3	Root type
4	Body part
5	Contrast
6	Qualifier
7	Qualifier

Imaging codes are found in Section B, so they have a first-character value of B. Similar to the Medical and Surgical section, the second-character value identifies the body system. Instead of root operation, the third character identifies the type of imaging procedure. The root types are as follows:

- **Plain Radiography (0):** planar display of an image developed from the capture of external ionizing radiation on photographic or photoconductive plate.
- **Fluoroscopy (1):** single-plane or bi-plane real-time display of an image developed from the capture of external ionizing radiation on a fluorescent screen. The image may also be stored by either digital or analog means.

- **Computerized tomography (CT scans) (2):** computer reformatted digital display of multiplanar images developed from the capture of multiple exposures of external ionizing radiation.
- **Magnetic resonance imaging (MRI) (3):** computer reformatted digital display of multiplanar images developed from the capture of radio-frequency signals emitted by nuclei in a body site excited within a magnetic field.
- **Ultrasonography (4):** real-time display of images of anatomy or flow information developed from the capture of reflected and attenuated high frequency sound waves.

The fourth character specifies the body part, and the fifth character identifies whether the contrast material used is high or low osmolar when applicable. The sixth and seventh characters identify various qualifiers necessary to provide more information about a specific imaging procedure.

EXAMPLE

CT abdomen and pelvis without contrast, BW21ZZZ

SECTION	BODY SYSTEM	TYPE	BODY REGION	CONTRAST	QUALIFIER	QUALIFIER
Imaging	Anatomical Regions	Computed Tomography	Abdomen and Pelvis	None	None	None
B	W	2	1	Z	Z	Z

Nuclear Medicine

Nuclear medicine procedures include nuclear medicine scans and PET scans. Radiation therapy is not included in this section. All ICD-10-PCS codes are seven characters, each representing a particular aspect of the procedure. The meanings of the nuclear medicine procedure characters are as follows:

CHARACTER	REPRESENTS
1	Section
2	Body system
3	Root type
4	Body part
5	Radionuclide
6	Qualifier
7	Qualifier

Nuclear medicine codes are found in Section C, so they have a first-character value of C. Similar to the Medical and Surgical section, the second character here specifies the body system. Instead of root operation, the third character identifies the type of nuclear medicine procedure. The root types are as follows:

- **Planar nuclear medicine imaging (1):** introduction of radioactive materials into the body for single-plane display of images developed from the capture of radioactive emissions.
- **Tomographic nuclear medicine imaging (2):** introduction of radioactive materials into the body for three-dimensional display of images developed from the capture of radioactive emissions.
- **Positron emission tomography (PET) (3):** introduction of radioactive materials into the body for three-dimensional display of images developed from the simultaneous capture, 180 degrees apart, of radioactive emissions.
- **Nonimaging nuclear medicine uptake (4):** introduction of radioactive materials into the body for measurements of organ functions, from detection of radioactive emissions.
- **Nonimaging nuclear medicine probe (5):** introduction of radioactive materials into the body for the study of distribution and fate of certain substances by the detection of radioactive emissions from an external source.

- **Nonimaging nuclear medicine assay (6):** introduction of radioactive materials into the body for the study of body fluids and blood elements, by the detection of radioactive emissions.
- **Systemic nuclear medicine therapy (7):** introduction of unsealed radioactive materials into the body for treatment.

The fourth character specifies body part or body region. The fifth character value identifies the radionuclide or radiation source. The sixth and seventh characters are for qualifiers, but they are not used in the Nuclear Medicine section at this time, so the value is always None.

EXAMPLE

Whole Body PET Scan, other radionuclide, CW3NYZZ

SECTION	BODY SYSTEM	TYPE	BODY REGION	RADIONUCLIDE	QUALIFIER	QUALIFIER
Nuclear Medicine	Anatomical Regions	PET	Whole Body	Other Radionuclide	None	None
C	W	3	N	Y	Z	Z

Radiation Therapy

Radiation therapy includes procedures that introduce radioactive material for the treatment of cancer. All ICD-10-PCS codes used here are seven characters, each representing a particular aspect of the procedure. The meanings of the radiation therapy procedure characters are as follows:

CHARACTER	REPRESENTS
1	Section
2	Body system
3	Root type
4	Body part
5	Modality qualifier
6	Isotope
7	Qualifier

Radiation therapy codes are found in Section D, so they have a first-character value of D. Similar to the Medical and Surgical section, the second character specifies the body system. Instead of root operation, the third character identifies the general modality used (e.g., beam radiation, brachytherapy, or stereotactic radiosurgery). The fourth character value specifies the body part that is the focus of the radiation therapy. The fifth character value, the modality qualifier, specifies the radiation modality used (e.g., photons, electrons). The sixth character specifies the isotopes introduced during the procedure, if applicable. The seventh character is used for other qualifiers.

EXAMPLE

HDR Brachytherapy of prostate using Palladium 103, DV109BZ

SECTION	BODY SYSTEM	MODALITY	TREATMENT SITE	MODALITY QUALIFIER	ISOTOPE	QUALIFIER
Radiation Therapy	Male Reproductive System	Brachytherapy	Prostate	High Dose Rate	Palladium 103 (Pd-103)	None
D	V	1	0	9	B	Z

EXERCISE 7-5

Answer the following questions or assign ICD-10-PCS codes.

1. MRI procedures are located in the Nuclear Medicine section.
A. True
B. False

2. Radionuclide is the fifth character in the Nuclear Medicine section.
   A. True
   B. False
3. The first-character value for an imaging procedure is B.
   A. True
   B. False
4. The fourth character in the radiation therapy section specifies the body part that is the focus of the radiation therapy.
   A. True
   B. False
5. Isotope is the seventh-character qualifier in the Radiation Therapy section.
   A. True
   B. False
6. Ultrasonic guidance for catheter placement is superior vena cava (code ultrasonic guidance only) ______________
7. Tomographic Nuclear imaging, right lower extremity using Technetium 99m ______________
8. External beam radiation to the brain using photons 1-10 MeV ______________

Physical Rehabilitation and Diagnostic Audiology

Physical rehabilitation procedures include physical therapy, occupational therapy, and speech-language pathology. Diagnostic audiology is also included in this section. All ICD-10-PCS codes are seven characters, each representing a particular aspect of the procedure. The meanings of the physical rehabilitation and diagnostic audiology procedure characters are as follows:

CHARACTER	REPRESENTS
1	Section
2	Section qualifier
3	Root type
4	Body system and region
5	Type qualifier
6	Equipment
7	Qualifier

Physical rehabilitation and diagnostic audiology codes are found in Section F, so they have a first-character value of F. There is a change from body system to section qualifier for the second-character value (e.g., rehabilitation or diagnostic audiology). Instead of root operation, the third character identifies the type of physical rehabilitation and diagnostic audiology procedure. There are 14 different root values. The root values are as follows:

- **Speech assessment (0):** measurement of speech and related functions
- **Motor and/or nerve function assessment (1):** measurement of motor, nerve, and related functions.
- **Activities of daily living assessment (2):** measurement of functional level for activities of daily living.
- **Hearing assessment (3):** measurement of hearing and related functions.
- **Hearing aid assessment (4):** measurement of the appropriateness and/or effectiveness of a hearing device.
- **Vestibular assessment (5):** measurement of vestibular system and related functions.
- **Speech treatment (6):** application of techniques to improve, augment, or compensate for speech and related functional impairment.
- **Motor treatment (7):** exercise or activities to increase or facilitate motor function.
- **Activities of daily living treatment (8):** exercise or activities to facilitate functional competence for activities of daily living.

- **Hearing treatment (9):** application of techniques to improve, augment, or compensate for hearing and related functional impairment.
- **Hearing aid treatment (B):** application of techniques to improve the communication abilities of individuals with cochlear implants.
- **Vestibular treatment (C):** application of techniques to improve, augment, or compensate for vestibular and related functional impairment.
- **Device fitting (D):** fitting of a device designed to facilitate or support achievement of a higher level of function.
- **Caregiver training (F):** training in activities to support patient's optimal level of function.

Treatment procedures include swallowing dysfunction exercises, bathing and showering techniques, wound management, gait training, and a host of activities typically associated with rehabilitation. The assessments are further classified into more than 100 different tests or methods. The majority of these focus on hearing and speech, but others focus on various aspects of body function, such as muscle performance, neuromotor development, and reintegration skills.

The fourth character specifies body part and body region. The fifth character, or type qualifier, further specifies the procedure performed. The sixth character identifies specific equipment used. Character seven is for a qualifier, but it is not used in this section at this time, so the value is always None.

EXAMPLE

Bedside swallow assessment, F00ZJWZ

SECTION	SECTION QUALIFIER	TYPE	BODY SYSTEM/ REGION	TYPE QUALIFIER	EQUIPMENT	QUALIFIER
Physical Rehabilitation and Diagnostic Audiology	Rehabilitation	Speech Assessment	None	Instrumental Swallowing and Oral Function	Swallowing	None
F	0	0	Z	J	W	Z

Mental Health

Mental health procedures are coded in this section. All ICD-10-PCS codes are seven characters, each representing a particular aspect of the procedure. The meanings of the mental health procedure characters are as follows:

CHARACTER	REPRESENTS
1	Section
2	Body system
3	Root type
4	Type qualifier
5	Qualifier
6	Qualifier
7	Qualifier

Mental health codes are found in Section G, so they have a first-character value of G. The second-character value, for body system, has a value of None in this section. And instead of root operation, the third character identifies the type of mental health procedure. The root types are as follows:

- Psychological tests (1)
- Crisis intervention (2)
- Medication management (3)
- Individual psychotherapy (5)
- Counseling (6)
- Family psychotherapy (7)

- ECT (B)
- Biofeedback (C)
- Hypnosis (F)
- Narcosynthesis (G)
- Group psychotherapy (H)
- Light therapy (J)

The fourth-character value is a type qualifier (e.g., educational or vocational counseling). Values for Characters 5, 6, and 7 are for qualifiers but are not used in the Mental Health section at this time, so the value is always None.

EXAMPLE

Family psychotherapy session, GZ72ZZZ

SECTION	BODY SYSTEM	TYPE	QUALIFIER	QUALIFIER	QUALIFIER	QUALIFIER
Mental Health	None	Family Psychotherapy	Other Family Psychotherapy	None	None	None
G	Z	7	2	Z	Z	Z

Substance Abuse Treatment Section

Treatments for substance abuse are coded in this section. All ICD-10-PCS codes are seven characters, each representing a particular aspect of the procedure. The meanings of the substance abuse procedure characters are as follows:

CHARACTER	REPRESENTS
1	Section
2	Body system
3	Root type
4	Type qualifier
5	Qualifier
6	Qualifier
7	Qualifier

Substance abuse treatment codes are found in Section H, so they have a first-character value of H. The second-character value for body system has a value of None in this section. And instead of root operation, the third-character value identifies the type of substance abuse procedure. The root types are as follows:

- Detoxification services (2)
- Individual counseling (3)
- Group counseling (4)
- Individual psychotherapy (5)
- Family counseling (6)
- Medication management (8)
- Pharmacotherapy (9)

The fourth-character value is a type qualifier (e.g., cognitive behavioral, 12-step, interpersonal). Values for Characters 5, 6, and 7 are for qualifiers but are not used in the Substance Abuse section at this time, so the value is always None.

EXAMPLE

Medication management for methadone maintenance, HZ81ZZZ

SECTION	BODY SYSTEM	TYPE	QUALIFIER	QUALIFIER	QUALIFIER	QUALIFIER
Substance Abuse Treatment	None	Medication Management	Methadone Maintenance	None	None	None
H	Z	8	1	Z	Z	Z

EXERCISE 7-6

Answer the following questions or assign ICD-10-PCS codes.

1. The seventh character in the Physical Rehabilitation and Diagnostic Audiology section identifies whether the procedure is a physical rehabilitation procedure or a diagnostic audiology procedure.
   A. True
   B. False
2. Equipment is the sixth character in the physical rehabilitation and diagnostic audiology section.
   A. True
   B. False
3. The first-character value for a physical rehabilitation or diagnostic audiology procedure is B.
   A. True
   B. False
4. Hypnosis is a procedure that can be coded in the Mental Health section.
   A. True
   B. False
5. In the Substance Abuse section, Characters 5, 6, and 7 are for qualifiers.
   A. True
   B. False
6. The first-character value for a mental health procedure is G.
   A. True
   B. False
7. Rehabilitation with feeding/eating treatment using assistive equipment ____________
8. Psychological testing with personality and behavioral tests ____________

NEW TECHNOLOGY SECTION

The New Technology section was added to ICD-10-PCS beginning on October 1, 2015. This section X was created in response to public comments for new technology proposals presented to the ICD-10 Coordination and Maintenance Committee Meetings. As the ICD-10-PCS guidelines state, Section X codes are standalone codes. They are not supplemental or adjunctive codes. When a code from Section X is assigned, no additional code is needed. The codes for new technology can be easily found in the index under the name of the new device, substance or technology plus under the main term New Technology. The format of the codes is in keeping with the other sections of ICD-10-PCS. The seventh character is the qualifier, and this will change each year as new technology codes are added. See Figure 7-1, the seventh character value 1 stands for New Technology Group 1. The following year, the seventh character of 2 was assigned for New Technology Group 2.

EXAMPLE Patient was admitted for a complicated acute pyelonephritis and is treated with IV (peripheral vein) ceftazidime-avibactam antibiotic due to gram-negative multidrug-resistant organism, N10, B96.89, Z16.24, XW03321.

Section **X** New Technology Body System **W** Anatomical Regions Operation **0** Introduction: Putting in or on a therapeutic, diagnostic, nutritional, physiological, or prophylactic substance except blood or blood products			
Body Part	**Approach**	**Device / Substance / Technology**	**Qualifier**
3 Peripheral Vein 4 Central Vein	3 Percutaneous	2 Ceftazidime-Avibactam Anti-infective 3 Idarucizumab, Dabigatran Reversal Agent 4 Isavuconazole Anti-infective 5 Blinatumomab Antineoplastic Immunotherapy	1 New Technology Group 1 ←

FIGURE 7-1. New Technology Table XW0

CHAPTER REVIEW EXERCISE

Complete the following review exercises using ICD-10-PCS.

1. CT procedures are located in the Nuclear Medicine section.
   A. True
   B. False
2. Detoxification services can be coded in the Mental Health section.
   A. True
   B. False
3. Obstetric tables include procedures performed on the products of conception only.
   A. True
   B. False
4. In ICD-10-PCS, *abortion* is defined as "spontaneous termination of a pregnancy."
   A. True
   B. False
5. Irrigation is defined as "the putting in or on of a cleansing substance."
   A. True
   B. False
6. Monitoring is defined as "determining the level of physiological or physical function repetitively over a period of time."
   A. True
   B. False
7. Extracorporeal therapy uses equipment outside the body for a therapeutic purpose that does not involve the assistance or performance of a physiological function.
   A. True
   B. False
8. The approach for an osteopathic treatment is always external.
   A. True
   B. False

Assign the appropriate ICD-10-PCS codes to the following procedures in accordance with the coding guidelines.

9. Placement of nasal packing, right nare ______________
10. Packing wound, abdomen wall ______________
11. Nonautologous bone marrow transplant via central venous catheter ______________
12. Mechanical ventilation, less than 24 hours ______________
13. ECMO, circulatory, continuous oxygenation, central membrane ______________
14. Robotic assisted laparoscopic abdominal hysterectomy ______________
15. Chiropractic treatment to cervical spine using short lever specific contact ______________
16. Phototherapy with Bili-Lite, single treatment ______________
17. MRI brain ______________
18. Proton radiation therapy of the brain ______________
19. Physical therapy treatment to increase ROM, right shoulder ______________
20. Hypnosis ______________
21. Twelve-step group therapy for alcohol addiction ______________

CHAPTER GLOSSARY

It is important to note that most of these definitions are as defined by ICD-10-PCS.

Abortion: artificially terminating a pregnancy.

Activities of daily living assessment: measurement of functional level for activities of daily living.

Activities of daily living treatment: exercise or activities to facilitate functional competence for activities of daily living.

Assistance: taking over a portion of a physiological function by extracorporeal means.

Atmospheric control: extracorporeal control of atmospheric pressure and composition.

Autologous: originating from the recipient, rather than from a donor; tissue transferred from the same individual's body (e.g., a skin graft taken from one part of the body is transferred to another part of the body on the same individual).

Caregiver training: training in activities to support patient's optimal level of function.

Compression: putting pressure on a body region.

Computerized tomography (CT scans): computer reformatted digital display of multiplanar images developed from the capture of multiple exposures of external ionizing radiation.

Decompression: extracorporeal elimination of undissolved gas from body fluids.

Delivery: assisting the passage of the products of conception from the genital canal.

Device fitting: fitting of a device designed to facilitate or support achievement of a higher level of function.

Dressing: putting material on a body region for protection.

Electromagnetic therapy: extracorporeal treatment by electromagnetic rays.

Fluoroscopy: single-plane or bi-plane real-time display of an image developed from the capture of external ionizing radiation on a fluorescent screen. The image may also be stored by either digital or analog means.

Hearing aid assessment: measurement of the appropriateness and/or effectiveness of a hearing device.

Hearing aid treatment: application of techniques to improve the communication abilities of individuals with cochlear implants.

Hearing assessment: measurement of hearing and related functions.

Hearing treatment: application of techniques to improve, augment, or compensate for hearing and related functional impairment.

Hyperthermia: extracorporeal raising of body temperature.

Hypothermia: extracorporeal lowering of body temperature.

Immobilization: limiting or preventing motion of a body region.

Introduction: putting in or on a therapeutic, diagnostic, nutritional, physiological, or prophylactic substance except blood or blood products.

Irrigation: putting in or on a cleansing substance.

Magnetic resonance imaging (MRI): computer reformatted digital display of multiplanar images developed from the capture of radio-frequency signals emitted by nuclei in a body site excited within a magnetic field.

Manipulation: manual procedures that involve a directed thrust to move a joint past the physiological range of motion without exceeding the anatomical limit.

Measurement: determining the level of a physiological or physical function at a point in time.

Monitoring: determining the level of a physiological or physical function repetitively over a period of time.

Motor and/or nerve function assessment: measurement of motor, nerve, and related functions.

Motor treatment: exercise or activities to increase or facilitate motor function.

Nonimaging nuclear medicine assay: introduction of radioactive materials into the body for the study of body fluids and blood elements, by the detection of radioactive emissions.

Nonimaging nuclear medicine probe: introduction of radioactive materials into the body for the study of distribution and fate of certain substances by the detection of radioactive emissions from an external source.

Nonimaging nuclear medicine uptake: introduction of radioactive materials into the body for measurements of organ functions, from detection of radioactive emissions.

Other procedures: methodologies that attempt to remediate or cure a disorder or disease.

Packing: putting material in a body region or orifice.

Performance: completely taking over a physiological function by extracorporeal means.

Perfusion: extracorporeal treatment by diffusion of therapeutic fluid.

Pheresis: extracorporeal separation of blood products.

Phototherapy: extracorporeal treatment by light rays.

Plain Radiography: planar display of an image developed from the capture of external ionizing radiation on photographic or photoconductive plate.

Planar nuclear medicine imaging: introduction of radioactive materials into the body for single-plane display of images developed from the capture of radioactive emissions.

Positron emission tomography (PET): introduction of radioactive materials into the body for three-dimensional display of images developed from the simultaneous capture, 180 degrees apart, of radioactive emissions.

Products of conception: all physical components of a pregnancy including the fetus, amnion, umbilical cord, and placenta, regardless of gestational age.

Restoration: returning, or attempting to return, a physiological function to its original state by extracorporeal means.

Shock wave therapy: extracorporeal treatment by shock waves.

Speech assessment: measurement of speech and related functions.

Speech treatment: application of techniques to improve, augment, or compensate for speech and related functional impairment.

Systemic nuclear medicine therapy: introduction of unsealed radioactive materials into the body for treatment.

Tomographic nuclear medicine imaging: introduction of radioactive materials into the body for three-dimensional display of images developed from the capture of radioactive emissions.

Traction: exerting a pulling force on a body region in a distal direction.

Transfusion: putting in blood or blood products.

Treatment: manual treatment to eliminate or alleviate somatic dysfunction and related disorders.

Ultrasound therapy: extracorporeal treatment by ultrasound.

Ultrasonography: real-time display of images of anatomy or flow information developed from the capture of reflected and attenuated high frequency sound waves.

Ultraviolet light therapy: extracorporeal treatment by ultraviolet light.

Vestibular assessment: measurement of vestibular system and related functions.

Vestibular treatment: application of techniques to improve, augment, or compensate for vestibular and related functional impairment.

8

Coding Medical and Surgical Procedures

CHAPTER OUTLINE

LEARNING OBJECTIVES

1. Define principal procedure
2. Define significant procedures
3. Assign codes for canceled, converted to open procedures, and bilateral procedures
4. Explain the purpose of a facility policy for procedure coding
5. Define the root operations for the medical and surgical section of ICD-10-PCS
6. Apply and assign the correct ICD-10-PCS codes in accordance with the conventions and ICD-10-PCS Coding Guidelines

ABBREVIATIONS/ ACRONYMS

CABG coronary artery bypass graft
CMS Centers for Medicare and Medicaid Services
COPD chronic obstructive pulmonary disease
D&C Dilation and Curettage
ECMO extracorporeal membrane oxygenation
EGD esophagogastroduodenoscopy
ER Emergency Room
ERCP endoscopic retrograde cholangiopancreatogram
ESWL extracorporeal shock wave lithotripsy
ICD-10-CM *International Classification of Diseases, 10th Revision, Clinical Modification*
ICD-10-PCS *International Classification of Diseases, 10th Revision, Procedure Coding System*
ICU intensive care unit
IUD intrauterine contraceptive device
IVF in vitro fertilization
LAD left anterior descending
MCE Medicare Code Editor
NPI National Provider Identifier
OR Operating Room
ORIF open reduction internal fixation
PACU post-anesthesia care unit
PTCA percutaneous transluminal coronary angioplasty
RUQ right upper quadrant
SLNB sentinel lymph node biopsy
TACE transarterial chemoembolization
TKR total knee replacement
TRAM transverse rectus abdominis muscle
UHDDS Uniform Hospital Discharge Data Set
VP ventriculoperitoneal

UHDDS DEFINITIONS

Uniform Hospital Discharge Data Set (UHDDS) definitions are used by acute care, short-term hospitals to report inpatient data elements in a standardized manner. Definitions that pertain to the assignment of procedure codes are presented in the following sections.

Principal Procedure

The UHDDS definition for **principal procedure** is one that was performed for definitive treatment rather than for diagnostic or exploratory purposes, or one that is necessary to take care of a complication. If two or more procedures appear to meet this definition, the one most related to the principal diagnosis should be selected as the principal procedure.

The following was added to the 2014 ICD-10-PCS Official Guidelines for Coding and Reporting. It helps to clarify the selection of the principal procedure when more than one procedure is performed.

F. Selection of Principal Procedure:
The following instructions should be applied in the selection of principal procedure and clarification on the importance of the relation to the principal diagnosis when more than one procedure is performed:

1. Procedure performed for definitive treatment of both principal diagnosis and secondary diagnosis.
   a. Sequence procedure performed for definitive treatment most related to principal diagnosis as principal procedure.
2. Procedure performed for definitive treatment and diagnostic procedures performed for both principal diagnosis and secondary diagnosis.
   a. Sequence procedure performed for definitive treatment most related to principal diagnosis as principal procedure.
3. A diagnostic procedure was performed for the principal diagnosis and a procedure is performed for definitive treatment of a secondary diagnosis.
   a. Sequence diagnostic procedure as principal procedure, since the procedure most related to the principal diagnosis takes precedence.
4. No procedures performed that are related to the principal diagnosis; procedure performed for definitive treatment and diagnostic procedures were performed for secondary diagnosis.
   a. Sequence procedure performed for definitive treatment of secondary diagnosis as principal procedure, since there are no procedures (definitive or nondefinitive treatment) related to principal diagnosis.

Significant Procedure

To qualify as a **significant procedure**, one of the following criteria must be met:

- Is surgical in nature
- Carries a procedural risk
- Carries an anesthetic risk
- Requires specialized training

It should be noted that a significant procedure does not have to be performed in an operating room (OR). Procedures can be done in the Emergency Room (ER) before admission, at the patient's bedside, in a treatment room, or in an interventional radiology department. These procedures can be easily missed because an operative report describing the procedure may not have been completed. Often, these procedures are documented with a brief, handwritten note on the ER record or in a progress note. Consent for treatment may assist the coder in attempting to verify a procedure, but not all procedures require consent forms. Also, a signed consent form does not confirm that the procedure was actually performed. A complete review of the entire health record is necessary to ensure that all completed procedures have been coded.

Other UHDDS data elements that must be coded include the date of the procedure and the National Provider Identifier (NPI) of the person who performed the procedure. It may be the coder's responsibility to abstract these data elements.

PROCEDURE CODES THAT SHOULD BE REPORTED

Any procedures that affect payment or reimbursement must be reported. Other procedures may be reported at a hospital's discretion or in accordance with hospital policy. Encoders (coding software) may also have special popup notices that alert the coder about noncovered or limited coverage OR procedures.

After assigning procedure codes, the coder should review the diagnosis codes to ensure the assignment of diagnosis codes that support the performance of a procedure.

EXAMPLE

If it was determined that lysis of peritoneal adhesions was sufficient to warrant a procedure code in this male patient, it would make sense that a diagnosis code should be assigned to identify the peritoneal adhesions.

Procedure: Lysis of peritoneal adhesions (via open approach), 0DNW0ZZ

SECTION	BODY SYSTEM	ROOT OPERATION	BODY PART	APPROACH	DEVICE	QUALIFIER
Medical and Surgical	Gastrointestinal System	Release	Peritoneum	Open	No Device	No Qualifier
0	D	N	W	0	Z	Z

The Centers for Medicare and Medicaid Services (CMS) has categorized procedures into different classifications through the Medicare Code Editor (MCE). In some code books, these procedures may be highlighted to facilitate assignment of procedure codes. The **Medicare Code Editor** is software that detects errors in coding on Medicare claims. For example, it would identify a male-only procedure coded on a female patient's record.

FACILITY POLICY

Each facility should have its own written policy regarding the assignment of ICD-10 procedure codes. This policy should consider reimbursement, but it should also take into account other uses of a procedure database and how that information can be extracted. It may be necessary to determine what types of procedures are being performed for physician profiles and credentialing. Research is an important aspect of data collection.

As has been stated previously, because not all procedures are performed in the operating room, it may be difficult to locate documentation of all procedures performed. Procedures that are easy to overlook include mechanical ventilation, debridement, lumbar puncture, suturing, ECMO (extracorporeal membrane oxygenation), and procedures performed by interventional radiology. Just because there is a code for a procedure does not necessarily mean that it should be coded. Some examples of procedures that are performed and it is not necessary to code include Foley catheter insertion, nasogastric tube insertion, insertion of arterial lines, and removal of PICC lines.

BILATERAL PROCEDURES

A **bilateral procedure** occurs when the same procedure is performed on paired anatomic organs or tissues (i.e., eyes, ears, joints such as shoulder or knee). According to ICD-10-PCS guidelines, if the identical procedure is performed on contralateral body parts, and a bilateral body part value exists for that body part, a single procedure code using the bilateral body part value is assigned. If no bilateral body part value exists, each procedure is coded separately.

As procedures become less invasive, more bilateral procedures may be performed during the same operative episode.

EXAMPLE

Open repair of bilateral direct and indirect inguinal hernia with synthetic prosthesis, 0YUA0JZ.

SECTION	BODY SYSTEM	ROOT OPERATION	BODY PART	APPROACH	DEVICE	QUALIFIER
Medical and Surgical	Anatomical Regions, Lower Extremities	Supplement	Inguinal Region, Bilateral	Open	Synthetic Substitute	No Qualifier
0	Y	U	A	0	J	Z

EXAMPLE

Primary osteoarthritis knees for bilateral total knee synthetic substitute replacement, 0SRC0JZ, 0SRD0JZ.

SECTION	BODY SYSTEM	ROOT OPERATION	BODY PART	APPROACH	DEVICE	QUALIFIER
Medical and Surgical	Lower Joints	Replacement	Knee Joint, Right	Open	Synthetic Substitute	No Qualifier
0	S	R	C	0	J	Z

SECTION	BODY SYSTEM	ROOT OPERATION	BODY PART	APPROACH	DEVICE	QUALIFIER
Medical and Surgical	Lower Joints	Replacement	Knee Joint, Left	Open	Synthetic Substitute	No Qualifier
0	S	R	D	0	J	Z

CLOSED SURGICAL PROCEDURES AND CONVERSION TO OPEN PROCEDURES

As technology has advanced, procedures are increasingly being performed through scopes, which are less invasive than open procedures. This has resulted in quicker recoveries, shorter hospital stays, and fewer complications.

Common closed surgical approaches include laparoscopic, thoracoscopic, and arthroscopic procedures. The **laparoscopic approach** involves use of a laparoscope to examine and perform closed procedures within the abdomen. With a **thoracoscopic approach**, a thoracoscope is used to examine and perform closed procedures within the thorax. The **arthroscopic approach** requires the use of an arthroscope to examine and perform closed procedures within a joint. Closed procedures may be diagnostic and/or therapeutic in nature.

A surgical procedure may start with an endoscopic approach that may need to be converted to an open procedure. Some reasons for conversion to an open procedure include adhesions, bleeding, technical difficulties due to anatomic body structure and/or inflammatory changes, and injury to an organ. The reason for converting to an open procedure may need to be coded, along with the appropriate Z53.- code, which identifies that an endoscopic procedure has been converted to an open procedure. According to ICD-10-PCS guidelines, two procedure codes are necessary: one for the endoscopic procedure and one for the open procedure. The root operation for the endoscopic procedure code may be inspection.

EXAMPLE

A patient was admitted for a laparoscopic cholecystectomy for chronic cholecystitis with cholelithiasis. Because of extensive adhesions of the gallbladder, the procedure was converted to an open cholecystectomy and the bleeding was controlled.

Laparoscopic cholecystectomy converted to open, 0FT40ZZ, 0FJ44ZZ

SECTION	BODY SYSTEM	ROOT OPERATION	BODY PART	APPROACH	DEVICE	QUALIFIER
Medical and Surgical	Hepatobiliary System and Pancreas	Resection	Gallbladder	Open	No Device	No Qualifier
0	F	T	4	0	Z	Z

SECTION	BODY SYSTEM	ROOT OPERATION	BODY PART	APPROACH	DEVICE	QUALIFIER
Medical and Surgical	Hepatobiliary System and Pancreas	Inspection	Gallbladder	Percutaneous Endoscopic	No Device	No Qualifier
0	F	J	4	4	Z	Z

Occasionally, a surgical procedure will be started that for whatever reason cannot be completed. The surgical procedure should be coded to the root operation that was performed. If the procedure was aborted before any root operation could be performed, assign the code for "inspection" of the body part or region that was inspected. These circumstances are different from those surrounding a procedure that is canceled, in that the patient received anesthesia and surgery was begun.

EXAMPLE

A patient was admitted for colon resection because of cancer of the descending colon. A laparotomy incision through subcutaneous tissue and fascia was made, and the patient became unstable with atrial fibrillation. It was decided that the procedure should be terminated and the patient transferred to the ICU for further management. The incision was closed before any definitive surgery could be performed.

Laparotomy incision through subcutaneous tissue and fascia, 0JJT0ZZ

SECTION	BODY SYSTEM	ROOT OPERATION	BODY PART	APPROACH	DEVICE	QUALIFIER
Medical and Surgical	Subcutaneous Tissue and Fascia	Inspection	Subcutaneous Tissue and Fascia, Trunk	Open	No Device	No Qualifier
0	J	J	T	0	Z	Z

PLANNED AND CANCELED PROCEDURES

When patients are admitted to the hospital for a scheduled procedure(s), under some circumstances, the procedure(s) may be canceled or not completed. If a patient's procedure is canceled prior to the time that he or she presents to the hospital, no code will be required because no services were provided, no bill was generated, and there is no health record. On some occasions, a patient presents to have a procedure performed, but for whatever reason the procedure has to be canceled. The principal diagnosis in this case is the reason why the patient was going to have the procedure performed. If a complication arose that resulted in the cancellation, a diagnosis code for that condition would be assigned as a secondary diagnosis. Also, Z codes describe the reason for the cancellation. They can be located in the Index under the main term, procedure (surgical) not done.

Z53. 01 Procedure and treatment not carried out due to patient smoking
Z53. 09 Procedure and treatment not carried out because of other contraindication
Z53.1 Procedure and treatment not carried out because of patient's decision for reasons of belief and group pressure
Z53.20 Procedure and treatment not carried out because of patient's decision for unspecified reasons
Z53.21 Procedure and treatment not carried out due to patient leaving prior to being seen by health care provider
Z52.29 Procedure and treatment not carried out because of patient's decision for other reasons
Z53.8 Procedure and treatment not carried out for other reasons
Z53.9 Procedure and treatment not carried out, unspecified reason

EXAMPLE

A patient was admitted for hysterectomy because of uterine fibroids. Shortly after admission, the patient told the nurse that she was having second thoughts and had decided not to go through with the procedure; the patient was discharged, D25.9, Z53.29. No procedure code is assigned because the procedure was never started.

EXAMPLE

A patient was admitted for coronary artery bypass grafting because of coronary atherosclerosis of the native arteries. The cardiac surgeon became ill, and the surgery was rescheduled. The patient was discharged, I25.10, Z53.8.

EXAMPLE

A patient was admitted for laparoscopic cholecystectomy for cholelithiasis of the gallbladder. It was noted that the patient was having an acute exacerbation of his COPD. The patient was treated with steroids and nebulizer treatments and was discharged. The cholecystectomy was rescheduled for the next week, K80.20, J44.1, Z53.09.

BIOPSY PROCEDURES

Biopsy specimens can be obtained in several ways. The approach used varies with the location of the mass, the age of the patient, and the technology that is available. A **biopsy** consists of removal of a representative sample of a tumor mass for pathologic examination and diagnosis. A biopsy is a diagnostic procedure. Biopsies can be coded to the following root operations:

- **Excision** – cutting out or off, without replacement, a portion of a body part
- **Extraction** – pulling or stripping out or off all or a portion of a body part by the use of force
- **Drainage** – taking or letting out fluids and/or gases from a body part

Sometimes a surgeon will remove the entire specimen and call it a biopsy. When the entire specimen such as a breast lump or colon polyp is removed, this is a therapeutic procedure and is not assigned a biopsy code.

If a biopsy is followed by more definitive treatment during the same encounter, both the biopsy and the code for the more-definitive treatment are assigned.

When procedures are performed for malignant neoplasms, often surrounding lymph nodes will be sampled or removed. If the intent is to remove all the lymph nodes in an area, code to root operation resection. Also, if a chain of lymph nodes is excised, code to root operation resection. Lymph nodes may be described by the level where they are located. Each level is considered a chain. If an entire level of lymph nodes is removed, this also is coded to a resection. Sometimes an axillary node dissection or removal is performed when a woman has breast cancer. There are three levels of axillary lymph nodes. Each level would be considered an entire chain.

A **sentinel lymph node** is defined as the first lymph node to which cancer cells are most likely to spread. A **sentinel lymph node biopsy** (SLNB) is a procedure that identifies the sentinel lymph node(s) for removal and pathologic examination. This spares the patient from having lymph nodes removed when it may not be necessary because the cancer has not spread to the sentinel node(s). This procedure is most often used to help stage melanoma and breast cancer patients.

EXAMPLE

Patient is admitted with breast mass (RUQ) has an open biopsy with immediate total mastectomy with removal of sentinel lymph nodes. Pathology of the biopsy showed carcinoma. Nodes were negative for malignancy.

Open biopsy breast mass with total mastectomy with removal of sentinel lymph nodes, 0HTT0ZZ, 07B50ZX, 0HBT0ZX

SECTION	BODY SYSTEM	ROOT OPERATION	BODY PART	APPROACH	DEVICE	QUALIFIER
Medical and Surgical 0	Skin and Breast H	Resection T	Breast, Right T	Open 0	No Device Z	No Qualifier Z

SECTION	BODY SYSTEM	ROOT OPERATION	BODY PART	APPROACH	DEVICE	QUALIFIER
Medical and Surgical 0	Lymphatic and Hemic Systems 7	Excision B	Lymphatic, Right Axillary 5	Open 0	No Device Z	Diagnostic X

SECTION	BODY SYSTEM	ROOT OPERATION	BODY PART	APPROACH	DEVICE	QUALIFIER
Medical and Surgical 0	Skin and Breast H	Excision B	Breast, Right T	Open 0	No Device Z	Diagnostic X

MEDICAL AND SURGICAL SECTION

Now that you have been introduced to the format and the structure of ICD-10-PCS codes and the guidelines that are associated with ICD-10-PCS, it is time to practice. A coder can no longer code an operative procedure based on the title of the procedure. It is also important for a coder to understand something about the procedure being performed. There are a number of videos on the Internet that help explain the details of a particular procedure. Keep in mind that a procedure can have various approaches or variances in the way they are accomplished. It requires reviewing the operative report for further details of the procedure, i.e., the root operation, what body part was involved, the operative approach, any device used, and/or a particular qualifier. Let's review the following operative report and assign the appropriate ICD-10-PCS code based on the documentation. What is a hemiarthroplasty of the hip? It is a surgical procedure in which the ball portion of the hip joint is replaced with a prosthesis. A hemiarthroplasty of the hip is used most often to treat a fractured hip. When coding a replacement procedure, the removal of a body part is integral to the procedure. Also the closure of the operative site is integral to the procedure and not coded separately. There is no alphabetic index term for "hemiarthroplasty." To get to the 0SR Table you can look up replacement, joint, hip, left, femoral surface 0SRS or arthroplasty, replacement, lower joints 0SR.

Operative Report for Left Hip Uncemented Hemiarthroplasty

Title of Operation. Left hip uncemented hemiarthroplasty.

Indications for Surgery. The patient is a very pleasant 92-year-old woman who fell and sustained a left femoral neck fracture. When she was cleared by medicine, she was taken for surgery. Informed consent was obtained. Risks include pain, bleeding, infection, damage to blood vessels and nerves, dislocations, and leg length discrepancy, among others.

Preoperative Diagnosis. Left femoral neck fracture.

Postoperative Diagnosis. Left femoral neck fracture.

Anesthesia. General endotracheal anesthetic.

Specimen (Bacteriologic, Pathologic, or Other). Her femoral neck **(BODY PART REMOVED)** was sent.

Prosthetic Device/Implant (DEVICE). Uncemented **(QUALIFIER)** Stryker Howmedica Accolade Bipolar system, using a size-3 femoral neck and 41 head.

Surgeon's Narrative. The patient was brought back to the operating theater, where she was given general endotracheal anesthetic. She was placed in the right lateral decubitus position with her left hip up. The patient was prepped and draped in the usual sterile fashion. Incision was carried down to the posterior hip; this was carried down through the gluteus maximus to the posterior capsule of the hip **(OPEN APPROACH)**. We used a cobra to retract the gluteus medius out of the way. We then incised the hip capsule, piriformis, and short external rotators all in one. This was tied with a tagging stitch. The femoral neck **(BODY PART)** was then taken out using the Christmas tree. We used the cookie cutter to lateralize the femur. We then broached up to a size 3. This fit well. We then measured the head, measured at 38. The smallest size Accolade head was a 41; therefore we trialed a 41, and this did well. It was somewhat tight, but it did stay.

We decided therefore to go with the 3 and a size 41 head. We thoroughly irrigated the hip capsule and debrided soft tissues away. The real implant was placed **(REPLACEMENT ROOT OPERATION)** and reduced, it fit well, it was stable to full flexion and extension, and the leg lengths were compatible. The wound was then thoroughly irrigated. The rotators were attached using 0 Vicryl, closing the remaining soft tissue. The fascia was closed using #1. We then closed the skin with 2-0 and skin staples. Overall, it went well and the patient was extubated and brought to PACU.

Section	0	Medical and Surgical	
Body System	S	Lower Joints	
Operation	R	Replacement: Putting in or on biological or synthetic material that physically takes the place and/or function of all or a portion of a body part	
Body Part	*Approach*	*Device*	*Qualifier*
R Hip Joint, Femoral Surface, Right **S** Hip Joint, Femoral Surface, Left	**0** Open	**1** Synthetic Substitute, Metal **3** Synthetic Substitute, Ceramic **J** Synthetic Substitute	**9** Cemented **A** Uncemented **Z** No Qualifier

FIGURE 8-1. Table 0SR.

EXAMPLE

Left Hip uncemented hemiarthroplasty, 0SRS0JA (see Table 0SR, Figure 8-1)

SECTION	BODY SYSTEM	ROOT OPERATION	BODY PART	APPROACH	DEVICE	QUALIFIER
Medical and Surgical	Lower Joints	Replacement	Hip Joint, Femoral Surface, Left	Open	Synthetic Substitute	Uncemented
0	S	R	S	0	J	A

Root Operations

According to the guidelines, procedures that are performed and are necessary to reach the operative site are not coded separately. Also closure of the operative site, including anastomosis of any tubular body parts, is not coded separately.

The most important character in a procedure code is the root operation. The root operation is the objective or the intent of the procedure. The full definition of the root operation as defined in the PCS Tables must be applied. There are 31 root operations in the Medical and Surgical Section. As discussed in chapter 6, these root operations are divided into nine different categories that have similar attributes. These categories are:

- Root operations to remove some/all of a body part
- Root operations to remove solids/fluids/gases from a body part
- Root operations that involve cutting or separation only
- Root operations that put in/put back or move some/all of a body part
- Root operations that alter the diameter/route of a tubular body part
- Root operations that always involve a device
- Root operations that involve examination only
- Root operations that include other repairs
- Root operations that include other objectives

Root Operations to Remove Some/All of a Body Part

The root operations that involve removing some or all of a body part are:

- Destruction
- Detachment
- Excision
- Extraction
- Resection

The two root operations that may cause some confusion are excision and resection. Resection is the root operation when "all" of a body part is removed (cut out or off). There are some body parts that are that are further subdivided. For example, the lobes of the liver have been divided into the right lobe and the left lobe (see Figure 8-2). If the entire left lobe of the liver were removed, it would be coded to the root operation resection instead of excision because there is a body part for left lobe of the liver, and all of it was removed,

Section	0 Medical and Surgical		
Body System	F Hepatobiliary System and Pancreas		
Operation	T Resection: Cutting out or off, without replacement, all of a body part		
Body Part	*Approach*	*Device*	*Qualifier*
0 Liver **1** Liver, Right Lobe **2** Liver, Left Lobe **4** Gallbladder **G** Pancreas	**0** Open **4** Percutaneous Endoscopic	**Z** No Device	**Z** No Qualifier
5 Hepatic Duct, Right **6** Hepatic Duct, Left **7** Hepatic Duct, Common **8** Cystic Duct **9** Common Bile Duct **C** Ampulla of Vater **D** Pancreatic Duct **F** Pancreatic Duct, Accessory	**0** Open **4** Percutaneous Endoscopic **7** Via Natural or Artificial Opening **8** Via Natural or Artificial Opening Endoscopic	**Z** No Device	**Z** No Qualifier

FIGURE 8-2. Table 0FT.

which corresponds with the definition for resection – cutting out or off, without replacement, all of a body part. Other body parts that are further subdivided include the lobes of the lungs and thyroid gland and the regions of the intestine.

EXAMPLE

Open removal of left lobe of the liver, 0FT20ZZ (See Table 0FT, Figure 8-2)

SECTION	BODY SYSTEM	ROOT OPERATION	BODY PART	APPROACH	DEVICE	QUALIFIER
Medical and Surgical	Hepatobiliary System and Pancreas	Resection	Liver, Left Lobe	Open	No Device	No Qualifier
0	F	T	2	0	Z	Z

The root operation excision covers a variety of surgical procedures. Excision is one of the root operations that can be used for biopsies. If a biopsy is performed, the qualifier for "diagnostic" should be assigned. The root operation excision involves the removal of only a portion of a body part. Some examples include partial nephrectomy, excision of lesions, polypectomy, wedge resections, or excisional debridement.

EXAMPLE

Partial right laparoscopic nephrectomy, 0TB04ZZ

SECTION	BODY SYSTEM	ROOT OPERATION	BODY PART	APPROACH	DEVICE	QUALIFIER
Medical and Surgical	Urinary System	Excision	Kidney, Right	Percutaneous Endoscopic	No Device	No Qualifier
0	T	B	0	4	Z	Z

In ICD-10-PCS, if an autograft is obtained from a different body part in order to complete the objective of the procedure, a separate procedure is coded. Some examples include the harvesting of iliac bone during a spinal fusion procedure or the excision of a saphenous vein graft to be used in a coronary artery bypass graft procedure (CABG).

EXAMPLE

Harvesting of right greater saphenous vein via percutaneous endoscopic approach, 06BP4ZZ

SECTION	BODY SYSTEM	ROOT OPERATION	BODY PART	APPROACH	DEVICE	QUALIFIER
Medical and Surgical	Lower Veins	Excision	Greater Saphenous Vein, Right	Percutaneous Endoscopic	No Device	No Qualifier
0	6	B	P	4	Z	Z

Destruction is a root operation that falls into the category to remove some/all of a body part. The PCS definition is physical eradication of all or a portion of a body part by the direct use of energy, force, or a destructive agent. Some terms that may qualify as destruction include ablation, cauterization, coagulation, cryosurgery, electrocautery, fulguration, and obliteration. Some examples may include destruction of a wart, ablation of heart tissue, pleurodesis, or cautery of a varicose vein.

EXAMPLE

EGD with control of bleeding ulcer with electrocautery, stomach, 0D568ZZ

SECTION	BODY SYSTEM	ROOT OPERATION	BODY PART	APPROACH	DEVICE	QUALIFIER
Medical and Surgical 0	Gastrointestinal System D	Destruction 5	Stomach 6	Via Natural or Artificial Opening Endoscopic 8	No Device Z	No Qualifier Z

The PCS definition for detachment is cutting off all or a portion of the upper or lower extremities. Because the only body parts that are involved in this root operation are the extremities, the codes can be found under the anatomical regions X and Y for upper and lower extremities. An amputation involves overlapping body layers including skin, subcutaneous, muscles, and bones, so that is the reason for appearing in the code tables 0Y6 and 0X6 (See Figure 8-3)

Section	**0** Medical and Surgical		
Body System	**Y** Anatomical Regions, Lower Extremities		
Operation	**6** Detachment: Cutting off all or a portion of the upper or lower extremities		
Body Part	*Approach*	*Device*	*Qualifier*
2 Hindquarter, Right **3** Hindquarter, Left **4** Hindquarter, Bilateral **7** Femoral Region, Right **8** Femoral Region, Left **F** Knee Region, Right **G** Knee Region, Left	**0** Open	**Z** No Device	**Z** No Qualifier
C Upper Leg, Right **D** Upper Leg, Left **H** Lower Leg, Right **J** Lower Leg, Left	**0** Open	**Z** No Device	**1** High **2** Mid **3** Low
M Foot, Right **N** Foot, Left	**0** Open	**Z** No Device	**0** Complete **4** Complete 1st Ray **5** Complete 2nd Ray **6** Complete 3rd Ray **7** Complete 4th Ray **8** Complete 5th Ray **9** Partial 1st Ray **B** Partial 2nd Ray **C** Partial 3rd Ray **D** Partial 4th Ray **F** Partial 5th Ray
P 1st Toe, Right **Q** 1st Toe, Left **R** 2nd Toe, Right **S** 2nd Toe, Left **T** 3rd Toe, Right **U** 3rd Toe, Left **V** 4th Toe, Right **W** 4th Toe, Left **X** 5th Toe, Right **Y** 5th Toe, Left	**0** Open	**Z** No Device	**0** Complete **1** High **2** Mid **3** Low

FIGURE 8-3. 0Y6 Table for Detachment.

The qualifier for the root operation detachment is the specific port of the body part that was amputated. Some definititions that are helpful for correct code assignment include:

- High – amputation at the proximal (upper) port of the shaft of the body part or the proximal phalanx of the phalanges
- Mid – amputation at the middle portion of the shaft of the body part or the middle phalanx or through the proximal interphalangeal joint
- Low – amputation of the distal (lower) portion of the shaft of the body part or the distal phalanx of the phalanges or distal interphalangeal joint
- Complete – amputation that includes the metacarpophalangeal or metatarsalphalangeal joint

The term ray is used to designate the fingers and corresponding metacarpals and the toes and corresponding metatarsals. The first ray of the hand is the thumb and first metacarpal and the first ray of the foot is the great toe and metatarsal.

EXAMPLE

Right above-knee amputation – at the distal shaft, 0Y6C0Z3

SECTION	BODY SYSTEM	ROOT OPERATION	BODY PART	APPROACH	DEVICE	QUALIFIER
Medical and Surgical	Anatomical Regions, Lower Extremities	Detachment	Upper Leg, Right	Open	No Device	Low
0	Y	6	C	0	Z	3

The PCS definition for extraction is pulling or stripping out or off all or a portion of a body part by the use of force. Some examples include varicose vein stripping, D&C, and nonexcisional debridement. Bone marrow and endometrial biopsies are coded to the root operation "extraction" because they involve the removal of tissue by pulling or stripping. Because a biopsy is for diagnostic purposes, an X diagnostic qualifier is assigned to bone marrow and endometrial biopsies.

EXAMPLE

Pulse lavage debridement of skin, 0HDKXZZ

SECTION	BODY SYSTEM	ROOT OPERATION	BODY PART	APPROACH	DEVICE	QUALIFIER
Medical and Surgical	Skin and Breast	Extraction	Skin, Right Lower Leg	External	No Device	No Qualifier
0	H	D	K	X	Z	Z

EXERCISE 8-1

Assign codes for the procedures only.

1. Endometrial ablation via natural opening, endoscopic __________
2. Above-knee amputation, right mid-shaft femoral region __________
3. Removal of mole, right upper arm __________
4. Excision of the entire right upper lobe of the lung via open approach __________
5. Nonexcisional debridement of skin right forearm __________

Root Operations to Remove Solids/Fluids/Gases from a Body Part

The root operations that involve removing solids/fluids/gases from a body part:

- Drainage — lets out fluids or gases
- Extirpation — takes out solid matter
- Fragmentation — breaks solid matter into pieces

A drainage procedure in ICD-10-PCS is one that takes or lets out fluids and/or gases from a body part. Examples include incision and drainage procedures, thoracentesis, or spinal tap. It is possible for a drainage procedure to be diagnostic in nature. Fluid from a thoracentesis may be sent for pathology and/or cytologic examination if a malignancy is suspected. A drainage procedure can also be performed for therapeutic reasons. An example may be a patient who needs paracentesis performed every couple of weeks to relieve discomfort from accumulating ascitic fluid. In this instance, they are not trying to determine a cause of the ascites, and the procedure is performed for patient comfort or therapeutic reasons. There may be some instances when a drainage device or tube needs to be left place to provide ongoing drainage of a particular body part.

EXAMPLE

Lumbar puncture to rule out meningitis (diagnostic), 009U3ZX

SECTION	BODY SYSTEM	ROOT OPERATION	BODY PART	APPROACH	DEVICE	QUALIFIER
Medical and Surgical	Central Nervous System	Drainage	Spinal Canal	Percutaneous	No Device	No Qualifier
0	0	9	U	3	Z	X

EXAMPLE

Therapeutic right thoracentesis, 0W993ZZ (see Figure 8-4)

SECTION	BODY SYSTEM	ROOT OPERATION	BODY PART	APPROACH	DEVICE	QUALIFIER
Medical and Surgical	Anatomical Regions, General	Drainage	Pleural Cavity, Right	Percutaneous	No Device	No Qualifier
0	W	9	9	3	Z	Z

EXAMPLE

Percutaneous insertion of right chest tube, 0W9930Z (see Figure 8-4)

SECTION	BODY SYSTEM	ROOT OPERATION	BODY PART	APPROACH	DEVICE	QUALIFIER
Medical and Surgical	Anatomical Regions, General	Drainage	Pleural Cavity, Right	Percutaneous	Drainage Device	No Qualifier
0	W	9	9	3	0	Z

The next root operation is extirpation, which is the taking or cutting out of solid matter from a body part. Physicians don't usually use the term extirpation. It is the coder's responsibility to take the documentation presented in the medical record and correlate it to the PCS definitions to assign the appropriate codes. Solid matter can be the abnormal by-product of a biological function such as a kidney stone or a blood clot. It also includes foreign bodies that are embedded in a body part or the lumen of a tubular body part.

EXAMPLE

ERCP with removal of stone from common bile duct, 0FC98ZZ

SECTION	BODY SYSTEM	ROOT OPERATION	BODY PART	APPROACH	DEVICE	QUALIFIER
Medical and Surgical	Hepatobiliary System and Pancreas	Extirpation	Common Bile Duct	Via Natural or Artificial Opening Endoscopic	No Device	No Qualifier
0	F	C	9	8	Z	Z

Section 0 Medical and Surgical			
Body System W Anatomical Regions, General			
Operation 9 Drainage: Taking or letting out fluids and/or gases from a body part			
Body Part	*Approach*	*Device*	*Qualifier*
0 Head **1** Cranial Cavity **2** Face **3** Oral Cavity and Throat **4** Upper Jaw **5** Lower Jaw **6** Neck **8** Chest Wall **9** Pleural Cavity, Right **B** Pleural Cavity, Left **C** Mediastinum **D** Pericardial Cavity **F** Abdominal Wall **G** Peritoneal Cavity **H** Retroperitoneum **K** Upper Back **L** Lower Back **M** Perineum, Male **N** Perineum, Female	**0** Open **3** Percutaneous **4** Percutaneous Endoscopic	**0** Drainage Device	**Z** No Qualifier
0 Head **1** Cranial Cavity **2** Face **3** Oral Cavity and Throat **4** Upper Jaw **5** Lower Jaw **6** Neck **8** Chest Wall **9** Pleural Cavity, Right **B** Pleural Cavity, Left **C** Mediastinum **D** Pericardial Cavity **F** Abdominal Wall **G** Peritoneal Cavity **H** Retroperitoneum **K** Upper Back **L** Lower Back **M** Perineum, Male **N** Perineum, Female	**0** Open **3** Percutaneous **4** Percutaneous Endoscopic	**Z** No Device	**X** Diagnostic **Z** No Qualifier

FIGURE 8-4. Table 0W9 (upper half).

Fragmentation is a root operation that involves breaking solid matter in a body part into pieces. In fragmentation procedures, the material is not removed or taken out. If the material is removed or taken out, it is coded to extirpation procedure only. The small pieces of matter may be able to pass out of the body on its own. Sometimes the pieces will be removed at a later date.

EXAMPLE

Percutaneous nephrostomy for fragmentation of left kidney stone, 0TF43ZZ

SECTION	BODY SYSTEM	ROOT OPERATION	BODY PART	APPROACH	DEVICE	QUALIFIER
Medical and Surgical	Urinary System	Fragmentation	Kidney, Left	Percutaneous	No Device	No Qualifier
0	T	F	4	3	Z	Z

According to the guidelines, if a procedure is performed percutaneously via a device placed for the procedure it is coded to "percutaneous" approach as in the placement of a nephrostomy device to assist with the fragmentation of the kidney stone.

EXERCISE 8-2

Assign codes for the procedures only.

1. ESWL, stone right ureter ____________
2. Diagnostic paracentesis ____________
3. Craniotomy with evacuation of subdural hematoma (clot) ____________
4. Incision and drainage of abscess on buttock (skin) ____________

Root Operations That Involve Cutting or Separation Only

The root operations that involve cutting or separation only:

- Division
- Release

Division is the cutting into a body part without drawing fluids and/or gases from the body part in order to separate or transect a body part. Some examples include osteotomy, neurotomy, spinal cordotomy, and an episiotomy (division of the perineum).

Release is the freeing of a body part from an abnormal physical constraint by cutting or by the use of force. Examples includes carpal tunnel release or lysis of adhesions. In a lysis of adhesions of the ileum, the body part is the ileum because that is the body part that is being freed. The ileum was not manipulated or cut into, but the adhesions that were around the ileum were cut to release the constraint on the ileum. The guidelines explain the difference between division and release. Division is when the body part is actually separated or divided. Cutting a nerve root to relieve pain is division, whereas freeing a nerve root by manipulation of the surrounding scar tissue is coded to release.

EXAMPLE Episiotomy, 0W8NXZZ

SECTION	BODY SYSTEM	ROOT OPERATION	BODY PART	APPROACH	DEVICE	QUALIFIER
Medical and Surgical 0	Anatomical Regions, General W	Division 8	Perineum, Female N	External X	No Device Z	No Qualifier Z

EXAMPLE Open right carpal tunnel release, 01N50ZZ

SECTION	BODY SYSTEM	ROOT OPERATION	BODY PART	APPROACH	DEVICE	QUALIFIER
Medical and Surgical 0	Peripheral Nervous System 1	Release N	Median Nerve 5	Open 0	No Device Z	No Qualifier Z

EXERCISE 8-3

Assign codes for the procedures only.

1. Laparoscopic lysis of adhesions small intestine ____________
2. Open release of trigger finger on the right ____________
3. Frenulotomy to release tongue tie ____________
4. Open lumbar spinal cordotomy ____________

Root Operations That Put In/Put Back or Move Some/All of a Body Part

The root operations that involve putting in or back or moving some or all of a body part:

- Reattachment
- Reposition

- Transfer
- Transplant

The root operation for reattachment would only be used for completely severed body parts. If a partial amputation is being operated on, the root operation is going to be repair for the reconnection of the partial amputation. Reattachment is assigned as the root operation when a completely severed body part is reattached. The restoration of the blood and nerve supply is included in the reattachment procedure. These types of procedures are very specialized and may not be performed at some facilities.

EXAMPLE

Reattachment of amputated right thumb, 0XML0ZZ

SECTION	BODY SYSTEM	ROOT OPERATION	BODY PART	APPROACH	DEVICE	QUALIFIER
Medical and Surgical	Anatomical Regions, Upper Extremities	Reattachment	Thumb, Right	Open	No Device	No Qualifier
0	X	M	L	0	Z	Z

Reposition is the moving to its normal location or other suitable location all or a portion of a body part. Some examples include relocating an undescended testicle into the scrotal sac, reduction of a displaced fracture or dislocated joint, or repositioning of a nerve.

EXAMPLE

ORIF left humeral shaft, 0PSG04Z

SECTION	BODY SYSTEM	ROOT OPERATION	BODY PART	APPROACH	DEVICE	QUALIFIER
Medical and Surgical	Upper Bones	Reposition	Humeral Shaft, Left	Open	Internal Fixation Device	No Qualifier
0	P	S	G	0	4	Z

When a reduction of a displaced fracture is coded, the application of a cast or splint in conjunction with the reposition procedure is not coded separately. For treatment of a fracture that is not displaced, the root operation reposition does not fit. If a nondisplaced fracture is casted, the root operation is immobilization, which is found in the Placement section of ICD-10-PCS. If a fixation device such as a pin is placed in a nondisplaced fracture, the root operation is insertion.

Transfer is the moving of all or a portion of a body part to another location to take over the function of all or a portion of that body part. The body part moved or transferred still remains connected to its vascular and nerve supply. There are no devices used in a transfer procedure, so the device value is always Z for no device. There are also some body systems such as the Heart and Great Vessels that do not have transfer procedures, so therefore there is no PCS table available. Examples of transfer procedures include pedicle skin flaps/grafts, nerve and tendon transfers, or skin advancement flap closures.

In transfer procedures that involve more than one layer as in the example below, the body part represents the deepest tissue layer in the flap/pedicle graft, and the qualifier identifies any other tissue layers that are involved in the transfer (see Figure 8-5).

EXAMPLE

Open pedicle skin and subcutaneous tissue graft, left buttock, 0JX90ZB

SECTION	BODY SYSTEM	ROOT OPERATION	BODY PART	APPROACH	DEVICE	QUALIFIER
Medical and Surgical	Subcutaneous Tissue and Fascia	Transfer	Subcutaneous Tissue and Fascia, Buttock	Open	No Device	Skin and Subcutaneous Tissue
0	J	X	9	0	Z	B

Section	0	Medical and Surgical	
Body System	J	Subcutaneous Tissue and Fascia	
Operation	X	Transfer: Moving, without taking out, all or a portion of a body part to another location to take over the function of all or a portion of a body part	
Body Part	**Approach**	**Device**	**Qualifier**
0 Subcutaneous Tissue and Fascia, Scalp 1 Subcutaneous Tissue and Fascia, Face 4 Subcutaneous Tissue and Fascia, Anterior Neck 5 Subcutaneous Tissue and Fascia, Posterior Neck 6 Subcutaneous Tissue and Fascia, Chest 7 Subcutaneous Tissue and Fascia, Back 8 Subcutaneous Tissue and Fascia, Abdomen 9 Subcutaneous Tissue and Fascia, Buttock B Subcutaneous Tissue and Fascia, Perineum C Subcutaneous Tissue and	0 Open 3 Percutaneous	Z No Device	B Skin and Subcutaneous Tissue C Skin, Subcutaneous Tissue and Fascia Z No Qualifier

FIGURE 8-5. Table 0JX.

The final root operation in this category is transplant, which is the putting in or on all or a portion of a living body part taken from another individual or animal to physically take the place and/or function of all or a portion of a similar body part. There are only a limited number of options available for transplant procedures. Some of the most common transplants are kidney, heart, lungs, liver, and pancreas.

EXAMPLE

Open kidney transplant with spouse's left kidney, 0TY10Z0

SECTION	BODY SYSTEM	ROOT OPERATION	BODY PART	APPROACH	DEVICE	QUALIFIER
Medical and Surgical	Urinary System	Transplantation	Kidney, Left	Open	No Device	Allogeneic
0	T	Y	1	0	Z	0

The qualifier for transplant has the following options:

- Allogeneic – tissue or cells transplanted from different individuals of the same species
- Syngeneic – individuals or tissues that have identical genes, such as identical twins
- Zooplastic – tissue from an animal

Bone marrow, stem cells, and pancreatic islet cells are not coded as transplantation but are coded in the Administration section with the root operation of transfusion according to the ICD-10-PCS guidelines.

When a kidney transplant is performed, they often leave the native kidneys in place. When a heart transplant is performed and they remove the heart and replace it with the donor heart, it is not necessary to code the removal of the organ that is being transplanted.

EXERCISE 8-4

Assign codes for the procedures only.

1. Reattachment of amputated right index finger ______________
2. Bilateral lung transplant, cadaver donor ______________
3. Closed reduction of dislocated right phalangeal joint (finger) ______________
4. Breast reconstruction with pedicled TRAM flap, open approach ______________

Root Operations That Alter the Diameter/Route of a Tubular Body Part

The root operations that alter the diameter/route of a tubular body part:

- Bypass
- Dilation
- Occlusion
- Restriction

The root operation bypass is the altering of the route of passage of the contents of a tubular body part. For the most part, the coder needs to identify the body part bypassed from and the body part bypassed to. Another way to look at it is, the contents of a body part are being rerouted in a downward stream. There may also be procedures that reroute contents to a totally different area of the body. An example is cerebrospinal fluid from the brain being rerouted with a ventriculoperitoneal shunt to the peritoneum to be absorbed into the body. Other examples include creation of a colostomy, CABG, gastric bypass, femoral-popliteal artery bypass, or urinary diversion with ileal conduit.

EXAMPLE

Insertion of ventriculoperitoneal shunt via open approach, 00160J6

SECTION	BODY SYSTEM	ROOT OPERATION	BODY PART	APPROACH	DEVICE	QUALIFIER
Medical and Surgical	Central Nervous System	Bypass	Cerebral Ventricle	Open	Synthetic Substitute	Peritoneal Cavity
0	0	1	6	0	J	6

According to the ICD-10-PCS guidelines, the coronary bypass procedures are coded differently from other bypass procedures. The body part identifies the number of coronary artery sites bypassed to, and the qualifier identifies the vessel bypassed from. The most common bypass is from the aorta to the coronary artery.

EXAMPLE

CABG of three coronary arteries using a graft from the greater saphenous vein left leg, which was harvested via percutaneous endoscopic approach, 021209W, 06BQ4ZZ

SECTION	BODY SYSTEM	ROOT OPERATION	BODY PART	APPROACH	DEVICE	QUALIFIER
Medical and Surgical	Heart and Great Vessels	Bypass	Coronary Artery, Three Sites	Open	Autologous Venous Tissue	Aorta
0	2	1	2	0	9	W

SECTION	BODY SYSTEM	ROOT OPERATION	BODY PART	APPROACH	DEVICE	QUALIFIER
Medical and Surgical	Lower Veins	Excision	Greater Saphenous Vein, Left	Percutaneous Endoscopic	No Device	No Qualifier
0	6	B	Q	4	Z	Z

The next root operation is dilation, which involves expanding an orifice or the lumen of a tubular body part. The intent of the procedure is to make the orifice or lumen larger. This can be accomplished either within the lumen of a tubular body part (intraluminal) or outside of the lumen (extraluminal).

If dilation is part of the approach for a given procedure and not the intent of the procedure, then dilation is not the root operation. An example of this is Dilation and Curettage (D&C), where the dilation is part of the approach to access the endometrium, which is then extracted which is the intent of the procedure. Extraction is the root operation for a non-obstetric D&C.

Some examples of a dilation procedure are PTCA, esophageal dilation, dilation of common bile duct, dilation of ureteral stricture, or dilation of old anastomotic site.

EXAMPLE

PTCA of the LAD (coronary artery) and insertion of drug-eluting stent, 027034Z

SECTION	BODY SYSTEM	ROOT OPERATION	BODY PART	APPROACH	DEVICE	QUALIFIER
Medical and Surgical	Heart and Great Vessels	Dilation	Coronary Artery, One Site	Percutaneous	Intraluminal Device, Drug-eluting	No Qualifier
0	2	7	0	3	4	Z

EXAMPLE

EGD with dilation of stricture at the esophagogastric junction, 0D748ZZ

SECTION	BODY SYSTEM	ROOT OPERATION	BODY PART	APPROACH	DEVICE	QUALIFIER
Medical and Surgical	Gastrointestinal System	Dilation	Esophagogastric Junction	Via Natural or Artificial Opening Endoscopic	No Device	No Qualifier
0	D	7	4	8	Z	Z

The root operation occlusion is the complete closing of an orifice or the lumen of a tubular body part. An important term in this definition is "complete." That is what differentiates this root operation from the root operation "restriction," which is to partially close an orifice or tubular body part. These procedures may use intraluminal or extraluminal devices or sutures/ligation to totally occlude the body part. Some examples of occlusions are fallopian tube ligation, ligation of a blood vessel, or some embolization procedures in which the intent is to totally occlude the body part.

EXAMPLE

Bilateral tubal ligation, 0UL70ZZ

SECTION	BODY SYSTEM	ROOT OPERATION	BODY PART	APPROACH	DEVICE	QUALIFIER
Medical and Surgical	Female Reproductive System	Occlusion	Fallopian Tubes, Bilateral	Open	No Device	No Qualifier
0	U	L	7	0	Z	Z

The last root operation in the category is restriction, which is the partial closing of an orifice or lumen of a tubular body part. Some examples include a Nissen fundoplication, gastric banding, cervical cerclage, clipping of a cerebral aneurysm, aneurysm repair with stent graft, and some embolization procedures.

EXAMPLE

Laparoscopic gastric banding with extraluminal device 0DV64CZ

SECTION	BODY SYSTEM	ROOT OPERATION	BODY PART	APPROACH	DEVICE	QUALIFIER
Medical and Surgical	Gastrointestinal System	Restriction	Stomach	Percutaneous Endoscopic	Extraluminal Device	No Qualifier
0	D	V	6	4	C	Z

EXERCISE 8-5

Assign codes for the procedures only.

1. Laparoscopic Nissen fundoplication __________
2. Right femoral artery to right popliteal artery bypass using synthetic substitute __________
3. Percutaneous ligation of varicose vein, left foot __________
4. PTCA of two vessels __________

Root Operations That Always Involve a Device

The root operations that always involve a device:

- Change
- Insertion
- Replacement
- Removal
- Revision
- Supplement

If there is no device involved, the root operation cannot be one of the above root operations, and the device has to be involved in the procedure.

Let's start with the root operation change, which is taking out or off a device from a body part and putting back an identical or similar device in or on the same body part without cutting or puncturing the skin or mucous membrane. Because you cannot cut or puncture the skin or mucous membrane, the only possible approach is external. Examples of a change procedure are change of a gastrostomy tube/catheter, change of chest tube, change of tracheostomy tube, or IUD removal with replacement.

EXAMPLE

Change of tracheostomy tube, 0B21XFZ

SECTION	BODY SYSTEM	ROOT OPERATION	BODY PART	APPROACH	DEVICE	QUALIFIER
Medical and Surgical	Respiratory System	Change	Trachea	External	Tracheostomy Device	No Qualifier
0	B	2	1	X	F	Z

The root operation insertion is putting in a nonbiological device that monitors, assists, performs, or prevents a physiological function but does not physically take the place of a body part. To be coded to the insertion root operation, the main objective/intent of the procedure must be the insertion of the device. There are instances where the device is not the main objective of the procedure; then the procedure should be coded to the appropriate root operation and not to insertion. For example, a chest tube is inserted and left in to drain a pleural effusion. The intent of the procedure is the drainage, and the device is then identified by the sixth character, drainage device.

EXAMPLE

Insertion of single array subcutaneous chest generator and percutaneous lead insertion, 0JH60BZ, 00H03MZ

SECTION	BODY SYSTEM	ROOT OPERATION	BODY PART	APPROACH	DEVICE	QUALIFIER
Medical and Surgical	Subcutaneous Tissue and Fascia	Insertion	Subcutaneous Tissue and Fascia, Chest	Open	Stimulator Generator, Single Array	No Qualifier
0	J	H	6	0	B	Z

SECTION	BODY SYSTEM	ROOT OPERATION	BODY PART	APPROACH	DEVICE	QUALIFIER
Medical and Surgical	Central Nervous System	Insertion	Brain	Percutaneous	Neurostimulator Lead	No Qualifier
0	0	H	0	3	M	Z

The root operation replacement is the putting in or on biological or synthetic material to physically take the place and/or function of all or a portion of a body part. Examples include joint replacement, heart valve replacement, free skin graft, keratoplasty, or prosthetic lens insertion. In replacement procedures, the removal of the native body part is included in the initial replacement procedure. Any subsequent replacement procedure would require a separate code for the removal and one for the replacement. An example is a patient who has a previous total knee replacement. The hardware has failed and needs to be replaced. A code would be assigned for the removal of the TKR and a code for the replacement of the knee joint.

When a device such as a heart valve is composed of animal tissue and synthetic material for support, such as a bioprosthesis, it is coded to the device value for Zooplastic.

EXAMPLE

Open aortic valve replacement with bioprosthetic valve, 02RF08Z

SECTION	BODY SYSTEM	ROOT OPERATION	BODY PART	APPROACH	DEVICE	QUALIFIER
Medical and Surgical	Heart and Great Vessels	Replacement	Aortic Valve	Open	Zooplastic Tissue	No Qualifier
0	2	R	F	0	8	Z

If a breast reconstruction is performed during the same operative episode as a mastectomy, only the replacement or breast reconstruction code is assigned. The removal of the body part during a replacement procedure is considered part of the replacement procedure

EXAMPLE

Total mastectomy with immediate TRAM reconstruction, right breast, 0HRT076

SECTION	BODY SYSTEM	ROOT OPERATION	BODY PART	APPROACH	DEVICE	QUALIFIER
Medical and Surgical	Skin and Breast	Replacement	Breast, Right	Open	Autologous Tissue Substitute	Transverse Rectus Abdominis Myocutaneous Flap
0	H	R	T	0	7	6

Removal is the taking out or off a device from a body part. Examples of removal include removal of a central line, removal of a chest tube or other drainage device, or removal of fixation devices. The main objective of the procedure is to remove the device. The insertion codes may have more description device values than are available in the removal tables.

EXAMPLE

Open removal of internal fixation device left upper femur, 0QP704Z

SECTION	BODY SYSTEM	ROOT OPERATION	BODY PART	APPROACH	DEVICE	QUALIFIER
Medical and Surgical	Lower Bones	Removal	Upper Femur, Left	Open	Internal Fixation Device	No Qualifier
0	Q	P	7	0	4	Z

The root operation revision is the correcting, to the extent possible, a malfunctioning or displaced device. Examples include adjustments to pacemaker leads or adjustment to a knee prosthesis. Sometimes physicians will document revision when they are completely redoing a procedure. This is not a revision and should be coded to the root operation being performed.

EXAMPLE

Pacemaker lead is repositioned percutaneously with the use of a guide wire, 02WA3MZ

SECTION	BODY SYSTEM	ROOT OPERATION	BODY PART	APPROACH	DEVICE	QUALIFIER
Medical and Surgical 0	Heart and Great Vessels 2	Revision W	Heart A	Percutaneous 3	Cardiac Lead M	No Qualifier Z

Supplement procedures are defined as putting in or on biologic or synthetic material that physically reinforces and/or augments the function of a portion of a body part. Some examples include herniorrhaphy with mesh, resurfacing of a joint, aortic valve annuloplasty, vertebroplasty, colporrhaphy with mesh, and Dacron patches used to reinforce a vessel.

EXAMPLE

Percutaneous vertebroplasty (synthetic substitute), 0PU43JZ

SECTION	BODY SYSTEM	ROOT OPERATION	BODY PART	APPROACH	DEVICE	QUALIFIER
Medical and Surgical 0	Upper Bones P	Supplement U	Thoracic Vertebra 4	Percutaneous 3	Synthetic Substitute J	No Qualifier Z

EXERCISE 8-6

Assign codes for the procedures only.

1. Open right inguinal herniorrhaphy with mesh ______________
2. Total right hip replacement with metal-on-metal prosthesis, open ______________
3. Removal of chest tube drainage device from right pleural cavity, external ______________
4. Change of gastrostomy tube ______________
5. Insertion of endotracheal tube ______________
6. Revision of VP shunt catheter at the peritoneal site (removed kink from tubing—no new tubing inserted) via laparotomy ______________

Root Operations That Involve Examination Only

The root operations that involve examination only:

- Inspection
- Map

There are only two root operations in this category, and the root operation, map, is limited to the central nervous system and the cardiac conduction mechanism.

Inspection is defined as visually and/or manually exploring a body part. Examples of inspection procedures include bronchoscopy, arthroscopy, colonoscopy, and EGD. There are a couple of guidelines that apply to inspection procedures:

- If the inspection procedure is performed in order to achieve the objective of the procedure, it should not be coded separately. For example, a colonoscopy is performed to removal a polyp. The polypectomy was the main intent of the procedure, and the colonoscopy is identified by the approach.
- If multiple tubular body parts are inspected, the most distal body part or the body part furthest from the starting point is coded. For example, a cystoureteroscopy with inspection of bladder and the ureters is coded to the ureter.
- If multiple nontubular body parts in a region are inspected, the body part that specifies the entire region should be coded. For example, an exploratory

laparotomy with inspection of the abdominal contents is coded to the peritoneal cavity.

- When both an inspection procedure and another procedure are performed on the same body part during the same operative episode, if the inspection is performed using a different approach than the other procedure, the inspection procedure is coded separately.
- If the intended root operation is attempted using one approach but is converted to a different approach, it is acceptable to code both procedures; for example, laparoscopic visualization of the gallbladder with subsequent conversion to open resection of the gallbladder.

EXAMPLE

Laparoscopic cholecystectomy which was converted to open procedure, 0FT40ZZ, 0FJ44ZZ

SECTION	BODY SYSTEM	ROOT OPERATION	BODY PART	APPROACH	DEVICE	QUALIFIER
Medical and Surgical	Hepatobiliary System and Pancreas	Resection	Gallbladder	Open	No Device	No Qualifier
0	F	T	4	0	Z	Z

SECTION	BODY SYSTEM	ROOT OPERATION	BODY PART	APPROACH	DEVICE	QUALIFIER
Medical and Surgical	Hepatobiliary System and Pancreas	Inspection	Gallbladder	Percutaneous Endoscopic	No Device	No Qualifier
0	F	J	4	4	Z	Z

Map is limited to the central nervous system and the cardiac conduction mechanism, so there are only two tables available to code from, 00K and 02K. Examples of mapping procedures include intraoperative brain mapping and intraoperative cardiac mapping.

EXAMPLE

Cardiac mapping, 02K83ZZ

SECTION	BODY SYSTEM	ROOT OPERATION	BODY PART	APPROACH	DEVICE	QUALIFIER
Medical and Surgical	Heart and Great Vessels	Map	Conduction Mechanism	Percutaneous	No Device	No Qualifier
0	2	K	8	3	Z	Z

EXERCISE 8-7

Assign codes for the procedures only.

1. Diagnostic bronchoscopy ______________
2. EGD ______________
3. Mapping of the basal ganglia, open approach ______________
4. Exploratory laparotomy (peritoneum) ______________

Root Operations That Include Other Repairs

The root operations that include other repairs:

- Control
- Repair

The root operation control is used when stopping, or attempting to stop, postprocedural or other acute bleeding. Only three tables are available for control procedures, 0W3,

0X3, and 0Y3. Examples include ligation of bleeding arteries, drainage of a postoperative hemorrhage, or clipping of a bleeding duodenal ulcer. A procedure code should not be assigned for control of intraoperative bleeding that would be integral to the procedure.

If the attempt to control the bleeding is unsuccessful and a definitive root operation such as bypass, detachment, excision, extraction, reposition, replacement or resection is required, the root operative for control should not be assigned, and the definitive root operation should be assigned instead. For example, if a splenectomy had to be performed to control the postoperative bleeding, the root operation for resection should be assigned.

There are times that physicians will document the performance of various procedures to control bleeding. For example, an EGD is performed and the bleeding gastric ulcer is cauterized to control bleeding; this should be coded to the root operation control instead of destruction.

The root operation repair is restoring, to the extent possible, a body part to its normal anatomic structure and function. An example of this is a herniorrhaphy without prosthesis and suturing of lacerations. The root operation for repair should only be selected when no other root operation applies. No devices would be left in place at the end of a repair procedure.

EXAMPLE

Repair of second-degree perineal laceration, 0KQM0ZZ

SECTION	BODY SYSTEM	ROOT OPERATION	BODY PART	APPROACH	DEVICE	QUALIFIER
Medical and Surgical	Muscles	Repair	Perineum Muscle	Open	No Device	No Qualifier
0	K	Q	M	0	Z	Z

EXERCISE 8-8

Assign codes for the procedures only.

1. Right femoral hernia repair (no mesh) via open approach ______________
2. Repair right Achilles tendon with sutures, open approach ______________
3. Control of postoperative bleeding in peritoneal cavity by suturing bleeding artery, via open approach ______________

Root Operations That Include Other Objectives

The root operations that include other objectives:

- Alteration
- Creation
- Fusion

The root operation alteration means modifying the natural anatomic structure of a body part without affecting the function of the body part. Alteration procedures are reserved for procedures that are performed for cosmetic purposes only. Some examples include brow lift, face lift, breast augmentation, and otoplasty. There are a number of procedures that alter appearance but are performed for medical reasons. A blepharoplasty can be performed for obstructed vision, and another root operation would be appropriate, depending on how the procedure was performed.

The root operation creation is used for the making of new genital structure that does not physically take the place of a body part. The root operation for sex change procedures are available on Table, 0W4. The body part describes the body part that is present at the start of the procedure and the qualifier is the body structure that has been created. The root operation creation can be used for limited corrective procedures in patients with congenital anomalies.

The final root operation is fusion. Fusion is the joining together a portion of an articular body part, thereby rendering the articular body part immobile. The root operation fusion is only available in code tables that deal with the joints, ORG upper joints, and OSG lower joints. The most common fusion procedure is spinal fusions. There are a couple of points to consider when coding spinal fusions:

- The body part is based on joints, C1 to C2 is one joint, C1-C3 is two joints.
- There are specific guidelines for the device designations.
- The qualifier includes the approach and which column.
- If multiple joints are fused, a separate procedure is coded for each vertebral joint that uses a different device and/or qualifier.
- When a combination of devices and materials are used on the same vertebral joint, the guidelines outline a coding hierarchy that should be followed.
- If an autograft is obtained from a different body part in order to complete the objective of the procedure, a separate procedure is coded.

EXAMPLE

Anterior cervical spinal fusion C3-C5 using interbody fusion device, 0RG20A0

SECTION	BODY SYSTEM	ROOT OPERATION	BODY PART	APPROACH	DEVICE	QUALIFIER
Medical and Surgical	Upper Joints	Fusion	Cervical Vertebral Joints, Two or More	Open	Interbody Fusion Device	Anterior Approach, Anterior Column
0	R	G	2	0	A	0

EXERCISE 8-9

Assign codes for the procedures only.

1. Female patient undergoing gender reassignment surgery with creation of penis with autologous tissue __________
2. Open bilateral breast augmentation with synthetic substitute (for cosmetic purposes) __________
3. Open posterior approach with spinal fusion at L5-S1 with autologous tissue, posterior column __________
4. Fusion of left ankle joint with bone tissue from the bone bank, open approach __________

CHAPTER REVIEW EXERCISE

Assign the appropriate ICD-10-PCS codes to the following procedures in accordance with the coding guidelines.

1. Thoracoscopic mechanical pleurodesis, right __________
2. Bronchoscopy with removal of mucous plug in right main bronchus __________
3. Replacement of drainage device in peritoneal cavity __________
4. Epistaxis controlled by cauterization __________
5. Punch biopsy of skin on the left shoulder __________
6. Laparoscopic pyloromyotomy for pyloric stenosis in infant __________
7. Diagnostic arthroscopic examination of right ankle joint __________
8. Percutaneous drainage of abscess left psoas muscle __________
9. Excision of the entire left lobe of the thyroid via open approach __________
10. Exploratory laparotomy with partial cholecystectomy __________
11. Laparoscopic-assisted right hemicolectomy with end-to-end anastomosis __________

12. Gastric (stomach) lavage via nasogastric tube ______________

13. Transarterial chemoembolization (TACE) for hepatocellular carcinoma via hepatic artery ______________

14. Open insertion of bone growth stimulator, right tibial shaft ______________

15. Percutaneous harvesting of ova for future IVF ______________

CHAPTER GLOSSARY

Allogenic: tissue or cells transplanted from different individuals of the same species.

Arthroscopic approach: requires the use of an arthroscope to examine and perform closed procedures within a joint.

Bilateral procedure: occurs when the same procedure is performed on paired anatomic organs or tissues (i.e., eyes, ears, joints such as shoulder or knee).

Biopsy: removal of a representative sample of a tumor mass for pathologic examination and diagnosis.

Drainage: defined in chapter 6.

Episiotomy: division of the perineum.

Excision: defined in chapter 6.

Extraction: defined in chapter 6.

Extraluminal: outside of the lumen of a tubular body part.

Intraluminal: within the lumen of a tubular body part.

Laparoscopic approach: use of a laparoscope to examine and perform closed procedures within the abdomen.

Medicare Code Editor: software that detects errors in coding on Medicare claims.

Principal Procedure: performed for definitive treatment rather than for diagnostic or exploratory purposes, or one necessary to take care of a complication.

Ray: used to designate the fingers and corresponding metacarpals and the toes and corresponding metatarsals.

Sentinel lymph node: the first lymph node to which cancer cells are most likely to spread.

Sentinel lymph node biopsy (SLNB): a procedure that identifies the sentinel lymph node(s) for removal and pathologic examination.

Significant procedure: surgical in nature, carries a procedural risk, carries an anesthetic risk, or requires specialized training.

Syngeneic: individuals or tissues that have identical genes, such as identical twins.

Thoracoscopic approach: a thoracoscope is used to examine and perform closed procedures within the thorax.

Zooplastic: tissue from an animal.

9

Symptoms, Signs, and Abnormal Clinical and Laboratory Findings Not Elsewhere Classified, and Z Codes

(ICD-10-CM Chapters 18 and 21, Codes R00-R99, Z00-Z99)

CHAPTER OUTLINE

ICD-10-CM Official Guidelines for Coding and Reporting
Anatomy and Physiology
Disease Conditions
- Symptoms and Signs (R00-R69)
- Abnormal Findings and Abnormal Tumor Markers (R70-R97)

Factors Influencing Health Status and Contact With Health Services (Z Codes Z00-Z99)
Procedures
Chapter Review Exercise
Chapter Glossary

LEARNING OBJECTIVES

1. Apply and assign the correct ICD-10-CM/PCS codes in accordance with Official Guidelines for Coding and Reporting
2. Determine when to assign signs and symptoms codes
3. Assign the correct Z codes and procedure codes

ABBREVIATIONS/ ACRONYMS

BMI body mass index
CEA carcinoembryonic antigen
COPD chronic obstructive pulmonary disease
CT computerized tomography
FUO fever of unknown origin
HGSIL high-grade squamous intraepithelial lesion
HIV human immunodeficiency virus
ICD-10-CM *International Classification of Diseases, 10th Revision, Clinical Modification*
ICD-10-PCS *International Classification of Diseases, 10th Revision, Procedure Coding System*
OR Operating Room
PSA prostate-specific antigen
UTI urinary tract infection

ICD-10-CM

Official Guidelines for Coding and Reporting (2021-2022)

Please refer to the companion Evolve site for the most current 2021-2022 guidelines.

18. Chapter 18: Symptoms, signs, and abnormal clinical and laboratory findings, not elsewhere classified (R00-R99)

Chapter 18 includes symptoms, signs, abnormal results of clinical or other investigative procedures, and ill-defined conditions regarding which no diagnosis classifiable elsewhere is recorded. Signs and symptoms that point to a specific diagnosis have been assigned to a category in other chapters of the classification.

a. Use of symptom codes

Codes that describe symptoms and signs are acceptable for reporting purposes when a related definitive diagnosis has not been established (confirmed) by the provider.

EXAMPLE Fever of unknown origin, R50.9.

b. Use of a symptom code with a definitive diagnosis code

Codes for signs and symptoms may be reported in addition to a related definitive diagnosis when the sign or symptom is not routinely associated with that diagnosis, such as the various signs and symptoms associated with complex syndromes. The definitive diagnosis code should be sequenced before the symptom code.

Signs or symptoms that are associated routinely with a disease process should not be assigned as additional codes, unless otherwise instructed by the classification.

EXAMPLE Hematuria due to calculus of kidney, N20.0.

EXAMPLE Ascites due to cirrhosis of the liver, K74.60, R18.8.

c. Combination codes that include symptoms

ICD-10-CM contains a number of combination codes that identify both the definitive diagnosis and common symptoms of that diagnosis. When using one of these combination codes, an additional code should not be assigned for the symptom.

EXAMPLE Acute cystitis with hematuria, N30.01.

d. Repeated falls

Code R29.6, Repeated falls, is for use for encounters when a patient has recently fallen and the reason for the fall is being investigated.

Code Z91.81, History of falling, is for use when a patient has fallen in the past and is at risk for future falls. When appropriate, both codes R29.6 and Z91.81 may be assigned together.

e. Coma scale

The coma scale codes (R40.2-) can be used in conjunction with traumatic brain injury codes. These codes are primarily for use by trauma registries, but they may be used in any setting where this information is collected. The coma scale may also be used to assess the status of the central nervous system for other non-trauma conditions, such as monitoring patients in the intensive care unit regardless of medical condition. The coma scale codes should be sequenced after the diagnosis code(s).

These codes, one from each subcategory, are needed to complete the scale. The 7th character indicates when the scale was recorded. The 7th character should match for all three codes.

At a minimum, report the initial score documented on presentation at your facility. This may be a score from the emergency medicine technician (EMT) or in the emergency department. If desired, a facility may choose to capture multiple coma scale scores.

Assign code R40.24, Glasgow coma scale, total score, when only the total score is documented in the medical record and not the individual score(s).

Do not report codes for individual or total Glasgow coma scale scores for a patient with a medically induced coma or a sedated patient.

See Section I.B.14 for coma scale documentation by clinicians other than patient's provider.

EXAMPLE

Patient had an accident and was admitted in a coma (Glasgow coma score was 5) due to traumatic subdural hemorrhage. Patient expired without regaining consciousness, due to brain injury, S06.5x7A, R40.2433, X58.xxxA.

f. Functional quadriplegia

GUIDELINE HAS BEEN DELETED EFFECTIVE OCTOBER 1, 2017.

g. SIRS due to Non-Infectious Process

The systemic inflammatory response syndrome (SIRS) can develop as a result of certain non-infectious disease processes, such as trauma, malignant neoplasm, or pancreatitis. When SIRS is documented with a noninfectious condition, and no subsequent infection is documented, the code for the underlying condition, such as an injury, should be assigned, followed by code R65.10, Systemic inflammatory response syndrome (SIRS) of non-infectious origin without acute organ dysfunction, or code R65.11, Systemic inflammatory response syndrome (SIRS) of non-infectious origin with acute organ dysfunction. If an associated acute organ dysfunction is documented, the appropriate code(s) for the specific type of organ dysfunction(s) should be assigned in addition to code R65.11. If acute organ dysfunction is documented, but it cannot be determined if the acute organ dysfunction is associated with SIRS or due to another condition (e.g., directly due to the trauma), the provider should be queried.

EXAMPLE

Patient was admitted with acute pancreatitis. Documentation by the physician indicated the patient met SIRS criteria, K85.90, R65.10.

h. Death NOS

Code R99, Ill-defined and unknown cause of mortality, is only for use in the very limited circumstance when a patient who has already died is brought into an emergency department or other healthcare facility and is pronounced dead upon arrival. It does not represent the discharge disposition of death.

i. NIHSS Stroke Scale

The NIH stroke scale (NIHSS) codes (R29.7- -) can be used in conjunction with acute stroke codes (I63) to identify the patient's neurological status and the severity of the stroke. The stroke scale codes should be sequenced after the acute stroke diagnosis code(s).

At a minimum, report the initial score documented. If desired, a facility may choose to capture multiple stroke scale scores.

See Section I.B.14. for NIHSS stroke scale documentation by clinicians other than patient's provider.

EXAMPLE

Patient was admitted to the hospital for treatment of acute cerebral infarction. At the time of admission, the patient's NIHSS score was 25. I63.9, N29.725.

ANATOMY AND PHYSIOLOGY

Signs, symptoms, and abnormal clinical and laboratory findings, and Z codes can affect any of the body systems. The anatomy and physiology of these body systems are outlined in their respective chapters.

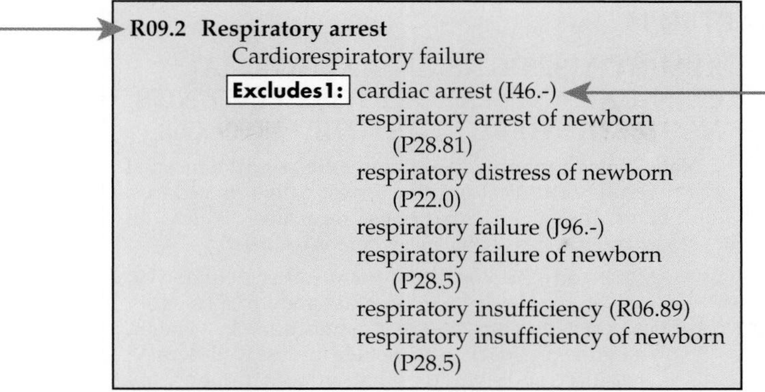
R09.2 Respiratory arrest
Cardiorespiratory failure
Excludes1: cardiac arrest (I46.-)
respiratory arrest of newborn (P28.81)
respiratory distress of newborn (P22.0)
respiratory failure (J96.-)
respiratory failure of newborn (P28.5)
respiratory insufficiency (R06.89)
respiratory insufficiency of newborn (P28.5)

FIGURE 9-1. Excludes1 note in ICD-10-CM.

DISEASE CONDITIONS

Chapter 18 in the ICD-10-CM code book is divided into the following categories:

CATEGORY	SECTION TITLES
R00-R09	Symptoms and signs involving the circulatory and respiratory systems
R10-R19	Symptoms and signs involving the digestive system and abdomen
R20-R23	Symptoms and signs involving the skin and subcutaneous tissue
R25-R29	Symptoms and signs involving the nervous and musculoskeletal systems
R30-R39	Symptoms and signs involving the genitourinary system
R40-R46	Symptoms and signs involving cognition, perception, emotional state, and behavior
R47-R49	Symptoms and signs involving speech and voice
R50-R69	General symptoms and signs
R70-R79	Abnormal findings on examination of blood, without diagnosis
R80-R82	Abnormal findings on examination of urine, without diagnosis
R83-R89	Abnormal findings on examination of other bloody fluids, substances, and tissues, without diagnosis
R90-R94	Abnormal findings on diagnostic imaging and in function studies, without diagnosis
R97	Abnormal tumor markers
R99	Ill-defined and unknown cause of mortality

See Figure 9-2 for details on an instructional note that appears at the very beginning of Chapter 18 of the Tabular List and applies to the entire chapter. This note provides information on the appropriate use of signs and symptoms codes.

Chapter 21 (Z codes) in the ICD-10-CM code book is divided into the following categories:

CATEGORY	SECTION TITLES
Z00-Z13	Persons encountering health services for examinations
Z14-Z15	Genetic carrier and genetic susceptibility to disease
Z16	Resistance to antimicrobial drugs
Z17	Estrogen receptor status
Z18	Retained foreign body fragments
Z20-Z29	Persons with potential health hazards related to communicable disease
Z30-Z39	Persons encountering health services in circumstances related to reproduction
Z40-Z53	Encounters for other specific health care
Z55-Z65	Persons with potential health hazards related to socioeconomic and psychosocial circumstances
Z66	Do Not Resuscitate status
Z67	Blood type
Z68	Body mass index (BMI)
Z69-Z76	Persons encountering health services in other circumstances
Z79-Z99	Persons with potential health hazards related to family and personal history and certain conditions influencing health status

CHAPTER 18

SYMPTOMS, SIGNS AND ABNORMAL CLINICAL AND LABORATORY FINDINGS, NOT ELSEWHERE CLASSIFIED (R00-R99)

Note: This chapter includes symptoms, signs, abnormal results of clinical or other investigative procedures, and ill-defined conditions regarding which no diagnosis classifiable elsewhere is recorded.

Signs and symptoms that point rather definitely to a given diagnosis have been assigned to a category in other chapters of the classification. In general, categories in this chapter include the less well-defined conditions and symptoms that, without the necessary study of the case to establish a final diagnosis, point perhaps equally to two or more diseases or to two or more systems of the body. Practically all categories in the chapter could be designated 'not otherwise specified', 'unknown etiology' or 'transient'. The Alphabetical Index should be consulted to determine which symptoms and signs are to be allocated here and which to other chapters. The residual subcategories, numbered .8, are generally provided for other relevant symptoms that cannot be allocated elsewhere in the classification.

The conditions and signs or symptoms included in categories R00-R94 consist of:

(a) cases for which no more specific diagnosis can be made even after all the facts bearing on the case have been investigated;
(b) signs or symptoms existing at the time of initial encounter that proved to be transient and whose causes could not be determined;
(c) provisional diagnosis in a patient who failed to return for further investigation or care;
(d) cases referred elsewhere for investigation or treatment before the diagnosis was made;
(e) cases in which a more precise diagnosis was not available for any other reason;
(f) certain symptoms, for which supplementary information is provided, that represent important problems in medical care in their own right.

Excludes2 abnormal findings on antenatal screening of mother (O28.-)
certain conditions originating in the perinatal period (P04-P96)
signs and symptoms classified in the body system chapters
signs and symptoms of breast (N63, N64.5)

FIGURE 9-2. Instructional note that appears at the beginning of Chapter 18.

A few Z code guidelines are explained within the various chapter guidelines; these will be addressed in those chapters. Some of them are repeated in the guidelines for Z codes and are reviewed in this chapter. These codes are addressed at the beginning of the book because they apply to all body systems. Z codes and signs and symptoms are common throughout this text.

Symptoms and Signs (R00-R69)

A **symptom** is subjective evidence of a disease or of a patient's condition as perceived by the patient.

Examples are fatigue, headache, and some types of pain. Symptoms may not be apparent to a physician on physical examination.

EXAMPLE

The patient presents to the ER complaining of a severe headache. The headache is an example of a symptom because it is a description of the patient's condition as perceived by the patient, R51.9.

A **sign** is objective evidence of a disease or of a patient's condition as perceived by the patient's examining physician.

Examples are elevated blood pressure, which can be measured or icterus and edema of the legs, which can be seen on physical examination.

EXAMPLE

The patient has a fever. This can be discerned by noting the patient's elevated temperature, R50.9.

It can be difficult to determine whether a sign or a symptom from Chapter 18 is routinely associated with the disease. It may be necessary to access resource books, such as *Merck's Manual,* or the Internet to find the most common symptoms of a disease or condition. As was previously stated in Chapter 5 of this text, signs and symptoms codes are acceptable to code:

- When no definitive diagnosis has been established
- When they are not an integral part of the disease process
- When directed by the classification to assign an additional code
- When a sign or symptom affects the patient's condition or the treatment given

It is not acceptable to code signs or symptoms:

- When a definitive diagnosis has been established
- When they are an integral part of the disease process

There are some ICD-10-CM combination codes that include a common symptom of that diagnosis. For example, cystitis with hematuria is coded to N30.91 cystitis, unspecified with hematuria. The symptom hematuria is part of this combination code.

EXAMPLE

Fever due to pneumonia, J18.9.

Fever is one of the symptoms of pneumonia that is integral to the disease process. Only the pneumonia should be coded.

EXAMPLE

Dehydration due to pneumonia, J18.9, E86.0.

Although many patients who are admitted to the hospital may be dehydrated, not all patients who have pneumonia become dehydrated.

EXAMPLE

Patient was admitted with right lower quadrant abdominal pain with nausea and vomiting. Patient has a low-grade fever. A diagnosis of acute appendicitis was confirmed upon removal of the patient's appendix via open approach in the Operating Room (OR), K35.80, 0DTJ0ZZ. The fever, abdominal pain, and nausea/vomiting are all symptoms of appendicitis and are not coded.

EXAMPLE

Patient has Type 1 diabetes and was admitted with diabetic ketoacidosis and was in a coma E10.11. The coma is included in the diabetic combination code, and a symptom code R40.20 would not be separately assigned.

Refer to Chapter 5 for general coding guidelines that relate to the coding of signs and symptoms. Also review the guidelines for selection of a principal diagnosis when a symptom is involved.

National Institutes of Health Stroke Scale (NIHSS)

The National Institutes of Health Stroke Scale score is a clinical assessment tool used to evaluate and monitor the neurologic status in acute stroke patients. The scale can be useful in measuring the severity of a stroke and as a predictor of short- and long-term outcomes. The NIHSS scale is a 15-item neurologic exam that assesses levels of consciousness, language, neglect, visual-field loss, extraocular movement, motor strength, ataxia, dysarthria, and sensory loss.

There is an instructional note in the Tabular under code R29.7- that states to code first the type of cerebral infarction. The NIHSS scores range from 0–42, with a corresponding code for each score. A code may be assigned based on clinician documentation as long as the acute stroke is documented by a healthcare provider.

EXAMPLE

Patient was admitted with acute cerebrovascular accident due to embolism of the right middle cerebral artery. An NIHSS score of 30 is documented by the ER nurse, I63.411, R29.730.

Glasgow Coma Scale (GCS)

The Glasgow Coma Scale was developed to describe the level of consciousness in patients with an acute brain injury. The scoring is based on the response to defined stimuli in relation to eye opening, verbal response, and motor response. According to the *Official Coding Guidelines for Coding and Reporting*, it is acceptable to assign codes from subcategory R40.2- for conditions other than acute brain injury or acute cerebrovascular disease or sequelae. The GCS may be used as an assessment tool to monitor patients with all types of central nervous system conditions regardless of the cause. A GCS code requires a 7th character to indicate when the scale was recorded. The 7th characters include:

0	unspecified time
1	in the field (EMT or ambulance)
2	at arrival to emergency department
3	at hospital admission
4	24 hours or more after hospital admission

It is recommended that the initial score documented on arrival at the hospital be assigned. Additional GCS codes may be assigned based on a facility's policy. A code may be assigned based on clinician documentation. If the documentation is available to assign individual scores for motor response, opening of eyes, and verbal response, all three codes should be assigned, and the 7th character should be the same for all three. When the individual scores are not documented or only partially documented, it is acceptable to assign the total score.

EXAMPLE

Patient was admitted in a coma due to viral hepatitis C. GCS documented by ICU nurse on admission to the hospital was 10, B19.21, R40.2423.

EXERCISE 9-1

Assign codes to the following conditions.

1. Alteration in mental status ____________
2. Fever of unknown origin (FUO) ____________
3. Right upper quadrant abdominal pain ____________
4. Ascites due to cirrhosis of liver ____________
5. Oliguria ____________
6. Palpitations ____________

7. Change in bowel habits ______________
8. Precordial chest pain ______________
9. Loss of appetite ______________
10. Ataxia ______________
11. Cerebrovascular accident (stroke) with NIHSS score 35 ______________
12. Type 1 diabetes with hypoglycemic coma. Nursing documents GCS 8 at the time of admission ______________

Abnormal Findings and Abnormal Tumor Markers (R70-R97)

Many times, an abnormality or elevation in a test result will lead to further investigation or repeat performance of certain tests. The patient may be without any signs or symptoms, and no definitive diagnosis may explain the abnormality. Some of the main terms that may be used to assist with location of these codes include "abnormal," "abnormality," "abnormalities," "elevation," and "findings, abnormal, inconclusive, without diagnosis." These abnormal findings must be documented by the physician to be coded. A coder should not code an abnormal finding on the basis of a review of laboratory results or reports of other diagnostic procedures.

EXAMPLE

Patient was seen by urologist because of an elevated PSA, R97.20.

EXAMPLE

Abnormal lung x-ray. Patient will be scheduled for a computerized tomography (CT) of the chest, R91.8.

EXERCISE 9-2

Assign codes to the following conditions.

1. Significant drop in hematocrit ______________
2. Abnormal coagulation profile ______________
3. Proteinuria ______________
4. Abnormal Pap smear (cervix) with atypical squamous cells of undetermined significance (ASCUS) ______________
5. Abnormal mammogram ______________
6. Bacteremia ______________
7. Abnormal lead levels in blood ______________
8. Positive Mantoux test ______________
9. Elevated CA-125 ______________
10. Transaminasemia ______________

FACTORS INFLUENCING HEALTH STATUS AND CONTACT WITH HEALTH SERVICES (Z CODES Z00-Z99)

The Z codes are located in Chapter 21. According to the guidelines, ICD-10-CM provides codes that should be assigned to encounters for circumstances other than a disease or injury. The Z codes are provided to deal with occasions when circumstances other than a disease or injury are recorded as a diagnosis or problem.

Assignment of Z codes can be problematic because some can be used only as the principal diagnosis, others can be used as both principal and secondary diagnoses, and some can be used only as secondary diagnoses. It can be difficult to locate Z codes in the Alphabetic Index. Coders will often say, "I did not know there was a Z code for that." It is very important to be familiar with the different types and uses of Z codes. Because appropriate main terms are difficult to find in the Alphabetic Index, some common main terms are as follows:

Admission	Donor	Procedure (surgical)
Aftercare	Examination	Prophylactic
Attention to	Fitting of	Removal
Boarder	Healthy	Replacement
Care (of)	History	Screening
Carrier	Maintenance	Status
Checking	Maladjustment	Supervision (of)
Contraception	Observation	Test
Counseling	Problem	Transplant
Dialysis		Unavailability (of)
		Vaccination

Guidelines for Z codes provide a lot of detail and descriptions of the various sections of Z codes. It may be necessary to review these guidelines frequently; Z codes will also be addressed in most of the following chapters because some Z codes are specific to certain body systems.

Screening Z codes should be assigned only when the service fits the definition of a screening. A **screening examination** is one that occurs in the absence of any signs or symptoms. It consists of examination of an asymptomatic individual to detect a given disease, typically by means of an inexpensive diagnostic test. There are Z codes for prophylactic organ removal. A **prophylactic** measure is the use of medication or treatment to prevent a disease from occurring. A patient who has a bilateral mastectomy because of a strong family history of breast cancer and genetic susceptibility is an example of prophylactic treatment.

EXAMPLE

Encounter for screening mammogram for 45-year-old female patient, Z12.31.

EXAMPLE

Encounter for screening mammogram in a 45-year-old female patient with nipple discharge, N64.52.

In the second example, even though it was documented as a screening mammogram, it does not fit the definition because the nipple discharge is a symptom and a reason for the test. It would be inappropriate to assign the screening Z code.

Several Z codes identify the history of certain conditions. Documentation of a patient's medical and surgical history may be found within the History and Physical or the Admit Note. Sometimes, documentation in the health record may indicate a history of a particular disease or condition, and the disease or condition is actually a current or active problem. If any question arises as to whether a condition is currently an active problem, a physician query may be necessary.

Relevant family history is often documented. It may be important to code a family history of malignant neoplasm of the breast when a patient has been admitted with breast cancer and is having a mastectomy. In the Index under "History," "Family history" is a subterm, and it is found before the personal history Index entries (Figure 9-3).

EXAMPLE

Patient has a past history of chronic obstructive pulmonary disease (COPD). You would not assign a Z code to indicate a previous history of a respiratory condition but the code for the active disease. COPD is a chronic condition that cannot be cured, J44.9.

Histoplasmosis *(Continued)*
  capsulati B39.4
    disseminated B39.3
    generalized B39.3
    pulmonary B39.2
      acute B39.0
      chronic B39.1
  Darling's B39.4
  duboisii B39.5
  lung NEC B39.2
History
  family (of) —*see also* History, personal (of)
    alcohol abuse Z81.1
    allergy NEC Z84.89
    anemia Z83.2
    arthritis Z82.61
    asthma Z82.5
    blindness Z82.1
    cardiac death (sudden) Z82.41
    carrier of genetic disease Z84.81
    chromosomal anomaly Z82.79
    chronic
      disabling disease NEC Z82.8
      lower respiratory disease Z82.5
    colonic polyps Z83.71
    congenital malformations and deformations Z82.79
      polycystic kidney Z82.71
    consanguinity Z84.3
    deafness Z82.2
    diabetes mellitus Z83.3
    disability NEC Z82.8
    disease or disorder (of)
      allergic NEC Z84.89
      behavioral NEC Z81.8
      blood and blood-forming organs Z83.2
      cardiovascular NEC Z82.49
      chronic disabling NEC Z82.8
      digestive Z83.79
      ear NEC Z83.52
      endocrine NEC Z83.49
      eye NEC Z83.518
        glaucoma Z83.511
      genitourinary NEC Z84.2
      glaucoma Z83.511
      hematological Z83.2
      immune mechanism Z83.2
      infectious NEC Z83.1
      ischemic heart Z82.49
      kidney Z84.1
      mental NEC Z81.8
      metabolic Z83.49
      musculoskeletal NEC Z82.69
      neurological NEC Z82.0
      nutritional Z83.49
      parasitic NEC Z83.1
      psychiatric NEC Z81.8
      respiratory NEC Z83.6
      skin and subcutaneous tissue NEC Z84.0
      specified NEC Z84.89
    drug abuse NEC Z81.3
    elevated lipoprotein(a) Z83.430
    epilepsy Z82.0
    genetic disease carrier Z84.81
    glaucoma Z83.511
    hearing loss Z82.2
    human immunodeficiency virus (HIV) infection Z83.0
    Huntington's chorea Z82.0
    intellectual disability Z81.0
    leukemia Z80.6

Family history index entries

History *(Continued)*
  family *(Continued)*
    malignant neoplasm (of) NOS Z80.9
      bladder Z80.52
      breast Z80.3
      bronchus Z80.1
      digestive organ Z80.0
      gastrointestinal tract Z80.0
      genital organ Z80.49
        ovary Z80.41
        prostate Z80.42
        specified organ NEC Z80.49
        testis Z80.43
      hematopoietic NEC Z80.7
      intrathoracic organ NEC Z80.2
      kidney Z80.51
      lung Z80.1
      lymphatic NEC Z80.7
      ovary Z80.41
      prostate Z80.42
      respiratory organ NEC Z80.2
      specified site NEC Z80.8
      testis Z80.43
      trachea Z80.1
      urinary organ or tract Z80.59
        bladder Z80.52
        kidney Z80.51
    mental
      disorder NEC Z81.8
    multiple endocrine neoplasia (MEN) syndrome Z83.41
    osteoporosis Z82.62
    polycystic kidney Z82.71
    polyps (colon) Z83.71
    psychiatric disorder Z81.8
    psychoactive substance abuse NEC Z81.3
    respiratory condition NEC Z83.6
      asthma and other lower respiratory conditions Z82.5
    self-harmful behavior Z81.8
    skin condition Z84.0
    specified condition NEC Z84.89
    stroke (cerebrovascular) Z82.3
    substance abuse NEC Z81.4
      alcohol Z81.1
      drug NEC Z81.3
      psychoactive NEC Z81.3
      tobacco Z81.2
    sudden cardiac death Z82.41
    tobacco abuse Z81.2
    violence, violent behavior Z81.8
    visual loss Z82.1
  personal (of) —*see also* History, family (of)
    abuse
      adult Z91.419
        physical and sexual Z91.410
        psychological Z91.411
      childhood Z62.819
        physical Z62.810
        psychological Z62.811
        sexual Z62.810
    alcohol dependence F10.21
    allergy (to) Z88.9
      analgesic agent NEC Z88.6
      anesthetic Z88.4
      antibiotic agent NEC Z88.1
      anti-infective agent NEC Z88.3
      contrast media Z91.041
      drugs, medicaments and biological unspecified substances Z88.9
        specified NEC Z88.8

Personal history index entries

FIGURE 9-3. Family and personal history Alphabetic Index entries.

EXAMPLE

The patient has a history of urinary tract infections (UTIs). In this case, no documentation, such as antibiotic therapy, to indicate that the patient currently has a UTI, so a history of UTI Z code is appropriate, Z87.440.

EXAMPLE

Family history of polycystic kidney disease, Z82.71.

EXAMPLE

Personal history of exposure to asbestos, Z77.090.

ICD-10-CM

Official Guidelines for Coding and Reporting (2021-2022)

Please refer to the companion Evolve site for the most current 2021-2022 guidelines.

21. Chapter 21: Factors influencing health status and contact with health services (Z00-Z99)

Note: The chapter specific guidelines provide additional information about the use of Z codes for specified encounters.

a. Use of Z codes in any healthcare setting

Z codes are for use in any healthcare setting. Z codes may be used as either a first-listed (principal diagnosis code in the inpatient setting) or secondary code, depending on the circumstances of the encounter. Certain Z codes may only be used as first-listed or principal diagnosis.

b. Z Codes indicate a reason for an encounter

Z codes are not procedure codes. A corresponding procedure code must accompany a Z code to describe any procedure performed.

EXAMPLE

A female patient was admitted for elective sterilization and percutaneous endoscopic bilateral tubal occlusion with Falope ring was performed, Z30.2, 0UL74CZ.

c. Categories of Z Codes

1) Contact/Exposure

Category Z20 indicates contact with, and suspected exposure to, communicable diseases. These codes are for patients who are suspected to have been exposed to a disease by close personal contact with an infected individual or are in an area where a disease is epidemic.

Category Z77, Other contact with and (suspected) exposures hazardous to health, indicates contact with and suspected exposures hazardous to health.

Contact/exposure codes may be used as a first-listed code to explain an encounter for testing, or, more commonly, as a secondary code to identify a potential risk.

EXAMPLE

Exposure to anthrax, Z20.810.

2) Inoculations and vaccinations

Code Z23 is for encounters for inoculations and vaccinations. It indicates that a patient is being seen to receive a prophylactic inoculation against a disease. Procedure codes are required to identify the actual administration of the injection and the type(s) of immunizations given. Code Z23 may be used as a secondary code if the inoculation is given as a routine part of preventive health care, such as a well-baby visit.

EXAMPLE

Vaccination for influenza (intramuscular), Z23, 3E0234Z.

3) Status

Status codes indicate that a patient is either a carrier of a disease or has the sequelae or residual of a past disease or condition. This includes such things as the presence of prosthetic or mechanical devices resulting from past treatment. A status code is informative, because the status may affect the course of treatment and its outcome. A status code is distinct from a history code. The history code indicates that the patient no longer has the condition.

A status code should not be used with a diagnosis code from one of the body system chapters, if the diagnosis code includes the information provided by the status code. For example, code Z94.1, Heart transplant status, should not be used with a code from subcategory T86.2, Complications of heart transplant. The status code does not provide additional information. The complication code indicates that the patient is a heart transplant patient.

For encounters for weaning from a mechanical ventilator, assign a code from subcategory J96.1, Chronic respiratory failure, followed by code Z99.11, Dependence on respirator [ventilator] status.

The status Z codes/categories are:

Z14 Genetic carrier
Genetic carrier status indicates that a person carries a gene, associated with a particular disease, which may be passed to offspring who may develop that disease. The person does not have the disease and is not at risk of developing the disease.

Z15 Genetic susceptibility to disease
Genetic susceptibility indicates that a person has a gene that increases the risk of that person developing the disease.
Codes from category Z15 should not be used as principal or first-listed codes. If the patient has the condition to which he/she is susceptible, and that condition is the reason for the encounter, the code for the current condition should be sequenced first. If the patient is being seen for follow-up after completed treatment for this condition, and the condition no longer exists, a follow-up code should be sequenced first, followed by the appropriate personal history and genetic susceptibility codes. If the purpose of the encounter is genetic counseling associated with procreative management, code Z31.5, Encounter for genetic counseling, should be assigned as the first-listed code, followed by a code from category Z15. Additional codes should be assigned for any applicable family or personal history.

Z16 Resistance to antimicrobial drugs
This code indicates that a patient has a condition that is resistant to antimicrobial drug treatment. Sequence the infection code first.

Z17 Estrogen receptor status

Z18 Retained foreign body fragments

Z19 Hormone sensitivity malignancy status

Z21 Asymptomatic HIV infection status
This code indicates that a patient has tested positive for HIV but has manifested no signs or symptoms of the disease.

Z22 Carrier of infectious disease
Carrier status indicates that a person harbors the specific organisms of a disease without manifest symptoms and is capable of transmitting the infection.

Z28.3 Underimmunization status

Z33.1 Pregnant state, incidental
This code is a secondary code only for use when the pregnancy is in no way complicating the reason for visit. Otherwise, a code from the obstetric chapter is required.

Z66 Do not resuscitate
This code may be used when it is documented by the provider that a patient is on do not resuscitate status at any time during the stay.

Z67 Blood type

Z68 Body mass index (BMI)
BMI codes should only be assigned when there is an associated, reportable diagnosis (such as obesity). Do not assign BMI codes during pregnancy.

See Section I.B.14 for BMI documentation by clinicians other than the patient's provider.

Z74.01	Bed confinement status
Z76.82	Awaiting organ transplant status
Z78	Other specified health status Code Z78.1, Physical restraint status, may be used when it is documented by the provider that a patient has been put in restraints during the current encounter. Please note that this code should not be reported when it is documented by the provider that a patient is temporarily restrained during a procedure.
Z79	Long-term (current) drug therapy Codes from this category indicate a patient's continuous use of a prescribed drug (including such things as aspirin therapy) for the long-term treatment of a condition or for prophylactic use. It is not for use for patients who have addictions to drugs. This subcategory is not for use of medications for detoxification or maintenance programs to prevent withdrawal symptoms in patients with drug dependence (e.g., methadone maintenance for opiate dependence). Assign the appropriate code for the drug use, abuse, or dependence instead. Assign a code from Z79 if the patient is receiving a medication for an extended period as a prophylactic measure (such as for the prevention of deep vein thrombosis) or as treatment of a chronic condition (such as arthritis) or a disease requiring a lengthy course of treatment (such as cancer). Do not assign a code from category Z79 for medication being administered for a brief period of time to treat an acute illness or injury (such as a course of antibiotics to treat acute bronchitis).
Z88	Allergy status to drugs, medicaments and biological substances Except: Z88.9, Allergy status to unspecified drugs, medicaments and biological substances status
Z89	Acquired absence of limb
Z90	Acquired absence of organs, not elsewhere classified
Z91.0-	Allergy status, other than to drugs and biological substances
Z92.82	Status post administration of tPA (rtPA) in a different facility within the last 24 hours prior to admission to a current facility Assign code Z92.82, Status post administration of tPA (rtPA) in a different facility within the last 24 hours prior to admission to current facility, as a secondary diagnosis when a patient is received by transfer into a facility and documentation indicates they were administered tissue plasminogen activator (tPA) within the last 24 hours prior to admission to the current facility. This guideline applies even if the patient is still receiving the tPA at the time they are received into the current facility. The appropriate code for the condition for which the tPA was administered (such as cerebrovascular disease or myocardial infarction) should be assigned first. Code Z92.82 is only applicable to the receiving facility record and not to the transferring facility record.
Z93	Artificial opening status
Z94	Transplanted organ and tissue status
Z95	Presence of cardiac and vascular implants and grafts
Z96	Presence of other functional implants
Z97	Presence of other devices
Z98	Other postprocedural states Assign code Z98.85, Transplanted organ removal status, to indicate that a transplanted organ has been previously removed. This code should not be assigned for the encounter in which the transplanted organ is removed. The complication necessitating removal of the transplant organ should be assigned for that encounter. *See section I.C.19. for information on the coding of organ transplant complications.*
Z99	Dependence on enabling machines and devices, not elsewhere classified **Note:** Categories Z89-Z90 and Z93-Z99 are for use only if there are no complications or malfunctions of the organ or tissue replaced, the amputation site or the equipment on which the patient is dependent.

EXAMPLE

A patient was admitted for myocardial infarction. The patient is status post (presence of) mitral valve replacement with porcine valve, I21.3, Z95.3.

Z79.- is assigned to identify the long-term use of a particular drug or medication. To locate these codes in the Alphabetic Index, the main term is "long-term drug therapy." These codes should not be used to identify drug abuse or dependence or to identify a medication that is used for a short period during an acute illness or injury. Drugs may be used to prevent a condition as a prophylactic measure or to treat a chronic condition. Sometimes a patient will need to have lab work to monitor the effectiveness of a particular medication or if the medication is causing any adverse effects. Code Z51.81 encounter for therapeutic drug monitoring would be assigned.

EXAMPLE

Patient has been taking Lipitor for hypercholesterolemia for one year. A hepatic function laboratory test was performed to assess any adverse effects on the patient's liver function. A fasting lipid profile was also done to assess the effectiveness of the Lipitor, Z51.81, Z79.899, E78.00.

In this example, the long-term use of Lipitor is identified with code Z79.899, long-term drug therapy of other medications, because the patient has been taking it for a year.

EXAMPLE

Patient was seen in the ER for acute bronchitis. The patient's family physician had seen the patient a couple of days ago and prescribed antibiotics. The patient was instructed to finish the antibiotics and follow-up with family physician, J20.9.

In this example the use of antibiotics is not assigned a Z code because it is only used for a short period of time to treat an acute illness.

4) History (of)

There are two types of history Z codes, personal and family. Personal history codes explain a patient's past medical condition that no longer exists and is not receiving any treatment, but that has the potential for recurrence, and therefore may require continued monitoring.

Family history codes are for use when a patient has a family member(s) who has had a particular disease that causes the patient to be at higher risk of also contracting the disease.

Personal history codes may be used in conjunction with follow-up codes and family history codes may be used in conjunction with screening codes to explain the need for a test or procedure. History codes are also acceptable on any medical record regardless of the reason for visit. A history of an illness, even if no longer present, is important information that may alter the type of treatment ordered.

The history Z code categories are:

Z80	Family history of primary malignant neoplasm
Z81	Family history of mental and behavioral disorders
Z82	Family history of certain disabilities and chronic diseases (leading to disablement)
Z83	Family history of other specific disorders
Z84	Family history of other conditions
Z85	Personal history of malignant neoplasm
Z86	Personal history of certain other diseases
Z87	Personal history of other diseases and conditions
Z91.4-	Personal history of psychological trauma, not elsewhere classified
Z91.5	Personal history of self-harm
Z91.81	History of falling
Z91.82	Personal history of military deployment
Z92	Personal history of medical treatment Except: Z92.0, Personal history of contraception Except: Z92.82, Status post administration of tPA (rtPA) in a different facility within the last 24 hours prior to admission to a current facility

EXAMPLE A patient was admitted with congestive heart failure and coronary artery disease. The patient has a history of coronary artery bypass graft (presence of) and a family history of coronary artery disease, I50.9, I25.10, Z95.1, Z82.49.

5) Screening

Screening is the testing for disease or disease precursors in seemingly well individuals so that early detection and treatment can be provided for those who test positive for the disease (e.g., screening mammogram).

The testing of a person to rule out or confirm a suspected diagnosis because the patient has some sign or symptom is a diagnostic examination, not a screening. In these cases, the sign or symptom is used to explain the reason for the test.

A screening code may be a first-listed code if the reason for the visit is specifically the screening exam. It may also be used as an additional code if the screening is done during an office visit for other health problems. A screening code is not necessary if the screening is inherent to a routine examination, such as a pap smear done during a routine pelvic examination.

Should a condition be discovered during the screening then the code for the condition may be assigned as an additional diagnosis.

The Z code indicates that a screening exam is planned. A procedure code is required to confirm that the screening was performed.

The screening Z codes/categories:

Z11	Encounter for screening for infectious and parasitic diseases
Z12	Encounter for screening for malignant neoplasms
Z13	Encounter for screening for other diseases and disorders
	Except: Z13.9, Encounter for screening, unspecified
Z36	Encounter for antenatal screening for mother

EXAMPLE Encounter for screening for colon cancer, Z12.11.

6) Observation

There are three observation Z code categories. They are for use in very limited circumstances when a person is being observed for a suspected condition that is ruled out. The observation codes are not for use if an injury or illness or any signs or symptoms related to the suspected condition are present. In such cases the diagnosis/symptom code is used with the corresponding external cause code.

The observation codes are primarily to be used as principal/first-listed diagnosis. An observation code may be assigned as a secondary diagnosis code when the patient is being observed for a condition that is ruled out and is unrelated to the principal/first-listed diagnosis (e.g., patient presents for treatment following injuries sustained in a motor vehicle accident and is also observed for suspected COVID-19 infection that is subsequently ruled out). Also, when the principal diagnosis is required to be a code from category Z38, Liveborn infants according to place of birth and type of delivery, then a code from category Z05, Encounter for observation and evaluation of newborn for suspected diseases and conditions ruled out, is sequenced after the Z38 code. Additional codes may be used in addition to the observation code, but only if they are unrelated to the suspected condition being observed.

Codes from subcategory Z03.7, Encounter for suspected maternal and fetal conditions ruled out, may either be used as a first-listed or as an additional code assignment depending on the case. They are for use in very limited circumstances on a maternal record when an encounter is for a suspected maternal or fetal condition that is ruled out during that encounter (for example, a maternal or fetal condition may be suspected due to an abnormal test result). These codes should not be used when the condition is confirmed. In those cases, the confirmed condition should be coded. In addition, these codes are not for use if an illness or any signs or symptoms related to the suspected condition or problem are present. In such cases the diagnosis/symptom code is used.

Additional codes may be used in addition to the code from subcategory Z03.7, but only if they are unrelated to the suspected condition being evaluated.

Codes from subcategory Z03.7 may not be used for encounters for antenatal screening of mother. *See Section I.C.21. Screening.*

For encounters for suspected fetal condition that are inconclusive following testing and evaluation, assign the appropriate code from category O35, O36, O40 or O41.

The observation Z code categories:

Z03	Encounter for medical observation for suspected diseases and conditions ruled out
Z04	Encounter for examination and observation for other reasons Except: Z04.9, Encounter for examination and observation for unspecified reason
Z05	Encounter for observation and evaluation of newborn for suspected diseases and conditions ruled out

EXAMPLE

The driver of a car was admitted for observation after a rollover on the highway, Z04.1.

7) Aftercare

Aftercare visit codes cover situations when the initial treatment of a disease has been performed and the patient requires continued care during the healing or recovery phase, or for the long-term consequences of the disease. The aftercare Z code should not be used if treatment is directed at a current, acute disease. The diagnosis code is to be used in these cases. Exceptions to this rule are codes Z51.0, Encounter for antineoplastic radiation therapy, and codes from subcategory Z51.1, Encounter for antineoplastic chemotherapy and immunotherapy. These codes are to be first-listed, followed by the diagnosis code when a patient's encounter is solely to receive radiation therapy, chemotherapy, or immunotherapy for the treatment of a neoplasm. If the reason for the encounter is more than one type of antineoplastic therapy, code Z51.0 and a code from subcategory Z51.1 may be assigned together, in which case one of these codes would be reported as a secondary diagnosis.

The aftercare Z codes should also not be used for aftercare for injuries. For aftercare of an injury, assign the acute injury code with the appropriate 7th character (for subsequent encounter).

The aftercare codes are generally first-listed to explain the specific reason for the encounter. An aftercare code may be used as an additional code when some type of aftercare is provided in addition to the reason for admission and no diagnosis code is applicable. An example of this would be the closure of a colostomy during an encounter for treatment of another condition.

Aftercare codes should be used in conjunction with other aftercare codes or diagnosis codes to provide better detail on the specifics of an aftercare encounter visit, unless otherwise directed by the classification. The sequencing of multiple aftercare codes depends on the circumstances of the encounter.

Certain aftercare Z code categories need a secondary diagnosis code to describe the resolving condition or sequelae. For others, the condition is included in the code title.

Additional Z code aftercare category terms include fitting and adjustment, and attention to artificial openings.

EXAMPLE

A patient was admitted for open takedown of a colostomy placed 3 months ago for diverticular disease. The descending colon was anastomosed to the rectum without any excision of colon. Patient still has diverticulosis of the colon, Z43.3, K57.30, 0DQM0ZZ.

Status Z codes may be used with aftercare Z codes to indicate the nature of the aftercare. For example code Z95.1, Presence of aortocoronary bypass graft, may be used with code Z48.812, Encounter for surgical aftercare following surgery on the circulatory system, to indicate the surgery for which the aftercare is being performed. A status code should not be used when the aftercare code indicates the type of status, such as using Z43.0, Encounter for attention to tracheostomy, with Z93.0, Tracheostomy status.

The aftercare Z category/codes:

Z42	Encounter for plastic and reconstructive surgery following medical procedure or healed injury
Z43	Encounter for attention to artificial openings
Z44	Encounter for fitting and adjustment of external prosthetic device
Z45	Encounter for adjustment and management of implanted device
Z46	Encounter for fitting and adjustment of other devices
Z47	Orthopedic aftercare
Z48	Encounter for other postprocedural aftercare
Z49	Encounter for care involving renal dialysis
Z51	Encounter for other aftercare and medical care

Palliative care or comfort care is a specialized type of treatment that is given to patients who are terminal. The focus of the treatment is symptom management and pain control. Palliative care can be provided in a variety of healthcare settings including hospitals and hospice/home care. If a patient receives palliative care during an encounter it is appropriate to assign Z51.5, Encounter for palliative care. Z51.5 is not assigned as the reason for the encounter, but the terminal condition or underlying disease should be sequenced first.

EXAMPLE Patient was admitted to hospice care for treatment of terminal ESRD, N18.6, Z51.5.

8) Follow-up

The follow-up codes are used to explain continuing surveillance following completed treatment of a disease, condition, or injury. They imply that the condition has been fully treated and no longer exists. They should not be confused with aftercare codes, or injury codes with a 7th character for subsequent encounter, that explain ongoing care of a healing condition or its sequelae. Follow-up codes may be used in conjunction with history codes to provide the full picture of the healed condition and its treatment. The follow-up code is sequenced first, followed by the history code.

A follow-up code may be used to explain multiple visits. Should a condition be found to have recurred on the follow-up visit, then the diagnosis code for the condition should be assigned in place of the follow-up code.

The follow-up Z code categories:

Z08	Encounter for follow-up examination after completed treatment for malignant neoplasm
Z09	Encounter for follow-up examination after completed treatment for conditions other than malignant neoplasm
Z39	Encounter for maternal postpartum care and examination

EXAMPLE Routine postpartum follow-up at 6 weeks. No problem or medical issues, Z39.2.

9) Donor

Codes in category Z52, Donors of organs and tissues, are used for living individuals who are donating blood or other body tissue. These codes are only for individuals donating for others, not for self-donations. They are not used to identify cadaveric donations.

EXAMPLE Patient is donating a kidney. A left laparoscopic nephrectomy was performed, Z52.4, 0TT14ZZ.

10) Counseling

Counseling Z codes are used when a patient or family member receives assistance in the aftermath of an illness or injury, or when support is required in coping with family or social problems.

The counseling Z codes/categories:

Z30.0-	Encounter for general counseling and advice on contraception
Z31.5	Encounter for procreative genetic counseling
Z31.6-	Encounter for general counseling and advice on procreation
Z32.2	Encounter for childbirth instruction
Z32.3	Encounter for childcare instruction
Z69	Encounter for mental health services for victim and perpetrator of abuse
Z70	Counseling related to sexual attitude, behavior and orientation
Z71	Persons encountering health services for other counseling and medical advice, not elsewhere classified Note: Code Z71.84, Encounter for health counseling related to travel, is to be used for health risk and safety counseling for future travel purposes.
Z76.81	Expectant mother prebirth pediatrician visit

EXAMPLE

Dietary counseling for diabetic diet. Patient was recently diagnosed with diabetes mellitus, type 2. Z71.3, E11.9.

11) Encounters for Obstetrical and Reproductive Services

See Section I.C.15. Pregnancy, Childbirth, and the Puerperium, for further instruction on the use of these codes.

Z codes for pregnancy are for use in those circumstances when none of the problems or complications included in the codes from the Obstetrics chapter exist (a routine prenatal visit or postpartum care). Codes in category Z34, Encounter for supervision of normal pregnancy, are always first listed and are not to be used with any other code from the OB chapter.

Codes in category Z3A, Weeks of gestation, may be assigned to provide additional information about the pregnancy. Category Z3A codes should not be assigned for pregnancies with abortive outcomes (categories O00-O08), elective termination of pregnancy (code Z33.2), nor for postpartum conditions, as category Z3A is not applicable to these conditions. The date of admission should be used to determine weeks of gestation for inpatient admissions that encompass more than one gestational week.

The outcome of delivery, category Z37, should be included on all maternal delivery records. It is always a secondary code. Codes in category Z37 should not be used on the newborn record.

Z codes for family planning (contraceptive) or procreative management and counseling should be included on an obstetric record either during the pregnancy or the postpartum stage, if applicable.

Z codes/categories for obstetrical and reproductive services:

Z30	Encounter for contraceptive management
Z31	Encounter for procreative management
Z32.2	Encounter for childbirth instruction
Z32.3	Encounter for childcare instruction
Z33	Pregnant state
Z34	Encounter for supervision of normal pregnancy
Z36	Encounter for antenatal screening of mother
Z3A	Weeks of gestation
Z37	Outcome of delivery
Z39	Encounter for maternal postpartum care and examination
Z76.81	Expectant mother prebirth pediatrician visit

EXAMPLE

Obstetric patent admitted at 40 weeks. Vaginal delivery of a single female infant with no complications, O80, Z3A.40, Z37.0, 10E0XZZ.

12) Newborns and Infants

See Section I.C.16. Newborn (Perinatal) Guidelines, for further instruction on the use of these codes.

Newborn Z codes/categories:

Z76.1	Encounter for health supervision and care of foundling
Z00.1-	Encounter for routine child health examination
Z38	Liveborn infants according to place of birth and type of delivery

EXAMPLE

Single liveborn female infant born via vaginal delivery, Z38.00

13) Routine and administrative examinations

The Z codes allow for the description of encounters for routine examinations, such as, a general check-up, or, examinations for administrative purposes, such as, a pre-employment physical. The codes are not to be used if the examination is for diagnosis of a suspected condition or for treatment purposes. In such cases the diagnosis code is used. During a routine exam, should a diagnosis or condition be discovered, it should be coded as an additional code. Pre-existing and chronic conditions and history codes may also be included as additional codes as long as the examination is for administrative purposes and not focused on any particular condition.

Some of the codes for routine health examinations distinguish between "with" and "without" abnormal findings. Code assignment depends on the information that is known at the time the encounter is being coded. For example, if no abnormal findings were found during the examination, but the encounter is being coded before test results are back, it is acceptable to assign the code for "without abnormal findings." When assigning a code for "with abnormal findings," additional code(s) should be assigned to identify the specific abnormal finding(s).

Pre-operative examination and pre-procedural laboratory examination Z codes are for use only in those situations when a patient is being cleared for a procedure or surgery and no treatment is given.

The Z codes/categories for routine and administrative examinations:

Z00	Encounter for general examination without complaint, suspected or reported diagnosis
Z01	Encounter for other special examination without complaint, suspected or reported diagnosis
Z02	Encounter for administrative examination Except: Z02.9, Encounter for administrative examinations, unspecified
Z32.0-	Encounter for pregnancy test

EXAMPLE

Preoperative examination for respiratory clearance for surgery. The patient has emphysema and is scheduled for cholecystectomy for cholelithiasis of the gallbladder, Z01.811, J43.9, K80.20.

14) Miscellaneous Z codes

The miscellaneous Z codes capture a number of other health care encounters that do not fall into one of the other categories. Certain of these codes identify the reason for the encounter; others are for use as additional codes that provide useful information on circumstances that may affect a patient's care and treatment.

Prophylactic Organ Removal

For encounters specifically for prophylactic removal of an organ (such as prophylactic removal of breasts due to a genetic susceptibility to cancer or a family history of cancer), the principal or first-listed code should be a code from category Z40, Encounter for prophylactic surgery, followed by the appropriate codes to identify the associated risk factor (such as genetic susceptibility or family history).

If the patient has a malignancy of one site and is having prophylactic removal at another site to prevent either a new primary malignancy or metastatic disease, a code for the malignancy should also be assigned in addition to a code from subcategory Z40.0, Encounter for prophylactic surgery for risk factors related to malignant neoplasms. A Z40.0 code should not be assigned if the patient is having organ removal for treatment of a malignancy, such as the removal of the testes for the treatment of prostate cancer.

Miscellaneous Z codes/categories:

Z28	Immunization not carried out Except: Z28.3, Underimmunization status
Z29	Encounter for other prophylactic measures
Z40	Encounter for prophylactic surgery
Z41	Encounter for procedures for purposes other than remedying health state Except: Z41.9, Encounter for procedure for purposes other than remedying health state, unspecified
Z53	Persons encountering health services for specific procedures and treatment, not carried out
Z55	Problems related to education and literacy
Z56	Problems related to employment and unemployment
Z57	Occupational exposure to risk factors
Z58	Problems related to physical environment
Z59	Problems related to housing and economic circumstances
Z60	Problems related to social environment

Z62 Problems related to upbringing
Z63 Other problems related to primary support group, including family circumstances
Z64 Problems related to certain psychosocial circumstances
Z65 Problems related to other psychosocial circumstances
Z72 Problems related to lifestyle
Note: These codes should be assigned only when the documentation specifies that the patient has an associated problem
Z73 Problems related to life management difficulty
Z74 Problems related to care provider dependency
Except: Z74.01, Bed confinement status
Z75 Problems related to medical facilities and other health care
Z76.0 Encounter for issue of repeat prescription
Z76.3 Healthy person accompanying sick person
Z76.4 Other boarder to healthcare facility
Z76.5 Malingerer [conscious simulation]
Z91.1- Patient's noncompliance with medical treatment and regimen
Z91.83 Wandering in diseases classified elsewhere
Z91.84- Oral health risk factors
Z91.89 Other specified personal risk factors, not elsewhere classified

See Section I.B.14 for Z55-Z65, Persons with potential health hazards related to socioeconomic and psychosocial circumstances, documentation by clinicians other than the patient's provider.

EXAMPLE

A patient was admitted for cosmetic surgery (bilateral silicone breast implants), Z41.1, 0H0V0JZ.

15) Nonspecific Z Codes

Certain Z codes are so non-specific, or potentially redundant with other codes in the classification, that there can be little justification for their use in the inpatient setting. Their use in the outpatient setting should be limited to those instances when there is no further documentation to permit more precise coding. Otherwise, any sign or symptom or any other reason for visit that is captured in another code should be used.

Nonspecific Z codes/categories:

Z02.9 Encounter for administrative examinations, unspecified
Z04.9 Encounter for examination and observation for unspecified reason
Z13.9 Encounter for screening, unspecified
Z41.9 Encounter for procedure for purposes other than remedying health state, unspecified
Z52.9 Donor of unspecified organ or tissue
Z86.59 Personal history of other mental and behavioral disorders
Z88.9 Allergy status to unspecified drugs, medicaments and biological substances
Z92.0 Personal history of contraception

16) Z Codes That May Only be Principal/First-Listed Diagnosis

The following Z codes/categories may only be reported as the principal/first-listed diagnosis, except when there are multiple encounters on the same day and the medical records for the encounters are combined:

Z00 Encounter for general examination without complaint, suspected or reported diagnosis Except: Z00.6
Z01 Encounter for other special examination without complaint, suspected or reported diagnosis
Z02 Encounter for administrative examination
Z04 Encounter for examination and observation for other reasons
Z33.2 Encounter for elective termination of pregnancy

Z31.81	Encounter for male factor infertility in female patient
Z31.83	Encounter for assisted reproductive fertility procedure cycle
Z31.84	Encounter for fertility preservation procedure
Z34	Encounter for supervision of normal pregnancy
Z39	Encounter for maternal postpartum care and examination
Z38	Liveborn infants according to place of birth and type of delivery
Z40	Encounter for prophylactic surgery
Z42	Encounter for plastic and reconstructive surgery following medical procedure or healed injury
Z51.0	Encounter for antineoplastic radiation therapy
Z51.1-	Encounter for antineoplastic chemotherapy and immunotherapy
Z52	Donors of organs and tissues Except: Z52.9, Donor of unspecified organ or tissue
Z76.1	Encounter for health supervision and care of foundling
Z76.2	Encounter for health supervision and care of other healthy infant and child
Z99.12	Encounter for respirator [ventilator] dependence during power failure

EXAMPLE

Single liveborn infant delivered by Cesarean section, Z38.01.

EXERCISE 9-3

Assign codes to the following conditions.

1. Patient receives long-term oxygen therapy for emphysema; patient has a history of tobacco dependence __________
2. Dietary counseling for morbid obesity in an adult patient; body mass index (BMI) is 41 __________
3. Screening for prostate cancer; patient has no signs or symptoms __________
4. Family history of ischemic heart disease __________
5. Personal history of malaria __________
6. History of urinary calculi __________
7. Personal history of diabetes mellitus, type 2; patient currently takes insulin for diabetes __________
8. Awaiting liver transplant for end-stage liver failure __________
9. Patient on Coumadin (anticoagulant) because of mechanical heart valve __________
10. Patient is noncompliant with diet and medications __________

Using the Z code guideline for principal/first-listed diagnosis, select the correct answer.

11. Z44.109 Fitting and adjustment of artificial leg
    A. First diagnosis only
    B. First and/or additional diagnosis
12. Z42.1 Encounter for breast reconstruction following mastectomy
    A. First diagnosis only
    B. First and/or additional diagnosis
13. Z41.2 Routine or ritual male circumcision
    A. First diagnosis only
    B. First and/or additional diagnosis

14. Z43.3 Attention to colostomy
   A. First diagnosis only
   B. First and/or additional diagnosis

15. Z34.01 Supervision of normal first pregnancy, first trimester
   A. First diagnosis only
   B. First and/or additional diagnosis

PROCEDURES

Procedures can be taken from any of the tables in ICD-10-PCS. When a Z code is used as a diagnosis for a given procedure or a reason for the encounter, a procedure code is still necessary to identify that the procedure was performed. It can be confusing when a Z code seems to describe a procedure.

Remember that ICD-10-PCS procedure codes only need to be assigned on inpatient encounters.

EXAMPLE

Patient was admitted for sterilization. A laparoscopic ligation of the fallopian tubes was performed, Z30.2, 0UL74ZZ.

EXAMPLE

Patient is donating a kidney. A left laparoscopic nephrectomy was performed, Z52.4, 0TT14ZZ.

EXERCISE 9-4

Assign codes for all diagnoses and procedures.

1. Admission for chemotherapy (via central vein) for ovarian cancer __________
2. Admission for replacement of tracheostomy tube __________
3. Admission following delivery in ambulance __________
4. Encounter for open removal of internal fixation device, right femoral shaft __________

CHAPTER REVIEW EXERCISE

Assign codes for all diagnoses and procedures.

1. Paresthesia of the skin __________
2. Abnormal Pap smear (cervix) with high-grade squamous intraepithelial lesion (HGSIL) __________
3. Previous history of cardiac arrest __________
4. Anasarca __________
5. Chest pain due to unstable angina __________
6. Adult failure to thrive __________
7. Insulin pump training for type 1 diabetic __________
8. Complex febrile seizure __________
9. Cachexia __________
10. Physical restraints were ordered by the physician __________
11. Debility __________
12. Patient has a gastrostomy tube and receives tube feedings __________
13. Headache due to migraine __________

14. Absence of kidney due to surgical removal ______________
15. History of falls ______________
16. Fussy baby ______________
17. Elevated blood pressure ______________
18. Encounter for screening mammogram in a high-risk patient with family history of breast cancer ______________
19. Anemia with drop in hematocrit ______________
20. Elevated carcinoembryonic antigen (CEA) ______________
21. Admission for elective circumcision ______________
22. Occult blood in stool ______________
23. Encounter for screening for bladder cancer in patient with gross hematuria ______________
24. Renal colic due to kidney stone ______________
25. Changing of gastrostomy tube in patient with dysphagia ______________
26. Diarrhea due to gastroenteritis ______________
27. Intramuscular vaccination for influenza ______________
28. Patient has type 1 diabetes mellitus and has an insulin pump ______________
29. Prophylactic removal of both ovaries due to strong family history of ovarian cancer and genetic susceptibility. An open bilateral salpingo-oophorectomy was performed ______________
30. Respiratory arrest ______________
31. Sudden infant death syndrome (SIDS) ______________
32. Decreased libido ______________
33. Hypoxia ______________
34. Nervousness ______________

CHAPTER GLOSSARY

Prophylactic: medication or treatment used to prevent a disease from occurring.

Screening examination: one that occurs in the absence of any signs or symptoms. It involves examination of an asymptomatic individual to detect a given disease, typically by means of an inexpensive diagnostic test.

Sign: objective evidence of a disease or of a patient's condition as perceived by the patient's examining physician.

Symptom: subjective evidence of a disease or of a patient's condition as perceived by the patient.

10

Certain Infectious and Parasitic Diseases

(ICD-10-CM Chapters 1 and 22, Codes A00-B99, U07.1)

CHAPTER OUTLINE

LEARNING OBJECTIVES

1. Apply and assign the correct ICD-10-CM/PCS codes in accordance with Official Guidelines for Coding and Reporting
2. Recognize infectious and parasitic diseases
3. Assign the correct Z codes and procedure codes related to infectious and parasitic diseases
4. Identify common treatments, medications, laboratory values, and diagnostic tests

ABBREVIATIONS/ ACRONYMS

AIDS acquired immunodeficiency syndrome

C. DIFF *Clostridium difficile*

CD4 Cluster of differentiation 4

CDC Centers for Disease Control and Prevention

COVID-19 Coronavirus disease 2019

ABBREVIATIONS/ ACRONYMS—*cont'd*

DMAC disseminated *Mycobacterium avium-intracellulare* complex

EGD esophogastroduodenoscopy

HAART highly active antiretroviral therapy

HFMD hand, foot, and mouth disease

HIV human immunodeficiency virus

HIVAN HIV-associated nephropathy

HPV Human papilloma virus

HSV herpes simplex virus

ICD-10-CM *International Classification of Diseases, 10th Revision, Clinical Modification*

ICD-10-PCS *International Classification of Diseases, 10th Revision, Procedure Coding System*

IVDU intravenous drug use

MAC *Mycobacterium avium-intracellulare* complex

MAI *Mycobacterium avium-intracellulare*

MDR multi-drug resistant

MOD multiple organ dysfunction

MRSA methicillin-resistant *Staphylococcus aureus*

MSSA methicillin-sensitive *Staphylococcus aureus*

PCP *Pneumocystis carinii* pneumonia

RPR rapid plasma reagin

SARS severe acute respiratory syndrome

SIRS systemic inflammatory response syndrome

STD sexually transmitted disease

STEC Shiga toxin-producing *E. coli*

TB tuberculosis

UTI urinary tract infection

VDRL Venereal Disease Research Laboratory

VRE vancomycin-resistant enterococcus

WBC white blood cells

ICD-10-CM Official Guidelines for Coding and Reporting (2021-2022)

Please refer to the companion Evolve website for the most current 2021-2022 guidelines.

1. Chapter 1: Certain Infectious and Parasitic Diseases (A00-B99), U07.1

a. Human Immunodeficiency Virus (HIV) Infections

1) Code only confirmed cases

Code only confirmed cases of HIV infection/illness. This is an exception to the hospital inpatient guideline Section II, H.

In this context, "confirmation" does not require documentation of positive serology or culture for HIV; the provider's diagnostic statement that the patient is HIV positive, or has an HIV-related illness is sufficient.

EXAMPLE

Patient with possible human immunodeficiency virus (HIV). Even though in the inpatient setting it is acceptable to code diagnoses that are possible or suspected, in the case of possible HIV, you would not assign B20. You would have to query the physician regarding the patient's exact HIV status. This is one of the exceptions to coding a diagnosis as if it exists when it is documented as possible or probable.

2) Selection and sequencing of HIV codes

(a) Patient admitted for HIV-related condition

If a patient is admitted for an HIV-related condition, the principal diagnosis should be B20, Human immunodeficiency virus [HIV] disease followed by additional diagnosis codes for all reported HIV-related conditions.

EXAMPLE

The patient was admitted for treatment of Kaposi's sarcoma of the skin. The patient's HIV has been symptomatic for the past year, B20, C46.0.

(b) Patient with HIV disease admitted for unrelated condition

If a patient with HIV disease is admitted for an unrelated condition (such as a traumatic injury), the code for the unrelated condition (e.g., the nature of injury code) should be the principal diagnosis. Other diagnoses would be B20 followed by additional diagnosis codes for all reported HIV-related conditions.

EXAMPLE

Initial encounter for accidental injury that resulted in traumatic closed-fracture of the left femur in a patient who has acquired immunodeficiency syndrome (AIDS), S72.92xA, B20, X58.xxxA.

(c) Whether the patient is newly diagnosed
Whether the patient is newly diagnosed or has had previous admissions/encounters for HIV conditions is irrelevant to the sequencing decision.

(d) Asymptomatic human immunodeficiency virus
Z21, Asymptomatic human immunodeficiency virus [HIV] infection status, is to be applied when the patient without any documentation of symptoms is listed as being "HIV positive," "known HIV," "HIV test positive," or similar terminology. Do not use this code if the term "AIDS" is used or if the patient is treated for any HIV-related illness or is described as having any condition(s) resulting from his/her HIV positive status; use B20 in these cases.

EXAMPLE The patient's HIV test last week was positive; the patient is asymptomatic, Z21.

(e) Patients with inconclusive HIV serology
Patients with inconclusive HIV serology, but no definitive diagnosis or manifestations of the illness, may be assigned code R75, Inconclusive laboratory evidence of human immunodeficiency virus [HIV].

(f) Previously diagnosed HIV-related illness
Patients with any known prior diagnosis of an HIV-related illness should be coded to B20. Once a patient has developed an HIV-related illness, the patient should always be assigned code B20 on every subsequent admission/encounter. Patients previously diagnosed with any HIV illness (B20) should never be assigned to R75 or Z21, Asymptomatic human immunodeficiency virus [HIV] infection status.

EXAMPLE HIV patient with prior history of *Pneumocystis carinii* pneumonia (PCP), B20. PCP is an opportunistic lung infection that has been identified as an AIDS-defining illness.

(g) HIV Infection in Pregnancy, Childbirth and the Puerperium
During pregnancy, childbirth or the puerperium, a patient admitted (or presenting for a health care encounter) because of an HIV-related illness should receive a principal diagnosis code of O98.7-, Human immunodeficiency [HIV] disease complicating pregnancy, childbirth and the puerperium, followed by B20 and the code(s) for the HIV-related illness(es). Codes from Chapter 16 always take sequencing priority.

Patients with asymptomatic HIV infection status admitted (or presenting for a health care encounter) during pregnancy, childbirth, or the puerperium should receive codes of O98.7- and Z21.

EXAMPLE The patient is 20 weeks pregnant and is admitted for treatment of esophageal candidiasis due to AIDS, O98.712, B20, B37.81, Z3A.20.

EXAMPLE A patient at 39 weeks delivered liveborn twins vaginally during her hospital stay. The mother's HIV has remained asymptomatic, O30.003, O98.712, Z21, Z37.2, Z3A.39, 10E0XZZ.

(h) Encounters for testing for HIV
If a patient is being seen to determine his/her HIV status, use code Z11.4, Encounter for screening for human immunodeficiency virus [HIV]. Use additional codes for any associated high risk behavior.

If a patient with signs or symptoms is being seen for HIV testing, code the signs and symptoms. An additional counseling code Z71.7, Human immunodeficiency virus [HIV] counseling, may be used if counseling is provided during the encounter for the test.

When a patient returns to be informed of his/her HIV test results and the test result is negative, use code Z71.7, Human immunodeficiency virus [HIV] counseling.

If the results are positive, see previous guidelines and assign codes as appropriate.

EXAMPLE

Because of high-risk homosexual behavior, the patient is seen in the clinic for HIV screening, Z11.4, Z72.52.

EXAMPLE

The patient returns for test results that are negative and is counseled regarding HIV prevention, Z71.7.

EXAMPLE

The patient returns for test results that are positive and is asymptomatic. She is instructed regarding symptoms to watch for and means of prevention, Z21, Z71.7.

b. Infectious agents as the cause of diseases classified to other chapters
Certain infections are classified in chapters other than Chapter 1 and no organism is identified as part of the infection code. In these instances, it is necessary to use an additional code from Chapter 1 to identify the organism. A code from category B95, Streptococcus, Staphylococcus, and Enterococcus as the cause of diseases classified to other chapters, B96, Other bacterial agents as the cause of diseases classified to other chapters, or B97, Viral agents as the cause of diseases classified to other chapters, is to be used as an additional code to identify the organism. An instructional note will be found at the infection code advising that an additional organism code is required.

EXAMPLE

Patient is admitted to the hospital with urinary tract infection due to E. coli, N39.0, B96.20.

c. Infections resistant to antibiotics
Many bacterial infections are resistant to current antibiotics. It is necessary to identify all infections documented as antibiotic resistant. Assign a code from category Z16, Resistance to antimicrobial drugs, following the infection code only if the infection code does not identify drug resistance.

EXAMPLE

Patient is admitted to the hospital with pneumonia due to MRSA, J15.212.

EXAMPLE

VRE acute endocarditis, I33.0, B95.2, Z16.21.

d. Sepsis, Severe Sepsis, and Septic Shock
1) Coding of Sepsis and Severe Sepsis
(a) Sepsis
For a diagnosis of sepsis, assign the appropriate code for the underlying systemic infection. If the type of infection or causal organism is not further specified, assign code A41.9, Sepsis, unspecified organism.

A code from subcategory R65.2, Severe sepsis, should not be assigned unless severe sepsis or an associated acute organ dysfunction is documented.

EXAMPLE

Patient presents with sepsis. After study the attending physician documents sepsis secondary to staph aureus found in the blood cultures. The patient also has staph aureus pneumonia, A41.01, J15.211.

(i) Negative or inconclusive blood cultures and sepsis
Negative or inconclusive blood cultures do not preclude a diagnosis of sepsis in patients with clinical evidence of the condition, however, the provider should be queried.

EXAMPLE

Patient presents to the ER with shaking chills, temperature of 104°F, and WBC of 14,000. Physician suspects sepsis and takes blood cultures. Blood cultures are negative for bacteria. Physician documents on discharge summary that the patient has sepsis, A41.9.

(ii) Urosepsis
The term urosepsis is a nonspecific term. It is not to be considered synonymous with sepsis. It has no default code in the Alphabetic Index. Should a provider use this term, he/she must be queried for clarification.

EXAMPLE Patient presents to the ER with fever and painful urination. The physician documents urosepsis and admits the patient to the hospital for IV antibiotics. Physician must be queried for clarification as to the condition as there is no ICD-10-CM code for this terminology.

(iii) Sepsis with organ dysfunction
If a patient has sepsis and associated acute organ dysfunction or multiple organ dysfunction (MOD), follow the instructions for coding severe sepsis.

EXAMPLE Patient is admitted to the hospital with sepsis and acute renal failure secondary to sepsis, A41.9, R65.20, N17.9.

(iv) Acute organ dysfunction that is not clearly associated with the sepsis
If a patient has sepsis and an acute organ dysfunction, but the medical record documentation indicates that the acute organ dysfunction is related to a medical condition other than the sepsis, do not assign a code from subcategory R65.2, Severe sepsis. An acute organ dysfunction must be associated with the sepsis in order to assign the severe sepsis code. If the documentation is not clear as to whether an acute organ dysfunction is related to the sepsis or another medical condition, query the provider.

EXAMPLE Patient is admitted to the hospital with sepsis, pneumonia, and acute respiratory failure, A41.9, J18.9, J96.00.

(b) Severe sepsis
The coding of severe sepsis requires a minimum of 2 codes: first a code for the underlying systemic infection, followed by a code from subcategory R65.2, Severe sepsis. If the causal organism is not documented, assign code A41.9, Sepsis, unspecified organism, for the infection. Additional code(s) for the associated acute organ dysfunction are also required (Figure 10-1).

Due to the complex nature of severe sepsis, some cases may require querying the provider prior to assignment of the codes.

2) Septic shock

(a) Septic shock generally refers to circulatory failure associated with severe sepsis, and therefore, it represents a type of acute organ dysfunction.

For cases of septic shock, the code for the systemic infection should be sequenced first, followed by code R65.21, Severe sepsis with septic shock or code T81.12, Postprocedural septic shock. Any additional codes for the other acute organ dysfunctions should also be assigned. As noted in the sequencing instructions in the Tabular List, the code for septic shock cannot be assigned as a principal diagnosis.

EXAMPLE The patient was admitted with septic shock and acute renal failure caused by a UTI due to *E. coli.* Discharge summary states sepsis due to *E. coli,* A41.51, N39.0, R65.21, N17.9.

3) Sequencing of severe sepsis
If severe sepsis is present on admission, and meets the definition of principal diagnosis, the underlying systemic infection should be assigned as principal diagnosis followed by the appropriate code from

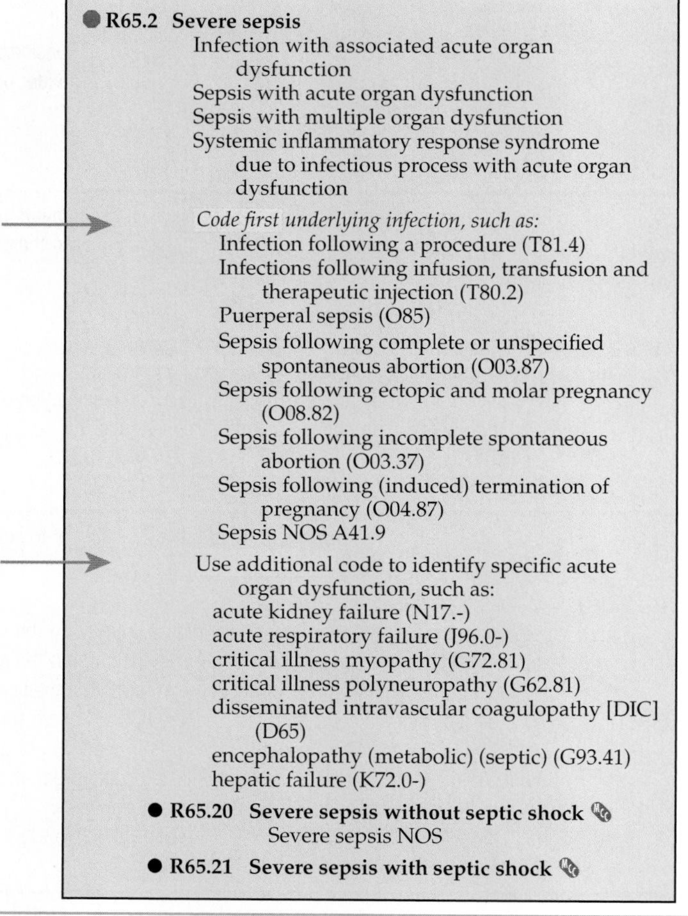

R65.2 Severe sepsis
Infection with associated acute organ dysfunction
Sepsis with acute organ dysfunction
Sepsis with multiple organ dysfunction
Systemic inflammatory response syndrome due to infectious process with acute organ dysfunction

Code first underlying infection, such as:
Infection following a procedure (T81.4)
Infections following infusion, transfusion and therapeutic injection (T80.2)
Puerperal sepsis (O85)
Sepsis following complete or unspecified spontaneous abortion (O03.87)
Sepsis following ectopic and molar pregnancy (O08.82)
Sepsis following incomplete spontaneous abortion (O03.37)
Sepsis following (induced) termination of pregnancy (O04.87)
Sepsis NOS A41.9

Use additional code to identify specific acute organ dysfunction, such as:
acute kidney failure (N17.-)
acute respiratory failure (J96.0-)
critical illness myopathy (G72.81)
critical illness polyneuropathy (G62.81)
disseminated intravascular coagulopathy [DIC] (D65)
encephalopathy (metabolic) (septic) (G93.41)
hepatic failure (K72.0-)

R65.20 Severe sepsis without septic shock
Severe sepsis NOS

R65.21 Severe sepsis with septic shock

FIGURE 10-1. Severe Sepsis.

subcategory R65.2 as required by the sequencing rules in the Tabular List. A code from subcategory R65.2 can never be assigned as a principal diagnosis.

When severe sepsis develops during an encounter (it was not present on admission) the underlying systemic infection and the appropriate code from subcategory R65.2 should be assigned as secondary diagnoses.

Severe sepsis may be present on admission but the diagnosis may not be confirmed until sometime after admission. If the documentation is not clear whether severe sepsis was present on admission, the provider should be queried.

EXAMPLE

The patient was admitted with pneumonia due to *Staphylococcus aureus*. Several days after admission, the patient developed septic shock due to staph aureus sepsis, J15.211, A41.01, R65.21.

4) Sepsis or severe sepsis with a localized infection

If the reason for admission is both sepsis or severe sepsis and a localized infection, such as pneumonia or cellulitis, a code(s) for the underlying systemic infection should be assigned first and the code for the localized infection should be assigned as a secondary diagnosis. If the patient has severe sepsis, a code from subcategory R65.2 should also be assigned as a secondary diagnosis. If the patient is admitted with a localized infection, such as pneumonia, and sepsis/severe sepsis doesn't develop until after admission, the localized infection should be assigned first, followed by the appropriate sepsis/severe sepsis codes.

EXAMPLE

The patient was admitted in acute respiratory failure due to *Staphylococcus aureus* pneumonia. The patient also presented with sepsis due to staph aureus infection associated with respiratory failure, A41.01, J15.211, J96.00, R65.20.

5) Sepsis due to a postprocedural infection

(a) Documentation of causal relationship

As with all postprocedural complications, code assignment is based on the provider's documentation of the relationship between the infection and the procedure.

(b) Sepsis due to a postprocedural infection

For infections following a procedure, a code from T81.40 to T81.43, Infection following a procedure, or code from O86.00 to O86.03, Infection of obstetric surgical wound, that identifies the site of the infection should be coded first, if known. Assign an additional code for sepsis following a procedure (T81.44) or sepsis following an obstetrical procedure (O86.04). Use an additional code to identify the infectious agent. If the patient has severe sepsis, the appropriate code from subcategory R65.2 should also be assigned with the additional code(s) for any acute organ dysfunction.

For infections following infusion, transfusion, therapeutic injection, or immunization, a code from subcategory T80.2, Infections following infusion, transfusion, and therapeutic injection, or code T88.0-, Infection following immunization, should be coded first, followed by the code for the specific infection. If the patient has severe sepsis, the appropriate code from subcategory R65.2 should also be assigned, with the additional code(s) for any acute organ dysfunction.

(c) Postprocedural infection and postprocedural septic shock

If a postprocedural infection has resulted in postprocedural septic shock, assign the codes indicated above for sepsis due to a postprocedural infection, followed by code T81.12-, Postprocedural septic shock. Do not assign code R65.21, Severe sepsis with septic shock. Additional code(s) should be assigned for any acute organ dysfunction.

EXAMPLE

Patient is admitted through the ER with an infection of her operative wound. The patient has sepsis due to the operative wound infection. Two weeks ago she had an open appendectomy, T81.4xxA, A41.9, Z90.49, Y83.6.

6) Sepsis and severe sepsis associated with a noninfectious process (condition)

In some cases a noninfectious process (condition), such as trauma, may lead to an infection which can result in sepsis or severe sepsis. If sepsis or severe sepsis is documented as associated with a noninfectious condition, such as a burn or serious injury, and this condition meets the definition for principal diagnosis, the code for the noninfectious condition should be sequenced first, followed by the code for the resulting infection. If severe sepsis, is present a code from subcategory R65.2 should also be assigned with any associated organ dysfunction(s) codes. It is not necessary to assign a code from subcategory R65.1, Systemic inflammatory response syndrome (SIRS) of non-infectious origin, for these cases.

If the infection meets the definition of principal diagnosis, it should be sequenced before the non-infectious condition. When both the associated non-infectious condition and the infection meet the definition of principal diagnosis, either may be assigned as principal diagnosis.

Only one code from category R65, Symptoms and signs specifically associated with systemic inflammation and infection, should be assigned. Therefore, when a non-infectious condition leads to an infection resulting in severe sepsis, assign the appropriate code from subcategory R65.2, Severe sepsis. Do not additionally assign a code from subcategory R65.1, Systemic inflammatory response syndrome (SIRS) of non-infectious origin.

See Section I.C.18. SIRS due to non-infectious process

EXAMPLE

Patient is admitted to the hospital with severe sepsis secondary to noninfectious acute pancreatitis, K85.90, R65.20.

7) Sepsis and septic shock complicating abortion, pregnancy, childbirth, and the puerperium

See Section I.C.15. Sepsis and septic shock complicating abortion, pregnancy, childbirth and the puerperium

8) Newborn sepsis

See Section I.C.16.f. Bacterial sepsis of Newborn

e. Methicillin Resistant *Staphylococcus aureus* (MRSA) Conditions

1) Selection and sequencing of MRSA codes

(a) Combination codes for MRSA infection

When a patient is diagnosed with an infection that is due to methicillin resistant *Staphylococcus aureus* (MRSA), and that infection has a combination code that includes the causal organism (e.g.,

sepsis, pneumonia) assign the appropriate combination code for the condition (e.g., code A41.02, Sepsis due to Methicillin resistant Staphylococcus aureus or code J15.212, Pneumonia due to Methicillin resistant Staphylococcus aureus). Do not assign code B95.62, Methicillin resistant Staphylococcus aureus infection as the cause of diseases classified elsewhere, as an additional code because the combination code includes the type of infection and the MRSA organism. Do not assign a code from subcategory Z16.11, Resistance to penicillins, as an additional diagnosis.
See Section I.C.1. for instructions on coding and sequencing of sepsis and severe sepsis.

(b) Other codes for MRSA infection
When there is documentation of a current infection (e.g., wound infection, stitch abscess, urinary tract infection) due to MRSA, and that infection does not have a combination code that includes the causal organism, assign the appropriate code to identify the condition along with code B95.62, Methicillin resistant Staphylococcus aureus infection as the cause of diseases classified elsewhere for the MRSA infection. Do not assign a code from subcategory Z16.11, Resistance to penicillins.

(c) Methicillin susceptible Staphylococcus aureus (MSSA) and MRSA colonization
The condition or state of being colonized or carrying MSSA or MRSA is called colonization or carriage, while an individual person is described as being colonized or being a carrier. Colonization means that MSSA or MRSA is present on or in the body without necessarily causing illness. A positive MRSA colonization test might be documented by the provider as "MRSA screen positive" or "MRSA nasal swab positive".

Assign code Z22.322, Carrier or suspected carrier of Methicillin resistant Staphylococcus aureus, for patients documented as having MRSA colonization. Assign code Z22.321, Carrier or suspected carrier of Methicillin susceptible Staphylococcus aureus, for patient documented as having MSSA colonization. Colonization is not necessarily indicative of a disease process or as the cause of a specific condition the patient may have unless documented as such by the provider.

(d) MRSA colonization and infection
If a patient is documented as having both MRSA colonization and infection during a hospital admission, code Z22.322, Carrier or suspected carrier of Methicillin resistant Staphylococcus aureus, and a code for the MRSA infection may both be assigned.

EXAMPLE Pneumonia due to MRSA, J15.212.

EXAMPLE UTI due to MRSA, N39.0, B95.62.

EXAMPLE Patient is nasal swab positive for MRSA, Z22.322.

f. Zika virus infections

1) Code only confirmed cases
Code only a confirmed diagnosis of Zika virus (A92.5, Zika virus disease) as documented by the provider. This is an exception to the hospital inpatient guideline Section II, H.

In this context, "confirmation" does not require documentation of the type of test performed; the provider's diagnostic statement that the condition is confirmed is sufficient. This code should be assigned regardless of the stated mode of transmission.

If the provider documents "suspected," "possible," or "probable" Zika, do not assign code A92.5. Assign a code(s) explaining the reason for encounter (such as fever, rash, or joint pain) or Z20.821, Contact with and (suspected) exposure to Zika virus.

EXAMPLE Patient was admitted to the hospital after confirmation of Zika virus A92.5.

Coronavirus disease 2019, COVID-19, is an infectious disease caused by severe acute respiratory syndrome coronavirus 2 (SARS-CoV-2). Common symptoms include cough, fever, shortness of breath, fatigue, and loss of taste and smell. Chapter 22 includes codes for special purposes (U00-U85). New diseases of uncertain etiology or emergency are to be reported with codes U00-U49. Category U07, Conditions of uncertain etiology, contains additional subcategories U07.0, Vaping-related disorder, and U07.1, COVID-19.

Subcategory code U07.1, COVID-19, provides guidance with directing the use of additional codes to identify pneumonia or other manifestations. Excludes 1 notes specifically exclude coronavirus infection unspecified (B34.2), Coronavirus as the cause of disease classified elsewhere (B97.2-), and Pneumonia due to SARS-associated coronavirus (J12.81). COVID-19 infections can manifest in a broad range of issues, from patients presenting with little or no symptoms to those presenting with serious illness or terminal condition. Symptoms may appear from 2 – 14 days after exposure. According to the Guidelines, a copy of the positive test result is not required for a COVID-19 case to be considered "confirmed," as the provider's diagnostic statement that the patient has the condition is sufficient in order to establish a confirmed diagnosis.

g. Coronavirus Infections

1) COVID-19 Infection (Infection due to SARS-CoV-2)

(a) Code only confirmed cases

Code only a confirmed diagnosis of the 2019 novel coronavirus disease (COVID-19) as documented by the provider or documentation of a positive COVID-19 test result. For a confirmed diagnosis, assign code U07.1, COVID-19. This is an exception to the hospital inpatient guideline Section II, H. In this context, "confirmation" does not require documentation of a positive test result for COVID-19; the provider's documentation that the individual has COVID-19 is sufficient.

If the provider documents "suspected," "possible," "probable," or "inconclusive" COVID-19, do not assign code U07.1. Instead, code the signs and symptoms reported. See guideline I.C.1.g.1.g.

(b) Sequencing of codes

When COVID-19 meets the definition of principal diagnosis, code U07.1, COVID-19, should be sequenced first, followed by the appropriate codes for associated manifestations, except when another guideline requires that certain codes be sequenced first, such as obstetrics, sepsis, or transplant complications.

For a COVID-19 infection that progresses to sepsis, see Section I.C.1.d. Sepsis, Severe Sepsis, and Septic Shock

See Section I.C.15.s. for COVID-19 infection in pregnancy, childbirth, and the puerperium

See Section I.C.16.h. for COVID-19 infection in newborn

For a COVID-19 infection in a lung transplant patient, see Section I.C.19.g.3.a. Transplant complications other than kidney

(c) Acute respiratory manifestations of COVID-19

When the reason for the encounter/admission is a respiratory manifestation of COVID-19, assign code U07.1, COVID-19, as the principal/first-listed diagnosis and assign code(s) for the respiratory manifestation(s) as additional diagnoses.

The following conditions are examples of common respiratory manifestations of COVID-19:

(i) Pneumonia

For a patient with pneumonia confirmed as due to COVID-19, assign codes U07.1, COVID-19, and J12.89, Other viral pneumonia.

(ii) Acute bronchitis

For a patient with acute bronchitis confirmed as due to COVID-19, assign codes U07.1, and J20.8, Acute bronchitis due to other specified organisms.

Bronchitis not otherwise specified (NOS) due to COVID-19 should be coded using code U07.1 and J40, Bronchitis, not specified as acute or chronic.

(iii) Lower respiratory infection

If the COVID-19 is documented as being associated with a lower respiratory infection, not otherwise specified (NOS), or an acute respiratory infection, NOS, codes U07.1 and J22, Unspecified acute lower respiratory infection, should be assigned.

If the COVID-19 is documented as being associated with a respiratory infection, NOS, codes U07.1 and J98.8, Other specified respiratory disorders, should be assigned.

(iv) Acute respiratory distress syndrome

For acute respiratory distress syndrome (ARDS) due to COVID-19, assign codes U07.1, and J80, Acute respiratory distress syndrome.

(v) Acute respiratory failure

For acute respiratory failure due to COVID-19, assign code U07.1, and code J96.0-, Acute respiratory failure.

(d) Non-respiratory manifestations of COVID-19

When the reason for the encounter/admission is a non-respiratory manifestation (e.g., viral enteritis) of COVID-19, assign code U07.1, COVID-19, as the principal/first-listed diagnosis and assign code(s) for the manifestation(s) as additional diagnoses.

(e) Exposure to COVID-19

For asymptomatic individuals with actual or suspected exposure to COVID-19, assign code Z20.828, Contact with and (suspected) exposure to other viral communicable diseases.

For symptomatic individuals with actual or suspected exposure to COVID-19 and the infection has been ruled out, or test results are inconclusive or unknown, assign code Z20.828, Contact with and (suspected) exposure to other viral communicable diseases. See guideline I.C.21.c.1., Contact/Exposure, for additional guidance regarding the use of category Z20 codes.

If COVID-19 is confirmed, see guideline I.C.1.g.1.a.

(f) Screening for COVID-19

During the COVID-19 pandemic, a screening code is generally not appropriate. For encounters for COVID-19 testing, including preoperative testing, code as exposure to COVID-19 (guideline I.C.1.g.1.e.). Coding guidance will be updated as new information concerning any changes in the pandemic status becomes available.

(g) Signs and symptoms without definitive diagnosis of COVID-19

For patients presenting with any signs/symptoms associated with COVID-19 (such as fever, etc.) but a definitive diagnosis has not been established, assign the appropriate code(s) for each of the presenting signs and symptoms such as:

- R05 Cough
- R06.02 Shortness of breath
- R50.9 Fever, unspecified

If a patient with signs/symptoms associated with COVID-19 also has an actual or suspected contact with or exposure to COVID-19, assign Z20.828, Contact with and (suspected) exposure to other viral communicable diseases, as an additional code.

(h) Asymptomatic individuals who test positive for COVID-19

For asymptomatic individuals who test positive for COVID-19, see guideline I.C.1.g.1.a. Although the individual is asymptomatic, the individual has tested positive and is considered to have the COVID-19 infection.

(i) Personal history of COVID-19

For patients with a history of COVID-19, assign code Z86.19, Personal history of other infectious and parasitic diseases.

(j) Follow-up visits after COVID-19 infection as resolved

For individuals who previously had COVID-19 and are being seen for follow-up evaluation, and COVID-19 test results are negative, assign codes Z09, Encounter for follow-up examination after completed treatment for conditions other than malignant neoplasm, and Z86.19, Personal history of other infectious and parasitic diseases.

(k) Encounter for antibody testing

For an encounter for antibody testing that is not being performed to confirm a current COVID-19 infection, nor is a follow-up test after resolution of COVID-19, assign Z01.84, Encounter for antibody response examination.

Follow the applicable guidelines above if the individual is being tested to confirm a current COVID-19 infection.

For follow-up testing after a COVID-19 infection, see guideline I.C.1.g.1.j.

15. Chapter 15: Pregnancy, Childbirth, and the Puerperium (O00-O9A)

s) COVID-19 infection in pregnancy, childbirth, and the puerperium

During pregnancy, childbirth or the puerperium, when COVID-19 is the reason for admission/encounter, code O98.5-, Other viral diseases complicating pregnancy, childbirth and the puerperium, should be sequenced as the principal/first-listed diagnosis, and code U07.1, COVID-19, and the appropriate codes for associated manifestation(s) should be assigned as additional diagnoses. Codes from Chapter 15 always take sequencing priority.

If the reason for admission/encounter is unrelated to COVID-19 but the patient tests positive for COVID-19 during the admission/encounter, the appropriate code for the reason for admission/encounter should be sequenced as the principal/first-listed diagnosis, and codes O98.5- and U07.1, as well as the appropriate codes for associated COVID-19 manifestations, should be assigned as additional diagnoses.

EXAMPLE

Patient has pneumonia confirmed as due to COVID-19, U07.1, J12.89

ANATOMY AND PHYSIOLOGY

This chapter focuses on diseases that are **communicable** (easily spread from one to another) and **parasitic** (organism taking nourishment from another organism) and the organisms that are responsible for the disease conditions. Many times, two codes are required. If a condition is not considered communicable, it will be found in a body system chapter; in this case, an additional code from category B95-B97 may be assigned to identify causative organisms or infectious agents.

EXAMPLE

Acute *Staphylococcus* vaginitis, N76.0, B95.8.

To locate the code for *Staphylococcus*, the coder can look under the main term, "Infection," and then under the subterm "*Staphylococcus*." Sometimes, the organism and the disease condition have a combination code; this is the case for many of the pneumonia codes.

Klebsiella pneumonia, J15.0.

There is no one body system that causes or is affected by infectious disease. These organisms can be found in any or all of the body systems.

DISEASE CONDITIONS

Certain Infectious and Parasitic Diseases (A00-B99), Chapter 1 in the ICD-10-CM code book, is divided into the following categories:

CATEGORY	SECTION TITLE
A00-A09	Intestinal infectious diseases
A15-A19	Tuberculosis
A20-A28	Certain zoonotic bacterial diseases
A30-A49	Other bacterial diseases
A50-A64	Infections with a predominantly sexual mode of transmission
A65-A69	Other spirochetal diseases
A70-A74	Other diseases caused by *Chlamydiae*
A75-A79	Rickettsioses
A80-A89	Viral and prion infections of the central nervous system
A90-A99	Arthropod-borne viral fevers and viral hemorrhagic fevers
B00-B09	Viral infections characterized by skin and mucous membrane lesions
B10	Other human herpesviruses
B15-B19	Viral hepatitis
B20	Human immunodeficiency virus (HIV) disease
B25-B34	Other viral diseases
B35-B49	Mycoses
B50-B64	Protozoal diseases
B65-B83	Helminthiases
B85-B89	Pediculosis, acariasis, and other infestations
B90-B94	Sequelae of infectious and parasitic diseases
B95-B97	Bacterial and viral, infectious agents
B99	Other infectious diseases
U07.1	Coronavirus disease 2019 (COVID-19)

This chapter focuses on diseases that are **communicable** (easily spread from one to another) and **parasitic** (organism taking nourishment from another organism) and the organisms that are responsible for the disease conditions. It is important to note that codes from this chapter take precedence over codes in other chapters for the same condition. Likewise, when two subterms exist in the Alphabetic Index to describe a condition, the organism subterm takes precedence over the general subterm. Sometimes a condition is not considered to be easily transmissible, and then those conditions may be found in other body-system–related chapters and use an additional code from category B95-B97 to indicate the organism responsible for that condition. To find the organism responsible, if it is not listed under the main term for the condition, the coder should look under the main term Infection or the main term for the organism.

The notes related to this chapter also advise that influenza and other acute respiratory conditions are not coded in Chapter 1 but found in the respiratory chapter. Also, in following the guidelines, all infectious or parasitic diseases that complicate pregnancy should be assigned codes from the pregnancy chapter.

There is advice at the beginning of this chapter to use an additional code to identify resistance to antimicrobial drugs using the Z16 category. The exception to this would be Methicillin-resistant *Staphylococcus aureus* (MRSA). There are unique codes to identify susceptible (MSSA) and resistant (MRSA) *Staphylococcus aureus.* Both of these categories allow for the selection of a code for infection (A49.01 and A49.02), sepsis (A41.02 and A41.01), and as the cause of diseases classified elsewhere (B95.61 and B95.62). There are also combination codes that include the susceptibility and resistance of organisms. If a combination code is used it is not necessary to use an additional code from the B95.6- category.

EXAMPLE Methicillin-resistant staph aureus pneumonia J15.212

EXAMPLE Methicillin-resistant staph aureus urinary tract infection N39.0, B95.62

EXAMPLE Methicillin-resistant staph aureus sepsis A41.02

EXAMPLE Multidrug (antimicrobial) resistant tuberculosis A15.9, Z16.35

If a patient is a carrier or suspected carrier of an infectious disease, code from Z22.- would be assigned. The terminology for carrier or colonized simply signifies that an organism is present in the body but it does not necessarily cause disease or mean an active infection. With the increasing frequency of MRSA being found in the population, many facilities will test a patient with a nasal swab when admitted. If the findings come back positive the documentation may say MRSA screen positive. In the case where a patient has a positive MRSA screen and an active infection, both codes would be assigned.

Intestinal Infectious Diseases (A00-A09)

Clostridium difficile

Clostridium difficile, which is also known as *C. diff,* is a leading cause of pseudomembranous colitis. It can be found in the Index under “Enteritis, clostridium *difficile.*”

C. diff is one of the most common **nosocomial** infections (hospital acquired). In the hospital setting, it may be spread from healthcare worker to patient. Spores associated with this disease can survive up to 70 days. It can also be caused by antibiotic use. This disease is characterized by watery diarrhea and abdominal cramping. The intestinal tract has usually been altered in some way to allow *C. diff* bacteria to flourish.

If a physician suspects *C. diff* (often seen in elderly hospitalized patients), a stool specimen is tested for *C. diff* toxins (cytotoxicity assay). The test results can take between 24 and 48 hours to complete. Treatment depends on the severity of infection. Often, antibiotics are changed or discontinued; however, in severe cases, a patient is treated with metronidazole (Flagyl). Patients with *C. diff* are usually placed on isolation protocol.

EXAMPLE *Clostridium difficile* colitis, A04.7.

Gastroenteritis

Gastroenteritis is the inflammation of the stomach, small intestine, and large intestine. Infectious gastroenteritis is the most common cause. It can be caused by viruses, bacteria, or parasites. In the United States viruses are most often the cause of gastroenteritis, with norovirus and rotavirus being the most common. Bacterial gastroenteritis is less common than viral gastroenteritis. It is most often caused by salmonella, campylobacter, shigella, and *E. coli.* The most common parasites causing gastroenteritis are giardia or cryptosporidium.

Gastroenteritis may be treated with fluid replacement to treat any hypotension and fluid depletion. Vomiting and diarrhea can cause metabolic acidosis or alkalosis as well as renal failure, hyponatremia, and hypokalemia. Antibiotics may be used in some cases.

EXAMPLE Patient is diagnosed with gastroenteritis due to salmonella, A02.0.

Tuberculosis (A15-A19)

Tuberculosis (TB) is an infection caused by *Mycobacterium tuberculosis* (Figure 10-2). These bacteria can attack any part of the body but most often attack the lungs. TB was the leading cause of death in the United States prior to the discovery of medicines to treat the disease. TB was almost eradicated but made a resurgence in the late 1980s.

TB is spread through the air via coughing or sneezing. TB of the lung is the only infectious form of TB. If TB occurs in the bones or kidney, it is not likely to be contagious. TB can be infectious only if it is an active disease. It may be necessary to isolate a patient who is suspected of having this condition, pending confirmation. A form of TB called "latent TB" occurs when a person breathes the bacteria but the immune system fights them off, and they remain alive in the body but are inactive. Latent TB can become active TB. Persons with latent TB usually have a positive TB test result.

Active TB usually occurs in the population whose immune systems are too weak to fight off this disease. This group would include individuals with human immunodeficiency virus (HIV), leukemia, substance abusers, young children, and organ transplant recipients.

EXAMPLE Patient admitted for pneumonia due to tuberculosis, A15.0.

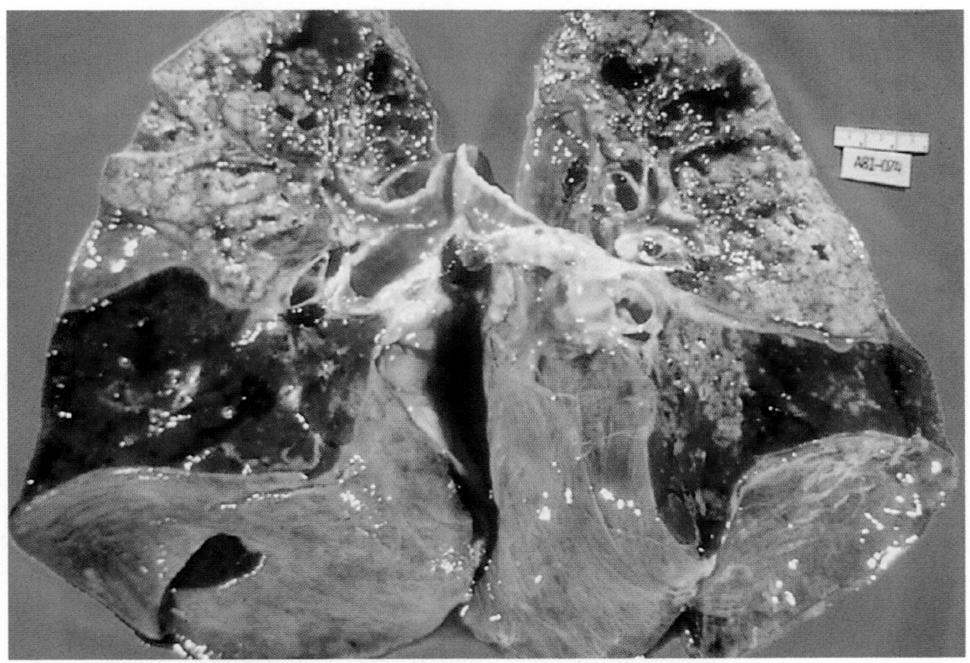

FIGURE 10-2. Tuberculosis.

EXERCISE 10-1

Assign codes to the following conditions.

1. Tubercular pyelonephritis __________
2. Acute miliary tuberculosis __________
3. Interstitial keratitis caused by tuberculosis __________
4. Cavitation of the lung caused by tuberculosis __________
5. *Salmonella* sepsis __________
6. Food poisoning caused by *Salmonella* resulting in gastroenteritis __________
7. Enteritis caused by the rotavirus __________
8. Norwalk virus __________
9. Dysentery __________
10. Giardiasis __________

Certain Zoonotic Bacterial Diseases (A20-A28)

Anthrax

Anthrax is a bacterial infection that is usually found in wild or domestic animals. It is most common in agricultural regions of Central America, Africa, Asia, and the Caribbean. Anthrax occurs in three forms: cutaneous, inhalation, and gastrointestinal. The most serious form is the inhalation type, which causes severe breathing problems that are most often fatal. Since the 9/11 attack on the United States and threats of anthrax attacks, a code was developed for contact or exposure to anthrax.

EXAMPLE Contact with or exposure to anthrax, Z20.810.

This code can be used for anyone who has been exposed to anthrax, or who is closely linked to persons with known exposure.

EXAMPLE Patient is discharged from hospital with possible inhalation anthrax, A22.1.

Other Bacterial Diseases (A30-A49)

Mycobacterium Avium *Complex*

Mycobacterium avium complex (MAC) or ***Mycobacterium avium-intercellulare*** (MAI) is a bacterium which attacks immunocompromised individuals. This bacterium is found in soil and water; an individual who is not immunocompromised does not succumb to the disease. This has been classified as an acquired immunodeficiency syndrome (AIDS)–defining illness. Tests that show high blood levels of the liver enzyme alkaline phosphatase may indicate MAC. Symptoms of this disease include night sweats, weight loss, and diarrhea. Prior to the advent of highly active antiretroviral therapy (**HAART**), which is a group of drugs given to patients with AIDS for prophylaxis, a high incidence of this condition was reported. It generally affects individuals whose T4 cell count is under 50. A variety of antibiotics are used to treat patients with this disease. Individuals with advanced AIDS often develop disseminated *Mycobacterium avium-intracellulare* complex (DMAC). A unique presentation of patients with DMAC is severe anemia.

EXAMPLE Infection from *Mycobacterium avium*, A31.0.

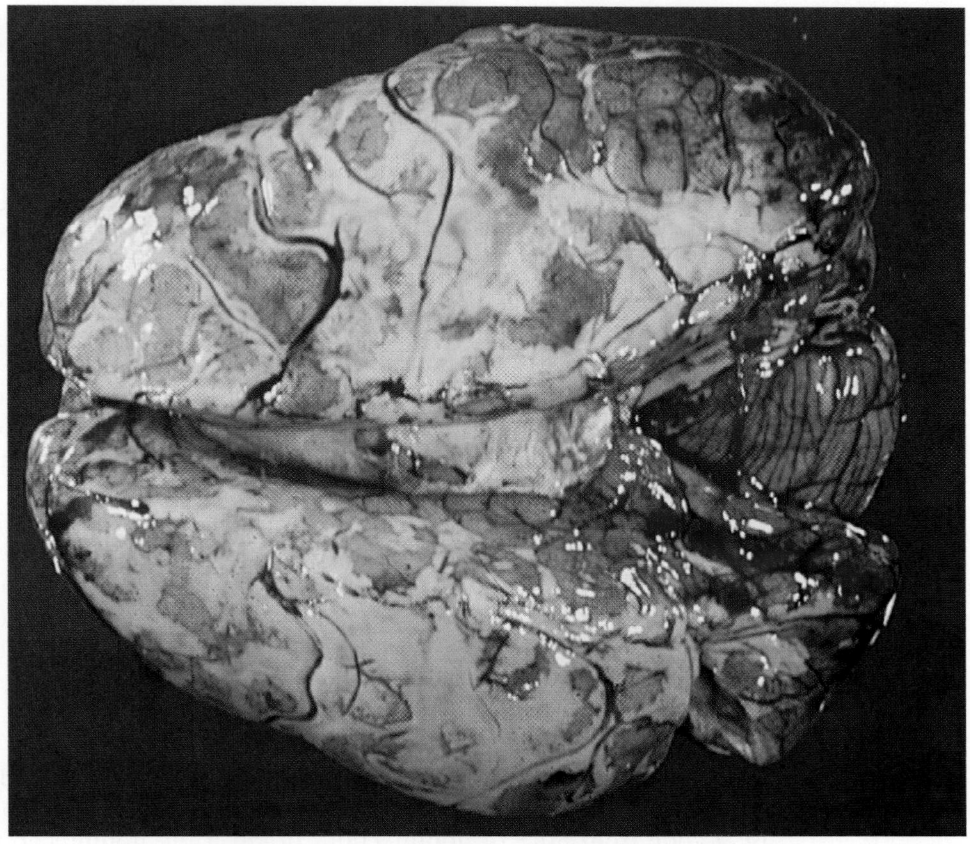

FIGURE 10-3. Bacterial meningitis. The surface of the brain is covered with pus.

Meningococcal Infection

Meningococcal infections are caused by the bacterium meningococcus (Figure 10-3). These bacteria may be found in around 10% of the population (in the nose or throat) and cause no ill effects. These people are known as asymptomatic carriers. This bacterium can cause **meningitis**, which is an infection in the fluid of a person's spinal cord and brain. It also can cause septicemia (blood infection), which is known as meningococcal septicemia.

EXAMPLE Meningococcal meningitis, A39.0.

EXAMPLE Meningococcemia, A39.4.

Sepsis

Sepsis is a medical condition in which the immune system goes into overdrive, releasing chemicals that trigger widespread inflammation into the blood to combat infection. When coding sepsis in ICD-10-CM it is appropriate to assign the code for the systemic infection. If the causal organism or type of infection is not further specified, assign code A41.9.

Some patients may have sepsis without positive blood cultures. If a physician documents urosepsis a query must be initiated for clarification. There is no Alphabetic Index term for this condition. If a patient has acute organ dysfunction and sepsis, and the organ dysfunction is not directly attributed to the sepsis, and there is no other underlying cause documented, a query should be initiated. Acute organ dysfunction attributable to sepsis should be assigned a code for severe sepsis. **Septic shock** represents a type of acute organ dysfunction and therefore should have a code for severe sepsis assigned.

Sequencing of the codes for *sepsis with a localized infection* (i.e., pneumonia, cellulitis) meeting the definition of principal diagnosis should be assigned in the following order:

- Assign the code for the systemic infection
- Assign the code for the localized infection
- Assign the code for severe sepsis, if applicable
- Assign a code for any applicable acute organ dysfunction

Sequencing of codes for *sepsis due to a postprocedural infection*, which is an infection due to a complication of medical care, should be assigned in the following order:

- Assign the postprocedural infection code first.
- Assign code for the specific infection
- Assign a code for severe sepsis, if applicable
- Assign a code for any applicable acute organ dysfunction

Systemic inflammatory response syndrome (SIRS) refers to a systemic response to infection, trauma/burns, pancreatitis, or cancer. The symptoms include some or all of the following:

- Hypothermia (temperature lower than 36° C/97° F) or fever (higher than 38° C/100° F)
- Tachycardia (heart rate greater than 100 beats/min)
- Tachypnea (more than 20 breaths/min) or hypocapnia (arterial CO_2 less than 32 mm Hg)
- WBC greater than 12,000 or less than 4000 or greater than 10% bands

SIRS due to a noninfectious process (such as trauma, surgery, or burn) that meets the definition of principal diagnosis should have codes assigned in the following order:

- Assign the code for the noninfectious condition
- Assign a code from R65.1-
- Assign a code for any applicable acute organ dysfunction

When a patient is admitted with a noninfectious condition and an infectious condition that both meet the definition of principal diagnosis, either may be sequenced first. Do not use a code from SIRS of noninfectious origin if the noninfectious condition leads to an infection resulting in severe sepsis.

EXAMPLE

Patient admitted with pneumonia, fever, and tachycardia with elevated WBC. Physician suspects sepsis and orders blood cultures. Two days after admittance, cultures are positive for pneumococcal bacteria and physician confirms pneumococcal sepsis, A40.3, J18.9.

EXERCISE 10-2

Assign codes to the following conditions.

1. Respiratory anthrax ______
2. Cutaneous anthrax ______
3. *Mycobacterium kansasii* ______
4. MAI ______
5. DMAC ______
6. Whooping cough ______
7. Meningococcal conjunctivitis ______
8. Meningococcal infection in the myocardium ______
9. Sepsis due to meningococcal bacteria ______
10. Gonococcal sepsis ______
11. Severe sepsis with acute respiratory failure ______
12. Patient presents with fever, chills, and elevated WBC. ______
    The physician orders blood cultures for suspected sepsis.
    The discharge summary lists sepsis due to *Escherichia coli.* Patient also had a UTI.
13. Patient with sepsis secondary to pneumonia ______

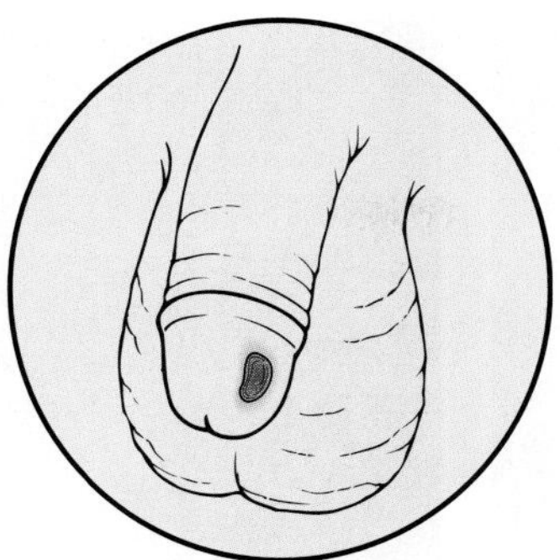

FIGURE 10-4. Chancre of primary syphilis.

Infections With a Predominantly Sexual Mode of Transmission (A50-A64)

Syphilis

Syphilis is a sexually transmitted disease (STD) that is caused by bacteria. Syphilis is passed through direct contact with syphilis sores. Sores occur in the vagina, penis, anus, or rectum. They can also occur on the lips and in the mouth. Syphilis can be passed on to babies through pregnant women. Syphilis occurs in three stages: primary, secondary, and late.

Primary syphilis is revealed by sores called "**chancres**" (Figure 10-4). These sores can last for 3 to 6 weeks. Treatment with a single injection of penicillin can cure the patient at this stage of the disease.

Secondary syphilis, which usually presents as a rash on the palms of the hands and feet, may be accompanied by fever, sore throat, headache, and fatigue. Lesions also may appear in the mouth, vagina, or penis. Sometimes, warty patches called "**condylomata** lata" may appear on the genitalia. These secondary signs eventually disappear even without treatment, but the infection then progresses to late stages.

Late syphilis is the hidden stage of the disease. No signs or symptoms are noted until it begins to damage internal organs, which may occur years later.

A blood test is performed to test for syphilis. This test is called VDRL (Venereal Disease Research Laboratory), or RPR (rapid plasma reagin).

EXAMPLE Late neurosyphilis with ataxia, A52.19.

EXAMPLE Two-year-old presents with syphilitic pemphigus, A50.06.

EXAMPLE Genital chancre, A51.0.

Gonorrhea

Gonorrhea is caused by a bacterium and transmitted by sexual contact. Women may have no symptoms, but men usually report burning while urinating and discharge from the penis. Gonorrhea is treated with an antibiotic. If gonorrhea is not treated, complications usually occur.

EXAMPLE Female patient presents with acute gonococcal cervicitis, A54.03.

EXAMPLE Male patient presents with chronic prostatitis due to gonorrhea, A54.22.

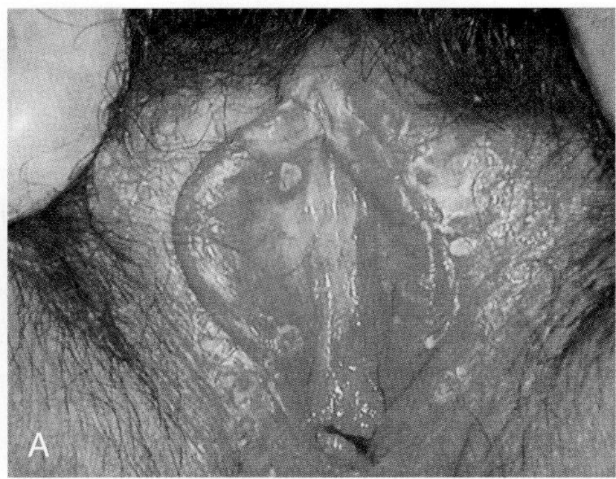

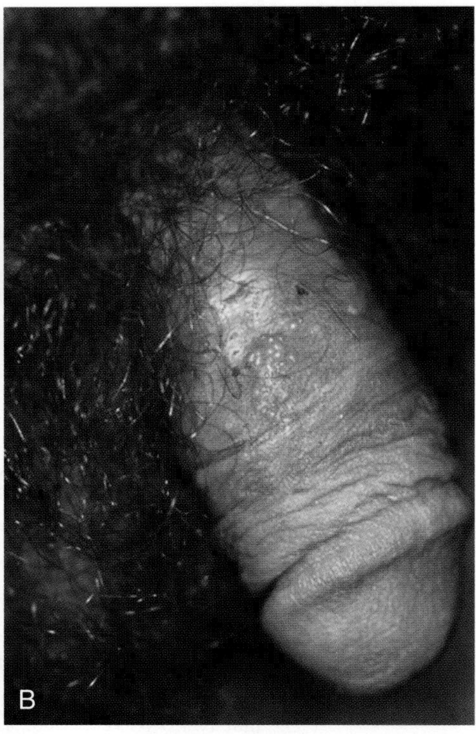

FIGURE 10-5. Genital herpes in the female patient **(A)** and the male patient **(B)**.

Herpes Simplex I and II

Herpes simplex virus is another name for a cold sore or fever blister, also known as HSV type I. The disease manifests as small fluid-filled blisters. It usually occurs on the face but occasionally is noted in the genital area. People usually acquire HSV I during infancy or childhood from people who kiss them or share towels or eating utensils. In type II or genital herpes, sores appear on the vagina, penis, or buttocks (Figure 10-5). Type II is transmitted via sexual intercourse. Antiviral medications are being used to suppress recurrences of herpes.

Genital herpes is considered an STD. It is highly unlikely that the virus is spread through contact with toilet seats or hot tubs. Herpes remains in the nerve cells of the body for life and can become active at any given time. There is no cure for herpes, but there are medicines such as acyclovir (Zovirax), Famciclovir (Famvir), and valacyclovir (Valtrex). Valtrex is also used as a preventive medicine.

EXAMPLE

Patient presents to physician's office with complaints of blisters on penis. Physician makes diagnosis of herpes infection of the penis, A60.01.

EXERCISE 10-3

Assign codes to the following conditions.

1. Patient has a chancre on the penis. ________
2. Patient presents with condyloma latum. ________
3. Latent syphilis with unknown date of infection ________
4. Neurosyphilitic dementia ________
5. Early congenital syphilis ________
6. Herpes simplex vaginitis ________
7. Gonococcal conjunctivitis ________
8. Pelvic inflammatory disease due to chlamydia ________

Other Spirochetal Diseases (A65-A69)

Lyme disease, also known as borreliosis, is an inflammatory disease caused by bacteria carried by ticks. Ticks acquire this bacterium through biting deer that are infected. It was first reported in the Northeast United States but now has spread throughout the Midwest, as well as the Pacific Coast. The symptoms of this disease resemble the flu and include headache, fever, and muscle aches. Sometimes, a bull's-eye rash appears at the site of the tick bite.

A blood test can be performed to look for antibodies to the bacteria that cause Lyme disease. Treatment for Lyme disease consists of antibiotics and anti-inflammatory medicines. If this disease is left untreated, complications such as Lyme arthritis, heart problems, or neurologic disorders can occur.

EXAMPLE A patient presents with severe joint pain. Blood work reveals Lyme disease. The physician documents that the patient has arthritis due to Lyme disease, A69.23.

Viral and Prion Infections of the Central Nervous System (A80-A89)

Poliomyelitis (polio) is a viral disease that affects the nerves and is caused by the poliovirus. It is also known as infantile paralysis. This disease has been nearly eradicated in the United States as the result of mandatory vaccination.

If people are unvaccinated, this disease may be contracted through direct contact with infected persons. The virus usually enters the body through the mouth or nose. Symptoms can resemble the flu, and a person may or may not become paralyzed. Treatment consists of alleviating the symptoms and letting the virus run its course. Essentially three types of polio infection may occur: subclinical infection, nonparalytic, and paralytic. If the spinal cord or the brain is not affected (which is the case 90% of the time), then complete recovery can occur.

EXAMPLE A patient presents to the hospital with headache, muscle weakness, fever, and muscle spasms of the neck. After a battery of testing, it is determined that the patient has acute poliomyelitis, A80.9.

Viral meningitis, also known as aseptic meningitis, is an infection of the fluid in the spinal cord and the fluid around the brain. Viral meningitis is far less serious than bacterial meningitis and is rarely fatal.

No treatment is available for viral meningitis other than relieving the symptoms, which usually consist of headache, stiff neck, and photophobia. Many different viruses may cause meningitis, but most cases are caused by the enteroviruses, and these viruses may be associated with other diseases. Meningitis also may be transmitted via mosquito bites.

EXAMPLE A patient presents to the hospital with severe headache and stiff neck. A lumbar puncture is performed, and it is determined that the patient has meningitis due to Echovirus, A87.0, 009U3ZX.

Arthropod-Borne Viral Fevers and Viral Hemorrhagic Fevers (A90-A99)

Dengue Fever

Dengue fever is a virus transmitted by an infected mosquito. It is not spread from person to person. Although very few cases have been reported in the United States, it is endemic to Puerto Rico and many tourist destinations in the Caribbean and Central America. According to the CDC there are 100 million cases worldwide each year. The symptoms of this disease include high fever, severe headache, and mild bleeding of the nose or gums. The more severe form of the disease, dengue hemorrhagic fever, includes severe abdominal pain and vomiting and capillary permeability, which can lead to ascites, pleural effusion, and shock. There is no vaccine or specific medicine to treat this disease.

West Nile

West Nile virus is a disease that is spread to individuals by a mosquito bite. People with healthy immune systems may be infected with this disease and have only mild symptoms such as fever or headache. Those people with weakened immune systems and the elderly may experience complications.

EXAMPLE West Nile virus, A92.30.

EXAMPLE West Nile encephalitis, A92.31.

ZIKA Virus

The Zika virus is a disease that is mainly spread by infected *Aedes* mosquitoes. It may also be transmitted via blood transfusion or by having sex with an infected person. The most common symptoms are fever, rash, conjunctivitis, and joint pain. The Zika virus can also be transmitted from a pregnant woman to her fetus, which could result in certain birth defects such as microcephaly and other defects of the eye, hearing deficits, and impaired growth. At this time, there is no vaccination available and no medicine to treat the virus. The treatment consists of treating the symptoms. According to the *Official Coding Guidelines for Coding and Reporting*, only confirmed cases should be coded to A92.5.

EXAMPLE Patient was seen in at the urgent care center with a fever. Patient recently traveled to Brazil with suspected exposure to mosquitoes carrying the Zika virus. Lab tests were performed to rule out Zika. R50.9, Z20.828.

Viral Infections Characterized by Skin and Mucous Membrane Lesions (B00-B09)

Hand, Foot, and Mouth Disease

Hand, foot, and mouth disease (HFMD) is a common viral illness in children. The symptoms include eruptions of blisters in the mouth and a rash usually found on the hands and feet. This is an infectious disease that is spread usually from infected hands. There is no specific treatment except to treat the symptoms. It is important to note that this disease is not the same as foot and mouth disease, which rarely occurs in humans.

EXAMPLE Child is seen by pediatrician and is diagnosed with HFMD, B08.4.

Herpes Zoster

Herpes zoster, or shingles, is a disease that is caused by the same virus that causes chickenpox. Once a person has contracted chickenpox, the virus remains dormant in the body in certain nerves. Shingles usually occurs in people over 50 years of age but sometimes is reported in younger people. It is caused by conditions that weaken the body's immune system such as cancer, aging, and stress.

Shingles starts as a rash that turns into fluid-filled blisters that may become very painful. Sometimes, a case of shingles results in long-term pain, known as "postherpetic neuralgia."

EXAMPLE Shingles with blepharitis, B02.39.

EXAMPLE Trigeminal neuralgia as a result of shingles, B02.22.

EXERCISE 10-4

Assign codes to the following conditions.

1. Shingles ____________
2. Stomatitis due to herpes simplex ____________
3. Acute polio ____________
4. West Nile virus ____________
5. Ebola virus ____________
6. Chickenpox ____________
7. Monkeypox ____________
8. German measles with pneumonia ____________
9. Verruca plantaris ____________
10. Molluscum contagiosum ____________
11. Fifth disease ____________

Viral Hepatitis (B15-B19)

Hepatitis

Hepatitis is inflammation of the liver and can be caused by, among other things, several different viruses, namely, A, B, C, D, and E. All of these strains of hepatitis cause acute viral hepatitis. Only B, C, and D viruses cause chronic hepatitis. In chronic hepatitis, the infection may last a lifetime. Symptoms of hepatitis include fatigue, jaundice, nausea and vomiting, headache, diarrhea, and fever.

Hepatitis A is most commonly spread via food or water that has been contaminated by feces from an infected person. International travelers are at risk for this disease. A vaccine is available. If contracted, this disease usually resolves on its own.

Hepatitis B is spread through contact with infected blood, via sex with an infected person, or during childbirth. A hepatitis B vaccine is available. In the past, this disease may have been acquired during a blood transfusion, but in 1992, testing was instituted to control infection transmitted through the blood supply. Acute hepatitis B usually resolves on its own, but chronic cases require drug treatment. Hepatitis B may cause cirrhosis of the liver, liver failure, and liver cancer. About 10% of those infected with the B virus may become carriers. A carrier will have B virus in his or her blood for 6 months or longer after the original infection subsides.

Hepatitis C is spread through infected blood, sexual contact, and childbirth. No vaccine is available for this disease; the only way to prevent it is through avoidance of risky behaviors such as needle sharing. There are new medications that can now cure hepatitis C.

Hepatitis D is spread through infected blood. To acquire hepatitis D, a patient must already have hepatitis B infection. Those with chronic hepatitis D are treated with medications. This form was formerly known as delta.

Hepatitis E is spread through food or water that has been contaminated by feces from an infected person; it is unusual in the United Sates. No vaccine is available, and an outbreak usually resolves on its own.

EXAMPLE Patient admitted is jaundiced and has chronic hepatitis B, B18.1.

Human Immunodeficiency Virus (HIV) Disease (B20)

It is important to note that codes within this section are used only when the diagnosis has been confirmed. This is an exception to the hospital inpatient guideline that allows the coding of possible, probable, or suspected diagnoses.

AIDS is an incurable disease of the immune system caused by the human immunodeficiency **(HIV)** virus, and it is the final stage of HIV disease. It first appeared in the United States in 1981. In the beginning this virus was seen in the homosexual and intravenous drug user (IVDU) population and later spread to the heterosexual population. The virus is found in and transmitted by blood, semen, vaginal secretions, and breast milk. Transmission occurs through sexual contact, blood transfusions, needle sharing, or breastfeeding.

People who are infected with the HIV virus may not have any symptoms for up to 10 years. Once the immune system becomes weakened, they become susceptible to opportunistic infections. When HIV infects a person it most commonly attacks the CD4 cells, which are a type of lymphocyte (white blood cell). Over time in a person infected with HIV the number of CD4 cells decreases, which means the immune system is weakened. Normal CD4 counts are between 500 and 1600. Often CD4 percentages are used as a basis for determining AIDS. These are the percentages of total lymphocytes. Once a CD4 count goes below 350 cells/mL a patient may be at risk to develop herpes, TB, Kaposi's sarcoma, or non-Hodgkin's lymphoma. When the count goes below 50 a patient may develop *Mycobacterium avium* or cytomegalovirus (CMV).

AIDS may be treated with HAART (highly active antiretroviral therapy). Sometimes drugs are given on a prophylactic basis to prevent opportunistic infections. With the use of today's drugs, a patient's CD4 count can rebound above 200. For example, it may be documented that a patient's CD4 nadir is 150. **Nadir** means the lowest level this patient's CD4 count has ever been.

Once a patient develops AIDS, from then on he or she is always assigned code B20. When a patient is admitted for treatment of an HIV-related condition, the principal diagnosis should always be B20.

EXAMPLE Patient admitted with Kaposi's sarcoma of connective tissue, B20, C46.1.

If a patient is admitted with an AIDS-defining illness (Box 10-1), the principal diagnosis is B20. When a patient is admitted with a condition unrelated to AIDS, then the code for the unrelated condition is the principal diagnosis.

EXAMPLE A patient with a history of AIDS is admitted in alcohol withdrawal, F10.230, B20.

Sometimes, patients test HIV positive but have no symptoms. Z21 is the code that should be used for these patients. Tests may have inconclusive results; then, the code R75 should be assigned, nonspecific serologic evidence of HIV. This code can be found in the Alphabetic Index under Human immunodeficiency virus disease, laboratory evidence.

EXAMPLE Patient is being treated for oral thrush and is HIV positive, B37.0, Z21.

AIDS and Pregnancy

If a woman has AIDS and is pregnant, code O98.7- should be used, along with B20. Codes from Chapter 15 in the code book always take precedence.

Encounters for Testing for HIV

- Encounter for determining HIV status, Z11.4, Screening for other specified viral disease
- Encounter for counseling for an HIV-negative patient, Z71.7
- Encounter for an HIV-positive patient who is asymptomatic, Z21; counseling code may also be used
- Encounter for HIV-positive patient who is symptomatic, B20; counseling code may also be used

BOX 10-1 LIST OF AIDS-DEFINING CONDITIONS[1]

The Centers for Disease Control and Prevention (CDC) considers a patient to have acquired immunodeficiency syndrome (AIDS) if a CD4+ T-cell count is below 200 cells/μl (or a CD4+ T-cell percentage of total lymphocytes is less than 14%), or if the patient has one of the following defining illnesses:

Conditions included in the 1993 AIDS surveillance case definition

- Candidiasis of bronchi, trachea, or lungs
- Candidiasis, esophageal
- Cervical cancer, invasive
- Coccidioidomycosis, disseminated or extrapulmonary
- Cryptococcosis, extrapulmonary
- Cryptosporidiosis, chronic intestinal (longer than 1 month duration)
- Cytomegalovirus disease (other than liver, spleen, or nodes)
- Cytomegalovirus retinitis (with loss of vision)
- Encephalopathy, human immunodeficiency virus (HIV)-related
- Herpes simplex: chronic ulcer(s) (longer than 1 month duration); or bronchitis, pneumonitis, or esophagitis
- Histoplasmosis, disseminated or extrapulmonary
- Isosporiasis, chronic intestinal (longer than 1 month duration)
- Kaposi's sarcoma
- Lymphoma, Burkitt's (or equivalent term)
- Lymphoma, immunoblastic (or equivalent term)
- Lymphoma, primary, of brain
- *Mycobacterium avium* complex or *Mycobacterium kansasii,* disseminated or extrapulmonary
- *Mycobacterium tuberculosis,* any site (pulmonary or extrapulmonary)
- *Mycobacterium,* other species or unidentified species, disseminated or extrapulmonary
- *Pneumocystis carinii* pneumonia
- Pneumonia, recurrent
- Progressive multifocal leukoencephalopathy
- *Salmonella* septicemia, recurrent
- Toxoplasmosis of brain
- Wasting syndrome due to HIV

EXERCISE 10-5

Assign codes to the following conditions.

1. Patient with HIV and CD4 nadir of 100. Currently being treated for HIV dementia. ____________
2. Patient has HIV and a history of invasive cervical cancer. ____________
3. Patient is admitted with *Pneumocystis* pneumonia (PCP) and has a history of AIDS. ____________
4. Patient is admitted with dehydration and has AIDS. ____________
5. Patient is tested for HIV in the physician's office, and the results are inconclusive. ____________
6. Patient is in the first trimester of pregnancy and is positive for AIDS. ____________
7. Patient is admitted with bacteremia and is an AIDS patient. ____________
8. Patient is admitted with pulmonary tuberculosis and has AIDS. ____________
9. Patient is admitted with *E. coli* sepsis and a CD4 count of 32, with known AIDS. ____________

10. Patient is admitted with difficulty swallowing; after an esophagogastroduodenoscopy (EGD) was performed, it was discovered that the patient had candidal esophagitis and a history of being HIV positive. __________
11. Acute hepatitis B with hepatitis delta __________
12. Patient has chronic hepatitis C. __________

Other Viral Diseases (B25-B34)

Infectious Mononucleosis

Infectious mononucleosis is often caused by the Epstein Barr virus. This virus is often called the kissing disease as it is spread through saliva. It can occur at any age but most often occurs during the teenage years. Symptoms include fever, sore throat, and swollen glands. A blood test can confirm a diagnosis and treatment consists of treating the symptoms.

EXAMPLE

Patient is seen in doctor's office complaining of sore throat and swollen glands. Testing is done and confirms infectious mono, B27.90.

Mycoses (B35-B49)

Candidiasis

Candidiasis is caused by *Candida* fungi. These fungi often live harmlessly within the body until a patient's immune system becomes weak, or until he or she is taking medications that reduce the native bacteria that control this fungus. Usual spots in which *Candida* infections are found include the following:

Mouth—Thrush is found as white plaques on lips, cheeks, or tongue. It can be seen in babies, people with cancer, and diabetics.

Esophagus—often found in patients with AIDS and those on chemotherapy

Cutaneous—found in warm, moist areas that receive little ventilation, such as diaper areas, buttocks, and skin folds of the abdomen, breasts, or groin

Vaginal yeast infections are often caused by birth control pills, pregnancy, or frequent douching.

Candidal infections are treated according to the area infected. Patients with oral thrush are generally treated with nystatin swish and swallow, whereas those with candidal esophagitis are treated with fluconazole. Patients with vaginal yeast infection are treated with antifungals such as Monistat, nystatin, or Vagistat. A common mistake that coders will make is to code candidiasis of the groin or other specified areas of the skin to B37.89, other sites of candidiasis. The groin area is really the skin or cutaneous candidiasis and should be coded to B37.2, candidiasis of skin and nail.

EXAMPLE

Patient is being treated for candidal intertrigo under breast, B37.2.

Histoplasmosis

Histoplasmosis is a fungal disease that primarily affects the lungs. If it affects other organs, it is termed "disseminated histoplasmosis." The fungus causing this disorder is found in soil and material that is contaminated with bat and/or bird droppings. It is treated with antifungals, and mild forms of this disease can resolve on their own.

EXAMPLE

Patient is being treated for acute pulmonary histoplasmosis, B39.0.

Protozoal Diseases (B50-B64)

Toxoplasmosis

Toxoplasmosis is caused by a parasite. Many people have the parasite, but the majority do not get sick. If a person is immunocompromised, they are more likely to contract the disease. Pregnant women are at risk for this disease, and if it is passed on to the baby there can be severe consequences either at birth or later in life. Symptoms can include headache, confusion, seizures, or lung problems. The disease can be transmitted from the waste of an infected cat, contaminated or raw meat, cutting boards that have been in contact with raw meat, or blood transfusions. This condition is treated with Pyrimethamine, an antimalarial medication, and Sulfadiazine, an antibiotic.

EXAMPLE Patient was admitted and is being treated for myocarditis due toxoplasmosis, B58.81

Helminthiases (B65-B83)

Helminthiases

Helminthiases is another word for diseases caused by parasitic worms. The most common parasitic worms are tapeworms, pin worms, round worms, and hook worms, and all are acquired in a variety of ways. Worms live in the intestines.

Tapeworms are acquired by eating undercooked meat or fish that have tapeworms. They can cause stomach aches, diarrhea, and loss of appetite. They can grow to 15-30 feet in length and can live for 20 years. When an invasive infection occurs, the larvae migrate to tissues or organs in the body and can cause other disorders such as seizures, hydrocephalus, or dementia.

Pinworms are a type of roundworm and the eggs are usually spread under the fingernails and then contaminate food, dishes, or play things. They are threadlike and found in the rectum and colon.

Roundworms are a type of worm that resemble an earthworm. They can be transmitted by eggs in human waste used as fertilizer or by pets. Hook worms are usually caused by unsanitary conditions. They can be transmitted through infected soil and walking barefoot.

EXAMPLE Child is in pediatrician's office with complaints of anal itching. The doctor diagnoses pinworms, B80.

EXAMPLE Patient had been working in Guatemala and acquired an infection with a pork tapeworm, B68.0.

Pediculosis, Acariasis, and Other Infestations (B85-B89)

Maggots can infest humans in areas of open sores or open body cavities. The condition is termed myiasis, and it occurs when flies lay eggs in areas of the body.

Contagious dermatitis caused by mites is known as **scabies**. The mite burrows under the skin and lays eggs (Figure 10-6). It causes a skin rash and intense itching, usually at night. Scabies is spread rapidly from skin-to-skin contact. Outbreaks often occur in institutions such as nursing homes and child care facilities. Scabies is treated with a scabicide, which is a form of pesticide.

EXAMPLE A homeless man presented to the ER with an open traumatic wound of the right calf of the leg that was infested with maggots, S81.801A, B87.1, Z59.0, X58.XXXA.

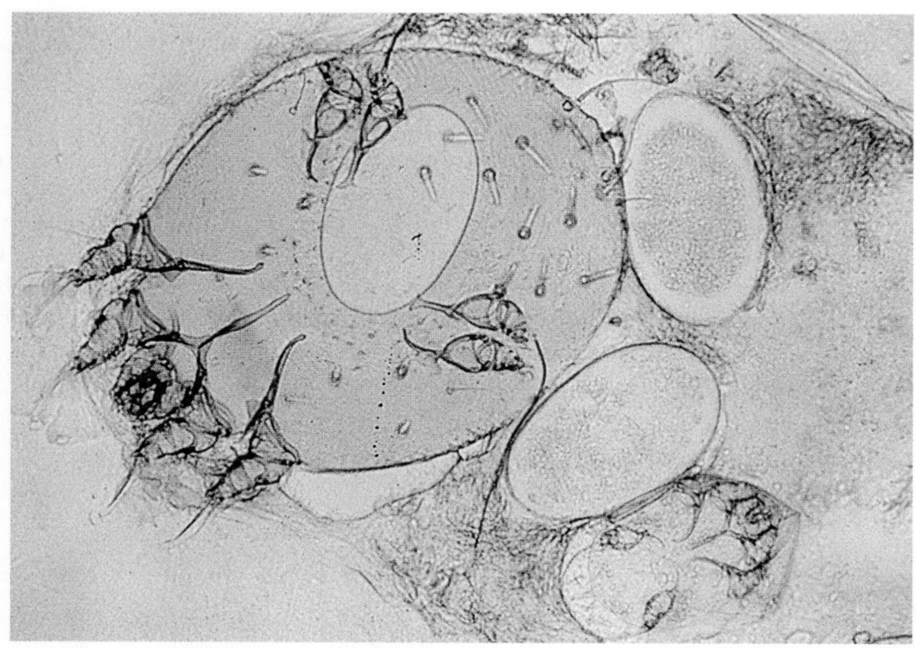

FIGURE 10-6. Scabies mite.

Sequelae of Infectious and Parasitic Diseases (B90-B94)

Some infections result in **sequelae** or late effects of an acute disease or that may be due to an inactive condition. Codes in this category (B90-B94) are used for late effects of conditions from categories A00-B89. Sequelae are residuals of diseases from A00-B89. Codes from categories B90-B94 are not to be used for chronic current infections. When coding sequelae, two codes are required. The first code would be the condition resulting from the infectious or parasitic disease, and then the sequelae code would be second.

EXAMPLE Patient is seen for chronic uveitis of the right eye, which is a late effect of leprosy, H20.11, B92.

EXAMPLE Patient with left-sided hemiplegia following acute poliomyelitis, G81.94, B91.

Bacterial and Viral Infectious Agents (B95-B97)

The codes in these categories are supplementary codes. They should be used to identify infectious agents in diseases that are classified elsewhere (Figure 10-7). There will be an instructional note found at the infection code advising the coder that an additional code, if known, should be assigned to identify the organism. Practitioners sometimes define organisms as resistant to certain antibiotics. MRSA is methicillin-resistant *Staphyloccus aureus.* If a patient has pneumonia caused by *Staphylococcus aureus* and the organism is resistant to methicillin, it would be coded as J15.212. Likewise, practitioners may identify organisms that are sensitive to antibiotics, such as MSSA, which is methicillin-sensitive *Staphylococcus aureus.* If a patient has pneumonia caused by *Staphylococcus aureus* that is susceptible to methicillin, it would be coded to J15.211.

EXAMPLE Patient with UTI. Physician documents UTI due to *E. coli,* N39.0, B96.20.

EXAMPLE UTI due to strep group D resistant to vancomycin, N39.0, B95.2, Z16.21.

N39.0 Urinary tract infection, site not specified

Use additional code (B95-B97), to identify infectious agent

Excludes1 candidiasis of urinary tract (B37.4-)
neonatal urinary tract infection (P39.3)
urinary tract infection of specified site, such as:
cystitis (N30.-)
urethritis (N34.-)

FIGURE 10-7. Use additional code to identify infectious agent.

EXERCISE 10-6

Assign codes to the following conditions.

1. Patient has jock itch. ______________
2. Patient has oral thrush. ______________
3. Patient presents to the physician's office with hemoptysis. Diagnosis is determined to be aspergillosis of the lung. ______________
4. Patient with a history of being HIV positive is admitted to the hospital and diagnosed with *Pneumocystis carinii* pneumonia. ______________
5. A patient was recently working in Ecuador and returns with a diagnosis of river blindness. ______________
6. A child presents to the pediatrician with an itchy scalp. She is diagnosed with head lice. ______________
7. Croup caused by RSV ______________
8. Patient is seen by physician for chronic pulmonary histoplasmosis. ______________
9. Patient is admitted to the hospital with severe abdominal pain. Discharge diagnosis is intestinal myiasis. ______________
10. Patient has impetigo due to *Staphylococcus aureus.* ______________

FACTORS INFLUENCING HEALTH STATUS AND CONTACT WITH HEALTH SERVICES (Z CODES)

As was discussed in Chapter 9, it may be difficult to locate Z codes in the Index. Coders often say, "I did not know there was a Z code for that." Refer to Chapter 9 for a listing of common main terms to locate Z codes.

A review of the Tabular reveals that some Z codes pertain to infectious and parasitic diseases:

CHAPTER 10: INFECTIOUS AND PARASITIC DISEASES

Z03.810	Encounter for observation for suspected exposure to anthrax ruled out
Z11.0	Encounter for screening for intestinal infectious diseases
Z11.1	Encounter for screening for respiratory tuberculosis
Z11.2	Encounter for screening for other bacterial diseases
Z11.3	Encounter for screening for infections with a predominantly sexual mode of transmission
Z11.4	Encounter for screening for human immunodeficiency virus [HIV]
Z11.5	Encounter for screening for other viral diseases
Z11.6	Encounter for screening for other protozoal diseases and helminthiases

Z11.8	Encounter for screening for other infectious and parasitic diseases
Z11.9	Encounter for screening for infectious and parasitic diseases, unspecified
Z16.10	Resistance to unspecified beta lactam antibiotics
Z16.11	Resistance to penicillins Resistance to amoxicillin Resistance to ampicillin
Z16.12	Extended spectrum beta lactamase (ESBL) resistance
Z16.19	Resistance to other specified beta lactam antibiotics Resistance to cephalosporins
Z16.20	Resistance to unspecified antibiotic Resistance to antibiotics NOS
Z16.21	Resistance to vancomycin
Z16.22	Resistance to vancomycin related antibiotics
Z16.23	Resistance to quinolones and fluoroquinolones
Z16.24	Resistance to multiple antibiotics
Z16.29	Resistance to other single specified antibiotic Resistance to aminoglycosides Resistance to macrolides Resistance to sulfonamides Resistance to tetracyclines
Z16.30	Resistance to unspecified antimicrobial drugs Drug resistance NOS
Z16.31	Resistance to antiparasitic drug(s) Resistance to quinine and related compounds
Z16.32	Resistance to antifungal drug(s)
Z16.33	Resistance to antiviral drug(s)
Z16.34	Resistance to antimycobacterial drug(s) Resistance to tuberculostatics
Z16.341	Resistance to single antimycobacterial drug Resistance to antimycobacterial drug NOS
Z16.342	Resistance to multiple antimycobacterial drugs
Z16.35	Resistance to multiple antimicrobial drugs Excludes1: Resistance to multiple antibiotics only (Z16.24)
Z16.39	Resistance to other specified antimicrobial drug
Z20.01	Contact with and (suspected) exposure to intestinal infectious diseases due to *Escherichia coli* (*E. coli*)
Z20.09	Contact with and (suspected) exposure to other intestinal infectious diseases
Z20.1	Contact with and (suspected) exposure to tuberculosis
Z20.2	Contact with and (suspected) exposure to infections with a predominantly sexual mode of transmission
Z20.3	Contact with and (suspected) exposure to rabies
Z20.4	Contact with and (suspected) exposure to rubella
Z20.5	Contact with and (suspected) exposure to viral hepatitis
Z20.6	Contact with and (suspected) exposure to human immunodeficiency virus [HIV]
Z20.7	Contact with and (suspected) exposure to pediculosis, acariasis, and other infestations
Z20.810	Contact with and (suspected) exposure to anthrax
Z20.811	Contact with and (suspected) exposure to meningococcus
Z20.818	Contact with and (suspected) exposure to other bacterial communicable diseases
Z20.820	Contact with and (suspected) exposure to varicella
Z20.821	Contact with and (suspected) exposure to Zika virus
Z20.828	Contact with and (suspected) exposure to other viral communicable diseases
Z20.89	Contact with and (suspected) exposure to other communicable diseases
Z20.9	Contact with and (suspected) exposure to unspecified communicable disease
Z21	Asymptomatic human immunodeficiency virus [HIV] infection status

Z22.0	Carrier of typhoid
Z22.1	Carrier of other intestinal infectious diseases
Z22.2	Carrier of diphtheria
Z22.31	Carrier of bacterial disease due to meningococci
Z22.32	Carrier of bacterial disease due to staphylococci
Z22.330	Carrier of Group B streptococcus
Z22.338	Carrier of other streptococcus
Z22.39	Carrier of other specified bacterial diseases
Z22.4	Carrier of infections with a predominantly sexual mode of transmission
Z22.5	Carrier of viral hepatitis
Z22.6	Carrier of human T-lymphotropic virus type 1 [HTLV-1]
Z22.8	Carrier of other infectious diseases
Z22.9	Carrier of infectious disease, unspecified
Z29.11	Encounter for prophylactic immunotherapy for respiratory syncytial virus (RSV)
Z29.14	Encounter for prophylactic rabies immune globin
Z71.7	Human immunodeficiency virus [HIV] counseling
Z83.0	Family history of human immunodeficiency virus [HIV] disease
Z83.1	Family history of other infectious and parasitic diseases
Z86.11	Personal history of tuberculosis
Z86.12	Personal history of poliomyelitis
Z86.13	Personal history of malaria
Z86.19	Personal history of other infectious and parasitic diseases

EXAMPLE

Student presents to health clinic after exposure to meningitis, Z20.811.

EXAMPLE

Patient is seen in doctor's office after handling a package in a mail facility suspected to be contaminated by anthrax, Z03.810.

EXERCISE 10-7

Assign codes to the following condition.

1. History of malaria ____________
2. Exposure to chickenpox at daycare ____________
3. Patient returning from China; was exposed to SARS ____________
4. Patient needs vaccination for cholera ____________
5. Influenza vaccination not administered because patient is hospitalized with pneumonia ____________

COMMON TREATMENTS

See Table 10-1 for drugs commonly used to treat infectious diseases.

PROCEDURES

There are multiple therapeutic and diagnostic procedures that can be performed for infectious and parasitic diseases. There are no specific procedure tables for infectious and parasitic diseases.

TABLE 10-1 DRUGS FOR INFECTIOUS DISEASES[2]

Drug Category	Drug Action	Examples	Side Effects	Comments
Antibiotics	Destroy or inhibit the growth of bacterial strains or microorganisms but have not been found to be effective for viral infections	Penicillin V Potassium (Pen-V-K) Tetracycline (Sumycin) Amoxicillin (Amoxil) Cephalosporins (Keflex, Ceclor) Ciprofloxacin (Cipro) Metronidazole (Flagyl) Azithromycin (Zithromax)	Common side effects of any are nausea, GI upset, urticaria	Caution must be used when administering penicillin IM regarding observation after infection for potential of anaphylaxis Cipro: acute infections and prophylactic postanthrax exposure
Antifungals	Inhibit and kill fungal growth	Griseofulvin (Grisactin) Ketoconazole (Nizoral) Clotrimazole (Lotrimin) Fluconazole (Diflucan)	Nausea, vomiting, abdominal, pain, itching, urticaria	Some are available in oral form for systemic treatment, others are available in topical form
Antivirals	Inhibit viral growth	Acyclovir (Zovirax) Zidovudine (Retrovir) Amantadine (Symmetrel)	GI disturbances, headache, malaise, insomnia, dizziness	Should be taken at first sign of onset of viral attack for best relief of symptoms
Antiretrovirals	Treat infection by retroviruses	NRTIs (Retrovir, AZT, Epivir, Abacavir) NNRTIs (Sustiva, Viramunde) Protease inhibitors (Kaletra, Norvir)	Often have severe side effects; side effects are many and varied and can include anemia, GI problems, wasting, acidosis, bone problems	These drugs are given in combination
Antiprotozoals	Inhibit protozoal infections	Chloroquine HCI (Aralen HCI)	Headache, pruritus, GI disturbances, tinnitus	Also known as antimalarials
Antipyretics	Reduce fever	Acetaminophen (Tylenol) Acetylsalicylic acid (aspirin) Ibuprofen (Motrin)	Toxic doses of acetaminophen may cause irreversible and fatal liver damage	Caution must be exercised when administering Tylenol drops and syrup to infants and children; check dosage for either before administering
Antitubercular	Suppress mycobacterium causing tuberculosis	Isoniazid (INH) Ethambutol (Myambutol)	GI disturbances and hepatic disturbances	These drugs usually are given in combination

CHAPTER REVIEW EXERCISE

Where applicable, assign codes for diagnoses and procedures.

1. Gastroenteritis due to *Salmonella* __________
2. Food poisoning, bacterial __________
3. UTI due to candidiasis __________
4. Diarrhea due to *Clostridium difficile* __________
5. Enteritis due to rotavirus __________
6. Infectious colitis __________
7. Primary TB; patient in isolation __________
8. TB of the hip bone __________
9. Tuberculosis lichenoides __________
10. Acute respiratory distress due to COVID-19 __________
11. Gastrointestinal anthrax __________
12. Whooping cough with pneumonia __________
13. DMAC __________
14. Meningococcal endocarditis __________

15. MSSA sepsis ____________

16. *Haemophilus influenzae* sepsis ____________

17. Acute prostatitis due to *E. coli* ____________

18. HIV positive ____________

19. HIV positive with Burkitt's lymphoma ____________

20. Postherpetic neuralgia ____________

CHAPTER GLOSSARY

AIDS: Acquired Immunodeficiency Syndrome, an incurable disease of the immune system caused by a virus.

Anthrax: a bacterial infection usually found in wild or domestic animals.

Candidiasis: a fungal infection; also known as a yeast infection.

Chancre: an ulcer that forms during the first stage of syphilis.

Clostridium difficile: microorganisms that are a leading cause of pseudomembranous colitis; also known as *C. diff.*

Communicable: easily spread from one person to another.

Condylomata: wart-type growth found usually in the genital or anal area.

Coronavirus disease 2019: Infectious disease caused by severe acute respiratory syndrome coronavirus 2 (SARS-CoV-2).

Dengue fever: a virus transmitted by an infected mosquito.

Gastroenteritis: inflammation of the stomach, small intestine and large intestine.

Gonorrhea: disease caused by a bacterium and transmitted by sexual contact.

HAART: highly active antiretroviral therapy, a group of drugs given to AIDS patients for prophylaxis.

Helminthiases: diseases caused by parasitic worms.

Hepatitis: an inflammation of the liver.

Herpes simplex: a virus also known as a *cold sore* or *fever blister.*

Herpes zoster: a disease caused by the same virus that causes chickenpox.

Histoplasmosis: a fungal disease that primarily affects the lungs

HIV: Human Immunodeficiency Virus; the virus that affects the immune system and can progress to AIDS.

Lyme disease: an inflammatory disease caused by bacteria carried by ticks.

Meningitis: an infection in the fluid of a person's spinal cord and brain.

Mycobacterium avium-intercellulare: a mycobacteria found in soil and water.

Nadir: the lowest level.

Nosocomial: hospital-acquired infection.

Parasitic: organism that lives on or takes nourishment from another organism.

Poliomyelitis: a viral disease that affects the nerves.

Scabies: contagious dermatitis caused by mites.

Sepsis: medical condition in which the immune system goes into overdrive, releasing chemicals into the blood to combat infection that trigger widespread inflammation.

Septic shock: a condition caused by *infection* and *sepsis.* It can cause *multiple organ failure* and *death.*

Sequelae: late effect or residual of an acute disease.

SIRS: systemic inflammatory response syndrome, which can be caused by infection or trauma.

Syphilis: a sexually transmitted disease (STD) that is caused by bacteria.

Tuberculosis (TB): an infection caused by *Mycobacterium tuberculosis.*

Urosepsis: infection of urinary site.

Viral meningitis: a viral infection of the fluid in the spinal cord and around the brain.

West Nile: a viral disease that is spread to individuals by a mosquito bite.

REFERENCES

1. Castro KG, Ward JW, Slutsker L, et al: 1993 revised classifi cation system for HIV infection and expanded surveillance: Case defi nition for AIDS among adolescents and adults. *Morb Mortal Wkly Rep* 41(RR–17), December 18, 1992. Bethesda, MD. Centers for Disease Control and Prevention. Available at: <http://www.cdc.gov/mmwr/preview/mmwrhtml/00018871.htm>. Accessed April 4. 2008.
2. Modifi ed from Frazier ME, Drzymkowki JW: Essentials of Human Diseases and Conditions, ed 3, St. Louis, 2004, Saunders, Appendix II, pp 766–767.

11

Neoplasms

(ICD-10-CM Chapter 2, Codes C00-D49)

CHAPTER OUTLINE

LEARNING OBJECTIVES

1. Apply and assign the correct ICD-10-CM/PCS codes in accordance with Official Guidelines for Coding and Reporting
2. Identify pertinent anatomy and physiology of neoplasms
3. Identify neoplastic diseases
4. Assign the correct Z codes and procedure codes related to neoplasms
5. Identify common treatments, medications, laboratory values, and diagnostic tests

ABBREVIATIONS/ ACRONYMS

AIDS acquired immunodeficiency syndrome

ALL acute lymphoblastic leukemia

BCC basal cell carcinoma

BMT bone marrow transplant

CC chief complaint

CDC Centers for Disease Control and Prevention

CML chronic myelogenous leukemia

DCIS ductal carcinoma in situ

FNA fine needle aspiration

GIST gastrointestinal stromal tumor

HCC hepatocellular carcinoma

ICD-10-CM *International Classification of Diseases, 10th Revision, Clinical Modification*

ICD-10-PCS *International Classification of Diseases, 10th Revision, Procedure Coding System*

KS Kaposi's sarcoma

NHL non-Hodgkin's lymphoma

NSCLC non–small cell lung cancer

RCC renal cell carcinoma

SCLC small cell lung cancer

SCC squamous cell carcinoma

SLNB sentinel lymph node biopsy

ICD-10-CM

Official Guidelines for Coding and Reporting (2021-2022)

Please refer to the companion Evolve website for the most current 2021-2022 guidelines.

2. Chapter 2: Neoplasms (C00-D49)

General guidelines

Chapter 2 of the ICD-10-CM contains the codes for most benign and all malignant neoplasms. Certain benign neoplasms, such as prostatic adenomas, may be found in the specific body system chapters. To properly code a neoplasm it is necessary to determine from the record if the neoplasm is benign, in-situ, malignant, or of uncertain histologic behavior. If malignant, any secondary (metastatic) sites should also be determined.

Primary malignant neoplasms overlapping site boundaries

A primary malignant neoplasm that overlaps two or more contiguous (next to each other) sites should be classified to the subcategory/code .8 ('overlapping lesion'), unless the combination is specifically indexed elsewhere. For multiple neoplasms of the same site that are not contiguous such as tumors in different quadrants of the same breast, codes for each site should be assigned.

Malignant neoplasm of ectopic tissue

Malignant neoplasms of ectopic tissue are to be coded to the site of origin mentioned, e.g., ectopic pancreatic malignant neoplasms involving the stomach are coded to malignant neoplasm of pancreas, unspecified (C25.9).

The neoplasm table in the Alphabetic Index should be referenced first. However, if the histological term is documented, that term should be referenced first, rather than going immediately to the Neoplasm Table, in order to determine which column in the Neoplasm Table is appropriate. For example, if the documentation indicates "adenoma," refer to the term in the Alphabetic Index to review the entries under this term and the instructional note to "see also neoplasm, by site, benign." The table provides the proper code based on the type of neoplasm and the site. It is important to select the proper column in the table that corresponds to the type of neoplasm. The Tabular List should then be referenced to verify that the correct code has been selected from the table and that a more specific site code does not exist.

See Section I.C.21. Factors influencing health status and contact with health services, Status, for information regarding Z15.0, codes for genetic susceptibility to cancer.

a. Treatment directed at the malignancy

If the treatment is directed at the malignancy, designate the malignancy as the principal diagnosis.

The only exception to this guideline is if a patient admission/encounter is solely for the administration of chemotherapy, immunotherapy or external beam radiation therapy, assign the appropriate Z51.– code as the first-listed or principal diagnosis, and the diagnosis or problem for which the service is being performed as a secondary diagnosis.

EXAMPLE

Patient was admitted for surgical treatment of primary cancer of the cervix. An open total abdominal hysterectomy was performed, C53.9, 0UT90ZZ, 0UTC0ZZ

b. Treatment of secondary site

When a patient is admitted because of a primary neoplasm with metastasis and treatment is directed toward the secondary site only, the secondary neoplasm is designated as the principal diagnosis even though the primary malignancy is still present.

EXAMPLE

Three months ago, the patient was given a diagnosis of small cell lung carcinoma with metastasis to the liver. The patient's primary neoplasm is lung carcinoma; the secondary neoplasm is located in the liver. The patient underwent open wedge resection for liver metastasis, C78.7, C34.90, 0FB00ZZ.

c. Coding and sequencing of complications

Coding and sequencing of complications associated with the malignancies or with the therapy thereof are subject to the following guidelines:

1) Anemia associated with malignancy

When admission/encounter is for management of an anemia associated with the malignancy, and the treatment is only for anemia, the appropriate code for the malignancy is sequenced as the principal or first-listed diagnosis followed by the appropriate code for the anemia (such as code D63.0, Anemia in neoplastic disease).

EXAMPLE

Anemia due to metastatic bone cancer. The patient has a history of primary breast cancer, which was treated with mastectomy 4 years ago. The patient was admitted for transfusion of packed red blood cells (percutaneous peripheral vein), C79.51, D63.0, Z85.3, Z90.10, 30233N1. ICD-10-CM instructs to code neoplasm first when anemia is due to neoplasm.

2) Anemia associated with chemotherapy, immunotherapy and radiation therapy

When the admission/encounter is for management of an anemia associated with an adverse effect of the administration of chemotherapy or immunotherapy and the only treatment is for the anemia, the anemia code is sequenced first followed by the appropriate codes for the neoplasm and the adverse effect (T45.1X5-, Adverse effect of antineoplastic and immunosuppressive drugs).

When the admission/encounter is for management of an anemia associated with an adverse effect of radiotherapy, the anemia code should be sequenced first, followed by the appropriate neoplasm code and code Y84.2, Radiological procedure and radiotherapy as the cause of abnormal reaction of the patient, or of later complication, without mention of misadventure at the time of the procedure.

EXAMPLE

Aplastic anemia due to radiation. The patient is being treated for cancer of the brain. The patient was transfused with 2 units of packed red blood cells (percutaneous peripheral vein), D61.2, C71.9, Y84.2, 30233N1.

3) Management of dehydration due to the malignancy

When the admission/encounter is for management of dehydration due to the malignancy and only the dehydration is being treated (intravenous rehydration), the dehydration is sequenced first, followed by the code(s) for the malignancy.

EXAMPLE

The patient was admitted for severe dehydration due to esophageal cancer. The patient was treated with IV fluids, E86.0, C15.9.

4) Treatment of a complication resulting from a surgical procedure

When the admission/encounter is for treatment of a complication resulting from a surgical procedure, designate the complication as the principal or first-listed diagnosis if treatment is directed at resolving the complication.

EXAMPLE

Hernia of colostomy with open repair of parastomal hernia. The colostomy was performed 1 year ago during colon cancer resection. The patient is no longer receiving treatment, and the cancer was completely resected, K43.5, Z85.038, Z90.49, 0WQF0ZZ.

d. Primary malignancy previously excised

When a primary malignancy has been previously excised or eradicated from its site and there is no further treatment directed to that site and there is no evidence of any existing primary malignancy, a code from category Z85, Personal history of malignant neoplasm, should be used to indicate the former site of the malignancy. Any mention of extension, invasion, or metastasis to another site is coded as a secondary malignant neoplasm to that site. The secondary site may be the principal or first-listed diagnosis with the Z85 code used as a secondary code.

EXAMPLE The patient had a melanoma removed from his back 4 years ago. The patient is currently being treated for metastatic melanoma of the right lung, C78.01, Z85.820.

e. Admissions/Encounters involving chemotherapy, immunotherapy and radiation therapy

1) Episode of care involves surgical removal of neoplasm

When an episode of care involves the surgical removal of a neoplasm, primary or secondary site, followed by adjunct chemotherapy or radiation treatment during the same episode of care, the code for the neoplasm should be assigned as principal or first-listed diagnosis.

EXAMPLE The patient had a modified radical mastectomy for malignant neoplasm of the right (upper outer quadrant) breast with mets to right axillary nodes with adjunct chemotherapy administration (percutaneous central vein), C50.411, C77.3, 0HTT0ZZ, 07T50ZZ, 3E04305.

2) Patient admission/encounter solely for administration of chemotherapy, immunotherapy and radiation therapy

If a patient admission/encounter is solely for the administration of chemotherapy, immunotherapy or external beam radiation therapy assign code Z51.0, Encounter for antineoplastic radiation therapy, or Z51.11, Encounter for antineoplastic chemotherapy, or Z51.12, Encounter for antineoplastic immunotherapy as the first-listed or principal diagnosis. If a patient receives more than one of these therapies during the same admission more than one of these codes may be assigned, in any sequence.

The malignancy for which the therapy is being administered should be assigned as a secondary diagnosis.

If a patient admission/encounter is for the insertion or implantation of radioactive elements (e.g., brachytherapy) the appropriate code for the malignancy is sequenced as the principal or first-listed diagnosis. Code Z51.0 should not be assigned.

EXAMPLE The patient was admitted for chemotherapy (percutaneous central vein) treatment of acute lymphoblastic leukemia (ALL), Z51.11, C91.00, 3E04305.

3) Patient admitted for radiation therapy, chemotherapy or immunotherapy and develops complications

When a patient is admitted for the purpose of external beam radiotherapy, immunotherapy or chemotherapy and develops complications such as uncontrolled nausea and vomiting or dehydration, the principal or first-listed diagnosis is Z51.0, Encounter for antineoplastic radiation therapy, or Z51.11, Encounter for antineoplastic chemotherapy, or Z51.12, Encounter for antineoplastic immunotherapy followed by any codes for the complications.

When a patient is admitted for the purpose of insertion or implantation of radioactive elements (e.g., brachytherapy) and develops complications such as uncontrolled nausea and vomiting or dehydration, the principal or first-listed diagnosis is the appropriate code for the malignancy followed by any codes for the complications.

EXAMPLE The patient was admitted for chemotherapy (percutaneous central vein) for lymphoma. Because of nausea and severe vomiting due to the chemotherapy, the patient was also treated for dehydration with IV fluids, Z51.11, C85.90, E86.0, T45.1x5A, R11.2, 3E04305.

f. Admission/encounter to determine extent of malignancy

When the reason for admission/encounter is to determine the extent of the malignancy, or for a procedure such as paracentesis or thoracentesis, the primary malignancy or appropriate metastatic site is designated as the principal or first-listed diagnosis, even though chemotherapy or radiotherapy is administered.

EXAMPLE

Patient has known carcinoma of the left kidney and left pleural effusion. Patient is admitted to determine if the renal cancer has spread and a thoracentesis is done, which confirms metastasis to the pleura with malignant pleural effusion, C78.2, J91.0, C64.2, 0W9B3ZX.

g. Symptoms, signs, and abnormal findings listed in Chapter 18 associated with neoplasms

Symptoms, signs, and ill-defined conditions listed in Chapter 18 characteristic of, or associated with, an existing primary or secondary site malignancy cannot be used to replace the malignancy as principal or first-listed diagnosis, regardless of the number of admissions or encounters for treatment and care of the neoplasm.

See Section I.C.21. Factors influencing health status and contact with health services, Encounter for prophylactic organ removal.

EXAMPLE

The patient was admitted with a first-time seizure due to brain cancer. The code R56.9 for seizure can be found in Chapter 18, so the brain cancer code would be sequenced as the principal diagnosis, C71.9, R56.9. Not all patients with brain cancer develop seizures, so it is appropriate to code the seizure code as a secondary diagnosis.

h. Admission/encounter for pain control/management

See Section I.C.6. for information on coding admission/encounter for pain control/management.

i. Malignancy in two or more noncontiguous sites

A patient may have more than one malignant tumor in the same organ. These tumors may represent different primaries or metastatic disease, depending on the site. Should the documentation be unclear, the provider should be queried as to the status of each tumor so that the correct codes can be assigned.

EXAMPLE

Primary cancer of right lung with metastasis to the left lung, C34.91, C78.02.

j. Disseminated malignant neoplasm, unspecified

Code C80.0, Disseminated malignant neoplasm, unspecified, is for use only in those cases where the patient has advanced metastatic disease and no known primary or secondary sites are specified. It should not be used in place of assigning codes for the primary site and all known secondary sites.

k. Malignant neoplasm without specification of site

Code C80.1, Malignant (primary) neoplasm, unspecified, equates to Cancer, unspecified. This code should only be used when no determination can be made as to the primary site of a malignancy. This code should rarely be used in the inpatient setting.

l. Sequencing of neoplasm codes

1) Encounter for treatment of primary malignancy

If the reason for the encounter is for treatment of a primary malignancy, assign the malignancy as the principal/first listed diagnosis. The primary site is to be sequenced first, followed by any metastatic sites.

EXAMPLE

Patient has papillary thyroid cancer that has spread to the cervical lymph nodes, C73, C77.0.

2) Encounter for treatment of secondary malignancy

When an encounter is for a primary malignancy with metastasis and treatment is directed toward the metastatic (secondary) site(s) only, the metastatic site(s) is designated as the principal/first listed diagnosis. The primary malignancy is coded as an additional code.

EXAMPLE

Patient is admitted for open wedge resection of metastatic liver cancer. The metastatic lesion was totally removed. Patient had a colorectal cancer removed 3 months ago and is undergoing treatment, C78.7, C19, 0FB00ZZ.

3) Malignant neoplasm in a pregnant patient

When a pregnant woman has a malignant neoplasm, a code from subcategory O9A.1-, Malignant neoplasm complicating pregnancy, childbirth, and the puerperium, should be sequenced first, followed by the appropriate code from Chapter 2 to indicate the type of neoplasm.

EXAMPLE Patient is in her second trimester (16 weeks) and was found to have follicular thyroid cancer, O9A.112, Z3A.16, C73.

4) Encounter for complication associated with a neoplasm

When an encounter is for management of a complication associated with a neoplasm, such as dehydration, and the treatment is only for the complication, the complication is coded first, followed by the appropriate code(s) for the neoplasm.

The exception to this guideline is anemia. When the admission/encounter is for management of an anemia associated with the malignancy, and the treatment is only for anemia, the appropriate code for the malignancy is sequenced as the principal or first-listed diagnosis followed by code D63.0, Anemia in neoplastic disease.

EXAMPLE Patient admitted for treatment of anemia due to gastric cancer with 2 units of packed red cells (percutaneously into peripheral vein), C16.9, D63.0, 30233N1.

5) Complication from surgical procedure for treatment of a neoplasm

When an encounter is for treatment of a complication resulting from a surgical procedure performed for the treatment of the neoplasm, designate the complication as the principal/first-listed diagnosis. See the guideline regarding the coding of a current malignancy versus personal history to determine if the code for the neoplasm should also be assigned.

EXAMPLE Patient developed an abdominal wall wound infection following surgery for colon cancer. Cellulitis was present. Cultures were negative. The patient is scheduled to begin chemo next week, T81.4xxA, L03.311, C18.9, Y83.2.

6) Pathologic fracture due to a neoplasm

When an encounter is for a pathological fracture due to a neoplasm, and the focus of treatment is the fracture, a code from subcategory M84.5, Pathological fracture in neoplastic disease, should be sequenced first, followed by the code for the neoplasm.

If the focus of treatment is the neoplasm with an associated pathological fracture, the neoplasm code should be sequenced first, followed by a code from M84.5 for the pathological fracture.

EXAMPLE The patient is being treated for pathologic vertebral fractures due to multiple myeloma, M84.58xA, C90.00.

m. Current malignancy versus personal history of malignancy

When a primary malignancy has been excised but further treatment, such as an additional surgery for the malignancy, radiation therapy or chemotherapy is directed to that site, the primary malignancy code should be used until treatment is completed.

When a primary malignancy has been previously excised or eradicated from its site, there is no further treatment (of the malignancy) directed to that site, and there is no evidence of any existing primary malignancy, a code from category Z85, Personal history of malignant neoplasm, should be used to indicate the former site of the malignancy.

Subcategories Z85.0 - Z85.7 should only be assigned for the former site of a primary malignancy, not the site of a secondary malignancy. Codes from subcategory Z85.8- may be assigned for the former site(s) of either a primary or secondary malignancy.

See Section I.C.21. Factors influencing health status and contact with health services, History (of)

EXAMPLE

Patient had a lobectomy for lung cancer 6 months ago. The patient will receive the fifth cycle of chemotherapy next week, C34.90, Z90.2.

EXAMPLE

Patient had a mastectomy 5 years ago for breast cancer. She is not being actively treated, Z85.3, Z90.10.

n. Leukemia, Multiple Myeloma, and Malignant Plasma Cell Neoplasms in remission versus personal history

The categories for leukemia, and category C90, Multiple myeloma and malignant plasma cell neoplasms, have codes indicating whether or not the leukemia has achieved remission. There are also codes Z85.6, Personal history of leukemia, and Z85.79, Personal history of other malignant neoplasms of lymphoid, hematopoietic and related tissues. If the documentation is unclear, as to whether the leukemia has achieved remission, the provider should be queried.

See Section I.C.21. Factors influencing health status and contact with health services, History (of)

EXAMPLE

The patient's acute myeloid leukemia is in remission, C92.01.

o. Aftercare following surgery for neoplasm

See Section I.C.21. Factors influencing health status and contact with health services, Aftercare

p. Follow-up care for completed treatment of a malignancy

See Section I.C.21. Factors influencing health status and contact with health services, Follow-up

There are Z code categories for aftercare following surgery for a neoplasm and for follow-up care after treatment of a malignancy. Many of these services are performed in the outpatient setting. Aftercare codes are generally listed first and explain the reason for the encounter. Aftercare codes are used following the initial treatment of a disease when the patient requires continued care during the healing and recovery stages or because of the long-term effects of the disease.

EXAMPLE

Patient admitted to a long-term care facility to recover from major surgery for colon cancer. Patient will undergo chemotherapy after discharge, Z48.3, C18.9.

Even after a patient has been successfully treated for a malignancy, periodic, routine follow-up examinations may be necessary to determine if there has been any recurrence of the cancer. When there is no evidence of any type of recurrence, a code from the Z08 follow-up examination should be assigned. A Z code to identify the history of a neoplasm should also be assigned to show the reason for the follow-up examination. There is an instructional note to identify any acquired absence of organs. If there is any evidence of recurrence at the primary site and/or metastasis to a secondary site, the appropriate neoplasm code(s) are assigned.

EXAMPLE

Patient had a surveillance cystoscopy done because of previous bladder cancer that was surgically removed. No evidence of recurrence was found. The patient will follow-up in 3 months, Z08, Z85.51, 0TJB8ZZ.

q. Prophylactic organ removal for prevention of malignancy

See Section I.C.21. Factors influencing health status and contact with health services, Prophylactic organ removal

r. Malignant neoplasm associated with transplanted organ

A malignant neoplasm of a transplanted organ should be coded as a transplant complication. Assign first the appropriate code from category T86.-, Complications of transplanted organs and tissue, followed by code C80.2, Malignant neoplasm associated with transplanted organ. Use an additional code for the specific malignancy.

EXAMPLE

Patient was diagnosed with hepatocellular carcinoma. Patient had a liver transplant 2 years ago, T86.49, C80.2, C22.0, Y83.0.

6. Chapter 6: Diseases of the Nervous System (G00-G99)

5) Neoplasm Related Pain

Code G89.3 is assigned to pain documented as being related, associated or due to cancer, primary or secondary malignancy, or tumor. This code is assigned regardless of whether the pain is acute or chronic.

This code may be assigned as the principal or first-listed code when the stated reason for the admission/encounter is documented as pain control/pain management. The underlying neoplasm should be reported as an additional diagnosis.

When the reason for the admission/encounter is management of the neoplasm and the pain associated with the neoplasm is also documented, code G89.3 may be assigned as an additional diagnosis. It is not necessary to assign an additional code for the site of the pain.

See Section I.C.2. for instructions on the sequencing of neoplasms for all other stated reasons for the admission/encounter (except for pain control/pain management).

When a patient has pain due to a previously identified neoplasm, code G89.3 is assigned. This code can be assigned as either principal or secondary, depending on the circumstances of the admission.

If a patient is admitted for pain management or pain control, the G89.3 code is assigned as the principal diagnosis, and the malignancy code(s) is assigned as a secondary code(s).

EXAMPLE

Patient was admitted for control of back pain due to vertebral metastasis. Patient has a history of prostate cancer. After pain medications were adjusted and pain was controlled, he was discharged, G89.3, C79.51, Z85.46.

If a patient is admitted for management of the malignancy and the pain associated with the malignancy, the malignancy code is assigned as the principal diagnosis with the G89.3 pain code assigned as a secondary diagnosis.

EXAMPLE

Patient was admitted for back pain due to vertebral metastasis. An MRI indicates that the disease has progressed. Patient has a history of prostate cancer. Beam radiation with heavy particles was administered, C79.51, G89.3, Z85.46, DP0C4ZZ.

ANATOMY AND PHYSIOLOGY

Neoplasms can affect any of the body systems. The anatomy and physiology of these body systems are outlined in their respective chapters. It is important to understand some of the terminology that is specific to neoplasms and their behavior. According to the National Cancer Institute, the most common cancers in the United States include the following:

- Bladder
- Breast
- Colon and rectal
- Endometrial
- Kidney (renal cell)
- Leukemia
- Lung
- Melanoma
- Non-Hodgkin's lymphoma
- Pancreatic
- Prostate
- Skin (nonmelanoma)
- Thyroid

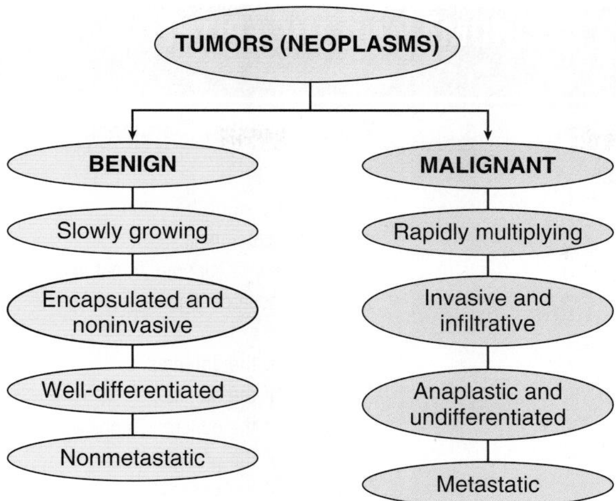

FIGURE 11-1. Differences between benign and malignant neoplasms.

A **neoplasm** is an abnormal tissue that grows by cellular proliferation more rapidly than normal tissue. Neoplasms show partial or complete lack of structural organization and functional coordination with normal tissue, and they usually form a distinct mass of tissue that may be benign (benign tumor) or malignant (cancer) (Figure 11-1). Both benign and malignant neoplasms are classified according to the type of tissue in which they are found. **Benign** neoplasms are tumors that are not malignant. **Malignancy** is a neoplasm that has the ability to invade adjacent structures and spread to distant sites. **Fibromas** are benign neoplasms of fibrous connective tissue, and **melanomas** are malignant changes of melanin cells. Malignant tumors originating from epithelial tissue (e.g., skin, bronchi, stomach) are called **carcinomas** (Table 11-1). Malignancies of epithelial glandular tissue such as those found in the breast, prostate, and colon are known as **adenocarcinomas**. Malignant growths of connective tissue (e.g., muscle, cartilage, bone) are called **sarcomas** (Table 11-2). **Lymphomas** form in lymphatic tissue, and **leukemias** are malignancies that arise from white blood cells. A **myeloma** originates within the bone marrow.

The **primary site** is the location at which the neoplasm begins, or originates. It is important for the treating physician to identify the site of origin so that the best treatment course and prognosis can be determined. **Metastasis** is the spread of cancer from one part of the body to another, as is seen when neoplasms occur in parts of the body separate from the site of the primary tumor. Metastasis occurs through dissemination of tumor cells by the lymphatics or blood vessels, or by direct extension through serous cavities or other spaces.

Grading involves pathologic examination of tumor cells. The degree of abnormality of cells determines the grade of cancer (Table 11-3). When the level of cell abnormality is greater, the cancer is of higher grade. Cells that are **well-differentiated** closely resemble mature, specialized cells. Tumor cells that are **undifferentiated** are highly abnormal (i.e., immature and primitive).

Cancerous tissue is classified according to degree of malignancy, from grade 1—barely malignant—to grade 4—highly malignant. In practice, it is not always possible for the pathologist to determine the degree of malignancy, and sometimes it may be difficult even to determine whether a particular tumor tissue is benign or malignant.

Staging, a means of categorizing a particular cancer, helps the clinician to determine a particular patient's treatment plan and the need for further therapy. Each type of cancer is staged according to specific characteristics:

- In situ cancers have been diagnosed at the earliest possible stage.
- Stage I or "local" cancers have been diagnosed early and have not spread.
- Stage II has spread into surrounding tissues but not beyond the location of origin.
- Stage III or "regional" cancer has spread to nearby lymph nodes.
- Stage IV or "distant" cancers have spread to other parts of the body and are the most difficult to treat.

TABLE 11-1 CARCINOMA AND THE EPITHELIAL TISSUES FROM WHICH THEY DERIVE[1]

Types of Epithelial Tissue	Malignant Tumor (Carcinoma)
Gastrointestinal Tract	
Colon	Adenocarcinoma of the colon
Esophagus	Esophageal carcinoma
Liver	Hepatocellular carcinoma (hepatoma)
Stomach	Gastric adenocarcinoma
Glandular Tissue	
Adrenal glands	Carcinoma of the adrenals
Breast	Carcinoma of the breast
Pancreas	Carcinoma of the pancreas (pancreatic adenocarcinoma)
Prostate	Carcinoma of the prostate
Thyroid	Carcinoma of the thyroid
Kidney and Bladder	
	Renal cell carcinoma (hypernephroma)
	Transitional cell carcinoma of the bladder
Lung	
	Adenocarcinoma (bronchioloalveolar)
	Large cell carcinoma
	Small (oat) cell carcinoma
	Squamous cell (epidermoid)
Reproductive Organs	
	Adenocarcinoma of the uterus
	Carcinoma of the penis
	Choriocarcinoma of the uterus or testes
	Cystadenocarcinoma (mucinous or serous) of the ovaries
	Seminoma and embryonal cell carcinoma (testes)
	Squamous cell (epidermoid) carcinoma of the vagina or cervix
Skin	
Basal cell layer	Basal cell carcinoma
Melanocyte	Malignant melanoma
Squamous cell layer	Squamous cell carcinoma

See Table 11-4 for an example of how the TNM (tumor-node-metastasis) staging system would be used to classify a lung cancer.

Neoplasm Table

The coding of most neoplasms requires an extra step, which involves use of the Neoplasm Table (Figure 11-2). The main term for the type of neoplasm is located in the Alphabetic Index. All subterms must be reviewed to facilitate assignment of proper codes. One must follow all instructions, such as *see* Neoplasm, by site, benign, or *see* Neoplasm, by site, malignant. It is important to follow all steps to ensure correct code assignment. The temptation to go directly to the Neoplasm Table should be avoided.

In the following examples, a step-by-step explanation will be given for coding of neoplasms.

EXAMPLE

Basal cell carcinoma left cheek (primary site) (Figure 11-3).

1. Look up "Carcinoma" in Alphabetic Index.
2. Review subterms; "basal cell" is a subterm.
3. Follow instructions to *see also* Neoplasm, skin, malignant.
4. Go to the Neoplasm Table.
5. Locate the site—skin—and review subterms under "skin."
6. Locate the subterm "cheek," and find the code under the appropriate column, which, in this case, is a primary malignancy of the cheek due to basal cell carcinoma.
7. Assign code C44.319.

TABLE 11-2 SARCOMAS AND THE CONNECTIVE TISSUES FROM WHICH THEY DERIVE[2]

Types of Connective Tissue	Malignant Tumor
Bone	
	Osteosarcoma (osteogenic sarcoma)
	Ewing's sarcoma
Muscle	
Smooth (visceral) muscle	Leiomyosarcoma
Striated (skeletal) muscle	Rhabdomyosarcoma
Cartilage	
	Chondrosarcoma
Fat	
	Liposarcoma
Fibrous Tissue	
	Fibrosarcoma
Blood Vessel Tissue	
	Angiosarcoma
Blood-Forming Tissue	
All leukocytes	Leukemias
Lymphocytes	Hodgkin's disease
Plasma cells	Non-Hodgkin's lymphoma
	Burkitt's lymphoma
	Multiple myeloma
Nerve Tissue	
Embryonic nerve tissue	Neuroblastoma
Glial tissue	Astrocytoma (tumors of glial cells, called "astrocytes")
	Glioblastoma multiforme

TABLE 11-3 GRADES OF NEOPLASMS

Grade 1	Cells slightly abnormal and well-differentiated
Grade 2	Cells more abnormal and moderately differentiated
Grade 3	Cells very abnormal and poorly differentiated
Grade 4	Cells immature and undifferentiated

EXAMPLE

Squamous cell in situ carcinoma of the endocervix, D06.0.

1. Look up carcinoma-in-situ in the Alphabetic Index.
2. Review subterms; "squamous cell" is a subterm.
3. Follow instructions, specified site—*see also* Neoplasm, by site, in situ.
4. Go to the Neoplasm Table.
5. Locate the site—cervix—and review subterms under "Cervix."
6. Locate the subterm "endocervix," and find the code under the appropriate column, which, in this case, is a carcinoma in situ of the endocervix.
7. Assign codes (in situ) D06.0.

EXERCISE 11-1

Assign codes to the following conditions.

1. Malignant melanoma, skin left foot ____________
2. Leukemia ____________
3. Adenoma of the prostate ____________
4. Renal cell carcinoma, right ____________

TABLE 11-4 INTERNATIONAL TNM STAGING SYSTEMS FOR LUNG CANCER[3]

Stage	TNM Description	5-Year Survival, %
I	T1-T2, N0, M0	60-80
II	T1-T2, N1, M0	25-50
IIIA	T3, N0-N1, M0	25-40
IIIB	T1-T3, N2, M0	10-30
IV	Any T4 or N3, M0	<5
	Any M1	<5
Primary Tumor (T)		
T1	Tumor <3 cm in diameter	
T2	Tumor <3 cm in diameter or with associated atelectasis–obstructive pneumonitis extending to the hilar region	
T3	Tumor with direct extension into the chest wall, diaphragm, mediastinum, pleura, or pericardium	
T4	Tumor invades the mediastinum, or presence of a malignant pleural effusion	
Regional Lymph Nodes (N)		
N0	No node involvement	
N1	Metastasis to lymph nodes in the peribronchial and ipsilateral (same side as the primary tumor) hilar regions	
N2	Metastasis to ipsilateral hilar and subcarinal (under the bifurcation of the trachea into the lungs) lymph nodes	
N3	Metastasis to contralateral mediastinal or hilar nodes or any nodes new to the clavicular (collar) bone	
Distance Metastasis (M)		
M0	No known metastasis	
M1	Distant metastasis present with site specified (e.g., brain, tumor)	

Primary and Secondary Neoplasms

Sometimes incomplete documentation makes it difficult to determine whether a neoplasm is primary or secondary. It is possible to have more than one primary cancer. At times, a secondary or metastatic cancer has been found, and the primary is unknown or has yet to be determined. Documentation in the health record may be incomplete and the terminology confusing.

As was described previously, a metastatic neoplasm is a secondary neoplasm that has spread from the original or primary site. The site of the metastasis may be close to the original site (e.g., breast spread to axillary lymph nodes) or to distant sites (e.g., lung spread to the brain). Neoplasms can metastasize to more than one site. If this is the case, codes are assigned to each metastatic site. Terminology used to describe metastatic sites varies greatly, depending on the documenting physician. For example, if a patient has a non–small cell primary lung carcinoma with secondary malignancy of the brain, it may be documented in the health record as follows:

EXAMPLE Lung cancer with metastasis to the brain, C34.90, C79.31.

The code that would be assigned is primary lung cancer with a secondary code assigned for the metastatic brain malignancy.

EXAMPLE Lung cancer metastatic to the brain, C34.90, C79.31.

The codes assigned are the same as in the preceding example.

EXAMPLE Brain cancer metastatic from the lung, C34.90, C79.31.

ICD-10-CM TABLE of NEOPLASMS

The list below gives the code numbers for neoplasms by anatomical site. For each site there are six possible code numbers according to whether the neoplasm in question is malignant, benign, in situ, of uncertain behavior, or of unspecified nature. The description of the neoplasm will often indicate which of the six columns is appropriate; e.g., malignant melanoma of skin, benign fibroadenoma of breast, carcinoma in situ of cervix uteri.

Where such descriptors are not present, the remainder of the Index should be consulted where guidance is given to the appropriate column for each morphological (histological) variety listed; e.g., Mesonephroma—see Neoplasm, malignant; Embryoma—see also Neoplasm, uncertain behavior; Disease, Bowen's—see Neoplasm, skin, in situ. However, the guidance in the Index can be overridden if one of the descriptors mentioned above is present; e.g., malignant adenoma of colon is coded to C18.9 and not to D12.6 as the adjective "malignant" overrides the Index entry "Adenoma—see also Neoplasm, benign."

Codes listed with a dash -, following the code have a required additional character for laterality. The tabular must be reviewed for the complete code.

N

	Malignant Primary	Malignant Secondary	Ca in situ	Benign	Uncertain Behavior	Unspecified Behavior
	N					
Neoplasm, neoplastic	C80.1	C79.9	D09.9	D36.9	D48.9	D49.9
abdomen, abdominal	C76.2	C79.8-	D09.8	D36.7	D48.7	D49.89
cavity	C76.2	C79.8-	D09.8	D36.7	D48.7	D49.89
organ	C76.2	C79.8-	D09.8	D36.7	D48.7	D49.89
viscera	C76.2	C79.8-	D09.8	D36.7	D48.7	D49.89
wall—*see also Neoplasm, abdomen, wall, skin*	C44.509	C79.2-	D04.5	D23.5	D48.5	D49.2
connective tissue	C49.4	C79.8-	—	D21.4	D48.1	D49.2
skin	C44.509					
basal cell carcinoma	C44.519	—	—	—	—	—
specified type NEC	C44.599	—	—	—	—	—
squamous cell carcinoma	C44.529	—	—	—	—	—
abdominopelvic	C76.8	C79.8-	—	D36.7	D48.7	D49.89
accessory sinus—*see Neoplasm, sinus*						
acoustic nerve	C72.4-	C79.49	—	D33.3	D43.3	D49.7

FIGURE 11-2. Excerpt from the Neoplasm Table.

The codes assigned are the same as in the preceding example.

EXAMPLE Non–small cell carcinoma of lung and brain, C34.90, C79.31.

Non–small cell carcinoma is a malignancy that originates in the lung, so the lung is primary. If a cancer that originates in the lung has spread to the brain, that is a metastasis.

EXAMPLE Metastatic lung cancer, C34.90, C79.9.

If a morphology type is not stated, assign the site qualified as "metastatic" to the primary malignant code for that site. The code assigned is primary lung cancer (C34.90), with an unknown secondary malignancy site (C79.9) because the metastatic site was not documented in this example.

If the documentation in the health record only identifies one site and it is identified as metastatic, then a determination has to be made as to whether to code the site as a primary malignancy or secondary malignancy. The following steps are followed to make that determination:

1. If the morphology type is documented, refer to the morphology type in the Alphabetic Index and code to the primary condition of that site.

Carcinoma (malignant) —*see also* Neoplasm, by site, malignant
- acidophil
  - specified site —*see* Neoplasm, malignant, by site
  - unspecified site C75.1
- acidophil-basophil, mixed
  - specified site —*see* Neoplasm, malignant, by site
  - unspecified site C75.1
- adnexal (skin) —*see* Neoplasm, skin, malignant
- adrenal cortical C74.0-
- alveolar —*see* Neoplasm, lung, malignant
  - cell —*see* Neoplasm, lung, malignant
- ameloblastic C41.1
  - upper jaw (bone) C41.0
- apocrine
  - breast —*see* Neoplasm, breast, malignant
  - specified site NEC —*see* Neoplasm, skin, malignant
  - unspecified site C44.99
- basal cell (pigmented) (*see also* Neoplasm, skin, malignant) C44.91
  - fibro-epithelial —*see* Neoplasm, skin, malignant
  - morphea —*see* Neoplasm, skin, malignant
  - multicentric —*see* Neoplasm, skin, malignant
- basaloid
- basal-squamous cell, mixed —*see* Neoplasm, skin, malignant
- basophil
  - specified site —*see* Neoplasm, malignant, by site
  - unspecified site C75.1
- basophil-acidophil, mixed
  - specified site —*see* Neoplasm, malignant, by site
  - unspecified site C75.1
- basosquamous —*see* Neoplasm, skin, malignant
- bile duct
  - with hepatocellular, mixed C22.0
  - liver C22.1
  - specified site NEC —*see* Neoplasm, malignant, by site
  - unspecified site C22.1
- branchial or branchiogenic C10.4
- bronchial or bronchogenic —*see* Neoplasm, lung, malignant

Carcinoma *(Continued)*
- bronchiolar —*see* Neoplasm, lung, malignant
- bronchioloalveolar —*see* Neoplasm, lung, malignant
- C cell
  - specified site —*see* Neoplasm, malignant, by site
  - unspecified site C73
- ceruminous C44.29-
- cervix uteri
  - in situ D06.9
    - endocervix D06.0
    - exocervix D06.1
    - specified site NEC D06.7
- chorionic
  - specified site —*see* Neoplasm, malignant, by site
  - unspecified site
    - female C58
    - male C62.90
- chromophobe
  - specified site —*see* Neoplasm, malignant, by site
  - unspecified site C75.1
- cloacogenic
  - specified site —*see* Neoplasm, malignant, by site
  - unspecified site C21.2
- diffuse type
  - specified site —*see* Neoplasm, malignant, by site
  - unspecified site C16.9
- duct (cell)
  - with Paget's disease —*see* Neoplasm, breast, malignant
  - infiltrating
    - with lobular carcinoma (in situ)
      - specified site —*see* Neoplasm, malignant, by site
      - unspecified site (female) C50.91-
        - male C50.92-
    - specified site —*see* Neoplasm, malignant, by site
    - unspecified site (female) C50.91-
      - male C50.92-
- ductal
  - with lobular
    - specified site —*see* Neoplasm, malignant, by site
    - unspecified site (female) C50.91-
      - male C50.92-
- ductular, infiltrating
  - specified site —*see* Neoplasm, malignant, by site
  - unspecified site (female) C50.91-
    - male C50.92-
- embryonal
  - liver C22.7
- endometrioid
  - specified site —*see* Neoplasm, malignant, by site
  - unspecified site
    - female C56.9
    - male C61
- eosinophil
  - specified site —*see* Neoplasm, malignant, by site
  - unspecified site C75.1

FIGURE 11-3. Index entry for main term "Carcinoma."

EXAMPLE

Metastatic islet cell carcinoma of the pancreas, C25.4, C79.9.

In the preceding example, the carcinoma is documented as metastatic. The first step is to locate the morphology type in the Alphabetic Index. There are subterms for islet cell of the pancreas with code C25.4, so that code should be assigned. If no specific site is listed as a subterm, assign the code for primary neoplasm of an unspecified site (C80.1). When a primary site has been determined, a code must be assigned to identify a secondary (metastatic) site. If no metastatic site is specified, then the code C79.9, unknown site, secondary, is assigned.

2. If the process in step 1 leads to code C80.0 or C80.1, or if the morphology is not stated, the site should be coded as a primary malignancy, unless it is included in the following list of exceptions.

Malignant neoplasms of the following sites are exceptions, and instead of coding to an unknown primary or to the morphology, the following sites are always coded as secondary neoplasms of that site:

- Bone
- Brain
- Diaphragm
- Heart
- Liver
- Lymph nodes
- Mediastinum
- Meninges
- Peritoneum
- Pleura
- Retroperitoneum
- Spinal cord
- Sites classifiable to C76

EXAMPLE

Metastatic carcinoma of the breast (female), C50.919, C79.9.

In the preceding example, there is no subterm for breast or unspecified site. In the Neoplasm Table, unspecified site, primary is coded to C80.1. When code C80.1 is obtained, then a review of the exception list is performed. Because breast is not on the list, it is assigned as the primary site, C50.919, and the code C79.9 is used to identify the unknown secondary.

EXAMPLE

Metastatic brain cancer (depending on the reason for the patient's admission) C80.1, C79.31 or C79.31, C80.1.

In this example, the brain is on the list of secondary neoplasms, and the morphology type is not stated; therefore the code (C79.31) is assigned for secondary neoplasm of the brain and (C80.1) for unknown primary. Sequencing of the primary and secondary neoplasms would depend on the focus of treatment.

EXAMPLE

Renal cell carcinoma (RCC) with metastasis to the adrenal glands
Primary neoplasm: Renal cell carcinoma (kidney)
Secondary neoplasm: Adrenal glands

EXAMPLE

Metastatic bone cancer
Primary neoplasm: Unknown primary site
Secondary neoplasm: Bones

Specific instructions are provided at the beginning of the "Neoplasm" chapter in the code book (Figure 11-4).

EXERCISE 11-2

Identify the following neoplasms in terms of primary or secondary, as in the earlier examples.

1. Colorectal adenocarcinoma with metastatic liver cancer
   Primary neoplasm ______________________
   Secondary neoplasm ______________________
2. Thyroid malignancy with mets to the lymph nodes of the neck
   Primary neoplasm ______________________
   Secondary neoplasm ______________________
3. Metastatic ovarian cancer
   Primary neoplasm ______________________
   Secondary neoplasm ______________________
4. Pancreatic cancer with extension into the liver
   Primary neoplasm ______________________
   Secondary neoplasm ______________________
5. Recurrence of cancer in the bladder
   Primary neoplasm ______________________
   Secondary neoplasm ______________________
6. Adenocarcinoma sigmoid colon with pericolic nodal involvement
   Primary neoplasm ______________________
   Secondary neoplasm ______________________
7. Inflammatory breast cancer with spread to the axillary lymph nodes
   Primary neoplasm ______________________
   Secondary neoplasm ______________________
8. Metastatic bone cancer from the prostate
   Primary neoplasm ______________________
   Secondary neoplasm ______________________
9. Endometrial adenocarcinoma with metastasis to the ovary
   Primary neoplasm ______________________
   Secondary neoplasm ______________________
10. Acinic cell carcinoma of the parotid gland
    Primary neoplasm ______________________
    Secondary neoplasm ______________________

Contiguous Sites

As is pointed out in the instructional note (see Figure 11-4), a neoplasm can overlap two or more subcategories, and determination of the exact point of origin may be difficult. These would be assigned to subcategory 8, "Other," unless the combination is specifically indexed elsewhere.

It is important to code any alterations to the functional activity of an organ caused by the neoplasm. Neoplasms of the endocrine glands or organs that secrete hormones are more likely to have disturbances in their functional activity because hormone production may increase or decrease because of the neoplasm.

EXAMPLE

Malignant neoplasm of the thyroid with hyperthyroidism, C73, E05.90.

CHAPTER 2

NEOPLASMS (C00-D49)

This chapter contains the following blocks:

C00-C14	Malignant neoplasms of lip, oral cavity and pharynx
C15-C26	Malignant neoplasms of digestive organs
C30-C39	Malignant neoplasms of respiratory and intrathoracic organs
C40-C41	Malignant neoplasms of bone and articular cartilage
C43-C44	Melanoma and other malignant neoplasms of skin
C45-C49	Malignant neoplasms of mesothelial and soft tissue
C50	Malignant neoplasms of breast
C51-C58	Malignant neoplasms of female genital organs
C60-C63	Malignant neoplasms of male genital organs
C64-C68	Malignant neoplasms of urinary tract
C69-C72	Malignant neoplasms of eye, brain and other parts of central nervous system
C73-C75	Malignant neoplasms of thyroid and other endocrine glands
C7A	Malignant neuroendocrine tumors
C7B	Secondary neuroendocrine tumors
C76-C80	Malignant neoplasms of ill-defined, other secondary and unspecified sites
C81-C96	Malignant neoplasms of lymphoid, hematopoietic and related tissue
D00-D09	In situ neoplasms
D10-D36	Benign neoplasms, except benign neuroendocrine tumors
D3A	Benign neuroendocrine tumors
D37-D48	Neoplasms of uncertain behavior, polycythemia vera and myelodysplastic syndromes
D49	Neoplasms of unspecified behavior

Notes: Functional activity

All neoplasms are classified in this chapter, whether they are functionally active or not. An additional code from Chapter 4 may be used, to identify functional activity associated with any neoplasm.

Morphology [Histology]

Chapter 2 classifies neoplasms primarily by site (topography), with broad groupings for behavior, malignant, in situ, benign, etc. The Table of Neoplasms should be used to identify the correct topography code. In a few cases, such as for malignant melanoma and certain neuroendocrine tumors, the morphology (histologic type) is included in the category and codes.

Primary malignant neoplasms overlapping site boundaries

A primary malignant neoplasm that overlaps two or more contiguous (next to each other) sites should be classified to the subcategory/code .8 ('overlapping lesion'), unless the combination is specifically indexed elsewhere. For multiple neoplasms of the same site that are not contiguous, such as tumors in different quadrants of the same breast, codes for each site should be assigned.

Malignant neoplasm of ectopic tissue

Malignant neoplasms of ectopic tissue are to be coded to the site mentioned, e.g., ectopic pancreatic malignant neoplasms are coded to pancreas, unspecified (C25.9).

FIGURE 11-4. Instructional notes at the beginning of the "Neoplasm" chapter in the Tabular List.

DISEASE CONDITIONS

Chapter 2 in the ICD-10-CM code book is divided into the following categories:

CATEGORY	SECTION TITLE
C00-C14	Malignant neoplasm of lip, oral cavity, and pharynx
C15-C26	Malignant neoplasm of digestive organs
C30-C39	Malignant neoplasm of respiratory and intrathoracic organs
C40-C41	Malignant neoplasm of bone and articular cartilage
C43-C44	Melanoma and other malignant neoplasms of skin
C45-C49	Malignant neoplasm of mesothelial and soft tissue
C50	Malignant neoplasm of breast
C51-C58	Malignant neoplasm of female genital organs
C60-C63	Malignant neoplasm of male genital organs
C64-C68	Malignant neoplasm of urinary tract
C69-C72	Malignant neoplasm of eye, brain, and other parts of the central nervous system
C73-C75	Malignant neoplasm of thyroid and other endocrine glands
C7A	Malignant neuroendocrine tumors
C7B	Secondary neuroendocrine tumors
C76-C80	Malignant neoplasm of ill-defined, secondary, and unspecified sites
C81-C96	Malignant neoplasm of lymphoid, hematopoietic, and related tissue
D00-D09	In situ neoplasms
D10-D36	Benign neoplasms, except benign neuroendocrine tumors
D3A	Benign neuroendocrine tumors
D37-D48	Neoplasms of uncertain behavior, polycythemia vera and myelodysplastic syndromes
D49	Neoplasms of unspecified behavior

The coding of neoplasms is determined by the behavior of the neoplasm and the anatomical site. The behaviors are classified as malignant, neuroendocrine, in situ, benign, uncertain behavior, or unspecified behavior.

Malignant Neoplasm of Lip, Oral Cavity, and Pharynx (C00-C14)

Several types of oral cancers have been identified; 90% of these are squamous cell carcinomas. Cancers are often discovered after they have already spread, usually to the lymph nodes of the neck. Smoking has been associated with about 70% to 80% of oral cancers. Also, heavy alcohol use adds to the risk. The lips and tongue are most commonly affected (Figure 11-5).

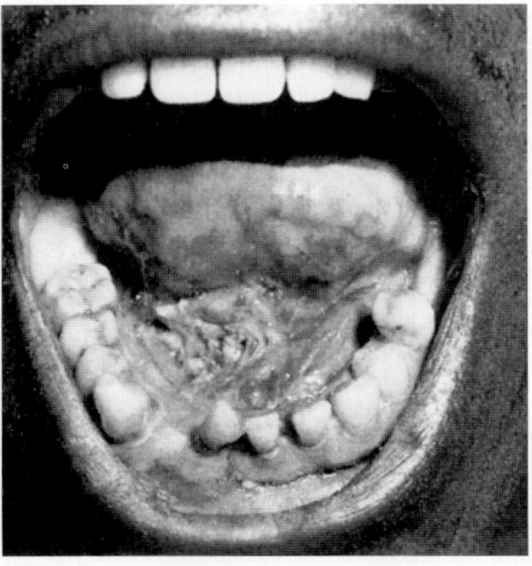

FIGURE 11-5. Squamous cell carcinoma of the mouth.

EXAMPLE

The patient is being treated for squamous cell carcinoma of the hypopharynx, C13.9.

EXERCISE 11-3

Assign codes to the following conditions.

1. Squamous cell carcinoma, base of tongue ______________
2. Adenocarcinoma of parotid gland ______________
3. Biopsy-proven squamous cell carcinoma, right tonsil ______________
4. Cancer, lower lip ______________

Malignant Neoplasm of Digestive Organs (C15-C26)

According to the Centers for Disease Control and Prevention (CDC), colorectal cancer (Figure 11-6) primarily affects men and women aged 50 years or older. For men, colorectal cancer is the third most common cancer after prostate cancer and lung cancer. For women, colorectal cancer is the third most common cancer after breast cancer and lung cancer. The best prevention is regular screening.

Hepatocellular carcinoma is a primary neoplasm of the liver (Figure 11-7). Patients who develop primary liver cancer often have some type of chronic liver disease such as cirrhosis. The liver is also a common site for metastasis. Malignant neoplasm of the liver that is not specified as primary or secondary (metastatic) is coded to C22.9.

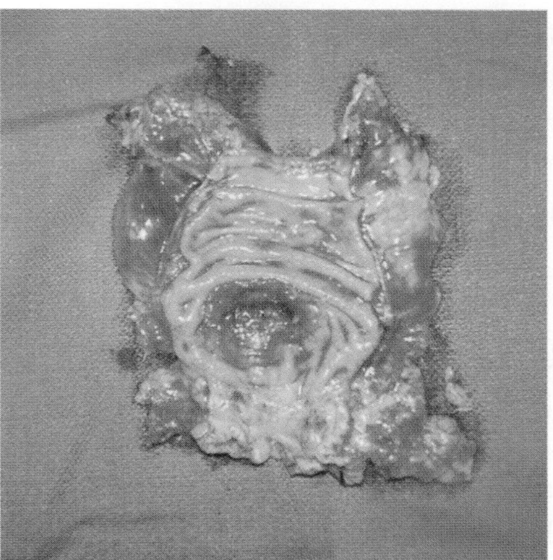

FIGURE 11-6. Adenocarcinoma distal rectum.

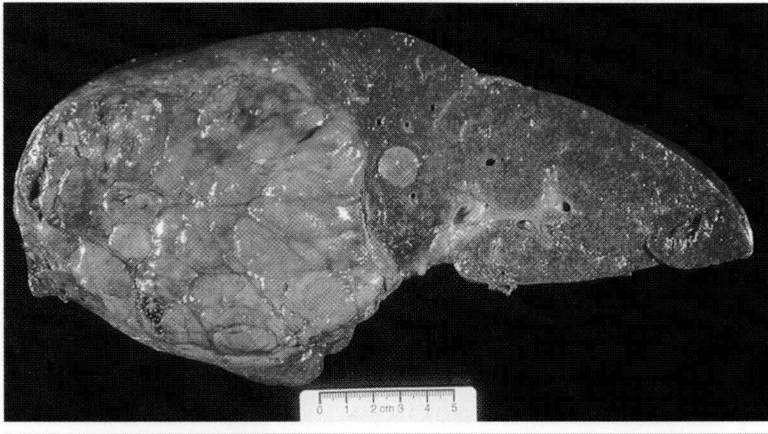

FIGURE 11-7. Hepatocellular carcinoma.

Malignant ascites is a condition in which excess fluid that contains malignant cells accumulates in the abdomen or peritoneum. A diagnostic paracentesis can be performed to determine if cancer cells are present. Patients with breast, ovarian, uterine, colon, stomach, intestinal, and pancreatic cancers are more likely to develop malignant ascites. Ascites can be very uncomfortable for the patient and a therapeutic paracentesis may be necessary to drain the fluid and provide relief. There is an instructional note in the code book to code the responsible neoplasm first. As the code for malignant ascites is a symptom code from Chapter 18, there is a guideline that states that a code from this chapter, when associated with an existing primary or secondary malignancy site, cannot be used as a principal or first-listed diagnosis. In a patient with cancer and multiple metastatic sites, it may be necessary to query the physician as to which cancer site is causing the ascites.

EXAMPLE Patient presented to the ER with shortness of breath due to extensive malignant ascites. She has inoperable ovarian cancer. A therapeutic percutaneous peritoneal cavity paracentesis was performed, C56.9, R18.0, 0W9G3ZZ.

EXAMPLE The patient has adenocarcinoma of the rectosigmoid junction, C19.

EXERCISE 11-4

Assign codes to the following conditions.

1. Hepatocellular carcinoma ______________
2. Adenocarcinoma, head of pancreas ______________
3. Fibrosarcoma of spleen ______________
4. Adenocarcinoma of the duodenum ______________
5. Gastric adenocarcinoma ______________
6. Cholangiocarcinoma of the extrahepatic bile ducts ______________

Malignant Neoplasm of Respiratory and Intrathoracic Organs (C30-C39)

Lung cancer, which is one of the most common types of cancer, is classified into two main categories: small cell lung cancer (SCLC) and non–small cell lung cancer (NSCLC). More than 85% of lung cancers are caused by smoking. Bronchogenic carcinoma is the most common type of malignant lung cancer (Figure 11-8). The lung is frequently a site for metastasis. Benign tumors of the lung are rare.

Malignant pleural effusion is a condition in which fluid accumulates in the pleural space and contains malignant cells. Malignant pleural effusions can result from lymphomas, breast cancer, and small cell lung cancer. Pleural effusions can be very uncomfortable for the patient and a therapeutic thoracentesis may be necessary to drain the fluid and provide relief. There is an instructional note in the code book to code first malignant neoplasm, if known. In the past, malignant pleural effusions were coded to secondary neoplasm of the pleura, but metastasis to the pleura is not always present in a patient with malignant pleural effusions.

EXAMPLE Patient presented to the ER with shortness of breath due to right-sided malignant pleural effusion due to right SCLC. A therapeutic thoracentesis was performed, C34.91, J91.0, 0W993ZZ.

EXAMPLE The patient was diagnosed with adenocarcinoma, right lower lobe of lung, C34.31.

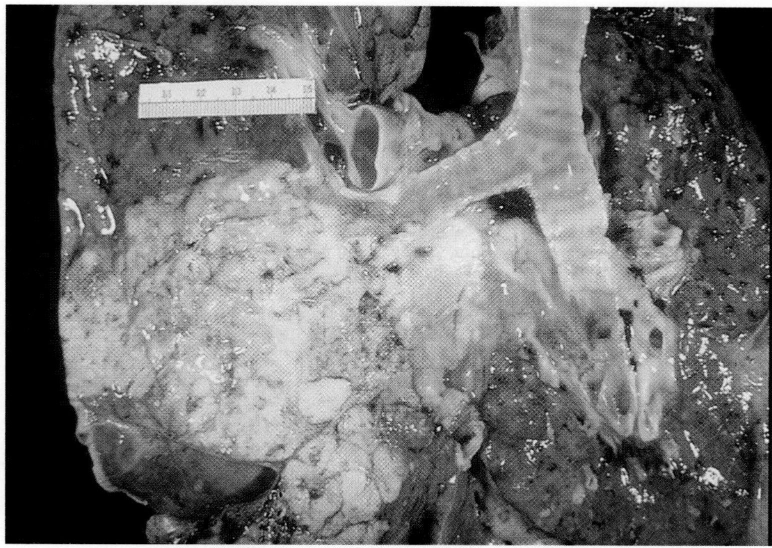

FIGURE 11-8. Bronchogenic carcinoma. The tumor, a squamous cell carcinoma, appears gray-white and infiltrates the lung tissue.

EXERCISE 11-5

Assign codes to the following conditions.

1. Malignancy of supraglottis __________
2. Cancer of the larynx __________
3. Oat cell cancer of right main bronchus __________
4. Squamous cell carcinoma of thymus __________
5. Cancer, maxillary sinus __________

Malignant Neoplasm of Bone, Articular Cartilage, and Skin (C40-C44)

Cancers of the connective tissue develop in the muscles, fat, blood and lymph vessels, and nerves. There are three main types of skin cancer:

- **Basal cell carcinoma (BCC)** is the most common type of skin cancer. Most cases occur in areas of the body that have been exposed to the sun, such as the head and neck. It usually does not metastasize.
- **Squamous cell carcinoma (SCC)** is the second most common type of skin cancer and also occurs in areas of the body that have been exposed to the sun. SCC of the lip and ears have high metastatic and recurrence rates.
- **Malignant melanoma** is a malignant neoplasm of the melanocytes, and the most common place of occurrence is the skin. Melanoma is the most dangerous skin cancer and is responsible for 75% of deaths due to skin cancer. Early signs of melanoma are summarized by "ABCDE":
  - **A**symmetry
  - **B**orders (irregular)
  - **C**olor (variegated)
  - **D**iameter (greater than 6 mm—about the size of a pencil eraser)
  - **E**volving over time

Osteosarcoma is the most common primary malignant cancer of the bone and usually occurs in young people between the age of 10 and 30. These tumors develop most often in bones of the arms, legs, or pelvis.

EXAMPLE The patient is being seen for Ewing's sarcoma distal left femur, C40.22.

EXERCISE 11-6

Assign codes to the following conditions.

1. Ewing's sarcoma, 7th rib __________
2. Basal cell carcinoma, right ear __________
3. Osteosarcoma, left humerus __________
4. Lentigo malignant melanoma, sole of left foot __________

Malignant Neoplasm of Mesothelial and Soft Tissue (C45-C49)

Malignant mesothelioma is a rare, aggressive cancer that develops in the protective lining or mesothelium that surrounds and protects the internal organs. The most common site for occurrence is the pleura, which is the outer lining of the lungs. Other sites include the peritoneum, which is the lining of the abdominal cavity, the pericardium, which surrounds the heart, and the tunica vaginalis, which surrounds the testicles. The most common cause is exposure to asbestos. Symptoms will vary depending on the site of occurrence. Symptoms of pleural mesothelioma may include:

- Chest/rib pain
- Cough
- Shortness of breath
- Unusual nodules under the skin on chest
- Unexplained weight loss

EXAMPLE Patient is being treated for malignant mesothelioma of the pleura, C45.0.

Kaposi's sarcoma (KS) is a cancer that develops from the lining of lymph or blood vessels. Purple, red, or brown blotches or lesions may form on the skin. Kaposi's can also occur in internal organs such as the lungs and gastrointestinal tract. Patients with HIV and those who have had organ transplants are at high risk for this malignancy. Both types of patients would be immunocompromised. KS may occur in more than one site. Each site should be coded separately and should be assigned codes for primary neoplasm instead of coding additional sites as a secondary neoplasm. If the Kaposi's sarcoma is due to HIV disease, B20 is coded first.

EXAMPLE Patient is seen in the clinic because of Kaposi's sarcoma lesions on the skin of the left leg. Patient has AIDS, B20, C46.0.

Gastrointestinal stromal tumors (GISTs) are a type of tumor that occurs in the gastrointestinal tract, usually in the stomach or small intestine. These tumors can be either benign or malignant in nature. The default code is to primary malignancy.

EXAMPLE Patient had an EGD with biopsy of stomach neoplasm and was found to have a malignant gastrointestinal stromal tumor, C49.A2, 0DB68ZX.

EXERCISE 11-7

1. Kaposi's sarcoma palate in patient with HIV __________
2. Mesothelioma of lung __________
3. Fibrosarcoma, right tibia __________
4. Malignant schwannoma, left sciatic nerve __________

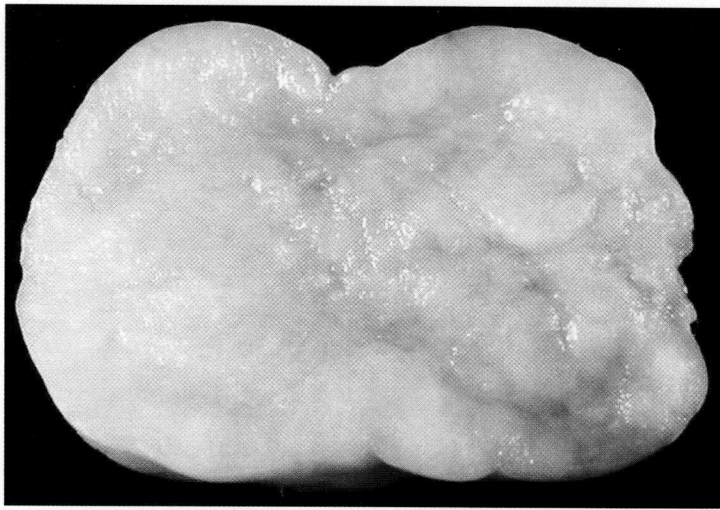

FIGURE 11-9. Breast carcinoma.

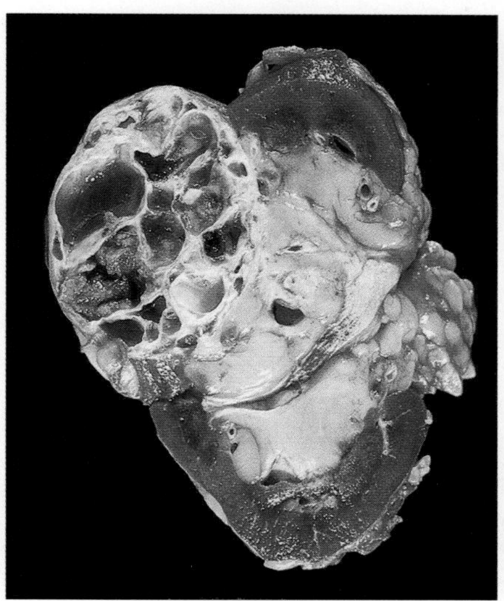

FIGURE 11-10. Renal cell carcinoma.

Malignant Neoplasm of Breast, Female and Male Genitourinary Organs (C50-C68)

One woman in eight has or will develop breast cancer in her lifetime (Figure 11-9). The 5-year survival rate exceeds 95% if detected early. Infiltrating or invasive ductal carcinoma is the most common type of breast cancer.

Malignancy can affect any organ in the genitourinary system. Many neoplasms are related to age; for example, Wilms' tumor is a common childhood tumor of the kidney. Testicular cancer usually affects young men, and the incidence of prostate cancer increases with age. Most kidney (Figure 11-10) and bladder (Figure 11-11) malignancies occur in adults between 60 and 70 years of age. As with many cancers, genetic, environmental, and behavioral risk factors may contribute to the cause.

EXAMPLE The patient is being treated for a malignancy of his right testis (descended), C62.11.

EXERCISE 11-8

Assign codes to the following conditions.

1. Endometrial carcinoma __________
2. Renal cell carcinoma, left __________

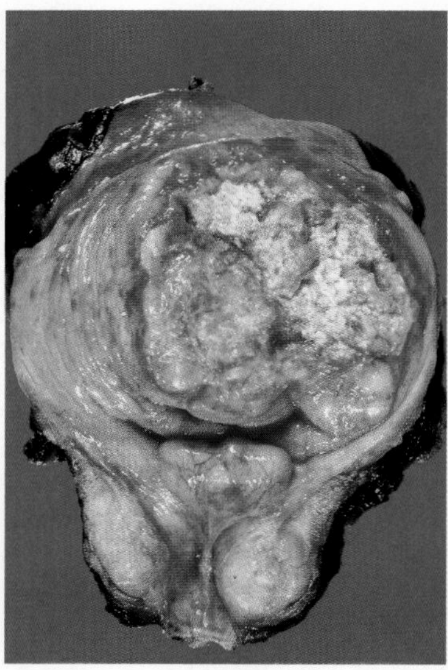

FIGURE 11-11. Bladder cancer.

3. Tubo-ovarian cancer ______________
4. Transitional cell carcinoma, lower neck of bladder, causing urinary obstruction ______________
5. Leiomyosarcoma of uterus ______________
6. Upper outer quadrant malignancy, right breast (female) ______________
7. Malignant neoplasm, left breast (male) ______________

Malignant Neoplasm of Eye, Brain, and Other Parts of Central Nervous System (C69-C72) and Malignant Neoplasm of Thyroid and Other Endocrine Glands (C73-C75)

These sections contain a variety of neoplasms including those of the eye, brain, spinal cord, thyroid, and other endocrine glands. The most common type of primary malignant brain neoplasm is a **glioma**. This means that the malignancy has started in the glial cells of the central nervous system. Gliomas are classified into four grades. Grades I and II are low-grade and slow-growing, while grade III grows at a moderate rate, and grade IV is the most aggressive. There are different types of glial cells in which gliomas form. Some of these include:

- Pilocytic astrocytoma
- Diffuse astrocytoma
- Anaplastic astrocytoma
- Glioblastoma multiforme (GBM)
- Oligodendroglioma
- Ependymoma

EXAMPLE

Patient was seen in the clinic and the results of recent biopsy were discussed. The patient has a pilocytic astrocytoma of the cerebellum, C71.6.

There are four major types of thyroid cancer:

- Papillary
- Follicular
- Medullary
- Anaplastic

The most common types are papillary and follicular cancer. Prior irradiation to the head and neck may be a risk factor for the development of thyroid cancer. There is an instructional note under category C73, malignant neoplasm of the thyroid gland, to use an additional code to identify any functional activity.

EXAMPLE Hypothyroidism due to malignancy of the thyroid gland, C73, E03.8.

EXERCISE 11-9

Assign codes to the following conditions.

1. Seizure due to carcinoma of parietal lobe of the brain ____________

2. Glioblastoma multiforme, brain ____________

3. Left orbital rhabdomyosarcoma ____________

4. Anaplastic astrocytoma spinal cord with metastasis to the vertebral bodies ____________

Neuroendocrine Tumors (C7A, C7B and D3A)

Code categories C7a and C7b include codes for primary and secondary malignant carcinoid neoplasms. Neuroendocrine tumors can be benign and/or malignant neoplasms that arise in the endocrine or neuroendocrine cells throughout the body. These neoplasms are usually slow growing. There are two groups of neuroendocrine neoplasms:

- Carcinoid
- Pancreatic neuroendocrine tumors

The most common sites for carcinoid neoplasms are the bronchi, stomach, small intestine, appendix, and rectum. They are classified according to the embryonic site of origin such as:

- **Foregut**—bronchi and stomach
- **Midgut**—small intestine and appendix
- **Hindgut**—colon and rectum

Malignant tumors are larger than benign tumors and do metastasize. The most common metastatic sites are lymph nodes, liver, lung, bone, and skin.

EXAMPLE Malignant carcinoid neoplasm of the appendix, C7a.020.

EXAMPLE Benign carcinoid neoplasm of the rectum, D3a.026.

EXERCISE 11-10

Assign codes to the following conditions.

1. Malignant carcinoid tumor, foregut ____________

2. Carcinoid neoplasm, small intestine, malignant ____________

3. Neuroblastoma, left adrenal gland ____________

4. Teratocarcinoma, pineal gland ____________

5. Benign carcinoid tumor of the appendix ____________

Malignant Neoplasm of Ill-defined, Secondary, and Unspecified Sites (C76-C80)

This section is where secondary or metastatic neoplasm codes are located. The C77 category is used to identify the spread of cancer to the lymph nodes. In contrast, code C79.51 is the code assigned to metastasis to the bone, and in this case specificity is not necessary for code assignment. It does not matter whether this is a vertebral bone, a pelvic bone, or the humerus.

EXAMPLE

The patient has metastatic lung cancer; no known primary, C78.00, C80.1 (sequencing will depend on reason for the encounter).

EXERCISE 11-11

1. Metastatic melanoma to the brain; melanoma skin lesion excised 5 years ago ____________
2. Carcinomatosis ____________
3. Metastasis to the mastectomy site; left mastectomy performed 1 year ago ____________

Malignant Neoplasm of Lymphoid, Hematopoietic, and Related Tissue (C81-C96)

Lymphoma is cancer of the lymphatic system. Two main types have been identified: Hodgkin's disease (HD) (Figure 11-12) or **lymphoma**, and **non-Hodgkin's lymphoma** (NHL). The incidence of non-Hodgkin's is greater than that of Hodgkin's disease. The lymphatic system follows the blood vessels, and groups are located in areas of the neck, axillary, groin, abdomen, and pelvic regions. Some organs contain lymphatic tissue and may be affected. These organs include the spleen, thymus gland, bone marrow, tonsils, and adenoids. Although lymphoma may be present in different or multiple areas of the body, this is not considered metastatic. Lymphomas should not be confused with solid tumors (malignancies) that have metastasized to the lymph nodes.

If a patient is in remission, he or she is considered to have lymphoma. There are different classifications of remission. **Complete remission** means there are no signs or symptoms of the cancer. **Partial remission** means there are still a few signs and symptoms of the cancer, and the cancer cells have significantly decreased.

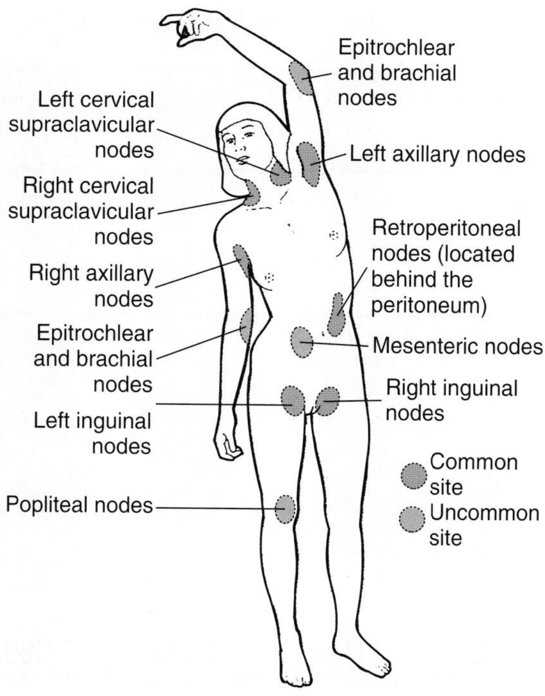

FIGURE 11-12. Lymph node sites for Hodgkin's disease.

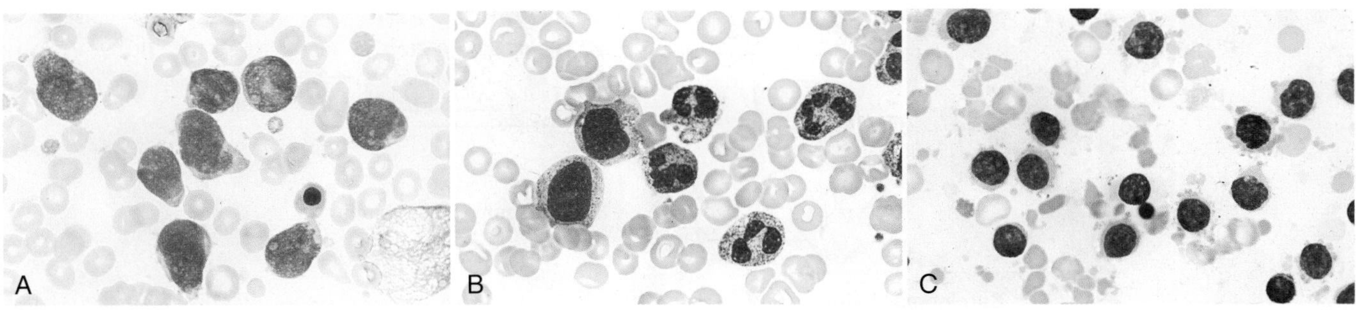

FIGURE 11-13. Peripheral blood smears. **A,** Acute lymphoblastic leukemia. **B,** Chronic myelogenous leukemia. **C,** Chronic lymphocytic leukemia.

Leukemia is cancer of the white blood cells that begins in the blood-forming cells of the bone marrow. As the disease progresses, leukemic cells invade other parts of the body, such as the lymph nodes, spleen, liver, and central nervous system. Various types of leukemia have been identified (Figure 11-13). Some develop suddenly and are acute leukemias; others are of the chronic variety.

EXAMPLE

The patient was diagnosed with nodular sclerosis Hodgkin's, C81.10.

EXERCISE 11-12

Assign codes to the following conditions.

1. Acute lymphocytic leukemia (ALL), relapsed __________
2. Acute promyelocytic leukemia __________
3. Chronic myelogenous leukemia (CML) __________
4. Lymphoma, ileum __________
5. Burkitt's lymphoma in remission __________

In Situ Neoplasms (D00-D09)

Carcinoma in situ consists of malignant cells that remain within the original site with no spread or invasion to neighboring tissues (Figure 11-14). Usually, the physician or the pathology report will confirm that the condition is "in situ." These tumors are usually curable because they are at the earliest stage of development.

EXAMPLE

Patient has Bowen's disease, right thigh, D04.71.

EXERCISE 11-13

Assign codes to the following conditions.

1. Carcinoma in situ of the cervix __________
2. Carcinoma in situ of the urinary bladder __________
3. Cervical intraepithelial neoplasia III __________
4. Ductal carcinoma in situ (DCIS) left breast __________

Benign Neoplasms (D10-D36)

A benign neoplasm or tumor is not malignant. It will not metastasize to other parts of the body, but it could continue to grow and may cause damage to neighboring organs and structures. It may be necessary to remove a benign neoplasm. Benign neoplasms may recur.

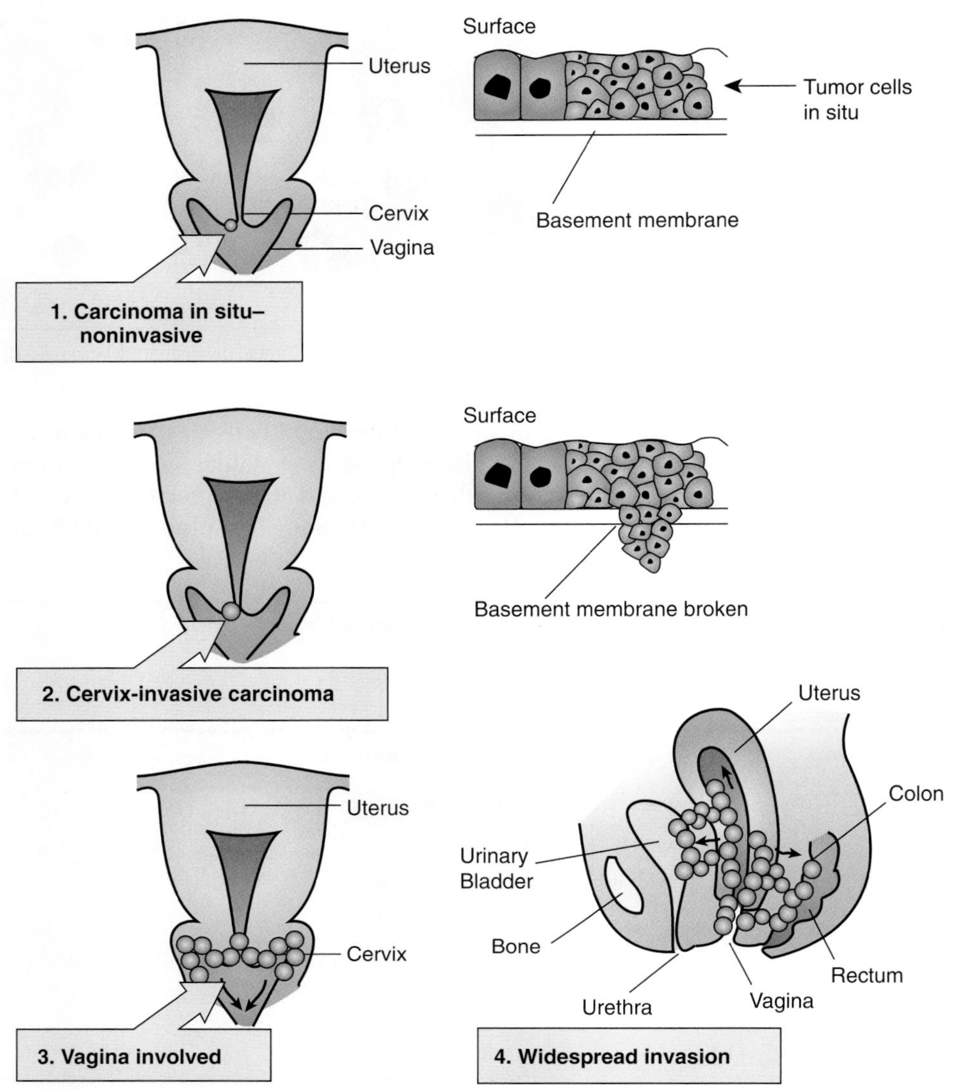

FIGURE 11-14. Invasive carcinoma of the cervix.

Lipoma is a growth of fat cells within a capsule that is usually found just below the skin. Lipomas are the most common benign soft tissue growths. For the most part, lipomas are small and movable, and they remain the same size and are not painful. It may be necessary to excise a lipoma if it becomes painful or infected, if it limits function or mobility, or if it increases in size.

Leiomyoma or uterine fibroids are tumors or growths within the walls of the uterus. These are the most common benign tumors in women of childbearing age. Not all fibroids cause symptoms. When fibroids become symptomatic, the following symptoms may be present:

- Heavy bleeding
- Painful periods
- Feeling of fullness in the pelvic region
- Urinary frequency
- Pain during sex
- Infertility, miscarriage, or early onset of labor

Treatment will depend on the severity of symptoms, the size and location of the fibroids, and the patient's age and desired fertility.

EXAMPLE

Patient is being seen because of a cavernous lymphangioma, D18.1.

EXERCISE 11-14

Assign codes to the following conditions.

1. Warthin's tumor ____________
2. Adenoma of the pituitary gland ____________
3. Chondromyxoid fibroma of the left tibia ____________
4. Squamous papilloma, soft palate ____________
5. Osteoma, proximal right femur ____________
6. Enchondroma, right fifth metacarpal ____________
7. Lipoma spermatic cord ____________
8. Rhabdomyoma, left ventricle of heart ____________
9. Hemangioma of liver ____________
10. Submucosal uterine fibroid ____________

Neoplasms of Uncertain Behavior, Polycythemia and Myelodysplastic Syndromes (D37-D48)

Neoplasms that fall into the categories of uncertain behavior are neither malignant nor benign. On pathologic examination, the behavior cannot be determined or predicted. In some instances, progression to some type of malignancy may occur. For example, myelodysplastic syndrome has been known to progress to leukemia.

EXAMPLE

Patient was being seen in the clinic and the findings of her path were discussed. The path showed granulosa cell tumors of the right ovary (undetermined behavior), D39.11.

Terms such as "growth," "neoplasm," or "tumor" are used to describe a medical finding. At times, this condition may require further investigation and testing. Sometimes, these findings are not investigated because the patient is elderly and has other chronic conditions, and aggressive treatment would not be pursued.

On occasion, a physician will document a patient as having a mass with no further specification other than site or location of the mass. Usually, this occurs when no pathology report is available when the physician is documenting details in the health record. According to *Coding Clinic for ICD-9-CM* (2006:1Q:p4),[4] if the diagnosis is documented as "mass" or "lesion," it would be incorrect to select a code for neoplasm of unspecified behavior.

EXAMPLE

Mass of the liver, R16.0.

The *Coding Clinic for ICD-9-CM* states that if there is no index entry for a specific site, go to the main term "disease." If terms such as lump or lesion are used, the same logic is applied. If a subterm cannot be found under "lump," "lesion," or "mass," go to the main term "disease."

EXAMPLE

Patient will need to follow up for definitive diagnosis of neoplasm sigmoid colon D49.0.

EXERCISE 11-15

Assign codes to the following conditions.

1. Intracranial tumor ____________
2. Neoplasm, bladder ____________
3. Growth, left ovary ____________
4. Mass, right lung ____________
5. Right breast lump ____________
6. Brain lesion was identified by MRI ____________
7. Myelodysplastic syndrome (MDS) ____________
8. Polycythemia vera ____________
9. Refractory anemia ____________
10. Paraganglioma of carotid body ____________

Coding and Sequencing of Neoplasms

In addition to assigning neoplasm codes, it is important to know how these codes are sequenced in accordance with the guidelines. The principal diagnosis is determined according to the reason the patient is admitted and the treatment provided. Documentation by physicians may be confusing in determining the principal diagnosis. They often will document the cancer as the reason for admission. Physicians may document cancers that have been previously removed. Physicians are not trained to document in accordance with coding guidelines. They may document the reason for admission as the cancer when the patient is receiving treatment for a complication of the cancer or of the cancer treatments.

Malignancy as Principal Diagnosis

When a patient is admitted for determination of whether a malignancy is present and a malignancy is found, the code for the primary malignancy is the principal diagnosis.

EXAMPLE

Patient was admitted for total thyroidectomy. Fine needle aspiration biopsy on an outpatient basis was inconclusive. Open total thyroidectomy was performed, and a diagnosis of anaplastic cancer was determined, C73, 0GTK0ZZ.

As in the previous example, during the course of determining whether a malignancy is present, a malignancy is found and a secondary malignancy is identified. The code for the primary neoplasm is the principal diagnosis, and the secondary malignancy is assigned as an additional code.

EXAMPLE

Patient has papillary thyroid cancer that has spread to the cervical lymph nodes, C73, C77.0.

Recurrence of Primary Malignancy

If a primary malignancy was previously excised or eradicated but has now recurred at the site of origin, the malignancy is coded to a primary malignant neoplasm.

EXAMPLE

Recurrence of transitional cell bladder cancer, posterior wall, C67.4.

Physicians may document a malignancy as recurrent at a site where a malignancy and the organ has been previously excised. This cannot be an actual recurrent neoplasm if the organ is no longer present. It may be necessary to query the physician to determine the metastatic site(s).

EXAMPLE

Recurrent ovarian cancer. Patient had open total abdominal hysterectomy and bilateral salpingo-oophorectomy 3 years ago, C79.9, Z85.43, Z90.722, Z90.710, Z90.79 (may need to query site of recurrence).

When a patient is admitted for removal of a known malignancy, the malignancy is the principal diagnosis. In some cases, a biopsy may have been performed previously that confirms the presence of a malignancy. The patient is readmitted for more definitive surgery. The pathology report following the surgery may report negative findings for malignancy. If the physician documents the malignancy as shown on the biopsy, the malignancy is assigned as the principal diagnosis for the definitive surgery even though no further evidence of malignancy is seen on the pathology report.

EXAMPLE

Patient has a fine needle aspiration biopsy that shows Hürthle carcinoma of the left lobe of the thyroid. Patient is admitted for a partial open thyroidectomy with removal of the left lobe. The pathology report from the thyroidectomy shows no evidence of malignancy, C73, 0GTG0ZZ.

When a patient is admitted with a sign or symptom (which codes to Chapter 18) related to a known primary or secondary malignancy, the primary or secondary malignancy code is the principal diagnosis.

EXAMPLE

Convulsion due to glioblastoma multiforme temporal lobe of brain, C71.2, R56.9 (the convulsion is coded as an additional code because convulsions are not integral to the brain neoplasm).

When a patient is admitted with a primary neoplasm and a metastatic neoplasm, and treatment is directed to the metastatic neoplasm, the metastatic neoplasm is the principal diagnosis.

EXAMPLE

Patient is admitted for open wedge resection of metastatic liver cancer.
Patient had a colorectal cancer removed 3 months ago and is undergoing treatment, C78.7, C19, 0FB00ZZ.

According to *Coding Clinic for ICD-9-CM* (1988:1Q:p4-5),[5] when a patient is admitted to the hospital for treatment by brachytherapy, the principal diagnosis is the malignancy that is being treated (which could be either a primary or a secondary malignancy).

EXAMPLE

Patient was admitted for implantation of brachytherapy (high dose rate Iridium 192) for cancer of cervix, C53.9, DU1198Z.

Complications as Principal Diagnosis

Often, complications are associated with malignancies or the treatment of malignancies. When the complication is the reason for admission or treatment, the complication is the principal diagnosis. The guidelines address some of the most common examples such as neutropenic fever and dehydration.

EXAMPLE

Patient has become extremely dehydrated due to her breast cancer. Patient is admitted for IV fluids, E86.0, C50.919.

EXAMPLE

Neutropenic fever with neutropenia due to chemotherapy for acute lymphocytic leukemia, D70.1, R50.81, T45.1x5A, C91.00.

Principal Diagnosis for Encounters for Chemotherapy/Immunotherapy and Radiation

When a patient is admitted solely for the administration of chemotherapy, chemoembolization, immunotherapy, and/or radiation, the principal diagnosis will be a Z51.- code. In cases where chemotherapy, chemoembolization, immunotherapy, or radiation is performed in conjunction with surgical removal of a neoplasm, the primary or secondary neoplasm code is the principal diagnosis, and no Z51.- code is assigned.

If a patient is admitted for both radiation and chemotherapy during the same encounter, either Z code can be sequenced as the principal with the other Z code used as a secondary diagnosis code.

If complications occur during an encounter for chemotherapy/immunotherapy/radiation treatment, codes to identify the complications are assigned as secondary diagnosis codes.

EXAMPLE

Patient was admitted for chemotherapy (percutaneous central vein) for osteosarcoma of right humerus. Patient became dehydrated and was treated with additional IV fluids, Z51.11, C40.01, E86.0, 3E04305.

EXAMPLE

Patient is admitted for chemotherapy (percutaneous central vein) for Burkitt's lymphoma, Z51.11, C83.70, 3E04305.

EXAMPLE

Patient is admitted for beam radiation therapy (heavy particle) for prostate cancer, Z51.0, C61, DV004ZZ.

Coding of Previously Excised Malignancies

If a primary malignancy has been previously excised and is no longer being treated, it is assigned a Z code for history of personal malignancy.

EXAMPLE

Patient had a mastectomy 5 years ago for breast cancer. She is not being actively treated, Z85.3, Z90.10.

However, if a previously excised malignancy is still being treated actively, it is appropriate to assign the neoplasm code.

EXAMPLE

Patient had a lobectomy for lung cancer 6 months ago. The patient will receive the fifth cycle of chemotherapy next week, C34.90, Z90.2.

EXERCISE 11-16

Complete the following exercises.

1. If a patient is admitted and treated for dehydration due to a malignancy, the malignancy code is the principal diagnosis.
   A. True
   B. False
2. If a patient has a complication during an encounter for chemotherapy, the complication code is the principal diagnosis.
   A. True
   B. False

3. If a malignancy of the bladder has been previously excised and now there is a recurrence of a malignancy within the bladder, the recurrence is coded as a primary malignancy.
   A. True
   B. False
4. A personal history Z code is assigned for a history of a primary malignancy when it is no longer being treated.
   A. True
   B. False
5. The primary neoplasm is always principal even if the treatment is directed at the secondary neoplasm.
   A. True
   B. False
6. If a patient is admitted for treatment of dehydration due to a malignancy, the dehydration is the principal diagnosis.
   A. True
   B. False
7. When a patient is admitted for immunotherapy, the Z51.12 is assigned as the principal diagnosis.
   A. True
   B. False
8. When a patient is admitted for brachytherapy, the Z51.0 is assigned as the principal diagnosis.
   A. True
   B. False

FACTORS INFLUENCING HEALTH STATUS AND CONTACT WITH HEALTH SERVICES (Z CODES)

As was discussed in Chapter 9, it may be difficult to locate Z codes in the Index. Coders often say, "I did not know there was a Z code for that." Refer to Chapter 9 for a listing of common main terms used to locate Z codes.

The guidelines provide instructions for the use and sequencing of some important Z codes. If a patient is admitted solely for administration of chemotherapy, immunotherapy, or radiation therapy, a code from category Z51.- should be the principal diagnosis followed by codes for the malignancies being treated. If they are admitted for more than one type of therapy, either code can be principal.

Z codes that may be used with neoplasms include the following:

Z08	Encounter for follow-up examination after completed treatment for malignant neoplasm
Z12.0	Encounter for screening for malignant neoplasm of stomach
Z12.10	Encounter for screening for malignant neoplasm of intestinal tract, unspecified
Z12.11	Encounter for screening for malignant neoplasm of colon
Z12.12	Encounter for screening for malignant neoplasm of rectum
Z12.13	Encounter for screening for malignant neoplasm of small intestine
Z12.2	Encounter for screening for malignant neoplasm of respiratory organs
Z12.31	Encounter for screening mammogram for malignant neoplasm of breast
Z12.39	Encounter for other screening for malignant neoplasm of breast
Z12.4	Encounter for screening for malignant neoplasm of cervix
Z12.5	Encounter for screening for malignant neoplasm of prostate
Z12.6	Encounter for screening for malignant neoplasm of bladder
Z12.71	Encounter for screening for malignant neoplasm of testis
Z12.72	Encounter for screening for malignant neoplasm of vagina
Z12.73	Encounter for screening for malignant neoplasm of ovary
Z12.79	Encounter for screening for malignant neoplasm of other genitourinary organs
Z12.81	Encounter for screening for malignant neoplasm of oral cavity

Z12.82	Encounter for screening for malignant neoplasm of nervous system
Z12.83	Encounter for screening for malignant neoplasm of skin
Z12.89	Encounter for screening for malignant neoplasm of other sites
Z12.9	Encounter for screening for malignant neoplasm, site unspecified
Z15.01	Genetic susceptibility to malignant neoplasm of breast
Z15.02	Genetic susceptibility to malignant neoplasm of ovary
Z15.03	Genetic susceptibility to malignant neoplasm of prostate
Z15.04	Genetic susceptibility to malignant neoplasm of endometrium
Z15.09	Genetic susceptibility to other malignant neoplasm
Z17.0	Estrogen receptor positive status [ER+]
Z17.1	Estrogen receptor negative status [ER-]
Z19.1	Hormone sensitive malignancy status
Z19.2	Hormone resistant malignancy status
Z40.00	Encounter for prophylactic removal of unspecified organ
Z40.01	Encounter for prophylactic removal of breast
Z40.02	Encounter for prophylactic removal of ovary
Z40.09	Encounter for prophylactic removal of other organ
Z42.1	Encounter for breast reconstruction following mastectomy
Z51.0	Encounter for antineoplastic radiation therapy
Z51.11	Encounter for antineoplastic chemotherapy
Z51.12	Encounter for antineoplastic immunotherapy
Z79.810	Long term (current) use of selective estrogen receptor modulators (SERMs)
Z79.811	Long-term (current) use of aromatase inhibitors
Z79.818	Long-term (current) use of other agents affecting estrogen receptors and estrogen levels
Z80.0	Family history of malignant neoplasm of digestive organs
Z80.1	Family history of malignant neoplasm of trachea, bronchus and lung
Z80.2	Family history of malignant neoplasm of other respiratory and intrathoracic organs
Z80.3	Family history of malignant neoplasm of breast
Z80.41	Family history of malignant neoplasm of ovary
Z80.42	Family history of malignant neoplasm of prostate
Z80.43	Family history of malignant neoplasm of testis
Z80.49	Family history of malignant neoplasm of other genital organs
Z80.51	Family history of malignant neoplasm of kidney
Z80.52	Family history of malignant neoplasm of bladder
Z80.59	Family history of malignant neoplasm of other urinary tract organ
Z80.6	Family history of leukemia
Z80.7	Family history of other malignant neoplasms of lymphoid, hematopoietic and related tissues
Z80.8	Family history of malignant neoplasm of other organs or systems
Z80.9	Family history of malignant neoplasm, unspecified
Z85.00	Personal history of malignant neoplasm of unspecified digestive organ
Z85.01	Personal history of malignant neoplasm of esophagus
Z85.020	Personal history of malignant carcinoid tumor of stomach
Z85.028	Personal history of other malignant neoplasm of stomach
Z85.030	Personal history of malignant carcinoid tumor of large intestine
Z85.038	Personal history of other malignant neoplasm of large intestine
Z85.040	Personal history of malignant carcinoid tumor of rectum
Z85.048	Personal history of other malignant neoplasm of rectum, rectosigmoid junction, and anus
Z85.05	Personal history of malignant neoplasm of liver
Z85.060	Personal history of malignant carcinoid tumor of small intestine
Z85.068	Personal history of other malignant neoplasm of small intestine
Z85.07	Personal history of malignant neoplasm of pancreas
Z85.09	Personal history of malignant neoplasm of other digestive organs

Z85.110	Personal history of malignant carcinoid tumor of bronchus and lung
Z85.118	Personal history of other malignant neoplasm of bronchus and lung
Z85.12	Personal history of malignant neoplasm of trachea
Z85.20	Personal history of malignant neoplasm of unspecified respiratory organ
Z85.21	Personal history of malignant neoplasm of larynx
Z85.22	Personal history of malignant neoplasm of nasal cavities, middle ear, and accessory sinuses
Z85.230	Personal history of malignant carcinoid tumor of thymus
Z85.238	Personal history of malignant neoplasm of thymus
Z85.29	Personal history of malignant neoplasm of other respiratory and intrathoracic organs
Z85.3	Personal history of malignant neoplasm of breast
Z85.40	Personal history of malignant neoplasm of unspecified female genital organ
Z85.41	Personal history of malignant neoplasm of cervix uteri
Z85.42	Personal history of malignant neoplasm of other parts of uterus
Z85.43	Personal history of malignant neoplasm of ovary
Z85.44	Personal history of malignant neoplasm of other female genital organs
Z85.45	Personal history of malignant neoplasm of unspecified male genital organ
Z85.46	Personal history of malignant neoplasm of prostate
Z85.47	Personal history of malignant neoplasm of testis
Z85.48	Personal history of malignant neoplasm of epididymis
Z85.49	Personal history of malignant neoplasm of other male genital organs
Z85.50	Personal history of malignant neoplasm of unspecified urinary tract organ
Z85.51	Personal history of malignant neoplasm of the bladder
Z85.520	Personal history of malignant carcinoid tumor of kidney
Z85.528	Personal history of other malignant neoplasm of kidney
Z85.53	Personal history of malignant neoplasm of renal pelvis
Z85.54	Personal history of malignant neoplasm of ureter
Z85.59	Personal history of malignant neoplasm of other urinary tract organ
Z85.6	Personal history of leukemia
Z85.71	Personal history of Hodgkin lymphoma
Z85.72	Personal history of non-Hodgkin lymphomas
Z85.79	Personal history of other malignant neoplasms of lymphoid, hematopoietic and related tissues
Z85.810	Personal history of malignant neoplasm of tongue
Z85.818	Personal history of malignant neoplasm of other sites of lip, oral cavity, and pharynx
Z85.819	Personal history of malignant neoplasm of unspecified site of lip, oral cavity, and pharynx
Z85.820	Personal history of malignant melanoma of skin
Z85.821	Personal history of Merkel cell carcinoma
Z85.828	Personal history of other malignant neoplasm of skin
Z85.830	Personal history of malignant neoplasm of bone
Z85.831	Personal history of malignant neoplasm of soft tissue
Z85.840	Personal history of malignant neoplasm of eye
Z85.841	Personal history of malignant neoplasm of brain
Z85.848	Personal history of malignant neoplasm of other parts of nervous tissue
Z85.850	Personal history of malignant neoplasm of thyroid
Z85.858	Personal history of malignant neoplasm of other endocrine glands
Z85.89	Personal history of malignant neoplasm of other organs and systems
Z85.9	Personal history of malignant neoplasm, unspecified
Z86.000	Personal history of in-situ neoplasm of breast
Z86.001	Personal history of in-situ neoplasm of cervix uteri
Z86.008	Personal history of in-situ neoplasm of other site
Z86.010	Personal history of colonic polyps
Z86.011	Personal history of benign neoplasm of the brain
Z86.012	Personal history of benign carcinoid tumor

Z86.018	Personal history of other benign neoplasm
Z86.03	Personal history of neoplasm of uncertain behavior
Z92.21	Personal history of antineoplastic chemotherapy
Z92.22	Personal history of monoclonal drug therapy
Z92.23	Personal history of estrogen therapy
Z92.25	Personal history of immunosupression therapy
Z92.3	Personal history of irradiation

There are some important Z code categories related to neoplasms and the treatment and follow-up of neoplasms. First, there are a number of screening codes and codes for family history of malignancies. A screening examination occurs in the absence of any signs or symptoms. The patient is asymptomatic.

EXAMPLE Patient has no symptoms. Screening for prostate cancer, Z12.5.

EXAMPLE Patient has a family history of leukemia, Z80.6.

EXERCISE 11-17

Assign codes to the following conditions.

1. History of adenocarcinoma of the prostate __________
2. Encounter for screening mammogram for patient with strong family history of breast cancer __________
3. Personal history of benign brain neoplasm previously removed __________
4. Admission for open takedown of colostomy; previous colon resection for malignancy __________

COMMON TREATMENTS

Cancer is treated by various modalities (i.e., surgery, chemotherapy, radiation, immunotherapy, or other methods). The type of treatment will depend on the location, grading, and stage of the neoplasm and the health of the patient. Chemotherapy destroys cancer cells, but may also target fast-growing healthy tissue. Often chemotherapy drugs are used in combinations because the drugs work better together than separately. Immunotherapy agents stimulate the immune system's response against tumors. Radiation therapy uses ionizing radiation to destroy cancer cells and shrink tumors. It is administered externally by external beam therapy or internally via brachytherapy.

CONDITION	MEDICATION/TREATMENT
Malignancies	Chemotherapy drugs are often given in combination with other chemotherapy drugs or hormonal therapy. The treatment will depend on the type of cancer. Some common drugs include carboplatin (Paraplatin), cisplatin (Platinol), cyclophosphamide (Cytoxan, Neosar), docetaxel (Taxotere), doxorubicin (Adriamycin), erlotinib (Tarceva), etoposide (VePesid, Toposar, Etopophos), fluorouracil (5-FU), gemcitabine (Gemzar), ifosfamide (Ifex), imatinib mesylate (Gleevec), irinotecan (Camptosar), methotrexate (Folex, Mexate, Amethopterin), mitomycin (Mitomycin-C), paclitaxel (Taxol, Abraxane), rituximab (Rituxan), sorafenib (Nexavar), sunitinib (Sutent), topotecan (Hycantin), vinblastine (Velban), vincristine (Oncovin, Vincasar PFS).
Melanoma and kidney cancer	Immunotherapy with interleukin and interferon
Superficial bladder cancer	Intravesical Bacillus Calmette-Guerin (BCG) immunotherapy

CONDITION	MEDICATION/TREATMENT
Certain types of breast or colon cancer	Capecitabine (Xeloda)—interferes with cancer cell growth and reproduction
Certain types of breast cancer	Tamoxifen (Nolvadex)—interferes with estrogen activity
Advanced prostate cancer in men and uterine fibroid tumors in women	Leuprolide acetate for depot suspension (Lupron Depot)
Certain types of leukemia (CML) and certain gastrointestinal stromal tumors	Imatinib (Gleevec) prevents the growth of cancer cells
Neutropenia due to chemotherapy	Pegfilgrastim (Neulasta) or filgrastim (Neupogen) builds up or stimulates white cell counts
Anemia due to malignancy	Epoetin alfa (Procrit, Epogen), darbepoetin alfa (Aranesp)
Symptoms of malignancy and treatment	Pain medications (narcotics), antiemetics to suppress nausea and vomiting
Human papilloma virus	Vaccination for prevention

PROCEDURES

Neoplasms can affect any body system, so for ICD-10-PCS, any of the tables in the Medical and Surgical section may be used. There may also be procedures that can be located in the Radiation Oncology, Placement, and Administration sections.

Chemotherapy/Immunotherapy/Radiation

Operative procedures are often performed to biopsy and resect or excise areas or organs that are affected by neoplastic conditions. At times, a neoplasm is considered unresectable, and other treatments are necessary. Sometimes, patients will receive chemotherapy or radiation therapy to shrink the tumor before surgery is performed. **Chemotherapy** consists of administration of drugs or medications to treat disease. In cancer patients, antineoplastic drugs are used. These drugs can be given intravenously, orally, subcutaneously, intramuscularly, or intrathecally. The introduction of chemotherapy is found in the Administration section of ICD-10-PCS. **Chemoembolization** is the intra-arterial administration of chemotherapy with collagen particles to enhance the delivery of chemotherapy to the targeted area. This should be treated as an encounter for chemotherapy, and Z51.11 should be assigned as the principal diagnosis. An additional diagnosis code is assigned for the malignancy. **Radiation** treatment involves the use of high-energy radiation to treat patients with cancer. **Brachytherapy** is the placement of radioactive material directly into or near the cancer. The radiation is delivered by needles, wires, or catheters and may be in the form of seeds. When a patient is admitted for treatment of a malignancy by implantation or insertion of radioactive elements, the principal diagnosis is the neoplastic condition (malignancy) being treated with the radioactive element. Radiation and brachytherapy are found under the Radiation Oncology section of ICD-10-PCS. **Immunotherapy** is the administration of agents that stimulate the immune system's response against tumors. **Biological response modifiers (BRMs)** are a type of immunotherapy and are used to fight certain cancers and even conditions such as rheumatoid arthritis. They can destroy cancer cells, stimulate the immune system to destroy cancer cells, or change cancer cells to normal cells. Immunotherapy is found in the Administration section of ICD-10-PCS.

The Guidelines provide instructions for the use and sequencing of some important Z codes. If a patient is admitted solely for administration of chemotherapy, immunotherapy, or radiation therapy, a code from category Z51.- should be the principal diagnosis followed by codes for the malignancies being treated. If they are admitted for more than one type of therapy, either code can be principal.

EXAMPLE

Patient was admitted for the administration of chemotherapy (percutaneous central vein) for osteosarcoma of upper end of the right tibia, Z51.11, C40.21, 3E04305.

SECTION	BODY SYSTEM	ROOT OPERATION	BODY SYSTEM/ REGION	APPROACH	SUBSTANCE	QUALIFIER
Administration	Physiological Systems and Anatomical Regions	Introduction	Central Vein	Percutaneous	Antineoplastic	Other Antineoplastic
3	E	0	4	3	0	5

EXAMPLE

Radioactive brachytherapy within Iodine 125 at high dose rate for treatment of prostate cancer, C61, DV1099Z.

SECTION	BODY SYSTEM	MODALITY	TREATMENT SITE	MODALITY QUALIFIER	ISOTOPE	QUALIFIER
Radiation Therapy	Male Reproductive System	Brachytherapy	Prostate	High Dose Rate	Iodine 125 (I-125)	None
D	V	1	0	9	9	Z

Palliative procedures may be performed to correct a condition that is causing problems or pain for the patient. It is not meant to cure. Palliative surgery may be performed to relieve an obstruction caused by a tumor. Sometimes radiation is administered for palliative treatment.

Biopsy

Biopsy specimens can be obtained in several ways. The approach used varies with the location of the mass, the age of the patient, and the technology that is available. A **biopsy** consists of removal of a representative sample of a tumor mass for pathologic examination and diagnosis. A biopsy is a diagnostic procedure. Biopsies can be coded to the following root operations:

- **Excision**–cutting out or off, without replacement, a portion of a body part
- **Extraction**–pulling or stripping out or off all or a portion of a body part by the use of force
- **Drainage**–taking or letting out fluids and/or gases from a body part

Sometimes a surgeon will remove the entire specimen and call it a biopsy. When the entire specimen such as a breast lump or colon polyp is removed, this is a therapeutic procedure and is not assigned a biopsy code.

If a biopsy is followed by more definitive treatment during the same encounter, both the biopsy and the code for the more definitive treatment are assigned.

- **Incisional biopsy:** This is the removal of a small piece of tumor or mass.
- **Core biopsy:** This procedure is less invasive than surgical biopsy. A large needle is used to extract a core sample.
- **Fine needle aspiration (FNA):** This method, which requires use of a very small needle, works best for masses that are superficial or easily accessible. The specimen is small, and sometimes, findings are inconclusive.
- **Endoscopic biopsy:** This is a biopsy that is performed during an endoscopic examination.

EXAMPLE

Patient had an FNA biopsy of a thyroid mass last week; this confirmed papillary thyroid cancer. Patient underwent total thyroidectomy (open), C73, 0GTK0ZZ.

SECTION	BODY SYSTEM	ROOT OPERATION	BODY PART	APPROACH	DEVICE	QUALIFIER
Medical and Surgical	Endocrine System	Resection	Thyroid Gland	Open	No Device	No Qualifier
0	G	T	K	0	Z	Z

EXAMPLE

Patient (female) was taken to the operating room for an open biopsy of a breast mass in the right upper outer quadrant. Frozen section showed invasive ductal carcinoma; a total mastectomy with removal of sentinel nodes was performed during the same operative episode for diagnostic purposes. Nodes were negative for malignancy, C50.411, 0HTT0ZZ, 07B50ZX, 0HBT0ZX.

SECTION	BODY SYSTEM	ROOT OPERATION	BODY PART	APPROACH	DEVICE	QUALIFIER
Medical and Surgical	Skin and Breast	Resection	Breast, Right	Open	No Device	No Qualifier
0	H	T	T	0	Z	Z

SECTION	BODY SYSTEM	ROOT OPERATION	BODY PART	APPROACH	DEVICE	QUALIFIER
Medical and Surgical	Lymphatic and Hemic Systems	Excision	Lymphatic, Right Axillary	Open	No Device	Diagnostic
0	7	B	5	0	Z	X

SECTION	BODY SYSTEM	ROOT OPERATION	BODY PART	APPROACH	DEVICE	QUALIFIER
Medical and Surgical	Skin and Breast	Excision	Breast, Right	Open	No Device	Diagnostic
0	H	B	T	0	Z	X

When procedures are performed for malignant neoplasms, often surrounding lymph nodes will be sampled or removed. If the intent is to remove all the lymph nodes in an area, code to root operation resection. Also, if a chain of lymph nodes is excised, code to root operation resection. Lymph nodes may be described by the level that they are located. Each level is considered a chain. If an entire level of lymph nodes is removed, this also is coded to a resection. Sometimes an axillary node dissection or removal is performed when a woman has breast cancer. There are three levels of axillary lymph nodes. Each level would be considered an entire chain.

A **sentinel lymph node** is defined as the first lymph node to which cancer cells are most likely to spread. A **sentinel lymph node biopsy** (SLNB) is a procedure that identifies the sentinel lymph node(s) for removal and pathologic examination. This spares the patient from having lymph nodes removed when it may not be necessary because the cancer has not spread to the sentinel node(s). This procedure is most often used to help stage melanoma and breast cancer patients.

Surgery

Endoscopic procedures are minimally invasive procedures during which a scope is used to examine the inside of the body. It is also possible for the clinician to perform a biopsy, remove a small polyp or foreign body, or control bleeding with the use of an endoscope.

Preventive or prophylactic surgery is performed to remove tissue that has the potential to become cancerous. A woman may have a prophylactic mastectomy as the result of a strong family history of breast cancer and/or a positive breast cancer gene (*BRCA1* or *BRCA2*).

The principal or first-listed diagnosis should be a code from subcategory Z40.-, prophylactic organ removal. The appropriate Z codes to identify the reason for the removal should also be assigned. If a patient has a malignancy of the breast and decides to have the other breast removed also as a prophylactic measure, the malignancy code should be assigned first with a Z40.01 code for the prophylactic removal of the other breast. **Staging surgeries** are performed to determine the extent of the disease and are generally more accurate than laboratory and imaging tests. **Debulking** procedures are performed when it is impossible to remove the tumor entirely. In many of these cases a number of organs may be involved and may also have to be removed. The tumor is removed to as great an extent as is possible, and adjunctive treatment such as chemotherapy or radiation may be used to treat the remaining disease. **Restorative or reconstructive** surgery is performed to restore function and enhance aesthetic appearance after surgery. Breast reconstruction is commonly performed after a mastectomy. Breast reconstruction procedures will be covered in Chapter 21.

EXAMPLE

Patient was admitted for prophylactic removal of ovaries and fallopian tubes due to genetic susceptibility and positive family history of ovarian cancer with laparoscopic removal, Z40.02, Z80.41, Z15.02, 0UT24ZZ, 0UT74ZZ.

SECTION	BODY SYSTEM	ROOT OPERATION	BODY PART	APPROACH	DEVICE	QUALIFIER
Medical and Surgical	Female Reproductive System	Resection	Ovaries, Bilateral	Percutaneous Endoscopic	No Device	No Qualifier
0	U	T	2	4	Z	Z

SECTION	BODY SYSTEM	ROOT OPERATION	BODY PART	APPROACH	DEVICE	QUALIFIER
Medical and Surgical	Female Reproductive System	Resection	Fallopian Tubes, Bilateral	Percutaneous Endoscopic	No Device	No Qualifier
0	U	T	7	4	Z	Z

EXERCISE 11-18

Assign codes for all diagnoses and procedures.

1. Refractory aplastic anemia with excess blasts (RAEB-2) for bone marrow transplant (BMT) via central vein; donor is the patient's sister ____________
2. Transitional cell carcinoma of the bladder with transurethral excision of tumor (via cystoscopy) ____________
3. Renal cell cancer of the right kidney with right laparoscopic nephrectomy ____________
4. Cervical brachytherapy with high dose rate Iridium 192 for cervical carcinoma ____________
5. Acoustic neuroma with hearing loss; craniotomy for removal of tumor ____________
6. Wide excision of melanoma right shoulder with skin grafting; split-thickness graft taken from left thigh ____________
7. Diagnostic percutaneous biopsy of intrathoracic lymph node showed non-Hodgkin's lymphoma in patient who has had a kidney transplant ____________
8. Admission for chemotherapy via central vein; patient has a malignancy of the esophagus ____________
9. Open wedge resection liver for HCC ____________
10. Ascending colon cancer with right open hemicolectomy ____________

CHAPTER REVIEW EXERCISE

Assign codes for all diagnoses and procedures.

1. Adenocarcinoma of the prostate with excision of prostate and seminal vesicles and partial regional pelvic lymph nodes ____________
2. Adenocarcinoma of the distal esophagus; patient is status post-laparoscopic jejunostomy prior to radiation treatments ____________
3. Chronic lymphocytic leukemia (CLL) ____________
4. Splenectomy showed non-Hodgkin's lymphoma of the spleen ____________
5. Benign carcinoid right lung ____________
6. Hydrocephalus due to malignant ependymoma fourth ventricle; the patient was admitted for ventriculoperitoneal shunt placement via craniotomy ____________
7. Diagnostic percutaneous needle biopsy of the right adrenal gland; physician documented pheochromocytoma (benign) ____________
8. Fibrosarcoma of the soft tissue of left thigh with mets to brain ____________
9. Malignant melanoma left thigh previously excised; patient admitted for immunotherapy with high-dose interleukin-2 via central venous infusion because of spread to inguinal lymph nodes ____________
10. Intraperitoneal metastatic carcinoma; unknown primary; treatment focused on determining primary source ____________
11. Short-term memory loss due to tumor frontal lobe ____________
12. Hodgkin's lymphoma in cervical lymph node. Admitted for chemotherapy, which is administered via central vein ____________
13. Admission for red blood cell transfusion (peripheral venous) due to anemia caused by renal cell carcinoma ____________
14. Dehydration due to chemotherapy in a female patient with carcinoma of breast with metastasis to axillary lymph nodes ____________
15. Recurrent seizures due to metastasis to brain from lung cancer ____________
16. Cerebral meningioma (benign) ____________
17. Right choroidal melanoma (malignant) ____________
18. Admission for chemoembolization of hepatocellular carcinoma (HCC) via hepatic artery ____________
19. Neutropenic fever in a patient who is undergoing treatment for leukemia; patient is anemic due to chemotherapy ____________
20. Intestinal obstruction due to peritoneal metastasis from inoperable colorectal cancer ____________
21. Impending hip fracture due to metastasis to bone; patient has a previous history of left breast cancer treated with mastectomy; internal fixation of upper right femur ____________
22. Patient's myelodysplastic syndrome has progressed to acute myelogenous leukemia ____________
23. Prophylactic removal of both breasts due to positive genetic susceptibility and positive family history of breast cancer; a bilateral simple mastectomy was performed ____________
24. Chronic myeloproliferative disease ____________
25. Falx cerebri meningioma surgically removed via crainiotomy ____________
26. Basophil adenoma of the pituitary gland causing Cushing's syndrome ____________
27. Carcinoma of the breast in the right upper and lower quadrant (overlapping site in female patient) ____________
28. Metastatic ovarian cancer admitted for pain control ____________

29. Cancer head of pancreas with spread to the liver __________

30. Endometrial adenocarcinoma with mets to right ovary __________

31. Open parotidectomy (partial excision of gland) for Warthin's tumor of the left parotid gland __________

32. Adenocarcinoma of the upper stomach with spread to the lower esophagus and lungs __________

CHAPTER GLOSSARY

Adenocarcinomas: malignancies of epithelial glandular tissue such as those found in the breast, prostate, and colon.

Basal cell carcinoma (BCC): most common type of skin cancer.

Benign: neoplasm or tumor; means that it is not malignant.

Biological response modifier (BRM): immunotherapy that can destroy cancer cells, stimulate the immune system to destroy cancer cells, or change cancer cells to normal cells.

Biopsy: removal of a representative sample for pathologic examination and diagnosis.

Brachytherapy: placement of radioactive material directly into or near the cancer.

Carcinomas: malignant tumors originating from epithelial tissue (e.g., in the skin, bronchi, and stomach).

Carcinoma in situ: malignant cells that remain within the original site with no spread or invasion into neighboring tissue.

Chemoembolization: intra-arterial administration of chemotherapy with collagen particles to enhance the delivery of chemotherapy to the targeted area.

Chemotherapy: the use of drugs or medications to treat disease.

Complete remission: there are no signs or symptoms of the cancer.

Core biopsy: procedure in which a large needle is used to extract a core sample.

Debulking: procedures performed when it is impossible to remove the tumor entirely.

Dissection: a tear in wall of a vessel.

Endoscopic biopsy: biopsy that is performed during endoscopic examination.

Excision: removal by surgical cutting.

Extraction: pulling or stripping out or off all or portion of a body part by force (e.g., bone marrow biopsy).

Fibromas: neoplasms of fibrous connective tissue.

Fine needle aspiration: procedure in which a very small needle is used; works best for masses that are superficial or easily accessible.

Foregut: bronchi and stomach (sites of carcinoid neoplasms).

Gastrointestinal stromal tumor: a type of tumor that occurs in the gastrointestinal tract, usually in the stomach or small intestine.

Glioma: a primary malignant brain neoplasm that starts in the glial cells of the central nervous system.

Grading: pathologic examination of tumor cells. Degree of cell abnormality determines the grade of cancer.

Hindgut: colon and rectum (sites of carcinoid neoplasms).

Immunotherapy: administration of agents that stimulate the immune system's response against tumors.

Incisional biopsy: procedure in which a representative sample of a tumor mass is removed to permit pathologic examination.

Kaposi's sarcoma (KS): cancer that develops from the lining of lymph or blood vessels.

Leiomyoma: tumor or growth within the walls of the uterus. Also called *uterine fibroid.*

Leukemia: cancer of the white blood cells that begins in the blood-forming cells of the bone marrow.

Lipoma: growth of fat cells within a capsule that is usually found just below the skin.

Lymphoma: cancer of the lymphatic system.

Malignancy: neoplasm that has the ability to invade adjacent structures and spread to distant sites.

Malignant ascites: excess fluid that contains malignant cells accumulates in the abdomen or peritoneum.

Malignant melanoma: malignant neoplasm of the melanocytes, and the most common place of occurrence is the skin.

Malignant mesothelioma: rare, aggressive cancer that develops in the protective lining or mesothelium that surrounds and protects the internal organs.

Malignant pleural effusion: fluid accumulates in the pleural space and contains malignant cells.

Melanomas: malignant changes of melanin cells.

Metastasis: spread of a cancer from one part of the body to another, as in the appearance of neoplasms in parts of the body separate from the site of the primary tumor.

Midgut: small intestine and appendix (sites of carcinoid neoplasms).

Myeloma: malignancy that originates in the bone marrow.

Neoplasm: abnormal growth.

Non-Hodgkin's lymphoma: a type of cancer of the lymphatic system.

Palliative: procedure performed to correct a condition that is causing problems for the patient.

Partial remission: there are still a few signs and symptoms of the cancer, and the cancer cells have significantly decreased.

Preventive or prophylactic surgery: procedure performed to remove tissue that has the potential to become cancerous.

Primary site: site at which the neoplasm begins or originates.

Radiation: use of high-energy radiation to treat cancer.

Restorative or reconstructive: surgery performed to restore function and enhance aesthetic appearance after surgery.

Sarcomas: malignant growths of connective tissue (e.g., muscle, cartilage, lymph tissue, and bone).

Sentinel lymph node: first lymph node to which cancer cells are most likely to spread.

Sentinel lymph node biopsy: a procedure that identifies the sentinel lymph node(s) for removal and pathologic examination.

Staging: means of categorizing a particular cancer that assists in determination of a patient's treatment plan and the need for further therapy.

Staging surgeries: procedures performed to help the clinician determine the extent of disease; these are generally more accurate than laboratory and imaging tests.

Squamous cell carcinoma (SCC): second most common type of skin cancer that also occurs in areas of the body that have been exposed to the sun.

Undifferentiated: tumor cells that are highly abnormal (e.g., immature, primitive).

Well-differentiated: tumor cells that closely resemble mature, specialized cells.

REFERENCES

1. Chabner D: The Language of Medicine, ed 8, St. Louis, 2007, Saunders, Table 19-2, p 776.
2. Chabner D: The Language of Medicine, ed 8, St. Louis, 2007, Saunders, Table 19-3, p 777.
3. Modified from Harrison' s Manual of Medicine, ed 15, New York, 2002, McGraw-Hill Professional, p 284.
4. American Hospital Association. *Coding Clinic for ICD-9-CM* 2006:1Q:p4. Correct coding of mass or lesion.
5. American Hospital Association. *Coding Clinic for ICD-9-CM* 1988:1Q:p4-5. Implantation or insertion of radioactive elements.

12

Diseases of the Blood and Blood-Forming Organs and Certain Disorders Involving the Immune Mechanism

(ICD-10-CM Chapter 3, Codes D50-D89)

CHAPTER OUTLINE

LEARNING OBJECTIVES

1. Apply and assign the correct ICD-10-CM/PCS codes in accordance with Official Guidelines for Coding and Reporting
2. Identify pertinent anatomy and physiology of the blood and blood-forming organs and immune mechanism
3. Identify diseases of the blood and blood-forming organs and immune mechanism
4. Assign the correct Z codes and procedure codes related to the blood-forming organs and immune mechanism
5. Identify laboratory values and diagnostic tests

ABBREVIATIONS/ ACRONYMS

ASA aspirin

CBC complete blood count

DIC disseminated intravascular coagulation

ESRD end-stage renal disease

GVHD graft-versus-host disease

Hct hematocrit

Hgb hemoglobin

HIV human immunodeficiency virus

ICD-10-CM *International Classification of Diseases, 10th Revision, Clinical Modification*

ICD-10-PCS *International Classification of Diseases, 10th Revision, Procedure Classification System*

ITP idiopathic thrombocytopenic purpura

PT prothrombin time

PTT partial thromboplastin time

SCID severe combined immunodeficiency

WBC white blood cell

ICD-10-CM Official Guidelines for Coding and Reporting (2021-2022)

Please refer to the companion Evolve website for the most current 2021-2022 guidelines.

3. **Chapter 3: Disease of the blood and blood-forming organs and certain disorders involving the immune mechanism (D50-D89)**
   Reserved for future guideline expansion.

Although there are no ICD-10-CM guidelines specifically for Chapter 3, there are a couple of guidelines that affect the coding and sequencing of anemia when it is associated with a malignancy or the treatment of a malignancy.

2. **Chapter 2: Neoplasms (C00-D49)**
   c. **Coding and sequencing of complications**
   Coding and sequencing of complications associated with the malignancies or with the therapy thereof are subject to the following guidelines:
   1) **Anemia associated with malignancy**
   When admission/encounter is for management of an anemia associated with the malignancy, and the treatment is only for anemia, the appropriate code for the malignancy is sequenced as the principal or first-listed diagnosis followed by the appropriate code for the anemia (such as code D63.0, Anemia in neoplastic disease).

EXAMPLE

Anemia due to metastatic bone cancer. The patient has a history of primary right breast cancer that was treated with mastectomy 4 years ago, C79.51, D63.0, Z85.3, Z90.11.

2) **Anemia associated with chemotherapy, immunotherapy and radiation therapy**
When the admission/encounter is for management of an anemia associated with an adverse effect of the administration of chemotherapy or immunotherapy and the only treatment is for the anemia, the anemia code is sequenced first followed by the appropriate codes for the neoplasm and the adverse effect (T45.1X5-, Adverse effect of antineoplastic and immunosuppressive drugs).

When the admission/encounter is for management of an anemia associated with an adverse effect of radiotherapy, the anemia code should be sequenced first, followed by the appropriate neoplasm code and code Y84.2, Radiological procedure and radiotherapy as the cause of abnormal reaction of the patient, or of later complication, without mention of misadventure at the time of the procedure.

EXAMPLE

Patient is being treated for anemia due to chemotherapy. The patient has primary rectal cancer, D64.81, T45.1x5A, C20.

ANATOMY AND PHYSIOLOGY

Blood is a viscous fluid that circulates through the vessels of the circulatory system as a result of the pumping action of the heart. Blood has three major functions. First, it transports oxygen, nutrients, hormones, enzymes, waste products, and carbon dioxide to and from cells. Second, blood promotes homeostasis and regulates body temperature. **Homeostasis** means balance or equilibrium. It is the ability of an organism or cell to maintain internal equilibrium by adjusting its physiologic processes. Third, blood provides a protective mechanism that combats foreign materials and assists in the body's defense against disease. Blood loss is prevented by clotting mechanisms within the body.

Blood is composed of plasma and formed elements or corpuscles. Corpuscles include erythrocytes (red blood cells), leukocytes (white blood cells), and platelets or thrombocytes. All of these components differ in terms of appearance, structure and type, function, life span, numbers, and means of production. **Erythrocytes**, or red blood cells, are made within the marrow of the bones; their main responsibility is to carry oxygen throughout the body and remove carbon dioxide. These are the cells that give blood its red color. **Leukocytes**, or white blood cells, increase in number to battle infection, inflammation, and other diseases. Five different types of white blood cells have been identified, and each has a role in fighting infection. White cells are comprised of neutrophils, monocytes, lymphocytes, eosinophils, and basophils. **Platelets** or **thrombocytes** circulate in the blood and assist in the clotting process.

Complete blood count (CBC) is a blood test that is commonly used to evaluate a patient's overall health; it detects a variety of disorders such as anemia, infection, and leukemia. This test measures the following:

- Hemoglobin (Hgb), a protein in red blood cells that carries oxygen to body tissues
- Hematocrit (Hct), the percentage of blood volume made up of red blood cells
- White blood cells (WBCs), which fight infection
- Platelets, which are essential to blood clotting

See Table 12-1 for normal values.

The **immune system,** the body's major defense mechanism, responds to invasion of the body by foreign substances. The immune system consists of lymphoid tissues such as thymus, bone marrow, tonsils, adenoids, spleen, and appendix. When the immune system malfunctions and homeostasis is interrupted, the response may be classified as one of the following:

- Hyperactive responses (such as allergies)
- Immunodeficiency in which the response is inadequate (such as acquired immunodeficiency syndrome [AIDS])

TABLE 12-1 NORMAL LABORATORY VALUES[1]

WBC 5000-10,000 mm^3 or μL	
Differential:	
Segs (polyps)	54%-62%
Lymphs	20%-40%
Eos	1%-3%
Baso	0%-1%
Mono	3%-7%
RBC	(M) 4.5-6.0 million per mm^3 or μL
	(F) 4.0-5.5 million per mm^3 or μL
Hct	(M) 40%-50%
	(F) 37%-47%
HGB	(M) 14-16 g/dL
	(F) 12-14 g/dL
Platelets	150,000-350,000/mm^3 or μL

Baso, Basophils; *Eos*, eosinophils; *Hct*, hematocrit; *HGB*, hemoglobin; *Lymphs*, lymphocytes; *Mono*, monocytes; *RBC*, red blood cell; *Segs*, segments; *WBC*, white blood cell.

- Autoimmune disorders in which the immune response is misdirected (such as systemic lupus erythematosus)
- Attacks on beneficial foreign tissues (such as transplants or blood transfusion)

DISEASE CONDITIONS

Chapter 3 in ICD-10-CM focuses on Diseases of the Blood and Blood-Forming Organs and Certain Disorders Involving the Immune Mechanism (D50-D89). Of interest is an Excludes2 note that appears at the beginning of the chapter (Figure 12-1). This note applies to the entire chapter. An Excludes2 note means that these conditions are not coded within this chapter, but it is possible for a patient to have one of these conditions with a condition from this chapter. The Excludes1 note under category D58 is a pure Excludes note. This means codes from category P55.- cannot be assigned with any codes from category D58.- (Figure 12-2). This chapter also includes conditions involving the immune mechanism.

Diseases of the Blood and Blood-Forming Organs and Certain Disorders Involving the Immune Mechanism (D50-D89), Chapter 3 in the ICD-10-CM code book, is divided into the following categories:

CATEGORY	SECTION TITLES
D50-D53	Nutritional anemias
D55-D59	Hemolytic anemias
D60-D64	Aplastic and other anemias and other bone marrow failure syndromes
D65-D69	Coagulation defects, purpura, and other hemorrhagic conditions
D70-D77	Other disorders of blood and blood-forming organs
D78	Intraoperative and postprocedural complications of the spleen
D80-D89	Certain disorders involving the immune mechanism

Nutritional Anemias (D50-D53)

Anemia occurs when hemoglobin drops, which interrupts the transport of oxygen throughout the body. The most common type of anemia is iron deficiency anemia. In women, this condition is often due to heavy blood loss during menstrual periods. In older men and

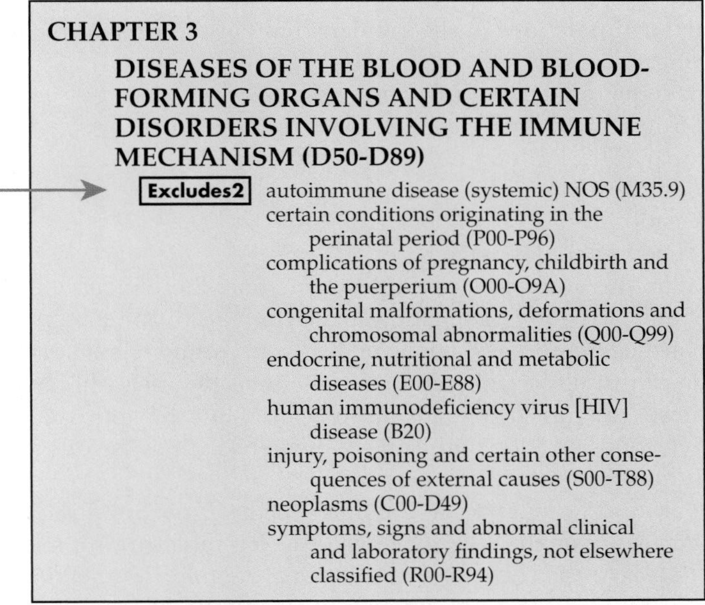

CHAPTER 3

DISEASES OF THE BLOOD AND BLOOD-FORMING ORGANS AND CERTAIN DISORDERS INVOLVING THE IMMUNE MECHANISM (D50-D89)

Excludes2 autoimmune disease (systemic) NOS (M35.9)
certain conditions originating in the perinatal period (P00-P96)
complications of pregnancy, childbirth and the puerperium (O00-O9A)
congenital malformations, deformations and chromosomal abnormalities (Q00-Q99)
endocrine, nutritional and metabolic diseases (E00-E88)
human immunodeficiency virus [HIV] disease (B20)
injury, poisoning and certain other consequences of external causes (S00-T88)
neoplasms (C00-D49)
symptoms, signs and abnormal clinical and laboratory findings, not elsewhere classified (R00-R94)

FIGURE 12-1. Excludes2 note that affects the entire chapter.

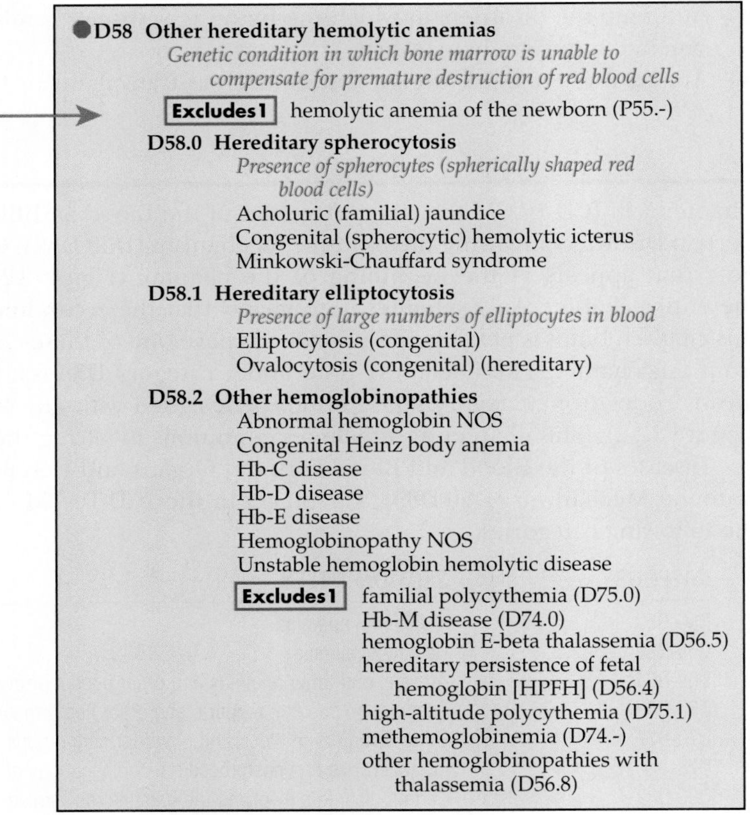

●D58 Other hereditary hemolytic anemias
Genetic condition in which bone marrow is unable to compensate for premature destruction of red blood cells
Excludes1 hemolytic anemia of the newborn (P55.-)

D58.0 Hereditary spherocytosis
Presence of spherocytes (spherically shaped red blood cells)
Acholuric (familial) jaundice
Congenital (spherocytic) hemolytic icterus
Minkowski-Chauffard syndrome

D58.1 Hereditary elliptocytosis
Presence of large numbers of elliptocytes in blood
Elliptocytosis (congenital)
Ovalocytosis (congenital) (hereditary)

D58.2 Other hemoglobinopathies
Abnormal hemoglobin NOS
Congenital Heinz body anemia
Hb-C disease
Hb-D disease
Hb-E disease
Hemoglobinopathy NOS
Unstable hemoglobin hemolytic disease
Excludes1 familial polycythemia (D75.0)
Hb-M disease (D74.0)
hemoglobin E-beta thalassemia (D56.5)
hereditary persistence of fetal hemoglobin [HPFH] (D56.4)
high-altitude polycythemia (D75.1)
methemoglobinemia (D74.-)
other hemoglobinopathies with thalassemia (D56.8)

FIGURE 12-2. Excludes1 note that affects category D58.-.

women, it may be an indication of gastrointestinal blood loss. Pregnant women and children need more iron, so a deficiency is likely due to insufficient iron in the diet. Testing may be necessary to determine a cause.

If a particular cause were determined, it would be appropriate to code the underlying condition. The sequencing of diagnoses would be determined by the coding guidelines and instructional notations in the tabular. Some of the reasons for iron deficiency include the following:

- Inadequate intake of iron in the diet
- Chronic blood loss
- Impaired absorption during digestion
- Liver disease
- Infection
- Cancers (neoplasms)

Numerous symptoms can indicate anemia; these include pallor, fatigue, lethargy, cold intolerance, irritability, stomatitis, headache, loss of appetite, numbness and tingling sensations, brittle hair, spoon-shaped and brittle nails, and edema, especially of the ankles. Severe anemia can result in tachycardia, palpitations, dyspnea (difficulty breathing), and syncope (fainting). Treatment depends on the cause, but the approach may be as simple as eating iron-rich foods or taking an iron supplement such as ferrous sulfate or ferrous gluconate. Blood transfusions may be necessary.

Look up the main term "Anemia" in the Index, and see the many subterms for the various types of anemia. "Deficiency" is also a subterm with many subterms, as is shown in Figure 12-3. At the subterm "in," entries are found for anemia in end-stage renal disease/chronic kidney disease and anemia in neoplastic disease (Figure 12-4). The term *chronic anemia* is not equated to "chronic simple anemia" or "anemia in chronic disease." Chronic

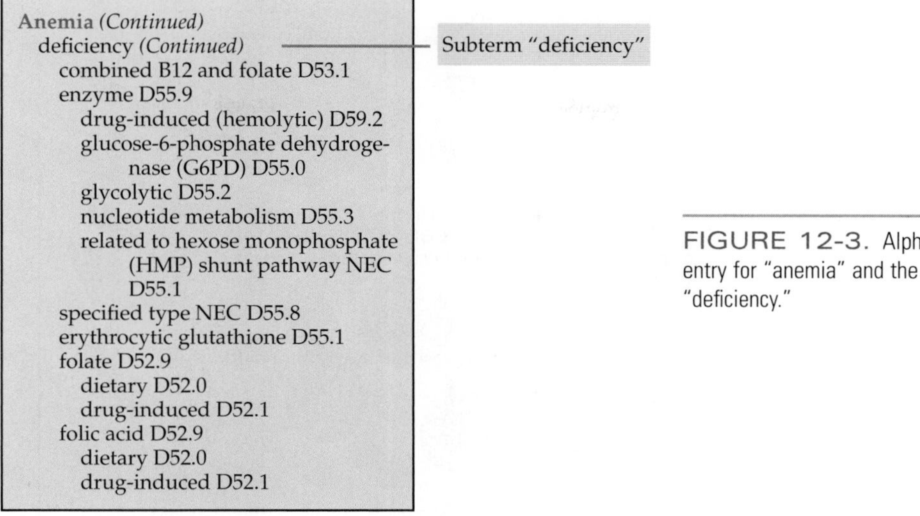

Anemia *(Continued)*
  deficiency *(Continued)*
    combined B12 and folate D53.1
    enzyme D55.9
      drug-induced (hemolytic) D59.2
      glucose-6-phosphate dehydrogenase (G6PD) D55.0
      glycolytic D55.2
      nucleotide metabolism D55.3
      related to hexose monophosphate (HMP) shunt pathway NEC D55.1
    specified type NEC D55.8
    erythrocytic glutathione D55.1
    folate D52.9
      dietary D52.0
      drug-induced D52.1
    folic acid D52.9
      dietary D52.0
      drug-induced D52.1

FIGURE 12-3. Alphabetic Index entry for "anemia" and the subterm "deficiency."

Anemia *(Continued)*
  in (due to) (with)
    chronic kidney disease D63.1
    end stage renal disease D63.1
    failure, kidney (renal) D63.1
    neoplastic disease (*see also* Neoplasm) D63.0

FIGURE 12-4. Anemia due to certain chronic diseases.

anemia is coded to D64.9 because no specific subterm is available for chronic, so the default code for anemia code is assigned.

EXAMPLE

Patient is being treated as an outpatient for anemia due to inadequate dietary iron intake, D50.8.

EXAMPLE

Patient is being treated for folate deficiency anemia, D52.9.

EXERCISE 12-1

Assign codes to the following conditions.

1. Iron deficiency anemia due to chronic blood loss ______________
2. Vitamin B_{12} deficiency anemia ______________
3. Megaloblastic anemia ______________

Hemolytic Anemias (D55-D59)

The hemolytic anemias are assigned to hereditary and acquired code categories (Figure 12-5). **Hemolytic anemia** results from abnormal or excessive destruction of red blood cells. **Sickle cell anemia** is one of the more common types of hereditary hemolytic anemia; it is found often in the African American population and among people living in Africa, the Mediterranean, Arabia, and South Asia. Red blood cells change from a disc shape to a crescent or "sickle" shape. This causes obstruction of the small blood vessels and eventual damage from thrombus formation, repeated organ infarctions, and tissue necrosis throughout the body. Varying degrees of disease severity and symptoms have been reported. Symptoms include severe anemia, hyperbilirubinemia or jaundice, splenomegaly, delayed and impaired growth and development, vascular occlusion, and infarctions, which can result in permanent damage, pain, frequent infection, and congestive heart failure. ICD-10-CM uses

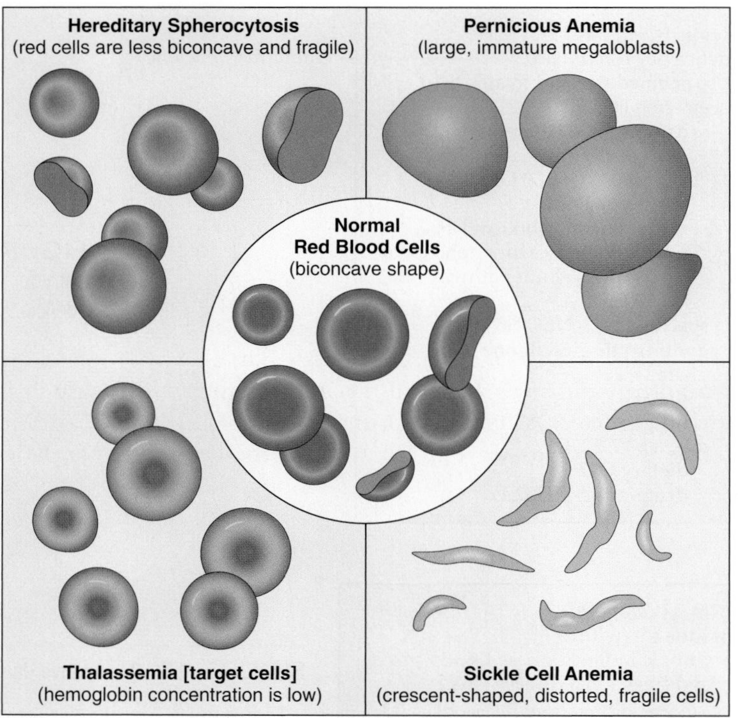

FIGURE 12-5. Normal red blood cells and red blood cells in several types of anemia.

combination code(s) that identifies the sickle cell crisis along with a manifestation such as acute chest syndrome or splenic sequestration. Most treatment is supportive in nature. A drug called Hydrea (hydroxyurea) has reduced the number of crises.

Code D57.3 for sickle cell trait is assigned when a patient is a carrier and the disease has remained asymptomatic. When both sickle cell trait and sickle cell anemia are present, only sickle cell anemia is coded.

EXAMPLE Patient was admitted with sickle cell crisis with acute chest syndrome. Patient has Hb-SS disease, D57.01.

Another hereditary disease that is prevalent among people from Greece and Italy (Mediterranean countries), the Middle East, South Asia, and Africa is **thalassemia**. Similar to sickle cell anemia, the disease manifests in varying degrees. Cooley's anemia is another name that is used to describe the beta thalassemias. Frequent blood transfusions are administered, along with treatment with an iron chelation drug, which helps the body get rid of excess iron resulting from repeated transfusions. Occasionally, bone marrow transplant is performed, but this is a risky procedure, and a suitable donor is required.

EXAMPLE Patient admitted with sickle cell thalassemia with vaso-occlusive pain crisis, D57.419.

EXERCISE 12-2

Assign codes to the following conditions.

1. Cooley's anemia ______________
2. Sickle cell trait with sickle cell anemia ______________
3. Acholuric jaundice ______________
4. Sickle cell Hb-C with vaso-occlusive crisis ______________
5. Sickle cell thalassemia crisis with splenic sequestration ______________

Aplastic and Other Anemias and Other Bone Marrow Failure Syndromes (D60-D64)

Aplastic anemia is characterized by a reduction in new blood cells due to impairment or failure of bone marrow function. Decreased production of erythrocytes (red blood cells), leukocytes (white blood cells), and thrombocytes (platelets), also defined as pancytopenia, can lead to many complications. In 50% of cases, the cause of aplastic anemia is unknown or **idiopathic** in nature. Some drugs, industrial agents, chemicals, or radiation can affect the function of the bone marrow. If the causative factor can be identified and eliminated, the bone marrow possibly can recover. Viruses such as hepatitis C may also cause aplastic anemia.

If a patient has the following three conditions—neutropenia, thrombocytopenia, and anemia, also known as **pancytopenia**—the code D61.81- would be assigned. According to *Coding Clinic for ICD-10* (2014:4Q:p22-23),[2] an exception occurs when a patient is admitted with neutropenic fever and is also pancytopenic; in this case, it is acceptable to assign the neutropenia code D70.- as the principal diagnosis, with an additional code D61.81- used to describe the pancytopenia and R50.81 for the fever. When a patient is admitted for neutropenic fever, investigations for any infectious source(s) are performed. Blood, sputum, and urine, and other sites may be cultured to try to identify an infection. The patient will be started on antibiotics, blood counts will be monitored, and neutropenic precautions will be implemented. If an infectious source is identified, treatment will be adjusted for that infection and the infection should be the principal diagnosis. Take note of the excludes1 note under subcategory code D61.81. You would not assign a code from this subcategory if the pancytopenia is due to, or with, aplastic anemia (D61.9), bone marrow infiltration (D61.82), congenital (pure) red cell aplasia (D61.01), hairy cell leukemia (C91.4-), HIV disease B20), leukoerythroblastic anemia (D61.82), or myeloproliferative disease (D47.1).

EXAMPLE Patient has pancytopenia due to oral methotrexate, which is taken for treatment of rheumatoid arthritis, initial encounter, D61.811, T45.1x5A, M06.9.

EXAMPLE Infant was seen for follow up for congenital aplastic anemia, D61.09.

Category D62 includes acute posthemorrhagic anemia or anemia due to acute blood loss. Acute blood loss anemia can occur due to a surgical procedure, due to trauma, or due to a medical condition such as excessive gastrointestinal bleeding. Anemia due to acute blood loss following surgery should not be coded as a postoperative complication unless documented as such by the physician. Procedures such as joint replacements are often associated with blood loss, and the resultant anemia is an expected outcome, not a complication. If only postop anemia is documented and there is no documentation of blood loss, code D64.9 anemia, unspecified, should be assigned. Whenever doubt occurs, the coder should query the physician. If acute and chronic blood loss anemia is present, only a code for the acute blood loss anemia is assigned because of the Excludes1 notes for D62 and D50.0.

EXAMPLE Patient treated for anemia due to acute blood loss, D62.

Category D63 includes codes that are assigned when anemia is due to neoplastic disease or malignancy, chronic kidney disease (CKD), or other chronic diseases that are classified elsewhere. In the ICD-10-CM Tabular, there are Instructional notes to code the chronic condition that is responsible for the anemia first (Figure 12-6). Sometimes a physician will document anemia due to chronic disease but will not specify which disease is responsible. A query may be necessary to identify the underlying disease.

EXAMPLE Patient is seen in the clinic for anemia due to hypothyroidism, E03.9, D63.8.

EXAMPLE Patient has anemia due to gastric cancer, C16.9, D63.0.

● **D63 Anemia in chronic diseases classified elsewhere**

● ***D63.0 Anemia in neoplastic disease***

Code first neoplasm (C00-D49)

Excludes1 anemia due to antineoplastic chemotherapy (D64.81)
aplastic anemia due to antineoplastic chemotherapy (D61.1)

● ***D63.1 Anemia in chronic kidney disease***

Erythropoietin resistant anemia (EPO resistant anemia)

Code first underlying chronic kidney disease (CKD) (N18.-)

● ***D63.8 Anemia in other chronic diseases classified elsewhere***

Code first underlying disease, such as:
diphyllobothriasis (B70.0)
hookworm disease (B76.0-B76.9)
hypothyroidism (E00.0-E03.9)
malaria (B50.0-B54)
symptomatic late syphilis (A52.79)
tuberculosis (A18.89)

FIGURE 12-6. Tabular instructional notes for anemia in chronic diseases.

EXERCISE 12-3

Assign codes to the following conditions.

1. Aplastic anemia due to hepatitis C __________
2. Idiopathic aplastic anemia __________
3. Fanconi's anemia __________
4. Anemia due to end-stage renal disease (ESRD) __________
5. Normocytic anemia __________
6. Sideroblastic anemia __________
7. Anemia due to rheumatoid arthritis __________
8. Pancytopenia in patient with aplastic anemia __________

Coagulation Defects, Purpura, and Other Hemorrhagic Conditions (D65-D69)

Excessive bleeding that occurs after a minor injury may be a sign of a **coagulation defect**, which is a breakdown in the blood clotting process. Multiple reasons may account for excessive bleeding:

- Acute viral infection in children
- Autoimmune reactions in adults
- End-stage renal failure
- Ingestion of aspirin (acetylsalicylic acid [ASA])
- Vitamin K deficiency
- Liver disease
- Inherited disorders
- Hemorrhagic fever viruses

Multiple warning signs may indicate a coagulation defect; these include bleeding from gums or repeated nosebleeds, petechiae (Figure 12-7), ecchymoses (bruises), hemarthroses (bleeding into a joint), hemoptysis (coughing up blood), hematemesis (vomiting blood), melena (blood in feces), anemia, feeling faint and anxious, low blood pressure, and increased pulse. Blood tests that involve bleeding time, prothrombin time (PT), or partial thromboplastin time (PTT) can measure the coagulation of blood. Occasionally, patients

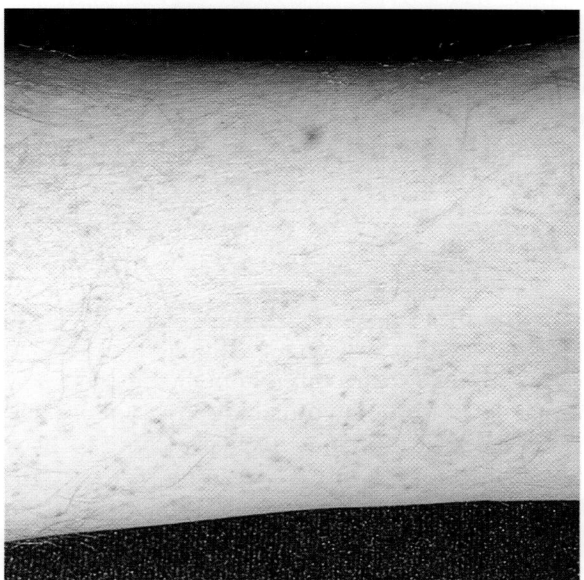

FIGURE 12-7. Petechiae.

who take anticoagulants such as warfarin (Coumadin) will have complications. Some common complications include gastrointestinal bleeding, epistaxis, hematuria, or hemorrhage from any tissue. According to *Coding Clinic for ICD-10* (2016:1Q:p14), any bleeding that is associated with a drug, including anticoagulation therapy, should be coded to D68.32, Hemorrhagic disorder due to extrinsic circulating anticoagulants. In the Tabular, under D68.32, there is an inclusion term for drug-induced hemorrhagic disorder. There is also a note to use an additional code for adverse effects, if applicable, to identify the drug. The sequencing of the D68.32 and the codes describing the type or site of bleeding will depend on the circumstances and focus of the encounter. Patients who are on anticoagulant therapy are at increased risk for bleeding. The Z code Z79.01 is assigned to identify the long-term use of anticoagulant medication such as Coumadin, which is located in the Alphabetic Index under the main term "Long-term drug therapy." A code may also be assigned for the diagnosis for which the patient is on anticoagulation therapy.

Prolonged prothrombin time or other abnormal coagulation profiles results are not coded to a coagulation defect. When a patient is on anticoagulation therapy, a prolonged prothrombin time is the desired result, so it is not coded to R79.1, abnormal coagulation profile.

EXAMPLE Patient was admitted with melena. Tests were undertaken to determine the source of the melena. After study, it was determined that the patient had a bleeding duodenal ulcer due to Coumadin that is taken for persistent atrial fibrillation. K26.4, D68.32, T45.515A, I48.11 (The focus was to determine the site of the bleeding, no mention of any treatment for the coagulopathy).

EXAMPLE Patient is taking Coumadin for previous history of pulmonary embolism, Z86.711, Z79.01.

EXAMPLE Patient was treated for coagulopathy due to chronic liver disease, D68.4, K76.9.

Disseminated intravascular coagulation (DIC) is a disorder that causes depletion of clotting factors in the blood. Risk factors include recent sepsis, severe injury or trauma, recent surgery and anesthesia, complications of labor and delivery, cancer, transfusion reaction, and liver disease. Treatment may include transfusion of coagulation factors with fresh frozen plasma; the underlying cause must be determined so the appropriate treatment can be provided.

Hemophilia is an inherited clotting disorder. **Hemophilia A**, the most common form, is a deficiency or abnormality of clotting factor VIII. **Hemophilia B** (Christmas disease) is the result of a deficiency of factor IX, and **Hemophilia C** is a mild form characterized by a decrease in factor XI. As with some of the other diseases of the blood, varying degrees of severity are reported. A common treatment consists of replacement therapy for factor VIII with cryoprecipitate. Unfortunately, transmission of viruses such as hepatitis and human immunodeficiency virus (HIV) has resulted from this treatment. Currently, blood products are treated in an effort to destroy known viruses, but risk of unknown infection or immune reaction is still present.

EXAMPLE

Patient has classical hemophilia, D66.

Purpura is characterized by ecchymoses or small hemorrhages in the skin, mucous membranes, or serosal surfaces that are due to blood disorders, vascular abnormalities, or trauma. A patient with idiopathic thrombocytopenic purpura (ITP) experiences a decrease in the number of platelets with no identifiable cause. Following laboratory testing, a bone marrow biopsy may be necessary. Treatments may include corticosteroids, immunosuppressive therapy, and possibly splenectomy.

Secondary thrombocytopenia is characterized by a decrease in the number of platelets; it is due to specific diseases such as congestive splenomegaly, Felty's syndrome, tuberculosis, sarcoidosis, lupus erythematosus, and chronic alcoholism. Some external causes include drugs, blood transfusions, extracorporeal circulation of blood, and overhydration.

EXAMPLE

Thrombocytopenia due to chronic alcoholism, D69.59, F10.20.

EXAMPLE

Patient admitted with idiopathic thrombocytopenic purpura, D69.3.

EXERCISE 12-4

Assign codes to the following conditions.

1. Rosenthal's hemophilia ____________
2. Hemophilia A ____________
3. Christmas disease ____________
4. DIC ____________
5. von Willebrand's disease ____________
6. Idiopathic nonthrombocytopenic purpura ____________
7. Thrombocytopenia due to systemic lupus erythematosus ____________
8. Schönlein-Henoch purpura ____________
9. Low platelets ____________
10. Factor V Leiden mutation ____________

Other Disorders of Blood and Blood-Forming Organs (D70-D77)

Leukocytosis (neutrophilia or granulocytosis) is characterized by an increase in the number of white cells in the blood. Usually, no treatment is required. If leukocytosis persists, investigation to rule out a neoplastic process or infection may become necessary. Leukocytosis may also be related to certain drugs or may occur in response to stress. The most common white blood cell condition is agranulocytosis, or **neutropenia**, which is an abnormal decrease in granular leukocytes in the blood. Radiation therapy, drugs used for chemotherapy, and other chemicals may cause neutropenia. With severe neutropenia, a patient may become immunocompromised; his or her ability to fight infection may be hampered, and treatment often consists of antibiotics. Testing may be necessary to determine cause and select appropriate treatment.

EXAMPLE

Infant is being treated for congenital agranulocytosis, D70.0.

The spleen serves as a blood reservoir, filters the blood and removes old or defective blood cells, and serves as part of the immune system by helping to fight infection. The spleen can become enlarged (**splenomegaly**) due to infections or other diseases. A swollen spleen is at risk for rupturing, which could result in significant blood loss.

EXAMPLE

Physician documents that the ultrasound exam showed that the patient has a splenic infarction, D73.5.

EXERCISE 12-5

Assign codes to the following conditions.

1. Neutropenic fever __________
2. Leukocytosis __________
3. Eosinophilia __________
4. Leukopenia __________

Certain Disorders Involving the Immune Mechanism (D80-D89)

Disorders that are coded in this section include acquired hypogammaglobulinemia, selective immunoglobulin A deficiency, X-linked agammaglobulinemia, severe combined immunodeficiency (SCID), sarcoidosis, and thymic hypoplasia or DiGeorge's syndrome.

Patients may become immunocompromised by medications; this is seen when patients undergo transplantation and are taking antirejection drugs, or when a patient undergoes chemotherapy treatment for cancer. A patient may also be in an immunocompromised state that is associated with a disease process. According to *Coding Clinic for ICD-9-CM* (1992:3Q:p13-14),[3] an expected side effect for transplant patients or chemotherapy patients is a comprised immune system, and codes should not be assigned for the immunocompromised state. However, if the cause of that state is not identified, code D89.9, unspecified disorder of immune mechanism, should be assigned.

EXAMPLE

Patient has a diagnosis of Wiskott-Aldrich syndrome, D82.0.

Sarcoidosis is an inflammatory disease that can affect multiple organs in the body. The most common sites are the lungs and lymph nodes. The exact cause is unknown, but it is believed to be a type of autoimmune disease. People with sarcoidosis develop abnormal nodules called *granulomas* made up of inflamed tissues in various organs of the body. The symptoms vary greatly from one person to the next depending on which organ(s) are involved. There is no cure for sarcoidosis, and treatment will vary depending on the organ(s) involved and the severity of the patient's symptoms. ICD-10 does provide numerous codes under code category D86.- for the most common sites affected.

EXAMPLE

The patient is being treated for pulmonary sarcoidosis, D86.0

Graft-versus-host disease (GVHD) is a common complication that can occur after a stem cell or bone marrow transplant in which the newly transplanted material attacks the transplant recipient's body. GVHD can sometimes occur following blood transfusion or any organ transplant where white blood cells are present. There is less risk of GVHD when the match between donor and recipient is optimal. The greater the mismatch, the greater the risk of GVHD.

There are two types of graft-versus-host disease:

- Acute—usually occurs during the first 3 months following a transplant.
- Chronic—usually occurs after the third month following a transplant.

It is possible to develop acute on chronic GVHD.

Symptoms in acute GVHD include:

- Abdominal pain and cramps
- Diarrhea
- Fever
- Jaundice
- Skin rash and/or desquamation
- Vomiting
- Weight loss

Symptoms in chronic GVHD include:

- Dry eye and dry mouth
- Hair loss
- Hepatitis
- Lung and digestive tract disorders
- Skin rash
- Skin thickening

In both acute and chronic GVHD, the patient is more susceptible to infections. Treatment includes corticosteroids, immunosuppressants, antibiotics, and immunoglobulins.

EXAMPLE

Patient was seen in the clinic for desquamation of skin with dermatitis. He had a bone marrow transplant 2 months ago. The physician is treating him for acute GVHD, T86.09, D89.810, L30.8.

EXERCISE 12-6

Assign codes to the following conditions.

1. Pulmonary sarcoidosis __________
2. Selective deficiency of IgA __________
3. Severe combined immunodeficiency disorder __________
4. Common variable immunodeficiency __________
5. Interstitial pneumonitis due to chronic GVHD in patient who is status post bone marrow transplant 8 months ago __________

FACTORS INFLUENCING HEALTH STATUS AND CONTACT WITH HEALTH SERVICES (Z CODES)

As was discussed in Chapter 9, it may be difficult to locate Z codes in the Index. Coders often say, "I did not know there was a Z code for that." Refer to Chapter 9 for a listing of common main terms used to locate Z codes.

A review of the Tabular reveals that some Z codes pertain diseases of the blood and blood-forming organs and immune mechanism:

Note the Z codes that specify a patient's blood type.

Z01.83	Encounter for blood typing
Z01.84	Encounter for antibody response examination
Z13.0	Encounter for screening for diseases of the blood and blood-forming organs and certain disorders involving the immune mechanism
Z14.01	Asymptomatic hemophilia A carrier
Z14.02	Symptomatic hemophilia A carrier
Z52.000	Unspecified donor, whole blood
Z52.001	Unspecified donor, stem cells
Z52.008	Unspecified donor, other blood

Z52.010	Autologous donor, whole blood
Z52.011	Autologous donor, stem cells
Z52.018	Autologous donor, other blood
Z52.090	Other blood donor, whole blood
Z52.091	Other blood donor, stem cells
Z52.098	Other blood donor, other blood
Z52.3	Bone marrow donor
Z67.10	Type A blood, Rh positive
Z67.11	Type A blood, Rh negative
Z67.20	Type B blood, Rh positive
Z67.21	Type B blood, Rh negative
Z67.30	Type AB blood, Rh positive
Z67.31	Type AB blood, Rh negative
Z67.40	Type O blood, Rh positive
Z67.41	Type O blood, Rh negative
Z67.90	Unspecified blood type, Rh positive
Z67.91	Unspecified blood type, Rh negative
Z79.01	Long-term (current) use of anticoagulants
Z79.02	Long-term (current) use of antithrombotics/antiplatelets
Z79.82	Long-term (current) use of aspirin
Z83.2	Family history of diseases of the blood and blood-forming organs and certain disorders involving the immune mechanism
Z86.2	Personal history of diseases of the blood and blood-forming organs and certain disorders involving the immune mechanism
Z90.81	Acquired absence of spleen
Z94.81	Bone marrow transplant status
Z94.84	Stem cells transplant status

Some Z codes describe the long-term use of a particular type of medication such as anticoagulants or antiplatelets/antithrombotics. **Anticoagulants** are medications that are used to prevent venous thrombi. They can be administered parenterally with heparin, or warfarin (Coumadin) can be taken orally. **Parenteral** drug administration is when medications are administered other than through the digestive tract, such as by intravenous or intramuscular injections. **Antiplatelet medications** are used to prevent clumping of platelets or formation of an arterial thrombus. Medications that are used as antiplatelet therapy include clopidogrel (Plavix), ticlopidine (Ticlid), dipyridamole (Persantine), and aspirin (ASA).

EXAMPLE

Screening for iron deficiency anemia, Z13.0.

EXAMPLE

Long-term use of ASA due to family history of stroke, Z79.82, Z82.3.

EXERCISE 12-7

Assign codes to the following conditions.

1. History of stem cell transplant __________
2. Long-term use of Coumadin __________
3. Screening for sickle cell disease __________
4. Long-term use of Plavix __________

COMMON TREATMENTS

CONDITION	MEDICATION/TREATMENT
Anemia	Treatment depends on the cause
Anemia due to chronic kidney disease	Epoetin alfa (Epogen, Procrit)
Iron deficiency anemia	Iron supplements, ferrous sulfate (FeoSol)
Pernicious anemia	B_{12} injections
Anemia of chronic disease	Treatment of the underlying cause/disease
Sickle cell anemia	Hydroxyurea (Droxia, Hydrea)
Hemophilia A	Desmopressin acetate (DDAVP), recombinant or plasma concentrate factor VIII, cryoprecipitate
Neutropenia	Filgrastim (Neupogen)

PROCEDURES

Procedures related to the blood and blood-forming organs in ICD-10-PCS can be located in the following tables:

072-07Y	Lymphatic and Hemic Systems
302-3EI	Administration
4A0-4B0	Measuring and Monitoring

Blood transfusion, which can be performed for many reasons, is the administration of donor blood cells into a patient. The root operation in ICD-10-PCS for transfusion is transfusion (putting in blood or blood products). The most common types of transfusions consist of red blood cells, plasma, and platelets. Sometimes, before undergoing an elective surgery, a patient will donate his or her own blood to be used in the event a transfusion is needed. This is known as an **autologous transfusion**.

The administration section includes services for transfusion and peripheral stem cell and bone marrow transplants. The documentation that may be difficult to find in the record is the body system. As noted in the 302 table (Figure 12-8) the body system that is necessary is the site of the administration of the transfusion, i.e. peripheral or central vein. Usually the approach for a transfusion is going to be percutaneous. The substance that is being transfused is identified by the 6th character substance and the qualifier is either autologous or nonautologous.

Section **3** Administration *Body System* **0** Circulatory *Operation* **2** Transfusion: Putting in blood or blood products			
Body System/Region	*Approach*	*Substance*	*Qualifier*
3 Peripheral Vein **4** Central Vein	**0** Open **3** Percutaneous	**A** Stem Cells, Embryonic	**Z** No Qualifier
3 Peripheral Vein **4** Central Vein	**0** Open **3** Percutaneous	**C** Hematopoietic Stem/ Progenitor Cells, Genetically Modified **G** Bone Marrow **H** Whole Blood **J** Serum Albumin **K** Frozen Plasma **L** Fresh Plasma **M** Plasma Cryoprecipitate **N** Red Blood Cells **P** Frozen Red Cells **Q** White Cells **R** Platelets **S** Globulin **T** Fibrinogen **V** Antihemophilic Factors **W** Factor IX **X** Stem Cells, Cord Blood **Y** Stem Cells, Hematopoietic	**0** Autologous **1** Nonautologous

FIGURE 12-8 Table for transfusion.

EXAMPLE

Transfusion of red blood cells, nonautologous via peripheral vein, 30233N1

SECTION	BODY SYSTEM	ROOT OPERATION	BODY SYSTEM/ REGION	APPROACH	SUBSTANCE	QUALIFIER
Administration 3	Circulatory 0	Transfusion 2	Peripheral Vein 3	Percutaneous 3	Red Blood Cells N	Nonautologous 1

Apheresis is a procedure that separates the different components of the blood and removes a certain part of the blood, such as occurs in leukapheresis, plateletpheresis, and plasmapheresis. A therapeutic plasmapheresis or plasma exchange occurs when the plasma is removed and is replaced with fresh plasma. The root operation in ICD-10-PCS for plasmaphersis is pheresis (extracorporeal separation of blood products). Pheresis is performed to treat diseases in which too much of a particular blood component if produced or to remove a blood component from a donor. Character 5 idenitifies the duration which can be either single or multiple times.

EXAMPLE

Plasmapheresis, single, 6A550Z3

SECTION	BODY SYSTEM	ROOT OPERATION	BODY SYSTEM	DURATION	QUALIFIER	QUALIFIER
Extracorporeal 6	Therapies A	Physiological Systems 5	Pheresis Circulatory 5	Single 0	No Qualifier Z	Plasma 3

Bone marrow biopsy is a diagnostic procedure that can be used to identify types of blood disorders. The root operation in ICD-10-PCS for bone marrow biopsy is extraction (pulling or stripping out/off without replacement some or all of a body part).

Peripheral stem cell and bone marrow transplants (Figure 12-9) are used to treat patients with certain leukemias and cancers, bone marrow failure syndromes, and genetic disease. Prior to transplant, the patient is prepared with radiation and/or chemotherapy to get rid of the defective or malignant cells and reduce the body's immunity so it will not reject the transplanted cells. According to the ICD-10-PCS Guidelines, the putting in of autologous or nonautologous bone marrow, pancreatic islet cells, or stem cells is coded in the Administration section (see Figure 12-8).

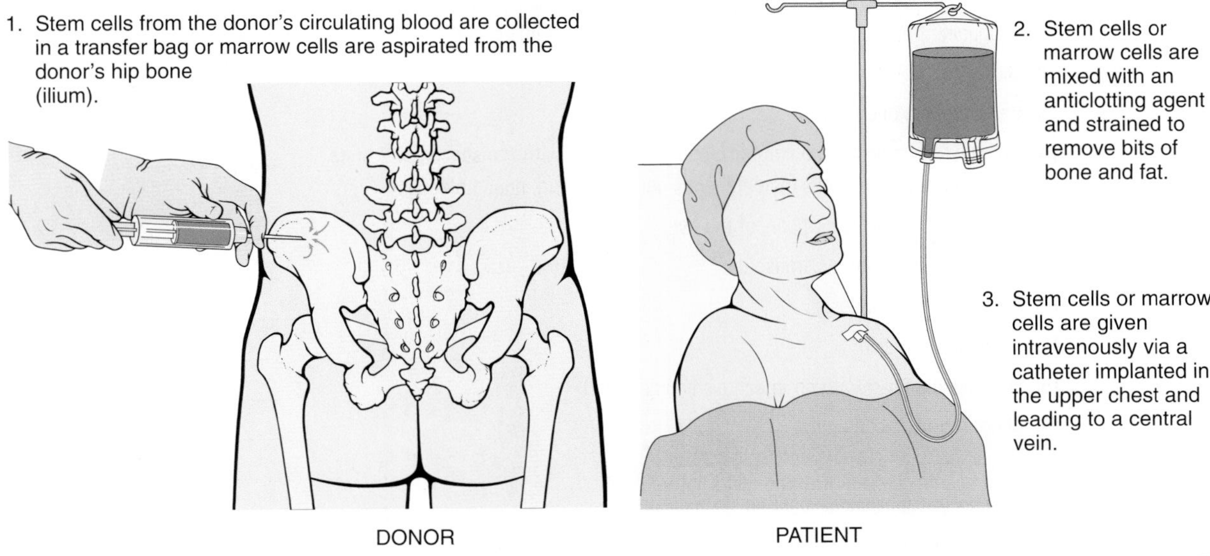

1. Stem cells from the donor's circulating blood are collected in a transfer bag or marrow cells are aspirated from the donor's hip bone (ilium).
2. Stem cells or marrow cells are mixed with an anticlotting agent and strained to remove bits of bone and fat.
3. Stem cells or marrow cells are given intravenously via a catheter implanted in the upper chest and leading to a central vein.
DONOR
PATIENT

FIGURE 12-9. Peripheral stem cell and bone marrow transplants.

EXAMPLE

Nonautologous bone marrow transplant via central vein, 30243G4

SECTION	BODY SYSTEM	ROOT OPERATION	BODY SYSTEM/ REGION	APPROACH	SUBSTANCE	QUALIFIER
Administration	Circulatory	Transfusion	Central Vein	Percutaneous	Bone Marrow	Allogenic, Unspecified
3	0	2	4	3	G	4

EXERCISE 12-8

Assign codes for all diagnoses and procedures.

1. Patient with profound pancytopenia had a diagnostic percutaneous bone marrow biopsy iliac crest ____________
2. Thrombocytopenia was treated with transfusion of platelets (nonautologous infusion in peripheral vein) ____________
3. Therapeutic single plasmapheresis performed on patient with thrombotic thrombocytopenic purpura ____________
4. DIC with transfusion of frozen plasma (percutaneous infusion, central vein, nonautologous) ____________
5. Postoperative blood loss anemia with autologous transfusion of red blood cells (percutaneous via peripheral vein) ____________

CHAPTER REVIEW EXERCISE

Assign codes for all diagnoses and procedures.

1. Bandemia ____________
2. Pernicious anemia ____________
3. Sickle cell trait ____________
4. Hemophilia A carrier ____________
5. DiGeorge's syndrome ____________
6. Polycythemia, benign ____________
7. Severe congenital aplastic anemia treated with bone marrow transplant, allogeneic from related donor (percutaneous central vein) ____________
8. Sickle cell Hb-SS disease with crisis ____________
9. Pancytopenia due to AIDS ____________
10. Anemia due to acute and chronic blood loss treated with transfusion of 2 units of packed red blood cells (percutaneous peripheral vein, nonautologous) ____________
11. Coagulopathy due to cirrhosis of the liver ____________
12. History of bone marrow transplant ____________
13. Chronic agranulocytosis ____________
14. Sarcoidosis of skin ____________
15. Neutropenic fever with no infectious source found ____________
16. Congestive splenomegaly ____________
17. Vegan anemia ____________
18. Lymphocytic leukemoid reaction ____________
19. Lupus anticoagulant syndrome ____________
20. Neutropenia due to infection ____________

Write the correct answer(s) in the space(s) provided.

21. Which blood component is essential for clotting?

____

22. Describe apheresis.

____

23. List two warning signs of a coagulation disorder.

____

24. Which cells fight infection, inflammation, and other diseases?

____

25. Define idiopathic.

____

CHAPTER GLOSSARY

Anemia: occurs when hemoglobin drops, which interrupts the transport of oxygen throughout the body.

Anticoagulants: medications that are used to prevent venous thrombi.

Antiplatelet medications: medications that are used to prevent clumping of platelets or formation of an arterial thrombus.

Apheresis: procedure that separates different components of blood and removes a certain part of the blood, such as occurs in leukapheresis, plateletpheresis, and plasmapheresis.

Aplastic anemia: reduction in new blood cells due to impairment or failure of bone marrow function.

Autologous transfusion: transfusion of a patient's own blood. Blood may have been donated prior to an elective procedure.

Blood: viscous fluid that circulates through the vessels of the circulatory system as a result of the pumping action of the heart.

Bone marrow biopsy: diagnostic procedure that is used to identify types of anemia and cell deficiencies and to detect leukemia.

Coagulation defect: breakdown in the clotting process of the blood.

Disseminated intravascular coagulation: disorder that results in depletion of clotting factors in the blood.

Erythrocytes: another name for red blood cells that are made in the marrow of bones; their main responsibility is to carry oxygen around the body and remove carbon dioxide. These are the cells that give blood its red color.

Graft-versus-host disease (GVHD): common complication that can occur after a stem cell or bone marrow transplant in which the newly transplanted material attacks the transplant recipient's body.

Hemolytic anemias: result from abnormal or excessive destruction of red blood cells.

Hemophilia A: most common type of hemophilia; deficiency or abnormality in clotting factor VIII.

Hemophilia B: another name for Christmas disease, which results from a deficiency of factor IX.

Hemophilia C: mild form of hemophilia with decreased factor XI.

Homeostasis: the ability of an organism or cell to maintain internal equilibrium by adjusting its physiologic processes.

Idiopathic: causative factor is unknown.

Immune system: includes the bone marrow, lymph nodes, thymus, and spleen. Its purpose is to protect the body from all types of infections, toxins, neoplastic cell growth, and foreign blood or tissues from another person.

Leukocytes: white blood cells increase in number to battle infection, inflammation, and other diseases.

Leukocytosis: increase in the number of white cells in the blood; it may be a sign of infection or may indicate stress on the body.

Neutropenia: abnormal decrease in granular leukocytes in the blood.

Pancytopenia: decrease in production of erythrocytes (red blood cells), leukocytes (white blood cells), and thrombocytes (platelets).

Parenteral: when medications are administered other than through the digestive tract, such as by intravenous or intramuscular injection.

Platelets: another name for thrombocytes. Platelets circulate in the blood and assist in the clotting process.

Purpura: ecchymoses or small hemorrhages in the skin, mucous membranes, or serosal surfaces due to blood disorders, vascular abnormalities, or trauma.

Sarcoidosis: inflammatory disease that can affect multiple organs in the body.

Secondary thrombocytopenia: decrease in the number of platelets due to specific diseases or external causes, such as drugs, blood transfusions, and overhydration.

Sickle cell anemia: one of the most common hemolytic anemias, in which the shape of the red blood cell changes from a disc to a crescent or "sickle," causing obstruction of small blood vessels and eventual damage throughout the body.

Splenomegaly: enlarged spleen.

Thalassemia: hereditary disease that is similar to sickle cell anemia and occurs in varying degrees.

Thrombocytes: another name for platelets. Thrombocytes circulate in the blood and assist in the clotting process.

REFERENCES

1. Chabner D: The Language of Medicine, ed 8, St. Louis, 2007, Saunders, p 506.
2. American Hospital Association: *Coding Clinic for ICD-10* 2014:4Q:p22-23. Neutropenic fever with anemia and thrombocytopenia.
3. American Hospital Association: *Coding Clinic for ICD-9-CM* 1992:3Q:p13-14. Immunocompromised state due to medication.
4. American Hospital Association: *Coding Clinic for ICD-10* (2016:1Q:p14). Duodenal ulcer with hemorrhage due to Coumadin therapy.

13

Endocrine, Nutritional, and Metabolic Diseases

(ICD-10-CM Chapter 4, Codes E00-E89)

CHAPTER OUTLINE

LEARNING OBJECTIVES

1. Apply and assign the correct ICD-10-CM/PCS codes in accordance with Official Guidelines for Coding and Reporting
2. Identify pertinent anatomy and physiology of the endocrine, nutritional, and metabolic diseases
3. Identify endocrine, nutritional, and metabolic diseases
4. Assign the correct Z codes and procedure codes related to the endocrine, nutritional, and metabolic diseases
5. Identify common treatments, medications, laboratory values, and diagnostic tests

ABBREVIATIONS/ ACRONYMS

AML acute myeloid leukemia

BMI body mass index

BPD biliopancreatic diversion

CDC Centers for Disease Control and Prevention

CF cystic fibrosis

CKD chronic kidney disease

DI diabetes insipidus

DM diabetes mellitus

hGH human growth hormone

ICD-10-CM *International Classification of Diseases, 10th Revision, Clinical Modification*

ICD-10-PCS *International Classification of Diseases, 10th Revision, Procedure Coding System*

IDDM insulin-dependent diabetes mellitus

IV intravenous

MEN multiple endocrine neoplasia

NIDDM non–insulin-dependent diabetes mellitus

ABBREVIATIONS/ ACRONYMS—*cont'd*

SIADH syndrome of inappropriate antidiuretic hormone secretion
TLS tumor lysis syndrome
TPN total parenteral nutrition
TSH thyroid-stimulating hormone
UTI urinary tract infection
VBG vertical banded gastroplasty

ICD-10-CM Official Guidelines for Coding and Reporting (2021-2022)

Please refer to the companion Evolve website for the most current 2021-2022 guidelines.

4. Chapter 4: Endocrine, Nutritional, and Metabolic Diseases (E00-*E89*)

a. Diabetes mellitus

The diabetes mellitus codes are combination codes that include the type of diabetes mellitus, the body system affected, and the complications affecting that body system. As many codes within a particular category as are necessary to describe all of the complications of the disease may be used. They should be sequenced based on the reason for a particular encounter. Assign as many codes from categories E08-E13 as needed to identify all of the associated conditions that the patient has.

1) Type of diabetes

The age of a patient is not the sole determining factor, though most type 1 diabetics develop the condition before reaching puberty. For this reason type 1 diabetes mellitus is also referred to as juvenile diabetes.

EXAMPLE

Juvenile diabetes, E10.9.

EXAMPLE

The patient is a 16-year-old with obesity and diabetes mellitus, type 2, uncontrolled, E11.65, E66.9.

In ICD-10-CM, out-of-control and poorly controlled diabetes are coded to the type of diabetes with hyperglycemia per the Alphabetic Index.

2) Type of diabetes mellitus not documented

If the type of diabetes mellitus is not documented in the medical record the default is E11.-, Type 2 diabetes mellitus.

EXAMPLE

The patient takes daily insulin for diabetes, E11.9, Z79.4.

3) Diabetes mellitus and the use of insulin and oral hypoglycemics

If the documentation in a medical record does not indicate the type of diabetes but does indicate that the patient uses insulin, code E11- Type 2 diabetes mellitus, should be assigned. An additional code should be assigned from category Z79 to identify the long-term (current) use of insulin or oral hypoglycemic drugs. If the patient is treated with both oral medications and insulin, only the code for long-term (current) use of insulin should be assigned. If the patient is treated with both insulin and an injectable non-insulin antidiabetic drug, assign codes Z79.4, Long-term (current) use of insulin, and Z79.899, Other long term (current) drug therapy. If the patient is treated with both oral hypoglycemic drugs and an injectable non-insulin antidiabetc drug, assign codes Z79.84, Long-term (current) use of oral hypoglycemic drugs, and Z79.899, Other long-term (current) drug therapy. Code Z79.4 should not be assigned if insulin is given temporarily to bring a type 2 patient's blood sugar under control during an encounter.

EXAMPLE

A patient with type 2 diabetes has been undergoing changes to daily insulin dosages. The patient's diabetes is uncontrolled, E11.65, Z79.4.

4) Diabetes mellitus in pregnancy and gestational diabetes

See Section I.C.15. Diabetes mellitus in pregnancy.

See Section I.C.15. Gestational (pregnancy induced) diabetes

5) Complications due to insulin pump malfunction

(a) Underdose of insulin due *to* insulin pump failure

An underdose of insulin due to an insulin pump failure should be assigned to a code from subcategory T85.6, Mechanical complication of other specified internal and external prosthetic devices, implants and grafts, that specifies the type of pump malfunction, as the principal or first-listed code, followed by code T38.3x6-, Underdosing of insulin and oral hypoglycemic [antidiabetic] drugs. Additional codes for the type of diabetes mellitus and any associated complications due to the underdosing should also be assigned.

(b) Overdose of insulin due to insulin pump failure

The principal or first-listed code for an encounter due to an insulin pump malfunction resulting in an overdose of insulin, should also be T85.6-, Mechanical complication of other specified internal and external prosthetic devices, implants and grafts, followed by code T38.3x1-, Poisoning by insulin and oral hypoglycemic [antidiabetic] drugs, accidental (unintentional).

EXAMPLE Patient has type 1 diabetes with hyperglycemia due to mechanical breakdown of insulin pump, which resulted in underdosing, T85.614A, T38.3x6A, E10.65.

EXAMPLE Patient has type 1 diabetes with hypoglycemia due to mechanical breakdown of insulin pump, which resulted in overdosing, T85.614A, T38.3x1A, E10.649.

6) Secondary diabetes mellitus

Codes under categories E08, Diabetes mellitus due to underlying condition, E09, Drug or chemical induced diabetes mellitus, and E13, Other specified diabetes mellitus, identify complications/manifestations associated with secondary diabetes mellitus. Secondary diabetes is always caused by another condition or event (e.g., cystic fibrosis, malignant neoplasm of pancreas, pancreatectomy, adverse effect of drug, or poisoning).

(a) Secondary diabetes mellitus and the use of insulin or oral hypoglycemic drugs

For patients with secondary diabetes mellitus who routinely use insulin or oral hypoglycemic drugs, an additional code from category Z79 should be assigned to identify the long-term (current) use of insulin or oral hypoglycemic drugs. If the patient is treated with both oral medications and insulin, only the code for long-term (current) use of insulin should be assigned. If the patient is treated with both insulin and an injectable non-insulin antidiabetic drug, assign codes Z79.4, Long-term (current) use of insulin, and Z79.899, Other long-term (current) drug therapy. If the patient is treated with both oral hypoglycemic drugs and an injectable non-insulin antidiabetic drug, assign codes Z79.84, Long-term (current) use of oral hypogylcemic drugs, and Z79.899, Other long-term (current) drug therapy. Code Z79.4 should not be assigned if insulin is given temporarily to bring a secondary diabetic patient's blood sugar under control during an encounter.

(b) Assigning and sequencing secondary diabetes codes and its causes

The sequencing of the secondary diabetes codes in relationship to codes for the cause of the diabetes is based on the Tabular List instructions for categories E08, E09 and E13.

(i) Secondary diabetes mellitus due to pancreatectomy

For postpancreatectomy diabetes mellitus (lack of insulin due to the surgical removal of all or part of the pancreas), assign code E89.1, Postprocedural hypoinsulinemia. Assign a code from category E13 and a code from subcategory Z90.41-, Acquired absence of pancreas, as additional codes.

(ii) Secondary diabetes due to drugs

Secondary diabetes may be caused by an adverse effect of correctly administered medications, poisoning or sequela of poisoning.

See Section I.C.19.e for coding of adverse effects and poisoning, and Section I.C.20 for external cause code reporting.

EXAMPLE Uncontrolled diabetes mellitus due to Cushing's syndrome. Patient has been on insulin for the last year, E24.9, E08.65, Z79.4.

ANATOMY AND PHYSIOLOGY

The **endocrine system** (Figure 13-1) works with the nervous system to maintain body functions and homeostasis, and to respond to stress. The endocrine system is composed of many glands that are located throughout the body. These glands secrete **hormones** that can regulate bodily functions such as urinary output, cellular metabolic rate, growth, and development.

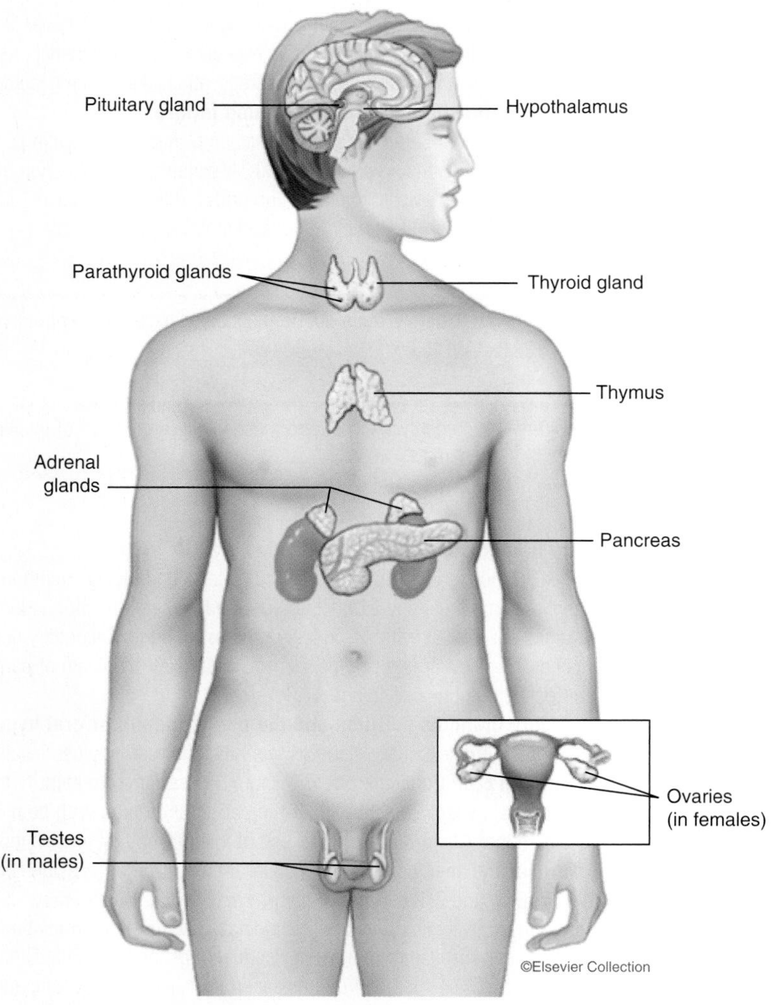

FIGURE 13-1. The endocrine system.

Major endocrine glands include the following:

- Anterior pituitary
- Posterior pituitary
- Thyroid
- Parathyroid
- Adrenal cortex
- Adrenal medulla
- Pancreas
- Ovaries
- Testes
- Thymus
- Pineal gland

See Table 13-1 for a listing of the glands, corresponding hormones, and expected hormonal response.

Endocrine diseases may result from an abnormal decrease or increase in hormone production. Changes in the size of a gland can alter hormone production. If the gland becomes larger, this is called **hyperplasia** and/or **hypertrophy**. If the gland becomes smaller, this is called **hypoplasia** and/or **atrophy**. Infection, inflammation, radiation, trauma, and surgical procedures can produce changes in the gland and hormonal dysfunction.

TABLE 13-1 MAJOR ENDOCRINE GLAND SECRETIONS AND FUNCTIONS[1]

Endocrine Gland	Hormone	Target Action
Anterior pituitary	Growth hormone (GH)	Promotes bone and tissue growth
	Thyrotropin (thyroid-stimulating hormone [TSH])	Stimulates thyroid gland and production of thyroxine
	Corticotropin (adrenocorticotropic hormone [ACTH])	Stimulates adrenal cortex to produce glucocorticoids
	Gonadotropin	Initiates growth of eggs in ovaries; stimulates spermatogenesis in testes
	Follicle-stimulating hormone (FSH)	
	Luteinizing hormone (LH)	Causes ovulation; stimulates ovaries to produce estrogen and progesterone; stimulates testosterone production
	Prolactin	Stimulates breast development and formation of milk during pregnancy and after delivery
	Melanocyte-stimulating hormone (MSH)	Regulates skin pigmentation
Posterior pituitary	Vasopressin (antidiuretic hormone [ADH])	Stimulates water resorption by renal tubules; has antidiuretic effect
	Oxytocin	Stimulates uterine contractions; stimulates ejection of milk in mammary glands; causes ejection of secretions in male prostate gland
Thyroid	Thyroxine (T_4) and triiodothyronine (T_3)—thyroid hormone (TH)	Regulates rate of cellular metabolism (catabolic phase)
	Calcitonin	Promotes retention of calcium and phosphorus in bone; opposes effect of parathyroid hormone
Parathyroid	Parathyroid hormone (parathormone, PTH)	Regulates metabolism of calcium; elevates serum calcium levels by drawing calcium from bones
Adrenal cortex	Mineralocorticoids (MCs), primarily aldosterone	Promote retention of sodium by kidneys; regulate electrolyte and fluid homeostasis
	Glucocorticoids (GCs): cortisol, corticosterone, cortisone	Regulate metabolism of carbohydrates, proteins, and fats in cells
	Gonadocorticoids: androgens, estrogens, progestins	Govern secondary sex characteristics and masculinization
Adrenal medulla	Catecholamines: epinephrine and norepinephrine	Produce quick-acting "fight or flight" response during stress; increase blood pressure, heart rate, and blood glucose level; dilate bronchioles
Pancreas	Insulin	Regulates metabolism of glucose in body cells; maintains proper blood glucose level
	Glucagon	Increases concentration of glucose in blood by causing conversion of glycogen to glucose
Ovaries	Estrogens	Cause development of female secondary sex characteristics
	Progesterone	Prepares and maintains endometrium for implantation and pregnancy
Testes	Testosterone	Stimulates and promotes growth of male secondary sex characteristics and is essential for erections
Thymus	Thymosin	Promotes development of immune cells (gland atrophies during adulthood)
Pineal gland	Melatonin	Regulates daily patterns of sleep and wakefulness; inhibits hormones that affect ovaries; other functions unknown

Some common mental and physical symptoms include the following:

- Growth abnormalities
- Emotional disturbances
- Skin, hair, and nail changes
- Edema
- Hypertension or hypotension
- Cardiac arrhythmias
- Changes in urine output
- Muscle weakness or atrophy
- Menstrual irregularities
- Impotence
- Changes in libido
- Infertility
- Fatigue

DISEASE CONDITIONS

Diseases of the endocrine system and nutritional and metabolic disorders (E00 to E89), covered in Chapter 4 of the ICD-10-CM code book, are divided into the following categories:

CATEGORY	SECTION TITLES
E00-E07	Disorders of the thyroid gland
E08-E13	Diabetes mellitus
E15-E16	Other disorders of glucose regulation and pancreatic internal secretion
E20-E35	Disorders of other endocrine glands
E36	Intraoperative complications of endocrine system
E40-E46	Malnutrition
E50-E64	Other nutritional deficiencies
E65-E68	Overweight, obesity, and other hyperalimentation
E70-E88	Metabolic disorders
E89	Postprocedural endocrine and metabolic complications and disorders, not elsewhere classified

Disorders of Thyroid Gland (E00-E07)

Goiter

Goiter is an enlargement of the thyroid gland (Figure 13-2). This enlargement may be uniform throughout the gland or diffuse. Enlargement may also occur in the form of nodules or nodular goiter. A goiter can cause difficulties in swallowing and/or breathing and may or may not be associated with hormonal disturbances. The most common cause is lack of iodine in the diet. Goiters due to iodine deficiency are rare in the United States since the introduction of iodized salt.

EXAMPLE Patient has a multinodular goiter, E04.2.

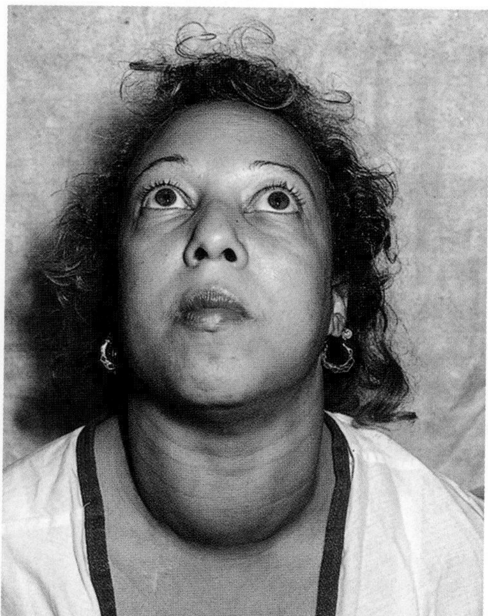

FIGURE 13-2. Goiter. Note the enlarged neck due to enlargement of the thyroid gland.

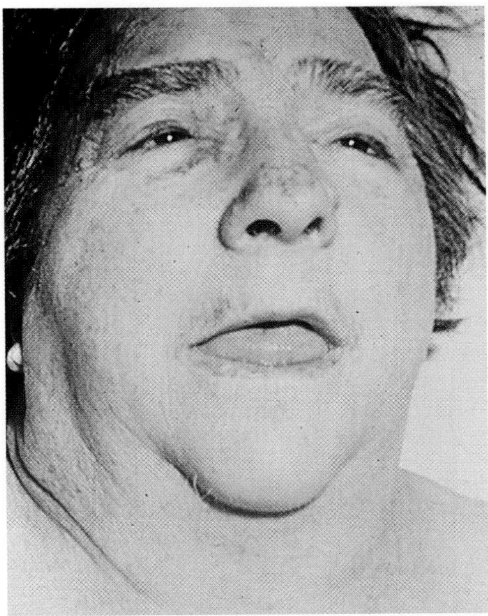

FIGURE 13-3. Myxedema.

Hypothyroidism

Hypothyroidism is diminished production of thyroid hormone, manifested by low metabolic rate, tendency toward weight gain, somnolence, and sometimes myxedema. **Myxedema** is a skin and tissue disorder that is usually due to severe, prolonged hypothyroidism (Figure 13-3). Symptoms include dull, puffy, yellowed skin; coarse, sparse hair; periorbital edema; and prominent tongue.

EXAMPLE Patient has hypothyroidism, E03.9.

Hashimoto's disease is an inflammation of the thyroid gland that often results in hypothyroidism. It is most common in women and individuals who have a family history of thyroid disease. Onset of Hashimoto's is slow, and it may not be detected for years. The most common signs and symptoms of Hashimoto's disease include the following:

- Intolerance to cold
- Weight gain
- Fatigue
- Constipation
- Goiter
- Dry skin
- Hair loss
- Heavy or irregular menses
- Difficulty with concentration

EXAMPLE Patient has autoimmune thyroiditis, E06.3.

Hyperthyroidism/Graves' Disease

Hyperthyroidism (Figure 13-4) is an abnormality of the thyroid gland in which secretion of thyroid hormone is usually increased and is no longer under the regulatory control of hypothalamic-pituitary centers.

Graves' disease, the most common form of hyperthyroidism, occurs as the result of an autoimmune response that attacks the thyroid gland, resulting in overproduction of the

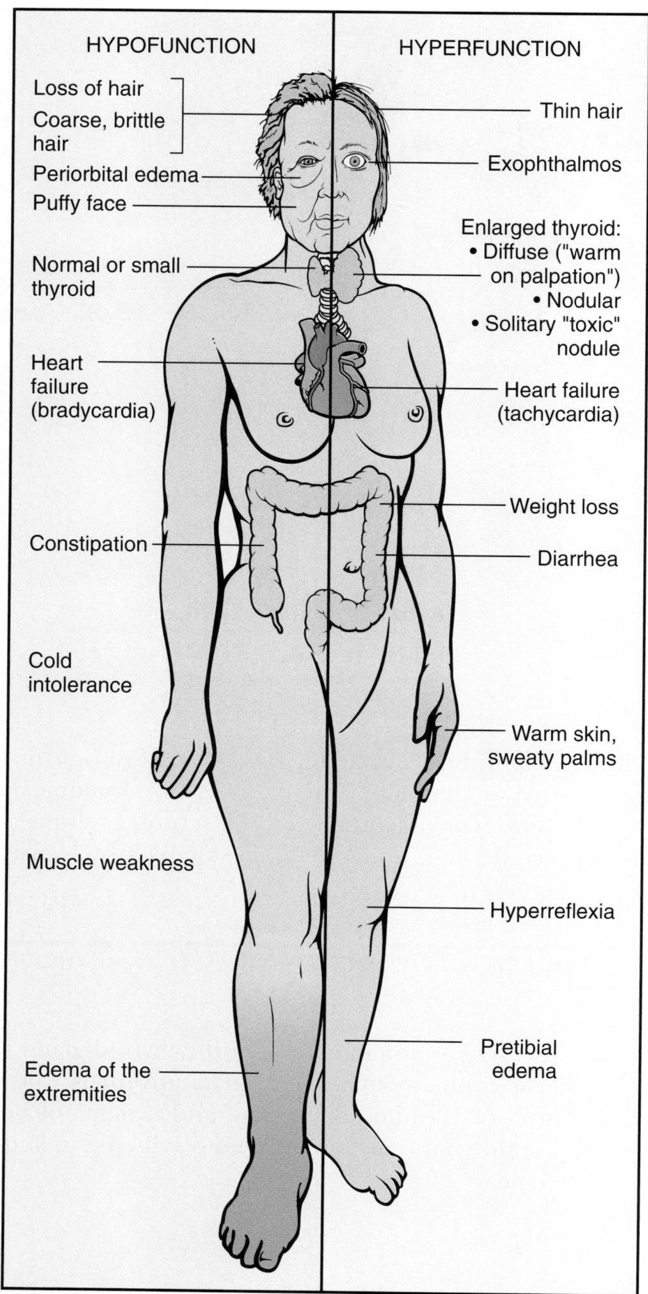

FIGURE 13-4. Comparison of hyperthyroidism and hypothyroidism.

thyroid hormone thyroxine. Graves' disease is most common among women between 20 and 40 years of age. The most common signs and symptoms include the following:

- Anxiety
- Irritability
- Difficulty sleeping
- Rapid or irregular heartbeat
- Tremor of hands or fingers
- Increased perspiration
- Sensitivity to heat
- Weight loss
- Brittle hair
- Goiter

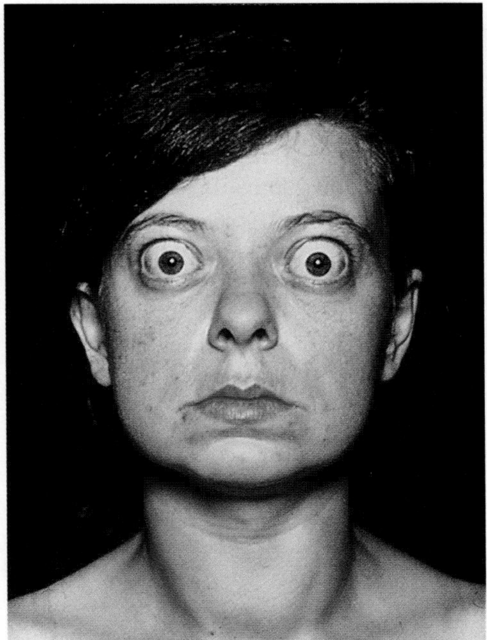

FIGURE 13-5. Exophthalmos in Graves' disease.

- Light menstrual periods
- Frequent bowel movements

Graves' ophthalmopathy is also fairly common and may result in **exophthalmos**, or bulging eyes (Figure 13-5). A complication of hyperthyroidism is **thyrotoxic crisis or storm**. This is a sudden intensification of symptoms combined with fever, rapid pulse, and delirium. Medical attention is required when a crisis episode occurs.

Common causes of a thyrotoxic storm or crisis include a medical illness or infection. Other causes include the following:

- Emotional stress
- Diabetic ketoacidosis
- Hypoglycemia
- Cerebrovascular accident
- Pulmonary embolism
- Bowel infarct
- Trauma
- Increase in thyroid hormone from surgery, radioiodine therapy, or iodinated contrast dye

EXAMPLE

Weight loss due to Graves' disease, E05.00.

EXERCISE 13-1

Assign codes to the following conditions.

1. Thyroid nodule ______________
2. Sick-euthyroid syndrome ______________
3. Graves' disease with thyrotoxic crisis ______________
4. Hashimoto's disease ______________
5. Congenital hypothyroidism ______________

Diabetes Mellitus (E08-E13) and Other Disorders of Glucose Regulation and Pancreatic Internal Secretion (E15-E16)

Diabetes Mellitus

Diabetes mellitus is a chronic syndrome of impaired carbohydrate, protein, and fat metabolism caused by insufficient production of insulin by the pancreas or faulty utilization of insulin by the cells. There are three major types of diabetes: type 1, type 2, and secondary diabetes. In ICD-10-CM the following code categories are available to code diabetes mellitus:

- E08 Diabetes mellitus due to underlying condition
- E09 Drug or chemical induced diabetes mellitus
- E10 Type 1 diabetes mellitus
- E11 Type 2 diabetes mellitus
- E13 Other specified diabetes mellitus

Types 1 and 2 vary in origin, pathology, genetics, age of onset, and treatment (Table 13-2). Patients with type 1 diabetes are insulin dependent; this condition usually develops early in life. The pancreas produces insulin in very small amounts or not at all. Type 2 diabetes usually is of adult onset. The pancreas continues to produce insulin, but it is not properly metabolized. Occasionally, patients with type 2 diabetes must be treated with insulin so that acceptable glucose levels are maintained; the fact that they are taking insulin does not mean that they are dependent on insulin, or that they have type 1 diabetes. Type 2 diabetes is much more common than type 1; 90% to 95% of diabetic patients have type 2 diabetes. Type 2 diabetes in adolescents and children is a relatively new phenomenon, and statistics are still being collected. Sometimes, diabetes is documented as insulin-dependent diabetes mellitus (IDDM) or non–insulin-dependent diabetes mellitus (NIDDM). Documentation of insulin dependence does not determine the type of diabetes, because a patient with type 2 diabetes may be on insulin. If only IDDM is documented, and type 1 or type 2 is not specified, according to coding guidelines, the default is type 2 diabetes.

Two types of complications may occur with diabetes mellitus. One of these is the acute metabolic complication that is part of diabetes itself. The other is the complication or manifestation that occurs in another body system due to the diabetes (Figure 13-6).

EXAMPLE

The patient is treated for diabetic ketoacidosis. Patient has type 1 DM, E10.10.

Acidosis would not be coded as an additional code in a diabetic patient with ketoacidosis, per the Excludes1 note under code E87.2.

Code E11.9, Diabetes mellitus without mention of complication, would have no additional diabetic codes or manifestation codes (Figure 13-7).

There are subcategories for metabolic complications that require no additional manifestation code (Figure 13-8). Subcategories are available for the following diabetic complications and manifestations (Figure 13-9).

TABLE 13-2 COMPARISON OF TYPE 1 AND TYPE 2 DIABETES MELLITUS[2]

	Type 1	Type 2
Clinical Features	Usually occurs before age 30	Usually occurs after age 30
	Abrupt, rapid onset	Gradual onset; asymptomatic
	Little or no insulin production	Insulin usually present
	Thin or normal body weight at onset	85% are obese
	Ketoacidosis often occurs	Ketoacidosis seldom occurs
Symptoms	Polyuria (glycosuria promotes loss of water)	Polyuria sometimes seen
	Polydipsia (dehydration causes thirst)	Polydipsia sometimes seen
	Polyphagia (tissue breakdown causes hunger)	Polyphagia sometimes seen
Treatment	Insulin	Diet (weight loss); oral hypoglycemics or insulin

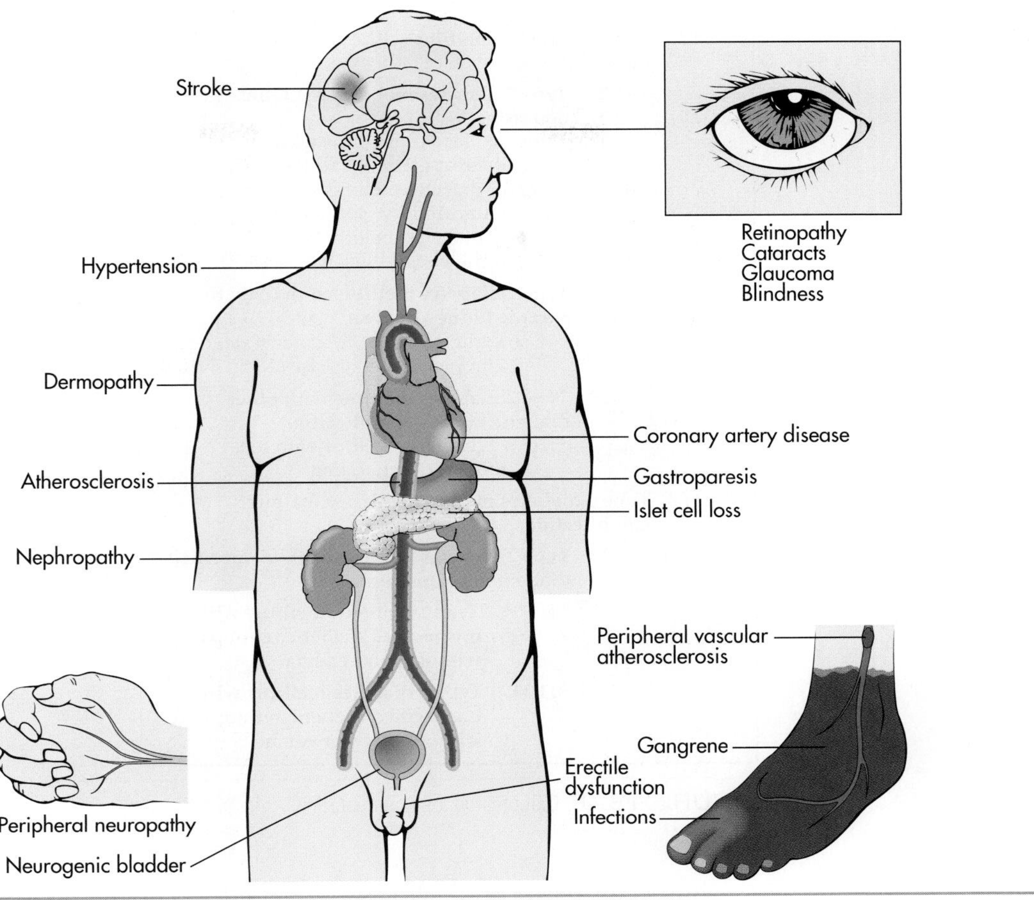

FIGURE 13-6. Possible manifestations/complications of diabetes mellitus.

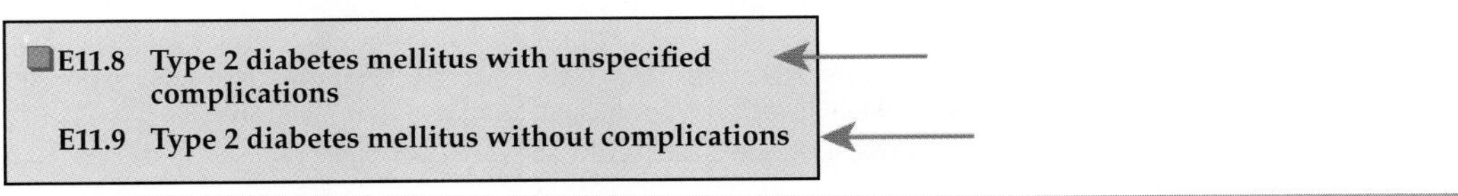

E11.8	**Type 2 diabetes mellitus with unspecified complications**
E11.9	**Type 2 diabetes mellitus without complications**

FIGURE 13-7. Type 2 diabetes mellitus without complications or unspecified complication.

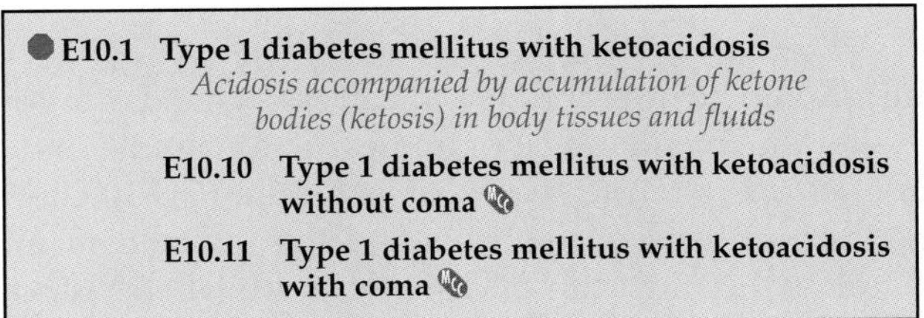

E10.1 Type 1 diabetes mellitus with ketoacidosis
Acidosis accompanied by accumulation of ketone bodies (ketosis) in body tissues and fluids
E10.10 Type 1 diabetes mellitus with ketoacidosis without coma
E10.11 Type 1 diabetes mellitus with ketoacidosis with coma

FIGURE 13-8. Diabetes type 1 with metabolic complication (ketoacidosis).

Subcategory E11.8 is reserved for diabetes with unspecified complication (Figure 13-7). It may be beneficial to query the physician for specific documentation regarding any diabetic complications and/or manifestations.

If a patient's diabetes is documented as being poorly controlled or out of control, the Alphabetic Index gives instructions to code the type of diabetes with hyperglycemia.

It is possible for a diabetic patient to have more than one complication and/or manifestation of diabetes, so it is necessary for the coder to use as many codes as necessary to

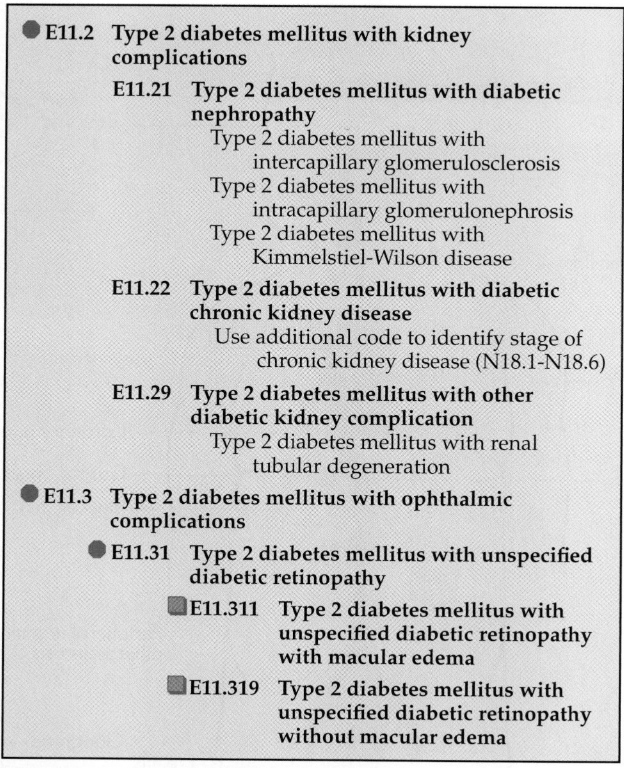

E11.2 Type 2 diabetes mellitus with kidney complications

E11.21 Type 2 diabetes mellitus with diabetic nephropathy
Type 2 diabetes mellitus with intercapillary glomerulosclerosis
Type 2 diabetes mellitus with intracapillary glomerulonephrosis
Type 2 diabetes mellitus with Kimmelstiel-Wilson disease

E11.22 Type 2 diabetes mellitus with diabetic chronic kidney disease
Use additional code to identify stage of chronic kidney disease (N18.1-N18.6)

E11.29 Type 2 diabetes mellitus with other diabetic kidney complication
Type 2 diabetes mellitus with renal tubular degeneration

E11.3 Type 2 diabetes mellitus with ophthalmic complications

E11.31 Type 2 diabetes mellitus with unspecified diabetic retinopathy

E11.311 Type 2 diabetes mellitus with unspecified diabetic retinopathy with macular edema

E11.319 Type 2 diabetes mellitus with unspecified diabetic retinopathy without macular edema

FIGURE 13-9. Diabetes type 2 manifestations.

completely describe the patient's diabetic conditions. It is very important to follow the guidelines with regard to coding and sequencing of manifestation codes.

EXAMPLE

A patient is admitted with diabetic gangrene of the left little toe. The toe was completely amputated. The patient has uncontrolled type 1 diabetes, E10.52, E10.65, 0Y6Y0Z0.

EXAMPLE

Patient is admitted with diabetic ketoacidosis. Patient also has diabetic gastroparesis (type 1), E10.10, E10.43, K31.84.

The term "with" should be interpreted to mean "associated with" or "due to" when it appears in a code title, the Alphabetic Index, or an instructional note in the Tabular List. According to *Coding Clinic for ICD-10-CM* (2016:1Q:p11-13), the ICD-10 classification assumes a cause-and-effect relationship between diabetes and the indexed manifestation/conditions that are subterms, unless the physician documents that diabetes is not the underlying cause of the manifestation. If the documentation is unclear, a physician query may be necessary.[3] See Figure 13-10 for the list of subterms for which the ICD-10-CM classification assumes a cause-and-effect relationship when they are present in a diabetic patient. For example, osteomyelitis in a diabetic patient would be coded to E11.69 unless there was provider documentation that stated the osteomyelitis was due to another cause.

The most common body systems that are affected by diabetes include renal, ophthalmic, neurological, and the circulatory system. Other complications involve the joints and skin.

The fourth character of the 5 diabetes mellitus categories are as follows:

- Kidney—fourth character 2
- Ophthalmic—fourth character 3
- Neurological—fourth character 4

- Diabetes, diabetic (mellitus) (sugar) E11.9
  - with
    - amyotrophy E11.44
    - arthropathy NEC E11.618
    - autonomic (poly)neuropathy E11.43
    - cataract E11.36
    - Charcot's joints E11.610
    - chronic kidney disease E11.22
    - circulatory complication NEC E11.59
    - complication E11.8
      - specified NEC E11.69
    - dermatitis E11.620
    - foot ulcer E11.621
    - gangrene E11.52
    - gastroparalysis E11.43
    - gastroparesis E11.43
    - glomerulonephrosis, intracapillary E11.21
    - glomerulosclerosis, intracapillary E11.21
    - hyperglycemia E11.65
    - hyperosmolarity E11.00
      - with coma E11.01
    - hypoglycemia E11.649
      - with coma E11.641
    - kidney complications NEC E11.29
    - Kimmelsteil-Wilson disease E11.21
    - loss of protective sensation (LOPS)—*see* Diabetes, by type, with neuropathy
    - mononeuropathy E11.41
    - myasthenia E11.44
    - necrobiosis lipoidica E11.620
    - nephropathy E11.21
    - neuralgia E11.42
    - neurologic complication NEC E11.49
    - neuropathic arthropathy E11.610
    - neuropathy E11.40
    - ophthalmic complication NEC E11.39
    - oral complication NEC E11.638
    - osteomyelitis E11.69
    - periodontal disease E11.630
    - peripheral angiopathy E11.51
      - with gangrene E11.52
    - polyneuropathy E11.42
    - renal complication NEC E11.29
    - renal tubular degeneration E11.29
    - retinopathy E11.319
      - with macular edema E11.311
        - resolved following treatment E11.37
      - nonproliferative E11.329
        - with macular edema E11.321
        - mild E11.329
          - with macular edema E11.321
        - moderate EU.339
          - with macular edema E11.331
        - severe E11.349
          - with macular edema E11.341
      - proliferative E11.359
        - with
          - combined traction retinal detachment and rhegmatogenous
          - retinal detachment E11.354
          - macular edema E11.351
          - stable proliferative diabetic retinopathy E11.355
          - traction retinal detachment involving the macula E11.352
          - traction retinal detachment not involving the macula E11.353
    - skin complication NEC E11.628
    - skin ulcer NEC E11.622

FIGURE 13-10. Manifestations of diabetes.

- Circulatory—fourth character 5
- Other specified complications—fourth character 6
- Unspecified complications—fourth character 8
- Without complications—fourth character 9

Renal or kidney complications are common in patients with diabetes and often result in chronic kidney disease (CKD). If diabetic CKD is present, there is an instructional note that states an additional code to identify the stage of the CKD (N18.1-N18.6) should be assigned. Notice that N18.9 is not included in the range of codes in the instructional note. N18.9 is the code for unspecified CKD, so if the specific stage is not documented, no additional code is assigned. A physician query may be necessary to establish the stage of the chronic kidney disease. In patients who have diabetic chronic kidney disease and hypertension, three codes are required.

EXAMPLE Patient with diabetic CKD, stage 4 and hypertension, E11.22, I12.9, N18.4.

Retinopathy is a common ophthalmic complication in diabetic patients. There are specific diabetic retinopathy codes that identify the type of retinopathy, if macular edema is present or not, and the severity of nonproliferative diabetic retinopathy.

Diabetic neuropathy is caused by damage to nerves throughout the body. This may affect the peripheral, cranial, and/or autonomic nervous systems. The fifth characters identify if the neuropathy is:

- Unspecified
- Mononeuropathy
- Polyneuropathy
- Autonomic (poly)neuropathy
- Amyotrophy
- Other neurological complication

Secondary Diabetes

Secondary diabetes mellitus is a form of the disease that develops as a result of another disease or condition. Secondary diabetes can be caused by any condition that damages or interferes with the function of the pancreas. Common conditions that may cause secondary diabetes include pancreatitis, tumor of the pancreas, cystic fibrosis, hemochromatosis, acromegaly, Cushing's syndrome, pheochromocytoma, and drug usage (e.g., corticosteroids). If the underlying cause can be successfully treated, insulin production may improve or return to normal.

The codes for secondary or drug-induced diabetes are similar to the Type 1 and Type 2 diabetes codes. There are subcategory codes for metabolic complications and manifestations.

EXAMPLE Patient has uncontrolled diabetic nephropathy. Diabetes is due to chronic pancreatitis, K86.1, E08.21, E08.65.

Steroid-induced diabetes is a drug-induced diabetes that results from the use of steroids. Steroids enhance insulin resistance, making insulin less effective. If the pancreas cannot make enough insulin to keep blood glucose within a normal range and the patient is on steroids, this could be steroid-induced diabetes. Steroid-induced diabetes may go away when steroids are discontinued. If the patient has a condition that requires long-term treatment with steroids, diabetes may remain. An episode of steroid-induced diabetes may be an indicator that the patient is at risk for developing diabetes later in life.

EXAMPLE Patient with steroid-induced diabetes due to long-term use of prednisone taken for rheumatoid arthritis, E09.9, T38.0x5S, M06.9, Z79.52.

Hypoglycemia

Hypoglycemia occurs when glucose or blood sugar becomes abnormally low. This is a relatively common occurrence in a diabetic patient. Hypoglycemia can also occur in patients who do not have diabetes mellitus. Normal fasting blood glucose levels range from 70 to 99 mg/dL.

EXAMPLE Patient was seen in the ER with hypoglycemia, E16.2.

EXAMPLE Patient who has type 2 diabetes with hypoglycemia, E11.649.

Hyperglycemia

Hyperglycemia occurs when glucose or blood sugar becomes abnormally high. This also is a relatively common occurrence in a diabetic patient. Patients who do not have diabetes may have episodes of hyperglycemia. Sometimes, medication such as steroids can cause hyperglycemia.

EXAMPLE

Patient with diabetes and hyperglycemia, E11.65.

EXAMPLE

Patient with hyperglycemia due to long-term use of prednisone taken for rheumatoid arthritis, R73.9, T38.0x5A, M06.9, Z79.52.

Gestational Diabetes

Gestational diabetes is discussed in Chapter 22, Complications of Pregnancy, Childbirth, and the Puerperium.

EXERCISE 13-2

Assign codes to the following conditions.

1. Diabetic with episode of hypoglycemia ____________
2. Diabetic retinopathy, DM type 2 ____________
3. Diabetic hyperosmolar coma ____________
4. Zollinger-Ellison syndrome ____________
5. Diabetic gangrene, left big toe ____________
6. Diabetes type 2, uncontrolled. Patient also has peripheral vascular disease ____________
7. Steroid-induced diabetes (sequela of long term steroid use) in patient with Crohn's disease ____________
8. Charcot's arthropathy right foot due to diabetes, type 1 uncontrolled ____________
9. Hypoglycemic coma in type 1 diabetes ____________
10. Overactive bladder due to diabetes ____________
11. Diabetic patient with hyperglycemia treated with insulin. Patient is normally on oral medication for diabetes. ____________
12. Syncope caused by autonomic neuropathy due to diabetes mellitus. The patient has type 2 diabetes. ____________

Disorders of Other Endocrine Glands (E20-E35)

Hypoparathyroidism

Hypoparathyroidism is caused by an underactive parathyroid gland that results in decreased levels of circulating calcium. The primary manifestation is **tetany**, a continuous muscle spasm. Vitamin D and calcium supplements are often used to treat this condition.

EXAMPLE

The patient had tetany due to hypoparathyroidism. The patient is treated with calcium supplements, E20.9.

Hyperparathyroidism

Hyperparathyroidism results from an overactive parathyroid gland that secretes excessive parathyroid hormone, causing increased levels of circulating calcium due to loss of calcium in the bone.

Hyperparathyroidism may be primary or secondary. In most cases, primary hyperparathyroidism is caused by a parathyroid adenoma. Secondary hyperparathyroidism is often related to chronic kidney disease.

EXAMPLE

The patient was treated for primary hyperparathyroidism. The patient was hypercalcemic, E21.0. Note the Excludes note under E83.5. Disorders of calcium metabolism (Figure 13-11). Hypercalcemia or hypocalcemia would not be coded as an additional code with any hyperparathyroidism, E21.0-E21.3.

Hyperpituitarism

Hyperpituitarism results from increased production of pituitary hormones, particularly of human growth hormone (hGH). **Gigantism** or **acromegaly** may occur, depending on the time of life when hormonal dysfunction begins (Figure 13-12).

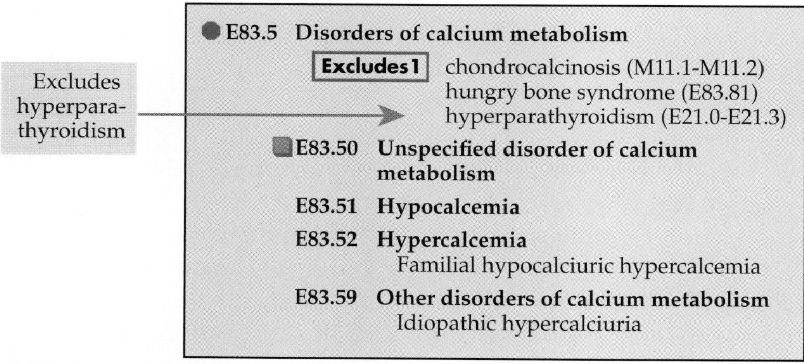

E83.5 Disorders of calcium metabolism

Excludes1 chondrocalcinosis (M11.1-M11.2)
hungry bone syndrome (E83.81)
hyperparathyroidism (E21.0-E21.3)

E83.50 Unspecified disorder of calcium metabolism

E83.51 Hypocalcemia

E83.52 Hypercalcemia
Familial hypocalciuric hypercalcemia

E83.59 Other disorders of calcium metabolism
Idiopathic hypercalciuria

FIGURE 13-11. Disorders of calcium metabolism Excludes1 note.

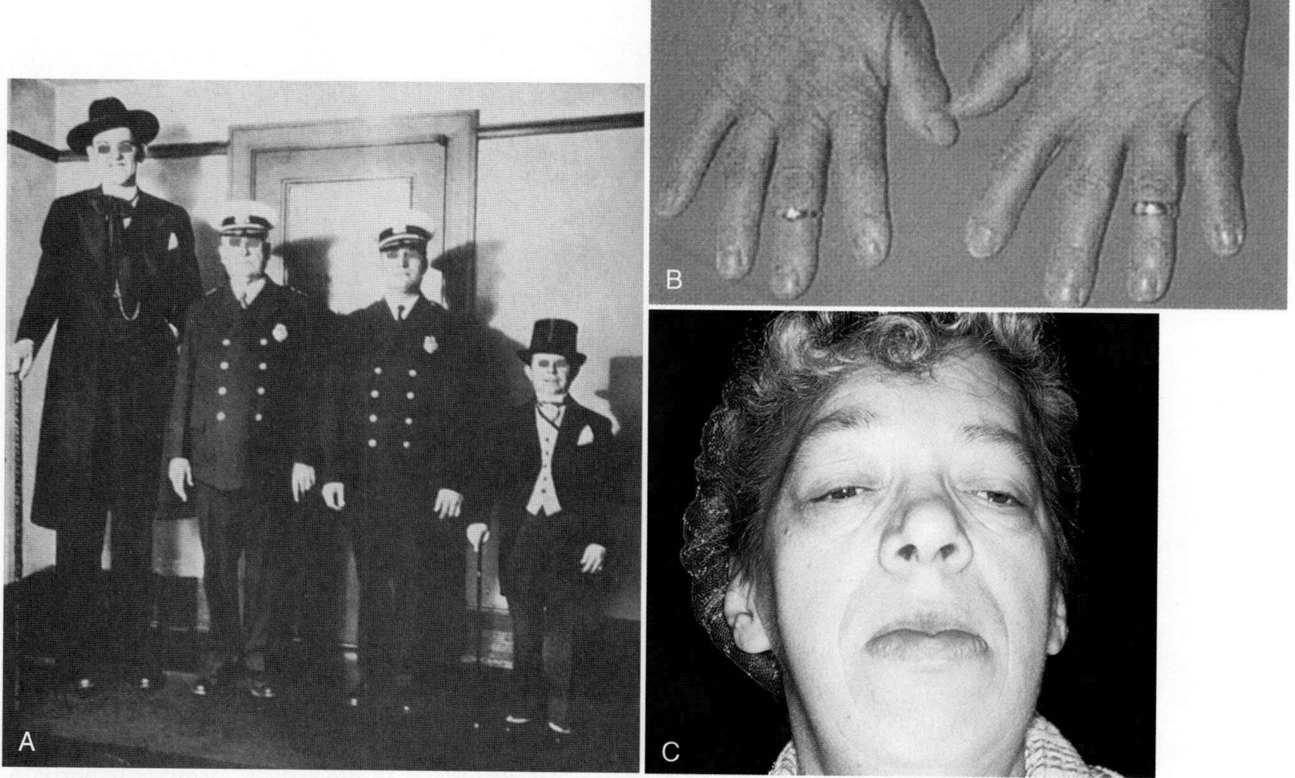

FIGURE 13-12. Effects of growth hormone. ***A,*** Comparison of gigantism, normal growth, and dwarfism. ***B,*** Hands with clinical signs of acromegaly. ***C,*** Face with clinical signs of acromegaly.

Gigantism occurs when hypersecretion of hGH occurs before puberty, along with proportionate overgrowth of all body tissues, especially of the long bones. Often, a pituitary adenoma results from oversecretion of hGH. Acromegaly results when hypersecretion of hGH occurs after puberty, along with overgrowth of the face, hands, feet, and soft tissues. Pituitary adenoma is often the cause.

EXAMPLE Patient has hypersecretion of growth hormone, E22.0.

Hypopituitarism

Hypopituitarism is a condition that is caused by low levels of pituitary hormones. Hormones secreted by the pituitary gland may affect the function of other glands. Lack of thyroid-stimulating hormone (TSH) affects the function of the thyroid gland. Hypopituitarism may be caused by a variety of conditions, such as the following:

- Tumor
- Head trauma
- Brain surgery
- Stroke
- Infections of brain

Occasionally, immune system or metabolic disease such as sarcoidosis, histiocytosis X, and hemochromatosis can cause hypopituitarism.

EXAMPLE The patient has hypopituitarism due to pituitary adenoma, D35.2, E23.0.

EXAMPLE The patient has hypopituitarism due to abscess of the brain, G06.0, E23.0.

Diabetes Insipidus

Diabetes insipidus (DI) or water diabetes is a deficiency in the release of vasopressin by the posterior pituitary gland. The patient excretes volumes of dilute urine and experiences excessive thirst, fatigue, and dehydration. The underlying cause needs to be identified and treated.

Underlying causes of DI include the following:

- Stroke
- Neoplasm
- Polycystic kidney disease
- Neurosurgery

Although DI and DM both include the term diabetes in their names, the two conditions are not related.

EXAMPLE The patient suffers from diabetes insipidus, E23.2.

Cushing's Syndrome

Cushing's syndrome is a condition that results in excessive circulating cortisol levels due to chronic hypersecretion of the adrenal cortex. Common signs and symptoms include the following:

- Fatigue
- Muscle weakness
- Changes in body appearance with fat deposits in the scapular and abdominal areas
- Moon face
- Hypertension
- Edema

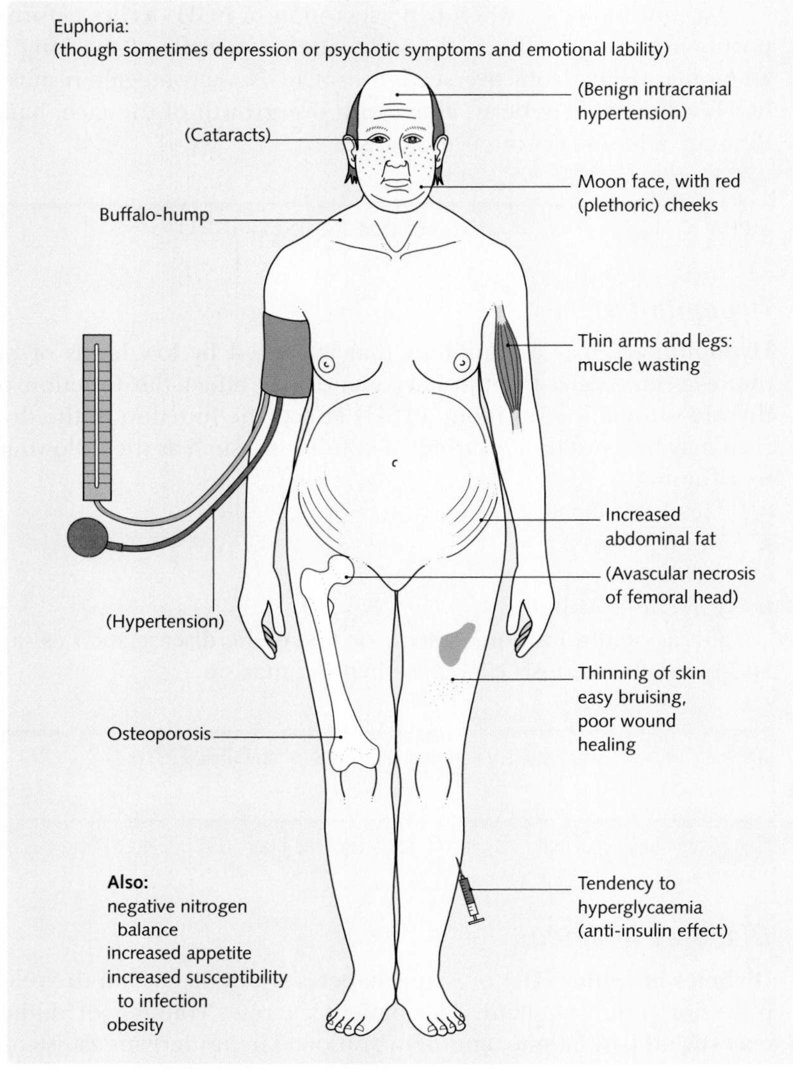

FIGURE 13-13. Cushingoid features.

Other complications include hyperlipidemia, osteoporosis, diabetes, excessive hair growth, amenorrhea, impotence, and psychiatric disturbances (Figure 13-13). The skin becomes thin and bruises easily, and red or purple stretch marks develop.

Administration of glucocorticoids (steroids) to treat other diseases can result in **iatrogenic** (treatment-induced) Cushing's. The patient's appearance may be described as "cushingoid" (see Figure 13-13).

EXAMPLE Patient has Cushing's syndrome and hyperlipidemia, E24.9, E78.5.

Addison's Disease

Addison's disease is an adrenocortical insufficiency that may be caused by neoplasms, surgical removal of the adrenal gland, autoimmune processes, tuberculosis, hemorrhage, and/or infection. Addison's is characterized by the following symptoms:

- Hypotension
- Weight loss
- Anorexia
- Weakness
- Bronze skin coloring

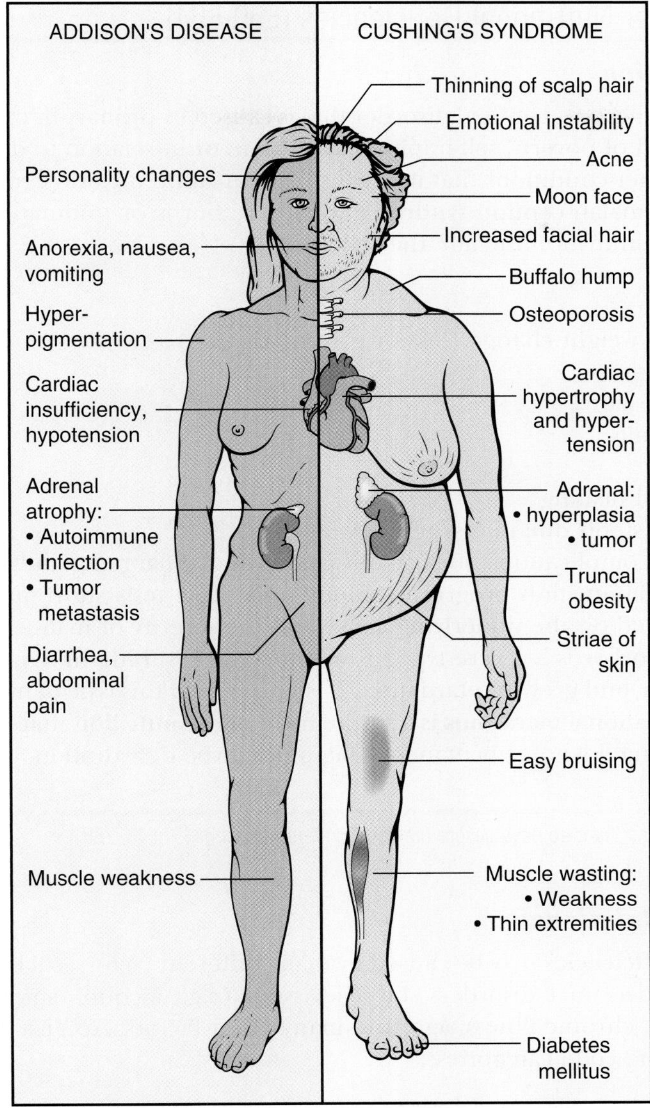

FIGURE 13-14. Comparison of adrenocortical hyperfunction and hypofunction.

Other complications include cardiovascular problems such as irregular pulse, reduced cardiac output, and orthostatic hypotension (Figure 13-14). Emotional disturbances such as depression and anxiety are common. When dehydration and electrolyte imbalances occur, medical attention is required to prevent a life-threatening situation.

EXAMPLE

Patient was admitted to the hospital for treatment of dehydration and for prevention of Addison's crisis, E86.0, E27.1.

EXERCISE 13-3

Assign codes to the following conditions.

1. Hyperparathyroidism __________
2. Syndrome of inappropriate antidiuretic hormone secretion (SIADH) __________
3. Vasopressin deficiency __________
4. Multiple endocrine neoplasia, type 1 __________
5. Precocious puberty __________

Malnutrition (E40-E46) and Other Nutritional Deficiencies (E50-E64)

Malnutrition

Malnutrition is a nutritional disorder that is caused by primary deprivation of protein energy as the result of poverty, self-imposed starvation, or in relation to deficiency diseases such as cancer. Other conditions that may cause malnutrition include Crohn's disease, short bowel syndrome, malabsorption syndrome, or severe burns or traumatic injury. Signs and symptoms of malnutrition include the following:

- Loss of energy
- Diarrhea
- Drastic weight change (loss or gain)
- Skin lesions
- Loss of hair
- Poor nails
- Edema
- Delayed healing
- Greasy stools due to loss of body fat

Other complications, such as muscle wasting, enlarged glands, and hepatomegaly, may occur as malnutrition progresses. Blood and urine tests show many abnormalities. Treatment is based on the underlying cause and the severity of malnutrition.

Kwashiorkor is a severe type of malnutrition resulting in dyspigmentation of skin and hair, edema, and growth retardation. It is rare to find this type of malnutrition in the United States. **Nutritional marasmus** is a severe form of malnutrition that is characterized by severe tissue wasting, loss of subcutaneous fat, and maybe dehydration.

EXAMPLE

The patient was found to have severe malnutrition with a BMI of 17, E43, Z68.1.

Vitamin Deficiencies

Vitamin deficiencies may be caused by many different factors, such as poor nutrient absorption, digestive tract disorders, lifestyle issues (e.g., alcohol, smoking, medications, overexercising), chronic illness, age, and many other factors. Applicable codes are included in the following code categories:

E50	Vitamin A deficiency
E51-E52	Thiamine and niacin deficiency states
E53	Deficiency of B complex components
E54	Ascorbic acid deficiency
E55	Vitamin D deficiency
E63	Other nutritional deficiencies

A diagnosis can be stated as a vitamin deficiency, or a specific name may be used for that particular deficiency (Figure 13-15). Another name for vitamin C deficiency is scurvy.

EXAMPLE

Rickets due to vitamin D deficiency, E55.0.

EXERCISE 13-4

Assign codes to the following conditions.

1. Wernicke's encephalopathy ______________
2. Vitamin B_{12} deficiency ______________
3. Night blindness due to vitamin A deficiency ______________
4. Severe protein calorie malnutrition ______________

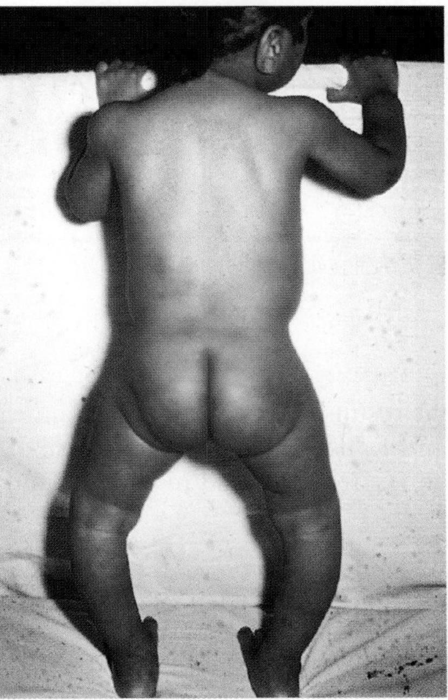

FIGURE 13-15. Rickets. The bowing of legs in a toddler due to formation of poorly mineralized bones.

Overweight, Obesity, and Other Hyperalimentation (E65-E68)

Obesity

Obesity is defined as an increase in body weight beyond the limitations of skeletal and physical requirements, as a result of excessive accumulation of fat in the body. In the United States, obesity has reached epidemic proportions, with two-thirds of American adults being overweight, and one in three considered obese. **Body mass index** (BMI) uses weight and height to estimate body fat.

According to the Centers for Disease Control and Prevention (CDC), for adults, body mass index (BMI) is defined as follows:

Below 18.5	Underweight
Between 18.5 and 24.9	Healthy weight or normal
Between 25.0 and 29.0	Overweight
30.0 and above	Obese

Z codes should be used in combination with overweight and obesity codes to indicate a patient's BMI, if documented. Assignment of codes for overweight or obesity must be based on documentation provided by the physician. According to General Coding Guidelines, it is acceptable to assign a body mass index (BMI) code based on medical record documentation from clinicians who are not the patient's provider. BMI is often documented in nurse or dietician notes. There are different BMI codes for pediatric and adult patients. The pediatric BMI codes are for use for persons 2 to 20 years of age. The adult BMI codes are for use for persons 21 years of age and older.

EXAMPLE

Adult patient is obese with a BMI of 31, E66.9, Z68.31.

Morbid obesity is the term that applies to patients who are 100 pounds overweight or over 50% above their ideal body weight. A BMI of 40 or higher defines morbid obesity. Many complications may be related to obesity, including the following:

- Diabetes
- Hypertension

- Heart disease
- Stroke
- Certain cancers such as breast and colon
- Depression
- Osteoarthritis

EXAMPLE

Adult patient is morbidly obese with a BMI of 41 and suffers from DM, E66.01, E11.9, Z68.41.

Hypervitaminosis

Hypervitaminosis is toxicity that results from an excess of any vitamin, but especially fat-soluble vitamins such as A, D, and K. If toxicity occurs because of an overdose, a poisoning code would be assigned. Poisonings are discussed in Chapter 25.

EXAMPLE

Hypervitaminosis (vitamin D), E67.3.

EXERCISE 13-5

Assign codes to the following conditions.

1. Adult patient with severe obesity with BMI of 40 __________
2. Hypoventilation syndrome in morbidly obese patient __________
3. Localized adiposity __________

Metabolic Disorders (E70-E88)

Cystic Fibrosis

Cystic fibrosis (CF) or mucoviscidosis is a **genetic** (inherited) condition that affects the cells that produce mucus, sweat, saliva, and digestive juices (Figure 13-16). Instead of being thin and slippery, these secretions are thick and sticky, plugging up tubes, ducts, and passageways, especially in the pancreas and lungs. No cure is available, and treatment is directed at the complications and manifestations of the disease. The most frequent complications are respiratory infections such as pneumonia, bronchitis, and bronchiectasis. Asthma may also develop. Although the organism *Pseudomonas aeruginosa* does not cause problems in a healthy person, it is a common infective organism in the patient with CF. Presence of *Pseudomonas* organism in the patient's sputum does not necessarily indicate that the patient has pneumonia due to *Pseudomonas.*

The codes E84.0, cystic fibrosis with pulmonary manifestations, and E84.19, cystic fibrosis with intestinal manifestations, identify the two major systems that are affected by the disease. If the patient has both respiratory and intestinal manifestations, both cystic fibrosis codes are used.

EXAMPLE

Patient who suffers from CF is admitted because of acute bronchitis, J20.9, E84.0.

Disorders of Fluid, Electrolyte, and Acid-Base Balance

Fluid balance occurs when the amount of fluid taken in is equal to the amount that is lost from the body. **Euvolemia** is the state of normal body fluid volume. A patient's fluid balance

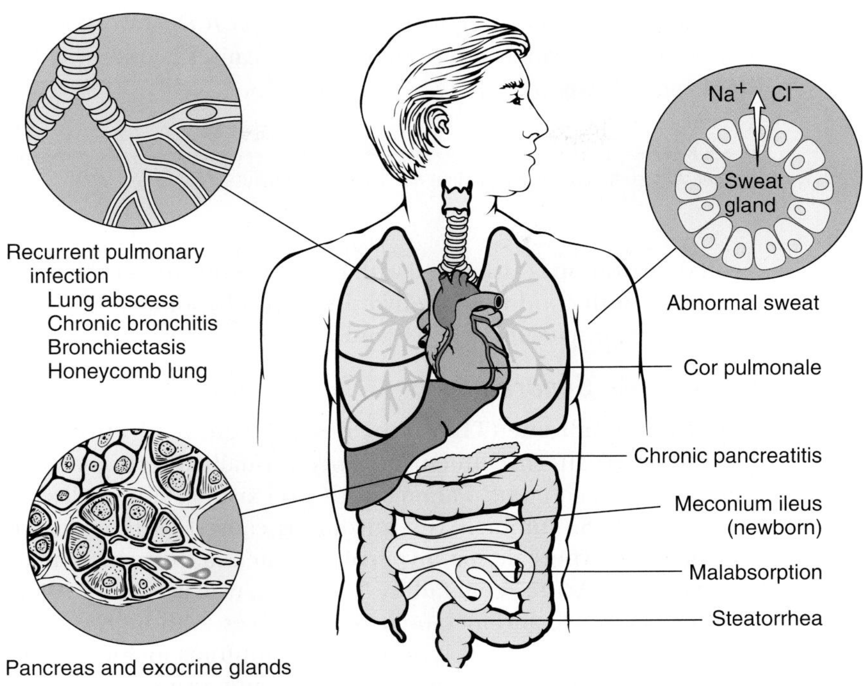

FIGURE 13-16. Abnormal chloride transport associated with cystic fibrosis affects the secretions of all exocrine glands, especially the pancreas, intestine, and bronchi.

provides important information about their hydration, as well as their renal and cardiovascular function. **Fluid overload** or **hypervolemia** occurs when there is too much fluid in the body. Fluid overload may be the result of too much sodium intake, due to IVs or blood transfusions, or a side effect of medication. Some conditions of the heart, kidney, and liver can affect fluid balance. The chief cause of fluid overload is heart failure. When fluid overload is due to congestive heart failure, it is not coded separately. Fluids can build up in various parts of the body causing edema. Peripheral edema is swelling that occurs in the lower extremities. Fluid can also build up in the lungs, causing pulmonary edema, or in the abdomen, causing ascites.

EXAMPLE

Patient has volume overload due to noncompliance with dialysis for end-stage renal disease, E87.70, N18.6, Z91.15.

Hypovolemia occurs due to decreased plasma volume. **Dehydration** is when the body does not have enough water or fluids. Dehydration can be caused by losing too much fluid (e.g., vomiting, diarrhea), not drinking enough water or fluids, or both. **Volume depletion** may be the result of either dehydration or hypovolemia.

EXAMPLE

Patient was seen in the Emergency Room and treated with IV fluids due to dehydration from gastroenteritis, E86.0, K52.9.

Dehydration occurs frequently as the result of other medical conditions, and principal diagnosis selection and sequencing may be confusing. According to the neoplasm guidelines, if an admission occurs for the management of dehydration due to malignancy or therapy for the malignancy, or a combination of both, and only dehydration is being treated, then dehydration is designated as the principal diagnosis, followed by the code(s) for malignancy. According to *Coding Clinic for ICD-9-CM* (2002:3Q:p21-22; 2003:1Q:p22),[4,5] in admissions in which severe dehydration causes acute renal failure, acute renal failure is the principal diagnosis.

EXAMPLE

Patient was admitted for dehydration and acute renal failure, N17.9, E86.0.

If dehydration is associated with hyponatremia or hypernatremia, two codes are assigned to capture both conditions, dehydration with hyponatremia (E86.0 and E87.1) or dehydration with hypernatremia (E86.0 and E87.0).

Tumor Lysis Syndrome

Tumor lysis syndrome (TLS) is the development of electrolyte and metabolic disturbances that can occur after treatment of cancer, usually lymphoma and leukemia, and sometimes even without treatment. Patients with preexisting kidney disease are at increased risk for developing TLS. Tumor lysis syndrome is caused by the breakdown of dying cancer cells and includes hyperkalemia, hyperphosphatemia, hyperuricemia and hyperuricosuria, and hypocalcemia. Acute renal failure and acute uric acid nephropathy can develop as a result of these electrolyte and metabolic disturbances. Although a patient may not have any symptoms in the early stages, as it progresses, symptoms include nausea and vomiting, shortness of breath, irregular heartbeat, lethargy, cloudy urine, and/or joint discomfort. Preventive measures can be taken before and during treatment that include IV hydration, medications such as allopurinol or rasburicase, and alkalinization of urine with sodium bicarbonate. If TLS is untreated or it progresses, it can cause acute kidney failure, cardiac arrhythmias, seizures, loss of muscle control, and death.

EXAMPLE

Patient was admitted to the hospital due to possible acute myeloid leukemia. After confirmation of his AML, it was decided to administer chemotherapy (via central vein). His labs were followed and showed tumor lysis syndrome due to the chemo, C92.00, E88.3, T45.1x5A, 3E04305.

Dysmetabolic Syndrome X

Dysmetabolic Syndrome X is characterized by abdominal obesity, insulin resistance, dyslipidemia, and elevated blood pressure or hypertension. Patients with these conditions are considered to be at greater risk for type 2 diabetes, cardiovascular disease, and stroke. Other names for dysmetabolic syndrome X include metabolic syndrome, syndrome X, insulin resistance syndrome, obesity syndrome, and Reaven's syndrome. In the ICD-10-CM code book, there is an Instructional note to use additional codes for any associated conditions.

EXAMPLE

Adult patient was seen in the clinic for dietary counseling for dysmetabolic syndrome X. Patient is obese with a BMI of 35 and has hypertriglyceridemia and hypertension, Z71.3, E88.81, E66.9, Z68.35, E78.1, I10.

EXERCISE 13-6

Assign codes to the following conditions.

1. Hypocalcemia ____________
2. Hypovolemia ____________
3. Alpha 1–antitrypsin deficiency ____________
4. Metabolic acidosis ____________

FACTORS INFLUENCING HEALTH STATUS AND CONTACT WITH HEALTH SERVICES (Z CODES)

As was discussed in Chapter 9, it is difficult to locate Z codes in the index. Coders will often say, "I did not know there was a Z code for that."

Refer to Chapter 9 for a listing of common main terms to locate Z codes. Z codes that may be used with diseases of the endocrine glands, nutritional, and metabolic diseases include the following:

Z13.1	Encounter for screening for diabetes mellitus
Z13.21	Encounter for screening for nutritional disorder
Z13.220	Encounter for screening for lipoid disorders
Z13.228	Encounter for screening for other metabolic disorders
Z13.29	Encounter for screening for other suspected endocrine disorders
Z14.1	Cystic fibrosis carrier
Z15.81	Genetic susceptibility to multiple endocrine neoplasia
Z46.51	Encounter for fitting and adjustment of gastric lap band
Z46.81	Encounter for fitting and adjustment of insulin pump
Z68.1	Body mass index (BMI) 19.9 or less, adult
Z68.20	Body mass index (BMI) 20.0-20.9, adult
Z68.21	Body mass index (BMI) 21.0-21.9, adult
Z68.22	Body mass index (BMI) 22.0-22.9, adult
Z68.23	Body mass index (BMI) 23.0-23.9, adult
Z68.24	Body mass index (BMI) 24.0-24.9, adult
Z68.25	Body mass index (BMI) 25.0-25.9, adult
Z68.26	Body mass index (BMI) 26.0-26.9, adult
Z68.27	Body mass index (BMI) 27.0-27.9, adult
Z68.28	Body mass index (BMI) 28.0-28.9, adult
Z68.29	Body mass index (BMI) 29.0-29.9, adult
Z68.30	Body mass index (BMI) 30.0-30.9, adult
Z68.31	Body mass index (BMI) 31.0-31.9, adult
Z68.32	Body mass index (BMI) 32.0-32.9, adult
Z68.33	Body mass index (BMI) 33.0-33.9, adult
Z68.34	Body mass index (BMI) 34.0-34.9, adult
Z68.35	Body mass index (BMI) 35.0-35.9, adult
Z68.36	Body mass index (BMI) 36.0-36.9, adult
Z68.37	Body mass index (BMI) 37.0-37.9, adult
Z68.38	Body mass index (BMI) 38.0-38.9, adult
Z68.39	Body mass index (BMI) 39.0-39.9, adult
Z68.41	Body mass index (BMI) 40.0-44.9, adult
Z68.42	Body mass index (BMI) 45.0-49.9, adult
Z68.43	Body mass index (BMI) 50.0-59.9, adult
Z68.44	Body mass index (BMI) 60.0-69.9, adult
Z68.45	Body mass index (BMI) 70 or greater, adult
Z68.51	Body mass index (BMI) pediatric, less than 5th percentile for age
Z68.52	Body mass index (BMI) pediatric, 5th percentile to less than 85th percentile for age
Z68.53	Body mass index (BMI) pediatric, 85th percentile to less than 95th percentile for age
Z68.54	Body mass index (BMI) pediatric, greater than or equal to 95th percentile for age
Z71.3	Dietary counseling and surveillance
Z79.4	Long-term (current) use of insulin
Z79.84	Long term (current) use of oral hypoglycemic drugs
Z83.3	Family history of diabetes mellitus

Z83.41	Family history of multiple endocrine neoplasia [MEN] syndrome
Z83.42	Family history of familial hypercholesterolemia
Z83.49	Family history of other endocrine, nutritional, and metabolic diseases
Z86.31	Personal history of diabetic foot ulcer
Z86.32	Personal history of gestational diabetes
Z86.39	Personal history of other endocrine, nutritional, and metabolic disease
Z94.83	Pancreas transplant status
Z96.41	Presence of insulin pump (external) (internal)
Z96.49	Presence of other endocrine implants
Z98.84	Bariatric surgery status

EXAMPLE Patient has a family history of diabetes, Z83.3.

EXAMPLE Patient is a type 2 diabetic who has been treated with insulin, E11.9, Z79.4.

EXERCISE 13-7

Assign codes to the following conditions.

1. Status post pancreas transplant ____________
2. Dietary counseling for patient with new diagnosis of DM ____________
3. Family history of Graves' disease ____________
4. History of rickets as a child ____________

COMMON TREATMENTS

CONDITION	MEDICATION/TREATMENT
Goiter	Small doses of iodine if due to iodine deficiency; otherwise, radioactive iodine or surgical treatment if symptomatic
Hypothyroidism/Hashimoto's disease	Levothyroxine, Levothroid, and Synthroid, which is the most common thyroid hormone replacement medication
Hyperthyroidism/Graves' disease	Antithyroid medications such as Tapazole; radioactive iodine or surgery
Diabetes	Diet, monitoring of blood sugars, and insulins such as Regular, Lente, Humalog, NPH; oral medications such as Glyburide, Micronase, Diabeta, Glucophage, etc.
Hyperpituitarism	Decrease the amount of hormone secreted, usually with radiation or surgery
Hypopituitarism	Removal of tumor if that is the cause, or hormone replacement therapy
Diabetes insipidus	Depending on cause, vasopressin medication
Hyperparathyroidism	Treatment depends on the cause
Hypoparathyroidism	Replacement therapy with calcium and vitamin D
Cushing's syndrome	Removal of tumor if that is the cause, or medication to suppress the production of cortisol
Addison's disease	Replacement therapy with corticosteroids
Malnutrition	Treat symptoms and/or underlying cause; nutritional supplements; replace missing nutrients, possibly with TPN (total parenteral nutrition)
Vitamin deficiencies	Treat symptoms and/or underlying cause; replace missing vitamins
Hypokalemia	Replace with potassium supplement, such as K-Dur, K-Lyte, K-Tab, K-Lor, Micro-K
Hyperkalemia	Remove potassium from body with Kayexalate, diuretics, sodium bicarbonate, intravenous calcium, glucose, or insulin
Cystic fibrosis	Postural drainage and chest percussion treatments, pancreatic enzymes and vitamins, antibiotics for infection, and possibly lung transplant
Obesity	Diet, exercise, behavior modification, and bariatric surgery
Hypervitaminosis	Stop taking specific vitamin

PROCEDURES

Procedures related to the endocrine system in ICD-10-PCS can be located in the following tables:

0F1-0FY	Gastrointestinal System
0F1-0FY	Hepatobiliary System and Pancreas
0G2-0GW	Endocrine System

EXAMPLE Goiter with complete thyroidectomy (open), E04.9, 0GTK0ZZ.

EXAMPLE Conn's syndrome due to adenoma of right adrenal gland with diagnostic percutaneous biopsy of adrenal gland D35.01, E26.01, 0GB33ZX.

Bariatric Surgery

Bariatric surgery is surgery performed for weight loss on people who are obese, usually with a BMI (Body Mass Index) of greater than 40. To achieve weight loss the stomach must be reduced. There are several different types of surgical procedures performed to achieve this result. The four most common types being offered in the U.S. are (Figure 13-17):

- Biliopancreatic diversion (BPD-DS) is rarely used because of troubles with malnourishment, and a modification known as a duodenal switch is now used. This procedure includes three features. The first is that a large part of the stomach is removed creating a pouch. The second is that the food is rerouted away from much of the small intestine limiting the amount of food absorbed by the body. Lastly, the third feature changes how bile affects the body's ability to digest and absorb food. The distal part of the small intestine is connected to the pouch bypassing the duodenum and jejunum.
- Roux-en-Y (RYGB) is a gastric bypass procedure. This procedure both restricts food intake and decreases how food is absorbed. The food is restricted because a small pouch is created by a stapler. A section of the small intestine is attached to the pouch, which bypasses the duodenum and part of the jejunum. Portions of the stomach are not removed in this procedure as they are in the BPD. This procedure

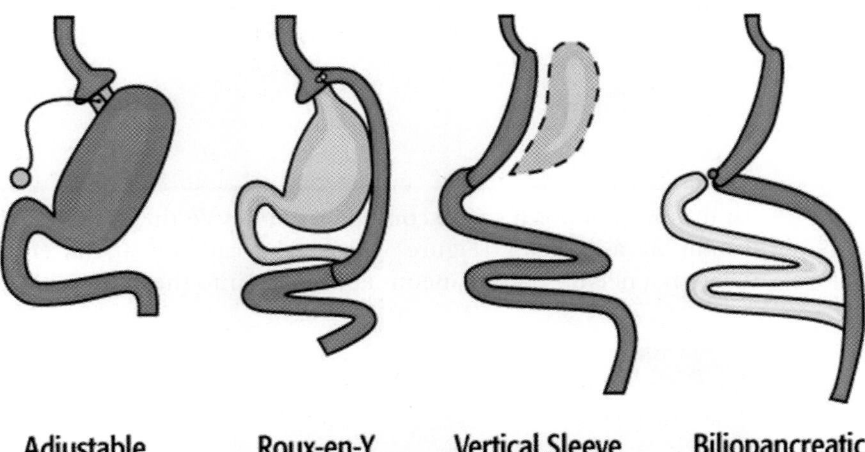

FIGURE 13-17. Types of bariatric surgery.

may be performed both laparoscopically as well as open. In ICD-10-PCS, when coding bypass procedures it is important to know which body part is "bypassed from" and which body part is "bypassed to." In this procedure the 4th character would represent the from (stomach), and the 7th character would represent the body part bypassed to (jejunum).

EXAMPLE

Open Roux-en-Y for gastric bypass (stomach to jejunum) 0D160ZA

SECTION	BODY SYSTEM	ROOT OPERATION	BODY PART	APPROACH	DEVICE	QUALIFIER
Medical and Surgical 0	Gastrointestinal System D	Bypass 1	Stomach 6	Open 0	No Device Z	Jejunum A

- Adjustable gastric banding (AGB) is a restrictive procedure. A band with an inflatable inner collar is placed around the upper stomach to restrict food intake. This makes the patient feel full earlier. Most often, this procedure is performed laparoscopically. In ICD-10-PCS the root operation is restriction.
- Vertical Sleeve Gastrectomy (VSG) both restricts food intake and decreases the amount of food used. In this procedure most of the stomach is removed. The hormone ghrelin that affects appetite appears to be decreased in this type of surgery. A special qualifier is available to identify a vertical sleeve excision.

EXAMPLE

Open vertical sleeve gastrectomy 0DB60Z3

SECTION	BODY SYSTEM	ROOT OPERATION	BODY PART	APPROACH	DEVICE	QUALIFIER
Medical and Surgical 0	Gastrointestinal System D	Excision B	Stomach 6	Open 0	No Device Z	Vertical 3

EXAMPLE

Morbidly obese adult patient (BMI 42) with diabetes mellitus. A laparoscopic gastric banding with extraluminal device was performed E66.01, E11.9, Z68.41, 0DV64CZ.

SECTION	BODY SYSTEM	ROOT OPERATION	BODY PART	APPROACH	DEVICE	QUALIFIER
Medical and Surgical 0	Gastrointestinal System D	Restriction V	Stomach 6	Percutaneous Endoscopic 4	Extraluminal Device C	No Qualifier Z

Insulin Pumps

An insulin pump is a small, computerized device that is attached to the body and delivers insulin via a catheter (Figure 13-18). The catheter at the end of the pump is inserted through a needle (percutaneous approach) into the abdominal fat or subcutaneous tissue.

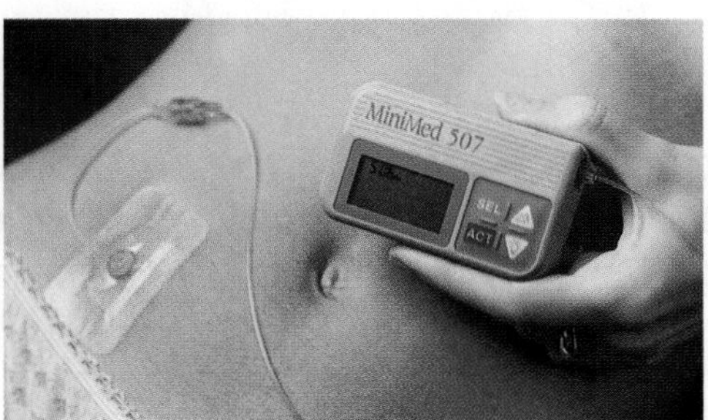

FIGURE 13-18. Insulin pump.

This pump provides a continuous drip of insulin throughout the day. The patient may also administer a bolus of insulin by pushing a button.

EXAMPLE

Patient has brittle Type 1 diabetes and is admitted for implantation of insulin pump catheter into subcutaneous tissue of abdominal wall, E10.9, 0WHF33Z.

SECTION	BODY SYSTEM	ROOT OPERATION	BODY PART	APPROACH	DEVICE	QUALIFIER
Medical and Surgical 0	Anatomical Regions, General W	Insertion H	Abdominal Wall F	Percutaneous 3	Infusion Device 3	No Qualifier Z

EXERCISE 13-8

Assign codes for all diagnoses and procedures.

1. Multinodular goiter which is symptomatic for dysphagia. Total thyroidectomy (open) was performed. ______________
2. Pheochromocytoma (benign) with laparoscopic excision right adrenal gland ______________
3. Adult with morbid obesity with BMI of 40. Laparoscopic VBG was performed. ______________

CHAPTER REVIEW EXERCISE

Assign codes for all diagnoses and procedures.

1. Homocystinemia ______________
2. Conn's syndrome ______________
3. Myxedema ______________
4. Idiopathic Cushing's syndrome ______________
5. Testicular hypogonadism ______________
6. Overproduction of growth hormone ______________
7. Hypertonic dehydration ______________
8. Asymptomatic hyperuricemia ______________
9. Symptomatic premature menopause ______________
10. Respiratory acidosis with metabolic alkalosis ______________
11. Overweight adult with BMI of 26.0 ______________
12. Volume depletion ______________
13. Patient with cystic fibrosis admitted with exacerbation of respiratory symptoms ______________
14. Hyperthyroidism with exophthalmos ______________
15. Poorly controlled diabetes (type 2) with diabetic gastroparesis; patient is on insulin ______________
16. Albinism ______________
17. Amyloidosis ______________
18. Proliferative retinopathy due to DM, type 2, out of control ______________
19. Diabetes due to prednisone (sequela due to long term use of a prescribed drug) ______________

20. Hyperlipidemia due to Cushing's syndrome ______________
21. Thiamine deficiency due to chronic alcoholism ______________
22. Phenylketonuria (PKU) ______________
23. Chronic kidney disease, stage 3 due to diabetic nephropathy, juvenile-onset diabetes ______________
24. Adult patient with severe obesity with BMI 43 and obstructive sleep apnea; patient had open Roux-en-Y gastric bypass to jejunum ______________
25. Erectile dysfunction due to diabetes mellitus, type 2 ______________
26. Inanition ______________
27. Methylenetetrahydrofolate reductase deficiency ______________

Write the correct answer(s) in the space(s) provided.

28. List a couple of conditions that qualify a person as morbidly obese.

____

____

29. What type of diabetes is the most common?

____

30. What organism may cause complications for a patient with cystic fibrosis?

____

CHAPTER GLOSSARY

Acromegaly: condition that results when hypersecretion of hGH occurs after puberty, along with overgrowth of the face, hands, feet, and soft tissues.

Addison's disease: adrenocortical insufficiency that may be caused by neoplasms, surgical removal of the adrenal gland, autoimmune processes, tuberculosis, hemorrhage, and/or infection.

Atrophy: when a gland becomes smaller.

Body mass index: uses weight and height to estimate body fat.

Cushing's syndrome: condition that results in excessive circulating cortisol levels caused by chronic hypersecretion of the adrenal cortex.

Cystic fibrosis: genetic (inherited) condition that affects the cells that produce mucus, sweat, saliva, and digestive juices. Instead of being thin and slippery, these secretions are thick and sticky, plugging up tubes, ducts, and passageways, especially in the pancreas and lungs.

Dehydration: when the body does not have enough water or fluids.

Diabetes insipidus: deficiency in the release of vasopressin by the posterior pituitary gland.

Diabetes mellitus: chronic syndrome of impaired carbohydrate, protein, and fat metabolism caused by insufficient production of insulin by the pancreas or faulty utilization of insulin by the cells.

Dysmetabolic Syndrome X: is characterized by abdominal obesity, insulin resistance, dyslipidemia, and elevated blood pressure or hypertension.

Endocrine system: body system composed of many glands that secrete hormones that regulate bodily functions; it works with the nervous system to maintain body activities and homeostasis and to respond to stress.

Euvolemia: is the state of normal body fluid volume.

Exophthalmos: bulging of the eyes.

Fluid overload: occurs when there is too much fluid in the body.

Genetic: inherited.

Gigantism: condition that occurs when hypersecretion of hGH occurs before puberty, along with proportionate overgrowth of all bodily tissues, especially the long bones.

Goiter: enlargement of the thyroid gland.

Graves' disease: the most common form of hyperthyroidism; it occurs through an autoimmune response that attacks the thyroid gland, resulting in overproduction of the thyroid hormone thyroxine.

Hashimoto's disease: inflammation of the thyroid gland that often results in hypothyroidism.

Hormones: substances secreted by glands that can regulate bodily functions, such as urinary output, cellular metabolic rate, and growth and development.

Hyperglycemia: condition that results when glucose or blood sugar becomes abnormally high. This is a relatively common event in patients with diabetes.

Hyperparathyroidism: condition that results when an overactive parathyroid gland secretes excessive parathyroid hormone, causing increased levels of circulating calcium associated with loss of calcium in the bone.

Hyperpituitarism: increased production of the pituitary hormones, particularly the human growth hormone (hGH).

Hyperplasia: enlargement of a gland.

Hyperthyroidism: abnormality of the thyroid gland in which secretion of thyroid hormone is usually increased and is no longer under the regulatory control of hypothalamic-pituitary centers.

Hypertrophy: enlargement of a gland.

Hypervitaminosis: toxicity resulting from an excess of any vitamin, especially fat-soluble vitamins such as A, D, and K.

Hypervolemia: occurs when there is too much fluid in the body.

Hypoglycemia: condition that results when glucose or blood sugar becomes abnormally low.

Hypoparathyroidism: underactive parathyroid gland that results in decreased levels of circulating calcium.

Hypopituitarism: condition caused by low levels of pituitary hormones. Hormones secreted by the pituitary gland can affect the functions of other glands.

Hypoplasia: atrophy; condition that results when a gland becomes smaller.

Hypothyroidism: condition caused by low levels of pituitary hormones. Hormones secreted by the pituitary gland can affect the functions of other glands.

Hypovolemia: occurs due to decreased plasma volume.

Iatrogenic: caused by medical treatment.

Kwashiorkor: severe type of malnutrition resulting in dyspigmentation of skin and hair, edema, and growth retardation.

Malnutrition: nutrition disorder caused by primary deprivation of protein energy caused by poverty or self-imposed starvation, or associated with deficiency diseases such as cancer.

Morbid obesity: applies to patients who are 50% to 100% or 100 pounds above their ideal body weight. A BMI of 40 or higher defines morbid obesity.

Myxedema: skin and tissue disorder that is usually due to severe prolonged hypothyroidism.

Nutritional marasmus: severe form of malnutrition that is characterized by severe tissue wasting, loss of subcutaneous fat, and maybe dehydration.

Obesity: condition defined as an increase in body weight beyond the limitation of skeletal and physical requirements, caused by excessive accumulation of fat in the body.

Secondary diabetes mellitus: form of the disease that develops as a result of another disease or condition.

Steroid-induced diabetes: diabetes that is caused by the use of steroids.

Tetany: a continuous muscle spasm.

Thyrotoxic crisis or storm: complication of hyperthyroidism associated with a sudden intensification of symptoms combined with fever, rapid pulse, and delirium.

Tumor lysis syndrome (TLS): the development of electrolyte and metabolic disturbances that can occur after treatment of cancer, usually lymphoma and leukemia, and sometimes even without treatment.

Vitamin deficiencies: conditions caused by many different factors, such as poor nutrient absorption, digestive tract disorders, lifestyle issues (e.g., alcohol, smoking, medication, overexercising), chronic illness, age, and many other factors.

Volume depletion: may be the result of either dehydration or hypovolemia.

REFERENCES

1. Frazier ME, Drzymkowski JW: Essentials of Human Diseases and Conditions, ed 4, St. Louis, 2009, Saunders, Table 4-1, p 158.
2. Chabner D: The Language of Medicine, ed 10, St. Louis, 2014, Saunders, Table 18-3, p 771.
3. American Hospital Association: *Coding Clinic for ICD-10-CM* 2016:1Q:p11-13. Diabetes Mellitus with Associated Conditions and Diabetic Foot Ulcer.
4. American Hospital Association: *Coding Clinic for ICD-9-CM* 2002:3Q:p21-22. ARF due to dehydration and treated with IV hydration only.
5. American Hospital Association: *Coding Clinic for ICD-9-CM* 2003:1Q:p22. Clarification—Renal failure due to dehydration with IV hydration.

14

Mental, Behavioral, and Neurodevelopmental Disorders

(ICD-10-CM Chapter 5, Codes F01-F99)

CHAPTER OUTLINE

LEARNING OBJECTIVES

1. Apply and assign the correct ICD-10-CM/PCS codes in accordance with Official Guidelines for Coding and Reporting
2. Identify pertinent anatomy and physiology of mental, behavioral, and neurodevelopmental disorders
3. Identify various mental, behavioral, and neurodevelopmental disorders
4. Assign the correct Z codes and procedure codes related to mental, behavioral, and neurodevelopmental disorders
5. Identify common treatments and medications

ABBREVIATIONS/ ACRONYMS

ADD attention deficit disorder

ADHD attention deficit hyperactivity disorder

AUD alcohol use disorder

CC complication/comorbidity

DSM-IV-TR *Diagnostic and Statistical Manual of Mental Disorders, Fourth Edition, Text Revision*

DSM-5 Diagnostic and Statistical Manual of Mental Disorders, Fifth Edition

DTs delirium tremens

ECT electroconvulsive therapy

ICD-9-CM *International Classification of Diseases, 9th Revision, Clinical Modification*

ABBREVIATIONS/ ACRONYMS—*cont'd*

ICD-10-CM *International Classification of Diseases, 10th Revision, Clinical Modification*

ICD-10-PCS *International Classification of Diseases, 10th Revision, Procedure Coding System*

IQ intelligence quotient

LD learning disability/difficulty

MDD major depressive disorder

OBS organic brain syndrome

PKU phenylketonuria

PTSD posttraumatic stress disorder

ICD-10-CM Official Guidelines for Coding and Reporting (2021-2022)

Please refer to the companion Evolve website for the most current 2021-2022 guidelines.

5. Chapter 5: Mental, Behavioral and Neurodevelopmental disorders (F01-F99)

a. Pain disorders related to psychological factors

Assign code F45.41, for pain that is exclusively related to psychological disorders. As indicated by the Excludes 1 note under category G89, a code from category G89 should not be assigned with code F45.41

Code F45.42, Pain disorders with related psychological factors, should be used with a code from category G89, Pain, not elsewhere classified, if there is documentation of a psychological component for a patient with acute or chronic pain.

See Section I.C.6. Pain

EXAMPLE

Patient is receiving behavioral therapy for treatment of chronic pain syndrome with associated psychological factors, G89.4, F45.42.

b. Mental and behavioral disorders due to psychoactive substance use

1) In Remission

Selection of codes for "in remission" for categories F10-F19, Mental and behavioral disorders due to psychoactive substance use (categories F10-F19 with -.11, -.21) requires the provider's clinical judgment. The appropriate codes for "in remission" are assigned only on the basis of provider documentation (as defined in the Official Guidelines for Coding and Reporting), unless otherwise instructed by the classification.

Mild substance use disorders in early or sustained remission are classified to the appropriate codes for substance abuse in remission, and moderate or severe substance use disorders in early or sustained remission are classified to the appropriate codes for substance dependence in remission.

EXAMPLE

Patient has a history of alcohol dependence, currently in remission, F10.21.

2) Psychoactive Substance Use, Abuse And Dependence

When the provider documentation refers to use, abuse and dependence of the same substance (e.g. alcohol, opioid, cannabis, etc.), only one code should be assigned to identify the pattern of use based on the following hierarchy:

- If both use and abuse are documented, assign only the code for abuse
- If both abuse and dependence are documented, assign only the code for dependence
- If use, abuse and dependence are all documented, assign only the code for dependence
- If both use and dependence are documented, assign only the code for dependence

EXAMPLE

The ER physician documents daily alcohol use. The attending documents alcohol abuse on discharge summary, F10.10.

3) Psychoactive Substance Use, Unspecified

As with all other unspecified diagnoses, the codes for unspecified psychoactive substance use (F10.9-, F11.9-, F12.9-, F13.9-, F14.9-, F15.9-, F16.9-, F18.9-, F19.9-) should only be assigned based on provider documentation and when they meet the definition of a reportable diagnosis (see Section III, Reporting Additional Diagnoses). The codes are to be used only when the psychoactive substance use is associated with a physical disorder included in Chapter 5 (such as sexual dysfunction and sleep disorder), mental or behavioral disorder, and such a relationship is documented by the provider.

c. Factitious Disorder

Factitious disorder imposed on self or Munchausen's syndrome is a disorder in which a person falsely reports or causes his or her own physical or psychological signs or symptoms. For patients with documentation factitious disorder on self or Munchausen's syndrome, assign the appropriate code from subcategory F68.1-, Factitious disorder imposed on self.

Munchausen's syndrome by proxy (MSBP) is a disorder in which a caregiver (perpetrator) falsely reports or causes an illness or injury in another person (victim) under his or her care, such as a child, an elderly adult, or a person who has a disability. The condition is also referred to as "factitious disorder imposed on another" or "factitious disorder by proxy." The perpetrator, not the victim, receives this diagnosis. Assign code F68.A, Factitious disorder imposed on another, to the perpetrators's record. For the victim of a patient suffering from MSBP, assign the appropriate code from categories T74, Adult and child abuse, neglect and other maltreatment, confirmed, or T76, Adult and child abuse, neglect and other maltreatment, suspected.

See Section I.C.19.f. Adult and child abuse, neglect and other maltreatment

ANATOMY AND PHYSIOLOGY

No one body system is known to cause or be affected by mental disorders because the causes of mental illness are not always known. Stress can be a contributing factor in mental disorders. Psychological issues can and do affect one's physical health.

DISEASE CONDITIONS

Mental Disorders, found in Chapter 5 in the ICD-10-CM code book, are divided into the following categories:

CATEGORY	SECTION TITLES
F01-F09	Mental disorders due to known physiological conditions
F10-F19	Mental and behavioral disorders due to psychoactive substance abuse
F20-F29	Schizophrenia, schizotypal, delusional, and other non-mood psychotic disorders
F30-F39	Mood (affective) disorders
F40-F48	Anxiety, dissociative, stress-related, somatoform, and other nonpsychotic mental disorders
F50-F59	Behavioral syndromes associated with physiological disturbances and physical factors
F60-F69	Disorders of adult personality and behavior
F70-F79	Intellectual disabilities
F80-F89	Pervasive and specific developmental disorders
F90-F98	Behavioral and emotional disorders with onset usually occurring in childhood and adolescence
F99	Unspecified mental disorder

The *Diagnostic and Statistical Manual of Mental Disorders* is used by healthcare professionals to diagnose psychiatric and mental disorders on the basis of specific criteria. A multiaxial assessment system is used to assess clinical disorders, personality disorders and intellectual disabilities, medical conditions that may affect psychological condition, psychosocial and environmental factors (stressors such as homelessness or unemployment), and global assessment of functioning.

The DSM-5 was published in 2013 and replaces the DSM-IV-TR. It includes ICD-10-CM codes that should be assigned to the psychiatric and mental disorders. Many healthcare providers will use these codes within their documentation. It is always recommended to verify the code with the code book and documentation in the health record to ensure accurate code assignment.

Mental Disorders due to Known Physiological Conditions (F01-F09)

Organic psychosis occurs as the result of deterioration in the brain. It is usually progressive and irreversible, as in senile dementia and Alzheimer's disease. Organic brain damage may be produced by a variety of conditions, including arteriosclerosis, thrombi, metabolic conditions, infection, toxins, tumors, alcohol, and drugs. The onset and severity of damage depend on the cause. **Organic brain syndrome** (OBS) or disease is a general term that is used to describe the decrease in mental function caused by other physical disease(s).

Dementia

Dementia is a progressive deterioration of mental faculties that is characterized by impairment of memory and one or more cognitive impairments in areas such as language, reasoning, judgment, calculation, and problem-solving abilities. **Cognitive impairment** is a decline in mental activities associated with thinking, learning, and memory. Dementia can occur at any age but is more prevalent in the elderly. Disease processes that may be associated with dementia include the following:

- Alzheimer's disease
- Lewy body disease
- Alcoholism
- AIDS
- Parkinson's disease
- Normal pressure hydrocephalus with dementia
- Genetic or metabolic disease (e.g., thyroid)
- Toxic or traumatic injury
- Malignant disease and treatment

Although the term "senile" may be associated with those who are 65 years of age or older, it should not be assumed that because a patient is older than 65, a condition is due to senility. The physician must document within the health record the specific type of dementia. For many of the dementia codes, code assignment may depend on the presence of behavioral disturbances such as aggressiveness, combativeness, violence, or wandering off. There is a Z code, Z91.83, that should also be assigned to identify that the patient has a tendency to wander off.

EXAMPLE Patient is 70 years old and has dementia with delirium, F03.90, F05.

EXAMPLE Patient is 60 years old and has senile dementia, F03.90.

EXERCISE 14-1

Assign codes to the following conditions.

1. Pre-senile dementia __________
2. Organic brain syndrome __________
3. Dementia due to neurosyphilis with behavioral disturbances __________
4. Dementia due to Pick's disease __________
5. Multiple sclerosis with dementia __________
6. Postconcussion syndrome due to previous head trauma __________
7. AIDS-related dementia __________

Mental and Behavioral Disorders due to Psychoactive Substance Abuse (F10-F19)

Alcohol/Drug Dependence and Abuse and Associated Psychoses

Alcohol dependence, or alcoholism, is a chronic disease that is characterized by a strong compulsion to drink, increasing tolerance, the inability to stop drinking once the person has started, and physical dependence and withdrawal symptoms. If alcohol dependence is associated with alcoholic psychosis, drug dependence or abuse, or physical complications, all diagnoses should be coded.

Drug dependence or addiction is similar to dependence on alcohol. It includes a compulsion to take the drug, increased tolerance, an inability to stop using, and physical withdrawal if the person does not have the drug.

It may be difficult for a healthcare provider to determine whether a patient is actually dependent on alcohol or drugs, so abuse codes tend to be used more often. It is possible that a patient is dependent on one drug and is abusing another drug or alcohol. Abuse and dependence codes of different substances can be used for the same patient.

Dependence is not limited to illegal substances and can occur with prescription drugs. Because drugs have generic and brand names, and since these are used interchangeably, it may be difficult to determine which category is assigned for a particular drug dependence. A drug reference book or an Internet search can be used to determine the generic name or category of the drug.

With the implementation of DSM-5, alcohol abuse and dependence were combined into a single disorder called *alcohol use disorder* (AUD) and can be further specified as mild, moderate, and severe.

- Mild alcohol use disorder codes to alcohol abuse
- Moderate alcohol use disorder codes to alcohol dependence
- Severe alcohol use disorder codes to alcohol dependence

The same terminology and code assignments are used for drug abuse and dependence. For example, cannabis use disorder is as follows:

- Mild cannabis use disorder codes to cannabis abuse
- Moderate cannabis use disorder codes to cannabis dependence
- Severe cannabis use disorder codes to cannabis dependence

Take note that alcohol use indexes to Z72.89, Other problems related to lifestyle and in accordance with the *Official Coding Guidelines for Coding and Reporting* any codes from category Z72 should only be assigned when the documentation specifies that the patient has an associated problem. The exception to coding alcohol use is when it is associated with pregnancy.

When a patient is admitted for a medical condition, they may have a comorbidity of alcohol dependence. Along with treating the medical condition, the patient's alcohol dependence may need to be stabilized with drugs to prevent withdrawal. Because they are treating to prevent withdrawal does not mean that the patient is experiencing withdrawal and therefore withdrawal is not coded.

EXAMPLE

Alcoholic gastritis with alcohol abuse, K29.20, F10.10. Upon verification of code K29.20 in the Tabular, there are instructions to use an additional code to identify alcohol abuse and dependence.

Drug or alcohol abuse indicates a problem with the substance that occurs without craving and physical dependence. However, it is likely that substance abuse can still cause problems with work, school, and home responsibilities and can interfere with relationships.

Psychosis is an impairment in mental state by which one's perception of reality becomes distorted. It may include visual or auditory hallucinations, paranoia or delusions, personality changes, and disorganized thinking. The use of alcohol or drugs could lead to alcohol- or drug-related psychosis. Psychotic episodes vary from person to person.

Alcohol withdrawal symptoms vary in severity from mild shakiness and sweating to the worst form, **delirium tremens** (DTs). Delirium tremens may involve severe mental or neurologic changes such as delirium and/or hallucinations. This is a life-threatening condition. People who have gone through withdrawal once are more likely to have withdrawal symptoms again when they stop drinking. Seizures are also a common form of withdrawal.

When a patient is admitted for withdrawal symptoms, the withdrawal code is assigned as the principal diagnosis. In the Alphabetic Index under the term "withdrawal state," there is a cross reference to *see also* Dependence, drug by type, with withdrawal (Figure 14-1).

Withdrawal state– *see also* Dependence, drug by type, with withdrawal
newborn
correct therapeutic substance properly administered P96.2
infant of dependent mother P96.1
therapeutic substance, neonatal P96.2

FIGURE 14-1. Cross reference for withdrawal.

EXAMPLE

Seizure due to alcohol withdrawal. Patient is an alcoholic who usually drinks every day but hasn't had a drink in 2 days, F10.230, R56.9.

EXAMPLE

Patient is being treated for withdrawal due to dependence on Valium, F13.230.

Admissions to the hospital for drug psychosis are on the rise. A number of drugs can induce psychosis; cocaine and methamphetamine are the most common.

EXAMPLE

Paranoia due to methamphetamine (meth). Patient is dependent on meth, F15.259.

When a patient is on a maintenance program for drug dependence, the appropriate code for drug dependence is assigned. For example, suboxone treatment is used to reduce withdrawl symptoms and cravings in people who are addicted to heroin or narcotics. It is not necessary to assign a Z code for long-term drug therapy.

At the beginning of category F10 Alcohol related disorders, there is an instructional note to use additional code for blood alcohol level if applicable (Y90.-).

The assignment of code F10.21 for Alcohol dependence "in remission" should be based on physician documentation.

EXERCISE 14-2

Assign codes to the following conditions.

1. Delirium tremens due to chronic alcoholism ____________
2. Morphine-induced delirium (adverse effect) ____________
3. Addiction to heroin and OxyContin ____________
4. Cirrhosis of liver due to chronic alcoholism ____________
5. Wernicke-Korsakoff syndrome due to chronic alcohol dependence ____________
6. Acute alcohol intoxication with blood alcohol level of 200 mg/100 mL ____________
7. Cocaine dependence in patient who abuses marijuana ____________

Schizophrenia, Schizotypal, Delusional, and Other Non-mood Psychotic Disorders (F20-F29)

Schizophrenia

Schizophrenia is a disorder of the brain. A person with schizophrenia may have trouble differentiating between real and unreal experiences and may not demonstrate logical thinking, normal emotional responses to others, and appropriate behavior in social situations.

A genetic component is associated with the disease, in that people who have family members with the disease are more likely to exhibit the disease themselves. Schizophrenia usually has its onset during young adulthood, and it affects men and women equally. Five types of schizophrenia have been identified:

- Catatonic—withdrawn, in one's own world
- Paranoid—suspicious of others
- Disorganized—disorganized thought process, unable to communicate coherently
- Undifferentiated—mixed types of schizophrenia
- Residual—has milder symptoms that come and go

EXAMPLE The patient has been in a chronic catatonic state of schizophrenia, F20.2.

Schizoaffective Disorders

Schizoaffective disorder is a condition in which a person experiences a combination of schizophrenia symptoms while exhibiting mood disorder symptoms, such as mania or depression. It can be difficult to differentiate a schizoaffective disorder from schizophrenia and from a mood disorder. Also, symptoms of schizoaffective disorder vary and may range from mild to severe.

Symptoms of schizoaffective disorder may include:

Depression

- Poor appetite
- Weight loss or gain
- Changes in sleeping patterns
- Agitation or restlessness
- Lack of energy
- Loss of interest in usual activities
- Feelings of worthlessness or hopelessness
- Guilt or self-blame
- Inability to think or concentrate
- Thoughts of death or suicide

Mania

- Increased activity (e.g., work, social, and sexual activity)
- Increased and/or rapid talking
- Rapid or racing thoughts
- Little need for sleep
- Agitation or restlessness
- Inflated self-esteem
- Distractibility
- Self-destructive or dangerous behavior (spending sprees, driving recklessly, or unsafe sex)

Schizophrenia

- Delusions
- Hallucinations
- Disorganized thinking
- Odd or unusual behavior
- Slow movements or total immobility
- Lack of emotion in facial expression and speech
- Poor motivation
- Problems with speech and communication

EXAMPLE Patient is being treated as an outpatient for schizoaffective disorder with depression, F25.1.

EXERCISE 14-3

Assign codes to the following conditions.

1. Paranoid schizophrenia ____________
2. Delusional disorder ____________
3. Schizo affective disorder, mixed type ____________

Mood [Affective] Disorders (F30-F39)

Mood Disorders

Mood disorders occur when a change in mood has been present for a prolonged time. The two most common mood disorders (**affective disorders**) are major depression and bipolar disorder (manic-depressive illness). Mood disorders can be triggered by a life event or by a chemical imbalance. The type of depression that is included in categories F32-F33 is different than depression, not otherwise specified (F32.9). **Bipolar disorder** is characterized by mood swings. Onset of symptoms is most likely to occur in early adulthood. A person with bipolar can have four main types of mood "episodes":

1. **Depression**—a feeling of sadness that can go on for a long period of time; lack of enjoyment of the things one would normally do
2. **Mania**—the other side of depression, in which a person feels so good, it is like a "high"; may do risky things
3. **Hypomania**—milder form of mania, but this "feel good" mood can change to depression or mania
4. **Mixed mood**—alternating between mania and depression very quickly

Major depressive disorder (MDD) is characterized by one or more major depressive episodes with a history of mania, hypomania, or mixed episodes. In major depression, more numerous symptoms of depression may be present, and usually, the symptoms are more severe. Major depression is most likely to occur in persons between the ages of 25 and 44; an episode may last from 6 to 9 months. MDD is classified to F32.- for single episode and F33.- for recurrent episodes. Categories are further subdivided to identify the severity of the major depressive disorder.

EXAMPLE The patient was diagnosed with major depressive disorder of moderate severity, single episode, F32.1.

EXAMPLE The patient is in a severe manic phase of bipolar I disorder, F31.13.

EXERCISE 14-4

Assign codes to the following conditions.

1. Bipolar disorder, currently depressed, without psychotic features ____________
2. Major depressive disorder, recurrent ____________
3. Bipolar disorder in full remission ____________
4. Bipolar II disorder ____________

Anxiety, Dissociative, Stress-related, Somatoform, and Other Nonpsychotic Mental Disorders (F40-F48)

Anxiety Disorders

Following is a breakdown of the different types of anxiety disorders:

- Generalized anxiety disorder
- Panic disorder

- Phobias
- Posttraumatic stress disorder

Most people experience mild anxiety and nervousness at various times during their lives, such as during a job interview, a business presentation, or social events.

Generalized anxiety disorder refers to chronic, exaggerated worry, tension, and irritability that may occur without cause or may be more intense than is warranted by the situation. Physical symptoms include restlessness, sleeping problems, headache, trembling, twitching, muscle tension, and sweating.

Panic disorder is a terrifying experience that occurs suddenly without warning. Physical symptoms include pounding heart, chest pains, dizziness, nausea, shortness of breath, trembling, choking, fear of dying, sweating, feelings of unreality, numbness, hot flashes or chills, and a feeling of going out of control or "crazy." Because panic attacks are unpredictable, many people live in fear of when the next one will occur.

Phobias are irrational anxieties or fears that can interfere with one's everyday life or daily routine. For example, if fear of heights would keep a person from visiting relatives who live on the 13th floor of an apartment building, the fear is excessive and disproportionate to the situation. A person without a phobia but with a fear of heights would still be able to go to visit the relatives. If situations are avoided because of fear, or if fear prevents one from enjoying life or preoccupies one's thinking, hindering ability to work, sleep, or do other things, then it becomes irrational.

Posttraumatic stress disorder (PTSD) is an anxiety disorder that is triggered by memories of a traumatic event. This disorder commonly affects survivors of traumatic events, such as sexual or physical assault, war, torture, a natural disaster, an automobile accident, or an airplane crash. In addition, PTSD can affect rescue workers at the site of an airplane crash or a mass shooting or someone who witnessed a tragic accident.

EXAMPLE The patient suffers from chronic PTSD, F43.12.

EXAMPLE The patient has generalized anxiety, F41.1.

Conversion disorder is a condition in which a person has some type of sensory or motor (neurologic) symptom(s) that cannot be explained. These physical symptom(s) appear suddenly and may be the result of psychological stress or emotional conflict. Three criteria must be met to diagnosis a conversion disorder:

- Neurological disease is ruled out
- Feigning illness is ruled out
- Psychological stress or emotional conflict is determined

Conversion disorder can present with many neurological symptoms. The following are some common symptoms:

- Weakness or paralysis of an extremity or the entire body (also known as hysterical paralysis)
- Vision impairment (hysterical blindness) or hearing impairment
- Alteration of sensation
- Impairment or loss of speech (hysterical aphonia)
- Psychogenic nonepileptic seizures
- Various movement disorders
- Problems with gait
- Fainting

EXAMPLE Following numerous tests, the patient was diagnosed with conversion disorder with seizures, F44.5.

EXERCISE 14-5

Assign codes to the following conditions.

1. Obsessive-compulsive disorder ____________
2. Posttraumatic stress syndrome ____________
3. Panic attack ____________
4. Fear of thunderstorms ____________
5. Hysterical blindness ____________

Behavioral Syndromes Associated with Physiological Disturbances and Physical Factors (F50-F59)

Eating Disorders

Eating disorders refer to a group of conditions characterized by abnormal eating habits that may affect an individual's physical and psychological well-being. The most common disorders include:

- Binge-eating disorder, characterized by eating binges without compensatory behavior.
- Bulimia nervosa, is characterized by eating binges followed by compensatory behavior such as purging (self-induced vomiting, fasting, excessive use of laxatives/diuretics, and/or excessive exercise)
- Anorexia nervosa, characterized by an unhealthy body weight and the fear of gaining weight. It is not about the food but is an unhealthy means of coping with emotional issues.

These disorders can have serious physical consequences and may even be life-threatening. Treatments for eating disorders usually involve psychotherapy, including family counseling, nutrition education, medications, and even hospitalization.

Sexual Problems

Sexual problems may be due to organic or medical conditions or to psychological dysfunction. Alcohol and drug use can also affect sexual function. After medical problems have been ruled out, a psychological cause can be explored.

EXAMPLE Patient is treated for impotence due to psychogenic cause, F52.21.

EXAMPLE Patient treated for erectile dysfunction, N52.9.

If a patient has erectile dysfunction it has to be specified as due to psychogenic causes to be coded to F52.21.

EXAMPLE Patient is being seen for psychogenic dyspareunia, F52.6.

EXAMPLE Female patient is being seen for dyspareunia, N94.10.

EXERCISE 14-6

Assign codes to the following conditions.

1. Anorexia nervosa with binging/purging ____________
2. Adult patient was seen in the clinic because of pagophagia; tests were ordered to evaluate for iron deficiency anemia ____________
3. Night terrors ____________
4. Laxative abuse ____________

Disorders of Adult Personality and Behavior (F60-F69)

Personality Disorders

A **personality disorder** is a pattern of behavior that can disrupt many aspects of a person's life. Personality disorders range from mild to severe and are often exacerbated during times of stress or external pressure. If a personality disorder is associated with neuroses, psychosis, or a physical condition, this should be coded. Personality disorders are divided into three clusters:

1. Cluster A—patients appear odd or eccentric, socially awkward
   - Paranoid—are suspicious of and do not trust others
   - Schizoid—loners who lack or do not show emotion
   - Schizotypal—seek isolation
2. Cluster B—patients appear dramatic, emotional, or erratic
   - Antisocial—disregard and tend to violate the rights of others, fail to conform to societal norms
   - Borderline—have difficulty coping with minor stress, have unstable relationships, and are self-destructive
   - Histrionic—are overly dramatic with a need to be the center of attention
   - Narcissistic—have an inflated sense of self-importance
3. Cluster C—patients appear anxious and fearful
   - Avoidant—avoid social situations because of fear of criticism, disapproval, or rejection; view themselves as inferior
   - Dependent—rely on others to make decisions for them; fear losing the support and approval of others
   - Obsessive-compulsive—are excessively preoccupied with orderliness, perfection, and mental and interpersonal control

EXAMPLE Patient has an obsessive-compulsive personality disorder, F60.5.

EXAMPLE Patient has a passive-aggressive personality, F60.89.

Sexual Disorder

Sexual activities that are not practiced by the majority of the population have been characterized as "deviant" or "variant" behavior. Although some may experiment with a variety of sexual behaviors, it is not until a person begins to rely on the deviant behavior as a means of sexual gratification that it becomes a more permanent trait. "Unconventional" sexual behaviors or paraphilias are coded to category 302 and include some of the following:

Transvestism—assuming the appearance, manner, or roles traditionally associated with members of the opposite sex (cross-dressing)

Exhibitionism—recurrent intense sexual urges and fantasies of exposing the genitals to an unsuspecting stranger

Fetishism—recurrent intense sexual urges and fantasies of using inanimate objects for sexual arousal or orgasm. Objects commonly used include female clothing such as shoes, earrings, or undergarments

Voyeurism—recurrent intense sexual urges and fantasies involving observing unsuspecting people who are naked, disrobing, or engaging in sexual activity

Sadism—the act or sense of gaining pleasure from inflicting physical or psychological pain on another

Masochism—the act or sense of gaining pleasure from experiencing physical or psychological pain

EXAMPLE Patient is an exhibitionist, F65.2.

EXERCISE 14-7

Assign codes to the following conditions.

1. Borderline personality ____________
2. Pedophile ____________
3. Kleptomania ____________
4. Voyeurism ____________

Intellectual Disabilities (F70-F79)

Intellectual disability is a disorder in which a person's overall intellectual functioning is well below average, and intelligence quotient (IQ) is around 70 or less. The term intellectual disability is now preferred instead of mental retardation. Rosa's Law, which required replacing the term mental retardation with intellectual disability in United States official documents, was passed on October 6, 2010. Individuals with intellectual disability also may have a significantly impaired ability to cope with common life demands and lack some of the daily living skills that are expected of people in their age group and culture. Impairment may interfere with learning, communication, self-care, independent living, social interaction, play, work, and safety. It appears in childhood, before age 18. There are a variety of causes for intellectual disability; however, often the cause is not documented. Causes of intellectual disability are discussed in the following paragraphs.

Genetic Causes

- Defective genes, as in Fragile X syndrome, which is the most common inherited cause of intellectual disability
- Chromosomal disorders such as Down's syndrome that are characterized by an abnormal number of chromosomes
- Congenital hypothyroidism, which can result in intellectual disability and stunted growth if the patient is not treated with thyroid replacement
- Inborn errors of metabolism may result in intellectual disability. More than 300 gene disorders involve inborn errors of metabolism. These include the following:
  - Phenylketonuria (PKU)
  - Tay-Sachs disease
  - Galactosemia
  - Homocystinuria
  - Maple syrup urine disease
  - Biotinidase deficiency

External Causes

- During pregnancy, the following factors can result in intellectual disability:
  - Malnutrition
  - Mother's use of alcohol and drugs
  - Environmental toxins such as lead and mercury
  - Viral infections such as rubella and cytomegalovirus
  - Untreated diabetes mellitus
- During birth, the following conditions can result in intellectual disability:
  - Low birth weight
  - Premature birth
  - Deprivation of oxygen
- After birth, the following conditions can result in intellectual disability:
  - Complications from infectious diseases such as measles, chickenpox, and whooping cough
  - Exposure to lead and mercury
  - Accidental injury to the brain
  - Severe child abuse
  - Poverty

At the beginning of this section, instructions state an additional code(s) should be assigned to identify any associated psychiatric or physical condition(s). A number of congenital syndromes may have some form of associated intellectual disability. The most common severity level is mild mental retardation; 85% of those affected have the mild type.

ICD-10-CM codes for intellectual disability are classified by IQ, as follows:

IQ 50-55 to 70	Mild intellectual disability
IQ 35-40 to 50-55	Moderate intellectual disability
IQ 20-25 to 35-40	Severe intellectual disability
IQ below 20-25	Profound intellectual disability

Documentation of intellectual disability in the health record may not include the IQ, but the condition often is described by severity.

EXAMPLE

Fragile X syndrome with mild intellectual disability, Q99.2, F70.

EXERCISE 14-8

Assign codes to the following conditions.

1. Shaken baby syndrome with profound intellectual disability; injury happened 2 years ago ______________
2. Trisomy 21 with moderate intellectual disability ______________
3. Severe intellectual disability due to Angelman's syndrome ______________
4. Mild intellectual disability due to Lesch-Nyhan syndrome ______________
5. Cerebral palsy with intellectual disability ______________

Pervasive and Specific Developmental Disorders (F80-F89) and Behavioral and Emotional Disorders With Onset Usually Occurring in Childhood and Adolescence (F90-F98)

Learning Disorders

Learning disabilities or differences (LDs) affect a person's ability to understand or use spoken or written language (**dyslexia**), to do mathematical calculations (**dyscalculia**), to coordinate movements such as writing (**dysgraphia**), or to direct attention. Although LDs may occur in very young children, these disorders usually are not recognized until the child reaches school age.

EXAMPLE

Patient's test results show a developmental mathematics disorder, F81.2.

Attention Deficit Disorder

Attention deficit disorder (ADD) and **attention deficit hyperactivity disorder** (ADHD) are common childhood disorders. ADHD and ADD are not learning disabilities, but they are characterized by inattention, hyperactivity, and impulsivity. Three subtypes of ADHD have been identified:

1. Hyperactive/impulsive type—patient does not show significant inattention
2. Inattentive type—patient does not show significant hyperactive-impulsive behavior; sometimes called ADD
3. Combined type—patient displays both inattentive and hyperactive-impulsive symptoms

Other disorders that sometimes accompany ADHD include Tourette's syndrome, oppositional defiant disorder, conduct disorder, anxiety and depression, and bipolar disorder. Attention deficit hyperactivity disorder continues into adulthood in about 50% of persons with childhood ADHD.

EXAMPLE

Patient takes medication for ADHD, combined type, F90.2.

Oppositional Defiant Disorder

Oppositional defiant disorder is defined as a pattern of uncooperative, defiant, and hostile behavior toward authority figures that does not involve major antisocial violations, is not normal for the patient's developmental stage, and results in significant functional impairment. A certain level of oppositional behavior is common in children and adolescents. It should be considered a disorder only when behaviors are more frequent and intense than in unaffected peers, and when they cause dysfunction in social, academic, or work-related arenas.

EXERCISE 14-9

Assign codes to the following conditions.

1. Attention deficit disorder with overactivity ____________
2. Dyslexia, developmental ____________
3. Asperger's syndrome ____________
4. Conduct disorder ____________

FACTORS INFLUENCING HEALTH STATUS AND CONTACT WITH HEALTH SERVICES (Z CODES)

As discussed in Chapter 9, it may be difficult for the coder to locate Z codes in the index. Coders often say, "I did not know there was a Z code for that." Refer to Chapter 9 for a listing of common main terms used to locate Z codes.

A review of the Tabular reveals that some Z codes pertain to mental and behavioral disorders.

Z02.83	Encounter for blood-alcohol and blood-drug test
Z04.6	Encounter for general psychiatric examination, requested by authority
Z13.40	Encounter for screening for unspecified developmental delays
Z13.41	Encounter for autism screening
Z13.42	Encounter for screening for global developmental delays (milestones)
Z55.0	Illiteracy and low-level literacy
Z55.1	Schooling unavailable and unattainable
Z55.2	Failed school examinations
Z55.3	Underachievement in school
Z55.4	Educational maladjustment and discord with teachers and classmates
Z55.8	Other problems related to education and literacy
Z55.9	Problems related to education and literacy, unspecified
Z56.0	Unemployment, unspecified
Z56.1	Change of job
Z56.2	Threat of job loss
Z56.3	Stressful work schedule
Z56.4	Discord with boss and workmates
Z56.5	Uncongenial work environment
Z56.6	Other physical and mental strain related to work
Z56.81	Sexual harassment on the job
Z56.82	Military deployment status
Z56.89	Other problems related to employment
Z56.9	Unspecified problems related to employment

Z59.0	Homelessness
Z59.1	Inadequate housing
Z59.2	Discord with neighbors, lodgers, and landlord
Z59.3	Problems related to living in residential institution
Z59.4	Lack of adequate food and safe drinking water
Z59.5	Extreme poverty
Z59.6	Low income
Z59.7	Insufficient social insurance and welfare support
Z59.8	Other problems related to housing and economic circumstances
Z59.9	Problem related to housing and economic circumstances, unspecified
Z60.0	Problems of adjustment to life-cycle transitions
Z60.2	Problems related to living alone
Z60.3	Acculturation difficulty
Z60.4	Social exclusion and rejection
Z60.5	Target of (perceived) adverse discrimination and persecution
Z60.8	Other problems related to social environment
Z60.9	Problem related to social environment, unspecified
Z62.0	Inadequate parental supervision and control
Z62.1	Parental overprotection
Z62.21	Child in welfare custody
Z62.22	Institutional upbringing
Z62.29	Other upbringing away from parents
Z62.3	Hostility towards and scapegoating of child
Z62.6	Inappropriate (excessive) parental pressure
Z62.810	Personal history of physical and sexual abuse in childhood
Z62.811	Personal history of psychological abuse in childhood
Z62.812	Personal history of neglect in childhood
Z62.813	Personal history of forced labor or sexual exploitation in childhood
Z62.819	Personal history of unspecified abuse in childhood
Z62.820	Parent-biological child conflict
Z62.821	Parent-adopted child conflict
Z62.822	Parent-foster child conflict
Z62.890	Parent-child estrangement NEC
Z62.891	Sibling rivalry
Z62.898	Other specified problems related to upbringing
Z62.9	Problem related to upbringing, unspecified
Z63.0	Problems in relationship with spouse or partner
Z63.1	Problems in relationship with in-laws
Z63.31	Absence of family member due to military deployment
Z63.32	Other absence of family member
Z63.4	Disappearance and death of family member
Z63.5	Disruption of family by separation and divorce
Z63.6	Dependent relative needing care at home
Z63.71	Stress on family due to return of family member from military deployment
Z63.72	Alcoholism and drug addiction in family
Z63.79	Other stressful life events affecting family and household
Z63.8	Other specified problems related to primary support group
Z63.9	Problem related to primary support group, unspecified
Z64.0	Problems related to unwanted pregnancy
Z64.1	Problems related to multiparity
Z64.4	Discord with counselors

Z65.0	Conviction in civil and criminal proceedings without imprisonment
Z65.1	Imprisonment and other incarceration
Z65.2	Problems related to release from prison
Z65.3	Problems related to other legal circumstances
Z65.4	Victim of crime and terrorism
Z65.5	Exposure to disaster, war, and other hostilities
Z65.8	Other specified problems related to psychosocial circumstances
Z65.9	Problem related to unspecified psychosocial circumstances
Z69.010	Encounter for mental health services for victim of parental child abuse
Z69.011	Encounter for mental health services for perpetrator of parental child abuse
Z69.020	Encounter for mental health services for victim of nonparental child abuse
Z69.021	Encounter for mental health services for perpetrator of nonparental child abuse
Z69.11	Encounter for mental health services for victim of spousal or partner abuse
Z69.12	Encounter for mental health services for perpetrator of spousal or partner abuse
Z69.81	Encounter for mental health services for victim of other abuse
Z69.82	Encounter for mental health services for perpetrator of other abuse
Z70.0	Counseling related to sexual attitude
Z70.1	Counseling related to patient's sexual behavior and orientation
Z70.2	Counseling related to sexual behavior and orientation of third party
Z70.3	Counseling related to combined concerns regarding sexual attitude, behavior, and orientation
Z70.8	Other sex counseling
Z70.9	Sex counseling, unspecified
Z71.41	Alcohol abuse counseling and surveillance of alcoholic
Z71.42	Counseling for family member of alcoholic
Z71.51	Drug abuse counseling and surveillance of drug abuser
Z71.52	Counseling for family member of drug abuser
Z71.6	Tobacco abuse counseling
Z71.81	Spiritual or religious counseling
Z71.89	Other specified counseling
Z71.9	Counseling, unspecified
Z72.0	Tobacco use
Z72.3	Lack of physical exercise
Z72.4	Inappropriate diet and eating habits
Z72.51	High-risk heterosexual behavior
Z72.52	High-risk homosexual behavior
Z72.53	High-risk bisexual behavior
Z72.6	Gambling and betting
Z72.810	Child and adolescent antisocial behavior
Z72.811	Adult antisocial behavior
Z72.820	Sleep deprivation
Z72.821	Inadequate sleep hygiene
Z72.89	Other problems related to lifestyle
Z72.9	Problem related to lifestyle, unspecified
Z73.0	Burn-out
Z73.1	Type A behavior pattern
Z73.2	Lack of relaxation and leisure
Z73.3	Stress, not elsewhere classified
Z73.4	Inadequate social skills, not elsewhere classified
Z73.5	Social role conflict, not elsewhere classified
Z73.6	Limitation of activities due to disability
Z73.810	Behavioral insomnia of childhood, sleep-onset association type
Z73.811	Behavioral insomnia of childhood, limit-setting type

Z73.812	Behavioral insomnia of childhood, combined type
Z73.819	Behavioral insomnia of childhood, unspecified type
Z73.82	Dual sensory impairment
Z73.89	Other problems related to life management difficulty
Z73.9	Problem related to life management difficulty, unspecified
Z76.5	Malingerer [conscious simulation]
Z81.0	Family history of intellectual disability
Z81.1	Family history of alcohol abuse and dependence
Z81.2	Family history of tobacco abuse and dependence
Z81.3	Family history of other psychoactive substance abuse and dependence
Z81.4	Family history of other substance abuse and dependence
Z81.8	Family history of other mental and behavioral disorders
Z87.890	Personal history of sex reassignment
Z87.891	Personal history of nicotine dependence
Z91.410	Personal history of adult physical and sexual abuse
Z91.411	Personal history of adult psychological abuse
Z91.412	Personal history of adult neglect
Z91.419	Personal history of unspecified adult abuse
Z91.42	Personal history of forced labor or sexual exploitation
Z91.49	Other personal history of psychological trauma, not elsewhere classified
Z91.5	Personal history of self-harm

EXAMPLE Adjustment disorder with depressed mood due to unemployment, F43.21, Z56.0.

EXAMPLE Counseling regarding marital problems, Z71.89, Z63.0.

EXERCISE 14-10

Assign codes to the following conditions.

1. Screening for depression ____________
2. Malingerer ____________
3. Examination for blood alcohol test ____________
4. Counseling for mother and son due to son's ADHD ____________
5. Laboratory testing (liver function tests) on patient who takes Cognex for Alzheimer's disease with dementia ____________

COMMON TREATMENTS

Many of the mental disorders can be treated with psychotherapy. Often, a combination of psychotherapy and medication is necessary for effective treatment.

CONDITION	MEDICATIONS
Dementia	Depends on type of dementia
Alcohol withdrawal	Benzodiazepam, such as diazepam (Valium) or chlordiazepoxide (Librium or Libritabs), may be used to reduce anxiety Multivitamin; thiamine and folate Beta blockers such as propranolol (Inderal) or atenolol (Tenormin) reduce heart rate and tremors Phenytoin (Dilantin), carbamazepine (Tegretol), and divalproex sodium (Depakote) are antiseizure medications that can be used to treat or prevent seizures

CONDITION	MEDICATIONS
Drug withdrawal	Treatment would depend on the drug
Schizophrenia	Often requires a combination of antipsychotic, antidepressant, and antianxiety medications such as haloperidol (Haldol), chlorpromazine (Thorazine), thioridazine (Mellaril), fluphenazine (Prolixin), Serentil, Seroquel, Clozaril, and Zyprexa
Depression	Antidepressants such as fluoxetine (Prozac), paroxetine (Paxil), sertraline hydrochloride (Zoloft), citalopram hydrobromide (Celexa), nefazodone (Serzone), mirtazapine (Remeron), venlafaxine (Effexor), and bupropion hydrochloride (Wellbutrin)
Bipolar disorder	Medications include lithium; anticonvulsants such as carbamazepine (Tegretol), divalproex sodium (Depakote), gabapentin (Neurontin), and lamotrigine (Lamictal); antidepressants such as bupropion hydrochloride (Wellbutrin) or sertraline hydrochloride (Zoloft); neuroleptics (e.g., Haldol); and benzodiazepines (e.g., lorazepam)
Anxiety	Diazepam (Valium), lorazepam (Ativan), clorazepate (Tranxene), alprazolam (Xanax), paroxetine (Paxil), buspirone (Buspar)
Panic disorder	Alprazolam (Xanax), paroxetine (Paxil)
Phobias	Amitriptyline (Elavil), desipramine (Norpramin), imipramine (Tofranil), nortriptyline (Pamelor), phenelzine (Nardil)
PTSD	Medications to reduce anxiety, depression, and insomnia associated with PTSD
ADD/ADHD	Methylphenidate (Ritalin, Concerta), amphetamine dextroamphetamine (Adderall), pemoline (Cylert), atomoxetine (Strattera)

PROCEDURES

Procedures related to mental disorders in ICD-10-PCS can be located in the following tables:

GZ1-GZJ	Mental Health
HZ2-HZ9	Substance Abuse

Some procedures would be appropriate for mental disorders such as detoxification and/or rehabilitation for alcohol and drug abuse. Sometimes, a patient's medical condition is stabilized in a hospital setting, and then the patient is transferred to a facility that is better equipped to offer specialized mental health care. Facility policy may determine which procedures are coded or assigned by the facility.

Electroconvulsive Therapy

Electroconvulsive therapy (ECT) is a treatment in which electricity is used to induce seizures. The procedure root type is electroconvulsive therapy. ECT is usually only considered when patients have not responded well to drug therapies. It is primarily used to treat severe depression and other disorders such as schizophrenia, mania, or catatonia. A course of treatments usually consists of 6-12 treatments, but may be more or may be less. To code an ECT treatment, the root operation is electroconvulsive therapy, and character 4 is the qualifier that identifies the treatment as:

- 0 Unilateral – single seizure
- 1 Unilateral – multiple seizure
- 2 Bilateral – single seizure
- 3 Bilateral – multiple seizure
- 4 Other ECT

EXAMPLE

ECT treatment which bilateral single seizure GZB2ZZZ

SECTION	BODY SYSTEM	TYPE	QUALIFIER	QUALIFIER	QUALIFIER	QUALIFIER
Mental Health	None	Electroconvulsive Therapy	Bilateral-Single Seizure	None	None	None
G	Z	B	2	Z	Z	Z

Detoxification and Rehabilitation

Detoxification is the active management of withdrawal symptoms in a patient who is physically dependent on alcohol or drugs. The procedure root type for detoxification is detoxification services. It consists of evaluation, observation, and monitoring, along with administration of thiamine, multivitamins, and other medications as needed. Detoxification for alcohol may require a 4- to 5-day period; depending on the drug, it may go on for days or months.

Rehabilitation is a structured program with the goal to stop and recover from the use of alcohol and/or drugs. The procedure root type for rehabilitation is counseling and/or psychotherapy. Many different types of programs are available in a variety of settings; these include inpatient, outpatient, day treatment, residential treatment, half-way houses, and so forth.

Facility policy will determine the coding of these procedures. In the hospital setting, a patient may be treated to prevent alcohol and drug withdrawal, or to alleviate symptoms of withdrawal, but this may not constitute true detoxification.

EXERCISE 14-11

Assign codes for all diagnoses and procedures.

1. Electroconvulsive therapy for schizophrenia __________
2. Detoxification and rehabilitation (12-step group counseling) for chronic alcoholism, continuous __________
3. Detoxification for heroin dependence, daily use __________

CHAPTER REVIEW EXERCISE

Assign codes for all diagnoses and procedures.

1. Dysthymic disorder __________
2. Panic disorder with agoraphobia __________
3. Fragile X syndrome with IQ of 25; family history of intellectual disability __________
4. Inhalant abuse __________
5. Tourette's syndrome __________
6. Malnutrition due to anorexia nervosa __________
7. Alcoholism, in remission with 1 year sobriety __________
8. Intellectual disability due to chickenpox 2 years ago __________
9. Alcoholic cardiomyopathy __________
10. Holiday heart syndrome with atrial fibrillation; patient had a drinking binge over Labor Day weekend. Patient abuses alcohol __________
11. Depression with anxiety __________
12. Social phobia __________
13. Dementia with wandering __________
14. Adjustment disorder with conduct disturbance due to parents' divorce __________
15. Hypochondria __________
16. Gambling addiction __________
17. Psychogenic asthma __________
18. Pica in an adult patient __________
19. Enuresis, psychogenic __________
20. Fear of flying __________

21. Adult patient with history of emotional abuse ______________
22. Parkinson's disease with dementia and related behavioral disturbances ______________
23. Suicidal ideation ______________
24. Unable to tolerate CT scan due to claustrophobia ______________

Write the correct answer(s) in the space(s) provided.

25. List four types of Cluster B personality disorders.

____

____

____

____

26. When are learning disabilities usually recognized?

____

27. List four causes of intellectual disability.

____

____

____

____

CHAPTER GLOSSARY

Affective disorders: category of mental health problems that include major depressive disorders and bipolar disorders.

Attention deficit disorder: common childhood disorder characterized by inattention and impulsivity.

Attention deficit hyperactivity disorder: common childhood disorder characterized by inattention, hyperactivity, and impulsivity.

Bipolar disorder: brain disorder that causes unusual shifts in a person's mood, energy, and ability to function; different from the normal ups and downs that everyone goes through; symptoms of bipolar disorder can be severe.

Cognitive impairment: decline in mental activities associated with thinking, learning, and memory.

Conversion disorder: condition in which a person has some type of sensory or motor (neurologic) symptom(s) that cannot be explained.

Delirium tremens: life-threatening condition that may involve severe mental or neurologic changes such as delirium and/or hallucinations.

Dementia: progressive deterioration of mental faculties characterized by impairment of memory and one or more cognitive impairments such as language, reasoning and judgment, and calculation and problem-solving abilities.

Depression: affective disorder that is characterized by sadness, lack of interest in everyday activities and events, and a sense of worthlessness.

Detoxification: active management of withdrawal symptoms in a patient who is physically dependent on alcohol or drugs.

Dyscalculia: learning disability that affects a child's ability to do mathematical calculations.

Dysgraphia: learning disability that affects a child's ability to coordinate movements such as writing.

Dyslexia: learning disability that affects a child's ability to understand or use spoken or written language.

Eating disorders: group of conditions characterized by abnormal eating habits that may affect an individual's physical and psychological well-being. The most common eating disorders are binge-eating disorder, bulimia nervosa, and anorexia nervosa.

Electroconvulsive therapy: psychiatric treatment in which electricity is used to induce seizures.

Exhibitionism: recurrent intense sexual urges and fantasies of exposing the genitals to an unsuspecting stranger.

Fetishism: recurrent intense sexual urges and fantasies of using inanimate objects for sexual arousal or orgasm. Objects commonly used include female clothing such as shoes, earrings, or undergarments.

Generalized anxiety disorder: chronic, exaggerated worry, tension, and irritability that may be without cause or may be more intense than the situation warrants.

Hypomania: milder form of mania, but this "feel good" mood can change to depression or mania.

Intellectual disability: disorder in which a person's overall intellectual functioning is well below average, with an intelligence quotient (IQ) around 70 or less.

Major depressive disorder: characterized by one or more major depressive episodes with a history of mania, hypomania, or mixed episodes.

Mania: the other side of depression, in which a person feels so good, it is like a "high"; may do risky things.

Masochism: the act or sense of gaining pleasure from experiencing physical or psychological pain.

Mixed mood: alternating between mania and depression very quickly.

Mood disorder: condition that occurs with a change in mood over a prolonged period.

Oppositional defiant disorder: pattern of uncooperative, defiant, and hostile behavior toward authority figures that does not involve major antisocial violations, is not accounted for by the child's developmental stage, and results in significant functional impairment.

Organic brain syndrome: general term used to describe a decrease in mental function due to other physical disease(s).

Panic disorder: terrifying experience that occurs suddenly without warning. Physical symptoms include pounding heart, chest pains, dizziness, nausea, shortness of breath, trembling, choking, fear of dying, sweating, feelings of unreality, numbness, hot flashes or chills, and a feeling of going out of control or "crazy."

Personality disorder: a pattern of behavior that can disrupt many aspects of a person's life.

Phobia: irrational anxiety or fear that can interfere with one's everyday life or daily routine.

Posttraumatic stress disorder: anxiety disorder that is triggered by memories of a traumatic event.

Psychosis: impairment in mental state in which perception of reality has become distorted.

Rehabilitation: structured program with the goal of stopping and recovering from the use of alcohol and/or drugs.

Sadism: the act or sense of gaining pleasure from inflicting physical or psychological pain on another.

Schizoaffective disorder: condition in which a person experiences a combination of schizophrenia symptoms while exhibiting mood disorder symptoms, such as mania or depression.

Schizophrenia: disorder of the brain characterized by trouble differentiating between real and unreal experiences, along with problems with logical thinking, normal emotional responses to others, and appropriate behavior in social situations.

Transvestism: assuming the appearance, manner, or roles traditionally associated with members of the opposite sex (cross-dressing).

Voyeurism: recurrent intense sexual urges and fantasies involving observing unsuspecting people who are naked, disrobing, or engaging in sexual activity.

15

Diseases of the Nervous System, Diseases of the Eye and Adnexa, and Diseases of the Ear and Mastoid Process

(ICD-10-CM Chapter 6, Codes G00-G99, Chapter 7, Codes H00-H59, and Chapter 8, Codes H60-H95)

CHAPTER OUTLINE

LEARNING OBJECTIVES

1. Apply and assign the correct ICD-10-CM/PCS codes in accordance with Official Guidelines for Coding and Reporting
2. Identify pertinent anatomy and physiology of the nervous system and sense organs
3. Identify diseases of the nervous system and sense organs
4. Assign the correct Z codes and procedure codes related to the nervous system and sense organs
5. Identify common treatments, medications, laboratory values, and diagnostic tests

ABBREVIATIONS/ ACRONYMS

CNS central nervous system
CPAP continuous positive airway pressure
CSF cerebrospinal fluid
CVA cerebrovascular accident
DBS deep brain stimulation
EEG electroencephalogram
EMG electromyelogram
ICD-10-CM *International Classification of Diseases, 10th Revision, Clinical Modification*
ICD-10-PCS *International Classification of Diseases, 10th Revision, Procedure Coding System*
IOL intraocular lens
IOP intraocular pressure
IV intravenous
LP lumbar puncture
MCI mild cognitive impairment
MRI magnetic resonance imaging
NPH normal pressure hydrocephalus
OM otitis media
OSA obstructive sleep apnea
PDT photodynamic therapy
SIRS systemic inflammatory response syndrome
SOM serous otitis media
TIA transient ischemic attack
VPS ventriculoperitoneal shunt
VNS vagal nerve stimulator

ICD-10-CM Official Guidelines for Coding and Reporting (2021-2022)

Please refer to the companion Evolve website for the most current 2021-2022 guidelines.

6. Chapter 6: Diseases of the Nervous System (G00-G99)

a. Dominant/nondominant side

Codes from category G81, Hemiplegia and hemiparesis, and subcategories, G83.1, Monoplegia of lower limb, G83.2, Monoplegia of upper limb, and G83.3, Monoplegia, unspecified, identify whether the dominant or nondominant side is affected. Should the affected side be documented, but not specified as dominant or nondominant, and the classification system does not indicate a default, code selection is as follows:

- For ambidextrous patients, the default should be dominant.
- If the left side is affected, the default is non-dominant.
- If the right side is affected, the default is dominant.

EXAMPLE

Patient is admitted to the hospital for treatment of a CVA. Patient has hemiparesis of the right side, I63.9, G81.91.

b. Pain—Category G89

1) General coding information

Codes in category G89, Pain, not elsewhere classified, may be used in conjunction with codes from other categories and chapters to provide more detail about acute or chronic pain and neoplasm-related pain, unless otherwise indicated below.

If the pain is not specified as acute or chronic, post-thoracotomy, postprocedural, or neoplasm-related, do not assign codes from category G89.

A code from category G89 should not be assigned if the underlying (definitive) diagnosis is known, unless the reason for the encounter is pain control/ management and not management of the underlying condition.

When an admission or encounter is for a procedure aimed at treating the underlying condition (e.g., spinal fusion, kyphoplasty), a code for the underlying condition (e.g., vertebral fracture, spinal stenosis) should be assigned as the principal diagnosis. No code from category G89 should be assigned.

EXAMPLE

The patient is admitted with acute chest pain due to pneumonia, J18.9. Only the code for pneumonia would be assigned.

EXAMPLE

The patient is admitted for acute pain control after failing off a ladder and suffering two broken ribs on the right side. The patient was admitted for pain control, G89.11, S22.41xA, W11.xxxA.

(a) Category G89 Codes as Principal or First-Listed Diagnosis

Category G89 codes are acceptable as principal diagnosis or the first-listed code:

- When pain control or pain management is the reason for the admission/encounter (e.g., a patient with displaced intervertebral disc, nerve impingement and severe back pain presents for injection of steroid into the spinal canal). The underlying cause of the pain should be reported as an additional diagnosis, if known.

EXAMPLE

Patient is admitted to the hospital with acute testicular pain. The patient had a vasectomy yesterday, and the physician documents postprocedural pain, G89.18, N50.819.

- When a patient is admitted for the insertion of a neurostimulator for pain control, assign the appropriate pain code as the principal or first-listed diagnosis. When an admission or encounter is for a procedure aimed at treating the underlying condition and a neurostimulator is inserted for pain control during the same admission/encounter, a code for the underlying condition should be assigned as the principal diagnosis and the appropriate pain code should be assigned as a secondary diagnosis.

EXAMPLE

Patient has chronic intractable pain secondary to lumbar spinal stenosis. She is admitted for insertion of a neurostimulator (single array) for pain control. The generator is inserted into the back pocket, and the leads are inserted into the spinal canal via percutaneous approach, G89.29, M48.06, 0JH70BZ, 00HU3MZ.

(b) Use of Category G89 Codes in Conjunction with Site Specific Pain Codes

(i) Assigning Category G89 and Site-Specific Pain Codes

Codes from category G89 may be used in conjunction with codes that identify the site of pain (including codes from chapter 18) if the category G89 code provides additional information. For example, if the code describes the site of the pain, but does not fully describe whether the pain is acute or chronic, then both codes should be assigned.

EXAMPLE

Patient is admitted with acute back pain after being rear-ended by a car while driving her children to school in her car, M54.9, G89.11, V43.52xA.

(ii) Sequencing of Category G89 Codes with Site-Specific Pain Codes

The sequencing of category G89 codes with site-specific pain codes (including chapter 18 codes), is dependent on the circumstances of the encounter/admission as follows:

- If the encounter is for pain control or pain management, assign the code from category G89 followed by the code identifying the specific site of pain (e.g., encounter for pain management for acute neck pain from trauma is assigned code G89.11, Acute pain due to trauma, followed by code M54.2, Cervicalgia, to identify the site of pain).

- If the encounter is for any other reason except pain control or pain management, and a related definitive diagnosis has not been established (confirmed) by the provider, assign the code for the specific site of pain first, followed by the appropriate code from category G89.

EXAMPLE

Patient presents to the ER with acute chest pain secondary to being kicked in the chest by a horse, R07.9, G89.11, W55.12xA.

2) Pain due to devices, implants and grafts

See Section I.C.19. Pain due to medical devices

3) Postoperative Pain

The provider's documentation should be used to guide the coding of postoperative pain, as well as *Section III. Reporting Additional Diagnoses* and *Section IV. Diagnostic Coding and Reporting in the Outpatient Setting.*

The default for post-thoracotomy and other postoperative pain not specified as acute or chronic is the code for the acute form.

Routine or expected postoperative pain immediately after surgery should not be coded.

EXAMPLE

Patient presents to physician's office complaining of chest pain. Patient recently had a lesion removed from the lung. The physician's diagnosis is post-thoracotomy pain, G89.12, R07.9.

(a) Postoperative pain not associated with specific postoperative complication

Postoperative pain not associated with a specific postoperative complication is assigned to the appropriate postoperative pain code in category G89.

(b) Postoperative pain associated with specific postoperative complication

Postoperative pain associated with a specific postoperative complication (such as painful wire sutures) is assigned to the appropriate code(s) found in Chapter 19, Injury, poisoning, and certain other consequences of external causes. If appropriate, use additional code(s) from category G89 to identify acute or chronic pain (G89.18 or G89.28).

EXAMPLE

Patient is 1 month status post TURP. Patient presents to physician's office with acute abdominal pain. After examination and assessment the physician documents acute post–TURP pain, G89.18, R10.9.

4) Chronic pain

Chronic pain is classified to subcategory G89.2. There is no time frame defining when pain becomes chronic pain. The provider's documentation should be used to guide use of these codes.

EXAMPLE

Patient is 2 years status post lumbar laminectomy and is being seen again for chronic low back pain due to the lumbar surgery, G89.28, M54.5.

5) Neoplasm Related Pain

Code G89.3 is assigned to pain documented as being related, associated or due to cancer, primary or secondary malignancy, or tumor. This code is assigned regardless of whether the pain is acute or chronic.

This code may be assigned as the principal or first-listed code when the stated reason for the admission/encounter is documented as pain control/pain management. The underlying neoplasm should be reported as an additional diagnosis.

When the reason for the admission/encounter is management of the neoplasm and the pain associated with the neoplasm is also documented, code G89.3 may be assigned as an additional diagnosis. It is not necessary to assign an additional code for the site of the pain.

See Section I.C.2 for instructions on the sequencing of neoplasms for all other stated reasons for the admission/encounter (except for pain control/pain management).

EXAMPLE

Patient is admitted for pain control due to metastatic bone cancer. Patient has a past history of breast cancer treated with surgical removal of the left breast, G89.3, C79.51, Z85.3, Z90.12.

EXAMPLE

Patient was admitted for back pain due to vertebral metastasis. An MRI indicates that the disease has progressed. Patient has a history of prostate cancer with surgical removal, C79.51, G89.3, Z85.46. Patient's bone mets treated with external beam radiation via the linear accelerator using electrons, DP0C3ZZ.

6) Chronic pain syndrome

Central pain syndrome (G89.0) and chronic pain syndrome (G89.4) are different than the term "chronic pain," and therefore codes should only be used when the provider has specifically documented this condition.

See Section I.C.5. Pain disorders related to psychological factors

7. Chapter 7: Diseases of the Eye and Adnexa (H00-H59)

a. Glaucoma

1) Assigning Glaucoma Codes

Assign as many codes from category H40, Glaucoma, as needed to identify the type of glaucoma, the affected eye, and the glaucoma stage.

2) Bilateral glaucoma with same type and stage

When a patient has bilateral glaucoma and both eyes are documented as being the same type and stage, and there is a code for bilateral glaucoma, report only the code for the type of glaucoma, bilateral, with the seventh character for the stage.

When a patient has bilateral glaucoma and both eyes are documented as being the same type and stage, and the classification does not provide a code for bilateral glaucoma (i.e. subcategories H40.10 and H40.20) report only one code for the type of glaucoma with the appropriate seventh character for the stage.

3) Bilateral glaucoma stage with different types or stages

When a patient has bilateral glaucoma and each eye is documented as having a different type or stage, and the classification distinguishes laterality, assign the appropriate code for each eye rather than the code for bilateral glaucoma.

When a patient has bilateral glaucoma and each eye is documented as having a different type, and the classification does not distinguish laterality (i.e. subcategories H40.10 and H40.20), assign one code for each type of glaucoma with the appropriate seventh character for the stage.

When a patient has bilateral glaucoma and each eye is documented as having the same type, but different stage, and the classification does not distinguish laterality (i.e. subcategories H40.10 and H40.20), assign a code for the type of glaucoma for each eye with the seventh character for the specific glaucoma stage documented for each eye.

4) Patient admitted with glaucoma and stage evolves during the admission

If a patient is admitted with glaucoma and the stage progresses during the admission, assign the code for highest stage documented.

5) Indeterminate stage glaucoma

Assignment of the seventh character "4" for "indeterminate stage" should be based on the clinical documentation. The seventh character "4" is used for glaucomas whose stage cannot be clinically determined. This seventh character should not be confused with the seventh character "0", unspecified, which should be assigned when there is no documentation regarding the stage of the glaucoma.

b. Blindness

If "blindness" or "low vision" of both eyes is documented but the visual impairment category is not documented, assign code H54.3, Unqualified visual loss, both eyes. If "blindness" or "low vision" in one eye is documented but the visual impairment category is not documented, assign a code from H54.6-, Unqualified visual loss, one eye. If "blindness" or "visual loss" is documented without any information about whether one or both eyes are affected, assign code H54.7, Unspecified visual loss.

EXAMPLE

Patient presents to ophthalmologist's office and is diagnosed with bilateral chronic angle closure glaucoma. Both eyes are mild stage, H40.2231.

EXAMPLE

Patient presents to ophthalmologist's office with bilateral acute angle closure glaucoma, right eye with moderate stage and left eye with severe, H40.213.

EXAMPLE

Glaucoma suspect in both eyes, H40.003.

8. Chapter 8: Diseases of Ear and Mastoid Process (H60-H95)
Reserved for future guideline expansion

ANATOMY AND PHYSIOLOGY

The nervous system is composed of specialized tissue that controls the actions and reactions of the body and the way it adjusts to changes that occur inside and outside the body. The nervous system is divided into two main systems: the central nervous system and the peripheral nervous system (Figures 15-1 and 15-2). The central nervous system and the peripheral nervous system are each further divided into two parts. The central nervous system is made up of the brain and the spinal cord, and the peripheral nervous system is made up of the somatic nervous system and the autonomic nervous system.

Central Nervous System

Different areas of the brain are in control of different functions of the body (Figure 15-3). For example, the cerebral cortex controls thought, language, and reasoning; the brain stem is in control of breathing and blood pressure; and the hippocampus is in control of memory and learning. The spinal cord serves as a pathway for information passing from the brain to the peripheral nervous system. Both the brain and the spinal cord are covered by bone—the brain by the skull, and the spinal cord by the vertebral column; both are covered by membranes called the meninges. The meninges (Figure 15-4) are made up of three layers: dura, arachnoid, and pia. In the spinal column, the dura is not attached to the vertebrae but is separated from them by the epidural space. The purpose of these membranes is to protect the brain and the spinal cord.

The spinal cord, which is located in the vertebral foramen, consists of 31 segments, each of which has a pair of spinal nerves that exit from the segment. The purpose of the spinal cord is to conduct nerve impulses and spinal reflexes.

Peripheral Nervous System

The peripheral nervous system connects the central nervous system to other parts of the body. It may be broken down into two parts: the somatic nervous system and the autonomic nervous system. The **somatic nervous system** sends sensory information (taste, hearing, smell, and vision) to the central nervous system (CNS) and motor nerve impulses to the skeletal muscles.

The **autonomic nervous system** has both sensory and motor functions that involve the CNS and the internal organs. Actions produced by this system, such as beating of the heart muscle, are for the most part involuntary.

DISEASE CONDITIONS

Diseases of the Nervous System (G00-G99), Chapter 6 in the ICD-10-CM code book, Diseases of the Eye and Adnexa (H00-H59), Chapter 7 in the ICD-10-CM code book, and Diseases of the Ear and Mastoid Process (H60-95), Chapter 8 in the ICD-10-CM code book, are divided into the following categories:

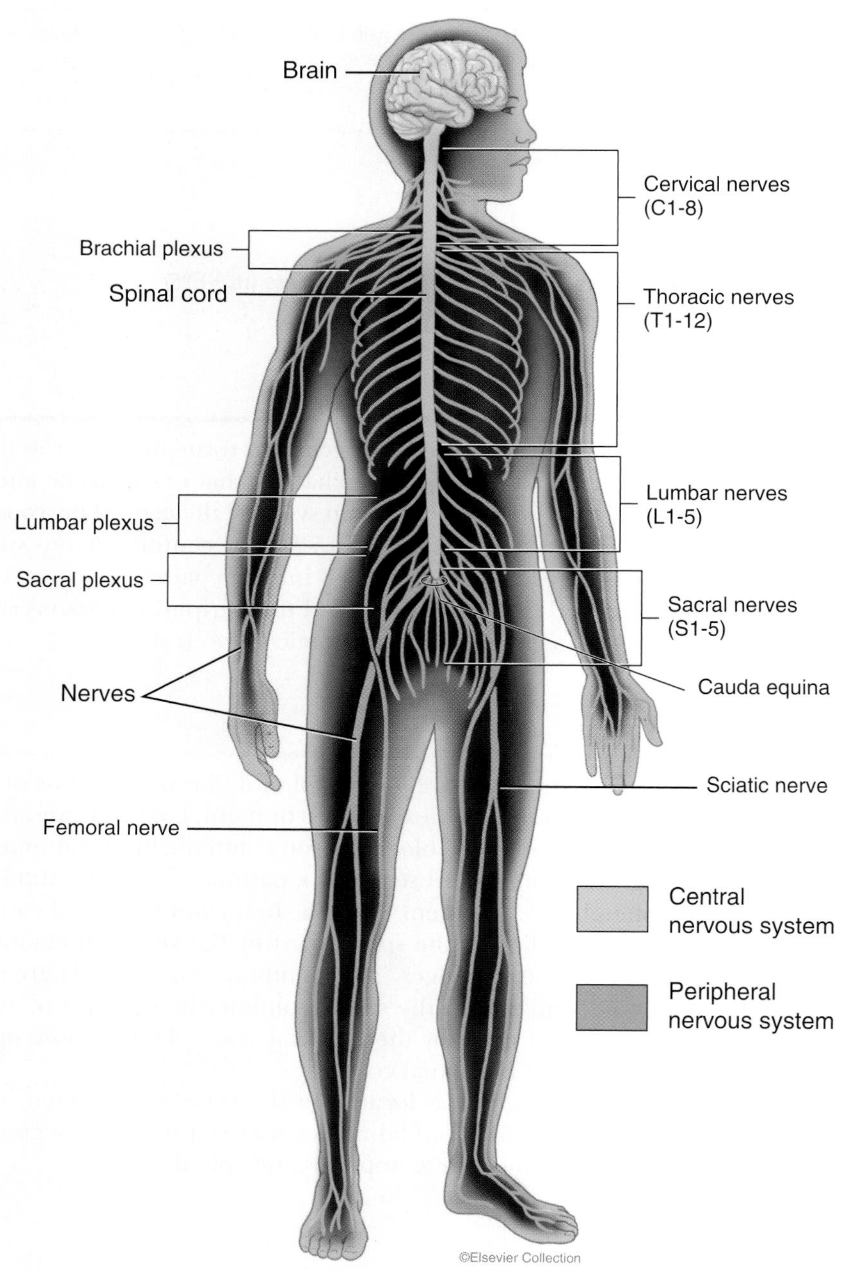

FIGURE 15-1. The brain and the spinal cord, spinal nerves, and spinal plexuses.

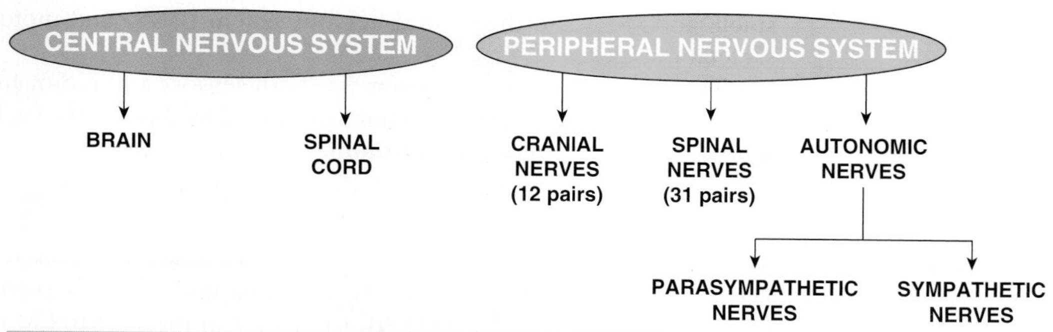

FIGURE 15-2. Divisions of the central nervous system (CNS) and peripheral nervous system (PNS). The autonomic nervous system is a part of the peripheral nervous system.

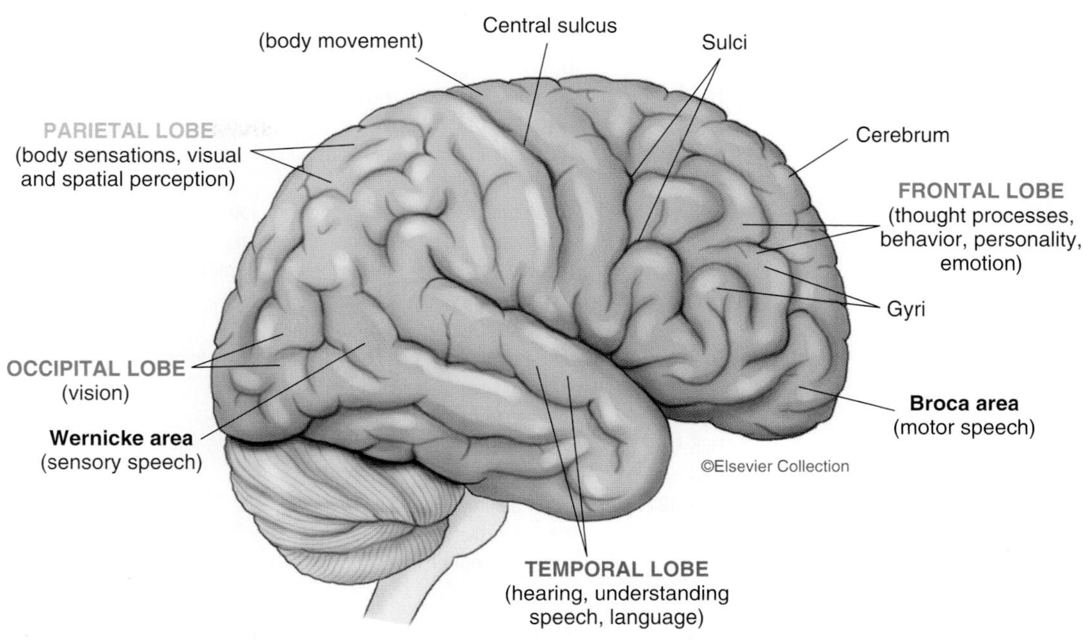

FIGURE 15-3. Left cerebral hemisphere (lateral view). Gyri (convolutions) and sulci (fissures) are indicated. Note the lobes of the cerebrum and the functional centers that control speech, vision, movement, hearing, thinking, and other processes.

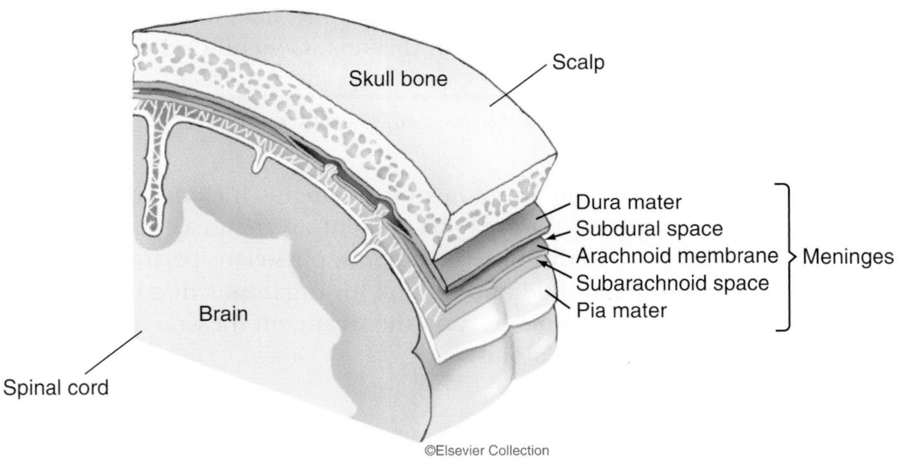

FIGURE 15-4. Meninges.

CATEGORY	SECTION TITLE
G00-G09	Inflammatory diseases of the central nervous system
G10-G14	Systemic atrophies primarily affecting the central nervous system
G20-G26	Extrapyramidal and movement disorders
G30-G32	Other degenerative diseases of the nervous system
G35-G37	Demyelinating diseases of the central nervous system
G40-G47	Episodic and paroxysmal disorders
G50-G59	Nerve, nerve root, and plexus disorders
G60-G65	Polyneuropathies and other disorders of the peripheral nervous system
G70-G73	Diseases of myoneural junction and muscle
G80-G83	Cerebral palsy and other paralytic syndromes
G89-G99	Other disorders of the nervous system
H00-H05	Disorders of eyelid, lacrimal system, and orbit

CATEGORY	SECTION TITLE
H10-H11	Disorders of the conjunctiva
H15-H22	Disorders of sclera, cornea, iris, and ciliary body
H25-H28	Disorders of the lens
H30-H36	Disorders of the choroid and retina
H40-H42	Glaucoma
H43-H44	Disorders of the vitreous body and globe
H46-H47	Disorders of the optic nerve and visual pathways
H49-H52	Disorders of ocular muscles, binocular movement, accommodation, and refraction
H53-H54	Visual disturbances and blindness
H55-H57	Other disorders of eye and adnexa
H59	Intraoperative and postprocedural complications and disorders of eye and adnexa, not elsewhere classified
H60-H62	Diseases of external ear
H65-H75	Diseases of middle ear and mastoid
H80-H83	Diseases of the inner ear
H90-H94	Other disorders of ear
H95	Intraoperative and postprocedural complications and disorders of ear and mastoid process, not elsewhere classified

Inflammatory Diseases of the Central Nervous System (G00-G09)

Meningitis is an infection or inflammation of the meninges. Meningitis is caused by a viral or bacterial organism and may be treated with antibiotics. Vaccines are available to prevent meningitis that is due to *Streptococcus pneumoniae.* It should be noted that often, coding of meningitis requires two codes, and in most cases, the Tabular List instructs to code the underlying condition first. For more information on coding guidelines for underlying conditions, refer to Chapter 5 in this text, General Coding Guidelines.

EXAMPLE

The patient was treated for meningitis due to Lyme disease, A69.21.

The signs and symptoms of meningitis include high fever, headache, and stiff neck. Other symptoms that may be present are nausea, vomiting, sleepiness, and sensitivity to bright lights. To diagnose meningitis, physicians perform a lumbar puncture (Figure 15-5) to obtain spinal fluid and to look for organisms that may be present. Bacterial meningitis is treated with antibiotics, and the treatment for viral meningitis (aseptic) is usually limited to treating the symptoms.

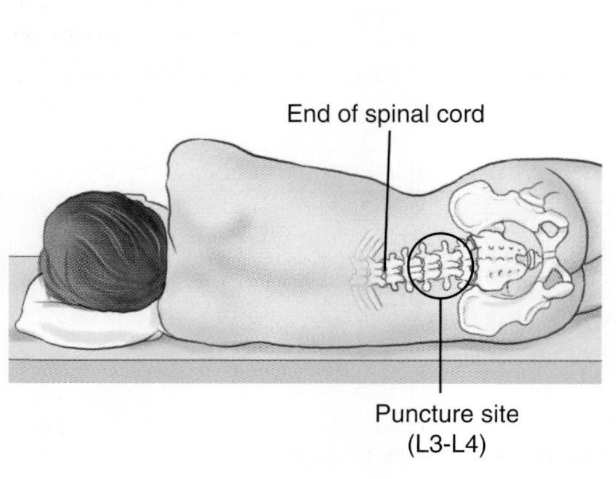

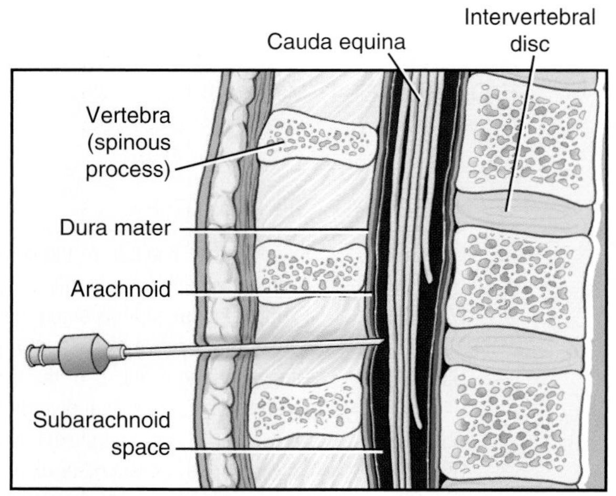

FIGURE 15-5. Lumbar (spinal) puncture. The patient lies laterally, with the knees drawn up to the abdomen and the chin brought down to the chest. This position increases the spaces between the vertebrae. The lumbar puncture needle is inserted between the third and fourth (or fourth and fifth) lumbar vertebrae, and it enters the subarachnoid space.

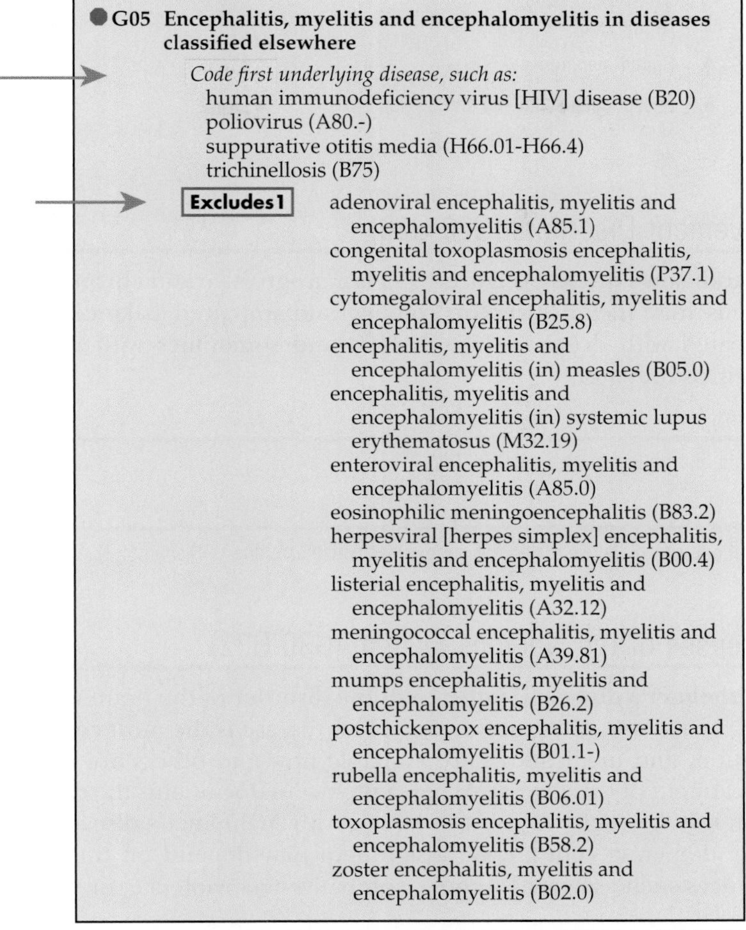

● **G05 Encephalitis, myelitis and encephalomyelitis in diseases classified elsewhere**

Code first underlying disease, such as:
human immunodeficiency virus [HIV] disease (B20)
poliovirus (A80.-)
suppurative otitis media (H66.01-H66.4)
trichinellosis (B75)

Excludes1 adenoviral encephalitis, myelitis and encephalomyelitis (A85.1)
congenital toxoplasmosis encephalitis, myelitis and encephalomyelitis (P37.1)
cytomegaloviral encephalitis, myelitis and encephalomyelitis (B25.8)
encephalitis, myelitis and encephalomyelitis (in) measles (B05.0)
encephalitis, myelitis and encephalomyelitis (in) systemic lupus erythematosus (M32.19)
enteroviral encephalitis, myelitis and encephalomyelitis (A85.0)
eosinophilic meningoencephalitis (B83.2)
herpesviral [herpes simplex] encephalitis, myelitis and encephalomyelitis (B00.4)
listerial encephalitis, myelitis and encephalomyelitis (A32.12)
meningococcal encephalitis, myelitis and encephalomyelitis (A39.81)
mumps encephalitis, myelitis and encephalomyelitis (B26.2)
postchickenpox encephalitis, myelitis and encephalomyelitis (B01.1-)
rubella encephalitis, myelitis and encephalomyelitis (B06.01)
toxoplasmosis encephalitis, myelitis and encephalomyelitis (B58.2)
zoster encephalitis, myelitis and encephalomyelitis (B02.0)

FIGURE 15-6. Refer to the Excludes notes for further instruction if an underlying disease is causing encephalitis, myelitis, and encephalomyelitis.

EXAMPLE Patient is admitted for meningitis due to chickenpox, B01.0.

EXAMPLE Patient is being treated for *Pseudomonas* meningitis, G00.8, B96.5.

Additional disease conditions found in the section on Inflammatory Diseases of the Central Nervous System often require the use of two codes and include the instruction to code first the underlying condition. It is also important to follow the Excludes notes for further instruction (Figure 15-6).

EXAMPLE Patient is being treated for encephalitis due to AIDS, B20, G05.3.

EXAMPLE The patient was admitted with herpes encephalitis, B00.4.

EXERCISE 15-1

Assign codes to the following conditions.

1. Meningitis due to *Salmonella* ____________
2. *Klebsiella pneumoniae* meningitis ____________

3. Gram-negative meningitis ______________
4. Spinal meningitis ______________
5. Encephalitis following chickenpox ______________

Extrapyramidal and Movement Disorders (G20-G26)

Parkinson's disease (Figure 15-7) is a progressive and chronic motor system disorder. Symptoms may include tremor, rigidity, and impaired balance or coordination. It is usually treated with drugs such as L-dopa and sometimes with implantation of an intracranial neurostimulator.

EXAMPLE Patient with Parkinson's disease, G20.

EXAMPLE Patient was diagnosed one year ago with parkinsonism due to Risperdal, G21.11, T43.595S.

Other Degenerative Diseases of the Nervous System (G30-G32)

Alzheimer's disease (Figure 15-8) is a disorder of the brain that causes a progressive decline in mental and physical function. This disease is the most common cause of mental deterioration, and medications are available now and others are in development to assist in the treatment of this disease. When a physician documents the condition as Alzheimer's dementia, it is necessary to use two codes, with Alzheimer's disease sequenced first. For many of the dementia codes, code assignment may depend on the presence of behavioral disturbances such as aggressiveness, combativeness, violence, or wandering off.

EXAMPLE Patient has Alzheimer's dementia without behavioral disturbance, G30.9, F02.80.

Cognitive impairment is characterized by problems with memory or thinking beyond that explained by normal aging. There is a higher risk for developing Azheimer's for those diagnosed with mild cognitive impairment. The symptoms of MCI include forgetting recent

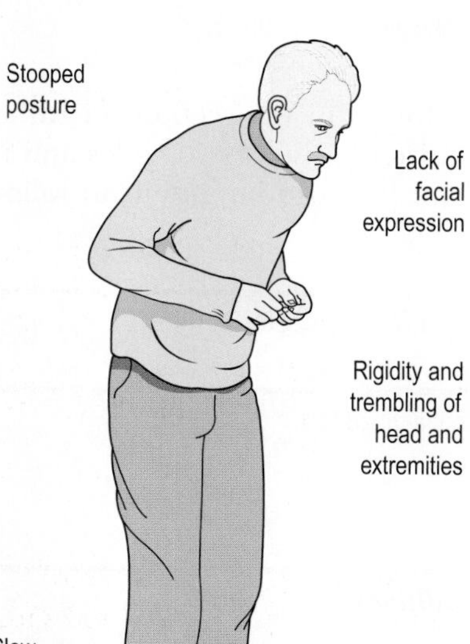

FIGURE 15-7. Typical shuffling gait and posture of patients with Parkinson's disease.

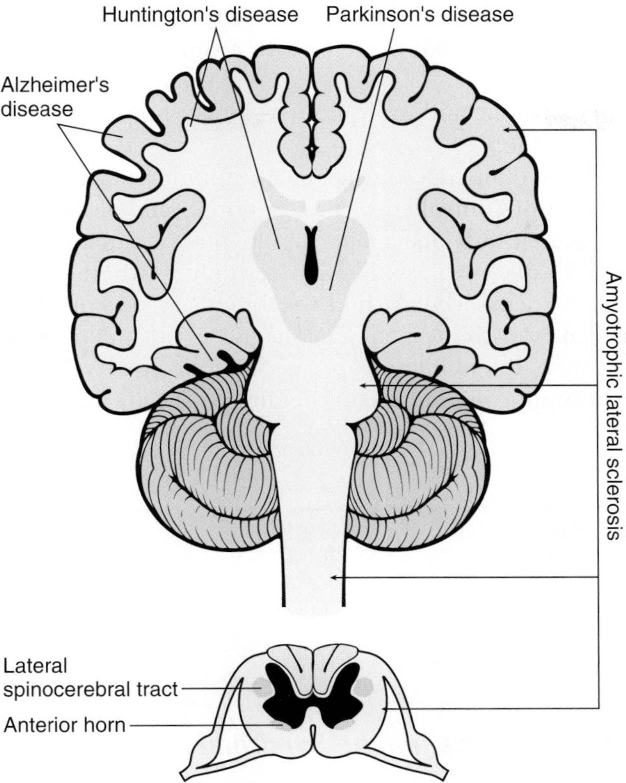

FIGURE 15-8. Degenerative diseases of the brain preferentially involve various parts of the brain. Alzheimer's disease causes atrophy of the frontal and occipital cortical gyri. Huntington's disease affects the frontal cortex and basal ganglia. Parkinson's disease is marked by changes in the substantia nigra. Amyotrophic lateral sclerosis affects the motor neurons in the anterior horn of the spinal cord, brain stem, and frontal cortex of the brain.

events or conversations, diffictulty performing more than one task at a time, difficulty solving problems, and taking a longer time to perform difficult mental activities.

Episodic and Paroxysmal Disorders (G40-G47)

Epilepsy is a disorder of the brain that is characterized by abnormal electrical discharges from the brain cells. Recurrent seizures are the main symptom of epilepsy. Two major types of seizures can occur: generalized and partial. Seizures may present in a variety of forms; patients may lose consciousness, their arms and legs may jerk, they may become incontinent, or they may stare blankly, unaware of their surroundings.

Epilepsy has many causes; however, in approximately half of the cases, the cause is unknown. Epilepsy may be inherited, or it may be caused by injury to the brain, metabolic disturbances, alcohol and drug abuse, brain tumor, infection, stroke, fever, or it may occur in pregnancy. Epilepsy is generally treated with anticonvulsants such as Dilantin or Depakote, although in severe uncontrolled cases, surgery may be performed on the brain to remove the area of the brain where seizures originate. The most common diagnostic test for epilepsy is an electroencephalogram (EEG).

Different Types of Seizures

- Localization-related (begin in a specific part of the brain)
    - Simple partial—a seizure that presents with abnormal sensations (jerking, smells, abnormal motor movements) where the patient does not lose consciousness
    - Complex partial—a seizure that presents with alteration in consciousness causing confusion

- Generalized seizures (affect both hemispheres of the brain)
  - Absence—a seizure that presents with a short lapse of consciousness, most often seen in children
  - Atonic, myoclonic, and tonic-clonic—loss of muscle control resulting in collapse or jerking movements

Epilepsy may be defined as intractable or not intractable. **Intractable** epilepsy is defined as epilepsy that is not controlled by medication. Some of the other terms that are synonymous with intractable are pharmacoresistant, treatment resistant, refractory, and poorly controlled. In ICD-10-CM the sixth character defines whether the patient has status epilepticus. Status epilepticus occurs when the brain is in a continous state of seizure. Status epilepticus is a medical emergency. A diagnosis of epilepsy may have legal or personal implication, such as the ability to operate machinery or vehicles. Just as in all diagnoses, documentation supporting the use of the diagnosis code should be recorded by the healthcare provider.

EXAMPLE Patient was admitted for intractable epilepsy, G40.919.

EXAMPLE Patient is being treated for progressive myoclonic epilepsy, G40.309.

Migraines and Other Headache Syndromes

Migraines are a chronic condition with recurrent headaches that are often associated with neurological symptoms such as nausea and vomiting, sensitivity to light and sound, visual disturbances, numbness, tingling, and fatigue/weakness. A migraine can last from an hour up to 72 hours. Migraines with aura account for 25% of all migraines. Aura is the neurological symptoms that are like a warning sign that start about an hour or so of the migraine. Women between the ages of 25 to 55 are more likely to suffer from migraines than men. The menstrual migraine is thought to occur due to the drop in hormones just before a woman's period. Migraines can be further classified as intractable and with or without status migrainosus. As with intractable epilepsy, other terms that are considered equivalent to intractable are pharmacoresistant, treatment resistant, refractory, and poorly controlled. Status migrainosus should be documented by the provider and usually indicates that the migraine has lasted for more than 72 hours.

Category G44 Other headache syndromes classifies the following types of headaches:

- Cluster headaches
- Vascular headaches
- Tension-type headaches
- Post-traumatic headaches
- Drug-induced headaches
- Complicated headache syndromes
- Other specified headache syndromes

EXAMPLE Patient was seen in the ER for severe headache that started yesterday. Patient was diagnosed and treated for intractable chronic tension headache, G44.221.

Transient Ischemic Attack

A **transient ischemic attack** (TIA) is a stroke that lasts for only a few minutes. Patients who present with a TIA usually have the same symptoms as occur with a stroke. Most symptoms of a TIA are gone within an hour, but they may last up to 24 hours. A TIA does not result in a cerebral infarction.

Sleep Disorders

Some typical sleep problems include **insomnia**, (difficulty falling asleep, staying asleep, wakefulness, and early morning awakening) and **hypersomnia** (excessive sleep). These problems are classified in this section when they are caused by a physiological condition.

EXAMPLE The patient is being treated for insomnia, G47.00.

Sleep apnea is a disorder that is characterized by breathing interruption during sleep. These patients awaken many times during the night to regain their breathing. This disorder results in sleep deprivation and can be life threatening. Sleep apnea can result in a drop in the oxygen saturation of blood and is a cause of daytime **somnolence** (sleepiness). A person is more likely to have obstructive sleep apnea (OSA) if they are overweight, snore loudly, are hypertensive, or have a family history of sleep apnea. This obstruction occurs when there is a blockage in the airway. Obstructive sleep apnea is diagnosed by a sleep study or polysomnogram. Patients may be treated with a CPAP (continuous positive airway pressure) mask. This mask helps push air into the breathing pathway. There are also surgical procedures to correct the obstruction.

Central sleep apnea occurs when the brain does not signal the muscles to breathe. This might occur in a stroke victim that has nervous system dysfunction or in patients that have neurodegenerative illnesses such as Lou Gehrig's disease.

EXAMPLE Patient has obstructive sleep apnea, G47.33.

Polyneuropathy and Other Disorders of the Peripheral Nervous System (G60-G65)

Critical illnesses polyneuropathy and myopathy are diseases of the nerves and muscles that occur as a complication of severe trauma or infection. These conditions are often diagnosed when there is an unexplained difficulty in weaning the patient from mechanical ventilation. These conditions are often associated with sepsis and are thought to be a manifestation of the systemic inflammatory response syndrome (SIRS).

EXAMPLE Patient is diagnosed with critical illness polyneuropathy, G62.81.

Diseases of the Myoneural Junction and Muscle (G70-G73)

Myasthenia gravis is a chronic **autoimmune disorder** that manifests as muscle weakness of varying degrees. The most frequently affected muscles are those that control the eye, eyelid, face, and swallowing. Myasthenia gravis may be treated with medication, thymectomy, and/or plasmapheresis. Patients who present in crisis may have difficulty breathing and require a ventilator to assist with breathing. These crises may be brought on by many different events, such as infection, stress, or fever.

EXAMPLE Patient was admitted for an acute exacerbation of myasthenia gravis, G70.01.

Muscular dystrophy is a type of myopathy. **Myopathies** are general disorders that affect muscles and usually result in muscle weakening or atrophy. Many disease processes involve myopathies.

EXAMPLE Patient has Graves' myopathy, E05.00, G73.7.

Cerebral Palsy and Other Paralytic Syndromes (G80-G83)

Hemiplegia and hemiparesis (Figure 15-9) describe paralysis of the body that could have a number of causes. One of the most common causes of hemiplegia is a cerebrovascular accident (CVA) (Figure 15-10). When a patient is admitted with an acute CVA and has hemiplegia, it is appropriate to code this condition. According to *Coding Clinic for ICD-10-CM/PCS* (2015:1Q:p25), unilateral weakness that is clearly documented as being associated with a stroke is considered synonymous with hemiparesis/hemiplegia.

EXAMPLE Patient has right-sided dominant spastic hemiparesis, G81.11.

Codes in category G81 and G83.1-G83.3 hemiplegia, hemiparesis, and monoplegia have a fifth character that identifies whether the dominant or non-dominant side is affected. If dominance is not documented in the record but the affected side is documented and there is no default indicated in the classification system, then the default would be as follows:
If the left side is affected, the default is non-dominant.
If the right side is affected, the default is dominant.

Hemiplegia is total paralysis of one side of the body, either of the leg or arm. Hemiparesis is incomplete paralysis of one side of the body or a generalized weakness. Flaccid hemiplegia results in muscle loss, whereas spastic hemiplegia will be defined by uncontrollable muscle spasms.

Sometime hemiplegia/hemiparesis may be a sequela of a stroke. This is not always the case, and sometimes it is just transient in that it rapidly clears. If it were a sequela (late effect) of a stroke, codes would be assigned from category I69. This will be described in more detail in Chapter 16, the circulatory chapter of this book.

Other Disorders of the Nervous System (G89-G99)

To use codes from category G89 the pain should be specified as:

- Pain due to trauma
- Postthoracotomy
- Postprocedural
- Neoplasm-related
- Central pain syndrome or chronic pain syndrome

These codes may be used with other codes to provide more detail about acute or chronic pain. If the cause of the pain (i.e, the underlying condition) is known, then a code from G89 is not used unless the purpose of the encounter is strictly for pain control or management and not for management of the underlying condition.

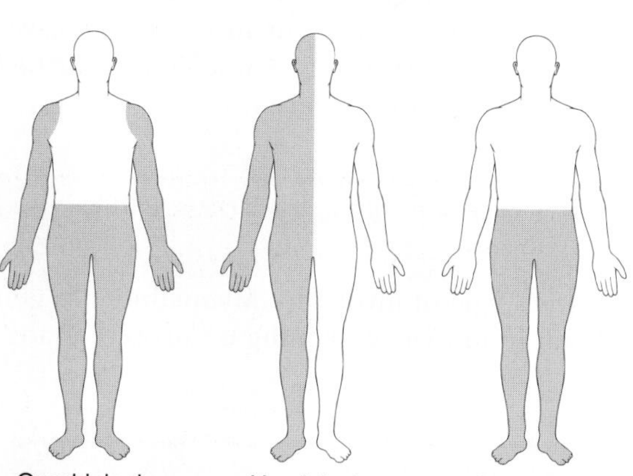

FIGURE 15-9. Types of paralysis.

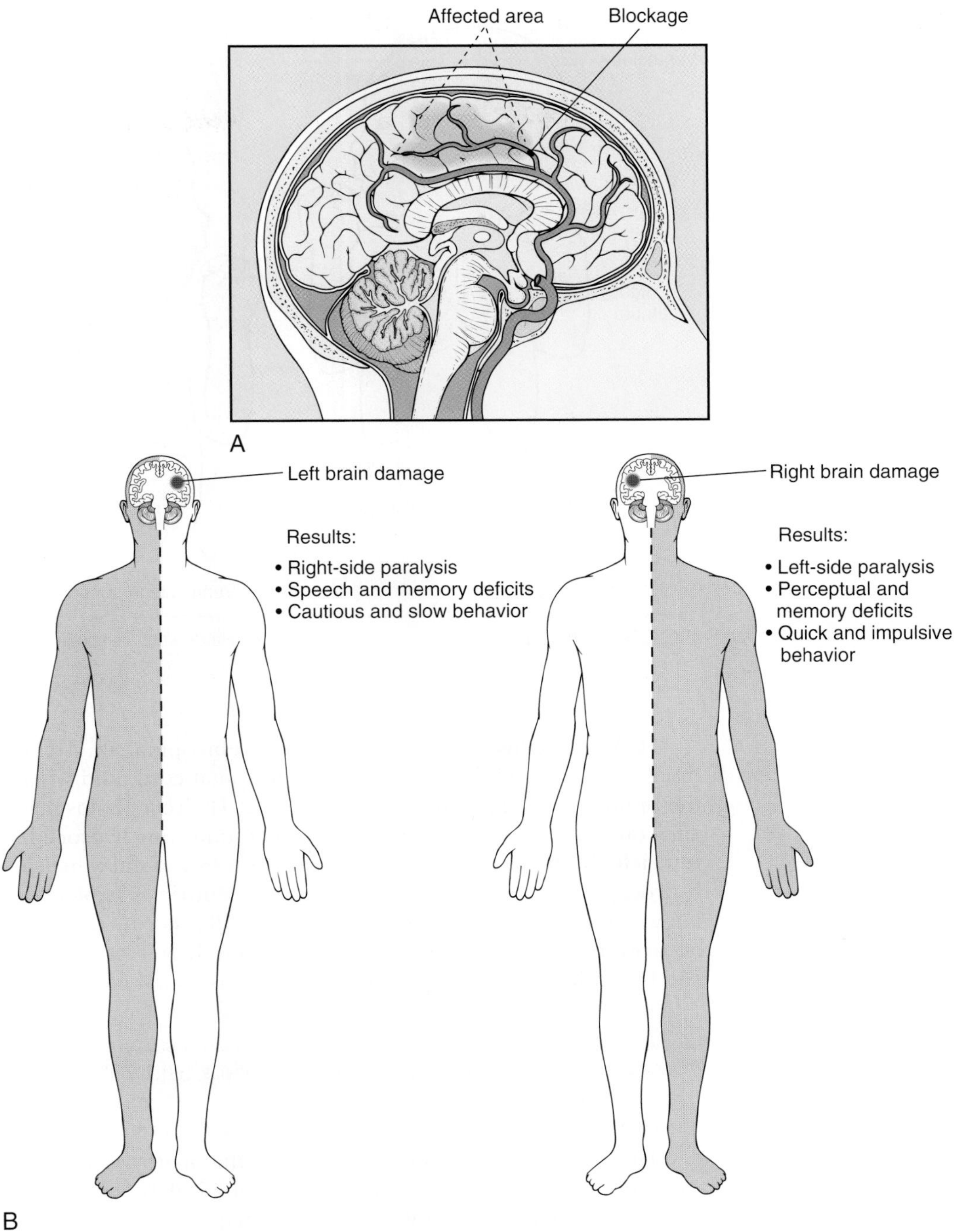

FIGURE 15-10. **A,** Cerebrovascular accident (CVA). **B,** Areas of the body affected by CVA.

Use category G89 codes as the principal or first-listed diagnosis when:

- The patient is admitted for pain management or control that is posttraumatic, postprocedural, postthoracotomy, or neoplasm-related (assign the specific site of the pain secondarily)
- The patient is admitted for the insertion of a neurostimulator for pain control

EXAMPLE

The patient has chronic low back pain secondary to an old automobile accident and is now admitted for pain control, G89.21, M54.5, V89.2xxS.

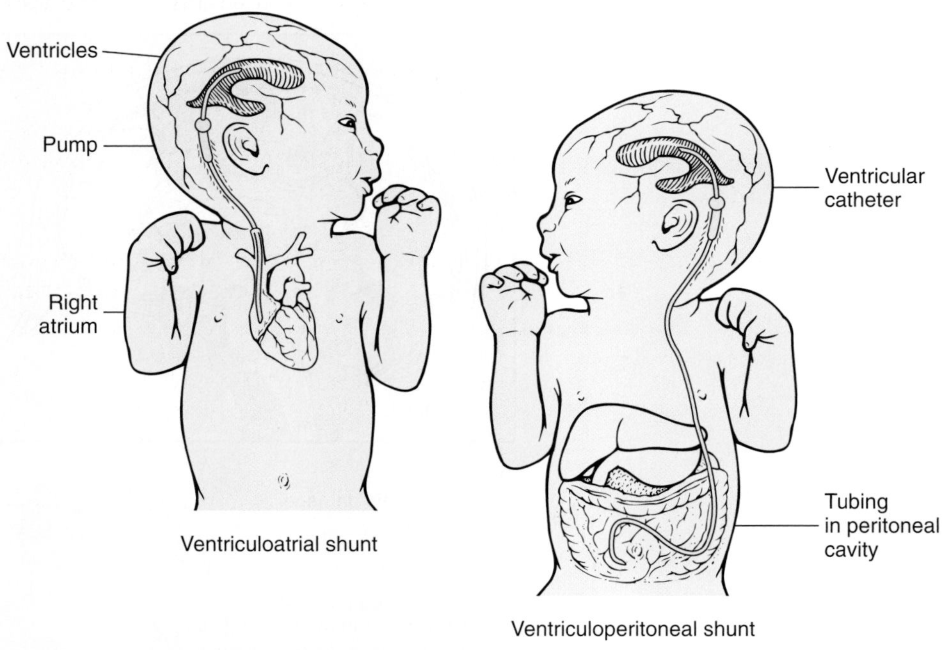

FIGURE 15-11. Shunting procedures for hydrocephalus. Ventriculoperitoneal shunt is the preferred procedure.

Hydrocephalus is excessive water (cerebrospinal fluid) on the brain. Cerebrospinal fluid (CSF) surrounds the brain and the spinal cord, and when this fluid accumulates on the brain, it causes pressure on brain tissue. Hydrocephalus may be acquired or congenital and communicating or obstructive. In communicating hydrocephalus, CSF can flow between ventricles of the brain, but it is blocked upon exit of the ventricle, as opposed to obstructive hydrocephalus, in which the flow between ventricles is blocked. In addition, a condition known as normal pressure hydrocephalus (NPH) occurs in the elderly population and often occurs with dementia. Hydrocephalus is most often treated with a ventricular shunt (Figure 15-11). Hydrocephalus that is left untreated is a fatal condition.

EXAMPLE

The patient has a shunt for noncommunicating hydrocephalus, G91.1, Z98.2.

There are many different types of encephalopathy, so it is important to review the documentation and the subterms in the Alphabetical Index to assign the appropriate code. Usually the encephalopathy is not the principal or first listed diagnosis because it is often due to an underlying cause. Encephalopathy that occurs due to postictal state following a seizure is not coded separately because it is integral to the seizure. Other types of encephalopathy include:

- Anoxic encephalopathy
- Alcoholic encephalopathy
- Hepatic encephalopathy
- Metabolic encephalopathy
- Toxic encephalopathy

Metabolic encephalopathy is temporary or permanent damage to the brain due to lack of glucose, oxygen, metabolic agents, or organ dysfunction. Another term used by physicians to describe this disorder may be acute confusional state. A patient with this condition usually presents with a change in mental status that could denote delirium and may be confused or agitated. Metabolic encephalopathy is a medical emergency. The causes of metabolic encephalopathy include brain tumors, cerebral infarcts, nutritional deficiency, poisoning, alcohol withdrawal, and systemic infection, to name a few. The treatment depends on the underlying cause.

Cerebral edema is an accumulation of water on the brain either intracellular or extracellular. Vasogenic cerebral edema may be caused by malignant hypertension, brain cancer, altitude sickness, or hypertensive encephalopathy. There are other forms of cerebral edema that may be caused by SIADH (syndrome of inappropriate antidiuretic hormone), acidosis, hydrocephalus, and pseudotumor cerebri, and stroke, to name a few. Cerebral edema is not always clinically significant. If a patient has undergone brain surgery, some amount of cerebral edema may be expected and therefore no code would be assigned. If there is any doubt as to the significance of this condition, it is best to query the health care provider.

EXAMPLE

Patient is admitted to the hospital with acute mental status changes. The physician documents that the patient has metabolic encephalopathy secondary to hypernatremia, E87.0, G93.41.

EXAMPLE

Patient has a known glioblastoma multiforme. They are being seen in the ER for severe headache and neck pain. The patient is admitted with cerebral edema due to glioblastoma, C71.9, G93.6.

EXERCISE 15-2

Assign codes to the following conditions.

1. Dementia with Parkinsonism ____________
2. Normal pressure hydrocephalus ____________
3. Seizure disorder ____________
4. Epilepsy, visual type ____________
5. Uncontrolled grand mal epilepsy ____________
6. Status epilepticus ____________
7. Organic hypersomnia ____________
8. Febrile seizures ____________
9. Patient has right-sided hemiplegia, which is a late effect of a stroke ____________
10. Patient is left handed and has hemiparesis affecting the nondominant side ____________
11. Patient is admitted for pain control with acute abdominal pain related to pancreatic cancer ____________
12. Patient is being treated for acute back pain due to previous trauma ____________
13. Patient is admitted for acute neck pain after an automobile accident. Attending plans magnetic resonance imaging (MRI) of the neck to rule out fracture ____________
14. Patient is readmitted for postoperative pain control after emergency appendectomy ____________
15. Patient is admitted for narcotics to treat chronic pain syndrome ____________

DISEASES OF THE EYE AND ADNEXA (H00-H59)

Many eye disorders are treated in the outpatient setting. Some of the conditions commonly found in inpatient records involve injuries to the eye (Figure 15-12), glaucoma, cataracts, macular degeneration, and visual impairment such as blindness. Injuries to the eye are covered in Chapter 20.

Disorders of the Lens (H25-H28)

Cataract (Figure 15-13) is a clouding of the lens of the eye that can cause obstructed vision. Most cataracts are related to the aging process; however, do not use the code for senile cataract just because of a patient's age. The physician must document the type of cataract the patient has. Other risk factors for development of cataracts include smoking, diabetes, and prolonged exposure to sunlight. Cataracts are most often treated by surgery. Possible complications of cataract surgery include retinal detachment, anterior capsule contracture, and aftercataract.

EXAMPLE Patient has a mature senile cataract, H25.89.

Disorders of the Choroid and the Retina (H30-H36)

Macular degeneration (Figure 15-14) is the leading cause of vision loss in the United States. Persons affected by this disease tend to be elderly; vision is lost in the central portion of the eye, leaving the patient with peripheral vision or low vision. Two common types of this disease have been identified: dry and wet. The dry form is more common and is less aggressive than the wet type.

EXAMPLE Patient has exudative macular degeneration, H35.3290.

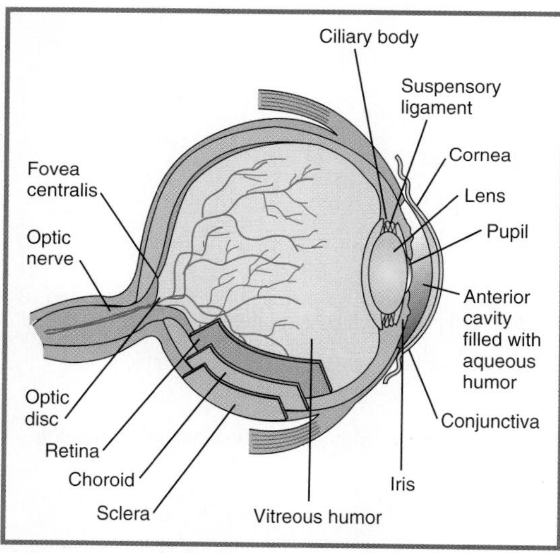

FIGURE 15-12. Normal eye anatomy.

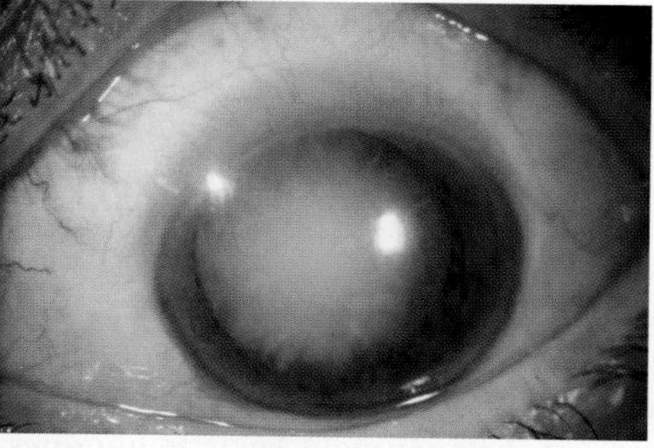

FIGURE 15-13. Cataract. The lens appears cloudy.

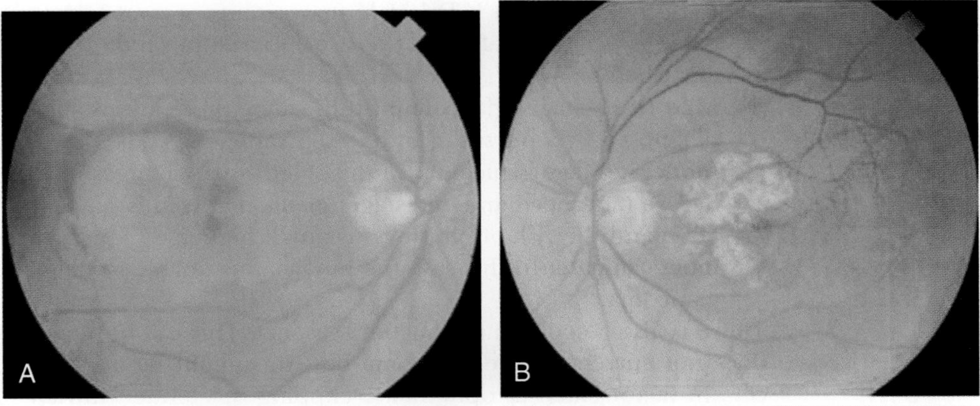

FIGURE 15-14. Macular degeneration. **A,** Wet, atrophic, age-related macular degeneration. **B,** Dry, atrophic, age-related macular degeneration.

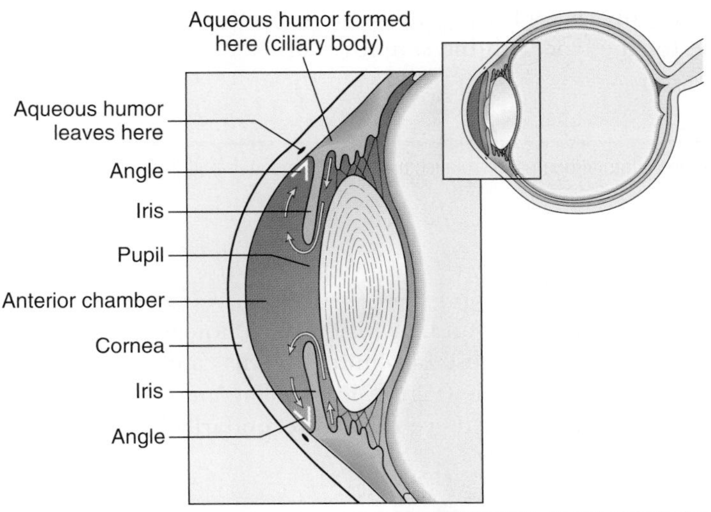

FIGURE 15-15. Glaucoma and circulation of aqueous humor. Circulation is impaired in glaucoma, so that aqueous fluid builds up in the anterior chamber.

Glaucoma (H40-H42)

Glaucoma (Figure 15-15) is a disorder of the optic nerve that may result in vision loss. The most common form is primary open angle glaucoma, in which the drainage canals of the eye become clogged over time and cause intraocular pressure (IOP) to rise; this damages the optic nerve. The four major types of glaucoma are:

- **Open-angle glaucoma** is most common type and is a chronic condition. This disease tends to run in families, and the cause is unknown. Treatment most often consists of eye drops.
- **Angle-closure glaucoma** is an acute form of the disease that occurs when the exit of the aqueous fluid is blocked. This condition causes painful pressure in the eye. Medications and dilating eye drops can cause this condition. Since this is an emergent condition, it may be treated with an iridotomy or IV medications.
- **Congenital glaucoma** is present at birth and is caused by abnormal eye development. Surgery is used most often to correct this condition.
- **Secondary glaucoma** can be caused by a variety of condition, such as trauma, drugs, and systemic diseases

Coding of glaucoma in ICD-10-CM may require several codes. The type of glaucoma and the stage, as well as the affected eye, are important to code selection. The stages of glaucoma are described below:

- **Mild (early-stage) glaucoma:** In this stage there are usually no vision changes. It is diagnosed by a physician by an eye exam.
- **Moderate-stage glaucoma:** In this stage visual changes may be noted.
- **Severe (advanced and end-stage) glaucoma:** In this stage peripheral vision may be gone and the risk of blindness is much higher
- **Indeterminate:** In this case the physician is unable to determine the stage of glaucoma.

There is also a code for a glaucoma suspect. This is a term used to describe a person who does not currently have glaucoma but who might be at risk of developing it because of certain factors such as optic nerve cupping or elevated intraocular pressure. Often these patients are treated by monitoring the risk factors.

The guidelines instruct for coding bilateral glaucoma of the same type and stage to code for bilateral with the seventh character for the stage. If the bilateral glaucoma is of different types or stages and the classification allows for laterality, then code each eye separately. If the bilateral glaucoma is of a different type and there is no laterality distinction, assign a code for each type; the same is true for the same type but different stages. Assign a code for the type with the seventh character for the stage for each eye.

EXAMPLE Patient has bilateral open-angle glaucoma of a mild stage in both eyes, H40.10X1.

Visual Disturbances and Blindness (H53-H54)

Category H54, Blindness and low vision has a note which instructs the coder to list first any associated underlying cause of blindness. This category also refers the coder to the visual impairment category table (Figure 15-16). The most severely affected eye is first in the code title, and the least affected eye is listed secondarily in the code title.

EXAMPLE Blind in the right eye and normal vision in the left eye, H54.41.

EXAMPLE Low vision, both eyes, H54.2.

DISEASES OF THE EAR AND THE MASTOID PROCESS (H60-H95)

Diseases of the Middle Ear and Mastoid (H65-H75)

As with eye conditions, many disorders of the ear (Figure 15-17) are treated in the outpatient setting. At times, inpatient coders see patients with the diagnoses of otitis media, mastoiditis, vertigo, and cholesteatoma, and of course, patients with hearing loss.

Otitis media (OM) is a middle ear infection. It is the most common illness among children and babies. OM often occurs after another illness such as a cold. If the physician describes OM as suppurative, it is purulent or is expressing pus.

EXAMPLE Patient has acute allergic serous otitis media, right ear, H65.111.

Category of visual impairment	Visual acuity with best possible correction	
	Maximum less than:	***Maximum equal to or better than:***
1	6/18 3/10 (0.3) 20/70	6/60 1/10 (0.1) 20/200
2	6/60 1/10 (0.1) 20/200	3/60 1/20 (0.05) 20/400
3	3/60 1/20 (0.05) 20/400	1/60 (finger counting of 1 meter) 1/50 (0.02) 5/300 (20/1200)
4	1/60 (finger counting of meter) 1/50 (0.02) 5/300	Light perception
5	No light perception	
9	Undetermined or unspecfied	

FIGURE 15-16. Visual impairment category table.

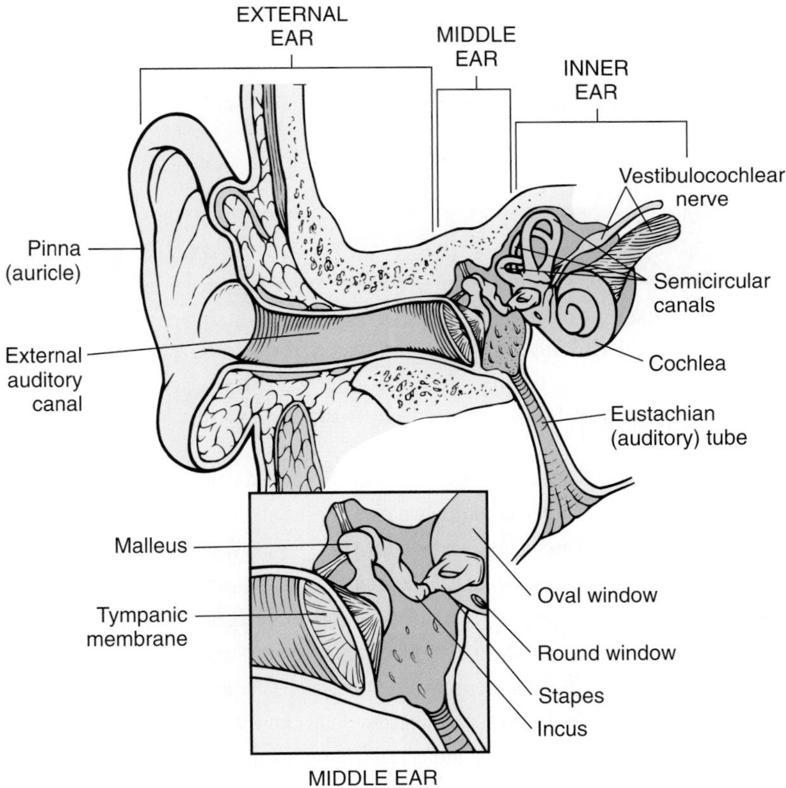

FIGURE 15-17. Normal ear anatomy.

Mastoiditis is an infection of the mastoid bone of the skull. It is often the consequence of untreated OM and may be difficult to treat. Treatment usually consists of antibiotics and, as a last resort, a mastoidectomy to drain and remove the mastoid.

EXAMPLE Patient is being treated for chronic recurrent mastoiditis in left ear, H70.12.

A **cholesteatoma** is a growth in the middle ear that usually results from repeated ear infections. Cholesteatomas may cause hearing loss or dizziness and may require surgery.

EXAMPLE Patient was diagnosed with a right attic cholesteatoma, H71.01.

EXERCISE 15-3

Answer the following questions and assign codes to the following conditions as appropriate.

1. What is the leading cause of vision loss in the United States? ____________
2. Bilateral SOM (serous otitis media) ____________
3. Acute and chronic mastoiditis, right ear ____________
4. Glaucoma suspect, left eye ____________
5. Cataract due to diabetes ____________
6. Meniere's disease, bilateral ____________
7. Papilledema ____________
8. Acquired aphakia, bilateral ____________
9. Acute uveitis ____________
10. Unstable keratoconus of the left eye ____________

FACTORS INFLUENCING HEALTH STATUS AND CONTACT WITH HEALTH SERVICES (Z CODES)

As was discussed in Chapter 9, it is difficult to locate Z codes in the Index. Coders will often say, "I did not know there was a Z code for that." Refer to Chapter 9 for a listing of common main terms used to locate Z codes. A review of the Tabular reveals that some Z codes pertain to diseases of the nervous system.

Z01.00	Encounter for examination of eyes and vision without abnormal findings
Z01.01	Encounter for examination of eyes and vision with abnormal findings
Z01.10	Encounter for examination of eyes and vision without abnormal findings
Z01.110	Encounter for hearing examination following failed hearing screening
Z01.118	Encounter for examination of ears and hearing with other abnormal findings
Z01.12	Encounter for hearing conservation and treatment
Z13.5	Encounter for screening for eye and ear disorders
Z13.858	Encounter for screening for other nervous system disorders
Z44.20	Encounter for fitting and adjustment of artificial eye, unspecified
Z44.21	Encounter for fitting and adjustment of artificial right eye
Z44.22	Encounter for fitting and adjustment of artificial left eye
Z45.320	Encounter for adjustment and management of bone conduction device
Z45.321	Encounter for adjustment and management of cochlear device
Z45.328	Encounter for adjustment and management of other implanted hearing device

Z45.41	Encounter for adjustment and management of cerebrospinal fluid drainage device
Z45.42	Encounter for adjustment and management of neuropacemaker (brain) (peripheral nerve) (spinal cord)
Z45.49	Encounter for adjustment and management of other implanted nervous system device
Z45.82	Encounter for adjustment or removal of myringotomy device (stent) (tube)
Z46.0	Encounter for fitting and adjustment of spectacle and contact lenses
Z46.1	Encounter for fitting and adjustment of hearing aid
Z46.2	Encounter for fitting and adjustment of other devices related to nervous system and special senses
Z52.5	Cornea donor
Z57.0	Occupational exposure to noise
Z79.891	Long-term (current) use of opiate analgesic
Z82.0	Family history of epilepsy and other diseases of the nervous system
Z82.1	Family history of blindness and visual loss
Z82.2	Family history of blindness and hearing loss
Z82.3	Family history of stroke
Z83.511	Family history of glaucoma
Z83.518	Family history of other specified eye disorders
Z83.52	Family history of ear disorders
Z86.61	Personal history of infections of the central nervous system
Z86.69	Personal history of other diseases of the nervous system and sense organs
Z90.01	Acquired absence of eyes
Z94.7	Corneal transplant status
Z96.1	Presence of intraocular lens
Z96.20	Presence of otological and audiological implant, unspecified
Z96.21	Cochlear implant status
Z96.22	Myringotomy tube(s) status
Z96.29	Presence of other otological and audiological implants
Z97.0	Presence of artificial eye
Z97.3	Presence of spectacles and contact lenses
Z97.4	Presence of external hearing aid
Z98.2	Presence of cerebrospinal fluid drainage device
Z98.41	Cataract extraction status, right eye
Z98.42	Cataract extraction status, left eye
Z98.49	Cataract extraction status, unspecified eye
Z98.83	Filtering (vitreous) bleb after glaucoma surgery status

EXAMPLE

Patient with previous cornea transplant, Z94.7.

EXERCISE 15-4

Assign codes to the following conditions.

1. Encounter for fitting of glasses __________
2. Patient is status cataract removal and has a history of cornea transplant __________
3. Patient previously had enucleation of right eye __________
4. Patient was screened for glaucoma __________

COMMON TREATMENTS

CONDITION	MEDICATION/TREATMENT
Alzheimer's	Tacrine (Cognex), donepezil hydrochloride (Aricept), rivastigmine tartrate (Exelon), galantamine (Reminyl), memantine HCl (Namenda)
Parkinson's	Entacapone (Comtan), pramipexole dihydrochloride (Mirapex), ropinirole hydrochloride (Requip), Carbidopa-Levodopa (Sinemet)
Epilepsy	Carbamazepine (Tegretol), clonazepam (Klonopin), phenytoin (Dilantin), sodium valproate and valproic acid (Depakote), levetiracetam (Keppra), topiramate (Topamax)
Myasthenia gravis	Neostigmine bromide—oral (Prostigmin), Pyridostigmine (Regonol), (Mestinon)
Muscular dystrophy	Phenytoin (Dilantin), phenytoin (Phenytek), Deltasone
Macular degeneration	Vitamins/Photodynamic surgery
Glaucoma	Eye drops such as Xalatan (prostaglandins), Iopidine (adrenergics), Carbachol (miotic), Timoptic (beta blocker), and Diamox (carbonic anhydrase inhibitors)

PROCEDURES

Procedures related to the nervous system and sense organs in ICD-10-PCS may be found in the following tables:

Central Nervous System	001-00X
Peripheral Nervous System	012-01X
Eye	080-08Y
Ear, Nose, Sinus	090-09W

Lumbar Puncture

Lumbar puncture (LP), also known as spinal tap or spinal puncture (Figure 15-5), is performed both diagnostically and therapeutically. The root operation in ICD-10-PCS for a lumbar puncture is drainage. When LP is performed for diagnosis, the cerebrospinal fluid (CSF) is analyzed for infection, inflammatory diseases such as multiple sclerosis, subarachnoid hemorrhage, and certain types of carcinoma. When LP is done therapeutically, it may be done to decrease spinal fluid pressure in conditions such as normal pressure hydrocephalus, benign intracranial hypertension, or pseudotumor cerebri. The code is listed in the index under "Drainage, spinal canal."

EXAMPLE

Patient presents to the ER with high fever and neck pain. The physician performs a lumbar puncture to rule out meningitis, R50.9, M54.2, 009U3ZX.

SECTION	BODY SYSTEM	ROOT OPERATION	BODY PART	APPROACH	DEVICE	QUALIFIER
Medical and Surgical	Central Nervous System	Drainage	Spinal Canal	Percutaneous	No Device	No Qualifier
0	0	9	U	3	Z	X

Deep Brain Stimulation

A brain stimulator, also known as an intracranial neurostimulator, a **deep brain stimulator** (DBS), or a thalamic stimulator, is used to control tremors in patients with Parkinson's and in those who have the condition of essential tremor. The root operation in ICD-10-PCS for insertion of a neurostimulator is insertion. An electrode is implanted, usually into the thalamus, and then is connected by a wire under the skin to a pulse generator implanted in the chest. Electrical impulses are sent to the thalamus, which in turn, controls tremors.

EXAMPLE

Patient had a deep brain neurostimulator implanted with single array generator placed in the subcutaneous tissue of the chest and percutaneous lead insertion for treatment of intractable essential tremor, G25.0, 0JH60BZ, 00H03MZ.

SECTION	BODY SYSTEM	ROOT OPERATION	BODY PART	APPROACH	DEVICE	QUALIFIER
Medical and Surgical	Subcutaneous Tissue and Fascia	Insertion	Subcutaneous Tissue and Fascia, Chest	Open	Stimulator Generator, Single Array	No Qualifier
0	J	H	6	0	B	Z

SECTION	BODY SYSTEM	ROOT OPERATION	BODY PART	APPROACH	DEVICE	QUALIFIER
Medical and Surgical	Central Nervous System	Insertion	Brain	Percutaneous	Neurostimulator Lead	No Qualifier
0	0	H	0	3	M	Z

Ventricular Shunting

Shunting treatment of hydrocephalus is done to drain fluid from the brain to relieve pressure. The most common type of shunting (ventriculoperitoneal shunt [VPS]) occurs between the ventricles of the brain and the peritoneal cavity. The root operation in ICD-10-PCS for insertion of a ventricular shunt is bypass of the ventricle, cerebral. The excess fluid is drained from the ventricles into the peritoneal cavity, where it is reabsorbed. Sometimes, complications can occur in either the ventricular or the peritoneal part of the shunt. It may be necessary to perform surgery only at the site with the complication.

To correct a complication, it may involve a change of the device which is the taking out or off a device from a body part and putting back an identical or similar device. A revision would involve correcting, to the extent possible, a portion of a malfunctioning device or the position of a displaced device. It is possible that a removal of the device may be necessary.

EXAMPLE

Patient admitted for insertion of ventriculoperitoneal shunt via open aproach for communicating hydrocephalus, G91.0, 00160J6.

SECTION	BODY SYSTEM	ROOT OPERATION	BODY PART	APPROACH	DEVICE	QUALIFIER
Medical and Surgical	Central Nervous System	Bypass	Cerebral Ventricle	Open	Synthetic Substitute	Peritoneal Cavity
0	0	1	6	0	J	6

Vagal Nerve Stimulation

A **vagal nerve stimulator** is a device that is used to treat intractable epilepsy. The root operation in ICD-10-PCS for a vagal nerve stimulator is insertion of a stimulator and insertion of an electrode. This device, which is similar to a heart pacemaker, is inserted into the upper chest and sends electrical current to the vagus nerve in the neck, which in turn travels to the brain and reduces or controls seizures.

EXAMPLE

A patient with intractable epilepsy presents for implantation of a single array neurostimulator pulse generator with leads. The generator was placed in the chest via open procedure and the leads were placed in the neck via percutaneous procedure attached to the vagus nerve, G40.919, 0JH60BZ, 00HE3MZ.

SECTION	BODY SYSTEM	ROOT OPERATION	BODY PART	APPROACH	DEVICE	QUALIFIER
Medical and Surgical	Subcutaneous Tissue and Fascia	Insertion	Subcutaneous Tissue and Fascia, Chest	Open	Stimulator Generator, Single Array	No Qualifier
0	J	H	6	0	B	Z

SECTION	BODY SYSTEM	ROOT OPERATION	BODY PART	APPROACH	DEVICE	QUALIFIER
Medical and Surgical	Central Nervous System	Insertion	Cranial Nerve	Percutaneous	Neurostimulator Lead	No Qualifier
0	0	H	E	3	M	Z

Cataract Extraction

Cataract extraction is usually performed by **phacoemulsification** (Figure 15-18), wherein an incision is made on the side of the cornea and the lens material is softened, broken, and suctioned out. Usually after the lens is removed, an artificial lens is inserted (intraocular lens [IOL]). If the cataract is removed without replacement, the root operation is extraction. If a cataract removal is performed with synchronous replacement of the lens, only the root operation replacement is assigned for lens insertion.

EXAMPLE

Patient is admitted for a mature senile cataract in the right eye to be removed by phacoemulsification with IOL replacement, H25.89, 08RJ3JZ.

SECTION	BODY SYSTEM	ROOT OPERATION	BODY PART	APPROACH	DEVICE	QUALIFIER
Medical and Surgical	Eye	Replacement	Lens, Right	Percutaneous	Synthetic Substitute	No Qualifier
0	8	R	J	3	J	Z

It is important to remember that when bilateral procedures are coded, the procedure code should be coded twice, unless a code is classified as bilateral.

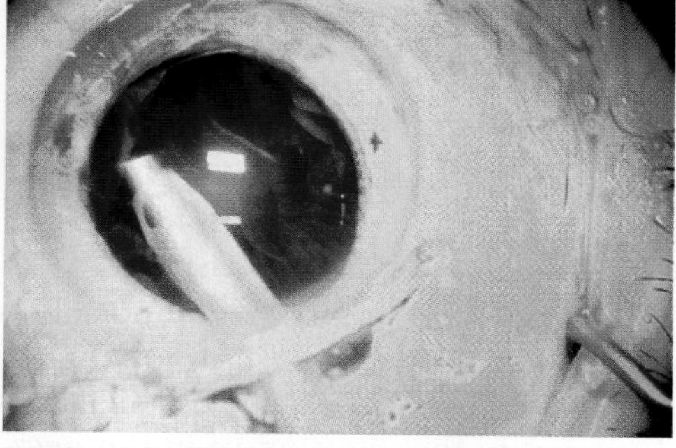

FIGURE 15-18. Phacoemulsification of a cataractous lens through a small, self-sealing, scleral tunnel incision.

EXERCISE 15-5

Answer the following questions, and code all diagnoses and procedures as appropriate.

1. Patient with pseudotumor cerebri is treated with a therapeutic spinal tap. ______________
2. Patient with obstructive hydrocephalus presents with malfunctioning ventriculoperitoneal shunt. The entire shunt was replaced via open approach. ______________
3. Patient with Parkinson's disease is admitted for insertion of a thalamic neurostimulator. Single array generator inserted in the chest via open approach. The lead was inserted via percutaneous approach. ______________
4. Patient admitted with nuclear senile cataract in the left eye and an extracapsular cataract extraction with Yag laser with lens implant was performed. ______________
5. A patient who had a cornea transplant on his right eye now has glaucoma in his left eye. He is admitted for a trabeculectomy ab externo. ______________

CHAPTER REVIEW EXERCISE

Answer the following questions and where applicable, assign codes for diagnoses, procedures, Z codes, and external cause codes.

1. Candidal meningitis ______________
2. Meningitis with a headache due to herpes zoster virus ______________
3. Aseptic meningitis ______________
4. Normal pressure hydrocephalus treated with an open ventriculocisternal shunt (synthetic) ______________
5. Congenital hydrocephalus with lumbosacral spina bifida ______________
6. Parkinsonism in Shy-Drager syndrome ______________
7. Benign essential tremor ______________
8. Lou Gehrig's disease ______________
9. Hemiplegia of the right side ______________
10. Recurrent seizures ______________
11. Family history of epilepsy ______________
12. Jacksonian seizure ______________
13. Intractable epileptic convulsions ______________
14. Addison's disease with myopathy ______________
15. Intensive care unit myopathy ______________
16. Chronic closed angle glaucoma, left eye mild stage, right eye moderate stage ______________
17. Aftercataract ______________
18. Right eye blind, the other eye normal vision ______________
19. Diagnostic lumbar puncture performed on a patient with probable diagnosis of multiple sclerosis. The patient is currently inpatient ______________

Write the correct answer(s) in the space(s) provided.

20. What procedure would a surgeon use to treat tremors in Parkinson's disease?

____

CHAPTER GLOSSARY

Alzheimer's disease: disorder of the brain that causes a progressive decline in mental and physical function.

Autoimmune disorder: disorder that occurs when the immune system attacks itself inappropriately.

Autonomic nervous system: consists of both sensory and motor functions that involve the central nervous system and internal organs.

Cataract: clouding of the lens of the eye causing obstructed vision.

Cerebral edema: an accumulation of water on the brain; can be either intracellular or extracellular.

Cholesteatoma: growth in the middle ear that usually results from repeated ear infections.

Cognitive impairment: decline in mental activities associated with thinking, learning, and memory.

Deep brain stimulator: a device implanted to control tremors.

Electromyelogram: test that measures electrical activity in muscles and nerves.

Epilepsy: disorder of the brain that is characterized by abnormal electrical discharges from the brain cells.

Glaucoma: disorder of the optic nerve that may result in vision loss.

Hemiplegia: paralysis of half of the body.

Hydrocephalus: cerebrospinal fluid collection in the skull.

Hypersomnia: excessive sleep.

Insomnia: difficulty falling asleep, wakefulness, and early morning awakening.

Intractable: not manageable.

Macular degeneration: vision loss in the central portion of the eye, leaving the patient with peripheral vision or low vision.

Mastoiditis: infection of the mastoid bone of the skull.

Meningitis: infection or inflammation of the meninges.

Metabolic encephalopathy: temporary or permanent damage to the brain due to lack of glucose, oxygen, metabolic agents, or organ dysfunction.

Muscular dystrophy: type of myopathy.

Myasthenia gravis: chronic autoimmune disorder that manifests as muscle weakness of varying degrees.

Myopathies: disorders that affect muscles, usually resulting in weakness or atrophy.

Otitis media: middle ear infection.

Parkinson's disease: progressive and chronic motor system disorder.

Phacoemulsification: incision is made on the side of the cornea and the lens material is softened, broken, and suctioned out.

Shunting: procedure to drain fluid from the brain to relieve pressure.

Sleep apnea: disorder characterized by breathing interruption during sleep.

Somatic nervous system: sends sensory (taste, hearing, smell) information to the central nervous system.

Somnolence: sleepiness.

Transient ischemic attack: a stroke that lasts only for a few minutes.

Vagal nerve stimulator: a device to control seizures.

REFERENCE

1. American Hospital Association: *Coding Clinic for ICD-10-CM/PCS* 2015:1Q:p25. Residual right-sided weakness due to previous cerebral infarction.

16

Diseases of the Circulatory System

(ICD-10-CM Chapter 9, Codes I00-I99)

CHAPTER OUTLINE

LEARNING OBJECTIVES

1. Apply and assign the correct ICD-10-CM/PCS codes in accordance with Official Guidelines for Coding and Reporting
2. Identify pertinent anatomy and physiology of the circulatory system
3. Identify diseases of the circulatory system
4. Assign the correct Z codes and procedure codes related to the circulatory system
5. Identify common treatments, medications, laboratory values, and diagnostic tests

ABBREVIATIONS/ ACRONYMS

ACS acute coronary syndrome

AF atrial fibrillation

AICD automatic implantable cardioverter-defibrillator

AIDS acquired immunodeficiency syndrome

AMI acute myocardial infarction

AV atrioventricular

AVM arteriovenous malformation

AVR aortic valve replacement

BNP brain natriuretic peptide

BP blood pressure

CAB coronary artery bypass

CABG coronary artery bypass graft

CAD coronary artery disease

CHB complete heart block

CHF congestive heart failure

CKD chronic kidney disease

COPD chronic obstructive pulmonary disease

CPK creatine phosphokinase

CPK-MB creatine phosphokinase, isoenzyme MB

CRT cardiac resynchronization therapy

CRT-D cardiac resynchronization treatment defibrillator

CRT-P cardiac resynchronization treatment pacemaker

CT computerized tomography

CVA cerebrovascular accident

CVL central venous line

CXR chest x-ray

DES drug-eluting stent

DOE dyspnea on exertion

DM diabetes mellitus

DVT deep vein thrombosis

EKG/ECG electrocardiogram

EP electrophysiologic

ER Emergency Room

HCVD hypertensive cardiovascular disease

HFpEF heart failure preserved ejection fraction

HFrEF heart failure reduced ejection fraction

HTN hypertension

ICD internal cardiac defibrillator

ICD-10-CM *International Classification of Diseases, 10th Revision, Clinical Modification*

ICD-10-PCS *International Classification of Diseases, 10th Revision, Procedure Coding System*

ICV implantable cardioverter

IV intravenous

IVDU intravenous drug user

LAD left anterior descending

LCA left coronary artery

MI myocardial infarction

MRI magnetic resonance imaging

MUGA multiple-gated acquisition

MVR mitral valve replacement

NQMI non–Q wave myocardial infarction

NSTEMI non–ST elevation myocardial infarction

OM obtuse marginal

OSA obstructive sleep apnea

PCI percutaneous coronary intervention

PDA posterior descending artery

PHT pulmonary hypertension

PICC peripherally inserted central catheter

PPH primary pulmonary hypertension

PTCA percutaneous transluminal coronary angioplasty

RA right atrium

RBBB right bundle branch block

RCA right coronary artery

RFA radiofrequency ablation

RW relative weight

SOB shortness of breath

SSS sick sinus syndrome

STEMI ST elevation myocardial infarction

SVT supraventricular tachycardia

TIA transient ischemic attack

TPA tissue plasminogen activator

TPN total parenteral nutrition

USA unstable angina

ICD-10-CM

Official Guidelines for Coding and Reporting (2021-2022)

Please refer to the companion Evolve website for the most current 2021-2022 guidelines.

9. Chapter 9: Diseases of Circulatory System (I00-I99)

a. Hypertension

The classification presumes a causal relationship between hypertension and heart involvement and between hypertension and kidney involvement, as the two conditions are linked by the term "with" in the Alphabetic Index. These conditions should be coded as related even in the absence of provider documentation explicitly linking them, unless the documentation clearly states the conditions are unrelated.

For hypertension and conditions not specifically linked by relational terms such as "with," "associated with," or "due to" in the classification, provider documentation must link the conditions in order to code them as related.

1) Hypertension with Heart Disease

Hypertension with heart conditions classified to I50.- or I51.4-I51.7, I51.89, I51.9, are assigned to a code(s) from category I11, Hypertensive heart disease. Use additional code(s) from category I50, Heart failure, to identify the type(s) of heart failure in those patients with heart failure.

The same heart conditions (I50.-, I51.4-I51.7, I51.89, I51.9) with hypertension are coded separately if the provider has specifically documented a different cause. Sequence according to the circumstances of the admission/encounter.

EXAMPLE Congestive heart failure due to hypertensive heart disease, I11.0, I50.9.

EXAMPLE Congestive heart failure in a patient with hypertension, I11.0, I50.9.

2) Hypertensive Chronic Kidney Disease

Assign codes from category I12, Hypertensive chronic kidney disease, when both hypertension and a condition classifiable to category N18, Chronic kidney disease (CKD), are present. CKD should not be coded as hypertensive if the provider indicates the CKD is not related to the hypertension.

The appropriate code from category N18 should be used as a secondary code with a code from category I12 to identify the stage of chronic kidney disease.

See Section I.C.14. Chronic kidney disease.

If a patient has hypertensive chronic kidney disease and acute renal failure, the acute renal failure should also be coded. Sequence according to the circumstances of the admission/encounter.

Hypertensive Heart and Chronic Kidney Disease.

Assign codes from combination category I13, Hypertensive heart and chronic kidney disease, when there is hypertension with both heart and kidney involvement. If heart failure is present, assign an additional code from category I50 to identify the type of heart failure.

The appropriate code from category N18, Chronic kidney disease, should be used as a secondary code with a code from category I13 to identify the stage of chronic kidney disease.

See Section I.C.14. Chronic kidney disease.

The codes in category I13, Hypertensive heart and chronic kidney disease, are combination codes that include hypertension, heart disease and chronic kidney disease. The Includes note at I13 specifies that the conditions included at I11 and I12 are included together in I13. If a patient has hypertension, heart disease and chronic kidney disease then a code from I13 should be used, not individual codes for hypertension, heart disease and chronic kidney disease, or codes from I11 or I12.

For patients with both acute renal failure and chronic kidney disease, the acute renal failure should also be coded. Sequence according to the circumstances of the admission/encounter.

EXAMPLE The patient was admitted with acute renal failure. The patient also has diagnoses of benign hypertension and chronic kidney disease, stage 3, N17.9, I12.9, N18.3.

EXAMPLE Patient has stage 3 chronic kidney disease. They are admitted with acute on chronic diastolic congestive heart failure which is hypertensive in nature, I13.0, 150.33, N18.3.

3) Hypertensive Cerebrovascular Disease

For hypertensive cerebrovascular disease, first assign the appropriate code from categories I60-I69, followed by the appropriate hypertension code.

EXAMPLE Cerebrovascular accident in a patient with malignant hypertension, I63.9, I10.

4) Hypertensive Retinopathy

Subcategory H35.0, Background retinopathy and retinal vascular changes, should be used with a code from category I10 – I15, Hypertensive disease to include the systemic hypertension. The sequencing is based on the reason for the encounter.

EXAMPLE The patient is being treated for bilateral retinopathy due to labile hypertension, H35.033, I10.

5) Hypertension, Secondary

Secondary hypertension is due to an underlying condition. Two codes are required: one to identify the underlying etiology and one from category I15 to identify the hypertension. Sequencing of codes is determined by the reason for admission/encounter.

EXAMPLE Hypertension due to periarteritis nodosa, M30.0, I15.8 or I15.8, M30.0.

6) Hypertension, Transient
Assign code R03.0, Elevated blood pressure reading without diagnosis of hypertension, unless patient has an established diagnosis of hypertension. Assign code O13.-, Gestational [pregnancy-induced] hypertension without significant proteinuria, or O14.-, Pre-eclampsia, for transient hypertension of pregnancy.

EXAMPLE The patient has an elevated blood pressure caused by pain, R03.0.

7) Hypertension, Controlled
This diagnostic statement usually refers to an existing state of hypertension under control by therapy. Assign the appropriate code from categories I10-I15, Hypertensive diseases.

8) Hypertension, Uncontrolled
Uncontrolled hypertension may refer to untreated hypertension or hypertension not responding to current therapeutic regimen. In either case, assign the appropriate code from categories I10-I15, Hypertensive diseases.

EXAMPLE The patient's benign hypertension has been well controlled since the patient lost 20 pounds and started a regular exercise program, I10.

EXAMPLE The patient's hypertension has been uncontrolled for the past 2 months in spite of changes in medication, I10.

9) Hypertensive Crisis
Assign a code from category I16, Hypertensive crisis, for documented hypertensive urgency, hypertensive emergency, or unspecified hypertensive crisis. Code also any identified hypertensive disease (I10-I15). The sequencing is based on the reason for the encounter.

10) Pulmonary Hypertension
Pulmonary hypertension is classified to category I27, Other pulmonary heart diseases. For secondary pulmonary hypertension (I27.1, I27.2-), code also any associated conditions or adverse effects of drugs or toxins. The sequencing is based on the reason for the encounter, except for adverse effects of drugs (See Section I.C.19.e.).

EXAMPLE Patient was admitted with hypertensive crisis. Patient also has CKD, stage 3, I16.9, I12.9, N18.3.

b. Atherosclerotic Coronary Artery Disease and Angina
ICD-10-CM has combination codes for atherosclerotic heart disease with angina pectoris. The subcategories for these codes are I25.11, Atherosclerotic heart disease of native coronary artery with angina pectoris and I25.7, Atherosclerosis of coronary artery bypass graft(s) and coronary artery of transplanted heart with angina pectoris.

When using one of these combination codes it is not necessary to use an additional code for angina pectoris. A causal relationship can be assumed in a patient with both atherosclerosis and angina pectoris, unless the documentation indicates the angina is due to something other than the atherosclerosis.

If a patient with coronary artery disease is admitted due to an acute myocardial infarction (AMI), the AMI should be sequenced before the coronary artery disease.

See Section I.C.9. Acute myocardial infarction (AMI)

EXAMPLE Patient with a previous coronary artery bypass is admitted with unstable angina. It is determined that the patient's angina is due to a blockage in the bypass grafts, I25.700.

c. Intraoperative and Postprocedural Cerebrovascular Accident
Medical record documentation should clearly specify the cause-and-effect relationship between the medical intervention and the cerebrovascular accident in order to assign a code for intraoperative or postprocedural cerebrovascular accident.

Proper code assignment depends on whether it was an infarction or hemorrhage and whether it occurred intraoperatively or postoperatively. If it was a cerebral hemorrhage, code assignment depends on the type of procedure performed.

EXAMPLE The patient had a postoperative cerebrovascular accident, which was embolic of right middle cerebral artery and due to the surgery. The patient had initially been admitted for treatment of coronary artery arteriosclerosis with CABG (two open saphenous vein grafts from the left greater saphenous vein were used). Cardiopulmonary bypass was used during the surgery. I25.10, I97.820, I63.411, Y83.2, Y92.239, 021109W, 06BQ0ZZ, 5A1221Z.

d. Sequelae of Cerebrovascular Disease

1) Category I69, Sequelae of Cerebrovascular disease

Category I69 is used to indicate conditions classifiable to categories I60-I67 as the causes of sequela (neurologic deficits), themselves classified elsewhere. These "late effects" include neurologic deficits that persist after initial onset of conditions classifiable to categories I60-I67. The neurologic deficits caused by cerebrovascular disease may be present from the onset or may arise at any time after the onset of the condition classifiable to categories I60-I67.

Codes from category I69, Sequelae of cerebrovascular disease, that specify hemiplegia, hemiparesi, and monoplegia identify whether the dominant or nondominant side is affected. Should the affected side be documented but not specified as dominant or nondominant, and the classification system does not indicate a default, code selection is as follows:

- For ambidextrous patients, the default should be dominant.
- If the left side is affected, the default is non-dominant.
- If the right side is affected, the default is dominant.

2) Codes from category I69 with codes from I60-I67

Codes from category I69 may be assigned on a health care record with codes from I60-I67, if the patient has a current cerebrovascular disease and deficits from an old cerebrovascular disease.

3) Codes from category I69 and Personal history of transient ischemic attack (TIA) and cerebral infarction (Z86.73)

Codes from category I69 should not be assigned if the patient does not have neurologic deficits.

See Section I.C.21. 4. History (of) for use of personal history codes

EXAMPLE Aphasia due to cerebrovascular accident 3 months ago, I69.320.

EXAMPLE The patient was admitted with left-sided hemiplegia due to a cerebrovascular accident. The patient has a history of previous CVA with residual facial droop, I63.9, G81.94, I69.392.

EXAMPLE The patient had a CVA in 2002 with no residuals, Z86.73.

e. Acute myocardial infarction (AMI)

1) Type 1 ST elevation myocardial infarction (STEMI) and non-ST elevation myocardial infarction (NSTEMI)

The ICD-10-CM codes for type 1 myocardial infarction (AMI) identify the site, such as anterolateral wall or true posterior wall. Subcategories I21.0-I21.2 and code I21.3 are used for type 1 ST elevation myocardial infarction (STEMI). Code I21.4, Non-ST elevation (NSTEMI) myocardial infarction, is used for type 1 non-ST elevation myocardial infarction (NSTEMI) and nontransmural MIs.

If a type 1 NSTEMI evolves to STEMI, assign the STEMI code. If a type 1 STEMI converts to NSTEMI due to thrombolytic therapy, it is still coded as STEMI.

For encounters occurring while the myocardial infarction is equal to, or less than, four weeks old, including transfers to another acute setting or a postacute setting, and the myocardial infarction meets the definition for "other diagnoses" (see Section III, Reporting Additional Diagnoses), codes from category I21 may continue to be reported. For encounters after the 4 week time frame and the patient is still receiving care related to the myocardial infarction, the appropriate aftercare code should be assigned, rather than a code from category I21. For old or healed myocardial infarctions not requiring further care, code I25.2, Old myocardial infarction, may be assigned.

EXAMPLE The patient was admitted with NSTEMI, I21.4.

EXAMPLE The patient was admitted with anterolateral wall STEMI, I21.09.

2) **Acute myocardial infarction, unspecified**
Code I21.9, Acute myocardial infarction, unspecified, is the default for unspecified acute myocardial infarction or unspecified type. If only type 1 STEMI or transmural MI without the site is documented, assign code I21.3 ST elevation (STEMI) myocardial infarction of unspecified site.

3) **AMI documented as nontransmural or subendocardial but site provided**
If an AMI is documented as nontransmural or subendocardial, but the site is provided, it is still coded as a subendocardial AMI.
See Section I.C.21.3 for information on coding status post administration of tPA in a different facility within the last 24 hours.

EXAMPLE Patient is admitted with an NSTEMI of the anterolateral wall, I21.4.

4) **Subsequent acute myocardial infarction**
A code from category I22, Subsequent ST elevation (STEMI) and non ST elevation (NSTEMI) myocardial infarction, is to be used when a patient who has suffered a type 1 or unspecified AMI within the 4 week time frame of the initial AMI. A code from category I22 must be used in conjunction with a code from category I21. The sequencing of the I22 and I21 codes depends on the circumstances of the encounter.
Do not assign code I22 for subsequent myocardial infarctions other than type 1 or unspecified. For subsequent type 2 AMI assign only I21.A1. For subsequent type 4 or type 5 AMI, assign only code I21.A9.
If a subsequent myocardial infarction of one type occurs within 4 weeks of a myocardial infarction of a different type, assign the appropriate codes from category I21 to identify each type. Do not assign a code from I22. Codes from category I22 should only be assigned if both the initial and subsequent myocardial infarctions are type 1 or unspecified.

5) **Other Types of Myocardial Infarction**
The ICD-10-CM provides codes for different types of myocardial infarction. Type 1 myocardial infarctions are assigned to codes I21.0-I21.4.
Type 2 myocardial infarction (myocardial infarction due to demand ischemia or secondary to ischemic imbalance) is assigned to code I21.A1, Myocardial infarctions type 2, with the underlying cause coded first. Do not assign code I24.8, Other forms of acute ischemic heart disease, for the demand ischemia. If a type 2 AMI is described as NSTEMI or STEMI, only assign code I21.A1. Codes I21.01-I21.4 should only be assigned for type 1 AMIs.
Acute myocardial infarctions type 3, 4a, 4b, 4c and 5 are assigned to code I21.A9, Other myocardial infarction type.
The "Code also" and "Code first" notes should be followed related to complications, and for coding of postprocedural myocardial infarctions during or following cardiac surgery.

EXAMPLE Patient is admitted with an STEMI of the anterolateral wall. During initial recovery in the hospital, the patient experiences a subsequent NSTEMI, I21.09, I22.2.

EXAMPLE Patient was discharged 3 weeks ago following an inferolateral STEMI. She presents today with unstable angina determined to be a posterolateral STEMI, I22.8, I21.19.

ANATOMY AND PHYSIOLOGY

The circulatory system is composed of the heart and blood vessels (Figure 16-1). Its function is to supply tissue in the body with oxygen and nutrients. This function is accomplished when the arteries carry blood (oxygen) to the cells. The largest artery, the aorta, branches off the heart and divides into many smaller arteries. The veins carry deoxygenated blood to the lungs to acquire oxygen and then to the heart, which pumps oxygenated blood back to the arteries.

The Heart

The function of the heart is to pump oxygen-rich blood to the cells of the body. The heart itself receives oxygenated blood from the coronary arteries; the two major coronary arteries branch off the aorta.

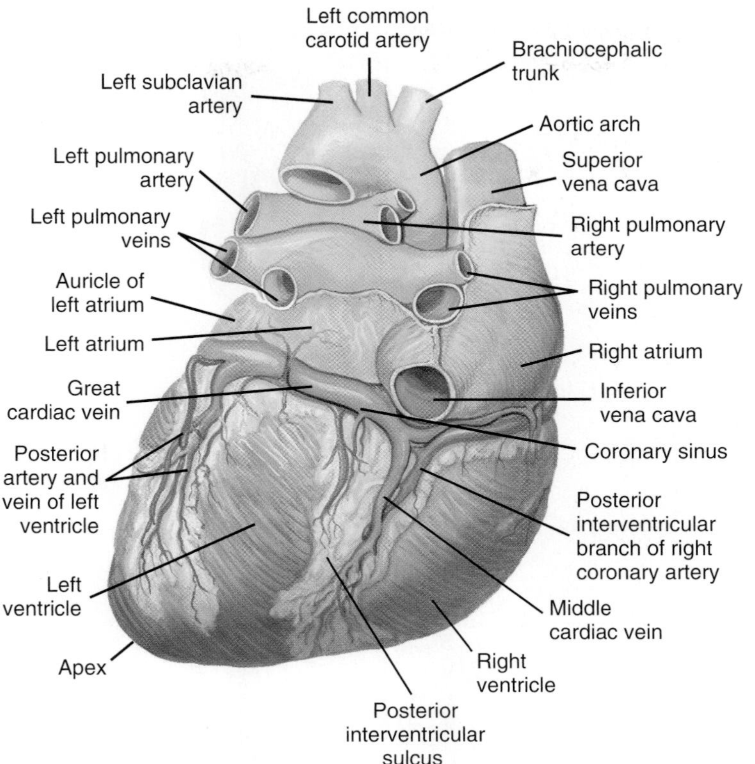

FIGURE 16-1. The heart and great vessels, posterior view.

The heart is enclosed laterally by the lungs, posteriorly by the backbone, and anteriorly by the sternum. The wall of the heart is composed of three layers: epicardium, myocardium, and endocardium (Figure 16-2). The epicardium is the outer protective layer, the myocardium is the middle layer and is composed of cardiac muscle, and the endocardium is the inner layer that lines all the heart chambers and covers the heart valves.

The heart consists of four chambers: right atrium, left atrium, right ventricle, and left ventricle. The atrium and the ventricle on the right side are separated from the left by a septum. The top two chambers, the atria, receive blood via the veins from the body or the lungs. The right ventricle pumps blood to the lungs to pick up oxygen, and the left ventricle pumps blood to the rest of the body. Within the heart are four valves (Figure 16-3), and their job is to direct blood flow. The tricuspid valve is located between the right atrium and the right ventricle. The valve between the left atrium and the left ventricle is the mitral or bicuspid valve. The aortic valve is located in the aorta at the point at which the left ventricle empties into the aorta. The pulmonary valve is located in the pulmonary artery at the point of exit from the right ventricle.

Blood Vessels

Blood vessels are the tubes that transport blood from the heart to the cells and back to the heart. Most arteries (Figure 16-4) carry oxygenated blood away from the heart. They continue to get smaller the farther away they are from the heart (arterioles). At this point, arterioles lead to **capillaries**, and exchange is made between blood and body cells; venules and veins (Figure 16-5) return blood back to the heart. The circulation of blood that moves throughout the body is referred to as systemic circulation. Blood pressure measured at the arm indicates systemic pressures.

Lymphatic System

The lymphatic system is closely related to the circulatory system. The lymphatic drainage system returns back to the bloodstream products that have leaked out from the capillaries. The lymph system is made up of lymph nodes, as well as spleen, thymus, tonsils, and adenoids. The lymph system fights infection by filtering out viruses and bacteria by attacking them with lymphocytes.

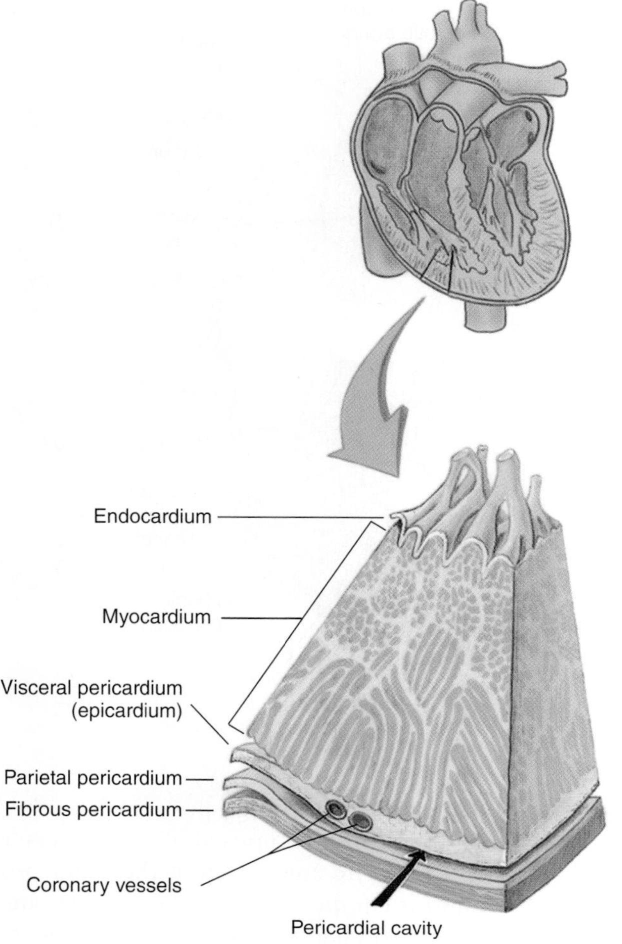

FIGURE 16-2. Layers of the heart wall.

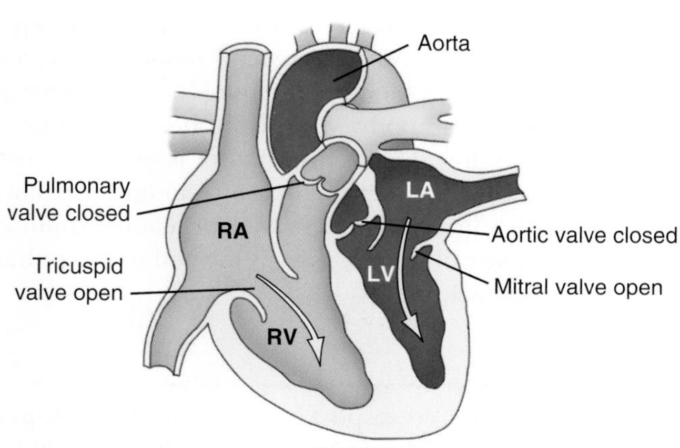

FIGURE 16-3. Cardiac valves.

DISEASE CONDITIONS

Diseases of the Circulatory System (I00-I99), Chapter 9 in the ICD-10-CM code book, is divided into the following categories:

CATEGORY	SECTION TITLES
I00-I02	Acute rheumatic fever
I05-I09	Chronic rheumatic heart disease
I10-I16	Hypertensive diseases
I20-I25	Ischemic heart diseases

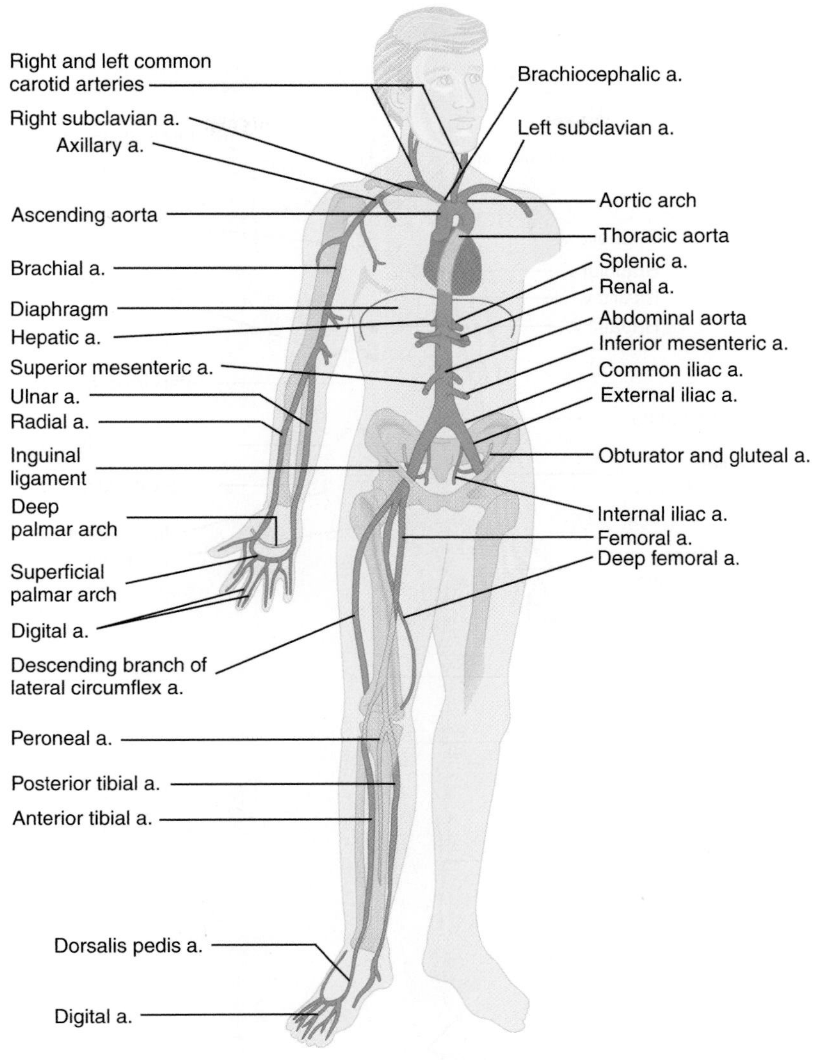

FIGURE 16-4. The arteries.

CATEGORY	SECTION TITLES
I26-I28	Pulmonary heart disease and diseases of pulmonary circulation
I30-I52	Other forms of heart disease
I60-I69	Cerebrovascular diseases
I70-I79	Diseases of arteries, arterioles, and capillaries
I80-I89	Diseases of veins, lymphatic vessels, and lymph nodes, not elsewhere classified
I95-I99	Other and unspecified disorders of the circulatory system

Acute Rheumatic Fever (I00-I02) and Chronic Rheumatic Heart Disease (I05-I09)

Acute rheumatic fever is an inflammatory disease usually found in children that may affect the heart, joints, skin, or brain following an infection with streptococcal bacteria such as strep throat or scarlet fever.

EXAMPLE Patient was admitted with acute rheumatic fever with endocarditis, I01.1.

EXAMPLE Patient has rheumatic chorea without heart involvement, I02.9.

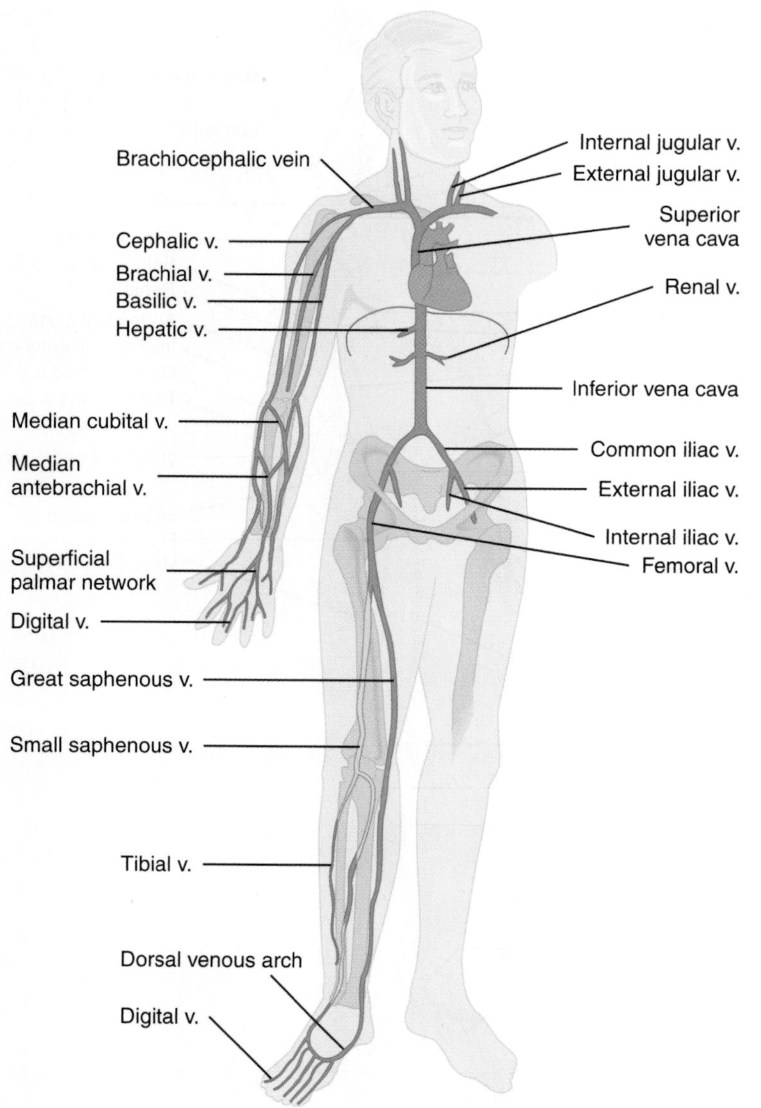

FIGURE 16-5. The veins.

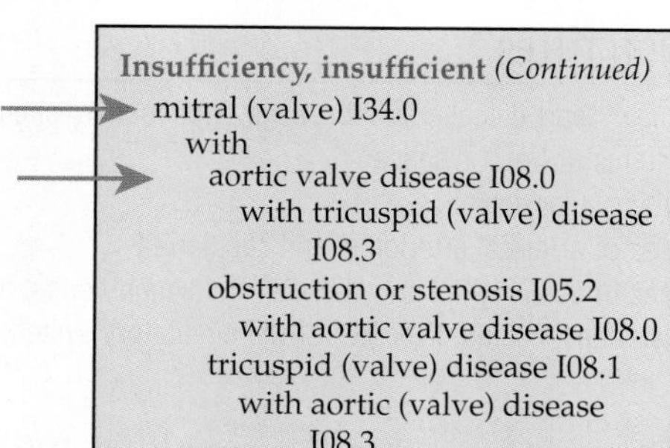

Insufficiency, insufficient *(Continued)*
mitral (valve) I34.0
with
aortic valve disease I08.0
with tricuspid (valve) disease I08.3
obstruction or stenosis I05.2
with aortic valve disease I08.0
tricuspid (valve) disease I08.1
with aortic (valve) disease I08.3

FIGURE 16-6. Mitral insufficiency with aortic valve disease.

Chronic rheumatic heart disease is a chronic condition that is usually a late effect of attacks of acute rheumatic fever and most often involves the heart valves. When mitral and aortic valves are involved, ICD-10-CM assumes a causal relationship to rheumatic heart disease unless specified as nonrheumatic. ICD-10-CM also presumes a causal relationship for certain mitral valve disorders of unspecified etiology. Tricuspid valve disorders are assumed rheumatic unless specified as nonrheumatic in origin (Figure 16-6).

EXAMPLE Stenosis, mitral, I05.0.

Hypertensive Diseases (I10-I15)

Hypertension is classified as primary (essential) or secondary. Primary hypertension, or high **blood pressure** (BP), is a condition that is defined as abnormally high blood pressure in the arterial system. The American Heart Association defines hypertension as pressures exceeding 140/90. A diagnosis of hypertension can be made only by a physician and should not be assigned on the basis of BP readings alone. Essential hypertension has no known origin, and its symptoms are insidious.

Secondary hypertension is a consequence of other diseases such as kidney diseases, brain tumor, or polycythemia. When secondary hypertension is documented, two codes are required. The additional code required for secondary hypertension is the underlying condition code. The sequencing of these two codes depends on the circumstances of the admission.

EXAMPLE

Patient is admitted with hypercalcemia due to hyperparathyroidism. The patient also has hypertension due to the hyperparathyroidism, E21.3, I15.2.

EXAMPLE

Patient has hypertension due to Cushing's disease, E24.9, I15.2.

Medications often used for treating hypertension include Accupril, Aldomet, captopril, Cardizem, diltiazem, Cozaar, losartan, Coreg, dyazide, Hytrin, Inderal, Lopressor, Norvasc, Procardia, Tenormin, atenolol, Vasotec, Toprol, Calan, verapamil, Zestril, and lisinopril.

EXAMPLE

Patient has a past history of hypertension, currently taking verapamil, I10.

For a variety of reasons, patients may have elevated blood pressure readings. Unless a patient has an established diagnosis of hypertension, the code R03.0 elevated blood pressure, should be assigned.

EXAMPLE

The patient has high blood pressure; will recheck at next clinic visit. No medications were given, R03.0.

Hypertensive Heart, Renal, and Heart and Renal Disease

ICD-10-CM assumes a cause-and-effect relationship and classifies chronic kidney disease with hypertension as hypertensive renal disease. This indicates to the coder that any time hypertension and chronic kidney disease (codes from category N18) occur in a patient, category (I12) should be assigned. The only time the (I12) category code would not be selected is when the physician has specifically documented a different cause for the CKD. On occasion, a patient will have CKD due to diabetes and also have hypertension; diabetic kidney disease and hypertensive kidney disease would both be assigned in these cases.

Because of the linking term within the Alphabetic Index, the classification also presumes a causal relationship between hypertension and heart involvement. The provider does not have to link these conditions in the medical record documentation. Provider documentation must clearly state that the heart condition is due to another condition to not code I11.- or if the patient has renal involvement I13.-. It is important to note that if a patient has hypertensive congestive heart failure, at least two codes—I11.0 and I50.-—are required; if known, the codes for systolic (I50.2-), diastolic (I50.3-), or a combination systolic and diastolic (I50.4-) should also be assigned.

EXAMPLE

Patient is admitted with acute on chronic diastolic and systolic congestive heart failure due to long history of hypertension, I11.0, I50.43.

Hypertensive heart and renal disease requires that the condition be classified to I13.–. It is important to become familiar with the Includes as well as Excludes notes in all of the above categories. It is also important to note that if a patient also has acute renal failure with any of the above conditions, an additional code for the acute renal failure is also assigned.

EXAMPLE

Patient is admitted with acute renal failure and hypertensive chronic kidney disease. The patient also has hypertensive heart disease, N17.9, I13.10, N18.9.

EXERCISE 16-1

Assign codes to the following conditions.

1. Patient is admitted with a diagnosis of hypertensive urgency ______________
2. Aortic stenosis with mitral insufficiency ______________
3. Malignant hypertension ______________
4. Labile hypertension ______________
5. Congestive heart failure due to hypertensive heart disease ______________
6. Cardiomegaly with hypertension ______________
7. Hypertension secondary to coarctation of aorta ______________
8. Essential hypertension ______________
9. HCVD (hypertensive cardiovascular disease) with chronic renal failure ______________
10. High blood pressure reading ______________

Ischemic Heart Disease (I20-I25)

Acute Myocardial Infarction

Acute **myocardial infarction** (AMI, or MI) in layman's terms is known as a heart attack. An MI occurs when complete blockage of blood flow occurs in a coronary artery. When this occurs, blood is prevented from reaching the heart muscle (Figure 16-7). Blockage may be caused by fatty deposits (also known as plaque or atherosclerosis) or blood clots. When the blood cannot reach the heart, the heart muscle may become damaged. Signs of a heart attack include chest pain, shortness of breath, nausea, and pain in the arms and chest.

To determine whether a patient is having a heart attack, several tests, including various types of blood tests, may be performed. One of these tests is called CPK (creatine phosphokinase, or creatine kinase). CPK is an isoenzyme that occurs in high concentration in the heart and skeletal muscle. The level of CPK-MB (creatine phosphokinase, MB isoenzyme) in the blood rises 3 to 6 hours after an MI and returns to normal 12 to 48 hours after the infarct. Usually, CPK is measured every 8 to 12 hours, and patterns are determined. The normal value for males is 25 to 90; for females, it is 10 to 70. Another type of blood test that is often performed is the measurement of cardiac muscle proteins called troponins. Testing for troponin levels and CPK levels is performed serially. Troponin levels are usually very low, and elevated levels can indicate damage to the heart. Healthcare providers also perform electrocardiograms (EKGs) to determine whether an MI has occurred.

Types of MI may be classified as to the area of heart that suffers damage or the extent of damage, as evidenced by an EKG (Figure 16-8). The most common areas are the following:

- Anterior
- Inferior
- Lateral
- Posterior
- Right ventricular

STEMI (ST elevation MI) occurs when complete obstruction of the coronary artery causes damage involving the full thickness of the heart muscle. This type of MI is also known as an ST elevation MI or a Q wave MI. **NSTEMI** (non–ST elevation) occurs when a coronary artery is partially obstructed and damage does not involve the full thickness of the heart

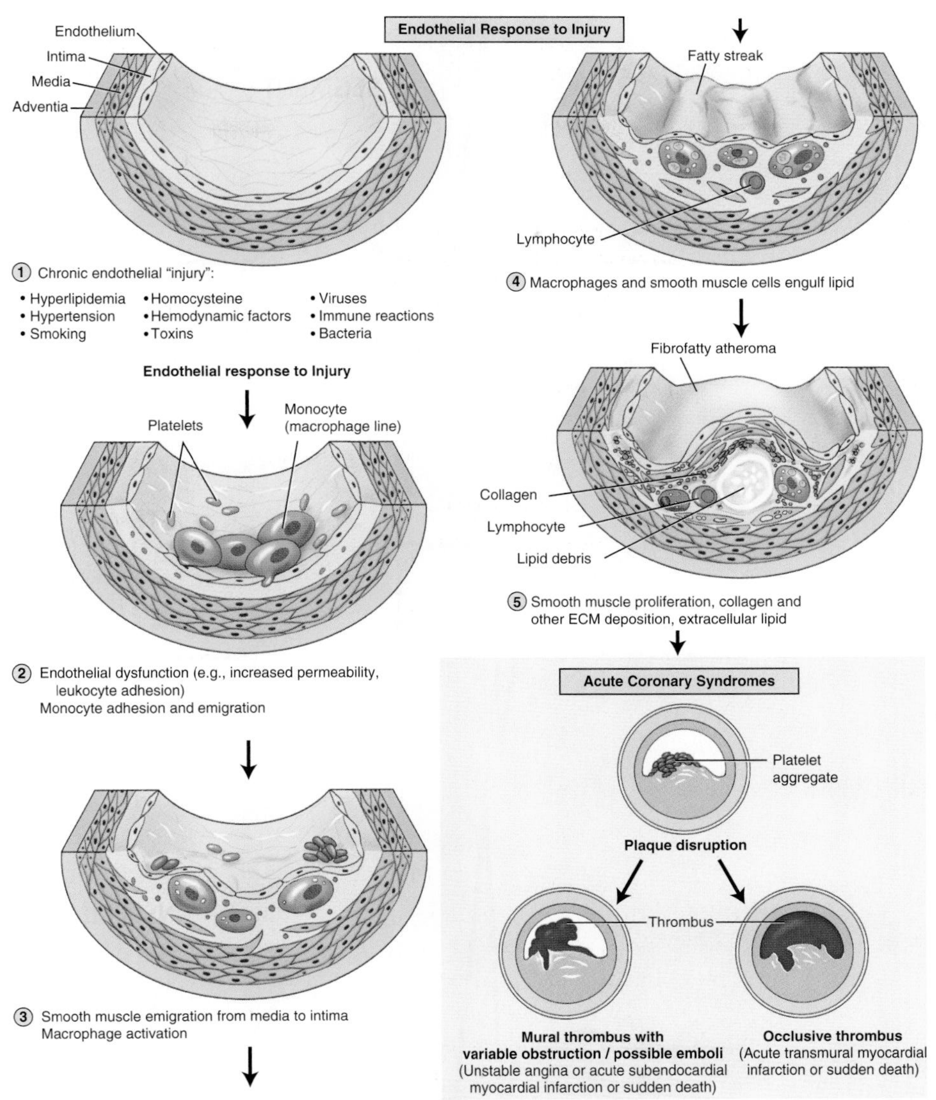

FIGURE 16-7. Development of an atheroma, leading to arterial occlusion.

muscle. This type of MI is often referred to as non–Q wave MI. Old terminology for transmural or nontransmural MI has been replaced by Q or non–Q MI.

Patients suspected of having an MI are usually treated with a combination of medications and/or procedures. Procedures performed to treat the causes of MI include coronary angioplasty (percutaneous transluminal coronary angioplasty [PTCA]), stenting (percutaneous coronary intervention [PCI]), and possibly coronary artery bypass surgery (CABG or CAB). Often, upon presentation of the patient to the Emergency Room (ER), thrombolytic therapy is initiated. Thrombolytics (tissue plasminogen activator [TPA], streptokinase) are used to dissolve blood clots that may be blocking a coronary artery. Thrombolytics must be administered within 6 hours of the onset of chest pain to avoid heart damage. A potential adverse effect of the use of these drugs is severe bleeding; for this reason, they are contraindicated in many patients. All of these procedures are discussed in greater detail in the procedure section of this chapter.

When assigning a code for an acute MI in ICD-10-CM, it is important to find documentation of the site of the MI for a STEMI. It is also important to note that a code from I21 is assigned for an MI that has occurred within 28 days of the current admission. If the MI is older than 28 days, then code I25.2 is assigned.

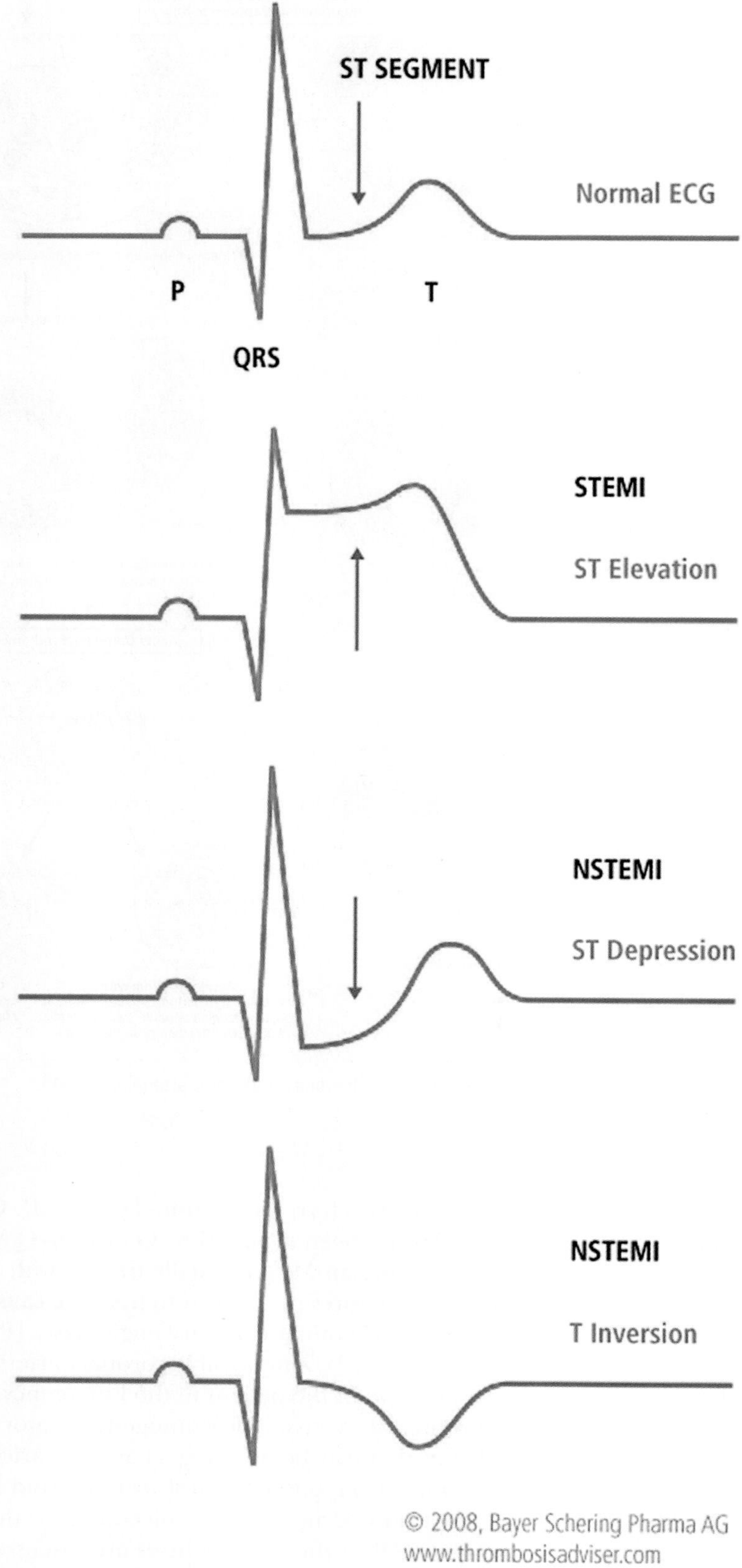

FIGURE 16-8. Illustration of normal ECG as well as STEMI and NSTEMI.

EXAMPLE

Patient was admitted with NSTEMI, I21.4.

ICD-10-CM also has codes for subsequent MIs that occur within 28 days of the previous MI. The code category assigned for these subsequent MIs is I22. Category I22 can never be assigned without a code from I21 for the original. The sequencing of these codes is dependent upon the conditions of the admission to the hospital.

EXAMPLE

Patient is admitted to the hospital with chest pain. After testing, it is determined that the patient has suffered a NSTEMI. Patient is discharged home. Two weeks later, patient returns to the hospital with severe chest pain. It is now determined that the patient has suffered a STEMI of the inferolateral wall, I22.1, I21.4.

EXAMPLE

Patient is admitted to the hospital with chest pain. Five weeks ago, the patient had been admitted for a NSTEMI, R07.9, I25.2.

Prior to having an MI, a patient may have had symptoms such as unstable angina (USA), which is often described as acute coronary syndrome, or ACS. A patient with this condition requires immediate medical treatment, but a patient with chronic angina may be treated with medications on a long-term basis as necessary. Patients with ACS may have unstable angina or could possibly have a non–Q MI. It may at times be necessary to query the provider for more specificity when ACS has been documented. Patients with angina may be prescribed sublingual nitroglycerin to relieve pain symptoms. Often, the underlying condition of chest pain, or angina, is coronary artery disease.

Coronary artery disease is indexed in ICD-10-CM as shown in Figure 16-9. ICD-10-CM assumes a causal relationship in a patient with both angina and coronary atherosclerosis unless it is documented that the angina is due to another cause. There is a note under category I25.1 to use an additional code if applicable for lipid rich plaque. Lipid rich plaque is the accumulation of lipids within coronary plaques. When coding an acute MI where the underlying cause is coronary artery disease, the acute MI is sequenced first.

When CAD is present in a patient with a previous CABG but it is not known whether the CAD is of a graft or a native artery, the code I25.10 should be used. Also assign code Z95.1 to show that the patient had coronary artery bypass surgery. When there is no documentation that the patient had a CABG procedure in the past, then the code for CAD should be assigned to native arteries I25.10.

Identification of plaque as being lipid rich or non–lipid rich is important diagnostic information for the interventional cardiologist. This diagnostic information can assist the

Disease, diseased *(Continued)*
heart *(Continued)*
hyperthyroid (*see also* Hyperthyroidism) E05.90 [I43]
with thyroid storm E05.91 [I43]
ischemic (chronic or with a stated duration of over 4 weeks) I25.9
→ atherosclerotic (of) I25.10
with angina pectoris - *see* Arteriosclerosis, coronary (artery)
coronary artery bypass graft - *see* Arteriosclerosis, coronary (artery),
cardiomyopathy I25.5
diagnosed on ECG or other special investigation, but currently presenting no symptoms I25.6
silent I25.6
specified form NEC I25.89

FIGURE 16-9. Coronary artery disease in ICD-10-CM Alphabetic Index.

cardiologist in determining the most appropriate type of stent (i.e., drug-eluting vs. bare metal) to use based on the present location and amount of lipid-rich plaque. The code for coronary atherosclerosis is sequenced before the code for lipid-rich plaque.

EXERCISE 16-2

Assign codes to the following conditions.

1. Patient had an MI 1 year ago ______________
2. Patient had a nontransmural MI 6 weeks ago and now presents with chest pain ______________
3. Patient has CAD and a history of CABG. Recent coronary catheterization shows coronary artery disease of the native arteries ______________
4. Patient has CAD and a previous MI and history of PCTA ______________
5. Patient with an anterolateral MI is transferred to this hospital for further evaluation and treatment ______________

Pulmonary Heart Disease and Diseases of Pulmonary Circulation (I26-I28)

Pulmonary Embolism

A **pulmonary embolism** is a blood clot(s) in the pulmonary artery that causes blockage in the artery. Most often, clots originate in the legs and then travel to the lung. A blood clot that forms and remains in a vein is a **thrombus**. A clot that travels to another part of the body is an **embolus**. Common symptoms of pulmonary embolism include shortness of breath, chest pain, and cough.

A pulmonary embolism may be diagnosed via lung scan or computed tomography (CT) scan. A pulmonary embolism can be life threatening, and once you have had one, the risk for recurrence is increased.

An acute pulmonary embolism may be treated with anticoagulant therapy (heparin or Coumadin) for 3 to 6 months and generally does not cause chronic disease. Once the embolism dissolves, therapy is discontinued. When a patient has a chronic pulmonary embolism, treatment may be longstanding, and sometimes surgery is performed to remove the clot.

EXAMPLE

Patient is admitted to the hospital with chest pain. The patient was diagnosed with an acute saddle pulmonary embolism, I26.92.

Pulmonary Hypertension

Pulmonary hypertension (PHT) is high blood pressure in the arteries that supply blood to the lungs. Normal pulmonary systolic pressure is 18 to 25 mm Hg. Two types of pulmonary hypertension—primary and secondary—have been identified. Primary pulmonary hypertension (PPH) is a rare condition of unknown origin that is both progressive and ultimately fatal. This condition has been linked with the use of anti-obesity drugs such as Fen/Phen. Secondary pulmonary hypertension is caused by other conditions such as chronic obstructive pulmonary disease (COPD), emphysema, pulmonary embolism, or obstructive sleep apnea (OSA). Patients who have prolonged untreated pulmonary hypertension often develop right ventricular failure. Doppler echocardiography is the most useful test for determining the diagnosis of pulmonary hypertension.

Symptoms of pulmonary hypertension may include dyspnea on exertion (DOE), syncope, fatigue, and chest pain. Treatment for this disease may involve correcting the underlying cause, if possible. Medical treatments may include vasodilators, diuretics, anticoagulants, oxygen, and digoxin. In some cases, lung transplantation may be considered.

EXAMPLE Patient has pulmonary hypertension due to COPD, I27.2, J44.9.

Other Forms of Heart Disease (I30-I52)

Pericarditis

Pericarditis is inflammation of the covering of the heart. It is often a complication of viral infection and systemic disease such as acquired immunodeficiency syndrome (AIDS). Sometimes, pericarditis follows an MI; it may also arise from bacterial infection. The disease presents with symptoms such as chest pain, breathing difficulties, fever, and cough. The heart sound heard through the stethoscope by the physician in cases of pericarditis is called a pericardial rub. Pericarditis is diagnosed through the use of chest x-ray (CXR), echocardiography, and magnetic resonance imaging (MRI). Usually, these patients also have abnormal EKG results.

EXAMPLE Acute pericardial effusion, I30.9.

EXAMPLE Uremic pericarditis, N18.9, I32.

EXAMPLE Acute viral pericarditis, I30.1, B97.89.

Endocarditis

Endocarditis is inflammation of the lining of the heart chambers and valves. Most often, bacterial infection is the cause of endocarditis. Patients with intravenous drug use (IVDU), central venous lines, and valve replacements (aortic valve replacement [AVR], mitral valve replacement [MVR]) are at greater risk for developing endocarditis. Patients with endocarditis might present with fever, shortness of breath (SOB), fatigue, night sweats, and muscle aches. In determining this diagnosis, physicians order blood cultures and perform echocardiograms. Treatment always consists of intravenous (IV) antibiotics; therefore, the patient may be hospitalized. IV antibiotic treatment may take up to 6 weeks.

EXAMPLE Patient admitted for antibiotics for subacute endocarditis, I33.9.

EXAMPLE Patient admitted for endocarditis caused by typhoid, A01.02.

Non–rheumatic Valve Disorders

Non–rheumatic valve disorders of incompetence, insufficiency, and regurgitation may be classified to categories I35-I39. A leaking valve is another name for regurgitation, incompetence, or insufficiency. When this occurs, blood flows backward within the valve. If a valve's opening is blocked or flow of blood is diminished, this is called **stenosis**. Coding of valve disorders requires the coder to pay close attention to the Alphabetic Index and all Instruction notes. When coding a combination of mitral, aortic, or tricuspid valve disorders together, ICD-10-CM assumes a causal relationship and defaults to rheumatic.

EXAMPLE Non-rheumatic tricuspid stenosis, I36.0.

EXAMPLE Mitral insufficiency, I34.0.

EXAMPLE Mitral valve prolapse, I34.1.

Cardiomyopathy

Cardiomyopathy is a disorder of the muscle of the heart chambers that impedes the functioning of the heart. Another term for congestive cardiomyopathy is dilated cardiomyopathy. Cardiomyopathy can be caused by disorders such as CAD, infection, diabetes, or alcohol abuse. Two codes may be required to code cardiomyopathy—one for the underlying condition and one for cardiomyopathy. Cardiomyopathy is diagnosed by echocardiography and is treated with antibiotics if due to an infection or treatment may be targeted to the underlying cause. Congestive cardiomyopathy may be associated with congestive heart failure. When they occur together, congestive heart failure would be the principal diagnosis, because it is often the focus of treatment. The cardiomyopathy would be assigned as an additional code.

EXAMPLE Obstructive hypertrophic cardiomyopathy, I42.1.

EXAMPLE Alcoholic cardiomyopathy, I42.6, F10.20.

EXAMPLE Cardiomyopathy due to amyloidosis, E85.4, I43.

Conduction Disorders

A **conduction disorder** is a problem that occurs in the electrical impulses that regulate heartbeat. A heartbeat begins when an electrical impulse is sent through the upper chambers of the heart. A human heart usually beats from 60 to 100 times per minute. **Tachycardia** (fast heart rate) means the heartbeat is greater than 100 beats per minute; **bradycardia** (slow heart rate) is a heartbeat of fewer than 60 beats per minute.

Electrophysiologic studies are often performed after a device is implanted to test if the device is working. If an arrhythmia is induced to test a device, the arrhythmia is not coded. If however, the arrhythmia or condition is discovered during testing, then this diagnosis would be coded.

Heart blocks occur when impulses originating in the upper chambers are unable to pass to the lower chambers at the correct rate. Three types of blocks have been observed:

- First degree: Conduction of beats from upper to lower is slower than normal.
- Second degree: Not all beats pass from upper to lower.
- Third degree: Impulses cannot pass from upper to lower.

EXAMPLE The patient has a bifascicular block, I45.2.

Cardiac arrhythmias (Table 16-1) occur when the normal sequence of electrical impulses changes, or the rhythm of the heartbeat is disturbed. (Normal sequence = RA [right atrium] through atrioventricular [AV] node through His bundle to ventricles.)

EXAMPLE Atrial fibrillation (AF), I48.91.

EXAMPLE Sick sinus syndrome (SSS), I49.5.

EXAMPLE Supraventricular tachycardia (SVT), I47.1.

Cardiac arrest, the sudden loss of heart function, is assigned code I46.9. This may be coded as the principal diagnosis in only two instances:

1. When the patient presents to the ER in cardiac arrest and dies before the underlying cause of the arrest has been established

TABLE 16-1 **ARRYTHMIAS**[1]

Types	Symptoms and Signs	Etiology	Diagnosis	Treatment
Normal sinus rhythm	Rate of 60-100 bpm, regular, P wave uniform	Impulse originates in SA node, conduction normal	Normal	None indicated
Sinus tachycardia	Rate >100 bpm, regular, P wave uniform	Rapid impulse originates in SA node, conduction normal	Rapid rate	Beta blockers, calcium channel blockers
Sinus brachycardia	Rate <60 bpm, regular, P wave uniform	Slow impulse originates in SA node, conduction normal	Slow rate	Atropine
Premature atrial contraction	Rate depends on underlying rhythm, usually normal P wave, morphology different from other P waves	Irritable atrium, single ectopic beat that arises prematurely, conduction through ventricle normal	Irregular heartbeat, diagnosis by ECG	Treatment usually unnecessary; if needed, antiarrhythmic drugs
Atrial tachycardia	Rate of 150-250 bpm, rhythm normal, sudden onset	Irritable atrium, firing at rapid rates, normal conduction	Rapid rate with atrial and ventricular rates identical, diagnosis by ECG	Reflex vagal stimulation, calcium channel–blocking drugs (verapamil), cardioversion
Atrial fibrillation	Atrial rate >350 bpm, ventricular rate <100 bpm (controlled) or ≥100 bpm (rapid ventricular response)	Atrial ectopic foci discharging at too rapid and chaotic a rate for muscles to respond and contract, resulting in quivering of atrium; AV node blocks some impulses, and ventricle responds irregularly	ECG show no P waves, grossly irregular ventricular rate	IV verapamil; if unsuccessful, procainamide; if unsuccessful, cardioversion
First-degree heart block	Rate depends on rate of underlying rhythm, PR interval >0.20 second	Delay at AV node, impulse eventually conducted	ECG shows PR interval >0.20 second	Atropine; if unsuccessful, artificial pacemaker insertion
Second-degree heart block, Wenckebach block	Intermittent block with progressively longer delay in conduction until one beat is blocked; atrial rate normal, ventricular rate slower than normal, rhythm irregular	SA node initiates impulse, conduction through AV node is blocked intermittently	ECG shows normal P waves, some P waves not followed by QRS complex; PR interval progressively longer, followed by block of impulse	Mild forms, no treatment; severe, insertion of artificial pacemaker
Classic second-degree heart block	Ventricular rate slow (½, ⅓, or ¼ of atrial rate); rhythm, regular; P waves normal, QRS complex dropped every 2nd, 3rd, or 4th beat	SA node initiates impulse, conduction through AV node is blocked	ECG shows P waves present, QRS complex blocked every 2nd, 3rd, or 4th impulse	Artificial pacemaker is inserted
Third-degree heart block	Atrial rate normal, ventricular rate 20-40 or 40-60 bpm; no relationship between P wave and QRS complex	SA node initiates impulse, which is completely blocked from conduction, causing atria and ventricles to beat independently	ECG shows P waves and QRS complexes with no relationship to each other; rhythms are regular but independent of each other	Insertion of artificial pacemaker is needed
Premature ventricular contraction (single focus)	Single ectopic beat, arising from ventricle, followed by compensatory pause	Ectopic beat originates in irritable ventricle	ECG shows a wide, bizarre QRS complex >0.12 second, usually followed by a compensatory pause	Usually, no treatment if <6 per minute and single focus
Multifocal arrhythmia Coupling, 2 in a row Bigeminy, every other beat Trigeminy, every 3rd beat Quadrigeminy, every 4th beat	Rate dependent on underlying rhythm; rhythm regular or irregular; P wave absent before ectopic beat	Same as single focus	Same as single focus	Same as single focus

AV, Atrioventricular; *bpm,* beats per minute; *ECG,* electrocardiogram; *IV,* intravenous; *PR,* pulse rate; *PVC,* premature ventricular contraction; *SA,* sinoatrial.

Continued

TABLE 16-1 ARRYTHMIAS[1]—cont'd

Types	Symptoms and Signs	Etiology	Diagnosis	Treatment
Ventricular tachycardia	Rate of 150-250 bpm, rhythm usually regular; focus of pacemaker normally single; patient experiences palpitations, dyspnea, and anxiety followed by chest pain	Four or more consecutive PVCs at a rapid rate due to advanced irritability of myocardium, indicating ventricular command of heart rate	ECG show runs of four or more PVCs; P was buried in QRS complex	Often forerunner of ventricular fibrillation; immediate intervention necessary; IV lidocaine; if unsuccessful, follow by cardioversion; procainamide or bretylium may be used
Ventricular fibrillation (lethal arrhythmia)	Patient loses consciousness immediately after onset; no peripheral pulses palpable, no heart sounds, no blood pressure	Ventricular fibers twitch rather than contract; reason unknown	Pulseless, unconscious patient; ECG shows rapid, repetitive, chaotic waves originating in ventricle	Recognize and terminate rhythm; precordial shock (defibrillation)

AV, Atrioventricular; *bpm,* beats per minute; *ECG,* electrocardiogram; *IV,* intravenous; *PR,* pulse rate; *PVC,* premature ventricular contraction; *SA,* sinoatrial.

2. When the patient presents to the hospital in cardiac arrest, is resuscitated, admitted as an inpatient, and subsequently dies before the underlying cause of the arrest has been established

Cardiac arrest may be coded as a secondary diagnosis when a patient has a cardiac arrest and is resuscitated on arrival or during the inpatient stay. The arrest is not coded when a physician documents cardiac arrest as the cause of death and there is no resuscitation.

Heart failure is impaired function of the heart's pumping ability. The heart is unable to pump with enough force or to fill with enough blood. This damage to the heart muscle may be caused by a variety of heart conditions such as CAD, MI, cardiomyopathy, hypertension (HTN), valve disease, diabetes mellitus (DM), and chronic kidney disease (CKD). This impaired pumping function in turn results in insufficient blood reaching the kidneys, which causes the body to retain fluid (Figure 16-10). Symptoms of heart failure include congested lungs, edema, fatigue, and irregular heartbeat.

Two types of heart failure may occur: systolic and diastolic. Systolic heart dysfunction, also known as systolic heart failure, occurs when the heart muscles are not contracting with enough force, and therefore, not enough blood is being pumped to the body. Diastolic cardiac dysfunction, also known as diastolic heart failure, occurs when the contraction is normal but the ventricle does not allow enough blood to enter the heart. Physicians can measure the percentage of blood that is pumped out of a filled ventricle with each heartbeat (known as ejection fraction) to determine how the heart is functioning. A normal ejection fraction measures 55% to 70%. Ejection fraction can be determined in several ways: echocardiography, MRI, multiple-gated acquisition (MUGA scan), or computerized tomography (CT) scan. Another test used to determine whether a patient is in heart failure is the brain natriuretic peptide (BNP) test. **BNP** is a hormone that is produced by the heart; a BNP test measures the amount of BNP that is found in the blood. Normally, levels of BNP are low, but in heart failure, these levels become elevated. A normal value of BNP would be 0 to 99 pg/mL. If this level is greater than 100, heart failure is indicated. Sometimes a provider will document the stage of heart failure. This may be described by a classification of the New York Heart Association (NYHA):

- NYHA Class I — Asymptomatic
- NYHA Class II — Symptoms with moderate exertion
- NYHA Class III — Symptoms with minimal exertion
- NYHA Class IV — Symptoms at rest

When coding heart failure, if the clinician documents systolic or diastolic heart failure along with congestive heart failure, only one code for the diastolic and/or systolic is

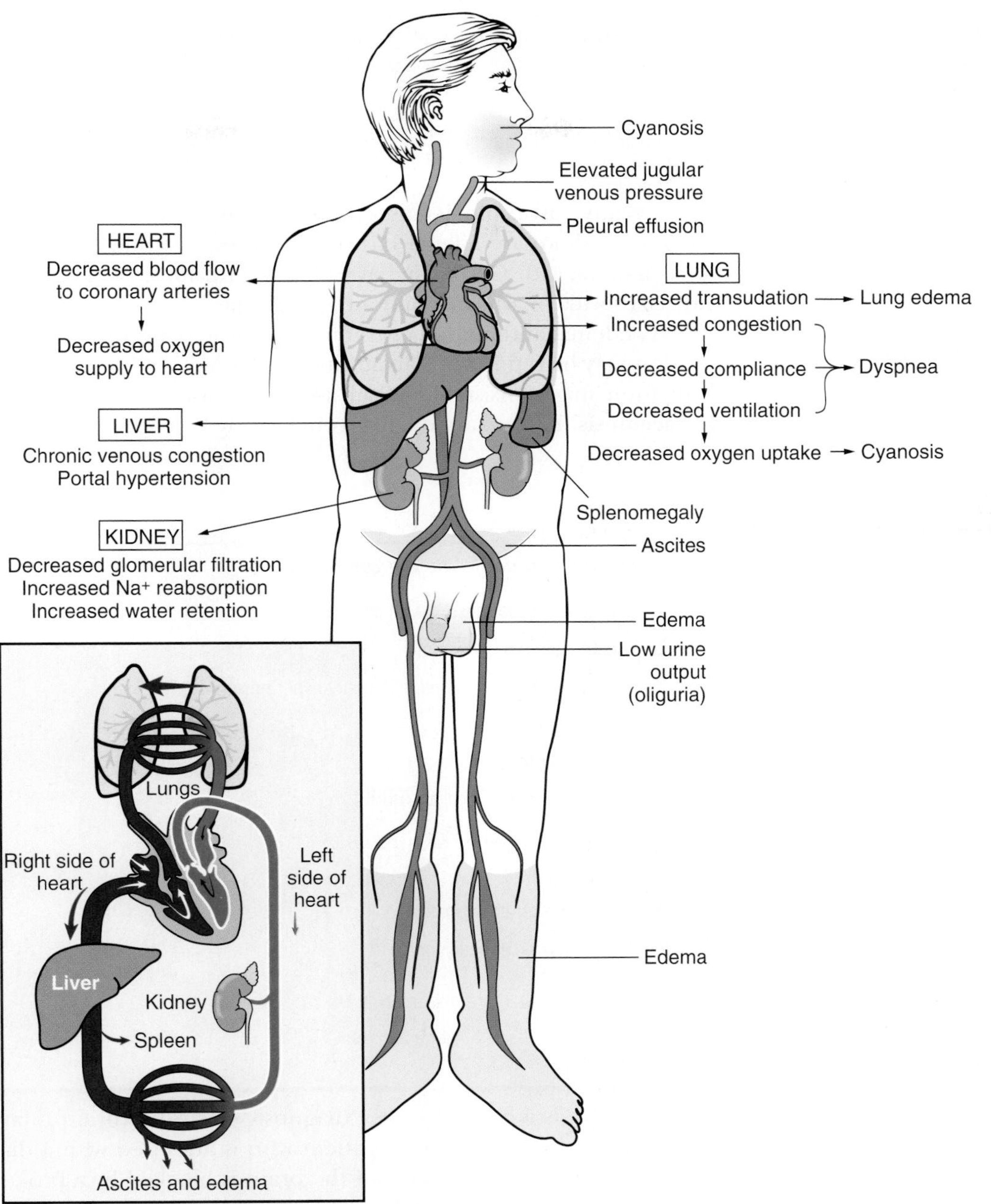

FIGURE 16-10. Chronic passive congestion. Left-sided heart failure leads to pulmonary edema. Right ventricular failure causes peripheral edema that is most prominent in the lower extremities.

assigned. The congestive heart failure is included in the codes of diastolic, systolic, or a combination. It is also important to look for documentation of acute, chronic, or acute on chronic. It is important to recognize that the terms "exacerbated" and "decompensated" indicate that a chronic condition is now in an acute phase. Patients may be treated for CHF as a chronic condition and may never be hospitalized. To assign a code for rheumatic congestive heart failure, the heart failure must be classified as rheumatic, or the physician must document that the heart failure is rheumatic in nature.

Providers may use terms such as heart failure with preserved ejection fraction (HFpEF) and heart failure with reduced ejection fraction (HFrEF). According to *Coding Clinic for ICD-10-CM/PCS* (2016:1Q:p10-11) HFrEF can be interpreted and coded to systolic heart failure and HFpEF can be interpreted and coded to diastolic heart failure.[2]

EXAMPLE Patient admitted with decompensated diastolic congestive heart failure, I50.33. The term decompensated means acute on chronic diastolic failure and should be coded as such.

EXAMPLE Patient admitted with congestive heart failure, acute on chronic combined systolic and diastolic, I50.43.

In many cases, physicians will refer to heart failure as pulmonary edema or volume overload. Pulmonary edema has other causes, but one of its main causes is heart failure. Also, patients with CHF may have pleural effusions. A pleural effusion is commonly seen with CHF with or without pulmonary edema. In cases in which the patient has CHF, pulmonary edema, and pleural effusions, CHF would always be the principal diagnosis. Pleural effusion may be reported as an additional diagnosis if it was specifically evaluated or treated. Evaluation may consist of special x-rays to confirm presence, treatment, or a diagnostic **thoracentesis**. Pulmonary edema would rarely be coded in addition to CHF.

EXERCISE 16-3

Assign codes to the following conditions.

1. Pulmonary hypertension with cor pulmonale ____________
2. Acute bacterial endocarditis ____________
3. Chronic hypertension and pulmonary hypertension ____________
4. Aortic regurgitation ____________
5. Dilated cardiomyopathy ____________
6. Right bundle branch block (RBBB) ____________
7. Wenckebach heart block ____________
8. Atrial flutter ____________
9. Thyrotoxic cardiomyopathy ____________
10. Hypertensive cardiomyopathy ____________

Cerebrovascular Diseases (I60-I69)

A patient who is admitted with a diagnosis of **stroke** (brain infarction or cerebrovascular accident [CVA]) is similar to a patient who is admitted with a diagnosis of heart attack or MI. The blood supply to a part of the brain is blocked by a broken blood vessel, ischemia, or blood clots (Figure 16-11). When the blood supply is cut off, brain cells die. Several types

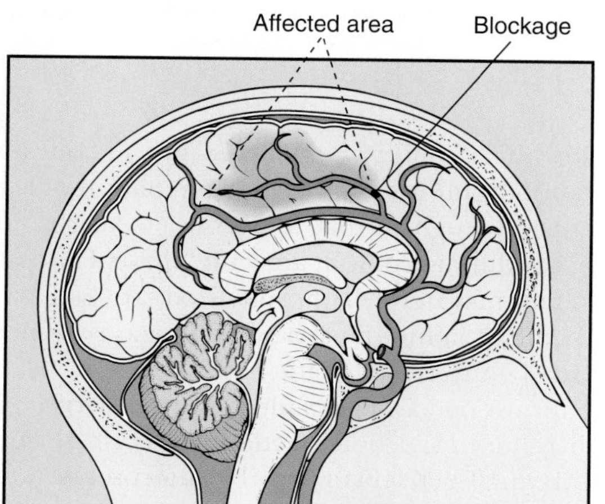

FIGURE 16-11. Cerebrovascular accident (CVA).

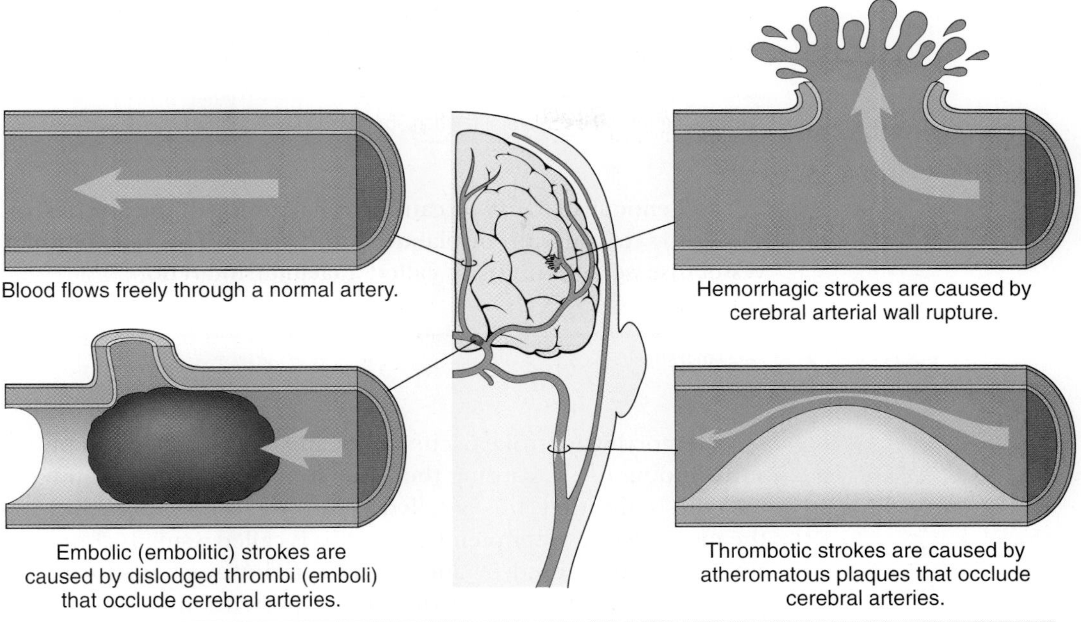

Blood flows freely through a normal artery.
Hemorrhagic strokes are caused by cerebral arterial wall rupture.
Embolic (embolitic) strokes are caused by dislodged thrombi (emboli) that occlude cerebral arteries.
Thrombotic strokes are caused by atheromatous plaques that occlude cerebral arteries.

FIGURE 16-12. Types of stroke: ischemic (thrombotic and embolic) and hemorrhagic.

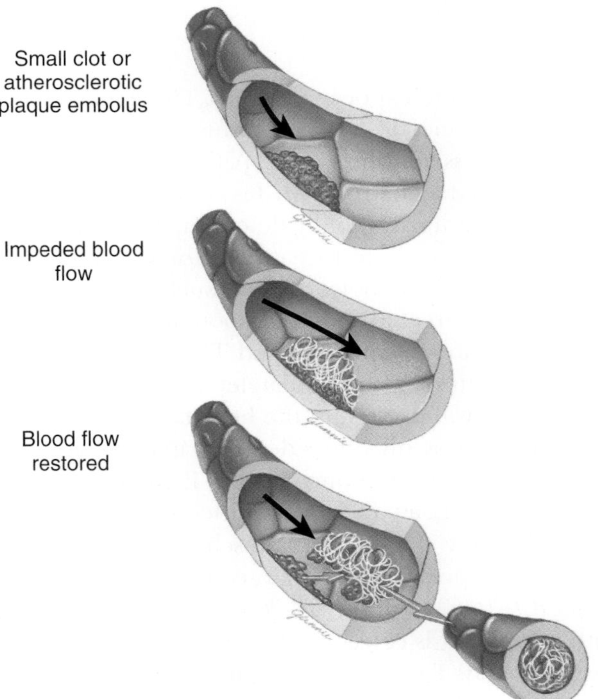

FIGURE 16-13. Embolus.

of stroke or brain infarcts may occur (Figure 16-12). Ischemic stroke, which accounts for 80% of all strokes, happens when blockage to the brain, usually by a blood clot, occurs. A clot that develops in another part of the body and then becomes wedged in a brain artery is a free-roaming clot or an embolus (Figure 16-13).

The most common type of stroke is ischemic (thrombotic/embolic). An ischemic stroke occurs when a blood clot or a piece of plaque breaks loose from an artery and lodges in a blood vessel of the brain, which then cuts off the blood supply to that area of the brain. A blood clot that forms and remains in a vein is called a thrombus, whereas a clot that travels to another part of the body is an **embolus**. Sometimes plaque is dislodged and becomes an embolus. The other type of stroke is hemorrhagic.

EXAMPLE Embolic right middle cerebral infarction, I63.411.

Ischemic stroke may be caused by narrowing of the arteries, or **stenosis**. Stenosis is often caused by the buildup of plaque in the artery. This may be referred to as small- or large-vessel disease. Often, this is called a lacunar infarction.

EXAMPLE Ischemic stroke, I63.9.

Hemorrhagic stroke occurs when an artery in the brain bursts and blood seeps into the surrounding tissue, causing the tissue to malfunction. When bleeding from the artery goes into the brain itself, this is called an intracerebral hemorrhage. When bleeding seeps into the meninges or outer membranes, this is called a subarachnoid hemorrhage. Hemorrhagic stroke may be caused by aneurysms, arteriovenous malformations (AVMs), and, possibly, plaque-encrusted walls that rupture. Hypertension can increase the risk of rupture of the artery wall.

EXAMPLE Nontraumatic subarachnoid hemorrhage, I60.9.

Symptoms of a stroke often appear suddenly. These may occur as weakness or numbness of one side of the body, arm, leg, or face; confusion; difficulty talking or speaking; trouble walking or seeing; dizziness; and headache. A CT scan is often used to determine whether a patient has had a hemorrhagic stroke; MRI is another useful tool in the diagnosis of stroke. The benefit of MRI is that it can rapidly detect small infarcts.

Medication is the most common treatment for stroke patients. Patients with ischemic stroke may be treated with thrombolytic agents such as TPA. Similar to heart attack victims, stroke patients need to be treated with TPA soon after onset of symptoms. There is a code (Z92.82) for a patient who was administered TPA at a different facility. Most patients are treated with anticoagulants or with antiplatelet agents.

Sometimes a patient will present to the hospital with symptoms of a stroke, such as difficulty speaking or weakness on one side. TPA may be administered with considerable improvement in the patient's symptoms. If the TPA aborts the patient's cerebral infarction code I63.9 is assigned. Often, a patient is admitted with a stroke with deficits. These deficits are often gone by the time the patient is discharged. Any deficits that a patient exhibits from the stroke, whether present at discharge or not, should be assigned codes. According to *Coding Clinic for ICD-10-CM and ICD-10-PCS (2015:1Q:pp:25-26)*, when unilateral weakness if associated with a stroke, it is considered to the same as hemiparesis/hemiplegia and it is acceptable to assign a code from G81 code category. Unilateral weakness that is not associated with some type of brain disorder or injury is not assumed to be hemiparesis/hemiplegia.

EXAMPLE Patient suffered an embolic stroke in the left middle cerebral artery. She presented with weakness of the right side and aphasia, both of which were not present at discharge, I63.412, R47.01, G81.91.

EXAMPLE Acute subdural hemorrhage, with dysphagia at time of discharge, I62.01, R13.10.

EXAMPLE Stenosis of the left carotid artery with cerebral infarction, I63.232.

Carotid artery stenosis is indexed in ICD-10-CM under occlusion, artery, carotid (Figures 16-14 and 16-15). It is important to take note of laterality if a patient has an infarct as a result of this stenosis and a known history of bilateral carotid stenosis—two codes are required.

EXAMPLE

> Patient with a history of bilateral carotid stenosis is admitted to the hospital with symptoms of a stroke. A workup is initiated, and it is determined that the patient had a ischemic stroke due to a thrombosis of the right carotid artery. The left carotid was recorded as a 65% blockage, I63.031, I65.22.

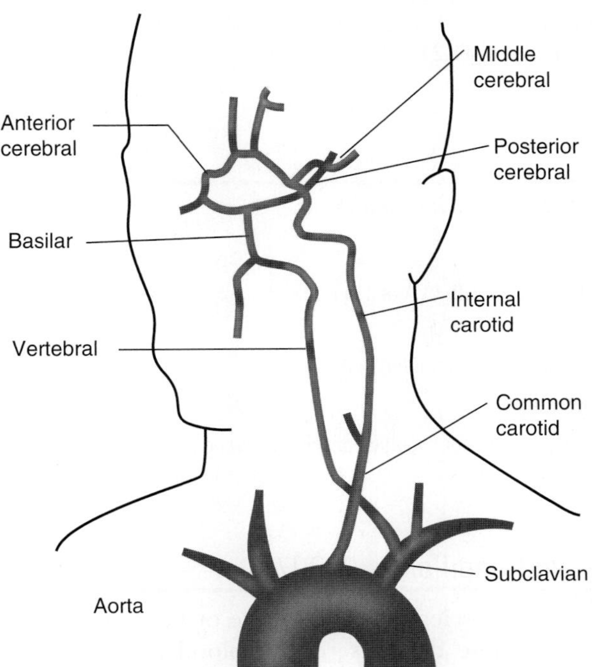

FIGURE 16-14. Cerebral and precerebral arteries.

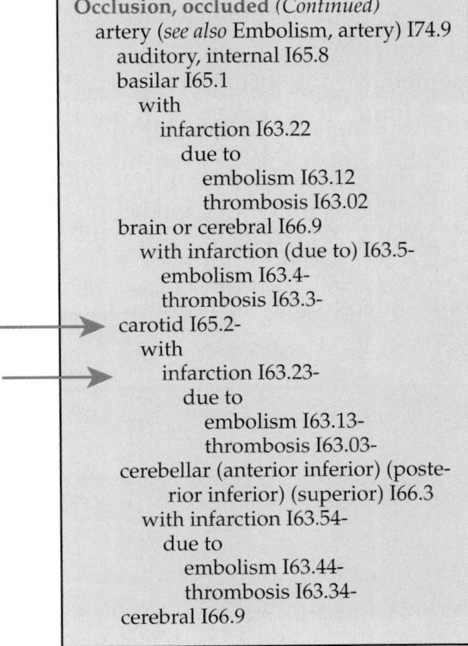
Occlusion, occluded *(Continued)*
artery (*see also* Embolism, artery) I74.9
auditory, internal I65.8
basilar I65.1
with
infarction I63.22
due to
embolism I63.12
thrombosis I63.02
brain or cerebral I66.9
with infarction (due to) I63.5-
embolism I63.4-
thrombosis I63.3-
carotid I65.2-
with
infarction I63.23-
due to
embolism I63.13-
thrombosis I63.03-
cerebellar (anterior inferior) (posterior inferior) (superior) I66.3
with infarction I63.54-
due to
embolism I63.44-
thrombosis I63.34-
cerebral I66.9

FIGURE 16-15. Carotid artery stenosis with infarction.

Sequelae of Cerebrovascular Disease

Stroke is one of the leading causes of disability in the United States. Types of disability that may result from stroke consist of paralysis, particularly on one side of the body (hemiplegia), or weakness on one side (hemiparesis). Other disabilities include **cognitive deficits**, **aphasia** (impairment of language comprehension and production), emotional problems, and pain. When an inpatient has had a stroke, has current deficits, and also has late effects from a previous stroke, all codes should be assigned. Late effect codes may be listed as principal diagnoses when the purpose of the admission is to treat the late effect. The code for a history of CVA with no residuals is Z86.73.

EXAMPLE Patient presents with left carotid artery stenosis with infarct and current right hemiparesis. Patient has residual aphasia from a previous stroke, I63.232, G81.91, I69.320.

EXERCISE 16-4

Assign codes to the following conditions.

1. Cerebral hemorrhage __________
2. Patient was admitted with CVA and aphasia; the aphasia cleared before discharge __________
3. Cerebral thrombosis without infarction __________
4. Ruptured berry aneurysm __________
5. Patient is being treated for cognitive deficits following a previous stroke __________

Diseases of the Arteries, Arterioles, and Capillaries (I70-I79)

Atherosclerosis or arteriosclerosis is a stricture or hardening of the artery that is caused by deposits of plaque. These deposits restrict blood flow through the artery; plaques can rupture and travel to other parts of the body or can form blood clots that block a blood vessel. If a blood vessel to the heart is blocked, this causes a heart attack; if a vessel to the brain is blocked, this causes a stroke; and if vessels to the extremities are blocked, this can cause claudication, ulcers, and eventually, gangrene. Codes found in subcategory I70.2 are hierarchical. For example, if a patient has atherosclerosis of a native artery of the right leg with ulceration of the heel, rest pain, and claudication of the right leg, then only the code from I70.234 would be assigned, for the ulceration.

Atherosclerosis may continue to progress and in that case code only the most severe form:

- I70.21- atherosclerosis of the extremity with intermittent claudication
- I70.22- atherosclerosis of the extremity with intermittent claudication and rest pain
- I70.23-, I70.24-, I70.25- atherosclerosis of the extremity with intermittent claudication, rest pain, and ulceration
- I70.26- atherosclerosis of the extremity with intermittent claudication, rest pain, ulceration, and gangrene

EXAMPLE Stenosis of renal artery, I70.1.

EXAMPLE Atherosclerosis of left leg autologous bypass graft with intermittent claudication, I70.412.

An **aneurysm** is a bulging or ballooning out of a vessel. Aneurysms are often caused by atherosclerosis and tend to have no symptoms, unless dissection occurs. **Dissection** is typically accompanied by severe pain in the area of dissection. Aneurysms tend to form in areas

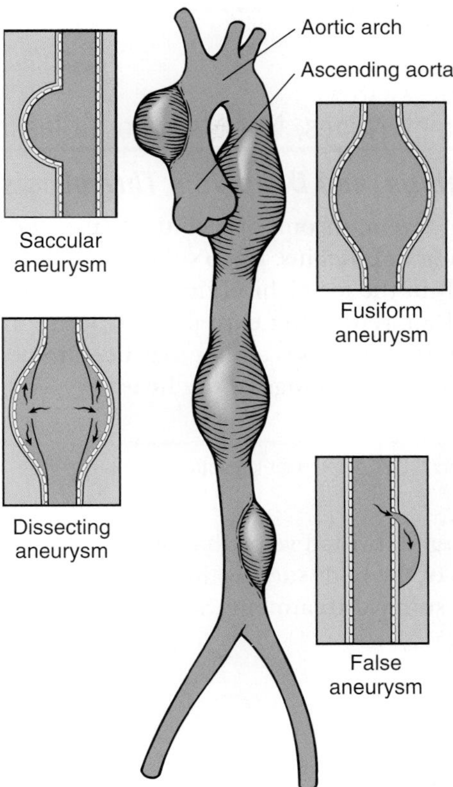

FIGURE 16-16. Types of aortic aneurysm.

where vessels branch out. Aortic aneurysms (Figure 16-16) can occur anywhere along the aorta, which is the largest artery in the body; it runs from the heart through the chest into the abdominal area and then divides into vessels that supply blood to the legs. The most common aneurysms occur in the abdominal area. Rupture of an aneurysm is a life-threatening event. The risk of rupture increases as the aneurysm becomes larger. Sometimes, an aneurysm becomes dissecting, which means a tear begins in the wall of the vessel that causes layers to separate. Physicians use the terms type I, type II, and type III to describe dissecting aneurysms.

EXAMPLE Patient presents to hospital with Type I dissecting thoracoabdominal aneurysm, I71.03.

Aneurysms are usually not treated until they reach a certain size or begin to enlarge quickly. Treatment for an aneurysm consists of open or endovascular surgery, which is discussed in the Procedure section of this chapter.

EXAMPLE Abdominal aortic aneurysm, I71.4.

EXAMPLE Ruptured thoracic aneurysm (aorta), I71.1.

EXAMPLE Femoral aneurysm, I72.4.

An arteriovenous **fistula** is an abnormal passage between an artery and a vein. Blood typically flows from arteries into capillaries and then to veins; however, when blood bypasses the capillaries and goes directly to the vein, an arteriovenous fistula results.

EXAMPLE Patient has an arteriovenous fistula, acquired, I77.0.

Diseases of Veins, Lymphatic Vessels, and Lymph Nodes, Not Elsewhere Classified (I80-I89)

Phlebitis, Thrombophlebitis, and Deep Vein Thrombosis

Phlebitis is inflammation of a vein; thrombophlebitis occurs when a clot forms in the vein and then causes inflammation or phlebitis. **Deep vein thrombosis** (DVT) is a blood clot that forms in a deep vein, usually in the leg or hip (Figures 16-17 and 16-18). A DVT is indexed in ICD-10-CM under Embolism, vein, lower extremity. DVTs are treated with anticoagulants such as heparin or warfarin. In some cases a filter may need to be inserted in the vena cava to prevent clots from traveling to the lungs or the heart.

EXAMPLE Patient admitted with an acute femoral DVT of the right leg with inflammation, I82.411.

Varicose veins are enlarged, twisted veins that usually occur in the legs. Varicose veins can be found in other areas of the body such as the esophagus. Varicose veins often develop complications that require surgical treatment. Stasis dermatitis with varicose veins of the leg is assigned code I83.10.

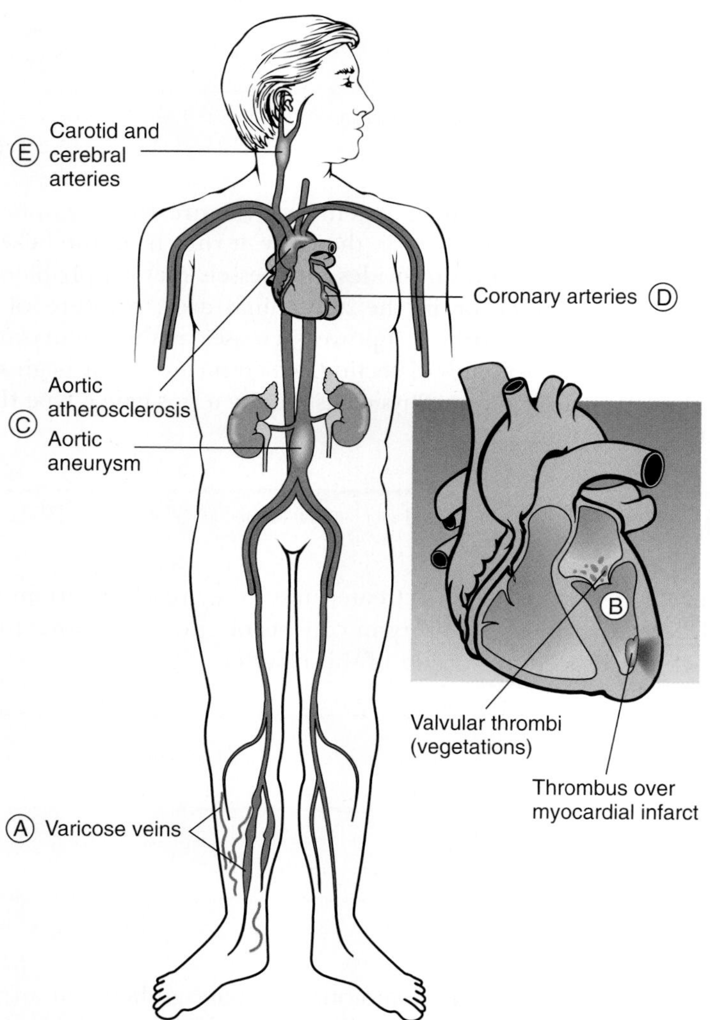

FIGURE 16-17. Common sites of thrombus formation.

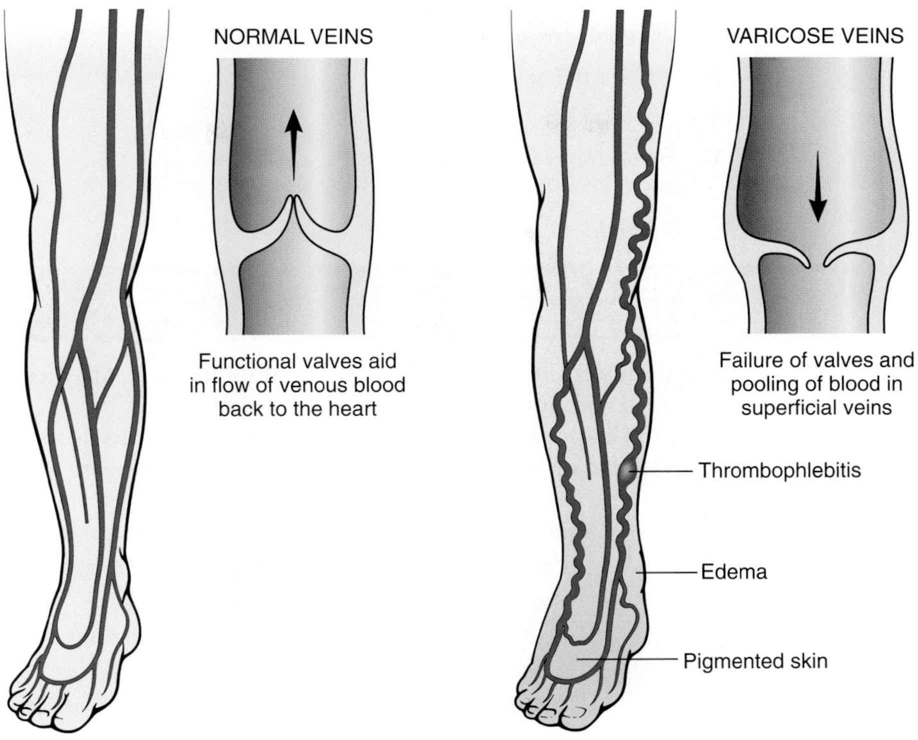

FIGURE 16-18. Normal and varicose veins. Slow flow in the veins makes an individual susceptible to clot formation. Thrombotic occlusion of varicose veins is known as thrombophlebitis. If a thrombus becomes loosened from its place in a vein, it can travel to the lungs (pulmonary embolism) and block a blood vessel there. Then blood pools in the lower part of the leg and fluid leaks from distended small capillaries, causing edema.

Stasis dermatitis is a skin condition caused by poor circulation (venous insufficiency) that is characterized by swelling, skin discoloration, weeping, itching, and scaly skin. The legs and particularly the ankles are the areas most often affected. This condition is often seen in the elderly, and risk for developing this condition increases when any of the following conditions is present: obesity, high blood pressure, varicose veins and heart, and/or kidney failure. A common complication of stasis dermatitis is cellulitis.

EXAMPLE Patient with varicose veins and stasis dermatitis of the left leg with a calf ulcer (skin breakdown), I83.222, L97.221.

EXAMPLE Patient with alcoholic cirrhosis of the liver with esophageal varices with bleeding, K70.30, I85.11, F10.20.

EXERCISE 16-5

Assign codes to the following conditions.

1. Atherosclerosis of bilateral legs with rest pain and gangrene ______________
2. Atherosclerosis of a nonautologous bypass graft of the left leg ______________
3. Dissection of the thoracic aorta ______________
4. Type II dissection of the abdominal aorta ______________
5. Iliac artery aneurysm ______________
6. Buerger's disease ______________
7. Embolic infarction of the abdominal aorta ______________
8. Thrombosis of the subclavian artery ______________

9. Deep vein thrombosis of the right lower extremity ______________
10. Peroneal DVT of the left leg ______________
11. Scrotal varices ______________
12. Bilateral lower extremity varicose veins, asymptomatic ______________

FACTORS INFLUENCING HEALTH STATUS AND CONTACT WITH HEALTH SERVICES (Z CODES)

As was discussed in Chapter 9, it may be difficult to locate Z codes in the index. Coders often say, "I did not know there was a Z code for that."

Refer to Chapter 9 for a listing of common main terms used to locate Z codes. A review of the Tabular reveals that some Z codes pertain to diseases of the circulatory system:

Z01.30	Encounter for examination of blood pressure without abnormal findings
Z01.31	Encounter for examination of blood pressure with abnormal findings
Z13.6	Encounter for screening for cardiovascular disorders
Z45.010	Encounter for checking and testing of cardiac pacemaker pulse generator [battery]
Z45.018	Encounter for adjustment and management of other part of cardiac pacemaker
Z45.02	Encounter for adjustment and management of automatic implantable cardiac defibrillator
Z45.09	Encounter for adjustment and management of other cardiac device
Z45.1	Encounter for adjustment and management of infusion pump
Z45.2	Encounter for adjustment and management of vascular access device
Z82.41	Family history of sudden cardiac death
Z82.49	Family history of ischemic heart disease and other diseases of the circulatory system
Z86.711	Personal history of pulmonary embolism
Z86.718	Personal history of other venous thrombosis and embolism
Z86.72	Personal history of thrombophlebitis
Z86.73	Personal history of transient ischemic attack (TIA) and cerebral infarction without residual deficits
Z86.74	Personal history of sudden cardiac arrest
Z86.79	Personal history of other diseases of the circulatory system
Z92.82	Status post administration of tPA (rtPA) in a different facility within the last 24 hours prior to admission to current facility
Z94.1	Heart transplant status
Z94.3	Heart and lungs transplant status
Z95.0	Presence of cardiac pacemaker
Z95.1	Presence of aortocoronary bypass graft
Z95.2	Presence of prosthetic heart valve
Z95.3	Presence of xenogenic heart valve
Z95.4	Presence of other heart-valve replacement
Z95.5	Presence of coronary angioplasty implant and graft
Z95.810	Presence of automatic (implantable) cardiac defibrillator
Z95.811	Presence of heart-assist device
Z95.812	Presence of fully implantable artificial heart
Z95.818	Presence of other cardiac implants and grafts
Z95.820	Presence vascular angioplasty status with implants and grafts
Z95.828	Presence of other vascular implants and grafts
Z95.9	Presence of cardiac and vascular implant and graft, unspecified
Z98.61	Coronary angioplasty status
Z98.62	Peripheral vascular angioplasty status

EXAMPLE

Patient admitted with chest pain. Has a history of PTCA, R07.9, Z98.61.

EXAMPLE

Patient admitted to Hospital A with a CVA and tPA was administered percutaneously via a peripheral vein. The patient was stabilized and 8 hours later transferred to Hospital B for treatment of CVA.

Hospital A: I63.9; 3E03317.

Hospital B: I63.9, Z92.82.

EXERCISE 16-6

Assign codes to the following conditions.

1. Patient is admitted to the hospital with chest pain; the only risk factor he has is a family history of CAD ____________
2. Patient has a history of a heart valve replaced by a prosthesis ____________
3. Patient has a history of a five-vessel CABG ____________
4. Patient has a history of angioplasty ____________
5. Patient has a previously inserted cardiac pacemaker ____________
6. Patient is awaiting a heart transplant and is on a heart assist device ____________

COMMON TREATMENTS

CONDITION	MEDICATION/TREATMENT
Angina	Nitroglycerin, beta blockers, and calcium channel blockers Coreg, Lopressor, Norvasc, Verapamil, Procardia
Atrial fibrillation	Blood thinners (Coumadin, Plavix, Ticlid) Rate control: calcium channel blockers: Cardizem, verapamil Beta blockers: atenolol, Lopressor, Inderal, Digoxin, Lanoxin, Amiodarone
Congestive heart failure	Diuretics such as Lasix, Bumex, Zaroxolyn, Furosemide Beta blockers: Dyazide, Lanoxin, HCTZ
Hypertension	Diuretics, Aldactone Beta blockers: atenolol, Vasotec, Cozaar, Calan, Cardizem, Aldomet (for additional antihypertensive drugs)
Stroke/CVA (nonhemorrhagic)	Blood thinners (Coumadin, Plavix, Ticlid) and clot busting agents such as tPA and streptokinase

PROCEDURES

Procedures related to the cardiovascular system in ICD-10-PCS may be found in the following tables:

Heart and Great Vessels	021-02Y
Upper Arteries	031-03W
Lower Arteries	041-04W
Upper Veins	051-05W
Lower Veins	061-06W

Diagnostic Cardiac Catheterization

Diagnostic cardiac catheterization (Figure 16-19) is a procedure that may be performed on a patient with chest pain, angina, or an acute MI to determine if coronary artery disease is present. This procedure allows the physician to view the heart chambers, valves, and arteries. A hollow needle or catheter is inserted into the vein for a right heart catheterization and into an artery in the arm or groin for a left heart catheterization. Usually, this catheter is inserted into the groin in the femoral artery and winds its way up into the heart.

Once the catheter is in place, various pressure measurements can be taken, and contrast dye can be injected into the arteries and with the use of fluoroscopy (angiocardiograph)

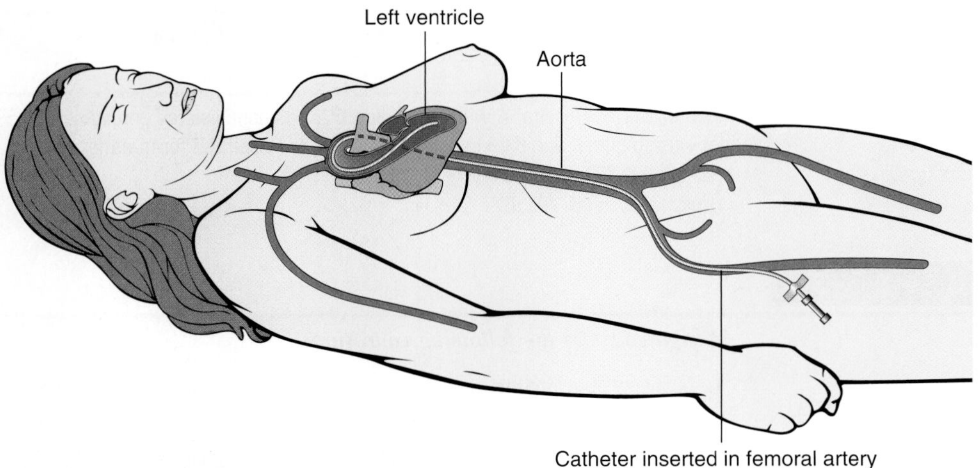

FIGURE 16-19. Left-sided cardiac catheterization. The catheter is passed retrograde (backward) from the femoral artery into the aorta and then into the left ventricle. For right-sided cardiac catheterization, the cardiologist inserts a catheter through the femoral vein and advances it to the right atrium and right ventricle and into the pulmonary artery.

TABLE 16-2 COMMON PROCEDURE CODES FOR CARDIAC CATHETERIZATION

Test	Procedure	Comment
Left heart cath	4A023N7	Most commonly done alone when used to diagnose coronary artery disease (CAD)
Right heart cath	4A023N6	This is used most commonly for assessment of ventricular function, especially for patients who also have congestive heart failure (CHF)
Combined right and left heart catherization	4A023N8	

detect blockages in the arteries. See Table 16-2 for coding of the different types of heart caths. In ICD-10-PCS cardiac caths are found in the measurement and monitoring section, with the root operation being measurement (determining the level of a physiologic function at a point in time).

During a heart catheterization other procedures such as biopsy, angioplasty, and stenting may be performed. Intravascular ultrasound (IVUS) may also be used during a cardiac cath.

EXAMPLE

Patient was admitted with chest pain. A left heart cath was performed which showed clean coronary arteries. No cause for the chest pain was found, R07.9, 4A023N7

SECTION	BODY SYSTEM	ROOT OPERATION	BODY PART	APPROACH	FUNCTION/ DEVICE	QUALIFIER
Measurement and Monitoring 4	Physiological Systems A	Measurement 0	Cardiac 2	Percutaneous 3	Sampling and Pressure N	Left Heart 7

Angioplasty

Angioplasty is a procedure for widening a diseased vessel, which is usually either obstructed or narrowed. The device is inserted, the balloon inflated, and the plaque is compressed against the wall of the artery (Figure 16-20). Angioplasty can be performed on both coronary and noncoronary vessels. In ICD-10-PCS the vessels are determined to be upper if they are above the diaphragm or lower if they are below the diaphragm. When angioplasty is

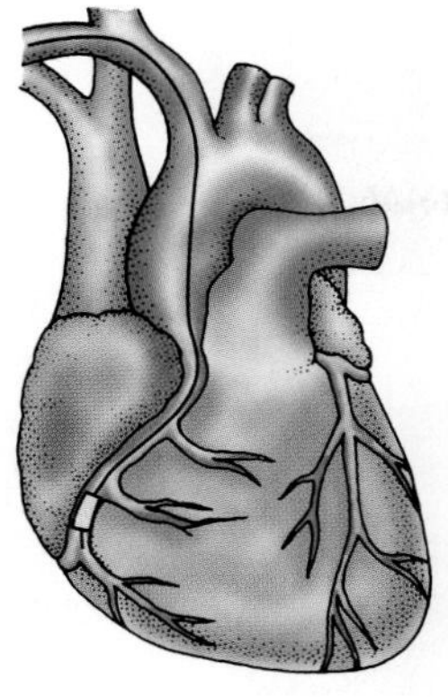

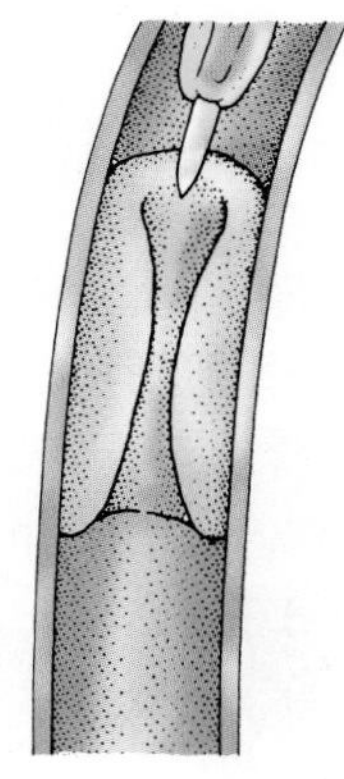

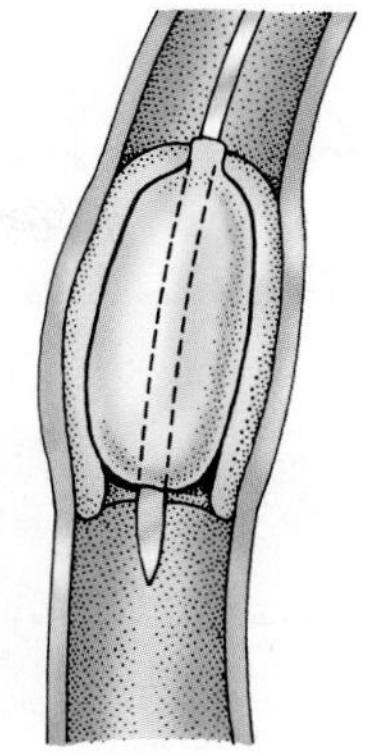

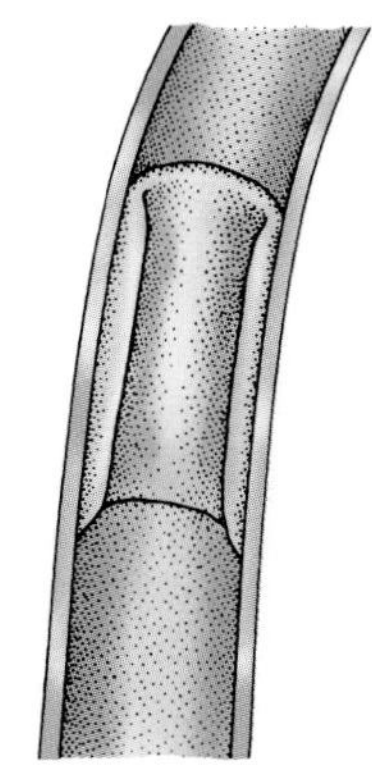

1. The balloon-tipped catheter is positioned in the artery.
2. The uninflated balloon is centered in the obstruction.
3. The balloon is inflated, which flattens plaque against the artery wall.
4. The balloon is removed, and the artery is left unoccluded.

FIGURE 16-20. Angioplasty.

performed on the coronary arteries it is often abbreviated PTCA (percutaneous transluminal coronary angioplasty). The root operation for an angioplasty procedure in ICD-10-PCS is dilation (expanding an orifice or lumen). In ICD-10-PCS it is important to know that coronary arteries are classified as a single body part. Attention must be paid to the number of arteries being treated. In ICD-10-PCS, character 6 identifies whether the stent being inserted is drug eluting, non–drug eluting, radioactive, or no device. If different types of stents are inserted, two codes would be required to identify the different stent types.

One of the most common complications of angioplasty is restenosis, which occurs in about one-third of cases. To try to avoid restenosis, physicians may use a stent. Sometimes, they also treat a restenosed patient with intravascular radiation therapy. Most often, an angioplasty is performed prior to insertion of a stent.

Atherectomy is the removal of plaque from a vessel. This may be done with the use of a catheter with a shaver or rotablator on the end. A laser is also used to perform atherectomy.

Stent insertion into the coronary artery is a procedure that may be performed after completion of an angioplasty (Figure 16-21). The stent helps to keep the artery open. Inserted stents may be drug-eluting (DES) or non–drug-eluting.

Three types of drug-eluting stents that are currently used in the United States are a paclitaxel-eluting stent, a sirolimus-eluting stent, and an everolimos. These drug-eluting stents are not to be confused with a stent that may be coated with antiplatelet drug.

EXAMPLE

Patient with CAD has a PTCA of the LAD and LCD with a drug-eluting stent placed in the LCD, I25.10, 027034Z, 02703ZZ.

SECTION	BODY SYSTEM	ROOT OPERATION	BODY PART	APPROACH	DEVICE	QUALIFIER
Medical and Surgical	Heart and Great Vessels	Dilation	Coronary Artery, One Artery	Percutaneous	Intraluminal Device, Drug-eluting	No Qualifier
0	2	7	0	3	4	Z

SECTION	BODY SYSTEM	ROOT OPERATION	BODY PART	APPROACH	DEVICE	QUALIFIER
Medical and Surgical	Heart and Great Vessels	Dilation	Coronary Artery, One Artery	Percutaneous	No Device	No Qualifier
0	2	7	0	3	Z	Z

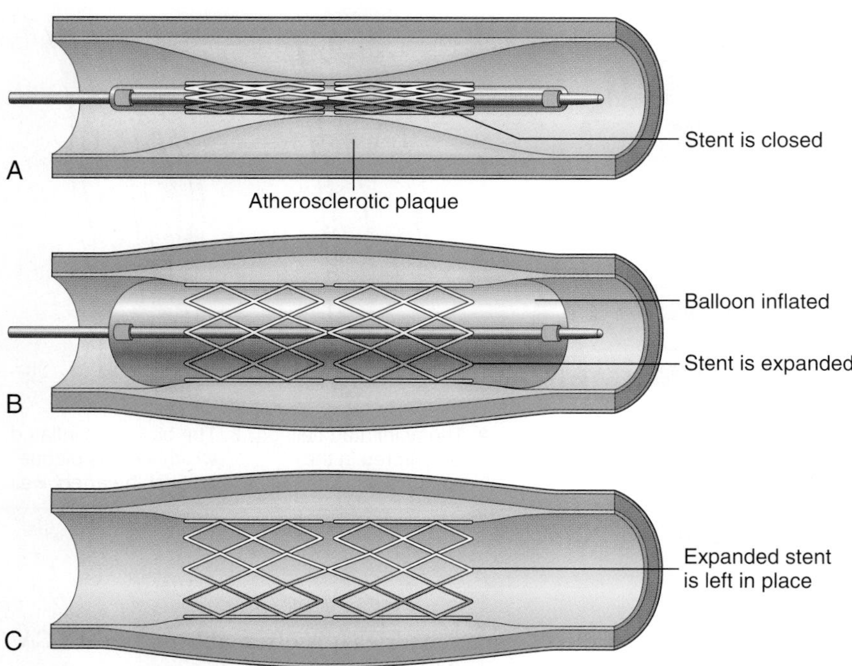

FIGURE 16-21. Placement of an intracoronary stent. **A,** The stent is positioned at the site of the lesion. **B,** The balloon is inflated, thereby expanding the stent. **C,** The balloon is then deflated and removed, and the implanted stent is left in place. Coronary stents are stainless steel scaffolding devices that help hold open arteries such as the coronary, renal, and carotid arteries.

EXAMPLE

Patient with CAD presents for PTCA of left anterior descending and left circumflex with atherectomy of the left anterior descending artery, I25.10, 02713ZZ, 02C03ZZ.

SECTION	BODY SYSTEM	ROOT OPERATION	BODY PART	APPROACH	DEVICE	QUALIFIER
Medical and Surgical	Heart and Great Vessels	Dilation	Coronary Artery, Two Arteries	Percutaneous	No Device	No Qualifier
0	2	7	1	3	Z	Z

SECTION	BODY SYSTEM	ROOT OPERATION	BODY PART	APPROACH	DEVICE	QUALIFIER
Medical and Surgical	Heart and Great Vessels	Extirpation	Coronary Artery, One Artery	Percutaneous	No Device	No Qualifier
0	2	C	0	3	Z	Z

Angioplasty of non-coronary vessels is also coded to the root operation dilation. The area of dilation must be indentified (i.e., of arteries or veins) and then the particular body system of the circulatory system, must also be identified (i.e., upper arteries, lower arteries, heart and great vessels). If a thrombolytic agent is used in these procedures, and an additional code must be added from the Administration Section using the root operation, introduction. New ICD-10-PCS codes have been implemented for the use of drug-coated balloons that are used during peripheral angioplasties. There is a new qualifier in table 047 Dilation of Lower Arteries. These drug-coated balloons are not a device as they are not left in after the procedure.

EXAMPLE

Angioplasty of a left external iliac artery with a non-drug-eluting stent, percutaneous approach, 047J3DZ.

SECTION	BODY SYSTEM	ROOT OPERATION	BODY PART	APPROACH	DEVICE	QUALIFIER
Medical and Surgical	Lower Arteries	Dilation	External Iliac Artery, Left	Percutaneous	Intraluminal Device	No Qualifier
0	4	7	J	3	D	Z

EXAMPLE

Patient has atherosclerosis of the left leg with intermittent claudication and rest pain. A left femoral artery angioplasty with drug-coated balloon was performed, 170.222, 047L3Z1

SECTION	BODY SYSTEM	ROOT OPERATION	BODY PART	APPROACH	DEVICE	QUALIFIER
Medical and Surgical	Lower Arteries	Dilation	Femoral Artery, Left	Percutaneous	No Device	Drug-Coated Balloon
0	4	7	L	3	Z	1

Coronary Artery Bypass Graft

Coronary artery bypass graft (CABG or CAB) is surgery that is performed to bypass blood around the clogged arteries to the heart (Figure 16-22). The procedure is done by taking a healthy blood vessel from another part of the body, usually the internal mammary artery or the saphenous vein. Surgeons should document in their operative notes the number of arteries bypassed and the types of blood vessels used. The root operation for a CABG in ICD-10-PCS is bypass (altering a root of passage of a tubular body part).

When reading a bypass operative report, it is helpful to know the coronary arteries that may be bypassed (Figure 16-23 and Figure 16-24). Two main coronary arteries are located on the left (LCA) and on the right (RCA). The LCA divides into two arteries: the LAD and

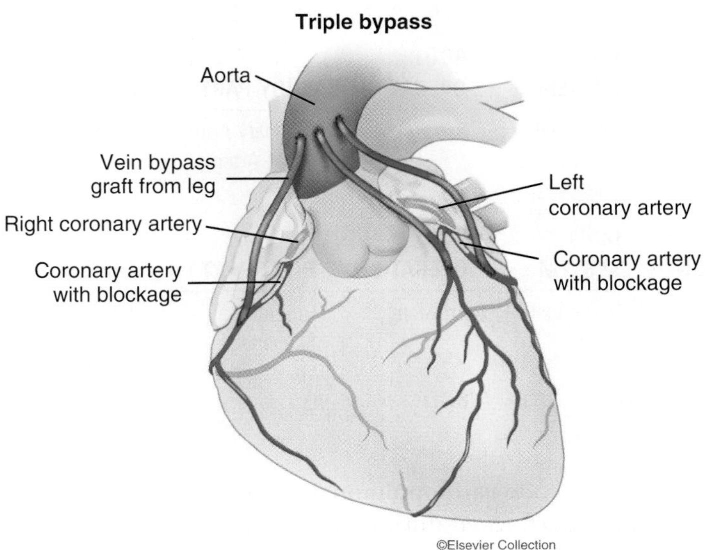

FIGURE 16-22. Coronary artery bypass graft (CABG) surgery with anastomosis of vein and arterial grafts. Section of a vein is removed from the leg and is anastomosed (upside down because of its directional valves) to a coronary artery to bypass the area of arteriosclerotic blockage.

SECTION: 0 MEDICAL AND SURGICAL
BODY SYSTEM: 2 HEART AND GREAT VESSELS
OPERATION: 1 BYPASS: *(on multiple pages)*
Altering the route of passage of the contents of a tubular body part

Body Part	Approach	Device	Qualifier
0 Coronary Artery, One Artery 1 Coronary Artery, Two Arteries 2 Coronary Artery, Three Arteries 3 Coronary Artery, Four or More Arteries	0 Open	8 Zooplastic Tissue 9 Autologous Venous Tissue A Autologous Arterial Tissue J Synthetic Substitute K Nonautologous Tissue Substitute	3 Coronary Artery 8 Internal Mammary, Right 9 Internal Mammary, Left C Thoracic Artery F Abdominal Artery W Aorta
0 Coronary Artery, One Artery 1 Coronary Artery, Two Arteries 2 Coronary Artery, Three Arteries 3 Coronary Artery, Four or More Arteries	0 Open	Z No Device	3 Coronary Artery 8 Internal Mammary, Right 9 Internal Mammary, Left C Thoracic Artery F Abdominal Artery

FIGURE 16-23. Coronary artery bypass table.

the circumflex. The RCA divides into the posterior descending artery (PDA) and the marginal branch. Smaller branches consist of the acute marginal, the obtuse marginal (OM), and the diagonals.

To code coronary artery bypasses in ICD-10-CM, the coder must review the operative report for the number of arteries bypassed. A separate procedure is coded for each coronary artery that uses a different device (i.e., saphenous vein, internal mammary). The most common bypass is from the aorta to the coronary artery. According to the ICD-10-PCS guidelines, the coronary bypass procedures are coded differently from other bypass procedures. The body part identifies the number of coronary arteries bypassed to, and the qualifier identifies the vessel bypassed from. A separate code is assigned for the harvesting of the bypass graft.

EXAMPLE

Patient has CABG of three coronary arteries, using a greater saphenous vein from the left leg (vein harvested by percutaneous endoscopic approach), 021209W, 06BQ4ZZ (Figure 16-23).

SECTION	BODY SYSTEM	ROOT OPERATION	BODY PART	APPROACH	DEVICE	QUALIFIER
Medical and Surgical 0	Heart and Great Vessels 2	Bypass 1	Coronary Artery, Three Arteries 2	Open 0	Autologous Venous Tissue 9	Aorta W

SECTION	BODY SYSTEM	ROOT OPERATION	BODY PART	APPROACH	DEVICE	QUALIFIER
Medical and Surgical 0	Lower Veins 6	Excision B	Greater Saphenous Vein, Left Q	Percutaneous Endoscopic 4	No Device Z	No Qualifier Z

It is acceptable to code cardiopulmonary bypass for heart procedures. Other auxiliary procedures that are performed during heart surgery such as hypothermia, cardioplegia, intraoperative cardiac pacing, and chest tube insertions are integral to the surgery and should not be coded separately. Some heart procedures are now being performed without cardiopulmonary bypass. These procedures may be documented as off pump or beating heart surgery.

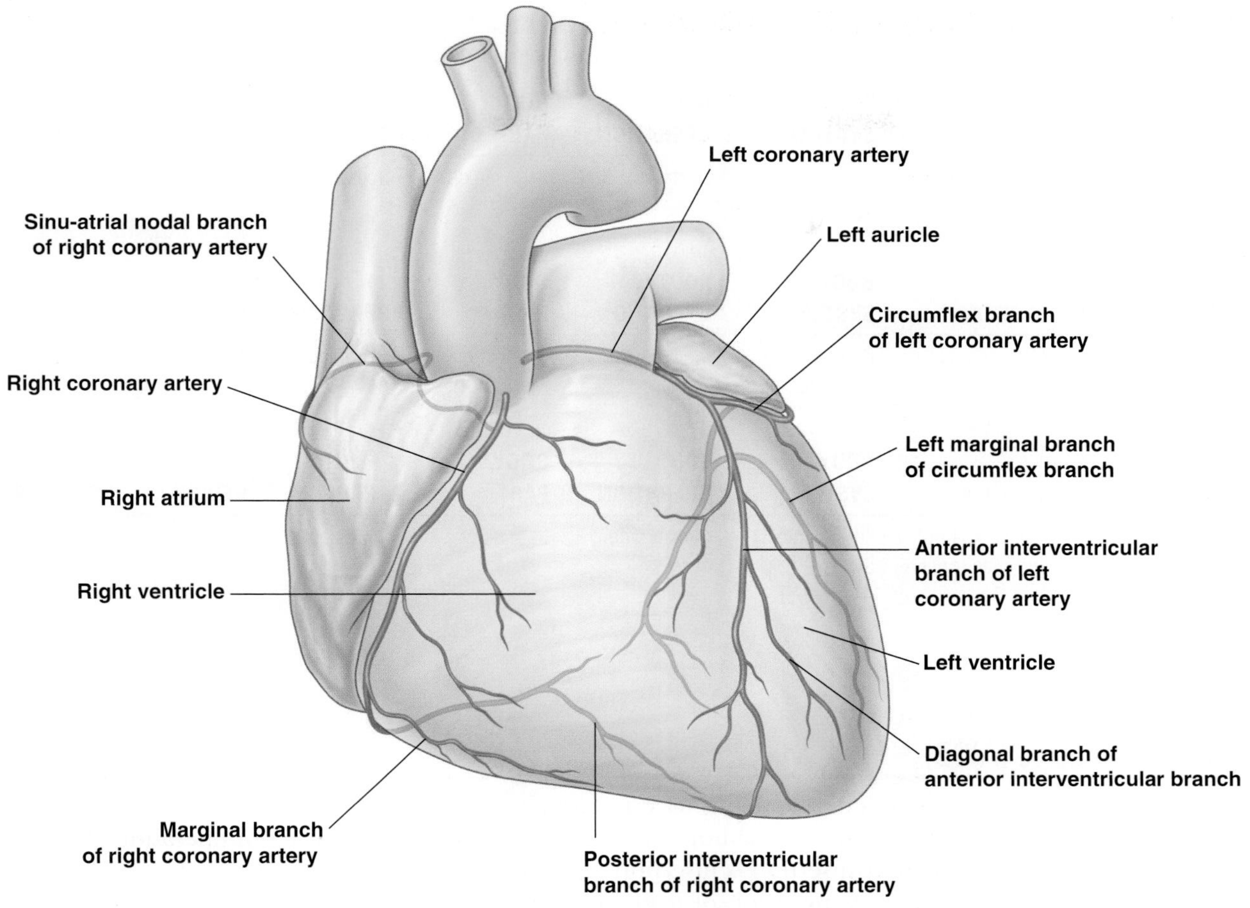

FIGURE 16-24. Anterior view of coronary arterial system.

Electrophysiologic Studies/Procedures

Electrophysiologic studies (EPS) are used to analyze the electrical conduction system of the heart. The root operation for eletrophysiologic studies is found in the medical- and surgical-related sections under measurement and monitoring (with a root operation of measurement, which is determining the level of a physiological or physical function at a point in time). Patients with symptoms such as light-headedness, palpitations, or syncope may have EP tests done to determine the cause of these symptoms. Other patients with known heart rhythm disturbances may have EP studies so that the severity of the heart disturbance can be determined. During these studies, catheters are inserted into a vein in the leg and are threaded to the heart. They measure electrical signals and conduction of these signals and look for abnormal heart rhythms. The **electrophysiologist** (physician trained in electrical disorders of the heart) may administer electrical stimuli to check the heart's response.

Ablation is correction of abnormal heart rhythm by destroying of abnormal heart tissue through radiofrequency or other methods such as laser, microwave, or freezing. Radiofrequency ablation (RFA) can be performed with the use of an EP catheter. The root operation for ablation in ICD-10-PCS is destruction (eradicating all or a portion of a body part by energy, force, or a destructive agent).

EXAMPLE

Patient is admitted through the ER with chronic atrial fibrillation. She is taken to the EPS lab for EPS testing, mapping, and ablation of the left atrium (percutaneous approach), I48.2, 02573ZZ, 02K83ZZ, 4A023FZ.

SECTION	BODY SYSTEM	ROOT OPERATION	BODY PART	APPROACH	DEVICE	QUALIFIER
Medical and Surgical	Heart and Great Vessels	Destruction	Atrium, Left	Percutaneous	No Device	No Qualifier
0	2	5	7	3	Z	Z

SECTION	BODY SYSTEM	ROOT OPERATION	BODY PART	APPROACH	DEVICE	QUALIFIER
Medical and Surgical	Heart and Great Vessels	Map	Conduction Mechanism	Percutaneous	No Device	No Qualifier
0	2	K	8	3	Z	Z

SECTION	BODY SYSTEM	ROOT OPERATION	BODY PART	APPROACH	DEVICE	QUALIFIER
Measurement and Monitoring	Physiological Systems	Measurement	Cardiac	Percutaneous	Rhythm	No Qualifier
4	A	0	2	3	F	Z

Pacemaker/Defibrillators (AICD)

A pacemaker is a device that is used to correct abnormally slow heartbeats, complete heart blocks (CHB), and other abnormalities of heart conduction. The root operation for pacemaker generator insertion is insertion of device into subcutaneous tissue of the chest. The root operation for insertion of leads (electrodes) is insertion of intraluminal device into the atrium (putting in a non–biologic device that monitors, assists, performs, or prevents a physiological function but does not take the place of a body part). Using the Index to locate the pacemaker insertion, the coder would look in the Alphabetic Index under insertion, subcutaneous, chest, pacemaker. Under the root operation, insertion, in the Alphabetic Index, not only are there Index listings for body system, but there are also subterms for the device being inserted. Patients who present with syncope and studies determined that they have a heart block often require a pacemaker. A pacemaker has two functions: sensing and pacing. Pacing is the sending of electrical signals to the heart from the pacemaker via the lead. If the rhythm of the heart is too slow, the pacemaker paces the heart to a faster rhythm. Sensing involves monitoring the heart's electrical activity; when the heart is functioning normally, no pacing is required.

The pacemaker system consists of the pulse generator (device, battery) and the leads (electrodes) (Figure 16-25). Leads are placed into the heart chambers and are then attached to the generator. An intraoperative pacemaker should only be reported if it remains in place and continues beyond the operative episode. A temporary pacemaker is used for emergencies or intraoperatively. Code assignment for a temporary pacemaker does not require codes for the leads or codes for removal.

A permanent pacemaker is usually implanted through an incision near the collarbone. Wires are inserted into a vein and are advanced into the heart; they are then connected to a generator, which is implanted under the skin. Coding of initial insertion of permanent pacemakers requires two codes: one for the insertion of the generator/device, and one for insertion of the leads or electrodes. Leads can be placed inside the heart or outside the heart (epicardially). Pacemaker pockets for epicardial leads are usually placed in the abdominal wall; this is typically done for children who are still growing.

Insertion/replacement/revision requires that the coder must know the type of device that is being inserted. Codes for initial insertion and replacement require knowledge as to whether this is a single-chamber or a dual-chamber device and whether the device is rate

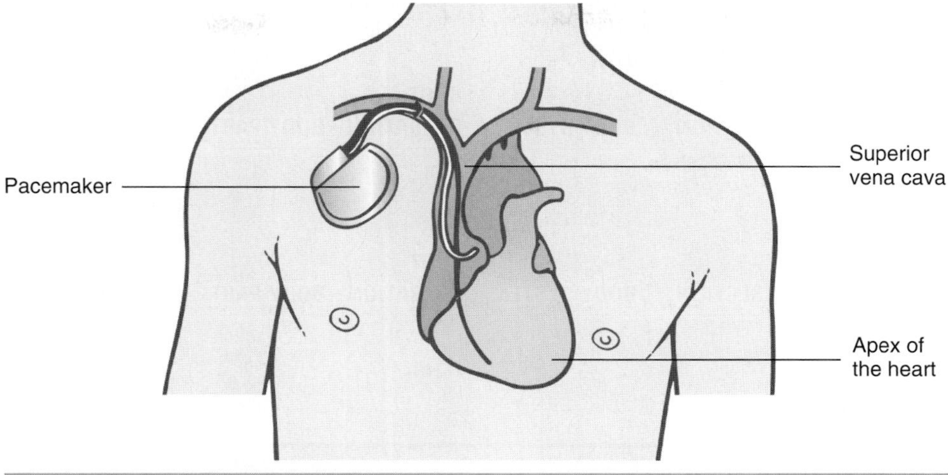

FIGURE 16-25. Cardiac leads in the atrium and in the ventricle enable a dual-chamber pacemaker to sense and pace in both heart chambers.

responsive. A rate-responsive device has a sensor that detects changes in movement of the body and reacts accordingly.

EXAMPLE

Patient with sick sinus syndrome is admitted for initial open insertion of a dual-chamber pacemaker into the subcutaneous tissue of the chest with percutaneous insertion of leads into the right atrium and right ventricle, I49.5, 0JH606Z, 02H63JZ, 02HK3JZ.

SECTION	BODY SYSTEM	ROOT OPERATION	BODY PART	APPROACH	DEVICE	QUALIFIER
Medical and Surgical	Subcutaneous Tissue and Fascia	Insertion	Subcutaneous Tissue and Fascia, Chest	Open	Pacemaker, Dual Chamber	No Qualifier
0	J	H	6	0	6	Z

SECTION	BODY SYSTEM	ROOT OPERATION	BODY PART	APPROACH	DEVICE	QUALIFIER
Medical and Surgical	Heart and Great Vessels	Insertion	Atrium, Right	Percutaneous	Cardiac Lead, Pacemaker	No Qualifier
0	2	H	6	3	J	Z

SECTION	BODY SYSTEM	ROOT OPERATION	BODY PART	APPROACH	DEVICE	QUALIFIER
Medical and Surgical	Heart and Great Vessels	Insertion	Ventricle, Right	Percutaneous	Cardiac Lead, Pacemaker	No Qualifier
0	2	H	K	3	J	Z

Separate codes are used for replacement of devices and leads and removal of devices and leads. When a patient is admitted for removal, replacement, or reprogramming the codes Z45.010 (Encounter for checking and testing of cardiac pacemaker pulse generator) or Z45.018 (Encounter for adjustment and management of other part of cardiac pacemaker) are assigned if there is no complication. Often, surgeons document that a patient is being admitted for end of life of the battery or pacemaker. In ICD-10-PCS the removal of a pacemaker and leads is found under the root operation removal (taking out a device). It is important to remember that if a device is removed and then a new device reinserted, both removal and insertion are assigned codes in ICD-10-PCS.

EXAMPLE

Admission for removal of a pacemaker and leads. Leads removed percutaneously and device via open approach, Z45.018, 02PA3MZ, 0JPT0PZ.

SECTION	BODY SYSTEM	ROOT OPERATION	BODY PART	APPROACH	DEVICE	QUALIFIER
Medical and Surgical 0	Heart and Great Vessels 2	Removal P	Heart A	Percutaneous 3	Cardiac Lead M	No Qualifier Z

SECTION	BODY SYSTEM	ROOT OPERATION	BODY PART	APPROACH	DEVICE	QUALIFIER
Medical and Surgical 0	Subcutaneous Tissue and Fascia J	Removal P	Subcutaneous Tissue and Fascia, Trunk T	Open 0	Cardiac Rhythm Related Device P	No Qualifier Z

EXAMPLE

Replacement of a single-chamber pacemaker with a dual-chamber device, with retention of the atrial lead and open removal of the single chamber generator in the chest with percutaneous right ventricle lead insertion, 0JH606Z, 0JPT0PZ, 02HK3JZ.

SECTION	BODY SYSTEM	ROOT OPERATION	BODY PART	APPROACH	DEVICE	QUALIFIER
Medical and Surgical 0	Subcutaneous Tissue and Fascia J	Insertion H	Subcutaneous Tissue and Fascia, Chest 6	Open 0	Pacemaker, Dual Chamber 6	No Qualifier Z

SECTION	BODY SYSTEM	ROOT OPERATION	BODY PART	APPROACH	DEVICE	QUALIFIER
Medical and Surgical 0	Subcutaneous Tissue and Fascia J	Removal P	Subcutaneous Tissue and Fascia, Trunk T	Open 0	Cardiac Rhythm Related Device P	No Qualifier Z

SECTION	BODY SYSTEM	ROOT OPERATION	BODY PART	APPROACH	DEVICE	QUALIFIER
Medical and Surgical 0	Heart and Great Vessels 2	Insertion H	Ventricle, Right K	Percutaneous 3	Cardiac Lead, Pacemaker J	No Qualifier Z

An automatic implantable cardioverter-defibrillator (AICD) is a device that is used for treating patients with tachyarrhythmias. Similar to a pacemaker, it has a pulse generator and electrodes that both sense and defibrillate. The root operation for insertion of an AICD is insertion for both the leads and the generator (putting in a nonbiologic device). Defibrillators give shocks that attempt to convert the heart rhythm.

EXAMPLE

Patient is admitted with ventricular tachycardia and has an AICD placed in the chest in the subcutaneous tissue, via open approach with leads inserted percutaneously in the right atrium and right ventricle, I47.2, 0JH608Z, 02H63KZ, 02HK3KZ.

SECTION	BODY SYSTEM	ROOT OPERATION	BODY PART	APPROACH	DEVICE	QUALIFIER
Medical and Surgical 0	Subcutaneous Tissue and Fascia J	Insertion H	Subcutaneous Tissue and Fascia, Chest 6	Open 0	Defibrillator Generator 8	No Qualifier Z

SECTION	BODY SYSTEM	ROOT OPERATION	BODY PART	APPROACH	DEVICE	QUALIFIER
Medical and Surgical 0	Heart and Great Vessels 2	Insertion H	Atrium, Right 6	Percutaneous 3	Cardiac Lead, Defibrillator K	No Qualifier Z

SECTION	BODY SYSTEM	ROOT OPERATION	BODY PART	APPROACH	DEVICE	QUALIFIER
Medical and Surgical 0	Heart and Great Vessels 2	Insertion H	Ventricle, Left K	Percutaneous 3	Cardiac Lead, Defibrillator K	No Qualifier Z

Biventricular pacing is also known as cardiac resynchronization therapy (CRT). Biventricular pacemakers come as a stand-alone device or with a built-in implantable cardioverter (ICV). They are used primarily to treat heart failure. Similar to a pacemaker, a generator and leads are included. The biventricular pacemaker uses a third lead. This third lead, which is attached to the wall of the left ventricle in the vein of the coronary sinus, causes both ventricles to contract at the same time or in sync. In contrast to regular pacemakers, biventricular pacemakers do not increase heart rate. Some biventricular pacers include internal cardiac defibrillators (ICDs) for patients with fast irregular rhythms. These systems have biventricular pacing, anti-tachycardia pacing, and internal defibrillators. There are codes for implantation and replacement of both systems, with the ICD and without. The root operation for insertion of a biventricular pacemaker and leads is insertion (putting in a nonbiologic device). The root operation for insertion of a cardiac resynchronization defibrillator pulse generator and the insertion of leads is insertion.

EXAMPLE

Open implantation of cardiac resynchronization treatment defibrillator (CRT-D) or total system CRT-D into chest with percutaneous insertion of leads into right atrium, right ventricle, and coronary sinus, 0JH609Z, 02HK3KZ, 02H63KZ, 02H43KZ.

SECTION	BODY SYSTEM	ROOT OPERATION	BODY PART	APPROACH	DEVICE	QUALIFIER
Medical and Surgical	Subcutaneous Tissue and Fascia	Insertion	Subcutaneous Tissue and Fascia, Chest	Open	Cardiac Resynchronization Defibrillator Pulse Generator	No Qualifier
0	J	H	6	0	9	Z

SECTION	BODY SYSTEM	ROOT OPERATION	BODY PART	APPROACH	DEVICE	QUALIFIER
Medical and Surgical	Heart and Great Vessels	Insertion	Ventricle, Right	Percutaneous	Cardiac Lead, Defibrillator	No Qualifier
0	2	H	K	3	K	Z

SECTION	BODY SYSTEM	ROOT OPERATION	BODY PART	APPROACH	DEVICE	QUALIFIER
Medical and Surgical	Heart and Great Vessels	Insertion	Atrium, Right	Percutaneous	Cardiac Lead, Defibrillator	No Qualifier
0	2	H	6	3	K	Z

SECTION	BODY SYSTEM	ROOT OPERATION	BODY PART	APPROACH	DEVICE	QUALIFIER
Medical and Surgical	Heart and Great Vessels	Insertion	Coronary Vein	Percutaneous	Cardiac Lead, Defibrillator	No Qualifier
0	2	H	4	3	K	Z

Aneurysm Repair

Aneurysms can be repaired either by resection using an open approach, with either an anastomosis or graft repair or endovascular repair where an endograft is introduced through the femoral artery via a catheter, which avoids the major abdominal incision. The root operations for an abdominal aortic aneurysm repair depend on the type of procedure performed. If the aneurysm is repaired openly by replacement with a graft, the root operation is replacement (putting in a device that replaces some or all of a body part). Taking out the body part is included in replacement. If the aneurysm is repaired openly by an anastomosis, the root operation is excision of an abdominal aorta (cutting out or off without replacement). Lastly, if the repair is performed endovascularly, the root operation is restriction of the abdominal aorta (partially closing off an orifice of a tubular body), if done with stent insertion or if done by synthetic or biologic graft, the root operation is supplement.

EXAMPLE

Patient presents for repair of an abdominal aortic aneurysm. The repair is performed endovascularly with restriction by an intraluminal device, I71.4, 04V03DZ.

SECTION	BODY SYSTEM	ROOT OPERATION	BODY PART	APPROACH	DEVICE	QUALIFIER
Medical and Surgical	Lower Arteries	Restriction	Abdominal Aorta	Percutaneous	Intraluminal Device	No Qualifier
0	4	V	0	3	D	Z

Central Lines/Catheters

Central venous lines (CVLs) are used for several purposes. They may be used to administer chemotherapy, total parenteral nutrition (TPN), antibiotics, and for dialysis. Hickman, Groshong, triple lumen, and double lumen are all types of central lines. Usually, central venous catheters are inserted into the subclavian or jugular vein and are then advanced into the vena cava. The root operation for insertion of a central line is insertion (putting in a non-biological device). A central line has a catheter that is NOT totally implanted under the skin. A peripherally inserted central catheter (PICC) (Figure 16-26) is assigned the same code as a central line. It is inserted in a slightly different manner. The correct body part depends on the site where the tip of the catheter ends up. If there is documentation that the tip of the catheter is at the cavoatrial junction, it is coded to 02HV33Z. The cavoatrial junction does not mean the tip is in the atrium. It is acceptable to use documentation from a radiology report for location of the tip.

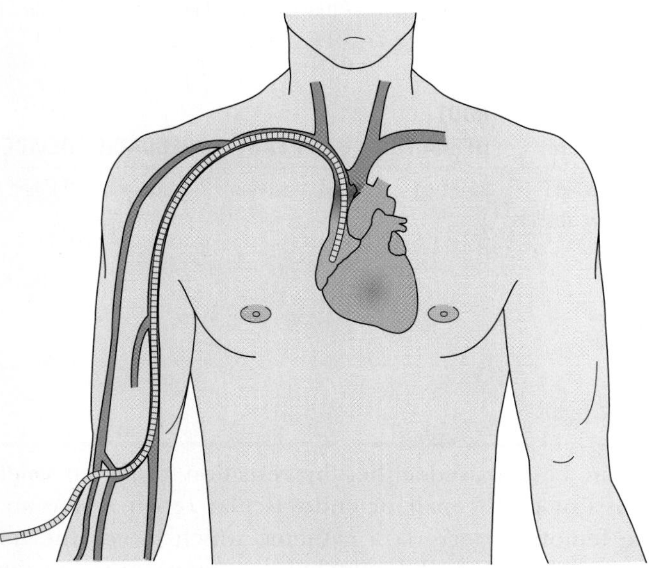

FIGURE 16-26. A peripherally inserted central catheter is threaded through the vein until the end is near the heart.

EXAMPLE

Patient is admitted to the hospital for bacterial endocarditis. A central line is inserted into the superior vena cava for administration of antibiotics to treat the endocarditis, I33.0, 02HV33Z, 3E04329.

SECTION	BODY SYSTEM	ROOT OPERATION	BODY PART	APPROACH	DEVICE	QUALIFIER
Medical and Surgical	Heart and Great Vessels	Insertion	Superior Vena Cava	Percutaneous	Infusion Device	No Qualifier
0	2	H	V	3	3	Z

SECTION	BODY SYSTEM	ROOT OPERATION	BODY PART	APPROACH	DEVICE	QUALIFIER
Administration	Physiological Systems and Anatomical Regions	Introduction	Central Vein	Percutaneous	Anti-infective	Other Anti-infective
3	E	0	4	3	2	9

EXERCISE 16-7

Assign codes to the following conditions.

1. Patient is admitted for a diagnostic left cardiac catheterization with a diagnosis of chest pain __________
2. Patient is admitted with a diagnosis of CAD for a PTCA with CYPHER stent insertion into the LAD __________
3. Patient is admitted 3 days status post angioplasty with restenosis of a stent; a non–drug-eluting stent is inserted into the RCA __________
4. Patient is admitted with atrial fibrillation, and percutaneous radiofrequency ablation of the AV node is performed __________
5. Patient is admitted with bradycardia, and a complete dual-chamber pacemaker system is inserted. The generator is inserted into a chest pocket and one lead is inserted in the right atrium, and the other lead is inserted into the right ventricle via a percutaneous approach __________
6. Patient is admitted for a single chamber pacemaker battery change for the end of life of the battery. The generator is inserted into a subcutaneous chest pocket __________
7. Patient is admitted with cerebral aneurysm, and a craniotomy with clipping is performed __________
8. Patient with ventricular fibrillation has a total AICD placed. The generator is placed in a chest pocket, and leads are placed percutaneously in the right atrium and right ventricle __________

CHAPTER REVIEW EXERCISE

Assign codes for all diagnoses and procedures including all applicable Z codes and external cause codes.

1. Patient has atrial fibrillation with rapid ventricular response __________
2. Patient had a previous CVA and now has left hemiparesis __________
3. Patient has orthostatic hypotension __________

4. Patient has mitral and tricuspid insufficiency ______
5. Patient has congestive heart failure, rheumatic ______
6. Patient has both acute and chronic renal failure and a history of hypertension; patient is currently taking verapamil ______
7. Patient has congestive heart failure with pleural effusion and hypertension ______
8. Patient has chest pain and elevated troponins ______
9. Patient presents with a non–Q wave myocardial infarction (NQMI), is taken to the cath lab for a left heart cath, and has a drug-eluting stent inserted in RCA for coronary artery disease ______
10. Patient with CAD and previous CABG presents to the hospital with USA ______
11. Patient with ACS presents to the hospital; patient has a diagnosis of CAD, the patient was immediately taken to surgery, where a 2-vessel CABG is performed LIMA to LAD and an autologous saphenous vein graft to RCA. Procedure performed under cardiopulmonary bypass and the right lesser saphenous vein was harvested via an open approach ______
12. Patient has a left anterior fascicular block ______
13. Patient is admitted through the ER with chest pain that is determined to be coronary artery disease following a left heart cath ______
14. Patient has congestive systolic and diastolic heart failure ______
15. Patient presents to the hospital with pulmonary edema and a history of hypertensive congestive heart failure for which the patient currently takes Lasix and verapamil ______
16. Patient is admitted for a stroke with left side hemiplegia and dysphagia. Upon discharge the hemiplegia has resolved ______
17. Patient has a history of stroke and is currently admitted with atrial fibrillation and dysphagia due to the old stroke ______
18. Patient has arteriosclerosis of the extremities and is admitted with a stage 1 (skin breakdown) ulcer and gangrene of the right foot ______
19. Patient is admitted to the hospital with deep vein thrombosis of the left calf and a pulmonary embolism ______
20. History of heart valve replaced with porcine valve ______
21. Patient had a percutaneous atherectomy of the right coronary artery for CAD ______
22. Patient had a dual chamber pacemaker inserted for syncope, which was attributed to bradycardia. Generator inserted into the chest and leads into the right atrium and right ventricle (generator inserted into chest via open approach and leads inserted percutaneously) ______
23. Patient had congestive heart failure and was treated with a cardiac resynchronization pacemaker with leads inserted into both ventricles and the right atrium (generator inserted into the chest via open approach, leads inserted via a transvenous approach) ______
24. Patient had an abdominal aortic aneurysm (AAA) and was treated with endovascular repair with a stent graft ______
25. Patient was admitted with bacterial endocarditis and had a Hickman catheter inserted into the left subclavian after subclavian insert (central vein) percutaneously for antibiotic administration ______

CHAPTER GLOSSARY

Ablation: correction of abnormal heart rhythm by burning of abnormal heart tissue through radiofrequency or other methods such as laser, microwave, or freezing.

Aneurysm: bulging or ballooning out of a vessel.

Angioplasty: a procedure performed to treat coronary artery disease. An inflated balloon compresses plaque against artery walls.

Aphasia: impairment of speech expression and/or word understanding.

Atherosclerosis: type of arteriosclerosis wherein fatty substances such as plaque block or clog the arteries.

Blood pressure: the force that blood puts on the arterial walls when the heart beats.

BNP: (brain natriuretic peptide) a hormone that is produced by the heart; a BNP test measures the amount of BNP that is found in the heart.

Bradycardia: slow heart rate, generally fewer than 60 beats per minute.

Capillaries: smallest blood vessel through which material passes to and from the bloodstream.

Cardiac arrest: sudden loss of heart function.

Cardiomyopathy: a disorder of the muscles of the heart chambers that impedes heart function.

Cognitive deficit: disorder in thinking, learning, awareness, or judgment.

Conduction disorder: abnormalities of cardiac impulses.

Coronary artery bypass graft: surgery performed to bypass an occluded coronary artery.

Deep vein thrombosis: a blood clot that forms in a deep vein.

Dissection: a tear in wall of a vessel.

Electrophysiologist: physician trained in electrical disorders of the heart.

Embolus: clot that travels to another part of the body.

Endocarditis: inflammation of the lining of the heart chambers and valves.

Heart failure: impaired function of the heart's pumping ability.

Myocardial infarction: heart attack.

NSTEMI: non–ST elevation myocardial infarction.

Pericarditis: inflammation of the covering of the heart.

Phlebitis: inflammation of a vein.

Pulmonary embolism: a blood clot(s) in the pulmonary artery that causes blockage in the artery.

Pulmonary hypertension: high blood pressure in the arteries that supply blood to the lungs.

Stasis dermatitis: skin condition due to poor circulation (venous insufficiency) that is characterized by swelling, skin discoloration, weeping, itching, and scaly skin.

STEMI: ST elevation myocardial infarction.

Stenosis: abnormal narrowing.

Stroke: cerebrovascular accident or brain infarction.

Tachycardia: fast heart rate, generally greater than 100 beats per minute.

Thoracentesis: puncture of the chest wall to remove fluid (pleural effusion) from the space between the lining of the outside of the lungs (pleura) and the wall of the chest.

Thrombus: a blood clot that forms and remains in a vein.

Varicose veins: enlarged, twisted veins that usually occur in the legs.

REFERENCES

1. Frazier ME, Drzymkowski JW: *Essentials of Human Diseases and Conditions*, ed 5, St. Louis, 2013, Saunders, Table 10-1, pp 508–509.
2. American Hospital Association: *Coding Clinic for ICD-10-CM/PCS* 1Q:10–11, 2016. Heart failure with preserved ejection fraction and heart failure with reduced ejection fraction.

17

Diseases of the Respiratory System

(ICD-10-CM Chapters 10 and 22, Codes J00-J99, U07.0)

CHAPTER OUTLINE

LEARNING OBJECTIVES

1. Apply and assign the correct ICD-10-CM/PCS codes in accordance with Official Guidelines for Coding and Reporting
2. Identify pertinent anatomy and physiology of the respiratory system
3. Identify diseases of the respiratory system
4. Assign the correct Z codes and procedure codes related to the respiratory system
5. Identify common treatments, medications, laboratory values, and diagnostic tests

ABBREVIATIONS/ ACRONYMS

ABG arterial blood gas
AIDS acquired immunodeficiency syndrome
BIPAP bilevel positive airway pressure
CAP community-acquired pneumonia
CC complication/comorbidity
CHF congestive heart failure
COPD chronic obstructive pulmonary disease
CPAP continuous positive airway pressure
CVA cerebrovascular accident

ABBREVIATIONS/ ACRONYMS—*cont'd*

E. coli *Escherichia coli*

ER Emergency Room

GERD gastroesophageal reflux disease

H. flu *Haemophilus influenzae*

HIV human immunodeficiency virus

ICD-10-CM *International Classification of Diseases, 10th Revision, Clinical Modification*

ICD-10-PCS *International Classification of Diseases, 10th Revision, Procedure Coding System*

IPPV intermittent positive pressure ventilation

IV intravenous

LLL left lower lobe

NEC not elsewhere classifiable

NOS not otherwise specified

NPPV noninvasive positive pressure ventilation

O_2 oxygen

OR Operating Room

$Paco_2$ partial pressure of carbon dioxide in arterial blood

Pao_2 partial pressure of oxygen in arterial blood

PCP *Pneumocystis carinii pneumonia*

RAD reactive airway disease

RSV respiratory syncytial virus

RUL right upper lobe

RW relative weight

STAPH aureus *Staphylococcus aureus*

VATS video-assisted thoracic surgery

ICD-10-CM Official Guidelines for Coding and Reporting (2021-2022)

Please refer to the companion Evolve website for the most current 2021-2022 guidelines.

10. Chapter 10: Diseases of Respiratory System (J00-J99, U07.0)

a. Chronic Obstructive Pulmonary Disease [COPD] and Asthma

1) Acute exacerbation of chronic obstructive bronchitis and asthma

The codes in categories J44 and J45 distinguish between uncomplicated cases and those in acute exacerbation. An acute exacerbation is a worsening or a decompensation of a chronic condition. An acute exacerbation is not equivalent to an infection superimposed on a chronic condition, though an exacerbation may be triggered by an infection.

EXAMPLE

Patient is seen by the pulmonologist for management of exacerbation of COPD. The exacerbation was triggered by the patient's acute bronchitis J44.0, J20.9.

EXAMPLE

Patient has asthma and is being treated for pneumonia, J18.9, J45.909.

b. Acute Respiratory Failure

1) Acute respiratory failure as principal diagnosis

A code from subcategory J96.0, Acute respiratory failure, or subcategory J96.2, Acute and chronic respiratory failure, may be assigned as a principal diagnosis when it is the condition established after study to be chiefly responsible for occasioning the admission to the hospital, and the selection is supported by the Alphabetic Index and Tabular List. However, chapter-specific coding guidelines (such as obstetrics, poisoning, HIV, newborn) that provide sequencing direction take precedence.

EXAMPLE

The patient presented to the ER in acute respiratory failure and was intubated and admitted to ICU. Following admission, the patient was started on antibiotics for pneumonia. The patient was on mechanical ventilation for 24 hours, J96.00, J18.9, 5A1945Z, 0BH17EZ.

(Per guidelines, if respiratory failure and another acute condition are equally responsible for occasioning the admission, the guidelines regarding two or more diagnoses that equally meet the definition for principal diagnoses may be applied.)

2) Acute respiratory failure as secondary diagnosis

Respiratory failure may be listed as a secondary diagnosis if it occurs after admission, or if it is present on admission, but does not meet the definition of principal diagnosis.

EXAMPLE

The patient was admitted from the clinic for IV antibiotics for pneumonia. A couple of hours after admission, the patient's condition deteriorated and acute respiratory failure developed, J18.9, J96.00.

3) Sequencing of acute respiratory failure and another acute condition

When a patient is admitted with respiratory failure and another acute condition, (e.g., myocardial infarction, cerebrovascular accident, aspiration pneumonia), the principal diagnosis will not be the same in every situation. This applies whether the other acute condition is a respiratory or nonrespiratory condition. Selection of the principal diagnosis will be dependent on the circumstances of admission. If both the respiratory failure and the other acute condition are equally responsible for occasioning the admission to the hospital, and there are no chapter-specific sequencing rules, the guideline regarding two or more diagnoses that equally meet the definition for principal diagnosis *(Section II, C.)* may be applied in these situations.

If the documentation is not clear as to whether acute respiratory failure and another condition are equally responsible for occasioning the admission, query the provider for clarification.

EXAMPLE Patient was admitted to the hospital in acute respiratory failure due to congestive heart failure. The patient was intubated and placed on mechanical ventilation for 2 days. The patient responded well to IV diuretics, J96.00, I50.9, 5A1945Z, 0BH17EZ.

c. Influenza due to certain identified influenza viruses

Code only confirmed cases of influenza due to certain identified influenza viruses (category J09), and due to other identified influenza virus (category JI0). This is an exception to the hospital inpatient guideline Section II, H. (Uncertain Diagnosis).

In this context, "confirmation" does not require documentation of positive laboratory testing specific for avian or other novel influenza A or other identified influenza virus. However, coding should be based on the provider's diagnostic statement that the patient has avian influenza, or other novel influenza A, for category J09, or has another particular identified strain of influenza, such as HINI or H3N2, but not identified as novel or variant, for category J10.

If the provider records "suspected" or "possible" or "probable" avian influenza, or novel influenza, or other identified influenza, then the appropriate influenza code from category J11, Influenza due to unidentified influenza virus, should be assigned. A code from category J09, Influenza due to certain identified influenza viruses, should not be assigned nor should a code from category J10, Influenza due to other identified influenza virus.

EXAMPLE Patient was admitted with a confirmed case of avian influenza, J09.X2.

EXAMPLE Patient was admitted with possible H1N1 influenza, J11.1.

d. Ventilator associated Pneumonia

1) Documentation of Ventilator associated Pneumonia

As with all procedural or postprocedural complications, code assignment is based on the provider's documentation of the relationship between the condition and the procedure.

Code J95.851, Ventilator associated pneumonia, should be assigned only when the provider has documented ventilator associated pneumonia (VAP). An additional code to identify the organism (e.g., Pseudomonas aeruginosa, code B96.5) should also be assigned. Do not assign an additional code from categories J12-J18 to identify the type of pneumonia.

Code J95.851 should not be assigned for cases where the patient has pneumonia and is on a mechanical ventilator and the provider has not specifically stated that the pneumonia is ventilator-associated pneumonia. If the documentation is unclear as to whether the patient has a pneumonia that is a complication attributable to the mechanical ventilator, query the provider.

2) Ventilator associated Pneumonia Develops after Admission

A patient may be admitted with one type of pneumonia (e.g., code J13, Pneumonia due to Streptococcus pneumonia) and subsequently develop VAP. In this instance, the principal diagnosis would be the appropriate code from categories J12-J18 for the pneumonia diagnosed at the time of admission. Code J95.851, Ventilator associated pneumonia, would be assigned as an additional diagnosis when the provider has also documented the presence of ventilator associated pneumonia.

e. Vaping-related disorders

For patients presenting with condition(s) related to vaping, assign code U07.0, Vaping-related disorder, as the principal diagnosis. For lung injury due to vaping, assign only code U07.0. Assign additional codes for other manifestations, such as acute respiratory failure (subcategory J96.0-) or pneumonitis (code J68.0).

Associated respiratory signs and symptoms due to vaping, such as cough, shortness of breath, etc., are not coded separately when a definitive diagnosis has been established. However, it would be appropriate to code separately any gastrointestinal symptoms, such as diarrhea and abdominal pain.

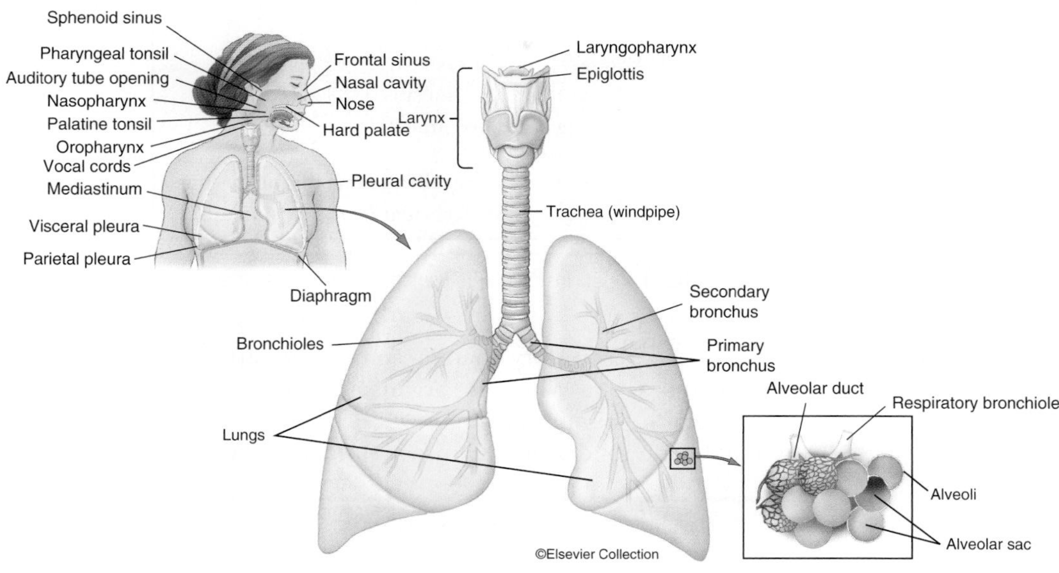

FIGURE 17-1. Anatomy of the respiratory system.

ANATOMY AND PHYSIOLOGY

The primary function of the **respiratory system** (Figure 17-1) is to supply the body with oxygen (O_2). Respiration occurs through the nose and mouth, bringing oxygen through the larynx and trachea and into the lungs, where oxygen is delivered and carbon dioxide is exhaled. Dome-shaped muscles at the bottom of the lungs, or the **diaphragm**, assist in the process of breathing and in the exchange of oxygen/carbon dioxide. The lungs are the major organ of the respiratory system. The right lung is made up of three lobes; the left lung is smaller and contains two lobes. The **bronchi** are the two air tubes that branch off the trachea and deliver air to both lungs. The **trachea**, or windpipe, is responsible for filtering the air that we breathe.

DISEASE CONDITIONS

Diseases of the Respiratory System, Chapter 10 in the ICD-10-CM code book, are divided into the following categories:

CATEGORY	SECTION TITLES
J00-J06	Acute upper respiratory infections
J09-J18	Influenza and pneumonia
J20-J22	Other acute lower respiratory infections
J30-J39	Other diseases of upper respiratory tract
J40-J47	Chronic lower respiratory diseases
J60-J70	Lung diseases due to external agents
J80-J84	Other respiratory diseases principally affecting the interstitium
J85-J86	Suppurative and necrotic conditions of the lower respiratory tract
J90-J94	Other diseases of the pleura
J95	Intraoperative and postprocedural complications and disorders of respiratory system, not elsewhere classified
J96-J99	Other diseases of the respiratory system

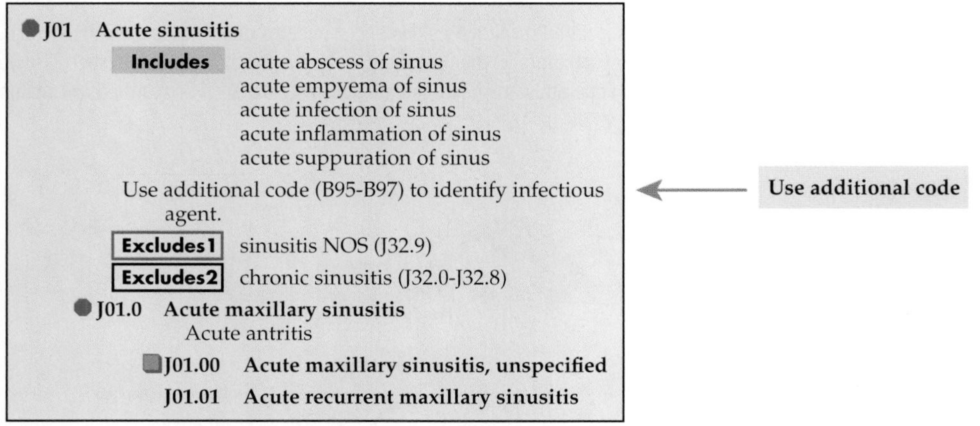
J01 Acute sinusitis

Includes acute abscess of sinus
acute empyema of sinus
acute infection of sinus
acute inflammation of sinus
acute suppuration of sinus

Use additional code (B95-B97) to identify infectious agent.

Excludes1 sinusitis NOS (J32.9)

Excludes2 chronic sinusitis (J32.0-J32.8)

J01.0 Acute maxillary sinusitis
Acute antritis

J01.00 Acute maxillary sinusitis, unspecified

J01.01 Acute recurrent maxillary sinusitis

FIGURE 17-2. Instruction to use additional code to identify infectious agent.

In the Respiratory chapter, some codes are provided that do include the organisms or infectious agent. When the organism is included, it is not necessary to assign an additional code for the organism. There will be an Instructional note if it is necessary to use an additional code to identify the infectious agent (Figure 17-2).

EXAMPLE Pneumonia due to respiratory syncytial virus, J12.1.

This is a combination code that includes the disease process, pneumonia, and the causative organism, respiratory syncytial virus (RSV). No additional code is necessary to identify the organism.

EXAMPLE Acute laryngitis due to *Haemophilus influenzae*, J04.0, B96.3.

In this case, laryngitis is due to *Haemophilus influenzae* bacteria *(H flu)*. The code for acute laryngitis, J04.0, makes no mention of the causative bacteria; therefore, code B96.3 is assigned as an additional code to identify the bacteria.

Infection is invasion of the body by organisms that have the potential to cause disease. In the respiratory chapter there are infections and/or inflammations of the upper and lower respiratory tract. It is possible that an acute infection may be superimposed upon a chronic infection or inflammation. Following general guidelines, "If the same condition is described as both acute (subacute) and chronic, and separate subentries exist in the Alphabetic Index at the same indentation level, code both and sequence the acute (subacute) code first" (Figure 17-3).

ICD-10-CM also has some codes to identify an infection that is acute and recurrent. An infection would be classified as recurrent if a patient has had multiple episodes within a year. Recurrent does not necessarily mean the condition is chronic. In a patient with recurrent acute infection a different approach in treating the infection may be necessary. For example, a patient with acute recurrent tonsillitis may require a tonsillectomy. A patient with acute tonsillitis may be treated with antibiotics.

EXAMPLE Acute and chronic bronchitis, J20.9, J42.

Acute Upper Respiratory Infections (J00-J06) and Other Diseases of Upper Respiratory Tract (J30-J39)

Acute **sinusitis** occurs when the linings of one or more sinuses become infected, usually because of viruses or bacteria. Sinuses may swell, causing an obstruction and interfering with the normal drainage of mucus. This may occur as the result of a cold. Sinusitis can cause considerable discomfort and may lead to more serious infection.

Acute → acute or subacute (with bronchospasm or obstruction) J20.9

Chronic → chronic J42

Bronchitis (diffuse) (fibrinous) (hypostatic) (infective) (membranous) J40
- with
  - influenza, flu or grippe —*see* Influenza, with, respiratory manifestations NEC
  - obstruction (airway) (lung) J44.9
  - tracheitis (15 years of age and above) J40
    - acute or subacute J20.9
    - chronic J42
    - under 15 years of age J20.9
- acute or subacute (with bronchospasm or obstruction) J20.9
  - with
    - bronchiectasis J47.0
    - chronic obstructive pulmonary disease J44.0
  - chemical (due to gases, fumes or vapors) J68.0
  - due to
    - fumes or vapors J68.0
    - Haemophilus influenzae J20.1
    - Mycoplasma pneumoniae J20.0
    - radiation J70.0
    - specified organism NEC J20.8
    - Streptococcus J20.2
    - virus
      - coxsackie J20.3
      - echovirus J20.7
      - parainfluenzae J20.4
      - respiratory syncytial J20.5
      - rhinovirus J20.6
  - viral NEC J20.8
- allergic (acute) J45.909
  - with
    - exacerbation (acute) J45.901
    - status asthmaticus J45.902
- arachidic T17.528
- aspiration (due to fumes or vapors) J68.0
- asthmatic J45.9
  - chronic J44.9
    - with
      - acute lower respiratory infection J44.0
      - exacerbation (acute) J44.1
- capillary —*see* Pneumonia, broncho
- caseous (tuberculous) A15.5
- Castellani's A69.8
- catarrhal (15 years of age and above) J40
  - acute —*see* Bronchitis, acute
  - chronic J41.0
  - under 15 years of age J20.9
- chemical (acute) (subacute) J68.0
  - chronic J68.4
  - due to fumes or vapors J68.0
    - chronic J68.4
- chronic J42
  - with
    - airways obstruction J44.9
    - tracheitis (chronic) J42
  - asthmatic (obstructive) J44.9
  - catarrhal J41.0

FIGURE 17-3. Alphabetic Index for acute and chronic bronchitis.

EXAMPLE

Acute maxillary sinusitis, J01.00.

Chronic sinusitis occurs when the sinuses become inflamed and swollen. Chronic sinusitis may be caused by an infection but could also be due to conditions such as nasal polyps or a deviated nasal septum. It can be difficult to treat and may last 12 weeks or longer.

EXAMPLE

Chronic maxillary sinusitis, J32.0.

EXERCISE 17-1

Assign codes to the following conditions.

1. Headache due to acute pansinusitis ______________
2. Laryngotracheitis ______________
3. Acute streptococcal pharyngitis ______________
4. Nasal polyp ______________
5. Upper respiratory infection ______________
6. Acute and chronic maxillary sinusitis ______________
7. Deviated nasal septum ______________
8. Paralysis, vocal cords, bilateral ______________
9. Allergic rhinitis ______________
10. Spasm larynx ______________

Influenza and Pneumonia (J09-J18)

Influenza is a contagious viral infection of the respiratory tract that causes coughing, difficulty breathing, headache, muscle aches, and weakness. Possible complications include pneumonia, encephalitis, bronchitis, and sinus and ear infections. Three types of influenza virus have been identified: Types A, B, and C. Types A and B cause flu epidemics each winter and are the types that may be prevented with a flu shot. Type A is the most common and the most serious type. Influenza C is a very mild respiratory illness that is not thought to be responsible for epidemics.

H1N1 influenza is an influenza virus that is a subtype of influenza A. Because it is a newer virus, people may not have any immunity to it. H1N1 influenza poses a greater risk to certain groups of people such as:

- Pregnant women
- Persons who are 6 months to 24 years of age
- Persons who are 25 to 64 years who have health conditions that put them at risk for medical complications due to influenza

Bacterial pneumonia is the most common complication of influenza.

EXAMPLE

Influenza with *Klebsiella* pneumonia, J11.08, J15.0.

Pneumonia is an infection of the lungs that can be caused by a variety of organisms, including viruses, bacteria, and parasites. Pneumonia frequently follows an upper respiratory infection, and symptoms depend on age and cause of the pneumonia. More than 50 different types of pneumonia have been identified. High-risk individuals include the elderly, the very young, and those with underlying health problems such as chronic obstructive pulmonary disease (COPD), diabetes mellitus, congestive heart failure, asthma, and sickle cell anemia. Those with impaired immune systems as the result of human immunodeficiency virus (HIV) or acquired immunodeficiency syndrome (AIDS), cancer therapy, steroid therapy, or anti-rejection medications are also at risk for developing pneumonia.

TABLE 17-1 COMMON CAUSES OF PNEUMONIA[1]

Causative Agents	Percentage of All Diagnosed Cases
Bacteria	50
Streptococcus pneumoniae	10
Haemophilus influenzae	5
Staphylococcus aureus	5
Mycobacterium tuberculosis	10
Viruses	
Influenza virus	–
Fungi*	
Aspergillus fumigatus	–
Candida albicans	–
Pneumocystis jiroveci	–
Bacterium-like organisms	
Mycoplasma pneumoniae	10

*Opportunistic infection: rare except in immunosuppressed, debilitated, or terminally ill patients.

Some common symptoms of pneumonia include the following:

- Fever/chills
- Cough
- Chest pain
- Shortness of breath
- Rapid breathing and heart rate

Community-acquired pneumonia (CAP) is a broad term that is used to refer to pneumonias that are contracted outside of the hospital or nursing home setting. The most common cause of CAP is *Streptococcus pneumoniae.* **Nosocomial pneumonia** refers to a pneumonia that is acquired while the patient is hospitalized. Hospital patients are most susceptible to Gram-negative bacteria and staphylococcal pneumonia. **Nursing home–acquired pneumonia** refers to a pneumonia that is acquired in a nursing home or extended care facility. More than one organism may be responsible for pneumonia. In this case, pneumonia codes would be assigned to identify both types of pneumonia. If this was the reason for the hospital stay, either could be sequenced as the principal diagnosis. See Table 17-1 for other pathogens responsible for pneumonia. Complications of pneumonia include the formation of abscesses, respiratory failure, bacteremia, pleural effusion, empyema, and pneumothorax.

A diagnostic workup may be performed to determine the infectious agent that is responsible for the patient's condition. This could include various cultures, x-rays, and invasive tests, such as bronchoscopy, or a lung biopsy, if necessary. A sputum culture from a healthy person would generally have no growth. A mixture of microorganisms, normally found in or on a patient's body, may be identified in a culture. This does not necessarily mean that this organism is responsible for a particular infection. A physician may document that a particular organism is a **contaminant**. This means that the physician does not believe that this organism is responsible for causing the infection. No code would be assigned for an organism that was described as a contaminant. Coders should not assume a causal organism on the basis of laboratory findings alone. All code assignments should be based on the physician's documentation. A physician query may be necessary to confirm whether the culture findings identify the causative agent or identify a contaminant.

Sometimes, pneumonia may be described as to the lobe that it is located in; for example, right upper lobe (RUL) pneumonia or left lower lobe (LLL) pneumonia. Occasionally, a patient will be diagnosed with multilobar pneumonia (pneumonia that affects more than one lobe). If no organism is identified, pneumonia of a particular lobe, lobar pneumonia or multilobar pneumonia is coded to J18.1, lobar pneumonia, unspecified organism.

Often, **empiric** treatment (initiation of treatment prior to making a definite diagnosis) with antibiotic will be administered before the organism has been identified or the type of pneumonia determined. For example, patients with HIV may be treated empirically with antibiotics that treat both *Pneumocystis carinii* pneumonia (PCP) and CAP. Once PCP has been ruled out, the treatment and the type of antibiotic used may be modified. Because *Pneumocystis carinii* pneumonia was ruled out, it cannot be coded, even though the condition was treated as such until test results were complete.

EXAMPLE Pneumonia due to Gram-negative bacteria, J15.6.

EXAMPLE Bronchopneumonia, J18.0.

EXERCISE 17-2

Assign codes to the following conditions.

1. Influenza with *Staph aureus* pneumonia ________
2. Viral pneumonia ________
3. *Mycoplasma* pneumonia ________
4. Possible Avian influenza ________
5. Pneumonia due to *E. coli* ________
6. Cough and fever due to pneumonitis ________
7. Community-acquired pneumonia; empiric treatment was started for *Pneumocystis carinii* pneumonia. PCP was ruled out. Patient has AIDS. ________
8. Headache and weakness due to influenza A ________

Other Acute Lower Respiratory Infections (J20-J22)

Acute **bronchitis** is a lower respiratory tract or bronchial tree infection that may be characterized by cough, sputum production, and wheezing. Most cases of acute bronchitis are caused by viruses such as RSV, influenza, and parainfluenza. Bacterial infection with *Mycoplasma pneumoniae, Chlamydia pneumoniae,* and *Bordetella pertussis* (whooping cough), particularly in young adults, can lead to acute bronchitis. Bronchitis may progress to pneumonia or may aggravate respiratory symptoms in those who have chronic respiratory conditions.

EXAMPLE Subacute bronchitis with bronchospasm, J20.9.

EXERCISE 17-3

Assign codes to the following conditions.

1. Acute bronchiolitis due to RSV ________
2. Acute bronchitis due to *Hemophilus influenzae* ________
3. Acute on chronic bronchitis ________

Chronic Lower Respiratory Diseases (J40-J47)

COPD, or **chronic obstructive pulmonary disease**, is a general term that is used to describe a lung disease in which the airways become obstructed, making it difficult for air to get into and out of the lungs. Although cigarette smoking is the most common culprit, other irritants such as pollution, chemicals, or dust can also play a role. Various diseases can be classified as COPD; these include chronic asthmatic bronchitis, chronic obstructive bronchitis, and emphysema. All three affect the bronchial tree and result in wheezing, coughing, and shortness of breath. It may be clinically difficult to distinguish among these disorders.

Code J44.0, chronic obstructive pulmonary disease with acute lower respiratory infection, includes infections such as acute bronchitis and pneumonia (except for aspiration pneumonia and ventilator-associated pneumonia). Influenza is not considered a lower respiratory infection. Additional codes should be assigned to specify the infection. It is possible to have a COPD exacerbation, J44.1, and COPD with acute lower respiratory infection, J44.0, coded together. The sequencing should be based on the reason for admission. For code J44.0, chronic obstructive pulmonary disease with acute lower respiratory infection, there is an instructional note in the Tabular that will provide guidance for the sequencing of the J44.0 and a code for the acute lower respiratory infection.

Chronic bronchitis is characterized by a mucus-producing cough most days of the month, 3 months out of a year, for 2 successive years, with no other underlying disease that explains the cough. Smoking cigarettes is the most common cause of chronic bronchitis. Chronic bronchitis often remains untreated because it is thought to be just a "smoker's cough."

Emphysema is a chronic lung disease of gradual onset that can be attributed to chronic infection and inflammation or irritation from cigarette smoke (Figure 17-4).

EXAMPLE

Patient was admitted with exacerbation of chronic obstructive bronchitis, J44.1.

Asthma is a disease that affects the airways that carry air into and out of the lungs. Asthma can be controlled to minimize serious symptoms or attacks. Physicians use the terms "asthma" and "reactive airway disease" (RAD) interchangeably.

Asthma can be classified into four severity stages based on the frequency of symptoms, the frequency of nocturnal symptoms, and the results of spirometry testing. Those stages are:

- Mild intermittent asthma
- Mild persistent asthma

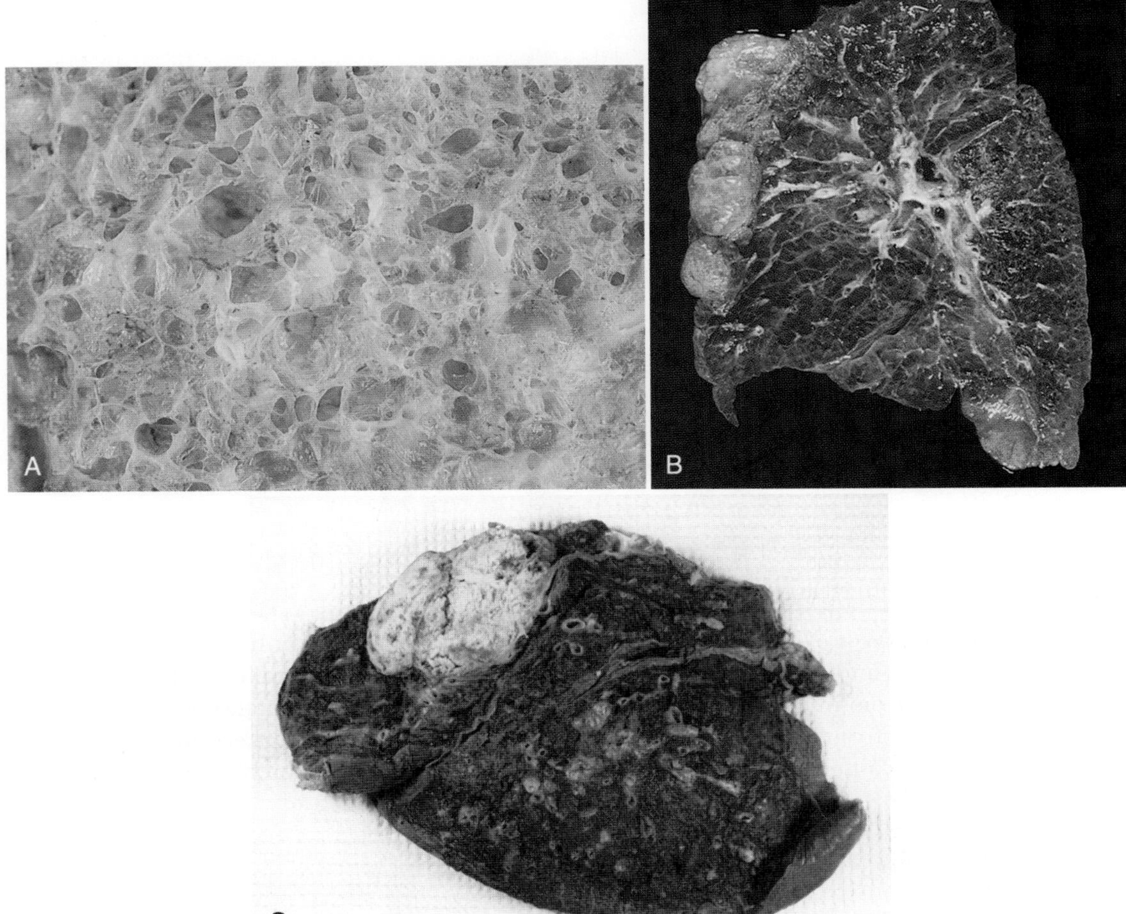

FIGURE 17-4. **A,** Emphysema. **B,** Bullous emphysema with large subpleural bullae. **C,** Emphysematous lung with tumor.

- Moderate persistent asthma
- Severe persistent asthma

Status asthmaticus can be described with the following terms:

- Intractable asthmatic attack
- Refractory asthma
- Severe, prolonged asthmatic attack
- Airway obstruction (mucous plug) not relieved by bronchodilators
- Severe, intractable wheezing

The presence of status asthmaticus should be queried if it is not documented by the physician. If respiratory failure occurs, it should also be coded, and sequencing would depend on whether respiratory failure was present on admission and meets the criteria for principal diagnosis. If both an acute exacerbation and status asthmaticus are documented, only a code identifying the status asthmaticus is necessary.

Asthmatic bronchitis refers to an underlying asthmatic problem in patients in whom asthma has become so persistent that clinically significant chronic airflow obstruction is present, despite antiasthmatic therapy. Symptoms of chronic bronchitis are generally also present.

EXAMPLE

Patient was admitted in acute hypoxemic respiratory failure caused by severe persistent asthma with status asthmaticus, J96.01, J45.52.

(Per guidelines, if both the respiratory failure and another acute condition are equally responsible for occasioning the admission, the guidelines regarding two or more diagnoses that equally meet the definition for principal diagnosis may be applied.)

EXAMPLE

Patient was admitted with acute exacerbation of chronic asthmatic bronchitis. The patient went into acute respiratory failure 6 hours after admission, J44.1, J96.00.

EXERCISE 17-4

Assign codes to the following conditions.

1. Mild persistent asthma ____________
2. Bronchiectasis ____________
3. Asthma exacerbation with pneumonia ____________
4. Emphysema with chronic bronchitis ____________
5. Asthma with allergic rhinitis ____________
6. Acute bronchitis with COPD ____________
7. Decompensated COPD ____________
8. Moderate persistent asthma with exacerbation of COPD ____________

Lung Diseases Due to External Agents (J60-J70)

Pneumoconioses are lung diseases that are caused by chronic inhalation of inorganic (mineral) dust and are often due to occupational exposure. Examples include **siderosis**, which results from inhalation of iron oxide; **baritosis**, caused by inhalation of barium; **stannosis**, resulting from inhalation of tin particles; **black lung or coal workers' pneumoconiosis** (Figure 17-5), caused by inhalation of coal dust; and **asbestosis**, which is caused by inhalation of asbestos.

EXAMPLE

Patient has silicosis, caused by working as a sandblaster for many years, J62.8.

Category J67.–, Extrinsic allergic alveolitis, includes conditions that are due to inhalation of organic materials such as grain dust, cotton dust, or animal dander.

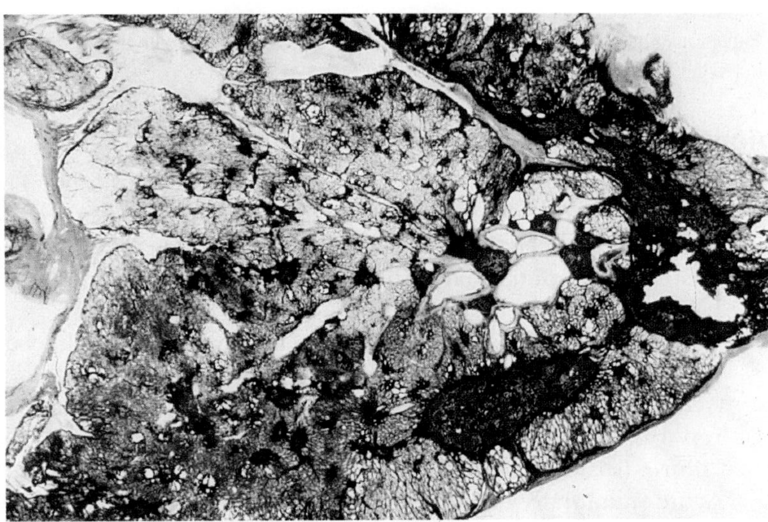

FIGURE 17-5. Coal workers' lung shows deposits of carbon particles *(black areas)*.

EXAMPLE

Patient was diagnosed with farmers' lung, J67.0.

Aspiration pneumonia is an inflammation of the lungs and bronchial tubes that is due to the aspiration of foreign material (e.g., food, saliva, vomit) into the lung. Disorders that affect normal swallowing include disorders of the esophagus, decreased or absent gag reflex, old age, dental problems, use of sedative drugs, anesthesia, coma, and excessive alcohol consumption. These disorders may cause aspiration.

If both aspiration pneumonia and bacterial pneumonia are present, it is acceptable to assign codes for both.

EXAMPLE

Aspiration pneumonia with superimposed pneumonia due to *Staphylococcus aureus*, J69.0, J15.211.
If both were present on admission, either could be sequenced as the principal diagnosis.

Several respiratory conditions can be induced by chemical fumes and vapors. These range from acute conditions such as bronchitis and pneumonitis to chronic respiratory conditions such as emphysema and pulmonary fibrosis.

EXERCISE 17-5

Assign codes to the following conditions.

1. Aspiration pneumonia; patient has dysphagia due to old CVA ______________
2. Fibrosis lung due to radiation treatments ______________
3. Black lung disease ______________
4. Pleural effusion due to asbestosis ______________
5. Ventilation (air conditioner) pneumonitis ______________
6. Mushroom worker's lung ______________

Other Respiratory Diseases Principally Affecting the Interstitium (J80-J84)

Pulmonary Edema

Pulmonary edema is a condition whereby fluid accumulates in the lungs. In most cases, heart problems are the cause. Pulmonary edema that is associated with heart failure is included in the heart failure codes and should not be assigned as an additional code.

EXAMPLE

Patient admitted with exacerbation of left ventricular heart failure with pulmonary edema confirmed by chest x-ray, I50.1.

Acute Pulmonary Edema of Noncardiac Origin

Pulmonary edema is not always related to a cardiac condition. The "noncardiogenic" type of acute pulmonary edema may also be caused by lung disease or related to patient trauma, and occurs in a variety of conditions. Some of these conditions include the following:

- Postoperative pulmonary edema that is not caused by left ventricular failure or CHF, both of which are cardiac in nature.
- Postoperative pulmonary edema specifically caused by fluid overload is reported with J81.0 and E87.70.
- Acute pulmonary edema caused by bacterial pneumonia, or viral pneumonia, is reported with J81.0 unless caused by left ventricular failure or congestive heart failure, because the latter conditions are cardiac in nature.
- Acute pulmonary edema is reported with an additional code when in conjunction with endotoxic shock, uremia, or septicemia.

EXERCISE 17-6

Assign codes to the following conditions.

1. Patient with hypertensive heart disease with pulmonary edema ____________
2. Acute pulmonary edema due to pneumonia ____________
3. Acute pulmonary edema in patient with no history of CHF ____________
4. Acute pulmonary edema following surgery ____________

Suppurative and Necrotic Conditions of the Lower Respiratory Tract (J85-J86) and Other Diseases of the Pleura (J90-J94)

Empyema and Lung Abscess

A **lung abscess** is an infection that forms in the lung parenchyma. It occurs more often in the right lung and often develops following an aspiration event. An **empyema** forms when pus collects in the pleural space. An empyema can be a complication of pneumonia. Many patients with pneumonia will develop a parapneumonic effusion in the pleural space. If this fluid becomes infected and turns to pus, it is called an empyema. Both of these conditions are more common in children and the elderly.

Pleural Effusion

Pleural effusion is accumulation of fluid in the pleural space caused by trauma or disease. If blood is present in the accumulating fluid, the condition is called **hemothorax**; if pus is present, it is called **empyema**; if chyle (milky fluid consisting of lymph and fat) is present, it is called **chylothorax**. The most common causes of pleural effusion include the following:

- Cardiac: congestive heart failure
- Liver: liver failure
- Kidney: nephrotic syndrome, peritoneal dialysis, uremia
- Lung: infection, pulmonary embolism, pulmonary infarction, cancer (primary lung and metastatic), asbestosis
- Vascular: collagen vascular disease (systemic lupus erythematosus, rheumatoid arthritis)
- Trauma: hemothorax, chylothorax, rupture of the esophagus
- Miscellaneous: pancreatitis, post abdominal or coronary artery bypass graft surgery, and drug reactions

According to *Coding Clinic for ICD-9-CM* (1991:3Q:p19-20),[2] pleural effusion is not usually reported if it appears in conjunction with congestive heart failure because the condition is not separately treated. When the only documentation is a diagnostic x-ray, the coder should not report the condition. However, in certain cases, "special x-rays such as decubitus views are required to confirm the presence of pleural effusion or diagnostic thoracentesis may be performed to identify its etiology. In other cases, it may be necessary to address the effusion by therapeutic thoracentesis or chest tube drainage. In any of these situations, it is acceptable to report pleural effusion as an additional diagnosis since the condition was specifically evaluated or treated, but reporting is not required."

EXAMPLE

Hemothorax due to pulmonary embolism, I26.99, J94.2.

Pneumothorax

When air enters the pleural space, this is called **pneumothorax**. A pneumothorax may be classified as spontaneous (not caused by trauma), traumatic, or iatrogenic. **Spontaneous pneumothorax** may occur in individuals who have no history of lung disease and often is the result of a ruptured subpleural bleb. **Iatrogenic** pneumothorax is the result of a complication of a diagnostic or therapeutic intervention or procedure. Traumatic pneumothorax occurs as the result of an injury and is assigned an injury code.

EXAMPLE

Spontaneous pneumothorax, no specific cause found, J93.83.

EXERCISE 17-7

Assign codes to the following conditions.

1. Empyema due to *streptococcus pneumoniae* __________
2. Pleural plaque with asbestos __________
3. Hemopneumothorax __________
4. Lung abscess due to *pseudomonas aeruginosa* __________

Other Diseases of the Respiratory System (J96-J99)

Respiratory Failure

Respiratory failure is a general term that describes ineffective gas exchange across the lungs by the respiratory system. An arterial blood gas (ABG) measurement may be used to detect the presence of respiratory failure. A partial pressure of oxygen in arterial blood (Pao_2) of less than 60 torr and a partial pressure of carbon dioxide in arterial blood ($Paco_2$) greater than 50 torr indicate respiratory failure.

Some of the most common causes of respiratory failure include the following:

- Obstruction of the airways (chronic bronchitis, emphysema, cystic fibrosis, etc.)
- Weak breathing due to drugs and alcohol, extreme obesity, or sleep apnea
- Muscle weakness from muscular dystrophy, polio, stroke, spinal cord injury, or Lou Gehrig's disease
- Abnormality of lung tissue such as pneumonia, fluid in lungs, lung cancer, pulmonary fibrosis, sarcoidosis, and radiation
- Abnormal chest wall from scoliosis or severe injury to chest wall

Respiratory failure is classified on the basis of acuity. Acute respiratory failure is the result of a sudden, catastrophic event. Chronic respiratory failure is the result of a gradual worsening of respiratory function. Acute on chronic respiratory failure occurs when a patient has chronic respiratory failure that has decompensated or deteriorated.

EXAMPLE

Patient presents to the emergency room (ER) in acute respiratory failure and is admitted. Following admission, the patient was started on antibiotics for pneumonia, J96.00, J18.9.

(Per guidelines, if both the respiratory failure and another acute condition are equally responsible for occasioning the admission, the guidelines regarding two or more diagnoses that equally meet the definition for principal diagnosis may be applied in these situations.)

EXAMPLE

Patient is admitted from the clinic for intravenous (IV) antibiotics for pneumonia. A couple of hours after admission, the patient deteriorated and developed acute respiratory failure, J18.9, J96.00.

EXAMPLE

Patient is admitted to the hospital in acute respiratory failure and is found to have suffered a myocardial infarction, I21.3, J96.00 or J96.00, I21.3.

(Per guidelines, if both the respiratory failure and another acute condition are equally responsible for occasioning the admission, the guidelines regarding two or more diagnoses that equally meet the definition for principal diagnosis may be applied in these situations.)

There are some chapter-specific guidelines that provide sequencing instruction when respiratory failure is also present. Obstetric, newborn, HIV, sepsis, and poisonings will have precedence over the acute respiratory failure codes.

EXAMPLE

Patient is admitted with acute respiratory failure due to severe sepsis and pneumonia A41.9, R65.20, J96.00, J18.9.

Respiratory Disorders in Diseases Classified Elsewhere

Code J99 identifies respiratory disorders in diseases that are classified elsewhere. There is a *code first* Instructional note that states the underlying disease should be coded first (Figure 17-6). There may be some combination codes such as systemic lupus erythematosus that involve the lung that are coded elsewhere. The Excludes1 note shows some of the more common conditions that are coded elsewhere (see Figure 17-6).

EXAMPLE

Systemic lupus erythematosus that has affected the patient's lungs, M32.13.

●◗ *J99* ***Respiratory disorders in diseases classified elsewhere***

Code first underlying disease, such as:
amyloidosis (E85-)
ankylosing spondylitis (M45)
congenital syphilis (A50.5)
cryoglobulinemia (D89.1)
early congenital syphilis (A50.0)
schistosomiasis (B65.0-B65.9)

Excludes1 respiratory disorders in:
amebiasis (A06.5)
blastomycosis (B40.0-B40.2)
candidiasis (B37.1)
coccidioidomycosis (B38.0-B38.2)
cystic fibrosis with pulmonary manifestations (E84.0)
dermatomyositis (M33.01, M33.11)
histoplasmosis (B39.0-B39.2)
late syphilis (A52.72, A52.73)
polymyositis (M33.21)
sicca syndrome (M35.02)
systemic lupus erythematosus (M32.13)
systemic sclerosis (M34.81)
Wegener's granulomatosis (M31.30-M31.31)

FIGURE 17-6. Code-first Instructional note and Excludes1 note.

EXERCISE 17-8

Assign codes to the following conditions.

1. Sickle cell disease with vaso-occlusive crisis with acute chest syndrome ______
2. Acute respiratory failure due to pneumonia; patient was intubated and was placed on mechanical ventilation for 48 hours; the respiratory failure developed after admission ______
3. Acute respiratory failure due to Lou Gehrig's disease ______
4. Acute pulmonary insufficiency following thoracic surgery ______
5. Acute on chronic respiratory failure in patient with severe emphysema; patient is oxygen dependent ______
6. Respiratory failure due to exacerbation of COPD ______

FACTORS INFLUENCING HEALTH STATUS AND CONTACT WITH HEALTH SERVICES (Z CODES)

As was discussed in Chapter 9, it is difficult to locate Z codes in the Index. Coders will often say, "I did not know there was a Z code for that." Refer to Chapter 9 for a listing of common main terms to locate Z codes.

Z codes that may be used with diseases of the respiratory system include the following:

Z01.811	Encounter for preprocedural respiratory examination
Z13.83	Encounter for screening for respiratory disorder NEC
Z43.0	Encounter for attention to tracheostomy
Z48.24	Encounter for aftercare following lung transplant
Z48.813	Encounter for surgical aftercare following surgery on the respiratory system
Z57.2	Occupational exposure to dust
Z57.31	Occupational exposure to environmental tobacco smoke
Z57.39	Occupational exposure to other air contaminants
Z71.6	Tobacco abuse counseling
Z77.090	Contact with and (suspected) exposure to asbestos
Z77.110	Contact with and (suspected) exposure to air pollution
Z77.22	Contact with and (suspected) exposure to environmental tobacco smoke (acute) (chronic)
Z82.5	Family history of asthma and other chronic lower respiratory diseases
Z83.6	Family history of other diseases of the respiratory system
Z87.01	Personal history of pneumonia (recurrent)
Z87.09	Personal history of other diseases of the respiratory system
Z90.02	Acquired absence of larynx
Z90.2	Acquired absence of lung [part of]
Z92.81	Personal history of extracorporeal membrane oxygenation (ECMO)
Z93.0	Tracheostomy status
Z94.2	Lung transplant status
Z94.3	Heart and lungs transplant status
Z96.3	Presence of artificial larynx
Z98.3	Post therapeutic collapse of lung status
Z99.0	Dependence on aspirator
Z99.11	Dependence on respirator [ventilator] status
Z99.12	Encounter for respirator [ventilator] dependence during power failure
Z99.81	Dependence on supplemental oxygen

EXAMPLE

Exposure to asbestos, Z77.090.

EXERCISE 17-9

Assign codes to the following conditions.

1. Status post lung transplant ____________
2. Preoperative examination to assess COPD status prior to elective surgery for cholelithiasis ____________
3. Patient has a tracheostomy and is dependent on a respirator ____________
4. Personal history of lung cancer with previous surgery to remove lung; no recurrence ____________
5. Family history of asthma ____________

COMMON TREATMENTS

Smoking cessation may be beneficial in the prevention of exacerbations and progression of many respiratory conditions. Annual vaccinations against influenza and a once-only vaccination against bacterial pneumococcal pneumonia may help prevent the pulmonary complications of infection.

CONDITION	MEDICATION/TREATMENT
Sinusitis	Decongestant to help sinuses drain; antibiotics
Bronchitis	If viral—rest, fluids, cough medicine If bacterial—an antibiotic may be prescribed
Asthmatic bronchitis	Bronchodilators, steroids, and antibiotics for acute infection
Chronic bronchitis	Bronchodilators, steroids, and antibiotics for acute infection
Emphysema	Bronchodilators, steroids, oxygen therapy, and antibiotics for acute infection
Asthma	Corticosteroids, albuterol (Proventil, Ventolin), theophylline (TheoDur, Slo-Bid, Uniphyl), Serevent, Xopenex, Azmocort, Advair, Singulair, and Symbicort
COPD	Prednisone, albuterol (Proventil, Ventolin), Combivent, Serevent, Alupent, and Atrovent
Pneumonia	Sputum culture and antibiotics, if suspected to be bacterial
Influenza	Influenza vaccination, nasal swab, amantadine, zanamivir, and treatment of symptoms
Respiratory failure	Oxygen, mechanical ventilation, treatment of underlying cause
Pleural effusion	Treatment of underlying cause
Pulmonary edema	Treatment of underlying cause

PROCEDURES

Procedures related to the respiratory system in ICD-10-PCS can be located in the following tables:

0B1-0BY	Respiratory System
0C0-0CX	Mouth and Throat
5A0-5A2	Extracorporeal Assistance and Performance

Mechanical Ventilation

Mechanical ventilation is the use of a machine to induce alternating inflation and deflation of the lungs for the purpose of regulating the exchange rate of gases in the blood. The root operation for mechanical ventilation is performance (completely taking over a physiological function by extracorporeal means). The most common type of ventilator (or respirator) delivers inspiratory gases directly into the person's airway. Mechanical ventilation codes are time-based as follows:

- Less than 24 consecutive hours
- 24 to 96 consecutive hours
- Greater than 96 consecutive hours

To calculate the number of hours (duration) of continuous mechanical ventilation during a hospitalization, begin the count from the start of the (endotracheal) intubation. The duration ends with (endotracheal) extubation. If a patient is intubated prior to admission, begin counting the duration from time of admission. If a patient is transferred (discharged) while intubated, the duration would end at the time of transfer (discharge).

For patients who have been (endotracheal) intubated and subsequently undergo a tracheostomy, duration begins with the (endotracheal) intubation and ends when the mechanical ventilation is turned off (after the weaning period).

In a patient with a tracheostomy, to calculate the number of hours of continuous mechanical ventilation during hospitalization, begin counting the duration when mechanical ventilation is started. Duration ends when the mechanical ventilator is turned off (after the weaning period). If a patient has received a tracheostomy prior to admission and is on mechanical ventilation at the time of admission, begin counting the duration from the time of admission. If a patient is transferred (discharged) while still on mechanical ventilation via tracheostomy, duration would end at the time of transfer (discharge).

For certain procedures or for particular patients, mechanical ventilation may be used during surgery and in the immediate postoperative period. Mechanical ventilation during surgery does not require a code assignment, unless the ventilation is required for "an extended period (several days)" during the post surgical period. *Coding Clinic for ICD-9-CM* (2004:3Q:p11)[3] states "the term 'several' is defined as more than two. Therefore, unless the physician has clearly documented an unexpected extended period of mechanical ventilation (several days), do not assign a code for the mechanical ventilation."

If ventilation is required for a longer period than normal, a medical reason for continuing ventilation should be documented. If this is not well documented, the coder may have to query the physician. To calculate the hours, begin counting from the time of intubation.

If a patient has been extubated and is no longer on mechanical ventilation, but his or her condition deteriorates, requiring reintubation and mechanical ventilation, this would begin a new ventilation period, and a second code based on hours of ventilation would be assigned.

According to Coding Clinic for ICD-10 (2014:4Q:pp5-6), the endotracheal intubation should be coded in addition to the mechanical ventilation code. It is important to note that when BIPAP or CPAP is administered via endotracheal tube or tracheostomy, it becomes invasive ventilation and is coded as mechanical ventilation.

EXAMPLE

Patient was intubated and placed on mechanical ventilation for respiratory failure due to myasthenia gravis in crisis. Patient was ventilated for 3 days, J96.90, G70.01, 5A1945Z, 0BH17EZ.

SECTION	BODY SYSTEM	ROOT OPERATION	BODY SYSTEM	DURATION	FUNCTION	QUALIFIER
Extracorporeal Assistance and Performance	Physiological Systems	Performance	Respiratory	24-96 Consecutive Hours	Ventilation	No Qualifier
5	A	1	9	4	5	Z

SECTION	BODY SYSTEM	ROOT OPERATION	BODY PART	APPROACH	DEVICE	QUALIFIER
Medical and Surgical	Respiratory System	Insertion	Trachea	Via Natural or Artificial Opening	Intraluminal Device, Endotracheal Airway	No Qualifier
0	B	H	1	7	E	Z

Noninvasive Ventilation

Noninvasive ventilation is a form of ventilation without an invasive artificial airway (endotracheal tube or tracheostomy). The root operation for noninvasive ventilation is assistance (taking over a portion of a physiological function by extracorporeal means). The use of noninvasive ventilation preserves the speech, swallowing, and cough functions of the patient. Noninvasive ventilation is divided into two categories:

- Negative-pressure ventilation
- Noninvasive positive-pressure ventilation (NPPV)

Negative-pressure ventilators provide ventilatory support by reducing the pressure surrounding the chest wall during inspiration and reversing the pressure during expiration. Machines such as iron lungs and body ventilators are used.

Noninvasive positive-pressure ventilation is being used more often in the hospital setting. NPPV is delivered by a nasal or face mask and may be administered with the following devices:

- Intermittent positive-pressure ventilation (IPPV)
- Bilevel positive airway pressure (BIPAP)
- Continuous positive airway pressure (CPAP)

NPPV is more comfortable for the patient and complications that are associated with invasive ventilation such as pneumothorax, airway injury, and ventilator-associated pneumonia can be minimized.

EXAMPLE

Patient was admitted with COPD exacerbation. Patient was treated with BiPAP for 12 hours, J44.1, 5A09357

SECTION	BODY SYSTEM	ROOT OPERATION	BODY SYSTEM	DURATION	FUNCTION	QUALIFIER
Extracorporeal Assistance and Performance	Physiological Systems	Assistance	Respiratory	Less than 24 Consecutive Hours	Ventilation	Continuous Positive Airway Pressure
5	A	0	9	3	5	7

Bronchoscopy

Bronchoscopy is an endoscopic procedure in which a tube with a tiny camera on the end is inserted through the nose or mouth into the lungs (Figure 17-7). The root operation for

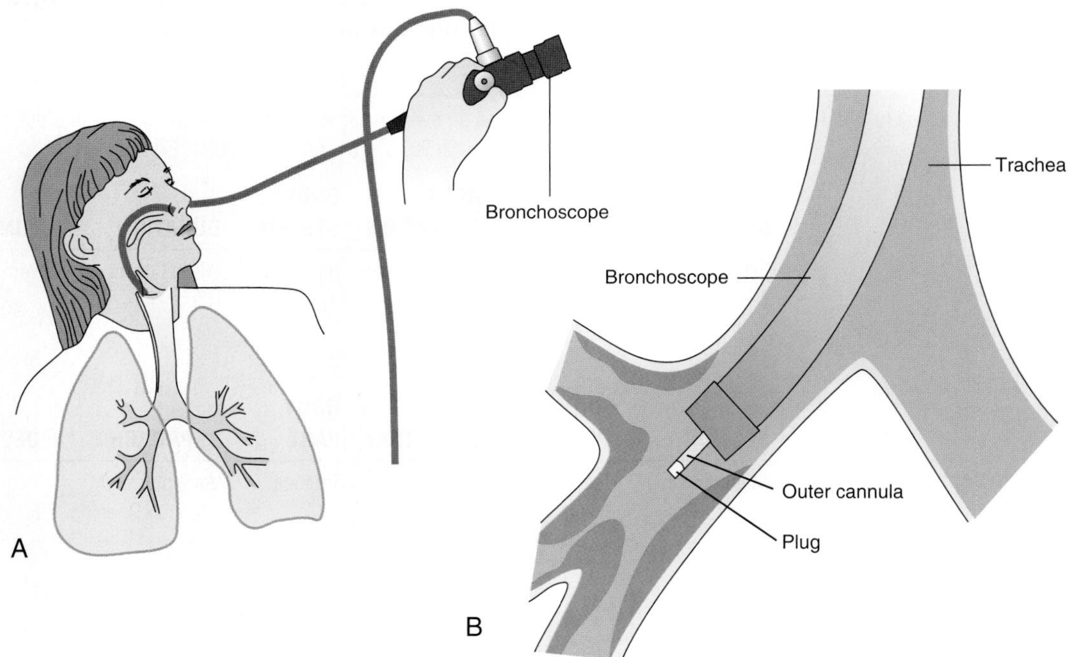

FIGURE 17-7. **A,** Fiberoptic bronchoscopy—a bronchoscope is passed through the nose, throat, larynx, and trachea into the bronchus. **B,** A bronchoscope, ready for biopsy of bronchial tissue.

a bronchoscopy is inspection (visual/manual exploration). This procedure provides a view of the airways of the lung and allows doctors to collect lung secretions or tissue specimens (biopsy). A biopsy of lung tissue during a bronchoscopic procedure may be performed. It is also possible to biopsy lymph nodes via bronchoscope. This may be referred to as a transbronchial needle aspiration (TBNA) biopsy. Sometimes it is difficult to tell by the documentation if the biopsy is of the lung tissue or a lymph node. When you see terminology such as nodal station, station 7, or station 4L, the surgeon is referring to intrathoracic lymph nodes or the stations in which the lymph nodes are located. Because it is a needle biopsy, the tissue may be sent to cytopathology instead of pathology.

Bronchoalveolar lavage (BAL) is very useful for diagnosing infections such as *P. carinii* pneumonia (PCP) in a patient with HIV. Fluid is squirted into a small part of the lung and is recollected for cytologic examination and culture. The root operation for BAL is drainage.

EXAMPLE

Bronchoalveolar lavage of right lower lobe bronchus (via bronchoscope) confirmed the diagnosis of PCP in a patient with HIV, B20, B59, 0B968ZX.

SECTION	BODY SYSTEM	ROOT OPERATION	BODY PART	APPROACH	DEVICE	QUALIFIER
Medical and Surgical	Respiratory System	Drainage	Lower Lobe Bronchus, Right	Via Natural or Artificial Opening Endoscopic	No Device	Diagnostic
0	B	9	6	8	Z	X

Thoracentesis

Thoracentesis is puncture of the chest wall to remove fluid (pleural effusion) from the space (cavity) between the lining of the outside of the lungs (pleura) and the wall of the chest (pleural cavity) (Figure 17-8). The root operation for thoracentesis is drainage (taking or letting out fluids or gases). Physicians may perform a diagnostic thoracentesis or a therapeutic thoracentesis. The fluid collected is sent to the laboratory for analysis. This may also relieve any shortness of breath caused by compression on the lung by the fluid.

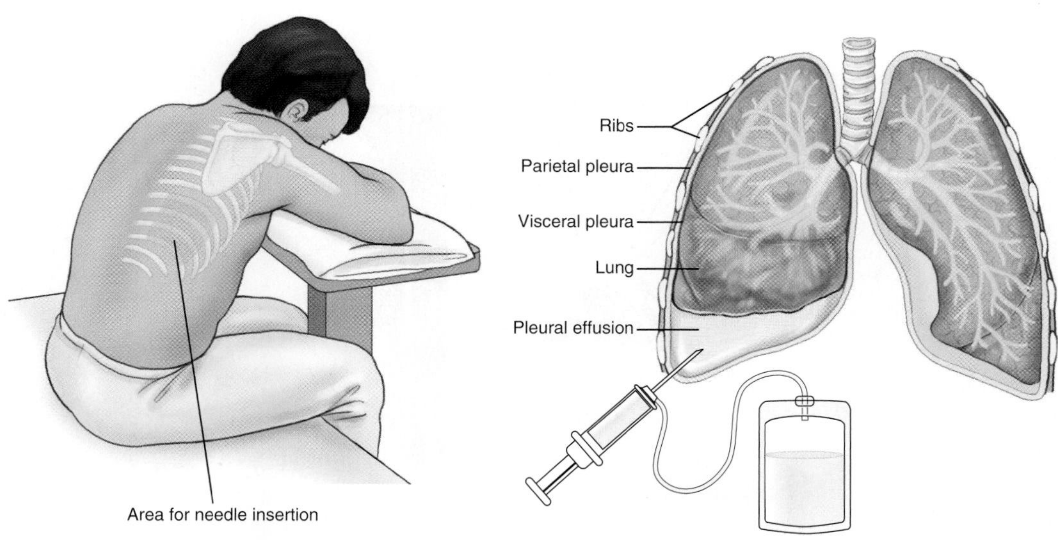

FIGURE 17-8. Thoracentesis. The needle is inserted close to the base of the effusion so that gravity will help with drainage.

EXAMPLE

Patient with pneumonia and large right parapneumonic effusion requiring therapeutic thoracentesis right pleural cavity, J18.9, J91.8, 0W993ZZ.

SECTION	BODY SYSTEM	ROOT OPERATION	BODY PART	APPROACH	DEVICE	QUALIFIER
Medical and Surgical 0	Anatomical Regions, General W	Drainage 9	Pleural Cavity, Right 9	Percutaneous 3	No Device Z	No Qualifier Z

Thoracostomy

Tube thoracostomy is the term used for insertion of chest tube(s) to drain blood, fluid, or air and to allow full expansion of the lungs. The root operation for tube thoracostomy is drainage (taking or letting out fluids or gases). A tube is placed between the ribs and into the space between the inner lining and the outer lining of the lung (pleural space); fluid is allowed to drain. A suction machine may be used to facilitate drainage. Reasons why chest tubes may be used include pneumothorax, hemothorax, abscess, empyema, and cancer; they also may be used after surgery.

EXAMPLE

Percutaneous insertion of chest tube on the right side for continuous drainage of empyema, J86.9, 0W9930Z.

SECTION	BODY SYSTEM	ROOT OPERATION	BODY PART	APPROACH	DEVICE	QUALIFIER
Medical and Surgical 0	Anatomical Regions, General W	Drainage 9	Pleural Cavity, Right 9	Percutaneous 3	Drainage Device 0	No Qualifier Z

Tracheostomy

Tracheostomy is a procedure in which an artificial opening is made in the front of the windpipe (trachea) through the skin of the neck (Figure 17-9). The root operation for tracheostomy is bypass (altering the route of passage of the contents of a tubular body part).

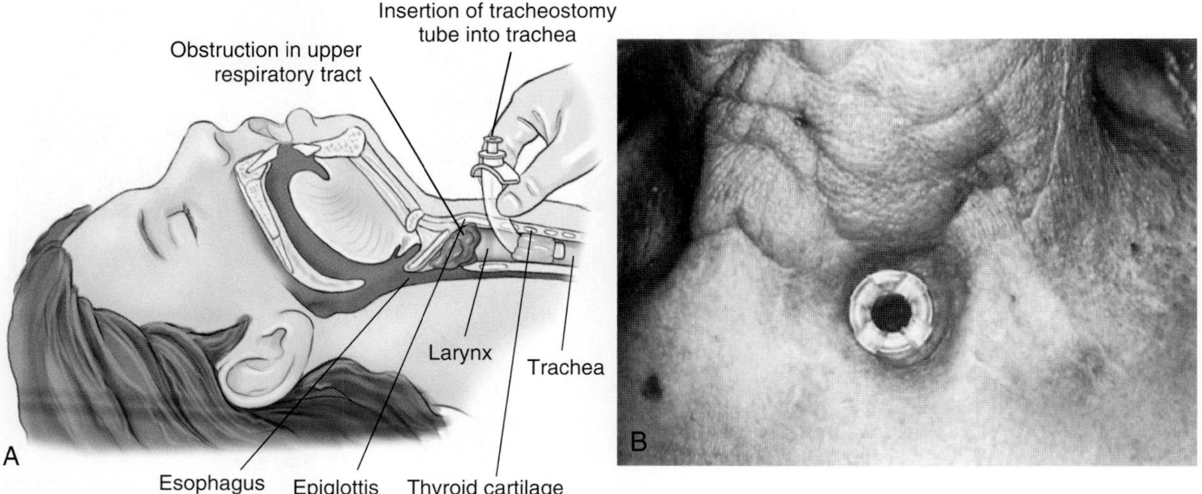

FIGURE 17-9. **A,** Tracheostomy with tube in place. **B,** Healed tracheostomy incision.

A tube is inserted, through which breathing may continue until the normal airway can be restored. A tracheostomy may be performed during an emergency at the patient's bedside. In some cases, a tracheostomy is planned and is performed in the Operating Room (OR).

EXAMPLE

Temporary open tracheostomy was performed in the OR because of the patient's recurrent aspiration pneumonitis, J69.0, 0B110F4.

SECTION	BODY SYSTEM	ROOT OPERATION	BODY PART	APPROACH	DEVICE	QUALIFIER
Medical and Surgical	Respiratory System	Bypass	Trachea	Open	Tracheostomy Device	Cutaneous
0	B	1	1	0	F	4

Pulmonary Resection

The type of pulmonary resection undertaken may depend on the condition that is being diagnosed and/or treated. Wedge resection (Figure 17-10, *A*) is the removal of a small, localized area of diseased tissue near the surface of the lung. Segmental resection

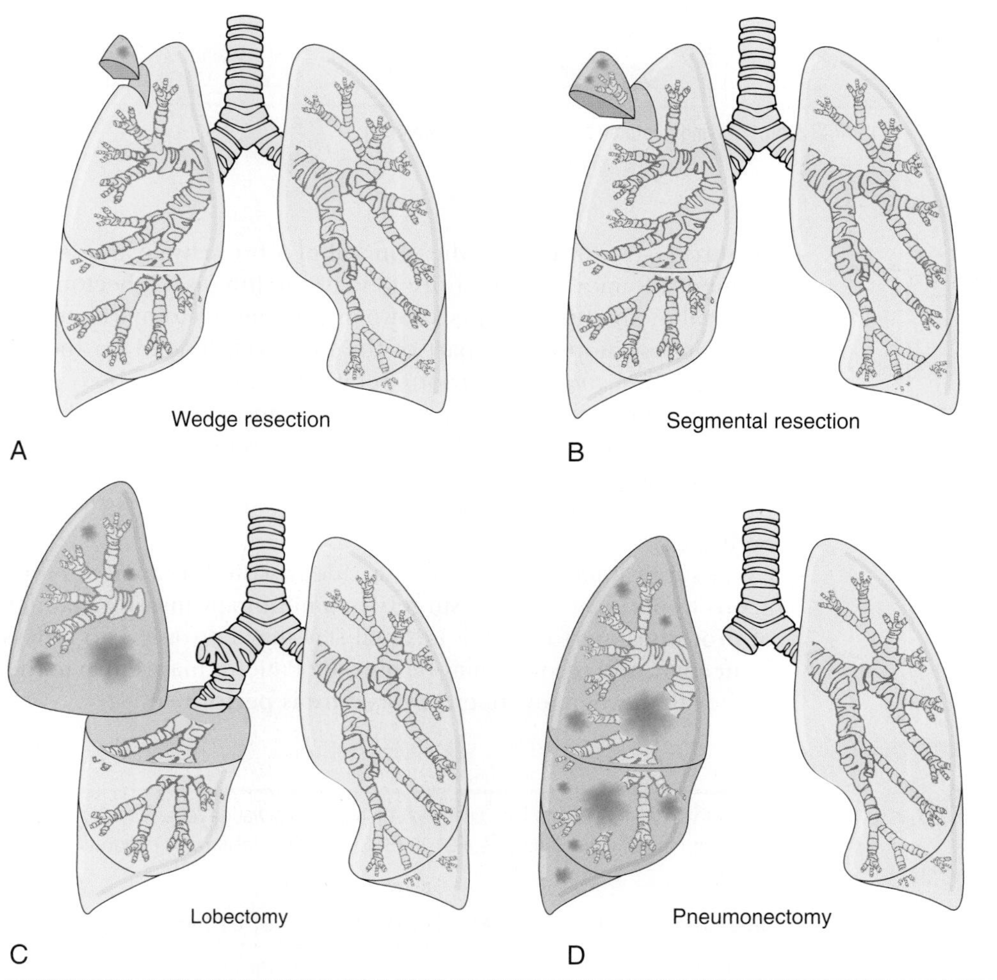

FIGURE 17-10. Pulmonary resections. **A,** Wedge resection. **B,** Segmental resection. **C,** Lobectomy. **D,** Pneumonectomy.

SECTION: 0 MEDICAL AND SURGICAL
BODY SYSTEM: B RESPIRATORY SYSTEM
OPERATION: T RESECTION: Cutting out or off, without replacement, all of a body part

Body Part	Approach	Device	Qualifier
1 Trachea 2 Carina 3 Main Bronchus, Right 4 Upper Lobe Bronchus, Right 5 Middle Lobe Bronchus, Right 6 Lower Lobe Bronchus, Right 7 Main Bronchus, Left 8 Upper Lobe Bronchus, Left 9 Lingula Bronchus B Lower Lobe Bronchus, Left C Upper Lung Lobe, Right D Middle Lung Lobe, Right F Lower Lung Lobe, Right G Upper Lung Lobe, Left H Lung Lingula J Lower Lung Lobe, Left K Lung, Right L Lung, Left M Lungs, Bilateral R Diaphragm, Right S Diaphragm, Left	0 Open 4 Percutaneous Endoscopic Anatomical subdivisions of the lung	Z No Device	Z No Qualifier

FIGURE 17-11. PCS table showing anatomical subdivisions of the lung.

(Figure 17-10, *B*) involves the removal of a bronchiole and its alveoli in one or more lung segments. Removal of an entire lobe of the lung is a lobectomy (Figure 17-10, *C*), and the removal of an entire lung is known as pneumonectomy (Figure 17-10, *D*). The root operation for resection of any part of the lung will depend on the portion of the lung that is resected. Resection is the root operation when all of a body part is cut out or off without replacement. "All of a body part" includes any anatomical subdivision that has its own body part value (Figure 17-11). Although a lobectomy is not the removal of the entire lung, it is the removal of a body part that has its own value, therefore it is a resection. For partial resections the root operation is excision (cutting out/off without replacement some of a body part).

A surgical technique known as video-assisted thoracic surgery (VATS) has allowed surgeons to perform thoracic surgery in a minimally invasive manner. Depending on the type of procedure performed, a hospital stay may last only 1 to 3 days, intensive care may not be needed, and recovery may be quicker. Patients may return to their normal activities much sooner than when an "open" procedure is performed.

EXAMPLE

Patient was admitted with lung nodule. A thoracoscopic wedge resection was performed with total removal of the lesion in the left upper lung lobe, R91.1, 0BBG4ZZ (entire lesion was removed so not diagnostic biopsy)

SECTION	BODY SYSTEM	ROOT OPERATION	BODY PART	APPROACH	DEVICE	QUALIFIER
Medical and Surgical	Respiratory System	Excision	Upper Lung Lobe, Left	Percutaneous Endoscopic	No Device	No Qualifier
0	B	B	G	4	Z	Z

EXERCISE 17-10

Assign codes for all diagnosis and procedures.

1. Thoracoscopy with excision of primary lung cancer from the left lower lobe (not a lobectomy) ______
2. Thorascopic pleurodesis with administration of talc for recurrent spontaneous pneumothorax on the right ______
3. Diagnostic thoracentesis for large right-sided pleural effusion ______
4. Bronchoscopy with bronchoalveolar lavage of right main bronchus to assess type of pneumonia ______
5. Temporary percutaneous tracheostomy in patient with laryngeal cancer who will be having surgery in a couple of weeks ______
6. Endotracheal intubation with mechanical ventilation for 3 days because of acute respiratory failure due to exacerbation of congestive heart failure ______
7. Open lobectomy for squamous cell carcinoma, right lung, upper lobe ______
8. Transbronchial biopsy of the left lung and mainstem bronchus (via bronchoscope); histologic exam confirms pulmonary tuberculosis ______

CHAPTER REVIEW EXERCISE

Assign codes for all diagnoses and procedures.

1. Cough due to *Streptococcus pneumoniae* pneumonia ______
2. Patient with severe emphysema who is dependent on oxygen; quit smoking 5 years ago. NPPV (48 hours) was initiated for the patient's chronic respiratory failure ______
3. Patient is high risk for lung disease due to on-the-job exposure to asbestos; patient has a 20–pack-year history of smoking cigarettes, currently active ______
4. Vaping-related disorder ______
5. Left tonsillar abscess; abscess was drained ______
6. Patient with whooping cough has pneumonia ______
7. *Haemophilus influenzae* pneumonia in a patient who is being treated for influenza ______
8. Edema, larynx ______
9. Status asthmaticus in patient with severe persistent asthma ______
10. Acute bronchitis with acute exacerbation of COPD ______
11. Acute on chronic respiratory failure due to sarcoidosis involving the lungs; endotracheal intubation and mechanical ventilation for 3 days ______
12. Reactive airway disease ______
13. Patient tested positive for H1N1 influenza ______
14. Bronchiolitis obliterans organizing pneumonia ______
15. Acute and chronic sinusitis ______
16. Chronic tonsillitis and adenoiditis; tonsillectomy with adenoidectomy performed ______
17. Nasal cavity polyps ______
18. Solitary pulmonary nodule ______
19. Empyema with insertion of left chest tube; empyema was due to *Staphylococcus aureus* ______

20. Double lung transplant for diffuse idiopathic pulmonary fibrosis; cardiopulmonary bypass was performed in this transplant from a cadaver ______________
21. Left pleural effusion that was treated with thoracentesis at bedside ______________
22. Granuloma lung ______________
23. Tension pneumothorax ______________
24. Acute bronchitis with chronic obstructive bronchitis ______________
25. Pulmonary edema ______________

Write the correct answer(s) in the space(s) provided.

26. Define contamination of a culture.

____

27. Define empiric treatment.

____

28. Define iatrogenic.

____

29. List two problems/conditions that could cause a patient to aspirate.

____

____

30. List two terms that describe status asthmaticus.

____

____

CHAPTER GLOSSARY

Asbestosis: lung disease due to inhalation of asbestos.

Aspiration pneumonia: inflammation of the lungs and bronchial tubes due to aspiration of foreign material into the lung.

Asthma: chronic disease that affects the airways that carry air into and out of the lungs.

Asthmatic bronchitis: underlying asthmatic problem in patients in whom asthma has become so persistent that clinically significant chronic airflow obstruction is present despite antiasthmatic therapy.

Baritosis: lung disease due to inhalation of barium.

Black lung: lung disease due to inhalation of coal dust.

Bronchi: the two air tubes that branch off the trachea and deliver air to both lungs.

Bronchitis: lower respiratory tract or bronchial tree infection characterized by cough, sputum production, and wheezing.

Bronchoscopy: diagnostic endoscopic procedure in which a tube with a tiny camera on the end is inserted through the nose or mouth into the lungs.

Chronic bronchitis: condition defined by a mucus-producing cough most days of the month, 3 months out of a year for 2 successive years, with no other underlying disease to explain the cough.

Chronic obstructive pulmonary disease: general term used to describe a lung disease in which the airways become obstructed, making it difficult for air to get into and out of the lungs.

Chronic sinusitis: occurs when the sinuses become inflamed and swollen.

Chylothorax: milky fluid consisting of lymph and fat (chyle) that accumulates in the pleural space.

Coal workers' pneumoconiosis: lung disease due to inhalation of coal dust.

Community-acquired pneumonia: broad term used to define pneumonias that are contracted outside of the hospital or nursing home setting.

Contaminant: a cultured organism that a physician does not believe is responsible for causing a particular infection.

Diaphragm: dome-shaped muscles at the bottom of the lungs that assist in the process of breathing and in the exchange of oxygen/carbon dioxide.

Emphysema: chronic lung disease of gradual onset that can be attributed to chronic infection and inflammation or irritation from cigarette smoke.

Empiric: initiation of treatment prior to making a definite diagnosis.

Empyema: pus that accumulates in the pleural space.

Hemothorax: blood that accumulates in the pleural space.

Iatrogenic: caused by medical treatment.

Infection: invasion of the body by organisms that have the potential to cause disease.

Influenza: contagious viral infection of the respiratory tract that causes coughing, difficulty breathing, headache, muscle aches, and weakness.

Lung abscess: infection that forms in the lung parenchyma.

Mechanical ventilation: use of a machine to induce alternating inflation and deflation of the lungs and to regulate the exchange rate of gases in the blood.

Noninvasive ventilation: ventilation without an invasion artificial airway (endotracheal tube or tracheostomy).

Nosocomial pneumonia: pneumonia that is acquired while the patient is residing in a hospital-type setting.

Nursing home–acquired pneumonia: pneumonia that is acquired in a nursing home or extended care facility.

Pleural effusion: fluid that accumulates in the pleural space because of trauma or disease.

Pneumoconioses: lung diseases due to chronic inhalation of inorganic (mineral) dust that are often due to occupational exposure.

Pneumonia: infection of the lungs that may be caused by a variety of organisms, including viruses, bacteria, and parasites.

Pneumothorax: air in space around the lung.

Pulmonary edema: condition in which fluid accumulates in the lungs.

Respiratory failure: general term that describes ineffective gas exchange across the lungs by the respiratory system.

Respiratory system: system that supplies the body with oxygen (O_2).

Siderosis: lung disease due to inhalation of iron oxide.

Sinusitis: a condition in which the linings of one or more sinuses become infected, usually because of viruses or bacteria.

Spontaneous pneumothorax: pneumothorax that is not caused by trauma.

Stannosis: lung disease due to inhalation of tin particles.

Thoracentesis: puncture of the chest wall to remove fluid (pleural effusion) from the space between the lining of the outside of the lungs (pleura) and the wall of the chest.

Trachea (windpipe): body part that is responsible for filtering the air that we breathe.

Tracheostomy: procedure in which an artificial opening is made in the front of the windpipe (trachea) through the skin of the neck.

Tube thoracostomy: insertion of chest tube(s) to drain blood, fluid, or air and allow full expansion of the lungs.

Vaping-related disorder: lung disorder(s) associated with inhaling vapors from electronic cigarettes.

REFERENCES

1. Damjanov I: Pathology for the Health Professions, ed 4, St. Louis, 2012, Saunders, Table 8-1, p 169.
2. American Hospital Association: *Coding Clinic for ICD-9-CM* 1991:3Q:p19-20. Pleural effusion with congestive heart failure.
3. American Hospital Association: *Coding Clinic for ICD-9-CM* 2004:3Q:p11. Clarification—Postoperative mechanical ventilation.

18

Diseases of the Digestive System

(ICD-10-CM Chapter 11, Codes K00-K95)

CHAPTER OUTLINE

LEARNING OBJECTIVES

1. Apply and assign the correct ICD-10-CM/PCS codes in accordance with Official Guidelines for Coding and Reporting
2. Identify pertinent anatomy and physiology of the digestive system
3. Identify diseases of the digestive system
4. Assign the correct Z codes and procedure codes related to the digestive system
5. Identify common treatments, medications, laboratory values, and diagnostic tests

ABBREVIATIONS/ ACRONYMS

EGD esophagogastroduodenoscopy

ERCP endoscopic retrograde cholangiopancreatography

ESWL extracorporeal shock wave lithotripsy

GERD gastroesophageal reflux disease

GI gastrointestinal

ICD-10-CM *International Classification of Diseases, 10th Revision, Clinical Modification*

ICD-10-PCS *International Classification of Diseases, 10th Revision, Procedure Coding System*

IV intravenous

LGIB lower gastrointestinal bleed

NSAID nonsteroidal antiinflammatory drug

ABBREVIATIONS/ ACRONYMS—*cont'd*

PEG percutaneous endoscopic gastrostomy

PUD peptic ulcer disease

TIPS transjugular intrahepatic portosystemic shunt

UGIB upper gastrointestinal bleed

ICD-10-CM OFFICIAL GUIDELINES FOR CODING AND REPORTING

There are currently no official guidelines for diseases of the digestive system.

Please refer to the companion Evolve website for the most current 2021-2022 guidelines.

ANATOMY AND PHYSIOLOGY

The digestive system (Figure 18-1) consists of the mouth, pharynx, esophagus, stomach, small intestine and large intestine (the **alimentary canal**), and accessory organs, which include the salivary glands, liver, gallbladder, and pancreas. The purpose of the digestive system is to process food so that it may be absorbed by cells.

The mouth is where digestion begins. The tongue (which is composed of muscle), the teeth, and saliva, facilitate **mastication** and assist in moving food to the pharynx, where swallowing occurs and food moves to the esophagus. **Peristalsis**, or the squeezing movement of food toward the stomach, occurs in the esophagus. Once the food arrives in the stomach, it is churned with gastric juices and begins the movement toward the small intestine.

The pancreas, the liver, and the gallbladder all aid in the digestive process. The purpose of the pancreas is to excrete juices that aid in the digestive process. The pancreatic duct connects with the duodenum in the same area in which the bile duct from the liver and the gallbladder intersect the duodenum. The liver secretes bile to aid in the digestive

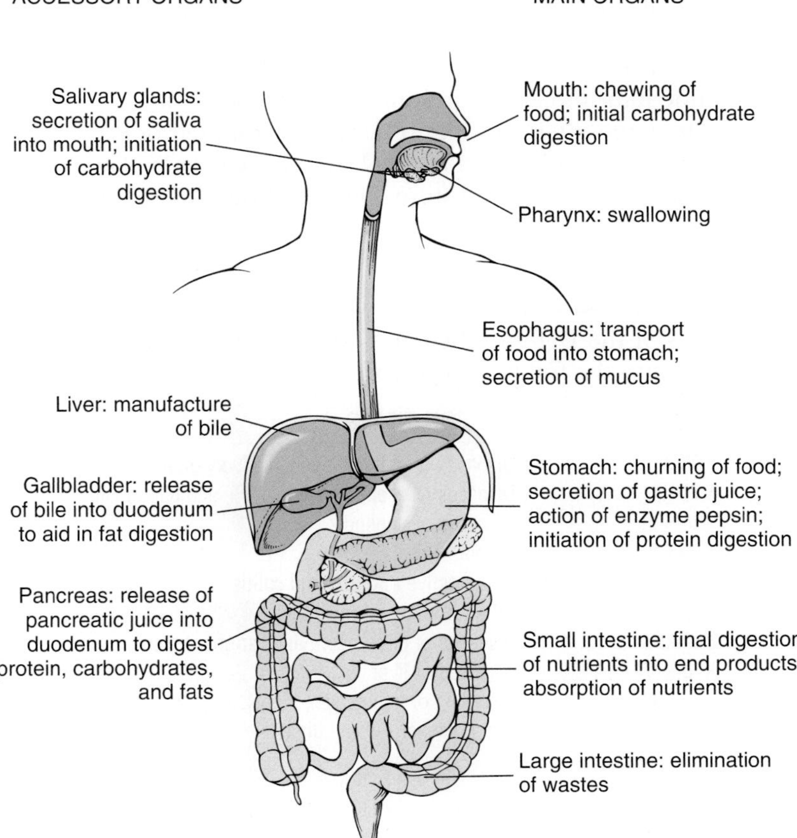

FIGURE 18-1. Main and accessory organs of the digestive system.

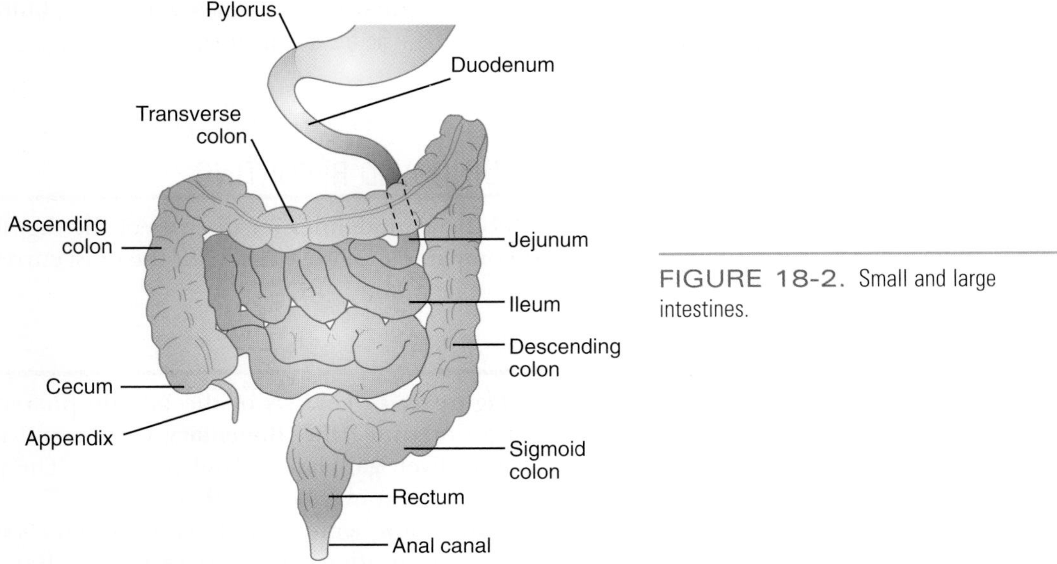

FIGURE 18-2. Small and large intestines.

process, and the gallbladder stores bile and releases it as needed. The gallbladder is attached to the liver by the cystic duct, which joins the hepatic duct. Together, they form the common bile duct, which enters into the duodenum.

The function of the liver, in addition to aiding the digestive process, is to remove poisons from the blood, produce immune agents to control infection, and remove germs and bacteria from the blood. The liver serves as a filter for the body; a person cannot live without a functioning liver.

The small intestine contains three areas: the duodenum, the jejunum, and the ileum. The small intestine completes the digestion begun in the stomach, absorbs products of digestion, and transports residue to the large intestine. The small intestine is suspended and is attached to the abdomen by a fold of peritoneum known as the mesentery. The small intestine joins the large intestine at the ileocecal valve.

The large intestine (Figure 18-2) is composed of the cecum, colon, rectum, and anal canal. The appendix is an appendage off the cecum. The purpose of the large intestine is to absorb electrolytes and store feces until the time of elimination.

DISEASE CONDITIONS

Diseases of the Digestive System (K00-K95), Chapter 11 in the ICD-10-CM code book, are divided into the following categories:

CATEGORY	SECTION TITLES
K00-K14	Diseases of oral cavity and salivary glands
K20-K31	Diseases of esophagus, stomach, and duodenum
K35-K38	Diseases of appendix
K40-K46	Hernia
K50-K52	Noninfective enteritis and colitis
K55-K64	Other diseases of intestines
K65-K68	Diseases of peritoneum and retroperitoneum
K70-K77	Diseases of liver
K80-K87	Disorders of gallbladder, biliary tract, and pancreas
K90-K95	Other diseases of the digestive system

Diseases of the Oral Cavity and Salivary Glands (K00-K14)

Many of the conditions in these categories concern the teeth and their structures. In the exam section of the record a healthcare provider might document whether the patient has dentures due to **edentulism**, which is the complete loss of teeth. The loss of teeth might affect the patient's ability to eat and therefore their nutritional state.

EXAMPLE

Patient is admitted to the hospital with severe malnutrition and dehydration. During the exam it is identified that the patient has Class I complete edentulism, E43, E86.0, K08.101.

Sialolithiasis is caused by stones in the salivary glands. Patients usually present with swollen, painful glands around the neck. When the stones are obstructing the gland, an infection, which is known as sialoadenitis, can result. Surgery may be required to remove the stone.

EXAMPLE

Patient with known sialolithiasis is admitted thru the ER with very painful glands in the neck and fever. After CT scan to determine the location of the stones and administration of antibiotics, the patient is taken to the OR for open removal of the stone from a minor salivary gland, K11.5, 0CCJ0ZZ.

Mucositis is an inflammation/ulceration of the digestive tract commonly occurring in the oral cavity. It can be found in up to 40% of patients being treated with chemotherapy. The condition can range from mild to severe. In the severest cases the patient may be unable to eat due to the pain caused by ulcerations in the mouth. It can be treated with viscous lidocaine.

EXAMPLE

Patient admitted for chemotherapy for pancreatic cancer and develops ulcerative oral mucositis due to chemo, which was administered via the central vein, Z51.11, K12.31, T45.1x5A, C25.9, 3E04305.

EXERCISE 18-1

Assign codes to the following conditions.

1. Canker sore ______________
2. Ulcerative stomatitis ______________
3. Hypertrophy of the salivary gland ______________
4. Impacted teeth ______________

Diseases of the Esophagus, Stomach, and Duodenum (K20-K31)

Esophageal Conditions

Esophageal varices (Figure 18-3), one of the most common causes of esophageal hemorrhage, are excluded from the code for gastrointestinal hemorrhage. The codes for esophageal hemorrhage due to esophageal varices are found in the Circulatory System chapter.

EXAMPLE

Patient has esophageal varices due to cirrhosis of the liver, K74.60, I85.10.

Mallory-Weiss is the name for bleeding laceration of the esophagogastric junction that usually occurs after severe vomiting. If the bleeding is severe, an EGD may be performed to control bleeding. One of the most common conditions is esophageal reflux, which is also known as gastroesophageal reflux disease (GERD). It is treated with proton pump inhibitors such as Prilosec or, in more severe cases, by Nissen fundoplication surgery.

Ulcers of the esophagus are often caused by drugs or medications (Figure 18-4).

Barrett's esophagus is a precancerous condition that usually occurs in people with chronic GERD. The normal cells lining the esophagus change type. Symptoms may include heartburn, indigestion, difficulty swallowing solid foods, and nocturnal regurgitation.

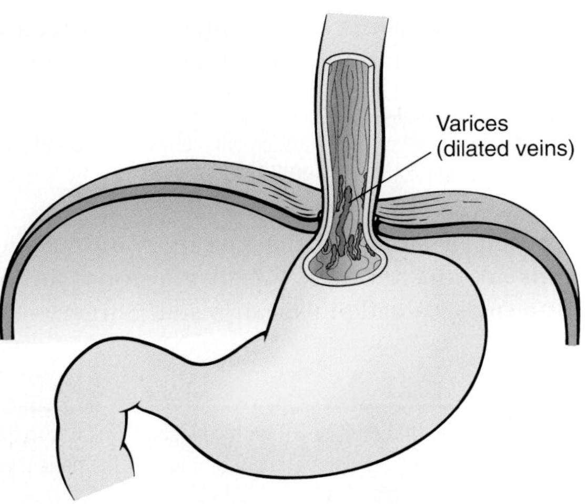

FIGURE 18-3. Esophageal varices.

K22.1 Ulcer of esophagus
Code first
poisoning due to drug or toxin, if applicable (T36-T65 with fifth or sixth character 1–4 or 6)
Use additional code for adverse effect if applicable to identify drug (T36-T50 with fifth or sixth character 5)
Excludes1: Barrett's esophagus (K22.87-)

FIGURE 18-4. If an esophageal ulcer is drug or chemical induced, use an additional code to identify the drug.

EXAMPLE

Patient with chronic GERD who is having difficulty swallowing is found to have Barrett's esophagus, K22.70, K21.9.

EXERCISE 18-2

Assign codes to the following conditions.

1. Esophageal ulcer due to ingestion of aspirin, initial encounter __________
2. Inflammation of the esophagus due to reflux __________
3. Mallory-Weiss tear __________
4. GERD __________

Ulcers of the Stomach and Small Intestine

An ulcer of the stomach or the intestine is an open sore in the lining of the stomach or intestine. An ulcer occurs when the lining is damaged. Damage to the lining may occur when production of stomach acid is increased, or it may be caused by a bacterium known as *Helicobacter pylori,* or *H. pylori.* When locating the code for a bacterium, the main term "Infection" should be referenced in the Alphabetic Index. Ulcers may be drug induced. The Tabular List contains instructions to use an additional code for adverse effect, if applicable to identify drug (T36-T50).

Symptoms of gastric ulcer may include pain when eating, vomiting, and tarry bowel movements. Ulcers can be diagnosed by means of an upper GI x-ray, blood tests that look for *H. pylori,* stool samples, or endoscopy. Treatment for ulcers may include antacids, drugs such as proton pump inhibitors or histamine receptor blockers, which stop the stomach from making acids, or antibiotics, and finally, in the worst case scenario, gastrectomy. Some conditions that may accompany ulcers are chronic or acute blood loss anemia and gastric outlet syndrome. A gastric ulcer is a stomach ulcer. A peptic ulcer can occur in the esophagus, stomach, duodenum, jejunum, and/or ileum.

EXAMPLE

Patient has a peptic ulcer of the esophagus, secondary to aspirin use, initial encounter, K22.10, T39.015A.

EXAMPLE

Patient is admitted for a bleeding gastric ulcer with perforation, K25.6.

Gastrointestinal Hemorrhage

Gastrointestinal (GI) hemorrhage is a common reason for a patient to seek medical attention. The healthcare provider must determine whether the bleed is lower or upper GI in origin, so appropriate treatment can be provided. To make this determination, the provider must evaluate how the patient presents.

- In lower GI bleeds (LGIB), the patient may present with the following:
  Hematochezia—bright red blood in stool
- In upper GI bleeds (UGIB), the patient may present with the following:
  Hematemesis—vomiting of blood

If a patient presents with **melena** (dark blood in stool) or **occult blood** in the stool (this can be found only by laboratory inspection), it is unknown without further workup whether this is an upper or a lower GI bleed. Often, when a patient presents with acute anemia without a causative condition, the healthcare provider may suspect a GI bleed.

EXAMPLE

Blood in feces, occult, lab finding, R19.5.

GI hemorrhage has many causes; the most common causes consist of gastric or intestinal ulcers, hemorrhoids, diverticulitis, and **angiodysplasia** (malformation characterized by dilated or fragile blood vessels).

EXAMPLE

Patient admitted with GI bleed caused by angiodysplasia of the stomach, K31.811.

EXAMPLE

Patient is being treated for diverticulitis of the sigmoid colon with hemorrhage, K57.33.

When a patient presents with a GI bleed and then undergoes diagnostic testing such as esophagogastroduodenoscopy (EGD) to determine the site of the bleed, unless the physician specifies a causal relationship between the findings on this test and the bleed, the code K92.2 should be assigned. Codes for any other findings such as gastritis should be coded as without hemorrhage. If melena (K92.1) or hematemesis (K92.0) is documented, these are more specific codes for GI bleeding and should be assigned instead of K92.2, GI hemorrhage, unspecified.

Sometimes endoscopic examination does not show active bleeding. If the physician documents GI bleeding based on the patient's history and other findings, it is acceptable to assign the code with mention of hemorrhage or a code from the K92 category, even though no active bleeding has occurred during a particular encounter.

EXERCISE 18-3

Assign codes to the following conditions.

1. Angiodysplasia with hemorrhage of the duodenum and chronic blood loss anemia __________
2. Acute penetrating peptic ulcer of the duodenum __________
3. GI bleed due to peptic ulcer __________
4. Dyspepsia, functional __________
5. Blood in stool __________

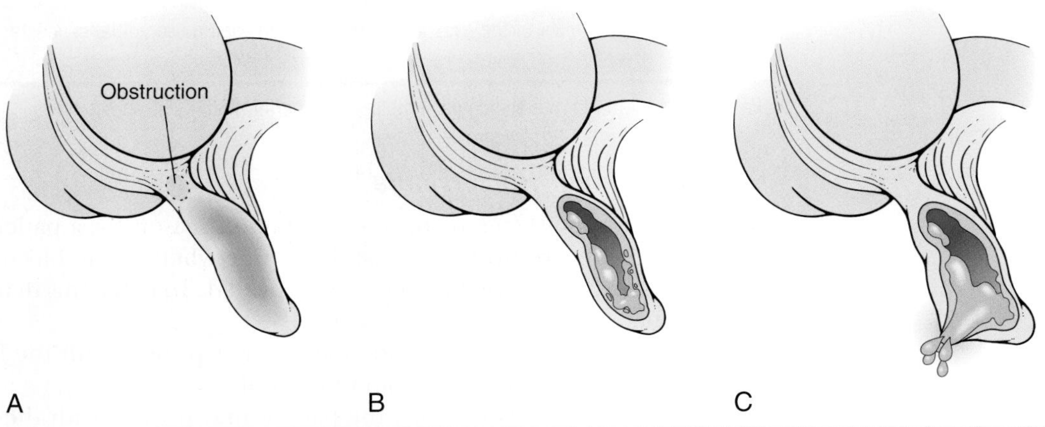

FIGURE 18-5. Stages of appendicitis. **A,** Obstruction that causes inflammation. **B,** Pus and bacteria invade the wall of the appendix. **C,** Pus perforates the wall of the appendix, leading to peritonitis.

Diseases of the Appendix (K35-K38)

Appendicitis is inflammation of the appendix that is usually caused by obstruction, which, in turn, results in infection (Figure 18-5). A patient who presents with appendicitis may have some or all of the following signs and symptoms: abdominal pain (right lower quadrant, also known as **McBurney's point**), vomiting, **anorexia** (loss of appetite), fever, constipation, and elevated white blood cell count.

If the appendix ruptures, peritonitis develops. Patients with appendicitis are usually treated with antibiotics and surgery (appendectomy). It is important to review the pathology report for documentation of abscess or perforation of appendix.

On occasion, all signs and symptoms lead the surgeon to believe that a patient has appendicitis, but the pathology report does not confirm this diagnosis.

EXAMPLE Patient admitted with acute appendicitis with peritoneal abscess, K35.3.

EXAMPLE Patient has a ruptured appendicitis, K35.2.

Hernia (K40-K46)

A **hernia** (Figure 18-6) is a protrusion of an organ or tissue through an abnormal opening in the body. Hernias can be present at birth or may develop over time. Most commonly, a hernia is a protrusion of the intestine through a weakness in the abdominal cavity. Hernias are classified by type or site. Once the site of the hernia is known, then it must be determined whether it is obstructed or gangrenous. An obstructed abdominal hernia is one in which the bowel is trapped and obstructed but viable (still working); when it becomes nonviable, it can become gangrenous (deficient blood supply to trapped bowel, making it **necrotic**). There is a note in ICD-10-CM that if a hernia is both obstructed and gangrenous, it should be classified to a hernia with gangrene. Some codes require documentation as to whether the hernia is unilateral or bilateral.

Some types of hernias:

- Inguinal—common in men, intestines protrude in the inguinal canal
- Femoral—more common in women, intestine protrudes through the femoral canal at the top of the thigh
- Umbilical—most common in children, abdominal wall is weakened at the point of the umbilical cord
- Incisional—this is when scar tissue in the abdominal wall weakens following surgery or trauma.

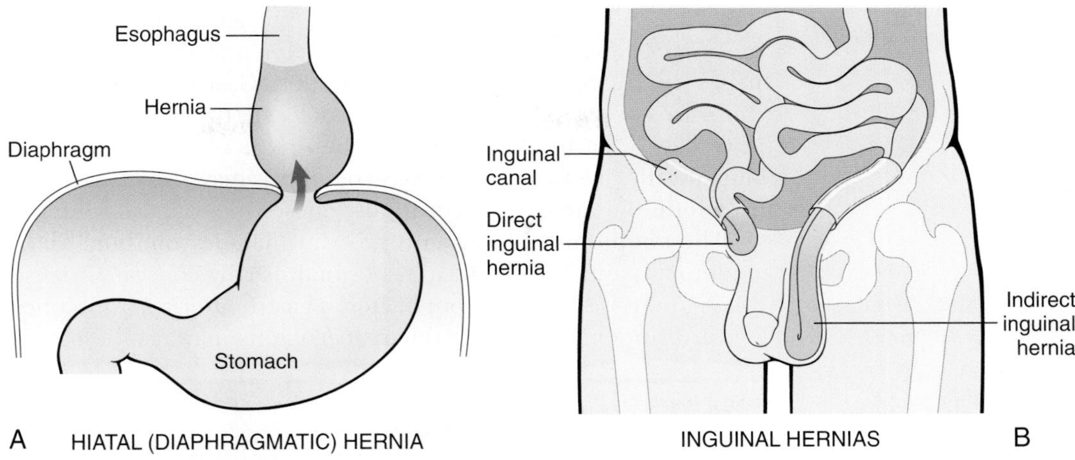

FIGURE 18-6. **A,** Hiatal hernia. **B,** Inguinal hernia. Direct inguinal hernia passes through the abdominal wall. Indirect hernia passes through the inguinal canal.

- Ventral—is a bulging in the abdominal wall, usually at the midline. It can occur spontaneously in a patient who does not have a surgical incision.
- Diaphragmatic—abnormal opening in the diaphragm that allows parts of organs from the abdominal cavity (i.e., intestines, stomach) to move into the chest cavity. Also known as a hiatal hernia

EXAMPLE

Patient was seen in consultation for an inguinal hernia, unilateral, recurrent, with obstruction, K40.31.

Noninfectious Enteritis and Colitis (K50-K52)

Crohn's Disease

Crohn's disease is characterized by inflammation of the GI tract, especially the small and large intestine. It is an inflammatory bowel disease that appears to run in families. It is typically diagnosed first at the age of 20 to 30. Often there is difficulty determining Crohn's versus ulcerative colitis. Crohn's may also be known as ileitis or enteritis. People presenting with Crohn's may exhibit symptoms of abdominal pain and diarrhea. Depending on the severity and location of the disease, patients may be treated with drugs to control inflammation, steroids, immunosuppressive agents, biologic response modifiers, antibiotics, and medications to control diarrhea, along with fluid replacement. Almost 75% of the patients with Crohn's require surgery at some point in their lives to remove the diseased intestine, and they often require an ostomy.

Ulcerative Colitis

Ulcerative colitis, like Crohn's disease, is an inflammatory bowel disease. Ulcerative colitis is a disease that produces ulcers in the lining of the rectum and colon, whereas Crohn's disease causes inflammation deep within the intestinal wall and can occur in other parts of the digestive system, including the small intestine, mouth, esophagus, and stomach.

EXAMPLE

Patient is admitted to the hospital with abdominal pain and dehydration. After testing is completed, a diagnosis of ulcerative enterocolitis is confirmed, K51.00, E86.0.

Gastroenteritis is an inflammation of the stomach and intestines. Two of the main causes of this condition are viruses and bacteria. Viral gastroenteritis usually runs its course in 1 to 2 days, whereas bacterial gastroenteritis can last for up to a week or more. The most common causes of viral gastroenteritis, which often spreads via poor handwashing habits in schools and daycare centers, are adenoviruses, rotaviruses, and norovirus. The noroviruses are the leading cause of acute gastroenteritis. The most common bacterial causes are *E. coli*, salmonella, campylobacter, and shigella. Gastroenteritis due to particular viruses or bacteria may be indexed under "Gastroenteritis" with a subterm for the bacterium/virus. If the bacterium/virus is not listed, the Index has an instruction to *see also* enteritis. Codes for gastroenteritis caused by viruses or bacteria may be located in the infectious and parasitic diseases chapter. Gastroenteritis may also be caused by chemical toxins such as those found in medications or foods. These types of gastroenteritis are not infectious.

The symptoms of gastroenteritis can include vomiting, diarrhea, low-grade fever, and abdominal pain. Treatment in a hospital usually consists of IV fluids for rehydration, and if the patient is suffering from bacterial gastroenteritis, antibiotics may be used. If vomiting is severe, antiemetics and antidiarrheal agents may also be used.

EXAMPLE

Patient is seen in physician's office with severe vomiting and diarrhea. After testing is performed it is determined that she is suffering from a bout of gastroenteritis, K52.9.

Other Diseases of Intestines and Peritoneum (K55-K68)

Intestinal Obstruction

This condition occurs when the content of the intestines cannot move forward. The intesines can be completely blocked or partially blocked. Obstruction may be mechanical or functional. Mechanical obstruction can be caused by a variety of conditions, such as neoplasm, **impaction**, stricture, adhesion, **intussusception**, **volvulus**, and herniation (Figure 18-7). When the obstruction is functional, it is called an **ileus.**

EXAMPLE

Patient with intestinal obstruction due to fecal impaction, K56.41.

EXAMPLE

Patient has intussusception of the intestine, K56.1.

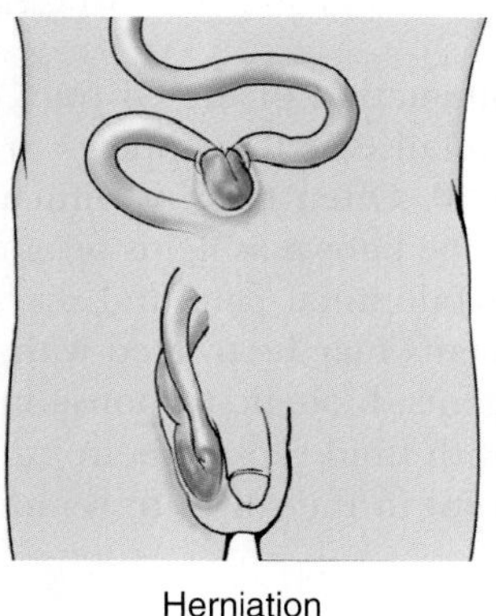

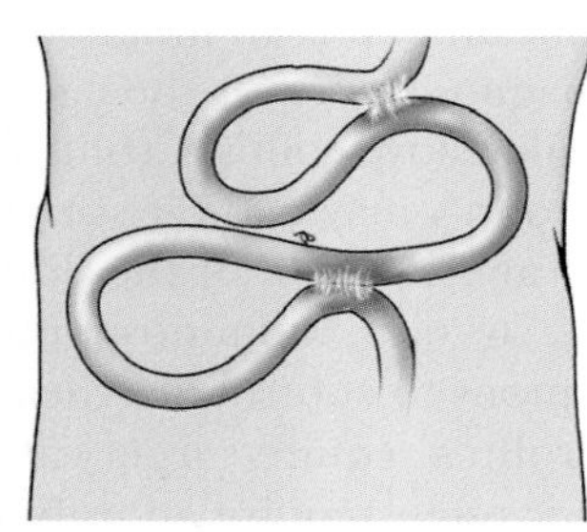

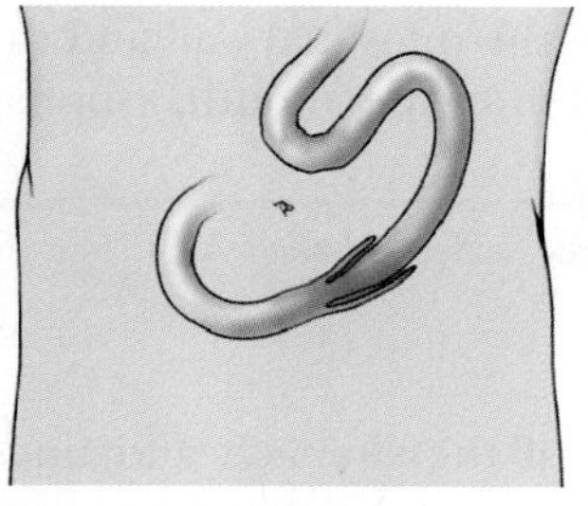

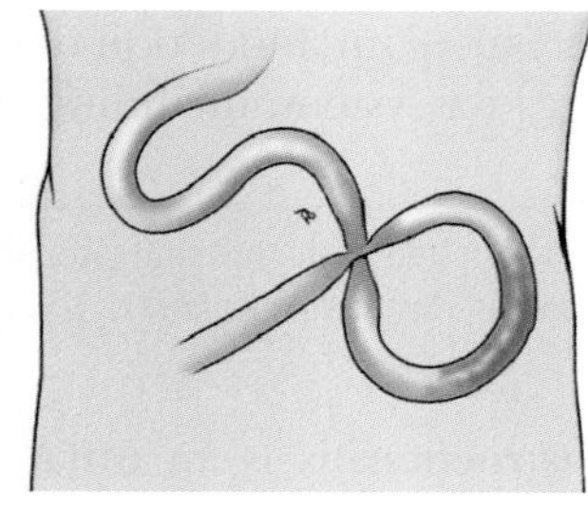

FIGURE 18-7. **A,** Herniation. **B,** Adhesions. **C,** Intussusception. **D,** Volvulus.

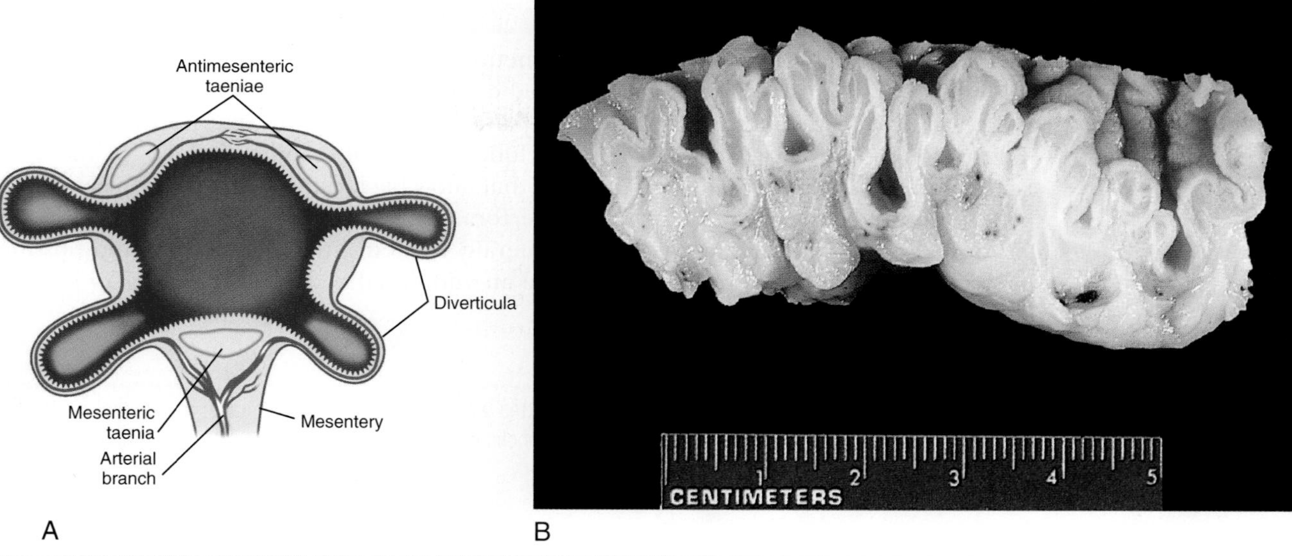

FIGURE 18-8. **A,** Diverticula. **B,** Diverticulosis.

Diverticulitis and Diverticulosis

Diverticula (Figure 18-8), also known as tics, are small pouches in the lining of the mucous membranes of an organ. When a patient has diverticula, the condition is referred to as diverticulosis. If these pouches become inflamed or infected, the condition becomes diverticulitis. Diverticulitis can result in peritonitis, perforation, fistula, bowel obstruction, or abscess. If a patient has diverticulitis, diverticula are assumed to be present and only the code for diverticulitis is assigned. Diverticulitis is an acute condition that usually is treated with antibiotics. If a patient has a history of diverticulitis, it may be acceptable to code diverticulosis, but the diverticulitis has likely resolved with prior treatment.

EXAMPLE

Patient has diverticulosis of the duodenum with diverticulitis and hemorrhage, K57.13.

EXERCISE 18-4

Assign codes to the following conditions.

1. Incisional hernia ____________
2. Gangrenous ventral hernia ____________
3. Diaphragmatic hernia ____________
4. Obstructed unilateral femoral hernia ____________
5. Abscess due to Crohn's ilietis ____________
6. Hemorrhagic diverticulitis of the large intestine ____________
7. Diverticulosis ____________
8. Volvulus causing intestinal obstruction ____________
9. Adhesions causing intestinal obstruction ____________
10. Regional enteritis of the colon ____________
11. Allergic gastroenteritis due to milk allergy ____________
12. Inflammatory polyps of the colon ____________

Diseases of Peritoneum and Retroperitoneum (K65-K68)

Peritonitis is an inflammation of the peritoneum (membrane covering the organs of the abdominal cavity), usually an infection caused either by bacteria or fungus. The symptoms of peritonitis can include fever, abdominal pain or distention, and nausea and vomiting. The most common causes of peritonitis include peritoneal dialysis, cirrhosis of the liver, ascites, and peritonitis caused by conditions that allow bacteria to get into the peritoneum such as ruptured appendix, stomach ulcer, perforated colon, pancreatitis, and diverticulitis. Peritonitis can be life threatening and is generally treated with IV antibiotics and possibly surgery. In ICD-10-CM there is a note to use an additional code from B95-B97 to identify the organism responsible for the peritonitis.

EXAMPLE Patient with known alcoholic cirrhosis of the liver is admitted with ascites and acute spontaneous bacterial peritonitis due to *Klebsiella pneumoniae*. Patient is a recovering alcoholic who has been in remission for 2 years, K65.2, K70.31, F10.21, B96.1.

Diseases of the Liver (K70-K77)

Cirrhosis of the Liver

Cirrhosis of the liver is degeneration of liver tissue that causes blockage of blood through the organ and inhibits the function of this organ. Cirrhosis may be caused by a variety of factors; alcoholism and hepatitis are the most common.

EXAMPLE Alcoholic cirrhosis of liver. Patient is a recovering alcoholic, in remission, K70.30, F10.21.

Hepatitis

Hepatitis, which is an inflammation of the liver, can last for a short time, or it may be chronic and last a lifetime. Most commonly, hepatitis is caused by a virus. When it is caused by a virus, hepatitis is coded from the infectious disease chapter of ICD-10-CM. However, other less common types of hepatitis are coded to the chapter on Digestive Diseases. Because the liver metabolizes both alcohol and drugs, a patient may develop alcoholic hepatitis or drug-induced hepatitis. When coding drug-induced hepatitis, it is important to also assign a code from T36-T65 to identify the responsible drug.

EXAMPLE Patient has chronic hepatitis C, B18.2.

EXAMPLE Patient has chronic hepatitis, K73.9.

Toxic hepatitis occurs when the liver is damaged by chemicals or drugs. Toxic hepatitis may come on very quickly or may take months of exposure to the drug or chemical. Likewise when the chemical or drug exposure stops the toxic hepatitis may clear, but sometimes permanent liver damage may have already occurred. Idiosyncratic toxins are those that cause damage in some people but not in others. Some common over the counter drugs can be toxic to the liver. These would include drugs such as Advil, Motrin, Aleve, and Tylenol. Some prescription drugs such as Isoniazid, methotrexate, and statins can potentially cause liver damage.

EXAMPLE Patient was admitted with acute toxic hepatitis due to accidental Tylenol overdose, T39.1x1A, K71.2

Disorders of the Gallbladder, Billiary Tract, and Pancreas (K80-K87)

Cholelithiasis and Cholecystitis

Cholelithiasis is an abnormal condition of stones in the gallbladder (gallstones). The condition is generally asymptomatic until gallstones block the cystic duct or the common bile duct, which does not allow the gallbladder to drain stored bile; the patient then develops acute cholecystitis (Figure 18-9). If the cystic duct is blocked, a patient generally has right upper quadrant crampy abdominal pain. This pain is often made worse by ingestion of fatty or greasy foods. When the common bile duct is blocked, a patient may develop cholangitis; when the stone is blocking the lower end of the common bile duct, secretion from the pancreas may be blocked, and pancreatitis may occur. **Choledocholithiasis** is the term used for a stone lodged in the bile duct. Endoscopic retrograde cholangiopancreatography (ERCP) may be used to detect the presence of gallstones.

In ICD-10-CM it is important to look for documentation of where the gallstones are located, i.e., in the gallbladder, the bile duct, or both; if cholecystitis is present and if it is acute or chronic; if the stone(s) are obstructing; and if there is cholangitis present.

EXAMPLE Patient has acute cholecystitis with cholelithiasis and choledocholithiasis, K80.62.

Pancreatitis is an inflammation of the pancreas often caused by gallstones or chronic heavy alcohol use. Pancreatitis can be acute or chronic. Acute pancreatitis often presents with upper abdominal pain that extends through the back and is often severe. When a

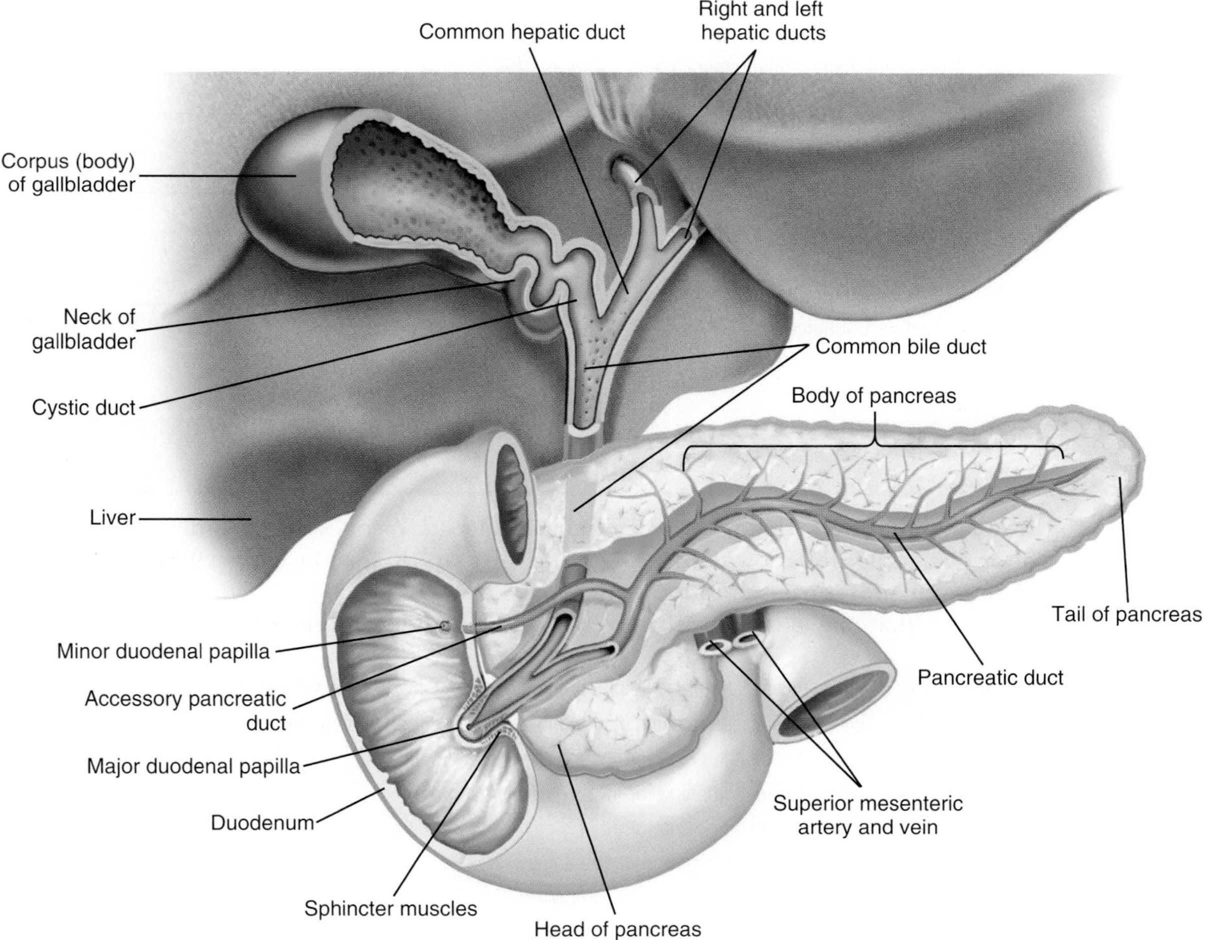

FIGURE 18-9. Ducts that carry bile from the liver and gallbladder. Obstruction of either the common hepatic duct or the common bile duct by a stone or spasm prevents bile from being ejected into the duodenum.

patient is experiencing acute pancreatitis, their bloodwork usually has elevated amylase and lipase, which are digestive enzymes found in the pancreas. Acute pancreatitis is treated with IV fluids and pain meds and by keeping the patient NPO. If the cause of the pancreatitis is not clear, an ERCP (endoscopic retrograde cholangiogram) may be peformed. During an ERCP a physician may perform one or more of the following procedures:

- Sphincterotomy—opens the pancreatic or bile duct
- Gallstone removal
- Stent placement—keeps the duct open
- Balloon dilation—opens or stretches the duct

Occasionally there can be complications related to acute pancreatitis. Systemic complications include hypotension, pulmonary edema, and adult respiratory distress syndrome. Inflammation may extend to surrounding organs causing additional problems. Localized complications include fluid collections, pancreatic pseudocysts, and pancreatic necrosis with or without infection.

Chronic pancreatitis is an inflammation that does not get better and most often gets worse and can lead to permanent damage. The most common cause of chronic pancreatitis is chronic heavy alcohol use. In chronic pancreatitis the pancreas may no longer be making the digestive enzymes, and then other complications may occur such as malabsorption or diabetes.

EXERCISE 18-5

Assign codes to the following conditions.

1. Alcoholic hepatitis __________
2. Type A viral hepatitis with coma __________
3. Hepatitis due to cytomegalovirus __________
4. Fatty liver __________
5. Laennec's cirrhosis of the liver with ascites. Patient is chronic alcoholic __________
6. Patient admitted to hospital with chronic cholecystitis for a laparoscopic cholecystectomy; during the surgery, the surgeon decides to convert to open __________
7. Patient is admitted with gallstone pancreatitis; this is treated and the patient is sent home __________

FACTORS INFLUENCING HEALTH STATUS AND CONTACT WITH HEALTH SERVICES (Z CODES)

As was discussed in Chapter 9, it is difficult to locate Z codes in the Index. Coders will often say, "I did not know there was Z code for that." Refer to Chapter 9 for a listing of common main terms used to locate Z codes.

Z codes that may be used with digestive system conditions include the following:

Z01.20	Encounter for dental examination and cleaning without abnormal findings
Z01.21	Encounter for dental examination and cleaning with abnormal findings
Z13.810	Encounter for screening for upper gastrointestinal disorder
Z13.811	Encounter for screening for lower gastrointestinal disorder
Z13.818	Encounter for screening for other digestive system disorders
Z43.1	Encounter for attention to gastrostomy
Z43.2	Encounter for attention to ileostomy
Z43.3	Encounter for attention to colostomy
Z43.4	Encounter for attention to other artificial openings of digestive tract
Z46.3	Encounter for fitting and adjustment of dental prosthetic device
Z46.4	Encounter for fitting and adjustment of orthodontic device

Z46.51	Encounter for fitting and adjustment of gastric lap band
Z46.59	Encounter for fitting and adjustment of other gastrointestinal appliance and device
Z52.6	Liver donor
Z83.71	Family history of colonic polyps
Z83.79	Family history of other diseases of the digestive system
Z87.11	Personal history of peptic ulcer disease
Z87.19	Personal history of other diseases of the digestive system
Z90.3	Acquired absence of stomach [part of]
Z90.410	Acquired total absence of pancreas
Z90.411	Acquired partial absence of pancreas
Z90.49	Acquired absence of other specified parts of digestive tract
Z93.1	Gastrostomy status
Z93.2	Ileostomy status
Z93.3	Colostomy status
Z93.4	Other artificial openings of gastrointestinal tract status
Z94.4	Liver transplant status
Z94.82	Intestine transplant status
Z94.83	Pancreas transplant status
Z96.5	Presence of tooth-root and mandibular implants
Z97.2	Presence of dental prosthetic device (complete) (partial)
Z98.0	Intestinal bypass and anastomosis status
Z98.810	Dental sealant status
Z98.811	Dental restoration status
Z98.818	Other dental procedure status
Z98.84	Bariatric surgery status

There are a number of different types of ostomies that can be present in the digestive system. There are three ways in which an ostomy can be coded.

- If there is a complication of the ostomy it is coded to the appropriate complication code.
- It there is no complication but the ostomy needs some type of attention such as closure (take-down), catheter change, etc., assign a code from the attention to Z43 category
- If there is no complication and no specific attention to the ostomy it would be appropriate to assign a status code from the Z93 code category.

EXAMPLE

Patient is admitted to donate a liver. An open right liver lobectomy is performed, Z52.6, OFT10ZZ.

EXERCISE 18-6

Assign codes to the following conditions.

1. Patient is admitted for open takedown of a colostomy, with trimming of the descending colon edges and end-to-end anastomosis ______________
2. Patient had gastric bypass 1 year ago ______________
3. Physician notes that the patient has a history of having the pancreas replaced by a transplant ______________
4. Patient has a remote history of PUD ______________

COMMON TREATMENTS

Many digestive disorders are treated with surgery.

CONDITION	MEDICATION
GERD	Propulsid, Reglan, Prilosec, Prevacid, Zantac, Tagamet
Crohn's disease	Azulfidine, Remicade, corticosteroids, Rowasa

CONDITION	MEDICATION
Diverticulitis	Metronidazole, Ciprofloxacin
Gastric ulcer	Pepcid, Axid, Prilosec, Nexium
Gastroenteritis	Antiemetics such as Promethazine (Phenergan), prochlorperazine (Compazine), ondansetron (Zofran)
	Antidiarrheals, such as diphenoxylate atropine (Lomotil, Lofene, Lonox) or loperamide hydrochloride (Imodium)
	IV fluids
Pancreatitis	Pain medications, IV fluids

PROCEDURES

Procedures related to the digestive system in ICD-10-PCS may be found in the following tables:

Mouth and Throat	0C0-0CX
Gastrointestinal System	0D1-0DY
Hepatobiliary System and Pancreas	0F1-0FY

Procedures of the Stomach

Nissen **fundoplication** (Figure 18-10) is a surgical treatment for GERD. The root operation in ICD-10-PCS for a Nissen fundoplication is restriction (meaning partially closing an orifice or lumen) of the esophagogastric junction. This procedure takes the fundus (the upper portion) of the stomach and wraps it around the lower portion of the esophagus to prevent the reflux of stomach contents back into the esophagus.

Percutaneous endoscopic gastrostomy (PEG) is the placement of a tube through the abdominal wall into the stomach with the use of a scope. The root operation for a PEG in ICD-10-PCS is insertion (putting in a nonbiological appliance that monitors, assists, performs, or prevents a physiological function but does not physically take the place of a body part) of a feeding device into the stomach. Because an endoscope is used does not mean that the approach is endoscopic via natural or artificial opening. The endoscope is only used to guide the insertion of the PEG tube. The tube, itself, is inserted "percutaneously" through the abdominal wall into the stomach. The endoscopic guidance is not coded separately. PEGs are used as feeding tubes for patients who are having difficulty eating (e.g., malnourished patients, patients who aspirate food). If a patient is admitted for insertion of a PEG tube because of carcinoma of the soft palate, and he or she now has dysphagia and dehydration, the principal diagnosis would be C05.1, carcinoma, and additional codes R13.10 for dysphagia and E86.0 for dehydration would be assigned.

If a patient presents to the hospital with a chief complaint of a PEG tube falling out, the principal diagnosis would be Z43.1, or attention to gastrostomy, because no complications resulted from the gastrostomy itself.

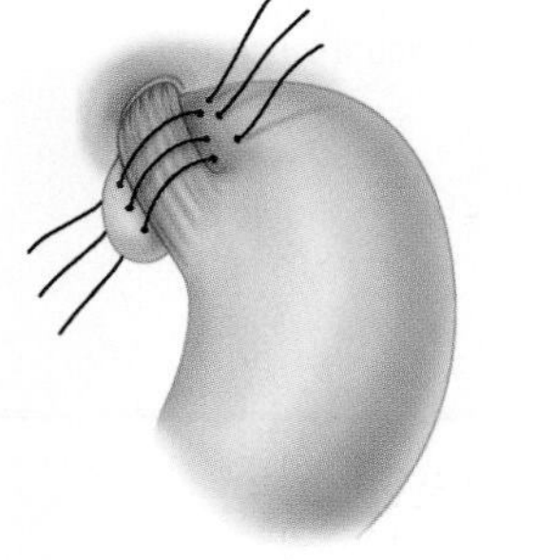
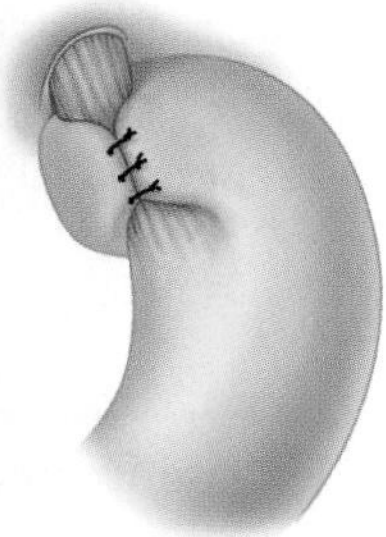

FIGURE 18-10. Nissen fundoplication.

EXAMPLE

Patient is admitted for insertion of a PEG tube because of carcinoma of the soft palate with resultant dysphagia and dehydration, C05.1, R13.10, E86.0, 0DH63UZ

SECTION	BODY SYSTEM	ROOT OPERATION	BODY PART	APPROACH	DEVICE	QUALIFIER
Medical and Surgical	Gastrointestinal System	Insertion	Stomach	Percutaneous	Feeding Device	No Qualifier
0	D	H	6	3	U	Z

Procedures of the Intestine

Esophagogastroduodenoscopy (EGD) (Figure 18-11) is a diagnostic procedure that is used to identify disease conditions in the esophagus, stomach, and duodenum. The root operation for an EGD in ICD-10-PCS is inspection (visual or manual exploration of a body part). Many times additional procedures are performed, such as biopsy, lesion removal, ablation, hemorrhage control, and dilations.

EXAMPLE

Patient with bleeding gastric ulcer taken to OR for EGD to control bleed; bleeding in the stomach controlled by electrocautery, K25.4, 0W3P8ZZ.

SECTION	BODY SYSTEM	ROOT OPERATION	BODY PART	APPROACH	DEVICE	QUALIFIER
Medical and Surgical	Anatomical Regions, General	Control	Gastrointestinal Tract	Via Natural or Artificial Opening Endoscopic	No Device	No Qualifier
0	W	3	P	8	Z	Z

Colostomy (Figure 18-12) is a procedure that uses the colon to create an artificial opening (**stoma**) to the exterior of the abdomen. The root operation for a colostomy in ICD-10-PCS is bypass (altering route of passage of the contents of a tubular body part). This artificial opening serves as a substitute anus through which the intestines excrete waste until the colon heals or other corrective surgery is performed. The location of the stoma depends on which part of the colon is involved in the surgery. Most colostomies are temporary. A sigmoid colostomy is the most commonly performed type.

When a patient is admitted for a colostomy closure (takedown), the principal diagnosis should be Z43.3. Most often when closing a colostomy, the surgeon makes an incision around the stoma and then trims the ends of the colon prior to completing the anastomosis. In this case, the root operation is excision. The anastomosis is inherent to the procedure and is not coded separately as well as the closure stoma since that was the manner in which

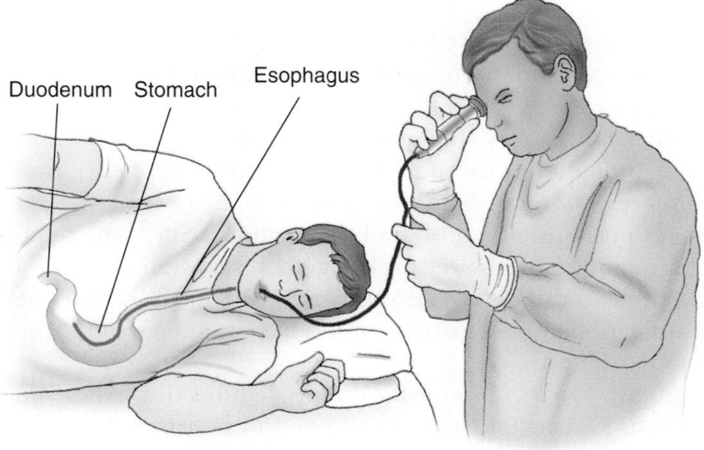

FIGURE 18-11. Esophagogastroduodenoscopy (EGD).

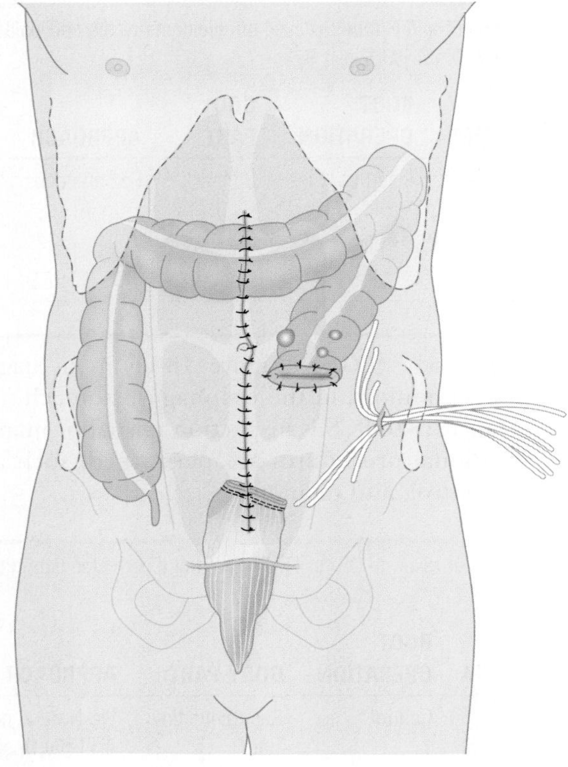

FIGURE 18-12. Colostomy. The opening of the colon is brought to the surface of the skin to divert feces into an external pouch worn by the patient.

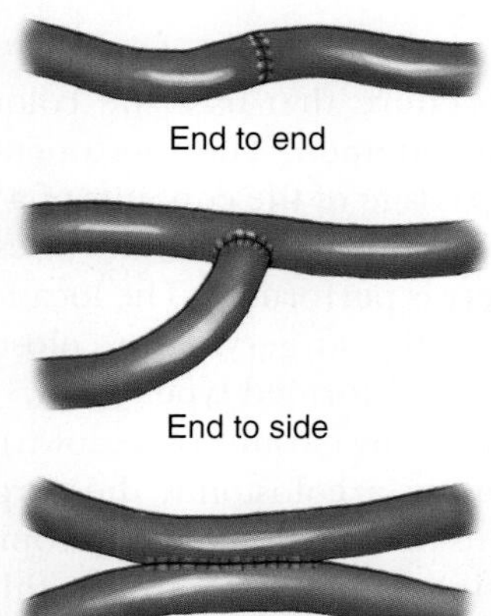

FIGURE 18-13. Types of anastomoses.

the operative site was entered. In some cases, the ends of the colon may be sutured together without any excision performed. Repair would be the appropriate root operation in this case.

An **ileostomy** is very similar to a colostomy, except that the end of the small intestine (ileum) is brought out through the abdominal wall.

Bowel resection can be performed for many reasons (i.e., neoplasms, severe diverticulitis, bowel perforation, and bowel obstruction). Surgeons remove a portion of the bowel and then connect the bowel back together (anastomosis). According to the ICD-10-PCS guidelines, procedural steps necessary to reach and close the operative site, including anastomosis of a tubular body part, are also not coded separately. Figure 18-13 illustrates various types of anastomoses.

There are many different surgical procedures that can be performed on the small and large intestines. Documentation will need to be carefully reviewed to determine whether the root operation should be excision versus resection. According to *Coding Clinic for ICD-10-CM/PCS* (2014:3Q:p6), the removal of an adjacent structure in order to resect an entire body part are inherent to the procedure and should not be coded separately.[1]

EXAMPLE

Patient was admitted to the hospital and underwent an open ileocecectomy (removal of the cecum, the terminal ileum, and appendix) for a malignant carcinoid tumor of the cecum, C7a.021, 0DTH0ZZ (the removal of a portion of the ileum and appendix are integral to the removal of the entire cecum).

EXAMPLE

Patient with malignant neoplasm of the descending colon is admitted for an open left hemicolectomy, and temporary colostomy (transverse colon), C18.6, 0DTG0ZZ, 0D1L0Z4.

SECTION	BODY SYSTEM	ROOT OPERATION	BODY PART	APPROACH	DEVICE	QUALIFIER
Medical and Surgical	Gastrointestinal System	Resection	Large Intestine, Left	Open	No Device	No Qualifier
0	D	T	G	0	Z	Z

SECTION	BODY SYSTEM	ROOT OPERATION	BODY PART	APPROACH	DEVICE	QUALIFIER
Medical and Surgical	Gastrointestinal System	Bypass	Transverse Colon	Open	No Device	Cutaneous
0	D	1	L	0	Z	4

Appendectomy is removal of the appendix. The root operation for an appendectomy in ICD-10-PCS is resection (cutting out or off without replacement all of a body part). Codes assigned will be different depending on the approach, i.e., open or laparoscopic. Often, when a surgeon is performing an abdominal operation, an incidental appendectomy may be performed. An **incidental appendectomy** is one that is performed at the time of another procedure with no known disease process in the appendix.

EXAMPLE

Patient with acute appendicitis is admitted for a laparoscopic appendectomy, K35.80, 0DTJ4ZZ.

SECTION	BODY SYSTEM	ROOT OPERATION	BODY PART	APPROACH	DEVICE	QUALIFIER
Medical and Surgical	Gastrointestinal System	Resection	Appendix	Percutaneous Endoscopic	No Device	No Qualifier
0	D	T	J	4	Z	Z

Procedures of the Gallbladder and Biliary System

Cholecystectomy, or removal of the gallbladder, can be performed by incision or by laparoscope (Figure 18-14). The root operation for a cholecystectomy in ICD-10-PCS is resection (cutting out or off without replacement, all of a body part). Cholecystostomy may also be performed to remove stones from the gallbladder or drain fluid. This can be performed by open incision as well as by scope or percutaneous approach.

EXAMPLE

Patient with acute cholecystitis with cholelithiasis has a laparoscopic cholecystectomy, which was converted to open procedure, K80.00, Z53.31, 0FT40ZZ, 0FJ44ZZ.

SECTION	BODY SYSTEM	ROOT OPERATION	BODY PART	APPROACH	DEVICE	QUALIFIER
Medical and Surgical	Hepatobiliary System and Pancreas	Resection	Gallbladder	Open	No Device	No Qualifier
0	F	T	4	0	Z	Z

SECTION	BODY SYSTEM	ROOT OPERATION	BODY PART	APPROACH	DEVICE	QUALIFIER
Medical and Surgical	Hepatobiliary System and Pancreas	Inspection	Gallbladder	Percutaneous Endoscopic	No Device	No Qualifier
0	F	J	4	4	Z	Z

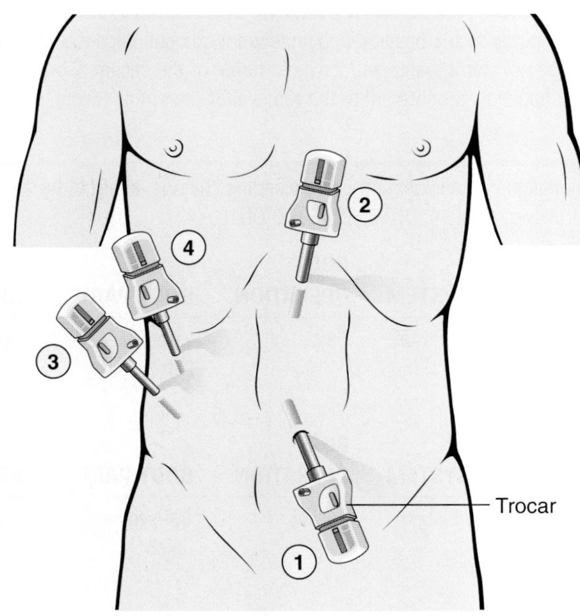

FIGURE 18-14. Trocar placement for laparoscopic cholecystectomy.

Common bile duct stones can be removed in three different ways (i.e., by incision, endoscopy, or percutaneously). Occasionally a cholecystectomy is performed along with removal of common duct stones. Codes should be assigned for both the cholecystectomy and the common bile duct stone removal. Fragmentation of stones of the gallbladder by extracorporeal shock wave lithotripsy, or ESWL, is the breaking apart of stones by shock waves.

An endoscopic retrograde cholangiopancreatography (ERCP) is often done for diagnosis, but it may be done for stent insertion, or may be done in combination with a sphincterotomy or for removal of stones. The root operation in ICD-10-PCS for a diagnostic ERCP is inspection of biliary and/or pancreatic ducts. If the ERCP is done for stent insertion, the root operation is dilation (expanding an orifice or lumen of a tubular body part). If the ERCP is done for stone removal, the root operation is extirpation (taking or cutting out solid matter from a body part).

EXAMPLE

Patient with common bile duct stones presents for stone removal by ERCP, K80.50, 0FC98ZZ.

SECTION	BODY SYSTEM	ROOT OPERATION	BODY PART	APPROACH	DEVICE	QUALIFIER
Medical and Surgical	Hepatobiliary System and Pancreas	Extirpation	Common Bile Duct	Via Natural or Artificial Opening Endoscopic	No Device	No Qualifier
0	F	C	9	8	Z	Z

Lysis of Adhesions

Lysis of adhesions is a procedure that is performed to destroy adhesions. The root operation in ICD-10-PCS for lysis of adhesions is release (freeing a body part from an abnormal physical constraint). **Adhesions**, which are very often found in the peritoneal area, are fibrous bands of tissue that adhere abdominal organs to one another or to the abdominal wall. Adhesions are often synonymous with scar tissue and can develop after surgery, often causing abdominal pain. Significant adhesions and the lysis thereof are to be assigned codes only if the significance is documented by the surgeon. The surgeon may document extensive adhesions, extensive lysis, or lysis requiring significant time. If there is any question as to the significance of the adhesions, the surgeon should be queried.

EXAMPLE

Patient with chronic cholecystitis admitted for laparoscopic cholecystectomy. The surgeon performed manual lysis of adhesions of the gallbladder, prior to laparoscopic cholecystectomy, K81.1, 0FT44ZZ. No code for lysis of adhesions required.

SECTION	BODY SYSTEM	ROOT OPERATION	BODY PART	APPROACH	DEVICE	QUALIFIER
Medical and Surgical 0	Hepatobiliary System and Pancreas F	Resection T	Gallbladder 4	Percutaneous Endoscopic 4	No Device Z	No Qualifier Z

EXAMPLE

Patient with abdominal pain is admitted. The surgeon performed laparoscopic lysis of adhesions of the peritoneum, K66.0, 0DNW4ZZ.

SECTION	BODY SYSTEM	ROOT OPERATION	BODY PART	APPROACH	DEVICE	QUALIFIER
Medical and Surgical 0	Gastrointestinal System D	Release N	Peritoneum W	Percutaneous Endoscopic 4	No Device Z	No Qualifier Z

Hernia Repair

Herniorrhaphy is repair of a hernia. The root operation in ICD-10-PCS for hernia repair is repair (restoring a body part to its normal structure and function). When the hernia is repaired with mesh, the root operation becomes supplement (putting in or on biological or synthetic material that physically reinforces and/or augments the function of a portion of a body part.) Coding hernia repairs requires attention to location, laterality, and whether performed with a prosthesis or a graft.

EXAMPLE

Patient had a bilateral inguinal hernia repair (open) with prosthesis, K40.20, 0YUA0JZ.

SECTION	BODY SYSTEM	ROOT OPERATION	BODY PART	APPROACH	DEVICE	QUALIFIER
Medical and Surgical 0	Anatomical Regions, Lower Extremities Y	Supplement U	Inguinal Region, Bilateral A	Open 0	Synthetic Substitute J	No Qualifier Z

Transjugular Intrahepatic Portosystemic Shunt (TIPS)

TIPS (transjugular intrahepatic portosystemic shunt): This procedure is often performed by interventional radiologists for patients with severe complications of liver disease. The root operation in ICD-10-PCS for a TIPS procedure is bypass (altering the route of passage of a tubular body part). The interventionalist percutaneously makes a tunnel through the liver with a needle and connects the portal vein to one of the hepatic veins. A stent is inserted into this tunnel to keep the tract open. This procedure does not improve the functioning of the liver but helps in treatment of the complications.

EXAMPLE

A patient with portal hypertension is admitted for a TIPS procedure (percutaneous), K76.6, 06183DY.

SECTION	BODY SYSTEM	ROOT OPERATION	BODY PART	APPROACH	DEVICE	QUALIFIER
Medical and Surgical 0	Lower Veins 6	Bypass 1	Portal Vein 8	Percutaneous 3	Intraluminal Device D	Lower Vein Y

EXERCISE 18-7

Assign codes to the following conditions.

1. Insertion of percutaneous endoscopic gastrostomy for dysphagia ______________
2. Incidental open appendectomy during open cholecystectomy for gallstones in the gallbladder ______________
3. Open repair of ventral hernia of the abdominal wall ______________
4. ERCP with endoscopic pancreatic sphincterotomy and stone removal from pancreatic duct, fluoroscopy performed with low osmolar contrast ______________
5. Patient with GERD admitted for laparoscopic Nissen fundoplication ______________

CHAPTER REVIEW EXERCISE

Where applicable, assign codes for diagnoses, procedures, Z codes, and external cause codes.

1. What makes up the alimentary canal?

   ____

2. What are the three areas of the small intestines?

   1. ____
   2. ____
   3. ____

3. What three organs assist the digestive process?

   1. ____
   2. ____
   3. ____

4. A patient is admitted to the hospital with severe indigestion. An EGD is performed, and it is discovered that the patient has acute gastritis due to *H. pylori*. ______________
5. A patient presents to the Emergency Room (ER) with hematochezia. The patient is admitted, and it is determined that acute blood loss anemia is caused by diverticulosis. ______________
6. A patient has a bleeding gastric ulcer caused by *Helicobacter pylori*. ______________
7. A patient is admitted to the hospital with what the surgeon believes to be acute appendicitis. The surgeon takes the patient to the Operating Room (OR) and removes the appendix via open approach; the postoperative diagnosis is ruptured appendix. ______________
8. A patient is admitted to the hospital with an incisional hernia (abdominal wall). The patient is taken to the OR, and open herniorrhaphy is performed with a graft. ______________
9. A patient is admitted to the hospital with a bilateral indirect inguinal hernia that is repaired via open approach with a mesh graft. ______________
10. A patient with diverticulitis and diverticulosis is taken to the OR for an endoscopic diverticulectomy of the large intestine. ______________
11. A patient with cholecystitis and cholelithiasis is admitted for surgery. The surgeon performs a laparoscopic partial cholecystectomy. ______________
12. A patient with severe Crohn's disease is taken to the OR for a Hartmann procedure on the left with an end-to-end anastomosis and colostomy via open approach using the transverse colon. ______________

13. A patient with cholelithaisis has an ESWL. ______________

14. A patient with severe chronic pancreatitis is admitted to the hospital. ______________

15. A patient with ascites due to alcoholic cirrhosis is admitted to the hospital for a TIPS procedure. Procedure was performed via a laproscopic approach. ______________

16. A patient with a bleeding duodenal ulcer is admitted to the hospital, where the gastroenterologist provides endoscopic control of the hemorrhage by ablation. ______________

17. A patient with severe malnutrition is admitted to the hospital for endoscopic placement of a gastrostomy tube. Enteral feedings were started prior to discharge. ______________

18. Acute hemorrhagic gastric ulcer caused by NSAID ______________

19. Retained gallstone, status post cholecystectomy 1 year ago ______________

20. Acute intestinal vascular insufficiency ______________

CHAPTER GLOSSARY

Adhesion: scar tissue that forms an abnormal connection between body parts.

Alimentary canal: comprises the mouth, pharynx, esophagus, stomach, small intestine, and large intestine.

Angiodysplasia: type of AVM characterized by dilated or fragile blood vessels.

Anorexia: loss of appetite.

Appendectomy: removal of the appendix.

Appendicitis: inflammation of the appendix.

Barrett's esophagus: precancerous condition that usually occurs in people with chronic GERD.

Bowel resection: removal of a portion of the bowel.

Choledocholithiasis: stone lodged in the bile duct.

Cholelithiasis: an abnormal condition of stones in the gallbladder.

Cirrhosis: liver disease wherein scar tissue replaces healthy tissue and blocks blood flow.

Colostomy: a procedure that uses the colon to create an artificial opening.

Crohn's disease: (Regional Enteritis) inflammation of the GI tract, especially the small and large intestine.

Diverticula: small pouches in the lining of the mucous membranes of an organ.

Edentulism: the complete loss of teeth.

Fundoplication: surgery in which the fundus of the stomach is wrapped around the esophagus.

Gastroenteritis: inflammation of the stomach and intestines.

Hematemesis: vomiting of blood.

Hematochezia: bright red blood in stool.

Hepatitis: an inflammation of the liver.

Hernia: protrusion of an organ or tissue through an abnormal opening in the body.

Herniorrhaphy: repair of a hernia.

Ileostomy: end of small intestine brought out through the abdominal wall.

Ileus: absence of normal movement within the intestine.

Impaction: condition that occurs when stool in the rectum becomes so hard that it cannot be passed normally.

Incidental appendectomy: appendectomy performed at the time of another procedure with no known disease process in the appendix.

Intussusception: bowel becomes obstructed when a portion of the intestine telescopes into another portion.

Lysis: destruction of adhesions.

Mallory-Weiss: bleeding laceration of the esophagogastric junction.

Mastication: chewing of food.

McBurney's point: area of the abdomen that, when touched, causes pain that may be indicative of appendicitis.

Melena: dark blood in stool.

Mucositis: an inflammation/ulceration of the digestive tract commonly occurring in the oral cavity.

Necrotic: dead tissue that lacks a blood supply.

Occult blood: blood only found by laboratory inspection.

Pancreatitis: inflammation of the pancreas often caused by gallstones or chronic heavy alcohol use.

Percutaneous endoscopic gastrostomy: a tube put through the abdominal wall into the stomach with the use of a scope.

Peristalsis: rhythmic muscle contractions that move food down the digestive tract.

Peritonitis: inflammation of the peritoneum usually caused by bacteria or fungus.

Sialolithiasis: stones in the salivary glands.

Stoma: an artificial opening.

TIPS (transjugular intrahepatic portosystemic shunt): a procedure in which the portal vein is connected to one of the hepatic veins and a stent is inserted.

Toxic hepatitis: when the liver is damaged by chemicals or drugs.

Ulcerative colitis: an inflammatory bowel disease.

Volvulus: an abnormal twisting of the intestine that may impair blood flow to the intestine.

REFERENCE

1. American Hospital Association: *Coding Clinic for ICD-10-CM/PCS* 2014:3Q:p6. Ileocecectomy including cecum, terminal ileum and appendix.

19

Diseases of the Skin and Subcutaneous Tissue

(ICD-10-CM Chapter 12, Codes L00-L99)

CHAPTER OUTLINE

LEARNING OBJECTIVES

1. Apply and assign the correct ICD-10-CM/PCS codes in accordance with Official Guidelines for Coding and Reporting
2. Identify pertinent anatomy and physiology of the skin and subcutaneous tissue
3. Identify diseases of the skin and subcutaneous tissue
4. Assign the correct Z codes and procedure codes related to the skin and subcutaneous tissue
5. Identify common treatments, medications, laboratory values, and diagnostic tests

ABBREVIATIONS/ ACRONYMS

FTSG full-thickness skin graft
ICD-10-CM *International Classification of Diseases, 10th Revision, Clinical Modification*
ICD-10-PCS *International Classification of Diseases, 10th Revision, Procedure Coding System*
I&D incision and drainage
SJS Stevens-Johnson Syndrome
STSG split-thickness skin graft
TEN toxic epidermal neurolysis

ICD-10-CM Official Guidelines for Coding and Reporting (2021-2022)

Please refer to the companion Evolve website for the most current 2021-2022 guidelines.

12. Chapter 12: Diseases of Skin and Subcutaneous Tissue (L00-L99)

a. Pressure ulcer stage codes

1) Pressure ulcer stages

Codes in category L89, Pressure ulcer, identify the site and stage of the pressure ulcer.

The ICD-10-CM classifies pressure ulcer stages based on severity, which is designated by stages 1-4, deep tissue pressure injury, unspecified stage and unstageable.

Assign as many codes from category L89 as needed to identify all the pressure ulcers the patient has, if applicable.

See Section I.B.14 for pressure ulcer stage documentation by clinicians other than patient's provider

EXAMPLE

The patient was admitted to the hospital from the nursing home. Upon examination the physician noted a stage II pressure ulcer on the sacrum, L89.152.

2) Unstageable pressure ulcers

Assignment of the code for unstageable pressure ulcer (L89.–0) should be based on the clinical documentation. These codes are used for pressure ulcers whose stage cannot be clinically determined (e.g., the ulcer is covered by eschar or has been treated with a skin or muscle graft) This code should not be confused with the codes for unspecified stage (L89.–9). When there is no documentation regarding the stage of the pressure ulcer, assign the appropriate code for unspecified stage (L89.–9).

EXAMPLE

Patient is seen in the physician's office for pneumonia. It is noted in the physical exam that the patient was recently treated for a pressure ulcer of the left heel by skin graft. The graft looks to be progressing as planned, and the ulcer is unstageable, J18.9, L89.620.

3) Documented pressure ulcer stage

Assignment of the pressure ulcer stage code should be guided by clinical documentation of the stage or documentation of the terms found in the Alphabetic Index. For clinical terms describing the stage that are not found in the Alphabetic Index, and there is no documentation of the stage, the provider should be queried.

EXAMPLE

Patient has stage IV pressure ulcers on both heels, L89.624, L89.614.

EXAMPLE

In a daily inpatient progress note, the physician documents that the patient has a pressure ulcer of the right heel with partial thickness skin loss, L89.612.

4) Patients admitted with pressure ulcers documented as healed

No code is assigned if the documentation states that the pressure ulcer is completely healed at the time of admission.

5) Pressure ulcers documented as healing

Pressure ulcers described as healing should be assigned the appropriate pressure ulcer stage code based on the documentation in the medical record. If the documentation does not provide information about the stage of the healing pressure ulcer, assign the appropriate code for unspecified stage.

If the documentation is unclear as to whether the patient has a current (new) pressure ulcer or if the patient is being treated for a healing pressure ulcer, query the provider.

For ulcers that were present on admission but healed at the time of discharge, assign the code for the site and stage of the pressure ulcer at the time of admission.

EXAMPLE

On the discharge summary, the provider documents the following discharge diagnoses: Exacerbation of COPD, hypertension, hyperlipidemia, and a healed sacral decubitus, J44.1, I10, E78.5.

EXAMPLE

On the discharge summary, the provider documents the following discharge diagnoses: Exacerbation of COPD, hypertension, hyperlipidemia, and a healing sacral decubitus, J44.1, I10, E78.5, L89.159.

6) **Patient admitted with pressure ulcer evolving into another stage during the admission**
If a patient is admitted to an inpatient hospital with a pressure ulcer at one stage and it progresses to a higher stage, two separate codes should be assigned: one code for the site and stage of the ulcer on admission and a second code for the same ulcer site and the highest stage reported during the stay.

7) **Pressure-induced deep tissue damage**
For pressure-induced tissue damage or deep tissue pressure injury, assign only the appropriate code for pressure-induced deep tissue damage (L89.–6).

b. Non-Pressure Chronic Ulcers

1) **Patients admitted with non-pressure ulcers documented as healed.**
No code is assigned if the documentation states that the non-pressure ulcer is completely healed at the time of admission.

2) **Non-pressure ulcers documented as healing.**
Non-pressure ulcers described as healing should be assigned the appropriate non-pressure ulcer code based on the documentation in the medical record. If the documentation does not provide information about the severity of the healing non-pressure ulcer, assign the appropriate code for unspecified severity.
If the documentation is unclear as to whether the patient has a current (new) non-pressure ulcer or if the patient is being treated for a healing non-pressure ulcer, query the provider.
For ulcers that were present on admission but healed at the time of discharge, assign the code for the site and severity of the non-pressure ulcer at the time of admission.

3) **Patient admitted with non-pressure ulcer that progresses to another severity level during the admission.**
If a patient is admitted to an inpatient hospital with a non-pressure ulcer at one severity level and it progresses to a higher severity level, two separate codes should be assigned: one code for the site and severity level of the ulcer on admission and a second code for the same ulcer site and the highest severity level reported during the stay.
See Section I.B.14 for pressure ulcer stage documentation by clinicians other than patient's provider

EXAMPLE

Patient is admitted to the hospital from the nursing home for aspiration pneumonia. The admitting provider documents that the patient has a stage II sacral ulcer. At the time of transfer back to the nursing home the provider documents the ulcer as stage III, J69.0, L89.152, L89.153.

ANATOMY AND PHYSIOLOGY

The skin and its accessory organs constitute the **integumentary** system (Figure 19-1), whose functions include protection, temperature regulation, sensory reception, and vitamin D synthesis.

The skin is composed of 3 layers: epidermis, dermis, and subcutaneous layers. The outer layer of the skin, or the **epidermis**, serves as a protective barrier and prevents the entrance of disease-causing organisms. The **dermis**, or middle layer, is composed of fibrous connective tissues that make it strong and elastic. This middle layer contains blood vessels, nerve fibers, sebaceous glands, and some hair follicles. The **subcutaneous** layer contains fat, sweat glands, and additional hair follicles.

The integumentary system also has accessory organs; these include hair, glands, and nails. Three types of glands are located in the skin: sweat glands, sebaceous glands, and mammary glands. The sweat glands assist in temperature regulation, and the sebaceous glands secrete an oily substance, **sebum**, which lubricates the hair and skin.

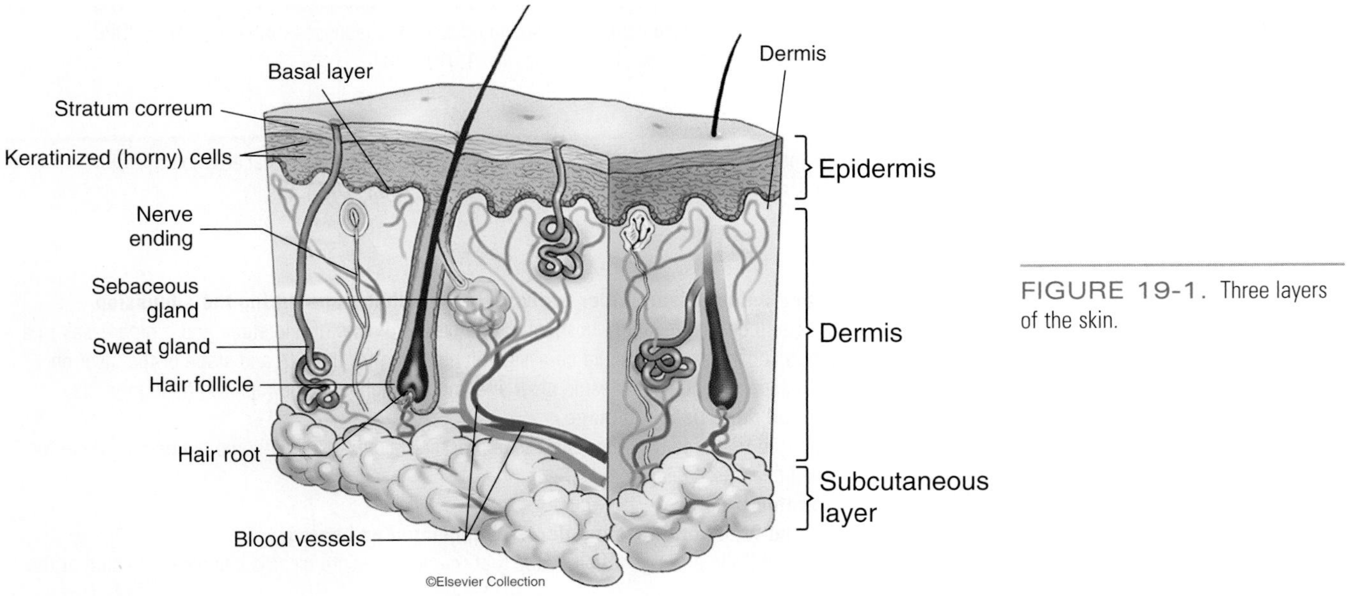

FIGURE 19-1. Three layers of the skin.

DISEASE CONDITIONS

Diseases of the Skin and Subcutaneous Tissue (L00-L99), Chapter 12 in the ICD-10-CM code book, are divided into the following categories:

CATEGORY	SECTION TITLES
L00-L08	Infections of the skin and subcutaneous tissue
L10-L14	Bullous disorders
L20-L30	Dermatitis and eczema
L40-L45	Papulosquamous disorders
L49-L54	Urticaria and erythema
L55-L59	Radiation-related disorders of the skin and subcutaneous tissue
L60-L75	Disorders of skin appendages
L76	Intraoperative and postprocedural complications of skin and subcutaneous tissue
L80-L99	Other disorders of the skin and subcutaneous tissue

Infections of the Skin and Subcutaneous Tissue (L00-L08)

It is important to note that this section has an Instructional note that advises the user to assign an additional code (B95-B97) to identify the infectious agent if known.

Carbuncle and Furuncle

Another name for a **furuncle** is a boil, and a cluster of boils is known as a **carbuncle** (Figure 19-2). The organism that is responsible for a boil is *Staphylococcus.* This organism enters the body through a hair follicle. The most common sites for furuncles to occur include the neck, breasts, face, and buttocks. An additional code is required to identify the organism responsible.

Cellulitis/Abscess of the Skin

Cellulitis is an acute inflammation of tissue that is characterized by swelling, redness, and tenderness that are most often caused by a bacterial infection. An **abscess** is a localized collection of pus that causes swelling. Cellulitis is generally treated with antibiotics; an abscess may be treated with antibiotics and also may require incision and drainage.

As is noted in these code categories, acute lymphangitis is included and is **NOT** coded separately in a patient with cellulitis or abscess. An additional code is used to identify the

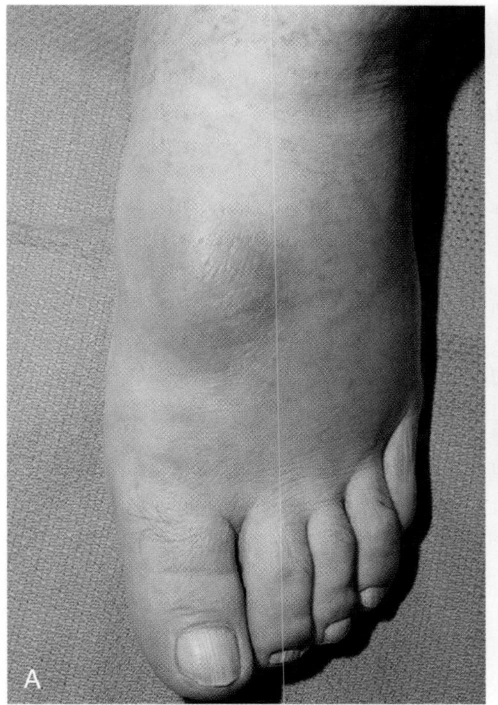

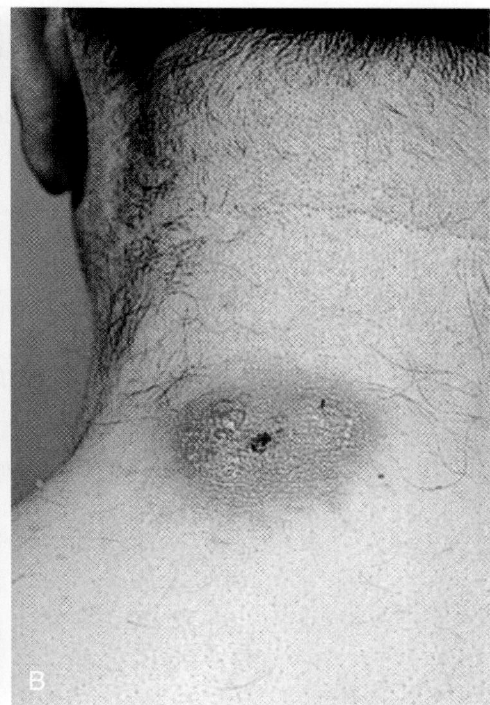

FIGURE 19-2. **A,** Furuncle. **B,** Carbuncle.

organism causing the cellulitis, when documented. In ICD-10-CM, if a patient has an abscess and cellulitis, two codes are required.

Cellulitis associated with a superficial injury, burn, or frostbite requires the use of two codes: one code for the injury/burn/frostbite and one code for the cellulitis. The sequence of these codes is dependent on the focus of treatment. For superficial injuries with cellulitis, it is likely that treatment will be focused on the cellulitis.

EXAMPLE

Patient with cat scratch of the right hand with localized cellulitis admitted for treatment of cellulitis, L03.113, S60.511A, W55.03xA.

Cellulitis associated with a traumatic open wound or laceration requires the use of two codes: one code for the open wound or laceration and one code for the cellulitis. The sequence of these codes is dependent on the focus of treatment. If the focus of treatment is the open wound, the code for the wound is sequenced first, followed by the code for cellulitis. If, on the other hand, the focus of the treatment is the cellulitis and the wound is trivial, or if the wound was treated on a separate occasion, the cellulitis would be sequenced first.

EXAMPLE

Patient stepped on a piece of glass and injured his foot 2 days ago. He is now being admitted to the hospital for treatment of cellulitis of the left foot laceration, L03.116, S91.312A, W25.xxxA.

Gangrenous cellulitis is assigned only the code for gangrene—NOT a code for cellulitis. Cellulitis associated with a skin ulcer requires the use of two codes: one for the ulcer and one for the cellulitis. The sequence of codes is dependent on the focus of treatment.

EXAMPLE

Patient has a chronic right leg ulcer with cellulitis. She is admitted to the hospital for treatment of the leg ulcer, L97.919, L03.115.

Cellulitis described as periorbital and/or preseptal is not cellulitis or abscess of the orbit but is coded to periorbital cellulitis, L03.213.

Cellulitis occurring in areas other than the skin are coded to the chapter that is most appropriate. An example is pelvic cellulitis. Code assignment depends on the patient's sex and if due to ectopic or molar pregnancy, abortion, or delivery.

EXAMPLE

Patient has cellulitis of the lip, K13.0.

EXERCISE 19-1

Assign codes to the following conditions.

1. Periorbital cellulitis ______________
2. Cellulitis with lymphangitis of the breast. *Staphylococcus aureus* infection ______________
3. Cellulitis of the left foot due to patient stepping on a nail with open puncture wound of the foot ______________
4. Gangrenous cellulitis of toe ______________
5. Neck abscess ______________

Bullous Disorders (L10-L14)

Pemphigus

Pemphigus is a rare autoimmune disorder that causes blistering of the skin and mucous membranes, such as the mouth, eyes, throat, and genitals. In people with this disorder, their immune systems attack cells of the epidermis or mucous membranes. This attack causes the formation of blisters that do not heal and can cover large areas of skin. This disorder is not contagious and may have a genetic predisposition. This disease often affects people of Mediterranean descent, and there is a particular form that is found in the rainforests of Brazil. Although this disorder can occur at any age, the most common onset is in middle age or older. There is a similar but different disorder called pemphigoid that causes blistering in areas below the dermis.

There are several different types of pemphigus:

- Pemphigus vulgaris—most common in the United States with sores usually starting in the mouth. The blisters form within the deep layer of the epidermis and are very painful
- Pemphigus vegetans—sores are usually found in the groin and under the arms
- Pemphigus foliaceus—sores on the face and scalp. This type of pemphigus is not found in the mouth
- Paraneoplastic pemphigus—this disorder is found in people with certain types of cancer

This disorder is treated by using steroids or a combination of steroids, anti-inflammatory medications, and at times immunosuppressive drugs. It is possible after a number of years of treatment that these patients can go into complete remissions.

EXAMPLE

The patient was seen for continued treatment of pemphigus vulgaris, L10.0.

Dermatitis and Eczema (L20-L30)

Dermatitis is an inflammation of the skin that is used to describe a variety of skin conditions that can be caused by infections, allergies, and substances either in contact with the skin or ingested. If the dermatitis is caused by contact with a substance, it is **exogenous** and if it is caused by ingestion of a substance, it is **endogenous.** The terms dermatitis and **eczema** are synonymous and can be used interchangeably. Stasis dermatitis is not included in this chapter and can be found in the chapter on diseases of the circulatory system.

The types of skin symptoms that may be caused by dermatitis include itchiness, reddening, crusting, scaling, and blisters, to name a few. In ICD-10-CM it should be noted that at categories L23.3 (Allergic contact dermatitis), L24-.4 (Irritant contact dermatitis), L25.1 (Unspecified contact dermatitis), and L27 (Dermatitis due to substances taken internally), there is an Instructional note to code T36-T65 to identify the drug, if this is an adverse effect. An adverse effect can occur as the result of taking a medication as prescribed. If the condition is due to a poisoning (incorrect use of a drug), the T36-T65 is coded first.

EXAMPLE Patient presents to physician's office with a red, crusty rash on her legs and arms. It is determined that she has irritant contact dermatitis due to using laundry detergent, L24.0.

Intertriginous dermatitis, a type of rash that is found in body folds, is a common condition in the overweight patient, possibly because of skin chafing and the inability of sweat to evaporate. This condition is not found under the Dermatitis heading in the Index but may be located under **Intertrigo**.

Papulosquamous Disorders (L40-L45)

Psoriasis is an inflammation of the skin caused by a fault in the immune system. There are several types of psoriasis, the most common of which is plaque psoriasis. The skin on the elbows, knees, lower back, and scalp are the most common areas plaques are found. Psoriasis usually itches, and the skin may crack and bleed. This is a life-long condition for which there is no cure. Some people develop psoriatic arthritis, which is a systemic rheumatic disease.

EXAMPLE Patient is seen by dermatologist for treatment of psoriasis vulgaris, L40.0.

Urticaria and Erythema (L49-L54)

"**Hives**" and "**urticaria**" are synonymous terms that refer to vascular reactions of the skin that present as wheals, welts, or reddened patches (Figure 19-3) and are associated with **pruritus** (itching). Hives usually occur as an allergic reaction to food, bug bites, or drugs.

Stevens-Johnson Syndrome (SJS) is a rare condition where the skin and mucous membranes react to medication or infection. It is characterized by rash and blisters, which can cause skin necrosis. The cause of this syndrome may be unknown, but a patient may be predisposed to this condition if they have diseases such as HIV or SLE that decrease their immunity. There is a gene called HLA-B12 that may make a patient more susceptible. This can be a life-threatening condition.

EXAMPLE Patient is treated for hives due to peanuts, L50.0.

EXAMPLE Patient presented with hives. No cause can be determined, L50.9.

EXAMPLE Patient is admitted to the hospital with probable SJS-TEN, Stevens-Johnson syndrome, toxic epidermal necrolysis. The patient has a fever, chills, blistering of the mouth and eyes, and large areas on the trunk of the body where skin is peeling off. The patient was recently placed on allopurinol for gout. The attending physician places the patient in the burn unit and documents that 30% of the body is affected by TENS, and the likely cause of this is the allopurinol, L51.3, T50.4x5A, L49.3, M10.9.

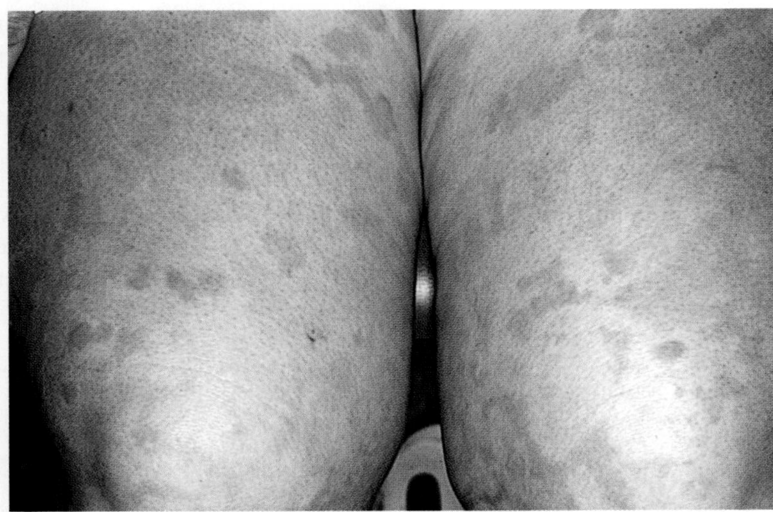

FIGURE 19-3. Urticaria.

EXERCISE 19-2

Assign codes to the following conditions.

1. Contact dermatitis due to mascara __________
2. Dermatitis due to ultraviolet rays from tanning bed __________
3. Irritant contact dermatitis due to detergent __________
4. Dermatitis, intertriginous __________
5. Fogo selvagem __________
6. Diaper rash __________
7. Patient has allergic contact dermatitis on the right hand secondary to latex gloves __________
8. Contact urticaria __________

Radiation-Related Disorders of the Skin and Subcutaneous Tissue (L55-L59)

Solar keratosis is also known as actinic keratosis and is a precancerous scaly or crusty growth often found on the areas of the body regularly exposed to sun. These lesions may be treated with medication or cryosurgery. This is a common condition in the United States.

EXAMPLE

A 32-year-old woman presents to dermatologist's office with solar keratosis. The physician documents that this patient has regularly been using tanning beds for the past 10 years, L57.0, W89.1xxA.

Disorders of Skin Appendages (L60-L75)

Alopecia is hair loss. There are many forms of hair loss, but the most common one is androgenic alopecia or male pattern baldness.

EXAMPLE

Physician documents in the record that the patient has male pattern baldness, L64.9.

Rosacea is a skin condition affecting the cheeks, nose, chin, and forehead. It can be characterized by redness, a bulbous nose, or an increased number of blood vessels in the face. Although it is not curable, it can be controlled by avoiding triggers such as alcohol, sun, spicy food, and wind, to name a few.

EXAMPLE Physician documents that the patient has rhinophyma, L71.1.

Hyperhidrosis is a condition characterized by excessive sweating. It can be secondary to a variety of disorders such as cancer, anxiety, medication, substance abuse, menopause, and Parkinson's disease. It can be treated with drugs, and in severe cases a procedure called an endoscopic thoracic sympathectomy may be performed.

EXAMPLE Patient with underarm localized primary hyperhidrosis, L74.510.

Other Disorders of Skin and Subcutaneous Tissue (L80-L99)

Skin **ulcers** are open sores of the skin (Figure 19-4). Ulcers may have a variety of causes such as diabetes, skin cancers, venous insufficiency, arteriosclerosis, and pressure sores (**decubitus ulcer**). When coding ulcers, care should be taken to closely follow instructions found under categories L89 and L97.

Pressure Ulcer

A pressure ulcer or decubitus ulcer (Figure 19-5) occurs over bony areas (e.g., heel, hip, sacrum, ankle, and elbow) of patients who are immobile. Conditions found under this heading are chronic in nature, although the ulcer may be described as infected. The fifth character identifies the site of the ulcer, and sixth character identifies the stage.

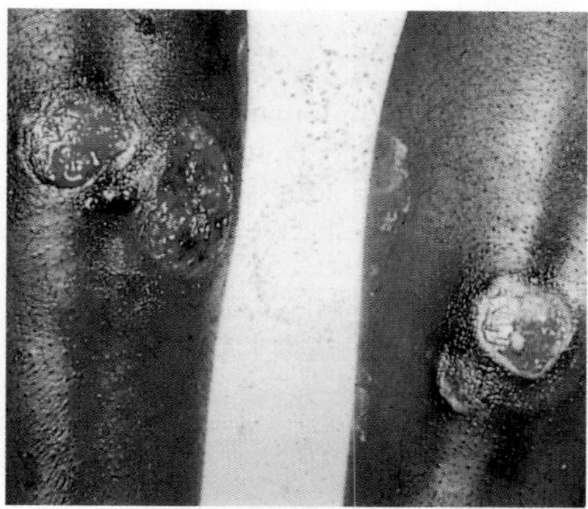

FIGURE 19-4. Ulcers.

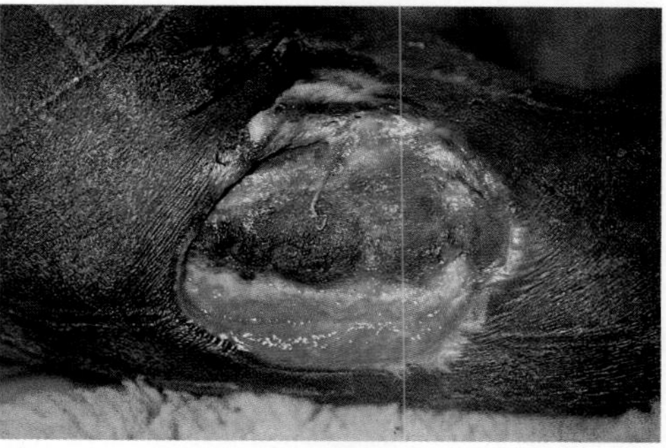

FIGURE 19-5. Decubitus ulcer.

An instructional note found under category L89 alerts the coder to code first any associated gangrene (I96). It is also important to note the Excludes2 note found under this section. For classification purposes these ulcers are identified by stages 1–4 and unstageable.

- Stage 1: Red skin with warmth—persistent focal erythema
- Stage 2: Skin swollen with abrasion, blister, and partial thickness skin loss
- Stage 3: Full-thickness skin loss with subcutaneous necrosis
- Stage 4: Necrosis of soft tissues through to underlying muscle/tendon/bone
- Unstageable: Ulcers that have either been previously treated or covered with an eschar and the clinician is unable to determine the stage or they are documented as deep tissue injury not due to trauma

Selecting the stage of the pressure ulcer may be determined by nursing documentation or terms listed in the Index. If a term describing an ulcer is not listed in the Index and there is no documentation of stage, the provider should be queried.

The National Pressure Ulcer Advisory Panel (NPUAP) has recently announced a change in terminology from "pressure ulcer" to "pressure injury." According to *Coding Clinic for ICD-10-CM/PCS* (2016:3Q:p38), if the term "pressure injury" means pressure ulcer, it is acceptable to code as a pressure ulcer by the site and documented stage.[1]

EXAMPLE

Patient has a decubitus ulcer on the left buttock with skin loss to bone, L89.324.

If a patient has a healed pressure ulcer documented, no code is assigned. However, if the pressure ulcer is documented as healing, then the ulcer and the stage of the ulcer are assigned codes. Should the documentation be unclear as to whether the patient has a healing or healed pressure ulcer the provider should be queried.

EXAMPLE

Patient is admitted with pneumonia. During the physical exam, the physician identifies a decubitus ulcer of the right heel that appears to be healing. The physician cannot give the ulcer a stage as it is covered by a skin graft, J18.9, L89.610.

If a patient has a pressure ulcer on admit that is documented as stage 2 and then during the admission this ulcer progresses to a stage 3, two separate codes should be assigned: one code for the site and stage of the ulcer on admission (with a POA status of Y) and a second code for the same ulcer site and the highest stage (with a POA status of N) reported during the stay.

EXAMPLE

Patient is admitted to the hospital with, among other conditions, a stage 1 decubitus ulcer of the left ankle. During this admission, this ankle ulcer progresses to a stage 3, L89.521, L89.523.

Non–Pressure Chronic Ulcer of the Lower Limb

A code from L97 may be used as the principal or first-listed diagnosis if there is no condition documented as the cause of the ulcer. If there is gangrene associated with the ulcer, the gangrene is to be coded first, which follows the same rule as with decubitus ulcers. This instruction goes on to say that if the ulcer is associated with any of the conditions listed below, the underlying condition should be coded first.

- Atherosclerosis of the lower extremities (I70.23-, J70.24-, I70.00-, I70.34-, I70.43-, I70.44-, I70.53-, I70.54-, I70.63-, I70.64-, I70.73-, I70.74-)
- Chronic venous hypertension (I87.01-, I87.33)
- Diabetic ulcers (E08.621, E08.622, E09.621, E09.622, E10.621, E10.622, E11.621, E11.622, E13.621, E13.622)
- Postphlebitic syndrome (I87.01-, I87.03-)
- Postthrombotic syndrome (I87.01-, I87.03-)
- Varicose ulcer (I83.0-, I83.2-)

EXAMPLE

Patient has a chronic ulcer of the second toe on the right with fat exposed, secondary to type 2 diabetes, E11.621, L97.512.

EXERCISE 19-3

Assign codes to the following conditions.

1. Decubitus ulcer of the right heel, stage 2 __________
2. Diabetic ulcer of the left toe, skin breakdown only __________
3. Arteriosclerotic ulcer of the left leg with gangrene, of native artery, with muscle necrosis __________
4. Ischemic ulcer of the right calf __________
5. Patient has a sacral stage 4 decubitus ulcer with gangrene __________
6. Patient has pressure ulcers on both buttocks. The buttock on the right has a stage 2 ulcer while the left buttock has a stage 3 ulcer __________
7. Patient is transferred from the nursing home with a fever and infected decubitus ulcers. There is an ulcer of the left hip stage 3 and ulcers of both elbows. The right elbow has a stage 1 ulcer and the left elbow has a stage 2 ulcer __________
8. Patient has a gangrenous ulcer of the left heel; he also has atherosclerosis of the left leg __________

FACTORS INFLUENCING HEALTH STATUS AND CONTACT WITH HEALTH SERVICES (Z CODES)

As was discussed in Chapter 9, it is difficult to locate Z codes in the Index. Coders will often say, "I did not know there was a Z code for that." Refer to Chapter 9 for a listing of common main terms used to locate Z codes.

Z codes that may be used with diseases of the skin and subcutaneous tissue include the following:

Z48.817	Encounter for surgical aftercare following surgery on skin and subcutaneous tissue
Z52.10	Skin donor, unspecified
Z52.11	Skin donor, autologous
Z52.19	Skin donor, other
Z84.0	Family history of diseases of the skin and subcutaneous tissue
Z87.2	Personal history of diseases of the skin and subcutaneous tissue
Z94.5	Skin transplant status
Z96.81	Presence of artificial skin

EXAMPLE

Patient presents to dermatologist's office for a rash on the cheeks and nose. Patient has a family history of skin disorders, R21, Z84.0.

EXERCISE 19-4

Assign codes to the following conditions.

1. Patient with a history of eczema __________
2. Patient with a family history of dermatitis __________

COMMON TREATMENTS

CONDITION	MEDICATION
Acne	Tetracycline (Achromycin), isotretinoin (Accutane)
Boils	Bacitracin, Neosporin
Cellulitis	Antibiotics such as nafcillin, oxacillin, cefazolin, vancomycin, linezolid
Psoriasis	Topical corticosteroids

PROCEDURES

Procedures related to the Diseases of the Skin and Subcutaneous Tissue section in ICD-10-PCS may be located in the following tables:

Skin and Breast	0H0-0HY
Subcutaneous Tissue and Fascia	0J0-0JX

Incision and Drainage

Incision and drainage (I&D) is a common form of treatment for abscesses of the skin. The physician cuts into the lining of the abscess, which allows the pus to drain. Usually, the physician cleans the cavity with warm saline. If the abscess is deep, the physician may insert a drainage device. It is important to be aware that I&D can also be used to describe incision and debridement. In cases in which the documentation is questionable, a physician query may be necessary. In ICD-10-PCS the root operation for incision and drainage is drainage (taking or letting out fluids and/or gases from a body part).

EXAMPLE

Incision and drainage of boil on left upper arm, L02.424, 0H9CXZZ

SECTION	BODY SYSTEM	ROOT OPERATION	BODY PART	APPROACH	DEVICE	QUALIFIER
Medical and Surgical	Skin and Breast	Drainage	Skin, Left Upper Arm	External	No Device	No Qualifier
0	H	9	C	X	Z	Z

Debridement

Excisional Debridement

Excisional debridement, the surgical removal or cutting away of devitalized tissue, necrosis, or slough. The root operation for an excisional debridement in ICD-10-PCS is excision (cutting out or off a portion of a body part) and extraction (pulling or stripping out or off all or a portion of a body part) if it is nonexcisional. Excisional debridements may be performed in a variety of settings (operating room, emergency room, or bedside) and by a variety of healthcare providers (physicians, nurse practitioners, physician assistants, and physical therapists). The provider must specify if the debridement is excisional, or the documentation must meet the root operation definition of "excision." If there is any question as to whether the debridement is excisional or nonexcisional, the provider should be queried.

Please see the ICD-10-PCS procedural guidelines for overlapping body layers. When an extensive debridement goes beyond the skin and subcutaneous tissue into the muscle, tendon, and/or bone, it is appropriate to assign only a code for the deepest layer of debridement when multiple layers of the same site are debrided. If a patient had a debridement of skin, subcutaneous tissue, muscle and bone, the bone is the deepest layer and debridement of the bone is the only procedure code assigned.

EXAMPLE

Patient with a stage 4 decubitus ulcer of the sacrum is taken to the OR for debridement. The debridement is performed through the skin, muscle, and sacral bone, L89.154, 0QB10ZZ.

SECTION	BODY SYSTEM	ROOT OPERATION	BODY PART	APPROACH	DEVICE	QUALIFIER
Medical and Surgical	Lower Bones	Excision	Sacrum	Open	No Device	No Qualifier
0	Q	B	1	0	Z	Z

Nonexcisional Debridement

Any debridement that does not meet the criteria described earlier for excisional debridement would be coded as nonexcisional. A nonexcisional debridement may be performed by brushing, irrigating, scrubbing, or washing to remove devitalized tissue. Documentation of sharp debridement or using a sharp instrument does not always mean that an excisional debridement was performed. Once again, this procedure may be performed in a variety of settings by a variety of healthcare providers.

It is important to remember that if debridement of the skin is performed in preparation for further surgery, the debridement should not be coded separately. For example, prior to reduction of an open fracture, a debridement may be performed.

EXAMPLE

Pulse lavage debridement of the skin is performed by wound care nurse on a patient with a stage 3 decubitus ulcer of the right ankle, L89.513, 0HDKXZZ.

SECTION	BODY SYSTEM	ROOT OPERATION	BODY PART	APPROACH	DEVICE	QUALIFIER
Medical and Surgical	Skin and Breast	Extraction	Skin, Right Lower Leg	External	No Device	No Qualifier
0	H	D	K	X	Z	Z

Excision of Lesion

There are two root operations that would be appropriate to assign for the removal or excision of a lesion. The root operations are:

- Excision—cutting out or off, without replacement, a portion of a body part
- Destruction—physical eradication of all or a portion of a body part by the direct use of energy, force or a destructive agent

Some terms that may qualify as destruction include ablation, cauterization, coagulation, cryosurgery, electrocautery, fulguration, and obliteration.

The next item to consider is if the procedure was performed on the skin or if it was a little deeper into the subcutaneous tissue and fascia. When a skin lesion is excised, the approach will usually be external. When the removal of a lesion goes deeper than the skin, the documentation will have to be thoroughly reviewed to determine the surgeon's approach.

EXAMPLE

Excision of nevus from the skin of the chest wall, D22.5, 0HB5XZZ

SECTION	BODY SYSTEM	ROOT OPERATION	BODY PART	APPROACH	DEVICE	QUALIFIER
Medical and Surgical	Skin and Breast	Excision	Skin, Chest	External	No Device	No Qualifier
0	H	B	5	X	Z	Z

EXAMPLE

Open excision of lipoma of the subcutaneous tissue left thigh, D17.24, 0JBM0ZZ

SECTION	BODY SYSTEM	ROOT OPERATION	BODY PART	APPROACH	DEVICE	QUALIFIER
Medical and Surgical	Subcutaneous Tissue and Fascia	Excision	Subcutaneous Tissue and Fascia, Left Upper Leg	Open	No Device	No Qualifier
0	J	B	M	0	Z	Z

Skin Grafts

Skin Grafts

Skin grafts are composed of pieces of skin that are removed from one body area (donor) and are used to cover a defect in another body area (recipient).

In ICD-10-PCS skin grafts are coded to the root operation replacement. Replacement is the putting in or on biological (autologous or nonautologous) or synthetic (man-made) material that physically takes the place and/or function of all or a portion of a body part.

- **Autologous**—donor and recipient are the same person
- Nonautologous—donor and recipient are different people or species
- Synthetic—man-made

SECTION: 0 MEDICAL AND SURGICAL
BODY SYSTEM: H SKIN AND BREAST
OPERATION: R REPLACEMENT: *(on multiple pages)*
Putting in or on biological or synthetic material that physically takes the place and/or function of all or a portion of a body part

Body Part	Approach	Device	Qualifier
0 Skin, Scalp 1 Skin, Face 2 Skin, Right Ear 3 Skin, Left Ear 4 Skin, Neck 5 Skin, Chest 6 Skin, Back 7 Skin, Abdomen 8 Skin, Buttock 9 Skin, Perineum A Skin, Genitalia B Skin, Right Upper Arm C Skin, Left Upper Arm D Skin, Right Lower Arm E Skin, Left Lower Arm F Skin, Right Hand G Skin, Left Hand H Skin, Right Upper Leg J Skin, Left Upper Leg K Skin, Right Lower Leg L Skin, Left Lower Leg M Skin, Right Foot N Skin, Left Foot	X External	7 Autologous Tissue Substitute K Nonautologous Tissue Substitute	3 Full Thickness 4 Partial Thickness

FIGURE 19-6. Example of skin graft table from ICD-10-PCS.

EXAMPLE

Patient presents for full-thickness skin graft to the left thigh from the abdomen to repair a skin contracture from third-degree burn of the left thigh. Patient spilled boiling water on himself several months ago, L90.5, T24.312S, X12.xxxS, 0HRJX73, 0HB7XZZ.

SECTION	BODY SYSTEM	ROOT OPERATION	BODY PART	APPROACH	DEVICE	QUALIFIER
Medical and Surgical	Skin and Breast	Replacement	Skin, Left Upper Leg	External	Autologous Tissue Substitute	Full Thickness
0	H	R	J	X	7	3

SECTION	BODY SYSTEM	ROOT OPERATION	BODY PART	APPROACH	DEVICE	QUALIFIER
Medical and Surgical	Skin and Breast	Excision	Skin, Abdomen	External	No Device	No Qualifier
0	H	B	7	X	Z	Z

Pedicle Grafts or Flaps

Pedicle grafts or **flaps** differ from split-thickness skin graft (STSG) and full-thickness skin graft (FTSG) (Figure 19-7) in that part of the graft or flaps remains attached to the donor site. A pedicle graft is a full-thickness skin and subcutaneous tissue flap/graft that is attached by tissue (Figure 19-8), through which it receives its blood supply.

The ICD-10-PCS root operation for a pedicle graft and for skin transfer flaps is transfer (moving, without taking out, all or a portion of a body part to another location to take over the function of all or a portion of a body part). The body part that is transferred remains connected to its vascular and nervous supply.

In transfer procedures that involve more than one layer as in the example below, the body part represents the deepest tissue layer in the flap/pedicle graft, and the qualifier identifies any other tissue layers that are involved in the transfer.

EXAMPLE

Open pedicle skin and subcutaneous tissue graft was performed on the patient's left buttock to aid in the healing of third degree pressure ulcer of the left buttock, L89.323, 0JX90ZB

SECTION	BODY SYSTEM	ROOT OPERATION	BODY PART	APPROACH	DEVICE	QUALIFIER
Medical and Surgical	Subcutaneous Tissue and Fascia	Transfer	Subcutaneous Tissue and Fascia, Buttock	Open	No Device	Skin and Subcutaneous Tissue
0	J	X	9	0	Z	B

EXERCISE 19-5

Assign codes to the following conditions.

1. STSG from patient's left thigh to cover scar contracture due to 2nd degree burn from fire on right forearm ______________
2. FTSG to left hand from buttock due to scar from necrotizing fasciitis ______________
3. Advancement flap to nose following surgery to remove skin cancer from nose ______________
4. Excisional debridement (skin) of decubitus ulcer of the left heel ______________
5. Skin tissue of lower left leg ulcer removed by scrubbing ______________
6. Debridement (nonexcisional) of a fungal infection of the nail bed of the index finger ______________
7. Incision and drainage of neck abscess ______________

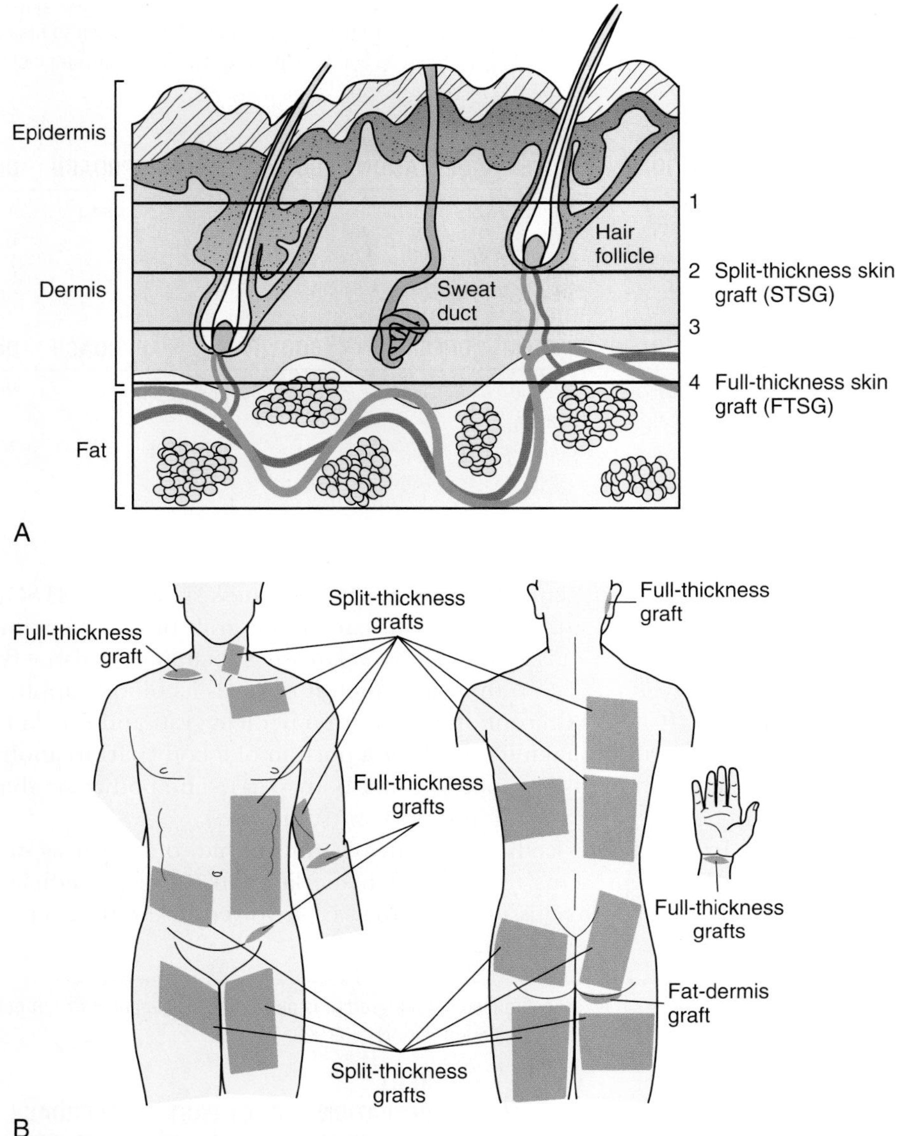

FIGURE 19-7. Split-thickness and full-thickness skin grafts.

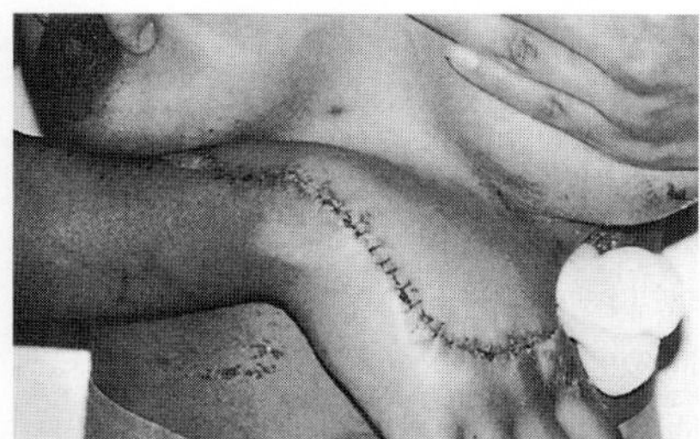

FIGURE 19-8. Pedicle graft.

CHAPTER REVIEW EXERCISE

Answer the following and assign codes to the following conditions.

1. Abscess of the right leg with cellulitis ____________
2. Pressure ulcer of the left heel with cellulitis, stage 3 ____________
3. Eczema ____________
4. Dermatitis caused by Cipro ____________
5. Allergic contact dermatitis due to poison sumac ____________
6. Stasis dermatitis with ulcer of the left calf ____________
7. Diabetic PVD with left foot ulcer with fat layer exposed ____________
8. Incision and drainage of abscess of the right lower leg ____________
9. Excision (skin) of a pilonidal cyst ____________
10. Excisional debridement including the fascia of decubitus ulcer of the right buttock (stage 4) by the attending physician ____________

Write the correct answer(s) in the space(s) provided.

11. What is the difference between a pedicle graft and a split-thickness skin graft?

    ____

12. What are the three accessory organs of the skin?

    ____

    ____

    ____

13. Where in ICD-10-CM would a coder find the skin condition herpes zoster?

    ____

14. What is another name for a decubitus ulcer?

    ____

15. Name and describe three types of skin grafts.

    ____

    ____

    ____

CHAPTER GLOSSARY

Abscess: a localized collection of pus that causes swelling.

Alopecia: hair loss.

Autologous graft: donor and recipient are the same person.

Carbuncle: cluster of boils.

Cellulitis: inflammation of the tissue with possible abscess.

Debridement: removal of devitalized tissue, necrosis, or slough.

Decubitus ulcer: skin ulcer also known as a bed sore.

Dermatitis: inflammation of the skin.

Dermis: layer of skin below the epidermis.

Eczema: type of dermatitis characterized by itching.

Endogenous: type of dermatitis caused by something taken internally, such as medication.

Epidermis: outermost layer of skin.

Excisional: removal by surgical cutting.

Exogenous: type of dermatitis caused by contact with a substance.

Furuncle: a boil.

Hives: skin condition also known as urticaria, wherein the skin reacts with welts; characterized by itching.

Hyperhidrosis: excessive sweating.

Integumentary: another name for skin.

Intertrigo: dermatitis in areas where friction may occur.

Pedicle graft or flap: involves identifying a flap that remains attached to its original blood supply and tunneling it under the skin to a particular area such as the breast.

Pemphigus: autoimmune disorder causing blistering of skin and mucous membranes.

Pruritus: itching.

Psoriasis: inflammation of skin caused by a fault in the immune system.

Rosacea: skin condition affecting cheeks, nose, chin, and forehead. It can be characterized by redness, a bulbous nose, or an increased number of blood vessels in the face.

Sebum: substance secreted from the sebaceous gland.

Solar Keratosis: precancerous scaly growth.

Stevens-Johnson Syndrome: skin necrosis caused by a reaction to medication or infection.

Subcutaneous: inner layer of the skin that contains fat and sweat glands.

Ulcer: open sore of skin.

Urticaria: another name for hives.

REFERENCE

1. American Hospital Association: *Coding Clinic for ICD-10-CM/PCS* 2016:3Q:p38. Pressure Injury.

20

Diseases of the Musculoskeletal System and Connective Tissue

(ICD-10-CM Chapter 13, Codes M00-M99)

CHAPTER OUTLINE

LEARNING OBJECTIVES

1. Apply and assign the correct ICD-10-CM/PCS codes in accordance with Official Guidelines for Coding and Reporting
2. Identify pertinent anatomy and physiology of the musculoskeletal system and connective tissue
3. Identify diseases of the musculoskeletal system and connective tissue
4. Assign the correct Z codes and procedure codes related to the musculoskeletal system and connective tissue
5. Identify common treatments, medications, laboratory values, and diagnostic tests

ABBREVIATIONS/ ACRONYMS

ALIF anterior lumbar interbody fusion

AxiaLIF axial lumbar interbody fusion

DJD degenerative joint disease

DLIF direct lateral lumbar interbody fusion

ICD-10-CM *International Classification of Diseases, 10th Revision, Clinical Modification*

ICD-10-PCS *International Classification of Diseases, 10th Revision, Procedure Coding System*

IV intravenous

ABBREVIATIONS/ ACRONYMS—*cont'd*

JRA juvenile rheumatoid arthritis
MRI magnetic resonance imaging
NSAIDs nonsteroidal anti-inflammatory drugs
OA osteoarthritis
PLIF posterior lumbar interbody fusion
PMR polymyalgia rheumatica
PV percutaneous vertebroplasty
RA rheumatoid arthritis
SLE systemic lupus erythematosus
TLIF transforaminal lumbar interbody fusion
XLIF extreme lateral lumbar interbody fusion

ICD-10-CM Official Guidelines for Coding and Reporting (2021-2022)

Please refer to the companion Evolve website for the most current 2021-2022 guidelines.

13. Chapter 13: Diseases of the Musculoskeletal System and Connective Tissue (M00-M99)

a. Site and laterality

Most of the codes within Chapter 13 have site and laterality designations. The site represents the bone, joint or the muscle involved. For some conditions where more than one bone, joint or muscle is usually involved, such as osteoarthritis, there is a "multiple sites" code available. For categories where no multiple site code is provided and more than one bone, joint or muscle is involved, multiple codes should be used to indicate the different sites involved.

1) Bone versus joint

For certain conditions, the bone may be affected at the upper or lower end, (e.g., avascular necrosis of bone, M87, Osteoporosis, M80, M81). Though the portion of the bone affected may be at the joint, the site designation will be the bone, not the joint.

EXAMPLE

The patient is being evaluated for hip replacement surgery because of idiopathic avascular necrosis of the right hip, M87.051.

b. Acute traumatic versus chronic or recurrent musculoskeletal conditions

Many musculoskeletal conditions are a result of previous injury or trauma to a site, or are recurrent conditions. Bone, joint or muscle conditions that are the result of a healed injury are usually found in chapter 13. Recurrent bone, joint or muscle conditions are also usually found in chapter 13. Any current, acute injury should be coded to the appropriate injury code from chapter 19. Chronic or recurrent conditions should generally be coded with a code from chapter 13. If it is difficult to determine from the documentation in the record which code is best to describe a condition, query the provider.

EXAMPLE

The patient was seen in the ER for recurrent dislocation of left little finger, M24.445.

c. Coding of Pathologic Fractures

7th character A is for use as long as the patient is receiving active treatment for the fracture. While the patient may be seen by a new or different provider over the course of treatment for a pathological fracture, assignment of the 7th character is based on whether the patient is undergoing active treatment and not whether the provider is seeing the patient for the first time.

7th character, D is to be used for encounters after the patient has completed active treatment for the fracture and is receiving routine care for the fracture during the healing or recovery phase. The other 7th characters, listed under each subcategory in the Tabular List, are to be used for subsequent encounters for treatment of problems associated with the healing, such as malunions, nonunions, and sequelae.

Care for complications of surgical treatment for fracture repairs during the healing or recovery phase should be coded with the appropriate complication codes.

See Section I.C.19. Coding of traumatic fractures.

EXAMPLE

The patient was seen for follow-up after vertebroplasty for pathologic fracture related to osteoporosis of the L1 vertebra, which is healing, M80.08xD.

d. Osteoporosis

Osteoporosis is a systemic condition, meaning that all bones of the musculoskeletal system are affected. Therefore, site is not a component of the codes under category M81, Osteoporosis without current pathological fracture. The site codes under category M80, Osteoporosis with current pathological fracture, identify the site of the fracture, not the osteoporosis.

1) Osteoporosis without pathological fracture

Category M81, Osteoporosis without current pathological fracture, is for use for patients with osteoporosis who do not currently have a pathologic fracture due to the osteoporosis, even if they have had a fracture in the past. For patients with a history of osteoporosis fractures, status code Z87.310, Personal history of (healed) osteoporosis fracture, should follow the code from M81.

2) Osteoporosis with current pathological fracture

Category M80, Osteoporosis with current pathological fracture, is for patients who have a current pathologic fracture at the time of an encounter. The codes under M80 identify the site of the fracture. A code from category M80, not a traumatic fracture code, should be used for any patient with known osteoporosis who suffers a fracture, even if the patient had a minor fall or trauma, if that fall or trauma would not usually break a normal, healthy bone.

EXAMPLE

The patient underwent a percutaneous vertebroplasty (synthetic substitute) for pathologic fracture of the L1 vertebra due to delayed healing. Patient has osteoporosis of vertebrae, M80.08xG, 0QU03JZ.

ANATOMY AND PHYSIOLOGY

The musculoskeletal system is made up of muscles, bones, ligaments, tendons, cartilage, and the joints they form. The purposes of the musculoskeletal system are to provide a framework and to protect the internal organs. Bones also are important for hematopoiesis and for storing calcium and phosphate. **Hematopoiesis** is the development of blood cells that occurs in the bone marrow and lymphatic tissue of normal adults.

A good grasp of anatomy is essential in coding conditions of the musculoskeletal system. It is important to know that the femur is the long bone in the thigh area, and that the radius and the ulna are two bones in the forearm. Pictures are best for illustrating the locations of the skeletal structures (Figure 20-1) and muscles (Figure 20-2). It is particularly important to understand the terms used in the musculoskeletal chapter to describe the location of structures relative to the body as a whole or to other body structures (Figure 20-3). **Anterior** or **ventral** describes the front of the body or an organ. **Posterior** or **dorsal** relates to the back of the body or an organ. The terms medial and lateral describe the position of the body or an organ relative to the median sagittal plane that divides the body in half. **Medial** refers to a structure that is closer to the median plane than is another structure in the body. The eyes are medial to the ears. **Lateral** refers to a structure that is to the side of the body. The ears are lateral to the eyes. The terms **superior** (above) and **inferior** (below) describe the position of the body or an organ relative to the vertical axis of the body. The shoulders are superior to the hips, and the ankles are inferior to the knees. Other terms that may be used are **cranial**, which means toward the head, and **caudal**, which means towards the tail. **Proximal** (closer to the point of reference) and **distal** (farther from the point of reference) are often used to describe a location in the limbs. The shoulder is proximal to the elbow, and the wrist is distal to the elbow. **Supine** refers to lying on the back, face up. **Prone** is lying on the stomach, face down.

The **joints** are the means of joining two bones together; they assist with body movement. **Ligaments** are dense fibrous bands of connective tissue that provide stability for the joint. Ligaments can be injured by overstretching or tearing (sprain). **Tendons** are the connective tissue that attaches muscle to bone. Tendons are susceptible to strain injuries. The **fascia** is the tissue just below the skin that covers and separates the underlying layers of muscle.

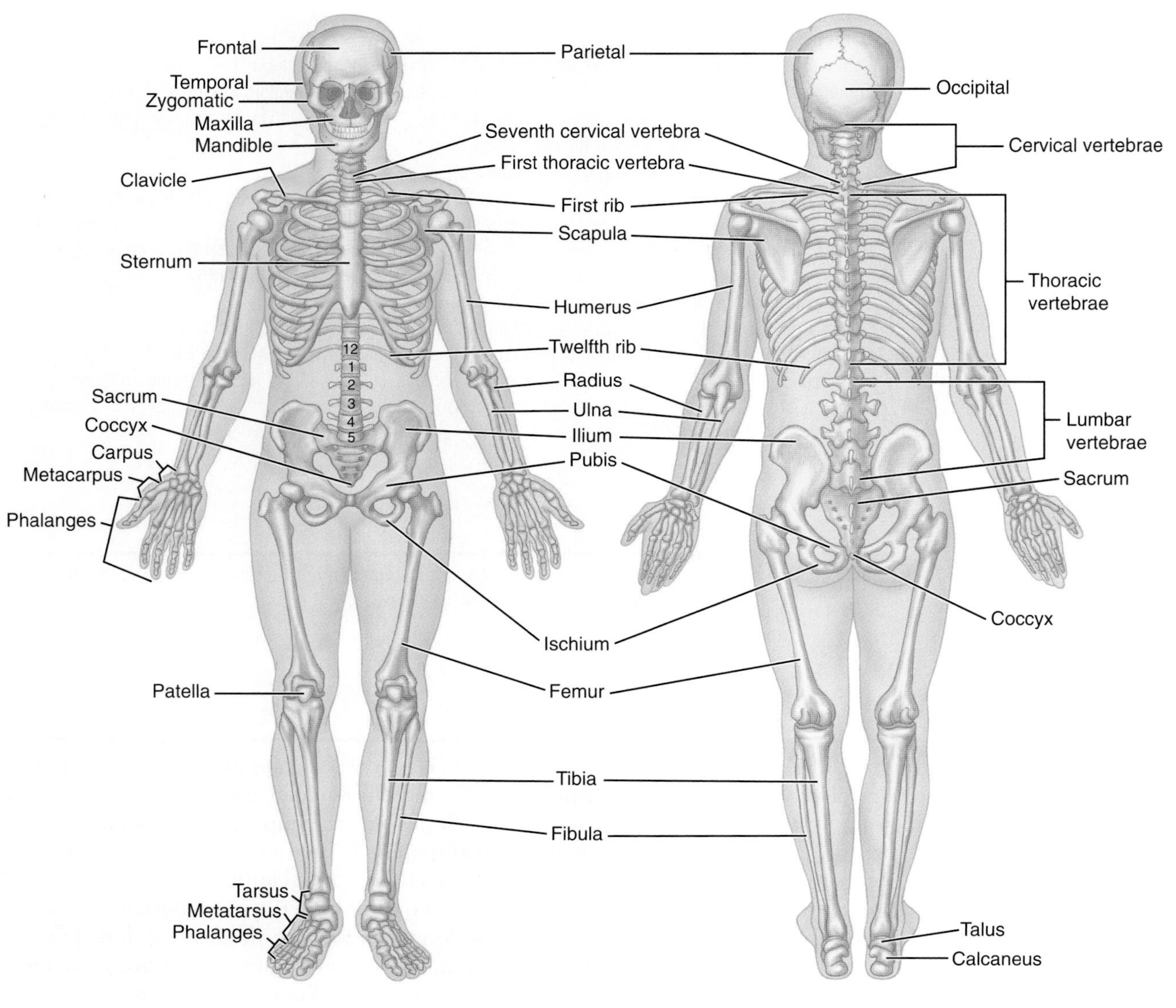

FIGURE 20-1. Anterior and posterior views of the human skeleton.

DISEASE CONDITIONS

Diseases of the Musculoskeletal System and Connective Tissue (M00-M99), Chapter 13 in the ICD-10-CM code book, are divided into the following categories:

CATEGORY	SECTION TITLES
M00-M02	Infectious arthropathies
M04	Autoinflammatory syndromes
M05-M14	Inflammatory polyarthropathies
M15-M19	Osteoarthritis
M20-M25	Other joint disorders
M26-M27	Dentofacial anomalies, including malocclusion, and other disorders of the jaw
M30-M36	Systemic connective tissue disorders
M40-M43	Deforming dorsopathies
M45-M49	Spondylopathies
M50-M54	Other dorsopathies
M60-M63	Disorders of muscles
M65-M67	Disorders of synovium and tendon
M70-M79	Other soft-tissue disorders

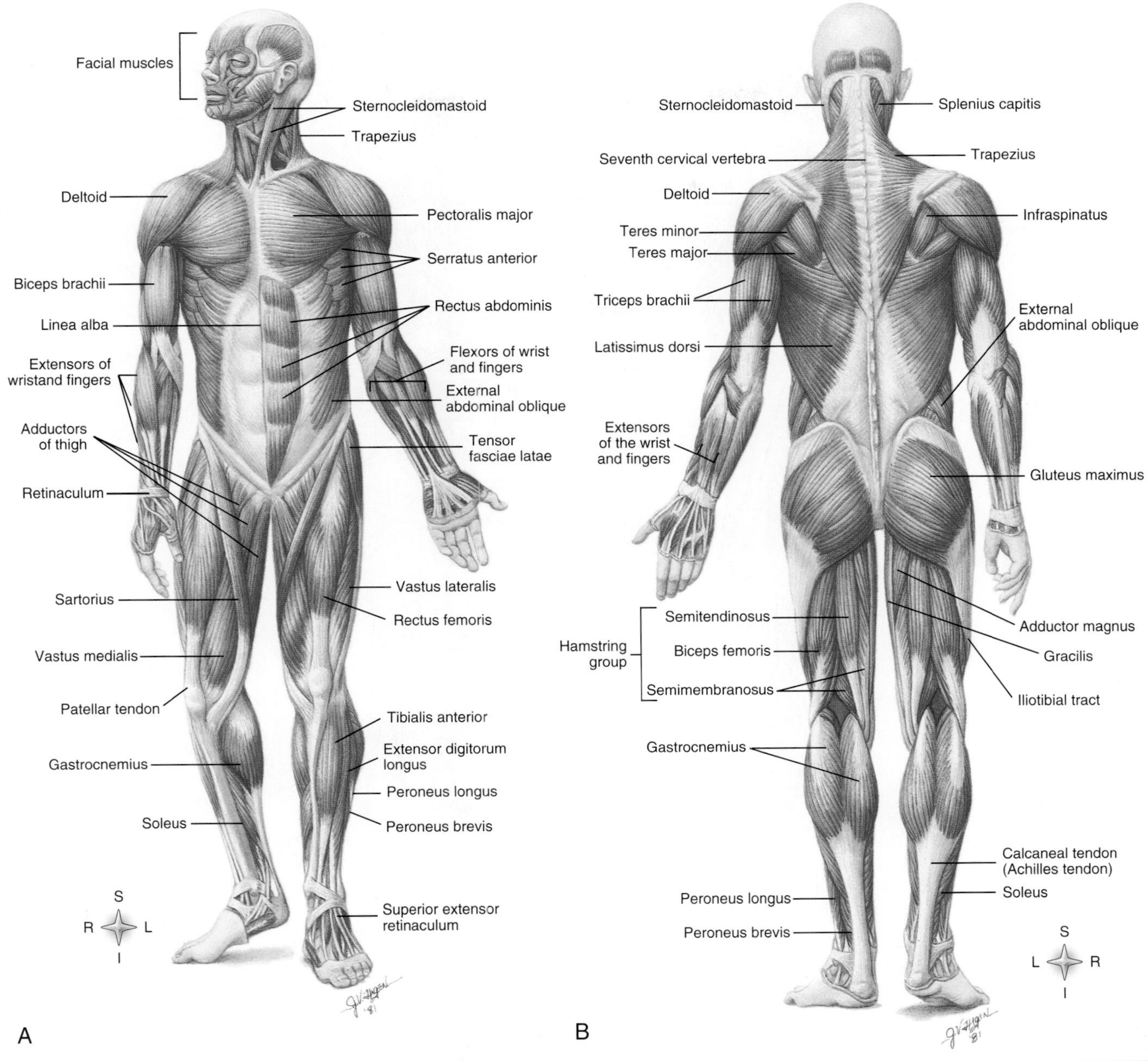

FIGURE 20-2. Normal muscular system. **A,** Anterior view. **B,** Posterior view.

CATEGORY	SECTION TITLES
M80-M85	Disorders of bone density and structure
M86-M90	Other osteopathies
M91-M94	Chondropathies
M95	Other disorders of the musculoskeletal system and connective tissue
M96	Intraoperative and postprocedural complications and disorders of musculoskeletal system, not elsewhere classified
M97	Periprosthetic fracture around internal prosthetic joint
M99	Biomechanical lesions, not elsewhere classified

Many of the conditions in Chapter 14 are coded based on site and laterality. Sites may include the bone, joint, or muscle involved. According to the guidelines, if a condition affects the portion of the bone at the joint, the site designation will be bone, not the joint.

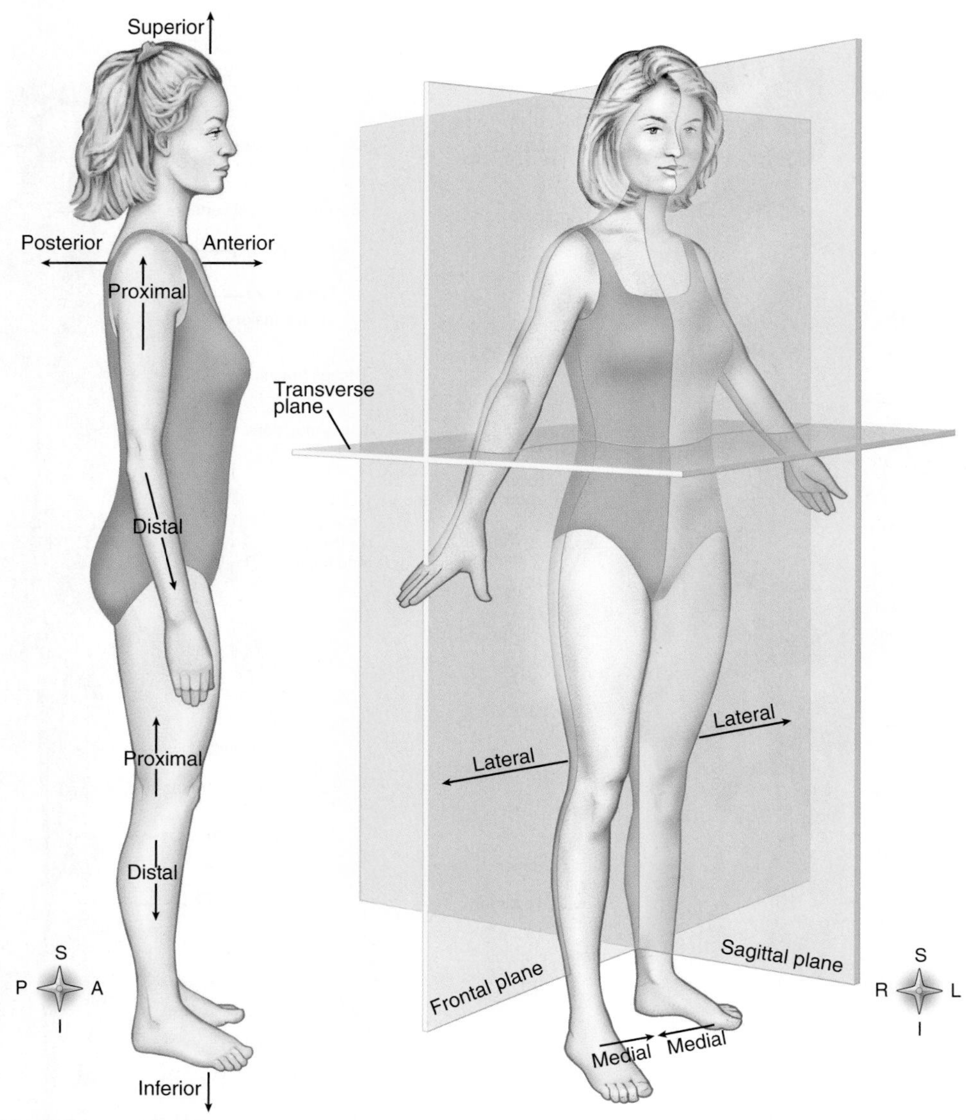

FIGURE 20-3. Directions and planes of the body.

Infectious (M00-M02) and Inflammatory Arthropathies (M05-M14)

Arthropathy is a disease that affects the joints. The term arthropathy is generic, and symptoms and treatment will depend on the cause of the arthropathy. Common causes include:

- Infectious—due to an infection of the joint
- Crystal—due to diseases such as gout that deposit crystals in the joint
- Diabetic—a manifestation of diabetes
- Neuropathic—a manifestation due to nerve damage around the joint
- Enteropathic—a type of arthritis that is related to colitis such a Crohn's or ulcerative colitis

Rheumatoid arthritis (RA) is a chronic, inflammatory, systemic disease that affects the joints, often causing deformity (Figure 20-4). RA is one of the most severe and disabling forms of arthritis. Damage may extend beyond the joints, affecting the heart and blood vessels and producing damage within the layers of skin.

Juvenile rheumatoid arthritis (JRA) affects children, usually between the ages of 2 and 5 years. Various forms of JRA may affect only a few joints, may affect many joints, or may be systemic in nature (also known as Still's disease).

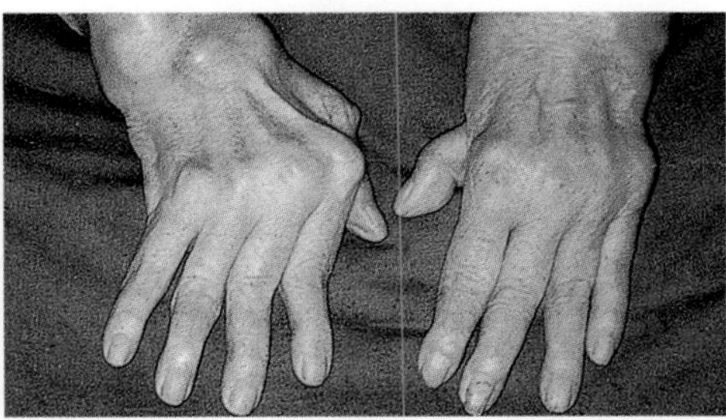

FIGURE 20-4. Joint deformity from rheumatoid arthritis.

EXAMPLE

Fourteen-year-old child is being treated for Still's disease, M08.20.

EXERCISE 20-1

Assign codes to the following conditions.

1. Juvenile RA, left knee ______________
2. Arthritis bilateral hips due to ulcerative colitis ______________
3. Rheumatoid lung disease ______________
4. Septic arthritis, right shoulder due to MRSA ______________
5. Idiopathic chronic gout, left wrist ______________

Osteoarthritis (M15-M19) and Other Joint Disorders (M20-M25)

Osteoarthritis

Osteoarthritis is a type of arthritis that develops as the result of wear and tear on the joints. It occurs because of breakdown and loss of cartilage within the joints (Figure 20-5). Osteoarthritis (OA) or degenerative joint disease (DJD), the most common form of arthritis, is more common in the elderly. Weight-bearing joints such as the knees and hips are often affected. The most common symptoms include sore and stiff joints, particularly in the morning or with changes of weather. Edema and deformity may also be present. Treatment depends on the severity of the condition and the success of conservative medical treatments (i.e., anti-inflammatory medications, exercise, steroid injections). In severe cases, surgery may be required to replace affected joints.

Primary osteoarthritis is an idiopathic condition that occurs in previously intact joints and has no apparent initiating factor. Primary osteoarthritis is related to the aging process and typically occurs in older individuals. **Secondary osteoarthritis** refers to degenerative disease of the joints that results from a predisposing condition such as trauma or disease. Secondary osteoarthritis may occur in relatively young individuals and usually affects the joints of one area. Osteoarthritis that involves multiple sites but is not specified in generalized is coded to polyosteoarthritis, unspecified M15.9.

EXAMPLE

Patient has primary osteoarthritis of both hips, M16.0.

EXAMPLE

Patient is being treated for osteoarthritis hands and wrists, M15.9.

Recurrent dislocations are not coded as an injury even if due to trauma. After the initial dislocation, the joint becomes less stable and requires less force to dislocate the joint again. The most common sites for recurrent dislocation to occur are shoulders, fingers, and knees.

EXAMPLE

Patient was treated in the ER for recurrent dislocation of left shoulder. A closed reduction was performed, M24.412, 0RSKXZZ.

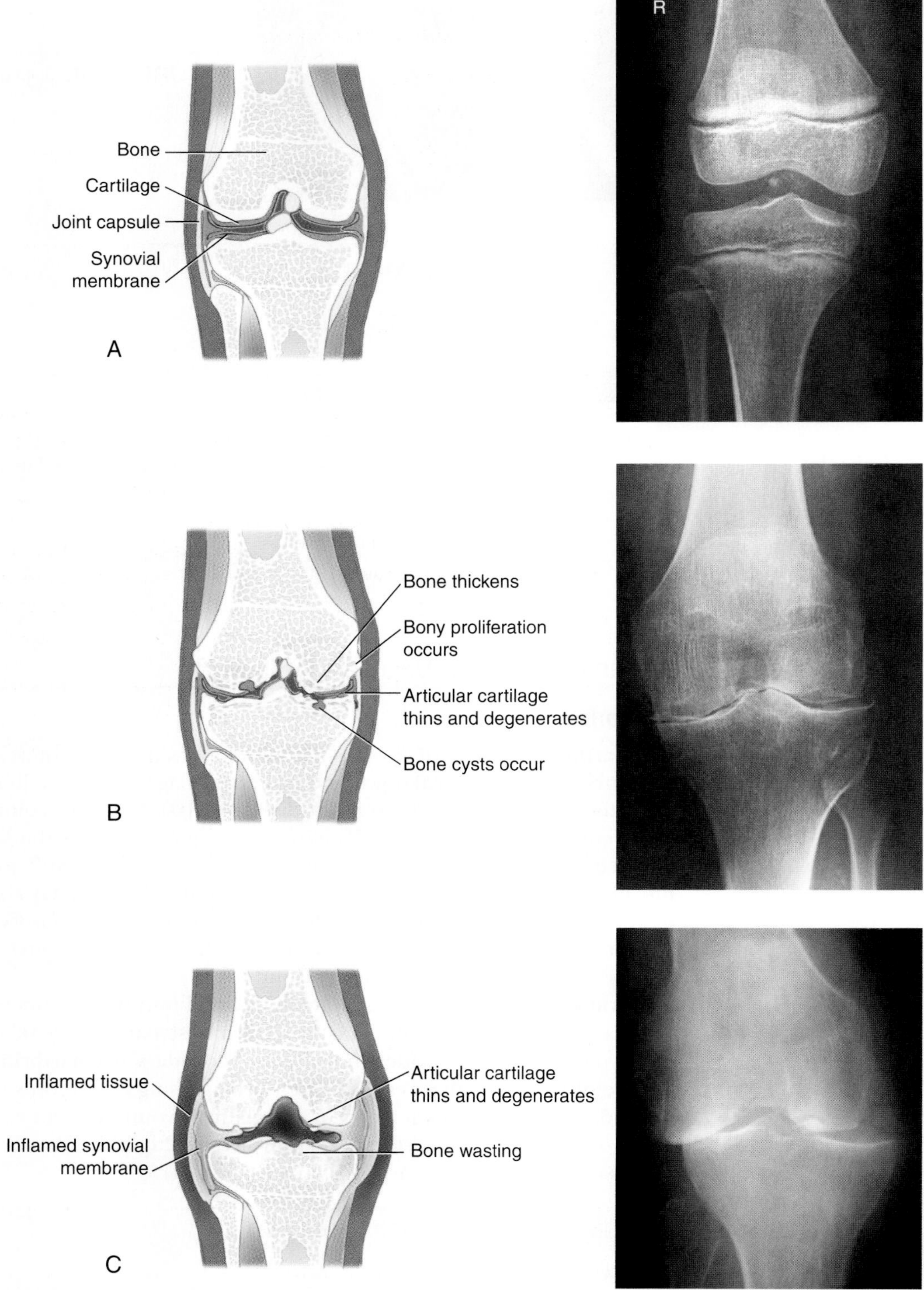

FIGURE 20-5. Pathologic changes of osteoarthritis.

EXERCISE 20-2

Assign codes to the following conditions.

1. Pain both knees due to DJD ____________
2. Loose body in left knee joint ____________
3. Talipes planus, right (acquired) ____________
4. Contracture, left hand ____________
5. Osteoarthritis, right shoulder ____________

Systemic Connective Tissue Disorders (M30-M36)

Collagen Diseases

The main component of connective tissue is collagen. Collagen diseases result from immune system malfunctions in which the immune system identifies the body's connective tissue as foreign and attacks it. A patient's heart, lungs, and kidneys may also suffer damage. No cure is known for these diseases. The most common conditions include systemic lupus erythematosus, scleroderma, and rheumatoid arthritis.

Systemic lupus erythematosus (SLE) is a chronic, inflammatory autoimmune disease that can damage connective tissue anywhere in the body. It causes inflammation of the skin, joints, nervous system, kidneys, lungs, and other organs. A butterfly rash that spreads from one cheek across the nose to the other cheek is a common symptom (Figure 20-6). Fever, fatigue, weight loss, and joint deformity may also be present.

Scleroderma is a chronic, progressive disease that is characterized by hardening of the skin and scarring of internal organs. No cure is known for scleroderma; treatment is supportive and varies according to the organs that are affected. CREST syndrome is a form of scleroderma that includes the following:

Calcinosis—calcification of the skin

Raynaud's phenomenon—a disorder that is characterized by vasospastic attacks in which blood vessels to the fingers, toes, and sometimes the ears and nose constrict, causing discoloration and pain

Esophageal dysfunction—such as reflux or difficulty in swallowing

Sclerodactyly—hardening of the skin of the fingers or toes

Telangiectasia—dilatation of tiny blood vessels, particularly of the skin

EXAMPLE Patient is being treated for CREST syndrome, M34.1.

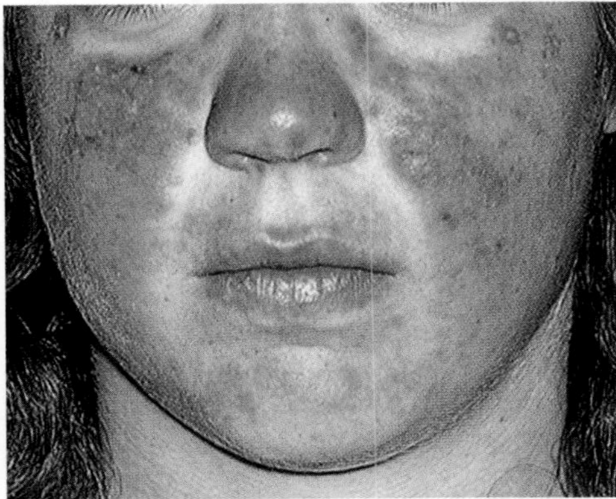

FIGURE 20-6. Butterfly rash that may accompany systemic lupus erythematosus.

Polymyalgia Rheumatica

Polymyalgia rheumatica, or PMR, is a syndrome that is characterized by severe aching and stiffness in the neck, shoulder girdle, and pelvic girdle. It is classified as a rheumatic disease, although its origin remains undetermined. It has been closely linked to temporal arteritis.

EXERCISE 20-3

Assign codes to the following conditions.

1. Sicca syndrome __________
2. SLE with nephrotic syndrome __________
3. Mixed connective tissue disease __________
4. Kawasaki disease __________
5. Giant cell arteritis __________

Deforming Dorsopathies (M40-M43), Spondylopathies (M45-M49), and Other Dorsopathies (M50-M54)

Spinal Deformities

Sometimes, the normal curvatures of the spine are altered. **Lordosis** is an exaggerated inward curvature of the spine that may be caused by increased abdominal girth due to obesity, pregnancy, or abdominal tumor (Figure 20-7, *A*). Improved posture, exercise, and weight loss can often alleviate symptoms. **Kyphosis** is an excessive posterior curvature of the thoracic spine that may not be detected until a hump in the upper back is noticeable (Figure 20-7, *B*). In older people, particularly women, osteoporosis is often the cause. If it occurs in children or adolescents, the exact cause may have to be determined, so that the best treatment approach can be selected. **Scoliosis** is a lateral or sideways curvature of the spine

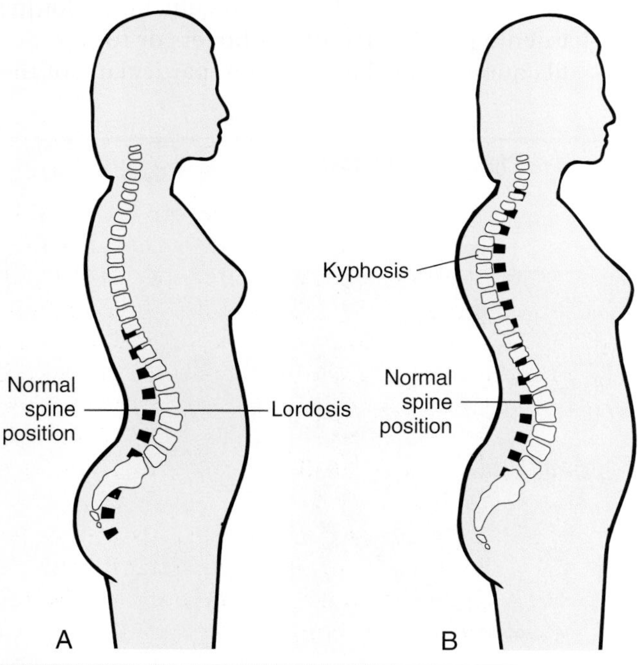

FIGURE 20-7. **A,** Lordosis. **B,** Kyphosis.

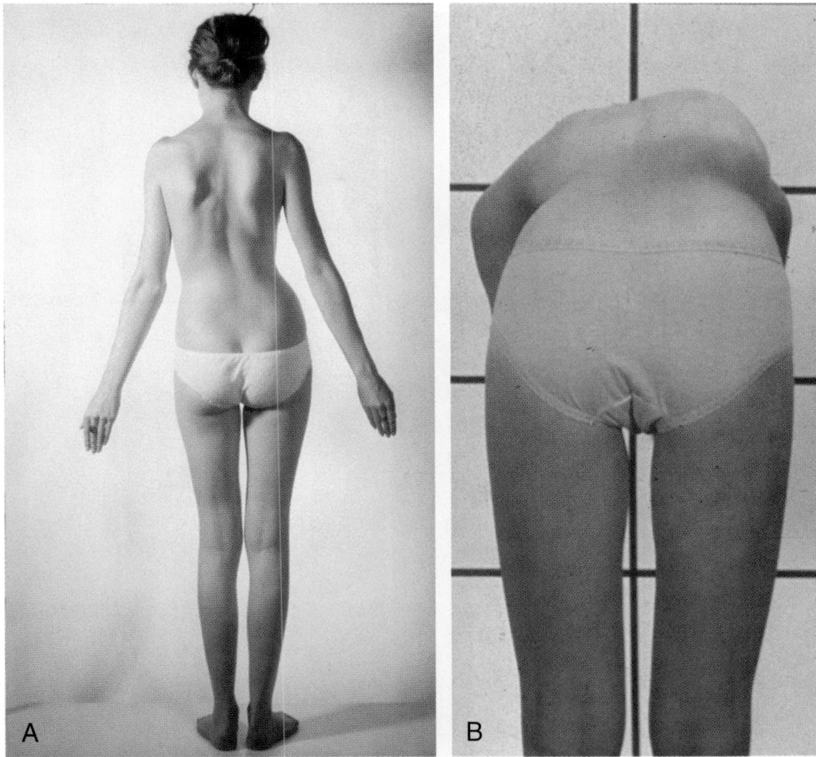

FIGURE 20-8. Scoliosis. **A,** Note scapular asymmetry in the upright position. **B,** Bending forward reveals a mild rib hump deformity.

(Figure 20-8). School screening programs may detect spinal abnormalities. Varying degrees of abnormality may be observed, and often, conservative medical management is attempted. In severe cases, the performance of procedures that fuse the vertebrae and the application of internal fixation devices such as rods, wires, plates, and/or screws may be necessary to correct the problem.

EXAMPLE

The patient is being treated conservatively for kyphoscoliosis, M41.9.

EXAMPLE

Patient has back, buttock, and leg pain due to acquired lumbar spondylolisthesis, M43.16.

Dorsopathies are conditions or diseases that affect the back or spine. Code assignment may depend on the location or region that is affected. The spinal column contains 33 vertebrae, as indicated in Figure 20-9. Seven cervical vertebrae are found in the neck. Twelve thoracic, or dorsal, vertebrae are found in the region of the chest, or thorax; these provide attachment for 12 pairs of ribs. Five lumbar vertebrae are located in the lower back. Five fused sacral vertebrae form the sacrum, a solid bone that fits like a wedge between the bones of the hip and the coccyx. The coccyx consists of three or four vertebrae fused together at the bottom of the sacrum. Between each vertebra is a thick, fibrous disc of cartilage known as an intervertebral disc. Intervertebral discs may become displaced, herniated, ruptured, and/or prolapsed with resultant pain.

Spondylosis (spinal osteoarthritis) is a degenerative disorder that may cause loss of normal spinal structure and function. Although aging is the primary cause, the location and rate of degeneration are individualized. The degenerative process of spondylosis may affect the cervical, thoracic, and/or lumbar regions of the spine, including the intervertebral discs and facet joints. **Facet joints** are small, stabilizing joints located between and behind adjacent vertebrae.

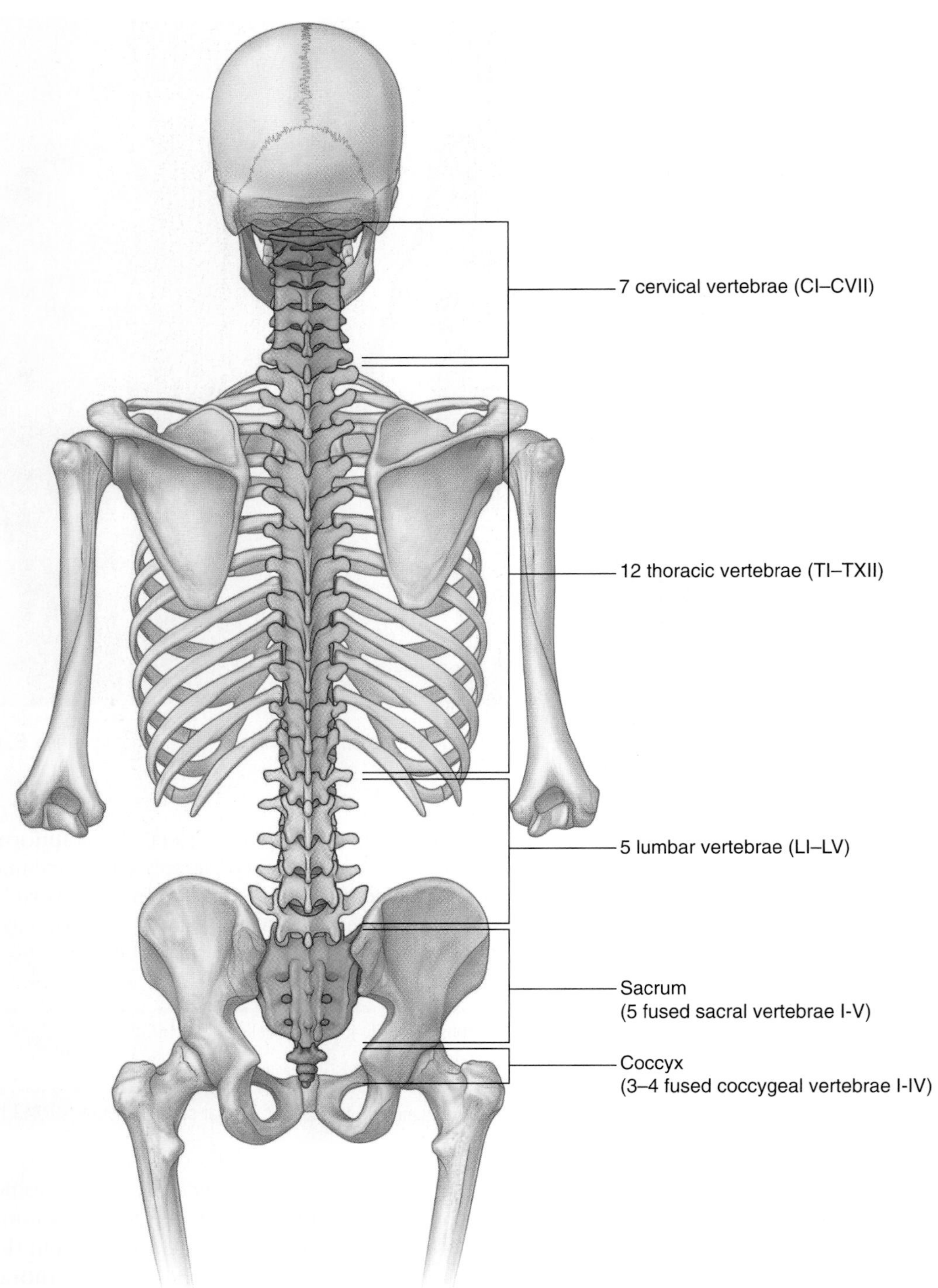

FIGURE 20-9. Vertebrae.

Spondylolisthesis occurs when one vertebra slips on another (Figure 20-10). Symptoms usually appear when the spinal nerves are pinched by the vertebrae. Symptoms such as back, buttock, and leg pain are often aggravated by activity and relieved with rest. The amount of slippage is identified by grades.

Spinal stenosis is a narrowing of the central spinal canal, or areas of the spine where the nerve roots exit (neuroforamina). This narrowing is often caused by arthritis and therefore is most often found in persons from older age groups. Spinal stenosis may be caused by other factors such as injury, infection, tumor, or congenital abnormality. Stenosis does

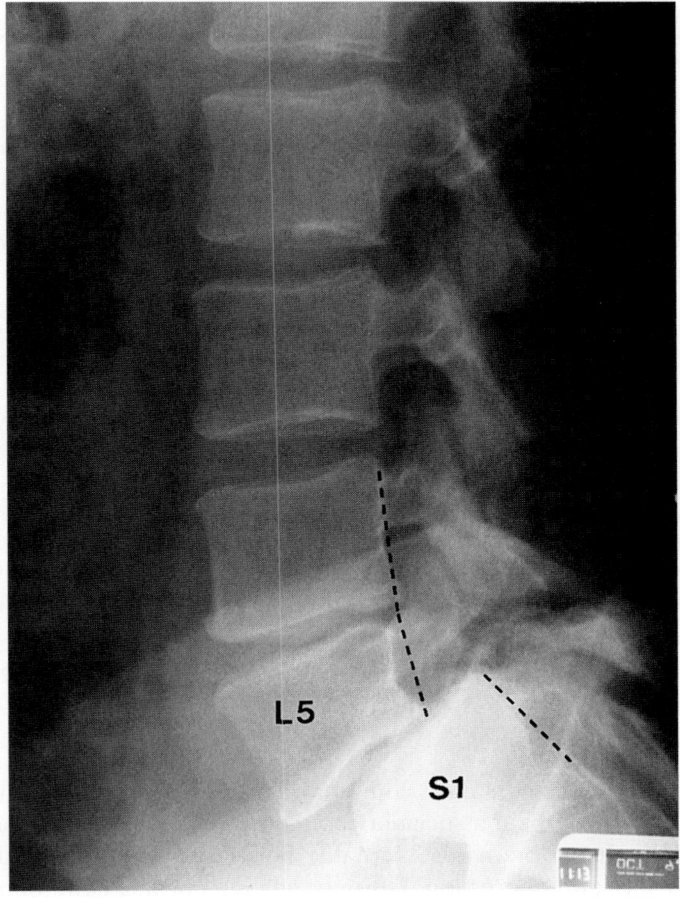

FIGURE 20-10. Spondylolysis with resulting grade 2 spondylolisthesis.

not necessarily cause symptoms; if symptoms do appear, they usually indicate the presence of **radiculopathy** (nerve root compression) or **myelopathy** (spinal cord compression).

EXAMPLE The patient's magnetic resonance imaging (MRI) showed stenosis cervical vertebrae, M48.02.

EXAMPLE Patient's CT shows spondylosis lumbar region with myelopathy, M47.16.

EXERCISE 20-4

Assign codes to the following conditions.

1. Cervical spondylosis without myelopathy ____________
2. Degenerative disc disease, lumbar spine ____________
3. Right-sided sciatica due to sitting on wallet ____________
4. Chronic low back pain ____________
5. Torticollis ____________
6. Pain in neck ____________
7. OA thoracic spine ____________
8. Stenosis, lumbosacral vertebra ____________
9. Lumbago due to disc herniation at L4-L5 ____________
10. Sacroiliitis ____________

Disorders of Muscles (M60-M63), Synovium, Tendon (M65-M67), and Other Soft Tissue (M70-M79)

Bursitis

Bursitis is inflammation of a bursa, which is a tiny, fluid-filled sac found between muscles, tendons, and bones designed to reduce friction and facilitate movement. Symptoms of bursitis include pain and tenderness when the affected body part is moved, limited range of motion, and edema or swelling. Areas most affected are the shoulders, elbows, hips, and knees. Bursitis may be caused by trauma, overuse of the joint, infection, or diseases such as gout and RA.

EXAMPLE

Patient is being seen for bursitis left olecranon process, M70.22.

EXAMPLE

Patient is being treated for right prepatellar bursitis, M70.41.

Necrotizing Fasciitis

Necrotizing fasciitis or "flesh-eating disease" is a rare but serious condition in which an infection occurs in the tissues below the skin. The tissues may quickly die because of poor blood supply, possibly leading to the death of the patient. Necrotizing fasciitis is usually caused by group A streptococcus (the same bacterium that causes strep throat) and is often preceded by an injury to the skin.

Fibromyalgia

Fibromyalgia, one of the most common diseases affecting the muscles, is characterized by widespread muscle pain associated with chronic fatigue. Other common symptoms of this condition include "brain fog," irritable bowel syndrome, sleep disorders, chronic headaches, anxiety, and depression. Fibromyalgia is a chronic condition that may be aggravated by weather conditions, infection, allergies, hormones, stress, and overexertion. Most available treatments focus on improving sleep and controlling pain.

EXERCISE 20-5

Assign codes to the following conditions.

1. Necrotizing fasciitis due to group A strep with gangrene right leg ____________
2. Pain due to bursitis, left shoulder ____________
3. Insomnia due to fibromyalgia ____________
4. De Quervain's disease ____________

Disorders of Bone Density and Structure (M80-M85), Other Osteopathies (M86-M90), Chondropathies (M91-M94), and Periprosthetic Fracture around Internal Prosthetic Joint (M97)

Osteoporosis

Osteoporosis is a metabolic bone disorder that results in decreased bone mass and density. Osteoporosis, which is most common in older persons, particularly postmenopausal women, may also occur as the result of other diseases such as hyperparathyroidism or Cushing's syndrome; use of steroids may contribute to bone loss. Individuals with osteoporosis are susceptible for pathologic fractures. These fractures most often occur in the vertebrae of the spine, wrists, and hips (Figure 20-11).

EXAMPLE

Patient is being treated for postmenopausal osteoporosis, M81.0.

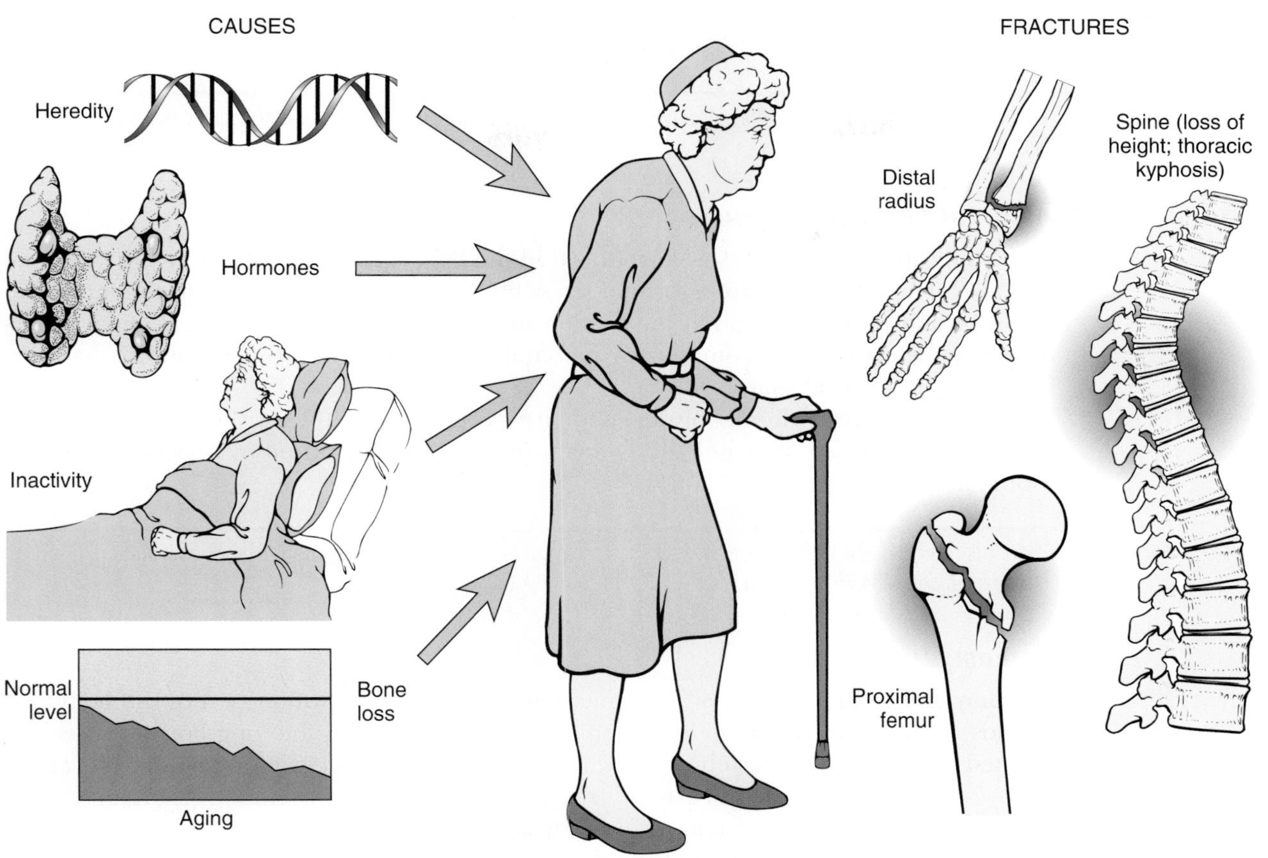

FIGURE 20-11. Causes and results of osteoporosis.

EXAMPLE

Patient has osteoporosis due to disuse, M81.8.

Pathologic Fractures and Fracture Aftercare

A **pathologic fracture** is a break in a bone that occurs because of underlying disorders that weaken the bone, including malignancy, benign bone tumors, metabolic disorders, infection, and osteoporosis. A pathologic fracture may result from normal stress placed on an abnormal bone. Fractures may occur spontaneously in individuals with diseased bones as the result of minor exertion or trauma. Because the bone is already diseased, the healing process of the fracture can be complicated by delayed healing, nonunion, pseudarthrosis, necrosis, and infection. A fracture cannot be coded as both a traumatic fracture and a pathologic fracture; it is one or the other. Only a physician can determine whether the severity of trauma corresponds with the injury. Compression fractures of the spine are often pathologic, but a thorough review of the record and/or a physician query may be necessary to determine the appropriate fracture code. Other terms that may indicate a pathologic fracture are stress fracture, fatigue fracture, or insufficiency fracture.

Active treatment for a pathologic fracture includes surgery, an Emergency Room encounter, and/or evaluation and continuing treatment by the same or a different physician. Assignment of the 7th character is based on active treatment and not whether the provider is seeing the patient for the first time. According to the guidelines, when a patient is receiving active treatment, the acute fracture code is assigned with a 7th character A. A 7th character D is used for encounters after the patient has completed active treatment. Some examples of "D" subsequent care are cast change or removal, an x-ray to check healing status of the fracture, removal of external or internal fixation device, medication adjustment or other aftercare, and follow-up visits.

EXAMPLE Patient had a cast change for pathologic right radial fracture, M84.433D, 2W0CX2Z.

EXAMPLE Patient was seen in the ER and diagnosed with a pathologic fracture distal left femur due to osteosarcoma femur, M84.552A, C40.22.

Atypical Femoral Fractures

A new subcategory, M84.75, was introduced in the 2017 updates to classify atypical femoral fractures. These fractures are a form of stress fracture that is associated with the long-term use of bisphosphonates or other medication such as glucocorticoids. Atypical femoral fractures may be classified as complete or incomplete and are located in the subtrochanteric region of the femoral shaft.

If the fracture is due to bisphosphonates, codes T45.8X5A, Adverse effect of other primarily systemic and hematologic agents, and Z79.83, Long-term use of bisphosphonates, should also be assigned.

EXAMPLE Patient is receiving active treatment for incomplete atypical femoral fracture of the right leg due to long-term use of bisphosphonate, M84.751A, T45.8X5A, Z79.83.

Osteomyelitis

Osteomyelitis is an infection of the bone that often starts in another part of the body and spreads to the bone via the blood (Figure 20-12). In children, the long bones are usually affected. In adults, the vertebrae and the pelvis are the most commonly affected areas. *Staphylococcus aureus* bacteria are usually the cause of acute osteomyelitis. This organism may enter the bloodstream through a wound or a contaminated intravenous needle. Chronic osteomyelitis results when bone tissue dies as a result of the lost blood supply. Risk factors include recent trauma, diabetes, hemodialysis, and intravenous (IV) drug abuse. People who have had a splenectomy are also at higher risk for osteomyelitis. Prolonged IV antibiotic therapy may be required.

EXAMPLE Subacute osteomyelitis sacrum with decubitus sacral ulcer, stage 3, M46.28, L89.153.

EXAMPLE Chronic osteomyelitis due to *staphylococcus aureus* left tibia, M86.662, B95.61.

Periprosthetic Fractures

A periprosthetic fracture is one that occurs around a joint prosthesis or implant. This is not a complication of the orthopedic prosthesis/implant because the prosthesis or implant has not been fractured. These fractures can occur either due to trauma or pathological causes

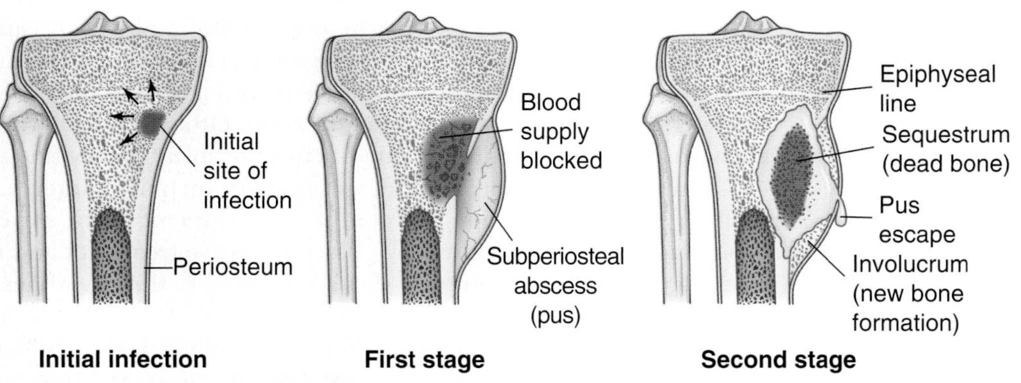

FIGURE 20-12. Progression of osteomyelitis. Bacterial growth results in bone destruction and abscess formation.

just like any other fractures. The treatment of these fractures may be more complex due to the presence of a prosthetic joint or other type of implant. The most common sites are around the hip and knee joints. If the reason for the admission or encounter is for the fracture, the type of fracture should be sequenced first, and the code to classify the fracture as periprosthetic should be added as a secondary diagnosis.

EXAMPLE

Patient was admitted for right femur periprosthetic fracture due to age-related osteoporosis. Patient had right total hip replacement 3 years earlier, M80.051A, M97.01XA.

EXERCISE 20-6

Assign codes to the following conditions.

1. Thoracic kyphosis due to osteoporosis ____________
2. Acute osteomyelitis, right tibia. Cultures did not grow any organisms. ____________
3. Osteochondritis dissecans ____________
4. Pathologic fracture, left wrist, due to osteoporosis ____________
5. Stress fracture, right tibia ____________
6. Chest pain due to costochondritis ____________
7. Cast change for pathologic fracture, right radius ____________
8. Nontraumatic slipped upper left femoral epiphysis ____________

FACTORS INFLUENCING HEALTH STATUS AND CONTACT WITH HEALTH SERVICES (Z CODES)

As was discussed in Chapter 9, it may be difficult to locate Z codes in the index. Coders often say, "I did not know there was a Z code for that." Refer to Chapter 9 for a listing of common main terms used to locate Z codes.

It is important for the coder to be familiar with different types and uses of Z codes.

Z13.820	Encounter for screening for osteoporosis
Z13.828	Encounter for screening for other musculoskeletal disorder
Z44.001	Encounter for fitting and adjustment of unspecified right artificial arm
Z44.002	Encounter for fitting and adjustment of unspecified left artificial arm
Z44.009	Encounter for fitting and adjustment of unspecified artificial arm, unspecified arm
Z44.011	Encounter for fitting and adjustment of complete right artificial arm
Z44.012	Encounter for fitting and adjustment of complete left artificial arm
Z44.019	Encounter for fitting and adjustment of complete artificial arm, unspecified arm
Z44.021	Encounter for fitting and adjustment of partial artificial right arm
Z44.022	Encounter for fitting and adjustment of partial artificial left arm
Z44.029	Encounter for fitting and adjustment of partial artificial arm, unspecified arm
Z44.101	Encounter for fitting and adjustment of unspecified right artificial leg
Z44.102	Encounter for fitting and adjustment of unspecified left artifical leg
Z44.109	Encounter for fitting and adjustment of unspecified artificial leg, unspecified leg
Z44.111	Encounter for fitting and adjustment of complete right artificial leg
Z44.112	Encounter for fitting and adjustment of complete left artificial leg
Z44.119	Encounter for fitting and adjustment of complete artificial leg, unspecified leg
Z44.121	Encounter for fitting and adjustment of partial artificial right leg
Z44.122	Encounter for fitting and adjustment of partial artificial left leg
Z44.129	Encounter for fitting and adjustment of partial artificial leg, unspecified leg

Z47.1	Aftercare following joint replacement surgery
Z47.2	Encounter for removal of internal fixation device
Z47.31	Aftercare following explantation of shoulder joint prosthesis
Z47.32	Aftercare following explantation of hip joint prosthesis
Z47.33	Aftercare following explantation of knee joint prosthesis
Z47.81	Encounter for orthopedic aftercare following surgical amputation
Z47.82	Encounter for orthopedic aftercare following scoliosis surgery
Z47.89	Encounter for other orthopedic aftercare
Z52.20	Bone donor, unspecified
Z52.21	Bone donor, autologous
Z52.29	Bone donor, other
Z53.33	Arthroscopic surgical procedure converted to open procedure
Z79.83	Long term (current) use of bisphosphonates
Z82.61	Family history of arthritis
Z82.62	Family history of osteoporosis
Z82.69	Family history of other diseases of the musculoskeletal system and connective tissue
Z87.310	Personal history of (healed) osteoporosis fracture
Z87.311	Personal history of (healed) other pathological fracture
Z87.312	Personal history of (healed) stress fracture
Z87.39	Personal history of other diseases of the musculoskeletal system and connective tissue
Z89.011	Acquired absence of right thumb
Z89.012	Acquired absence of left thumb
Z89.019	Acquired absence of unspecified thumb
Z89.021	Acquired absence of right finger(s)
Z89.022	Acquired absence of left finger(s)
Z89.029	Acquired absence of unspecified finger(s)
Z89.111	Acquired absence of right hand
Z89.112	Acquired absence of left hand
Z89.119	Acquired absence of unspecified hand
Z89.121	Acquired absence of right wrist
Z89.122	Acquired absence of left wrist
Z89.129	Acquired absence of unspecified wrist
Z89.201	Acquired absence of right upper limb, unspecified level
Z89.202	Acquired absence of left upper limb, unspecified level
Z89.209	Acquired absence of unspecified upper limb, unspecified level
Z89.211	Acquired absence of right upper limb below elbow
Z89.212	Acquired absence of left upper limb below elbow
Z89.219	Acquired absence of unspecified upper limb below elbow
Z89.221	Acquired absence of right upper limb above elbow
Z89.222	Acquired absence of left upper limb above elbow
Z89.229	Acquired absence of unspecified upper limb above elbow
Z89.231	Acquired absence of right shoulder
Z89.232	Acquired absence of left shoulder
Z89.239	Acquired absence of unspecified shoulder
Z89.411	Acquired absence of right great toe
Z89.412	Acquired absence of left great toe
Z89.419	Acquired absence of unspecified great toe
Z89.421	Acquired absence of other right toe(s)
Z89.422	Acquired absence of other left toe(s)
Z89.429	Acquired absence of other toe(s), unspecified side
Z89.431	Acquired absence of right foot
Z89.432	Acquired absence of left foot

Z89.439	Acquired absence of unspecified foot
Z89.441	Acquired absence of right ankle
Z89.442	Acquired absence of left ankle
Z89.449	Acquired absence of unspecified ankle
Z89.511	Acquired absence of right leg below knee
Z89.512	Acquired absence of left leg below knee
Z89.519	Acquired absence of unspecified leg below knee
Z89.521	Acquired absence of right knee
Z89.522	Acquired absence of left knee
Z89.529	Acquired absence of unspecified knee
Z89.611	Acquired absence of right leg above knee
Z89.612	Acquired absence of left leg above knee
Z89.619	Acquired absence of unspecified leg above knee
Z89.621	Acquired absence of right hip joint
Z89.622	Acquired absence of left hip joint
Z89.629	Acquired absence of unspecified hip joint
Z89.9	Acquired absence of limb, unspecified
Z94.6	Bone transplant status
Z96.60	Presence of unspecified orthopedic joint implant
Z96.611	Presence of right artificial shoulder joint
Z96.612	Presence of left artificial shoulder joint
Z96.619	Presence of unspecified artificial shoulder joint
Z96.621	Presence of right artificial elbow joint
Z96.622	Presence of left artificial elbow joint
Z96.629	Presence of unspecified artificial elbow joint
Z96.631	Presence of right artificial wrist joint
Z96.632	Presence of left artificial wrist joint
Z96.639	Presence of unspecified artificial wrist joint
Z96.641	Presence of right artificial hip joint
Z96.642	Presence of left artificial hip joint
Z96.643	Presence of artificial hip joint, bilateral
Z96.649	Presence of unspecified artificial hip joint
Z96.651	Presence of right artificial knee joint
Z96.652	Presence of left artificial knee joint
Z96.653	Presence of artificial knee joint, bilateral
Z96.659	Presence of unspecified artificial knee joint
Z96.661	Presence of right artificial ankle joint
Z96.662	Presence of left artificial ankle joint
Z96.669	Presence of unspecified artificial ankle joint
Z96.691	Finger-joint replacement of right hand
Z96.692	Finger-joint replacement of left hand
Z96.693	Finger-joint replacement, bilateral
Z96.698	Presence of other orthopedic joint implants
Z96.7	Presence of other bone and tendon implants
Z97.10	Presence of artificial limb (complete) (partial), unspecified
Z97.11	Presence of artificial right arm (complete) (partial)
Z97.12	Presence of artificial left arm (complete) (partial)
Z97.13	Presence of artificial right leg (complete) (partial)
Z97.14	Presence of artificial left leg (complete) (partial)
Z97.15	Presence of artificial arms, bilateral (complete) (partial)
Z97.16	Presence of artificial legs, bilateral (complete) (partial)
Z98.1	Arthrodesis status

EXAMPLE

Patient is status post bilateral knee replacements 1 year ago, Z96.653.

EXAMPLE

Patient with a family history of rheumatoid arthritis is being screened for rheumatoid arthritis, Z13.828, Z82.61.

EXERCISE 20-7

Assign codes to the following conditions.

1. Status post right knee replacement __________
2. Dual-energy x-ray absorptiometry (DEXA) scan screening for osteoporosis __________
3. Amputation status right foot __________
4. Previous amputation, left great toe __________

COMMON TREATMENTS

Many conditions or diseases of the musculoskeletal system cause pain and inflammation. Anti-inflammatory agents reduce inflammation in joints and muscles, antiarthritics are used to treat arthritic symptoms, and muscle relaxants may be helpful for acute low back pain and muscle spasms. Physical therapy and chiropractic treatment may be beneficial for many conditions. Medical treatment is usually tried before surgical intervention is considered.

CONDITION	MEDICATION/TREATMENT
Rheumatoid arthritis	Celecoxib (Celebrex), gold compounds such as Ridaura and Myochrysine
Osteoarthritis	Analgesics Nonsteroidal anti-inflammatory drugs (NSAIDs) for pain and inflammation (aspirin, ibuprofen [Motrin, Advil], nabumetone [Relafen], naproxen [Aleve, Naprosyn], diclofenac [Voltaren], indomethacin [Indocin], etodolac [Lodine], oxaprozin [Daypro], celecoxib [Celebrex])
Fibromyalgia	Analgesics for pain, muscle relaxants, antidepressants, and sleep aids
Bursitis	Rest, immobilization, ice, NSAIDs
Necrotizing fasciitis	Aggressive antibiotic therapy with surgical debridement
Osteomyelitis	Antibiotics depending on causative organism
Osteoporosis	Alendronate (Fosamax), Boniva (ibandronate), calcitonin, calcium with vitamin D

PROCEDURES

Procedures related to the musculoskeletal system and connective tissue in ICD-10-PCS can be located in the following tables:

0K2-0KX	Muscles
0L2-0LX	Tendons
0M2-0MX	Bursae and Ligaments
0N2-0NW	Head and Facial Bones
0P2-0PW	Upper Bones
0Q2-0QW	Lower Bones
0R2-0RW	Upper Joints
0S2-0S2	Lower Joints

Arthroscopic Surgery

Arthroscopic surgery is a minimally invasive surgery that involves the use of highly specialized instruments to perform surgery through very small incisions ($\frac{1}{2}$ inch) on joints. Advantages of arthroscopic surgery include small incisions, minimal scar tissue, and less pain after

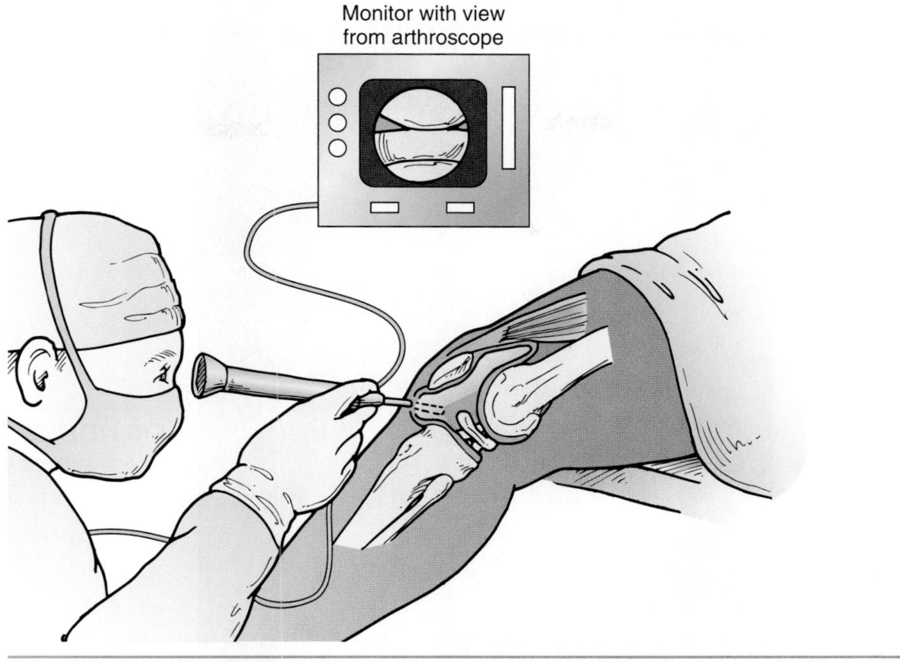

FIGURE 20-13. Arthroscopic examination of a joint.

surgery with quicker recovery. Arthroscopic procedures can be performed on any of the joints and joint structures. Occasionally, an arthroscopic procedure is performed for diagnostic purposes, and no additional therapeutic procedures are performed (Figure 20-13). The root operation for a diagnostic arthroscopic examination is inspection (visual/manual exploration).

EXAMPLE

Arthroscopic examination of the left knee for pain. All joint structures appear to be intact, M25.562, 0SJD4ZZ.

SECTION	BODY SYSTEM	ROOT OPERATION	BODY PART	APPROACH	DEVICE	QUALIFIER
Medical and Surgical	Lower Joints	Inspection	Knee Joint, Left	Percutaneous Endoscopic	No Device	No Qualifier
0	S	J	D	4	Z	Z

EXAMPLE

Arthroscopic meniscectomy (partial) for torn right medial meniscus (old injury) (knee), M23.203, 0SBC4ZZ.

SECTION	BODY SYSTEM	ROOT OPERATION	BODY PART	APPROACH	DEVICE	QUALIFIER
Medical and Surgical	Lower Joints	Excision	Knee Joint, Right	Percutaneous Endoscopic	No Device	No Qualifier
0	S	B	C	4	Z	Z

Joint Replacement

Joint replacement consists of removal of an arthritic or damaged joint and replacement with an artificial joint, which is also known as a prosthesis. Materials used in total joint replacement are designed to enable the joint to move similarly to a normal joint. The root operation for a total joint replacement is replacement (putting in or on biologic or synthetic

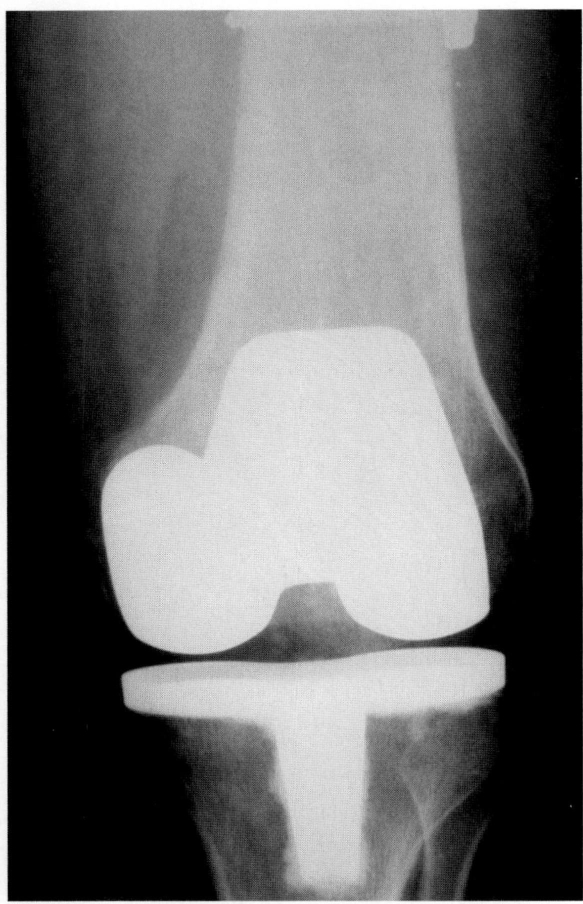

FIGURE 20-14. Total knee replacement for osteoarthritis.

material that replaces a body part). The prosthesis is generally composed of two parts; a metal piece fits closely into a matching sturdy plastic piece (Figure 20-14). Several metals, including stainless steel, alloys of cobalt and chrome, and titanium, are used. The plastic material is durable and wear-resistant (polyethylene). A plastic bone cement may be used to anchor the prosthesis into the bone. Hip and knee replacements are the most common joint replacements, but other joints, including the ankle, foot, shoulder, elbow, and fingers, can be replaced. In cases in which the disease process does not affect the entire joint, partial joint replacement may be performed. Other options besides total joint replacement procedures are available. A resurfacing procedure may be an option. A surface replacement procedure leaves more of the patient's bone in place with resurfacing of the affected area of the joint. As with replacement procedures, resurfacing can involve partial or total joint resurfacing. The root operation for a resurfacing procedure is supplement (putting in a device that reinforces or augments a body part).

Common complications of joint replacement include infection, blood clot, nerve injury, loosening, dislocation, wear and tear, and breakage of the prosthesis. It may be necessary to remove the prosthesis and insert a new prosthesis.

EXAMPLE

Primary osteoarthritis both knees. Patient is hospitalized for right partial knee replacement (femoral surface) with synthetic substitute (uncemented), M17.0, OSRTOJA.

SECTION	BODY SYSTEM	ROOT OPERATION	BODY PART	APPROACH	DEVICE	QUALIFIER
Medical and Surgical	Lower Joints	Replacement	Knee Joint, Femoral Surface, Right	Open	Synthetic Substitute	Uncemented
0	S	R	T	0	J	A

Vertebroplasty/Kyphoplasty

Percutaneous vertebroplasty (PV) is a technique that is used to treat pain caused by compression fractures of the vertebrae. The root operation for a vertebroplasty is supplement (putting in a device that reinforces or augments a body part). Under x-ray guidance, an acrylic cement is injected through a needle into a collapsed or weakened vertebra. This stabilizes the fracture, allowing the patient to resume normal activity and decrease the use of analgesics. PV does not reverse osteoporosis or prevent future compression fractures. This procedure is usually performed by interventional radiologists.

Kyphoplasty, similar to PV, is used to treat fractures of the spine; however, in kyphoplasty, a special balloon device is inserted into the compacted vertebrae in an attempt to restore vertebrae to a more normal state by improving the alignment of the spine. The root operations for a kyphoplasty are reposition (moving to its normal or other suitable location some or all of a body part) and supplement (putting in a device that reinforces or augments a body part). After the balloon has been removed, the cavity is filled with a cement-like material to stabilize the fracture. Kyphoplasty is usually performed under fluoroscopic guidance through a small incision in the back.

EXAMPLE

Compression fractures T11-T12 due to idiopathic osteoporosis. Percutaneous vertebroplasty (synthetic substitute) was performed in radiology, M80.88xA, 0PU43JZ.

SECTION	BODY SYSTEM	ROOT OPERATION	BODY PART	APPROACH	DEVICE	QUALIFIER
Medical and Surgical	Upper Bones	Supplement	Thoracic Vertebra	Percutaneous	Synthetic Substitute	No Qualifier
0	P	U	4	3	J	Z

Fusion Procedures of the Spine

Spinal decompression is a surgical procedure that frees space for nerves in the spinal canal. A number of different surgical methods, including laminectomy, laminotomy, laminoplasty, foraminotomy, and anterior discectomy, can be performed to accomplish a decompression. Although in many cases decompression involves removal of tissue that is constricting or compressing nerve structures, in some cases, the spine becomes unstable and spinal fusion is performed at the time of the decompression.

Spinal fusion is the creation of a solid bone bridge between two or more adjacent vertebrae to create stability between levels of the spine. The root operation for spinal fusion or refusion is fusion (rendering a joint immobile). Fusion is a gradual process (6 to 9 months or longer) in which bone is grown across desired areas to form a solid fusion. Bone grafts, interbody fusion, and other devices are used to facilitate and promote the fusion process. If a fusion fails to heal or fuse properly, this is called a nonunion or pseudarthrosis; repeat or refusion procedure may be required. A bone graft may be obtained from a variety of sources. Bone may be harvested from the patient's (autologous) spine or from the iliac crest. Bone graft material can also be obtained from a bone bank (harvested from cadavers [allograft]). Synthetic bone materials made from demineralized bone matrix (DBM) and calcium phosphates or hydroxyapatites (some derived from sea coral) may also be used. The use of metal devices (e.g. screws, rods, plates, cables, wires) can facilitate correction of a deformed spine and may increase the probability of attaining solid spinal fusion. Spinal instrumentation can be placed in the front or in the back portion of the spine. Devices are usually made of metal, commonly stainless steel or titanium. Spinal instrumentation is gradually covered by scar tissue and sometimes by new growth of bone. Even when the spine has healed solidly, the instrumentation is rarely removed. A 360-degree spinal fusion is a spinal fusion of both the anterior and posterior portions of the spine during the same operative episode. Using a lateral transverse approach, both the anterior and posterior

SECTION: 0 MEDICAL AND SURGICAL
BODY SYSTEM: S LOWER JOINTS
OPERATION: G FUSION: Joining together portions of an articular body part, rendering the articular body part immobile

Body Part	Approach	Device	Qualifier
0 Lumbar Vertebral Joint 1 Lumbar Vertebral Joint, 2-4 3 Lumbosacral Joint	0 Open 3 Percutaneous 4 Percutaneous Endoscopic	7 Autologous Tissue Substitute J Synthetic Substitute K Nonautologous Tissue Substitute	0 Anterior Approach, Anterior Column 1 Posterior Approach, Posterior Column J Posterior Approach, Anterior Column K Lateral Transverse Process Approach, Posterior Column
5 Sacrococcygeal Joint 6 Coccygeal Joint 7 Sacroiliac Joint, Right 8 Sacroiliac Joint, Left	0 Open 3 Percutaneous 4 Percutaneous Endoscopic	4 Internal Fixation Device 7 Autologous Tissue Substitute J Synthetic Substitute K Nonautologous Tissue Substitute	Z No Qualifier
9 Hip Joint, Right B Hip Joint, Left C Knee Joint, Right D Knee Joint, Left F Ankle Joint, Right G Ankle Joint, Left H Tarsal Joint, Right J Tarsal Joint, Left K Metatarsal-Tarsal Joint, Right L Metatarsal-Tarsal Joint, Left M Metatarsal-Phalangeal Joint, Right N Metatarsal-Phalangeal Joint, Left P Toe Phalangeal Joint, Right Q Toe Phalangeal Joint, Left	0 Open 3 Percutaneous 4 Percutaneous Endoscopic	3 Internal Fixation Device, Sustained Compression 4 Internal Fixation Device 5 External Fixation Device 7 Autologous Tissue Substitute J Synthetic Substitute K Nonautologous Tissue Substitute	Z No Qualifier

FIGURE 20-15. Table used to code lumbar fusion.

vertebral columns can be operated on through a single incision. Sometimes a spinal fusion is performed as a “staged procedure” with a posterior fusion performed one day and an anterior fusion is performed a few days later.

During any spinal fusion procedure, the documentation should be reviewed to ascertain the site of the fusion, the operative approach, the device or substitute used, and whether the fusion was on the anterior or posterior column of the spine (Figure 20-15). It is important to know that the placement of an interbody fusion device takes place only on the anterior spinal column. Other types of hardware can be placed along the posterior spine, but never an interbody fusion device. Not all character values within a row on a PCS table are possible code combinations. For example, 0SG0031 is an incorrect code because an interbody fusion device is not possible on the posterior spine. This is a common mistake made by coders.

There are some PCS guidelines specific to spinal fusions that state:

- The body part coded for a spinal vertebral joint(s) rendered immobile by a spinal fusion procedure is classified by the level of the spine (e.g. thoracic). There are distinct body part values for a single vertebral joint and for multiple vertebral joints at each spinal level.

EXAMPLE

Body part values specify lumbar vertebral joint, lumbar vertebral joints, 2 or more, and lumbosacral vertebral joint.

- If multiple vertebral joints are fused, a separate procedure is coded for each vertebral joint that uses a different device and/or qualifier.

EXAMPLE

Fusion of lumbar vertebral joint, posterior approach, anterior column, and fusion of lumbar vertebral joint, posterior approach, posterior column, are coded separately.

- Combinations of devices and materials are often used on a vertebral joint to render the joint immobile. When combinations of devices are used on the same vertebral joint, the device value coded for the procedure is as follows:
  - If an interbody fusion device is used to render the joint immobile (alone or containing other material like bone graft), the procedure is coded with the device value Interbody Fusion Device.
  - If bone graft is the only device used to render the joint immobile, the procedure is coded with the device value Nonautologous Tissue Substitute or Autologous Tissue Substitute.
  - If a mixture of autologous and nonautologous bone graft (with or without biological or synthetic extenders or binders) is used to render the joint immobile, code the procedure with the device value Autologous Tissue Substitute. Fusion of a vertebral joint using a cage-style interbody fusion device containing morselized bone graft is coded to the device Interbody Fusion Device.
  - Fusion of a vertebral joint using a bone dowel interbody fusion device made of cadaver bone and packed with a mixture of local morselized bone and demineralized bone matrix is coded to the device Interbody Fusion Device.
  - Fusion of a vertebral joint using both autologous bone graft and bone bank bone graft is coded to the device Autologous Tissue Substitute.

EXAMPLE

The patient was admitted for surgical intervention for cervical disc herniation with myelopathy. Partial discectomy at C3 and spinal fusion of C3-C4 and C4-C5 were performed via the anterior approach using interbody fusion device (anterior column), M50.01, M50.021, 0RG20A0, 0RB30ZZ.

SECTION	BODY SYSTEM	ROOT OPERATION	BODY PART	APPROACH	DEVICE	QUALIFIER
Medical and Surgical	Upper Joints	Fusion	Cervical Vertebral Joints, Two or more	Open	Interbody Fusion Device	Anterior Approach, Anterior Column
0	R	B	3	0	Z	Z

SECTION	BODY SYSTEM	ROOT OPERATION	BODY PART	APPROACH	DEVICE	QUALIFIER
Medical and Surgical	Upper Joints	Excision	Cervical Vertebral Disc	Open	No Device	No Qualifier
0	R	G	2	0	A	0

For spinal fusions, the incision site is identified as part of the qualifier. If the incision is anterior, that refers to the front of the body. A posterior incision is made in the back part of the body, and lateral refers to the side of the body. Many of the fusion procedures are described with an acronym. For example, an **A**nterior **L**umbar **I**nterbody **F**usion (ALIF) indicates anterior approach, the lumbar part of the body is the site of the procedure, and interbody fusion means within the disc space, which indicates anterior spinal column. PLIF is the same as ALIF with the exception of the approach, which would be posterior instead of anterior. Other common spinal fusion procedures are:

- AxiaLIF – axial lumbar interbody fusion
- DLIF – direct lateral lumbar interbody fusion
- TLIF – transforaminal lumbar interbody fusion
- XLIF – extreme lateral interbody fusion

EXERCISE 20-8

Assign codes for all diagnoses and procedures.

1. Open bone biopsy, left upper femur, which confirmed acute and chronic osteomyelitis ____________
2. Excision Baker's cyst, right ____________
3. Open partial hip replacement (femoral head) for OA right hip with metallic prosthesis ____________
4. Open removal of fixation device, lumbar spine ____________
5. Arthroscopy, right knee. Mild osteoarthritis ____________
6. Necrotizing fasciitis with excisional debridement of subcutaneous tissue and fascia, right forearm ____________
7. Pathologic fracture T12 due to postmenopausal osteoporosis. Percutaneous kyphoplasty with synthetic substitute was performed ____________

CHAPTER REVIEW EXERCISE

Assign codes for all diagnoses and procedures.

1. Osteitis deformans of skull ____________
2. Wry neck ____________
3. Hallux valgus, left big toe ____________
4. Frozen right shoulder ____________
5. Plantar fasciitis ____________
6. Recurrent dislocation, right thumb ____________
7. Osteoporosis (sequela) due to previous long-term use of steroids ____________
8. Instability, left ankle ____________
9. Ganglion tendon sheath of the right wrist with open removal ____________
10. Tennis elbow, right ____________
11. Polymyalgia rheumatica ____________
12. Myositis ____________
13. Pain in both wrists ____________
14. Avascular necrosis (left femur) due to sickle cell (hemoglobin SS) disease ____________
15. Stiffness, left elbow ____________
16. History of right above the knee amputation (AKA) ____________
17. Housemaid's knee (right) ____________
18. Scleroderma with lung involvement ____________
19. Enteropathic arthropathy due to Crohn's disease ____________
20. Felty's syndrome, right hand ____________
21. Pyogenic arthritis, left knee, due to *Staphylococcus aureus* ____________

22. Osteoarthritis right shoulder treated with intra-articular steroid injection ______________
23. Paget's disease, left femur ______________
24. Chondromalacia, right patella ______________

Write the correct answer(s) in the blank(s) provided.

25. Explain the difference between radiculopathy and myelopathy.

____

26. Another name for osteoarthritis.

____

27. List 4 symptoms of SLE.
    1. ____
    2. ____
    3. ____
    4. ____
28. Which individuals are at risk for osteoporosis?

____

29. List 3 examples of aftercare for a pathologic fracture.
    1. ____
    2. ____
    3. ____

CHAPTER GLOSSARY

Anterior: front of the body or an organ.

Arthropathy: disease that affects the joints.

Arthroscopic: minimally invasive surgery that involves the use of highly specialized instruments to perform surgery through very small incisions on joints.

Bursitis: inflammation of a bursa, which is a tiny, fluid-filled sac that is found between muscles, tendons, and bones that reduces friction and facilitates movement.

Caudal: toward the tail.

Cranial: toward the head.

Distal: farther from the median plane; term is often used to describe a location in the limbs.

Dorsal: back of the body or an organ.

Dorsopathies: conditions or diseases that affect the back or spine.

Facet joints: small, stabilizing joints located between and behind adjacent vertebrae.

Fascia: tissue just below the skin that covers and separates the underlying layers of muscle.

Fibromyalgia: one of the most common diseases affecting the muscles; it is characterized by widespread muscle pain associated with chronic fatigue.

Hematopoiesis: development of blood cells that occurs in the bone marrow and lymphatic tissue of normal adults.

Inferior: position of the body or an organ relative to the vertical axis of the body.

Joints: means of joining two bones together.

Juvenile rheumatoid arthritis: type of arthritis that affects children, usually between the ages of 2 and 5 years.

Kyphoplasty: procedure performed to treat and stabilize fractures of the spine.

Kyphosis: excessive posterior curvature of the thoracic spine that may not be detected until a hump in the upper back is noticeable.

Lateral: position of a structure that is to the side of the body.

Ligaments: dense, fibrous bands of connective tissue that provide stability for the joint.

Lordosis: exaggerated inward curvature of the spine that may be caused by increased abdominal girth due to obesity, pregnancy, or abdominal tumor.

Medial: position of a structure closer to the median plane than is another structure in the body.

Myelopathy: compression of the spinal cord.

Necrotizing fasciitis (or "flesh-eating disease"): a rare but serious condition in which an infection occurs in the tissues below the skin.

Osteoarthritis: type of arthritis that develops as the result of wear and tear on the joints.

Osteomyelitis: infection of the bone that often starts in another part of the body and spreads to the bone via the blood.

Osteoporosis: metabolic bone disorder that results in decreased bone mass and density.

Pathologic fracture: break in a bone that occurs because of underlying disorders that weaken the bone, including malignancy, benign bone tumor, metabolic disorder, infection, and osteoporosis.

Percutaneous vertebroplasty: technique in which x-ray guidance is used to inject an acrylic cement through a needle into a collapsed or weakened vertebra; procedure is performed to treat pain caused by compression fractures of the vertebrae.

Polymyalgia rheumatica: syndrome classified as a rheumatic disease that is characterized by severe aching and stiffness in the neck, shoulder girdle, and pelvic girdle.

Posterior: back of the body or an organ.

Primary osteoarthritis: idiopathic degenerative condition that occurs in previously intact joints, with no apparent initiating factor.

Prone: lying on the stomach, face down.

Proximal: closer to the median plane.

Radiculopathy: compression of a nerve root.

Rheumatoid arthritis: chronic, inflammatory systemic disease that affects the joints, often causing deformity.

Scleroderma: chronic, progressive disease characterized by hardening of the skin and scarring of internal organs.

Scoliosis: deviation of the vertical line of the spine.

Secondary osteoarthritis: degenerative disease of the joints that results from some predisposing condition such as trauma or disease.

Spinal decompression: surgical procedure that frees space for the nerves in the spinal canal.

Spinal fusion: the creation of a solid bone bridge between two or more adjacent vertebrae to enhance stability between levels of the spine.

Spinal stenosis: narrowing of the central spinal canal or the areas of the spine where the nerve roots exit (neuroforamina).

Spondylolisthesis: condition in which one vertebra slips on another.

Spondylosis (or spinal osteoarthritis): degenerative disorder that may cause loss of normal spinal structure and function.

Superior: position of the body or an organ relative to the vertical axis of the body.

Supine: lying on the back, face up.

Systemic lupus erythematosus: chronic, inflammatory autoimmune disease that can damage connective tissue anywhere in the body.

Tendons: connective tissue that attaches muscle to bone.

Ventral: front of the body or an organ.

21

Diseases of the Genitourinary System

(ICD-10-CM Chapter 14, Codes N00-N99)

CHAPTER OUTLINE

LEARNING OBJECTIVES

1. Apply and assign the correct ICD-10-CM/PCS codes in accordance with Official Guidelines for Coding and Reporting
2. Identify pertinent anatomy and physiology of diseases of the genitourinary system
3. Identify diseases of the genitourinary system
4. Assign the correct Z codes and procedure codes related to the genitourinary system
5. Identify common treatments, medications, laboratory values, and diagnostic tests

ABBREVIATIONS/ ACRONYMS

ARF acute renal failure
ARI acute renal insufficiency
AV arteriovenous
BUN blood urea nitrogen
CAPD continuous ambulatory peritoneal dialysis
CC Complication/comorbity
CCPD continuous cycling peritoneal dialysis
CIN cervical intraepithelial neoplasia
CKD chronic kidney disease
CRF chronic renal failure
CRI chronic renal insufficiency
DIEP deep inferior epigastric perforator
ESRD end-stage renal disease
ESWL extracorporeal shock wave lithotripsy
FSG focal segmental glomerulosclerosis
GAP gluteal artery perforator
GFR glomerular filtration rate
GN glomerulonephritis
HSIL high-grade squamous intraepithelial lesion
ICD-10-CM *International Classification of Diseases, 10th Revision, Clinical Modification*
ICD-10-PCS *International Classification of Diseases, 10th Revision, Procedure Coding System*
Ig immunoglobulin
LAVH laparoscopically assisted vaginal hysterectomy
LDMF latissimus dorsi musculocutaneous flap
LSIL low-grade squamous intraepithelial lesion
LUTS lower urinary tract symptoms
MRSA methicillin-resistant *Staphylococcus aureus*
MSSA methicillin-sensitive *Staphylococcus aureus*
NKF National Kidney Foundation
NOS not otherwise specified
PID pelvic inflammatory disease
PSA prostate-specific antigen
RPGN rapidly progressive glomerulonephritis
SIEA superficial inferior epigastric artery
SIL squamous intraepithelial lesion
TRAM transverse rectus abdominis musculocutaneous
TULIP transurethral ultrasound-guided laser-induced prostatectomy
TUMT transurethral microwave thermotherapy
TUNA transurethral needle ablation of prostate
TURP transurethral resection of the prostate
UTI urinary tract infection
VIN vulvular intraepithelial neoplasia
VLAP visual laser ablation of the prostate
VUR vesicoureteral reflux

ICD-10-CM Official Guidelines for Coding and Reporting (2021-2022)

Please refer to the companion Evolve website for the most current 2021-2022 guidelines.

14. Chapter 14: Diseases of Genitourinary System (N00-N99)

a. Chronic kidney disease

1) Stages of chronic kidney disease (CKD)

The ICD-10-CM classifies CKD based on severity. The severity of CKD is designated by stages 1-5. Stage 2, code N18.2, equates to mild CKD; stage 3, codes N18.30-N18.32, equate to moderate CKD; and stage 4, code N18.4, equates to severe CKD. Code N18.6, End stage renal disease (ESRD), is assigned when the provider has documented end-stage-renal disease (ESRD).

If both a stage of CKD and ESRD are documented, assign code N18.6 only.

EXAMPLE

Patient was admitted to the hospital for fluid overload due to noncompliance with attending renal dialysis sessions. Patient has stage 5 CKD. Prolonged intermittent dialysis was performed, E87.70, N18.6, Z91.15, 5A1D80Z.

2) Chronic kidney disease and kidney transplant status

Patients who have undergone kidney transplant may still have some form of chronic kidney disease (CKD) because the kidney transplant may not fully restore kidney function. Therefore, the presence of CKD alone does not constitute a transplant complication. Assign the appropriate N18 code for the patient's stage of CKD and code Z94.0, Kidney transplant status. If a transplant complication such as failure or rejection or other transplant complication is documented, see section I.C.19.g for information on coding complications of a kidney transplant. If the documentation is unclear as to whether the patient has a complication of the transplant, query the provider.

EXAMPLE

Patient had a kidney transplant last year but still has mild CKD, stage 2, N18.2, Z94.0.

3) Chronic kidney disease with other conditions

Patients with CKD may also suffer from other serious conditions, most commonly diabetes mellitus and hypertension. The sequencing of the CKD code in relationship to codes for other contributing conditions is based on the conventions in the Tabular List.

See I.C.9. Hypertensive chronic kidney disease.

See I.C.19. Chronic kidney disease and kidney transplant complications.

EXAMPLE

Patient has chronic kidney disease due to hypertension, I12.9, N18.9.

ANATOMY AND PHYSIOLOGY

Urinary Tract

The kidneys, ureters, urinary bladder, and urethra form the urinary tract (Figure 21-1). Its main function involves producing, storing, and excreting urine. The kidneys and ureters make up the upper urinary tract, and the bladder and urethra constitute the lower urinary tract. The kidneys are two bean-shaped organs that are located on either side of the spine or retroperitoneally. The kidneys form a complex filtration system that cleanses the blood of waste products that become urine. Each kidney has a ureter that allows the urine to travel to the bladder for storage. The bladder is expandable, and openings into the ureters close so that urine cannot flow backward or reflux into the kidneys. The urine is excreted out of the body through a tube called the urethra. It is easy to confuse the terminology for urethra and ureter. Less than half of a single kidney is needed to do all the work that can be accomplished by two kidneys. The main difference between the male and female urinary tracts is the length of the urethra. The male urethra is 20 cm long; the female urethra measures only 3 cm.

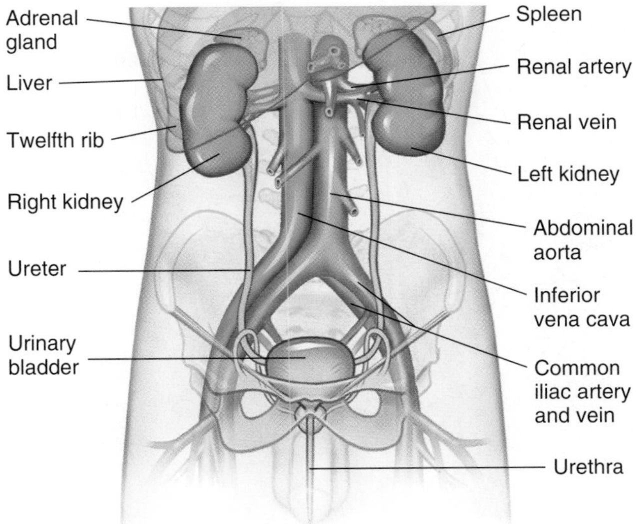

FIGURE 21-1. Gross anatomy of the urinary system (male).

Male Genital Tract

The main parts of the male genital or reproductive tract are the testes, epididymis, vas deferens, seminal vesicles, prostate, and penis (Figure 21-2). Its primary function is the production of sperm. The main diseases related to the male genital tract are infertility, infection, and tumor.

Female Genital Tract

The main parts of the female genital or reproductive tract are the vulva, vagina, uterus, fallopian tubes, and ovaries (Figure 21-3). Reproduction is its primary function. The main diseases and conditions of the female genital tract are related to infection, tumor, hormonal disorders, and pregnancy.

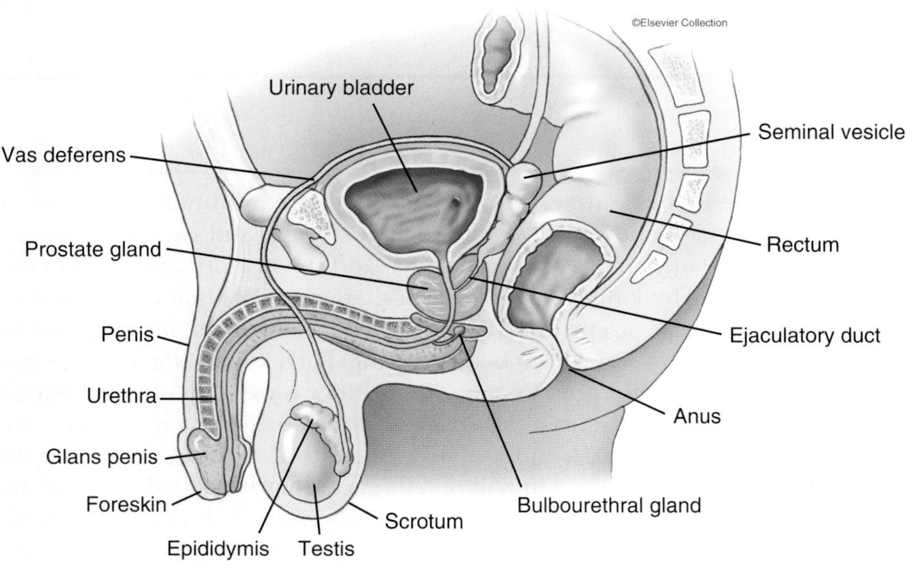

FIGURE 21-2. Normal male reproductive system.

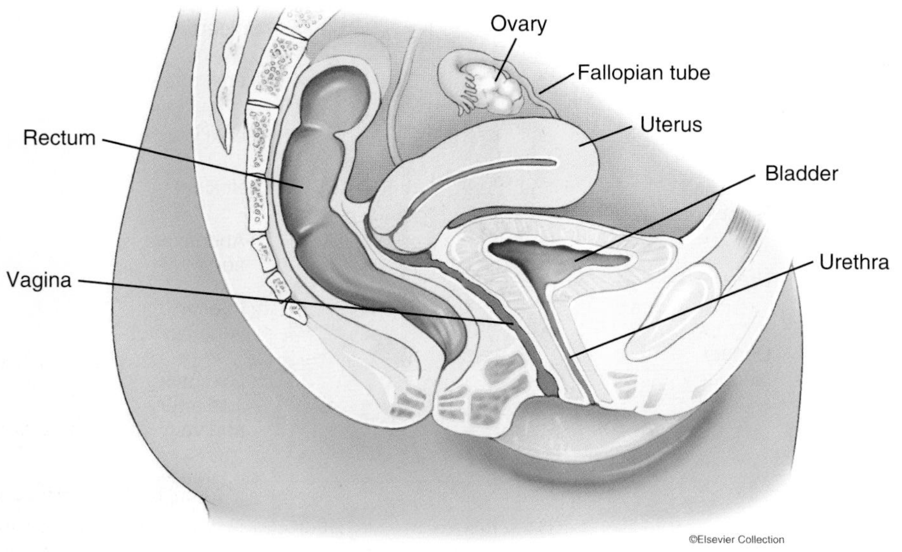

FIGURE 21-3. Normal female reproductive system.

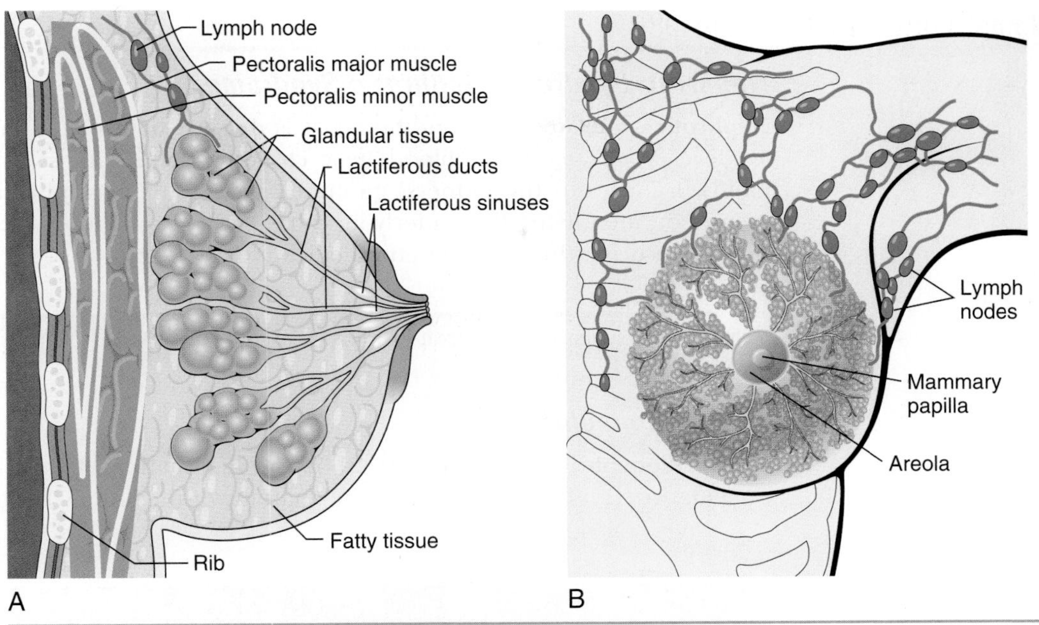

FIGURE 21-4. Views of the breast. **A,** Sagittal. **B,** Frontal. Notice the numerous lymph nodes.

Breast

Male and female breasts are similar in that they are formed embryologically from the same tissues. It is possible for males to have breast disorders also. The female breast (Figure 21-4) will start to develop during puberty due to the hormone estrogen. Female breasts are considered an accessory organ of reproduction and are composed of fat and fibrous tissue with mammary glands for the production of milk (**lactation**).

DISEASE CONDITIONS

Diseases of the Genitourinary System, Chapter 14 in the ICD-10-CM code book, are divided into the following categories:

CATEGORY	SECTION TITLES
N00-N08	Glomerular diseases
N10-N16	Renal tubulo-interstitial diseases
N17-N19	Acute renal failure and chronic kidney disease
N20-N23	Urolithiasis
N25-N29	Other disorders of the kidney and ureter
N30-N39	Other diseases of the urinary system
N40-N53	Diseases of male genital organs
N60-N65	Disorders of the breast
N70-N77	Inflammatory diseases of female pelvic organs
N80-N98	Noninflammatory disorders of the female genital tract
N99	Intraoperative and postprocedural complications and disorders of genitourinary system, not elsewhere classified

It is important to note that disorders of the breast are classified as Diseases of the Genitourinary System in ICD-10-CM.

Genitourinary diseases that are due to communicable infections may be classified in Chapter 1, Certain Infectious and Parasitic Diseases. Also, any genitourinary conditions that occur during pregnancy, childbirth, and the puerperium will be coded in accordance with the Obstetrical guidelines.

Glomerular Diseases (N00-N08)

Nephritic Syndrome/Nephrotic Syndrome

Nephrotic syndrome is a condition that is marked by **proteinuria** (protein in the urine), low levels of protein in the blood, hypercholesterolemia, and swelling of the eyes, feet, and hands. Damage to the kidneys' glomeruli can result in nephrotic syndrome. Treatment focuses on identifying the underlying cause and reducing cholesterol, blood pressure, and protein in urine through diet and medications.

EXAMPLE Acute nephritic syndrome with extracapillary glomerulonephritis, N00.7.

Glomerulonephritis

Glomerulonephritis (GN) (Figure 21-5) is inflammation of the glomeruli of the kidneys. (See Figure 21-6 for illustration of the anatomy of the kidney.) Glomerulonephritis can be

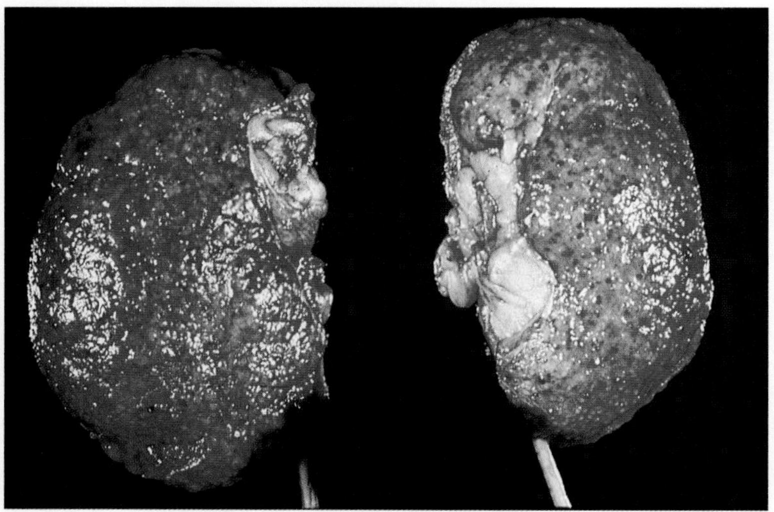

FIGURE 21-5. End-stage glomerulopathy–chronic glomerulonephritis.

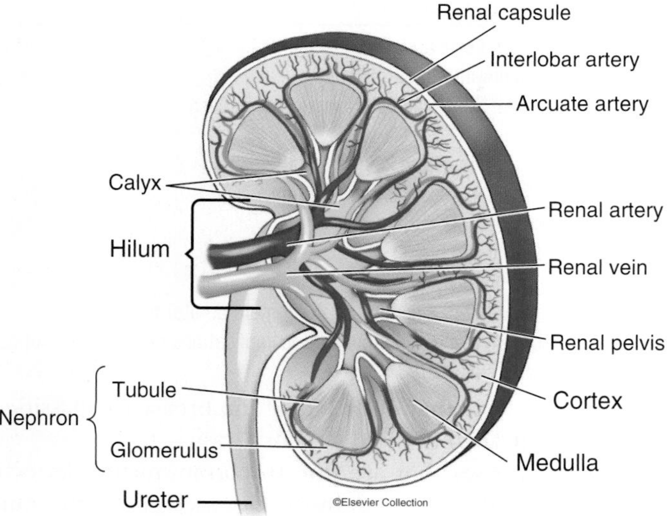

FIGURE 21-6. Anatomy of the kidney.

a temporary, reversible condition, or it may be a chronic progressive condition that results in chronic renal failure and end-stage renal disease. GN may cause hypertension and may not be discovered until the hypertension becomes difficult to control. Specific disorders that are associated with glomerulonephritis include the following:

- Focal segmental glomerulosclerosis (FSG)
- Goodpasture's syndrome
- Immunoglobulin (Ig)A nephropathy (Berger's disease)
- IgM mesangial proliferative glomerulonephritis
- Lupus nephritis
- Membranoproliferative glomerulonephritis I
- Membranoproliferative glomerulonephritis II
- Poststreptococcal glomerulonephritis
- Rapidly progressive (crescentic) glomerulonephritis
- Rapidly progressive glomerulonephritis (RPGN)

EXAMPLE Minimal change glomerulonephritis, N05.0.

EXAMPLE RPGN, N01.9.

EXERCISE 21-1

Assign codes to the following conditions.

1. Nephrotic syndrome __________
2. Nephritis due to systemic lupus erythematosus __________
3. Focal segmental glomerulonephritis __________

Renal Tubulo-Interstitial Diseases (N10-N16)

Renal tubulo-interstitial diseases involve the structures in the kidney outside the glomerulus. These conditions generally affect the tubules and/or the interstitium of the kidney and not the glomeruli. Some of the more common conditions in this section include acute pyelonephritis, hydronephrosis, and vesicoureteral reflux.

Pyelonephritis involves the kidneys and is an upper urinary tract infection. The most common cause is due to organisms from the intestinal tract (E. coli and *Enterococcus faecalis*) entering the urinary tract. It may initially start out as a lower urinary tract infection such as cystitis or prostatitis. Common symptoms include:

- Dysuria
- Flank pain
- Costovertebral angle tenderness

Chronic, recurrent infections can result in damage and scarring of the kidneys (Figure 21-7). In patients with recurrent infections, it may be necessary to do further testing to determine if there are some structural abnormalities such as vesicoureteral reflux, polycystic disease, or some other cause.

EXAMPLE Patient was seen in the ER with flank pain and dysuria. Patient was given antibiotics for acute pyelonephritis, N10.

Vesicoureteral reflux (VUR) is an abnormality in the flow of urine from the bladder into the ureters and/or kidneys. The normal flow is from the kidneys through the ureter into the bladder. In VUR the urine flows backwards. Damage to the kidney(s) may occur depending of the severity of the reflux and other complications such as recurrent urinary tract infections.

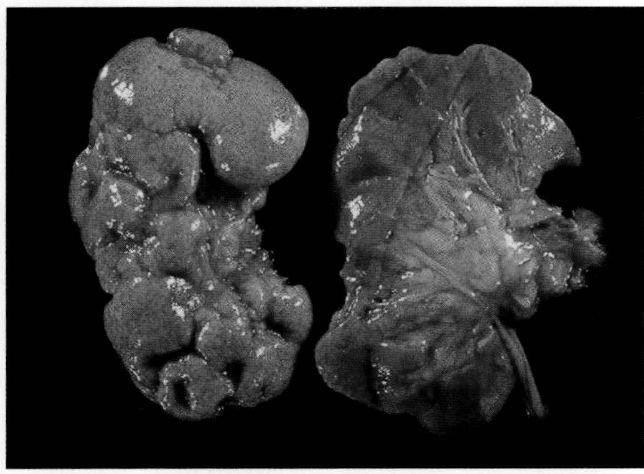

FIGURE 21-7. Gross appearance of an inflamed, small-sized kidney with irregular surface due to scarring resulting from recurrent or chronic pyelonephritis.

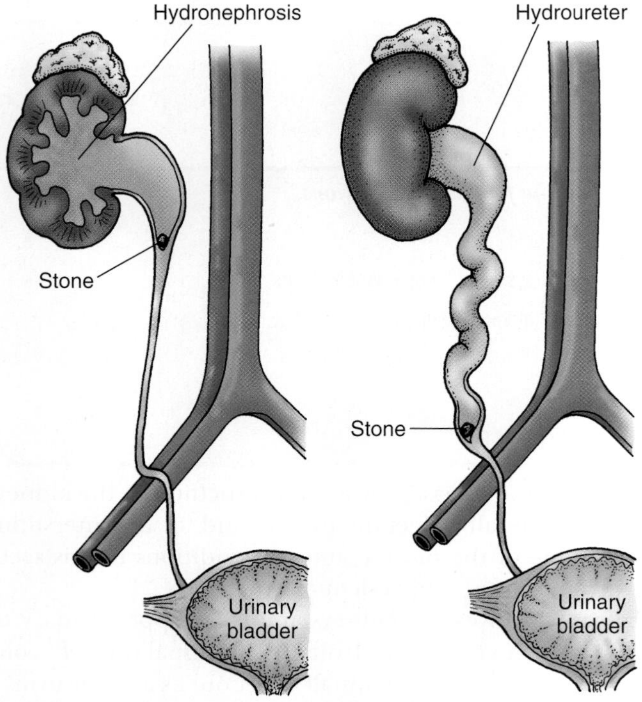

FIGURE 21-8. Hydronephrosis caused by a stone (obstruction) in the proximal part of the ureter and hydroureter with hydronephrosis caused by a stone in the distal part of the ureter.

EXAMPLE Patient is being followed by a urologist for VUR with nephropathy of the right kidney, N13.721.

Hydronephrosis is abnormal dilatation of the renal pelvis that is caused by pressure from urine that cannot flow past an obstruction in the urinary tract (Figure 21-8). **Hydroureter** is the accumulation of urine in the ureters. These conditions may be documented in x-ray reports, ultrasound, or other diagnostic tests, but they must be documented by a physician before code assignment. Obstruction can result from a stone, tumor, infection, prostatic hypertrophy, or congenital abnormalities.

EXAMPLE Hydronephrosis due to ureterolithiasis, N13.2.

EXERCISE 21-2

Assign codes to the following conditions.

1. Acute and chronic pyelonephritis due to *Pseudomonas* ______________
2. Hydronephrosis due to kinking of ureter ______________
3. Bilateral VUR with hydroureter ______________
4. Obstructive uropathy ______________

Acute Renal Failure and Chronic Kidney Disease (N17-N19) and Urolithiasis (N20-N23)

Acute Renal Failure

Acute renal failure (ARF) is sudden and severe impairment in renal function characterized by oliguria, increased serum urea, and acidosis. With treatment, ARF is usually reversible. ARF often occurs in hospitalized patients with serious systemic illness such as infection, low blood pressure, shock, and as an adverse effect of the use of certain antibiotics and drugs. Obstruction of the urinary tract and dehydration may also cause ARF. It is possible for a patient with chronic renal failure or chronic kidney disease to also develop ARF. In this case, codes are assigned for both the acute and chronic renal failure.

Physicians will sometimes use the term *acute kidney injury*. Usually this is not due to a traumatic event and is due to a nontraumatic injury, which codes to the same code as acute kidney failure N17.9.

Also physicians may use the terms *insufficiency* and *failure* or *injury* interchangeably. In ICD-10-CM, there are different codes for acute renal insufficiency and acute renal failure/injury. It may be necessary to query the physician for clarification of the correct diagnosis. The abbreviation AKI is also frequently used by physicians, so it may be necessary to query if the physician means acute kidney injury or acute kidney insufficiency.

EXAMPLE

Patient is admitted with an exacerbation of congestive heart failure. The patient is also in acute renal failure. This physician documents that the ARF is due to the patient's fluid overload, I50.9, N17.9.

When a patient is admitted to the hospital with acute renal failure and dehydration, according to *Coding Clinic for ICD-9-CM* (2002:3Q:p21-22),[1] ARF is the principal diagnosis, and the dehydration is a secondary diagnosis. Patients with both conditions are generally treated with IV fluids, and ARF is more serious than dehydration. A patient who is dehydrated and has no impairment in renal function may be given IV fluids and sent home instead of being admitted to the hospital.

EXAMPLE

Acute renal failure due to dehydration, N17.9, E86.0.

Another example in *Coding Clinic for ICD-9-CM (2002:3Q:p28)* is acute renal failure due to rhabdomyolysis in which the acute renal failure is the more significant problem and was responsible for the admission, so the acute renal failure should be sequenced as the principal diagnosis.

Chronic Kidney Disease (CKD)

Codes for chronic kidney disease (CKD) identify the various stages of CKD that were developed by the National Kidney Foundation (NKF) (Table 21-1). In the past, CKD has been documented with imprecise terms such as chronic kidney failure (CRF) and chronic renal insufficiency (CRI).

TABLE 21-1 FIVE STAGES OF CHRONIC KIDNEY DISEASE

Stage	Description	Glomerular Filtration Rate (GFR)
At increased risk	Risk factors for kidney disease (e.g., diabetes, high blood pressure, family history, older age, ethnic group)	Higher than 90
1	Kidney damage (protein in the urine) and normal GFR	Higher than 90
2	Kidney damage and mild decrease in GFR	60-89
3	Moderate decrease in GFR	30-59
4	Severe decrease in GFR	15-29
5	Kidney failure (dialysis or kidney transplant needed)	Less than 15

Data from the National Kidney Foundation.

Using these NKF guidelines, levels of kidney damage and kidney function must be determined to accurately assign the code for CKD. A patient's glomerular filtration rate (GFR) indicates the level of kidney function and indicates the stage of the disease, which may progress slowly over many years. Early detection through laboratory tests and proper treatment can limit the effects of CKD, if the disease is discovered in the early stages.

If CKD is left untreated, a patient will develop end-stage renal disease (ESRD). This condition is characterized by the near or complete failure of kidney function, which leaves the patient unable to process waste material. Dialysis or transplantation may be needed to treat the condition.

CKD can develop from ARF if renal function is not restored through dialysis or treatment. This may take several weeks or months. Documentation in the health record that might indicate the presence of renal failure could include the following:

1. Markedly elevated values of serum creatinine or blood urea nitrogen (BUN), or diminished creatinine clearance
2. Other clinical and laboratory manifestations of renal impairment are as follows:
   - Anemia
   - Hyperphosphatemia
   - Hypocalcemia
   - Hyperkalemia
   - Renal osteodystrophy
   - Uremic symptoms: nausea, vomiting, itching, hemorrhagic conditions, hypertension, edema, dyspnea, lethargy, coma, etc.

EXAMPLE Hyperkalemia due to chronic kidney disease (CKD), E87.5, N18.9.

Hypertension and Chronic Kidney Disease

ICD-10-CM presumes a cause-and-effect relationship with hypertension and chronic kidney disease. This is addressed in the coding guidelines. Code N18.– has instructions to code first hypertensive chronic kidney disease, if applicable. If the provider has specifically documented a different cause for the CKD, then the CKD should not be coded as hypertensive. Hypertension and hypertensive manifestations are discussed more extensively in Chapter 16, Diseases of the Circulatory System.

EXAMPLE Patient has chronic kidney disease, stage 3, and benign hypertension, I12.9, N18.30.

Urolithiasis

Calculi or stones (Figure 21-9) may develop anywhere in the urinary tract and can vary in size. "**Urolithiasis**" describes a stone in the urinary tract. The terms "**nephrolithiasis**" and "**ureterolithiasis**" provide greater specificity with regard to location of the stone. Patients

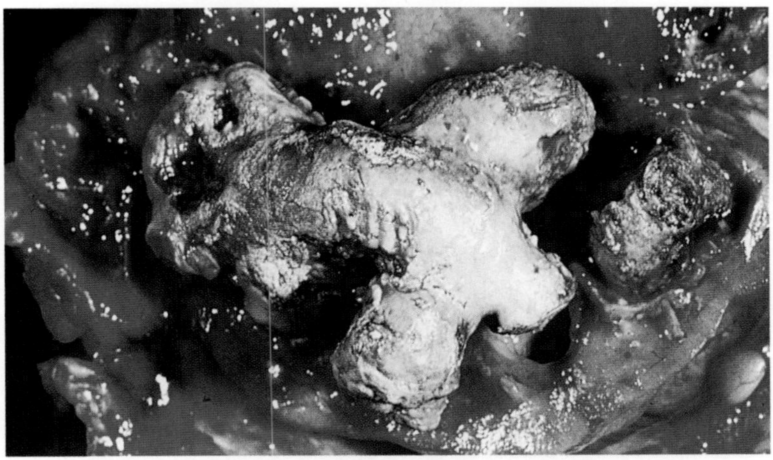

FIGURE 21-9. Irregularly shaped struvite stone in the renal pelvis.

with stones are often asymptomatic unless they result in infection or start to move and obstruct the flow of urine. Obstructions due to stones are very painful and may result in admission to the hospital for pain control, identification, and treatment of the stone. Procedures such as extracorporeal shock wave lithotripsy (ESWL) and laser lithotripsy can be used to break up larger stones. "**Renal colic**" describes the intense pain associated with the body's efforts to try to force the stone through the ureters. Renal colic is not coded separately from a renal or ureteral calculus. Pain or renal colic is integral to the presence of urinary tract calculus.

EXAMPLE

Hematuria due to renal stone, N20.0.

EXERCISE 21-3

Assign codes to the following conditions.

1. Acute on chronic renal failure ____________
2. Essential hypertension; stage 4 CKD ____________
3. Flank pain due to ureteral stone ____________

Other Disorders of the Kidney and Ureter (N25-N29) and Other Diseases of the Urinary System (N30-N39)

Urinary Tract Infections

Urinary tract infection (UTI) is a general term that is used to describe infection of any area of the urinary tract. **Cystitis** is a lower tract infection that affects the bladder (Figure 21-10), and **urethritis** affects the urethra. An upper tract infection that involves the kidneys is called pyelonephritis.

The term "urinary tract infection" is commonly used when referring to cystitis, urethritis, or pyelonephritis. UTIs are assigned codes based on the site of infection, if known, although it is not always possible to distinguish between the three conditions on clinical grounds alone. Only the code for cystitis should be assigned when the physician indicates the bladder as the infection site. Additional sites may be coded if the infection has spread. However, if the documentation includes both UTI and cystitis as diagnoses, only N30.90

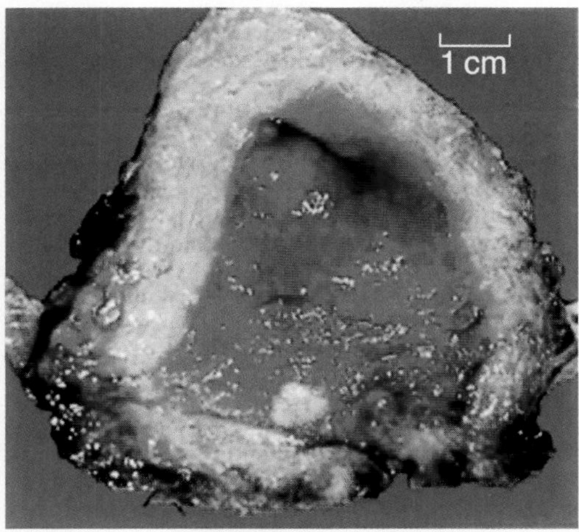

FIGURE 21-10. Acute cystitis. The mucosa of the bladder is red and swollen.

should be used. If the site of the UTI is not documented or identified, code N39.0, urinary tract infection, NOS, should be assigned; this code can ONLY be used if the site is not identified and not in combination with any other codes where the site is identified.

EXAMPLE

Urinary tract infection due to acute pyelonephritis, N10.

The code N39.0 is not assigned because the site of infection has been identified as the kidneys. No bacteria have been identified, so no organism code is assigned.

Most UTIs are due to bacteria. Urinalysis (Table 21-2) and culture and sensitivity tests may be performed to identify the causative organism and to determine which drugs are more effective in treating the infection. Less common are infections caused by viruses, fungi, or parasites. Infections that are due to sexually transmitted disease such as chlamydia or candidiasis are discussed in the infectious and parasitic disease chapter. An instructional note is provided about the use of an additional code to identify the organism as well as the code for the urinary tract infection (Figure 21-11). The following are the most common organisms responsible for UTIs:

- *Escherichia coli (E. coli)*
- *Proteus (mirabilis) (morganii)*
- Methicillin-susceptible *Staphylococcus aureus* (MSSA)
- Methicillin-resistant *Staphylococcus aureus* (MRSA)
- *Staphylococcus saprophyticus*
- Group B *Streptococcus*
- *Klebsiella pneumoniae*

If a causative organism or infectious agent is documented by the physician, this should be coded, in addition to the infection. It would not be appropriate to code an organism on the basis of a urine culture or sensitivity report only. Sometimes the documentation will indicate that the urine grew gram negative bacteria, awaiting sensitivity report. The next progress note will indicate that the urine culture is positive for *Escherichia coli (E. coli)*. The *E. coli* is the gram negative bacteria that was identified and the only code necessary to show the causative organism is B96.2- for the *E. coli*. It would be incorrect to also assign B96.89, other gram negative organisms.

EXAMPLE

Urinary tract infection due to *E. coli*, N39.0, B96.20.

TABLE 21-2 **ROUTINE URINALYSIS*[2]**

	Normal	Abnormal	Pathology
Characteristics			
Color and clarity	Pale to darker yellow, and clear	Very pale	Excessive water
		Cloudy, milky white blood cells	Pus, urinary tract infection
		Hematuria, red blood cells, reddish to reddish brown	Bleeding in infection, calculi, or cancer
Odor	Aromatic	Fishy	Cystitis
		Fruity	Diabetes mellitus
		Foul	Urinary tract infection
Chemical nature	pH is generally slightly acidic, 6.5	Alkaline	Infections cause ammonia to form
Specific gravity	1.003-1.030—reflects quantity of waste, minerals, and solids in urine	Higher—causes precipitation of solutes Lower—polyuria	Kidney stones, diabetes mellitus, diabetes insipidus
Constituent Compounds			
Protein	None, or small	Albuminuria	Nephritis, renal failure, amount infection
Glucose	None	Glycosuria	Faulty carbohydrate metabolism, as in diabetes mellitus
Ketone bodies	None	Ketonuria	Diabetic acidosis
Bile and bilirubin	None	Bilirubinuria	Hepatic or gallbladder disease
Casts	None—or small number of hyaline casts	Urinary casts composed of red or white blood cells, fat, or pus	Nephritis, renal disease, inflammation, metal poisoning
Nitrogenous wastes	Ammonia, creatinine, urea, and uric acid	Azoturia, creatinine, and urea clearance tests disproportionate to normal BUN/creatinine ratio	Hepatic disease, renal disease
Crystals	None to trace	Acidic urine, alkaline urine, hypercalcemia, metabolism error	Not significant unless the crystals are large (stones); certain types are interpreted by physician
Fat droplets	None	Lipoiduria	Nephrosis

BUN, Blood urea nitrogen.
*Routine urinalysis is the physical, chemical, and microscopic examination of urine for abnormal elements; this may help the clinician to estimate renal function and may provide clues of systemic disease. This table includes some important characteristics and elements that are screened for in basic urinalysis. Other normal constituents of urine that are studied routinely for diagnosis include calcium, potassium, sodium, phosphorus, creatinine, and volume in a 24-hour period.

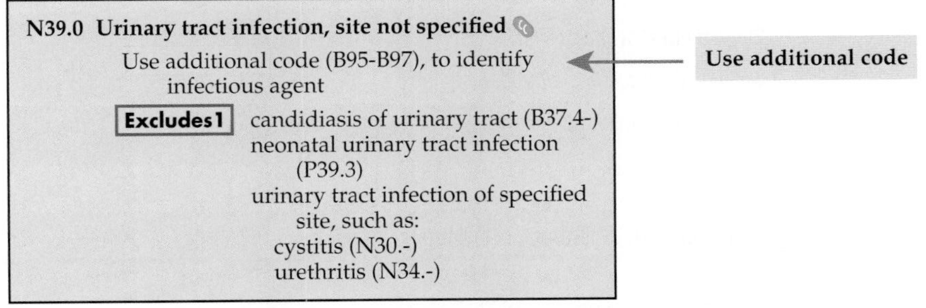

FIGURE 21-11. Instruction is given to use an additional code to identify the organism or infectious agent.

EXAMPLE

Acute cystitis due to *Proteus mirabilis,* N30.00, B96.4.

Some patients are plagued by recurrent and/or chronic UTIs. For this reason, they are sometimes treated with a daily dose of antibiotic to prevent an infection or for prophylactic measures. This should be coded as Z79.2, long-term (current) use of antibiotic, and Z87.41 to identify the personal history of urinary tract infection. It would be inappropriate to assign a code for an infection that is not a current condition.

The term "urosepsis" can cause confusion. Some physicians use the term "urosepsis" to mean an infection of the urinary tract without systemic infection. Other physicians may document urosepsis and mean that the patient has a UTI that has progressed to sepsis. In the Alphabetic Index of ICD-10-CM the term "urosepsis" does not have a code listed but does have an instruction to code to the condition. A physician query may be necessary to determine what that condition is.

EXAMPLE Urosepsis in patient with UTI due to *Proteus mirabilis,* N39.0. B96.4; ICD-10-CM Alphabetic Index entry for urosepsis instructs to code to condition. According to the guidelines, the physician should be queried.

EXAMPLE Sepsis due to *Staphylococcus aureus* with urinary tract infection as the source, A41.01, N39.0.

Urinary Incontinence

Urinary incontinence can be a significant health problem that interferes with a patient's activities of daily living. This problem is more common among women because of specific features of their anatomy and as the result of childbearing. Incontinence often occurs after radical prostatectomy but usually resolves in time.

Types of incontinence include stress, urge, mixed, and overflow incontinence. **Stress incontinence** is the involuntary loss of small amounts of urine due to increased pressure from coughing, sneezing, or laughing. **Urge incontinence** is the sudden and involuntary loss of large amounts of urine. **Mixed incontinence** is a combination of stress and urge incontinence. **Overflow incontinence** is the constant dribbling of urine. Treatments include diet, Kegel exercises, biofeedback, and bladder training.

Functional urinary incontinence is when a physical or mental condition prevents someone from making it to the bathroom in time. For example, if the patient has severe arthritis, they may not be able to get to the bathroom in time or have trouble removing their pants quickly enough.

EXAMPLE Neurogenic bladder with stress incontinence, N31.9, N39.3.

EXERCISE 21-4

Assign codes to the following conditions.

1. Neurogenic bladder ____________
2. Stricture of the urethra ____________
3. UTI due to *Klebsiella pneumoniae* ____________
4. Overflow incontinence associated with overactive bladder ____________

Diseases of the Male Genital Organs (N40-N53)

Prostate

The most common diseases of the male genitourinary tract are those that affect the prostate. The prostate gland can become inflamed or enlarged, causing urinary problems. The prostate surrounds the urethra, through which urine flows. The flow of urine can be obstructed by the prostate. **Benign prostatic hyperplasia** and **benign prostatic hypertrophy** are conditions that result in enlargement of the prostate gland; these conditions usually occur in men who are older than 50 years of age (Figure 21-12). Symptoms may include frequency, nocturia, difficulty starting urination, a weak stream of urine, and inability to completely empty the bladder. Within the N40.1 code category there are special instructions for coding lower urinary tract symptoms (LUTS) (Figure 21-13). This corresponds with the general coding guideline that signs and symptoms that are integral to the disease process should not be assigned as additional codes, *unless otherwise instructed by the classification.*

Prostatitis or inflammation of the prostate may be acute and/or chronic in nature and may be due to bacteria or to inflammation that is not caused by a bacterial infection.

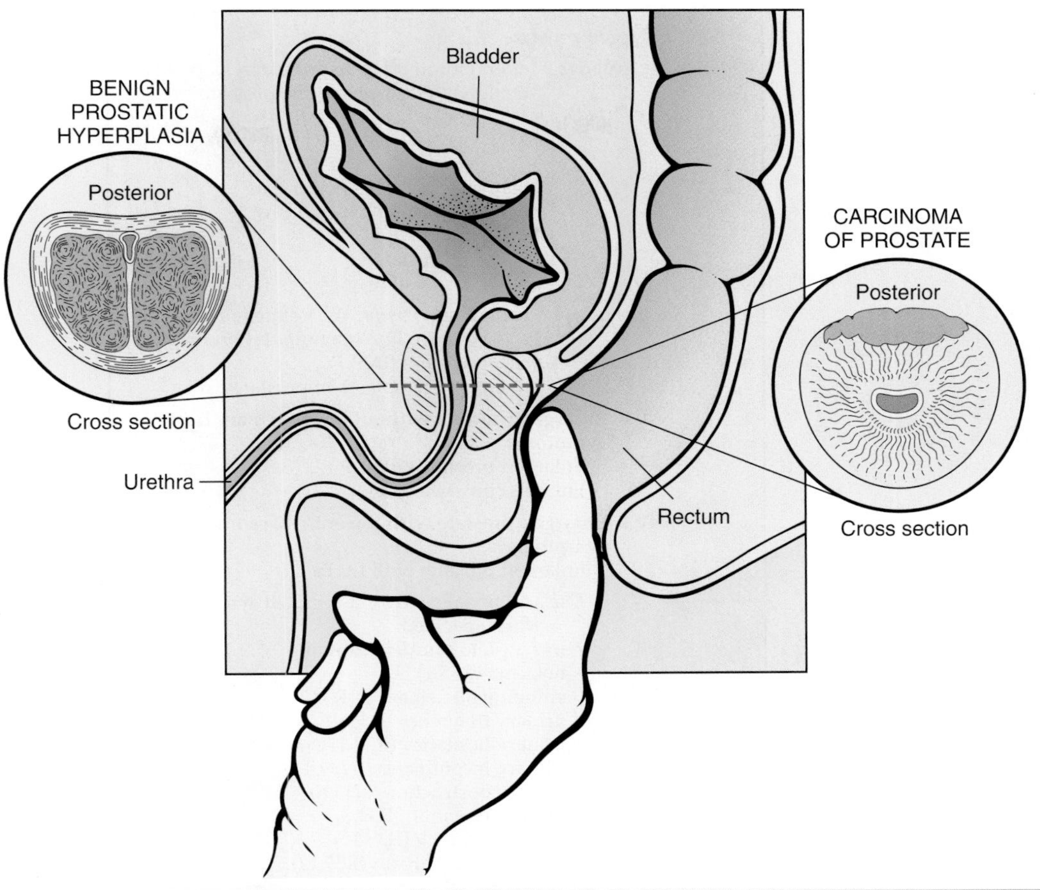

FIGURE 21-12. Digital prostate or rectal examination to identify prostatic abnormalities.

Bacterial infections can be easily treated with antibiotics. Nonbacterial prostatitis involves treatment of urinary symptoms, which may be ongoing. There is an instructional note to use an additional code to identify the infectious agent. Use the Index and the Tabular to verify the accuracy of organism codes as referenced in the Tabular instructional note.

EXAMPLE

Chronic prostatitis due to staphylococcus N41.1, B95.8.

Prostate-specific antigen (PSA) is a protein produced by the prostate gland. A blood test to measure PSA is a means of screening for prostate cancer. The risk of cancer is based on the following:

- PSA levels under 4 ng/mL: "normal"
- 4 to 10 ng/mL: 20% to 30% risk
- 10 to 20 ng/mL: 50% to 75% risk
- Above 20 ng/mL: 90%

Elevated levels do not always indicate cancer but may be elevated due to other prostate problems such as BPH or prostatitis.

EXAMPLE

Patient was seen in the clinic for an elevated PSA. It was determined that the patient's severe benign prostatic hypertrophy was the cause, N40.0.

EXAMPLE

Patient was referred to a urologist for elevated PSA, R97.20.

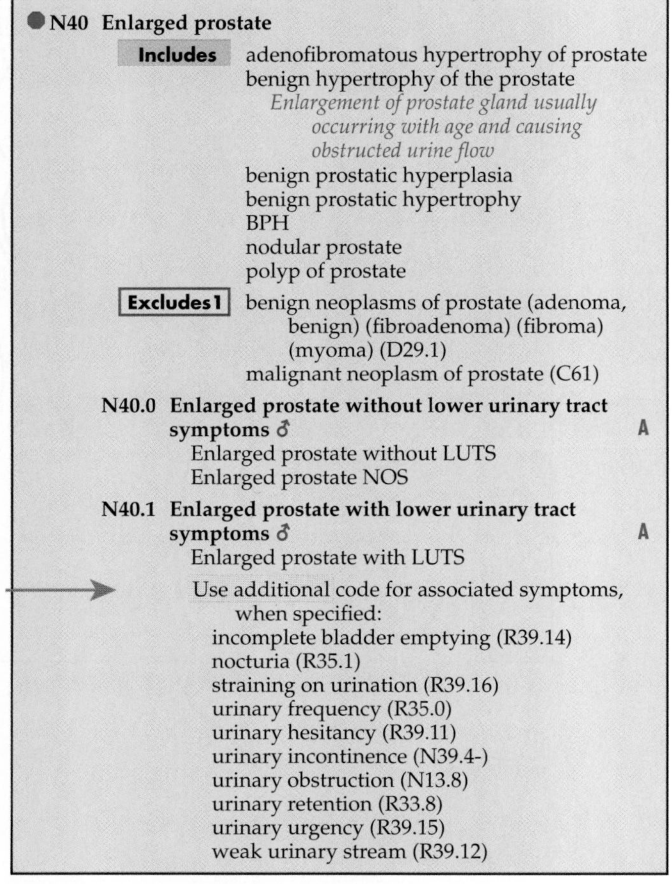

● **N40 Enlarged prostate**

Includes adenofibromatous hypertrophy of prostate
benign hypertrophy of the prostate
Enlargement of prostate gland usually occurring with age and causing obstructed urine flow
benign prostatic hyperplasia
benign prostatic hypertrophy
BPH
nodular prostate
polyp of prostate

Excludes1 benign neoplasms of prostate (adenoma, benign) (fibroadenoma) (fibroma) (myoma) (D29.1)
malignant neoplasm of prostate (C61)

N40.0 Enlarged prostate without lower urinary tract symptoms ♂ A
Enlarged prostate without LUTS
Enlarged prostate NOS

N40.1 Enlarged prostate with lower urinary tract symptoms ♂ A
Enlarged prostate with LUTS
Use additional code for associated symptoms, when specified:
incomplete bladder emptying (R39.14)
nocturia (R35.1)
straining on urination (R39.16)
urinary frequency (R35.0)
urinary hesitancy (R39.11)
urinary incontinence (N39.4-)
urinary obstruction (N13.8)
urinary retention (R33.8)
urinary urgency (R39.15)
weak urinary stream (R39.12)

FIGURE 21-13. Instructions to use additional code(s) for lower urinary tract symptoms (LUTS).

EXERCISE 21-5

Assign codes to the following conditions.

1. Nocturia due to benign prostatic hypertrophy ______________
2. Acute prostatitis due to *Escherichia coli* ______________
3. Scrotal pain and swelling due to epididymitis ______________
4. Hydrocele (male) ______________
5. Phimosis ______________

Disorders of Breast (N60-N65)

Breast

Conditions of the breast in a pregnant woman are coded in the obstetrical chapter, or Chapter 15, of the ICD-10-CM code book. Male patients can also have conditions that are classified to the breast. **Mastitis** is inflammation or infection of the breast (Figure 21-14). Swelling, redness, tenderness, and pain may be noted. A breast abscess may form if mastitis is not treated. An abscess may require incision and drainage.

Some patients undergo prophylactic breast removal because they have a strong family history of breast cancer and/or genetic susceptibility or a personal history of breast cancer. After breast reconstruction is performed, complications such as infection, pain, and malfunction or failure of the implant or tissue expander, may occur.

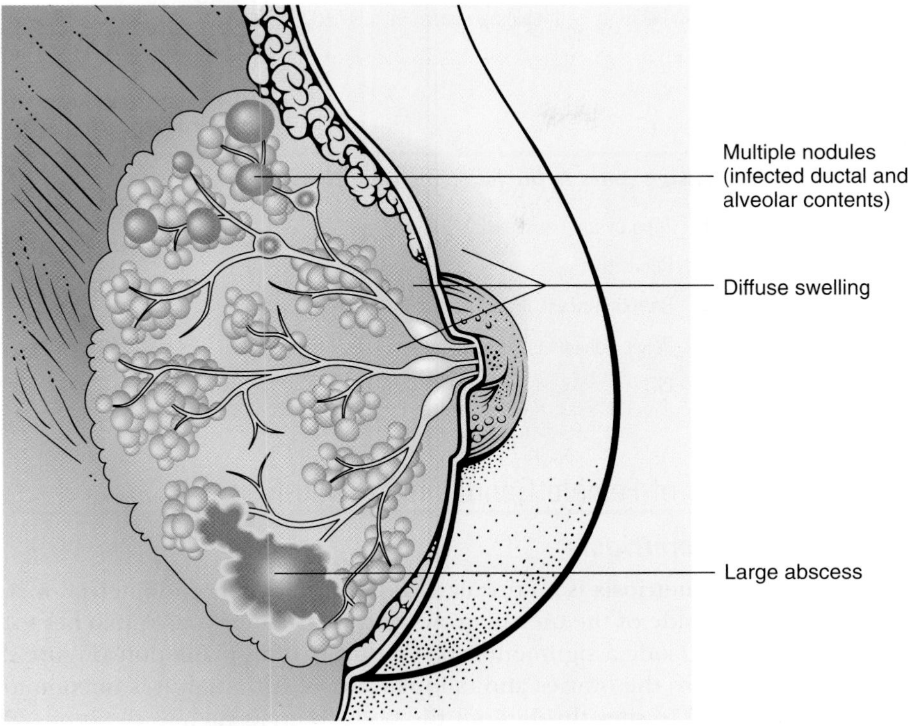

FIGURE 21-14. Acute mastitis typically occurs during lactation.

EXAMPLE

Patient has diffuse fibroadenosis of both breasts, N60.21, N60.22.

EXERCISE 21-6

Assign codes to the following conditions.

1. Fibrocystic disease of breast, bilateral ______
2. Nipple discharge, right breast ______
3. Male patient with gynecomastia ______
4. Mastodynia ______

Inflammatory Diseases of Female Pelvic Organs (N70-N77)

Pelvic Inflammatory Disease

Pelvic inflammatory disease (PID) occurs when vaginal or cervical infection spreads and involves the uterus, fallopian tubes, ovaries, and surrounding tissues. **Salpingitis** is inflammation of the fallopian tubes, which are the most common sites of pelvic inflammation. **Endometritis** is inflammation of the uterus, and **oophoritis** is inflammation of the ovaries. The most prevalent symptoms of these infections include vaginal discharge, pain, and possibly a fever. Complications that may result include infertility, chronic pain, tubal pregnancy, recurrent inflammation, and abscess.

EXAMPLE

Acute and chronic right salpingo-oophoritis, N70.03, N70.13.

EXERCISE 21-7

Assign codes to the following conditions.

1. Tubo-ovarian abscess __________
2. Cervicitis __________
3. Bartholin's cyst __________
4. Pelvic adhesions, female __________
5. PID __________

Noninflammatory Disorders of Female Genital Tract (N80-N98)

Endometriosis

Endometriosis is a chronic condition in which endometrial material, the tissue that lines the inside of the uterus, grows outside the uterus and attaches to other organs in the pelvic cavity. Code assignment is based on site of implantation (Figure 21-15). The most common sites are the ovaries and fallopian tubes. Although it is uncommon, endometrial tissue can spread to sites throughout the body to areas such as the lungs. Pain and infertility are the two most common symptoms.

EXAMPLE

Endometriosis of the uterus, N80.0.

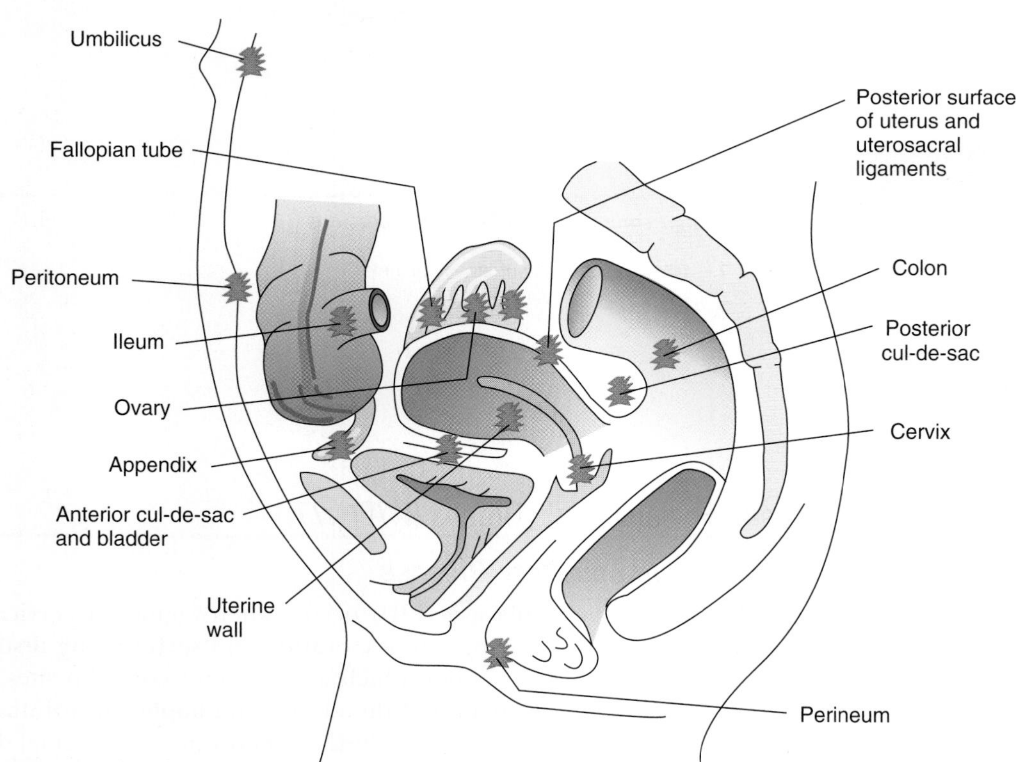

FIGURE 21-15. Possible sites for endometriosis implantation.

Genital Prolapse

Genital prolapse occurs when pelvic organs such as the uterus, bladder, and rectum shift from their normal anatomic positions and protrude into the vagina or press against the wall of the vagina (Figure 21-16). Weakening or damage to the ligaments, muscles, and connective tissues that support these organs is the cause of genital prolapse. It occurs commonly in postmenopausal women who have had children. Other contributing factors include genetics, pelvic surgery, and pressures within the abdomen that would weaken the pelvic floor. Different types of prolapse are usually graded on the basis of severity. **Uterine prolapse** is the descent of the uterus and cervix into the vaginal canal. **Cystocele** occurs when the bladder descends and presses into the wall of the vagina. **Urethrocele** results when the urethra presses into the vagina; it usually is reported in conjunction with a cystocele, which is then called a **cystourethrocele**. **Rectocele** is the descent of the rectum and pressing of the rectum against the vaginal wall. **Vaginal vault prolapse** may occur after a hysterectomy has been performed, when the top of the vagina descends into the vault.

EXAMPLE Examination of the patient showed a second degree uterine prolapse, N81.2.

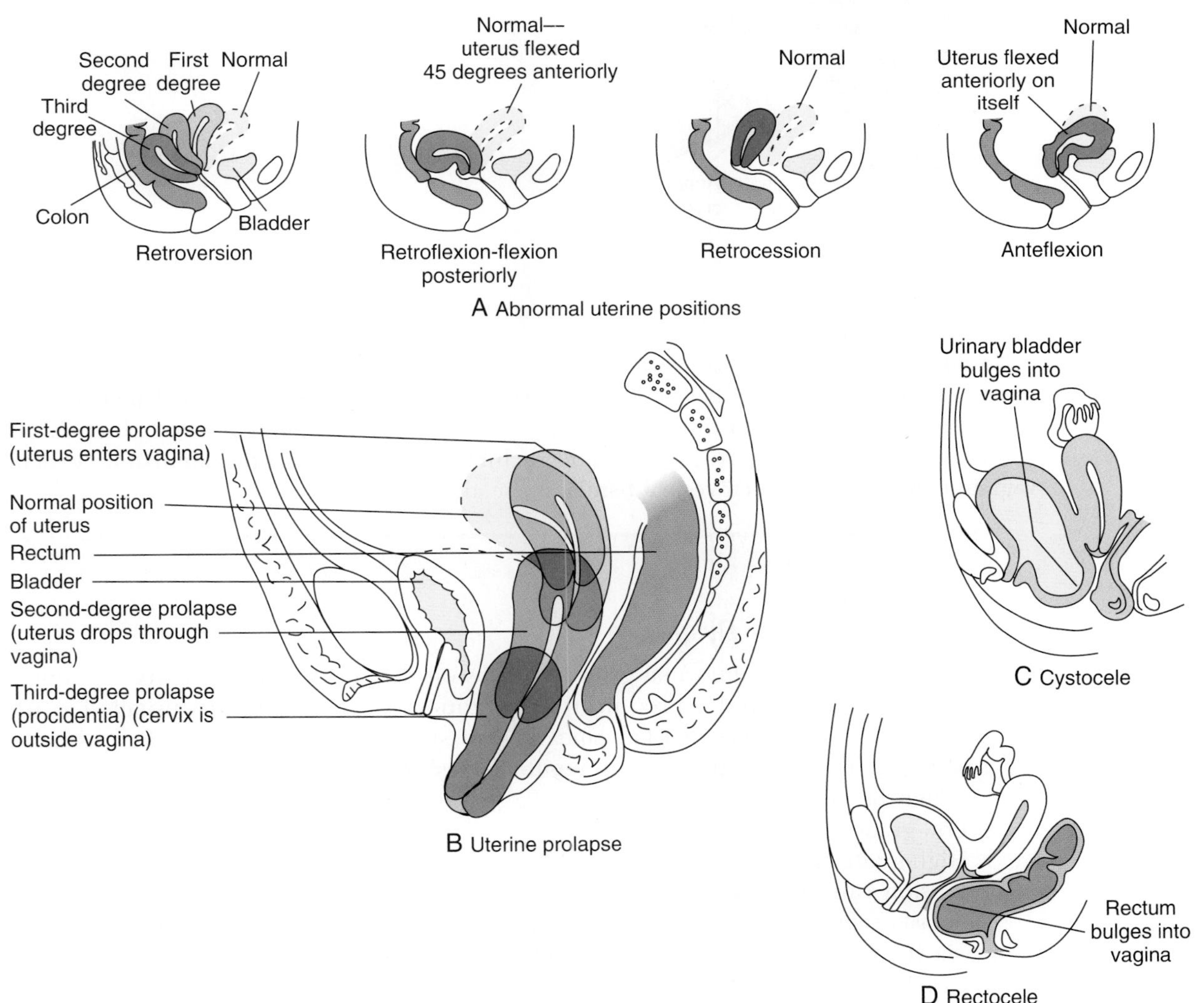

FIGURE 21-16. Structural abnormalities of the uterus.

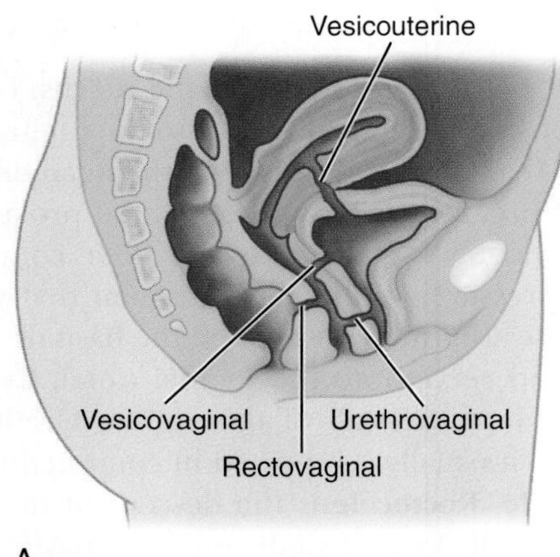

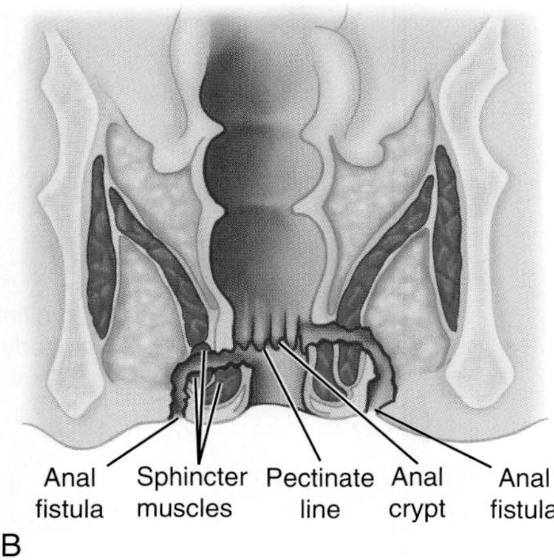

FIGURE 21-17. Various types of fistulas, designated according to site or to organs with which they communicate. **A,** Genitourinary fistulas. **B,** Anal fistulas.

Fistulas

A **fistula** is an abnormal passage or communication between two internal organs, or leading from an organ to the surface of the body (Figure 21-17). A **urethrovaginal fistula** is an abnormal passage between the urethra and the vagina. The bladder has the potential to communicate with the uterus, vagina, and rectum, forming a **vesicouterine fistula**, **vesicovaginal fistula**, and/or **rectovesical fistula**, respectively.

EXAMPLE

Rectovesicovaginal fistula, N82.3.

Cervical and Vulvular Dysplasia

Cervical dysplasia is the abnormal growth of cells on the surface of the cervix. Although not cancer, it is considered a precancerous condition. Cervical dysplasia usually has no symptoms and is discovered on a Pap smear. Dysplasia that is identified on a Pap smear is described using the term **squamous intraepithelial lesion (SIL)**. These abnormal Pap smear changes may be graded as:

- Low-grade (LSIL)
- High-grade (HSIL)
- Possibly cancerous (malignant)

Dysplasia that is seen on a biopsy of the cervix uses the term **cervical intraepithelial neoplasia (CIN)** and is grouped into the following three categories:

- CIN I—mild dysplasia
- CIN II—moderate to marked dysplasia
- CIN III—severe dysplasia to carcinoma in situ

Vulvar intraepithelial neoplasia (VIN) refers to certain changes that can occur in the skin that covers the vulva. It is similar to CIN or dysplasia of the cervix and can be diagnosed with a biopsy. VIN is grouped into the following three categories:

- VIN I—mild dysplasia
- VIN II—moderate to marked dysplasia
- VIN III—severe dysplasia to carcinoma in situ

If either of these conditions (CIN or VIN) are left untreated, it may result in invasive cancer.

EXAMPLE

Patient was seen in the clinic, and her cervical biopsy results showed CIN II, N87.1.

EXERCISE 21-8

Assign codes to the following conditions.

1. Endometriosis of fallopian tube ______________
2. Cystocele with female stress incontinence ______________
3. Corpus luteum cyst ______________
4. Chocolate cyst of the ovary ______________
5. Vaginal stenosis ______________

FACTORS INFLUENCING HEALTH STATUS AND CONTACT WITH HEALTH SERVICES (Z CODES)

As was discussed in Chapter 9, it may be difficult to locate Z codes in the Index. Coders often say, "I did not know there was a Z code for that." Refer to Chapter 9 for a listing of common main terms used to locate Z codes.

Z codes that may be used with diseases of the genitourinary system include the following:

Z01.411	Encounter for gynecological examination (general)(routine) with abnormal findings
Z01.419	Encounter for gynecological examination (general)(routine) without abnormal findings
Z01.42	Encounter for cervical smear to confirm findings of recent normal smear following initial abnormal smear
Z13.89	Encounter for screening of other disorder
Z41.2	Encounter for routine and ritual male circumcision
Z43.5	Encounter for attention to cystostomy
Z43.6	Encounter for attention to other artificial openings of urinary tract
Z43.7	Encounter for attention to artificial vagina
Z44.30	Encounter for fitting and adjustment of external breast prosthesis, unspecified breast
Z44.31	Encounter for fitting and adjustment of external right breast prosthesis
Z44.32	Encounter for fitting and adjustment of external left breast prosthesis
Z45.811	Encounter for adjustment or removal of right breast implant
Z45.812	Encounter for adjustment or removal of left breast implant
Z45.819	Encounter for adjustment or removal of unspecified breast implant
Z46.6	Encounter for fitting and adjustment of urinary device
Z49.01	Encounter for fitting and adjustment of extracorporeal dialysis catheter
Z49.02	Encounter for fitting and adjustment of peritoneal dialysis catheter
Z49.31	Encounter for adequacy testing for hemodialysis
Z49.32	Encounter for adequacy testing for peritoneal dialysis
Z52.4	Kidney donor
Z52.810	Egg (Oocyte) donor under age 35, anonymous recipient; Egg donor under age 35 NOS
Z52.811	Egg (Oocyte) donor under age 35, designated recipient

Z52.812	Egg (Oocyte) donor age 35 and over, anonymous recipient; Egg donor age 35 and over NOS
Z52.813	Egg (Oocyte) donor age 35 and over, designated recipient
Z52.819	Egg (Oocyte) donor, unspecified
Z78.0	Asymptomatic menopausal state
Z79.890	Hormone replacement therapy (postmenopausal)
Z82.71	Family history of polycystic kidney
Z84.1	Family history of disorders of kidney and ureter
Z84.2	Family history of other diseases of the genitourinary system
Z87.410	Personal history of cervical dysplasia
Z87.411	Personal history of vaginal dysplasia
Z87.412	Personal history of vulvar dysplasia
Z87.430	Personal history of prostatic dysplasia
Z87.438	Personal history of other disease of male genital organs
Z87.440	Personal history of urinary (tract) infections
Z87.441	Personal history of nephrotic syndrome
Z87.442	Personal history of urinary calculi
Z87.448	Personal history of other diseases of the urinary system
Z90.10	Acquired absence of unspecified breast and nipple
Z90.11	Acquired absence of right breast and nipple
Z90.12	Acquired absence of left breast and nipple
Z90.13	Acquired absence of bilateral breasts and nipples
Z90.5	Acquired absence of kidney
Z90.6	Acquired absence of other parts of urinary tract
Z90.710	Acquired absence of both cervix and uterus
Z90.711	Acquired absence of uterus with remaining cervical stump
Z90.712	Acquired absence of cervix with remaining uterus
Z90.721	Acquired absence of ovaries, unilateral
Z90.722	Acquired absence of ovaries, bilateral
Z90.79	Acquired absence of other genital organ(s)
Z91.15	Patient's noncompliance with renal dialysis
Z93.50	Unspecified cystostomy status
Z93.51	Cutaneous-vesicostomy status
Z93.52	Appendico-vesicostomy status
Z93.59	Other cystostomy status
Z93.6	Other artificial openings of urinary tract status
Z94.0	Kidney transplant status
Z96.0	Presence of urogenital implants
Z98.51	Tubal ligation status
Z98.52	Vasectomy status
Z98.82	Breast implant status
Z98.86	Personal history of breast implant removal
Z98.870	Personal history of in utero procedure during pregnancy
Z98.871	Personal history of in utero procedure while a fetus
Z98.891	History of uterine scar from previous surgery
Z99.2	Dependence on renal dialysis

EXAMPLE

Adult male is admitted for elective routine circumcision, Z41.2, 0VTTXZZ.

The Z code indicates that a procedure is going to be performed, but it is not the procedure code. A diagnosis code is not assigned because no medical condition is present.

EXAMPLE

Patient is admitted for kidney donation. A laparoscopic left nephrectomy is performed with partial left ureterectomy, Z52.4, 0TT14ZZ, 0TB74ZZ.

EXERCISE 21-9

Assign codes to the following conditions.

1. Status post kidney transplant ____________
2. Personal history of kidney stones ____________
3. Family history of polycystic kidney disease ____________
4. Acquired absence of uterus and cervix ____________

COMMON TREATMENTS

CONDITION	MEDICATION/TREATMENT
Glomerulonephritis	If due to infection, antibiotics Diuretics, antihypertensives, and diet Serious cases may be treated with corticosteroids and/or Cytoxan
Acute renal failure	Fluid management and treat the underlying cause Dialysis, if necessary
Chronic renal failure	Determine cause. Control blood pressure and diet
Cystitis	Fluids and possibly antibiotics
Urethritis	Antibiotics
Pyelonephritis	Antibiotics
Calculus of urinary tract	Fluids, pain control, blood pressure control, and antibiotics, if associated infection
Urinary incontinence	Kegel exercises, biofeedback, and medications such as Detrol
Prostatitis	Antibiotics
Benign prostatic hyperplasia	Medications such as tamsulosin hydrochloride (Flomax) and terazosin hydrochloride (Hytrin)
Mastitis	Compresses, massage, fluids, and possibly antibiotics
PID	Antibiotics
Endometriosis	Pain medication and/or hormonal therapy

PROCEDURES

Procedures related to the genitourinary system in ICD-10-PCS can be located in the following tables:

0H0-0HY	Skin and Breast
0T1-0TY	Urinary System
0U1-0UY	Female Reproductive System
0V1-0VW	Male Reproductive System
302-3E1	Administration
5A0-5A2	Extracorporeal Assistance and Performance

Cystoscopy is an endoscopic approach used for many procedures involving the urinary tract (Figure 21-18). Often, another diagnostic or therapeutic procedure, such as biopsy, removal of a stone, dilatation of a stricture, or control of hemorrhage, is performed during a cystoscopic examination.

EXAMPLE

Bladder lesion with diagnostic transurethral biopsy of the bladder via cystoscope, N32.9, 0TBB8ZX.

SECTION	BODY SYSTEM	ROOT OPERATION	BODY PART	APPROACH	DEVICE	QUALIFIER
Medical and Surgical	Urinary System	Excision	Bladder	Via Natural or Artificial Opening Endoscopic	No Device	Diagnostic
0	T	B	B	8	Z	X

Dialysis

Dialysis is needed when the kidneys can no longer filter the blood and form urine. Two basic types of dialysis are available. **Hemodialysis** uses a machine called a hemodialyzer to

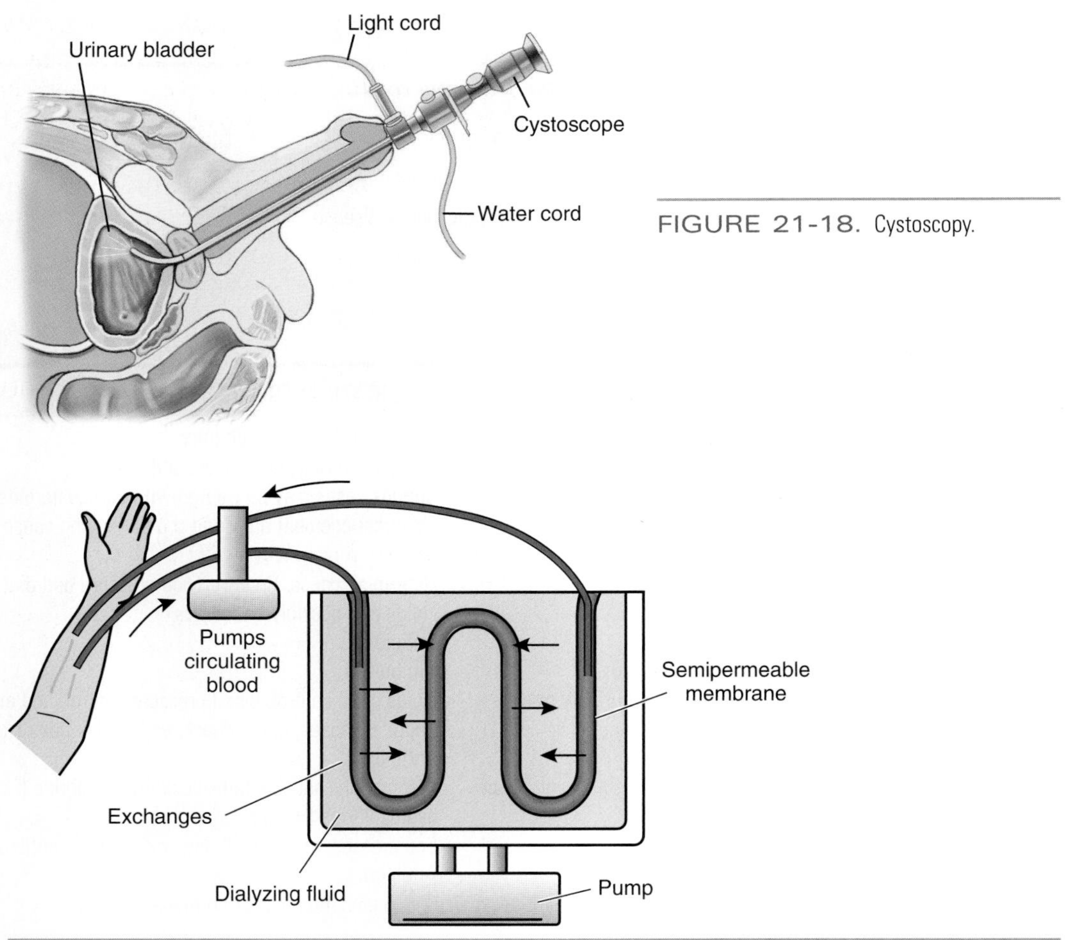

FIGURE 21-18. Cystoscopy.

FIGURE 21-19. Hemodialysis.

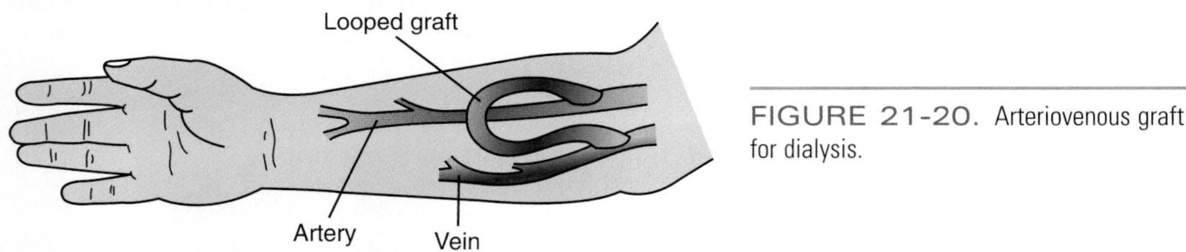

FIGURE 21-20. Arteriovenous graft for dialysis.

remove wastes from the blood (Figure 21-19). Access is obtained through a surgically created internal (arteriovenous [AV]) fistula that allows blood to pass from the body to the machine for cleansing. Sometimes, an AV graft (Figure 21-20) is used for permanent access. The root operation for creation of an AV fistula is bypass (altering the route of passage of the contents of a tubular body). If treatment must be begun before permanent access is ready or available, temporary access can be obtained through a catheter. Usually, hemodialysis is conducted at dialysis centers, and it is often scheduled 3 times per week. A dialysis session may take 3 to 5 hours to complete. The root operation for hemodialysis is performance (completely taking over a physiological function by extracorporeal means).

In cases where the patient is receiving treatment in preparation for dialysis (e.g., creation of an arteriovenous fistula or graft), the principal diagnosis will be the medical condition for which the dialysis is required. If the encounter is for a dialysis session, assign the appropriate code for the reason for the dialysis or the underlying disease. Just because a patient is receiving dialysis does not mean they have ESRD. Occasionally there are other reasons for hemodialysis, such as acute renal failure. Documentation of the actual dialysis method is required in order to determine the Duration value for hemodialysis treatment.

There are three types of dialysis treatments recognized. Intermittent hemodialysis (IHD) is the method of therapy provided typically for CKD/ESRD treatment, with the dialysis administered over 3-5 hours per day for 3 to 7 days per week. Prolonged intermittent renal replacement therapy (PIRRT), also known as Sustained Low Efficiency Dialysis (SLED), describes dialysis provided for 2-7 days per week over 6-18 hours per day. Continuous renal replacement therapy (CRRT), describes dialysis therapy provided for greater than 18 hours per day. Both PIRRT and CRRT are typically used for patients with acute renal failure.

EXAMPLE

Patient with ESRD and hypertension is admitted for creation of an AV fistula (left radiocephalic fistula using a synthetic graft). Patient has dialysis on M, W, and F. I12.0, N18.6, Z99.2, 031C0JF.

SECTION	BODY SYSTEM	ROOT OPERATION	BODY PART	APPROACH	DEVICE	QUALIFIER
Medical and Surgical	Upper Arteries	Bypass	Radial Artery, Left	Open	Synthetic Substitute	Lower Arm Vein
0	3	1	C	0	J	F

Peritoneal dialysis uses the peritoneal membrane in the patient's own body along with a dialysate solution to filter out wastes and excess fluid (Figure 21-21). Dialyzing fluid passes into the peritoneal cavity through a permanent indwelling peritoneal catheter (Tenckhoff catheter) and is then drained from the peritoneal cavity. **Continuous ambulatory peritoneal dialysis** (CAPD) takes about 15 minutes and is performed 3 to 4 times per day and once at

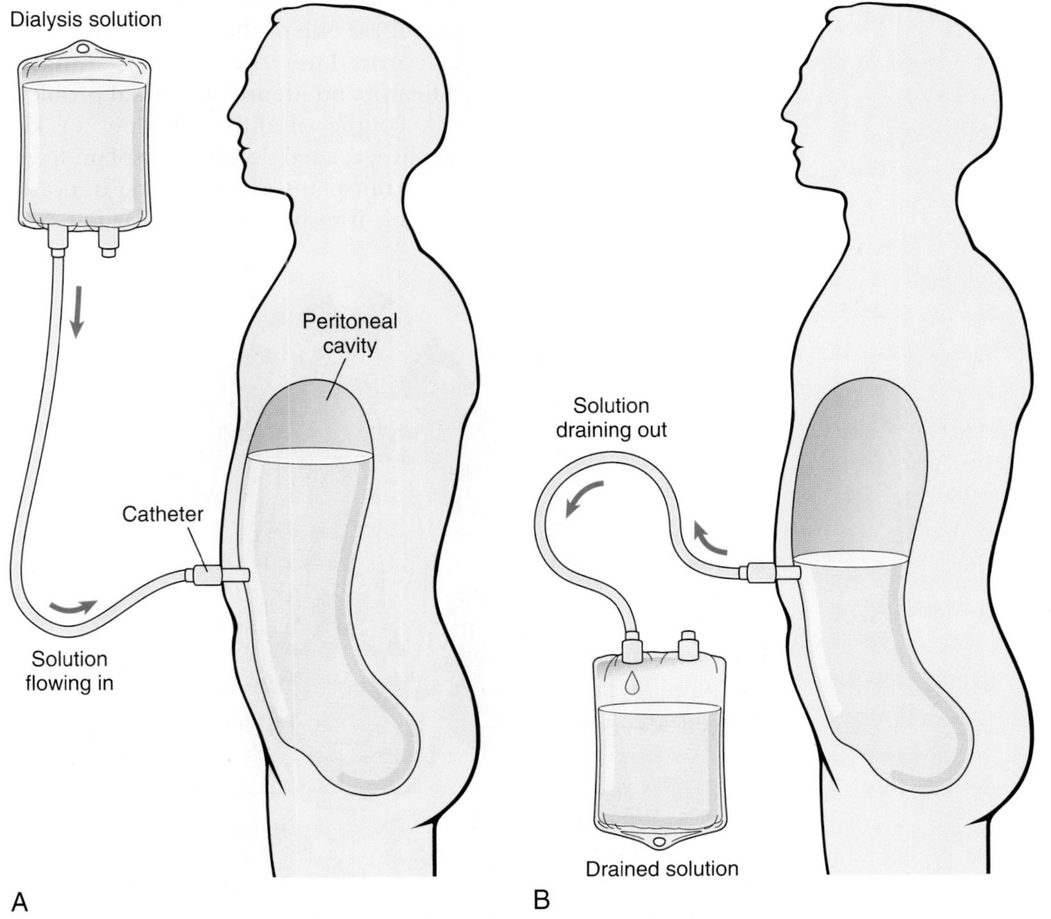

FIGURE 21-21. Continuous ambulatory peritoneal dialysis. **A,** The dialysis solution (dialysate) flows from a collapsible plastic bag through a Tenckhoff catheter into the patient's peritoneal cavity. The empty bag is folded and inserted into undergarments. **B,** After 4 to 8 hours, the bag is unfolded, and the fluid is allowed to drain into it with the help of gravity. The full bag is discarded, and a new bag of fresh dialysate is attached.

night. **Continuous cycling peritoneal dialysis** (CCPD) uses a cycling machine and is performed while the patient sleeps. In some cases, a combination of the two may be needed to achieve the best results. The root operation for peritoneal dialysis is irrigation (putting in or on a cleansing substance).

EXAMPLE

Patient with end-stage renal failure has peritoneal dialysis with Dialysate while hospitalized for acute prostatitis, N41.0, N18.6, Z99.2, 3E1M39Z.

SECTION	BODY SYSTEM	ROOT OPERATION	BODY SYSTEM/ REGION	APPROACH	SUBSTANCE	QUALIFIER
Administration	Physiological Systems and Anatomical Regions	Irrigation	Peritoneal Cavity	Percutaneous	Dialysate	No Qualifier
3	E	1	M	3	9	Z

Providers may document that a patient gets dialysis on MWF (Monday, Wednesday, Friday schedule). For patients who are maintained on dialysis, code Z99.2, dependence on renal dialysis, should be assigned as an additional code. Code Z91.15 should be assigned if the patient has been noncompliant with their dialysis treatments.

Kidney Transplantation

A kidney transplant (Figure 21-22) is one of the most common transplant operations. Prior to performance of a transplant procedure, a thorough pretransplant evaluation is necessary to assess the patient's overall health and identify potential problems to increase the chances of a successful transplant. A couple of different types of kidney transplants may be performed—transplant from a live, related donor; transplant from a live, nonrelated donor; and transplant from a cadaver. Transplants from a living donor are generally scheduled in advance, and the kidney may be transplanted immediately following removal from the

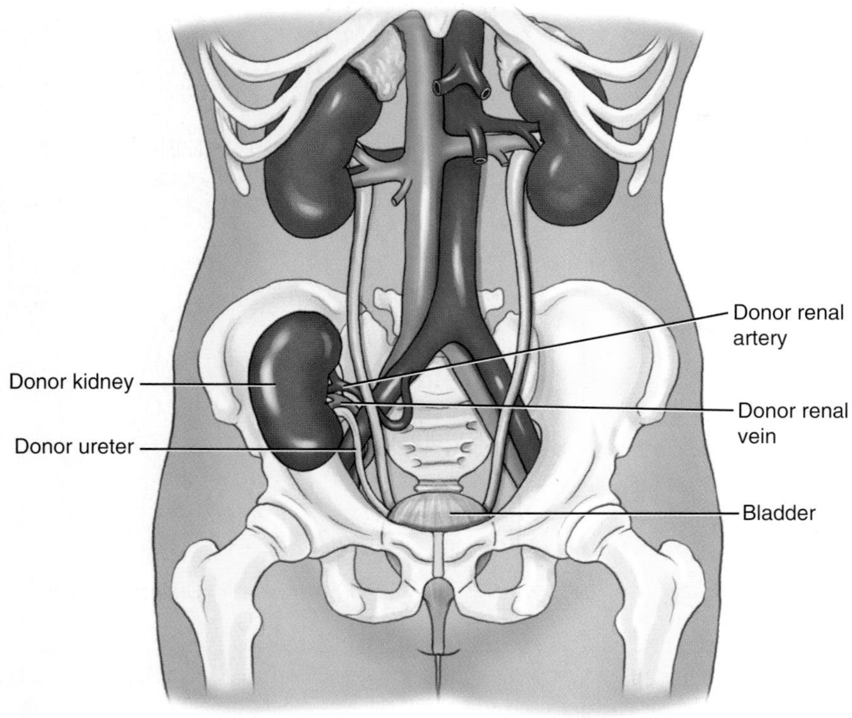

FIGURE 21-22. Kidney transplantation. The left kidney of the donor is removed and transplanted to the right pelvis of the recipient.

donor. The root operation for a kidney transplant is transplantation (putting in a living body part from a person/animal).

Patients who are on a waiting list for a kidney are notified when a kidney becomes available that is a good match; they must report to the hospital immediately. The transplanted kidney will usually start making urine as soon as the blood starts to flow through it, and most patients feel much better after their surgery has been completed. In most cases, only one kidney is necessary to take over for two failed kidneys. Most of the time, the diseased kidneys are left in place.

EXAMPLE

Patient was admitted for kidney transplant (open). Patient has CKD, stage 5 due to hypertension. Patient never did receive dialysis. The transplant was performed using the spouse's left kidney, I12.0, N18.5, 0TY10Z0.

SECTION	BODY SYSTEM	ROOT OPERATION	BODY PART	APPROACH	DEVICE	QUALIFIER
Medical and Surgical	Urinary System	Transplantation	Kidney, Left	Open	No Device	Allogeneic
0	T	Y	1	0	Z	0

Prostate Procedures

Prostate procedures are most often performed for benign prostatic hypertrophy or for prostate cancer. A biopsy is usually performed prior to a prostatectomy. Correct procedural code assignment depends on the method of the procedure performed. When **transurethral resection of the prostate** (TURP) is performed, it is not necessary to code the cystoscopy that is performed in the course of the surgical procedure. Cystoscopy is the approach that is used in transurethral procedures. Transurethral ultrasound-guided laser-induced prostatectomy (TULIP) and visual laser ablation of the prostate (VLAP) are two types of laser treatments used for ablation of prostatic tissue. Transurethral microwave thermotherapy (TUMT) and transurethral needle ablation (TUNA) of the prostate use radiofrequency energy to ablate obstructive prostatic tissue; these procedures can be performed in the physician's office. For the prostate procedures, if a biopsy is performed, the root operation is excision (cutting out or off without replacement some of a body part). If a prostatectomy with complete removal of the prostate gland is performed, resection is the root operation (cutting out or off without replacement all of a body part). If an ablation is done, destruction is the root operation (eradicating without replacement some or all of a body part [none of the body part is physically taken out]).

EXAMPLE

Cancer of the prostate with open radical prostatectomy (including bilateral seminal vesicles) with diagnostic pelvic lymph node sampling, C61, 0VT00ZZ, 0VT30ZZ, 07BC0ZX.

SECTION	BODY SYSTEM	ROOT OPERATION	BODY PART	APPROACH	DEVICE	QUALIFIER
Medical and Surgical	Male Reproductive System	Resection	Prostate	Open	No Device	No Qualifier
0	V	T	0	0	Z	Z

SECTION	BODY SYSTEM	ROOT OPERATION	BODY PART	APPROACH	DEVICE	QUALIFIER
Medical and Surgical	Male Reproductive System	Resection	Seminal Vesicles, Bilateral	Open	No Device	No Qualifier
0	V	T	3	0	Z	Z

SECTION	BODY SYSTEM	ROOT OPERATION	BODY PART	APPROACH	DEVICE	QUALIFIER
Medical and Surgical	Lymphatic and Hemic Systems	Excision	Lymphatic, Pelvis	Open	No Device	Diagnostic
0	7	B	C	0	Z	X

EXAMPLE Benign prostatic hypertrophy with urinary obstruction. Endoscopic transurethral partial prostatectomy, N40.1, N13.8, 0VB08ZZ.

SECTION	BODY SYSTEM	ROOT OPERATION	BODY PART	APPROACH	DEVICE	QUALIFIER
Medical and Surgical	Male Reproductive System	Excision	Prostate	Via Natural or Artificial Opening Endoscopic	No Device	No Qualifier
0	V	B	0	8	Z	Z

Breast Biopsies and Reconstruction

Breast biopsies are performed for diagnostic purposes to determine the nature of a breast abnormality or mass. The root operation for biopsy is excision (cutting out or off some of a body part without replacement). In a biopsy of the breast, a tissue sample is taken for diagnostic examination.

At times, breast biopsy is performed during the same operative episode as a therapeutic procedure or more definitive treatment such as a mastectomy. In these cases, the biopsy is coded in addition to the mastectomy.

Breast reconstructions are often performed following a mastectomy. Reconstruction may be done immediately or as a delayed procedure. The type of reconstruction and the timing of when it is done vary according to the patient's need for radiation and the type of mastectomy that is performed. Reconstruction may also be performed in stages. Implants and tissue expanders are sometimes used to create the breast. Tissue expanders are removed after the skin and muscles have been expanded to accommodate the breast implant or further reconstruction.

Tissue flap procedures use tissue from the abdomen, back, thighs, or buttocks to reconstruct the breast. Several flap procedures are currently used (Figure 21-23); these include the following:

- Transverse rectus abdominis musculocutaneous (TRAM)
- Latissimus dorsi musculocutaneous flap (LDMF)

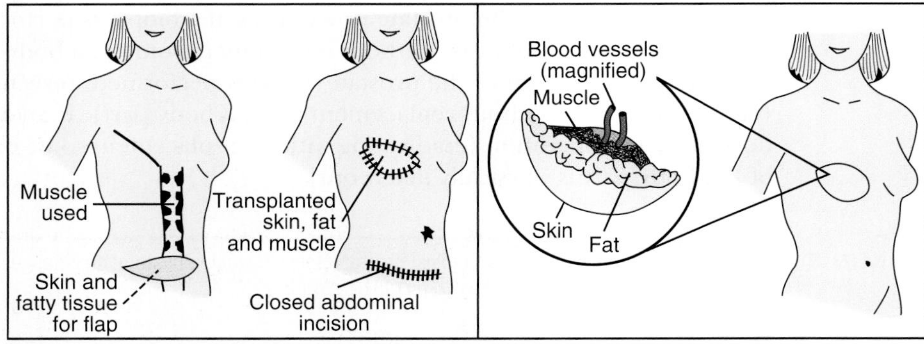

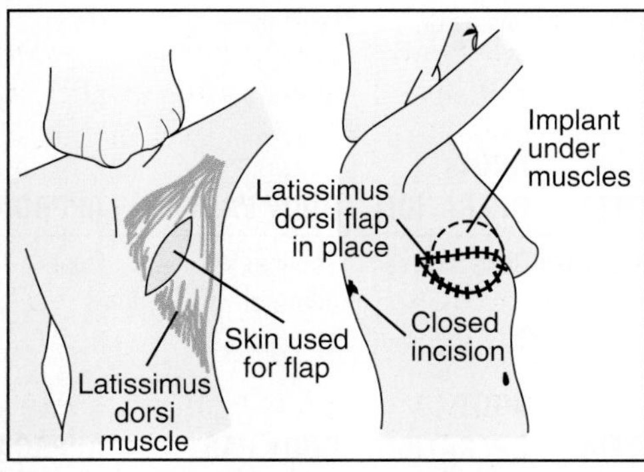

FIGURE 21-23. Various flaps used for breast reconstruction.

- Lateral transverse thigh flap
- Nipple—Areola reconstruction
- Deep inferior epigastric perforator (DIEP) flap free
- Superficial inferior epigastric artery (SIEA) flap free
- Gluteal artery perforator (GAP) flap free

A **pedicle flap** involves a flap that remains attached to its original blood supply and tunneling it under the skin to the breast area. A **free flap** involves the cutting of skin, fat, blood vessels, and muscle free from their locations and moving them to the chest area. Blood vessels are connected with the use of a microscope. A free flap takes more time to complete. The root operation for free flap reconstruction is replacement (putting in or on biologic or synthetic material that replaces a body part). The root operation for pedicle flap reconstruction is transfer (moving a body part with taking out to another location to take over the function of another body part). If a breast reconstruction is performed during the same operative episode as a mastectomy, only the replacement or breast reconstruction code is assigned. The removal of the body part during a replacement procedure is considered part of the replacement procedure.

EXAMPLE

Patient has right upper outer quadrant breast cancer. She was admitted for a right total mastectomy with immediate TRAM reconstruction, C50.411, 0HRT076

SECTION	BODY SYSTEM	ROOT OPERATION	BODY PART	APPROACH	DEVICE	QUALIFIER
Medical and Surgical	Skin and Breast	Replacement	Breast, Right	Open	Autologous Tissue Substitute	Transverse Rectus Abdominis Myocutaneous Flap
0	H	R	T	0	7	6

Removal of Stones

Extracorporeal shock wave lithotripsy (ESWL) is used to break up kidney stones into small particles that can then pass through the urinary tract in the urine. Different devices can be used to transmit shock waves, and usually, x-ray or ultrasound is used to reveal the exact location of the stone. The root operation for ESWL is fragmentation (breaking solid matter into pieces).

If the stone is quite large, or the location is such that ESWL is not very effective, a **percutaneous nephrolithotomy** is performed. The root operation for nephrolithotomy is extirpation (taking or cutting out solid matter). The stone is removed by the surgeon with the use of a nephroscope. At times, an ultrasonic or electrohydraulic probe is used to break up the stone, and the fragments are then removed. A nephrostomy tube may have to remain within the kidney during the postoperative phase.

Ureteroscopic stone removal is necessary when a kidney stone has traveled into one of the ureters. The ureteroscope is inserted through the urethra and bladder and into the ureter until the stone can be removed or is broken into pieces.

EXAMPLE

Patient was treated with percutaneous nephrostomy with removal of left kidney stone, N20.0, 0TC13ZZ.

SECTION	BODY SYSTEM	ROOT OPERATION	BODY PART	APPROACH	DEVICE	QUALIFIER
Medical and Surgical	Urinary System	Extirpation	Kidney, Left	Percutaneous	No Device	No Qualifier
0	T	C	1	3	Z	Z

EXERCISE 21-10

Assign codes for all diagnoses and procedures.

1. Right solitary renal cyst (acquired) with right partial laparoscopic nephrectomy ______
2. Transurethral needle ablation of prostate (endoscopic TUNA) in patient with benign prostatic hyperplasia ______
3. Laparoscopically assisted vaginal hysterectomy (LAVH) in patient with endometriosis of the uterus ______
4. Extracorporeal shock wave lithotripsy, bladder stone ______
5. Bilateral modified radical mastectomy, and breast reconstruction with latissimus dorsi musculocutaneous flap (LDMF) following prophylactic removal due to strong family history of breast cancer ______
6. Peritoneal dialysis in patient with ESRD and anemia of chronic renal disease ______
7. Open left kidney transplant in patient with hypertensive renal disease and end-stage renal failure. The patient's spouse was the donor. ______
8. Left breast cyst with percutaneous breast aspiration ______

CHAPTER REVIEW EXERCISE

Assign codes for all diagnoses and procedures.

1. Pelvic pain due to interstitial cystitis ______
2. Benign hyperplasia of the prostate with urinary obstruction ______
3. Patient with benign prostatic hypertrophy with urinary obstruction and history of renal calculi is admitted for TURP. After the procedure, the patient has slight hematuria. ______
4. Complete uterovaginal prolapse ______
5. Azotemia ______
6. Vesicoureteral reflux with nephropathy, unilateral ______
7. Menometrorrhagia with chronic blood loss anemia ______
8. Infertility due to tubal endometriosis ______
9. Hematuria with diagnostic cystoscope performed to inspect bladder ______
10. Acute tubular necrosis in patient with labile hypertension ______
11. Berger's disease ______
12. Rectovesical fistula ______
13. Chronic glomerulonephritis due to amyloidosis ______
14. Multinodular prostate ______
15. Infertility due to azoospermia ______
16. Incision and drainage of Bartholin's abscess ______
17. Open total abdominal hysterectomy (removal of uterus and cervix)with right salpingo-oophorectomy for symptomatic uterine fibroids and follicular cyst, right ovary. ______
    Family history of cervical cancer
18. Infertility due to dysmucorrhea ______
19. Urethroscrotal fistula ______
20. Nonfunctioning right kidney with laparoscopic nephrectomy ______

21. Postmenopausal bleeding. Therapeutic dilatation and curettage (D&C) of uterus ______________
22. Patient with ESRD following transplant nephrectomy who is noncompliant with dialysis sessions ______________
23. Descensus of uterus ______________
24. Left ureteral stent was placed (via cystoscopic approach) due to obstruction of the ureter due to stone ______________
25. Bilateral laparoscopic oophorectomy with bilateral salpingectomy due to polycystic ovarian syndrome ______________

Write the correct answer(s) in the space(s) provided.

26. What type of scope is used for procedures involving the urinary tract?

    ____

27. Define fistula.

    ____

28. Pyelonephritis involves what organ?

    ____

29. Describe the main difference in the female and male genitourinary tract.

    ____

30. Define ARF.

    ____

CHAPTER GLOSSARY

Acute renal failure: sudden and severe impairment of renal function characterized by oliguria, increased serum urea, and acidosis.

Benign prostatic hyperplasia: condition resulting in enlargement of the prostate gland; usually occurs in men older than 50 years of age.

Benign prostatic hypertrophy: condition resulting in enlargement of the prostate gland; usually occurs in men older than 50 years of age.

Calculus: a stone. Calculi, which vary in size, can develop anywhere in the urinary tract.

Cervical dysplasia: abnormal growth of cells on the surface of the cervix.

Cervical intraepithelial neoplasia (CIN): dysplasia that is seen on a biopsy of the cervix.

Continuous ambulatory peritoneal dialysis: type of peritoneal dialysis that takes about 15 minutes and is performed 3 to 4 times per day and once at night.

Continuous cycling peritoneal dialysis: type of peritoneal dialysis that uses a cycling machine and is performed while the patient sleeps.

Cystitis: lower tract infection that affects the bladder.

Cystocele: when the bladder descends and presses into the wall of the vagina.

Cystoscopy: approach used for many procedures of the urinary tract.

Cystourethrocele: a urethrocele in conjunction with a cystocele.

Endometriosis: a chronic condition in which endometrial material, the tissue that lines the inside of the uterus, grows outside the uterus and attaches to other organs in the pelvic cavity.

Endometritis: inflammation of the uterus.

Extracorporeal shock wave lithotripsy: used to break up kidney stones into small particles that can then pass through the urinary tract into the urine.

Fistula: abnormal passage or communication between two internal organs, or leading from an organ to the surface of the body.

Free flap: involves the cutting of skin, fat, blood vessels, and muscle free from its location and moving it to the chest area.

Functional urinary incontinence: when a physical or mental condition prevents someone from making it to the bathroom in time.

Genital prolapse: when pelvic organs such as the uterus, bladder, and rectum shift from their normal anatomic positions and protrude into the vagina or press against the wall of the vagina.

Glomerulonephritis: inflammation of the glomeruli of the kidneys.

Hemodialysis: process that uses a machine called a hemodialyzer to remove wastes from the blood.

Hydronephrosis: abnormal dilatation of the renal pelvis caused by pressure from urine that cannot flow past an obstruction in the urinary tract.

Hydroureter: accumulation of urine in the ureters.

Lactation: the secretion of milk from mammary glands.

Mastitis: inflammation or infection of the breast.

Mixed incontinence: combination of stress and urge incontinence.

Nephrolithiasis: kidney stone.

Nephrotic syndrome: condition marked by proteinuria (protein in the urine), low levels of protein in the blood, hypercholesterolemia, and swelling of the eyes, feet, and hands.

Oophoritis: inflammation of the ovaries.

Overflow incontinence: the constant dribbling of urine.

Pedicle flap: involves identifying a flap that remains attached to its original blood supply and tunneling it under the skin to a particular area such as the breast.

Pelvic inflammatory disease: when vaginal or cervical infections spread and involve the uterus, fallopian tubes, ovaries, and surrounding tissues.

Percutaneous nephrolithotomy: procedure in which the surgeon uses a nephroscope to remove a stone. At times, an ultrasonic or electrohydraulic probe is used to break up the stone, and the fragments are then removed.

Peritoneal dialysis: when the peritoneal membrane in the patient's own body is used with a dialysate solution to filter out the wastes and excess fluids.

Prostate-specific antigen (PSA): protein produced by the prostate gland.

Prostatitis: inflammation of the prostate that can be acute and/or chronic in nature and is due to a bacterium or inflammation that is not caused by a bacterial infection.

Proteinuria: protein in urine.

Pyelonephritis: upper tract infection that involves the kidneys.

Rectocele: descent of the rectum and pressing of the rectum against the vaginal wall.

Rectovesical fistula: a communication between the bladder and the rectum.

Renal colic: intense pain associated with the body's efforts to try to force the stone through the ureters.

Salpingitis: inflammation of the fallopian tubes, which are the most common site of pelvic inflammation.

Squamous intraepithelial lesion (SIL): dysplasia of the cervix that is identified on a Pap smear.

Stress incontinence: involuntary loss of small amounts of urine due to increased pressure resulting from coughing, sneezing, or laughing.

Transurethral resection of the prostate: endoscopic removal of prostate tissue.

Ureterolithiasis: ureter stone.

Urethritis: infection of the urethra.

Urethrocele: when the urethra presses into the vagina.

Urethrovaginal fistula: abnormal passage between the urethra and the vagina.

Urge incontinence: sudden and involuntary loss of large amounts of urine.

Urinary tract infection: general term used to describe infection in any area of the urinary tract.

Urolithiasis: a stone in the urinary tract.

Uterine prolapse: descent of the uterus and the cervix into the vaginal canal.

Vaginal vault prolapse: condition that may occur following a hysterectomy, when the top of the vagina descends.

Vesicoureteral reflux: abnormality in the flow of urine from the bladder into the ureters and/or kidneys.

Vesicouterine fistula: communication between the bladder and the uterus.

Vesicovaginal fistula: communication between the bladder and the vagina.

Vulvar intraepithelial neoplasia (VIN): certain changes that can occur in the skin that covers the vulva.

REFERENCES

1. American Hospital Association: *Coding Clinic for ICD-9-CM* 2002:3Q:p21-22. ARF due to dehydration and treated with IV hydration only.
2. American Hospital Association: *Coding Clinic for ICD-9-CM* 2002:3Q:p28. Acute renal failure due to rhabdomyolysis.
3. From Frazier ME, Drzymkowski JW: Essentials of Human Diseases and Conditions, ed 5, St. Louis, 2013, Saunders, Table 11-1, p 559.

22

Pregnancy, Childbirth, and the Puerperium

(ICD-10-CM Chapter 15, Codes O00-O9A)

CHAPTER OUTLINE

LEARNING OBJECTIVES

1. Apply and assign the correct ICD-10-CM/PCS codes in accordance with Official Guidelines for Coding and Reporting
2. Identify pertinent anatomy and physiology of pregnancy, childbirth, and the puerperium
3. Recognize conditions and complications of pregnancy, childbirth, and the puerperium
4. Assign the correct Z codes and procedure codes related to pregnancy, childbirth, and the puerperium
5. Identify common treatments, medications, laboratory values, and diagnostic tests

ABBREVIATIONS/ ACRONYMS

AROM artificial rupture of membranes
CPD cephalopelvic disproportion
D&C dilatation and curettage
EDC estimated date of confinement
GBS group B strep
GDM gestational diabetes mellitus
hCG human chorionic gonadotropin
HELLP hemolysis, elevated liver enzymes, and low platelet count
ICD-10-CM *International Classification of Diseases, 10th Revision, Clinical Modification*
ICD-10-PCS *International Classification of Diseases, 10th Revision, Procedure Coding System*
IOL induction of labor
LGA large for gestational age
LTCS low transverse cesarean section
NST nonstress test
OB obstetrics
PIH pregnancy-induced hypertension
POC products of conception
PROM premature rupture of membranes
PTA prior to admission
PTL preterm labor
SVD spontaneous vaginal delivery
UTI urinary tract infection
VBAC vaginal birth after cesarean section

ICD-10-CM Official Guidelines for Coding and Reporting (2021-2022)

Please refer to the companion Evolve website for the most current 2021-2022 guidelines.

15. Chapter 15: Pregnancy, Childbirth, and the Puerperium (O00-*O9A*)

a. General Rules for Obstetric Cases

1) Codes from chapter 15 and sequencing priority

Obstetric cases require codes from chapter 15, codes in the range O00-O9A, Pregnancy, Childbirth, and the Puerperium. Chapter 15 codes have sequencing priority over codes from other chapters. Additional codes from other chapters may be used in conjunction with chapter 15 codes to further specify conditions. Should the provider document that the pregnancy is incidental to the encounter, then code Z33.1, Pregnant state, incidental, should be used in place of any chapter 15 codes. It is the provider's responsibility to state that the condition being treated is not affecting the pregnancy.

In most cases, when a patient is pregnant, a code from Chapter 15 must be assigned regardless of what condition the patient presents with. The exception to this rule would occur when a physician documents that the pregnancy is incidental to the reason for this encounter. Almost ALWAYS, codes from the pregnancy chapter are to be assigned. This does not mean that codes from other chapters cannot be used to more fully describe a condition. The codes from Chapter 15 have sequencing priority.

EXAMPLE

Patient presents to physician office with pain and burning on urination. The physician documents that the patient is 26 weeks pregnant and has a UTI, O23.42, Z3A.26.

EXAMPLE

A patient with gastroenteritis is seen in the emergency room (ER). The ER physician documents that the pregnancy is incidental to her gastroenteritis, K52.9, Z33.1.

2) Chapter 15 codes used only on the maternal record

Chapter 15 codes are to be used only on the maternal record, never on the record of the newborn.

It can be confusing as to what can be reported on the mother's chart and what can be reported on the newborn's chart. If possible it may be helpful to code both charts at the same time.

If a pregnant woman has a UTI that in turn affects the care of the newborn, the code O23.42 would not be used on the newborn chart. The code P00.1 would be assigned to the newborn chart and is found in the index. See Figure 23-1 for an example of a condition that may complicate pregnancy.

Codes that are assigned to the newborn are discussed in Chapter 23.

3) Final character for trimester

The majority of codes in Chapter 15 have a final character indicating the trimester of pregnancy. The timeframes for the trimesters are indicated at the beginning of the chapter. If trimester is not a component of a code it is because the condition always occurs in a specific trimester, or the concept of trimester of pregnancy is not applicable. Certain codes have characters for only certain trimesters because the condition does not occur in all trimesters, but it may occur in more than just one.

Assignment of the final character for trimester should be based on the provider's documentation of the trimester (or number of weeks) for the current admission/encounter. This applies to the assignment of trimester for pre-existing conditions as well as those that develop during or are due to the pregnancy. The provider's documentation of the number of weeks may be used to assign the appropriate code identifying the trimester.

Whenever delivery occurs during the current admission, and there is an "in childbirth" option for the obstetric complication being coded, the "in childbirth" code should be assigned.

4) Selection of trimester for inpatient admissions that encompass more than one trimester

In instances when a patient is admitted to a hospital for complications of pregnancy during one trimester and remains in the hospital into a subsequent trimester, the trimester character for the antepartum complication code should be assigned on the basis of the trimester when the complication developed, not the trimester of the discharge. If the condition developed prior to the current admission/encounter or represents a pre-existing condition, the trimester character for the trimester at the time of the admission/encounter should be assigned.

5) Unspecified trimester

Each category that includes codes for trimester has a code for "unspecified trimester." The "unspecified trimester" code should rarely be used, such as when the documentation in the record is insufficient to determine the trimester and it is not possible to obtain clarification.

EXAMPLE

Patient in the third trimester of pregnancy is admitted with oligohydramnios, O41.03X0, Z3A.00.

6) *7th character for Fetus Identification*

Where applicable, a 7th character is to be assigned for certain categories (O31, O32, O33.3–O33.6, O35, O36, O40, O41, O60.1, O60.2, O64, and O69) to identify the fetus for which the complication code applies.

Assign 7th character "0":

- For single gestations
- When the documentation in the record is insufficient to determine the fetus affected and it is not possible to obtain clarification.
- When it is not possible to clinically determine which fetus is affected.

b. Selection of OB Principal or First-listed Diagnosis

1) Routine outpatient prenatal visits

For routine outpatient prenatal visits when no complications are present, a code from category Z34, Encounter for supervision of normal pregnancy, should be used as the first-listed diagnosis. These codes should not be used in conjunction with chapter 15 codes.

2) Supervision of High-Risk Pregnancy

Codes from category O09, Supervision of high-risk pregnancy, are intended for use only during the prenatal period. For complications during the labor or delivery episode as a result of a high-risk pregnancy, assign the applicable complication codes from Chapter 15. If there are no complications during the labor or delivery episode, assign code O80, Encounter for full-term uncomplicated delivery. For routine prenatal outpatient visits for patients with high-risk pregnancies, a code from category O09, Supervision of high-risk pregnancy, should be used as the first-listed diagnosis. Secondary chapter 15 codes may be used in conjunction with these codes if appropriate.

EXAMPLE

The patient is seen in her first trimester at 13 weeks for a routine prenatal visit. She also has a 2-year-old daughter, Z34.81, Z3A.13.

EXAMPLE

The patient is seen at 11 weeks for a routine prenatal visit. The physician documents that she has iron deficiency anemia, O99.011, D50.9, Z3A.11.

Pregnancy *(Continued)*
- infection(s) O98.91-
  - amniotic fluid or sac O41.10-
  - bladder O23.1-
  - carrier state NEC O99.830
    - streptococcus B O99.820
  - genital organ or tract O23.9-
    - specified NEC O23.59-
  - genitourinary tract O23.9-
  - gonorrhea O98.21-
  - hepatitis (viral) O98.41-
  - HIV O98.71-
  - human immunodeficiency [HIV] O98.71-
  - kidney O23.0-
  - nipple O91.01-
  - parasitic disease O98.91-
    - specified NEC O98.81-
  - protozoal disease O98.61-
  - sexually transmitted NEC O98.31-
  - specified type NEC O98.81-
  - syphilis O98.11-
  - tuberculosis O98.01-
  - urethra O23.2-
  - urinary (tract) O23.4-
    - specified NEC O23.3-

FIGURE 22-1. A urinary tract infection is an example of a condition that may complicate pregnancy.

For a patient at high risk, first-listed diagnoses should be selected from the O09 category for outpatient prenatal visits. ICD-10-CM has separate codes for different high-risk categories such as infertility, history of abortion, multiparity, history of preterm labor, poor reproductive history, insufficient prenatal care, elderly primigravida or multigravida, and young primigravida or multigravida. The *Merck Manual* reports that "high-risk" pregnancy has no formal or universally accepted definition, but it goes on to list the following risk factors:

- Weight of mother less than 100 lb
- Obese mother
- Short stature of mother
- Structural abnormalities such as double uterus or incompetent cervix
- Disorders of a mother that are present prior to pregnancy, such as heart disease, high blood pressure, and seizure

EXAMPLE A pregnant patient at 10 weeks presents for a routine prenatal visit. During her previous pregnancy, she had early pregnancy vomiting and the physician documents high-risk pregnancy, O09.891, Z3A.10.

EXAMPLE A gravid patient at 12 weeks presents for a routine prenatal visit. This patient had preeclampsia on her previous pregnancy and the physician documents high-risk pregnancy. She has blood work taken on this visit and is found to be anemic. The physician prescribes an iron supplement, O09.891, O99.011, D64.9, Z3A.12.

3) Episodes when no delivery occurs

In episodes when no delivery occurs, the principal diagnosis should correspond to the principal complication of the pregnancy which necessitated the encounter. Should more than one complication exist, all of which are treated or monitored, any of the complications codes may be sequenced first.

At times, a pregnant woman may have to be admitted to the hospital prior to delivery and sent home before delivery occurs. In these cases, the principal diagnosis is the reason the patient was admitted to the hospital.

EXAMPLE A pregnant patient at 13 weeks presents to the ER with dehydration related to hyperemesis gravidarum. The physician in the ER discovers that the patient has pregnancy-induced hypertension. The patient is admitted, O21.1, O13.1, Z3A.13.

4) When a delivery occurs

When an obstetric patient is admitted and delivers during that admission, the condition that prompted the admission should be sequenced as the principal diagnosis. If multiple conditions prompted the admission, sequence the one most related to the delivery as the principal diagnosis. A code for any complication of the delivery should be assigned as an additional diagnosis. In cases of cesarean delivery, if the patient was admitted with a condition that resulted in the performance of a cesarean procedure, that condition should be selected as the principal diagnosis. If the reason for the admission was unrelated to the condition resulting in the cesarean delivery, the condition related to the reason for the admission should be selected as the principal diagnosis.

EXAMPLE A patient is admitted to the hospital in labor at 40 weeks. She is 40 years old, and labor proceeds uneventfully. This is her sixth pregnancy, and the baby weighs 11 lb. She is delivered by a physician, who performs a midline episiotomy. Physician documents LGA, O36.63x0, Z3A.40, Z37.0, 0W8NXZZ, 10E0XZZ.

EXAMPLE A patient is admitted to the hospital for severe preeclampsia. She is 36 weeks pregnant, and there is no evidence of labor. A low transverse cervical cesarean section (LTCS) is performed immediately, and she delivers a healthy baby boy, O14.14, Z3A.36, Z37.0, 10D00Z1.

5) Outcome of delivery

A code from category Z37, Outcome of delivery, should be included on every maternal record when a delivery has occurred. These codes are not to be used on subsequent records or on the newborn record.

EXAMPLE Healthy 40-year-old primigravida presents to the hospital at 37 weeks and delivers twins vaginally, O30.003, Z3A.37, Z37.2, 10E0XZZ.

EXAMPLE A pregnant woman at 39 weeks presents to the hospital for delivery of known quadruplets. She is taken to the operating room for a cesarean section (LTCS). As the babies are delivered, it is discovered that one has died in utero, O30.203, O36.4xx0, Z3A.39, Z37.62, 10D00Z1.

c. Pre-existing conditions versus conditions due to the pregnancy

Certain categories in Chapter 15 distinguish between conditions of the mother that existed prior to pregnancy (pre-existing) and those that are a direct result of pregnancy. When assigning codes from Chapter 15, it is important to assess if a condition was pre-existing prior to pregnancy or developed during or due to the pregnancy in order to assign the correct code.

Categories that do not distinguish between pre-existing and pregnancy-related conditions may be used for either. It is acceptable to use codes specifically for the puerperium with codes complicating pregnancy and childbirth if a condition arises postpartum during the delivery encounter.

d. Pre-existing hypertension in pregnancy

Category O10, Pre-existing hypertension complicating pregnancy, childbirth and the puerperium, includes codes for hypertensive heart and hypertensive chronic kidney disease. When assigning one of the O10 codes that includes hypertensive heart disease or hypertensive chronic kidney disease, it is necessary to add a secondary code from the appropriate hypertension category to specify the type of heart failure or chronic kidney disease.

See Section I.C.9. Hypertension.

If a condition existed prior to the pregnancy, it is considered pre-existing, as opposed to a condition that develops as a direct result of a pregnancy. If there are categories that do not make a distinction between pre-existing and pregnancy-related, then it is acceptable to use them for either. If a condition arises postpartum, it is acceptable to assign codes specifically for the puerperium.

EXAMPLE

Patient is seen by the obstetrician at 30 weeks for lab work related to her diabetes. The patient has had diabetes type 1 since childhood, O24.013, E10.9, Z3A.30.

EXAMPLE

Patient has had varicose veins in her legs for years. She is now in the 22nd week of her pregnancy and complaining of pain in her lower extremities. Physician documents varicose veins, O22.02, Z3A.22.

e. Fetal Conditions Affecting the Management of the Mother

1) Codes from categories O35 and O36

Codes from categories O35, Maternal care for known or suspected fetal abnormality and damage, and O36, Maternal care for other fetal problems, are assigned only when the fetal condition is actually responsible for modifying the management of the mother, i.e., by requiring diagnostic studies, additional observation, special care, or termination of pregnancy. The fact that the fetal condition exists does not justify assigning a code from this series to the mother's record.

2) In utero surgery

In cases when surgery is performed on the fetus, a diagnosis code from category O35, Maternal care for known or suspected fetal abnormality and damage, should be assigned identifying the fetal condition. Assign the appropriate procedure code for the procedure performed.

No code from Chapter 16, the perinatal codes, should be used on the mother's record to identify fetal conditions. Surgery performed in utero on a fetus is still to be coded as an obstetric encounter.

EXAMPLE

Fetal chromosomal abnormality with elective termination of pregnancy at 14 weeks, with insertion of laminaria and aspiration abortion, with complete extraction of products of conception, Z33.2, O35.1xx0, 10A07Z6, 10A07ZW.

EXAMPLE

Mother presents for delivery at 40 weeks. The physician documents that the baby appears large for dates (LGA [large for gestational age]). The mother vaginally delivers a 7 lb baby girl without any complications, O80, Z3A.40, Z37.0.

In this case, the LGA code would not be used because it does not affect the management of the mother.

EXAMPLE

A fetus is known to have spina bifida. The parents find a surgeon trained in operating in utero and have this problem corrected at 20 weeks. Central nervous system malformation in fetus O35.0xx0, Z3A.20, 10Q00ZE, Open correction of fetal defect.

f. HIV Infection in Pregnancy, Childbirth and the Puerperium

During pregnancy, childbirth or the puerperium, a patient admitted because of an HIV-related illness should receive a principal diagnosis from subcategory O98.7-, Human immunodeficiency [HIV] disease complicating pregnancy, childbirth and the puerperium, followed by the code(s) for the HIV-related illness(es).

Patients with asymptomatic HIV infection status admitted during pregnancy, childbirth, or the puerperium should receive codes of O98.7- and Z21, Asymptomatic human immunodeficiency virus [HIV] infection status.

EXAMPLE

A 32-year-old female who is 23 weeks pregnant with known AIDS is admitted with severe diarrhea determined to be caused by cryptosporidium. She is treated with IV fluids, O98.712, B20, A07.2, Z3A.23.

EXAMPLE

A 23-year-old gravid female is admitted in preterm labor at 35 weeks. She has had an uneventful pregnancy, except for the fact that she has an asymptomatic human immunodeficiency virus (HIV) infection. She vaginally delivers a 7 lb 2 oz baby, O60.14x0, O98.72, Z37.0, Z21, Z3A.35, 10E0XZZ.

g. Diabetes mellitus in pregnancy

Diabetes mellitus is a significant complicating factor in pregnancy. Pregnant women who are diabetic should be assigned a code from category O24, Diabetes mellitus in pregnancy, childbirth, and the puerperium, first, followed by the appropriate diabetes code(s) (E08-E13) from Chapter 4.

h. Long term use of insulin and oral hypoglycemics

See Section I.C.4.a.3. for information on the long term use of insulin and oral hypoglycemics.

EXAMPLE

Patient is admitted to hospital in diabetic ketoacidosis. The admitting physician documents that the patient is 12 weeks pregnant with a history of type I diabetes. She is treated with sliding scale insulin, O24.011, E10.10, Z3A.12.

i. Gestational (pregnancy induced) diabetes

Gestational (pregnancy induced) diabetes can occur during the second and third trimester of pregnancy in women who were not diabetic prior to pregnancy. Gestational diabetes can cause complications in the pregnancy similar to those of pre-existing diabetes mellitus. It also puts the woman at greater risk of developing diabetes after the pregnancy. Codes for gestational diabetes are in subcategory O24.4, Gestational diabetes mellitus. No other code from category O24, Diabetes mellitus in pregnancy, childbirth, and the puerperium, should be used with a code from O24.4

The codes under subcategory O24.4 include diet-controlled, insulin-controlled, and controlled by oral hypoglycemic drugs. If a patient with gestational diabetes is treated with both diet and insulin, only the code for insulin-controlled is required. If a patient with gestational diabetes is treated with both diet and oral hypoglycemic medications, only the code for "controlled by oral hypoglycemic drugs" is required. Code Z79.4, Long-term (current) use of insulin or code Z79.84, Long-term (current) use of oral hypoglycemic drugs, should not be assigned with codes from subcategory O24.4.

An abnormal glucose tolerance in pregnancy is assigned a code from subcategory O99.81, Abnormal glucose complicating pregnancy, childbirth, and the puerperium.

EXAMPLE

A patient is admitted to the hospital in labor at 39 weeks. She has had a relatively uneventful pregnancy except for gestational diabetes which was diet controlled. She vaginally delivers a healthy 7 lb baby girl, O24.420, Z3A.39, Z37.0, 10E0XZZ.

j. Sepsis and septic shock complicating abortion, pregnancy, childbirth and the puerperium

When assigning a chapter 15 code for sepsis complicating abortion, pregnancy, childbirth, and the puerperium, a code for the specific type of infection should be assigned as an additional diagnosis. If severe sepsis is present, a code from subcategory R65.2, Severe sepsis, and code(s) for associated organ dysfunction(s) should also be assigned as additional diagnoses.

k. Puerperal sepsis

Code O85, Puerperal sepsis, should be assigned with a secondary code to identify the causal organism (e.g., for a bacterial infection, assign a code from category B95-B96, Bacterial infections in conditions classified elsewhere). A code from category A40, Streptococcal sepsis, or A41, Other sepsis, should not be used for puerperal sepsis. If applicable, use additional codes to identify severe sepsis (R65.2-) and any associated acute organ dysfunction.

Code O85 should not be assigned for sepsis following an obstetrical procedure (See Section I.C.1.d.5.b., Sepsis due to a postprocedural infection).

EXAMPLE

A 38-week primagravida spontaneously delivers an SGA baby. Following delivery the obstetrician manually removes fragments of the retained placenta. On the second day after delivery the patient develops a fever and foul-smelling discharge. Antibiotics are initiated and puerperal sepsis is documented, O73.1, O85, Z3A.38, Z37.0, 10D17ZZ, 10E0XZZ.

l. Alcohol, tobacco and drug use during pregnancy, childbirth and the puerperium

1) Alcohol use during pregnancy, childbirth and the puerperium

Codes under subcategory O99.31, Alcohol use complicating pregnancy, childbirth, and the puerperium, should be assigned for any pregnancy case when a mother uses alcohol during the pregnancy or postpartum. A secondary code from category F10, Alcohol related disorders, should also be assigned to identify manifestations of the alcohol use.

2) Tobacco use during pregnancy, childbirth and the puerperium

Codes under subcategory O99.33, Smoking (tobacco) complicating pregnancy, childbirth, and the puerperium, should be assigned for any pregnancy case when a mother uses any type of tobacco product during the pregnancy or postpartum. A secondary code from category F17, Nicotine dependence, should also be assigned to identify the type of nicotine dependence.

3) Drug use during pregnancy, childbirth and the puerperium

Codes under subcategory O99.32, Drug use complicating pregnancy, childbirth, and the puerperium, should be assigned for any pregnancy case when a mother uses drugs during the pregnancy or postpartum. This can involve illegal drugs, or inappropriate use of abuse of prescription drugs. Secondary code(s) from categories F11-F16 and F18-F19 should also be assigned to identify manifestations of the drug use.

EXAMPLE

Patient reports to the emergency room in labor. She is 30 weeks pregnant and admits to drinking daily during this pregnancy. She is admitted for administration of terbutaline. Physician documents early labor due to alcohol abuse, O60.03, O99.313, F10.10, Z3A.30.

m. Poisoning, toxic effects, adverse effects and underdosing in a pregnant patient

A code from subcategory O9A.2, Injury, poisoning and certain other consequences of external causes complicating pregnancy, childbirth, and the puerperium, should be sequenced first, followed by the appropriate injury, poisoning, toxic effect, adverse effect or underdosing code, and then the additional code(s) that specifies the condition caused by the poisoning, toxic effect, adverse effect or underdosing.

See Section I.C.19. Adverse effects, poisoning, underdosing and toxic effects.

EXAMPLE

Patient is 18 weeks pregnant. She presents to the ED in an altered mental state after taking a whole bottle of Valium. She was trying to kill herself after an argument with her mother, O9A.212, T42.4x2A, R41.82, Z3A.18.

n. Normal Delivery, Code O80

1) Encounter for full term uncomplicated delivery

Code O80 should be assigned when a woman is admitted for a full-term normal delivery and delivers a single, healthy infant without any complications antepartum, during the delivery, or postpartum during the delivery episode. Code O80 is always a principal diagnosis. It is not to be used if any other code from chapter 15 is needed to describe a current complication of the antenatal, delivery, or postnatal period. Additional codes from other chapters may be used with code O80 if they are not related to or are in any way complicating the pregnancy.

2) Uncomplicated delivery with resolved antepartum complication

Code O80 may be used if the patient had a complication at some point during the pregnancy, but the complication is not present at the time of the admission for delivery.

3) Outcome of delivery for O80

Z37.0, Single live birth, is the only outcome of delivery code appropriate for use with O80.

EXAMPLE

Patient is admitted to the hospital in labor. She is 40 weeks pregnant. She has had an uneventful pregnancy and vaginally delivers a 7 lb 2 oz baby boy. The doctor performs an episiotomy during delivery, O80, Z37.0, Z3A.40, 0W8NXZZ, 10E0XZZ.

EXAMPLE

Patient is admitted to the hospital in labor. She is 40 weeks pregnant. She has had an uneventful pregnancy and vaginally delivers a 7 lb 2 oz baby boy. The doctor performs an episiotomy and the baby is delivered with the use of a vacuum extractor due to maternal exhaustion, O75.81, Z3A.40, Z37.0, 10D07Z6, 0W8NXZZ.

The use of a vacuum extractor in the above example prohibits the use of code O80 for this delivery.

EXAMPLE

Patient is admitted to the hospital in labor. She is 40 weeks pregnant, has had an uneventful pregnancy, and vaginally delivers a 7 lb 2 oz baby boy. The patient has a first-degree perineal laceration that is repaired, O70.0, Z3A.40, Z37.0, 10E0XZZ, 0WQ9XZZ.

As in the previous example, the first-degree extension in this example prohibits the use of O80. When an extension of an episiotomy occurs, both the episiotomy and laceration repair are coded.

EXAMPLE

Patient is admitted to the hospital in labor. She is 40 weeks pregnant. She had a UTI early on in her pregnancy and was treated appropriately. She delivers a 7 lb 2 oz baby boy by spontaneous vaginal delivery, O80, Z3A.40, Z37.0, 10E0XZZ.

o. The Peripartum and Postpartum Periods

1) Peripartum and Postpartum periods

The postpartum period begins immediately after delivery and continues for six weeks following delivery. The peripartum period is defined as the last month of pregnancy to five months postpartum.

EXAMPLE

Patient is admitted to hospital for mastitis. She is 2 weeks postpartum and is given a course of intravenous (IV) antibiotics, O91.22.

2) Peripartum and postpartum complication

A postpartum complication is any complication occurring within the six-week period.

EXAMPLE

Patient is admitted to the hospital 3 weeks postpartum. She is having pain in her right calf and is given a diagnosis of deep vein thrombosis. The patient is treated with IV heparin, O87.1, I82.4Z1.

3) Pregnancy-related complications after 6 week period

Chapter 15 codes may also be used to describe pregnancy-related complications after the peripartum or postpartum period if the provider documents that a condition is pregnancy related.

EXAMPLE

Patient is admitted to the hospital with postpartum cholecystitis. She delivered 8 weeks prior to this presentation, O99.63, K81.9.

In this case, the physician documented that this was a postpartum condition; therefore it was coded as such even though it occurred beyond the 6-week time period.

4) Admission for routine postpartum care following delivery outside hospital

When the mother delivers outside the hospital prior to admission and is admitted for routine postpartum care and no complications are noted, code Z39.0, Encounter for care and examination of mother immediately after delivery, should be assigned as the principal diagnosis.

EXAMPLE

Patient delivers baby at 38 weeks in the car on the way to the hospital. She is admitted through the ER for examination, Z39.0.

5) Pregnancy associated cardiomyopathy
Pregnancy associated cardiomyopathy, code O90.3, is unique in that it may be diagnosed in the third trimester of pregnancy but may continue to progress months after delivery. For this reason, it is referred to as peripartum cardiomyopathy. Code O90.3 is only for use when the cardiomyopathy develops as a result of pregnancy in a woman who did not have pre-existing heart disease.

EXAMPLE

Patient is 2 weeks postpartum. She presents to physician's office complaining of shortness of breath, swollen ankles, and frequent awakening to urinate. The physician performs chest CT. His diagnosis is postpartum cardiomyopathy, O90.3.

p. Code O94, Sequelae of complication of pregnancy, childbirth, and the puerperium

1) Code O94
Code O94, Sequelae of complication of pregnancy, childbirth, and the puerperium, is for use in those cases when an initial complication of a pregnancy develops a sequelae requiring care or treatment at a future date.

2) After the initial postpartum period
This code may be used at any time after the initial postpartum period.

3) Sequencing of Code O94
This code, like all sequela codes, is to be sequenced following the code describing the sequelae of the complication.

EXAMPLE

The patient presents to the physician's office complaining of painful intercourse.
She is 6 months postpartum. The obstetrician determines that the patient is suffering from a late effect of the repair of the perineum, N94.10, O94, Y83.8.

q. Termination of Pregnancy and Spontaneous abortions

1) Abortion with Liveborn Fetus
When an attempted termination of pregnancy results in a liveborn fetus, assign code Z33.2, Encounter for elective termination of pregnancy and a code from category Z37, Outcome of Delivery.

EXAMPLE

A woman is admitted at 22 weeks for insertion of a laminaria for termination of pregnancy. She delivers a liveborn fetus, Z33.2, Z3A.22, Z37.0, 10A07ZW, 10E0XZZ.

2) Retained Products of Conception following an abortion
Subsequent encounters for retained products of conception following a spontaneous abortion or elective termination of pregnancy without complications are assigned O03.4, Incomplete spontaneous abortion without complication, or codes O07.4, Failed attempted termination of pregnancy without complication. This advice is appropriate even when the patient was discharged previously with a discharge diagnosis of complete abortion. If the patient has a specific complication associated with the spontaneous abortion or elective termination of pregnancy in addition to retained products of conception, assign the appropriate complication code (e.g., O03.-, O04.-, O07.-) instead of code O03.4 or O07.4.

EXAMPLE

Retained products of conception after spontaneous abortion at 8 weeks' gestation. The products of conception were initially passed at home 2 days earlier. D&C was performed, O03.4, 10D17ZZ.

3) Complications leading to abortion
Codes from Chapter 15 may be used as additional codes to identify any documented complications of the pregnancy in conjunction with codes in categories in O04, O07 and O08.

r. **Abuse in a pregnant patient**
For suspected or confirmed cases of abuse of a pregnant patient, a code(s) from subcategories O9A.3, Physical abuse complicating pregnancy, childbirth, and the puerperium, O9A.4, Sexual abuse complicating pregnancy, childbirth, and the puerperium, and O9A.5, Psychological abuse complicating pregnancy, childbirth, and the puerperium, should be sequenced first, followed by the appropriate codes (if applicable) to identify any associated current injury due to physical abuse, sexual abuse, and the perpetrator of abuse.
See Section I.C.19.f. Adult and child abuse, neglect and other maltreatment.

s. **COVID-19 infection in pregnancy, childbirth, and the puerperium**
During pregnancy, childbirth or the puerperium, when COVID-10 is the reason for admission/encounter, code O98.5-, Other viral diseases complicating pregnancy, childbirth and the puerperium, should be sequenced as the principal/first-listed diagnosis, and code U07.1, COVID-19, and the appropriate codes for associated manifestation(s) should be assigned as additional diagnoses. Codes from Chapter 15 always take sequencing priority.
If the reason for admission/encounter is unrelated to COVID-19 but the patient tests positive for COVID-19 during the admission/encounter, the appropriate code for the reason for admission/encounter should be sequenced as the principal/first-listed diagnosis, and codes O98.5- and U07.1, as well as the appropriate codes for associated COVID-19 manifestations, should be assigned as additional diagnoses.

EXAMPLE

Pregnant woman is admitted at 37 weeks in active labor after being physically abused by her spouse. She goes on to have a normal vaginal delivery, O9a.32, Z3A.37, Z37.0, Y07.01, 10E0XZZ.

ANATOMY AND PHYSIOLOGY

The organs of the female reproductive system include the ovaries, fallopian tubes, uterus, vagina, and cervix (Figure 22-2). These organs aid in reproduction and supply hormones that aid in the development of secondary female sex characteristics such as body hair and breasts.

The **vulva** is the external covering to the vagina. The **labia** surround the vaginal opening. The vagina is a muscular tube that extends from the vaginal opening to the uterus. The **vagina** serves three purposes: It is the receptacle for sperm during intercourse, it serves as the birth canal for childbirth, and it rids the body of menstrual blood during menstruation.

The **cervix** is the neck of the uterus and serves as an outlet from the uterus. The **uterus** is a muscular organ that serves as an incubator for the developing fetus. The wall of the uterus is composed of three layers. The inner layer, the endometrium, is where an egg grows if fertilized.

The **ovaries** produce female hormones and eggs. If the egg is fertilized and becomes a fetus, all the other female organs assist in development and expulsion of the fetus. When an egg becomes mature and is ready for fertilization, it travels through the **fallopian tube**

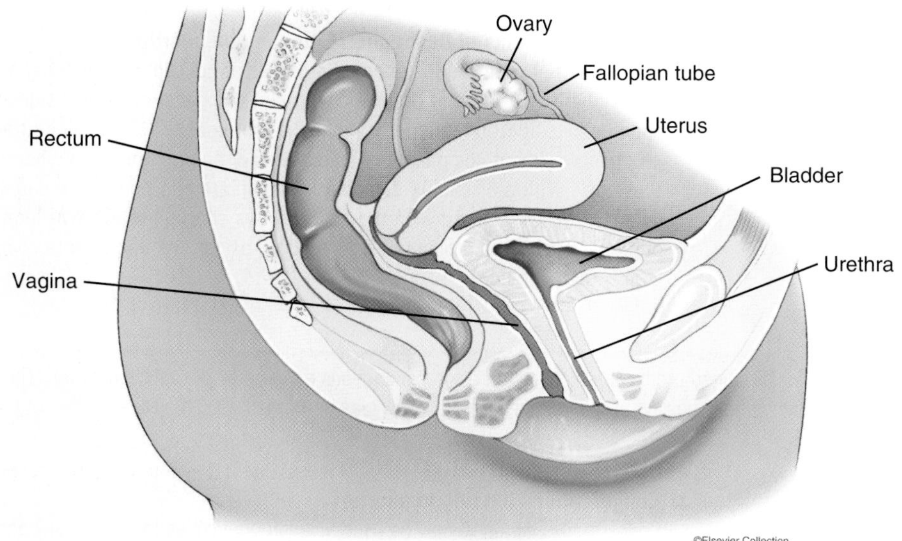

FIGURE 22-2. Normal female reproductive system.

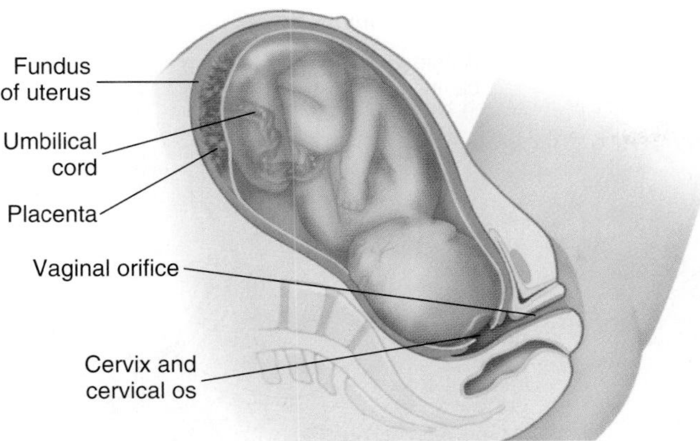

FIGURE 22-3. Normal uterine pregnancy.

to the uterus. The purpose of the fallopian tube is to deliver the mature egg to the uterus for fertilization. See Figure 22-3 for the anatomy of a normal uterine pregnancy.

To confirm a pregnancy, a woman's blood or urine may be tested for human chorionic gonadotropin (hCG). In the early months of pregnancy, secretion of hCG occurs at a high level.

Common Pregnancy Definitions

Antepartum: before delivery
Elderly obstetric patient: 35 years or older at date of delivery
Gravid: pregnant
Habitual aborter: a woman who miscarries at least three consecutive times
Lactation: process of milk production
Multigravida or **multiparity**: two or more pregnancies
Postpartum: after delivery
Postterm pregnancy: pregnancy longer than 40 weeks up to 42 weeks
Precipitate labor: rapid labor and delivery
Pregestational: condition present prior to pregnancy
Prenatal: before birth
Primigravida: first pregnancy
Prolonged pregnancy: beyond 42 weeks of pregnancy
Puerperium: time from delivery through first 6 weeks post partum
Stillbirth: dead at birth
Young obstetric patient: younger than 16 years at date of delivery

CONDITIONS OF PREGNANCY, CHILDBIRTH, AND PUERPERIUM

Pregnancy, Childbirth, and the Puerperium (O00-O9A), Chapter 15 in the ICD-10-CM code book, is divided into the following categories:

CATEGORY	SECTION TITLES
O00-O08	Pregnancy with abortive outcome
O09	Supervision of high-risk pregnancy
O10-O16	Edema, proteinuria, and hypertensive disorders in pregnancy, childbirth, and the puerperium
O20-O29	Other maternal disorders predominantly related to pregnancy
O30-O48	Maternal care related to the fetus and amniotic cavity and possible delivery problems
O60-O77	Complications of labor and delivery
O80-O82	Encounter for delivery
O85-O92	Complications predominantly related to the puerperium
O94-O9A	Other obstetric conditions, not elsewhere classified

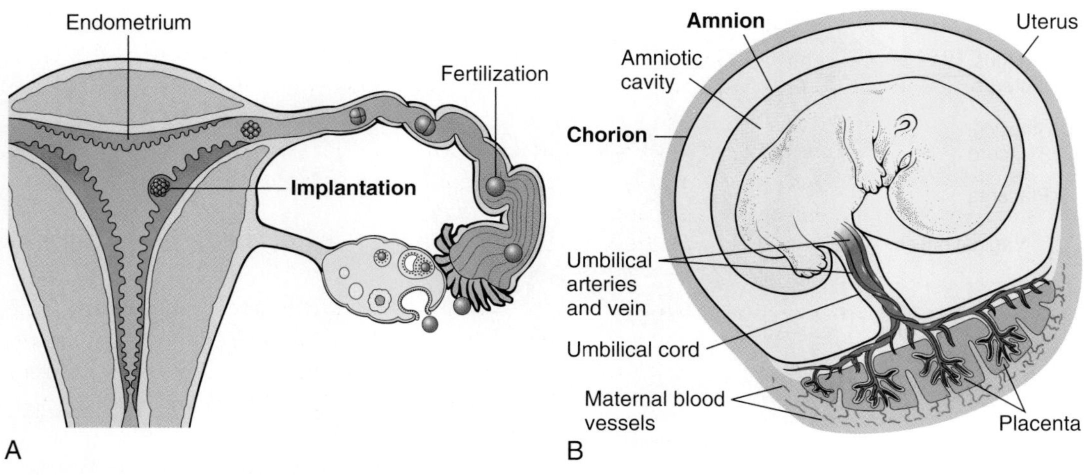

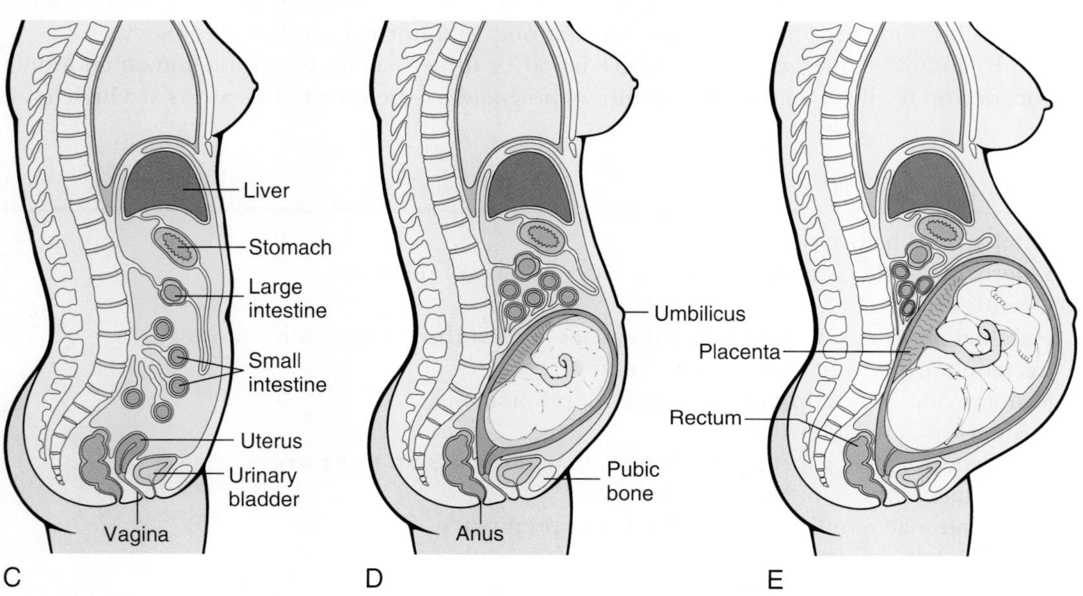

FIGURE 22-4. **A,** Implantation of the embryo in the endometrium. **B,** The placenta and membranes (chorion and amnion). **C–E,** Sagittal sections of pregnancy. **C,** Nonpregnant woman. **D,** Woman who is 20 weeks pregnant. **E,** Woman who is 30 weeks pregnant.

Coding of Pregnancy

A normal pregnancy (Figure 22-4) usually lasts anywhere from 37 to 40 weeks. These weeks are counted from the beginning of the last menstrual cycle. A normal pregnancy has three trimesters, counted from the first day of the last menstrual period. They are defined as follows:

- First trimester—less than 14 weeks 0 days
- Second trimester—14 weeks 0 days to less than 28 weeks 0 days
- Third trimester—28 weeks 0 days until delivery

When a pregnancy lasts longer than 40 weeks (post-term), complications can occur; and therefore this is no longer considered a normal pregnancy. Documentation of weeks/trimester should be made by the provider.

Labor is the process of expelling the products of conception from the uterus through the vagina to the outside world. There are four stages of labor:

- First Stage—Dilation

  Begins with cervical dilation and regular uterine contraction and ends when the patient is completely dilated and **effaced** (shortening or thinning of the cervix has occurred). The average length of time for this process is 10 to 14 hours.

- Second Stage—Expulsion
  Begins with complete dilation and effacement of the cervix and ends with the birth of the baby. The average length of time for this process is 1 to 4 hours.
- Third Stage—Placenta
  Begins with the birth of the baby and ends with the delivery of the placenta. The average length of time for this process is from 5 to 15 minutes.
- Fourth Stage—Return to normal
  Begins with the delivery of the placenta and ends 1 to 2 hours after delivery, when uterine tone is established.

All deliveries require an outcome of delivery code on the mother's record. The outcome of delivery is the code used to describe the number of newborns delivered and their status, i.e., live or stillborn. The outcome of delivery code is found in the Alphabetic Index under the main term "outcome of delivery." **It is important to note that if code O80 is selected, it cannot be used with any other code in Chapter 15.**

When codes are selected for complications of pregnancy, childbirth, and the puerperium, a variety of main terms in the index may be accessed. If the condition is affecting the pregnancy, the index term is pregnancy. Likewise if the condition is affecting labor, the index directs the coder to see delivery. The Alphabetic Index may be checked directly for a condition (Figure 22-5).

Other main terms in the Alphabetic Index that may be used to locate pregnancy-related codes include the following:

- Failure
- Laceration
- Puerperal
- Pregnancy
- Delivery
- Outcome

cardiorenal (disease) I13.10
  with heart failure I13.0
    with stage 1 through stage 4
        chronic kidney disease I13.0
    with stage 5 or end stage renal
        disease I13.2
  without heart failure I13.10
    with stage 1 through stage 4
        chronic kidney disease I13.10
    with stage 5 or end stage renal
        disease I13.11
cardiovascular
  disease (arteriosclerotic) (sclerotic) -
      see Hypertension, heart
  renal (disease) - *see* Hypertension,
      cardiorenal
  chronic venous - *see* Hypertension,
      venous (chronic)
  complicating
    childbirth (labor) O16.4
      pre-existing O10.92
        with
          heart disease O10.12
            with renal disease O10.32
          pre-eclampsia O11.4 4
          renal disease O10.22
            with heart disease O10.32
        essential O10.02
      secondary O10.42
    pregnancy O16.-

FIGURE 22-5. Alphabetic Index entry for hypertension complicating pregnancy.

EXERCISE 22-1

Answer the following questions.

1. The duration of a normal pregnancy is ______________________________
2. Can code O80 be used with O66.5xx0? ______________________________
3. What are the three most common areas of the Alphabetic Index to look under for codes related to Chapter 15?
   1. ______________________________
   2. ______________________________
   3. ______________________________
4. What are the organs of the female reproductive system? ______________________________
5. To confirm a pregnancy, what is tested for from a woman's blood or urine? ______________________________
6. If a woman is pregnant for the first time at age 36, what would be another term for her? ______________________________
7. If a woman delivers at 41 weeks, what would this be considered? ______________
8. How long does the puerperium last? ______________

Identify the main term(s) that would be used to locate the following in the Alphabetic Index.

9. Obstructed labor ______________
10. First-degree perineal laceration delivered single liveborn vaginally ______________
11. Arrested labor ______________
12. Fever due to amnionitis during labor ______________
13. Twin pregnancy ______________
14. Oligohydramnios ______________
15. Premature rupture of membranes ______________
16. Primary uterine inertia ______________
17. Postpartum hemorrhage ______________
18. Breech delivery ______________
19. Prolonged labor ______________
20. Precipitous delivery ______________

Pregnancy With Abortive Outcome (O00-O08)

Ectopic and Molar Pregnancy

Ectopic pregnancies usually occur when the egg is implanted outside the cavity of the uterus, most commonly in the fallopian tube (Figure 22-6). This type of pregnancy occurs in 1 of every 50 pregnancies. Pelvic infections may predispose a woman to having ectopic pregnancies.

EXAMPLE

Patient presents to physician's office with abdominal pain and vaginal bleeding. She is 10 weeks pregnant. An ultrasound performed in the office determines that the patient has an ectopic pregnancy of the right fallopian tube. She is scheduled for emergency surgery, O00.101.

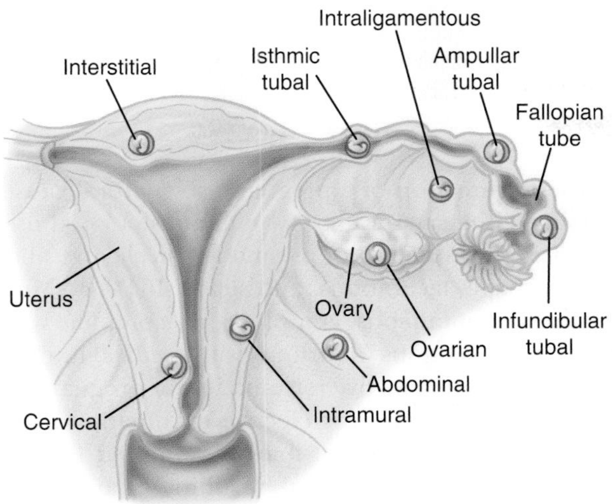

FIGURE 22-6. Diagram showing locations of ectopic (extrauterine) pregnancy.

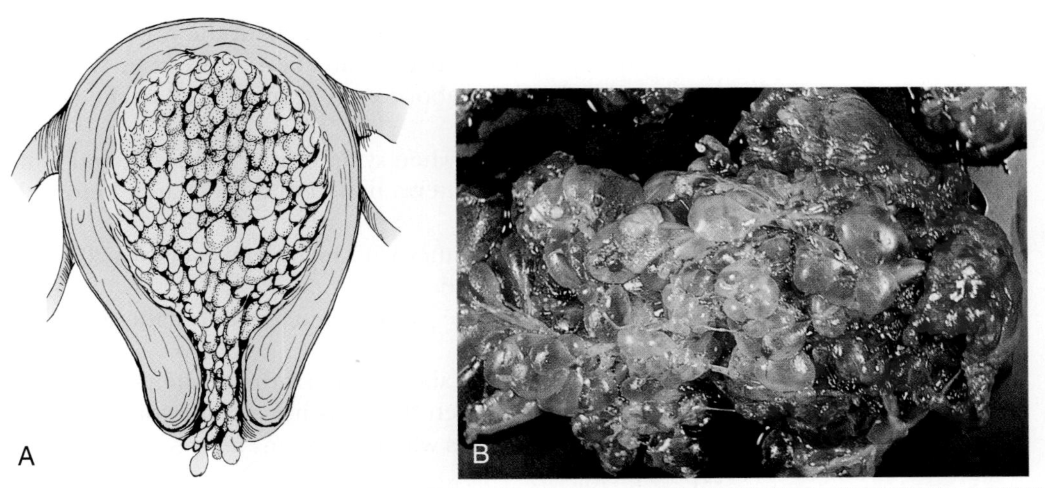

FIGURE 22-7. Hydatidiform mole.

Molar pregnancies are rare and occur in 1 in 1000 pregnancies. In a **molar pregnancy** the embryo does not form at all or is malformed. The early placenta develops into a mass of cysts within a hydatidiform mole (Figure 22-7). Occasionally, a molar pregnancy can turn into a rare pregnancy-related form of cancer.

EXAMPLE

Patient presents to her physician's office with a pregnancy in the 10th week. She comes in because she is experiencing dark brown vaginal bleeding. The physician identifies a molar pregnancy. The patient is admitted to the hospital for vacuum curettage to remove the hydatidiform molar tissue, O01.9, 10A07Z6.

Codes in category Z3A, weeks of gestation, should not be assigned for pregnancies with abortive outcomes (categories O00-O08), elective termination of pregnancy (code Z33.32), nor for postpartum conditions. It is appropriate to use codes from O08.– to describe any complications that may occur during an ectopic or molar pregnancy. According to the general rule for obstetric cases, additional codes from other chapters may be used in conjunction with Chapter 15 codes to further specify conditions.

EXAMPLE

Patient is admitted to the hospital at 8 weeks with a tubal pregnancy without intrauterine pregnancy. After the tubal pregnancy is removed with right salpingectomy via laparoscopic approach, the patient develops a urinary tract infection (UTI), O00.101, O08.83, N39.0, 10T24ZZ, 0UT54ZZ.

Abortion is the termination of a pregnancy by natural causes or medical intervention. Abortions occurring either naturally (spontaneously) or those performed with medical intervention (induced termination of pregnancy or elective abortion) may have complications such as hemorrhage, lacerations, and sepsis. ICD-10-CM contains codes that include two types of abortions: spontaneous/complete or incomplete with or without complications, and induced or elective abortions (abortions with medical intervention) with complications. If a patient is admitted for an elective termination of pregnancy and there are no complications, the code Z33.2 (Encounter for elective termination of pregnancy) is the principal diagnosis. In some instances a patient may be admitted for an elective abortion and the attempt to abort the fetus is unsuccessful, resulting in an incomplete elective abortion. In these cases a code Z33.2 Encounter for elective termination and a code from category Z73.- outcome of delivery are used. If there are any associated complication(s) the appropriate code from category O07 should be assigned.

Types of Abortion

Complete abortion is an abortion in which all the products of conception are expelled.

Elective abortion is the elective termination of pregnancy.

Incomplete abortion is an abortion in which not all of the products of conception are expelled.

Inevitable abortion occurs when symptoms are present, and a miscarriage will happen.

Miscarriage is spontaneous termination of a pregnancy before the fetus has reached 20 weeks.

Missed abortion is a pregnancy with fetal demise before 20 weeks, when no products of conception are expelled.

Spontaneous abortion is the loss of a fetus due to natural causes; it is also known as a miscarriage.

Therapeutic abortion is an abortion performed when the pregnancy is endangering the mother's health, or when the fetus has a condition that is incompatible with life.

Threatened abortion occurs when symptoms are present that indicate that a miscarriage is possible.

EXAMPLE

Patient presents to the hospital with known pregnancy. She is in her 11th week and is now complaining of severe back pain and vaginal bleeding. The physician examines the patient and determines that she has suffered an incomplete abortion. A dilation and curettage (D&C) is performed, and the patient is discharged, O03.4, 10D17ZZ.

EXAMPLE

Pregnant patient at 9 weeks presents to the hospital with vaginal bleeding and abdominal cramps. She is evaluated in the ER and is found to have a UTI. It is also determined that she has suffered a complete miscarriage. The patient is monitored for several hours and is discharged on a course of antibiotics, O03.88.

EXAMPLE

Spontaneous abortion at 12 weeks, incomplete, in patient with gestational hypertension. D&C was performed, O03.4, O13.1, 10D17ZZ.

EXAMPLE

Patient had a spontaneous abortion 2 weeks ago. She presents to the hospital with a high fever, chills, and elevated WBC. Sepsis due to abortion is diagnosed, and she is admitted, O03.87.

EXERCISE 22-2

Assign codes to the following conditions.

1. Ruptured ectopic pregnancy of the fallopian tube at 6 weeks ____________
2. Vesicular mole ____________
3. Ectopic pregnancy of the fallopian tube followed by oliguria ____________
4. Woman is admitted to the hospital after having a miscarriage. The physician performs a suction curettage to remove the products of conception. It is believed that the miscarriage occurred in association with placenta previa. ____________
5. Patient presents to the hospital at 8 weeks for an elective abortion. After the abortion is performed by suction, she spikes a high fever and is diagnosed with endometritis. ____________
6. Patient with missed abortion at 10 weeks was admitted to the hospital for a therapeutic abortion by D&C. ____________
7. Patient presents to the hospital for an elective abortion at 20 weeks because the fetus is hydrocephalic. An aspiration abortion is performed. ____________
8. Patient presents to the hospital with hemorrhage after a self-induced abortion at 6 weeks. Physician performs a D&C to control hemorrhage. ____________

Supervision of High-Risk Pregnancy (O09)

Every pregnancy contains some risk of problems. Pregnancies that are high-risk mean there is a greater chance of problems. Some of the codes in this category include previous pregnancies with history of molar pregnancy, ectopic pregnancy, pre-term labor, elderly obstetric patient, and history of in utero procedures. Codes from category O09 are intended for use only during the prenatal period.

EXAMPLE Patient presents today at 32 weeks. Patient is being seen weekly during this pregnancy secondary to a previous neonatal death, O09.293, Z3A.32.

Edema, Proteinuria, and Hypertensive Disorders in Pregnancy, Childbirth, and the Puerperium (O10-O16)

Hypertension in Pregnancy

Pregnancy can be complicated by high blood pressure. In the United States, approximately 6%–8% of pregnancies are complicated by high blood pressure. A patient may have had high blood pressure prior to conceiving or may develop high blood pressure (gestational) during the pregnancy. When it develops during the pregnancy, this may be referred to as pregnancy-induced hypertension (PIH). The effects of high blood pressure can cause low birth weight or early delivery and may affect the mother's kidneys. High blood pressure in pregnancy may lead to preeclampsia or eclampsia.

Preeclampsia is related to increased blood pressure and protein in the mother's urine that occurs in the second or third trimester of pregnancy. Preeclampsia may be referred to as **toxemia** of pregnancy. Risk factors for developing preeclampsia include obesity, multiple pregnancies, first pregnancy, under the age of 20 or over the age of 40, or women with chronic diseases such as diabetes, chronic hypertension, and lupus. Preeclampsia is detected by high blood pressure, protein in the urine, swelling of the hands and feet, and weight gain of more than 2 lbs per week. The only treatment for preeclampsia is delivery of the baby. Preeclampsia can be monitored in the early stages but should it develop into seizures (eclampsia) or HELLP (hemolytic anemia, elevated liver enzymes, low platelet count) syndrome, this becomes a life-threatening condition.

EXAMPLE

Patient presents to her doctor's office for routine check up at 24 weeks of pregnancy. Blood pressure is elevated and patient's hands and feet are quite swollen. The physician performs a lab test to look for protein in the urine. The test is positive. The physician documents PIH, O14.92, Z3A.24.

Other Maternal Disorders Predominantly Related to Pregnancy (O20-O29)

Hyperemesis gravidarum is a severe form of morning sickness, which presents with persistent vomiting and nausea. Many pregnant women develop morning sickness during the first 3 months of pregnancy. This is attributed to the rising blood levels of HCG, which is secreted by the placenta. When the vomiting gets severe, it can lead to metabolic disturbances such as electrolyte imbalance.

EXAMPLE

Patient in her 8th week presents to obstetrician's office with terrible nausea and vomiting. He diagnoses her with hyperemesis gravidarium and dehydration, O21.1, Z3A.08.

Another condition that occurs in about 5% of the pregnancies in the United States is gestational diabetes. Gestational diabetes (GDM) is diabetes brought on by pregnancy and typically occurs in the second trimester. GDM can affect the baby in several ways; the baby may be large for its gestational age, the baby may have hypoglycemia, and the baby may develop jaundice. Sometimes women have diabetes prior to becoming pregnant which may also complicate the pregnancy.

EXAMPLE

Patient is in her 24th week of pregnancy and has pre-existing type 1 diabetes, O24.012, E10.9, Z3A.24.

Maternal Care Related to the Fetus and Amniotic Cavity and Possible Delivery Problems (O30-O48)

In ICD-10-CM there are certain codes that require a seventh character that identifies which fetus is affected in multiple gestations by the condition code assigned. Categories using the 7th character are O31, O32, O33.3–O33.7, O35, O36, O40, O41, O60.1, O60.2, O64, and O69. When using a 7th character a code for multiple gestation must also be assigned.

Assign 7th character "0" in the following cases:

- For single gestations
- When the documentation in the record is not sufficient to determine the fetus affected and it is not possible to obtain clarification
- When it is not clinically possible to determine the fetus affected

EXAMPLE

Patient was delivered by low cervical cesarean section for a breech presentation for a single liveborn, 40-week gestation, code O32.1xx0, Z3A.40, Z37.0, 10D00Z1.

EXAMPLE

However, if the patient was being delivered by classic cesarean section at 39 weeks for a breech presentation for a twin pregnancy with Twin A in the vertex position and Twin B in the breech position, code O32.1xx2 would be assigned along with the code for twin pregnancy O30.003 and Z3A.39, Z37.2, 10D00Z0.

7th Character Identifying Fetus Affected	
0	not applicable or unspecified
1	fetus 1 or fetus A
2	fetus 2 or fetus B
3	fetus 3 or fetus C
4	fetus 4 or fetus D
5	fetus 5 or fetus E
9	other fetus

It is important to note that if there is a fetal problem and it does not affect the care of the mother, then a code is not assigned. It is also important to assign a code when the management of the mother is affected by the fetal condition. For example, if there are diagnostic studies required, observation, termination, or care this would affect the management of the mother.

Malpresentation of the fetus would include any presentation other than vertex. Malpresentation would include breech, face, brow, and shoulder. The most common malpresentation is breech, and it occurs in around 4% of deliveries. Malpresentation may be the reason a cesarean section is performed. Sometimes labor becomes obstructed due to fetal presentation. Figure 22-8 shows some examples of fetal presentation.

EXAMPLE

Pregnant patient at 20 weeks is tested for spina bifida with a maternal serum alpha-fetoprotein (MSAFP) test. The test is positive so the physician performs an amniocentesis, which is positive for spinal bifida, O35.0xx0, Z3A.20, 10903ZU.

Premature rupture of the membranes (PROM) is a condition that occurs when the membranes rupture more than an hour before the onset of labor. Usually labor will ensue; however, if left to go on too long, there becomes a high risk of infection.

EXAMPLE

Patient in the 35th week of pregnancy is seen in obstetrician's office in early labor. She reports that the evening before while making dinner, she suspected her water may have broken. She is sent to the hospital with a diagnosis of PROM, O42.013, Z3A.35.

EXERCISE 22-3

Answer the questions and assign codes to the following conditions. If not specified, presume liveborn.

1. Patient vaginally delivered at 35 weeks; single liveborn infant ____________
2. Patient presents with PIH at 32 weeks; she is treated and sent home. ____________
3. Patient presents at 39 weeks in labor; she had a previous cesarean section and delivered on this admit with no complications; vaginal delivery of single liveborn ____________
4. Patient is given pitocin to induce labor for post-dates (41 weeks); induction is unsuccessful and she is sent home. ____________
5. Patient presents at 35 weeks with premature rupture of membranes and delivers a healthy newborn vaginally. ____________
6. Patient with a history of preterm labor is seen in the OB office for a routine pregnancy visit. She is in her 18th week. ____________
7. An obese pregnant woman at 20 weeks presents to the hospital with extremely high blood pressure. The physician documents mild preeclampsia. She is put on medications and sent home. ____________
8. A pregnant woman at 40 weeks presents to the hospital with gestational diabetes; she delivers a single liveborn vaginally. ____________
9. A pregnant woman presents to the hospital in labor with a diagnosis of severe preeclampsia. She has smoked this entire pregnancy. She is 35 weeks pregnant and delivers a baby girl vaginally. ____________
10. A pregnant woman at 30 weeks presents to the hospital in labor; she has a twin pregnancy and vaginally delivers two baby girls. ____________
11. A 15-year-old girl at 37 weeks presents to the hospital in labor. She has a known twin pregnancy. A low cervical cesarean section is performed. One of the twins is stillborn. ____________

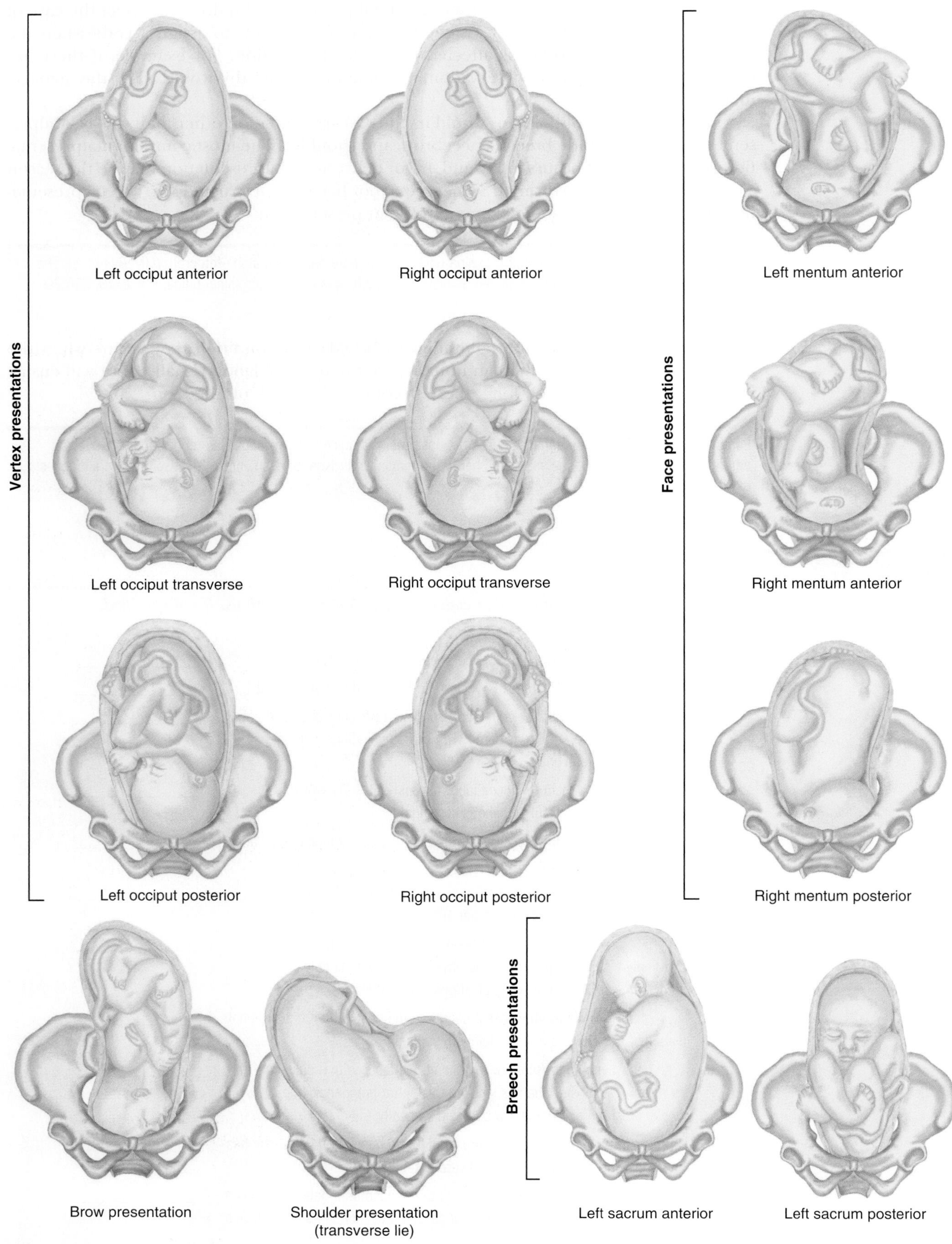
Vertex presentations
Left occiput anterior
Right occiput anterior
Left occiput transverse
Right occiput transverse
Left occiput posterior
Right occiput posterior
Face presentations
Left mentum anterior
Right mentum anterior
Right mentum posterior
Brow presentation
Shoulder presentation
(transverse lie)
Breech presentations
Left sacrum anterior
Left sacrum posterior

FIGURE 22-8. Fetal presentations.

12. The patient at 39 weeks had a low transverse cesarean section due to the baby being large for dates. ________________

13. The patient was induced with IV Pitocin at 39 weeks as the baby was suspected to have spina bifida; she vaginally delivered a 5 lb baby boy. ________________

14. The patient presents for delivery at 40 weeks. She is a known type 2 diabetic, treated with insulin at the onset of pregnancy. She delivers a large for dates baby via cesarean section. ________________

15. Pregnant woman at 20 weeks presents to doctor's office with complaints of blurred vision. Testing is done, and the diagnosis of gestational diabetes is made. ________________

Complications of Labor and Delivery (O60-O77)

A completely normal vaginal delivery is not all that common. There are many conditions that may complicate either or both labor and delivery. Some of the more common are listed below:

- Preterm labor—occurs when the onset of labor is before 37 completed weeks of pregnancy
- Precipitate labor—very rapid labor
- Failure to progress—labor does not progress as expected, slow cervical dilatation, or lack of descent
- Obstructed labor—could be due to malposition or malpresentation of fetus, pelvic abnormality, or fetopelvic disproportion
- Cord complications, such as entanglement, compression or cord around the neck of the fetus
- Lacerations during delivery (Figure 22-9).
- First degree—laceration to skin only
- Second degree—laceration to perineum involving perineal muscles but not involving anal sphincter
- Third degree—laceration to perineum involving anal sphincter complex
  - 3a—less than 50% of external anal sphincter thickness torn
  - 3B—more than 50% external anal sphincter thickness torn
  - 3C—both external and internal anal sphincter torn
- Fourth degree—laceration to perineum involving anal sphincter complex (external and internal anal sphincter) and anal epithelium
- Retained placenta—when the placenta is not totally expulsed
- Non reassuring fetal heart rate—abnormal fetal heart rate or rhythm (i.e., bradycardia, decelerations, irregularity)

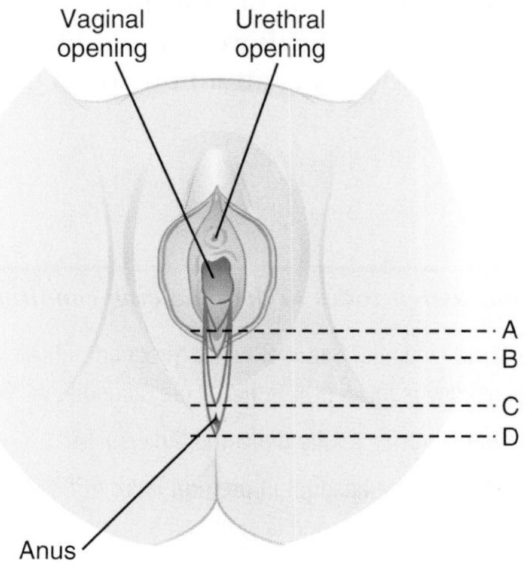

FIGURE 22-9. Perineal lacerations: **A,** First-degree is laceration of artificial tissues. **B,** Second-degree is limited to the pelvic floor and may involve the perineal or vaginal muscles. **C,** Third-degree involves the anal sphincter. **D,** Fourth-degree involves anal or rectal mucosa.

Encounter for Delivery (O80, O82)

When a delivery occurs where minimal or no assistance is required, a code from this category is assigned along with the code for outcome of delivery (Z37.0). Minimal assistance would include episiotomy, but otherwise the delivery would be spontaneous, cephalic, vaginal, full-term, single, liveborn fetus. This code is never used with any other codes from Chapter 15.

Code O82 is used when there is no indication for the reason a cesarean delivery is being performed. This case scenario would be highly unlikely.

EXAMPLE

Patient is admitted to the hospital at 39 weeks in labor. Labor progresses and patient goes on to spontaneously deliver a normal newborn, O80, Z3A.39, Z37.0, 10E0XZZ.

Complications Predominantly Related to the Puerperium (O85-O92)

The definition of puerperium is from the time of delivery through the first 6 weeks postpartum. This code category does include postpartum infections, complications of anesthesia occurring postpartum, complications of cesarean delivery, and issues with lactation.

EXAMPLE

Patient is 2 weeks post normal vaginal delivery. She presents to the physician's office with painful cracked nipples due to nursing, O92.13.

Other Obstetric Conditions, Not Elsewhere Classified (O94-O9a)

This category contains codes for sexually transmitted diseases, infections and viral conditions, as well as AIDS. There are codes for smoking, alcohol, and drug abuse that complicate pregnancy.

Group B strep (GBS) is a type of bacterial infection that can be found in the vagina and/or lower intestine of up to 30% of all healthy women. If a person has this bacteria but has no signs or symptoms of disease, it is called a colonization (carrier). The problem with being a carrier is that this infection can be passed on to the baby. Usually, a woman is tested late in her pregnancy for group B strep, and if the culture is positive she will be given antibiotics during labor to help prevent the spread of this bacteria to the baby.

EXAMPLE

Patient with asymptomatic HIV infection is seen in obstetrician's office at 16 weeks for a check-up, O98.712, Z21, Z3A.16.

Due to the fact that there is no known safe amount of alcohol to drink while pregnant, any pregnancy case where the mother uses alcohol during pregnancy should be assigned a code from subcategory O99.31. Use of alcohol in pregnancy can cause disorders ranging from miscarriage and stillbirth to low birth weight and lifelong disorders such as learning disabilities, poor memory, difficulty paying attention, low IQ, and speech or language delays to name a few.

EXERCISE 22-4

Answer the questions and assign codes to the following conditions.

1. Patient presents with acute sinusitis. She is 8 weeks pregnant. Physician documents that the pregnancy is incidental to her acute sinusitis. ______________
2. Patient has a postpartum hemorrhage; she delivered 5 days PTA. ______________
3. A pregnant woman presents to the hospital in preterm labor at 34 weeks; she is treated with tocolysis for 3 days and is sent home on bed rest. ______________

4. A pregnant woman presents to the hospital in labor at 32 weeks. After 2 weeks of treatment with tocolytics, she goes into heavy labor. Her cervix has failed to dilate, and a low transverse cesarean section is performed. She delivers a healthy baby boy. ______________
5. Pregnant woman at 20 weeks is admitted to the hospital with *Pneumocystis carinii* pneumonia and known AIDS; she is treated with high-dose antibiotics and is discharged. ______________
6. The patient has been dependent on methadone for the entire pregnancy. She delivers a baby girl on this admit at 38 weeks. She has no complications during delivery and has a normal spontaneous vaginal birth. ______________
7. Pregnant woman had pneumonia early in her pregnancy. She presents to the hospital in labor at 39 weeks with no other complaints. She vaginally delivers a healthy baby. ______________
8. Can code O80 be used as a secondary diagnosis? ______________
9. What is the only outcome of delivery that can be used with O80? ______________
10. If surgery is performed in utero, is this coded on the baby's chart or on the mother's chart? ______________
11. A woman delivers a 5-lb baby in her home at 39 weeks. She is brought by paramedics to the hospital, where they find that she has a first-degree perineal laceration. This is repaired, and the patient is admitted. ______________
12. A woman is admitted 6 weeks after a cesarean delivery with infection of the cesarean wound. ______________
13. A woman delivered 5 weeks ago. She is admitted for an abscess of the breast. ______________
14. A patient presents with abdominal pain 3 months after the birth of her first baby. The physician documents that she has cholelithiasis that is related to her pregnancy. ______________
15. Two weeks after delivery, a woman has terrible pain in her leg. Her physician diagnoses her with a superficial thrombophlebitis of the leg. ______________
16. Five months after delivery of her first born, an obese woman is diagnosed with postpartum cardiomyopathy. ______________

FACTORS INFLUENCING HEALTH STATUS AND CONTACT WITH HEALTH SERVICES (Z CODES)

As was discussed in Chapter 9, it is difficult to locate Z codes in the Index. Coders will often say, "I did not know there was a Z code for that."

Refer to Chapter 9 for a listing of common main terms used to locate Z codes. Z codes that may be used during pregnancy, childbirth, and the puerperium include the following:

Z codes are often used for encounters relating to pregnancy, childbirth, and the puerperium. Normal encounters for routine prenatal visits will use category Z34, Encounter for supervision of a normal pregnancy. These codes are first-listed and are not used with any other code from the OB chapter. Codes from category Z3A, Weeks of gestation, may be used to provide additional information about the pregnancy.

There are a number of Z codes that would be assigned as the first-listed diagnosis code on an outpatient encounter. Category Z30, Encounter for contraceptive management, is assigned for encounters dealing with the initiation, insertion, and/or surveillance of various contraceptive devices. Category Z31, Encounter for procreative management is for patients who have difficulty conceiving and are seeking healthcare services for this problem.

Z02.81	Encounter for paternity testing
Z02.82	Encounter for adoption services
Z03.71	Encounter for suspected problem with amniotic cavity and membrane ruled out
Z03.72	Encounter for suspected placental problem ruled out
Z03.73	Encounter for suspected fetal anomaly ruled out
Z03.74	Encounter for suspected problem with fetal growth ruled out
Z03.75	Encounter for suspected cervical shortening ruled out
Z03.79	Encounter for other suspected maternal and fetal conditions ruled out
Z30.011	Encounter for initial prescription of contraceptive pills
Z30.012	Encounter for prescription of emergency contraception
Z30.013	Encounter for initial prescription of injectable contraceptive
Z30.014	Encounter for initial prescription of intrauterine contraceptive device
Z30.015	Encounter for initial prescription of vaginal ring hormonal contraceptive
Z30.016	Encounter for initial prescription of transdermal patch hormonal contraceptive device
Z30.017	Encounter for initial prescription of implantable subdermal contraceptive
Z30.018	Encounter for initial prescription of other contraceptive
Z30.019	Encounter for initial prescription of contraceptives, unspecified
Z30.02	Counseling and instruction in natural family planning to avoid pregnancy
Z30.09	Encounter for other general counseling and advice on contraception
Z30.2	Encounter for sterilization
Z30.40	Encounter for surveillance of contraceptives, unspecified
Z30.41	Encounter for surveillance of contraceptive pills
Z30.42	Encounter for surveillance of injectable contraceptive
Z30.430	Encounter for insertion of intrauterine contraceptive device
Z30.431	Encounter for routine checking of intrauterine contraceptive device
Z30.432	Encounter for removal of intrauterine contraceptive device
Z30.433	Encounter for removal and reinsertion of intrauterine contraceptive device
Z30.44	Encounter for surveillance or vaginal ring hormonal contraceptive device
Z30.45	Encounter for surveillance of transdermal patch hormonal contraceptive device
Z30.46	Encounter for surveillance of implantable subdermal contraceptive
Z30.49	Encounter for surveillance of other contraceptives
Z30.8	Encounter for other contraceptive management
Z30.9	Encounter for contraceptive management, unspecified
Z31.0	Encounter for reversal of previous sterilization
Z31.41	Encounter for fertility testing
Z31.42	Aftercare following sterilization reversal
Z31.430	Encounter of female for testing for genetic disease carrier status for procreative management
Z31.438	Encounter for other genetic testing of female for procreative management
Z31.440	Encounter of male for testing for genetic disease carrier status for procreative management
Z31.441	Encounter for testing of male partner of habitual aborter
Z31.448	Encounter for other genetic testing of male for procreative management
Z31.49	Encounter for other procreative investigation and testing
Z31.5	Encounter for genetic counseling
Z31.61	Procreative counseling and advice using natural family planning
Z31.62	Encounter for fertility preservation counseling
Z31.69	Encounter for other general counseling and advice on procreation
Z31.7	Encounter for procreative management and counseling for gestational carrier
Z31.81	Encounter for male factor infertility in female patient
Z31.82	Encounter for Rh incompatibility status
Z31.83	Encounter for assisted reproductive fertility procedure cycle
Z31.84	Encounter for fertility preservation procedure

Z31.89	Encounter for other procreative management
Z31.9	Encounter for procreative management, unspecified
Z32.00	Encounter for pregnancy test, result unknown
Z32.01	Encounter for pregnancy test, result positive
Z32.02	Encounter for pregnancy test, result negative
Z32.2	Encounter for childbirth instruction
Z32.3	Encounter for childcare instruction
Z33.1	Pregnant state, incidental
Z33.2	Encounter for elective termination of pregnancy
Z33.3	Pregnant state, gestational carrier
Z34.00	Encounter for supervision of normal first pregnancy, unspecified trimester
Z34.01	Encounter for supervision of normal first pregnancy, first trimester
Z34.02	Encounter for supervision of normal first pregnancy, second trimester
Z34.03	Encounter for supervision of normal first pregnancy, third trimester
Z34.80	Encounter for supervision of other normal pregnancy, unspecified trimester
Z34.81	Encounter for supervision of other normal pregnancy, first trimester
Z34.82	Encounter for supervision of other normal pregnancy, second trimester
Z34.83	Encounter for supervision of other normal pregnancy, third trimester
Z34.90	Encounter for supervision of normal pregnancy, unspecified, unspecified trimester
Z34.91	Encounter for supervision of normal pregnancy, unspecified, first trimester
Z34.92	Encounter for supervision of normal pregnancy, unspecified, second trimester
Z34.93	Encounter for supervision of normal pregnancy, unspecified, third trimester
Z36	Encounter for antenatal screening of mother
Z3A	Weeks of gestation

Note: Codes from category Z3A are for use, only on the maternal record, to indicate the weeks of gestation of the pregnancy.

Code first	complications of pregnancy, childbirth and the puerperium (O00-O9A)	
Z3A.0	Weeks of gestation of pregnancy, unspecified or less than 10 weeks	
	Z3A.00	Weeks of gestation of pregnancy not specified
	Z3A.01	Less than 8 weeks gestation of pregnancy
	Z3A.08	8 weeks gestation of pregnancy
	Z3A.09	9 weeks gestation of pregnancy
Z3A.1	Weeks of gestation of pregnancy, weeks 10-19	
	Z3A.10	10 weeks gestation of pregnancy
	Z3A.11	11 weeks gestation of pregnancy
	Z3A.12	12 weeks gestation of pregnancy
	Z3A.13	13 weeks gestation of pregnancy
	Z3A.14	14 weeks gestation of pregnancy
	Z3A.15	15 weeks gestation of pregnancy
	Z3A.16	16 weeks gestation of pregnancy
	Z3A.17	17 weeks gestation of pregnancy
	Z3A.18	18 weeks gestation of pregnancy
	Z3A.19	19 weeks gestation of pregnancy
Z3A.2	Weeks of gestation of pregnancy, weeks 20-29	
	Z3A.20	20 weeks gestation of pregnancy
	Z3A.21	21 weeks gestation of pregnancy
	Z3A.22	22 weeks gestation of pregnancy
	Z3A.23	23 weeks gestation of pregnancy
	Z3A.24	24 weeks gestation of pregnancy
	Z3A.25	25 weeks gestation of pregnancy
	Z3A.26	26 weeks gestation of pregnancy
	Z3A.27	27 weeks gestation of pregnancy

	Z3A.28	28 weeks gestation of pregnancy
	Z3A.29	29 weeks gestation of pregnancy
Z3A.3	Weeks of gestation of pregnancy, weeks 30-39	
	Z3A.30	30 weeks gestation of pregnancy
	Z3A.31	31 weeks gestation of pregnancy
	Z3A.32	32 weeks gestation of pregnancy
	Z3A.33	33 weeks gestation of pregnancy
	Z3A.34	34 weeks gestation of pregnancy
	Z3A.35	35 weeks gestation of pregnancy
	Z3A.36	36 weeks gestation of pregnancy
	Z3A.37	37 weeks gestation of pregnancy
	Z3A.38	38 weeks gestation of pregnancy
	Z3A.39	39 weeks gestation of pregnancy
Z3A.4	Weeks of gestation of pregnancy, weeks 40 or greater	
	Z3A.40	40 weeks gestation of pregnancy
	Z3A.41	41 weeks gestation of pregnancy
	Z3A.42	42 weeks gestation of pregnancy
	Z3A.49	Greater than 42 weeks gestation of pregnancy
Z37.0	Single live birth	
Z37.1	Single stillbirth	
Z37.2	Twins, both liveborn	
Z37.3	Twins, one liveborn and one stillborn	
Z37.4	Twins, both stillborn	
Z37.50	Multiple births, unspecified, all liveborn	
Z37.51	Triplets, all liveborn	
Z37.52	Quadruplets, all liveborn	
Z37.53	Quintuplets, all liveborn	
Z37.54	Sextuplets, all liveborn	
Z37.59	Other multiple births, all liveborn	
Z37.60	Multiple births, unspecified, some liveborn	
Z37.61	Triplets, some liveborn	
Z37.62	Quadruplets, some liveborn	
Z37.63	Quintuplets, some liveborn	
Z37.64	Sextuplets, some liveborn	
Z37.69	Other multiple births, some liveborn	
Z37.7	Other multiple births, all stillborn	
Z37.9	Outcome of delivery, unspecified	
Z39.0	Encounter for care and examination of mother immediately after delivery	
Z39.1	Encounter for care and examination of lactating mother	
Z39.2	Encounter for routine postpartum follow-up	
Z76.81	Expectant parent(s) prebirth pediatrician visit	
Z79.3	Long-term (current) use of hormonal contraceptives	
Z86.32	Personal history of gestational diabetes	
Z87.51	Personal history of pre-term labor	
Z87.59	Personal history of other complications of pregnancy childbirth, and the puerperium	
Z92.0	Personal history of contraception	
Z97.5	Presence of (intrauterine) contraceptive device	

EXAMPLE Primigravida seen in OB office at 25 weeks for routine postpartum care, Z34.02, Z3A.25.

EXAMPLE Patient missed a period and is seen in physician office for a pregnancy test. The test is positive, Z32.01.

COMMON TREATMENTS

CONDITION	MEDICATION/TREATMENT
Narcotics for Labor Pain	Stadol (butorphanol), fentanyl Demerol (meperidine) Nubain (nalbuphine) Used for decreasing pain
Anesthesia for Labor Pain	Epidural is a regional anesthetic injected into the epidural space Spinal is also a regional anesthetic which is injected into the cerebrospinal fluid
Drugs for Inducing Labor	Pitocin is a synthetic oxytocin which is a natural hormone produced by a woman's body to cause the uterus to contract Cervidil (dinoprostone) is vaginally inserted and used for ripening of the cervix
Drugs Used to Inhibit Labor	Beta agonists (terbutaline, ritodrine, isoxsuprine), magnesium sulfate

PROCEDURES

Procedures that may be related to complications of pregnancy, childbirth, and the puerperium in ICD-10-PCS may be found in the following tables:

Obstetrics	102-10Y
Female Reproductive System	0U1-0UY

The obstetrics section includes only those procedures that are performed on the products of conception. The term **products of conception** refers to all physical components of a pregnancy, including the fetus, amnion, umbilical cord, and placenta, regardless of gestational age. Procedures performed on a pregnant female other than on products of conception are coded in the Medical and Surgical section.

All ICD-0-PCS codes are seven characters, each character representing a particular aspect of the procedure. The meanings of the obstetric procedure characters are as follows:

CHARACTER	REPRESENTS
1	Section
2	Body system
3	Root operation
4	Body part
5	Approach
6	Device
7	Qualifier

Obstetric codes are found in Section 1, so they have a first-character value of 1. The second-character value for body system is Pregnancy. The third character identifies the root operation. There are a total of 12 root operations in the Obstetrics section. Ten of these are taken from the Medical and Surgical section, and that includes:

CHARACTER	REPRESENTS
2	Change
9	Drainage
D	Extraction
H	Insertion
J	Inspection
P	Removal
Q	Repair
S	Reposition
T	Resection
Y	Transplantation

This section includes two additional root operations:

- **Abortion (A):** artificially terminating a pregnancy
- **Delivery (E):** assisting the passage of the products of conception from the genital canal

The fourth character classifies the body part. Body part values in this section are:

- Products of conception
- Products of conception, retained
- Products of conception, ectopic

The fifth character identifies the approach; these are defined in the Medical and Surgical section. The sixth character is for the device. The seventh character identifies various qualifiers, such as:

- Types of extraction (i.e., forceps, or type of cesarean section)
- Type of fluid removed (i.e., amniotic fluid, fetal cerebrospinal fluid)
- Body system of the products of conception on which the repair was done

EXAMPLE

Manually assisted vaginal delivery, 10E0XZZ

SECTION	BODY SYSTEM	ROOT OPERATION	BODY PART	APPROACH	DEVICE	QUALIFIER
Obstetrics	Pregnancy	Delivery	Products of Conception	External	No Device	No Qualifier
1	0	E	0	X	Z	Z

The root operation, Delivery, applies only to manually-assisted, vaginal delivery and is defined as assisting the passage of the products of conception from the genital canal. Cesarean deliveries are coded in this section to the root operation extraction.

Labor

Labor can be induced (IOL) in a variety of ways. Often, artificial rupture of the membranes (AROM) is performed to start labor (medical and surgical section, root operation, drainage). Pitocin is a drug used for medical induction of labor.

A nonstress test (NST) is performed to confirm the health of the baby. A mother is hooked up to a fetal monitor, and the test is performed without giving the mother medications. The test records the baby's heart rate while moving. This test may be performed throughout the pregnancy if the mother has medical conditions or if the pregnancy is considered high risk. Results of these tests are recorded as "reactive," meaning the baby moved and the heart rate increased appropriately, or "nonreactive," which means that either the baby did not move or the heart rate did not increase enough when the baby did move.

When the NST is abnormal, another test is performed. This test is called a CST, or a contraction stress test. In this test, which is done during fetal monitoring, a drug (Pitocin) may be administered to initiate contractions. The purpose is to see how the baby will handle the stress of labor. The baby's heart should speed up during a contraction; if this does not happen during this test, problems may occur during labor.

Amnioinfusion (administration of a substance) is the insertion of normal saline or lactated Ringer's solution into the amniotic sac. The injection may be done transabdominally or transcervically. This procedure is performed for a variety of reasons, such as oligohydramnios, variable decelerations, and thick meconium. The volume of amniotic fluid is increased, which increases the likelihood of better outcomes of delivery.

Delivery

In a normal pregnancy with no complications, a code of 10E0XZZ should be assigned for manually assisted delivery (Figure 22-10). Forceps and vacuum extraction may be used in cases in which the baby does not spontaneously deliver and assistance is needed (Figure 22-11).

Episiotomy is performed to facilitate delivery. The root operation in ICD-10-PCS for an episiotomy is division of the female perineum. This is not assigned a code from the obstetric

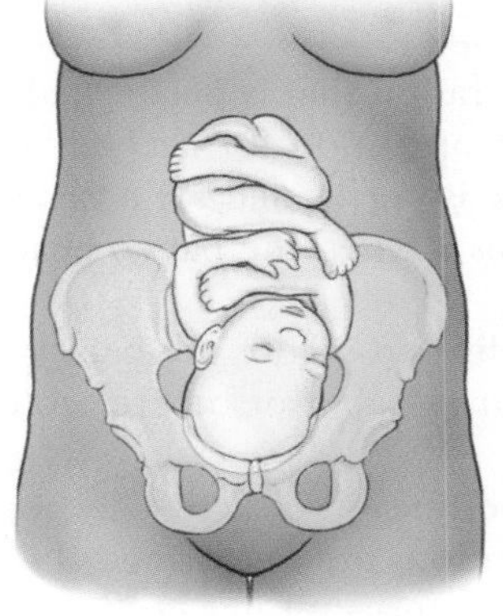

FIGURE 22-10. Cephalic presentation of the fetus during delivery from the vaginal (birth) canal during a normal delivery.

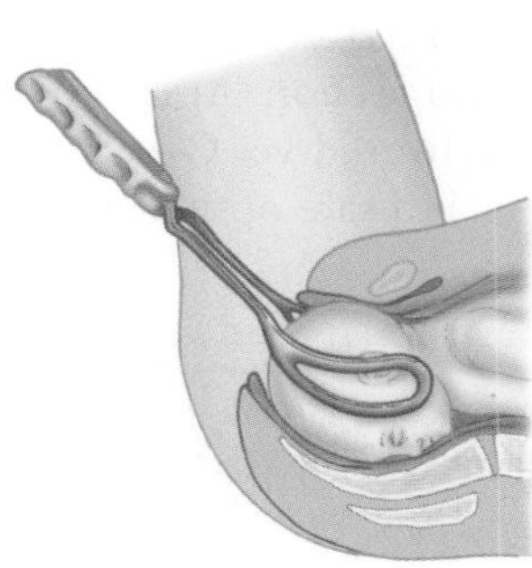

FIGURE 22-11. Forceps delivery.

table, but from the female reproductive system tables. The physician makes a cut in the perineum to make room for the baby's head to emerge. Repair of an episiotomy is included in the code for episiotomy. Sometimes, an episiotomy will extend and will become a laceration. If this happens, codes for both episiotomy and laceration repair are required. The degree of perineal laceration is coded under the diagnostic category of O70. If more than one degree is mentioned, only the highest degree should be assigned.

EXAMPLE

Patient is admitted to the hospital in labor. She is 40 weeks pregnant and delivers a healthy infant. The physician performs an episiotomy that extends to a second degree perineal laceration, which was repaired, O70.1, Z37.0, Z3A.40, 10E0XZZ, 0W8NXZZ, 0KQM0ZZ

SECTION	BODY SYSTEM	ROOT OPERATION	BODY PART	APPROACH	DEVICE	QUALIFIER
Obstetrics	Pregnancy	Delivery	Products of Conception	External	No Device	No Qualifier
1	0	E	0	X	Z	Z

SECTION	BODY SYSTEM	ROOT OPERATION	BODY PART	APPROACH	DEVICE	QUALIFIER
Medical and Surgical	Anatomical Regions, General	Division	Perineum, Female	External	No Device	No Qualifier
0	W	8	N	X	Z	Z

SECTION	BODY SYSTEM	ROOT OPERATION	BODY PART	APPROACH	DEVICE	QUALIFIER
Medical and Surgical	Muscles	Repair	Perineum Muscle	Open	No Device	No Qualifier
0	K	Q	M	0	Z	Z

Cesarean Section

A cesarean section (C-section) is an operation that is performed to deliver a baby through an incision in the abdomen. The root operation for a cesarean section is extraction of products of conception. This procedure is performed for a variety of reasons:

- *Cephalopelvic disproportion (CPD):* This is when the baby's head is too large to fit through the birth canal.
- *Prolapsed cord:* The cord is being delivered before the baby.
- *Fetal distress:* Distress of the fetus during labor or before, noted by low oxygen levels or the presence of meconium
- *Conditions of the mother:* Such as hypertension or active herpes

Three main types of cesarean operations are performed: 1) classical, which involves a vertical incision in the main body of the uterus; 2) low cervical or low transverse, which is the most common and is done via a horizontal incision in the lower uterus; and 3) extraperitoneal, which is an incision in the lower part of the uterus without entering the peritoneal cavity, which is performed to prevent infection.

Vaginal birth after cesarean section (VBAC) occurs when a woman delivers vaginally after having delivered previously via cesarean section. At one point in time, it was believed that it was unsafe for a woman who had delivered via C-section to deliver vaginally. Many variables go into deciding whether a VBAC is a safe option; however, it is being performed more and more frequently.

EXAMPLE

Patient is admitted to the hospital in labor at 39 weeks gestation. A low cervical C-section is performed due to obstructed labor because of footling breech presentation. A healthy infant is delivered, O64.8xx0, Z37.0, Z3A.39, 10D00Z1

SECTION	BODY SYSTEM	ROOT OPERATION	BODY PART	APPROACH	DEVICE	QUALIFIER
Obstetrics	Pregnancy	Extraction	Products of Conception	Open	No Device	Low Cervical
1	0	D	0	0	Z	1

Sterilization

Sterilization is a procedure performed for permanent birth control. Sterilization can be performed either on the male or female. Sterilization procedures may occur immediately following delivery or at a later date. When a patient (either male or female) is admitted for the purpose of sterilization the principal diagnosis code should be Z30.2 Encounter for sterilization. When a patient has delivered during the same encounter as the sterilization the Z30.2 code is a secondary code. Additional codes may be used along with the Z code to describe any additional conditions that may exist as a reason for the procedure being performed. The Z code is not assigned if the sterilization is performed incidental to other treatment.

The root operation for female sterilization procedures in ICD-10-PCS is classified according to the type of sterilization procedure performed. The most common female tubal sterilization procedures are:

- Sterilization performed by removing a portion of the fallopian tubes (Pomeroy). The root operation for this procedure is Excision.
- Sterilization performed by the use of mechanical devices to shut or close the fallopian tube such as clips, rings, or bands (Falope ring). The root operation for this procedure is Occlusion.
- Sterilization performed by electric current. The root operation for this procedure is Destruction.

In rare cases a sterilization procedure may be reversed. When a patient is admitted for a reverse tubal ligation the principal diagnosis would be Z31.0 Encounter for reversal of previous sterilization.

EXAMPLE

A patient is admitted at 38 weeks for an elective repeat c-section. This is her third pregnancy, and she has requested to have a sterilization procedure performed following the c-section. This pregnancy was complicated by a bout of morning sickness early on but otherwise has been uneventful. A repeat classical c-section was performed, and a single liveborn delivered. Following the delivery the surgeon performed a bilateral tubal ligation. O34.212, Z3A.38, Z37.0, Z30.2, 10D00Z0, 0UL70ZZ.

SECTION	BODY SYSTEM	ROOT OPERATION	BODY PART	APPROACH	DEVICE	QUALIFIER
Obstetrics	Pregnancy	Extraction	Products of Conception	Open	No Device	Classical
1	0	D	0	0	Z	0

SECTION	BODY SYSTEM	ROOT OPERATION	BODY PART	APPROACH	DEVICE	QUALIFIER
Medical and Surgical	Female Reproductive System	Occlusion	Fallopian Tubes, Bilateral	Open	No Device	No Qualifier
0	U	L	7	0	Z	Z

EXAMPLE

A patient is admitted for a tubal ligation. She has recently been diagnosed with cancer of the right breast and does not want to risk the chance of pregnancy while she receives chemotherapy. The surgeon performs laprascopic bilateral cauterization of the fallopian tubes. Z30.2, C50.911, 0U574ZZ.

SECTION	BODY SYSTEM	ROOT OPERATION	BODY PART	APPROACH	DEVICE	QUALIFIER
Medical and Surgical	Female Reproductive System	Destruction	Fallopian Tubes, Bilateral	Percutaneous Endoscopic	No Device	No Qualifier
0	U	5	7	4	Z	Z

EXERCISE 22-5

Assign codes for all diagnoses and procedures.

1. Patient is induced by pitocin for postdate pregnancy (41 weeks). She delivers a 6 lb 4 oz baby vaginally. ______________
2. Elderly multigravida at 39 weeks presents in labor. After 20 hours of labor, an LTCS is performed because of failure to progress. She delivers a normal newborn. ______________
3. A 22-year-old primigravida at 40 weeks presents for induction. She is known to have oligohydramnios. Pitocin is administered, and she goes on to vaginally deliver an SGA normal newborn. The physician performs an episiotomy to facilitate delivery, and a second-degree extension is repaired. ______________
4. Patient presents in active labor. She is in her 38th week of pregnancy. She labors for 8 hours, after which the physician decides to perform a low cervical C-section because of CPD. A normal newborn is delivered. ______________
5. Patient presents with severe preeclampsia. She is in her 39th week of pregnancy. She is taken directly to the operating room, where an LTCS is performed. She delivers a normal newborn. ______________

CHAPTER REVIEW EXERCISE

Assign codes for all diagnoses and procedures. If not otherwise specified, presume liveborn.

1. Breech presentation with obstructed labor at 39 weeks; delivery by cesarean section (LTCS); single liveborn ________
2. Patient admitted 2 weeks post delivery with postpartum depression ________
3. Patient at 40 weeks delivers 12 lb baby (LGA), requiring an episiotomy. ________
4. Patient at 37 weeks is admitted to the hospital for delivery; she is being treated with methadone for heroin dependence; vaginal delivery of single liveborn ________
5. Patient with a history of preterm labor and previous cesarean section is admitted in labor at 39 weeks; she has a vaginal birth after cesarean (VBAC) of single liveborn. ________
6. Patient at 36 weeks is admitted to hospital for HELLP (hemolytic anemia, elevated liver enzymes, and low platelet count) syndrome; she is taken to the operating room for delivery by cesarean section (LTCS) of single liveborn. ________
7. Patient is admitted to the hospital in preterm labor; she is 35 weeks pregnant; 3 days after admission, the patient vaginally delivers a small for gestational age (SGA) baby. ________
8. Patient presents to physician's office for a routine obstetric visit; she is in her 30th week of pregnancy; she had a stillborn 1 year ago. ________
9. Patient is admitted to the hospital at 33 weeks in preterm labor; she has a twin pregnancy and has a spontaneous vaginal delivery (SVD) of liveborn twins; a few hours after delivery, she hemorrhages due to uterine atony. ________
10. Patient is 8 weeks pregnant and has known uterine fibroids; the fibroids are so large that the physician recommends an abortion; patient presents to hospital for abortion to be performed by aspiration. ________
11. The patient was treated for a right sprained wrist. Incidentally, the patient is 10 weeks pregnant. ________
12. Urinary tract infection in patient who delivered 1 week ago ________
13. The patient was admitted for treatment of hyperemesis gravidarum. The patient is 12 weeks pregnant. ________
14. The patient has a high-risk pregnancy due to a previous stillbirth. She is currently at 28 weeks. ________
15. The patient is 16 weeks pregnant, and her condition is complicated by diabetes mellitus, type 2, which is uncontrolled. ________
16. The patient is admitted with HIV and *Pneumocystis carinii* pneumonia (PCP) and is 35 weeks pregnant. ________
17. The patient is 19 weeks pregnant and has hypothyroidism. ________
18. The patient delivered a baby 6 days ago. She is now being admitted because of dehiscence of the outer layer of skin of her cesarean wound. The wound was sutured. ________
19. Urinary tract infection in a patient who is 30 weeks pregnant ________
20. A 33-year-old presents at 40 weeks in labor. She has had an uneventful pregnancy, except for slight anemia which is still being treated with iron. She has an uncomplicated vaginal delivery of a 6 lb baby girl. ________
21. A 15-year-old pregnant female presents at 39 weeks in active labor. She has no past history, except for several bouts of asthma as a toddler. She had an uncomplicated delivery of a healthy baby boy. ________
22. A patient is admitted in labor at 39 weeks and delivers a 7 lb baby boy vaginally. The physician requests a social work consult because this mother has struggled with depression prior to and during this pregnancy. ________

23. Patient is 40 weeks pregnant. The physician documents that chlamydia was discovered early on in the pregnancy, and the patient now tests negative. Patient has a spontaneous vaginal delivery of an 8 lb baby girl. ______________

24. Patient is admitted to the hospital in labor at 39 weeks. She has had an uneventful pregnancy and goes on to a spontaneous vaginal delivery of twin boys. ______________

25. A patient is admitted to the hospital 1 week post partum with a high fever. The physician diagnosed endometritis. The patient is treated with IV antibiotics. ______________

CHAPTER GLOSSARY

Abortion: termination of a pregnancy by natural causes or by medical intervention.

Amnioinfusion: the insertion of normal saline or lactated Ringer's solution into the amniotic sac.

Antepartum: time from conception until delivery or childbirth with regard to the mother.

Cervix: the neck of the uterus that serves as an outlet from the uterus.

Complete abortion: abortion in which all the products of conception are expelled.

Ectopic: type of pregnancy that occurs when the egg is implanted outside the cavity of the uterus.

Effaced: cervical thinning.

Elderly obstetric patient: 35 years or older at date of delivery.

Elective abortion: the elective termination of pregnancy.

Fallopian tube: delivers the mature egg to the uterus for fertilization.

Gravid: pregnant.

Habitual aborter: a woman who miscarries at least three consecutive times.

Hyperemesis gravidarum: excessive vomiting in pregnancy.

Incomplete abortion: abortion in which not all of the products of conception are expelled.

Inevitable abortion: abortion that occurs when symptoms are present and a miscarriage will happen.

Labia: surrounds the vaginal opening.

Labor: process by which the products of conception are expelled from the uterus.

Lactation: process of milk production.

Miscarriage: spontaneous termination of pregnancy before the fetus has reached 20 weeks.

Missed abortion: pregnancy with fetal demise before 20 weeks; products of conception are not expelled.

Molar pregnancy: fertilized ovum is converted to a growing mass of cysts due to an extra set of paternal chromosomes.

Multigravida: a woman with two or more pregnancies.

Multiparity: a woman with two or more pregnancies.

Ovaries: produce female hormones and eggs.

Postpartum: after delivery or childbirth.

Postterm pregnancy: pregnancy longer than 40 weeks up to 42 weeks.

Precipitate labor: rapid labor and delivery.

Preeclampsia: pregnancy complication characterized by hypertension, edema, and/or proteinuria.

Pregestational: condition present prior to pregnancy.

Prenatal: before birth.

Primigravida: first pregnancy.

Prolonged pregnancy: beyond 42 weeks of pregnancy.

Puerperium: time from delivery through the first 6 weeks postpartum.

Spontaneous abortion: loss of a fetus due to natural causes; also known as *miscarriage*.

Stillbirth: born dead.

Therapeutic abortion: abortion performed when the pregnancy is endangering the mother's health, or when the fetus has a condition that is incompatible with life.

Threatened abortion: abortion that occurs when symptoms are present that indicate the possibility of a miscarriage.

Toxemia: another term for preeclampsia, which is pregnancy complicated by hypertension, edema, or proteinuria.

Uterus: a muscular organ that serves as an incubator for the developing fetus.

Vagina: a muscular tube that extends from the vaginal opening to the uterus.

Vulva: the external covering to the vagina.

Young obstetric patient: younger than 16 years at date of delivery.

KEY REFERENCE

1. From Chabner D: The Language of Medicine, ed 10, St. Louis, 2014, Saunders, p 804. Table 19-2.
2. From Chabner D: The Language of Medicine, ed 10, St. Louis, 2014, Saunders, p 805. Table 19-3.
3. Modified from Harrison's Manual of Medicine, ed 15, New York, 2002, McGraw-Hill Professional, p 284.

23

Certain Conditions Originating in the Perinatal Period, and Congenital Malformations, Deformations, and Chromosomal Abnormalities

(ICD-10-CM Chapter 16, Codes P00-P96 and Chapter 17, Codes Q00-Q99)

CHAPTER OUTLINE

LEARNING OBJECTIVES

1. Apply and assign the correct ICD-10-CM/PCS codes in accordance with Official Guidelines for Coding and Reporting
2. Identify perinatal conditions and congenital malformations, deformations, and chromosomal abnormalities
3. Assign the correct Z codes and procedure codes to perinatal conditions and congenital malformations, deformations, and chromosomal abnormalities
4. Identify common treatments, medications, laboratory values, and diagnostic tests

ABBREVIATIONS/ ACRONYMS

BPD bronchopulmonary dysplasia
CVS chorionic villus sampling
ICD-10-CM *International Classification of Diseases, 10th Revision, Clinical Modification*
IUGR intrauterine growth retardation
MSAFP maternal serum alpha-fetoprotein
NICU neonatal intensive care unit
OI osteogenesis imperfecta
PDA patent ductus arteriosus
PWS Prader-Willi syndrome
RDS respiratory distress syndrome
SGA small for gestational age
TOF tetralogy of Fallot
TTN transitory tachypnea of the newborn
VSD ventricular septal defect

ICD-10-CM Official Guidelines for Coding and Reporting (2021-2022)

Please refer to the companion Evolve website for the most current 2021-2022 guidelines.

16. Chapter 16: Certain Conditions Originating in the Perinatal Period (P00-P96)

For coding and reporting purposes the perinatal period is defined as before birth through the 28th day following birth. The following guidelines are provided for reporting purposes

a. General Perinatal Rules

1) Use of Chapter 16 Codes

Codes in this chapter are never for use on the maternal record. Codes from Chapter 15, the obstetric chapter, are never permitted on the newborn record. Chapter 16 codes may be used throughout the life of the patient if the condition is still present.

2) Principal Diagnosis for Birth Record

When coding the birth episode in a newborn record, assign a code from category Z38, Liveborn infants according to place of birth and type of delivery, as the principal diagnosis. A code from category Z38 is assigned only once, to a newborn at the time of birth. If a newborn is transferred to another institution, a code from category Z38 should not be used at the receiving hospital.

A code from category Z38 is used only on the newborn record, not on the mother's record.

3) Use of Codes from other Chapters with Codes from Chapter 16

Codes from other chapters may be used with codes from chapter 16 if the codes from the other chapters provide more specific detail. Codes for signs and symptoms may be assigned when a definitive diagnosis has not been established. If the reason for the encounter is a perinatal condition, the code from chapter 16 should be sequenced first.

EXAMPLE

An infant was delivered in the hospital via cesarean section. On discharge, the infant was examined and appeared completely healthy with the exception of neonatal jaundice. A bilirubin count should be performed in 2 days, Z38.01, P59.9.

4) Use of Chapter 16 Codes after the Perinatal Period

Should a condition originate in the perinatal period, and continue throughout the life of the patient, the perinatal code should continue to be used regardless of the patient's age.

EXAMPLE

A 3-year-old child is seen in the pediatrician's office with a diagnosis of bronchopulmonary dysplasia (BPD), P27.1.

5) Birth process or community acquired conditions

If a newborn has a condition that may be either due to the birth process or community acquired and the documentation does not indicate which it is, the default is due to the birth process and the code from Chapter 16 should be used. If the condition is community-acquired, a code from Chapter 16 should not be assigned.

For COVID-19 infection in a newborn, see guideline I.C.16.h.

EXAMPLE

A 1-week-old baby is admitted for cough and fever, and on the discharge summary the physician documents pneumonia, P23.9.

EXAMPLE

A 1-week-old baby is admitted for cough and fever, and on the discharge summary the physician documents congenital pneumonia, P23.9.

EXAMPLE

A 1-week-old baby is admitted for cough and fever, and on the discharge summary the physician documents community acquired pneumonia, J18.9.

6) Code all clinically significant conditions

All clinically significant conditions noted on routine newborn examination should be coded. A condition is clinically significant if it requires:

- clinical evaluation; or
- therapeutic treatment; or
- diagnostic procedures; or
- extended length of hospital stay; or
- increased nursing care and/or monitoring; or
- has implications for future health care needs

Note: The perinatal guidelines listed above are the same as the general coding guidelines for "additional diagnoses", except for the final point regarding implications for future health care needs. Codes should be assigned for conditions that have been specified by the provider as having implications for future health care needs.

EXAMPLE

The infant was born via vaginal delivery and suffered a fractured clavicle caused by the delivery, Z38.00, P13.4.

b. Observation and Evaluation of Newborns for Suspected Conditions not Found

1) Use of Z05 codes

Assign a code from category Z05, Observation and evaluation of newborns and infants for suspected conditions ruled out, to identify those instances when a healthy newborn is evaluated for a suspected condition that is determined after study not to be present. Do not use a code from category Z05 when the patient has identified signs or symptoms of a suspected problem; in such cases, code the sign or symptom.

2) Z05 on other than the birth record

A code from category Z05 may also be assigned as a principal or first-listed code for readmissions or encounters when the code from category Z38 code no longer applies. Codes from category Z05 are for use only for healthy newborns and infants for which no condition after study is found to be present.

3) Z05 on a birth record.

A code from category Z05 is to be used as a secondary code after the code from category Z38, Liveborn infants according to place of birth and type of delivery.

EXAMPLE

A male infant was born by a precipitous vaginal delivery and was observed for complications related to precipitate delivery, and no complications were found, Z38.00, Z05.8.

c. Coding Additional Perinatal Diagnoses

1) Assigning codes for conditions that require treatment

Assign codes for conditions that require treatment or further investigation, prolong the length of stay, or require resource utilization.

2) Codes for conditions specified as having implications for future health care needs

Assign codes for conditions that have been specified by the provider as having implications for future health care needs.

Note: This guideline should not be used for adult patients.

EXAMPLE

A male infant was born via vaginal delivery. The clinician will evaluate and review treatment options for his undescended right testicle at the 6-week appointment, Z38.00, Q53.10.

d. Prematurity and Fetal Growth Retardation

Providers utilize different criteria in determining prematurity. A code for prematurity should not be assigned unless it is documented. Assignment of codes in categories P05, Disorders of newborn related to slow fetal growth and fetal malnutrition, and P07, Disorders of newborn related to short gestation and low birth weight, not elsewhere classified, should be based on the recorded birth weight and estimated gestational age.

When both birth weight and gestational age are available, two codes from category P07 should be assigned, with the code for birth weight sequenced before the code for gestational age.

EXAMPLE A premature infant was born in the hospital via vaginal delivery. The infant weighed 4 pounds and was 33 weeks' gestational age, Z38.00, P07.17, P07.36.

e. Low birth weight and immaturity status

Codes from category P07, Disorders of newborn related to short gestation and low birth weight, not elsewhere classified, are for use for a child or adult who was premature or had a low birth weight as a newborn and this is affecting the patient's current health status.

See Section I.C.21. Factors influencing health status and contact with health services, Status.

f. Bacterial Sepsis of Newborn

Category P36, Bacterial sepsis of newborn, includes congenital sepsis. If a perinate is documented as having sepsis without documentation of congenital or community acquired, the default is congenital and a code from category P36 should be assigned. If the P36 code includes the causal organism, an additional code from category B95, Streptococcus, Staphylococcus, and Enterococcus as the cause of diseases classified elsewhere, or B96, Other bacterial agents as the cause of diseases classified elsewhere, should not be assigned. If the P36 code does not include the causal organism, assign an additional code from category B96. If applicable, use additional codes to identify severe sepsis (R65.2-) and any associated acute organ dysfunction.

EXAMPLE A 2-week-old infant is admitted to the hospital with high fever. The infant is diagnosed with group B strep sepsis, P36.0.

g. Stillbirth

Code P95, Stillbirth, is only for use in institutions that maintain separate records for stillbirths. No other code should be used with P95. Code P95 should not be used on the mother's record.

h. COVID-19 Infection in Newborn

For a newborn that tests positive for COVID-19, assign code U07.1, COVID-19, and the appropriate codes for associated manifestation(s) in neonates/newborns in the absence of documentation indicating a specific type of transmission. For a newborn that tests positive for COVID-19 and the provider documents the condition was contracted in utero or during the birth process, assign codes P35.8, Other congenital viral disease, and U07.1, COVID-19. When coding the birth episode in a newborn record, the appropriate code from category Z38, Liveborn infants according to place of birth and type of delivery, should be assigned as the principal diagnosis.

17. Chapter 17: Congenital malformations, deformations, and chromosomal abnormalities (Q00-Q99)

Assign an appropriate code(s) from categories Q00-Q99, Congenital malformations, deformations, and chromosomal abnormalities when a malformation/deformation or chromosomal abnormality is documented. A malformation/deformation/or chromosomal abnormality may be the principal/first-listed diagnosis on a record or a secondary diagnosis.

When a malformation/deformation/or chromosomal abnormality does not have a unique code assignment, assign additional code(s) for any manifestations that may be present.

When the code assignment specifically identifies the malformation/deformation/or chromosomal abnormality, manifestations that are an inherent component of the anomaly should not be coded separately. Additional codes should be assigned for manifestations that are not an inherent component.

Codes from Chapter 17 may be used throughout the life of the patient. If a congenital malformation or deformity has been corrected, a personal history code should be used to identify the history of the malformation or deformity. Although present at birth, a malformation/deformation/or chromosomal abnormality may not be identified until later in life. Whenever the condition is diagnosed by the provider, it is appropriate to assign a code from codes Q00-Q99.

For the birth admission, the appropriate code from category Z38, Liveborn infants, according to place of birth and type of delivery, should be sequenced as the principal diagnosis, followed by any congenital anomaly codes, Q00-Q99.

EXAMPLE Infant delivered vaginally was discovered to have a supernumerary finger of the left hand, Z38.00, Q69.0.

EXAMPLE Infant delivered via C-section with known Tetralogy of Fallot, Z38.01, Q21.3.

EXAMPLE Patient is a 40-year-old male complaining of nausea, vomiting, and abdominal pain. He is admitted to the hospital, and it is determined that he has Meckel's diverticulum, Q43.0.

EXERCISE 23-1

Answer the questions and assign codes to the following conditions.

1. A congenital anomaly is always listed second on a newborn record.
A. True
B. False

2. A congenital anomaly code can be assigned to an adult record.
A. True
B. False

3. Codes from Chapter 15 can be used on the newborn record.
A. True
B. False

4. Chapter 16 codes can be used anytime throughout the life of the patient.
A. True
B. False

5. Code P02.7 belongs on the mother's record.
A. True
B. False

6. If a newborn has a condition that has implications for future health care needs, that condition may be coded. The same is true for the adult population.
A. True
B. False

7. When a newborn is transferred to another hospital, the principal diagnosis should be a code from the Z38 series.
A. True
B. False

8. Codes in category P00 can be assigned as a principal diagnosis.
A. True
B. False

9. A coder should assign a code for prematurity on the basis of weeks and/or weight in grams.
A. True
B. False

10. If the mother of a newborn has hypertension, code P00.0 is assigned.
A. True
B. False

11. When the code P74.1 is used would it also be appropriate to use code E86.0? ______________

12. If it is not clearly documented on the infant's chart whether a condition is community acquired or is due to the birth process, which is the default? ______________

13. What makes a condition clinically significant?
____

14. What category of codes is used as the principal diagnosis for newborns? ______________

15. When a baby is born extremely prematurely at 25 weeks' gestation and has a birth weight of 950 grams, and physician documents extreme immatunity, what code or codes are assigned? ____________

16. When a newborn has a diagnosis of sepsis, what code or codes are assigned? ____________

17. What is the definition of "congenital"?

____

18. The principal diagnosis code for a single newborn who is delivered by a cesarean section is ____________

19. How long does the perinatal period last? ____________

20. It is permissible to use codes from other chapters with codes from Chapter 16. ____________

A. True

B. False

DISEASE CONDITIONS

Certain Conditions Originating in the Perinatal Period (P00-P96), Chapter 16 in the ICD-10-CM code book, and Congenital Malformations, Deformations, and Chromosomal Abnormalities (Q00-Q99), Chapter 17, is divided into the following categories:

CATEGORY	SECTION TITLES
P00-P04	Newborn affected by maternal factors and by complications of pregnancy, labor, and delivery
P05-P08	Disorders of the newborn related to length of gestation and fetal growth
P09	Abnormal findings on neonatal screening
P10-P15	Birth trauma
P19-P29	Respiratory and cardiovascular disorders specific to the perinatal period
P35-P39	Infections specific to the perinatal period
P50-P61	Hemorrhagic and hematological disorders of newborn
P70-P74	Transitory endocrine and metabolic disorders specific to newborn
P76-P78	Digestive system disorders of newborn
P80-P83	Conditions involving the integument and temperature regulation of newborn
P84	Other problems with newborn
P90-P96	Other disorders originating in the perinatal period
Q00-Q07	Congenital malformations of the nervous system
Q10-Q18	Congenital malformations of the eye, ear, face, and neck
Q20-Q28	Congenital malformations of the circulatory system
Q30-Q34	Congenital malformations of the respiratory system
Q35-Q37	Cleft lip and cleft palate
Q38-Q45	Other congenital malformations of the digestive system
Q50-Q56	Congenital malformations of genital organs
Q60-Q64	Congenital malformations of the urinary system
Q65-Q79	Congenital malformations and deformations of the musculoskeletal system
Q80-Q89	Other congenital malformations
Q90-Q99	Chromosomal abnormalities, not elsewhere classified

Coding the Birth of an Infant

All newborn charts must contain a code from Z38.- for the principal diagnosis on the baby's birth record. In ICD-10-CM the Z codes for the birth of an infant describe the place of birth as well as the type of delivery and the number of infants delivered. This Z code is only used one time. If the baby is transferred to another facility, these sets of Z codes are not used and the reason for admission at that facility is the principal diagnosis. If an infant is born outside the hospital, Z38.1 single liveborn infant, born outside hospital, should be assigned. If an infant is born outside of the hospital and the only reason for admission is due to a complication, then the complication code should be assigned as the principal diagnosis, and no code from category Z38 is assigned.

EXAMPLE Single liveborn, born in hospital, via cesarean section, Z38.01.

EXAMPLE Twin, mate liveborn, delivered vaginally in hospital, Z38.30.

EXAMPLE Single liveborn delivered by cesarean section at Hospital A. The infant was transferred to Hospital B because of bladder exstrophy.
Hospital A Z38.01, Q64.10
Hospital B Q64.10

The guidelines state that all clinically significant conditions noted on routine newborn examination should be coded. These follow the same general guidelines for assigning secondary diagnoses except for the guideline regarding implications for future healthcare needs.

A condition is clinically significant if it requires the following:

- Clinical evaluation, or
- Therapeutic treatment, or
- Diagnostic procedures, or
- Extended length of hospital stay, or
- Increased nursing care and/or monitoring; or if it has
- Implications for future healthcare needs (applies to newborn only)

Apgar Scores

Most babies are assessed after birth by what is known as an **Apgar** test (Figure 23-1). This test is usually given twice—once at 1 minute and again at 5 minutes. If problems are noted with the baby, the test may be done a third time. It is good to be familiar with this test because a low Apgar score is often indicative of problems.

Five factors are used for evaluation; the baby is given a score of 0 to 2 for each factor. These consist of the following:

1. Heart (pulse)
2. Breathing (rate and effort)
3. Activity and muscle tone
4. Grimace (reflex irritability)
5. Appearance (skin coloration)

If a baby scores 7 or above at 1 minute after birth, the baby is considered healthy. If a score between 4 and 6 is recorded at 1 minute, usually the baby needs immediate care with oxygen or suctioning.

APGAR SCORING CHART

SIGN	0	1	2
Heart rate	Absent	Below 100	Over 100
Respiratory effort	Absent	Slow, irregular	Good, crying
Muscle tone	Limp	Some flexion of extremities	Active motion
Response to catheter in nostril (tested after oropharynx is clear)	No response	Grimace	Cough or sneeze
Color	Blue, pale	Body pink, extremities blue	Completely pink

FIGURE 23-1. Apgar scoring chart.

Newborn Affected by Maternal Factors and by Complications of Pregnancy, Labor, and Delivery (P00-P04)

The codes in these categories are used when a maternal condition is specified as the cause for a confirmed or potential morbidity. As is stated in the guidelines, these conditions are assigned only if and when the maternal condition has actually affected the fetus or the newborn. Just because a mother has a condition does not necessarily mean that it affects the newborn. For example, a nuchal cord may affect the delivery and should be coded on the mother's chart, but a cord around the neck may not have had any physical effect on the infant, so it should not be coded.

EXAMPLE

Infant is delivered via vaginal delivery. The mother is addicted to heroin. The newborn has a positive drug screen but shows no signs of dependence or withdrawal, Z38.00, P04.14.

Disorders of the Newborn Related to Length of Gestation and Fetal Growth (P05-P08)

Prematurity must be documented by the provider in order to assign a code for this condition. Codes for (P05) Newborns light for gestational age should not be assigned with codes (P07) Disorders of the newborn related to short gestation and low birth weight, NEC. If both birth weight and gestational age are available, both should be coded with the birth weight sequenced first. Sometimes in later admissions or on later visits, a physician may document something such as "ex-25 week preemie," and in this case, even if the child is older, this code can be assigned as the fact that the child is a preemie may account for or contribute to the current condition. This also follows the rule that Chapter 16 codes may be used throughout a patient's life.

EXAMPLE

Infant delivered vaginally is premature as documented by provider. The baby is delivered at 28 weeks and weighs 1720 grams, Z38.00, P07.16, P07.31.

EXAMPLE

The physician documented that the baby was small for gestational age (SGA). The baby weighed 1850 grams. The infant was born in the hospital by vaginal delivery, Z38.00, P05.17.

Birth Trauma (P10-P15)

Cephalhematoma is a condition of blood between the skull and periosteum of a newborn. This condition is often caused by either a prolonged second stage of labor or injury to the skull during birth caused by instrumentation. In most cases this is a benign condition that requires no treatment, and the hematoma resolves on its own.

EXAMPLE

Newborn delivered via difficult vaginal birth. Infant suffered a cephalhematoma secondary to the use of a forceps delivery, Z38.00, P12.0.

Respiratory and Cardiovascular Disorders Specific to the Perinatal Period (P19-P29)

Respiratory Problems After Birth

If a baby is born by cesarean section, a pediatrician may be asked to be present for the birth. If an abnormal heart rate occurs during labor, or any indications suggest that the baby might be in trouble, a pediatrician may be called and is asked to be present for the delivery. Documentation by the physician should note any abnormal conditions.

Transitory Tachypnea of Newborn (TTN). This is a respiratory problem that is likely due to retained lung fluid. It usually resolves in 24 to 48 hours. The baby may be treated with oxygen.

Apnea of the Newborn. This tends to occur in premature infants and is defined as a pause in breathing for longer than 15 seconds that can result in cyanosis.

Respiratory Distress Syndrome (RDS). This syndrome rarely affects full-term infants. It is caused by lack of lung surfactant. Surfactant is a chemical that keeps the air sacs from collapsing. The more premature the baby is, the greater is the chance of RDS. Treatment for mild cases consists of oxygen. Patients with more severe disease must be ventilated; sometimes, an artificial lung surfactant is placed in the lungs of an infant who is at high risk, to try to prevent RDS.

EXAMPLE Respiratory distress syndrome in liveborn infant who was delivered vaginally, Z38.00, P22.0.

Meconium Aspiration Syndrome

Meconium is the fecal matter within a baby's intestines before birth. Normally, it is expelled after birth, but if problems occur during labor, the baby may expel meconium into the amniotic fluid. Meconium may be inhaled by the baby while within the uterus or during birth. Inhalation of meconium occurs most often in postterm babies.

A physician may suspect aspiration if the newborn is covered with meconium, or if thick meconium is found in the amniotic fluid. Aspiration of meconium can result in major problems for the newborn.

A variety of codes may be used to indicate the different ways in which meconium may be found.

- Meconium staining P96.83
- Meconium passage during delivery P03.82
- Meconium aspiration without respiratory symptoms P24.00
- Meconium aspiration with respiratory symptoms P24.01
- Fetal and newborn aspiration, unspecified P24.9

Bronchopulmonary Dysplasia (BPD)

Bronchopulmonary dysplasia (BPD) is a chronic lung disease that develops in babies during the first 4 weeks after birth. It occurs most often in premature babies; that is, those weighing less than 1500 grams. Sometimes, the ventilator that is keeping a baby alive may cause BPD. BPD may also be caused by infections such as pneumonia. Providers often document this as chronic lung disease instead of BPD, so a query may be necessary to ascertain the nature of the infant's or child's chronic lung disease.

EXAMPLE A 4-week old infant is diagnosed with bronchopulmonary dysplasia. Infant was on a ventilator following birth, P27.1.

Infections Specific to the Perinatal Period (P35-P39)

Infection in the Perinatal Period

Newborn Sepsis. To locate infections of the newborn in the index, it is best to look under the main term for the infection, and then to look for a subterm of newborn, fetal, or congenital.

For example, newborn sepsis codes to P36.-. It is also important to assign a code from category B96 to identify the organism responsible for the infection if not identified by another code in this category. Additional codes for severe sepsis (R65.2-) and any associated acute organ dysfunction should be assigned if applicable.

The guidelines also state that if a newborn has a condition that may be due to the birth process or may be community acquired, and the documentation is not clear regarding the underlying cause, the default is to the congenital condition.

EXAMPLE A 7-day-old infant presents to the ER with sepsis due to group B *Streptococcus*, P36.0.

Hemorrhagic and Hematological Disorders of Newborn (P50-P61)

Many newborns have jaundice. Jaundice results from too many red blood cells and the breakdown of these cells into bilirubin. A large amount of bilirubin causes the skin to take on a yellow color. The most common types of jaundice are:

Physiological (normal) jaundice: this occurs in most newborns. It is a mild form of jaundice that is due to the immaturity of the baby's liver. This type of jaundice usually occurs 2 to 4 days following birth and is gone by 2 weeks of age. It is the most common type of jaundice.

Jaundice of prematurity: this type of jaundice occurs in newborns who are born premature. Their systems are even more immature and, therefore, they are more likely to get jaundice.

Breastfeeding jaundice: this occurs when a breastfeeding baby is not getting enough breast milk because of difficulty with breastfeeding or because the mother's milk isn't in yet. This is not caused by a problem with the breast milk itself but by the baby not getting enough to drink.

Other factors may cause jaundice, but the next most common cause is Rh or ABO incompatibility. ABO incompatibility affects newborns whose blood type is A, B, or AB and whose mothers have a blood type of O.

A Coombs' test may be performed on newborns who are jaundiced. This is done to look for possible causes of **hemolysis** (the breaking down of red blood cells). Two common forms of hemolysis in the newborn are Rh incompatibility and ABO incompatibility. Rh incompatibility occurs when an Rh-negative (anti-Rh antibodies in blood) mom gives birth to an Rh-positive baby. If any maternal and fetal blood gets mixed during pregnancy or the birth process, the mother's Rh-negative antibodies will attack the baby's Rh-positive RBCs and destroy them. ABO incompatibility is very similar in mechanism.

Most often, jaundice is treated by putting a baby under "bili" lights. In very mild cases, a mother is instructed to put the baby in a sunlit window. In very severe cases, a transfusion may be required.

EXAMPLE Newborn with Rh incompatibility. Infant was delivered vaginally, Z38.00, P55.0.

Other Problems With the Newborn (P84)

Fetal Distress

Fetal distress occurs when the fetus develops a problem before or during labor. No exact consensus has been reached as to what constitutes fetal distress, but the term often refers to **hypoxia** (insufficient oxygen in blood), **bradycardia** (slow heartbeat), **tachycardia** (fast heartbeat), fetal acidosis, and/or the presence of thick meconium.

EXAMPLE Fetal distress first noted during labor, infant born vaginally, Z38.00, P84.

EXAMPLE Fetal hypoxia in infant born by C-Section, Z38.01, P84.

Other Disorders Originating in the Perinatal Period (P90-P96)

Feeding Problems in Newborns

Newborns are prone to a variety of minor feeding problems. Most newborns spit up, but if spitting up interferes with feeding and growing, it may be GERD. Vomiting could be the result of a more serious infectious condition. Projectile vomiting can occur because of a blockage in the stomach. Overfeeding, which is usually done in response to crying, can cause spitting up and diarrhea. Underfeeding may lead to failure to thrive. Underfeeding usually occurs when an infant has difficulty sucking or swallowing. Sometimes infants have a problem with breastfeeding. When they are not growing at the expected rate for their age, or if their weight is disproportionately low compared to their height and head circumference, they may be considered to have failure to thrive.

EXAMPLE

Newborn delivered vaginally has lost more weight than usual at discharge. Physician documents that a lactation consult should be ordered as there seems to be problems with breastfeeding, Z38.00, P92.5.

EXERCISE 23-2

Answer the following questions.

1. Should the first-listed code on newborn charts be from category Z37? ______
2. If a baby has a low Apgar score it would be indicative of no problems. T or F? ______
3. Mother had a urinary tract infection (UTI) during the pregnancy; this was treated, and no effect on the fetus was observed. Should code P00.1 be added to the baby's chart? ______
4. Mother had an automobile accident. She needed to undergo immediate surgery to correct the open fracture of her arm. It was decided that a cesarean section should be performed and the baby delivered prior to repair of the fracture. Should code P00.5 be added to the baby's chart? ______
5. A baby is born with spina bifida due to the mother taking statins during pregnancy. Should code P04.1 be used on the baby's chart? ______
6. A baby is born to a mother who used cocaine during the pregnancy. The baby experiences no signs of withdrawal but has a positive drug screen. Should P04.41 be used on this baby's chart? ______
7. A newborn is delivered via vacuum extractor. A large hematoma is located on the scalp. Should P03.3 be coded? ______

Assign codes to the following. Consider the birth to be a live birth unless otherwise specified.

8. Preterm baby born via vaginal delivery at 27 weeks at a weight of 950 grams ______
9. Baby was delivered via a difficult vaginal delivery at 40 weeks. Upon delivery the pediatrician noted a fractured clavicle ______
10. Mother used heroin during this pregnancy. Upon vaginal delivery, it is noted that the baby is jittery and is experiencing symptoms of withdrawal ______
11. Meconium aspiration syndrome ______
12. Neonatal bradycardia ______
13. Sepsis of the newborn due to group B strep ______
14. Neonatal jaundice due to preterm delivery ______
15. Anemia of the newborn due to prematurity ______
16. Hypomagnesemia of the newborn ______
17. Hypoxia of the newborn ______
18. Meconium staining ______
19. Neonatal abstinence syndrome ______
20. Floppy baby syndrome ______

Congenital Malformations of the Nervous System (Q00-Q07)

Chapter 17 *Congenital Malformations, Deformations, and Chromosomal Abnormalities*

A **congenital anomaly** is an abnormal condition that is present at birth. Sometimes, conditions that a person is born with do not appear until later in life. Some conditions are congenital by definition, such as Meckel's diverticulum. This condition is present at birth but may not manifest until later in life. Congenital anomalies may be located in the Alphabetic Index under the specific condition or anomaly and/or deformity.

Spina bifida is a disorder that involves incomplete development of the brain, spinal cord, and/or their protective coverings (Figure 23-2). It occurs in 1 in every 2000 births in the United States. Pregnant women can be tested with a blood test called MSAFP (maternal serum alpha-fetoprotein) to screen for spina bifida. This disorder occurs during the first month of pregnancy and is caused by the spine of the fetus not closing properly. This results in permanent nerve damage to various degrees, even though the opening can be closed in utero or after birth. Three types of spina bifida have been identified: (1) myelomeningocele, which is the most severe form; the spinal cord and the meninges protrude from the opening in the spine; (2) meningocele, which is the most rare form; the spinal cord is normally developed, but the meninges protrudes through the opening; and (3) occulta, which is the mildest form; one or more vertebrae are malformed; this type usually involves no treatment.

Children with spina bifida often have bowel and bladder complications and hydrocephalus (Figure 23-3). Spina bifida has no cure because nerve tissue cannot be repaired. Treatment is rendered according to the severity of the condition. Children born with spina bifida are usually treated through surgery that is performed to close the opening within 24 hours of birth. If a child is born with the most severe type, he or she often has **hydrocephalus**; this is treated by inserting a **ventriculoperitoneal shunt** into the brain to drain accumulating fluid (Figure 23-4). Another complication of a severe case of spina bifida is a tethered spinal cord. A tethered spinal cord is a cord that does not move up and down during movement, as it is designed to do. If a child has severe pain, surgery may be performed to untether the spinal cord.

EXAMPLE A child with Cockayne's Syndrome is seen by a physician who documents that the patient has mild intellectual disability, retinal atrophy, and microcephaly, Q87.1, H35.89, F70, Q02.

EXAMPLE Baby born by cesarean section is found to have spina bifida with hydrocephalus, Z38.01, Q05.4.

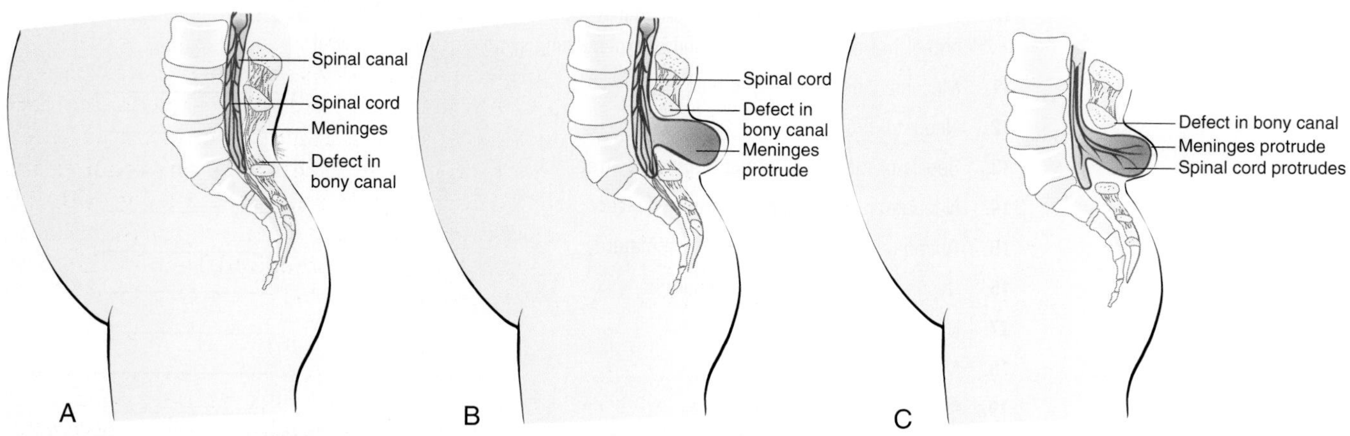

FIGURE 23-2. Congenital spinal cord defects.

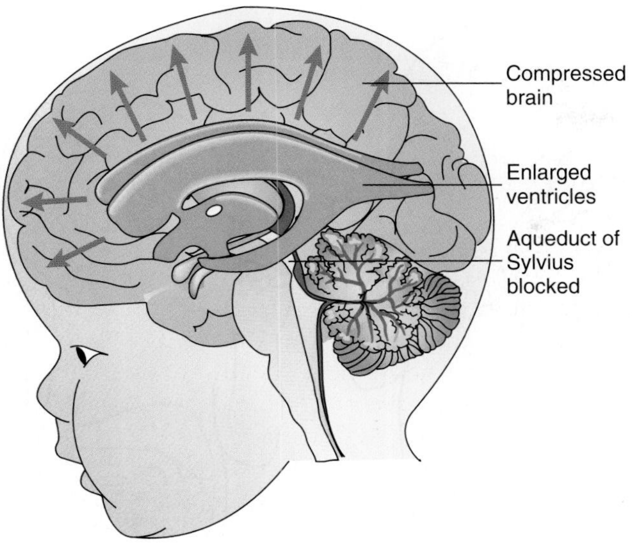

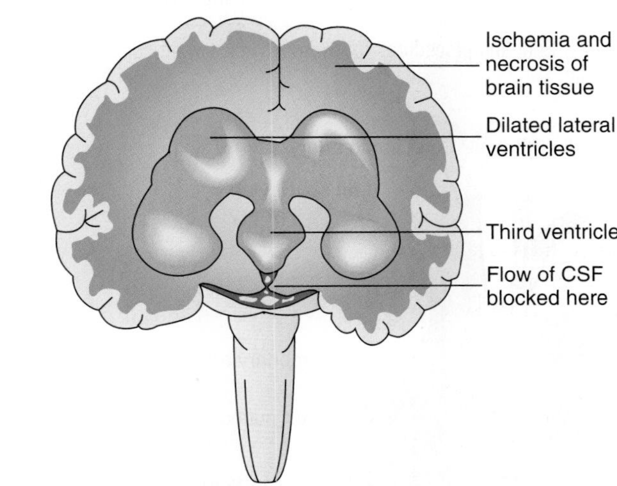

FIGURE 23-3. Hydrocephalus.

Congenital Malformations of the Circulatory System (Q20-Q28)

Tetralogy of Fallot

Tetralogy of Fallot (TOF) (Figure 23-5) is a congenital heart defect that manifests with four key features: (1) a hole between the ventricles (ventral septal defect [VSD]); (2) pulmonary stenosis; (3) aorta lying directly over the hole; and (4) thick, muscled right ventricle (hypertrophy). Treatment recommended for this condition is surgery. Often, surgery requires two stages. The first stage occurs when the infant is first born; a little later, after growth has occurred, the second stage is performed. Patients who have undergone repair often are at greater risk for arrhythmia; sometimes, additional surgery is required later in life. The operation performed to treat this condition is called the **Blalock-Taussig procedure**.

EXAMPLE

VSD is diagnosed in a newborn along with pulmonary stenosis and hypertrophy of the right ventricle, as well as dextroposition of the aorta. The baby is seen by a cardiac surgeon who diagnoses Tetralogy of Fallot. The surgeon recommends surgery, Q21.3.

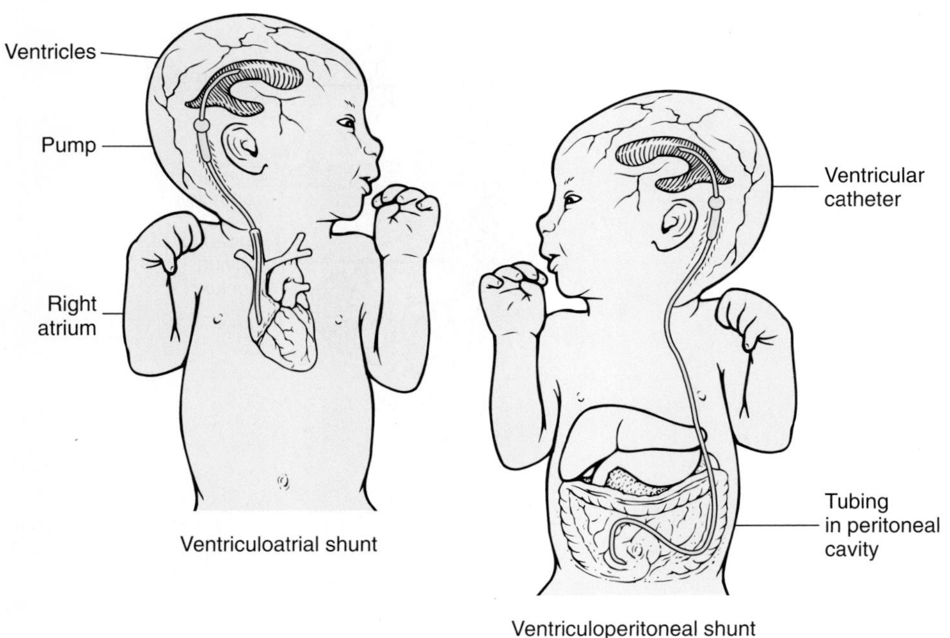

FIGURE 23-4. Shunting procedures for hydrocephalus. Ventriculoperitoneal shunt is the preferred procedure.

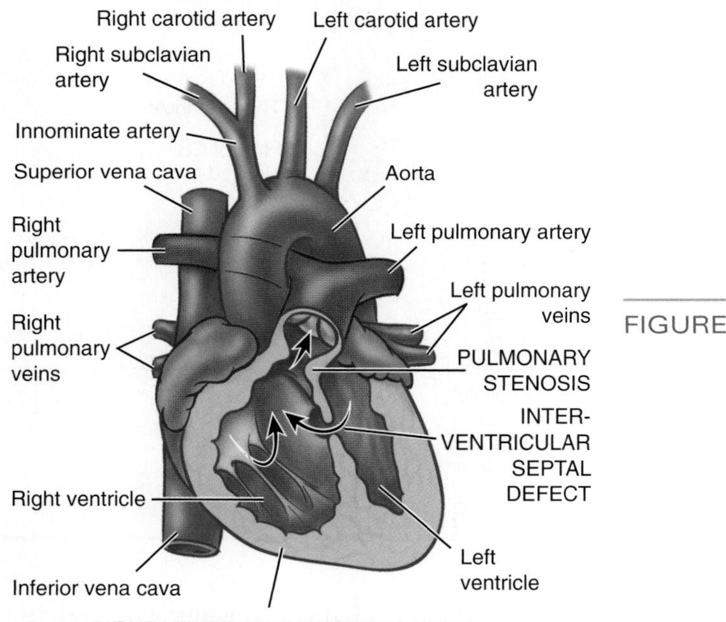

FIGURE 23-5. Tetralogy of Fallot.

Cleft Lip and Cleft Palate (Q35-Q37)

A **cleft lip/palate** is an opening in the lip or palate of an infant that occurs in utero.

Three different types of clefts can occur on one or both sides of the mouth:

1. Cleft lip without a cleft palate (Figure 23-6)
2. Cleft palate without a cleft lip
3. Cleft lip and cleft palate together

Approximately 1 in 600 babies is born with a cleft. Surgery is performed to repair the cleft; often, surgery is completed in several stages. The first surgery is usually done when a baby is 10 weeks of age or older and weighs at least 10 pounds.

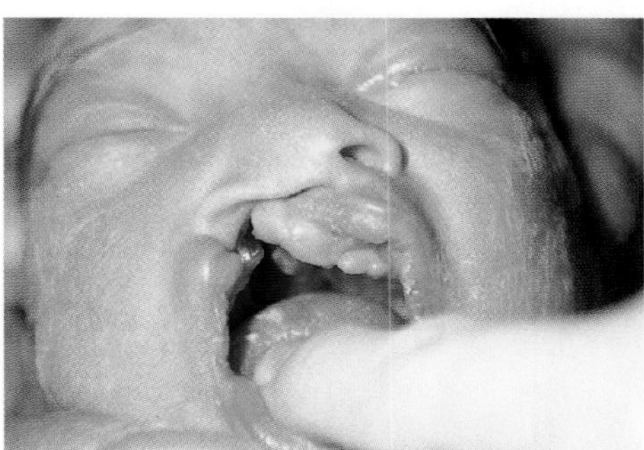

FIGURE 23-6. Unilateral cleft lip.

EXAMPLE

The child was admitted for repair of unilateral upper cleft lip and soft and hard palate. A repair of both the hard and soft palate and lip is performed by external approach, Q37.5, 0CQ0XZZ, 0CQ2XZZ, 0CQ3XZZ.

Other Congenital Malformations of the Digestive System (Q38-A45)

Meckel's Diverticulum

Meckel's diverticulum occurs during the fifth week of fetal development. This is a small pouch on the wall of the small bowel that contains ectopic tissue. It occurs in about 2% of the population, and most people who have this condition have no problems. Complications of Meckel's diverticulum include hematochezia in children and obstruction or diverticulitis in adults. Treatment varies but may require only observation and treatment of symptoms or surgery to remove the diverticulum.

EXAMPLE

A 60-year-old woman presents to the hospital with severe abdominal pain. A scan is performed, and Meckel's diverticulum is discovered. The surgeon is called in and performs an open ileal resection (partial), Q43.0, 0DBB0ZZ.

Hirschsprung's disease, a disease of the large intestine, causes intestinal obstruction or severe constipation. Infants with this disease are lacking in nerve cells in the large intestine. These nerve cells signal the muscles to push out the fecal matter in the intestine. If these cells are not present, then the stool remains in the intestine. The symptoms of this disease usually occur shortly after birth and include lots of gas, bloody diarrhea, and green or brown vomit. In order to correct this problem, sometimes surgery is performed to remove the part of the intestine that has no nerve cells.

EXAMPLE

Newborn is brought to pediatrician with symptoms of fussiness and gas. After examination, the doctor documents congenital megacolon, Q43.1.

Congenital Malformations of Genital Organs (Q50-Q56)

Undescended testes, also known as cryptorchism, is a common condition ocurring in approximately 3% of full term births and 30% of premature births. An undescended testicle is a condition where one of the testes is located outside of the scrotum; this may also be referred to as an ectopic testicle. Risk factors for this condition occurring include family with a history of this condition, premature birth, or low birth weight. In 80% of the cases, the testicle will travel to the correct position within the first year of birth. In some cases surgery termed orchipexy will need to be performed.

EXAMPLE

At birth the pediatrician examining the baby found that he had bilateral undescended testicles. He recommended that this be watched by the pediatrician, Q53.20.

Hypospadias is a condition where the opening of the urethra is not in the normal position at the end of the penis. Most often the opening can be found at the underside of the penis (Figure 23-7). Depending on how close or far the opening is from the normal

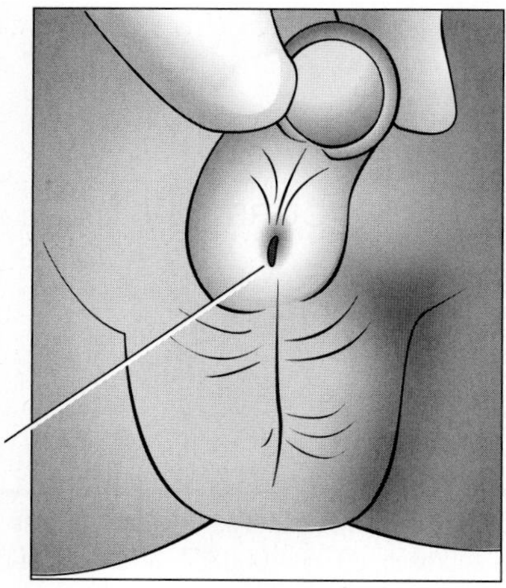

FIGURE 23-7. Hypospadias, urethral opening underside.

anatomic position will determine the symptoms. Some of the symptoms are abnormal spraying of urine and having to sit when urinating. When infants are diagnosed with hypospadias, they should not be circumcised as the foreskin can be used when surgical repair is performed. Often infants that have hypospadias also have chordee (downward curve of the penis). Surgery to repair these defects is usually performed before a child turns 2 years old.

EXAMPLE Baby was born with penile hypospadias, Q54.1.

Congenital Malformations of the Urinary System (Q60-Q64)

Exstrophy of the urinary bladder is a condition where a child is born with part of the urinary bladder outside of the body. This condition is a rare condition that most often occurs in males. It generally occurs with other urinary issues such as epispadias, undescended testicles, and a widening of the pubic symphysis. Surgery is used to repair this birth defect and often requires more than one surgery.

EXAMPLE Baby is born with cloacal exstrophy of the urinary bladder, Q64.12.

Congenital Malformations and Deformations of the Musculoskeletal System (Q65-Q79)

Congenital malformations of the musculoskeletal system are not uncommon. Some common deformities are:

- Clubfoot—foot turns inward and downward. It is the most common congenital disorder of the legs and can be repaired with a series of casts or in extreme cases with surgery
- Hip dislocations—often occur in breech births
- Funnel chest—chest appears sunken as breast bone is pushed abnormally inward
- Polydactyly—extra digits
- Syndactyly—webbed digits
- Oteogenesis imperfecta—congenital disease causing weak bones

EXAMPLE Baby born by C-section is diagnosed with pigeon chest, Z38.01, Q67.7.

Other Congenital Malformations (Q80-Q89)

Prader-Willi Syndrome (PWS) is a congenital condition caused by an abnormality of the 15th chromosome. The child with this condition will often be short in stature and have uncontrollable hunger. They never feel full, and they require fewer calories because they have less muscle mass. This is a disorder of the hypothalmus and has symptoms such as stubborness, temper tantrums, learning disabilities, hoarding, low sex hormone levels, and repetitive thoughts and verbalizations. People with this disorder can live a normal lifespan if the obesity can be controlled.

Marfan's Syndrome

Marfan's syndrome (Figure 23-8), which is caused by a gene mutation, is an inherited condition that affects the connective tissue. Because connective tissue is found throughout the body, Marfan's may affect many body systems. Often, patients with Marfan's have skeletal defects, such as spider-like fingers, pectus excavatum, and curvature of the spine. They also may have cardiovascular problems such as aortic regurgitation or prolapse of the mitral valve.

EXAMPLE Ectopia lentis in a patient with Marfan's syndrome, Q87.42, Q12.1.

Chromosomal Abnormalities, Not Elsewhere Classified (Q90-Q99)

One in 200 babies is born with a chromosomal abnormality. Each egg and sperm cell contains 23 chromosomes. When they unite, 23 pairs or 46 chromosomes are created. If a baby is born with too many, too few, or broken or rearranged chromosomes, birth defects may

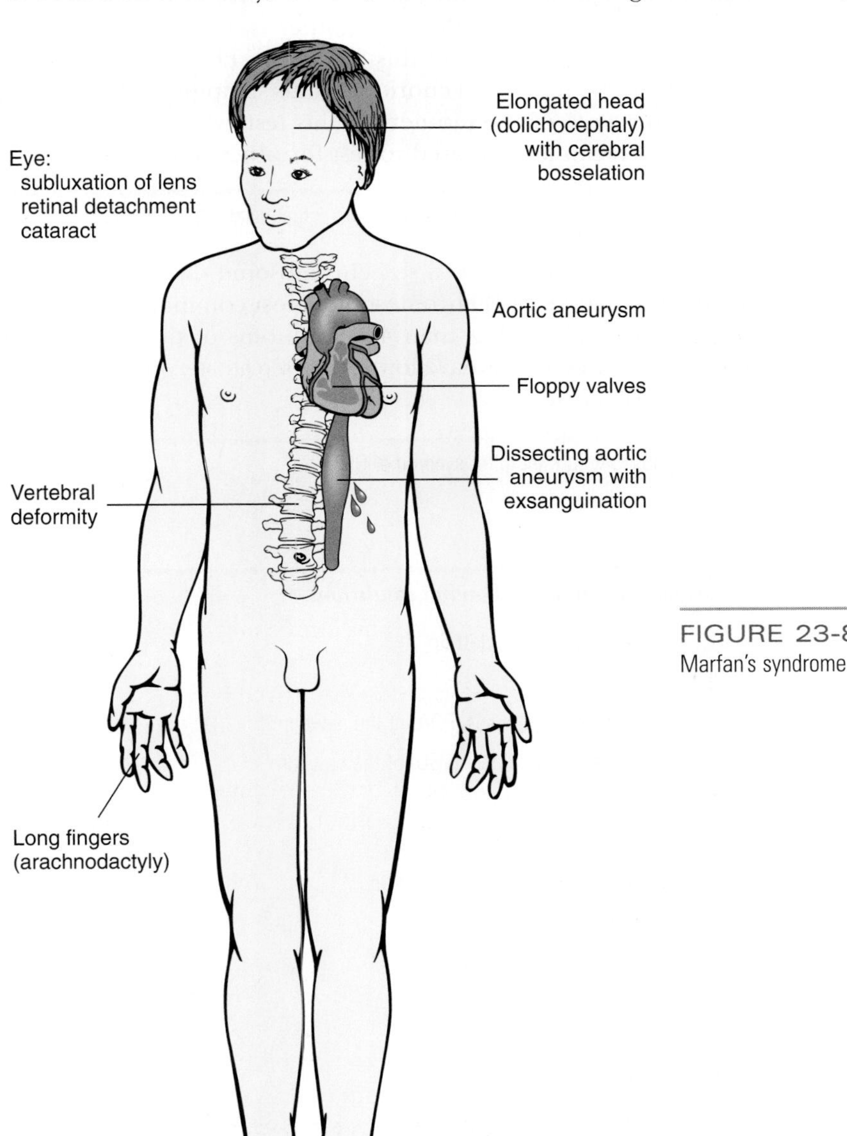

FIGURE 23-8. Typical features of Marfan's syndrome.

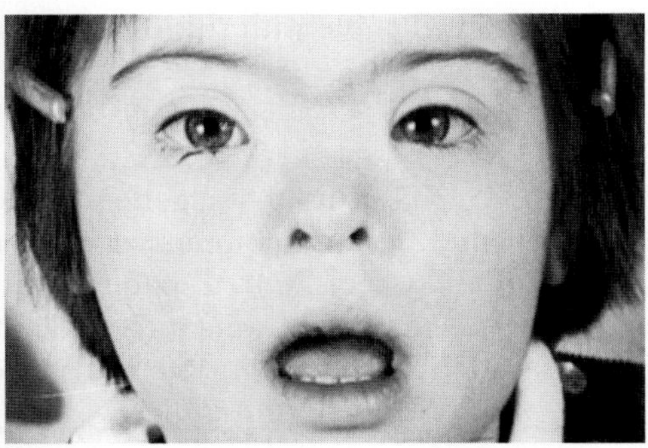

FIGURE 23-9. Photograph of 3½-year-old girl with typical facial appearance of Down syndrome.

occur. A chromosomal abnormality with three instead of two of a specific chromosome is called a **trisomy**. In most cases, when this occurs, the pregnancy ends in a miscarriage.

Down syndrome (Figure 23-9), the most common chromosomal abnormality, is also known as trisomy 21. Babies with Down syndrome have an extra chromosome 21. Children with Down syndrome can have a combination of birth defects. Some of these are characteristic facial features, intellectual disability, and heart defects. No cure is known for Down syndrome; however, the older the mother is, the greater the risk. Research suggests that folic acid can help to prevent this condition. Physicians can test for this condition during pregnancy with a test called chorionic villus sampling (CVS). A tiny sample of tissue is taken from the placenta of the mother for this test, which is performed transcervically or transvaginally. CVS can also be used to test for other disorders.

EXAMPLE Patient with Down syndrome with moderate intellectual disability, Q90.9, F71.

Klinefelter syndrome is a sex chromosome disorder which occurs only in males; the individual has an extra X chromosome. Most commonly, the child is born with 47 chromosomes in each cell, rather than 46. Symptoms of this condition generally do not appear until puberty. Individuals have low levels of testosterone and small testicles and may exhibit behavior problems.

EXAMPLE Patient diagnosed with Klinefelter syndrome, Q98.4.

EXERCISE 23-3

Assign codes to the following conditions.

1. Unilateral, complete cleft lip ____________
2. Tongue tie ____________
3. Patent ductus arteriosus (PDA) of the newborn ____________
4. Ventricular septal defect (VSD) of the newborn ____________
5. Preauricular cyst ____________
6. Transposition of the great vessels ____________
7. Ptosis of the eyelid present at birth ____________
8. Microcephalus ____________
9. Arnold-Chiari syndrome type II ____________
10. Cerebral cyst present at birth ____________
11. Supernumerary ear ____________
12. Branchial cleft cyst ____________
13. Microtia ____________
14. Micro-penis ____________
15. Conjoined twins ____________

FACTORS INFLUENCING HEALTH STATUS AND CONTACT WITH HEALTH SERVICES (Z CODES)

As was discussed in Chapter 9, it may be difficult to locate Z codes in the Index. Coders often say, "I did not know there was a Z code for that."

Refer to Chapter 9 for a listing of common main terms used to locate Z codes.

Z00.110	Health examination for newborn under 8 days old
Z00.111	Health examination for newborn 8 to 28 days old
Z05.0	Observation and evaluation of newborn for suspected cardiac condition ruled out
Z05.1	Observation and evaluation of newborn for suspected infectious condition ruled out
Z05.2	Observation and evaluation of newborn for suspected neurological condition ruled out
Z05.3	Observation and evaluation of newborn for suspected respiratory condition ruled out
Z05.41	Observation and evaluation of newborn for suspected genetic condition ruled out
Z05.42	Observation and evaluation of newborn for suspected metabolic condition ruled out
Z05.43	Observation and evaluation of newborn for suspected immunologic condition ruled out
Z05.5	Observation and evaluation of newborn for suspected gastrointestinal condition ruled out
Z05.6	Observation and evaluation of newborn for suspected genitourinary condition ruled out
Z05.71	Observation and evaluation of newborn for suspected skin and subcutaneous tissue condition ruled out
Z05.72	Observation and evaluation of newborn for suspected musculoskeletal condition ruled out
Z05.73	Observation and evaluation of newborn for suspected connective tissue condition ruled out
Z05.8	Observation and evaluation of newborn for other specified suspected condition ruled out
Z05.9	Observation and evaluation of newborn for unspecified suspected condition ruled out
Z13.71	Encounter for nonprocreative screening for genetic disease carrier status
Z13.79	Encounter for other screening for genetic and chromosomal anomalies
Z28.01	Immunization not carried out because of acute illness of patient
Z28.02	Immunization not carried out because of chronic illness or condition of patient
Z28.03	Immunization not carried out because of immune-compromised state of patient
Z28.04	Immunization not carried out because of patient allergy to vaccine or component
Z28.09	Immunization not carried out because of other contraindication
Z28.1	Immunization not carried out because of patient decision for reasons of belief or group pressure
Z28.20	Immunization not carried out because of patient decision for unspecified reason
Z28.21	Immunization not carried out because of patient refusal
Z28.29	Immunization not carried out because of patient decision for other reason
Z28.3	Underimmunization status
Z28.81	Immunization not carried out due to patient having had the disease
Z28.82	Immunization not carried out because of caregiver refusal
Z28.89	Immunization not carried out for other reason
Z28.9	Immunization not carried out for unspecified reason
Z38.00	Single liveborn infant, delivered vaginally
Z38.01	Single liveborn infant, delivered by cesarean
Z38.1	Single liveborn infant, born outside hospital
Z38.2	Single liveborn infant, unspecified as to place of birth
Z38.30	Twin liveborn infant, delivered vaginally
Z38.31	Twin liveborn infant, delivered by cesarean
Z38.4	Twin liveborn infant, born outside of hospital
Z38.5	Twin liveborn infant, unspecified as to place of birth
Z38.61	Triplet liveborn infant, delivered vaginally
Z38.62	Triplet liveborn infant, delivered by cesarean
Z38.63	Quadruplet liveborn infant, delivered vaginally
Z38.64	Quadruplet liveborn infant, delivered by cesarean

Z38.65	Quadruplet liveborn infant, delivered vaginally
Z38.66	Quadruplet liveborn infant, delivered by cesarean
Z38.68	Other multiple liveborn infant, delivered vaginally
Z38.69	Other multiple liveborn, delivered by cesarean
Z38.7	Other multiple liveborn infant, born outside hospital
Z38.8	Other multiple liveborn infant, unspecified as to place of birth
Z41.2	Encounter for routine and ritual male circumcision
Z82.71	Family history of polycystic kidney
Z82.79	Family history of other congenital malformations, deformations, and chromosomal abnormalities
Z87.71	Personal history of (corrected) congenital malformation of genitourinary system
Z87.710	Personal history of (corrected) hypospadias
Z87.718	Personal history of other specified (corrected) congenital malformations of genitourinary system
Z87.720	Personal history of (corrected) congenital malformations of eye
Z87.721	Personal history of (corrected) congenital malformations of ear
Z87.728	Personal history of other specified (corrected) congenital malformations of nervous system and sense organs
Z87.730	Personal history of (corrected) cleft lip and palate
Z87.738	Personal history of other specified (corrected) congenital malformations of digestive system
Z87.74	Personal history of (corrected) congenital malformations of heart and circulatory system
Z87.75	Personal history of (corrected) congenital malformations of respiratory system
Z87.76	Personal history of (corrected) congenital malformations of integument, limbs and musculoskeletal system
Z87.790	Personal history of (corrected) congenital malformations of face and neck
Z87.798	Personal history of other (corrected) congenital malformations

Often, a newborn is evaluated for a condition that may be suspected but is then ruled out. In cases in which this happens, it is appropriate to assign a code from the Z05.- category as a diagnosis in support of the testing and treatment that is being performed. Sometimes, a mother is running a fever during labor, and the physician must make sure that the infant does not have an infection. The physician orders tests, observation, and/or treatment until this condition can be ruled out. If the newborn is experiencing signs or symptoms, then a code from category Z05.- is not to be used. Likewise, a Z05.- code may be assigned as the principal diagnosis code for readmission when a condition is suspected and is subsequently ruled out. It is important to remember that this code can be used only during the neonatal period (the first 28 days of life).

EXAMPLE

During labor the mother develops a fever. After vaginal delivery the baby is monitored for infectious disease. All tests are negative, Z38.00, Z05.1.

EXAMPLE

Newborn is seen at 5 days for well baby check-up, Z00.110.

CHAPTER REVIEW EXERCISE

Where applicable, assign codes for diagnoses, procedures, Z codes, and external cause codes. Consider the birth to be a live birth unless otherwise specified.

1. Newborn delivered by cesarean section __________
2. Twins born in the parking lot of the hospital __________
3. Baby was born at 2200 grams; physician documented "small for dates"; delivered vaginally __________
4. Post-term newborn at 43 weeks' gestation, vaginal delivery. Birthweight is listed as 3500 grams __________

5. Newborn with IUGR (intrauterine growth retardation); delivered vaginally. Baby weighed 2200 grams and physician documented light for gestational age __________
6. Newborn fractured left femur during birth process; vaginal delivery __________
7. TTN (transitory tachypnea of the newborn); infant delivered by emergency C-section __________
8. 7-day-old with thrush; seen in physician office __________
9. Transfer from community hospital for treatment of interstitial pulmonary fibrosis of prematurity in a newborn __________
10. Baby is admitted 5 days after birth for jaundice due to breast milk __________
11. 7-day-old infant with infection of the navel cord __________
12. Newborn with a hydrocele following vaginal delivery __________
13. Baby delivered by cesarean section in respiratory failure and immediately transferred to NICU (neonatal intensive care unit) __________
14. Newborn aspirated meconium during vaginal delivery __________
15. Baby was delivered by C-section and initially had bradycardia, which was resolved prior to discharge __________
16. Newborn with fetal alcohol syndrome delivered vaginally __________
17. Newborn delivered vaginally to a mother with chorioamnionitis. The newborn has a fever and is being monitored for a suspected infection related to the mother's condition __________
18. Newborn with hypoglycemia, whose mother has diabetes, delivered vaginally __________
19. Newborn with apnea following vaginal delivery __________
20. Newborn delivered vaginally in the hospital; failed hearing test __________

CHAPTER GLOSSARY

Anomaly: a deviation from normal standards (e.g., as in congenital defects).

Apgar: test used to measure the condition of a newborn at birth.

Blalock-Taussig procedure: procedure used to treat patients with Tetralogy of Fallot who have insufficient pulmonary arterial flow.

Bradycardia: slow heart rate.

Bronchopulmonary dysplasia: chronic lung disease that develops in babies during the first 4 weeks after birth.

Cephalhematoma: a condition of blood between the skull and periosteum of a newborn.

Cleft lip/palate: opening in the lip or palate of an infant that occurs in utero.

Congenital anomaly: an abnormal condition present at birth.

Hemolysis: the breaking down of red blood cells.

Hydrocephalus: cerebrospinal fluid collection in the skull.

Hypoxia: insufficient oxygen in the blood.

Klinefelter syndrome: a sex chromosome disorder that occurs in males and is caused by an extra X chromosome.

Marfan's syndrome: an inherited condition that affects connective tissue and is caused by gene mutation.

Meconium: material in the intestine of a fetus.

Perinatal period: before birth through the first 28 days of life.

Prader-Willi Syndrome: a congenital condition caused by an abnormality of the 15th chromosome.

Trisomy: extra chromosome.

Ventriculoperitoneal shunt: procedure used to treat patient with hydrocephalus in whom drainage of the ventricle occurs through an artificial channel between the ventricle and the peritoneum.

24

Injury and Certain Other Consequences of External Causes and External Causes of Morbidity

(ICD-10-CM Chapter 19, Codes S00-T88 and Chapter 20, Codes V00-Y99)

CHAPTER OUTLINE

LEARNING OBJECTIVES

1. Apply and assign the correct ICD-10-CM/PCS codes in accordance with Official Guidelines for Coding and Reporting
2. Identify the various types of injuries
3. Assign the correct Z codes, External cause codes, and procedure codes related to injuries
4. Identify common treatments, medications, and diagnostic tests

ABBREVIATIONS/ ACRONYMS

CHI closed head injury
CT computerized tomography
FB foreign body
ICD-10-CM *International Classification of Diseases, 10th Revision, Clinical Modification*
ICD-10-PCS *International Classification of Diseases, 10th Revision, Procedure Coding System*
LOC loss of consciousness
MRI magnetic resonance imaging
MVA motor vehicle accident
OR Operating Room
ORIF open reduction with internal fixation
SCI spinal cord injury
SLAP superior labrum anterior-posterior
TBI traumatic brain injury

ICD-10-CM Official Guidelines for Coding and Reporting (2021-2022)

Please refer to the companion Evolve website for the most current 2021-2022 guidelines.

19. Chapter 19: Injury, poisoning, and certain other consequences of external causes (S00-T88)

a. Application of 7th Characters in Chapter 19

Most categories in chapter 19 have a 7th character requirement for each applicable code. Most categories in this chapter have three 7th character values (with the exception of fractures): A, initial encounter, D, subsequent encounter and S, sequela. Categories for traumatic fractures have additional 7th character values. While the patient may be seen by a new or different provider over the course of treatment for an injury, assignment of the 7th character is based on whether the patient is undergoing active treatment and not whether the provider is seeing the patient for the first time.

For complication codes, active treatment refers to treatment for the condition described by the code, even though it may be related to an earlier precipitating problem. For example, code T84.50XA, Infection and inflammatory reaction due to unspecified internal joint prosthesis, initial encounter, is used when active treatment is provided for the infection, even though the condition relates to the prosthetic device, implant or graft that was placed at a previous encounter.

7th character "A," initial encounter, is used for each encounter where the patient is receiving active treatment for the condition.

7th character "D," subsequent encounter, is used for encounters after the patient has completed active treatment of the condition and is receiving routine care for the condition during the healing or recovery phase.

The aftercare Z codes should not be used for aftercare for conditions such as injuries or poisonings, where 7th characters are provided to identify subsequent care. For example, for aftercare of an injury, assign the acute injury code with the 7th character "D" (subsequent encounter).

7th character "S", sequela, is for use for complications or conditions that arise as a direct result of a condition, such as scar formation after a burn. The scars are sequelae of the burn. When using 7th character "S", it is necessary to use both the injury code that precipitated the sequela and the code for the sequela itself. The "S" is added only to the injury code, not the sequela code. The 7th character "S" identifies the injury responsible for the sequela. The specific type of sequela (e.g. scar) is sequenced first, followed by the injury code. *See Section I.B.10 Sequelae, (Late Effects)*

EXAMPLE

Injury left wrist and dislocation right elbow from fall on escalator in public hall. Dislocation was reduced, S53.104A, S69.92xA, W10.0xxA, Y92.29, 0RSLXZZ.

EXAMPLE

The patient is seen in follow-up for healing blow-out fracture, S02.30xD, X58.xxxD.

EXAMPLE

Left wrist with keloid scar due to previous burns from fire (accidental), L91.0, T23.072S, X08.8xxS.

b. Coding of Injuries

When coding injuries, assign separate codes for each injury unless a combination code is provided, in which case the combination code is assigned. Code T07, Unspecified multiple injuries should not be assigned in the inpatient setting unless information for a more specific code is not available. Traumatic injury codes (S00-TI4.9) are not to be used for normal, healing surgical wounds or to identify complications of surgical wounds.

The code for the most serious injury, as determined by the provider and the focus of treatment, is sequenced first.

1) **Superficial injuries**
Superficial injuries such as abrasions or contusions are not coded when associated with more severe injuries of the same site.

EXAMPLE

Abrasion with laceration to the left knee, S81.012A, X58.xxxA.

2) **Primary injury with damage to nerves/blood vessels**
When a primary injury results in minor damage to peripheral nerves or blood vessels, the primary injury is sequenced first with additional code(s) for injuries to nerves and spinal cord (such as category S04), and/or injury to blood vessels (such as category S15). When the primary injury is to the blood vessels or nerves, that injury should be sequenced first.

3) **Iatrogenic injuries**
Injury codes from Chapter 19 should not be assigned for injuries that occur during, or as a result of, a medical intervention. Assign the appropriate complication code(s).

EXAMPLE

Minor laceration of splenic artery and fracture of right little finger due to trauma from being kicked and falling during a football game. Suture of laceration of splenic artery, S35.291A, S62.606A, W50.1xxA, Y92.321, Y93.61, 04Q40ZZ.

c. **Coding of Traumatic Fractures**
The principles of multiple coding of injuries should be followed in coding fractures. Fractures of specified sites are coded individually by site in accordance with both the provisions within categories S02, S12, S22, S32, S42, S49, S52, S59, S62, S72, S79, S82, S89, S92 and the level of detail furnished by medical record content.

A fracture not indicated as open or closed should be coded to closed. A fracture not indicated whether displaced or not displaced should be coded to displaced.

EXAMPLE

Closed fracture of right surgical neck of humerus and left open fracture of anatomic neck of humerus, S42.292B, S42.211A, X58.xxxA.

More specific guidelines are as follows:

1) **Initial vs. Subsequent Encounter for Fractures**
Traumatic fractures are coded using the appropriate 7th character for initial encounter (A, B, C) for each encounter where the patient is receiving active treatment for the fracture. The appropriate 7th character for initial encounter should also be assigned for a patient who delayed seeking treatment for the fracture or nonunion.

Fractures are coded using the appropriate 7th character for subsequent care for encounters after the patient has completed active treatment of the fracture and is receiving routine care for the fracture during the healing or recovery phase.

Care for complications of surgical treatment for fracture repairs during the healing or recovery phase should be coded with the appropriate complication codes.

Care of complications of fractures, such as malunion and nonunion, should be reported with the appropriate 7th character for subsequent care with nonunion (K, M, N,) or subsequent care with malunion (P, Q, R).

Malunion/nonunion: The appropriate 7th character for initial encounter should also be assigned for a patient who delayed seeking treatment for the fracture or nonunion.

The open fracture designations in the assignment of the 7th character for fractures of the forearm, femur, and lower leg, including ankle, are based on the Gustilo open fracture classification. When the Gustilo classification type is not specified for an open fracture, the 7th character for open fracture type I or II should be assigned (B, E, H, M, Q). A code from category M80, not a traumatic fracture code, should be used for any patient with known osteoporosis who suffers a fracture, even if the patient had a minor fall or trauma, if that fall or trauma would not usually break a normal, healthy bone.

See Section I.C.13. Osteoporosis.

The aftercare Z codes should not be used for aftercare for traumatic fractures. For aftercare of a traumatic fracture, assign the acute fracture code with the appropriate 7th character.

EXAMPLE
The patient suffered a blow-out fracture 1 week ago and is now being referred to a specialist for continued treatment, S02.30xA, X58.xxxA.

EXAMPLE
Subsequent encounter for malunion fracture of right tibia (traumatic), S82.201P, X58.xxxD.

2) Multiple fractures sequencing
Multiple fractures are sequenced in accordance with the severity of the fracture.

3) Physeal fractures
For physeal fractures, assign only the code identifying the type of physeal fracture. Do not assign a separate code to identify the specific bone that is fractured.

EXAMPLE
The patient had a fractured parietal bone of the skull and fracture of the left fifth rib, S02.0xxA, S22.32xA, X58.xxxA.

EXAMPLE
Fractures of multiple metacarpal bones of the right hand, S62.309A, X58.xxxA.

As with Z codes, detailed guidelines have been put forth for the use of external cause codes. The Alphabetic Index for these codes is located prior to the Tabular List and after the Table of Neoplasms and Table of Drugs and Chemicals. Codes are located by using the Alphabetic Index and then verifying the appropriate code in the Tabular List. The assignment of external cause codes may depend on facility policy, particular state requirements, and the following guidelines. For example, the assignment of external cause codes may be useful in determining the number of head injuries that occur as a result of bicycle accidents. This data may be used to support bicycle helmet programs in a particular city or state. Codes for external causes are never used as a principal or first-listed diagnosis. External cause codes are always assigned as an additional code(s). External cause codes are used to identify the cause, the intent, the place of occurrence, the activity, and the status at the time of the event.

The External cause guidelines are used for injuries, poisonings, adverse effects, and complications of surgical and medical care, which are covered in the next three chapters. Some of the external cause guidelines may be addressed in subsequent chapters so the numbering/lettering may not be sequential.

20. Chapter 20: External Causes of Morbidity (V00-Y99)
The external causes of morbidity codes should never be sequenced as the first-listed or principal diagnosis.

External cause codes are intended to provide data for injury research and evaluation of injury prevention strategies. These codes capture how the injury or health condition happened (cause), the intent (unintentional or accidental; or intentional, such as suicide or assault), the place where the event occurred, the activity of the patient at the time of the event, and the person's status (e.g., civilian, military).

There is no national requirement for mandatory ICD-10-CM external cause code reporting. Unless a provider is subject to a state-based external cause code reporting mandate or these codes are required by a particular payer, reporting of ICD-10-CM codes in Chapter 20, External Causes of Morbidity, is not required. In the absence of a mandatory reporting requirement, providers are encouraged to voluntarily report external cause codes, as they provide valuable data for injury research and evaluation of injury prevention strategies.

a. General External Cause Coding Guidelines

1) Used with any code in the range of A00.0-T88.9, Z00-Z99
An external cause code may be used with any code in the range of A00.0-T88.9, Z00-Z99, classification that represents a health condition due to an external cause. Though they are most applicable to injuries, they are also valid for use with such things as infections or diseases due to an external source, and other health conditions, such as a heart attack that occurs during strenuous physical activity.

EXAMPLE
Concussion without loss of consciousness due to accidental fall down steps at single-family house, S06.0X0A, W10.9xxA, Y92.019.

EXAMPLE
Patient was admitted and treated for an ST elevation myocardial infarction due to shoveling snow in the driveway of his single-family house, I21.3, Y92.014, Y93.H1, Y99.8.

2) External cause code used for length of treatment
Assign the external cause code, with the appropriate 7th character (initial encounter, subsequent encounter or sequela) for each encounter for which the injury or condition is being treated.

Most categories in chapter 20 have a 7th character requirement for each applicable code. Most categories in this chapter have three 7th character values: A, initial encounter; D, subsequent encounter; and S, sequela. While the patient may be seen by a new or different provider over the course of treatment for an injury or condition, assignment of the 7th character for external cause should match the 7th character of the code assigned for the associated injury or condition for the encounter.

3) Use the full range of external cause codes
Use the full range of external cause codes to completely describe the cause, the intent, the place of occurrence, and if applicable, the activity of the patient at the time of the event, and the patient's status, for all injuries, and other health conditions due to an external cause.

4) Assign as many external cause codes as necessary
Assign as many external cause codes as necessary to fully explain each cause. If only one external code can be recorded, assign the code most related to the principal diagnosis.

5) The selection of the appropriate external cause code
The selection of the appropriate external cause code is guided by the Alphabetic Index of External Causes and by Inclusion and Exclusion notes in the Tabular List.

6) External cause code can never be a principal diagnosis
An external cause code can never be a principal (first-listed) diagnosis.

7) Combination external cause codes
Certain of the external cause codes are combination codes that identify sequential events that result in an injury, such as a fall which results in striking against an object. The injury may be due to either event or both. The combination external cause code used should correspond to the sequence of events regardless of which caused the most serious injury.

8) No external cause code needed in certain circumstances
No external cause code from Chapter 20 is needed if the external cause and intent are included in a code from another chapter (e.g. T36.0x1- Poisoning by penicillins, accidental (unintentional)).

b. Place of Occurrence Guideline
Codes from category Y92, Place of occurrence of the external cause, are secondary codes for use after other external cause codes to identify the location of the patient at the time of injury or other condition.

Generally, a place of occurrence code is assigned only once, at the initial encounter for treatment. However, in the rare instance that a new injury occurs during hospitalization, an additional place of occurrence code may be assigned. No 7th characters are used for Y92.

Do not use place of occurrence code Y92.9 if the place is not stated or is not applicable.

EXAMPLE Injury to the left wrist occurred on the playground at the public park. Child fell off slide, S69.92xA, W09.0xxA, Y92.830, Y99.8.

c. Activity Code
Assign a code from category Y93, Activity code, to describe the activity of the patient at the time the injury or other health condition occurred.

An activity code is used only once, at the initial encounter for treatment. Only one code from Y93 should be recorded on a medical record.

The activity codes are not applicable to poisonings, adverse effects, misadventures or sequela.

Do not assign Y93.9, Unspecified activity, if the activity is not stated.

A code from category Y93 is appropriate for use with external cause and intent codes if identifying the activity provides additional information about the event.

EXAMPLE Injury left knee due to twisting movement while playing basketball at the YMCA gym, S89.92xA, Y93.67, Y92.310, Y99.8.

d. Place of Occurrence, Activity, and Status Codes Used with other External Cause Code
When applicable, place of occurrence, activity, and external cause status codes are sequenced after the main external cause code(s). Regardless of the number of external cause codes assigned, generally there should be only one place of occurrence code, one activity code, and one external cause status code

assigned to an encounter. However, in the rare instance that a new injury occurs during hospitalization, an additional place of occurrence code may be assigned.

e. If the Reporting Format Limits the Number of External Cause Codes

If the reporting format limits the number of external cause codes that can be used in reporting clinical data, report the code for the cause/intent most related to the principal diagnosis. If the format permits capture of additional external cause codes, the cause/intent, including medical misadventures, of the additional events should be reported rather than the codes for place, activity, or external status.

f. Multiple External Cause Coding Guidelines

More than one external cause code is required to fully describe the external cause of an illness or injury. The assignment of external cause codes should be sequenced in the following priority:

If two or more events cause separate injuries, an external cause code should be assigned for each cause. The first-listed external cause code will be selected in the following order:

External codes for child and adult abuse take priority over all other external cause codes.

See Section I.C.19., Child and Adult abuse guidelines.

External cause codes for terrorism events take priority over all other external cause codes except child and adult abuse.

External cause codes for cataclysmic events take priority over all other external cause codes except child and adult abuse and terrorism.

External cause codes for transport accidents take priority over all other external cause codes except cataclysmic events, child and adult abuse and terrorism.

Activity and external cause status codes are assigned following all causal (intent) external cause codes.

The first-listed external cause code should correspond to the cause of the most serious diagnosis due to an assault, accident, or self-harm, following the order of hierarchy listed above.

g. Child and Adult Abuse Guideline

Adult and child abuse, neglect and maltreatment are classified as assault. Any of the assault codes may be used to indicate the external cause of any injury resulting from the confirmed abuse.

For confirmed cases of abuse, neglect and maltreatment, when the perpetrator is known, a code from Y07, Perpetrator of maltreatment and neglect, should accompany any other assault codes.

See Section I.C.19. Adult and child abuse, neglect and other maltreatment.

EXAMPLE Laceration left wrist from sharp glass, suicide attempt, S61.512A, X78.0xxA.

h. Unknown or Undetermined Intent Guideline

If the intent (accident, self-harm, assault) of the cause of an injury or other condition is unknown or unspecified, code the intent as accidental intent. All transport accident categories assume accidental intent.

1) Use of undetermined intent

External cause codes for events of undetermined intent are only for use if the documentation in the record specifies that the intent cannot be determined.

EXAMPLE Laceration left wrist from sharp glass, intent unknown, S61.512A, Y28.0xxA.

i. Sequelae (Late Effects) of External Cause Guidelines

1) Sequelae external cause codes

Sequela are reported using the external cause code with the 7th character "S" for sequela. These codes should be used with any report of a late effect or sequela resulting from a previous injury. *See Section I.B.10 Sequela (Late Effects)*

2) Sequela external cause code with a related current injury

A sequela external cause code should never be used with a related current nature of injury code.

3) Use of sequela external cause codes for subsequent visits

Use a late effect external cause code for subsequent visits when a late effect of the initial injury is being treated. Do not use a late effect external cause code for subsequent visits for follow-up care (e.g., to assess healing, to receive rehabilitative therapy) of the injury when no late effect of the injury has been documented.

j. Terrorism Guidelines

1) Cause of injury identified by the Federal Government (FBI) as terrorism

When the cause of an injury is identified by the Federal Government (FBI) as terrorism, the first-listed external cause code should be a code from category Y38, Terrorism. The definition of terrorism employed by the FBI is found at the inclusion note at the beginning of category Y38. Use additional code for place of occurrence (Y92.-). More than one Y38 code may be assigned if the injury is the result of more than one mechanism of terrorism.

2) Cause of an injury is suspected to be the result of terrorism
When the cause of an injury is suspected to be the result of terrorism a code from category Y38 should not be assigned. Suspected cases should be classified as assault.

3) Code Y38.9, Terrorism, secondary effects
Assign code Y38.9, Terrorism, secondary effects, for conditions occurring subsequent to the terrorist event. This code should not be assigned for conditions that are due to the initial terrorist act.

It is acceptable to assign code Y38.9 with another code from Y38 if there is an injury due to the initial terrorist event and an injury that is a subsequent result of the terrorist event.

EXAMPLE The patient (civilian) had a head injury due to a terrorist explosion, S09.90xA, Y38.2x2A, Y99.8.

EXAMPLE The patient (civilian) has chronic posttraumatic stress syndrome following a terrorist attack, subsequent encounter, F43.12, Y38.9x2S.

k. External cause status
A code from category Y99, External cause status, should be assigned whenever any other external cause code is assigned for an encounter, including an Activity code, except for the events noted below. Assign a code from category Y99, External cause status, to indicate the work status of the person at the time the event occurred. The status code indicates whether the event occurred during military activity, whether a non-military person was at work, whether an individual including a student or volunteer was involved in a non-work activity at the time of the causal event.

A code from Y99, External cause status, should be assigned, when applicable, with other external cause codes, such as transport accidents and falls. The external cause status codes are not applicable to poisonings, adverse effects, misadventures or late effects.

Do not assign a code from category Y99 if no other external cause codes (cause, activity) are applicable for the encounter.

An external cause status code is used only once, at the initial encounter for treatment. Only one code from Y99 should be recorded on a medical record.

Do not assign code Y99.9, Unspecified external cause status, if the status is not stated.

Remember that External cause codes identify how an injury occurred and the intent. External cause codes also identify the place that an injury occurred and describe the activity that caused the injury or other health condition. At the beginning of Chapter 19 in the ICD-10-CM code book, special instructions state that codes from this chapter should be used as secondary codes and that a code from another chapter of the Classification should be assigned indicating the nature of the injury or health condition (Figure 24-1). Also remember, do NOT use code Y92.9 if the place of occurrence is not stated or Y93.9 if the activity was not stated. Physician documentation may not include the detail required to assign the place of occurrence, activity, and the patient's status at the time of the event.

EXERCISE 24-1

Assign only the External cause codes to the following. Remember that External cause codes provide information about the cause and intent of an injury. If the place of occurrence, the status of the patient at the time, and/or an activity code is applicable, assign the appropriate codes. Assume initial episode of care, unless otherwise specified.

1. Patient is employed doing data entry and has carpal tunnel syndrome from using computer keyboard ________________
2. Patient fell from a ladder while working as an employee at church ________________

CHAPTER 20

EXTERNAL CAUSES OF MORBIDITY (V00-Y99)

Note: This chapter permits the classification of environmental events and circumstances as the cause of injury, and other adverse effects. Where a code from this section is applicable, it is intended that it shall be used secondary to a code from another chapter of the Classification indicating the nature of the condition. Most often, the condition will be classifiable to Chapter 19, Injury, poisoning and certain other consequences of external causes (S00-T88). Other conditions that may be stated to be due to external causes are classified in Chapters I to XVIII. For these conditions, codes from Chapter 20 should be used to provide additional information as to the cause of the condition.

FIGURE 24-1. Instructional note regarding the use of External cause codes.

3. Patient was bitten by a dog while jogging at the public park ______________
4. Patient was injured in a motorcycle accident. Patient was the driver and lost control due to wet interstate highway ______________
5. Patient accidentally lacerated hand with hunting knife while hunting in the woods ______________
6. Patient fell out of bed at the nursing home and was injured ______________
7. Patient was injured during an assault with a baseball bat in public parking garage ______________
8. Patient was injured while playing in NHL hockey game. Patient was checked into the boards by another player and fell to the ice ______________
9. Patient was the victim of accidental drowning in lake while swimming ______________
10. Patient was the driver and was injured during a motor vehicle collision with a train ______________

ANATOMY AND PHYSIOLOGY

The musculoskeletal chapter outlines the anatomy and physiology that is pertinent to injury. Internal organs and the blood vessels may also be involved in an injury. These are outlined in their respective body system chapters.

DISEASE CONDITIONS

Injury, Poisoning, and Certain Other Consequences of External Causes (S00-T88), Chapter 19 in the ICD-10-CM code book, covers a wide range of codes that will be discussed in the next three chapters of this textbook. Categories marked with an asterisk (*) are covered in this chapter. Chapter 25 discusses burns, adverse effects, and poisonings and Chapter 26 is dedicated to complications associated with surgical and medical care.

Chapter 19 in the ICD-10-CM code book—Injury, Poisoning, and Certain Other Consequences of External Causes (S00-T88)—is divided into the following categories:

SECTION	SECTION TITLES
*S00-S09	Injuries to the head
*S10-S19	Injuries to the neck
*S20-S29	Injuries to the thorax
*S30-S39	Injuries to the abdomen, lower back, lumbar spine, pelvis, and external genitalia

SECTION	SECTION TITLES
*S40-S49	Injuries to the shoulder and upper arm
*S50-S59	Injuries to the elbow and forearm
*S60-S69	Injuries to the wrist, hand and fingers
*S70-S79	Injuries to the hip and thigh
*S80-S89	Injuries to the knee and lower leg
*S90-S99	Injuries to the ankle and foot
*T07	Injuries involving multiple body regions
*T14	Injury of unspecified body region
*T15-T19	Effects of foreign body entering through natural orifice
T20-T32	Burns and corrosions
T33-T34	Frostbite
T36-T50	Poisoning by, adverse effect of, and underdosing of drugs, medicaments, and biological substances
T51-T65	Toxic effects of substances chiefly nonmedicinal as to source
T66-T78	Other and unspecified effects of external causes
*T79	Certain early complications of trauma
T80-T88	Complications of surgical and medical care, not elsewhere classified

Chapter 20 is divided into the following categories:

V00-V09	Pedestrian injured in transport accident
V10-V19	Pedal cycle rider injured in transport accident
V20-V29	Motorcycle rider injured in transport accident
V30-V39	Occupant of three-wheeled motor vehicle injured in transport accident
V40-V49	Car occupant injured in transport accident
V50-V59	Occupant of pick-up truck or van injured in transport accident
V60-V69	Occupant of heavy transport vehicle injured in transport accident
V70-V79	Bus occupant injured in transport accident
V80-V89	Other land transport accidents
V90-V94	Water transport accidents
V95-V97	Air and space transport accidents
V98-V99	Other and unspecified transport accidents
W00-W19	Slipping, tripping, stumbling, and falls
W20-W49	Exposure to inanimate mechanical forces
W50-W64	Exposure to animate mechanical forces
W65-W74	Accidental non-transport drowning and submersion
W85-W99	Exposure to electric current, radiation and extreme ambient air temperature and pressure
X00-X08	Exposure to smoke, fire, and flames
X10-X19	Contact with heat and hot substances
X30-X39	Exposure to forces of nature
X50	Overexertion and strenuous or repetitive movements
X52-X58	Accidental exposure to other specified factors
X71-X83	Intentional self-harm
X92-Y09	Assault
Y21-Y33	Event of undetermined intent
Y35-Y38	Legal intervention, operations of war, military operations, and terrorism
Y62-Y69	Misadventures to patients during surgical and medical care
Y70-Y82	Medical devices associated with adverse incidents in diagnostic and therapeutic use
Y83-Y84	Surgical and other medical procedures as the cause of abnormal reaction of the patient, or of later complication, without mention of misadventure at the time of the procedure
Y90-Y99	Supplementary factors related to causes of morbidity classified elsewhere

TYPES OF INJURIES

The S section is for coding different types of injuries related to single body regions, and the T section is for injuries to unspecified body regions, poisonings, and certain other consequences of external causes. Many of the code categories in this chapter have seventh character values that are applicable. If a code is fewer than six characters and requires a seventh character value, a placeholder x is used to fill in the empty character value(s). There are a number of instructional notes throughout this chapter in the Tabular.

When a patient has multiple injuries, each injury is coded separately unless there is a combination code provided. When an injury code category contains the term "with," that means that both injuries must be documented to assign that code. The term "and" is interpreted as meaning "and/or." In other words, one or both injuries are present.

Superficial Injuries

Superficial injuries may manifest in the form of contusions, abrasions (Figure 24-2), nonthermal blisters, nonvenomous insect bites, and superficial foreign bodies or splinters and external constriction (Figure 24-3). The physician may not document the term "superficial," so supporting documentation must be used to determine whether the injury fits into the superficial categories. It is not necessary to code superficial injuries when a more serious injury has occurred at the same site.

EXAMPLE Corneal abrasion due to being struck by tree branch while hiking in the forest, S05.00xA, W22.8xxA, Y92.821, Y93.01, Y99.8.

EXAMPLE Laceration and abrasion right elbow due to fall from scooter, S51.011A, V00.141A. The abrasion is not coded separately because it occurred at the same site as a more severe injury.

EXAMPLE Sprain right ankle and abrasions left knee due to being knocked down while playing basketball in gym class, S93.401A, S80.212A, W03.xxxA, Y92.310, Y99.8. Abrasions are coded because they occurred at a different site from the sprain.

EXERCISE 24-2

Assign codes to the following conditions. Assume initial episode of care, unless otherwise specified. Do not assign external cause codes.

1. Blister, left heel, due to rubbing of shoe __________
2. Mosquito bites, both legs __________
3. Abrasions, right hand and right knee __________
4. Superficial wood splinter, right thumb __________
5. Abrasions and deep laceration of left elbow __________

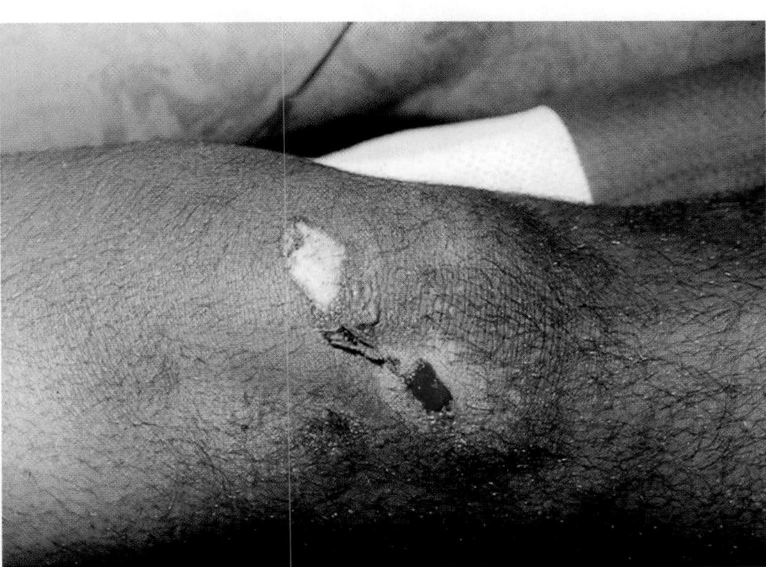

FIGURE 24-2. Abrasion wound of kneecap.

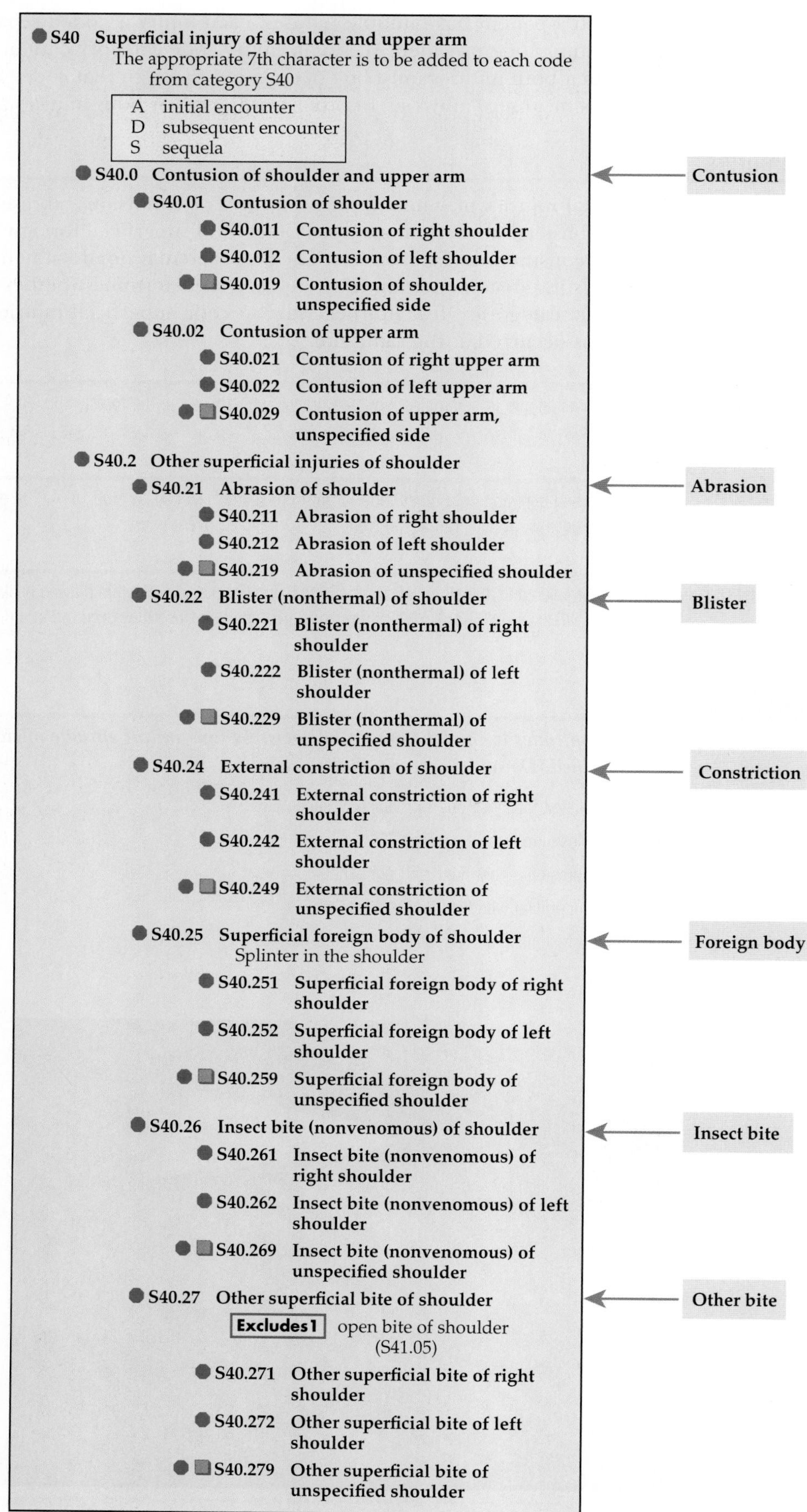

S40 Superficial injury of shoulder and upper arm
The appropriate 7th character is to be added to each code from category S40

A	initial encounter
D	subsequent encounter
S	sequela

S40.0 Contusion of shoulder and upper arm
S40.01 Contusion of shoulder
S40.011 Contusion of right shoulder
S40.012 Contusion of left shoulder
S40.019 Contusion of shoulder, unspecified side
S40.02 Contusion of upper arm
S40.021 Contusion of right upper arm
S40.022 Contusion of left upper arm
S40.029 Contusion of upper arm, unspecified side
S40.2 Other superficial injuries of shoulder
S40.21 Abrasion of shoulder
S40.211 Abrasion of right shoulder
S40.212 Abrasion of left shoulder
S40.219 Abrasion of unspecified shoulder
S40.22 Blister (nonthermal) of shoulder
S40.221 Blister (nonthermal) of right shoulder
S40.222 Blister (nonthermal) of left shoulder
S40.229 Blister (nonthermal) of unspecified shoulder
S40.24 External constriction of shoulder
S40.241 External constriction of right shoulder
S40.242 External constriction of left shoulder
S40.249 External constriction of unspecified shoulder
S40.25 Superficial foreign body of shoulder
Splinter in the shoulder
S40.251 Superficial foreign body of right shoulder
S40.252 Superficial foreign body of left shoulder
S40.259 Superficial foreign body of unspecified shoulder
S40.26 Insect bite (nonvenomous) of shoulder
S40.261 Insect bite (nonvenomous) of right shoulder
S40.262 Insect bite (nonvenomous) of left shoulder
S40.269 Insect bite (nonvenomous) of unspecified shoulder
S40.27 Other superficial bite of shoulder
Excludes1 open bite of shoulder (S41.05)
S40.271 Other superficial bite of right shoulder
S40.272 Other superficial bite of left shoulder
S40.279 Other superficial bite of unspecified shoulder

FIGURE 24-3. Superficial injuries.

Contusion With Intact Skin Surface

A **contusion** is any injury that results in hemorrhage beneath unbroken skin. Other terms for contusion include "bruise" and "hematoma." Contusions associated with more severe or serious injuries at the same site would not be coded. Occasionally, if a hematoma does not absorb on its own, it may have to be evacuated or aspirated.

EXAMPLE

Contusion right quadriceps after tackle in college football game, S70.11xA, W03.xxxA, Y92.321, Y93.61, Y99.8.

EXAMPLE

Contusion and severe sprain of left ankle after falling into a hole while hiking in the mountains, S93.402A, W17.2xxA, Y92.828, Y93.01, Y99.8.

EXERCISE 24-3

Assign codes to the following conditions. Assume initial episode of care, unless otherwise specified. Do not assign external cause codes.

1. Blackeye (right) ____________
2. Subungual hematoma, left thumb (traumatic) ____________
3. Bruise, left ankle ____________
4. Hematoma, right breast (traumatic) ____________
5. Contusion, right shin ____________

Laceration/Open Wounds

An open traumatic wound and/or **laceration** is an injury that results in a tear in the skin (Figure 24-4). Bruising and swelling can occur around the wound site. Common sites of laceration are body areas with underlying bony support, such as above the eyebrows, on the scalp and face, and over the knees. Traumatic injury codes should not be used to identify surgical wounds, nontraumatic wounds or ulcers, decubitus ulcers, and stasis ulcers. Laceration and open wound codes are assigned by location. Other factors that may make a difference in the code assignment include:

- If there is damage to nail (i.e., thumb nail damaged)
- If the wound is described as a puncture wound

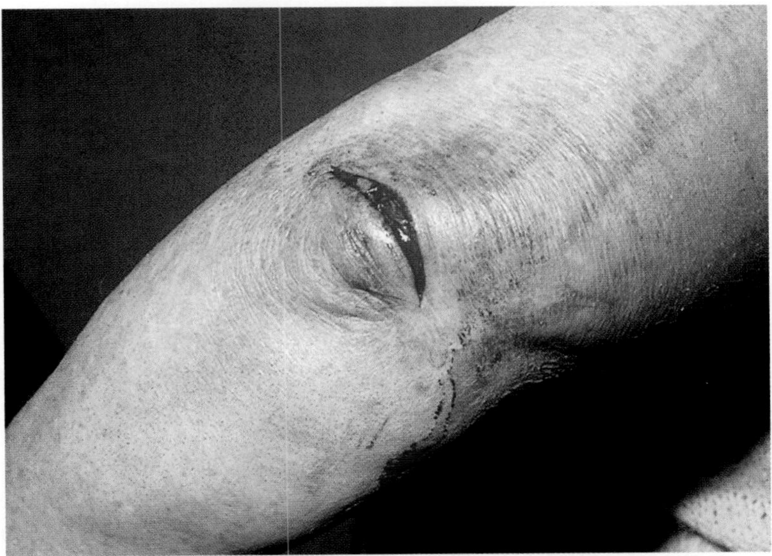

FIGURE 24-4. Laceration of elbow.

- If the wound is a bite wound that is not classified as superficial
- The presence of a foreign body
- Penetration into a body cavity (i.e., laceration abdominal wall with penetration into peritoneal cavity)

An additional code would be assigned to identify any associated wound infection and any responsible organism.

EXAMPLE

The patient cut his right eyebrow during fall while downhill skiing; patient fell while skiing at resort, S01.111A, V00.321A, Y92.838, Y93.23, Y99.8.

EXAMPLE

Patient presented to the emergency room with gravel embedded in laceration of left knee. Patient fell while hiking in the mountains 2 days ago. The wound was cleaned and dressing applied, S81.022A, W19.xxxA, Y92.828, Y93.01, Y99.8.

EXERCISE 24-4

Assign codes to the following conditions. Assume initial episode of care, unless otherwise specified. Do not assign external cause codes.

1. Puncture wound, left forearm ______________
2. Laceration, right calf which occurred 3 days ago, and no medical attention has been sought until now ______________
3. Laceration, left foot, with glass pieces in wound ______________

Fractures

A **fracture** is a break in a bone. Bones are rigid but will bend. However, if the impact or force is too great, the bone will break. There are different types of fractures (Figure 24-5) with varying degrees of complexity. In a minor injury, the bone may just crack and may not break all the way through. In a more severe injury, the bone may shatter, or it may break through the skin. Treatment provided for a fracture depends on the specific bone broken, the severity of the break, and whether it is an "open" or a "closed" fracture. If a fracture is not documented as displaced or not displaced, it should be assigned a displaced fracture code.

Fractures fall into two categories:

1. **Closed fracture** or **simple fracture** is diagnosed when the bone is broken, but the skin remains intact. Descriptive words used for a closed fracture include the following:
   - Comminuted—broken, splintered, or crushed into a number of pieces
   - Depressed—portion of the skull that is broken and driven inward
   - Fissured—incomplete fracture that does not split the bone
   - Fracture NOS—not otherwise specified
   - Greenstick—the bone is somewhat bent and is partially broken; occurs in children
   - Impacted—one fractured bone end is wedged into another broken end
   - Linear—straight line fracture
   - Simple—fracture that remains in alignment with little damage to surrounding tissue
   - Slipped epiphysis—separation of the growing end of the bone (epiphysis) from the shaft of the bone; occurs in children and young adults
   - Spiral—occurs when a bone has been twisted apart
2. **Open fracture** or **compound fracture** occurs when the bone exits and is visible through the skin, or a deep wound exposes the bone through the skin. If the wound is superficial and the fracture site is not exposed, the injury is coded as a closed

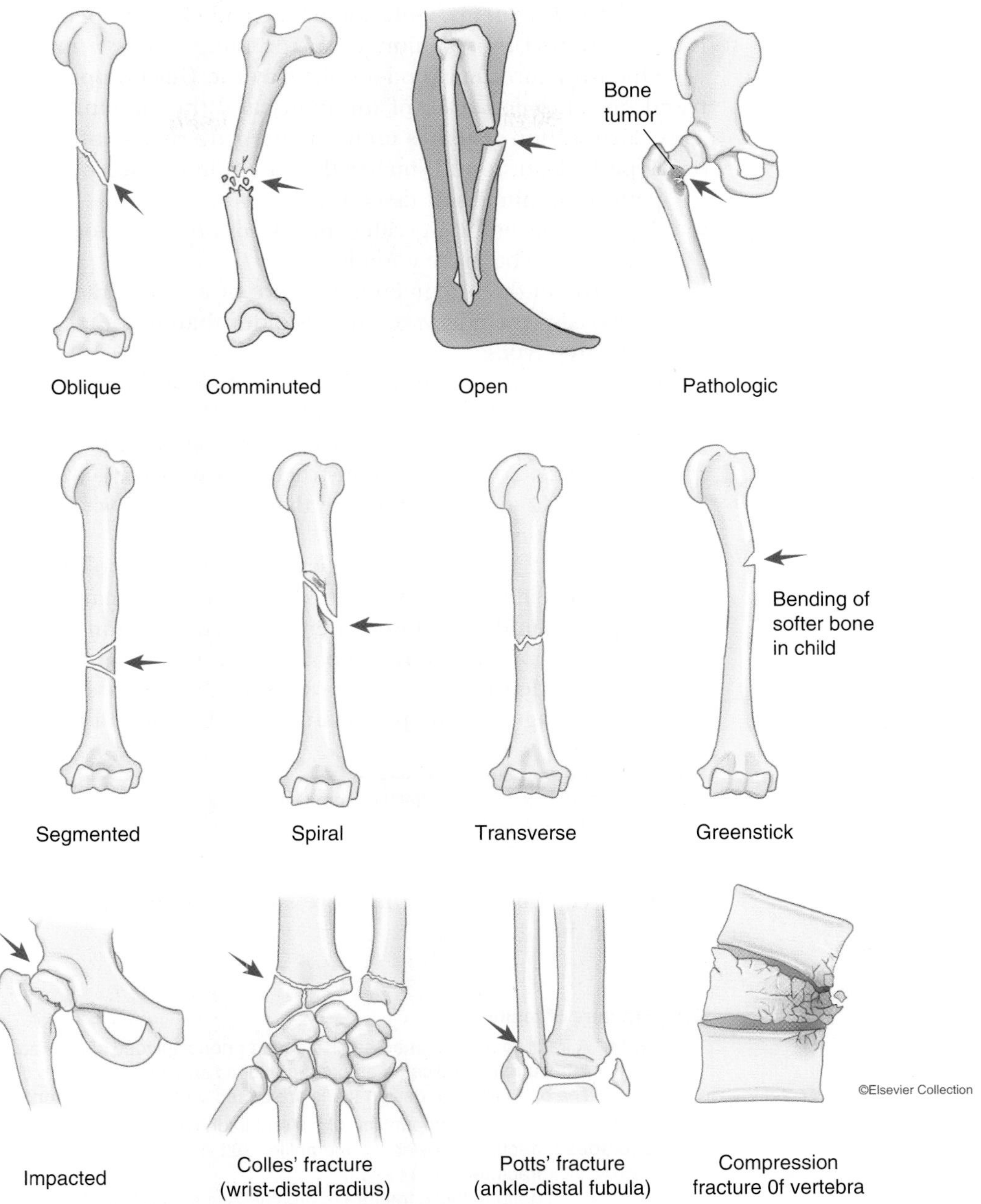

FIGURE 24-5. Types of fractures.

fracture—not an open fracture. Some descriptive words used for an open fracture include the following:

- Compound—fracture in which the bone is sticking through the skin
- Infected—condition in which the bone becomes infected by bacteria
- Missile—penetrating injuries resulting in fractures caused by bullets or stab wounds
- Puncture—a puncture wound is present. The wound may be related to the injury or to bone fragments
- Foreign body—presence of a foreign body within the fracture site

If a fracture is not specified as open or closed, it is coded as a closed fracture. If documentation in the record reveals an open wound around the fracture site, it may be necessary to query the physician as to whether this is an open or a closed fracture. In some instances, a fracture is documented as both open and closed. This usually occurs with a severe fracture with fracture fragments, and it should be coded as an open fracture. A **complicated fracture** is a fracture that causes injury to surrounding tissues; it may be open or closed.

Open fractures may be identified by the **Gustilo open fracture classification**, which is based on the mechanism of the injury and the amount of soft tissue and skeletal injury. This classification system is useful in assessing risk of infection and possible amputation.

- Type I: clean wound smaller than 1 cm in diameter, appears clean, simple fracture pattern, minimal soft tissue injury
- Type II: a laceration greater than 1 cm but with moderate soft tissue injury. Fracture pattern may be more complex
- Type III: an open segmental fracture or a single fracture with extensive soft tissue injury. Also included are injuries older than 8 hours. Type III injuries are subdivided into three types:
  - Type IIIA: adequate soft tissue coverage of the fracture despite high energy trauma or extensive laceration or skin flaps
  - Type IIIB: inadequate soft tissue coverage with periosteal stripping and bone exposure. Soft tissue reconstruction is necessary. Wound is contaminated
  - Type IIIC: any open fracture that is associated with vascular (major arterial) injury that requires repair

See Figure 24-6 for the 7th characters applicable to fracture of femur S72. The Gustilo classification is identified for the open fracture 7th characters.

If a physician does not document the exact location of a fracture, *Coding Clinic for ICD-9-CM* (1999:1Q:p5)[1] says it is acceptable to review the entire recording including the radiology report to identify the exact location of the fracture. If there is any question as to the appropriate diagnosis, the physician should be queried before assigning a diagnosis code.

EXAMPLE

The physician documents closed fracture right femur. The x-ray report indicates a fracture of the shaft of the right femur, S72.301A, X58.xxxA.

It is acceptable to use the more specific code S72.301A instead of S72.91xA as documented by the physician.

S72 Fracture of femur

Note: A fracture not indicated as displaced or nondisplaced should be coded to displaced
A fracture not indicated as open or closed should be coded to closed
The open fracture designations are based on the Gustilo open fracture classification

Excludes1: traumatic amputation of hip and thigh (S78.-)

Excludes2: fracture of lower leg and ankle (S82.-)
fracture of foot (S92.-)
periprosthetic fracture of prosthetic implant of hip (M97.01, M97.02)

The appropriate 7th character is to be added to all codes from category S72
A - initial encounter for closed fracture
B - initial encounter for open fracture type I or II
initial encounter for open fracture NOS
C - initial encounter for open fracture type IIIA, IIIB, or IIIC
D - subsequent encounter for closed fracture with routine healing
E - subsequent encounter for open fracture type I or II with routine healing
F - subsequent encounter for open fracture type IIIA, IIIB, or IIIC with routine healing
G - subsequent encounter for closed fracture with delayed healing
H - subsequent encounter for open fracture type I or II with delayed healing
J - subsequent encounter for open fracture type IIIA, IIIB, or IIIC with delayed healing
K - subsequent encounter for closed fracture with nonunion
M - subsequent encounter for open fracture type I or II with nonunion
N - subsequent encounter for open fracture type IIIA, IIIB, or IIIC with nonunion
P - subsequent encounter for closed fracture with malunion
Q - subsequent encounter for open fracture type I or II with malunion
R - subsequent encounter for open fracture type IIIA, IIIB, or IIIC with malunion
S - sequela

FIGURE 24-6. 7th characters for category S72.

EXAMPLE

The physician documents closed fracture right tibia. The x-ray report indicates a fracture through the shaft of the right tibia and fibula.

In this instance, the physician would need to be queried regarding the fracture of the fibula, S82.201A, X58.xxxA.

Specific coding guidelines assist with sequencing and coding of fractures. The most severe fracture is sequenced first. When a patient presents with multiple fractures, all fractures must be coded. It may be necessary to query the physician for more specific information.

A **pathologic fracture** is a break in a bone that occurs because of underlying disorders that weaken the bone, including malignancy, benign bone tumor, metabolic disorders, infection, and osteoporosis. A fracture can result from normal stress placed on an abnormal bone. Minor trauma can cause fracture. It is important to determine whether a fracture is pathologic or traumatic, so the appropriate code can be assigned. Coding of pathologic fractures is discussed in Chapter 20. Fractures that are due to a birth injury are classified as perinatal conditions.

Skull Fractures

Skull fracture may be associated with traumatic head injury. Injury to the brain may also occur. In most skull fractures, there is no displacement of broken bones. This is a closed or simple fracture. In severe cases, bone fragments are displaced, resulting in an open and/or depressed skull fracture. Fractures of the skull are frequently encountered after falls, crushing injuries, direct blows to the head, or motor vehicle accidents. A simple skull fracture may have little impact on eventual neurologic outcomes of head trauma. Neurological outcomes of a skull fracture are determined by the nature of the brain injury. Some trauma patients can have severe neurologic impairment without having a skull fracture. The cranium, which protects the brain, consists of eight bones: occipital, frontal, sphenoidal, ethmoidal, two parietal, and two temporal bones (Figure 24-7). There is an Instructional note at the beginning of category S02 to code also any associated intracranial injury (S06.-). The level of consciousness is identified within the S06.- codes. **Loss of consciousness** (LOC) occurs when a patient is unable to respond to people or to other stimuli. Unconsciousness and other sudden changes in mental status should be treated as a medical emergency.

EXAMPLE

Fracture frontal skull bone due to motor vehicle accident involving head-on collision with pick-up truck, unbelted car passenger. The patient did not lose consciousness, S02.0xxA, V43.63xA, Y92.410.

Spine Fractures

As was discussed in Chapter 20, vertebral fractures are often pathologic fractures, particularly in older women with osteoporosis. This chapter focuses on traumatic spinal fractures, which usually occur as the result of motor vehicle accidents, falls, acts of violence, or recreational and sporting activities. Spinal fracture does not necessarily indicate damage to the spinal cord, and a spinal cord injury can occur without a spinal fracture (Figure 24-8).

EXAMPLE

Clay shoveler's fracture C7 (nondisplaced) due to strain injury from shoveling while working at construction site, S12.601A, Y93.H1, Y92.69, Y99.0.

Upper Limb Fractures

Shoulder and upper arm (Figure 24-9) injuries, including fractures of the clavicle or the upper part of the humerus, are fairly common. Fractures of the scapula are less common. A **Colles' fracture** is a common fracture in adults. In this type of fracture, the lower end of the radius is fractured, and the wrist and the hand are displaced backward. Fractures of the ulna typically occur across the shaft or at the tip of the elbow. Sometimes, the radius is fractured at the same time. Fractures of the radius, which are among the most common of

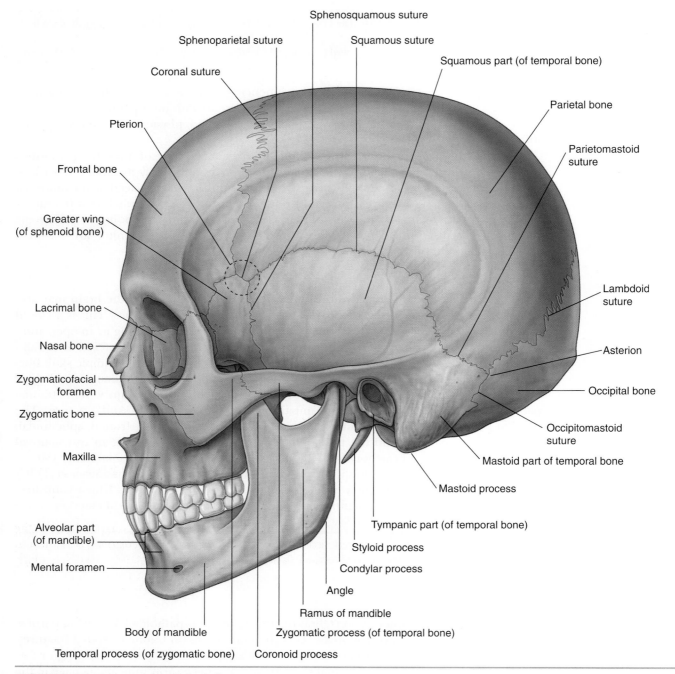

Sphenosquamous suture
Sphenoparietal suture
Squamous suture
Squamous part (of temporal bone)
Coronal suture
Parietal bone
Pterion
Parietomastoid suture
Frontal bone
Greater wing (of sphenoid bone)
Lambdoid suture
Lacrimal bone
Nasal bone
Asterion
Zygomaticofacial foramen
Occipital bone
Zygomatic bone
Occipitomastoid suture
Maxilla
Mastoid part of temporal bone
Mastoid process
Tympanic part (of temporal bone)
Alveolar part (of mandible)
Styloid process
Mental foramen
Condylar process
Angle
Ramus of mandible
Body of mandible
Zygomatic process (of temporal bone)
Temporal process (of zygomatic bone)
Coronoid process

FIGURE 24-7. Lateral view of the skull.

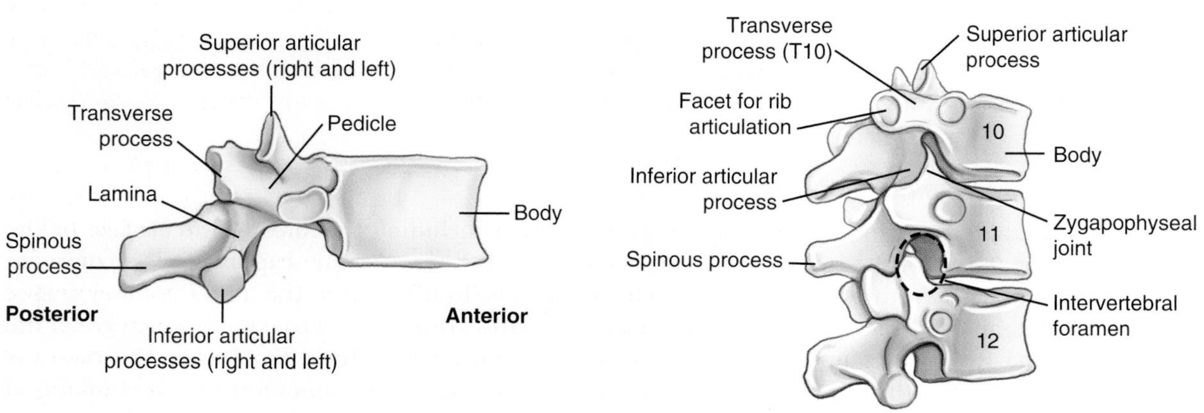

FIGURE 24-8. Lateral view of vertebrae.

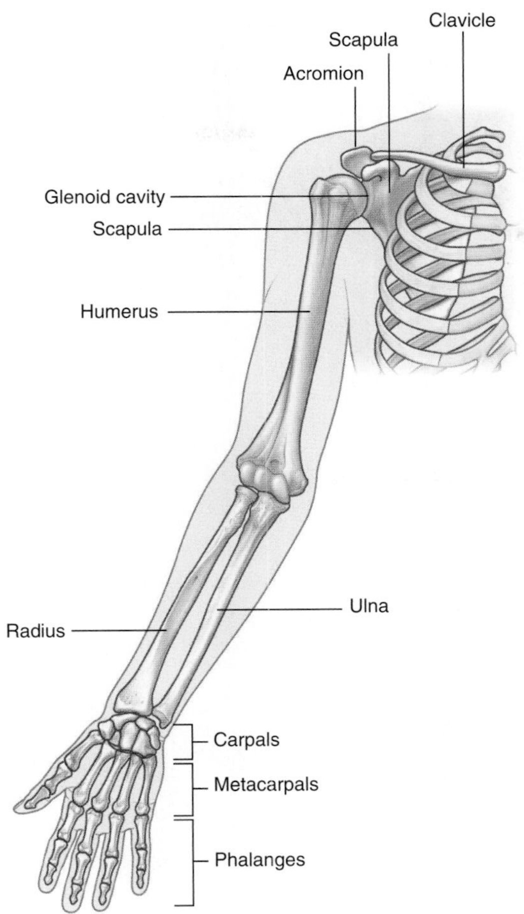

FIGURE 24-9. Bones of the upper limb.

fractures, usually are caused by a fall on an outstretched hand. The disc-shaped head of the bone just below the elbow joint is one of the most common sites of fracture in young adults. Fingers often sustain lacerations, fractures, and tendon ruptures. Fractures are particularly common at the knuckles, usually in the little finger, as the result of a blow.

EXAMPLE

Right Boxers' fracture (neck of the fifth metacarpal) due to brawl at nightclub. The patient was employed at the nightclub as a bouncer, S62.336A, Y04.0xxA, Y92.29, Y99.0.

Lower Limb Fractures

A fractured hip is usually a fracture of the head or neck of the femur. The nature, symptoms, treatment, and possible complications of a fractured femur depend on whether the bone has been broken across its neck or across the shaft. A fracture in the shaft of the femur usually occurs when the femur is subjected to extreme force, as occurs in a motor vehicle accident.

In most cases, the bone ends are considerably displaced, causing severe pain, tenderness, and swelling. The patella is the triangular bone that protects the knee joint. Fracture is usually caused by a direct blow. The tibia is one of the most commonly fractured bones. It may break across the shaft as the result of a direct blow to the front of the leg, or at the upper end from a blow to the outside of the leg below the knee. The fibula, a very common site of fracture, usually breaks just above the ankle as the result of a harsh twisting motion, such as occurs in severe ankle sprain. Injury to the foot commonly results in fractures of the bones in the toes, caused by stubbing or twisting them or as the result of a falling or

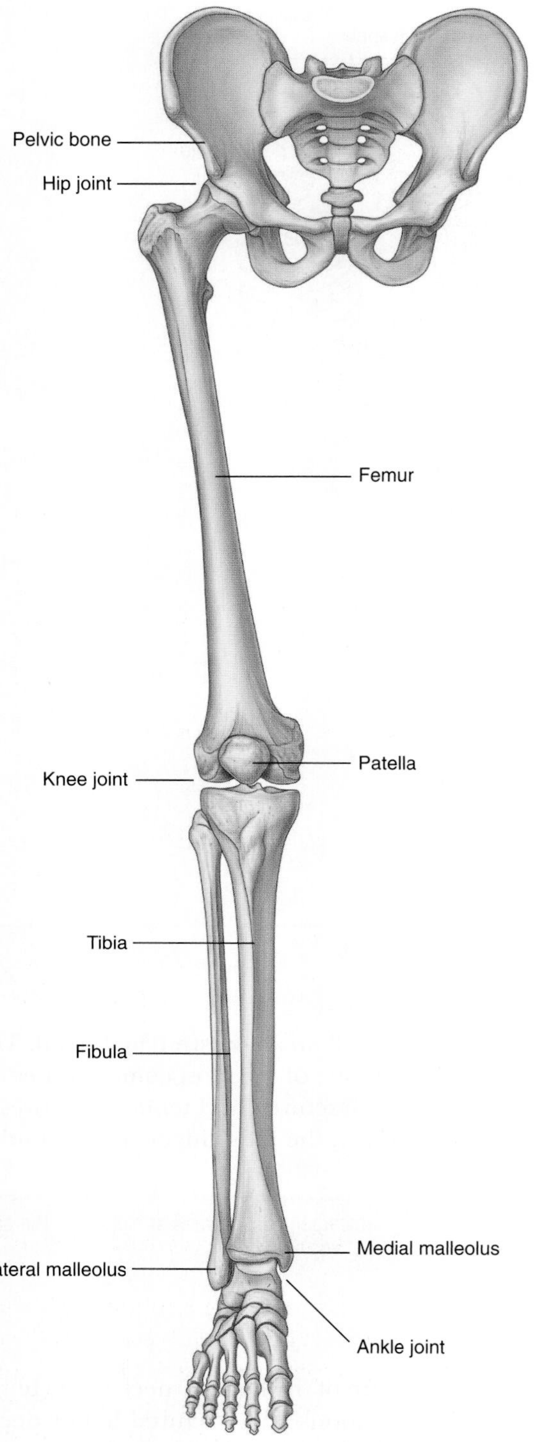

FIGURE 24-10. Bones and joints of the lower limb.

crushing injury. The calcaneus may fracture after a fall from a height onto a hard surface (Figures 24-10 and 24-11).

EXAMPLE Left Dupuytren's fracture due to fall from horse while riding in meadow, S82.62xA, V80.010A, Y92.828, Y93.52, Y99.8.

Traumatic Fractures and Fracture Aftercare

Active treatment of a traumatic fracture includes surgery, an emergency room encounter, and/or evaluation and continuing treatment by the same or a different physician.

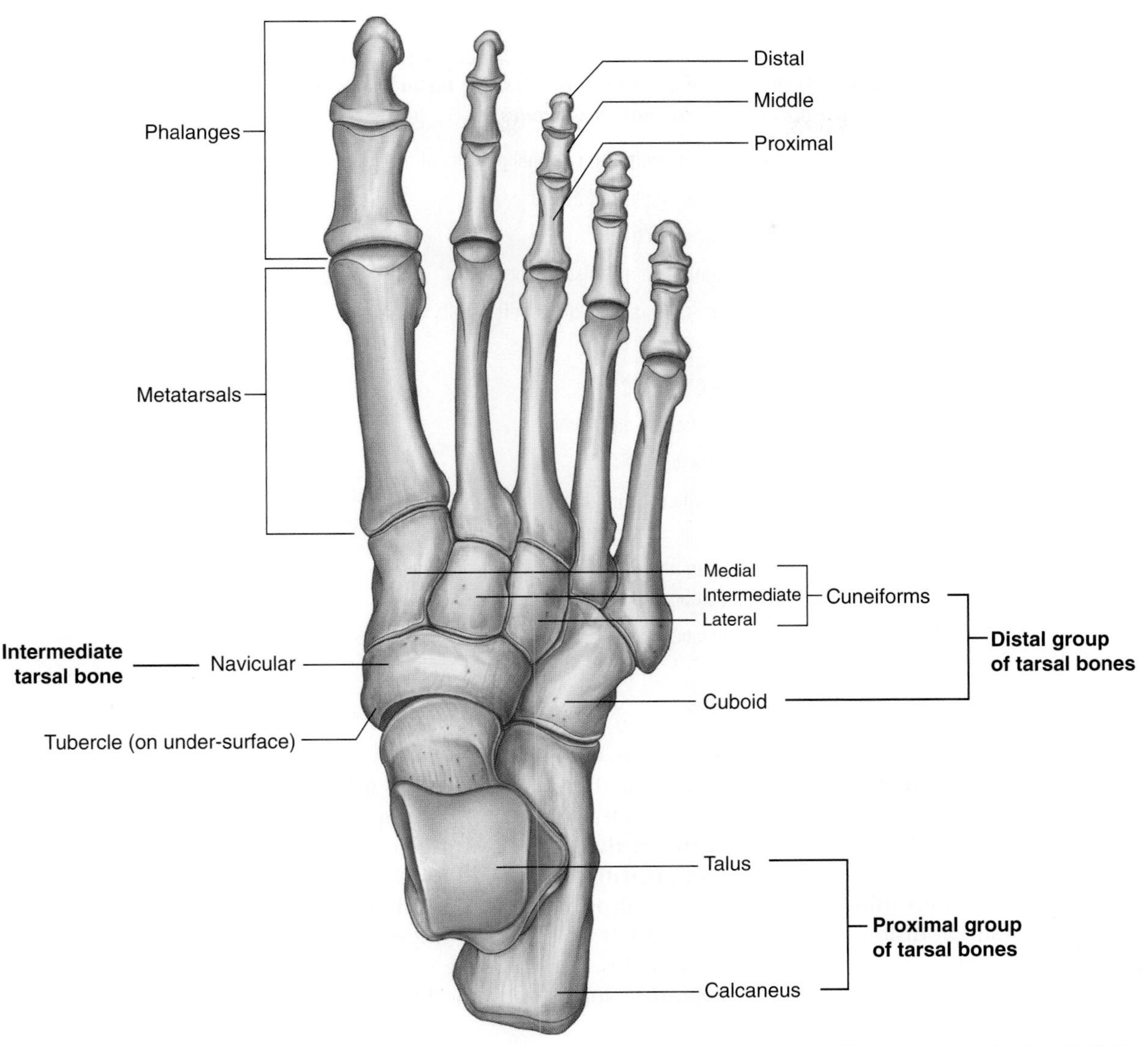

FIGURE 24-11. Dorsal view of right foot.

According to the guidelines, when a patient is receiving active treatment, the acute fracture code is assigned.

Following the period of active treatment of a traumatic fracture, other encounters may be necessary. Aftercare may include a cast change or removal, removal of a fixation device, medication adjustments, and other follow-up visits. The fracture code is assigned with the appropriate 7th character for subsequent care encounters. There are Z codes for encounters for orthopedic aftercare, Z47.-. These Z codes are for non-fracture–related orthopedic aftercare. The exception would be a hip fracture that has been treated with a joint replacement surgery. It would no longer be appropriate to assign the fracture code, as the fracture is no longer present.

EXAMPLE

Patient is admitted for open reduction of right orbital floor fracture. Patient was involved in a fight at a bar last week, and this was the initial encounter for treatment, S02.31xA, Y04.0xxA, Y92.29, 0NSP0ZZ.

EXAMPLE

Patient had a cast change for traumatic right radial shaft fracture, S52.301D, 2W0CX2Z.

EXERCISE 24-5

Assign codes to the following conditions. Assume initial episode of care, unless otherwise specified. Do not assign external cause codes.

1. Type II Salter Harris fracture, left fifth proximal phalanx of the hand ____________
2. Nondisplaced right lateral malleolus fracture ____________
3. Comminuted left calcaneal fracture ____________
4. Open fracture, distal right tibia, and distal right fibula ____________
5. Avulsion fracture of the medial aspect of the left patella ____________
6. LeFort I fracture ____________
7. Fracture, cervical spine C1 and C2 ____________
8. Compound fracture, midshaft of right femur ____________
9. Fracture, midshaft left clavicle ____________
10. Temporal skull fracture with subdural hemorrhage without loss of consciousness ____________
11. Patient was seen for open removal of internal fixation device from previous right traumatic tibial fracture ____________
12. Follow-up visit for traumatic pelvic fracture ____________

Dislocations

Dislocation is the displacement of the bones that form a joint. It is the separation of the end of a bone and the joint it meets. A partial or incomplete dislocation is called a **subluxation.** Dislocations may occur as the result of traumatic injury, or they may result from diseases such as rheumatoid arthritis, congenital joint defects, or weakened joints due to previous injury. The shoulder is especially prone to dislocation. The elbow is a common site of dislocation in toddlers. Other sites include fingers, hips, jaws, and spine. Soft tissues such as ligaments, tendons, muscles, and cartilage in and around the joint may stretch or tear as a result of the dislocation. Nerves and blood vessels may also be injured by the dislocated bone.

It is possible for a fracture and dislocation/subluxation to occur at the same anatomic site. In these instances, the index gives the coder instructions under the main term "Dislocation": It says, "with fracture—*see* Fracture" (Figure 24-12). This means that only the fracture code is assigned for fractures/dislocations at the same site. Reduction of fracture/dislocation is coded to reduction of fracture. No additional code is assigned for reduction of a dislocation.

Once a joint has been dislocated, it is not unusual for it to dislocate again; with each recurrence, less force is required to sustain a dislocation. Only the initial occurrence of the dislocation is coded with an injury code, and all subsequent dislocations of the same joint are coded as recurrent dislocations.

Dislocation (articular)
  with fracture - *see* Fracture
  acromioclavicular (joint) S43.10-
    with displacement
      100%-200% S43.12-
      more than 200% S43.13-
    inferior S43.14-
    posterior S43.15-
  ankle S93.0-

FIGURE 24-12. Instruction for dislocation with fracture—see Fracture.

EXAMPLE

The patient sustained an open dislocation distal interphalageal joint right little finger during tackle on school football field during game, S63.296A, S61.206A, W03.xxxA, Y92.321, Y93.61, Y99.8.

EXERCISE 24-6

Assign codes to the following conditions. Assume initial episode of care, unless otherwise specified. Do not assign external cause codes.

1. Dislocation, right patella ______________
2. Dislocation, proximal interphalangeal joint left index finger ______________
3. Recurrent dislocation, right shoulder ______________
4. Subluxation, left elbow ______________

Sprains and Strains

A **sprain** is a stretch and/or tear of a ligament. The severity of the injury depends on whether a tear is partial or complete and on the number of ligaments involved. A **strain** is an injury to a muscle or a tendon. Depending on the severity of the injury, a strain may be the result of an overstretched muscle or tendon, or it can be caused by a partial or complete tear. Often, the patient is unaware of any specific injury. Strains can be acute or chronic. Chronic strains usually result from overuse or prolonged repetitive movement.

EXAMPLE

The patient has an anterior cruciate ligament sprain due to injury of right knee, S83.511A, X58.xxxA.

EXERCISE 24-7

Assign codes to the following conditions. Assume initial episode of care, unless otherwise specified. Do not assign external cause codes.

1. Sprain, left hand ______________
2. Strain, lumbosacral spine ______________
3. Rupture of left Achilles tendon ______________
4. SLAP (superior labrum anterior-posterior) lesion on right shoulder ______________

Injury to Nerves/Spinal Cord and Blood Vessel

Spinal cord injury (SCI) is damage to the spinal cord that causes loss of sensation and motor control. The most common causes of SCI include MVAs, falls, acts of violence, and sporting accidents. SCIs tend to occur where the spine is most flexible, in the regions C5-C7 of the neck and T10-L2 at the base of the rib cage. If SCI is suspected, a computed tomography (CT) scan, magnetic resonance imaging (MRI), or a myelogram may be used as a diagnostic tool. Immediate medical treatment should focus on stabilizing the spine and providing aggressive treatment with corticosteroid drugs to limit damage. Surgery may also be necessary to stabilize the spine or fuse the spine with metal plates or pins. Once the initial injury heals, functional improvements may continue for at least 6 months. After this time, any remaining disability is likely to be permanent. Any nerve damage or injury should be coded, in addition to other injuries.

EXAMPLE

Spinal cord injury at C2 level due to tackle during NFL football game, S14.102A, W03.xxxA, Y92.321, Y93.61, Y99.0.

Often, injuries to the blood vessels occur in conjunction with other injuries such as fractures, dislocations, open wounds, or lacerations. It is appropriate to assign codes that identify injury to the blood vessels, in addition to fractures and dislocations. Sequencing of codes according to Coding Guidelines depends on which is the primary injury.

EXAMPLE

Injury to the thoracic aorta due to MVA involving collision with train. Patient was the driver of the car, S25.00xA, V45.5xxA, Y92.410.

EXERCISE 24-8

Assign codes to the following conditions. Assume initial episode of care, unless otherwise specified. Do not assign external cause codes.

1. Injury to ulnar nerve due to laceration left wrist ____________
2. Radial nerve injury due to fracture of right humerus ____________
3. Injury to sciatic nerve due to dislocation of left hip ____________
4. Spinal cord injury T10 ____________
5. Injury to abdominal aorta ____________
6. Injury to internal left jugular ____________
7. Rupture of right anterior tibial artery ____________
8. Dislocation of left femoral neck. Minor damage to the left femoral artery was noted ____________

Internal Injuries

Intracranial Injury, Excluding Those With Skull Fracture

A **concussion** is an injury to the brain that results from a significant blow to the head. Length of unconsciousness may relate to severity of the concussion. Most people recover with no ill effects. A patient may have to be admitted to the hospital for observation. It may be necessary to review the emergency room and ambulance records to determine the time that the patient was unconscious.

Traumatic brain injury (TBI) is injury to the brain that may affect the brain's normal functions. Penetrating injuries are injuries in which a foreign object such as a bullet enters the brain. Symptoms vary depending on the areas of the brain that are damaged.

Closed head injury (CHI) results from a blow to the head. Primary brain damage may occur at the time of the injury or accident. Secondary brain damage may result from complications of the injury such as brain swelling, increased intracranial pressure, seizure, infection, fever, hematoma, high or low blood pressure, anemia, and metabolic changes.

EXAMPLE

Patient was hospitalized with a concussion due to tripping while jumping rope at school. Unconscious for 5 minutes S06.0x1A, W01.0xxA, Y92.219, Y93.56, Y99.8.

EXERCISE 24-9

Assign codes to the following conditions. Assume initial episode of care, unless otherwise specified. Do not assign external cause codes.

1. Cerebral contusion due to fall. Positive for loss of consciousness ____________
2. Laceration, cerebral (left side), with loss of consciousness for 2 hours ____________
3. Subdural hemorrhage due to fall 1 week ago ____________
4. Traumatic subarachnoid hemorrhage without regaining consciousness. Patient died after 2 days due to the hemorrhage ____________

Internal Injury of Thorax, Abdomen, and Pelvis

Injury to the internal organs can occur with or without an open wound. Laceration of the spleen may result from blunt trauma without an open wound; injury to the spleen can occur from an open wound due to a gunshot. Types of internal injuries are as follows:

- Blast injuries of internal organs
- Blunt trauma of internal organs
- Bruise of internal organs
- Concussion injuries (except cerebral) of internal organs
- Crushing of internal organs
- Hematoma of internal organs
- Laceration of internal organs
- Puncture of internal organs
- Traumatic rupture of internal organs

The Organ Injury Scaling was developed by the Organ Injury Scaling Committee of the American Association for the Surgery of Trauma. This scale is graded from I through VI for each organ, with I being least severe and V the most severe injury from which the patient may survive. Grade VI injuries are by definition not salvageable. Scales are available for the following organ injuries:

- Thoracic vascular
- Lung
- Heart
- Chest wall
- Diaphragm
- Spleen
- Liver
- Abdominal vascular
- Kidney
- Ureter
- Bladder
- Urethra

Table 24-1 shows the organ injury scale for liver injuries.

These scales can be helpful in coding internal injuries more accurately. They may also be useful for querying the physician about the extent of an internal injury. See Figure 24-13 for liver laceration codes that are specified as minor, moderate, and major.

TABLE 24-1 ORGAN INJURY SCALING—LIVER[2]

Grade	Injury Description	
I	Hematoma	Subscapular, <10% surface area
	Laceration	Capsular tear, <1 cm parenchymal depth
II	Hematoma	Subscapular, 10%-50% surface area
		Intraparenchymal, <10 cm diameter
	Laceration	1-3 cm parenchymal depth, <10 cm length
III	Hematoma	Subscapular, >50% surface area or expanding. Ruptured subscapular or parenchymal hematoma
		Intraparenchymal hematoma >10 cm or expanding
	Laceration	>3 cm parenchymal depth
IV	Laceration	Parenchymal disruption involving 25%-75% of hepatic lobe, or 1-3 Coinaud's segments in a single lobe
V	Laceration	Parenchymal disruption involving >75% of hepatic lobe or >3 Coinaud's segments within a single lobe
	Vascular	Juxtahepatic venous injuries (i.e., retrohepatic vena cava/central major hepatic veins)
VI	Vascular	Hepatic avulsion

Advance one grade for multiple injuries to same organ up to grade III.

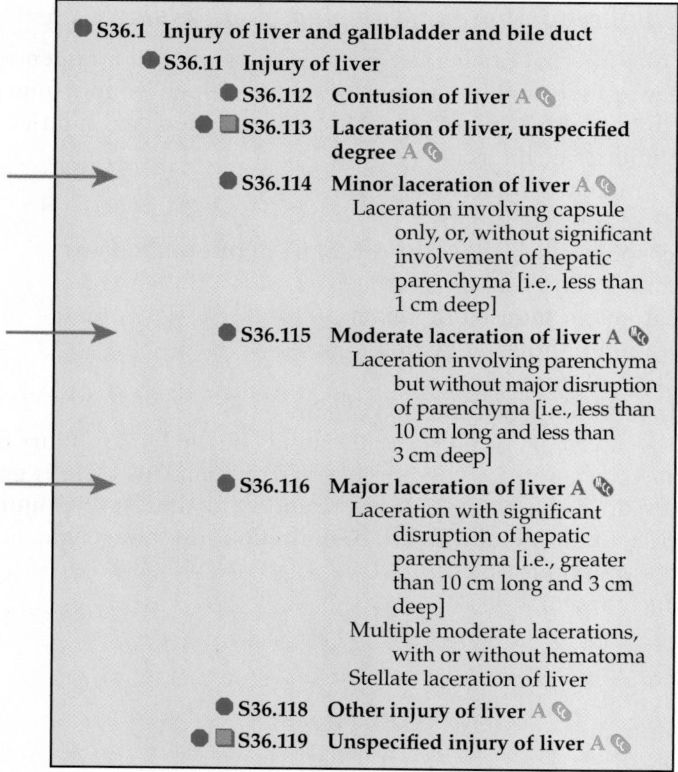

S36.1 Injury of liver and gallbladder and bile duct
S36.11 Injury of liver
S36.112 Contusion of liver A
S36.113 Laceration of liver, unspecified degree A
S36.114 Minor laceration of liver A
Laceration involving capsule only, or, without significant involvement of hepatic parenchyma [i.e., less than 1 cm deep]
S36.115 Moderate laceration of liver A
Laceration involving parenchyma but without major disruption of parenchyma [i.e., less than 10 cm long and less than 3 cm deep]
S36.116 Major laceration of liver A
Laceration with significant disruption of hepatic parenchyma [i.e., greater than 10 cm long and 3 cm deep]
Multiple moderate lacerations, with or without hematoma
Stellate laceration of liver
S36.118 Other injury of liver A
S36.119 Unspecified injury of liver A

FIGURE 24-13. Types of liver laceration.

EXAMPLE

Patient had laceration of right lung due to stab wound (laceration) right chest wall during fight at nightclub, S27.331A, S21.311A, X99.9xxA, Y92.29.

EXERCISE 24-10

Assign codes to the following conditions. Assume initial episode of care, unless otherwise specified. Do not assign external cause codes.

1. Pneumothorax due to stab wound (puncture) of the right chest wall __________
2. A superficial 5-cm laceration, spleen, due to blunt trauma __________
3. Grade III laceration, liver (involving parenchyma) __________
4. Minor contusion of the left kidney __________
5. Mediastinal hematoma due to trauma __________

Crush Injuries and Amputations

A **crush injury** occurs when a body part is subjected to a high degree of force or pressure, usually after it has been squeezed between two heavy or immobile objects. A crush injury can be more serious than other types of injury such as a fracture or a laceration. In a severe crush, the force of the trauma can damage the underlying tissues, bones, blood vessels, and nerves. Increased pressure from tissue swelling can also damage muscles, blood vessels, and nerves. Instructions say to use additional codes to identify all associated injuries such as the following:

- Fractures
- Internal organs injury
- Intracranial injury

In the Tabular List there is an instructional note under the crush injury codes to "use additional code for any/all associated injuries."

EXAMPLE

Crush injury left foot with metatarsal fractures due to dropping car battery on foot at industrial factory, S97.82xA, S92.302A, W20.8xxA, Y92.63, Y99.0.

EXAMPLE

Employee sustained a crush injury right index finger with 3-cm laceration which happened while fixing combine on the farm, S67.190A, S61.210A W30.0xxA, Y92.79, Y99.0.

EXERCISE 24-11

Assign codes to the following conditions. Assume initial episode of care, unless otherwise specified. Do not assign external cause codes.

1. Crush injury, left fingers, with fractures of distal phalanges ____________
2. Crush injury to abdomen with injury to bladder and pelvic fracture ____________
3. Crush injury, right foot ____________
4. Crush injury, left great toe ____________
5. Crush injury, right ankle, with 4-cm laceration ____________
6. Crush injury, abdomen, with minor injury to splenic artery ____________
7. Partial traumatic amputation, right little toe ____________

Certain Early Complications of Trauma

A variety of complications may occur as the result of injury. An **air embolism** is formed when air or gas bubbles get into the bloodstream and obstruct the circulation. Trauma to the lungs can cause an air embolism, as may occur in divers from rapid changes of pressure.

A **fat embolism** can occur when fat enters the circulatory system after long bone or pelvic fracture. It usually presents 12 to 48 hours after the injury with symptoms such as tachycardia, tachypnea, elevated temperature, hypoxemia, hypocapnia, thrombocytopenia, and occasionally with mild neurologic symptoms. A petechial rash also appears on the upper portions of the body, including the chest, neck, upper arm, axilla, shoulder, oral mucous membranes, and conjunctivae. Infection, shock, anuria, and subcutaneous emphysema are other examples of complications of trauma.

EXAMPLE

Patient was hospitalized for treatment of an open traumatic fracture, right femur (shaft) and developed a fat embolism, S72.301B, T79.1xxA, X58.xxxA.

EXERCISE 24-12

Assign codes to the following conditions. Assume initial episode of care, unless otherwise specified. Do not assign external cause codes.

1. Pain due to twisting injury to left knee ____________
2. Patient injured head ____________
3. Shoulder injury ____________
4. Injury to left hip ____________
5. Subcutaneous emphysema due to pneumothorax from a stab wound (laceration) into thorax ____________
6. Active treatment of MRSA infection due to second-degree burn on left thigh ____________
7. Traumatic shock due to blunt intraabdominal injury ____________

Effects of Foreign Body Entering Through Orifice

A foreign body (FB) can enter the body through natural openings or orifices such as eyes, ears, nose, and mouth. In some cases it may be necessary to seek emergency medical attention for possible removal. One of the most common sites that foreign bodies enter are the eyes. Young children and elderly patients, particularly those with neurologic disorders and/or decreased gag reflexes, are at risk for aspiration and food can become lodged in the esophagus.

EXAMPLE

Small piece of grass from mowing lawn at a single family house stuck on right cornea. Grass was removed, T15.01xA, Y92.017, Y93.H2, 08C8XZZ.

EXERCISE 24-13

Assign codes to the following conditions. Assume initial episode of care, unless otherwise specified. Do not assign external cause codes.

1. Hot dog lodged in distal esophagus of patient with dysphagia. EGD with removal of hot dog ____________
2. 1-year-old swallowed a penny, and x-rays showed that it was in the stomach ____________
3. Child put sunflower seed in right nostril; removed with forceps ____________
4. Patient with cough and hemoptysis was found to have a chicken bone lodged in right main stem bronchus of the lung; bronchoscopy with removal of chicken bone ____________
5. Malodorous vaginal discharge due to retained tampon in vagina; manually removed ____________

FACTORS INFLUENCING HEALTH STATUS AND CONTACT WITH HEALTH SERVICES (Z CODES)

As was discussed in Chapter 9, it may be difficult to locate Z codes in the index. Coders often say, "I did not know there was a Z code for that." Refer to Chapter 9 for a listing of common main terms used to locate Z codes.

Z codes that may be used with injuries include the following:

Z04.1	Encounter for examination and observation following transport accident
Z04.2	Encounter for examination and observation following work accident
Z04.3	Encounter for examination and observation following other accident
Z13.850	Encounter for screening for traumatic brain injury
Z18.10	Retained metal fragments, unspecified
Z18.11	Retained magnetic metal fragments
Z18.12	Retained nonmagnetic metal fragments
Z18.2	Retained plastic fragments
Z18.31	Retained animal quills or spines
Z18.32	Retained tooth
Z18.33	Retained wood fragments
Z18.39	Other retained organic fragments
Z18.81	Retained glass fragments
Z18.83	Retained stone or crystalline fragments
Z18.89	Other specified retained foreign body fragments
Z18.9	Retained foreign body fragments, unspecified material

Z42.8	Encounter for other plastic and reconstructive surgery following medical procedure or healed injury
Z48.00	Encounter for change or removal of nonsurgical wound dressing
Z48.02	Encounter for removal of sutures
Z87.81	Personal history of (healed) traumatic fracture
Z87.820	Personal history of traumatic brain injury
Z87.821	Personal history of retained foreign body fully removed
Z87.828	Personal history of other (healed) physical injury and trauma
Z91.81	History of falling

EXAMPLE

Patient has a history of traumatic brain injury, Z87.820.

Admission for Observation Following an Injury

According to the Guidelines, the observation codes should only be used in very limited circumstances, such as when a person is being observed for a suspected condition that is ruled out. The observation codes are not for use if an injury or illness or any signs or symptoms related to the suspected condition are present. In such cases the diagnosis/symptom code is used with the corresponding external cause code. If a patient has minor cuts, bruises, or other superficial injuries, these are coded as secondary diagnoses and the appropriate observation code as the principal.

This Z04.– code category is used for patients who are suspected of having an abnormal condition without a sign or a symptom that requires study. After examination and observation, no condition is determined to exist.

EXAMPLE

Patient has a minor contusion of the right chest wall and is admitted for observation to rule out a concussion. Patient was the driver of a motor vehicle that lost control while taking a curve on a state road and collided with a tree. Patient was discharged when they were able to rule out any type of head injury. Z04.1, S20.211A, V47.5xxA, Y92.413.

EXERCISE 24-14

Assign codes to the following conditions. Assume initial episode of care, unless otherwise specified. Do not assign external cause codes.

1. Observation following work accident ______________
2. Previous right knee joint replacement ______________
3. Observation after MVA for internal abdominal injuries. Internal injuries were ruled out, and patient was discharged with a diagnosis of contusion abdominal wall ______________
4. Encounter for open removal of screw used to stabilize left tibial fracture; fracture is well healed, and no complications of the fixation device or infections are reported ______________
5. Patient had a previous amputation of the left great toe ______________

COMMON TREATMENTS

Many injuries are diagnosed with the use of imaging procedures such as x-ray, MRI, CT scans, and ultrasound. Treatment depends on the severity of the injury. For very severe injuries, patients may have to be transferred to hospitals that specialize in the care of trauma patients. Surgical intervention may also be required to repair the specific injury or trauma.

Pain medications, anti-inflammatories, corticosteroids, and antibiotics may be necessary to alleviate pain and inflammation and to prevent or fight infection.

PROCEDURES

Procedures related to injuries in ICD-10-PCS can be located in many tables depending on the procedure performed and the body system involved.

Fracture Treatment

A fracture is classified as "open" or "closed." Treatments for fracture are also classified as "open" or "closed," and the coder should not confuse the type of fracture with the type of procedure. An open fracture may not require open treatment, and a closed fracture may need open reduction. The root operation for reduction of a displaced fracture is reposition (moving to its normal location or other suitable location some or all of a body part). The treatment provided will depend on other injuries and the type and location of the fracture. Reduction or manipulation of bone fragments to their proper anatomic position is necessary for appropriate healing. For fractures that are not displaced, stabilization or immobilization may be all that is necessary to promote healing. Reductions may be performed in the operating room or other areas of the hospital, such as the emergency room, fracture treatment room, and/or in radiology.

Closed reduction of a fracture occurs when the surgeon manipulates or reduces fractured bones into anatomic alignment without making an incision through the skin and subcutaneous tissue. The approach for a closed reduction without internal fixation is external. Closed reduction may include internal fixation. Small incision(s) may be made for placement of internal fixation device(s) such as pins, wires, screws, plates, and intramedullary nails. As long as the fracture is not exposed, it is considered a percutaneous fixation. Fixation devices are used to immobilize the fracture, but they do not manipulate or reduce the fracture. Sometimes radiologic guidance is needed for placement of the fixation device(s). It is also possible for a closed reduction to be performed prior to having an open reduction and fixation.

Open reduction of a fracture occurs when the surgeon makes an incision at the fracture site to reduce or manipulate the fracture into anatomic position. Open reduction and internal fixation (ORIF) is a procedure that is very commonly performed for fractures.

External skeletal fixation is another form of fracture treatment (Figure 24-14). This involves insertion of percutaneous pins proximal and distal to the fracture and application of a frame that connects the pins externally. The pins are located internally, except for the portion to which the frame is connected. The frame is located outside the body. These devices can be used to hold a reduced fracture or to assist the surgeon in reducing a fracture.

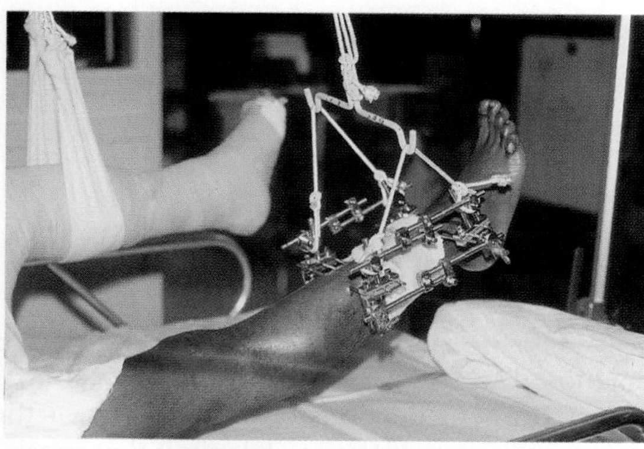

FIGURE 24-14. Example of an external fixation service on the right leg. The left is in a splint.

EXAMPLE

Open reduction and internal fixation of left humeral midshaft transverse fracture, S42.322A, X58.xxxA, 0PSG04Z

SECTION	BODY SYSTEM	ROOT OPERATION	BODY PART	APPROACH	DEVICE	QUALIFIER
Medical and Surgical	Upper Bones	Reposition	Humeral Shaft, Left	Open	Internal Fixation Device	No Qualifier
0	P	S	G	0	4	Z

Repair of Lacerations

Suture is a method used to close cutaneous lacerations. The root operation for suture of skin and subcutaneous tissue is repair (restoring a body part to its normal structure to the extent possible). The risks of bleeding and infection are reduced by approximating skin edges for an aesthetically pleasing and functional result. Routine debridement of wound edges prior to suturing of the wound is considered part of the suturing and should not be coded separately.

Sometimes, a combination of adhesive and sutures is used for wound repair.

EXAMPLE

Laceration nose due to being hit in nose by surfboard while at beach. Laceration of the skin was repaired, S01.21xA, W21.89xA, Y92.832, 0HQ1XZZ.

SECTION	BODY SYSTEM	ROOT OPERATION	BODY PART	APPROACH	DEVICE	QUALIFIER
Medical and Surgical	Skin and Breast	Repair	Skin, Face	External	No Device	No Qualifier
0	H	Q	1	X	Z	Z

EXERCISE 24-15

Assign codes for all diagnoses and procedures. Assume initial episode of care, unless otherwise specified. Do not assign external cause codes.

1. Patient sustained a major laceration to spleen with parenchymal disruption with open total splenectomy ______________
2. Cocoa Puff in left ear (auditory canal); removed by physician ______________
3. Closed reduction and percutaneous fixation of left supracondylar fracture elbow ______________
4. Manipulation of right shoulder dislocation ______________
5. Suture, laceration of the right hand ______________
6. Suture of laceration of the left upper eyelid ______________
7. Open reduction and internal fixation (femur) of left hip fracture (traumatic) ______________
8. Open manipulation and internal fixation of left acetabular fracture (traumatic) ______________
9. Healing traumatic fracture right tibia/fibula with application of short leg cast ______________
10. Closed reduction and percutaneous internal fixation of right Bennett's fracture (traumatic) ______________

CHAPTER REVIEW EXERCISE

Assign codes for all diagnoses and procedures. Assume initial episode of care, unless otherwise specified. Do not assign external cause codes.

1. Fracture/dislocation, right femur, with contusion right hip __________
2. Closed reduction of recurrent left shoulder dislocation __________
3. Inversion injury, right ankle, with severe sprain __________
4. Grade III laceration to the bladder due to gunshot wound (abdominal wall). Exploratory laparotomy with repair of the bladder laceration. __________
5. Crush injury with fracture of the right hand (multiple metacarpals) __________
6. Superficial wound, left calf, due to dog bite. Wound was cleansed and Steri-Strips applied __________
7. Closed head injury with concussion and brief loss of consciousness (10 minutes) __________
8. Pain caused by anterior dislocation of the distal humerus (ulnohumeral) __________
9. Contusion, right forearm __________
10. Sprain, right foot __________
11. Crush injury with laceration of left foot __________
12. Hemiarthroplasty due to displaced right femoral neck fracture (traumatic) with replacement of right femoral head with synthetic substitute. __________
13. Rib fractures on the left due to child abuse by foster mother __________
14. Open fractures of left tibial shaft with the fibula. Laceration, calf, which exposes the tibia __________
15. Flail chest __________
16. Lacerations of right upper arm with embedded gravel. Skin and subcutaneous tissue were repaired with sutures __________
17. Contusions, chest and forehead, with 2-cm laceration of forehead.Skin on forehead was sutured __________
18. Bilateral fractures of the radius. Right upper end and left distal end. Closed reductions bilaterally __________
19. Dislocation of left little finger. This is the third time the patient has dislocated this finger. Closed reduction was performed __________
20. Intertrochanteric fracture of left hip with ORIF __________
21. Fracture, temporal bone __________
22. Injury to right eye __________
23. Hangman's fracture (C2) __________
24. Laceration of scalp repaired with staples __________
25. Fracture of L3 (traumatic) __________
26. Closed head injury with brain contusion and LOC __________
27. Subdural hematoma with brief loss of consciousness (20 minutes). Hematoma was evacuated in the OR through burr hole __________
28. Peroneal nerve injury due to left fibular fracture (shaft) __________
29. Traumatic fractures of C1-C2 vertebra with spinal cord injury __________

Write the correct answer(s) in the space(s) provided.

30. Define open fracture. ____

CHAPTER GLOSSARY

Air embolism: when air or gas bubbles get into the bloodstream and obstruct the circulation.

Closed fracture: injury in which the bone is broken, but the skin remains intact.

Closed head injury: injury that results from a blow to the head.

Closed reduction: the surgeon manipulates or reduces fractured bones into anatomic alignment without making an incision through the skin and subcutaneous tissue.

Colles' fracture: common fracture in adults in which the lower end of the radius is fractured and the wrist and hand are displaced backward.

Complicated fracture: fracture that causes injury to surrounding tissues.

Compound fracture: when the broken bone exits and is visible through the skin, or a deep wound exposes the broken bone through the skin.

Concussion: injury to the brain that results from a significant blow to the head.

Contusion: any mechanical injury that results in hemorrhage beneath unbroken skin.

Crush injury: when a body part is subjected to a high degree of force or pressure, usually after it has been squeezed between two heavy or immobile objects.

Dislocation: displacement of the bones that form a joint; separation of the end of a bone from the joint it meets.

External skeletal fixation: form of fracture treatment that involves insertion of percutaneous pins proximal and distal to the fracture and application of a frame that connects the pins externally.

Fat embolism: when fat enters the circulatory system after long bone or pelvic fracture.

Fracture: break in a bone.

Gustilo open fracture classification: based on the mechanism of the injury and the amount of soft tissue and skeletal injury and is useful in assessing risk of infection and possible amputation.

Laceration: an injury that results in a tear in the skin.

Loss of consciousness: when a patient is unable to respond to people or other stimuli.

Open fracture: when the broken bone exits and is visible through the skin, or a deep wound exposes the broken bone through the skin.

Open reduction: when the surgeon makes an incision at the fracture site to reduce or manipulate the fracture into anatomic position.

Pathologic fracture: break in a bone that occurs because of underlying disorders that weaken the bone, including malignancy, benign bone tumor, metabolic disorder, infection, and osteoporosis.

Simple fracture: injury in which the bone is broken, but the skin remains intact.

Spinal cord injury: damage to the spinal cord that causes loss of sensation and motor control.

Sprain: stretch and/or tear of a ligament.

Strain: injury to a muscle or a tendon.

Subluxation: partial or incomplete dislocation.

Suture: method for closing cutaneous wounds.

Traumatic brain injury: injury to the brain that may result in interference with the brain's normal functions.

KEY REFERENCE

1. American Hospital Association: Coding Clinic for ICD-9-CM, vol 1Q, 1999, p 5. Fracture site specified in radiology report.
2. From American Association for the Surgery of Trauma, Chicago, Illinois.
3. American Hospital Association: Coding Clinic for ICD-9-CM, vol M-A, 1987, pp 1–5. Observation and evaluation for suspected conditions—Guidelines.

25

Burns, Adverse Effects, and Poisonings

(ICD-10-CM Chapters 19 and 20, Codes S00-Y99)

CHAPTER OUTLINE

LEARNING OBJECTIVES

1. Apply and assign the correct ICD-10-CM/PCS codes in accordance with Official Guidelines for Coding and Reporting
2. Identify the various types of burns
3. Differentiate between an adverse effect and a poisoning
4. Assign the correct Z codes, External cause codes, and procedure codes related to burns, adverse effects, and poisonings
5. Identify common treatments

ABBREVIATIONS/ACRONYMS

AKA above-knee amputation
CC complication/comorbidity
CHF congestive heart failure
COPD chronic obstructive pulmonary disease
HBOT Hyperbaric oxygen therapy
ICD-10-CM *International Classification of Diseases, 10th Revision, Clinical Modification*
ICD-10-PCS *International Classification of Diseases, 10th Revision, Procedure Coding System*
MVA motor vehicle accident
SIRS systemic inflammatory response syndrome
UTI urinary tract infection

ICD-10-CM

Official Guidelines for Coding and Reporting (2021-2022)

Please refer to the companion Evolve website for the most current 2021-2022 guidelines.

19. Chapter 19: Injury, poisoning, and certain other consequences of external causes (S00-T88)

d. Coding of Burns and Corrosions

The ICD-10-CM makes a distinction between burns and corrosions. The burn codes are for thermal burns, except sunburns, that come from a heat source, such as a fire or hot appliance. The burn codes are also for burns resulting from electricity and radiation. Corrosions are burns due to chemicals. The guidelines are the same for burns and corrosions.

Current burns (T20-T25) are classified by depth, extent and by agent (X code). Burns are classified by depth as first degree (erythema), second degree (blistering), and third degree (full-thickness involvement). Burns of the eye and internal organs (T26-T28) are classified by site, but not by degree.

1) Sequencing of burn and related condition codes

Sequence first the code that reflects the highest degree of burn when more than one burn is present.

a. When the reason for the admission or encounter is for treatment of external multiple burns, sequence first the code that reflects the burn of the highest degree.

b. When a patient has both internal and external burns, the circumstances of admission govern the selection of the principal diagnosis or first-listed diagnosis.

c. When a patient is admitted for burn injuries and other related conditions such as smoke inhalation and/or respiratory failure, the circumstances of admission govern the selection of the principal or first-listed diagnosis.

EXAMPLE Second-degree burns of the left hand and first-degree burns of the left forearm, T23.202A, T22.112A.

2) Burns of the same anatomic site

Classify burns of the same anatomic site and on the same side but of different degrees to the subcategory identifying the highest degree recorded in the diagnosis. (e.g., for second and third degree burns of right thigh, assign only code T24.311-).

EXAMPLE Second- and third-degree burns of the right thigh, T24.311A.

3) Non-healing burns

Non-healing burns are coded as acute burns.

Necrosis of burned skin should be coded as a non-healed burn.

EXAMPLE Active treatment for necrosis of third-degree burn on the buttock, T21.35xA.

4) Infected Burn

For any documented infected burn site, use an additional code for the infection.

EXAMPLE Active treatment of infected burn, right foot, T25.021A, L08.89.

5) Assign separate codes for each burn site

When coding burns, assign separate codes for each burn site. Category T30, Burn and corrosion, body region unspecified is extremely vague and should rarely be used.

Codes for burns of "multiple sites" should only be assigned when the medical record documentation does not specify the individual sites.

EXAMPLE Multiple burns over the entire body. The patient expired before he could be admitted, T30.0.

6) Burns and Corrosions Classified According to Extent of Body Surface Involved
Assign codes from category T31, Burns classified according to extent of body surface involved, or T32, Corrosions classified according to extent of body surface involved, when the site of the burn is not specified or when there is a need for additional data. It is advisable to use category T31 as additional coding when needed to provide data for evaluating burn mortality, such as that needed by burn units. It is also advisable to use category T31 as an additional code for reporting purposes when there is mention of a third-degree burn involving 20 percent or more of the body surface.

Categories T31 and T32 are based on the classic "rule of nines" in estimating body surface involved: head and neck are assigned nine percent, each arm nine percent, each leg 18 percent, the anterior trunk 18 percent, posterior trunk 18 percent, and genitalia one percent. Providers may change these percentage assignments where necessary to accommodate infants and children who have proportionately larger heads than adults, and patients who have large buttocks, thighs, or abdomen that involve burns.

EXAMPLE

The patient has second-degree (3%) and third-degree (5%) burns of the trunk and first-degree burns (2%) of the right arm, T21.30xA, T22.10xA, T31.10.

7) Encounters for treatment of sequela of burns
Encounters for the treatment of the late effects of burns or corrosions (i.e., scars or joint contractures) should be coded with a burn or corrosion code with the 7th character "S" for sequela.

8) Sequelae with a late effect code and current burn
When appropriate, both a code for a current burn or corrosion with 7th character "A" or "D" and a burn or corrosion code with 7th character "S" may be assigned on the same record (when both a current burn and sequelae of an old burn exist). Burns and corrosions do not heal at the same rate and a current healing wound may still exist with sequela of a healed burn or corrosion. *See Section I.B.10 Sequela (Late Effects)*

EXAMPLE

Contracture scar of the skin of the right index finger due to burn from fire injury 6 months ago, L90.5, T23.021S.

9) Use of an external cause code with burns and corrosions
An external cause code should be used with burns and corrosions to identify the source and intent of the burn, as well as the place where it occurred.

The place of occurrence codes can be assigned from category Y92. The following external cause categories indicate the source and the intent.

- X00-X08 Exposure to smoke, fire, and flames
- X10-X19 Contact with heat and hot substances
- X75 Intentional self-harm by explosive material
- X76 Intentional self-harm by smoke, fire, and flames
- X77 Intentional self-harm by steam, hot vapors, and hot objects
- X96 Assault by explosive material
- X97 Assault by smoke, fire, and flames
- X98 Assault by steam, hot vapors and hot objects

e. Adverse Effects, Poisoning, Underdosing and Toxic Effects
Codes in categories T36-T65 are combination codes that include the substance that was taken as well as the intent. No additional external cause code is required for poisonings, toxic effects, adverse effects and underdosing codes.

1) Do not code directly from the Table of Drugs
Do not code directly from the Table of Drugs and Chemicals. Always refer back to the Tabular List.

2) Use as many codes as necessary to describe
Use as many codes as necessary to describe completely all drugs, medicinal or biological substances.

3) If the same code would describe the causative agent
If the same code would describe the causative agent for more than one adverse reaction, poisoning, toxic effect or underdosing, assign the code only once.

4) If two or more drugs, medicinal or biological substances
If two or more drugs, medicinal or biological substances are taken, code each individually unless a combination code is listed in the Table of Drugs and Chemicals.

If multiple unspecified drugs, medicinal or biological substances were taken, assign the appropriate code from subcategory T50.91, Poisoning by, adverse effect of and underdosing of multiple unspecified drugs, medicaments and biological substances.

5) The occurrence of drug toxicity is classified in ICD-10-CM as follows:

(a) Adverse Effect
When coding an adverse effect of a drug that has been correctly prescribed and properly administered, assign the appropriate code for the nature of the adverse effect followed by the appropriate code for the adverse effect of the drug (T36-T50). The code for the drug should have a 5th or 6th character "5" (for example T36.0X5-) Examples of the nature of an adverse effect are tachycardia, delirium, gastrointestinal hemorrhaging, vomiting, hypokalemia, hepatitis, renal failure, or respiratory failure.

EXAMPLE Patient was treated for epistaxis which is due to the patient's long term use of Coumadin for atrial fibrillation. Patient was taking the Coumadin as prescribed, R04.0, D68.32, T45.515A, I48.91.

EXAMPLE Hypokalemia due to Lasix therapy for congestive heart failure, E87.6, T50.1x5A, I50.9.

(b) Poisoning
When coding a poisoning or reaction to the improper use of a medication (e.g., overdose, wrong substance given or taken in error, wrong route of administration), first assign the appropriate code from categories T36-T50. The poisoning codes have an associated intent as their 5th or 6th character (accidental, intentional self-harm, assault and undetermined). If the intent of the poisoning is unknown or unspecified, code the intent as accidental intent. The undetermined intent is only for use if the documentation in the record specifies that the intent cannot be determined. Use additional code(s) for all manifestations of poisonings.

If there is also a diagnosis of abuse or dependence of the substance, the abuse or dependence is assigned as an additional code.

EXAMPLE Chest pain due to accidental poisoning from cocaine. The patient abuses cocaine on a daily basis, T40.5x1A, R07.9, F14.10.

Examples of poisoning include:

(i) Error was made in drug prescription
Errors made in drug prescription or in the administration of the drug by provider, nurse, patient, or other person.

(ii) Overdose of a drug intentionally taken
If an overdose of a drug was intentionally taken or administered and resulted in drug toxicity, it would be coded as a poisoning.

EXAMPLE The patient intentionally overdosed with 20 Valium tablets. The patient is in a coma, T42.4x2A, R40.20.

(iii) Nonprescribed drug taken with correctly prescribed and properly administered drug
If a nonprescribed drug or medicinal agent was taken in combination with a correctly prescribed and properly administered drug, any drug toxicity or other reaction resulting from the interaction of the two drugs would be classified as a poisoning.

(iv) Interaction of drug(s) and alcohol
When a reaction results from the interaction of a drug(s) and alcohol, this would be classified as poisoning.

See Section I.C.4. if poisoning is the result of insulin pump malfunctions.

EXAMPLE

A patient combined prescription Percodan with beer and became stuporous and drowsy, T40.2x1A, T51.0x1A, R40.1, R40.0.

(c) Underdosing

Underdosing refers to taking less of a medication than is prescribed by a provider or a manufacturer's instruction. Discontinuing the use of a prescribed medication on the patient's own initiative (not directly by the patient's provider) is also classified as an underdosing. For underdosing, assign the code from categories T36-T50 (fifth or sixth character "6").

Codes for underdosing should never be assigned as principal or first-listed codes. If a patient has a relapse or exacerbation of the medical condition for which the drug is prescribed because of the reduction in dose, then the medical condition itself should be coded.

Noncompliance (Z91.12-, Z91.13- and Z91.14-) or complication of care (Y63.6-Y63.9) codes are to be used with an underdosing code to indicate intent, if known.

EXAMPLE

Patient was admitted to the hospital with an exacerbation of asthma. Patient has not been using Flovent inhaler on a daily basis as prescribed due to financial issues, J45.901, T49.1x6A, Z91.120.

(d) Toxic Effects

When a harmful substance is ingested or comes in contact with a person, this is classified as a toxic effect. The toxic effect codes are in categories T51-T65.

Toxic effect codes have an associated intent: accidental, intentional self-harm, assault and undetermined.

EXAMPLE

A 2-year-old accidentally drank lye, causing burns to the mouth and throat, T54.3x1A, T28.5xxA.

f. Adult and child abuse, neglect and other maltreatment

Sequence first the appropriate code from categories T74, Adult and child abuse, neglect and other maltreatment, confirmed or T76, Adult and child abuse, neglect and other maltreatment, suspected, for abuse, neglect and other maltreatment, followed by any accompanying mental health or injury code(s).

If the documentation in the medical record states abuse or neglect it is coded as confirmed (T74.-). It is coded as suspected if it is documented as suspected (T76.-).

For cases of confirmed abuse or neglect an external cause code from the assault section (X92-Y09) should be added to identify the cause of any physical injuries. A perpetrator code (Y07) should be added when the perpetrator of the abuse is known. For suspected cases of abuse or neglect, do not report external cause or perpetrator code.

If a suspected case of abuse, neglect or mistreatment is ruled out during an encounter code Z04.71, Encounter for examination and observation following alleged adult physical abuse, ruled out, or code Z04.72, Encounter for examination and observation following alleged child physical abuse, ruled out, should be used, not a code from T76.

If a suspected case of alleged rape or sexual abuse is ruled out during an encounter code Z04.41, Encounter for examination and observation following alleged adult rape or code Z04.42, Encounter for examination and observation following alleged child rape, should be used, not a code from T76.

If a suspected case of forced sexual exploitation or forced labor exploitation is ruled out during an encounter, code Z04.81, Encounter for examination and observation of victim following forced sexual exploitation, or code Z04.82, Encounter for examination and observation of victim following forced labor exploitation, should be used, not a code from T76.

See Section I.C.15. Abuse in a pregnant patient.

EXAMPLE

A wife was seen with head and face injuries due to spousal abuse. The patient had been hit repeatedly in the face and head, T74.11xA, S09.93xA, S09.90xA, Y04.0xxA, Y07.01.

CHAPTER 19

INJURY, POISONING AND CERTAIN OTHER CONSEQUENCES OF EXTERNAL CAUSES (S00-T88)

Note: Use secondary code(s) from Chapter 20, External causes of morbidity, to indicate cause of injury. Codes within the T section that include the external cause do not require an additional external cause code.

Use additional code to identify any retained foreign body, if applicable (Z18.-)

Excludes1 birth trauma (P10-P15)
obstetric trauma (O70-O71)

FIGURE 25-1. Instructional note regarding the use of External cause code(s).

20. Chapter 20: External Causes of Morbidity (V00-Y99)

g. Child and Adult Abuse Guideline

Adult and child abuse, neglect and maltreatment are classified as assault. Any of the assault codes may be used to indicate the external cause of any injury resulting from the confirmed abuse.

For confirmed cases of abuse, neglect and maltreatment, when the perpetrator is known, a code from Y07, Perpetrator of maltreatment and neglect, should accompany any other assault codes.

See Section I.C.19. Adult and child abuse, neglect and other maltreatment

At the beginning of Chapter 19 in the ICD-10-CM code book, special instructions say, "Use secondary code(s) from Chapter 20 to indicate cause of injury" (Figure 25-1).

ANATOMY AND PHYSIOLOGY

All areas of the body may be involved in an injury. These are outlined in their respective body system chapters.

DISEASE CONDITIONS

Injury, Poisoning, and Certain Other Consequences of External Causes (S00-T88), Chapter 19 in the ICD-10-CM code book, is divided into the following categories:

CATEGORY	SECTIDN TITLES
T20-T32	Burns and corrosions
T33-T34	Frostbite
T36-T50	Poisoning by, adverse effect of, and underdosing of drugs, medicaments, and biological substances
T51-T65	Toxic effects of substances chiefly nonmedicinal as to source
T66-T78	Other and unspecified effects of external causes

ICD-10-CM creates a distinction between burns and corrosions. Burns codes are for thermal injuries (except for sunburns), and corrosions identify burns that are due to chemicals. Many of the code categories in this chapter have seventh character values that are applicable. If a code is fewer than six characters and requires a seventh character value, a placeholder x is used to fill in the empty character value(s). There are a number of instructional notes throughout this chapter.

There are ICD-10-CM codes that can be used to identify underdosing. These would be used to code situations when a patient takes less of a medication than is prescribed or less than the manufacturer's instructions, with a negative effect on health.

Burns and Corrosions (T20-T32) and Frostbite (T33-T34)

It may be necessary to transport burn victims to a hospital that has a specialized unit for care of the burn patient. Plastic surgeons, anesthesiologists, nurses, dietitians, and physical and occupational therapists assist the burn patient through the acute and recovery phases of their injury. As a result, many facilities only stabilize the burn patient in the emergency room and then transport to a burn unit, or only less critical burn patients are admitted for care.

According to the ICD-10-CM guidelines, the burn codes are assigned for thermal burns, except for sunburns, that come from a heat source such as a fire or hot appliance. **Corrosion** is a burn that is due to a chemical. The guidelines are the same for both types of burns. As with other injuries, it is necessary to assign separate codes for each burn site. Codes are available for multiple sites, but these should be used only if the documentation is insufficient to allow assignment of more specific burn codes.

Burn severity is classified by degrees (Figure 25-2):

- First-degree burn: **erythema** or redness of the skin
- Second-degree burn: formation of blisters with epidermal loss
- Third-degree burn: full-thickness skin loss
- Fourth-degree burn: deep necrosis of underlying tissues or deep third-degree burn

The guidelines instruct the coder to sequence the code that reflects the highest degree of burn first.

EXAMPLE Patient was seen in the ER for second-degree burns of the left calf and first-degree burns of the right foot due to uncontrolled grass fire in forest, T24.232A, T25.121A, X01.0xxA, Y92.821.

Often, a burn will be described as having different degrees at the same site. It is only necessary to assign the code that identifies the highest degree of burn.

EXAMPLE Examination of the patient shows erythema and blisters to the right wrist due to burn from an iron. The accident occurred at the patient's house, T23.271A, X15.8xxA, Y92.019, Y93.e4.

EXAMPLE Patient was seen in the ER with erythema and blisters on left hand due to accidental chemical burn from hydrochloric acid. Patient works in an industrial factory, T54.2x1A, T23.602A, Y92.63, Y99.0.

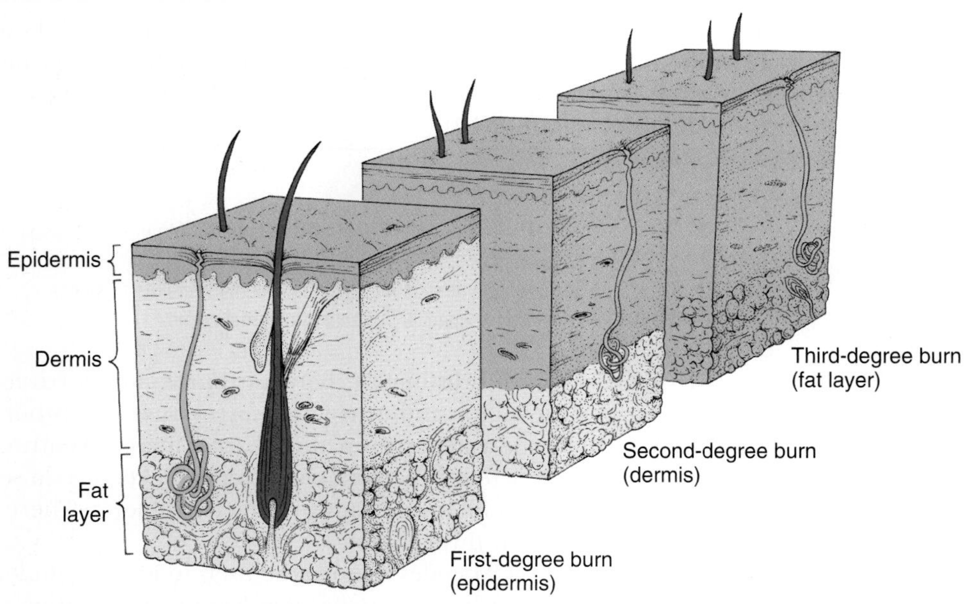

FIGURE 25-2. Depths of burns.

Although the physician did not state first- or second-degree burn, by the description, this burn is a first- (erythema) and second-degree (blister) burn, so it would be coded to the most severe burn, which is second-degree.

For a variety of reasons, a burn may not heal quickly, or it may become infected. A nonhealing burn is coded as an acute burn. It is possible to have burns that occurred at the same time, and some may have healed completely while others have not yet healed. If the burn contains necrotic tissue, it is coded as an acute burn. It is possible to have late effects (e.g., scar, contracture) of a burn along with a nonhealing burn. Sometimes, late effects remain after the burn has healed, and these still require treatment.

EXAMPLE

Patient has third-degree burn on chest wall due to house fire, T21.31xA, X00.0xxA, Y92.019.

EXAMPLE

Active treatment for patient who has a nonhealing third-degree burn of abdominal wall with keloid scar forming on right shoulder burn. Burns due to accidental injury in house fire, T21.32xA, L91.0, T22.051S, X00.0xxA, X00.0xxS, Y92.019.

EXAMPLE

Patient is being treated for an infected burn right palm from a hot light bulb, T23.051A, L08.89, X15.8xxA.

T31 and T32 categories are provided to identify the extent of body surface that is involved by burns and to indicate the percentage of body surface that has third-degree burns. According to the classic "rule of nines," in estimating involved body surface, head and neck are assigned 9%, each arm 9%, each leg 18%, anterior trunk 18%, posterior trunk 18%, and genitalia 1%. These percentage assignments may change as necessary to accommodate infants and children who have proportionately larger heads than adults and patients who have large buttocks, thighs, or abdomen that involve burns (Figure 25-3). The percentages of body surface involvement must be documented by a healthcare professional for code assignment. Percentages should not be calculated by the coder.

Category (T30) can be used when the site of the burn is not specified. In some instances, the burns may be so extensive that detailed documentation is not provided. A specialized burn assessment form to document burn location, type, and body percentage is often used in burn centers.

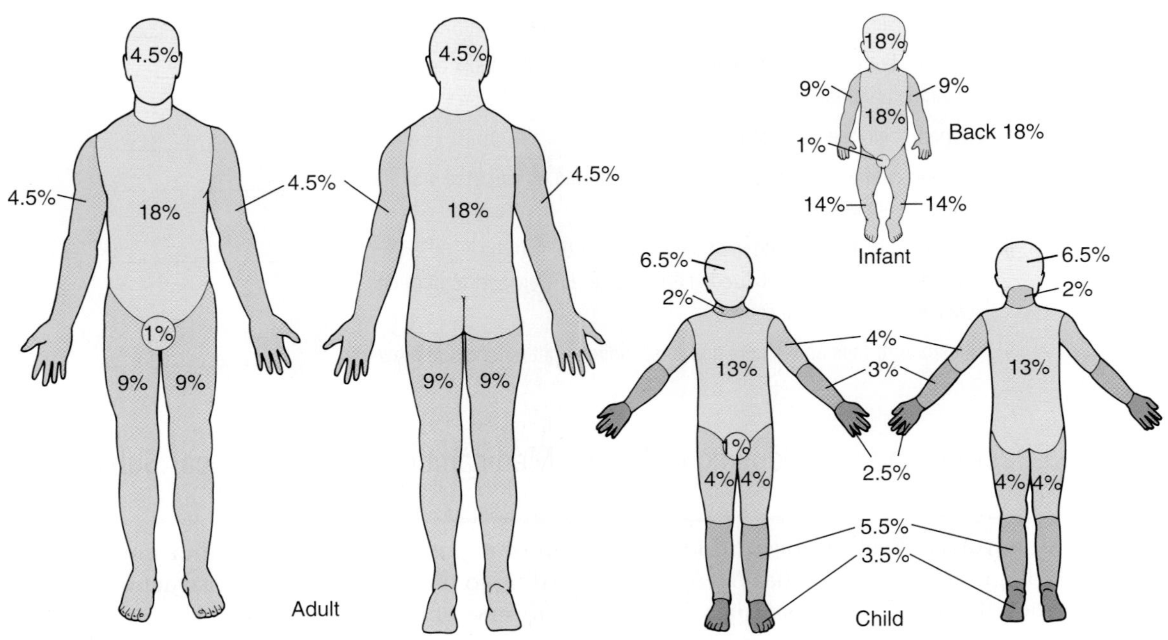

FIGURE 25-3. Rule of nines.

EXAMPLE

Patient has second- (3%) and third-degree (5%) burns of the trunk and first-degree burns (2%) of the right arm due to fire from a street car accident, T21.30xA, T22.10xA, T31.10, V82.8xxA, Y92.818.

Frostbite

Frostbite occurs when skin and the underlying tissues freeze due to extreme cold. The areas that are most likely to be affected are the cheeks, nose, ears, fingers, and toes. The blood vessels close to the skin start to constrict to sustain the core body temperature. The skin and underlying tissues are affected due to the lack of blood supply to these areas. There are four degrees of frostbite.

- First degree—only affects the skin surface. Usually no permanent damage but may be affected by heat and cold sensitivity.
- Second degree—blisters will form within 1 to 2 days. Blisters will become hard and are black. These areas will be insensitive to heat and cold.
- Third and fourth degree—the frostbite goes deep into the muscles, tendons, blood vessels, and nerves. Nerve damage will result in loss of feeling. Affected areas may develop gangrene, and amputation may be necessary.

EXAMPLE

Patient was seen in the ER for superficial frostbite, both ears. Patient was exposed to cold weather, T33.011A, T33.012A, X31.xxxA.

EXERCISE 25-1

Assign codes to the following conditions. (If percentage of the body burned is not documented do not assign a code from category T31 or T32).

1. Nonhealing second-degree burn to left thigh due to hot coffee spill, under active treatment ______________
2. Second- and third-degree burns to trunk, and second- and third-degree burns both to legs due to fire at night club; in all, 35% of the body was burned, 25% third degree ______________
3. First-degree burn right to wrist and second-degree burns to right fingers and right hand due to firework explosion while playing in backyard ______________
4. Infected second-degree burn to buttock, under active treatment ______________
5. Alkaline burn to left cornea due to caustic soda while working in a paper manufacturing factory ______________
6. Hypertrophic scar of burn to right cheek ______________
7. Friction burn to left elbow due to accidental fall on carpeted stairs at patient's home ______________
8. Patient in house fire with multiple burns over 60% of body, 30% third degree; patient was stabilized and prepared for transport to burn unit; fire was due to accidental causes ______________
9. Frostbite to toes and fingers due to spending night outdoors in blizzard ______________

Poisoning by, Adverse Effect of, and Underdosing of Drugs, Medicaments, and Biological Substances (T36-T50)

An **adverse effect** can occur due to ingestion or exposure to a drug or other medicinal or biologic substance that has been taken according to the prescription or instructions on the label of over-the-counter drugs. To code an adverse effect, at least two codes are required.

The Table of Drugs and Chemicals (Figure 25-4) is used to identify one code from categories T36-T50 to identify the drug and then additional code(s) to identify the

		External Cause (T-Code)				
Substance	Poisoning, Accidental (Unintentional)	Poisoning, Intentional Self-Harm	Poisoning, Assault	Poisoning, Undetermined	Adverse Effect	Underdosing
	#					
1-propanol	T51.3X1	T51.3X2	T51.3X3	T51.3X4	—	—
2-propanol	T51.2X1	T51.2X2	T51.2X3	T51.2X4	—	—
2,4-D (dichlorophen-oxyacetic acid)	T60.3X1	T60.3X2	T60.3X3	T60.3X4	—	—
2,4-toluene diisocyanate	T65.0X1	T65.0X2	T65.0X3	T65.0X4	—	—
2,4,5-T (trichloro-phenoxyacetic acid)	T60.1X1	T60.1X2	T60.1X3	T60.1X4	—	—
3,4-methylenedioxymethamphetamine	T43.641	T43.642	T43.643	T43.644	—	—
14-hydroxydihydro-morphinone	T40.2X1	T40.2X2	T40.2X3	T40.2X4	T40.2X5	T40.2X6
	A					
ABOB	T37.5X1	T37.5X2	T37.5X3	T37.5X4	T37.5X5	T37.5X6
Abrine	T62.2X1	T62.2X2	T62.2X3	T62.2X4	—	—
Abrus (seed)	T62.2X1	T62.2X2	T62.2X3	T62.2X4	—	—
Absinthe	T51.0X1	T51.0X2	T51.0X3	T51.0X4	—	—
beverage	T51.0X1	T51.0X2	T51.0X3	T51.0X4	—	—
Acaricide	T60.8X1	T60.8X2	T60.8X3	T60.8X4	—	—
Acebutolol	T44.7X1	T44.7X2	T44.7X3	T44.7X4	T44.7X5	T44.7X6
Acecarbromal	T42.6X1	T42.6X2	T42.6X3	T42.6X4	T42.6X5	T42.6X6
Aceclidine	T44.1X1	T44.1X2	T44.1X3	T44.1X4	T44.1X5	T44.1X6
Acedapsone	T37.0X1	T37.0X2	T37.0X3	T37.0X4	T37.0X5	T37.0X6
Acefylline piperazine	T48.6X1	T48.6X2	T48.6X3	T48.6X4	T48.6X5	T48.6X6
Acemorphan	T40.2X1	T40.2X2	T40.2X3	T40.2X4	T40.2X5	T40.2X6
Acenocoumarin	T45.511	T45.512	T45.513	T45.514	T45.515	T45.516
Acenocoumarol	T45.511	T45.512	T45.513	T45.514	T45.515	T45.516
Acepifylline	T48.6X1	T48.6X2	T48.6X3	T48.6X4	T48.6X5	T48.6X6
Acepromazine	T43.3X1	T43.3X2	T43.3X3	T43.3X4	T43.3X5	T43.3X6
Acesulfamethoxypyridazine	T37.0X1	T37.0X2	T37.0X3	T37.0X4	T37.0X5	T37.0X6
Acetal	T52.8X1	T52.8X2	T52.8X3	T52.8X4	—	—
Acetaldehyde (vapor)	T52.8X1	T52.8X2	T52.8X3	T52.8X4	—	—
liquid	T65.891	T65.892	T65.893	T65.894	—	—
P-Acetamidophenol	T39.1X1	T39.1X2	T39.1X3	T39.1X4	T39.1X5	T39.1X6
Acetaminophen	T39.1X1	T39.1X2	T39.1X3	T39.1X4	T39.1X5	T39.1X6
Acetaminosalol	T39.1X1	T39.1X2	T39.1X3	T39.1X4	T39.1X5	T39.1X6
Acetanilide	T39.1X1	T39.1X2	T39.1X3	T39.1X4	T39.1X5	T39.1X6
Acetarsol	T37.3X1	T37.3X2	T37.3X3	T37.3X4	T37.3X5	T37.3X6
Acetazolamide	T50.2X1	T50.2X2	T50.2X3	T50.2X4	T50.2X5	T50.2X6
Acetiamine	T45.2X1	T45.2X2	T45.2X3	T45.2X4	T45.2X5	T45.2X6
Acetic						
acid	T54.2X1	T54.2X2	T54.2X3	T54.2X4	—	—
with sodium acetate (ointment)	T49.3X1	T49.3X2	T49.3X3	T49.3X4	T49.3X5	T49.3X6
ester (solvent) (vapor)	T52.8X1	T52.8X2	T52.8X3	T52.8X4	—	—

FIGURE 25-4. Excerpt from the Table of Drugs and Chemicals.

manifestations of the adverse effect. The drug responsible for the adverse effect must first be identified and then located in the Table under the adverse effect column. If a specific drug cannot be located, the generic name should be determined or the category of the drug identified (e.g., antihypertensive, antianginal, antineoplastic). Once the drug or drug category has been located in the index, the T code from the adverse effect column is assigned after verification in the Tabular. Refer to the guidelines for assistance with sequencing of the manifestation(s) and assignment of the appropriate T code(s).

Because drugs have generic and brand names, and these are used interchangeably, it may be difficult to locate the drug in the index. A drug reference book or an Internet search can be used to determine the generic name or category of the drug.

EXAMPLE

Hematuria due to Coumadin, which is taken for atrial fibrillation, R31.9, D68.32, T45.515A, I48.91.

Hematuria in this case is the adverse effect of medication that was properly prescribed and properly taken.

EXAMPLE

Patient presented with hypokalemia due to long-term use of diuretics, E87.6, T50.2x5A. Hypokalemia is the adverse effect of the diuretic.

EXAMPLE

Dizziness caused by Claritin, which was taken per instructions on the label, R42, T45.0x5A. Claritin is not listed in the Table of Drugs and Chemicals, but an Internet search reveals that loratadine is the generic name, and this is not listed either. Claritin is classified as an antihistamine that can be located in the Table.

EXERCISE 25-2

Using a drug reference book or the Internet, specify drug category or generic name for the following drugs.

1. Lunesta ______________

2. Cardizem ______________

3. Bactrim ______________

4. Zoloft ______________

5. Ditropan ______________

It is possible that an adverse effect to some drugs may be based on an abnormal laboratory result. Sometimes a physician will document "toxicity" based on these laboratory results. For a drug toxicity with no documented adverse reaction assign code R89.2. The appropriate 7th character will need to be added to the code to identify whether this is an initial encounter, subsequent encounter, or a sequela of an adverse effect. If the patient has any symptoms, then the symptom codes are assigned along with the appropriate T code for adverse effect.

EXAMPLE

Dilantin toxicity per laboratory report. Patient is asymptomatic. The Dilantin dosage will be adjusted and Dilantin levels monitored. Patient takes Dilantin for seizure disorder, R89.2, T42.0x5A, G40.909.

Underdosing is taking less of a medication than is prescribed by a provider or a manufacturer's instructions. Occasionally a patient will be admitted to the hospital for a relapse or exacerbation of the medical condition for which that drug was prescribed. According to the guidelines, a code for the medical condition should be assigned first, then a code from categories T36-T50 to indicate underdosing. Additional codes to further explain the reason for underdosing such as noncompliance because of financial hardship should also be assigned.

EXERCISE 25-3

Assign codes to the following conditions.

1. Hives due to Bactrim taken to treat UTI (urinary tract infection) __________
2. Diarrhea due to erythromycin used to treat acute bronchitis __________
3. Headache due to Nitrostat taken for angina __________
4. Constipation due to narcotics used after surgery __________
5. Decreased sex drive due to treatment with Zoloft for depression __________
6. Dizziness and irregular heartbeat due to Inderal, which was taken for hypertension __________
7. Tachycardia due to albuterol, which was administered for asthma __________
8. CHF exacerbation due to noncompliance with lasix. Not taking required dosage because patient has trouble getting to bathroom due to osteoarthritis __________

Poisonings

It is sometimes confusing to determine the difference between an adverse effect and a poisoning. Poisoning from medication(s) occurs when:

- The wrong medication is taken—patient took a medication that is not currently prescribed for them
- The wrong dose is taken—patient took 2 tablets instead of 1 (double the dosage)
- Overdose—patient took large amount of medication or other drug or chemical
- Nonprescribed drug (including illegal drugs and alcohol) interacts with a prescription medication—patient took an over-the-counter medication that causes some reaction with prescribed medication

The poisoning T code is always sequenced first and is found in the Table of Drugs and Chemicals under the heading for "poisoning." It is possible to assign more than one poisoning code, to describe a poisoning if more than one substance or drug is responsible. A poisoning requires at least two codes.

The selection of the appropriate T code for poisonings can be confusing. Unlike adverse effects where the only option for T code assignment from the "adverse effect" column, poisoning T codes are assigned according to circumstances surrounding this poisoning. The circumstances (intent) include the following:

- Accidental
- Intentional Self-Harm
- Assault
- Undetermined

According to the guidelines:

- If the intent (accident, self-harm, assault) of the cause of an injury or poisoning is unknown or unspecified, code the intent as accidental.
- Undetermined intent is only for use if the documentation specifies that the intent cannot be determined.

If the manifestation(s) of the poisoning is documented, it should be coded as a secondary diagnosis. Manifestations could include chest pain, vomiting, lethargy, coma, and so forth.

Chronic medical conditions related to alcohol and/or drug abuse or dependence would not be considered a poisoning. In these cases, the chronic medical condition should be coded along with a code to identify the type of abuse or dependence.

EXAMPLE Alcoholic cardiomyopathy in patient with alcohol dependence, I42.6, F10.20.

EXAMPLE

Patient admitted for a suicide attempt with multiple medications, including Naproxen, Keppra, and acetaminophen mixed with beer. Patient was somnolent on arrival in the ER, T39.312A, T42.6x2A, T39.1x2A, T51.0x2A, R40.0.

EXAMPLE

Patient became weak, had labored breathing, and had altered mental status caused by an accidental overdose of codeine, T40.2x1A, R53.1, R06.4, R41.82.

The manifestations of the overdose are the weakness, breathing problems, and alteration in mental status.

EXERCISE 25-4

Assign codes to the following conditions.

1. Patient took ampicillin that belonged to his wife; patient developed hives caused by the ampicillin ______________
2. Patient became stuporous and lethargic after taking Valium according to prescription, then drinking a couple of beers; accidental intent ______________
3. The patient accidentally received the higher dosage of potassium resulting in hyperkalemia while in the hospital ______________
4. Cocaine-induced chest pain (atypical); patient is a known cocaine abuser with a daily habit; accidental intent ______________
5. Suicide attempt with acetaminophen; patient has nausea and vomiting with abdominal pain ______________
6. Toddler accidentally drank bottle of Visine; the toddler was having labored breathing and was very irritable ______________
7. Patient was taking extra doses of Lasix to reduce swelling of lower extremities; patient is hypokalemic and takes Lasix for congestive heart failure ______________
8. Patient became dizzy and very drowsy after taking one of spouse's Vicodin tablets and drinking a couple of alcoholic beverages and smoking marijuana; patient has abused marijuana for years ______________

Toxic Effects of Substances Chiefly Nonmedicinal as to Source (T51-T65)

Numerous toxic substances can cause ill effects. Categories T51 to T65 identify these types of reactions. Reactions range from mild events such as headache to life-threatening conditions. At the beginning of this section, instructions are provided on the use of additional codes for all associated manifestations of toxic effect.

EXAMPLE

Patient admitted with alcohol poisoning due to intake of vodka, T51.0x1A.

EXERCISE 25-5

Assign codes to the following conditions.

1. Nausea and vomiting due to ingestion of holly berries ______________
2. Accidental lead poisoning from paint with anemia and muscle weakness ______________
3. Unconscious due to carbon monoxide poisoning caused by motor vehicle fumes, suicide attempt ______________
4. Weight loss, and extreme fatigue due to mercury toxicity caused by exposure while working with dental fillings ______________

Other and Unspecified Effects of External Causes (T66-T78)

Categories T66 to T78 are used to identify the effects that external causes such as radiation, temperature, heat, light, and air pressure may have on the human body.

Adult/Child Abuse

Domestic violence, elder abuse, and child abuse occur more often than one might think. Healthcare providers are required to report to the proper authorities any suspicions of abuse and/or neglect. Four major types of abuse have been identified:

1. Physical abuse
2. Sexual abuse
3. Emotional or psychological abuse
4. Neglect or abandonment

There are specific ICD-10-CM T codes that identify "suspected" abuse or neglect. It is not necessary to assign external cause codes or perpetrator codes with these codes. If the suspected abuse or neglect has been ruled out during an encounter, Z04.71 should be assigned for adults and Z04.72 for children. A code from category T76 should not be assigned. Shaken infant syndrome is the exception to this rule and defaults to code T74.4.

ICD-10-CM classifies confirmed cases of abuse or neglect to code category T74. The fourth character of the T74 and T76 codes indicates the type of abuse. The fifth character identifies if the patient is a child or adult.

The code book gives instructions on the use of additional code(s), if applicable, to identify any associated injuries (Figure 25-5) and the appropriate External cause code to identify the perpetrator.

EXAMPLE

The child was admitted for moderate malnutrition because of neglect by the mother, T74.02xA, E44.0, Y07.12.

Systemic Inflammatory Response Syndrome (SIRS)

Systemic inflammatory response syndrome (SIRS) is a serious medical condition that can occur in response to an infection or to noninfectious causes, such as severe trauma, burns, and complications of surgery. It may also occur in diseases such as pancreatitis and AIDS.

SIRS may be diagnosed when two or more of the following criteria are present:

- Heart rate >90 beats per minute
- Body temperature <36°C or >38°C
- Tachypnea (high respiratory rate) >20 breaths per minute or, on blood gas, a $PaCo_2$ <4.3 kPa (32 mm Hg)
- White blood cell count <4000 cells/mm^3 or >12,000 cells/mm^3 ($<4 \times 10^9$ or $>12 \times 10^9$ cells/L), or the presence of greater than 10% immature neutrophils.

Because of instructional notes in the code book to "code first underlying condition," the SIRS codes will generally not be the principal diagnosis. In patients with trauma, the most severe injury would be the principal diagnosis and the SIRS code would be assigned as a secondary code. It is possible for organ dysfunction to occur as a result of trauma, and this would be coded to SIRS due to noninfectious process with acute organ dysfunction.

EXAMPLE

Patient has SIRS due to accidental burns in an accident in which a street car caught on fire. Patient has second- (3%) and third-degree (5%) burns of the trunk and first-degree burns of the right arm, T21.30xA, T22.10xA, T31.0, R65.10, V82.8xxA, Y92.818.

Rhadomyolysis

Rhadomyolysis is the breakdown of muscle fibers that results in the release of muscle fiber contents into the circulation. Some of these contents are toxic to the kidney, frequently resulting in kidney damage. Some inherited disorders such as carnitine palmityltransferase, phosphofructokinase deficiency, and phosphoglycerate kinase deficiency can lead to muscle

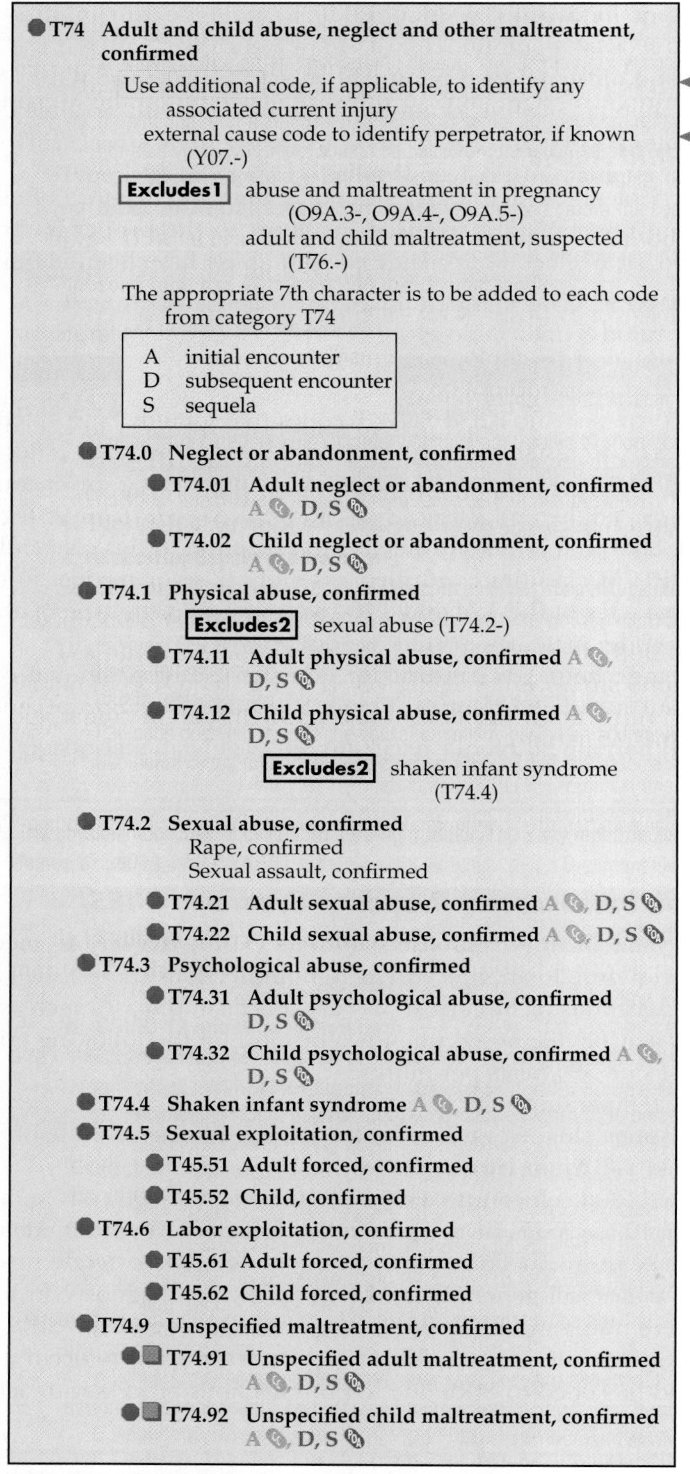

T74 Adult and child abuse, neglect and other maltreatment, confirmed

Use additional code, if applicable, to identify any associated current injury
external cause code to identify perpetrator, if known (Y07.-)

Excludes1 abuse and maltreatment in pregnancy (O9A.3-, O9A.4-, O9A.5-)
adult and child maltreatment, suspected (T76.-)

The appropriate 7th character is to be added to each code from category T74

A	initial encounter
D	subsequent encounter
S	sequela

T74.0 Neglect or abandonment, confirmed
T74.01 Adult neglect or abandonment, confirmed A, D, S
T74.02 Child neglect or abandonment, confirmed A, D, S
T74.1 Physical abuse, confirmed
Excludes2 sexual abuse (T74.2-)
T74.11 Adult physical abuse, confirmed A, D, S
T74.12 Child physical abuse, confirmed A, D, S
Excludes2 shaken infant syndrome (T74.4)
T74.2 Sexual abuse, confirmed
Rape, confirmed
Sexual assault, confirmed
T74.21 Adult sexual abuse, confirmed A, D, S
T74.22 Child sexual abuse, confirmed A, D, S
T74.3 Psychological abuse, confirmed
T74.31 Adult psychological abuse, confirmed D, S
T74.32 Child psychological abuse, confirmed A, D, S
T74.4 Shaken infant syndrome A, D, S
T74.5 Sexual exploitation, confirmed
T45.51 Adult forced, confirmed
T45.52 Child, confirmed
T74.6 Labor exploitation, confirmed
T45.61 Adult forced, confirmed
T45.62 Child forced, confirmed
T74.9 Unspecified maltreatment, confirmed
T74.91 Unspecified adult maltreatment, confirmed A, D, S
T74.92 Unspecified child maltreatment, confirmed A, D, S

FIGURE 25-5. Instructions to use additional code(s) to identify any current injury and external cause code for perpetrator.

injury with exercise and rhabdomyolysis. Some of the most common causes include the following:

- Muscle exertion (physical, related to convulsions or to heat injury)
- Trauma-crush syndromes and pseudo-crush syndrome
- Muscle ischemia related to arterial occlusion or insufficiency
- Burns
- Repetitive muscle injury (bongo drumming, torture)

- Status epilepticus
- Drug overdose
- Extended periods of muscle pressure

EXAMPLE

Traumatic rhabdomyolysis due to intractable status epilepticus
Patient was diagnosed with epilepsy 2 years ago, G40.911, T79.6xxA.

EXERCISE 25-6

Assign codes to the following conditions.

1. Heatstroke due to high temperature while at beach ______________
2. Anaphylactic shock due to peanut butter ______________
3. Seasickness while on cruise ______________
4. Bilateral retinal hemorrhages. ______________
5. Diarrhea, drowsiness, and seizure caused by arsenic poisoning. Wife was trying to harm the patient ______________

Late Effects of Injuries, Poisonings, Toxic Effects, and Other External Causes

Once the acute nature of an injury, adverse effect, or poisoning has resolved, some residual effects or sequela that have remained may require medical treatment. In Chapter 5, the coding and sequencing of late effects were discussed. Remember, a late effect may occur at any time after the acute injury has resolved. No specific time frames are required.

To assign a code for a late effect or sequela of a traumatic injury, adverse effect, or poisoning, the code that identifies the type of injury, adverse effect, or poisoning is assigned with a 7th character of "S" which identifies "sequela." Code(s) are also assigned to identify the late effect or sequela. Usually there will be at least two codes when coding a late effect with the sequela code(s) sequenced first. There are also external cause codes for late effects, which can be found under the main term sequelae in the Alphabetic Index for External Causes (Figure 25-6). A 7th character of "K" may be used to identify encounters for fractures with nonunion.

EXAMPLE

The patient was diagnosed five years ago with drug-induced Parkinson's due to perphenazine, which was taken for schizophrenia, G21.11, T43.3x5S, F20.9.

Sequelae (of)
accident NEC —*see* W00-X58 with 7th character S
assault (homicidal) (any means) —*see* X92-Y08 with 7th character S
homicide, attempt (any means) —*see* X92-Y08 with 7th character S
injury undetermined whether accidentally or purposely inflicted —*see* Y21-Y33 with 7th character S
intentional self-harm (classifiable to X71-X83) —*see* X71-X83 with 7th character S
legal intervention (*see* with 7th character S Y35)
motor vehicle accident —*see* V00-V99 with 7th character S
suicide, attempt (any means) —*see* X71-X83 with 7th character S
transport accident —*see* V00-V99 with 7th character S
war operations —*see* War operations

FIGURE 25-6. Alphabetic Index entry for Sequelae.

EXAMPLE Scar on left wrist due to previous burn by fire, L90.5, T23.072S.

EXAMPLE Patient is being treated for avascular necrosis following previous left scaphoid fracture (traumatic), M87.242, S62.002S.

EXERCISE 25-7

Assign codes to the following conditions.

1. Nonunion of left lateral humeral condylar fracture; patient fell 2 months ago (accidental injury), subsequent encounter ____________
2. Traumatic arthritis due to severe sprain of right ankle 3 years ago (accidental injury) ____________
3. Phantom limb pain due to traumatic AKA (above knee amputation); patient was in a motorcycle accident 6 months ago ____________
4. Spastic quadriplegia due to complete C3 spinal cord injury from diving accident 5 years ago ____________
5. Hypoxic brain injury due to suicide attempt by strangulation 1 year ago ____________

FACTORS INFLUENCING HEALTH STATUS AND CONTACT WITH HEALTH SERVICES (Z CODES)

As was discussed in Chapter 9, it may be difficult to locate Z codes in the index. Coders often say, "I did not know there was a Z code for that." It is important for the coder to be familiar with different types and uses of Z codes. Refer to Chapter 9 for a listing of common main terms used to locate Z codes. See Chapter 24 for Z codes used for injuries.

Z03.6	Encounter for observation for suspected toxic effect from ingested substance ruled out
Z03.810	Encounter for observation for suspected exposure to anthrax ruled out
Z03.818	Encounter for observation for suspected exposure to other biological agents ruled out
Z04.71	Encounter for examination and observation following alleged adult physical abuse
Z04.72	Encounter for examination and observation following alleged child physical abuse
Z04.81	Encounter for examination and observation of victim following forced sexual exploitation
Z04.82	Encounter for examination and observation of victim following forced labor exploitation
Z13.88	Encounter for screening for disorder due to exposure to contaminants
Z18.01	Retained depleted uranium fragments
Z18.09	Other retained radioactive fragments
Z57.1	Occupational exposure to radiation
Z57.39	Occupational exposure to other air contaminants
Z57.4	Occupational exposure to toxic agents in agriculture
Z57.5	Occupational exposure to toxic agents in other industries
Z57.6	Occupational exposure to extreme temperature
Z62.810	Personal history of physical and sexual abuse in childhood
Z62.811	Personal history of psychological abuse in childhood
Z62.812	Personal history of neglect in childhood
Z62.819	Personal history of unspecified abuse in childhood
Z77.010	Contact with and (suspected) exposure to arsenic
Z77.011	Contact with and (suspected) exposure to lead
Z77.012	Contact with and (suspected) exposure to uranium
Z77.018	Contact with and (suspected) exposure to other hazardous metals
Z77.020	Contact with and (suspected) exposure to aromatic amines

Z77.021	Contact with and (suspected) exposure to benzene
Z77.028	Contact with and (suspected) exposure to other hazardous aromatic compounds
Z77.090	Contact with and (suspected) exposure to asbestos
Z77.098	Contact with and (suspected) exposure to other hazardous, chiefly nonmedicinal, chemicals
Z77.110	Contact with and (suspected) exposure to air pollution
Z77.111	Contact with and (suspected) exposure to water pollution
Z77.112	Contact with and (suspected) exposure to soil pollution
Z77.118	Contact with and (suspected) exposure to other environmental pollution
Z77.120	Contact with and (suspected) exposure to mold (toxic)
Z77.121	Contact with and (suspected) exposure to harmful algae and algae toxins
Z77.123	Contact with and (suspected) exposure to radon and other naturally occurring radiation
Z77.128	Contact with and (suspected) exposure to other hazards in the physical environment
Z77.29	Contact with and (suspected) exposure to other hazardous substances
Z77.9	Other contact with and (suspected) exposures hazardous to health
Z87.892	Personal history of anaphylaxis
Z88.0	Allergy status to penicillin
Z88.1	Allergy status to other antibiotic agents
Z88.2	Allergy status to sulfonamides
Z88.3	Allergy status to other anti-infective agents
Z88.4	Allergy status to anesthetic agent
Z88.5	Allergy status to narcotic agent
Z88.6	Allergy status to analgesic agent
Z88.7	Allergy status to serum and vaccine
Z88.8	Allergy status to other drugs, medicaments, and biological substances
Z88.9	Allergy status to unspecified drugs, medicaments and biological substances
Z91.010	Allergy to peanuts
Z91.011	Allergy to milk products
Z91.012	Allergy to eggs
Z91.013	Allergy to seafood
Z91.018	Allergy to other foods
Z91.02	Food additives allergy status
Z91.030	Bee allergy status
Z91.038	Other insect allergy status
Z91.040	Latex allergy status
Z91.041	Radiographic dye allergy status
Z91.048	Other nonmedicinal substances allergy status
Z91.09	Other allergy status, other than to drugs and biological substances
Z91.120	Patient's intentional underdosing of medication regimen due to financial hardship
Z91.128	Patient's intentional underdosing of medication regimen for other reason
Z91.130	Patient's unintentional underdosing of medication regimen due to age-related debility
Z91.138	Patient's unintentional underdosing of medication regimen for other reason
Z91.14	Patient's other noncompliance with medication regimen
Z91.19	Patient's noncompliance with other medical treatment and regimen
Z91.410	Personal history of adult physical and sexual abuse
Z91.411	Personal history of adult psychological abuse
Z91.412	Personal history of adult neglect
Z91.419	Personal history of unspecified adult abuse
Z91.42	Personal history of forced labor or sexual exploitation
Z91.5	Personal history of self-harm

EXAMPLE

Patient was exposed to asbestos while working in a shipyard years ago, Z77.090.

EXAMPLE Patient wears a bracelet because of allergy to penicillin, Z88.0.

EXERCISE 25-8

Assign codes to the following conditions.

1. History of allergy to latex ______
2. History of allergy to Bactrim ______
3. Patient has a history of anaphylactic shock due to bee sting ______
4. History of rape. Patient is an adult ______
5. History of hives due to contrast media or radiologic dye ______
6. Observation for suspected physical abuse (adult), which was ruled out ______

COMMON TREATMENTS

Treatment will depend on the type and severity of the injury. Pain medications, anti-inflammatories, corticosteroids, and antibiotics may be necessary to alleviate pain and inflammation and to prevent or fight infection.

PROCEDURES

Debridement

Debridement of burns is probably the most common procedure that will be assigned in this chapter. The root operation for excisional debridement is excision (cutting out/off without replacement some of a body part). Debridements can be performed in many settings in the hospital including at the bedside, so documentation may be difficult to locate. Debridements do not have to be performed in the operating room. Debridements may also be performed by physical therapists, wound care nurses, and other healthcare professionals in addition to physicians.

According to the ICD-10-PCS guidelines, when an excision is performed on overlapping layers, the body part specifying the deepest layer is coded. If a patient had a debridement of skin, subcutaneous tissue, muscle, and bone, the bone is the deepest layer and debridement of the bone is the only procedure code assigned. (If a nonexcisional debridement is performed, the root operation is extraction.) Examples of nonexcisional debridement include brushing, irrigation, scrubbing, washing of tissue, or utilization of a Versajet device. Documentation of sharp debridement does not always mean that an excisional debridement was performed. Definite cutting away of tissue and not just removal of loose tissue fragments with a sharp instrument must be documented in order to code excisional debridement. The documentation for coding an excisional debridement must meet the root operation definition of "excision" and/or the provider documents excisional debridement. If there is any question as to whether the debridement is excisional or nonexcisional, the provider should be queried.

EXAMPLE Excisional debridement of infected burn right palm (skin) performed by physician. Patient was burned by hot light bulb, T23.051A, L08.89, X15.8xxA, 0HBFXZZ.

SECTION	BODY SYSTEM	ROOT OPERATION	BODY PART	APPROACH	DEVICE	QUALIFIER
Medical and Surgical	Skin and Breast	Excision	Skin, Right Hand	External	No Device	No Qualifier
0	H	B	F	X	Z	Z

EXAMPLE

Excisional debridement subcutaneous tissue of fourth-degree burn lower back by physician, T21.34xA, 0JB70ZZ.

SECTION	BODY SYSTEM	ROOT OPERATION	BODY PART	APPROACH	DEVICE	QUALIFIER
Medical and Surgical	Subcutaneous Tissue and Fascia	Excision	Subcutaneous Tissue and Fascia, Back	Open	No Device	No Qualifier
0	J	B	7	0	Z	Z

Hyperbaric Oxygen Therapy

Hyperbaric oxygen therapy (HBOT) is a treatment in which the patient's entire body is placed in a transparent, airtight chamber at increased atmospheric pressure. The patient breathes in 100% pure oxygen. This increased oxygen flow in the body helps to improve healing within the tissues and helps to get rid of toxic gases in the case of a poisoning. The ICD-10-PCS codes for HBOT can be found in the extracorporeal assistance and performance section.

HBOT is helpful in treating medical conditions such as the following:

- Air or gas embolism (in divers or following bypass surgery)
- Decompression sickness in divers (bends)
- Burns and other wounds
- Carbon monoxide poisoning
- Smoke inhalation
- Near drowning, near electrocution, or near hanging
- Diabetic ulcers/skin ulcers

EXAMPLE

Patient is being treated with a single HBOT for decompression sickness while surfacing while scuba diving in the ocean, T70.3xxA, W94.21xA, Y92.832, Y93.15, 6A150ZZ.

SECTION	BODY SYSTEM	ROOT OPERATION	BODY SYSTEM	DURATION	QUALIFIER	QUALIFIER
Extracorporeal Therapies	Physiological Systems	Decompression	Circulatory	Single	No Qualifier	No Qualifier
6	A	1	5	0	Z	Z

EXERCISE 25-9

Assign codes for all diagnoses and procedures.

1. Z-plasty to release scar contracture, left forearm ______________
2. Excisional debridement of skin in patient with second-degree burn, right knee ______________
3. Excisional debridement of subcutaneous tissue in patient with second- and third-degree burns to back, performed at the patient's bedside ______________
4. Excisional debridement to the soft tissue of deep burns, left thigh ______________
5. Full-thickness skin graft to deep third-degree burn area of the right hand. Graft from patient's left thigh ______________

CHAPTER REVIEW EXERCISE

Assign codes for all diagnoses and procedures. Explain why it is an adverse effect or a poisoning.

1. Alcoholic drank rubbing alcohol, undetermined circumstances ______________________________

____

2. Anaphylactic shock due to shellfish ______

3. Gastrointestinal bleeding due to excessive use of aspirin for chronic low back pain (accidental) ______

4. Orthostatic hypotension due to Nitro-Bid taken for stable angina ______

5. Depression due to Keppra, which was taken for a seizure disorder ______

6. Accidental ingestion of Drano with burns of the mouth and esophagus ______

7. Drug-induced dementia due to Lithium. Lithium is taken for bipolar disorder______

8. Coma due to accidental alcohol poisoning with blood alcohol of 400 mg/100 mL ______

9. Abnormal level of mercury in blood indicating poisoning. No symptoms______

10. Accidental injury with chemical burns to bilateral eyelids from Roundup chemical used on the job doing farm work ______

11. Weakness and tremor due to Lithium toxicity. Patient has bipolar type I, currently depressed with psychotic features. Lithium taken as prescribed______

12. Drug-induced hepatitis due to isoniazid, which is being taken because of exposure to tuberculosis ______

13. Bite by poisonous rattlesnake ______

14. Steroid-induced hyperglycemia due to prednisone ______

15. Paralytic ileus due to interaction of anticholinergics and codeine ______

16. Patient admitted with hyperglycemia with uncontrolled diabetes due to unintentional underdosing of metformin. Patient has dementia, which interferes with taking medications as prescribed ______

Assign codes for all diagnoses and procedures.

17. Chemical burn on right knee due to leaking ice pack that was used for knee injury. The skin is reddened with no blister formation ______

18. History of exposure to lead. No apparent symptoms ______

19. Malunion of left radial shaft fracture. Previous accidental injury ______

20. Firefighter suffers smoke inhalation after fighting warehouse fire ________________

21. Hypothermia due to cold weather. Patient is homeless ________________

22. Second-degree burns to left foot due to accidental scald injury with hot water from bathroom sink at home ________________

23. Toddler was admitted due to physical abuse with third- and fourth-degree burns on buttocks, lower legs, and feet. Patient was put into boiling water by the mother's boyfriend. Twenty percent of his body was affected ________________

24. Extensive burns 50% of body with 18% third degree. Patient was in a motor vehicle accident (MVA) that occurred on Interstate highway ________________

25. SIRS due to crush injury to chest. Patient driver of MV that hit deer on roadway________________

26. Second-degree burns to right hand and third-degree burns to left hand due to grease fire while working as employee at restaurant. Excisional debridement of the subcutaneous tissue of left hand done in the Operating Room________________

Write the correct answer(s) in the space(s) provided.

27. Define excisional debridement.

____

____

28. Describe the code assignment for underdosing of a medication.

____

29. What degree of burn results in full-thickness skin loss?

____

30. Define adverse effect of a drug.

____

CHAPTER GLOSSARY

Adverse effect: pathologic manifestation due to ingestion or exposure to drugs or other chemical substances.

Corrosion: burn due to a chemical.

Erythema: redness of the skin.

Frostbite: occurs when skin and underlying tissues freeze due to extreme cold.

Hyperbaric oxygen therapy (HBOT): treatment in which the patient's entire body is placed in a transparent, airtight chamber at increased atmospheric pressure.

Rhabdomyolysis: breakdown of muscle fibers that results in the release of muscle fiber contents into the circulation.

Systemic inflammatory response syndrome: a serious medical condition that can occur in response to infectious or noninfectious causes, such as severe trauma, burns, or complications of surgery.

Underdosing: taking less of a medication than is prescribed by a provider or a manufacturer's instructions.

26

Complications of Surgical and Medical Care

CHAPTER OUTLINE

LEARNING OBJECTIVES

1. Apply and assign the correct ICD-10-CM/PCS codes in accordance with Official Guidelines for Coding and Reporting
2. Identify complications of surgical and medical care
3. Assign the correct Z codes, codes, and procedure codes related to complications of surgical and medical care

ABBREVIATIONS/ ACRONYMS

CKD chronic kidney disease

ECT electroconvulsive therapy

ESRD end-stage renal disease

HAP hospital acquired pneumonia

ICD-10-CM *International Classification of Diseases, 10th Revision, Clinical Modification*

IUD intrauterine device

PE pulmonary embolism

UTI urinary tract infection

VAP ventilator assisted pneumonia

ICD-10-CM Official Guidelines for Coding and Reporting (2021-2022)

Please refer to the companion Evolve website for the most current 2021-2022 guidelines.

Section II. Selection of a Principal Diagnosis

G. Complications of surgery and other medical care

When the admission is for treatment of a complication resulting from surgery or other medical care, the complication code is sequenced as the principal diagnosis. If the complication is classified to the T80-T88 series and the code lacks the necessary specificity in describing the complication, an additional code for the specific complication should be assigned.

Section I. Conventions, general coding guidelines and chapter specific guidelines

C. Chapter-Specific Coding Guidelines

1. Chapter 1: Certain Infectious and Parasitic Diseases (A00-B99)

d. Sepsis, Severe Sepsis, and Septic Shock

5) Sepsis due to a postprocedural infection

(a) Documentation of causal relationship

As with all postprocedural complications, code assignment is based on the provider's documentation of the relationship between the infection and the procedure.

(b) Sepsis due to a postprocedural infection

For infections following a procedure, a code from T81.40 to T81.43, Infection following a procedure, or a code from O86.00 to O86.03, Infection of obstetric surgical wound, that identifies the site of the infection should be coded first, if known. Assign an additional code for sepsis following a procedure (T81.44) or sepsis following an obstetric procedure (O86.04). Use an additional code to identify the infectious agent. If the patient has severe sepsis the appropriate code from subcategory R65.2 should also be assigned with the additional code(s) for any acute organ dysfunction.

For infections following infusion, transfusion, therapeutic injection, or immunization, a code from subcategory T80.2, Infection following infusion, transfusion, and therapeutic injection, or code T88.0-, Infection following immunization, should be coded first, followed by the code for the specific infection. If the patient has severe sepsis, the appropriate code from subcategory R65.2- should also be assigned, with the additional code(s) for any acute organ dysfunction.

(c) Postprocedural infection and postprocedural septic shock

If a postprocedural infection has resulted in postprocedural septic shock, assign the codes indicated above for sepsis due to a postprocedural infection, followed by code T81.12-, Postprocedureal septic shock. Do not assign code R65.21, Severe sepsis with septic shock. Additional code(s) should be assigned for any acute organ dysfunction.

EXAMPLE

The patient was readmitted after undergoing surgery last week; the patient is being treated for sepsis due to previous surgery, T81.44xA, A41.9, Y83.9.

2. Chapter 2: Neoplasms (C00-D49)

c. Coding and sequencing of complications

4) Treatment of a complication resulting from a surgical procedure

When the admission/encounter is for treatment of a complication resulting from a surgical procedure, designate the complication as the principal or first-listed diagnosis if treatment is directed at resolving the complication.

l. Sequencing of neoplasm codes

5) Complication from surgical procedure for treatment of a neoplasm

When an encounter is for treatment of a complication resulting from a surgical procedure performed for the treatment of the neoplasm, designate the complication as the principal/first-listed diagnosis. See the guideline regarding the coding of a current malignancy versus personal history to determine if the code for the neoplasm should also be assigned.

r. Malignant neoplasm associated with transplanted organ

A malignant neoplasm of a transplanted organ should be coded as a transplant complication. Assign first the appropriate code from category T86.-, Complications of transplanted organs and tissue, followed by code C80.2, Malignant neoplasm associated with transplanted organ. Use an additional code for the specific malignancy.

EXAMPLE

Hernia of colostomy with laparoscopic repair of parastomal hernia. The colostomy was performed 1 year ago during colon cancer resection. The patient is no longer receiving treatment, and the cancer was completely resected, K43.5, Z85.038, Z90.49, Y83.3, 0WQF4ZZ.

EXAMPLE

Patient is admitted with abdominal pain. The patient had previously received a kidney transplant. After study it is determined that the patient had renal carcinoma of the transplanted kidney, T86.19, C80.2, C64.9.

4. Chapter 4: Endocrine, Nutritional, and Metabolic Diseases (E00-E89)

a. Diabetes mellitus

5) Complications due to insulin pump malfunction

(a) Underdose of insulin due to insulin pump failure

An underdose of insulin due to an insulin pump failure should be assigned to a code from subcategory T85.6, Mechanical complication of other specified internal and external prosthetic devices, implants and grafts, that specifies the type of pump malfunction, as the principal or first listed code, followed by code T38.3x6-, Underdosing of insulin and oral hypoglycemic [antidiabetic] drugs. Additional codes for the type of diabetes mellitus and any associated complications due to the underdosing should also be assigned.

(b) Overdose of insulin due to insulin pump failure

The principal or first-listed code for an encounter due to an insulin pump malfunction resulting in an overdose of insulin, should also be T85.6-, Mechanical complication of other specified internal and external prosthetic devices, implants and grafts, followed by code T38.3x1-, Poisoning by insulin and oral hypoglycemic [antidiabetic] drugs, accidental (unintentional).

6) Secondary diabetes mellitus

(b) Assigning and Sequencing secondary diabetes codes and its causes

(i) Secondary diabetes mellitus due to pancreatectomy

For postpancreatectomy diabetes mellitus (lack of insulin due to the surgical removal of all or part of the pancreas), assign code E89.1, Postprocedural hypoinsulinemia. Assign a code from category E13 and a code from subcategory Z90.41-, Acquired absence of pancreas, as additional codes.

EXAMPLE

Patient presents with a kink in the tubing of the insulin pump resulting in underdosing (type 1). This has resulted in diabetic ketoacidosis, T85.694A, E10.10, T38.3x6A, Y84.8.

6. Chapter 6: Diseases of Nervous System (G00-G99)

b. Pain—Category G89

2) Pain due to devices, implants and grafts

See Section I.C.19. Pain due to medical devices

3) Postoperative Pain

The provider's documentation should be used to guide the coding of postoperative pain, as well as *Section III. Reporting Additional Diagnoses* and *Section IV. Diagnostic Coding and Reporting in the Outpatient Setting.*

The default for post-thoracotomy and other postoperative pain not specified as acute or chronic is the code for the acute form.

Routine or expected postoperative pain immediately after surgery should not be coded.

(a) Postoperative pain not associated with specific postoperative complication

Postoperative pain not associated with a specific postoperative complication is assigned to the appropriate postoperative pain code in category G89.

(b) Postoperative pain associated with specific postoperative complication

Postoperative pain associated with a specific postoperative complication (such as painful wire sutures) is assigned to the appropriate code(s) found in Chapter 19, Injury, poisoning, and certain other consequences of external causes. If appropriate, use additional code(s) from category G89 to identify acute or chronic pain (G89.18 or G89.28).

EXAMPLE

Patient presents to doctor's office with the chief complaint of acute postoperative pain. Patient is 1 week status post laparoscopic appendectomy, G89.18, Z90.49.

9. Chapter 9: Diseases of Circulatory System (I00-I99)

c. Intraoperative and Postprocedural Cerebrovascular Accident

Medical record documentation should clearly specify the cause- and-effect relationship between the medical intervention and the cerebrovascular accident in order to assign a code for intraoperative or postprocedural cerebrovascular accident. Proper code assignment depends on whether it was an infarction or hemorrhage and whether it occurred intraoperatively or postoperatively. If it was a cerebral hemorrhage, code assignment depends on the type of procedure performed.

EXAMPLE

The patient had an intraoperative cerebrovascular accident, which was embolic in nature. The patient initially had been admitted for treatment of coronary artery arteriosclerosis with CABG, I25.10, I97.810, I63.40, Y83.2, (codes for procedure not included).

10. Chapter 10: Diseases of Respiratory System (J00-J99)

d. Ventilator associated Pneumonia

1) Documentation of Ventilator associated Pneumonia

As with all procedural or postprocedural complications, code assignment is based on the provider's documentation of the relationship between the condition and the procedure.

Code J95.851, Ventilator associated pneumonia, should be assigned only when the provider has documented ventilator associated pneumonia (VAP). An additional code to identify the organism (e.g., Pseudomonas aeruginosa, code B96.5) should also be assigned. Do not assign an additional code from categories J12-J18 to identify the type of pneumonia.

Code J95.851 should not be assigned for cases where the patient has pneumonia and is on a mechanical ventilator but the provider has not specifically stated that the pneumonia is ventilator-associated pneumonia. If the documentation is unclear as to whether the patient has a pneumonia that is a complication attributable to the mechanical ventilator, query the provider.

2) Ventilator associated Pneumonia Develops after Admission

A patient may be admitted with one type of pneumonia (e.g., code J13, Pneumonia due to Streptococcus pneumonia) and subsequently develop VAP. In this instance, the principal diagnosis would be the appropriate code from categories J12-J18 for the pneumonia diagnosed at the time of admission. Code J95.851, Ventilator associated pneumonia, would be assigned as an additional diagnosis when the provider has also documented the presence of ventilator associated pneumonia.

EXAMPLE

Patient was hospitalized last month and was on a ventilator for exacerbation of COPD. She presents to the hospital today with pneumonia, J18.9, J44.9.

EXAMPLE

Patient was recently admitted for an acute exacerbation of CHF for which she was placed on a ventilator. She presents to the hospital today with ventilator associated pneumonia. Sputum cultures were taken and this pneumonia was found to be due to MRSA, J95.851, I50.9, B95.62, Y84.8.

EXAMPLE

Patient was admitted to the hospital in acute respiratory failure due to pneumonia. She is placed in the ICU intubated and on a vent for 120 hours. She is transferred to the floor where she develops a high fever. The physician documents ventilator associated pneumonia due to *Pseudomonas aeruginosa,* J96.00, J18.9, J95.851, B96.5, Y84.8, Y92.230, 5A1955Z, 0BH17EZ.

19. Chapter 19: Injury, poisoning, and certain other consequences of external causes (S00-T88)

g. Complications of care

1) General guidelines for complications of care

(a) Documentation of complications of care

See Section I.B.16. for information on documentation of complications of care.

2) Pain due to medical devices

Pain associated with devices, implants or grafts left in a surgical site (for example painful hip prosthesis) is assigned to the appropriate code(s) found in Chapter 19, Injury, poisoning, and certain other consequences of external causes. Specific codes for pain due to medical devices are found in the T code section of the ICD-10-CM. Use additional code(s) from category G89 to identify acute or chronic pain due to presence of the device, implant or graft (G89.18 or G89.28).

EXAMPLE Patient presents with acute pain secondary to a displaced nail in the right femur, T84.124A, G89.18, M79.604, Y83.1.

3) Transplant complications

(a) Transplant complications other than kidney

Codes under category T86, Complications of transplanted organs and tissues, are for use for both complications and rejection of transplanted organs. A transplant complication code is only assigned if the complication affects the function of the transplanted organ. Two codes are required to fully describe a transplant complication: the appropriate code from category T86 and a secondary code that identifies the complication.

Pre-existing conditions or conditions that develop after the transplant are not coded as complications unless they affect the function of the transplanted organs.

See Section I.C.21. for transplant organ removal status

See Section I.C.2. for malignant neoplasm associated with transplanted organ.

EXAMPLE A patient with a previous intestinal transplant presents with diarrhea which has been diagnosed as acute graft-versus-host disease, T86.858, D89.810, R19.7, Y83.0.

(b) Kidney transplant complications

Patients who have undergone kidney transplant may still have some form of chronic kidney disease (CKD) because the kidney transplant may not fully restore kidney function. Code T86.1- should be assigned for documented complications of a kidney transplant, such as transplant failure or rejection or other transplant complication. Code T86.1- should not be assigned for post kidney transplant patients who have chronic kidney (CKD) unless a transplant complication such as transplant failure or rejection is documented. If the documentation is unclear as to whether the patient has a complication of the transplant, query the provider.

Conditions that affect the function of the transplanted kidney, other than CKD, should be assigned a code from subcategory T86.1, Complications of transplanted organ, Kidney, and a secondary code that identifies the complication.

For patients with CKD following a kidney transplant, but who do not have a complication such as failure or rejection, *see section I.C.14. Chronic kidney disease and kidney transplant status.*

EXAMPLE Patient with history of kidney transplant presents to the ER with gastroenteritis. His review of systems documents CKD and hypertension, K52.9, I12.9, N18.9, Z94.0.

EXAMPLE Patient with history of kidney transplant presents to hospital in acute renal failure due to rejection, T86.11, N17.9, Y83.0.

4) **Complication codes that include the external cause**
As with certain other T codes, some of the complications of care codes have the external cause included in the code. The code includes the nature of the complication as well as the type of procedure that caused the complication. No external cause code indicating the type of procedure is necessary for these codes.

5) **Complications of care codes within the body system chapters**
Intraoperative and postprocedural complication codes are found within the body system chapters with codes specific to the organs and structures of that body system. These codes should be sequenced first, followed by a code(s) for the specific complication, if applicable.

Complication codes from the body system chapters should be assigned for intraoperative and postprocedural complications (e.g., the appropriate complication code from Chapter 9 should be assigned for a vascular intraoperative or postprocedural complication(s) unless the complication is specifically indexed to a T code in Chapter 19.

EXAMPLE Patient recently had a below the knee amputation of his right leg. He now presents to the surgeon's office with an infection of the amputation stump, T87.43, Y83.5.

EXAMPLE Patient presents to the ER with a nonfunctioning colostomy, K94.03, Y83.3.

ANATOMY AND PHYSIOLOGY

Complications of surgical or medical care can affect any of the body systems. The anatomy and physiology of these body systems are outlined in their respective chapters. Find below some general guidelines that apply to complications.

CODING COMPLICATIONS

Several general guidelines should be kept in mind when coding complications.

- No time limit: can occur after medical care or surgery, either immediately or years later.
- Complications after surgery or medical care should be documented as such. Routine events such as fever in the immediate postoperative period are not considered postoperative complications.
- Coding of complications does not imply that poor care or improper care has been delivered.
- Codes for complications may be located in the chapter for specified body sites or under abortion and pregnancy.
- Codes for complications that affect multiple sites or body systems are usually located in codes T80-T88.
- "**Iatrogenic**" is a term that is used to signify that a condition is a result or complication of treatment.
- When in doubt as to whether the condition occurred as the result of a procedure or medical care, it is best practice to query the physician. Coders should not just assume that something is a complication because it occurred after a procedure.
- Complications of surgical and medical care may require an External cause code in the range of Y83-Y84 for abnormal reactions or later complications, or Y62-Y69 if misadventure is stated.
- When the admission is for treatment of a complication resulting from surgery or other medical care, the complication code is sequenced as the principal diagnosis.
- If the complication is classified to T80-T88 and the code lacks necessary specificity to fully describe the complication, an additional code should be assigned for the specific complication.

Obstruction, obstructed, obstructive *(Continued)*
intestine *(Continued)*
by gallstone K56.3
congenital (small) Q41.9
large Q42.9
specified part NEC Q42.8
neurogenic K56.0
Hirschsprung's disease or megacolon Q43.1
newborn P76.9
due to
fecaliths P76.8
inspissated milk P76.2
meconium (plug) P76.0
in mucoviscidosis E84.11
specified NEC P76.8
→ postoperative K91.3

FIGURE 26-1. Obstruction, intestine, postoperative.

Complication(s) *(Continued)*
suture, permanent (wire) NEC *(Continued)*
mechanical
breakdown T85.612
displacement T85.622
malfunction T85.612
malposition T85.622
obstruction T85.692
perforation T85.692
protrusion T85.692
specified NEC T85.692
pain T85.848
specified type NEC T85.898
stenosis T85.858
thrombosis T85.868
→ tracheostomy J95.00
granuloma J95.09
hemorrhage J95.01
infection J95.02
malfunction J95.03
mechanical J95.03
obstruction J95.03
specified type NEC J95.09
tracheo-esophageal fistula J95.04

FIGURE 26-2. Tracheostomy complication.

Locating Complication Codes in the Alphabetic Index

When looking for a complication code in the index, the condition for which the patient is admitted should be referred to first (Figures 26-1).

EXAMPLE Patient was readmitted for treatment of postoperative intestinal obstruction following appendectomy, K91.3, Z90.49, Y83.6.

When no entry is found under the main term for the condition, the term "complication" should be referenced along with the appropriate subterm (Figures 26-2 and 26-3).

EXAMPLE Patient is admitted with tracheal stenosis of tracheostomy site, J95.03, Y83.3. Note that this complication code is located in the respiratory chapter.

EXAMPLE Patient admitted with cystitis due to indwelling urinary catheter, T83.511A, N30.90, Y84.6.

urethral T83.9
  displacement T83.028
  embolism T83.81
  fibrosis T83.82
  hemorrhage T83.83
  indwelling
    breakdown T83.011
    displacement T83.021
    infection and inflammation T83.511
    leakage T83.031
    specified complication NEC T83.091
  infection and inflammation T83.511
  leakage T83.038
  malposition T83.028
  mechanical
    breakdown T83.011
  obstruction (mechanical) T83.091
  pain T83.84

FIGURE 26-3. Urinary catheter complications, indwelling.

Complication (delayed) **of or following** (medical or surgical procedure) Y84.9
  with misadventure - *see* Misadventure
  amputation of limb(s) Y83.5
  anastomosis (arteriovenous) (blood vessel) (gastrojejunal) (tendon) (natural or artificial material) Y83.2
  aspiration (of fluid) Y84.4
    tissue Y84.8
  biopsy Y84.8

FIGURE 26-4. Cross-reference to other index entries under *complication* in the External cause index.

Locating External Causes of Injury and Poisoning to Correspond With Complication Coding

To locate the corresponding external cause code for complications, begin by locating the Alphabetic Index to External Causes. This index follows the Alphabetic Index to Diseases. Locate the term *complication* to see the cross-references to other index entries (Figure 26-4).

For further detail on external cause codes, refer to Chapter 24 of this textbook.

EXAMPLE

During spinal surgery, the surgeon accidentally nicks the dura due to the amount of adhesions present in the spinal canal, G97.41, G96.12, Y83.8, Y92.234 (Figure 26-5).

CHAPTER-SPECIFIC COMPLICATIONS

In ICD-10-CM, many complications are found in specific chapters. Intraoperative and post-procedural complications may be found within the body system chapters. The coding of complications is one of the more challenging aspects of coding because of the effects on patient safety and quality, health grades, and reimbursement. Not all conditions that occur following a procedure are considered complications. For example, during a joint replacement surgery, there may be a significant amount of bleeding. This is an expected result and should not be coded as a surgical complication. The documentation with regard to a cause-and-effect relationship between the condition and the procedure may not be clear. The provider should be queried when the documentation is sketchy or unclear.

Complications of the Digestive System

Patients who have had some or part of their stomach removed or who have undergone gastric bypass surgery may be susceptible to a condition known as "**dumping syndrome**."

This condition occurs when undigested contents of the stomach are transported to the small intestine too quickly. The symptoms of this condition may include abdominal cramping, nausea, and diarrhea, to name a few. Dumping syndrome may in turn result in weight loss or malnutrition. This syndrome may be treated with dietary changes, as well as with medications.

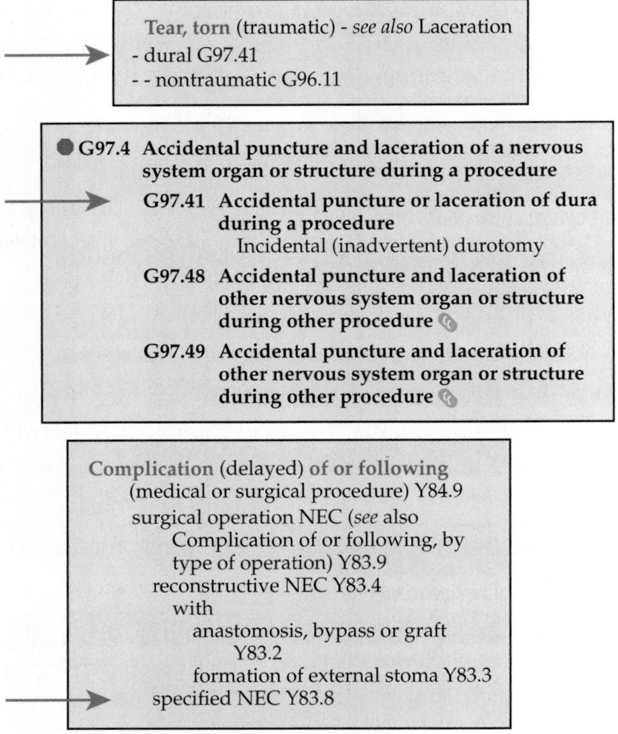

Tear, torn (traumatic) - *see also* Laceration
- dural G97.41
- - nontraumatic G96.11

G97.4 Accidental puncture and laceration of a nervous system organ or structure during a procedure
G97.41 Accidental puncture or laceration of dura during a procedure
Incidental (inadvertent) durotomy
G97.48 Accidental puncture and laceration of other nervous system organ or structure during other procedure
G97.49 Accidental puncture and laceration of other nervous system organ or structure during other procedure

Complication (delayed) of or following
(medical or surgical procedure) Y84.9
surgical operation NEC (*see* also Complication of or following, by type of operation) Y83.9
reconstructive NEC Y83.4
with
anastomosis, bypass or graft Y83.2
formation of external stoma Y83.3
specified NEC Y83.8

FIGURE 26-5. ICD-10-CM excerpts showing correct code assignment for accidental dural tear.

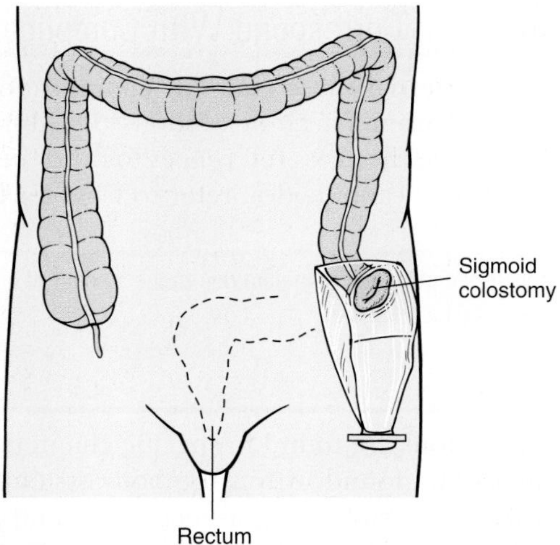

FIGURE 26-6. Colostomy. The opening in the colon is brought to the surface of the skin to divert feces into an external pouch worn by the patient.

EXAMPLE Patient presents with significant weight loss and abdominal pain following a gastric bypass performed for obesity. It is determined that she suffers from dumping syndrome, and dietary changes are suggested, K91.1, Z98.84, R63.4.

Complications of Gastrostomy, Colostomy, Enterostomy

Ostomies are surgically created openings into the body (Figure 26-6). Enterostomies and colostomies are created to discharge waste products from the body; gastrostomies are typically used for feeding or aspirating the contents of the stomach. Sometimes, these surgically created openings result in complications. Complications associated with these openings are caused by a variety of problems such as infection, blockage of the opening, drainage or leakage around the opening, breakage of the device, and granulation of tissue.

If a patient presents to the hospital with a chief complaint of a percutaneous endoscopic gastrostomy (PEG) tube falling out, the principal diagnosis would be Z43.1, or attention to gastrostomy, because no complications resulted from the gastrostomy itself.

EXAMPLE Patient is admitted for a clogged gastrostomy tube, Z43.1.

EXAMPLE Patient presents with cellulitis of the abdominal wall due to an infected colostomy site. The organism responsible for the cellulitis is *Staph aureus,* K94.02, L03.311, B95.61, Y83.3.

Complications of the Genitourinary System

Occasionally, hematuria occurs as the result of a traumatic injury due to forceful removal of a urinary catheter. This is coded as injury of the urethra. In some cases, it may be appropriate to assign an External cause code to indicate the cause and intent of the injury.

EXAMPLE Hematuria due to patient pulling out indwelling urinary catheter with injury to the urethra, S37.30xA, X58.xxxA.

Hematuria is expected after many urinary procedures and should not be coded unless it is excessive and has been documented as such by the physician.

Complications of Dialysis

Several complications may result from dialysis treatment. Many of these conditions are included in other chapters of the ICD-10-CM book. **Dialysis disequilibrium syndrome**, which is characterized by weakness, dizziness, headache, and, in severe cases, mental status changes, is a complication of dialysis. Electrolyte imbalances such as hyperkalemia, hyponatremia, hypocalcemia, hypermagnesemia, and acidosis may also occur. Hypotension and fluid overload can complicate the care of the patient on dialysis. Occasionally, some of these conditions occur because the patient has been noncompliant with dialysis treatment and/or medications and diet. Complications associated with dialysis catheters may be due to infection or mechanical malfunction. If an infection is present, an additional code may be needed to identify specified infections and causative organisms.

EXAMPLE Patient with ESRD was admitted to the hospital with noncardiogenic fluid overload due to noncompliance with dialysis treatment. Patient has a history of CHF and is on Lasix, E87.70, I50.9, N18.6, Z91.15.

EXAMPLE Leakage of peritoneal dialysis catheter. Patient is on dialysis for end-stage renal disease. Peritoneal catheter was removed, T85.631A, N18.6, Z99.2, Y84.1, 0WPGX3Z.

Complications of the Musculoskeletal System

Common complications of joint replacement include infection, blood clot, nerve injury, dislocation, wear and tear, and breakage of the prosthesis. It may be necessary to remove the prosthesis and insert a new prosthesis. According to *Coding Clinic for ICD-10-CM/PCS* (2015:2Q:p6), the removal of fixation hardware because of loose screws is not considered a complication because it is an expected outcome. When orthopedic devices are used to align and link two bones, the screws will hold the bones in position during the healing process, but, once the patient starts to bear weight, the screw is expected to break or loosen. It may be necessary to remove the device.

EXAMPLE Patient presents with dislocation of a right hip replacement. An open revision must be performed, T84.020A, Y83.1, 0SW90JZ (Figure 26-7).

joint prosthesis, internal T84.9
  breakage (fracture) T84.01-
  dislocation T84.02-
  fracture T84.01-
  instability T84.02-
  subluxation T84.02-
  infection or inflammation T84.50
    hip T84.5-
    knee T84.5-
    specified joint NEC T84.59
  malposition - *see* Complications, joint prosthesis, mechanical, displacement
  mechanical
    breakage, broken T84.01-
    dislocation T84.02-
    fracture T84.01-
    instability T84.02-
    subluxation T84.02-

FIGURE 26-7. Complication of hip replacement.

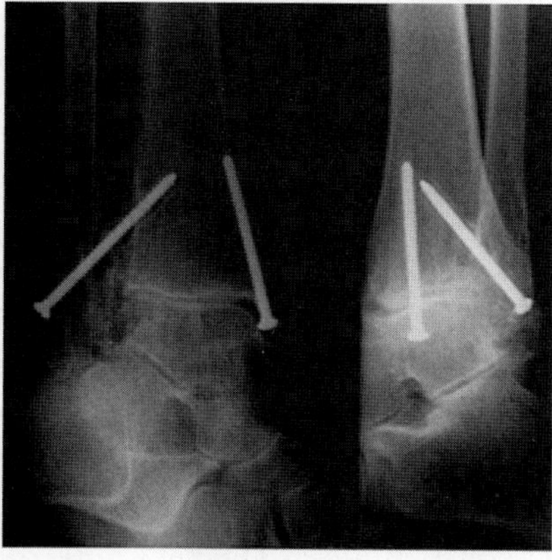

FIGURE 26-8. Surgical correction of malunion ankle fracture.

Malunion/Nonunion of Fractures

Malunion of a fracture occurs when the fracture fragments have united but are not properly aligned. Incorrectly positioned bones may demonstrate angulation, rotation, and shortening. The degree and severity of the malunion will determine the selection of treatment, which may include surgery (Figure 26-8).

Nonunion of a fracture occurs when bony healing is not achieved at the fracture site. A fracture site that fails to heal within approximately 6 to 9 months of the injury represents a nonunion (Figure 26-9).

Malunion or nonunion may occur as the result of insufficient or improper reduction and immobilization, infection, metabolic bone disease, poor nutrition, and/or inadequate blood supply. Improper healing may be noted in cases of traumatic fracture and pathologic fracture and is considered a "late effect" or sequela of a fracture.

EXAMPLE Patient's x-rays showed nonunion of left tibial shaft fracture, S82.202K.

EXAMPLE Patient presents with pain and swelling in the ankle status post casting 3 weeks ago. Patient suffered a closed fracture of the left ankle. It is determined that the patient has a malunion of the fracture, and the patient is scheduled next week for surgery to correct the malunion, S82.892P.

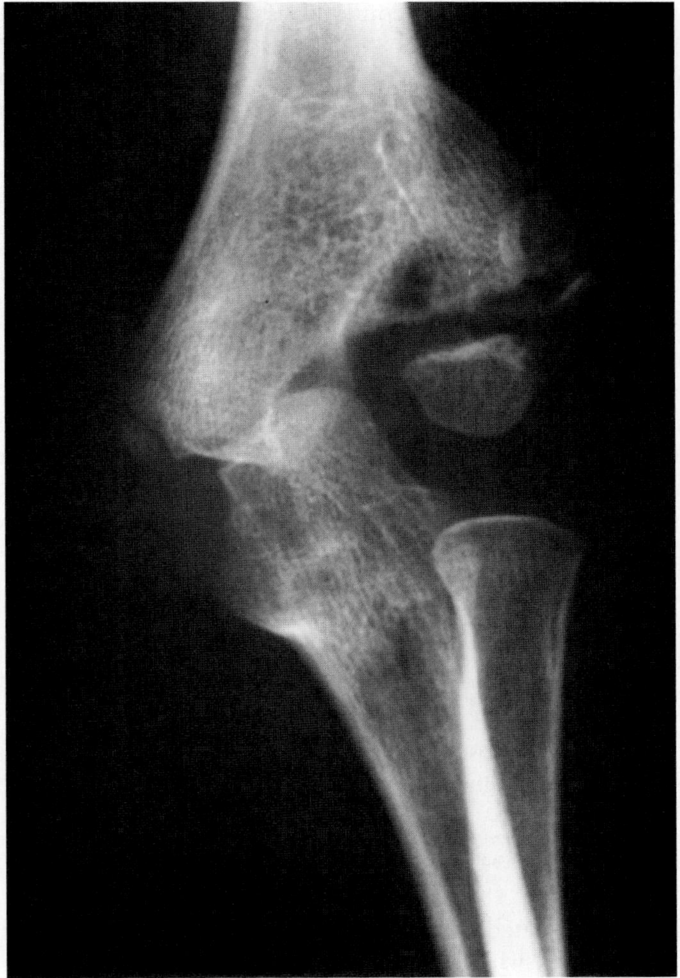

FIGURE 26-9. Nonunion of the lateral humeral condyle.

Complications of the Nervous System and Sense Organs

One of the most common complications discussed in this chapter is a spinal headache. A spinal headache, which is also known as a postdural puncture headache, may occur following a spinal tap (lumbar puncture) or spinal anesthesia. These headaches are caused by spinal fluid that is leaking from the puncture site of the procedure. The patient may experience nausea, vomiting, dizziness, ringing in the ears, and/or sensitivity to light. Treatment for the headache consists of lying flat and drinking fluids, particularly those that include caffeine. If these conservative treatments do not help, an epidural blood patch to seal the puncture hole may be required.

EXAMPLE

Patient develops a severe headache 1 day post lumbar puncture performed because of high fever and stiff neck to rule out meningitis, attending documents post-procedural headache, G97.1, R50.9, M43.6, Y84.4, 009U3ZX.

Complications of the Respiratory System

A **pulmonary embolism** (PE) is a blockage in an artery of the lung that can be life threatening. This blockage commonly is caused by a blood clot that started in the leg and then traveled to the lung. A pulmonary embolism may occur as a result of a surgical procedure. If a patient has recently had surgery and presents with sudden shortness of breath, chest pain, or cough, a pulmonary embolism may be suspected. To determine whether a patient has a PE, scans or angiograms may be performed. Treatment consists of anticoagulant drugs such as heparin. When a condition is the result of treatment or surgery, it is referred to as iatrogenic.

Pulmonary embolism and deep vein thrombosis may also be the result of immobilization following surgery. If this is the case, it is not a complication of the surgical procedure and should not be coded as such. Patients may even experience a DVT due to immobilization following an extended hospital stay. A provider query may be necessary if there is any question regarding the cause of the pulmonary embolism or deep vein thrombosis.

EXAMPLE

Patient presents with shortness of breath and chest pain. Two weeks before presentation, the patient had a right total hip replacement. A pulmonary angiogram is performed, as is a Doppler ultrasound of the legs. The attending documents that the patient is positive for both a pulmonary embolism in the pulmonary artery and a right lower leg deep vein thrombosis secondary to recent surgery, T81.718A, T81.72xA, I26.99, I82.4Z1, Z96.641, Y83.1.

A pneumothorax is another condition that can result from medical treatment. A **pneumothorax** is air in the space around the lung. Procedures such as central venous lines, chest tubes, and mechanical ventilation may inadvertently cause an iatrogenic pneumothorax. A patient may have symptoms of chest pain or shortness of breath. A chest x-ray or CT scan can be used to diagnose this condition.

EXAMPLE

Patient with a chronic cough undergoes a left transbronchial right lung biopsy. A chest x-ray is performed following this procedure, and a pneumothorax is noted. Attending physician decides that since the pneumothorax is small, the condition will be monitored by chest x-ray, R05, J95.811, Y83.8, Y92.234, 0BBK8ZX.

Patients with tracheostomies often develop complications related to the tracheostomy site. A patient can have infection or bleeding or mechanical complications at the site.

EXAMPLE

Patient presents with cellulitis of the neck secondary to an infected tracheostomy site, J95.02, L03.221, Y83.3.

Ventilator associated pneumonia is a type of hospital acquired pneumonia (HAP) that may occur in people who have been on a ventilator.

As with any postprocedural complication, code assignment must be based on provider documentation of the relationship between the procedure and condition. In the case of ventilator associated pneumonia, the provider must document the association of the use of a ventilator with the pneumonia. If the documentation is unclear about the association, the provider may be queried. An additional code may be used to identify the organism (B95-, B96-, B97-).

It is possible for a patient to be admitted with pneumonia and later develop ventilator associated pneumonia. In this case, the code for pneumonia would be assigned as the principal diagnosis with the complication code for the VAP assigned as a secondary diagnosis.

Ventilation pneumonitis is not the same as ventilator associated pneumonia. Ventilation pneumonitis is the result of inhalation of organisms growing in air conditioning systems.

EXAMPLE

Patient is admitted to the hospital with pneumonia. After reviewing the records from an outside hospital, the physician documents that it appears this pneumonia is due to the use of a ventilator on the previous admission, J95.851, Y84.8.

EXERCISE 26-1

Assign codes to the following conditions.

1. Patient is seen in the office for malfunctioning gastrostomy tube ____________
2. Two weeks prior to this admission patient had a resection of the intestine. The patient is now being seen for excessive vomiting following this surgery ____________
3. Patient presents following a hysterectomy with pelvic pain and is now diagnosed with residual ovary syndrome ____________

4. One month prior to this visit the patient had a left total knee replacement. The patient presents with pain and swelling of the knee and is diagnosed with an infection of the knee prosthesis __________
5. Patient is noted to have cerebral spinal fluid (CSF) leaking from the nose due to recent lumbar puncture __________
6. Patient with peritoneal dialysis catheter presents with inflammation of the skin around the catheter; patient has ESRD, initial encounter __________
7. Patient with pelvic inflammatory disease attributed to an intrauterine device (IUD) __________
8. Patient is admitted for removal of her intramedullary rod because of leg pain __________
9. Cellulitis of the skin of the right knee due to right knee replacement, initial encounter __________
10. Patient with bilateral lung transplant presents with pneumonia __________
11. Patient is rejecting transplanted kidney __________
12. Patient has graft-versus-host disease; status post bone marrow transplant __________
13. Patient with an intestine transplant presents with dehydration __________
14. Patient with a ventricular shunt presents with severe headache due to stenosis of the shunt; patient has hydrocephalus __________
15. Patient with an abscess of a gastrostomy tube site due to *Staph aureus* __________
16. Patient with left pleural effusion develops iatrogenic pneumothorax following insertion of a chest tube __________

COMPLICATIONS OF SURGICAL AND MEDICAL CARE NOT ELSEWHERE CLASSIFIED (T80-T88)

Complications of Surgical and Medical Care, codes T80-T88 are found in ICD-10-CM, in Chapter 19 (Figure 26-10).

It is important to note that the instructional notes for this section remind the user to use an additional code to identify the specified condition that results from the complication, as well as an additional code from Y62-Y82 to identify the devices involved and the details of the circumstances. It is also important to note the many Excludes2 notes in this section.

Complications Following Infusion, Transfusion, and Therapeutic Injection

There are many and varied risks that can be associated with infusions, transfusions, and injections. Some reactions may be minor and consist of fevers or urticarial reactions. Others can be more serious such as thrombosis, infections, and even shock.

There are codes in ICD-10-CM that cover the **extravasation** (i.e., the leakage of infused substances into the vasculature or into the subcutaneous tissue). If this occurs, there can be significant complications or tissue breakdown. Medicinal drugs that may cause only slight damage if extravasated are called irritants, and medicinal drugs that may cause severe damage, up to tissue necrosis, if extravasated are called vesicants. Common chemotherapeutic irritant drugs are bleomycin, carboplatin, cisplatin, and doxorubicin. Common chemotherapeutic vesicant drugs are doxorubicin, paclitaxel, and vinicristine.

EXAMPLE

Patient received her first infusion of chemotherapy yesterday. She returns to the office today with blistering on the right forearm. It appears that the chemotherapeutic agent has infiltrated, T80.810A, T22.611A, Y84.8.

EXAMPLE

After transfusion, patient presents with thrombophlebitis of right arm, T80.1xxA, I80.8, Y84.8.

Complications of surgical and medical care, not elsewhere classified (T80-T88)
Use additional code for adverse effect, if applicable, to identify drug (T36-T50 with fifth or sixth character 5)
Use additional code(s) to identify the specified condition resulting from the complication
Use additional code to identify devices involved and details of circumstances (Y62-Y82)
Excludes2: any encounters with medical care for postprocedural conditions in which no complications are present, such as:
artificial opening status (Z93.-)
closure of external stoma (Z43.-)
fitting and adjustment of external prosthetic device (Z44.-)
burns and corrosions from local applications and irradiation (T20-T32)
complications of surgical procedures during pregnancy, childbirth and the puerperium (O00-O9A)
mechanical complication of respirator [ventilator] (J95.850)
poisoning and toxic effects of drugs and chemicals (T36-T65 with fifth or sixth character 1-4 or 6)
postprocedural fever (R50.82)
specified complications classified elsewhere, such as:
cerebrospinal fluid leak from spinal puncture (G97.0)
colostomy malfunction (K94.0-)
disorders of fluid and electrolyte imbalance (E86-E87)
functional disturbances following cardiac surgery (I97.0-I97.1)
intraoperative and postprocedural complications of specified body systems (D78.-, E36.-, E89.-, G97.3-, G97.4, H59.3-, H59.-, H95.2-, H95.3, I97.4-, I97.5, J95.6-, J95.7, K91.6-, L76.-, M96.-, N99.-)
ostomy complicatons (J95.0-, K94-, N99.5-)
postgastric surgery syndromes (K91.1)
postlaminectomy syndrome NEC (M96.1)
postmastectomy lymphedema syndrome (197.2)
postsurgical blind-loop syndrome (K91.2)
ventilator associated pneumonia (J95.851)

FIGURE 26-10. Instruction notes for Complications of Surgical and Medical Care.

Complications of Procedures, Not Elsewhere Classified

This category describes complications that may occur as the result of procedures but are not described by other specific codes. A second code to identify the exact type of complication may be required with this category.

EXAMPLE Patient is admitted for treatment of postoperative wound infection following appendectomy. The patient has developed cellulitis of the abdominal wound, T81.43xA, L03.311, Y83.8.

EXAMPLE Dehiscence of an external abdominal wound following cholecystectomy, T81.31xA, Y83.6.

EXAMPLE Patient presents to the ER with terrible abdominal pain and fever. After performing abdominal x-rays it was discovered that she had a foreign object in her abdomen. She had a cesarean section 6 months prior to this presentation. The intestine has been perforated by this foreign object, T81.530A, K63.1, Y83.8.

EXAMPLE Patient has acute osteomyelitis of femur secondary to infected right hip replacement, T84.51xA, M86.151, Y83.1.

Complications of Internal Prosthetic Devices, Implants, and Grafts

Categories T82-T85 are concerned with mechanical complications of prosthetic devices, implants, and grafts, as well as infection and inflammatory reactions due to other internal prosthetic devices, implants, and grafts. **Mechanical complications** may include items such as breakdown, displacement, leakage, and obstruction of the device implant or graft. For example:

- T82 Complications of cardiac and vascular prosthetic devices, implants, and grafts
- T82.1- through T82.5- Mechanical complications of cardiac and vascular prosthetic devices, implants, and grafts
  - Breakdown
  - Displacement

- Leakage
- Obstruction
- T82.6- through T82.7- Infection and inflammatory reaction to cardiac and vascular devices, implants, and grafts
- T82.8- Other specified complications of cardiac and vascular devices, implants, and grafts
  - Embolism
  - Fibrosis
  - Hemorrhage
  - Pain
  - Stenosis
  - Thrombosis
  - Other
- T82.9- Unspecified complications of cardiac and vascular prosthetic devices, implants, and grafts

Mechanical Complications

Mechanical complications involve equipment malfunctions. If a device is causing a problem or complication such as breakdown, displacement, leakage, obstruction, perforation, or protrusion, the code assigned would be from the section on mechanical complications.

EXAMPLE Patient has ascending cholangitis related to clogged biliary stent, T85.590A, K83.0, Y83.8 (Figure 26-11).

EXAMPLE Patient has a leaking breast implant, T85.43xA, Y83.1.

Infections and Inflammatory Reactions Due to Prosthetic Device, Implants, and Grafts

The presence of a device, implant, or graft carries a risk of infection. It is important to note that the codes in this section may give instruction to use an additional code to identify specified infections.

EXAMPLE Patient has sepsis due to a central venous catheter, T80.211A, A41.9, Y84.8.

Complication(s) *(Continued)*
bile duct implant (prosthetic) T85.89
embolism T85.818
fibrosis T85.828
hemorrhage T85.838
infection and inflammation T85.79
mechanical
breakdown T85.510
displacement T85.520
malfunction T85.510
malposition T85.520
→ obstruction T85.590
perforation T85.590
protrusion T85.590
specified NEC T85.590
pain T85.848
specified type NEC T85.898
stenosis T85.858
thrombosis T85.868

FIGURE 26-11. Complications of devices.

Other Specified Complications

Devices can also cause embolisms, thrombosis, stenosis, and fibrosis, as well as hemorrhage and pain. When these conditions are documented they will be found in "Other specified complications."

EXAMPLE Patient is admitted to remove prosthetic right hip because of severe hip pain, T84.84xA, Y83.1, 0SP90JZ.

EXAMPLE Patient with CAD is admitted because of coronary artery stent restenosis and to percutaneously insert new drug-eluting stent, T82.855A, I25.10, Y83.8, 027034Z.

Complications of Transplanted Organs and Tissue

Complications of a transplanted organ include rejection or any posttransplant illnesses that affect the function of a transplanted organ. If illness affects the transplanted organ, two codes are required. The exceptions per guidelines are those patients with a kidney transplant and chronic kidney disease (CKD). In those cases, T86.1- should be used only for complications such as rejection, failure, or a medical condition such as infection affecting the transplanted organ. If documentation is unclear as to whether the CKD is a complication the provider should be queried.

EXAMPLE Acute pyelonephritis of transplanted kidney, T86.13, N10, Y83.0.

Posttransplant surgical complications that do not affect the function of the transplanted organ are coded to the specific surgical complications.

EXAMPLE Patient presents for heart transplant (donor is a victim of a car accident) due to primary cardiomyopathy and postoperatively develops renal failure, which is a complication of the surgery, I42.9, N99.0, N19, Y83.0, 02YA0Z0.
In this case, the complication is affecting the urinary system, not the heart, which is the transplanted organ.

Preexisting conditions or medical conditions that develop after transplant are not coded as complications unless they affect the transplanted organ. Code Z94.- is used as an additional code to identify transplant status when no complications are associated with the transplanted organ. Codes Z94.- and T86 are **NEVER** used together.

EXAMPLE Patient is admitted for treatment of primary liver cancer. Patient had a liver transplant 2 years ago, T86.49, C80.2, C22.8, Y83.0.

Complications Peculiar to Reattachment and Amputation

Some common complications of amputations include infections, neuromas, necrosis, and contractures.

- **Neuroma** is a growth made up of a bundle of nerve fibers.
- **Contracture** is a tightening of muscle and skin that prevents normal movement.
- **Necrosis** is the decay of tissue.

EXAMPLE Patient is seen in the physician's office following a below-the-knee amputation of the left leg. The patient is complaining of a burning pain in the leg. The physician documents a neuroma of the stump, T87.34, Y83.5.

Other Complications of Surgical and Medical Care, Not Elsewhere Classified

This category contains some anesthesia complications as well as some codes that don't fall into other more specified categories.

EXAMPLE

Hospitalist is called to the ER because of a difficult intubation, T88.4xxA.

EXERCISE 26-2

Assign diagnostic codes to the following conditions.

1. During a surgical procedure, patient goes into cardiac arrest __________
2. Patient develops aspiration pneumonia due to anesthesia __________
3. Patient has a hemicolectomy and is readmitted to the hospital for intractable postoperative vomiting __________
4. Oliguria due to surgical procedure __________
5. Patient is admitted for a *Staphylococcus aureus* infection of a right amputation stump of the lower extremity __________
6. Patient is admitted for removal of a sponge left in during a hysterectomy, initial encounter __________
7. Patient develops a hematoma of the operative wound, initial encounter, following an appendectomy __________
8. Patient develops anaphylactic shock after a blood transfusion, initial encounter __________

CHAPTER REVIEW EXERCISE

Where applicable, assign codes for diagnoses, procedures, and Z codes and external cause codes.

1. Postoperative septicemia, initial encounter __________
2. Internal abdominal surgical wound dehiscence, initial encounter __________
3. Patient with abdominal adhesions due to surgical instrument left in body cavity, initial encounter __________
4. Perforation of coronary artery due to coronary artery stent insertion __________
5. During hemicolectomy, doctor inadvertently makes a rent in the intestine, which is documented as a complication __________
6. Infection of the urostomy __________
7. Rejection of a skin graft __________
8. Mechanical breakdown of an insulin pump. Patient has type 1 diabetes, initial encounter __________
9. Thrombophlebitis of the superficial vessels, right lower extremity, as the result of saphenous vein graft harvest, initial encounter __________
10. Patient had an outpatient laparoscopic cholecystectomy today. She is admitted this evening suffering with a postoperative embolic stroke. __________
11. Shock due to surgery, initial encounter __________
12. Hematoma of surgical site __________
13. After a transfusion of PRBC via the peripheral left arm vein, done percutaneously, patient develops high fever __________

14. Cytomegalovirus infection in transplanted kidney ____________
15. Patient had a traumatic amputation of the right upper extremity 1 year ago after a farm accident. The patient had to have the amputation site surgically amputated at a higher level. He presents with a neuroma of the amputation stump ____________

CHAPTER GLOSSARY

Contracture: a tightening of muscle and skin that prevents normal movement.

Dialysis disequilibrium syndrome: characterized by weakness, dizziness, headache, and, in severe cases, mental status changes.

Dumping syndrome: occurs when undigested contents of the stomach are transported to the small intestine too quickly.

Extravasation: leakage of infused substance into vasculature or subcutaneous tissue.

Iatrogenic: caused by medical treatment.

Malunion: occurs when the fracture fragments have united but are not properly aligned. Incorrectly positioned bones may demonstrate angulation, rotation, and shortening.

Mechanical complication: when a device or equipment malfunctions.

Necrosis: the decay of tissue.

Neuroma: a growth made up of a bundle of nerve fibers.

Nonunion: occurs when bony healing is not achieved at the fracture site. A fracture site that fails to heal within approximately 6 to 9 months of the injury represents a nonunion.

Ostomies: surgically created openings in the body.

Pneumothorax: air in space around the lung.

Pulmonary embolism: blood clot(s) in the pulmonary artery that causes blockage in the artery.

REFERENCE

1. American Hospital Association: *Coding Clinic for ICD-10-CM/PCS* 2015:2Q:p6. Planned implant break.

Glossary

Ablation Correction of abnormal heart rhythm by burning of abnormal heart tissue through radiofrequency or other methods such as laser, microwave, or freezing.

Abortion Artificially terminating a pregnancy.

Abscess A localized collection of pus that causes swelling.

Abstracting Extracting data from the health record.

Acromegaly Condition that results when hypersecretion of human growth hormone (hGH) occurs after puberty, along with overgrowth of the face, hands, feet, and soft tissues.

Activities of daily living assessment Measurement of functional level for activities of daily living.

Activities of daily living treatment Exercise or activities to facilitate functional competence for activities of daily living.

Acute A short and relatively severe course.

Acute renal failure Sudden and severe impairment of renal function characterized by oliguria, increased serum urea, and acidosis.

Addison's disease Adrenocortical insufficiency that may be caused by neoplasms, surgical removal of the adrenal gland, autoimmune processes, tuberculosis, hemorrhage, and/or infection.

Adenocarcinomas Malignancies of epithelial glandular tissue such as those found in the breast, prostate, and colon.

Adhesion Scar tissue that forms an abnormal connection between body parts.

Adjunct codes Add-on codes to a primary procedure to provide additional information about the primary procedure that was performed.

Admission diagnosis Diagnosis that brings the patient to the hospital. This will often be a symptom.

Admitting diagnosis The condition that requires the patient to be hospitalized.

Adverse effect Pathologic manifestation due to ingestion or exposure to drugs or other chemical substances.

Affective disorders A category of mental health problems that includes major depressive disorders and bipolar disorders.

AIDS Acquired immunodeficiency syndrome, an incurable disease of the immune system caused by a virus.

Air embolism When air or gas bubbles get into the bloodstream and obstruct the circulation.

Alimentary canal Comprises the mouth, pharynx, esophagus, stomach, small intestine, and large intestine.

Allogenic Tissue or cells transplanted from different individuals of the same species.

Alopecia Hair loss.

Alphabetic Index The index found in the ICD-10-CM book for both disease conditions and procedures.

Alteration Modifying the natural anatomic structure of a body part without affecting the function of the body part (e.g., breast augmentation).

Alzheimer's disease Disorder of the brain that causes a progressive decline in mental and physical function.

Ambulatory Payment Classifications (APCs) Used for outpatient prospective payment.

Amnioinfusion The insertion of normal saline or lactated Ringer's solution into the amniotic sac.

Ancillary services Services provided by a hospital that are additional to a professional service, such as laboratory work and radiology and pathology services.

Anemia Occurs when hemoglobin drops, which interrupts the transport of oxygen throughout the body.

Aneurysm Bulging or ballooning out of a vessel.

Angiodysplasia Type of AVM characterized by dilated or fragile blood vessels.

Angioplasty A procedure performed to treat coronary artery disease. An inflated balloon compresses plaque against artery walls.

Anomaly A deviation from normal standards (e.g., as in congenital defects).

Anorexia Loss of appetite.

Antepartum Time from conception until delivery or childbirth with regard to the mother.

Anterior Front of the body or an organ.

Anthrax Bacterial infection usually found in wild or domestic animals.

Anticoagulants Medications that are used to prevent venous thrombi.

Antiplatelet medications Medications that are used to prevent clumping of platelets or formation of an arterial thrombus.

Apgar Test used to measure the condition of a newborn at birth.

Aphasia Impairment of speech expression and/or word understanding.

Apheresis Procedure that separates different components of blood and removes a certain part of the blood, such as occurs in leukapheresis, plateletpheresis, and plasmapheresis.

Aplastic anemia Reduction in red blood cells due to impairment or failure of bone marrow function.

Appendectomy Removal of the appendix.

Appendicitis Inflammation of the appendix.

Arthropathy Disease that affects the joints.

Arthroscopic Minimally invasive surgery that involves the use of highly specialized instruments to perform surgery through very small incisions on joints.

Arthroscopic approach Requires the use of an arthroscope to examine and perform closed procedures within a joint.

Asbestosis Lung disease due to inhalation of asbestos.

Aspiration pneumonia Inflammation of the lungs and bronchial tubes due to aspiration of foreign material into the lung.

Assistance Taking over a portion of a physiological function by extracorporeal means.

Asthma Chronic disease that affects the airways that carry air into and out of the lungs.

Asthmatic bronchitis Underlying asthmatic problem in patients in whom asthma has become so persistent that clinically significant chronic airflow obstruction is present despite antiasthmatic therapy.

Atherosclerosis Type of arteriosclerosis wherein fatty substances such as plaque block or clog the arteries.

Atmospheric control Extracorporeal control of atmospheric pressure and composition.

Atrophy When a gland becomes smaller.
Attention deficit disorder A common childhood disorder characterized by inattention and impulsivity.
Attention deficit hyperactivity disorder A common childhood disorder characterized by inattention, hyperactivity, and impulsivity.
Autoimmune disorder Disorder that occurs when the immune system attacks itself inappropriately.
Autologous graft Donor and recipient are the same person.
Autologous transfusion Transfusion of a patient's own blood. Blood may have been donated before an elective procedure.
Autonomic nervous system Consists of both sensory and motor functions that involve the central nervous system and internal organs.
Bacteremia Bacteria in blood, which is a laboratory finding.
Baritosis Lung disease due to inhalation of barium.
Barrett's esophagus Precancerous condition that usually occurs in people with chronic GERD.
Basal cell carcinoma (BCC) Most common type of skin cancer.
Benign Neoplasm or tumor; means that it is not malignant.
Benign prostatic hyperplasia Condition resulting in enlargement of the prostate gland; usually occurs in men older than 50 years of age.
Benign prostatic hypertrophy Condition resulting in enlargement of the prostate gland; usually occurs in men older than 50 years of age.
Bilateral procedure Occurs when the same procedure is performed on paired anatomic organs or tissues (i.e., eyes, ears, joints such as shoulder or knee).
Biological response modifiers (BRM) Immunotherapy that can destroy cancer cells, stimulate the immune system to destroy cancer cells, or change cancer cells to normal cells.
Biopsy Removal of a representative sample for pathologic examination and diagnosis.
Bipolar disorder Brain disorder that causes unusual shifts in a person's mood, energy, and ability to function. Different from the normal ups and downs that everyone goes through, the symptoms of bipolar disorder are severe.
Black lung Lung disease due to inhalation of coal dust.
Blalock-Taussig procedure Procedure used to treat patients with tetralogy of Fallot who have insufficient pulmonary arterial flow.
Blood Viscous fluid that circulates through the vessels of the circulatory system as a result of the pumping action of the heart.
Blood pressure The force that blood puts on the arterial walls when the heart beats.
BNP (Brain natriuretic peptide) A hormone that is produced by the heart; a BNP test measures the amount of BNP that is found in the heart.
Body mass index Uses weight and height to estimate body fat.
Body system An anatomic region or a general physiological system on which a procedure is performed.
Bone marrow biopsy Diagnostic procedure that is used to identify types of anemia and cell deficiencies, and to detect leukemia.
Bowel resection Removal of a portion of the bowel.
Brachytherapy Placement of radioactive material directly into or near the cancer.
Bradycardia Slow heart rate, generally fewer than 60 beats per minute.
Bronchi The two air tubes that branch off the trachea and deliver air to both lungs.
Bronchitis Lower respiratory tract or bronchial tree infection characterized by cough, sputum production, and wheezing.
Bronchopulmonary dysplasia Chronic lung disease that develops in babies during the first 4 weeks after birth.
Bronchoscopy Diagnostic endoscopic procedure in which a tube with a tiny camera on the end is inserted through the nose or mouth into the lungs.
Bursitis Inflammation of a bursa, which is a tiny, fluid-filled sac that is found between muscles, tendons, and bones that reduces friction and facilitates movement.
Bypass Altering the route of passage of the contents of a tubular body part (CABG).
Calculus A stone. Calculi, which vary in size, can develop anywhere in the urinary tract.
Candidiasis Fungal infection also known as a *yeast infection.*
Capillaries Smallest blood vessel through which material passes to and from the bloodstream.
Carbuncle Cluster of boils.
Carcinoma in situ Malignant cells that remain within the original site with no spread or invasion into neighboring tissue.
Carcinomas Malignant tumors originating from epithelial tissue (e.g., in the skin, bronchi, and stomach).
Cardiac arrest Sudden loss of heart function.
Cardiomyopathy A disorder of the muscles of the heart chambers that impedes heart function.
Caregiver training Training in activities to support patients' optimal level of function.
Carryover line Used when an entry will not fit on a single line.
Case-mix index A measurement used by hospitals to define how sick their patients are.
Cataract Clouding of the lens of the eye causing obstructed vision.
Category A single three-digit code that describes a disease or a similarly related group of conditions.
Caudal Toward the tail.
Cellulitis Inflammation of the tissue with possible abscess.
Cephalhematoma A condition of blood between the skull and periosteum of a newborn.
Cerebral edema An accumulation of water on the brain, either intracellular or extracellular.
Cervical dysplasia Abnormal growth of cells on the surface of the cervix.
Cervical intraepithelial neoplasia (CIN) Dysplasia that is seen on a biopsy of the cervix.
Cervix The neck of the uterus that serves as an outlet from the uterus.
Chancre An ulcer that forms during the first stage of syphilis.
Change To take out or off a device from a body part and put back an identical or similar device, in or on the same body part, without cutting or puncturing the skin or a mucous membrane (e.g., change gastrostomy tube).
Charge description number A number that designates a particular service or procedure, used to generate a charge on a patient bill.
Chargemaster or **Charge description master** A listing of the services, procedures, drugs, and supplies that can be applied to a patient's bill.
Chemoembolization Intra-arterial administration of chemotherapy with collagen particles to enhance the delivery of chemotherapy to the targeted area.
Chemotherapy Use of drugs or medications to treat disease.
Chief complaint The reason, in the patient's own words, for presenting to the hospital.
Choledocholithiasis Stone lodged in the bile duct.
Cholelithiasis An abnormal condition of stones in the gallbladder.
Cholesteatoma Growth in the middle ear that usually results from repeated ear infections.
Chronic Persistent over a long period.
Chronic bronchitis Condition defined by a mucus-producing cough most days of the month, 3 months out of a year for 2 successive years, with no other underlying disease to explain the cough.

Chronic obstructive pulmonary disease General term used to describe a lung disease in which the airways become obstructed, making it difficult for air to get into and out of the lungs.
Chronic sinusitis Occurs when the sinuses become inflamed and swollen.
Chylothorax Milky fluid consisting of lymph and fat (chyle) that accumulates in the pleural space.
Cirrhosis Liver disease wherein scar tissue replaces healthy tissue and blocks blood flow.
Classification Grouping together of items as for storage and retrieval.
Cleft lip/palate Opening in the lip or palate of an infant that occurs in utero.
Closed fracture Injury in which the bone is broken, but the skin remains intact.
Closed head injury An injury that results from a blow to the head.
Closed reduction The surgeon manipulates or reduces fractured bones into anatomic alignment without making an incision through the skin and subcutaneous tissue.
Clostridium difficile Microorganisms that are a leading cause of pseudomembranous colitis; also known as *C. diff.*
Coagulation defect Breakdown in the clotting process of the blood.
Coal workers' pneumoconiosis Lung disease due to inhalation of coal dust.
Cognitive deficit Disorder in thinking, learning, awareness, or judgment.
Cognitive impairment Decline in mental activities associated with thinking, learning, and memory.
Colles' fracture Common fracture in adults in which the lower end of the radius is fractured, and the wrist and the hand are displaced backward.
Colostomy A procedure that uses the colon to create an artificial opening.
Combination code A single code used to classify two diagnoses; or a diagnosis with an associated secondary process (manifestation); or a diagnosis with an associated complication.
Communicable Easily spread from one person to another.
Community-acquired pneumonia Broad term used to define pneumonias that are contracted outside of the hospital or nursing home setting.
Comorbidities Preexisting diagnoses or conditions that are present on admission.
Comorbidity A preexisting condition (it is present on admission) which may lead to increased resource use.
Complete abortion Abortion in which all the products of conception are expelled.
Complete remission There are no signs or symptoms of the cancer.
Compliance Adherence to accepted standards.
Complicated fracture Fracture that causes injury to surrounding tissues.
Complication A condition that arises during a patient's hospitalization which may lead to increased resource use.
Compound fracture When the broken bone exits and is visible through the skin, or a deep wound exposes the broken bone through the skin.
Compression Putting pressure on a body region.
Computer assisted surgery (CAS) Adjunctive procedure that allows increased visualization and more precise navigation while remaining minimally invasive.
Computerized tomography (CT scans) Computer reformatted digital display of multiplanar images developed from the capture of multiple exposures of external ionizing radiation.
Concussion Injury to the brain that results from a significant blow to the head.
Conduction disorder Abnormalities of cardiac impulses.
Condylomata Wart-type growth found usually in the genital or anal area.
Congenital anomaly An abnormal condition present at birth.
Connecting words Subterms that denote a relationship between a main term or a subterm and an associated condition or etiology.
Consultant Healthcare provider who is asked to see the patient to provide expert opinion outside the expertise of the requestor.
Contaminant A cultured organism that a physician does not believe is responsible for causing a particular infection.
Continuous ambulatory peritoneal dialysis Type of peritoneal dialysis that takes about 15 minutes and is performed 3 to 4 times per day and once at night.
Continuous cycling peritoneal dialysis Type of peritoneal dialysis that uses a cycling machine and is performed while the patient sleeps.
Contracture A tightening of muscle and skin that prevents normal movement.
Control Stopping, or attempting to stop, postprocedural bleeding or other acute bleeding (control of post-prostatectomy hemorrhage, control of bleeding duodenal ulcer, control of retroperitoneal hemorrhage).
Contusion Any mechanical injury that results in hemorrhage beneath unbroken skin.
Conventions General rules for use in classification that must be followed for accurate coding.
Conversion disorder Condition in which a person has some type of sensory or motor (neurologic) symptom(s) that cannot be explained.
Core biopsy Procedure in which a large needle is used to extract a core sample.
Coronary artery bypass graft Surgery performed to bypass an occluded coronary artery.
Coronavirus disease 2019 Infectious disease caused by severe acute respiratory syndrome coronavirus 2 (SARS-CoV-2).
Corrosion Burn due to a chemical.
Cranial Toward the head.
Creation Making a new structure that does not take the place of a body part (creation of vagina in males for sex reassignment).
Credential Degree, certificate, or award that recognizes a course of study taken in a specific field and that acknowledges the competency required.
Crohn's disease (Regional Enteritis) Inflammation of the GI tract, especially the small and large intestine.
Crush injury When a body part is subjected to a high degree of force or pressure, usually after it has been squeezed between two heavy or immobile objects.
Current Procedural Terminology (CPT) A coding system for reporting medical services and procedures.
Cushing's syndrome Condition that results in excessive circulating cortisol levels caused by chronic hypersecretion of the adrenal cortex.
Cystic fibrosis Genetic (inherited) condition that affects the cells that produce mucus, sweat, saliva, and digestive juices. Instead of being thin and slippery, these secretions are thick and sticky, plugging up tubes, ducts, and passageways, especially in the pancreas and lungs.
Cystitis Lower tract infection that affects the bladder.
Cystocele When the bladder descends and presses into the wall of the vagina.
Cystoscopy Approach used for many procedures of the urinary tract.
Cystourethrocele A urethrocele in conjunction with a cystocele.
Debridement Removal of devitalized tissue, necrosis, or slough.
Debulking Procedures performed when it is impossible to remove the tumor entirely.
Decompression Extracorporeal elimination of undissolved gas from body fluids.
Decubitus ulcer Skin ulcer also known as a bed sore.
Deep brain stimulator A device implanted to control tremors.
Deep vein thrombosis A blood clot that forms in a deep vein.
Deficit Reduction Act (DRA) Mandates all acute-care facilities reimbursed under MS-DRGs to identify and report diagnoses that are present at the time of a patient's admission.

Dehiscence Opening of a surgical wound.
Dehydration When the body does not have as much water or fluids as it should.
Delirium tremens Life-threatening condition that may involve severe mental or neurologic changes, such as delirium and/or hallucinations.
Delivery Assisting the passage of the products of conception from the genital canal.
Dementia Progressive deterioration of mental faculties characterized by impaired memory and one or more cognitive impairments such as language, reasoning and judgment, or calculation and problem-solving ability.
Dengue fever A virus transmitted by an infected mosquito.
Department number Ancillary departments (e.g., radiology, laboratory, ER) that have a specific hospital departmental number.
Depression Affective disorder that is characterized by sadness, lack of interest in everyday activities and events, and a sense of worthlessness.
Destruction Physical eradication of all or a portion of a body part by the direct use of energy, force, or a destructive agent (e.g., ablation of endometriosis).
Dermatitis Inflammation of the skin.
Dermis Layer of skin below the epidermis.
Detachment Cutting off all or a portion of the upper or lower extremities (e.g., above-knee amputation).
Detoxification Active management of withdrawal symptoms in a patient who is physically dependent on alcohol or drugs.
Device fitting Fitting of a device designed to facilitate or support achievement of a higher level of function.
Diabetes insipidus Deficiency in the release of vasopressin by the posterior pituitary gland.
Diabetes mellitus Chronic syndrome of impaired carbohydrate, protein, and fat metabolism caused by insufficient production of insulin by the pancreas or faulty utilization of insulin by the cells.
Diagnosis Identification of a disease through signs, symptoms, and tests.
Dialysis disequilibrium syndrome Characterized by weakness, dizziness, headache, and in severe cases, mental status changes.
Diaphragm Dome-shaped muscles at the bottom of the lungs that assist in the process of breathing and in the exchange of oxygen/carbon dioxide.
Differential diagnosis When a symptom may represent a variety of diagnoses.
Dilation Expanding an orifice or the lumen of a tubular body part (e.g., PTCA).
Discharge summary A review of the patient's hospital course. This summary details the reason for admission or tests or procedures performed and how the patient responded.
Dislocation Displacement of the bones that form a joint; separation of the end of a bone from the joint it meets.
Dissection A tear in wall of a vessel.
Disseminated intravascular coagulation Disorder that results in depletion of clotting factors in the blood.
Distal Farther from the median plane; term is often used to describe a location in the limbs.
Diverticula Small pouches in the lining of the mucous membranes of an organ.
Division Cutting into a body part, without draining fluids and/or gases from it, in order to separate or transect the part (e.g., osteotomy).
Dorsal Back of the body or an organ.
Dorsopathies Conditions or diseases that affect the back or spine.
Drainage Taking or letting out fluids and/or gases from a body part (e.g., paracentesis).
Dressing Putting material on a body region for protection.
Dumping syndrome Occurs when undigested contents of the stomach are transported to the small intestine too quickly.
Dyscalculia Learning disability that affects a child's ability to do mathematical calculations.
Dysgraphia Learning disability that affects a child's ability to coordinate movements such as writing.
Dyslexia Learning disability that affects a child's ability to understand or use spoken or written language.
Dysmetabolic Syndrome X Characterized by abdominal obesity, insulin resistance, dyslipidemia and elevated blood pressure or hypertension.
Eating disorders A group of conditions characterized by abnormal eating habits that may affect an individual's physical and psychological well-being. The most common eating disorders are binge-eating disorder, bulimia nervosa, and anorexia nervosa.
Eclampsia Complication of pregnancy characterized by hypertension, edema, proteinuria, and convulsions or seizures.
Ectopic Type of pregnancy that occurs when the egg is implanted outside the cavity of the uterus.
Eczema Type of dermatitis characterized by itching.
Edentulism The complete loss of teeth.
Effaced Cervical thinning.
Elderly obstetric patient 35 years or older at date of delivery.
Elective abortion Elective termination of pregnancy.
Electroconvulsive therapy Psychiatric treatment in which electricity is used to induce seizures.
Electromagnetic therapy Extracorporeal treatment by electromagnetic rays.
Electromyelogram Test that measures electrical activity in muscles and nerves.
Electrophysiologist Physician trained in electrical disorders of the heart.
Embolus Clot that travels to another part of the body.
Emphysema Chronic lung disease of gradual onset that can be attributed to chronic infection and inflammation or irritation from cigarette smoke.
Empiric Initiation of treatment prior to making a definite diagnosis.
Empyema Pus that accumulates in the pleural space.
Encoder Coding software that is used to assign diagnosis and procedure codes.
Encounter Face-to-face visit with a healthcare provider.
Endocarditis Inflammation of the lining of the heart chambers and valves.
Endocrine system Body system composed of many glands that secrete hormones that regulate bodily functions; it works with the nervous system to maintain body activities and homeostasis and to respond to stress.
Endogenous Type of dermatitis caused by something taken internally, such as medication.
Endometriosis A chronic condition in which endometrial material, the tissue that lines the inside of the uterus, grows outside the uterus and attaches to other organs in the pelvic cavity.
Endoscopic Examinations and procedures performed with an instrument that examines any cavity of the body with a rigid or a flexible scope.
Endoscopic biopsy Biopsy that is performed during endoscopic examination.
Epidermis Outermost layer of skin.
Epilepsy Disorder of the brain that is characterized by abnormal electrical discharges from the brain cells.
Episiotomy Division of the perineum.
Eponym Term for a disease, structure, procedure, or syndrome that has been named for a person.
Erythema Redness of the skin.
Erythrocytes Another name for red blood cells that are made in the marrow of bones; their main responsibility is to carry oxygen around the

body and remove carbon dioxide. These are the cells that give blood its red color.

Ethics Moral standard.

Etiology Cause or origin of a disease or condition.

Euvolemia State of normal body fluid volume.

Excision Cutting out or off, without replacement, a portion of a body part (e.g., partial nephrectomy).

Excision Removal by surgical cutting.

Excisional biopsy Total removal of local small masses or growths.

Exhibitionism Recurrent intense sexual urges and fantasies of exposing the genitals to an unsuspecting stranger.

Exogenous Type of dermatitis caused by contact with a substance.

Exophthalmos Bulging of the eyes.

External Procedures performed directly on the skin or mucous membrane, and procedures performed indirectly by the application of external force through the skin or mucous membrane (e.g., tonsillectomy).

External skeletal fixation Form of fracture treatment that involves insertion of percutaneous pins proximal and distal to the fracture and application of a frame that connects the pins externally.

Extirpation Taking or cutting out solid matter from a body part (e.g., thrombectomy).

Extracorporeal shock wave lithotripsy Used to break up kidney stones into small particles that can then pass through the urinary tract into the urine.

Extraction Pulling or stripping out or off all or portion of a body part by force (e.g., bone marrow biopsy).

Extraluminal Outside of the lumen of a tubular body part.

Extravasation Leakage of infused substance into vasculature or subcutaneous tissue.

Facet joints Small, stabilizing joints located between and behind adjacent vertebrae.

Fallopian tube Delivers the mature egg to the uterus for fertilization.

Fascia Tissue just below the skin that covers and separates the underlying layers of muscle.

Fat embolism When fat enters the circulatory system after long bone or pelvic fractures.

Federal Register The official daily publication for rules, proposed rules, and notices of U.S. federal agencies and organizations.

Fetishism Recurrent intense sexual urges and fantasies of using inanimate objects for sexual arousal or orgasm. Objects commonly used include female clothing such as shoes, earrings, or undergarments.

Fibromas Neoplasms of fibrous connective tissue.

Fibromyalgia One of the most common diseases affecting the muscles; it is characterized by widespread muscle pain associated with chronic fatigue.

Fine needle aspiration Procedure in which a very small needle is used; works best for masses that are superficial or easily accessible.

Fistula Abnormal passage or communication between two internal organs, or leading from an organ to the surface of the body. It can also be an abnormal passage between an artery and a vein.

Fluid overload Occurs when there is too much fluid in the body.

Fluoroscopy Single plane or bi-plane real time display of an image developed from the capture of external ionizing radiation on a fluorescent screen. The image may also be stored by either digital or analog means.

Foregut Bronchi and stomach (sites of carcinoid neoplasm).

Fracture Break in a bone.

Fragmentation Breaking solid matter in a body part into pieces (e.g., extracorporeal shock wave lithotripsy).

Free flap Involves the cutting of skin, fat, blood vessels, and muscle free from its location and moving it to the chest area.

Frostbite Occurs when skin and underlying tissues freeze due to extreme cold.

Functional urinary incontinence When a physical or mental condition prevents someone from making it to the bathroom in time.

Fundoplication Surgery in which the fundus of the stomach is wrapped around the esophagus.

Furuncle A boil.

Fusion Joining together portions of an articular body part, rendering the articular body part immobile (e.g., spinal fusion).

Gangrene Dead tissue usually associated with loss of vascular supply.

Gastroenteritis Inflammation of the stomach, small intestine, and large intestine.

Gastrointestinal stromal tumor A type of tumor that occurs in the gastrointestinal tract, usually in the stomach or small intestine.

Generalized anxiety disorder Chronic exaggerated worry, tension, and irritability that may occur without cause or that are more intense than the situation warrants.

Genetic Inherited.

Genital prolapse When pelvic organs such as the uterus, bladder, and rectum shift from their normal anatomic positions and protrude into the vagina or press against the wall of the vagina.

Gigantism Condition that occurs when hypersecretion of hGH occurs before puberty, along with proportionate overgrowth of all bodily tissues, especially the long bones.

Glaucoma Disorder of the optic nerve that may result in vision loss.

Glioma A primary malignant brain neoplasm that starts in the glial cells of the central nervous system.

Glomerulonephritis Inflammation of the glomeruli of the kidneys.

Goiter Enlargement of the thyroid gland.

Gonorrhea Disease caused by a bacterium and transmitted by sexual contact.

Grading Pathologic examination of tumor cells. Degree of cell abnormality determines the grade of cancer.

Graft-versus-host disease (GVHD) Common complication that can occur after a stem cell or bone marrow transplant in which the newly transplanted material attacks the transplant recipient's body.

Granulation Newly formed tissue that covers an open sore or a wound.

Graves' disease The most common form of hyperthyroidism; it occurs through an autoimmune response that attacks the thyroid gland, resulting in overproduction of the thyroid hormone thyroxine.

Gravid Pregnant.

Grouper Specialized software used to assign the appropriate MS-DRG.

Gustilo open fracture classification Based on the mechanism of the injury and the amount of soft tissue and skeletal injury; is useful in assessing risk of infection and possible amputation.

HAART Highly active antiretroviral therapy, a group of drugs given to AIDS patients for prophylaxis.

Habitual aborter A woman who miscarries at least three consecutive times.

Hashimoto's disease Inflammation of the thyroid gland that often results in hypothyroidism.

Health Maintenance Organizations (HMOs) Type of managed care in which hospitals, physicians, and other providers contract to provide health care for patients, usually at a discounted rate.

Healthcare provider Person who provides care to a patient.

Hearing aid assessment Measurement of the appropriateness and/or effectiveness of a hearing device.

Hearing aid treatment Application of techniques to improve the communication abilities of individuals with cochlear implant.

Hearing assessment Measurement of hearing and related functions.

Hearing treatment Application of techniques to improve, augment, or compensate for hearing and related functional impairment.

Heart failure Impaired function of the heart's pumping ability.
Helminthiases Another word for diseases caused by parasitic worms.
Hematemesis Vomiting of blood.
Hematochezia Bright red blood in stool.
Hematopoiesis Development of blood cells that occurs in the bone marrow and lymphatic tissue of normal adults.
Hemiplegia Paralysis of half of the body.
Hemodialysis Process that uses a machine called a hemodialyzer to remove wastes from the blood.
Hemolysis The breaking down of red blood cells.
Hemolytic anemias Result from abnormal or excessive destruction of red blood cells.
Hemophilia A Most common type of hemophilia; deficiency or abnormality in clotting factor VIII.
Hemophilia B Another name for Christmas disease, which results from a deficiency of factor IX.
Hemophilia C Mild form of hemophilia with decreased factor XI.
Hemothorax Blood that accumulates in the pleural space.
Hepatitis An inflammation of the liver.
Hernia Protrusion of an organ or tissue through an abnormal opening in the body.
Herniorrhaphy Repair of a hernia.
Herpes simplex A virus also known as a *cold sore* or *fever blister*.
Herpes zoster A disease caused by the same virus that causes chicken pox.
Hindgut Colon and rectum (sites of carcinoid neoplasms).
Histoplasmosis A fungal disease that primarily affects the lungs.
HIV Human immunodeficiency virus is the virus that affects the immune system and can progress to AIDS.
Hives Skin condition also known as urticaria, wherein the skin reacts with welts; characterized by itching.
Homeostasis The ability of an organism or cell to maintain internal equilibrium by adjusting its physiological processes.
Hormones Substances secreted by glands that can regulate bodily functions, such as urinary output, cellular metabolic rate, and growth and development.
Hybrid A combination of formats producing similar results (e.g., paper and electronic records).
Hydrocephalus Cerebrospinal fluid collection in the skull.
Hydronephrosis Abnormal dilatation of the renal pelvis caused by pressure from urine that cannot flow past an obstruction in the urinary tract.
Hydroureter Accumulation of urine in the ureters.
Hyperbaric oxygen therapy (HBOT) Treatment in which the patient's entire body is placed in a transparent, airtight chamber at increased atmospheric pressure.
Hyperemesis gravidarum Excessive vomiting in pregnancy.
Hyperglycemia Condition that results when glucose or blood sugar becomes abnormally high. This is a relatively common event in patients with diabetes.
Hyperhidrosis Excessive sweating.
Hyperparathyroidism Condition that results when an overactive parathyroid gland secretes excessive parathyroid hormone, causing increased levels of circulating calcium associated with loss of calcium in the bone.
Hyperpituitarism Increased production of the pituitary hormones, particularly the human growth hormone (hGH).
Hyperplasia Enlargement of a gland.
Hypersomnia Excessive sleep.
Hyperthermia Extracorporeal raising of body temperature.
Hyperthyroidism Abnormality of the thyroid gland in which secretion of thyroid hormone is usually increased and is no longer under the regulatory control of hypothalamic-pituitary centers.
Hypertrophy Enlargement of a gland.
Hypervitaminosis Toxicity resulting from an excess of any vitamin, especially fat-soluble vitamins such as A, D, and K.
Hypervolemia Occurs when there is too much fluid in the body.
Hypoglycemia Condition that results when glucose, or blood sugar, becomes abnormally low.
Hypomania Milder form of mania, but this "feel good" mood can change to depression or mania.
Hypoparathyroidism Underactive parathyroid gland that results in decreased levels of circulating calcium.
Hypopituitarism Condition caused by low levels of pituitary hormones. Hormones secreted by the pituitary gland can affect the functions of other glands.
Hypoplasia Atrophy; condition that results when a gland becomes smaller.
Hypothermia Extracorporeal lowering of body temperature.
Hypothyroidism Condition caused by low levels of pituitary hormones. Hormones secreted by the pituitary gland can affect the functions of other glands.
Hypovolemia Occurs due to decreased plasma volume.
Hypoxia Insufficient oxygen in the blood.
Iatrogenic Caused by medical treatment.
ICD-10-CM *International Classification of Diseases, 10th Revision Clinical Modification.*
ICD-10-PCS *International Classification of Diseases, 10th Revision-Procedure Coding System.*
Idiopathic Causative factor is unknown.
Ileostomy End of small intestine brought out through the abdominal wall.
Ileus Absence of normal movement within the intestine.
Immobilization Limiting or preventing motion of a body region.
Immune system Includes the bone marrow, lymph nodes, thymus, and spleen; its purpose is to protect the body from all types of infections, toxins, neoplastic cell growth and foreign blood or tissues from another person.
Immunotherapy Administration of agents that stimulate the immune system's response against tumors.
Impaction Condition that occurs when stool in the rectum becomes so hard that it cannot be passed normally.
Incidental appendectomy Appendectomy performed at the time of another procedure with no known disease process in the appendix.
Incisional biopsy Procedure in which a representative sample of a tumor mass is removed to permit pathologic examination.
Incomplete abortion Abortion in which not all of the products of conception are expelled.
Inevitable abortion Abortion that occurs when symptoms are present and a miscarriage will happen.
Infection Invasion of the body with organisms that have the potential to cause disease.
Inferior Position of the body or an organ relative to the vertical axis of the body.
Influenza Contagious viral infection of the respiratory tract that causes coughing, difficulty breathing, headache, muscle aches, and weakness.
Insertion Putting in a nonbiological appliance that monitors, assists, performs, or prevents a physiological function but does not physically take the place of a body part (e.g., insertion of pacemaker lead).
Insomnia Difficulty falling asleep, wakefulness, and early morning awakening.
Inspection Visually and/or manually exploring a body part (e.g., diagnostic arthroscopy).
Integral Essential part of a disease process.
Integumentary Another name for skin.
Intellectual disability Disorder in which a person's overall intellectual functioning is well below average, with an intelligence quotient (IQ) around 70 or less.

Intertrigo Dermatitis in areas where friction may occur.

Interventionalist Physician trained in disease treatment via the use of catheter-based technique.

Intractable Not manageable.

Intraluminal Within the lumen of a tubular body part.

Introduction Putting in or on a therapeutic, diagnostic, nutritional, physiological, or prophylactic substance except blood or blood products.

Intussusception Bowel becomes obstructed when a portion of the intestine telescopes into another portion.

Irrigation Putting in or on a cleansing substance.

Joints Means of joining two bones together.

Juvenile rheumatoid arthritis Type of arthritis which affects children usually between the ages of 2 and 5 years.

Kaposi's sarcoma (KS) Cancer that develops from the lining of lymph or blood vessels.

Klinefelter's syndrome A sex chromosome disorder that occurs in males and is caused by an extra X chromosome.

Kwashiorkor Severe type of malnutrition resulting in dyspigmentation of the skin and hair, edema, and growth retardation.

Kyphoplasty Procedure to treat and stabilize fractures of the spine.

Kyphosis Excessive posterior curvature of the thoracic spine that may not be detected until a hump in the upper back is noticeable.

Labia Surrounds the vaginal opening.

Labor Process by which the products of conception are expelled from the uterus.

Laceration An injury that results in a tear in the skin.

Lactation Process of milk production from mammary glands.

Laparoscopic approach Uses a laparoscope to examine and perform closed procedures within the abdomen.

Lateral Position of a structure that is to the side of the body.

Leiomyoma Tumor or growth within the walls of the uterus. Also called *uterine fibroid*.

Leukemia Cancer of the white blood cells that begins in the blood-forming cells of the bone marrow.

Leukocytes White blood cells increase in number to battle infection, inflammation, and other diseases.

Leukocytosis Increase in the number of white cells in the blood; it may be a sign of infection or may indicate stress on the body.

Level II of HCPCS Codes used to identify drugs, medical supplies, and durable medical equipment.

Ligaments Dense, fibrous bands of connective tissue that provide stability for the joint.

Limited coverage Procedures that are identified by the Medicare Code Editor as procedures covered under limited circumstances.

Lipoma Growth of fat cells within a capsule that usually is found just below the skin.

Lobar pneumonia Synonym for pneumococcal pneumonia or pneumonia due to *Streptococcus pneumoniae* pneumonia.

Local coverage determinations (LCDs) Local policy that may include certain time frames for testing, that a patient be a certain age, and that a particular diagnosis or condition is present to be considered medical necessary.

Lordosis Exaggerated inward curvature of the spine that may be caused by increased abdominal girth due to obesity, pregnancy, or abdominal tumor.

Loss of consciousness When a patient is unable to respond to people or other stimuli.

Lung abscess Infection that forms in the lung parenchyma.

Lyme disease An inflammatory disease caused by bacteria carried by ticks.

Lymphadenitis Inflammation of a lymph node that usually is caused by a bacterial infection.

Lymphoma Cancer of the lymphatic system.

Lysis Destruction of adhesions.

Macular degeneration Vision loss in the central portion of the eye, leaving the patient with peripheral vision or low vision.

Main term Term that identifies disease conditions or injuries, it is identified in bold print and set flush with the left margin of each column in the Alphabetic Index.

Magnetic resonance imaging (MRI) Computer reformatted digital display of multiplanar images developed from the capture of radio-frequency signals emitted by nuclei in a body site excited within a magnetic field.

Major depressive disorder Characterized by one or more major depressive episodes with a history of mania, hypomania, or mixed episodes.

Malignancy Neoplasm that has the ability to invade adjacent structures and spread to distant sites.

Malignant A neoplasm that invades surrounding structures and metastasizes to distant places in the body.

Malignant ascites Excess fluid that contains malignant cells and accumulates in the abdomen or peritoneum.

Malignant melanoma Malignant neoplasm of the melanocytes; the most common place of occurrence is the skin.

Malignant mesothelioma Rare aggressive cancer that develops in the protective lining or mesothelium that surrounds and protects the internal organs.

Malignant pleural effusion Fluid accumulates in the pleural space and contains malignant cells.

Mallory-Weiss Bleeding laceration of the esophagogastric junction.

Malnutrition Nutrition disorder caused by primary deprivation of protein energy resulting from poverty or self-imposed starvation or associated with deficiency diseases such as cancer.

Malunion Occurs when fracture fragments have united but are not properly aligned. Incorrectly positioned bones may demonstrate angulation, rotation, and shortening.

Mania The other side of depression, in which a person feels so good, it is like a "high"; may do risky things.

Manifestation Symptom or condition that is the result of a disease.

Manipulation Manual procedure that involves a directed thrust to move a joint past the physiological range of motion without exceeding the anatomical limit.

Map Locating the route of passage of electrical impulses and/or locating functional areas in a body part (e.g., cardiac mapping).

Marfan's syndrome An inherited condition that affects connective tissue and is caused by gene mutation.

Masochism The act or sense of gaining pleasure from experiencing physical or psychological pain.

Mastication Chewing of food.

Mastitis Inflammation or infection of the breast.

Mastoiditis Infection of the mastoid bone of the skull.

Maximization The manipulation of codes to result in maximum reimbursement without supporting documentation in the health record or with disregard for coding conventions, guidelines, and UHDDS definitions.

McBurney's point Area of the abdomen that, when touched, causes pain that may be indicative of appendicitis.

Measurement Determining the level of a physiological or physical function at a point in time.

Mechanical complication When a device or equipment malfunctions.

Mechanical ventilation Use of a machine to induce alternating inflation and deflation of the lungs, to regulate the exchange rate of gases in the blood.

Meconium Material in the intestine of a fetus.

Medial Position of a structure closer to the median plane than is another structure in the body.

Medical necessity Criteria or guidelines for what is determined to be reasonable and necessary for a particular medical service.

Medicare Code Editor Software that detects errors in coding on Medicare claims.

Melanomas Malignant changes of melanin cells.

Melena Dark blood in stool.

Meningitis An infection in the fluid of a person's spinal cord and brain.

Metabolic encephalopathy Temporary or permanent damage to the brain due to lack of glucose, oxygen, metabolic agents, or organ dysfunction.

Metastasis Spread of a cancer from one part of the body to another, as in the appearance of neoplasms in parts of the body separate from the site of the primary tumor.

Midgut Small intestine and appendix (sites of carcinoid neoplasms).

Miscarriage Spontaneous termination of pregnancy before the fetus has reached 20 weeks.

Missed abortion Pregnancy with fetal demise before 20 weeks; products of conception are not expelled.

Mixed incontinence Combination of stress and urge incontinence.

Mixed mania/mood Alteration from mania and depression, back and forth, very quickly.

Molar pregnancy Fertilized ovum is converted to a mass of cysts due to an extra set of paternal chromosomes.

Monitoring Determining the level of a physiological or physical function repetitively over a period of time.

Mood disorder Condition that occurs when there has been a change in mood for a prolonged time.

Morbid obesity Applies to patients who are 50% to 100% or 100 pounds above their ideal body weight. A BMI of 40 or higher defines morbid obesity.

Morbidity Pertaining to disease.

Mortality Pertaining to death.

Motor and/or nerve function assessment Measurement of motor, nerve, and related functions.

Motor treatment Exercise or activities to increase or facilitate motor function.

MS-DRG grouper Software that assigns MS-DRG using diagnosis and procedure codes.

Mucositis An inflammation/ulceration of the digestive tract commonly occurring in the oral cavity.

Multigravida/Multiparity A woman with two or more pregnancies.

Muscular dystrophy Type of myopathy.

Myasthenia gravis Chronic autoimmune disorder that manifests as muscle weakness of varying degrees.

Mycobacterium avium intercellulare Mycobacteria found in soil and water.

Mycosis Fungal infection.

Myeloma Malignancy that originates in the bone marrow.

Myelopathy Compression of the spinal cord.

Myocardial infarction Heart attack.

Myopathies Disorders that affect muscles, usually resulting in weakness or atrophy.

Myxedema Skin and tissue disorder that usually is due to severe prolonged hypothyroidism.

Nadir The lowest level.

National coverage determinations (NCDs) National policy that may include certain time frames for testing, certain age requirements, and that a particular diagnosis or condition be present for a procedure to be considered medically necessary.

NEC Abbreviation for "not elsewhere classifiable" that means "other specified."

Necrotic Dead tissue that lacks a blood supply.

Necrotizing fasciitis (or "flesh-eating disease") A rare but serious condition in which an infection occurs in the tissues below the skin.

Neoplasm Abnormal growth.

Nephrolithiasis Kidney stone.

Nephrotic syndrome Condition marked by proteinuria (protein in the urine), low levels of protein in the blood, hypercholesterolemia, and swelling of the eyes, feet, and hands.

Neuroma A growth made up of a bundle of nerve fibers.

Neutropenia Abnormal decrease in granular leukocytes in the blood.

Nomenclature System of names that are used as the preferred terminology.

Noncovered OR procedure A procedure code categorized by the Medicare Code Editor as a noncovered operating room procedure for which Medicare does not provide reimbursement.

Nonessential modifier Term that is enclosed in parentheses; its presence or absence does not affect code assignment.

Non-Hodgkin's lymphoma A type of cancer of the lymphatic system.

Nonimaging nuclear medicine assay Introduction of radioactive materials into the body for the study of body fluids and blood elements, by the detection of radioactive emissions.

Nonimaging nuclear medicine probe Introduction of radioactive materials into the body for the study of distribution and fate of certain substances by the detection of radioactive emissions from an external source.

Nonimaging nuclear medicine uptake Introduction of radioactive materials into the body for measurements of organ functions, from detection of radioactive emissions.

Noninvasive ventilation Ventilation without an invasive artificial airway (endotracheal tube or tracheostomy).

Non-OR procedure affecting DRG assignment Procedure code recognized by the MS-DRG Grouper as a non–operating room procedure that may affect MS-DRG assignment.

Nonunion Of a fracture occurs when the bony healing is not achieved at the fracture site. A fracture site that fails to heal within approximately 6 to 9 months of the injury represents a nonunion.

NOS Abbreviation for "not otherwise specified" that means "unspecified."

Nosocomial Hospital-acquired infection.

Nosocomial pneumonia Pneumonia that is acquired while the patient is residing in a hospital-type setting.

NSTEMI Non–ST elevation myocardial infarction.

Nursing home–acquired pneumonia Pneumonia that is acquired in a nursing home or extended care facility.

Nutritional marasmus Severe form of malnutrition that is characterized by severe tissue wasting, loss of subcutaneous fat, and maybe dehydration.

Obesity Condition defined as an increase in body weight beyond the limitation of skeletal and physical requirements, caused by excessive accumulation of fat in the body.

Observation unit Area outside the emergency department where unstable patients are admitted for a stay of less than 48 hours. The patient is observed for admission to the hospital or is discharged to home.

Occult blood Blood found only by laboratory inspection.

Occlusion Completely closing an orifice or lumen of a tubular body part (e.g., tubal ligation).

Omit code An instructional note found in Volume 3 that denotes that no code is to be assigned; it generally is used for coding approaches and closures that are integral to an operative procedure.

Oophoritis Inflammation of the ovaries.

Open Cutting through the skin, mucous membrane, and any other body layers necessary to expose the site of the procedure (e.g., abdominal hysterectomy).

Open fracture When the broken bone exits and is visible through the skin, or a deep wound exposes the broken bone through the skin.

Open reduction When the surgeon makes an incision at the fracture site to reduce or manipulate the fracture into anatomic position.

Oppositional defiant disorder Pattern of uncooperative, defiant, and hostile behavior toward authority figures that does not involve major antisocial violations, is not accounted for by the child's developmental stage, and results in significant functional impairment.

Optimization The process of striving to obtain optimal reimbursement or the highest possible payment to which a facility is legally entitled on the basis of documentation in the health record.

Organic brain syndrome General term used to describe the decrease in mental function caused by other physical disease(s).

Osteoarthritis Type of arthritis that develops as the result of wear and tear on the joints.

Osteomyelitis Infection of the bone that often starts in another part of the body and spreads to the bone via the blood.

Osteoporosis Metabolic bone disorder that results in decreased bone mass and density.

Ostomies Surgically created openings into the body.

Other procedures Methodologies that attempt to remediate or cure a disorder or disease.

Otitis media Middle ear infection.

Ovaries Produce female hormones and eggs.

Overflow incontinence The constant dribbling of urine.

Packing Putting material in a body region or orifice.

Palliative Procedure performed to correct a condition that is causing problems for the patient.

Pancreatitis Inflammation of the pancreas often caused by gallstones or chronic heavy alcohol use.

Pancytopenia Decrease in production of erythrocytes (red blood cells), leukocytes (white blood cells), and thrombocytes (platelets).

Panic disorder Terrifying experience that occurs suddenly without warning. Physical symptoms include pounding heart, chest pains, dizziness, nausea, shortness of breath, trembling, choking, fear of dying, sweating, feelings of unreality, numbness, hot flashes or chills, and a feeling of going out of control or "crazy."

Parasitic Organism that lives on or takes nourishment from another organism.

Parenteral When medications are administered other than through the digestive tract, such as by intravenous or intramuscular injection.

Parkinson's disease Progressive and chronic motor system disorder.

Partial remission There are still a few signs and symptoms of the cancer, and the cancer cells have significantly decreased.

Pathologic fracture Break in a bone that occurs because of underlying disorders that weaken the bone, including malignancy, benign bone tumor, metabolic disorder, infection, and osteoporosis.

Pedicle flap Involves identifying a flap that remains attached to its original blood supply and tunneling it under the skin to a particular area, such as the breast.

Pelvic inflammatory disease When vaginal or cervical infections spread and involve the uterus, fallopian tubes, ovaries, and surrounding tissues.

Pemphigus Autoimmune disorder causing blistering of skin and mucous membranes.

Percutaneous Entry of instrumentation, by puncture or minor incision, through the skin, mucous membrane, and any other body layers necessary to reach the site of the procedure (e.g., needle biopsy liver).

Percutaneous endoscopic Entry of instrumentation, by puncture or minor incision, through the skin, mucous membrane, and any other body layers necessary to reach and visualize the site of the procedure (e.g., laparoscopic cholecystectomy).

Percutaneous endoscopic gastrostomy A tube put through the abdominal wall into the stomach with the use of a scope.

Percutaneous nephrolithotomy Procedure in which the surgeon uses a nephroscope to remove a stone. At times, an ultrasonic or electrohydraulic probe is used to break up the stone, and the fragments are then removed.

Percutaneous vertebroplasty Technique in which x-ray guidance is used to inject an acrylic cement through a needle into a collapsed or weakened vertebra; procedure is performed to treat pain caused by compression fractures of the vertebrae.

Performance Completely taking over a physiological function by extracorporeal means.

Perfusion extracorporeal treatment by diffusion of therapeutic fluid.

Pericarditis Inflammation of the covering of the heart.

Perinatal period Before birth through the first 28 days of life.

Peristalsis Rhythmic muscle contractions that move food down the digestive tract.

Peritoneal dialysis When the peritoneal membrane in the patient's own body is used with a dialysate solution to filter out the wastes and excess fluids.

Peritonitis Inflammation of the peritoneum usually caused by bacteria or fungus.

Personality disorder A pattern of behavior that can disrupt many aspects of a person's life.

Phacoemulsification Incision that is made on the side of the cornea where the lens material is softened, broken, and suctioned out.

Pheresis Extracorporeal separation of blood products.

Phlebitis Inflammation of a vein.

Phobia Irrational anxiety or fear that can interfere with one's everyday life or daily routine.

Phototherapy Extracorporeal treatment by light rays.

Physician Licensed medical doctor.

Plain radiography Planar display of an image developed from the capture of external ionizing radiation on photographic or photoconductive plate.

Planar nuclear medicine imaging Introduction of radioactive materials into the body for single plane display of images developed from the capture of radioactive emissions.

Platelets Another name for thrombocytes. Platelets circulate in the blood and assist in the clotting process.

Pleural effusion Fluid that accumulates in the pleural space because of trauma or disease.

Pneumoconioses Lung diseases due to chronic inhalation of inorganic (mineral) dust that are often due to occupational exposure.

Pneumonia Infection of the lungs that may be caused by a variety of organisms, including viruses, bacteria, and parasites.

Pneumothorax Air in space around the lung.

Poliomyelitis A viral disease that affects the nerves.

Polymyalgia rheumatica Syndrome classified as a rheumatic disease that is characterized by severe aching and stiffness in the neck, shoulder girdle, and pelvic girdle.

Positron emission tomography (PET) Introduction of radioactive materials into the body for three-dimensional display of images developed from the simultaneous capture, 180 degrees apart, of radioactive emissions.

Posterior Back of the body or an organ.

Postlaminectomy syndrome Terms used to describe patients who have undergone spine surgery and have some degree of recurrent spinal and/or leg pain due to the build up of scar tissue.

Postpartum After delivery or childbirth.

Postterm pregnancy Pregnancy longer than 40 weeks up to 42 weeks.

Posttraumatic stress disorder Anxiety disorder that is triggered by memories of a traumatic event.

Prader-Willi Syndrome A congenital condition caused by an abnormality of the 15th chromosome.

Precipitate labor Rapid labor and delivery.

Preeclampsia Pregnancy complication characterized by hypertension, edema, and/or proteinuria.

Preferred Provider Organizations (PPO) Type of managed care in which hospitals, physicians, and other providers have an arrangement with a third-party payer to provide health care at discounted rates to third party payer clients.

Pregestational Condition present prior to pregnancy.

Prenatal Before birth.

Present on admission (POA) An indicator to differentiate between a condition that developed during a particular hospital encounter and a condition present at the time of admission.

Preventive or prophylactic surgery Procedure performed to remove tissue that has the potential to become cancerous.

Primary osteoarthritis Idiopathic degenerative condition that occurs in previously intact joints, with no apparent initiating factor.

Primary site Site at which the neoplasm begins or originates.

Primigravida First pregnancy.

Principal diagnosis Condition established after study to be chiefly responsible for occasioning admission of the patient to the hospital for care.

Principal procedure Performed for definitive treatment rather than for diagnostic or exploratory purposes, or one necessary to take care of a complication.

Procedure A diagnostic or therapeutic process performed on a patient.

Products of conception All physical components of a pregnancy including the fetus, amnion, umbilical cord, and placenta, regardless of gestational age.

Professional service Service rendered by a physician or a nonphysician practitioner.

Progress notes Daily recordings by health care providers of patient progress.

Prolonged pregnancy Beyond 42 weeks of pregnancy.

Prone Lying on the stomach, face down.

Prophylactic Medication or treatment used to prevent a disease from occurring.

Prospective payment system Method of reimbursement in which payment is made on the basis of a predetermined, fixed amount rather than for billed charges.

Prostate-specific antigen (PSA) Protein produced by the prostate gland.

Prostatitis Inflammation of the prostate that can be acute and/or chronic in nature and is due to a bacterium or inflammation that is not caused by a bacterial infection.

Proteinuria Protein in urine.

Proximal Closer to the median plane.

Pruritus Itching.

Psoriasis Inflammation of skin caused by a fault in the immune system.

Psychosis Impaired mental state in which the perception of reality has become distorted.

Puerperium Time from delivery through the first 6 weeks postpartum.

Pulmonary edema Condition in which fluid accumulates in the lungs.

Pulmonary embolism A blood clot(s) in the pulmonary artery that causes blockage in the artery.

Pulmonary hypertension High blood pressure in the arteries that supply blood to the lungs.

Purpura Ecchymoses or small hemorrhages in the skin, mucous membranes, or serosal surfaces due to blood disorders, vascular abnormalities, or trauma.

Pyelonephritis Upper tract infection that involves the kidneys.

Radiation Use of high-energy radiation to treat cancer.

Radiculopathy Compression of a nerve root.

Ray Used to designate the fingers and corresponding metacarpals and the toes and corresponding metatarsals.

Reattachment Putting back in or on all or a portion of a separated body part to its normal location or other suitable location.

Rectocele Descent of the rectum and pressing of the rectum against the vaginal wall.

Rectovesical fistula A communication between the bladder and the rectum.

Rehabilitation Structured program with the goal to stop and recover from the use of alcohol and/or drugs.

Reimbursement Payment for healthcare services.

Release Freeing a body part from an abnormal physical constraint (e.g., lysis of adhesions) or location to a more suitable location (e.g., reattachment of finger).

Removal Taking out or off a device from a body part (e.g., removal of a chest tube).

Renal colic Intense pain associated with the body's efforts to try to force the stone through the ureters.

Repair Restoring, to the extent possible, a body part to its normal anatomic structure and function (herniorrhaphy).

Replacement Putting in or on biological or synthetic material that physically takes the place and/or fuction of all or a portion of a body part (total knee replacement).

Reposition Moving to its normal location or other suitable location all or a portion of a body part (e.g., fracture reduction).

Resection Cutting out or off, without replacement, all of a body part (e.g., total lobectomy of lung).

Respiratory failure General term that describes ineffective gas exchange across the lungs by the respiratory system.

Respiratory system System that supplies the body with oxygen (O_2).

Restoration Returning, or attempting to return, a physiological function to its original state by extracorporeal means.

Restorative or reconstruction Surgery performed to restore function and enhance aesthetic appearance after surgery.

Restriction Partially closing an orifice or lumen of a tubular body part (e.g., Nissen fundoplication).

Revenue code A four-digit code that is utilized on the UB-04 to indicate a particular type of service.

Revision Correcting, to the extent possible, a malfunctioning of displaced device (e.g., adjustment of knee prosthesis).

Rhabdomyolysis Breakdown of muscle fibers resulting in the release of muscle fiber contents into the circulation.

Rheumatoid arthritis Chronic, inflammatory systemic disease that affects the joints, often causing deformity.

Robotic-assisted surgery Minimally invasive technique that utilizes robotic arms to manipulate the surgical equipment and tools.

Rosacea Skin condition affecting cheeks, nose, and chin. It can be characterized by redness, a bulbous nose, or an increased number of blood vessels in the face.

Sadism The act or sense of gaining pleasure from inflicting physical or psychological pain on another.

Salpingitis Inflammation of the fallopian tubes, which are the most common site of pelvic inflammation.

Sarcomas Malignant growths of connective tissue (e.g., muscle, cartilage, lymph tissue, bone).

Scabies Contagious dermatitis caused by mites.

Schizoaffective disorder Condition in which a person experiences a combination of schizophrenia symptoms while exhibiting mood disorder symptoms, such as mania or depression.

Schizophrenia Disorder of the brain characterized by difficulty differentiating between real and unreal experiences, as well as in logical thinking, normal emotional responses to others, and appropriate behavior in social situations.

Scleroderma Chronic, progressive disease characterized by hardening of the skin and scarring of internal organs.

Scoliosis Deviation of the vertical line of the spine.

Screening examination One that occurs in the absence of any signs or symptoms. It involves examination of an asymptomatic individual to detect a given disease, typically by means of an inexpensive diagnostic test.

Sebum Substance secreted from the sebaceous gland.

Secondary diabetes mellitus Form of the disease that develops as a result of another disease or condition.

Secondary osteoarthritis Degenerative disease of the joints that results from some predisposing condition such as trauma or disease.

Secondary thrombocytopenia Decrease in the number of platelets due to specific diseases or external causes, such as drugs, blood transfusions, and overhydration.

Section Consists of a group of three-digit categories that represent diseases or conditions that are similar.

See A mandatory cross-reference that advises the coder to go to another main term.

See also Cross-reference that instructs the coder about the possibility that there may be a better main term elsewhere in the Alphabetic Index.

Self-insured plans Self-insurance fund is set up by an employer to provide health claim benefits for employees.

Sentinel lymph node The first lymph node to which cancer cells are most likely to spread.

Sentinel lymph node biopsy (SLNB) A procedure that identifies the sentinel lymph node(s) for removal and pathologic examination.

Sepsis A medical condition in which the immune system goes into overdrive, releasing chemicals into the blood to combat infection that trigger widespread inflammation.

Septic shock A condition caused by infection and sepsis. It can cause multiple organ failure and death.

Septicemia The presence in the blood of pathologic microorganisms that cause systemic illness.

Sequelae Late effect or residual of an acute disease.

Shock wave therapy Extracorporeal treatment by shock waves.

Shunting Procedure to drain fluid from the brain to relieve pressure.

Sialolithiasis Stones in the salivary glands.

Sickle cell anemia One of the most common hemolytic anemias, in which the shape of the red blood cell changes from a disc to a crescent or "sickle," causing obstruction of small blood vessels and eventual damage throughout the body.

Siderosis Lung disease due to inhalation of iron oxide.

Sign Objective evidence of a disease or of a patient's condition as perceived by the patient's examining physician.

Significant procedure Surgical in nature, carries a procedural risk, carries an anesthetic risk, or requires specialized training.

Simple fracture Injury in which the bone is broken, but the skin remains intact.

Sinusitis A condition in which the linings of one or more sinuses become infected, usually because of viruses or bacteria.

SIRS Systemic inflammatory response syndrome, which can be caused by infection or trauma.

Sleep apnea Disorder characterized by breathing interruption during sleep.

Solar keratosis Precancerous scaly growth.

Somatic nervous system Sends sensory (taste, hearing, smell) information to the central nervous system.

Somnolence Sleepiness.

Specificity Coding to the greatest detail of a code. Coding to the fourth or fifth digit as necessary.

Speech assessment Measurement of speech and related functions.

Speech treatment Application of techniques to improve, augment, or compensate for speech and related functional impairment.

Spinal cord injury Damage to the spinal cord that causes loss of sensation and motor control.

Spinal decompression Surgical procedure that frees space for the nerves in the spinal canal.

Spinal fusion The creation of a solid bone bridge between two or more adjacent vertebrae to enhance stability between levels of the spine.

Spinal stenosis Narrowing of the central spinal canal or the areas of the spine where the nerve roots exit (neuroforamina).

Splenomegaly Enlarged spleen.

Spondylolisthesis Condition in which one vertebra slips on another.

Spondylosis (or spinal osteoarthritis) Degenerative disorder that may cause loss of normal spinal structure and function.

Spontaneous abortion Loss of a fetus due to natural causes; also known as *miscarriage*.

Spontaneous pneumothorax Pneumothorax that is not caused by trauma.

Sprain Stretch and/or tear of a ligament.

Squamous cell carcinoma (SCC) Second most common type of skin cancer and also occurs in areas of the body that have been exposed to the sun.

Squamous intraepithelial lesion (SIL) Dysplasia of the cervix that is identified on a Pap smear.

Staging Means of categorizing a particular cancer that assists in determination of a patient's treatment plan and the need for further therapy.

Staging surgeries Procedures performed to help the clinician determine the extent of disease; these generally are more accurate than laboratory and imaging tests.

Stannosis Lung disease due to inhalation of tin particles.

Stasis dermatitis Skin condition due to poor circulation (venous insufficiency) that is characterized by swelling, skin discoloration, weeping, itching, and scaly skin.

Stasis ulcer Ulcer associated with varicose veins.

STEMI ST elevation myocardial infarction.

Stenosis Abnormal narrowing.

Steroid-induced diabetes Diabetes that is caused by the use of steroids.

Stevens-Johnson Syndrome Skin necrosis caused by a reaction to medication or infection.

Stillbirth Born dead.

Stoma An artificial opening.

Strain Injury to a muscle or a tendon.

Stress incontinence Involuntary loss of small amounts of urine due to increased pressure resulting from coughing, sneezing, or laughing.

Stroke Cerebrovascular accident or brain infarction.

Subacute Somewhat acute; between chronic and acute.

Subcategory A fourth-digit code that provides additional information or specificity.

Subcutaneous Inner layer of the skin that contains fat and sweat glands.

Subluxation Partial or incomplete dislocation.

Subterm Gives more specific information about a main term. Subterms identify site, type, or etiology of a disease condition or injury, they are indented to the right of the main term.

Superior Position of the body or an organ relative to the vertical axis of the body.

Supine Lying on the back, face up.
Supplement Putting in or on biological or synthetic material that physically reinforces and/or augments the function of a portion of a body part (e.g., herniorrhaphy with mesh).
Suture Method for closing cutaneous wounds.
Symptom Subjective evidence of a disease or of a patient's condition as perceived by the patient.
Syngeneic Individuals or tissues that have identical genes, such as identical twins.
Syphilis A sexually transmitted disease (STD) that is caused by bacteria.
Systemic inflammatory response syndrome A serious medical condition that can occur in response to infectious or noninfectious causes, such as severe trauma, burns, or complications of surgery.
Systemic lupus erythematosus Chronic, inflammatory autoimmune disease that can damage connective tissue anywhere in the body.
Systemic nuclear medicine therapy Introduction of unsealed radioactive materials into the body for treatment.
Tabular List Section of the ICD-10-CM book that contains the code listing, along with exclusion or inclusion notes.
Tachycardia Fast heart rate, generally greater than 100 beats per minute.
Tendons Connective tissue that attaches muscle to bone.
Terminology Words and phrases that apply to a particular field.
Tetany A continuous muscle spasm.
Thalassemia Hereditary disease that is similar to sickle cell anemia and occurs in varying degrees.
Therapeutic Treating disease.
Therapeutic abortion Abortion performed when the pregnancy is endangering the mother's health, or when the fetus has a condition that is incompatible with life.
Third party payer Makes payments for health services on behalf of the patient; may be a government program, insurance company, or managed care plan.
Thoracentesis Puncture of the chest wall to remove fluid (pleural effusion) from the space between the lining of the outside of the lungs (pleura) and the wall of the chest.
Thoracoscopic approach A thoracoscope is used to examine and perform closed procedures within the thorax.
Threatened abortion Abortion that occurs when symptoms are present that indicate the possibility of a miscarriage.
Thrombocytes Another name for platelets. Thrombocytes circulate in the blood and assist in the clotting process.
Thrombus A blood clot that forms and remains in a vein.
Thyrotoxic crisis/storm Complication of hyperthyroidism associated with a sudden intensification of symptoms combined with fever, rapid pulse, and delirium.
TIPS (transjugular intrahepatic portosystemic shunt) A procedure in which the portal vein is connected to one of the hepatic veins and a stent is inserted.
Tomographic nuclear medicine imaging Introduction of radioactive materials into the body for three-dimensional display of images developed from the capture of radioactive emissions.
Toxemia Another term for preeclampsia, which is pregnancy complicated by hypertension, edema, or proteinuria.
Toxic effect When a harmful substance is ingested or comes in contact with a person, this is classified as a toxic effect.
Toxic hepatitis When the liver is damaged by chemicals or drugs.
Trachea (windpipe) Body part that is responsible for filtering the air that we breathe.
Tracheostomy Procedure in which an artificial opening is made in the front of the windpipe (trachea) through the skin of the neck.
Traction Exerting a pulling force on a body region in a distal direction.
Transfer Moving, without taking out, all or a portion of a body part to another location to take over the function of all or a portion of a body part (e.g., pedicle skin flap).
Transfusion Putting in blood or blood products.
Transient ischemic attack A stroke that lasts for only a few minutes.
Transplantation Putting in or on all or a portion of a living body part taken from another individual or animal to physically take the place and/or function of all or a portion of a similar body part (kidney transplant).
Transurethral resection of the prostate Endoscopic removal of prostate tissue.
Transvestism Assuming the appearance, manner, or roles traditionally associated with members of the opposite sex (cross-dressing).
Traumatic brain injury Injury to the brain that may result in interference with the brain's normal functions.
Treatment Manual treatment to eliminate or alleviate somatic dysfunction and related disorders.
Trisomy Extra chromosome.
Tube thoracostomy Insertion of chest tube(s) to drain blood, fluid, or air and allow full expansion of the lungs.
Tuberculosis (TB) An infection caused by *Mycobacterium tuberculosis*.
Tumor lysis syndrome (TLS) Development of electrolyte and metabolic disturbances that can occur after treatment of cancer, usually lymphoma and leukemia, and sometimes even without treatment.
Ulcer Open sore of the skin.
Ulcerative colitis An inflammatory bowel disease.
Ultrasonography Real time display of images of anatomy or flow information developed from the capture of reflected and attenuated high frequency sound waves.
Ultrasound therapy Extracorporeal treatment by ultrasound.
Ultraviolet light therapy Extracorporeal treatment by ultraviolet light.
Underdosing Taking less of a medication than is prescribed by a provider or a manufacturer's instructions.
Undifferentiated Tumor cells that are highly abnormal (e.g., immature, primitive).
Ureterolithiasis Ureter stone.
Urethritis Infection of the urethra.
Urethrocele When the urethra presses into the vagina.
Urethrovaginal fistula Abnormal passage between the urethra and the vagina.
Urge incontinence Sudden and involuntary loss of large amounts of urine.
Urinary tract infection General term used to describe infection in any area of the urinary tract.
Urolithiasis A stone in the urinary tract.
Urosepsis Infection of urinary site.
Urticaria Another name for hives.
Uterine prolapse Descent of the uterus and the cervix into the vaginal canal.
Uterus A muscular organ that serves as an incubator for the developing fetus.
Vagal nerve stimulator A device to control seizures.
Vagina A muscular tube that extends from the vaginal opening to the uterus.
Vaginal vault prolapse Condition that may occur following a hysterectomy, when the top of the vagina descends.
Valid OR procedure A procedure that may affect MSG-DRG assignment.
Vaping-related disorder lung disorder(s) associated with inhaling vapors from electronic cigarettes.
Varicose veins Enlarged, twisted veins that usually occur in the legs.
Ventral Front of the body or an organ.

Ventriculoperitoneal shunt Procedure used to treat patient with hydrocephalus in whom drainage of the ventricle occurs through an artificial channel between the ventricle and the peritoneum.

Vesicoureteral reflux Abnormality in the flow of urine from the bladder into the ureters and/or kidneys.

Vesicouterine fistula Communication between the bladder and the uterus.

Vesicovaginal fistula Communication between the bladder and the vagina.

Vestibular assessment Measurement of vestibular system and related functions.

Vestibular treatment Application of techniques to improve, augment, or compensate for vestibular and related functional impairment.

Via natural or artificial opening Entry of instrumentation through a natural or artificial external opening to reach the site of the procedure (e.g., endotracheal intubation).

Via natural or artificial opening endoscopic Entry of instrumentation through a natural or artificial external opening to reach and visualize the site of the procedure (e.g., colonoscopy).

Via natural or artificial opening with percutaneous endoscopic assistance Cutting through the skin, mucous membrane, and any other body layers necessary to expose the site of the procedure; and entry of instrumentation, by puncture or minor incision, through the skin, mucous membrane, and any other body layers necessary to aid in the performance of the procedure (laparoscopically assisted vaginal hysterectomy).

Viral meningitis An infection of the fluid in the spinal cord and around the brain.

Vitamin deficiencies Condition caused by many different factors, such as poor nutrient absorption, associated with digestive tract disorders, lifestyle issues (e.g., alcohol, smoking, medication, over-exercising), chronic illness, age, and many other factors.

Volume depletion May be the result of either dehydration or hypovolemia.

Volvulus An abnormal twisting of the intestine that may impair blood flow to the intestine.

Voyeurism Recurrent intense sexual urges and fantasies involving observing unsuspecting people who are naked, disrobing, or engaging in sexual activity.

Vulva The external covering to the vagina.

Vulvar intraepithelial neoplasia (VIN) Certain changes that can occur in the skin that covers the vulva.

Well-differentiated Tumor cells that closely resemble mature, specialized cells.

West Nile A viral disease that is spread to individuals by a mosquito bite.

Young obstetric patient Younger than 16 years at date of delivery.

Zooplastic Tissue from an animal.

Abbreviations/Acronyms

A&P anatomy and physiology
AAPC American Academy of Professional Coders
ABG arterial blood gas
ACS acute coronary syndrome
ADD attention deficit disorder
ADHD attention deficit hyperactivity disorder
AF atrial fibrillation
AHA American Hospital Association
AHIMA American Health Information Management Association
AHQA American Health Quality Association
AICD automatic implantable cardioverter-defibrillator
AIDS acquired immunodeficiency syndrome
AKA above-knee amputation
ALIF anterior lumbar interbody fusion
ALL acute lymphoblastic leukemia
AMI acute myocardial infarction
AML acute myeloid leukemia
ARF acute renal failure
ARI acute renal insufficiency
AROM artificial rupture of membranes
ASA aspirin
AUD alcohol use disorder
AV arteriovenous
AV atrioventricular
AVM arteriovenous malformation
AVR aortic valve replacement
AxiaLIF axial lumbar interbody fusion
BCC basal cell carcinoma
BIPAP bilevel positive airway pressure
BMI body mass index
BMT bone marrow transplant
BNP brain natriuretic peptide
BP blood pressure
BPD biliopancreatic diversion
BPD bronchopulmonary dysplasia
BPH benign prostatic hypertrophy
BUN blood urea nitrogen
C. DIFF *Clostridium difficile*
CAB coronary artery bypass
CABG coronary artery bypass graft
CAD coronary artery disease
CAP community-acquired pneumonia
CAPD continuous ambulatory peritoneal dialysis
CAS computer assisted surgery
CBC complete blood count
CC chief complaint
CC complication/comorbidity
CC Complication/comorbity
CCA Certified Coding Associate
CCPD continuous cycling peritoneal dialysis
CCS Certified Coding Specialist
CCS-P Certified Coding Specialist—Physician Based
CD4 Cluster of differentiation 4
CDC Centers for Disease Control and Prevention
CDIP Certified Documentation Improvement Practitioner
CEA carcinoembryonic antigen
CEUs continuing education units
CF cystic fibrosis
CHB complete heart block
CHF congestive heart failure
CHI closed head injury
CIC Certified Inpatient Coder
CIN cervical intraepithelial neoplasia
CKD chronic kidney disease
CML chronic myelogenous leukemia
CMS Centers for Medicare and Medicaid Services
CNS central nervous system
COC Certified Outpatient Coder
COC-A Certified Outpatient Coder-Apprentice
COPD chronic obstructive pulmonary disease
COVID-19 Coronavirus disease 2019
CPAP continuous positive airway pressure
CPB Certified Professional Biller
CPC Certified Professional Coder

CPC-A Certified Professional Coder-Apprentice
CPD cephalopelvic disproportion
CPK creatine phosphokinase
CPK-MB creatine phosphokinase, isoenzyme MB
CPMA Certified Professional Medical Auditor
CPPM Certified Physician Practice Manager
CPT *Current Procedural Terminology*
CRC Certified Risk Adjustment Coder
CRF chronic renal failure
CRI chronic renal insufficiency
CRT cardiac resynchronization therapy
CRT-D cardiac resynchronization treatment defibrillator
CRT-P cardiac resynchronization treatment pacemaker
CSF cerebrospinal fluid
CT computerized tomography
CVA cerebrovascular accident
CVL central venous line
CVS chorionic villus sampling
CXR chest x-ray
D&C dilatation and curettage
D&C Dilation and Curettage
DBS deep brain stimulation
DCIS ductal carcinoma in situ
DES drug-eluting stent
DHHS U.S. Department of Health and Human Services
DI diabetes insipidus
DIC disseminated intravascular coagulation
DIEP deep inferior epigastric perforator
DJD degenerative joint disease
DLIF direct lateral lumbar interbody fusion
DM diabetes mellitus
DMAC disseminated *Mycobacterium avium-intracellulare* complex
DOB date of birth
DOE dyspnea on exertion
DRGs diagnosis-related groups
DS discharge summary
DSM-5 Diagnostic and Statistical Manual of Mental Disorders, Fifth Edition
DSM-IV-TR *Diagnostic and Statistical Manual of Mental Disorders, Fourth Edition, Text Revision*
DTs delirium tremens
DVT deep vein thrombosis
E. coli *Escherichia coli*
ECMO extracorporeal membrane oxygenation
ECT electroconvulsive therapy
ED Emergency Department
EDC estimated date of confinement
EEG electroencephalogram
EGD esophagogastroduodenoscopy
EGD esophogastroduodenoscopy
EKG electrocardiogram
EKG/ECG electrocardiogram
EMG electromyelogram
EP electrophysiologic
ER Emergency Room
ERCP endoscopic retrograde cholangiopancreatogram
ERCP endoscopic retrograde cholangiopancreatography
ESRD end-stage renal disease
ESWL extracorporeal shock wave lithotripsy
FB foreign body
FNA fine needle aspiration
FSG focal segmental glomerulosclerosis
FTSG full-thickness skin graft
FUO fever of unknown origin
GAP gluteal artery perforator
GBS group B strep
GDM gestational diabetes mellitus
GERD gastroesophageal reflux disease
GFR glomerular filtration rate
GI gastrointestinal
GIST gastrointestinal stromal tumor
GN glomerulonephritis
GVHD graft-versus-host disease
H&P history and physical
H. flu *Haemophilus influenzae*
HAART highly active antiretroviral therapy
HAP hospital acquired pneumonia
HBOT Hyperbaric oxygen therapy
HCC hepatocellular carcinoma
HCC Hierarchical Condition Categories
hCG human chorionic gonadotropin
Hct hematocrit
HCVD hypertensive cardiovascular disease
HELLP hemolysis, elevated liver enzymes, and low platelet count
HFMD hand, foot, and mouth disease
HFpEF heart failure preserved ejection fraction
HFrEF heart failure reduced ejection fraction
Hgb hemoglobin
hGH human growth hormone
HGSIL high-grade squamous intraepithelial lesion
HIPAA Health Insurance Portability and Accountability Act
HIV human immunodeficiency virus
HIVAN HIV-associated nephropathy
HPI history of present illness
HPV Human papilloma virus
HSIL high-grade squamous intraepithelial lesion

HSV herpes simplex virus
HTN hypertension
I&D incision and drainage
ICD internal cardiac defibrillator
ICD-10-CM *International Classification of Diseases, 10th Revision, Clinical Modification*
ICD-10-PCS *International Classification of Diseases, 10th Revision, Procedure Coding System*
ICD-10-PCS *International Classification of Diseases, 10th Revision, Procedure Classification System*
ICU intensive care unit
ICV implantable cardioverter
IDDM insulin-dependent diabetes mellitus
Ig immunoglobulin
IOL induction of labor
IOL intraocular lens
IOP intraocular pressure
IPPV intermittent positive pressure ventilation
IQ intelligence quotient
IS *information systems*
ITP idiopathic thrombocytopenic purpura
IUD intrauterine contraceptive device
IUD intrauterine device
IUGR intrauterine growth retardation
IV intravenous
IVDU intravenous drug use
IVDU intravenous drug user
IVF in vitro fertilization
JRA juvenile rheumatoid arthritis
KS Kaposi's sarcoma
LAD left anterior descending
LAVH laparoscopically assisted vaginal hysterectomy
LCA left coronary artery
LD learning disability/difficulty
LDMF latissimus dorsi musculocutaneous flap
LGA large for gestational age
LGIB lower gastrointestinal bleed
LLL left lower lobe
LOC loss of consciousness
LP lumbar puncture
LSIL low-grade squamous intraepithelial lesion
LTCS low transverse cesarean section
LUTS lower urinary tract symptoms
MAC *Mycobacterium avium-intracellulare* complex
MAI *Mycobacterium avium-intracellulare*
MAR medication administration record
MCE Medicare Code Editor
MCI mild cognitive impairment
MDD major depressive disorder
MDR multi-drug resistant
MEN multiple endocrine neoplasia
MI myocardial infarction
MOD multiple organ dysfunction
MRA magnetic resonance angiography
MRI magnetic resonance imaging
MRSA methicillin-resistant *Staphylococcus aureus*
MSAFP maternal serum alpha-fetoprotein
MS-DRG Medicare Severity diagnosis-related group
MS-DRGs Medicare Severity diagnosis-related groups
MSSA methicillin-sensitive *Staphylococcus aureus*
MUGA multiple-gated acquisition
MVA motor vehicle accident
MVP mitral valve prolapse
MVR mitral valve replacement
NCHS National Center for Health Statistics
NEC not elsewhere classifiable
NHL non-Hodgkin's lymphoma
NICU neonatal intensive care unit
NIDDM non–insulin-dependent diabetes mellitus
NKF National Kidney Foundation
NOS not otherwise specified
NPH normal pressure hydrocephalus
NPI National Provider Identifier
NPPV noninvasive positive pressure ventilation
NQMI non–Q wave myocardial infarction
NSAID nonsteroidal antiinflammatory drug
NSAIDs nonsteroidal anti-inflammatory drugs
NSCLC non–small cell lung cancer
NST nonstress test
NSTEMI non–ST elevation myocardial infarction
O2 oxygen
OA osteoarthritis
OB obstetrics
OBS organic brain syndrome
OI osteogenesis imperfecta
OIG Office of the Inspector General
OM obtuse marginal
OM otitis media
OP Report operative report
OR Operating Room
ORIF open reduction internal fixation
ORIF open reduction with internal fixation
OSA obstructive sleep apnea
Paco2 partial pressure of carbon dioxide in arterial blood
PACU post-anesthesia care unit
Pao2 partial pressure of oxygen in arterial blood
PCI percutaneous coronary intervention

PCP *Pneumocystis carinii* pneumonia
PDA patent ductus arteriosus
PDA posterior descending artery
PDT photodynamic therapy
PE pulmonary embolism
PEG percutaneous endoscopic gastrostomy
PET positron emission tomography
PHT pulmonary hypertension
PICC peripherally inserted central catheter
PID pelvic inflammatory disease
PIH pregnancy-induced hypertension
PKU phenylketonuria
PLIF posterior lumbar interbody fusion
PMR polymyalgia rheumatica
POA present on admission
POC products of conception
PPH primary pulmonary hypertension
PROM premature rupture of membranes
PSA prostate-specific antigen
PT prothrombin time
PTA prior to admission
PTCA percutaneous transluminal coronary angioplasty
PTL preterm labor
PTSD posttraumatic stress disorder
PTT partial thromboplastin time
PUD peptic ulcer disease
PV percutaneous vertebroplasty
PWS Prader-Willi syndrome
RA rheumatoid arthritis
RA right atrium
RAD reactive airway disease
RBBB right bundle branch block
RCA right coronary artery
RCC renal cell carcinoma
RDS respiratory distress syndrome
RFA radiofrequency ablation
RHIA Registered Health Information Administrator
RHIT Registered Health Information Technician
RPGN rapidly progressive glomerulonephritis
RPR rapid plasma reagin
RSV respiratory syncytial virus
RUL right upper lobe
RUQ right upper quadrant
RW relative weight
SARS severe acute respiratory syndrome
SCC squamous cell carcinoma
SCI spinal cord injury
SCID severe combined immunodeficiency
SCLC small cell lung cancer
SGA small for gestational age
SIADH syndrome of inappropriate antidiuretic hormone secretion
SIEA superficial inferior epigastric artery
SIL squamous intraepithelial lesion
SIRS systemic inflammatory response syndrome
SJS Stevens-Johnson Syndrome
SLAP superior labrum anterior-posterior
SLE systemic lupus erythematosus
SLNB sentinel lymph node biopsy
SNOMED Systematized Nomenclature of Medicine
SOAP Subjective/Objective/Assessment/Plan
SOB shortness of breath
SOM serous otitis media
SSS sick sinus syndrome
STAPH aureus *Staphylococcus aureus*
STD sexually transmitted disease
STEC Shiga toxin-producing *E. coli*
STEMI ST elevation myocardial infarction
STSG split-thickness skin graft
SVD spontaneous vaginal delivery
SVT supraventricular tachycardia
TACE transarterial chemoembolization
TB tuberculosis
TBI traumatic brain injury
TEN toxic epidermal neurolysis
TIA transient ischemic attack
TIPS transjugular intrahepatic portosystemic shunt
TJC The Joint Commission
TKR total knee replacement
TLIF transforaminal lumbar interbody fusion
TLS tumor lysis syndrome
TOF tetralogy of Fallot
TPA tissue plasminogen activator
TPN total parenteral nutrition
TPR temperature, pulse, and respiration
TRAM transverse rectus abdominis muscle
TRAM transverse rectus abdominis musculocutaneous
TSH thyroid-stimulating hormone
TTN transitory tachypnea of the newborn
TULIP transurethral ultrasound-guided laser-induced prostatectomy
TUMT transurethral microwave thermotherapy
TUNA transurethral needle ablation of prostate
TURP transurethral resection of the prostate
UGIB upper gastrointestinal bleed
UHDDS Uniform Hospital Discharge Data Set
UPIN Unique Physician Identification Number
UR utilization review

USA unstable angina
UTI urinary tract infection
VAP ventilator assisted pneumonia
VATS video-assisted thoracic surgery
VBAC vaginal birth after cesarean section
VBG vertical banded gastroplasty
VDRL Venereal Disease Research Laboratory
VIN vulvular intraepithelial neoplasia
VLAP visual laser ablation of the prostate
VNS vagal nerve stimulator
VP ventriculoperitoneal
VPS ventriculoperitoneal shunt
VRE vancomycin-resistant enterococcus
VSD ventricular septal defect
VUR vesicoureteral reflux
WBC white blood cell
WBC white blood cells
WHO World Health Organization
XLIF extreme lateral lumbar interbody fusion

Illustration Credits

Chapter 1
Figure 1-1: Courtesy American Health Information Management Association. 1-2: Courtesy American Academy of Professional Coders.

Chapter 2
Figures 2-1, 2-9, 2-11, 2-12: From Abdelhak M, Grostick S, Hanken MA, Jacobs EB (eds). Health Information: Management of a Strategic Resource, 4th ed. St. Louis, Saunders, 2011.

Chapter 6
Figure 6-5: A & C from Rothrock J. Alexander's Care of the Patient in Surgery, 14th ed. St. Louis, Elsevier, 2011. B from Spiro SG, Albert RK, Jett JR. Clinical Respiratory Medicine, 4th ed. St. Louis, Elsevier, 2012. D from Sanders MJ, McKenna KD. Mosby's Paramedic Textbook, 3rd ed. St. Louis, Mosby/JEMS, 2007. E from Salvo SG. Mosby's Pathology for Massage Therapists, 3rd ed. St. Louis, Elsevier, 2013. F from Phillips N. Berry & Kohn's Operating Room Technique, 12th ed. St. Louis, Elsevier, 2013. G from Burkitt HG, Quick CRG: Essential Surgery, ed 3, Churchill Livingstone, 2002.

Chapter 10
Figure 10-2: From Kumar V, Cotran RS, Robbins SJ. Robbins Basic Pathology, 9th ed. Philadelphia, Saunders, 2013. 10-3: Courtesy Dr. John J. Kepers, Kansas City, Kansas. 10-4: From Behrman RE, Kleigman RM, Arvin AM. Slide set for Nelson Textbook of Pediatrics, 15th ed. Philadelphia, Saunders, 1996. 10-5A: From Mosby's Guide to Physical Examination, 6th ed. St. Louis, Mosby, 2006. 10-5B: From Marx J, Hockberger R, Walls R. Rosen's Emergency Medicine — Concepts and Clinicla Practice, 7th ed. Philadelphia, Mosby, 2009. 10-6: From Eichenfeld L. Textbook of Neonatal Dermatology, 2nd ed. Philadelphia, Saunders, 2008.

Chapter 11
Figure 11-5: From James WD, Berger TG. Andrews' Diseases of the Skin, 11th ed. Philadelphia, Saunders, 2011. 11-6: From Doughty DB, Jackson DB. Gastrointestinal Disorders — Mosby' s Clinical Nursing Series, 5th ed. St. Louis, Mosby, 1993. 11-7: From Cotran RS, Kumar V,Collins T. Robbins Pathologic Basis for Disease, 6th ed. Philadelphia, Saunders, 1999. 11-8: From Kumar V, Abbas AK, Fausto N. Robbins & Cotran Pathologic Basis of Disease, 9th ed. Philadelphia, Saunders, 2013. 11-9: From Crum C, Nucci M, Lee K. Diagnostic Gynecologic and Obstetric Pathology, 2nd ed. Philadelphia, Saunders, 2011. 11-10: From Rosai J. Rosai and Ackerman's Surgical Pathology, 10th ed. Philadelphia, Mosby, 2011. 11-11: From Salvo S. Mosby's Pathology for Massage Therapists, 2nd ed. St. Louis, Mosby, 2008. 11-13: From Damjanov I. Pathology for the Health Professions, 4th ed. St. Louis, Saunders, 2012. 11-12: From Huether SE, McCance KL. Understanding Pathophysiology, 5th ed. St. Louis, Mosby, 2013. 11-14: From Gould BE. Pathophysiology for the Health Professions, 4th ed. St. Louis, Saunders, 2011.

Chapter 12
Figure 12-5: From Chabner D. The Language of Medicine, 10th ed. St. Louis, Saunders, 2014. 12-7: From Lookingbill DP, Marks JG. Lookingbill and Marks' Principles of Dermatology, 5th ed. Philadelphia, Saunders, 2014.

Chapter 13
Figure 13-1: ©Elsevier Collection. 13-2: From Jarvis C: Physical Examination and Health Assessment, 3rd ed. Philadelphia, WB Saunders, 2000. 13-3: Courtesy Paul W. Ladenson, MD, The Johns Hopkins University and Hospital, Baltimore, Maryland. 13-4, 13-13: From Damjanov I. Pathology for the Health Professions, 4th ed. St. Louis, Saunders, 2012. 13-5: From Seidel HM, Ball JW, Dains JE, Flynn JA, Solomon BS, Stewart RW. Mosby's Guide to Physical Examination, 7th ed. St. Louis, Mosby, 2011. 13-6: From Chintamani. Lewis's Medical Surgical Nursing. Elsevier. 13-12A: From Thibodeau GA. Anatomy and Physiology. 6th ed. St. Louis, Mosby, 2007. 13-12B: From Beuschlein F, Strasburger CJ, Siegerstetter V, et al. Acromegaly caused by secretion of growth hormone by a non-Hodgkins lymphoma. N Engl J Med 2000;342:1871-1876. Copyright 2000, Massachusetts Medical Society. All rights reserved. 13-12C: From Little JW, Falace D, Miller C, Rhodus NL. Little and Falace's Dental Management of the Medically Compromised Patient, 8th ed. St. Louis, Mosby, 2013. 13-13: From Battista E. Crash Course: Pharmacology, 4th ed. St. Louis, Mosby, 2012. 13-15: From Zitelli BJ, McIntire SC, Nowalk AJ. Atlas of Pediatric Physical Diagnosis, 6th ed. St. Louis, Mosby, 2012. 13-16: From Kumar V, Abbas AK, Fausto N. Robbins & Cotran Pathologic Basis of Disease, 9th ed. Philadelphia, Saunders, 2013. 13-17: From Mahan LK, Escott-Stump S. Krause's Food & Nutrition Therapy. St. Louis, Elsevier, 2008. 13-18: Courtesy MiniMed Technologies, Sylmar, California; from Mosby's Medical, Nursing, and Allied Health Dictionary, 6th ed. St. Louis, Mosby, 2002.

Chapter 15
Figure 15-1, 15-3, 15-4: ©Elsevier Collection. 15-5: From LaFleur Brooks M. Exploring Medical Language: A Student-Directed Approach, 8th ed. St. Louis, Mosby, 2011. 15-8, 15-9, 15-10, 15-11, 15-12: From Proctor D, Adams A. Kinn's The Medical Assistant: An Applied Learning Approach, 11th ed. St. Louis, Saunders, 2010. 15-13: From Tietze K. Clinical Skills for Pharmacists: A Patient-Focused Approach, 3rd ed. St. Louis, Mosby, 2011. 15-14: Courtesy Ophthalmic Photography at the University of Michigan, WK Kellogg Eye Center, Ann Arbor, Michigan. 15-15: From Frazier MS, Drzymkowski JW. Essentials of Human Diseases and Conditions, 5th ed. St. Louis, Saunders, 2013. 15-17: Patton KT, Thibodeau GA. Anatomy and Physiology, 8th ed. St. Louis, Mosby, 2013. 15-18: From Lewis SM, Heitkemper MM, Dirksen SR. Medical-Surgical Nursing: Assessment and Management of Clinical Problems, 8th ed. St. Louis, Mosby, 2011.

Chapter 16
Figure 16-1: From Patton KT, Thibodeau GA. Mosby's Handbook of Anatomy and Physiology. St. Louis, Mosby, 2000. 16-2: From Applegate EJ. The Anatomy and Physiology Learning System, 4th ed. Philadelphia, Saunders, 2011. 16-3, 16-22: ©Elsevier Collection. 16-11, 16-13: From Gerdin J. Health Careers Today, 5th ed. St. Louis, Mosby, 2011. 16-16: From Frazier MS, Drzymkowski JW. Essentials of Human Diseases and Conditions, 5th ed. St. Louis, Saunders, 2013. 16-20: From Ignatavicius D,

Workman M.L. Medical-Surgical Nursing: Patient-Centered Collaborative Care, 6th ed. St. Louis, Saunders, 2009. 16-4, 16-5: From Black JM, Hawks JH: Medical-Surgical Nursing: Clinical Management for Positive Outcomes, 8th ed. Philadelphia, Saunders, 2008. 16-7: From Darby M, Walsh M. Dental Hygiene: Theory and Practice, 3rd ed. St. Louis, Saunders, 2009. 16-8: © Bayer Schering Pharma AG www.thrombosisadvisor.com. 16-10, 16-17: From Damjanov I. Pathology for the Health Professions, 4th ed. St. Louis, Saunders, 2012. 16-12: Modified from Ignatavicius DD, Workman ML. Medical-Surgical Nursing: Critical Thinking for Collaborative Care, 7th ed. Philadelphia, Saunders, 2013. 16-14: From Applegate EJ. The Sectional Anatomy Learning System, 3rd ed. Philadelphia, Saunders, 2010. 16-18, 16-19, 16-21: From Chabner D. The Language of Medicine, 10th ed. St. Louis, Saunders, 2014. 16-24: From Drake RL, Vogl W, Mitchell AWM. Gray's Anatomy for Students, 2nd ed. Philadelphia, Churchill Livingstone, 2009. 16-25: From Lewis SM, Heitkemper MM, Dirksen SR. Medical-Surgical Nursing: Assessment and Management of Clinical Problems, 8th ed. St. Louis, Mosby, 2011.

Chapter 17

Figure 17-1: ©Elsevier Collection. 17-4A, B: From Kumar V, Abbas AK, Fausto N. Robbins & Cotran Pathologic Basis of Disease, 9th ed. Philadelphia, Saunders, 2013. 17-4C: Courtesy Paul Emmerson and Seneca College of Applied Arts and Technology, Toronto, Ontario, Canada. 17-5: Courtesy Dr. W. Thurlback, Vancouver, BC, Canada. 17-7: From Forbes B, Sahm D, Weissfeld A. Bailey & Scott's Diagnostic Microbiology, 12th ed. Philadelphia, Mosby, 2007. 17-8: From LaFleur M. Exploring Medical Language: A Student-Directed Approach, 9th ed. St. Louis, Mosby, 2011. 17-9A: From LaFleur M. Exploring Medical Language: A Student-Directed Approach, 9th ed. St. Louis, Mosby, 2011. 17-10: From Chabner D. The Language of Medicine, 10th ed. St. Louis, Saunders, 2014. 17-9B: From Black JM, Hawks JH, Keene AM. Medical-Surgical Nursing: Clinical Management for Positive Outcomes, 8th ed. Philadelphia, Saunders, 2009.

Chapter 18

Figure 18-1: Redrawn from Miller M. Pathophysiology: Principles of Disease. Philadelphia, Saunders, 1983. 18-2: From Buck CJ. Saunders 2010 ICD-9-CM, Volumes 1, 2, and 3. St. Louis, Saunders, 2010. 18-3: From Damjanov I. Pathology for the Health-Related Professions, 2nd ed. Philadelphia, Saunders, 2000. 18-5: From Damjanov I. Pathology for the Health Professions, 4th ed. St. Louis, Saunders, 2013. 18-6, 18-8A: From Feldman M, Friedman L, Brandt L. Sleisenger and Fordtran's Gastrointestinal and Liver Disease, 9th ed. St. Louis, Saunders, 2010. 18-7: From Cotran RS, Kumar V, Collins T. Robbins Pathologic Basis for Disease, 6th ed. Philadelphia, Saunders, 1999. 18-8B: From Kumar V, Abbas AK, Fausto N. Robbins & Cotran Pathologic Basis of Disease, 9th ed. Philadelphia, Saunders, 2013. 18-9: From Patton KT, Thibodeau GA. Anatomy and Physiology, 8th ed. St. Louis, Mosby, 2013. 18-10: From Dorland's Illustrated Medical Dictionary, 31st ed. Philadelphia, Saunders, 2007. 18-11: From Leonard P. Building A Medical Vocabulary: with Spanish Translations, 6th ed. St. Louis, Saunders, 2005. 18-12: From Clinic C. Current Clinical Medicine 2009: Expert Consult Premium Edition, 1st ed. Philadelphia, Saunders, 2008. 18-13: From LaFleur M, LaFleur D. Exploring Medical Language: A Student-Directed Approach, 8th ed. St. Louis, Mosby, 2011. 18-14: From Chabner D. The Language of Medicine, 10th ed. St. Louis, Saunders, 2014.

Chapter 19

Figure 19-1: ©Elsevier Collection. 19-2A: From Lookingbill D, Marks J. Lookingbill and Marks' Principles of Dermatology, 5th ed. Philadelphia, Saunders, 2014. 19-2B: From Lawrence CM, Cox NH. Physical Signs in Dermatology: Color Atlas and Text. London, Mosby Europe, 1993. 19-3: From Murphy GF, Herzberg AJ. Atlas of Dermatopathology. Philadelphia, Saunders, 1996. 19-4: From Dorland's Illustrated Medical Dictionary, 31st ed. Philadelphia, Saunders, 2007. 19-5: From Callen J, Greer K, Hood A, et al. Color Atlas of Dermatology. Philadelphia, Saunders, 1993. 19-8: From McCarthy JG, et al (eds). Plastic Surgery, vol 7, Philadelphia, WB Saunders, 1990.

Chapter 20

Figures 20-1: From Dorland's Illustrated Medical Dictionary, 31st ed. Philadelphia, Saunders, 2007. 20-2: From LaFleur M. Exploring Medical Language: A Student-Directed Approach, 9th ed. St. Louis, Mosby, 2011. 20-8AB: From Frazier MS, Drzymkowski JW. Essentials of Human Diseases and Conditions, 5th ed. St. Louis, Saunders, 2013. 20-3: Thibodeau GA, Patton KT: The Human Body in Health and Disease, 6th ed. St. Louis, Mosby, 2014. 20-6: From Marx J, Hockberger R, Walls R. Rosen's Emergency Medicine - Concepts and Clinicla Practice, 7th ed. Philadelphia, Mosby, 2009. 20-4: From Gerdin J. Health Careers Today, 5th ed. St. Louis, Mosby, 2011. 20-5: From LaFleur M. Exploring Medical Language: A Student-Directed Approach, 9th ed. St. Louis, Mosby, 2011. 20-8A: From Grace S, Deal M. Textbook of Remedial Massage, 1st ed. Australia, 2012. 20-8B: From Glancy G. Advances in Idiopathic Scoliosis in Children and Adolescents. Advances in Pediatrics, Vol 54, Issue 1, Pages 55-66. Mosby, Colorado,2007. 20-11: From Damjanov I. Pathology for the Health Professions, 4th ed. St. Louis, Saunders, 2012. 20-12: From Huether S, McCance K. Understanding Pathophysiology, 5th ed. St. Louis, Mosby, 2012. 20-9: From Drake RL, Vogl W, Mitchell AWM. Gray' s Anatomy for Students, 2nd ed. Philadelphia, Churchill Livingstone, 2009. 20-10: From Mettler FA, Jr. Essentials of Radiology, 3rd ed. Philadelphia, Saunders, 2014. 20-13: From Buck CJ. Step-by-Step Medical Coding, 2010 edition. St. Louis, Saunders, 2010. 20-14: From Duthie EH Jr, Katz PR, Malone M. Practice of Geriatrics, 4th ed. Philadelphia, Saunders, 2007.

Chapter 21

Figure 21-1: From McCance K, Huether S, Brashers V, Rote N. Pathophysiology: The Biologic Basis for Disease in Adults and Children, 6th ed. St. Louis, Mosby, 2009. 21-2, 21-3, 21-6: ©Elsevier Collection. 21-14, 21-15, 21-16, 21-19: From Gould BE. Pathophysiology for the Health Professions, 4th ed. St. Louis, Saunders, 2011. 21-4, 21-10: From Bostwick D, Cheng L. Urologic Surgical Pathology: Expert Consult, 2nd ed. Philadelphia, Saunders, 2008. 21-18: From LaFleur M. Exploring Medical Language: A Student-Directed Approach, 9th ed. St. Louis, Mosby, 2011. 21-21: From Chabner D. The Language of Medicine, 10th ed. St. Louis, Saunders, 2014. 21-22: From LaFleur M. Exploring Medical Language: A Student-Directed Approach, 9th ed. St. Louis, Mosby, 2011. 21-5, 21-7: From Zitelli B, McIntire S, Nowalk A. Zitelli and Davis' Atlas of Pediatric Physical Diagnosis: Expert Consult, 6th ed. Philadelphia, Saunders, 2012. 21-8: From Saunders Comprehensive Review for the NCLEX-RN Examination, 5th ed. St. Louis, Saunders, 2011. 21-9, 21-12: From Damjanov I. Pathology for the Health Professions, 4th ed. St. Louis, Saunders, 2012. 21-17: From Dorland's Illustrated Medical Dictionary, 31st ed. Philadelphia, Saunders, 2007.

Chapter 22

Figure 22-2: ©Elsevier Collection. 22-3: From Thibodeau G, Patton K. Structure & Function of the Body, 14th ed. St. Louis, Mosby, 2011. 22-4: From Chabner D. The Language of Medicine, 10th ed. St. Louis, Saunders, 2014. 22-6, 22-11: From Dorland's Illustrated Medical Dictionary, 31st ed. Philadelphia, Saunders, 2007. 22-7A: From Leifer G. Introduction to Maternity & Pediatric Nursing, 6th ed. St. Louis, Saunders, 2010. 22-7B: From Damjanov I, Linder J. Pathology: A Color Atlas. St. Louis, Mosby, 1999. 22-8: From Murray S, McKinney E. Foundations of Maternal-Newborn and Women's Health Nursing, 5th ed. St. Louis, Saunders, 2009. 22-9: From Elsevier: Buck's 2021 ICD-10-CM for Physicians,

St. Louis, Elsevier, 2021. 22-10: From LaFleur M. Exploring Medical Language: A Student-Directed Approach, 7th ed. St. Louis, Mosby, 2008.

Chapter 23

Figure 23-1: Modified from O'Toole M (ed). Miller-Keane Encyclopedia of Medicine, Nursing, and Allied Health, 6th ed. Philadelphia, Saunders, 1997. 23-2: From Leifer G. Introduction to Maternity and Pediatric Nursing. Philadelphia, Saunders, 2002. 23-3: From Gould BE. Pathophysiology for the Health Professions, 4th ed. St. Louis, Saunders, 2011. 23-4: From Frazier MS, Drzymkowski JW. Essentials of Human Diseases and Conditions, 5th ed. St. Louis, Saunders, 2013. 23-5: From Dorland's Illustrated Medical Dictionary, 31st ed. Philadelphia, Saunders, 2007. 23-6: From Behrman RE, Kleigman RM, Arvin AM. Slide set for Nelson Textbook of Pediatrics, 15th ed. Philadelphia, Saunders, 1996. 23-8: From Damjanov I. Pathology for the Health Professions, 4th ed. St. Louis, Saunders, 2012. 23-9: From Baralos M, Baramki TA. Medical Cytogenics. Baltimore, Lippincott Williams and Wilkins, 1967.

Chapter 24

Figures 24-2, 24-4: From Henry MC, Stapleton ER.EMT Prehospital Care, 3rd ed. Philadelphia, Saunders, 2004. 24-5: ©Elsevier Collection. 24-7, 24-9, 24-10, 24-11: From Drake RL, Vogl W, Mitchell AWM. Gray's Anatomy for Students, 2nd ed. Philadelphia, Churchill Livingstone, 2010. 24-8: From Lampignano J, Bontrager K. Textbook of Radiographic Positioning and Related Anatomy, 7th ed. St. Louis, Mosby, 2009. 24-14: From McCance KL, Huether SE: Pathophysiology: The Biologic Basis for Disease in Adults and Children, ed 7, St. Louis, Mosby, 2014.

Chapter 25

Figure 25-2: From Schlenker E, Roth S. Williams' Essentials of Nutrition and Diet Therapy, 10th ed. St. Louis, Mosby, 2010. 25-3: From Frazier MS, Drzymkowski JW. Essentials of Human Diseases and Conditions, 5th ed. St. Louis, Saunders, 2013.

Chapter 26

Figure 26-6: From Frazier MS, Drzymkowski JW. Essentials of Human Diseases and Conditions, 5th ed. St. Louis, Saunders, 2009. 26-8: From Canale ST. Campbell's Operative Orthopaedics, 12th ed. Philadelphia, Mosby, 2013. 26-9: From Green NE, Swiontkowski MF. Skeletal Trauma in Children, 4th ed. Philadelphia, Saunders, 2009.

Index

Page numbers followed by "*f*" indicate figures, "*t*" indicate tables, and "*b*" indicate boxes.

B

H

I

N

O

T

U

V